THINKA

a division of ALM Global, LLC

THE TOOLS & TECHNIQUES OF ESTATE PLANNING, 21ST EDITION

Stephan R. Leimberg, L. Paul Hood, Jr., and Edwin P. Morrow, III

The Tools & Techniques of Estate Planning covers all aspects of estate planning, from behavioral and ethical issues to estate and gift tax planning, to planning for nontraditional couples and the risk of health issues for aging clients. With topics that are applicable for both large and small estates, this title enables estate planners to:

- **Help** clients plan every aspect of their estate, including tax, investment, insurance, and estate administration decisions;
- **Help** clients effectively preserve their assets under current law;
- **Handle** a wide variety of estates and specific circumstances; and
- **Save** significant amounts of time with exclusive estate planning tools.

This book features easy-to-understand, real-world examples from expert authors on which techniques are best suited for a wide variety of circumstances, and equally important advice on how to avoid future problems.

Highlights of the 21st Edition

This new 21st edition has been completely updated, including **five** new chapters, and featuring:

- **SECURE Act 2.0** Proposed Regulations and Secure 2.0 Act changes, such as:
  - the new required minimum distribution ages
  - Employee Stock Ownership Plan changes
  - when RMDs must be paid out after the death of the account holder
  - proposed regulations interpreting the 10 year rule differently when decedent dies *before* reaching the required beginning date versus after
  - starting in 2024, additional incentives if the trust is a conduit trust for a surviving spouse
  - stating in 2024, how Roth employer plans won't be subject to mandatory distributions during their lifetime
  - how SECURE Act 2.0 encourages expansion of vesting, eligibility and establishment of qualified retirement plans
  - a provision that incentivizes small employers to make military spouses eligible for plan participation and matching sooner than they would otherwise have to

- A **new** chapter 32, *Spousal Lifetime Access Trust (SLAT)*, including the advantages and disadvantages and potential uses

- A **new** chapter 35, *Beneficiary Deemed Owner Trusts*, explaining the advantages of a BDOT, including how they allow the shifting of the income tax burden to the powerholder without having to make a distribution

- A **new** chapter 44, *Using Formula Powers of Appointment/Optimal Basis Increase Trusts (OBITs)*, discussing how it can be used to avoid a step down in basis and an increase in estate or GST tax

- A **new** chapter 60, *Planning with Roth Retirement Accounts*, which explains the two key advantages of Roth IRAs over traditional IRAs, as well as the impact of conversions on the beneficiary designation and estate plan and how trusts for the two types of plans may be drafted differently

- A **new** chapter 66, *Community Property Trusts*, identifying the advantages and disadvantages of creating these trusts

- A fully revised chapter on Planning with S Corporations, including recent IRS taxpayer-friendly guidance on inadvertent S corporation terminations with simplified procedures

- An update on state laws, including the states that have adopted the Revised Uniform Limited Liability Company Act and states that still have inheritance and/or estate taxes, as well as states that now permit "legal suicide"

- Revisions to the chapter on planning opportunities for family members are not U.S. citizens, including a list of countries that have estate or gift tax treaties with the United States

As with all of the resources in the highly acclaimed Leimberg Library, every area covered in this book is accompanied by the tools, techniques, practice tips, and examples you can use to help your clients successfully navigate the complex course of estate planning and confidently meet their needs.

Related Titles Also Available:

- *The Tools & Techniques of Estate Planning for Modern Families*

- *The Tools & Techniques of Financial Planning*

- *The Tools & Techniques of Investment Planning*

- *The Tools & Techniques of Income Tax Planning*

- *Tax Facts on Insurance & Employee Benefits*

- *Tax Facts on Individuals & Small Business*

- *Tax Facts on Investments*

- *2024 Field Guide: Estate & Retirement Planning, Business Planning & Employee Benefits*

- *Tax Facts on Individuals & Small Business*

- *Tax Facts on Insurance & Employee Benefits*

21ST EDITION

The Tools & Techniques of
Estate Planning

LEIMBERG LIBRARY

Stephan R. Leimberg
L. Paul Hood, Jr.
Edwin P. Morrow, III

This publication is designed to provide accurate and authoritative information in regard to the subject matter covered. It is sold with the understanding that the publisher is not engaged in rendering legal, accounting or other professional service. If legal advice or other expert assistance is required, the services of a competent professional person should be sought.— From a Declaration of Principles jointly adopted by a Committee of the American Bar Association and a Committee of Publishers and Associations.

ISBN: 978-1-58852-810-0

Copyright © 1977, 1979, 1980, 1982, 1983, 1985, 1987, 1989, 1990, 1992, 1995, 1998, 2001, 2004, 2006, 2011, 2013, 2015, 2017, 2019, 2021, 2023, 2024

ALM Global, LLC
150 E. 42nd St.
New York, NY 10017

All rights reserved.
No part of this publication may be reproduced, stored in a retrieval system, or transmitted, in any form or by any means, electronic, mechanical, photocopying, recording, or otherwise, without prior written permission of the publisher.

Printed in the United States of America

DEDICATION

To our wives, parents, children, and grandchildren
and others
whom we love,
who have taught us –
and from whom
we will learn so much more.

Ed Morrow would like to dedicate his contribution in this edition to his late father, Edwin P. Morrow II (1939-2023), who was a true pioneer in the financial planning profession - https://www.wilsonschrammspaulding.com/obituaries/edwin-morrow-ii.

Paul dedicates his contributions to his dear friend and co-author, the late, great Steve Leimberg and those like-minded pilgrims who enthusiastically work toward the "good estate planning result."

ACKNOWLEDGEMENTS

We wish to thank the late Stephan R. Leimberg for his contribution to this volume and all the volumes in the *Tools and Techniques* series.

We wish to thank attorney Charles K. Plotnick for his chapters on selection of an executor, trustee, and attorney, and his probate primer.

NumberCruncher software illustrations throughout the book are courtesy of Leimberg and LeClair, Inc. (610-924-0515).

Most importantly, we would like to acknowledge you, our loyal readers, who have consistently contributed to the *Tools & Techniques of Estate Planning* being one of the most widely read professional books on estate planning of all time. Many of you have had every one of the previous eighteen editions on your shelves. To you, and to those of you for whom this edition is the first, we want you to know how very much we continue to appreciate your trust.

ABOUT THE AUTHORS

STEPHAN R. LEIMBERG

The late Stephan R. Leimberg was CEO of LISI, Leimberg Information Services, Inc., at leimbergservices.com, a provider of e-mail/internet news and commentary for professionals on recent cases, rulings, and legislation; CEO of Leimberg and LeClair, Inc., an estate and financial planning software company; and President of Leimberg Associates, Inc., a publishing and software company in Bryn Mawr, Pennsylvania at leimberg.com.

Leimberg was the author of numerous books on estate, financial, and employee benefit and retirement planning and a nationally known speaker. Leimberg was the creator and/or principal author of the entire nine book *Tools & Techniques* series including *The Tools & Techniques of Estate Planning, The Tools & Techniques of Financial Planning, The Tools & Techniques of Employee Benefit and Retirement Planning, The Tools & Techniques of Life Insurance Planning, The Tools & Techniques of Charitable Planning, The Tools & Techniques of Income Tax Planning, The Tools & Techniques of Investment Planning, The Tools & Techniques of Risk Management, and The Tools & Techniques of Practice Management*. Leimberg was co-author, with noted attorney Howard Zaritsky, of *Tax Planning with Life Insurance, The Book of Trusts* with attorneys Charles K. Plotnick and Daniel Evans, and *How to Settle an Estate* with Charles K. Plotnick, and *The Buy-Sell Handbook*.

Leimberg was creator or co-creator of many software packages for the financial services professional including *NumberCruncher* (estate planning), *IRS Factors Calculator* (actuarial computations), *Financial Analyzer II*, *Estate Planning Quickview* (Estate Planning Flow Charts), *Toward a Zero Estate Tax* (PowerPoint Estate Planning Client Seminar), *Gifts That Give, Gifts That Give Back* (Powerpoint Client Charitable Planning Seminar), and Long-Term Care (Powerpoint Client Seminar).

A nationally known speaker, Leimberg has addressed the Miami (Heckerling) Estate Planning Institute, the NYU Tax Institute, the Notre Dame Law School and Duke University Law School's Estate Planning Conference, The American Bar Association Planning Techniques for Large Estate and Sophisticated Planning Techniques courses of study, the National Association of Estate Planners and Councils, and the AICPA's National Estate Planning Forum. Leimberg has also spoken to the Federal Bureau of Investigation, and the National Aeronautics and Space Administration.

Leimberg, a 2004 recipient of the National Association of Estate Planners and Councils Distinguished Accredited Estate Planner award, was named 1998 Edward N. Polisher Lecturer of the Dickinson School of Law, and was awarded the Excellence in Writing Award of the American Bar Association's Probate and Property Section. He has been honored as Estate Planner of the Year by the Montgomery County Estate Planning Council and as Distinguished Estate Planner by the Philadelphia Estate Planning Council. He was also recipient of the President's Cup of the Philadelphia Life Underwriters, a three time Boris Todorovitch Lecturer, and the first Ben Feldman Lecturer.

L. PAUL HOOD, JR.

L. Paul Hood, Jr. received his J.D. from Louisiana State University Law Center in 1986 and Master of Laws in Taxation from Georgetown University Law Center in 1988. Paul is a frequent speaker, is widely quoted and his articles have appeared in a number of publications, including BNA Tax Management Memorandum, BNA Estates, Gifts & Trusts Journal, CCH Journal of Practical Estate Planning, Estate Planning, Valuation Strategies, Digest of Federal Tax Articles, Loyola Law Review, Louisiana Bar Journal, Tax Ideas, The Value Examiner and Charitable Gift Planning News. He has spoken at programs sponsored by a number of law schools, including Duke University, Georgetown University, New York University, Tulane University, Loyola (N.O.) University, and Louisiana State University, as well as many other professional organizations, including AICPA and NACVA. From 1996-2004, Paul served on the Louisiana Board of Tax Appeals, a three-member board that has jurisdiction over all State of Louisiana tax matters.

A self-described "recovering tax lawyer," Paul is the author or co-author of seven other books, and is the proud father of two boys who are the apples of his eye, Paul III and Evan. Happily married to Carol A. Sobczak, Paul lives with Carol in Toledo OH, where he serves as the Director of Planned Giving for The University of Toledo Foundation.

EDWIN P. MORROW, III

Edwin (Ed) Morrow, III is a Senior Wealth Strategist with Huntington National Bank's Wealth Strategy Group, a team of tax attorneys and accountants who work with high net worth clients and business owners, helping them with designing and implementing sophisticated wealth strategies as part of Huntington's personal investment, trust and family CFO services. These strategies include tax reduction, transactional tax, alternative risk management practices, philanthropy, asset protection, legacy planning as well as complex credit and leverage strategies. Ed is based in Cincinnati, Ohio.

Prior to joining Huntington, Ed was in similar roles at Key Private Bank and U.S. Bank and prior to working in the wealth management industry, was in private law practice focused on the areas of wealth preservation, business and trust planning, probate, tax litigation and ERISA retirement plans.

Ed has his Juris Doctor (J.D.) from the Northwestern School of Law at Lewis and Clark College in Portland, Oregon. He has a master's degree in business (MBA) from Xavier University in Cincinnati and a master's degree in tax law (LL.M.) from Capital University in Columbus, Ohio. Ed is a board-certified specialist in estate planning and trust law through the Ohio State Bar Association and a Fellow of the American College of Trusts and Estate Counsel (ACTEC), currently serving as the Chair of its Employee Benefits committee and serving on the Asset Protection committee. He recently participated in ACTEC's well-received submissions to the Treasury Department regarding regulations under the SECURE and Secure 2.0 Acts, encouraging and guiding them to issue clearer and more helpful regulations and examples for taxpayers. He is also a Certified Financial Planner (CFP®) and Certified Mergers and Acquisitions Advisor (CM&AA®).

An accomplished presenter and speaker at state and national conferences such as the Heckerling Estate Planning Institute, Notre Dame Estate Planning Institute, and the Southern Federal Tax Institute, he has taught thousands of attorneys, accountants and financial planners in various continuing education courses on estate, tax and asset protection planning. Ed also co-taught a capstone course on estate planning as an adjunct professor at the University of Cincinnati Law School.

TABLE OF CONTENTS

Part 1: The Purpose and Practice of Estate Planning

Chapter 1:	Overview of Estate Planning	1
Chapter 2:	Data Gathering and Analysis and Initial Client Interview	53
Chapter 3:	Human Side of Estate Planning	91
Chapter 4:	The Unauthorized Practice of Law	99
Chapter 5:	Ethics – A Practical Guideline	103
Chapter 6:	Malpractice in Estate Planning	109

Part 2: Ownership and Transfer of Property

Chapter 7:	Ownership and Transfer of Property	123
Chapter 8:	Gifts	135
Chapter 9:	Uniform Gifts/Transfers to Minors Acts	151
Chapter 10:	Wills	157
Chapter 11:	How to Review a Will: A Checklist for the Estate and Financial Planner	167
Chapter 12:	Powers of Appointment	181
Chapter 13:	Disclaimers	193
Chapter 14:	Selecting the Right People	203
Chapter 15:	Probate and Trust Administration	231
Chapter 16:	Executor's Primary Duties	249
Chapter 17:	Trusts in General	253

Part 3: Taxes

Chapter 18:	Estate Tax	277
Chapter 19:	Extensions of Time to Pay Estate Tax	295
Chapter 20:	Gift Tax	305
Chapter 21:	Generation-Skipping Transfer Tax	339
Chapter 22:	Federal Income Tax Issues	357
Chapter 23:	Qualified Business Income Deduction	377
Chapter 24:	Post Mortem Tax Elections	405
Chapter 25:	Death Tax Apportionment and Estate Tax Reimbursement	417
Chapter 26:	State Death Taxes	437

Part 4: Irrevocable Trusts

Chapter 27:	Marital Deduction and Bypass Trusts	445
Chapter 28:	Section 2503(b) and 2503(c) Trusts	463
Chapter 29:	Grantor Retained Interest Trusts (GRIT, GRAT, GRUT, QPRT)	471
Chapter 30:	Intentionally "Defective" Trust	485

Chapter 31:	Tax Basis Irrevocable Trust	495
Chapter 32:	Spousal Lifetime Access Trust (SLAT)	501
Chapter 33:	*Inter Vivos* QTIP Trusts	511

Part 5: Life Insurance

Chapter 34:	Life Insurance	521
Chapter 35:	Beneficiary Deemed Owner Trusts (BDOT)	545
Chapter 36:	Irrevocable Life Insurance Trust	551

Part 6: Charitable Giving

Chapter 37:	Charitable Contributions	561
Chapter 38:	Charitable Split Interest Trusts	579
Chapter 39:	Conservation Easement Exclusion	591

Part 7: Intra-family and Other Business Transfers Techniques

Chapter 40:	Intra-Family Loans	597
Chapter 41:	Installment Sales and SCINs	603
Chapter 42:	Private Annuity	617
Chapter 43:	Interest-Free and Below Market Rate Loans	629
Chapter 44:	Using Formula Powers of Appointment/Optimal Basis Increase Trusts (OBITS)	635
Chapter 45:	Split Interest Purchase of Property (SPLIT)	639
Chapter 46:	Sale (Gift) – Leaseback	645
Chapter 47:	Buy-Sell (Business Continuation) Agreement	655
Chapter 48:	Section 303 Stock Redemption	675
Chapter 49:	Family Limited Partnerships	683
Chapter 50:	Planning with C Corporations	705
Chapter 51:	Limited Liability Companies	721
Chapter 52:	Personal Holding Company	729
Chapter 53:	Planning with S Corporations	737

Part 8: Planning for Employee Benefits and Retirement

Chapter 54:	Deferred Compensation (Nonqualified)	751
Chapter 55:	Employee Stock Ownership Plan	769
Chapter 56:	Individual Retirement Plans (Including SEP and SIMPLE IRAs)	783
Chapter 57:	Profit Sharing/401(k)/Pension Plan	801
Chapter 58:	Survivor's Income Benefit Plan	827
Chapter 59:	Planning with IRAs and Qualified Retirement Plans	833
Chapter 60:	Planning with Roth Retirement Accounts	849

Part 9: Human Aspects of Estate Planning

Chapter 61:	Planning for Aging and Health Challenges	857
Chapter 62:	Durable Power of Attorney	869
Chapter 63:	Health-Care Documents	883
Chapter 64:	Revocable Trusts	907
Chapter 65:	Planning for Unmarried Partners	923
Chapter 66:	Community Property Trusts	937
Chapter 67:	Marriage Contracts and Property Agreements	943
Chapter 68:	Representing Blended Families for Estate Planning	959

Part 10: Valuation Issues

Chapter 69:	Planning for Digital Assets	979
Chapter 70:	Valuation Planning	995
Chapter 71:	Freezing Techniques – Corporations and Partnerships	1035
Chapter 72:	Non-U.S. Persons in the Estate Plan	1045

Index

Index	1055

OVERVIEW OF ESTATE PLANNING

CHAPTER 1

1.1 INTRODUCTION

Often, in order to encourage cooperation and full disclosure of pertinent data, it is necessary or helpful to explain to a client:

- what estate planning is
- who should be concerned with estate planning
- how the federal estate tax laws work
- the mistakes that are commonly made because of a lack of proper planning

This chapter is presented in plain language and in a format designed to help professionals present and highlight to the client the significance and urgency of estate planning. As part of this process, it is also important to explain to the client how assets actually pass. For example, not all assets pass by operation of the will. Many assets pass by virtue of titling or beneficiary designations. Therefore, it is important for the client to understand the importance of coordinating the disposition of these "automatically passing" assets with the overall estate plan.

1.2 ESTATE PLANNING PARADIGM SHIFT

The 2012 tax act changed the estate planning paradigm that had been in place since at least the 1976 tax act. The old estate paradigm was as follows:

- During life, use the applicable exclusion amount **sooner** rather than later.

- It was usually better to pay gift tax than estate tax because the gift tax was **cheaper** (tax-exclusive v. tax-inclusive).

- During life, transfer wealth as **quickly** as possible.

- Avoid estate tax inclusion at **every** generation.

- New basis at death is **less important** because of the relatively low capital gain tax rates, particularly relative to the **higher** federal estate tax rates.

- Income tax consequences are **secondary**.

- State of residence will **not** significantly affect the estate plan.

Since the 2012 tax act, the new paradigm, which represents a radical shift in thinking, is as follows:

- Estate planning is **significantly** more nuanced and complex and considers **many** more factors in the calculus.

- Clients should consider keeping as **much** low basis property as possible for the **new basis** at death.

- Paying gift tax doesn't make nearly as much sense **today.** What if there is **no** estate tax tomorrow?

- **"Zeroed-out"** transfers and **freezes** should be utilized instead.

- Income tax considerations must be considered **in tandem** with potential transfer taxes.

- **Tax basis management** will be a crucial part of "estate planning"-swaps of high basis assets for low basis assets in grantor trusts.

- Estate tax **inclusion** can save more in income taxes and should be used if the income tax savings are **greater** than the transfer tax cost.

- **State of residence** will give rise to very different types of estate planning, as far as how **active** versus **passive** the planning is.

This new paradigm requires much more intellectual rigor, as the new paradigm is much grainier than the old paradigm and is, in places, directly opposed to what was sound advice just five years ago. Estate planners must adapt quickly to this new paradigm-until the next so-called *permanent* law change is enacted.

1.3 WHAT IS ESTATE PLANNING?

Estate planning is the process of planning the accumulation, conservation, and distribution of an estate in the manner that most efficiently and effectively accomplishes your personal tax and nontax objectives. Every estate is planned – either by the individual or by the state and federal governments. By your actions now, you can strongly influence, if not determine, what will happen when...

Controlled estate planning is a systematic process for uncovering problems and providing solutions in clients' L.I.V.E.S. Planners should use this L.I.V.E.S. acronym to illustrate the seven major areas of estate planning and emphasize the significance and urgency of action to solve them:

1. Lack of liquidity: Insufficient cash to pay administrative costs including the costs of maintaining property, taxes, and other estate settlement expenses. A lack of liquidity can trigger a forced sale and result in the loss of an estate's most precious assets at pennies on the dollar. In other words, if there is not enough cash in an estate to pay for the demands as they come due, the estate's personal representative may be forced to sell the estate's prime assets under "fire sale" conditions. Liquidity can also become a problem when considering retirement assets. While on a superficial level, retirement assets are both available and liquid, it is important to keep in mind that when distributions are made from retirement accounts, these distributions are taxed at ordinary income tax rates. In addition, these assets are also subject to estate tax at their full value. Therefore, if the estate and/or beneficiaries take distributions from these accounts in order to pay taxes or administration expenses, these distributions will be subject to income tax and incur a significant cost for using these funds.

2. Improper disposition of assets: When the wrong asset goes at the wrong time to the wrong person in the wrong manner, the result is often disaster. For example, picture the proceeds of $100,000 of group life insurance or a $500,000 pension plan being paid to a twenty-one year-old child. All too many estates contain property that will pass outright to a person who has little, if any, training, experience, or desire to properly invest and manage that asset. This is particularly true where a family-owned business is concerned. Problems can also arise when trying to access these funds. For example, when distributions are payable directly to a minor, some states require that a court appoint a guardian when the assets passing to the minor exceed a certain amount. This creates additional costs and paperwork in order to access these assets.

3. Inflation (need to both diversify and inflation-proof portfolio): Many individuals have placed all their financial eggs in one basket or have not considered the diminished and diminishing purchasing power of life insurance or a retirement fund that may have been adequate only four or five years ago. The ravages of inflation and risk of placing all of a client's family financial security in one investment (or business) must be factored into the estate plan.

4. Inadequate income or capital at retirement/death/disability: Planners and clients often forget that cash demands for survivors' food, clothing, shelter, and schooling often will exhaust the funds that would otherwise be available for estate liquidity needs – and vice versa. And in an astounding number of cases, the principal necessary to maintain a given lifestyle is vastly

underestimated, often because of unrealistic assumptions of long-term net-after-tax growth or the actual cost of living at the scale the client and his family wish to maintain.

5. Value and values: Clients need to stabilize and maximize the value of their business and other assets. Clients, who own businesses should build key employee protection into their plans, establish "golden handcuffs" to attract, retain, and retire key employees and use their businesses more effectively to solve personal financial problems. Plans also need to be made to encourage and perpetuate core family values.

6. Excessive transfer costs: Simply put, many clients' families will pay a severe – and needless price – for the inaction of senior family members. The difference between an "I love you – all to my spouse" will and the use of a well-designed bypass and marital trust combination can sometimes be measured in millions of dollars of senseless federal estate tax payments. This is true even with the portability rules discussed in greater detail in Chapter 18.

7. Special problems: Clients must not overlook the extreme importance of planning for the spouse or child who cannot, should not, or does not want to, handle a family business or large investment portfolio, or for a physically handicapped or emotionally or mentally troubled spouse or child. Satisfying the desire to give back and to enrich and support charity is also often a strong planning need.

1.4 WHO NEEDS ESTATE PLANNING?

More sophisticated planning than a simple will is indicated for:

1. Individuals with estates exceeding the unified credit exemption equivalent (applicable exclusion). Currently, the federal estate, gift, and generation skipping tax exemptions are all $12,920,000 (for 2023, with such amounts being adjusted annually for inflation). Most clients will not have assets of a sufficient level to have to do a lot of planning to reduce or pay tax on gift, estate, or generation-skipping transfers. The planning considerations will begin for those clients who are close to the amount of the exemption. As your assets begin to exceed the estate tax exemption, it will be important to consider the extent to which you want to implement a traditional credit shelter arrangement, or to rely on the estate tax portability provisions. This is the point where more sophisticated estate tax planning starts to become warranted.

2. Individuals in combined state and federal income tax brackets in excess of 15 percent.

3. People with:

   a. Children who are minors.

   b. Children (or spouses or other dependents) who are exceptionally artistic or intellectually gifted or otherwise are expected to have their own wealth.

   c. Children (or spouses or other dependents) who are emotionally or mentally challenged, emotionally disturbed, or physically handicapped.

   d. Spouses (or children or other dependents) who can't, or don't want to, handle money, securities, or a business.

   e. Closely held business interests.

   f. Property in more than one state or persons who often move from state to state.

   g. Charitable objectives.

   h. Special property such as fine art, a coin, gun, or stamp collection.

   i. Pets that are particularly important to them.

   j. Asset protection concerns of heirs.

4. Nonresident aliens, resident aliens, aliens about to move to the U.S., individuals considering expatriation, and U.S. citizens with property interests in foreign countries. (See Chapter 72.)

1.5 THE MOST COMMON ESTATE PLANNING MISTAKES

(And How to Avoid Them)

This entire commentary is devoted to the types of problems that can cost you and your family dearly in terms of dollars and unbelievable heartache. Since it would be a shame to have to learn from your own mistakes, this commentary is dedicated to the wise man (and woman) who can profit from the lessons so many have expensively learned the hard way.

Here are a number of areas of common (and serious) mistakes that can be easily solved with the assistance of a financial services professional. While the following is addressed to clients, financial services professionals should be on the lookout for these common mistakes and periodically review clients' plans accordingly.

Mistake 1: Improper Use of Jointly-Held Property

If used excessively or by the wrong parties (especially by unmarried individuals, or where one spouse is not a United States citizen) the otherwise "poor man's will" becomes a poor will for an otherwise good man or woman. In short, jointly held property can become a nightmare of unexpected tax and nontax problems including:

A. When property is titled jointly, there is the potential for both federal and state gift tax, particularly with non-spouses and non-citizen spouses.

B. There is the possibility of double federal estate taxation; if the joint ownership is between individuals other than spouses, the entire property will be taxed in the estate of the first joint owner to die – except to the extent the survivor can prove contribution to the property. Then, whatever the survivor receives and does not consume or give away will be included (and taxed a second time) in the survivor's gross estate. With non-citizen spouses, the typical rules associated with the marital deduction do not apply, and the client may need to utilize a Qualified Domestic Trust (QDOT) to avoid the immediate imposition of the federal estate tax. See Chapter 72 for a further discussion of the QDOT.

C. Once jointly owned property with right of survivorship has passed to the survivor, the provisions of the decedent's will are ineffective. This means the property is left outright to the survivor who is then without the benefit of management protection or investment advice or the property could be left to a person not intended to be benefited.

D. Even when property is jointly owned by spouses, the surviving spouse can give away or at death leave the formerly jointly owned property to anyone the surviving spouse wants; regardless of the desires of the deceased spouse. In other words, holding property jointly results in a total loss of control at the first death since the surviving spouse can completely ignore (and in fact may not know) the decedent's wishes as to the ultimate disposition of the property. Whether this is an issue depends upon the specific facts of the situation. However, this loss of control can be especially horrendous when the joint owners are not related or are clearly not in agreement as to the ultimate recipient of the property.

E. Since the jointly held property passes directly to the survivor (who then could possibly squander, gamble, give away, or lose the property to creditors), the decedent's executor could be faced with a lack of adequate cash to pay estate taxes and other settlement expenses. By the same token, since joint assets pass directly to the survivor, it is important to keep in mind how the taxes associated with these assets are to be allocated among the other beneficiaries of the estate. It is entirely possible that the joint assets can pass to one person, and the taxes associated with these assets be charged to another.

F. A well-drawn estate plan is designed to avoid double taxation – often by passing at least a portion of the estate into a CEBT (Credit Equivalent Bypass Trust). In this manner, up to $12,920,000 in 2023, can be sheltered from federal estate tax at both the first decedent's death and then again (since the surviving spouse has only an income interest) escape estate tax at the death of the surviving spouse. But holding property in joint tenancy thwarts that objective. Instead of going to a bypass trust to avoid a second tax, the property goes directly to the survivor and will be taxed at the survivor's death. So the unified credit of the first spouse to die is wasted. See Chapter 13 related to disclaimers whereby with some difficulty, a planner may be able to fix the problem after death. In addition, see Chapter 18 discussing portability, where in some cases this problem can be overcome even if property is held jointly.

G Some clients title assets in joint names in order to increase the FDIC insurance limitations. This occurs because FDIC insurance provides for $250,000 of protection for each owner on an account at that particular financial institution.[1] Therefore, by titling assets in joint names, the amount of the protection is increased. However, by titling assets in joint names, these assets are bypassing the provisions of the estate documents, which can create other problems.

Mistake 2: Improperly Arranged Life Insurance

A. The proceeds of life insurance are often payable to a beneficiary at the wrong time (before that person is emotionally, physically, or legally capable of handling it) or in the wrong manner (outright instead of being paid over a period of years or paid into trust).

B. There is inadequate insurance on the life of the key person in a family (the breadwinner) or the key person in a corporation (the rainmaker).

C. Often, no contingent (backup) beneficiary has been named. The "Rule of Two" should be applied here. In every dispositive document (any legal instrument that will transfer property at death) there should be – for every name in the document – at least two backups. So, whenever possible, there should be not only back-up beneficiaries but also contingent executors, trustees, guardians, and trust protectors.

D. The proceeds of the policy are includable in the gross estate of the insured because the policy was owned by the insured and either never transferred, or it was transferred within three years of the insured's death. The solution is to have a responsible financially competent adult beneficiary (or a trust), acting without specific direction from the insured and using his (or its) own money, purchase and own the insurance from its inception. That party should also be named beneficiary (the insured and the insured's estate should not be named beneficiary).

E. When the policy owner of a policy on the life of another names a third party as beneficiary, at the death of the insured, the proceeds are treated as a gift to the beneficiary from the policy owner. For example, if a wife purchases a policy on her husband's life but names her children as beneficiaries, at the husband's death she is making a gift in the amount of the proceeds to the children.

F. If a corporation names someone other than itself (or its creditor) as the beneficiary of insurance on the life of a key employee, when the proceeds are paid, the IRS will argue that the proceeds are not income tax free and should be treated as either dividends, if paid to or on behalf of a shareholder, or compensation, if paid to an employee who is not a shareholder (assuming the premiums were never reported as income or there was no split dollar agreement or no Table 2001 income reported). Worse yet, if the insured owned more than 50 percent of the corporation's stock, he is deemed to have incidents of ownership (that means federal estate tax inclusion of the proceeds) in the policy on his life. So, for example, the same $1,000,000 proceeds could be taxed as a dividend for income tax purposes (as much as $396,000 of income tax for those in the highest tax bracket and also be taxed as an asset in the estate for estate tax purposes (as much as $400,000 of estate tax).

G. Whenever life insurance is paid to the insured's estate, it is needlessly subjected to the claims of the insured's creditors and in many states unnecessarily subjected to state inheritance tax costs. Probate costs are increased without reason and the proceeds are then subjected to the potential for an attack on the will or an election against the will. Although, in some rare cases, it may make sense for the estate to be named beneficiary of a modest amount of life insurance (e.g., an amount sufficient to pay estimated debts in an estate small enough to pay no federal estate tax), in most estate planning situations life insurance should be payable only to a named beneficiary, a trust, or a business entity.

H. If a life insurance policy – or any interest in a life insurance policy – is transferred for any kind of valuable consideration in money or money's worth, the proceeds may lose their income tax free status. For example, if a child buys the $1,000,000 term insurance policy owned on her father's life from his corporation or business partner, when she receives the proceeds, the entire $1,000,000 could be subjected to ordinary income tax. These rules are usually described as the transfer for value rules with respect to life insurance, and they are set forth in Code section 101(a)(2).

I. Where a husband is required by a divorce decree or separation agreement to purchase or maintain insurance on his life, he will receive no income tax deduction for premium payments if he owns the policy – even if his ex-wife is named as irrevocable beneficiary. No alimony deduction is allowed on the cash values in a policy the husband is required to transfer to his ex-wife under a divorce decree. The safest way to assure a deduction is for the husband to increase his tax deductible alimony and for the ex-wife to purchase new insurance on his life, which she owns and on which she is the beneficiary. It is extremely important for each spouse recently divorced to immediately review his own life, health, disability, and other insurance situation.

J. Failing to update beneficiary designation to reflect changes to the estate planning documents. If an individual names his estate as the beneficiary of life insurance policies, the manner in which the money is disbursed is automatically updated as the will is changed. However, when an individual maintains a revocable living trust, it is important to check if the beneficiary designation needs updating as the document is changed. For example, with a new will, the document will almost assuredly revoke all prior wills. But this is not the case with revocable trusts. If an insurance policy is paid to a particular revocable trust, it will be paid to that Trust even if the document is "abandoned" in favor of a new document. Therefore, when life insurance is paid to a revocable trust, it is better to make amendments to that Trust so that the beneficiary designation has a lesser chance of requiring updating. The problem with this approach is that if a person makes a lot of changes to their documents, you can wind up with a lot of amendments. At some point, it may make sense to truly start over with a new Trust; but when doing so, make sure all beneficiary designations are updated.

Mistake 3: Lack of Liquidity

A. Most people don't have the slightest idea of how much it will cost to settle their estates or how quickly the taxes and other expenses must be paid. Worse yet, they don't realize that a forced (and, possibly, fire) sale of their most precious assets, highest income producing property, or loss of control of their family business will result from an insufficiency of cash. (If you haven't checked, how do you know your executor will have enough cash to avoid a forced sale?)

B. Liquidity demands have increased significantly in the last few years and should be revisited by those who have not done a "what if ..." hypothetical probate. Among the expenses that demand cash from the estate's executor are:

- Federal estate taxes
- State death taxes
- Federal income taxes (including taxes on pension distributions)
- State income taxes (including taxes on pension distributions)
- Probate and administration costs
- Payment of maturing debts
- Maintenance and welfare of family
- Payment of specific cash bequests
- Funds to continue operation of family business, meet payroll and inventory costs, recruit replacement personnel, and pay for mistakes while new management is learning the business
- Generation-skipping transfer tax (top estate tax rate)

Most larger estates will be subjected to almost all of these taxes and costs.

Mistake 4: Choice of the Wrong Executor

A. Naming the wrong people to administer the estate can be disastrous. The person who administers the estate must – with dispatch – often without compensation, with great personal financial risk, and without conflict of interest:

- Collect all assets
- Pay all obligations
- Distribute the remaining assets to beneficiaries

Although this three step process seems simple, in reality these tasks are highly complex, time consuming, and, in some cases, technically demanding. Is the named executor capable of carrying out these tasks?

B. Selection of a beneficiary as an executor can result in a conflict of interest. That person may be forced to choose between his personal interest and that of the other beneficiaries. This problem can potentially be solved by adding an independent third party, such as a bank trust department, to serve alone or together with a family member.

C. Selection of a business associate may result in a conflict of interest. If the executor's job is to decide whether or not to sell the business interest or the task is to obtain the highest possible sales price, the executor will be responsible for the course of action that will best serve the beneficiaries' interests. Yet that may be diametrically opposed to the executor's personal interest. For example, if the business were to be sold, the executor may be selling himself out of a job. As such, the executor may demand a higher price for the business than he would expect a buyer to pay in order to discourage the business from being sold.

D. Sometimes the selected executor has neither the time nor the inclination to devote to the sometimes long and drawn out process of estate administration.

E. Another consideration is whether the executor lives in the state of the testator. This can become a problem in a state such as Florida (where the executor is referred to as the Personal Representative). In Florida, the Personal Representative must be a resident, or a close family member.

F. The appointment of executors who do not know, or get along well with, the family members they are to serve sometimes results in chaos. A similar problem can occur if more than one executor is chosen and the executors do not get along with each other.

Mistake 5: Will Errors

A. One of the greatest mistakes is dying without a valid will. This results in "intestacy," which is another way of saying that the state will force its own will upon the heirs it chooses.

B. Too many wills have not been updated. A will should be reviewed at least:

- At the birth, adoption, or death of a child
- Upon the marriage, divorce, or separation of anyone named in the will
- Upon every major tax law change
- Upon a move of the testator to a new state
- On a significant change in income or wealth of either the testator or a beneficiary
- On any major change in the needs, circumstances, or objectives of the testator or the beneficiaries

Mistake 6: Leaving Everything to Your Spouse

A. Far too many people feel that there will be no federal estate tax because of the unlimited estate tax marital deduction and so they leave their entire estates to their spouses. But upon the death of the surviving spouse, everything that the surviving spouse received (assuming it has not been consumed or given away) is then piled on top of the assets that spouse owns. It is then that the "second death wallop" occurs with federal estate tax starting on taxable amounts in excess of $12,920,000 in 2023. The solution can be simple: the establishment of a CEBT (credit equivalent bypass trust). Up to $12,920,000 in 2023 can be left to a trust that provides income to the surviving spouse as well as other financial security, but it will not be taxed in his estate no matter when he dies or no matter how large trust funds grow. The balance of the estate can go in trust or outright to the surviving spouse. If that amount together with the surviving spouse's own assets doesn't exceed the unified credit applicable exclusion amount for the survivor's year of death, this portion will also pass estate tax free when the surviving spouse dies. This is good planning even though the unused credit shelter amount of a spouse may be used by the survivor under the deceased spouses unused exclusion amount rules. For reasons discussed in Chapters 18 and 63, there may be technical issues with multiple marriages, lost opportunities, and lost generation skipping opportunities if property is held jointly with right of survivorship or left entirely to the surviving spouse, which makes the standard credit shelter planning still the best way to go for many taxpayers.[2]

B. Some individuals leave huge amounts outright to a surviving spouse, amounts that neither they nor their spouse have never managed on their own. (Few people have ever successfully managed huge amounts of assets, let alone successfully managed a spouse.) Often the surviving spouse doesn't have the slightest training or experience in handling and investing a large stock portfolio, real estate holdings, or running a family business.

C. Leaving everything to a spouse also wastes an opportunity to skip generations and potentially save future generations significant taxes.

Mistake 7: Improper Disposition of Assets

A. An improper disposition of assets occurs whenever the wrong asset goes to the wrong person in the wrong manner or at the wrong time. Leaving an entire estate to a surviving spouse or leaving a large or complex estate outright to a spouse unprepared or unwilling to handle it is a good example. Leaving a sizeable estate outright to a teenager or to an emotionally or mentally challenged person are also common examples.

B. Equal but inequitable distributions are common. If an estate is divided equally among four children who have drastically different income or capital needs, an equal distribution can be very unfair. Consider, for example, four children, the oldest of which is a brilliant and financially successful medical doctor and the youngest of which has serious learning disabilities and is still in junior high school. Think of a family with a physically handicapped child and three healthy children with no physical problems. Obviously, their needs and circumstances are not the same. Should each child receive an equal share? The proper solution may be a "sprinkle" or spray provision in a trust that empowers the trustee to provide extra income or additional principal to a child that needs or deserves more or who is in an unusually low income tax bracket in a given year.

C. Obvious examples of improper dispositions include the gift of a high powered sports car to a child, or to a senior citizen who no longer drives. "That can't happen in my estate," many people would be tempted to say. But upon the death of a primary beneficiary at the same time or soon after the testator, quite often there is no secondary beneficiary named, or the second beneficiary who is named shouldn't receive the asset in the same manner as the primary beneficiary. The solution is to consider a trust or custodial arrangements and to provide in the will or other dispositive instruments for young children and legally incompetent people. Consider also the importance of a well-planned "common disaster" or "simultaneous death" provision, so that the asset avoids needless second probates and double inheritance taxes and goes to the right person in the right manner.

Mistake 8: Failure to Stabilize and Maximize Value

A. Many business owners have not stabilized the value of their businesses in the event of the disability or death of key personnel. What economic "shock absorbers" have been put in place to cushion the blow caused if a key employee dies, becomes permanently disabled, or is lured away by competition at the absolutely worst possible time? Who will pay for the fixed expenses of the practice or business if the key employee is not there to generate income? Key employee life and disability insurance, coupled with good business overhead coverage, will certainly help.

B. Buy-sell agreements are essential to a business that is to survive the death of one of its owners. Yet many businesses have no such agreement. Or the agreement isn't in writing. Or the price (or price setting mechanism) doesn't reflect the current value of the business. Or the agreement isn't properly funded. So there is no guarantee that the heirs will receive the price they are entitled to – or no assurance that the surviving owners will have the cash they need to buy out the heirs (especially the dissident ones who want to tell them how to run their company).

C. Wills, trusts, life insurance contracts, qualified plans, IRAs, and tax deferred annuities without "backup" beneficiaries mean that money that could otherwise pass outside of the probate estate may instead be subjected unnecessarily to such costs and risks. The value of all those instruments and wealth transfer tools can be enhanced at no cost by merely naming secondary beneficiaries. It can also be a problem to name a minor child as the direct beneficiary of an asset. Since a minor cannot legally own assets, this may result in needing to have a guardian appointed for the minor child to help manage these assets. The guardian may have to be someone other than the minor's parent. The solution to this problem is to make sure that beneficiary designations are properly coordinated with the estate plan.

Mistake 9: Lack of Adequate Records

A. It can drive your executor crazy – and cost thousands of dollars of expenses – if estate and financial documents are difficult or impossible to find. Too many people hide assets such as cash in books or drawers, or even under mattresses. Take out a safe deposit box. Tell your executor where it is and make sure your executor has or can get the key and has access to it. Put all your important documents in that box. Each year, put an updated list of the names, phone numbers, and e-mail addresses of advisors your family can count on in the box. Check with your attorney on the rules that apply at death: some safe deposit boxes are frozen (the state requires that the bank seal the box from entry until the inheritance tax examiner can inventory the contents) and there can be lengthy delays in getting to the papers in the box. It is also advisable to maintain a personal inventory of important information such as account information; and insurance policy schedules.

B. It is possible for an executor to obtain new copies of old income tax returns from the IRS – but why put the executor to the trouble and expense? Be sure to keep tax returns and records at least six years.

C. Many survivors have never been told what the decedent's goals were, what assets they can rely on for income or capital needs, or how best to utilize the available resources. Most widows or surviving children never had a meaningful discussion with the decedent about their financial security if…

Mistake 10: Lack of a "Master Strategy" Game Plan

A. Do-it-yourself estate and financial planning is the closest thing to do-it-yourself brain surgery. Few people can do it successfully. Yet, even do-it-yourself planning – from taking courses, reading books, or listening to radio shows on the subject – is sometimes preferable to no planning. Actually, an intelligent layman can learn and do quite a bit if the time is taken at least once a year to quantify in dollar terms financial needs and objectives (here's what we must have and here's what we'd like to have), current financial status (here's where we are), and a game plan for getting to the goal in the most efficient and effective way. Using the right team of CPA, attorney, life insurance agent, trust officer, and other financial services professionals to conduct an annual "Financial Firedrill" to help formulate and execute that plan can make all the difference.

Mistake No. 11: Failure to Complete and Implement Estate Plan[3]

A. The best estate plan ever devised is worthless if it is not completed and implemented. This seems rather self-evident, many people walk around with incomplete estate plans. In other words, these people have started the estate-planning process but have not purchased the necessary life insurance, signed wills or trusts, or otherwise put their estate plans into effect. Estate planners must accept a part of the blame for this resistance; perhaps the documents and explanations were not sufficiently clear to give the client confidence that this estate plan was right for them or impressed them with the urgency and significance of action. Some estate planners are better at persuading clients to finish their estate plans than others. Many clients blithely say mañana and have done nothing at all but think about estate planning without coming to any conclusions. Too often, tomorrow comes earlier than anticipated.

B. Estate planning is a matter of inertia: Once the client starts, the client needs to keep going until it is finished. Unfortunately, we see an inordinately high number of blended family estate plans go uncompleted. It is suspected that this is because some tough choices have to be made that require forthright communication.

Mistake No. 12: Failure to Provide Complete and Accurate Information to Estate Planners

A. It is axiomatic that clients must provide complete and accurate information to their estate planners. However, the simple fact is that many people neglect, withhold or refuse to turn over key pieces of information that, had the estate planner been apprised of that information, would have changed the advice or recommendations given. The estate planner should maintain a healthy skepticism about the information that the client gives to them. Is it *all* of the material information?

B. Why would someone intentionally withhold important information? Perhaps the client thinks that the information is too embarrassing or will give too much financial information that will alert the taxing authorities. Perhaps the client does not trust the estate planner enough. Whatever the reason, it is the wrong approach because it has been our experience that all of the information comes out after the client is dead. Just like you cannot take your property with you when you die, you can rarely take everything you know about your affairs to your grave and bury it, especially if it affects someone still living. We also see a higher than average number of blended family estate plans fail due to withheld information, and we suspect that some of this is due to a number of different factors, including the following:

- There may not be enough trust and transparency between two partners who choose to use only one estate planner.

- The complexities of the estate-planning process get the couple bogged down, and they choose what they believe is "enough" information as a way to try to streamline the process instead of digging up all the information and data that is needed.

- There may be sufficient shame and guilt about past choices and decisions that have one or both partners unwilling or unable to openly share all their sordid details with their advisors.

- The estate planners may not have asked enough of the right questions in the right manner and at the right time.

C. The individuals may not know what to do about aspects of their estates so they end up not talking about it because they do not know where to begin.

Mistake No. 13: Failure to Coordinate Estate Plan

A. People often try to do piecemeal estate planning (e.g., a life insurance policy here, a will there) but have no coordinated estate plan. Here is an example of a failure to properly plan in a coordinated way. Suppose the clients' wills are drafted to pay estate tax at either death, but their life insurance policy is a second-to-die life insurance policy, which does not pay its benefits until *both* insured parties die. Another example of failure to properly coordinate is an elaborate will structure in an estate where most of the value of the estate passes via a beneficiary designation or via joint tenancy. A client's estate planning documents need to be coordinated with all of the client's other estate-planning, whether it's life insurance, lifetime trusts, retirement plans or buy-sell agreements. It is imperative that all of this estate planning be coordinated.

Mistake No. 14: Failure to Communicate about Estate Plan

A. It may not be evident exactly why communication of estate-planning intentions with a client's loved ones is so important, but our experience and research has shown us unquestionably that it is. The research from Roy Williams and Vic Preisser in their book *Preparing Heirs* claimed that the number one reason why 70 percent of estate plans fail is "lack of communication and trust" among family members as it related to the family's wealth, assets, finances and estate plan.

B. Family members and perhaps others have expectations about inheritance from the client, whether or not they should. When these expectations are not met after the client's death, many of them leap to some conclusions that may not be true and they may take some actions that were unnecessary. These actions can run the gamut from challenging the estate plan in court to simply cutting off communication with certain family members that are perceived to be "on the other side."

Example. The estate planner probably has had very wealthy and powerful clients break down and cry in their offices when telling them that they did not receive an equal share of their parents' estates — even in situations where the beneficiary clients were several times wealthier than their parents. Their conclusion: Their parents did not *love* them as much as the other children, as if the relative inheritances of the children was the barometer of the parent's love for each child. Had these parents simply told these clients either during their lifetime or by a letter at death (or inclusion in a will or living trust) what their reasons for the amounts or terms of the bequests were, the clients might not have been left for years wondering why their parents did what they did. One simple communication could have staved off years of, not only heartbreak, but possible resentment of their siblings, neither of which the parents probably intended.

C. Other possible unnecessary actions that people take after a person's death include resenting some or all of the receivers of power or property as well as litigation in contesting or simply prolonging the matter. We firmly believe that good communication can prevent or at least minimize these types of actions by reducing animosity and creating buy-in with all family members so that everyone is clear about what to expect at the time of the client's death.

D. When we say communication, we mean exactly that. The clients do not have to ask their loved ones for their input, although we have found that – at least the solicitation of some limited input – is a good idea in many cases. The clients' estate plans are theirs alone. It does not have to be a democracy. However, communicating *why* the clients are doing what they are doing in their estate plans can prevent broken relationships after their death as well as costly litigation where no one wins but the lawyers. In blended families, because of the complexity and tenuousness of some relationships to begin with, communication is even more encouraged because, again, more blended family estate plans seem to fail on this score. Communication can be made during the client's lifetime or shortly after the client's death. It can be in writing, recorded, or merely oral. The big thing is to just encourage clients to do it.

E. The estate planner may have experienced pushback from clients when they enthusiastically encouraged communication. Some clients thought that it was simply none of their heirs' business. Others were scared at the prospect of confrontation. However, after relating some horror stories of the things that can happen if they do not communicate the reason for the estate-planning decisions, the overwhelming majority did so, and most of them actually found the experience to be pleasant and gave them significant peace of mind. We also have seen that with a few key strategies to effectively open up a sense of safety in the communication process, couples learn things during the process that they were unaware of that had them re-evaluate and adjust their estate planning in ways that worked even better for all concerned.

Mistake No. 15: Incomplete or Incorrect Beneficiary Designations

A. It cannot be said too much that deficient or even missing beneficiary designations are the culprits for many failed estate plans. Too often, people do not give a lot of thought to the ramifications of their decisions about beneficiaries of life insurance, retirement plans, tax deferred annuities and IRAs, even though these constitute the majority of the wealth of most people. The beneficiary designation forms often are hurriedly completed without a lot of thought. The first step is to gather up all of the beneficiary designations that are on file with the company or plan provider. One cannot work from memory here.

B. Estate planners have experienced some horror stories where companies lost the original beneficiary forms, which caused some serious and unfortunate chaos. Or the beneficiary designations had not been reviewed for years and a named beneficiary has died (without a back-up being named), the client no longer wants that person as beneficiary, the beneficiary no longer needs the wealth, or the beneficiary is no longer married to or is estranged from the client.

C. After gathering all of the client's beneficiary designations, the estate planner needs to sit down with the client and coordinate their beneficiary designations with their overall estate plans. Clients also should also have contingent beneficiary designations in case the original beneficiary dies before they do or disclaims the interest. The client needs to spell out with specificity what is to happen if, for example, one of their beneficiaries dies but leaves children. Who gets that share? The surviving beneficiaries (which is what most plans provide)? Or do the children of the predeceased beneficiary, who often are grandchildren, get the share? There should always be not one but two or more tiers of "back-up" beneficiaries – including perhaps a charity.

Example. Suppose that Bill has three sons, Moe, Larry, and Curly and Moe dies before Bill.

Moe has a son, Shemp. When Bill dies, it is discovered that he has not changed his beneficiary designation to reflect Moe's death. What happens to Moe's share? Is it simply divided between Moe's surviving brothers, Larry and Curly, or does Shemp step in and take Moe's share? Bill's beneficiary form should describe his intentions in this regard, or the terms of the retirement plan will govern. The bottom line: Discover and specify what the client wants to have happen in given contingencies, and do not leave it to chance.

D. The client must give this significant thought and seek competent professional advice with these matters. As is the case with most of estate planning, this is not a do-it-yourself task. Unfortunately, blended family estate plans are more deficient in this area than most, again because of the complexity and often torn and highly emotionally charged agendas with yours, mine, and ours to look after.

Mistake No. 16: Failure to Keep Estate Plan Current

A. Even the best estate plans can go stale if not revisited regularly, sometimes it is due to law changes. Usually, though, it is due to life and business changes – both of the client and client's partner – and in the life or lives of the beneficiaries. In blended families, we have seen many situations where a *former* partner received a large share of the deceased partner's estate (i.e., the decedent), life insurance, or retirement plans because the decedent failed to update the estate plan after the separation. Some jurisdictions have laws that automatically drop a spouse as an heir (and also a personal representative) on divorce, but these laws may not apply to life insurance or retirement plans unless the statute specifically covers those assets.[4] In the case of qualified retirement plans, such a state law is probably preempted by federal ERISA law.[5] However, these laws only apply to married partners. Unmarried partners who separate are at a greater risk of having a former partner share in their estates without affirmative action on their part to change their estate plans on a split.

Mistake No. 17: Elections against a Will

A. This section applies to legally married partners only. It is especially relevant for those spouses who cannot agree on how to divide the estate in ways that feel fair to both of them. Depending on the client's jurisdiction, a surviving spouse may be able to claim rights in up to one-half of the client's estate unless that right has been properly waived in a valid marriage contract. The client will have to ask their estate-planning attorney the ins and outs of this area (e.g., how much the spouse can get, how he or she can get it, and what is covered in the estate that is potentially exposed to a spousal election). It also is imperative that the client get good advice from an expert in marriage contracts, since these often are challenged at death if, at the time of the marital agreement, there was not full and fair disclosure of the deceased spouse's assets, the parties were not represented by separate counsel and the surviving spouse does not get what he or she expects or thinks that he or she deserves.

Mistake No. 18: Post-Death Will and Trust Challenges

A. Few things delay the administration of an estate longer than post-death challenges to the estate plan. As we have discussed at several points in this book, it has been the estate planner's experience that a significant amount of post-death challenges almost always arise from a failure to meet the suing person's expectations of inheritance. However, there are some people who, out of pure spite, will challenge an estate, will or trust. The estate planner sees far more of both categories in blended family situations.

B. The vast majority of post-death challenges fall into two basic categories:

1. Challenges based on a claim that the decedent was not in his or her right mind when he or she made his or her estate plan.

2. A claim that someone unduly influenced the decedent to make the estate plan the way that it was made.

C. It is the latter category that more blended family estate planners have to be concerned about due to the frequency of discord between stepparents and stepchildren. This is one reason why many partners in blended families choose to do their estate planning independently of each other and their children. While this choice may cause the "undue influence" cause to be seen as unfounded, it does not preclude a disgruntled heir from suing anyway. As shown already, in addition to well-considered and drafted pre-relational agreements, effective communication before death to temper expectations often is the key to mitigating litigation in the end.

Mistake No. 19: Too Much Joint-Tenancy Property

A. Joint tenancy can be the prime enemy of estate plans because property that is titled as joint tenants automatically passes to the surviving joint tenant on the death of the first joint tenant to die, irrespective of the deceased joint tenant's will or trust. In situations where this may not be the client's intention, or if it conflicts with what the client's other estate planning documents provide, it will override them and they become irrelevant where those assets are concerned. This is why it is imperative to review the titles to all real estate and accounts and the latest beneficiary designations in life insurance and retirement plans. In the estate planner's judgment, it could be negligent to fail to do so during the estate planning process.

Mistake No. 20: Failure to Properly Plan for Disability

A. Just because the client has a living trust or a property power of attorney does not mean that the client is adequately prepared for disability. It is important that the power of attorney document, especially if it is a springing power of attorney, clearly describe a procedure for "springing" the power of attorney into effect. The same thing is true for the activation of a successor trustee in a living trust. If the document does not do that, the client's loved ones may have to go to court to open a conservatorship or guardianship and having to incur that expense and time delay. Additionally, if the client has a revocable living trust, the property power of attorney and the revocable living trust must be coordinated with each other.

Mistake No. 21: Overfunding of the Marital Deduction Portion

A. If the client has to worry about the federal estate tax and is married, overfunding what effectively passes to the surviving spouse could cause the client to underutilize the client's $12,920,000 (in 2023) estate-tax applicable exclusion amount. Of course, the new law of portability, which allows spouses to transfer unused estate-tax exemptions to the surviving spouse, may save the day, although the law of portability has a number of traps for the unwary. One of the biggest traps is what happens if the surviving spouse remarries; this law is somewhat complicated. We believe that it is strongly advisable for married partners in blended family relationships to each utilize separately their respective estate-tax applicable exclusions because their families often are different.

Mistake No. 22: Relying on Someone to Do the "Right Thing"

A. Believe it or not, there is a good percentage of people who simply wish to leave it up to someone else to determine who gets what out of their estates. For example, they leave their estates to their partners or to one of their children with nonbinding instructions as to how they wish the estate to be divided. Most of the time, these people truly believe that the designated person will do "the right thing" and divide the estate either equally amongst their heirs, or that they will know and do what the person wanted them to do with the property and simply follow those directions. Sadly, this rarely happens, so the designated person often ends up keeping (and sometimes then losing to creditors or a divorcing spouse) the entire estate. This type of attitude can be particularly dangerous in blended families since there is less incentive for the designated person, be it a child from a prior relationship or a surviving partner, to share property with their stepfamily. In the estate planner's experience, the "happy ever after" expected, rarely happens.

The Bottom Line

A. A key principle in estate planning is that *you can't eliminate the big mistakes in your estate plan until you've identified them.* Every family (and single person) – every year – should stage a "financial firedrill." Become informed. Educate yourself now. Educate your survivors – before they *are* the survivors! Teach them how to handle money and make decisions. Show them, by example, how to read the bottom line on where their financial security stands.

B. A "financial firedrill" means that, with the assistance of competent financial services professionals, you annually measure your needs. Establish an order of priorities and then develop and put into effect plans to make certain that you are on target to meet your financial security needs.

1.6 WHAT ARE SOME COMMON ESTATE PLANNING GOALS?

The first step in the estate-planning process is identifying what the client wants to accomplish--their estate planning goals. This step often befuddles people, and they almost always ask: What do other people in our situation do? It is not that easy. Every family is different, especially blended families.

In order to help the client along, we have included a laundry list of possible estate-planning goals for the client to consider, many in the context of a blended family. These potential goals are not in any particular order. Many of these goals can conflict with one another. A client will not have all of these goals either. The following sections are intended to give you some idea of possible goals and concerns so that you can have the client consider all of the possibilities. The clients also may even have a goal that is not discussed here, so it is important to include a "catch-all" blank for them to consider.

1. **Retain control over assets and business and health care decisions.**

First and foremost, most people want to retain control over their lives and their property as long as they possibly can, and they decide who will be in control when they are no longer capable or want to do so. The goal of control is a particularly important one in estate planning for the blended family because there are people whose interests can be widely divergent (e.g., children from a prior relationship and a current partner) and who are (or who seem to be) vying for that job. Therefore, a carefully thought out durable power of attorney, provisions for backup trustees for those who use revocable living trusts, and advance health-care directives are a must, even more so in the blended family.

If the client owns a business, the estate planner may also want to pay very close attention to the corporate documents to see what they provide regarding succession in offices. Failure to coordinate business documents with estate-planning documents can ruin or negatively affect the estate plan.

Example. If the client is being paid a salary by their company and becomes disabled, will the client's salary continue to be paid, and, if so, for how long? Who will make that determination? Who will succeed the client in their office in the company if the client is unable to serve? Will it be a child of the client, who may be adverse to their stepparent? Can the new person in charge fire someone in the client's family, such as a child? These and others are all very critical questions that need to be answered in advance of disability.

2. **Provide support for children and the surviving partner.**

Providing support for children and the surviving partner is not as easy to achieve in a blended family for many reasons, not the least of which could be conflicts between children, stepchildren and the surviving partner. Many people have a goal of wanting to provide support either for a period of time or through an endeavor such as the education of a minor child. The goal of providing support to someone in a blended family can conflict with other estate-planning goals, such as giving your children an inheritance. For instance, the client might want to provide lifetime support to the client's partner (who may be depending on it), even if it means that the client's own children must take a back seat and possibly even get nothing from the client. There are no easy answers here. That's why the estate planner and the client really must give this one some serious thought.

Sometimes, there are conflicts between older children, for whom the client already provided an education, and younger children, whose education may not have even started yet. This often is compounded in the blended family situation because the younger children might be with the client's current partner, whereas the client's older children are from a prior relationship. The client may feel obligated to support a child of another union even though their current partner might also need (and expect) support. This situation would clearly be a conflict for the client. However, do not allow these potential or actual conflicts to cause the client to stop or procrastinate on their estate planning; remember, intestacy or an incomplete estate plan is far worse.

OVERVIEW OF ESTATE PLANNING — CHAPTER 1

3. **Protect loved ones from predators and themselves.**

Loved ones who are young or vulnerable may need protection to ensure that their inheritance stays intact and is not reached by creditors or those who would unduly influence them and rob them of their money. In addition, with the high divorce rate, spendthrift trusts (a clause added to a trust that is intended to protect the beneficiaries from their creditors) may help otherwise capable loved ones from the ravages of a divorcing spouse even if they may not otherwise require trust protection.

In a blended family, this goal could be even more important because of the polarization that frequently occurs in these families after the death of a parent partner. Some children are too young or immature to handle responsibility or money. There may also be a child who has special needs that requires management of that child's property. Other instances that suggest the possible need for financial management, via a trust vehicle, are when a child has a drug or alcohol addiction or who has financial problems.

4. **Keep certain property in the family.**

Some families own property that has been in the family for a long time, and others own family businesses that they wish to keep in "*the* family." This requires special planning and can involve buy-sell agreements (discussed in Chapter 47) or co-tenancy arrangements, the latter of which can provide a method of sharing property use, revenues and expenses.

Some estate-planning goals may have to be changed to achieve keeping property in the family as opposed to being sold. This is particularly true when estate or capital gains tax will be owed. In the context of a blended family, this type of property, more often than not, consists of antiques, art, heirlooms or family vacation homes that have been passed down for generations. The estate planner has seen lots of problems and litigation over such assets, even family pictures or other items with little intrinsic value, especially in blended families. Sometimes, it is more important in a blended family to specifically provide who will receive the "emotional assets" (e.g., grandma's silver baby spoon)—which often have more sentimental value than actual value—than it is to provide for the financial assets. People will and do fight each other in court over items of very little marketable value, and this is much more common in blended families.

5. **Protect assets from creditors, lawsuits and undue influence.**

Many people do not consider asset protection to be an estate-planning goal, and a detailed discussion of asset protection is beyond the scope of this book. However, the litigious nature of our society today demands that we consider insuring against many of the risks of life. Life insurance is important, as is property and casualty insurance, including umbrella coverage. The client always should consider insuring against insurable losses (there is no such thing as lawsuit insurance) by using corporations or limited liability companies, or, in some cases, trusts.

In blended families, the risk of undue influence, most notably from the other parent of the stepchildren involved, is even greater than in other families, and trusts can protect the client against changes by others in favor of themselves late in life that the client would have never done on their own.

6. **Avoid probate.**

This may or may not be a reasonable or important goal, depending on where the client resides. The probate process in most jurisdictions has been generally streamlined and is now relatively easy, but there are jurisdictions, such as California, where probate is costly and complex. In fact, in the context of a blended family, we frequently recommend that a client make sure that their estate will go through formal probate because of the scrutiny and supervision that a judge would give. This may seem like radical advice, but it is not. There are lots of situations that require oversight by someone, and often prefer that person be a judge rather than an interested family member who may not have the other member's best interests at heart.

The converse side of probate for blended families – even when the time and expense of probate is relatively small – may be the loss of privacy. It may be important to use trusts, life insurance and other techniques to keep certain dispositions confidential.

7. **Maintain flexibility.**

A key goal in any estate plan, , is to be certain the client's estate plan is flexible enough to "work" in changed circumstances, such as changes to tax laws or relational changes. Frankly, no one really knows what the future will bring. For example, will there even be an estate tax in the United States in the future, and, if so, what are the rules going to be? Sometimes, our desire to retain flexibility outweighs all other estate-planning considerations, particularly in the area of lifetime gifting, which often makes sense in estate planning. Good estate planning documents build in as much flexibility as possible to anticipate reasonably foreseeable events. In a blended family situation, perhaps the couple is planning on having children of their own, which may prime other goals. The use of a trust protector can be very beneficial in this regard to give an estate plan additional flexibility.

8. **Retain access to capital.**

This is no doubt one of the most important goals for clients that unfortunately many estate planners neglect to consider. Estate planners too often over focus on estate-tax reduction. Gifting in any form, whether outright or in trust, causes the loss of access to the capital represented by the gifted property. Many people cannot really afford to part with access to capital, even though they may have a taxable estate.[6]

9. **Make lifetime gifts.**

Another goal may be that the client wants to enjoy the satisfaction of seeing family members and others enjoy gifts during the client's lifetime. The bad thing about transfers at death is that the donor is not around to see the donee enjoy the property. Some people like to see their loved ones enjoy financial security, learn to handle wealth and business decisions, or have a life-time standard of living they might not otherwise have. Such clients therefore often make significant gifts during their lifetimes. In blended families, the desire to make lifetime gifts can cause conflict because someone (e.g., your partner or one of your children, to whom a gift was not made) may be very unhappy that a gift was made for fear that this might work to their detriment.

10. **Transfer future appreciation.**

Maybe the client has property such as real estate or stock in a family business that is expected to appreciate significantly in value, and the client would like to get that property out of their estate before it appreciates and away from the reach of future potential creditors. This is an estate-planning goal for some. There are some very effective estate-planning techniques that can accomplish this, such as Grantor Retained Annuity Trusts (GRATs) or installment sales that are discussed in Chapter 29.

11. **Transfer an opportunity.**

Opportunities for wealth, such as an idea for a new business or a piece of property, often present themselves to a client. For some clients, they would like to transfer that opportunity to a loved one before the opportunity is taken, which keeps the value out of their estate, and they never have to estate plan with that asset.

12. **Move property to grandchildren or more remote descendants.**

Some clients believe that their children are well-provided for, so they are more concerned with benefiting their grandchildren. Some do like to make significant lifetime transfers to grandchildren or great-grandchildren. In blended families, this is definitely an area to discuss and consider how the client wants to plan, as they may have different grandchildren with different needs from prior relationships.

13. **Defer estate or income tax.**

Most clients have a goal to defer estate tax or paying income tax for as long as possible. This often makes no sense when it comes to the estate tax, but many people like to do so anyway because they lack the liquid cash to pay estate tax at the first death. Deferring estate tax can increase the amount of estate tax due when the survivor dies at a time that the federal estate tax has graduated tax rates, which is not the case presently. However, many people see this as the problem for their surviving loved ones.

Income tax deferral usually makes sense unless the client is deferring income into periods where the tax rate will be higher. Income tax deferral most often comes into play in the setting of beneficiary designations and distribution options for retirement plans and IRAs. There are ways to stretch out receipt of benefits from retirement plans and IRAs to maximize the income tax deferral.

14. **Avoid estate tax.**

Needless to say, a goal of most clients is to avoid as much estate tax as possible. The current law provides relatively few breaks from the estate tax. One of those, though, is the special use valuation provision of Code section 2032A. However, this is a very complex provision and only applies to estates that have a heavy concentration of certain types of real estate (e.g., farms and closely held business property). Sometimes, it makes sense to plan to retain that benefit by continuing that use, as opposed to doing something else with the property, such as sell or lease it.

There also is a break by paying estate tax in installments (it usually is due nine months after death) under Code section 6166. This break only applies to estates that have a heavy concentration of closely held business interests or real estate. Often, people lack the cash to pay their estate tax if they died today. Sometimes, it makes sense to plan a client's estate so that it retains the eligibility to pay the estate tax in installments. Of course, when the federal estate tax exclusion is high (i.e., in 2023 it is $12,920,000), very few people have to worry about the US federal estate tax.

15. Avoid gift tax.

For clients who wish to make lifetime gifts, one goal is to generally pay as little gift tax as possible while making the greatest amount of gifts. The federal gift tax contains several handy breaks that the federal estate tax does not have. One of them is the exclusion under Code section 2503(b) for gifts of up to $17,000 (in 2023) to an unlimited number of people, who do not even have to be related to the client. Another is the unlimited exclusion under Code section 2503(e) for transfers made directly to health-care providers or schools for someone else; this allows grandparents to pay for their grandchildren's tuition. It often makes sense for people to use these breaks.

There are some other breaks too. The "biggie," though, is the $12,920,000 applicable exclusion amount for gifts made during 2023. The client can use this exclusion during lifetime or at death. There are possibly more benefits to using it during your lifetime if the client can afford it. The biggest advantage to lifetime use is that all of the income and growth in value of the gifted property is out of your estate. This also is the downside: The client will no longer have that property in case the client needs it later in life.

16. Maximize usage of estate tax exclusions.

It almost always makes sense – if the client is sufficiently wealth – to fully use the $12,920,000 applicable exclusion amount (in 2023), which can be used either during lifetime or at death. Use of this exclusion usually is a goal for most people once they are aware that it can keep their estates from being subject to the estate tax.

17. Donate to favorite charities.

Some people have an estate-planning goal to make significant transfers to their favorite charities. There are estate-planning techniques that assist in facilitating charitable pursuits that are discussed in Chapters 37-39.

18. Achieve tax predictability or finality.

If the client is risk averse, it is important to discuss tax predictability and finality with the client at the outset. Some estate planning techniques are riskier than others, while others are very risk averse. These people are not interested in estate-planning techniques that create any form of risk of running afoul of the taxman. This is similar to a risk assessment that one would do for investments. It is important at the beginning of the estate-planning process for the client to tell their estate planner the client's estate planning risk sensitivity. Of course, some people want the most aggressive estate plan they can get, and these are available.

19. Provide tax-deferred diversification.

The estates of many people hold a significant part of their value in one or two assets (e.g., a family home or family business). This is an undiversified estate, which is much riskier than a diversified estate because in the undiversified estate, all of the estate's money is tied up in only one asset. As the lesson in an Aesop's Fable says, it is dangerous to put all of one's eggs in one basket because there is no safety net if the value of the asset drops drastically. This is why it frequently is said that wealth is created by non-diversification but retained by diversification.

At some point in their lives, some people want to reduce their risk of non-diversification. The major obstacle for those who desire this is the capital gains tax. There are estate-planning techniques, such as the charitable remainder trust, that permit diversification of assets without having to pay the capital gains tax upfront. In other words, the client can keep a significant part of the tax working for the client.

20. Provide guidance and management for the client's children.

A major goal of estate planning for many is to set up a system to protect loved ones from themselves when they are young or financially challenged. Or give them a way to a soft landing by doling out the money in parts. Trusts and some other estate-planning techniques can do a very good job of this. For example, instead of a child receiving all of their inheritance at once, a trust can be set up to give the inheritance out in "stages" such as a certain amount at age thirty-five, some more at age forty-five with a final distribution at age fifty, with discretion placed in the hands of a trustee to provide additional amounts in the event of emergencies or opportunities – and yet additional amounts that can be demanded by beneficiaries to provide for health, education, maintenance and basic support.

21. Encourage or discourage certain behaviors.

Most clients do not wish to encourage their children to become "trust babies." To the contrary, they want to reward their children for increasing their schooling, doing well in business or in a professional practice and other honest work and discourage them from using trust money to finance their indolence or using their wealth to engaging in unsavory or illegal activity. State law (which varies from state to state) permits people to create "incentive trusts" that give additional money or income to their loved ones for engaging in certain types of positive and productive behavior, such as working in a socially useful but undercompensated field like law enforcement, teaching, or in the not-for-profit sector.

State law, within limits, also may permit delaying or withholding an inheritance to discourage certain types of behavior, such as not working, marrying outside of the family faith (although this one often does not work) or substance abuse. This does not matter to most people, but to those to whom it matters, it seems to matter a lot.

We harbor mixed feelings about these types of clauses, and usually we sometimes counsel against their use because, in the estate planner's opinion, they often are inflexible, and there may be much better alternatives to achieve the same effective result. For example, a fully discretionary trust with some parameters can be very helpful in this regard.

22. Level the playing field.

In many families, beneficiaries will have extremely different needs, and many clients wish to provide appropriately for those beneficiaries while not excluding the others. Estate plans should identify those who could be vulnerable after the death of a parent or partner and take some steps to anticipate and minimize this vulnerability to the extent consistent with their overall estate-planning goals.

Leveling the playing field can be crucial in a blended family. For example, a father decides that his second wife will have voting control over a family business by virtue of being trustee. But then Dad's eldest son from his first marriage, who works in the business, becomes subject to the decision-making and potential whims of his stepmother and could even be fired from his job with the family company. There are ways to ensure that this either does not happen or is made so difficult or costly that it is unlikely. Sometimes, if it is decided that a bank or other institutional trustee will be used, giving the trust beneficiaries or a trust protector, the power to change institutional trustees could make that trustee more responsive to the beneficiaries' needs.

23. Provide a mechanism for resolution of disputes.

Even among family members who seem to get along well during life, disputes may, and generally do arise after the death of a parent, and this is particularly more so in blended families. Providing a mechanism for resolution of disputes can be critical in estates in which a fight is possible or even expected. A system for either arbitrating or mediating disputes should always be considered in estate-planning documents for a blended family because court fights in blended families are far more likely than in other families.

24. Keep certain assets away from certain people.

Some clients know that certain beneficiaries would not properly handle the inheritance of a particular asset such as an interest in a business. Some people want certain assets to be beyond the control of a former partner. This is a very common estate-planning goal in blended families. People often shudder if they think that their property could come into the hands or under the control of a former partner and are relieved when they learn about ways to keep that from happening. If the client, one of the fortunate few with a good relationship with a former spouse or partner, the client can always name the person in the client's estate plan if the client chooses to give them something or some fiduciary role. Life insurance is often used to "even things up" so that one person is given an interest in a family business while another receives life insurance proceeds of equal value.

1.7 THE CLIENT'S ESTATE PLANNING CONCERNS

After the estate planner has evaluated the client's estate planning goals and the client has chosen their estate planning desires, it is time to consider possible risks and concerns in estate planning. In blended families, these concerns can be daunting.

1. **Choosing between a partner and the children.**

Often, choosing between a partner and the children is the greatest concern in estate planning for blended families. Who should receive what and at what time? Trying to balance the interests of the children getting an inheritance and a partner being supported after their death usually is a matter of the size of their estate. If the client's estate is large, it may be possible to do both. However, if the client's estate is modest, the client may well have to choose. This is acceptable, even though it may be gut-wrenchingly hard. The best advice is, once the client has decided how they want the estate plan to look, the client should take time to explain their actions to all parties so that no one is surprised after the client's death.

2. **Plan for the payment and apportionment of estate taxes.**

If the client's estate is taxable (and due to the changes in federal tax laws, the client's estate may not be taxable today but it may be at some time in the future if tax laws change), how will the taxes be paid, and from which beneficiary's share will they be paid? Currently, very few estates have to worry about paying the federal estate tax (although it is essential to consider the amount and impact of state death taxes). However, for those who do have to pay, the federal estate tax presents a huge area for concern because of the possible amount of the tax, the short time frame from death at which it is due, and the fact that many estates do not – without life insurance – have the liquidity to pay it.

Some people whose estates will owe some estate tax choose not to worry about it and leave the problem to their loved ones. After all, they reason that they'll be dead and gone anyway. However, others realize that failure to minimize the estate tax could cause the sale of a family farm or business that they (and perhaps their parents) worked for years to build. These people are much more likely to make estate-tax reduction and funding a high priority. This is something that the client should discuss with their estate planning advisors because most just assume that everyone wants to reduce estate tax to the lowest possible amount, which is not always true. In blended families, having the estate tax on the share of one heir payable out of the share of another heir negatively impacts one side over the other, which greatly increases the likelihood of litigation. However, in blended family situations, it is not unusual for a client to divide an estate between their partner and the children from prior relationships, even if it increases the total amount of estate tax due, provided that each side gets an equal share of the estate.

3. **Dealing with problem children.**

Should the client leave assets outright to a child who has problems handling money or who has a problem partner or a drug or alcohol problem or who is just inept at handling money and who may easily fall prey to undue and badly intended influence of others? Some people consider their children who have not panned out in life to be problems. This usually means that a trust (which seems to really mean "don't trust") will be helpful to that child.

4. **Protecting young or disabled children.**

How can the client make sure that the new baby's inheritance is not totally used up by higher education while at the same time older beneficiaries are enjoying theirs? Also, how can the client provide funds to support a disabled child without the child losing federal or state disability benefits? These raise distinct and separate concerns. Perhaps a healthy youngster needs to be educated. However, a disabled child may need support and property management for the rest of his or her lifetime. In a yours, mine and ours blended family scenario, the "ours" children will be younger than the children from prior relationships. Quite often in these situations, the younger "ours" children may not have finished their education, so an additional share probably should be set aside to allow those children to finish their educations, which is only fair since the parent paid for the education of the older children.

5. **Caring for elderly parents.**

What if the client's parents outlive their own retirement savings? Suppose one or both of the client's parents survive the client. Does the client want to take care of their parents' financial needs in their estate plan? Can the client afford to take care of their parents' financial needs? Elderly parents can present a serious impact both on the client's lifestyle and on their estate planning.

1.8 WHY DO SOME BLENDED FAMILIES HAVE SO MUCH ANGST?

Divisions based upon divided loyalties are very common in blended families. Children often are still grieving the loss of their parents' relationship or the loss of a parent to death and holding on to the fact that, for example, "no one is going to replace momma"—jealousy of the new partner also can play a role. Distrust of a new partner's motives also factor into the mix. For this reason, extra care should go into the creation of an estate plan for a blended family couple, with a particular view toward how the plan would fare if the relationships go south after the death of the parent partner.

1.9 OPTIONAL CHECKLISTS FOR DISCUSSION

One or more of the following checklists can be given to a client to review and fill out prior to meeting with the planner or it can be reviewed and processed with the client. In addition, a planner may want to use these checklists to review potential estate planning issues to be considered.

RALPH GANO MILLER CLIENT_____

MILLER, MONSON, PESHEL, POLACEK & HOSHAW

A Partnership of Professional Law Corporations

OPTIONAL CHECKLIST FOR DISCUSSION

As an option in preparing for our meeting, you may wish to review the following, which covers many of the specific areas of potential benefit and some of the unique problems that relate to various circumstances in which clients find themselves. By reviewing the list and checking off those items that relate to your circumstances, we will be able to focus more clearly on your particular concerns at our estate planning conference. This will also provide you an opportunity to consider beforehand the matters that will come under discussion.

Please do not delay your meeting because of the fact that you have not had a chance to review the checklist, since there will be an opportunity in our discussions to cover any area in which you have an interest.

Checklist Index
CHECKLISTS FOR VARIOUS CIRCUMSTANCES

i.	How To Use The Checklists	Page 21
[ ] A.	All Husbands and Wives With Some Estate	Page 22
[ ] B.	Single Persons	Page 28
[ ] C.	Persons With a Potential Inheritance	Page 29
[ ] D.	Persons Moving From Other States or Countries	Page 30
[ ] E.	Owners of Private Corporations	Page 32
[ ] F.	Individual Proprietors	Page 37
[ ] G.	Partners and Members of LLCs	Page 39
[ ] H.	Business Persons in General	Page 41
[ ] I.	Rancher or Farmer	Page 42
[ ] J.	Professionals	Page 43
[ ] K.	Corporate Executives	Page 44
[ ] L.	Persons Planning for Retirement	Page 46
[ ] M.	Persons Planning for Marriage	Page 48
[ ] N.	Persons Planning for Separation or Divorce	Page 50

OVERVIEW OF ESTATE PLANNING

CHAPTER 1

Please recognize that the comments in this checklist are necessarily incomplete and that many important areas of potential benefit and detriment have not been covered. Therefore, you should not take any actions on the basis of the material in these lists without consulting with one of the attorneys in our office or with some other attorney.

[Some editing of the checklist has been done for this book.]

Copyright 2023

Ralph Gano Miller

1. HOW TO USE THE CHECKLISTS

To save you time, you will probably wish to review only those aspects of the checklist that actually relate to your circumstances, since some aspects are redundant. Using the list of topics below, check the ones that relate to your circumstances, or to areas in which you might be interested (such as incorporating a business which presently might be held as a sole proprietorship).

In every case, you will wish to review either Checklist A or B (depending on your marital status). In addition, as an example, if you have an incorporated business or professional practice, you may wish to review the following additional areas:

Owners of Private Corporations

Professionals

Once you have determined the topics you wish to review, you can then turn to the appropriate page for each topic as shown below and check off the individual items of interest that are listed under that topic. Please also use the check-off boxes at the bottom of each page of the checklists to indicate those pages that you wish to review at our conference.

In reviewing specific areas of potential benefit or problems, please note that those which relate to non-tax matters (N), estate, gift, or generation-skipping tax (E), or income or payroll tax (I) are indicated by the letter next to the check-off box to provide an easier means of identifying those areas which are of special interest to you.

The references to chapters after the heading of each item are to chapters of the 21st edition of *The Tools & Techniques of Estate Planning*.

Checklist Index
CHECKLISTS FOR VARIOUS CIRCUMSTANCES

[ ] A.	All Husbands and Wives With Some Estate	Page 22
[ ] B.	Single Persons	Page 28
[ ] C.	Persons With a Potential Inheritance	Page 29
[ ] D.	Persons Moving From Other States or Countries	Page 30
[ ] E.	Owners of Private Corporations	Page 32
[ ] F.	Individual Proprietors	Page 37
[ ] G.	Partners and Members of LLCs	Page 39
[ ] H.	Business Persons in General	Page 41
[ ] I.	Rancher or Farmer	Page 42
[ ] J.	Professionals	Page 43
[ ] K.	Corporate Executives	Page 44
[ ] L.	Persons Planning for Retirement	Page 46
[ ] M.	Persons Planning for Marriage	Page 48
[ ] N.	Persons Planning for Separation or Divorce	Page 50

CHECKLIST FOR VARIOUS CIRCUMSTANCES

A. ALL HUSBANDS AND WIVES WITH SOME ESTATE

AREAS OF POSSIBLE BENEFIT

[ ]N[1]* (1) Avoidance of Probate (Chapter 15): Use of a trust to both avoid the cost of probate and to eliminate the very substantial delays and restrictions of probate can be a benefit to even a very small estate. Although this course of planning is usually very beneficial, it may not apply if there are many potential liabilities of the decedent (e.g., a physician, engineer, or attorney with no malpractice coverage or coverage which may be inadequate) and a probate proceeding is the only method by which claims of creditors might be "scraped off." For most estates, avoidance of probate (and conservatorship) is a major benefit to consider. However, while it is often beneficial to avoid probate, clients sometimes have an unrealistic fear of probate. While it may add time and cost to the process, probate adds court oversight and provides a number of protections that would be absent without it.

[ ]N (2) Providing Assistance with Asset Management: Use of a trust may also provide financial planning assistance to a child or a spouse who is not experienced in handling funds and also delay distribution of trust principal until the beneficiary gains more experience in managing assets. Outright gifts to a minor child will usually be held by a court appointed guardian until age eighteen or twenty-one, and a distribution to a child at that age may destroy planning for college. This problem may be avoided by a trust to provide for education and living expenses and distribution of the proceeds at later dates (e.g., one-third each at ages twenty-five, thirty and thirty-five).

[ ]N (3) Broad Durable Power of Attorney (Chapter 62): Like most states, California permits one to give to another person a power of attorney which will be valid even if the person giving it becomes incompetent. This can aid greatly in the proper use of funds and avoid a conservatorship of the estate in some situations for a period of time. However, some people are unwilling to give someone else a power to deal broadly with their assets.

[ ]N (4) Limited Durable Power of Attorney (Chapter 62): Some people prefer to give someone else only the power to transfer property to a trust created by the grantor of the power. With this power, if the grantor is in a coma or otherwise unable to act, the holder of the power can shift the ownership of the grantor's assets to a revocable trust (previously created by the grantor) in order to avoid their being subject to probate at the grantor's death.

[ ]N (5) Advance Health Care Directive: California also allows one to designate a person who will have the power to make health care decisions, often permitting the avoidance of a conservatorship of the person. This document also allows one to indicate their wishes as to being placed in a rest home (as opposed to staying in their own home). It also provides a means of giving instructions as to any donation of body parts after death. This document is often accompanied by a "pull the plug" directive. Those persons who want to do so may have a directive created, strictly adhering to state requirements, which may direct a physician to not sustain their life when there is no reasonable expectation that they may regain the use of their faculties.

[ ]N (6) HIPAA Authorization: Taking its name from the Health Insurance Portability and Accountability Act of 1996, this document will indicate the persons who will have the right to information from your medical records, and generally would include your spouse, your adult children, and the person(s) named as the successor trustee under your revocable trust (if any).

---

* The letters N, I or E after each check-off box indicates whether the specific item is more related to non-tax matters (N), income or payroll tax (I) or estate gift or generation-skipping tax (E).

OVERVIEW OF ESTATE PLANNING
CHAPTER 1

[ ]N (7) <u>Clarification of Property Rights Through Property Agreement</u>: The actual ownership of property acquired before and during marriage is usually of importance, and often can be difficult to trace for either estate or income tax purposes or for marital rights purposes. A brief agreement can set forth and even change the form of title of their assets. This can be particularly important for people living in a community property state in order to receive a new stepped-up income tax basis (at one spouse's death) on both halves of property that they considered community property but which was titled as joint tenancy property.

[ ]N (8) <u>Provision of Liquidity Through Insurance</u> (Chapter 34): Where liquidity is important, it can be provided by life insurance, something that has become a "better buy" item in recent years.

[ ]E (9) <u>Full Use of Applicable Exclusion Amount</u> (Chapter 18): Since every citizen or resident has the unified credit available to offset either gift tax (credit protects up to $12,920,000 in 2023) during his or her lifetime (see Chapter 8), or estate tax (credit protects portion of estate ranging from $12,920,000 in 2023) at death (see Chapter 18), most estate planning for married couples since 1981 has been focused on the maximum use of the credit at the death of the first spouse to die so that, at the death of the second spouse, certain assets that have been already taxed and set aside (nearly always in a trust) will not be subject to tax again at the survivor's death.

[ ]E (10) <u>Measured Use of The Marital Deduction</u> (Chapter 27): Property left to a surviving spouse or to a trust that qualifies for the marital deduction will not be subject to tax at the death of the first spouse. A great bulk of estate planning for spouses calls for a measured amount of property to be taxed so as to result in a tax equal to the remaining unified credit applicable exclusion, with the balance of the property being subject to the marital deduction and thus deferred as to estate tax until the survivor's death. The property that has been taxed (with the tax offset by the unified credit) can escape taxation at the death of the surviving spouse.

With proper planning, the surviving spouse may have all of the assets available without any reduction for taxes to be paid to the federal government (i.e., having a zero net estate tax to pay) and thus have a more financially secure position for the remainder of her or his life. However this approach can result in more overall estate taxes for the spousal unit than might be the case if some estate tax were paid at the first spouse's death. Use of the qualified terminable interest property (QTIP) concept of obtaining the marital deduction can be flexible so as to permit payment of none, some or all of the estate tax due at the first death, to be decided after the first spouse's death.

[ ]E (11) <u>Use of Gift Tax Annual Exclusion</u> (Chapter 20): Outright gifts and other gifts qualifying as "present interests" with values up to $15,000 for 2021) can be made to each person in the world each year without creating any taxable gifts.

Where financial security permits, a program of annual gifts of $15,000-or-less can greatly reduce the amount of tax to be paid at the death of anyone. Currently, such gifts may be made even a few minutes before death and thus may also be a part of death-bed tax planning.

[ ]E (12) <u>Taxable Gifts of Appreciating Property</u> (Chapter 20): Where financial security permits, gifts made now of property which is expected to increase in value can be good planning even though such gift may be taxable.

Use of the applicable exclusion amount to offset such gift tax will essentially reduce the amount of exclusion left available for offsetting estate tax at death. However, giving an asset now that is worth $100,000 is much better than having that same asset included in one's estate if it is then expected to be worth $500,000.

If the gift is community property, it is divided between the two spouses. Where the property given is separate property, the availability of "gift splitting" (Chapter 20) permits the same result.

23

[ ]E (13) <u>Sales to Next Generation of Appreciating Property</u>: Future appreciation in a property may be avoided by a sale of the entire property to the persons who would otherwise inherit it. The potential estate tax benefits here must be weighed against the income taxes paid by the seller that would have never been paid if the property were retained until death.

[ ]E (14) <u>Gifts of Insurance</u>: A transfer of insurance, either outright or through the use of irrevocable trusts, may be an example of a gift with a high potential for appreciation since, for gift tax purposes, the gift is measured only by the value of the property at the time of the gift (usually the "interpolated terminal reserve value," approximately the same as the cash surrender value of the policy). Regardless of the gift value, the entire face amount of the policy will be paid over to the donee(s) at the insured's death. Besides being extremely effective in transferring values without significant transfer tax, such planning can often be done without any significant impairment of the financial security of the donor(s).

[ ]E (15) <u>Private Annuities</u> (Chapter 42): Private annuities are often used by children to purchase assets from their parents. One of the benefits of a private annuity is that the payments stop at the annuitant's death, so nothing remains to be taxed in the annuitant's estate at the annuitant's death. The monthly Section 7520 rate (120 percent of the mid-term applicable federal rate) applies for valuing such annuities.

[ ]E (16) <u>Sales of Remainder Interests in Property</u>: This is generally no longer feasible between family members due to Code section 2702. There are, however, some quite technical transactions that may be undertaken to accomplish this.

[ ]E (17) <u>Split Interest Purchases of Property</u> (Chapter 45): Generally, this technique is less feasible for family members than previously due to Code section 2702.

[ ]E (18) <u>Freezing Values of Assets</u> (Chapters 49 and 71): Partnership "freezes" and corporate arrangements with different classes of stock can in many circumstances shift the increase in value from one generation to the next; but such transactions are now generally subject to Code section 2701.

[ ]E/N (19) <u>Use of Generation-Skipping Trusts</u> (Chapter 21): Although the generation-skipping tax restricts what had been almost an open field for delaying tax through successive generations, it still leaves some very significant areas of benefit that should be considered.

Up to $12,920,000 (per donor in 2023, $25,840,000 for a married couple with proper planning) can benefit the children and go to their children (the grandchildren of the donors) without any tax at the death of each child, the child's spouse, or anyone else in the child's generation.

Apart from the estate tax benefits, this type of trust can also provide lifetime financial assistance and a measure of security to a child who is not "money wise."

[ ]E

[ ]I (20) <u>Grantor Retained Interest Trusts</u> (Chapters 29): Another technique used to reduce the transfer tax impact of a gift involves creating a trust which retains for the donor the right to payments from the gifted property for a certain number of years. Generally, grantor retained annuity trusts (GRATs) and grantor retained unitrusts (GRUTs) will be used instead of grantor retained income trusts (GRITs) due to Code section 2702.

[ ]I/E (21) <u>Charitable Remainder Trusts</u> (Chapter 38): In circumstances where one has an asset with a very low income tax basis that does not produce satisfactory income (or if another reason exists to dispose of it), it is possible to avoid tax on the gain on sale by creating a trust which will ultimately go to a charity, transferring the asset to the trust, and having the trust sell it. The original owner(s) may retain a payment stream from the newly invested sales proceeds, which have not been reduced by any income taxes. Insurance on the donor(s) may often be a basis for replacing the value of the assets which otherwise would have gone to the children of the donor(s).

OVERVIEW OF ESTATE PLANNING — CHAPTER 1

POTENTIAL PROBLEMS

[ ]N (1) <u>Possible Estate Liabilities</u>: To the extent that the decedent has a large amount of potential liabilities (e.g., an anesthesiologist, a civil engineer, a tax shelter attorney who has neglected to carry professional liability insurance, or a businessman who has found himself saddled with large debts), probate may be of some benefit in that most states provide a creditors claim period which cuts off liabilities to those creditors that do not file their claims in the proper way within that period. Similar procedures are available in some states for trusts.

Differences in state laws affect this, but there are some circumstances where most, if not all, of the assets, should be subjected to probate in order to "cleanse" them of potential liabilities of the decedent. The availability of adequate professional or business liability insurance is a factor to be considered in determining whether to have assets (other than insurance or retirement fund benefits) be probated.

[ ]N (2) <u>Diversion of Assets to Replacement Spouse</u>: Children are often unintentionally deprived of security and benefits where assets are held in joint tenancy with a surviving spouse or left outright to a surviving spouse and that surviving spouse remarries. Without a trust to protect the children, there is no way to be certain that the children will receive any benefits, particularly if the survivor remarries and is subject to pressure to prove his or her love and devotion to a new spouse by joint tenancy ownership or a new will.

[ ]N (3) <u>Distributions to Children at Early Ages</u>: An estate built with great care and effort may be wasted, with little or no real benefit to the next generation, by leaving the property outright to a child who has no experience or ability in managing the assets. Early distributions also usually have a very adverse effect on educational planning.

[ ]N (4) <u>Loss of Mental Capacity</u>: If no trust has been created to hold the assets and provide a successor trustee to manage the assets, or where no one has been given a broad durable power of attorney, incapacity may cause serious disruption of a business and also disrupt payment of normal expenses of living. In this circumstance, a relatively cumbersome and expensive court conservatorship of the estate is the only way to provide some management for the assets.

[ ]N (5) <u>Spouse's and Children's Ignorance of Estate Affairs</u>: Failure to provide information as to the existence and/or location of assets may seriously disrupt the process of garnering the estate assets and properly managing them.

[ ]N (6) <u>Lack of Liquidity</u>: Although liquidity for estate tax at the first spouse's death may not be required with current planning techniques, it may well be required for other purposes, particularly if the decedent was in business or farming. Further, for larger estates, at the death of the second spouse, there may be a need to either have cash liquidity or liquidate many of the estate assets at a loss in order to pay death taxes.

Although it is possible to have a zero estate tax liability at the death of the first-to-die spouse, there are circumstances where it may be beneficial to have funds available at the first death to pay estate taxes on assets at that time and avoid the increase in value which may take place during the lifetime of the surviving spouse. Where other liquidity may not be available, insurance on one or both of the spouses (or the survivor of them) may be the best answer.

[ ]E (7) <u>Having an Estate Plan Which Does Not Qualify For the Unlimited Marital Deduction</u> (Chapter 18): Many pre-1982 estate plans now result in payment of substantial federal estate tax at the death of the first spouse to die. The "totally tax-free transfer to a surviving spouse" simply doesn't happen under many pre-1982 estate plans, including some plans which use trusts to reduce estate taxes.

[ ]E   (8)   <u>Loss of Applicable Exclusion Amount</u> (Chapter 18): The most frequently encountered estate "problem" for married couples is that of the first spouse to die leaving all assets outright to a surviving spouse, although portability saves the day for many of these situations now.

A deduction is available for estate tax purposes as to any assets left to a surviving spouse. Thus, the decedent who leaves all assets to a surviving spouse has no tax to pay (since all the tax will be deferred until the survivor's death) and, thus, loses the advantage of the unified credit to reduce the overall estate taxes on the estates of the two spouses. This is true regardless of whether the decedent had separate property or community property. See Chapter 27 for a description of the use of a trust to create sufficient tax and take advantage of the applicable exclusion amount so that the property in that trust, taxed at the first spouse's death and segregated until the survivor's death, can avoid tax at the survivor's death. However, these issues are significantly reduced as a result of the portability of the estate tax applicable exclusion amount between spouses (also discussed in Chapter 18).

[ ]E/N   (9)   <u>Generation-Skipping Transfer Tax</u> (Chapter 21): Trusts with grandchildren and lower generations as beneficiaries may be subject to generation-skipping transfer tax. Also, direct gifts to grandchildren can trigger not only death taxes, but also generation-skipping taxes, and should be evaluated.

[ ]E   (10) <u>State Inheritance Taxes</u>: (Chapter 26) Not all state laws follow the federal tax rules allowing a total marital deduction for gifts to surviving spouses. Planning must also consider the applicable laws of the state since such inheritance taxes can be significant. Many states which previously had only a "pick-up" tax that took advantage of the federal credit for state death taxes have enacted their own transfer tax system now that the federal credit has been repealed. This can seriously impact nonresidents who own property in such a state.

[ ]E   (11) <u>Gifts with Retained Interests</u> (Chapter 20): Where the donor retains an interest in a property (either technically as by retaining a life estate in property deeded to someone else or practically as by continuing to live in and make use of a house given to someone else), the property will be brought back into the donor's estate for estate tax purposes. Proper planning, e.g., paying full market rent on the residence given away but still used, can avoid any adverse results in some situations.

[ ]E   (12) <u>Custodianship Gifts</u> (Chapter 9): A typical example of a retained right is the donor who makes a gift to a child and appoints himself or herself as the custodian of the gift until the child reaches maturity. Such gifts will be brought back into the taxable estate of the donor if he or she is the custodian of the gift.

[ ]E   (13) <u>State Gift Taxes</u>: As of the present, only Connecticut still has a state gift tax.

[ ]E   (14) <u>Accidental Gifts</u>: Although planned giving can be a most effective way of reducing transfer taxes, care should be taken to not create unintended taxable gifts.

Except as between husband and wife, nearly every creation of a co-ownership with any other person (e.g., putting a stock or piece of real property in joint tenancy with someone) creates a taxable gift. Obtaining competent tax advice is the only way to avoid such gifts.

Interest-free loans or below-market-rate loans are a potential area for unintended taxable gifts (Chapter 40).

[ ]E   (15) <u>Insurance Gifts Within Three Years of Death</u> (Chapter 34): Gifts within three years of death are generally not brought back into the taxable estate. However, direct or indirect gifts of insurance within that period can result in the taxability of the insurance proceeds in the donor's estate. Community property rules may often present unique problems in identifying the donor of insurance.

[ ]E	(16)	<u>Lack of a Qualifying Marriage</u>: The increasing frequency of absence of a formal marriage makes this a very real danger for couples who in other times would have married. Depending on state law, either a formal or a common law marriage can qualify a spouse for the marital deduction, but there must be a "marriage." Documentation for a marriage or a divorce in foreign countries must be examined by a competent attorney. Most states do not recognize "common law" marriages (those based on people living together).
[ ]E/I	(17)	<u>Failure to be Aware of Law Changes</u>: Although laws sometimes change in regard to wills and trusts, the changes are much more frequent with regard to estate, gift, and income taxes. Ignorance of such changes can have very adverse effects on an estate plan. Estate plans should be reviewed regularly with competent counsel.
[ ]E/I	(18)	<u>Property Tax Reassessment at Death</u>: Where state law (e.g., Proposition 13 in California) has prevented valuation increases for property tax purposes, death can lift the barrier to such increases in valuation and also to tax increases. Some exceptions to such increases often exist and estate planning must be done with property tax matters in mind.
[ ]E/I	(19)	<u>Retirement Plan Beneficiary Designation Forms (</u>: Where benefits built up in a qualified retirement plan are planned to be transmitted at death, this is generally accomplished by using a beneficiary designation form created for such a purpose, rather than by one's will or trust. In those circumstances where there is a gift to anyone other than the surviving spouse of a participant (perhaps a gift over to a trust in the event the spouse does not survive or disclaims the gift), great care must be taken to see that the laws created by the Retirement Equity Act of 1984 are not violated. This law generally restricts all transfers of benefit from a qualified plan other than in the form of annuity payments. Further, any spouse of at least one year has an immediate right to half of the value in the plan to be left to her or him in the form of an annuity. Beneficiary designation forms must be carefully reviewed to spot any violations of this law. The wording of the beneficiary designation form can also have an impact on the amount required to be withdrawn from the plan each year after the participant's death. These same issues relating to the importance of proper beneficiary designations also apply to 401(k) plans and IRAs.
[ ]E/I	(20)	<u>Possible Retirement Plan Control By Will</u>: A California court has surprisingly said that regardless of retirement plan rules and possible preemption of state law by federal law, an interest in a retirement plan may be controlled by one's will. Many other states follow California law. Therefore, until this matter is resolved, it may be necessary to have one's will reference and confirm the effect of plan beneficiary designation forms. Otherwise, planning for proper direction of such plan proceeds may be frustrated.

THE TOOLS & TECHNIQUES OF ESTATE PLANNING

CHECKLIST FOR VARIOUS CIRCUMSTANCES

B.   SINGLE PERSONS (Chapter 65)

AREAS OF POSSIBLE BENEFIT

    (1)   <u>Implications for the Single Client</u>: With the exception of a marital deduction, all the potential benefits described in the checklist for "Husbands and Wives" are available to a single person. This group includes persons who have never married, those who have had an annulment or divorce, and also survivors of marriage, both with and without children. However, the marital deduction is available only to the extent that there is an existing spouse who receives a lifetime gift or assets transmitted at death.

    With the possible exception of the annuity (discussed below), there are few unique estate planning benefits available for a single person, although income taxation rules may from time to time give some advantage to a single person as compared to one who is married.

[ ]N   (2)   <u>Use of Annuities</u>: For those persons who truly have no financial responsibility for anyone else, the purchase of commercial annuities may have some application in increasing the cash available each month during the person's lifetime. However, the need for protection of purchasing power from inflation often argues against putting the majority of one's assets into such investments. Certain annuities provide some degree of protection from inflation.

[ ]I   (3)   <u>Use of Charitable Remainder Trusts</u> (Chapter 38): Where the single person has no need for concern over leaving assets to children or other persons, consideration should be given to obtaining a current income tax deduction by giving to a charity the right to use property after the single person's death. Although the flexibility of sale and/or consumption of the asset is lost, a payment stream is retained and income tax lessened because of the deduction. Gain on sale of assets placed in the trust can escape taxation if placed in such a trust.

POTENTIAL PROBLEMS

    (1)   <u>Implications for the Single Client</u>: All the potential problems with regard to the above "All Husbands and Wives With Some Estate" apply to the single person. The exception is that there is no accidental loss of applicable exclusion amount by leaving all the assets to a surviving spouse since the marital deduction does not apply to a single person.

[ ]N   (2)   <u>Difficulty in Finding Conservator of Person or Estate</u>: For those single persons who have no children, it is often much more difficult to find someone in whom they have enough confidence to make decisions regarding their person and all their assets when the single person is no longer able to make such decisions well.

[ ]N   (3)   <u>The Lee Marvin Syndrome</u>: Unmarried persons who have a live-in companion but no written agreement as to ownership of property or rights to income have exposure to lawsuits that may reduce assets that would otherwise go to the beneficiaries of their estate plan. A written property agreement can solve this problem.

[ ]N   (4)   <u>Heirs' Lack of Knowledge of Estate</u>: Assets of a single person are frequently never all found since the executor, often an unrelated person and often a corporate fiduciary, may never have been given information as to the existence or location of assets.

[ ]N   (5)   <u>Single Parent Finding Guardian For Children</u>: Failure to direct some thought and effort toward the often difficult question of finding a suitable guardian for the children of a single parent often results in not only not finding a suitable guardian but also often causes the single parent to delay having a will or trust drafted.

[ ]E   (6)   <u>No Easy Way to Defer Estate Taxes</u> (Chapter 18): Without a surviving spouse, estate taxes must be faced and the single person's estate must be prepared to bear the brunt of such taxes.

CHECKLIST FOR VARIOUS CIRCUMSTANCES

C.   PERSONS WITH POTENTIAL INHERITANCE

AREAS OF POSSIBLE BENEFIT

[ ]N   (1)   Avoidance of Probate and/or Conservatorships for Parents: Probate of a parent's estate and particularly that of the surviving parent, puts the burden of such delays and costs directly on the client. Use of an *inter vivos* trust will permit the avoidance of such a probate. It also permits the avoidance of what may be an expensive and cumbersome conservatorship (or guardianship) proceeding where the parent is not managing assets well. A trust that is contained in one's will does not avoid probate at the death of the owner of the property.

[ ]E   (2)   Generation-Skipping Trust (Chapter 21): Where the client has an expectation of an inheritance, there should be a discussion of the possibility of receiving some or all of such inheritance in the form of a trust which typically gives the client (as trustee) the control over all the benefits from the assets to be inherited, but also permits the avoidance of the generation-skipping transfer tax and the estate tax.

POTENTIAL PROBLEMS

[ ]N   (1)   Reduction of Parental Control Over Children: Direct gifts to clients' children from the clients' parents may often interfere significantly with parental control, particularly as to education of the client's children. Use of a trust may avoid this problem and still provide the benefit the grandparents' desire.

[ ]N   (2)   Dissipation of Estate by Parent's New Spouse: Where the parent leaves all assets to a new spouse with the intent that she or he will leave it to the children of the prior marriage, the children often never receive any of the assets. Use of a trust by the parent to control the assets would avoid this problem. Often, such a trust can be best created before the death of either parent.

[ ]E   (3)   Loss of Generation-Skipping Exemption (Chapter 21): There is an exemption from generation-skipping transfer tax for $12,920,000 (in 2023) per donor, or $25,840,000 for a couple. However, without proper planning, the exemption of both parents and particularly that of the first parent to die can be lost. This is a very important aspect if generation-skipping for an inheritance is planned.

[ ]E   (4)   Accidental Application of Generation-Skipping Transfer Tax: Planning in which the parent of the client plans to benefit both the client and the client's children may often unwittingly cause application of the generation-skipping tax, resulting in a tax at the death of the client on assets which will go on to benefit the next generation. Under some circumstances, the generation-skipping tax may apply and the estate tax unified credit of the child is wasted.

CHECKLIST FOR VARIOUS CIRCUMSTANCES

D. <u>PERSONS MOVING FROM OTHER STATES OR COUNTRIES</u>

AREAS OF POSSIBLE BENEFIT

[ ]E (1) <u>Gifts to Permit Both Spouses to Use Applicable Exclusion Amount</u>: Where one spouse has more property (because of state laws or inheritance) than the other spouse, gifts to the spouse with the smaller estate should be considered in order to be certain that such spouse has sufficient estate to take advantage of the full amount of the unified credit applicable exclusion and/or generation-skipping exemption. Where the spouse with the larger amount of assets is unwilling to make outright gifts to the other spouse, consideration may be given to having the other spouse purchase and continue to own life insurance on his or her life in an amount which will take advantage of the opportunity to pass assets tax free because of the unified credit.

If the gift is of real property or some other asset that may be subject to the laws of another state, care must be taken to determine if that state imposes gift taxes on transfers between spouses.

[ ]E (2) <u>Change of Residence to Avoid State Death Taxes</u>: Since many states (e.g., Florida, Nevada, California, etc.) have no death taxes, changing one's residence to one of those or similar states may avoid significant death taxes.

[ ]E (3) <u>Possibility of Nonresidents Making Gifts Before Becoming Residents</u>: In some circumstances, nonresidents (e.g., an exile from San Salvador temporarily living in the U.S. but who is as yet not a U.S. citizen or resident) may be able to make gifts without being subject to U.S. gift taxes. In some such cases, planning may include gifts to family members made before becoming a resident of the U.S.

[ ]I (4) <u>Ownership Change to Community Property</u> (Chapter 7): Where one spouse has separate property (e.g., acquired through earnings in a separate property state or from inheritance) that has increased in value, consideration should be given to changing that property to community property. If the property is left as separate property and the non-owning spouse dies, the property will retain its present income tax basis. If the property is changed to community property, in a properly conceived estate plan, it is possible that the death of either spouse will provide the survivor with a new (and hopefully increased) income tax basis for the property equal to the fair market value of the property at the time of the death of the first spouse to die.

POTENTIAL PROBLEMS

[ ]N (1) <u>Ancillary Probate</u>: If a person retains ownership of real property in another state, there will probably have to be two probates, one for the state of residence and another for the state in which the retained real property is located. Use of a trust to hold such out-of-state property can usually avoid this costly and cumbersome circumstance.

[ ]N (2) <u>State Law Differences for Execution and Administration of Wills and Trusts</u>: A will drafted in one state is generally valid in another state, but it may be wise to have the will reviewed by an attorney in each state in which a person owns real property.

[ ]N (3) <u>Surviving Spouse's Rights Differ From State to State</u>: State laws also differ as to what rights the spouses have in property acquired during marriage (e.g., community property spouses each having a half interest in earnings during the marriage), rights in separate property at the death of a spouse, and also intestacy rules (which operate in the absence of a valid will). All of these differences may be magnified in comparing the laws of different states.

[ ]N (4) <u>Real Property in Other States Usually Subject to that State's Laws</u>: Even though the residence of the owners was considered in drafting their wills, laws of the state where the property is located will usually apply – including the aspects of the rights of surviving spouses and the rules of intestacy.

[ ]N (5) <u>Foreign Residents</u>: For those persons who have previously lived in, who are currently residents of, or who perhaps even have property in, other countries, there must be an examination of the law of the other country to see if a will must be drafted in accordance with its laws in order to be effective as to assets in that country.

[ ]E (6) <u>Accidental Gifts Prior to 1982</u> (Chapter 18): Transfers of ownership between husband and wife prior to 1982 may very well have resulted in taxable gifts for federal gift and estate tax purposes and for a state's gift tax purposes even though no gift was intended. Putting separate property (e.g., which was inherited or which was earned in a separate property state) of one spouse into co-ownership with the other in many cases resulted in a taxable gift, and the expanded marital deduction did not wipe out such prior gift tax liabilities. Such transfers should be reviewed to determine if any gift tax liability exists or if any steps should be taken to currently record the circumstances that argued against the transaction having been considered a gift.

[ ]E (7) <u>Possibility of Two State Death Taxes Applying</u>: By having indicia of residence (e.g., driver's license, lodge membership, income tax filings, etc.) in two or more states, it is possible to be subject to state death tax in each state.

[ ]E (8) <u>Different U.S. Estate and Gift Tax Rules for Nonresidents</u> (Chapter 72): Foreign citizens who are not U.S. residents do not have all of the estate tax benefits of U.S. citizens in relation to federal estate and gift tax, and also often with regard to state gift and death taxes. Such noncitizens with significant assets must have their estate plans prepared by an attorney who is aware of the impact of such differences on estate planning.

[ ]E (9) <u>Special Trust Required to Obtain Marital Deduction for Transfer to Noncitizens</u>: The benefit of the marital deduction for transfers to spouses who are not U.S. citizens is lost unless the transferred property is held in a qualified domestic trust (QDOT). A QDOT must have a trustee that is a citizen of, or a corporation created in, the United States. This rule will invalidate any prior estate plan involving noncitizens that is not amended to comply with these rules.

THE TOOLS & TECHNIQUES OF ESTATE PLANNING

CHECKLIST FOR VARIOUS CIRCUMSTANCES

E.   OWNERS OF PRIVATE CORPORATIONS

AREAS OF POSSIBLE BENEFIT

[ ]N   (1)   <u>Shield Against Corporate Liabilities</u> (Chapter 50): Wherever the business activity has some potential financial dangers, a business operated through a properly organized and operated corporation with sufficient capital may protect the other assets of a client.

[ ]N   (2)   <u>Pooling of Capital for Business</u> (Chapters 49-53): Issuance of shares to various persons permits the pooling of capital and thus raising of more funds than would otherwise be available to any individual proprietor for the capital needs of a business activity.

[ ]N   (3)   <u>Maintaining Value of Business – Buy and Sell Agreement</u> (Chapter 47): Often the most important aspect of estate planning is preserving the values built up in the private corporation. Executing a proper buy and sell agreement may be an effective way of doing this in many situations that involve private corporations.

[ ]N   (4)   <u>Capitalization to Permit Retention of Control</u>: In circumstances where gifts of stock to family members are contemplated, consideration might be given early to issuance of both voting and nonvoting stock.

[ ]N   (5)   <u>Use of a Voting Trust to Permit Retention of Control</u>: Where issuance of nonvoting stock is not practical, the possibility of maintaining control is feasible in some circumstances by the use of a voting trust.

[ ]E   (6)   <u>Early Gifts of Stock Within Family</u> (Chapter 20): Where it is likely the corporation will appreciate in value, gifts of stock at an early stage of the corporation's growth may permit the transfer of a much larger part of the future value without there being any significant gift tax consequences. The effect of Code section 2701 on such transfers must be considered.

[ ]E   (7)   <u>Capitalization to Permit Easier Corporate Freeze – A Lost Planning Tool</u> (Chapter 71): When an increase in the value of a corporation is a very significant possibility, consideration was previously given early to issuance of both preferred stock (which can be recovered by the corporation at stated prices) and common stock (to be given to the next generation) which will not have such restrictions, and thus will have the major potential for increase in value. The effect of Code section 2701 on such transfers must be considered.

[ ]E   (8)   <u>Corporation or Partnership May Qualify More Assets for Estate Tax Deferral</u> (Chapter 18): All of the "business assets" in a going business corporation may qualify at a client's death to meet the minimum percentage limits in order to achieve deferral of the related estate tax over a period of as long as fourteen years and with some of the tax bearing interest at a very low rate. Although the value of "passive assets" held by the business do not qualify for deferral, holding assets in a corporation or partnership may still result in a larger amount qualifying for deferral of tax than if such assets were owned by an individual proprietor.

[ ]I   (9)   <u>Retaining Rights at Original Incorporation of Business</u> (Chapter 50): As opposed to putting all the assets of a business into the corporation in exchange for stock, when forming a corporation consideration should be given to taking back a note in place of some of the stock so that some money or other assets can be later drawn out of the corporation against such note without recognition of income tax.

OVERVIEW OF ESTATE PLANNING   CHAPTER 1

[ ]I (10) <u>Fringe Benefit Planning</u>: The following are some of the most typically used fringe benefit planning techniques:

    (a) group term life insurance (Chapter 34)

    (b) disability insurance deductibility

    (c) cafeteria plans

    (d) split-dollar insurance coverage (Chapter 34)

    (e) education costs

    (f) financial counseling

    (g) prepaid group legal services

    (h) dependent care assistance

    (ij) auto and travel costs

[ ]I (11) <u>Use of High Profile Qualified Retirement Plans</u> (Chapters 54-60): Pension and profit sharing plans, both for corporations and for individual proprietors and partners, are recognized by tax experts as probably the most effective tax shelter for those persons in a business or profession.

[ ]I (12) <u>Use of Dividends Received Deduction</u>: When investment of corporate funds is considered, the deduction afforded corporations of 80 percent (70 percent in some circumstances) of any dividends received should be taken into consideration.

[ ]I (13) <u>Use of Corporation's Initial Low Income Tax Rate</u> (Chapter 50): Tax rates as low as 15 percent for income tax purposes makes the corporation a very useful tool for building capital for some businesses or professions. However, "personal service corporations" (e.g., most of those that practice law, medicine, or consulting using shareholders as employees) do not have the advantage of the lower corporate tax rate. Thus, all income of such corporations will be taxed at the 35 percent rate.

[ ]I (14) <u>Electing S Corporation Status</u> (Chapter 53): Where circumstances warrant, the corporation may be shifted to being taxed like a partnership through election into "S" status, thus having the income taxed at the shareholder's own individual rate. The ability to make this election is subject to a number of important rules. Relative tax brackets of corporations and shareholders should be considered.

Since stock of S corporations cannot be held for a significant period of time in most trusts without revocation of the S election, the existence of a possible future addition of such a corporation in one's estate must be brought to the attention of the estate planner. It is possible to draft trusts that can continue to hold S corporation stock without revocation of the "S" election.

[ ]I (15) <u>Shifting Income to Low Tax Bracket Family Members</u>: The S corporation election described above also permits the shifting of income to other family members by giving them ownership of stock. Relative tax brackets of each should be considered. Unearned income of children under age eighteen is generally taxed at the parent's marginal tax rate.

[ ]I (16) <u>Using an ESOP to Defer or Avoid Gain on Sale</u> (Chapter 55): The deferral of gain is permitted on a sale of the corporation stock in certain circumstances by the use of an employee stock ownership plan (ESOP) as the buyer and the reinvestment of sale proceeds in domestic stock on the open market. This is a potentially important benefit for many clients.

THE TOOLS & TECHNIQUES OF ESTATE PLANNING

[ ]I (17) <u>Using an ESOP to Redeem Stock with Pretax Dollars</u> (Chapter 55): The installation of an ESOP can provide the means, in some circumstances, to redeem stock by making deductible cash contributions to a qualified plan to build up a fund for the purchase. In some circumstances, this can also provide for acquisition of the stock in conjunction with a bank loan and the repayment of that loan with tax deductible funds contributed to the ESOP.

[ ]I (18) <u>Noncash Deductions Through Use of ESOP</u> (Chapter 55): Where taxable income may be high and cash resources low, the installation of the ESOP can provide for cash-free deductions by having the corporation issue stock to the ESOP. However, this planning also shifts some stock ownership to the employees of the corporation.

[ ]I (19) <u>Lifetime Stock Redemptions to Remove Cash</u>: Where some shareholders are not related, it may be possible to redeem stock of certain shareholders with the recognition of gain as a sale instead of dividend treatment. This will permit treatment as long-term capital gains.

[ ]I (20) <u>Avoiding Tax on Underlying Gains</u>: Even though the corporation may contain assets (e.g., unrecognized receivables, appreciated inventory, fixed assets which have been depreciated, etc.) that would normally produce income to the corporation when sold, under many circumstances all of the assets may be sold together through a sale of the corporation's stock, and thus a gain avoided at the corporation's level until the asset is sold or converted to cash. The selling shareholder, however, recognizes the gain that may exist with regard to his stock. However, item (27) below regarding the loss of the General Utilities doctrine should be reviewed.

[ ]I (21) <u>Stock Redemption at Death to Pay Death Taxes</u> (Chapter 48): Special rules permit redemption of stock under Code section 303 in an amount equal to the total of both federal and state death taxes without having the redemption treated as a dividend.

[ ]I (22) <u>Total Stock Redemption at Death of Community Property Shareholder</u> (Chapters 7 and 48): By holding property in community property form, the death of one spouse gives the surviving spouse an income tax basis in both halves of the stock equal to the then fair market value. The corporation can then be liquidated, and no gain is recognized at the shareholder level.

(However, corporations that have not elected S corporation status under certain specific rules are required to recognize any gain inherent in the assets upon liquidation (e.g., a building worth $100,000 with a cost basis to the corporation of only $30,000), as noted also in item (27) below.

[ ]I (23) <u>Shifting of Income Between Tax Years</u> (Chapter 50): By having a fiscal year of the corporation that overlaps the owner-employee's usual December 31st taxable year (e.g., having a January 31st year end for the corporation), it is possible to shift income from one year to the next. Holding back salary payments during the year and making them in January of the succeeding year may shift income from one taxable year of the owner-employee to his next taxable year, without creating any taxable income for the corporation. Generally, this is not available for S corporations and personal service corporations.

[ ]I (24) <u>$50,000 Borrowable from Qualified Retirement Plan</u> (Chapter 57): The amount of money that can be borrowed by a participant from a corporate qualified plan is generally limited to $50,000.

[ ]I (25) <u>Full Deduction for California Income Tax Purposes of Plan Contributions</u>: Several states restrict the deduction allowed for contributions allowed to noncorporate retirement plans (Keogh plans). Some states, like California, have conformed to federal law and permit a full deduction. However, this can be an important reason for using a corporation in those states that have income tax rules that restrict such deductions.

OVERVIEW OF ESTATE PLANNING — CHAPTER 1

[ ]I   (26)   <u>Rollover of Qualified Plan Account to IRA on Retirement or Death of Spouse</u> (Chapters 55-59): Recognition of income tax can be avoided by a "terminating" qualified retirement plan participant or spouse of a deceased participant by transferring – under certain conditions – the plan proceeds to an individual retirement account (IRA). Because such a transfer could have other ramifications, this should be carefully considered.

[ ]I   (27)   <u>Loss of the General Utilities Doctrine</u>: Liquidation of corporations other than S corporations will result in recognizing a tax at the corporate level on the excess of the value of any assets over the corporation's income tax basis in them. E.g., a real property owned by the corporation with a corporate tax basis (cost less depreciation) of $20,000 but which is worth $100,000 at time of liquidation, will result in a corporate tax on the $80,000 difference. Even some S corporations can recognize all or part of this corporate gain upon liquidation under the "built in gain" rules. Thus, a taxable gain can be recognized at both the corporate and shareholder levels upon liquidation of a corporation.

POTENTIAL PROBLEMS

[ ]N   (1)   <u>Wrong Choice of Form of Buy-and-Sell Agreement</u> (Chapter 47): Whether you use a stock redemption agreement or a cross purchase agreement depends on several factors which should be reviewed with a competent advisor to avoid loss of potential benefits.

[ ]N   (2)   <u>Buy-In Problems Created by High Stock Values</u>: Where future shareholders may not have much capital and where the corporation has accumulated a great deal of fair market value, many qualified prospective co-shareholders may be preempted from buying into the corporation. An example of this might be a large medical radiology group that over the years has accumulated in the operating corporation a very large amount of value related to accounts receivable and to the radiology equipment used in the practice. For a bright young doctor, it may simply cost too much to consider buying into such a corporation.

[ ]N   (3)   <u>Cash Problems in Redeeming Shares</u>: The same problem as described above of accumulating too much in the way of asset values in a corporation may make the redemption of shares a very difficult problem.

[ ]N   (4)   <u>Piercing of Corporate Veil by Creditors</u> (Chapter 50): Inadequate capitalization or failure to follow corporate procedures may result in a corporation failing to provide a shield for shareholders as to any liability for corporate debts.

[ ]N   (5)   <u>Securities Law Problems</u> (Chapter 50): Failure to observe legal requirements in creating a corporation may cause adverse civil results and even criminal penalties. The incorporation should be done by an experienced and competent attorney.

[ ]E   (6)   <u>Corporate Owned Insurance on Life of Majority Shareholder</u> (Chapter 34): Ownership by the corporation of insurance on the majority shareholder may result in that insurance being included in the taxable estate of the client-shareholder.

[ ]E   (7)   <u>Stock Valuation Problems</u> (Chapter 70): The various methods approved by the courts for valuation of corporations should be reviewed with a competent tax attorney in determining the value which estate tax authorities will place on the corporate stock. The client may be unpleasantly surprised to learn of the high value that will be assigned to a corporate ownership.

[ ]

[ ]I (8) <u>Double Taxation of Dividends</u>: (Chapter 50): Where a corporation accumulates earnings, it pays income tax on them (unless it has elected to be taxed as an S corporation). However, when the dividends are paid to the shareholder, the corporation receives no deduction or offset against taxable income but the shareholder is subject to income tax on the dividends received. For this reason, very few large dividends are paid to shareholders of privately owned C corporations.

[ ]I (9) <u>Real Property Owned by Corporation</u>: In many planning circumstances where the business activity itself is in a corporation, the ownership of the building in which the business is carried on is maintained outside the corporation. Failure to do this may cause recognition of gain at both corporate and individual levels, in those circumstances where either the business or the real property are to be sold separately or where C corporations (and even some S corporations) liquidate.

[ ]I (10) <u>Corporation Ignored as Sham by Taxing Authorities</u> (Chapter 50): Failure to observe the requirements for corporate meetings, salary arrangements, separation of ownership as between shareholder and corporation, etc., may result in all the corporate income being taxed to the individual shareholders.

[ ]I (11) <u>Possible Dividend Treatment for Payments or Benefits to Shareholder</u> (Chapter 50): Certain salary payments and other payments to or for the benefit of shareholders (e.g., personal use of a corporate auto) may be challenged by the IRS and denied as deductions to the corporation on the basis that they are "dividends."

[ ]I (12) <u>Special IRS Scrutiny for Corporate Partners</u> (Chapter 50): The IRS has a tool to use against those corporations that are partners of a partnership, e.g., medical or legal "incorporated partnerships." Corporations in this situation should review Code section 269A with competent tax counsel to see if changes in the form of business or practice should be considered.

[ ]I (13) <u>Limitation on Accumulation of Corporate Earnings</u> (Chapter 50): Accumulation of corporate earnings for purposes of avoiding income taxes may result in an additional tax equal to 20 percent. Avoidance of such tax on such accumulated earnings requires a showing that the earnings are required to be retained for the "reasonable needs of the business."

[ ]I (14) <u>Extra Tax on "Incorporated Pocketbooks"</u> (Chapter 52): Where 60 percent of the corporate income is from rents, royalties, dividends, interest, and certain personal service income (with some very significant exceptions), a large extra income tax may apply.

[ ]I (15) <u>No/Low Interest Loans from Corporation</u> (Chapter 50): Income is recognized as a dividend where a corporate owner has a loan from his corporation at no interest or at a rate lower than market. Since it is a dividend, the corporation gets no deduction.

[ ]I (16) <u>Payroll Taxes</u>: Income received as salary by a shareholder-employee is subject to social security tax paid by both the corporation and the employee. There is currently a special income tax deduction of 50 percent of the self-employment tax. Payment of rent or dividends is not subject to this tax or to any state payroll taxes.

[ ]I (17) <u>Possible Second Tax on Liquidations</u>: For C corporation liquidations, the corporation will be taxed to the extent that any assets have a value in excess of the corporation's basis in them (e.g., a building with $100,000 which has a tax basis of only $30,000). Certain S corporations can avoid this corporate level of tax, which is in addition to the tax on the shareholder to the extent that the net proceeds from the liquidation exceed his or her basis in the corporate stock.

OVERVIEW OF ESTATE PLANNING — CHAPTER 1

CHECKLIST FOR VARIOUS CIRCUMSTANCES

F. INDIVIDUAL PROPRIETORS

AREAS OF POSSIBLE BENEFIT

[ ]N (1) <u>No Corporate Creation or Operation Costs</u>: The individual proprietorship is the simplest form of doing business and avoids legal fees for incorporation as well as those for subsequent annual meetings, etc.

[ ]I (2) <u>Only One Level of Income Taxation</u>: By avoiding the corporation, one avoids the taxation of income at the corporate level and its subsequent second taxation where the payment to the shareholder is deemed to be a dividend, as opposed to being an expense deductible to the corporation (e.g., salary). One also avoids the corporate tax (which is in addition to the shareholder tax) on appreciation at the time of the sale of the business (followed by a liquidation).

[ ]I (3) <u>Assets Removable from Business without Tax</u>: Unlike the corporation or certain partnership circumstances, the individual proprietorship allows the taxpayer to remove assets or add assets without the recognition of any gain for income tax purposes.

[ ]I (4) <u>Avoidance of Social Security Tax for Family Employees</u>: Payments of salary to spouses or children permits shifting of income from an individual proprietor to other persons in the family without payment of social security taxes. This is becoming more important as social security taxes are increasing.

[ ]I (5) <u>Payroll Taxes</u>: There is a special income tax deduction of 50 percent of the self-employment tax.

[ ]I (6) <u>Ability to Produce Losses Which Can Offset Salary or Other Taxable Income</u>: Where the business is actively pursued by the owner (and thus is not a "passive" activity) and produces a tax loss, the amount of the loss can be used to reduce the amount of ordinary taxable income. However, if the taxpayer does not materially participate in an active business or the activity is considered passive, then any loss will be considered a passive loss and can only offset passive income. Passive income does not include portfolio income (e.g., interest, dividends). The allowance of passive losses is generally deferred until there is passive income to offset it. Tax shelters are the target of the passive loss rules. Material participation by the individual is now required in order to have the loss be currently applied to offset other income of the individual.

POTENTIAL PROBLEMS

[ ]N (1) <u>Lack of Shield against Liabilities</u> (Chapter 50): Unlike a corporation, the individual proprietor is liable for all debts of the business.

[ ]N (2) <u>More Difficult to Give Some of Business and Retain Control</u>: Unlike a corporate circumstance, it is very difficult to give interests in the individual proprietorship without having to deal with the possibility of some control shifting to the donee.

[ ]I (3) <u>All Inherent Gain in Assets Recognized on Sale of Business</u>: Sale of an individual proprietorship will result in the recognition of gain taxed as ordinary income with regard to sale of accounts receivable, inventory, and other assets which have a value in excess of income tax basis.

[ ]I (4) <u>Lack of Corporate Fringe Benefits</u>: The various corporate fringe benefits described above for corporations generally do not apply to an individual proprietorship.

[ ]I (5) <u>Low Keogh Plan Deduction Limit for Some State Income Taxes</u>: Some states permit only a small income tax deduction for contributions to Keogh plans. Some states, e.g., California, permit the full deduction for such contributions.

[ ]I (6) <u>All Income Taxable at Individual Rates</u>: None of the income developed by an individual proprietorship will be taxed at the often lower corporate rates or on the tax return of other family members.

[ ]I (7) <u>No Use of ESOP Available</u>: Unlike the corporation, the sale of an individual proprietorship may not have the gain deferred by sale to an ESOP and investment in corporate common stock.

[ ]I (8) <u>No Shifting of Income Between Tax Years</u>: All of the income earned in a taxable year will be subject to tax in that year as opposed to the circumstances of a corporation with a fiscal year different from that of its shareholder-employee.

[ ]I (9) <u>All Business Earnings Subject to Self-Employment Tax</u>: Unlike the corporation, where retained income may be subject only to income tax and not social security tax, earnings of an individual proprietor business are generally subject to both income tax and self-employment tax.

[ ]N (10) <u>No Pooling of Capital for Business Purposes</u> (Chapter 50): Since no other persons may be involved in the proprietorship, the individual may supply only his own or borrowed funds.

[ ]N (11) <u>Difficult to Create Market-At-Death for Business</u> (Chapter 47): Although buy-and-sell agreements may, under unusual circumstances, be created for individual proprietorships, the lack of a partner or other shareholders as a potential ready buyer is a disadvantage in creating a market for the business.

[ ]E (12) <u>Fewer Assets May Qualify for Estate Tax Deferral</u> (Chapter 18): In determining whether or not an estate meets the percentage requirements necessary to qualify for deferral of a portion of the estate tax, only those assets of an individual proprietorship which can be shown to relate directly to the business may be included in determining such percentages.

[ ]I (13) <u>No Shifting of Income to Children</u>: Unlike a partnership or an S corporation, the individual proprietorship income cannot be shifted to other persons but children can be hired as employees and paid a deductible salary if they perform needed tasks. Unearned income in excess of $2,300 (in 2023) shifted to children under age eighteen will be taxed at their parents' top marginal rate.

[ ]I (14) <u>No Operation of Individual Proprietorship in a Trust</u>: Unlike almost all other assets, there is a significant danger in holding and operating an individual proprietor business in a trust. The danger is that the IRS may be able to tax the entire trust as if it were a corporation, a very bad result! Therefore, any business operated in trusts, including revocable *inter vivos* family planning trusts, should be operated through a corporation or a partnership, which type of entity can be operated through the trust without this danger.

OVERVIEW OF ESTATE PLANNING — CHAPTER 1

CHECKLIST FOR VARIOUS CIRCUMSTANCES

G.   PARTNERS AND MEMBERS OF LLCS

AREAS OF POSSIBLE BENEFIT

[ ]N   (1)   Pooling of Capital for Business: Like a corporation, the assets of more than one person may be combined to meet the capital needs of the business.

[ ]N   (2)   Market for Business – Buy-and-Sell Agreement (Chapter 47): The existence of partners or members often creates a market for business interests which does not exist for an individual proprietorship.

[ ]N   (3)   Protection from Liability Available Through Limited Partnerships and LLCs (Chapters 49 and 51): Although the general partner(s) will always be liable for all debts and other liabilities of the partnership, a limited partnership may be created which will limit both the liability and control of a limited partner. In the case of an LLC, all members will be isolated from personal liability.

[ ]E   (4)   Reduced Value of Certain Partnerships and LLCs for Estate Tax Purposes (Chapters 49 and 70): The family partnership was a vehicle often used for attempting to "freeze" the value of real property and other assets including business interests; but such transactions are now generally subject to Code section 2701 (Chapter 71).

However, certain partnerships and LLCs which have restrictions on withdrawal of assets after the death of a partner or member can still be a very effective vehicle for reducing value of a partner's or member's interest in a partnership or LLC (But see the discussions of Code sections 2701 and 2704 in Chapter 71 and section 2703 in Chapter 47.)

[ ]I   (5)   Some Removal of Assets from Business or Even Liquidation Without Tax: Unlike a corporation, under proper circumstances, assets may sometimes be removed from a partnership or LLC, or the partnership or LLC may be liquidated without the recognition of any gain for income tax purposes. Gain may be recognized without competent advice.

[ ]I   (6)   Only One Level of Income Tax: Like an individual proprietorship, there is no double taxation of income (at both the corporate and an individual level). This benefit is really often a detriment where lower corporate income tax rates might otherwise apply (e.g., the 15 percent corporate rate for the first $50,000 of income each year for corporations which are not "personal service corporations").

[ ]I   (7)   Some Shifting of Income to Other Family Members (Chapters 49 and 51): By observing the relevant rules, some income may be shifted to other family members by giving interests in the ownership of the partnership or LLC.

[ ]I   (8)   Special Allocations of Income Between Partners or Members May Be Possible (Chapters 49 and 51): With a partnership or LLC agreement drafted by an attorney with experience in dealing with such "special allocations," it may be possible to allocate income and even income tax deductions among the partners or members in such a way as to optimize income tax planning.

[ ]I   (9)   Losses May Be Available to Offset Personal Income: Like an individual proprietorship, losses from active general partnerships flow through to the taxpayer and may offset personal income (e.g., salary, interest). However, losses from passive activities and activities in which the partner does not materially participate can only offset passive income. Passive income does not include portfolio income (e.g., interest, dividends).

THE TOOLS & TECHNIQUES OF ESTATE PLANNING

POTENTIAL PROBLEMS

(1-10) The numbered items listed for the potential problems of individual proprietors also apply to partnerships and LLCs (pages 26 & 27):

[ ]N (11) <u>Possible Liability for Actions of Partners</u>: Certain actions of a partner in relation to a general partnership may result in liability for all the other partners.

[ ]I (12) <u>Tax Due on Certain Removals of Assets from Business</u>: Certain assets (e.g., accounts receivable which have not been taken into income or highly appreciated inventory) may result in the recognition of income if withdrawn from the partnership or LLC under some circumstances.

[ ]I (13) <u>Greater Tax Shelter Audit Potential</u>: Because the partnership has been used so frequently for tax shelters, the IRS now seems to view all partnerships and LLCs with more suspicion.

[ ]I (14) <u>Disposition of Certain Partnership or LLC Interests May Trigger Recognition of Gain</u>: Where the income tax basis of the partner or member has been significantly reduced (as by depreciation expense), it may become impossible to even give away a partnership or LLC interest without the recognition of a large amount of gain.

[ ]I (15) <u>Accidental Loss of Right to Partnership or LLC Deductions</u>: In an attempt to deal with certain sophisticated tax shelter partnerships, rules may be imposed on all partnerships or LLCs which may cause a partner's or member's share of expense to be capitalized as opposed to being available to offset income.

[ ]I (16) <u>Passive Limited Partnerships</u>: The deduction of "passive losses" is generally disallowed. If the limited partner does not materially participate, losses from the limited partnership generally cannot be taken currently but must be deferred until there is "passive income" (which excludes dividends, interest, and certain other income) against which the passive loss can be offset.

[ ]I (17) <u>Inactive General Partners Not Allowed Current Partnership Loss Deductions</u>: In focusing on "passive income" as a likely way to deal with tax shelters, the passive loss rules require that there be "material participation" in the activity in order for even a general partner to currently deduct the loss from the partnership. A lower standard of "active participation" is required for real estate rental activity.

[ ]I (18) <u>Avoiding Corporate Classification</u>: In structuring both limited partnerships and LLCs, care must be taken to avoid at least two of the four corporate characteristics – limited liability, free transferability of interest, continuity of life, and centralized management.

OVERVIEW OF ESTATE PLANNING — CHAPTER 1

CHECKLIST FOR VARIOUS CIRCUMSTANCES

H. BUSINESS PERSONS IN GENERAL

AREAS OF POSSIBLE BENEFIT

[ ]N (1) <u>Creating and Maintaining Market for Business</u> (Chapter 47): Whether the business is in a corporate, partnership, LLC, or individual proprietorship form, planning can be done to create a market for the business whether that may be by creating a buy-and-sell agreement or whether it is accumulating information on other prospective purchasers of the business.

[ ]E (2) <u>Sharing of Name Goodwill within Family</u>: It may be possible to bestow benefits onto family members by permitting the use of a business name without the actual recognition of a gift or the application of a gift tax.

[ ]E (3) <u>Personal Financial Guarantees for Family Members</u>: Like the use of a family name, personal financial guarantees may currently permit the bestowing of real benefits on a family member or other person without the actual recognition of a gift or the application of a gift tax (but beware of continuing expansion of the *Dickman* deemed gift theory).

[ ]E (4) <u>Special Use (Low) Valuation for Estate Tax</u> (Chapter 70): Unlike investments in cash, securities, or investment real property, certain assets involved in a business (such as real property used for business) or farming may be subject to special rules which will permit use of lower values for estate tax purposes.

[ ]E (5) <u>Deferral and Installment Payments for Estate Tax</u> (Chapter 18): Again, unlike investments in cash, securities, or investment real property, investment of the assets in an active business may permit the payment of related estate tax over a period as long as fourteen years and at a very low interest rate for a portion of the tax.

POTENTIAL PROBLEMS

[ ]N (1) <u>Heirs Ignorant of Market for Business</u> (Chapter 47): Preservation of estate values argues strongly for communicating to one's spouse and heirs any plans for the business and especially potential markets for the sale of the business.

[ ]N (2) <u>Lack of Instruction to Heirs as to Disposition or Continuation of Business</u>: Often only the family member active in the business knows whether it should be continued or sold upon his death. Failure to communicate to other family members on this point may result in a tragically wrong decision as to the disposition or continuation of the business.

[ ]N (3) <u>Lack of Successor Management</u> (Chapter 47): Existence of a buy-and-sell agreement may provide for some successor management that otherwise would not be available for the business. The universal dislike for thinking of one's own death often results in no planning in this important area for maintenance of the value of the business.

[ ]N (4) <u>Lack of Cash Reserves at Owner's Death</u> (Chapter 34): Failure to provide for cash availability (e.g., through insurance) at the death of the person on whom the business depends often results in the complete collapse of the business.

CHECKLIST FOR VARIOUS CIRCUMSTANCES

I. <u>RANCHER OR FARMER</u>

AREAS OF POSSIBLE BENEFIT

[ ]E   (1)   <u>Special Use (Low) Valuation For Estate Tax</u> (Chapter 70): Ranches and farms actually worked by the client are subject to very favorable rules for valuation as farm land rather than their value for use as shopping centers, subdivisions, etc.

[ ]E   (2)   <u>Deferral and Installment Payments for Estate Tax</u> (Chapter 18): Ranchers and farmers are particularly favored in the application of rules for the deferral of tax and payment (at low interest rates) over a period as long as 14 years.

[ ]I   (3)   <u>No Income Recognized Until Sale of Product</u>: Special cash basis rules for farmers permit the reaping of crops without the recognition of the income until the time the crops are actually sold and value received by the seller.

[ ]I   (4)   <u>Some Greater Flexibility for Cash Deduction</u>: Although some restrictions have been placed on the deductibility of farm payments, the farmer generally has more flexibility in this regard than the average business man.

[ ]I   (5)   <u>Avoidance of Income Tax at Death on Some Products</u>: Certain crops and livestock may receive a new income tax basis at death so as to prevent any recognition of gain upon their being sold.

POTENTIAL PROBLEMS

[ ]N   (1)   <u>Liquidity Problems of Land Ownership</u>: Typically, a farmer or rancher has the greatest need for estate tax liquidity (often in the form of insurance) since so much of the total value of the farm is in the form of land that may not be readily saleable without destroying the farm as a viable unit.

[ ]N   (2)   <u>Loss of Political Power</u>: Because efficiency of operation and a number of other factors have drastically reduced the number of farmers in relation to the rest of the nation, the formerly very impressive political power of the American farmer or rancher has deteriorated greatly. This fact, combined with increasing free world trade in agriculture, has resulted in reductions in income received from certain areas of farming.

[ ]E   (3)   <u>Loss of Deferral of Estate Tax</u> (Chapter 18): Changing the farm operation to a cash rent basis can cause loss of this particularly important estate tax benefit.

CHECKLIST FOR VARIOUS CIRCUMSTANCES

J. PROFESSIONALS

General Comment: Usually the term "professional" is applied to those persons who have met certain educational goals and who usually perform services for others (e.g., architects, dentists, doctors, engineers, lawyers, etc.).

Although many of these people work for large companies as employees, a large proportion work essentially for themselves, as individual proprietors or partners and in corporate form. Thus, the professional should review the appropriate checklists for Individual Proprietorships, Partners and LLCs, or Owners of Private Corporations, or perhaps that of the Corporate Executive where the category may be appropriate (usually thought of as applying to highly paid employees of large corporations).

Over the years, many professionals have incorporated for income tax benefit reasons. While some of the incentives for such incorporations have been removed, there are many benefits of incorporation still available and the professional who is not yet incorporated should review the possible benefits and detriments listed in the checklist for Owners of Private Corporations to determine if his estate might be improved by incorporating.

Below are listed some specific areas of possible benefit or problems which generally apply to professionals, regardless of the form in which they practice their profession:

AREAS OF POSSIBLE BENEFIT

[ ]N (1) Cost Savings Available from Professional Groups: Frequently, membership in professional groups may provide medical or insurance coverage at lower rates than are generally available.

[ ]N (2) Market for Business/Practice Enhanced by Professional Group: Some groups provide special services for retirees or estates of deceased members in finding a purchaser for the practice or business. Although professional goodwill may often die with a practitioner, in many cases such services can be very beneficial.

POTENTIAL PROBLEMS

[ ]N (1) Licensing Limitation on Marketability of Business or Practice: Most states limit the practice of many professions only to those persons who are licensed by the state. Upon the death of someone practicing one of these professions, there is only the limited market of state licensees to whom the practice or business may be transferred. Such restrictions on marketability obviously will reduce the value that will be received from such a sale.

[ ]N (2) Licensing Restrictions on Transfers to Family Members: The same license restrictions typically often prevent shifting the value of the business or profession to the next generation over a period of years.

[ ]N (3) Personal Liability Even Where Corporate Form Used: Except for those professionals who perform work for the benefit of large corporations as opposed to benefiting the public, there is always some personal exposure of a professional who performs services for another person or entity. Although a sufficiently capitalized and properly operated corporation can shield the owner-employee from liability caused by the acts of other persons, each individual is still liable for his or her own acts regardless of the fact that the business may be carried on in a corporate form.

[ ]I (4) No Low Corporate Tax Rates: For most professionals who use the corporate form, there will be the disadvantage that income left in the corporation cannot be taxed at only 15 percent or 25 percent rates for lower levels of income. A personal service corporation is taxed at a flat 35 percent rate.

CHECKLIST FOR VARIOUS CIRCUMSTANCES

K.   CORPORATE EXECUTIVES

AREAS OF POSSIBLE BENEFIT

[ ]N   (1)   Sick Pay – Disability Pay: Executives working for large corporations whose welfare and profitability does not depend solely on their efforts have a very real benefit in the contract provisions usually available for continuation of pay regardless of whether they may be sick or disabled. Agreements to spread compensation over future years often produce income tax benefits for the employee. Typically, this is available in and feasible for large corporations where the lack of current deductibility for such future payments is not the significant problem that it is for the smaller, private corporations.

[ ]I   (2)   Income Tax Benefits Allowed to All Corporate Employees: The various possible benefits described in the Owners of Private Corporations check-list are all available to the extent that the corporation is willing to tailor its decisions to benefit the corporate executive. Often the cost of including other employees of a large corporation may limit flexibility in benefits available to executives but they may still be very substantial.

[ ]I   (3)   "Non-Qualified" Deferred Compensation (Chapter 54): The stability and good financial position of many large corporations permit many executives to enter, reasonably worry-free, into agreements which defer some portion of their compensation to future years (usually after a planned retirement date) when income tax can be expected to have less impact. Additionally, many such arrangements provide the equivalent of accumulation of "effective interest" (in the form of increase of the compensation based on how long it is deferred) that is not taxed until it is received.

[ ]I   (4)   Incentive Stock Options: Incentive stock options may both defer taxation and shift such benefits from ordinary income rates to capital gain rates. Strict rules must be adhered to in issuing such options.

[ ]I   (5)   Regular and Restricted Stock Options: Although they may not qualify for the special tax benefits afforded incentive stock options, options to buy stock of a very successful business may be very valuable. By having certain restrictions on such options, in some instances the amount of gain recognized may be substantially reduced without a proportionate reduction in real value to the corporate employee.

[ ]I   (6)   "Phantom Stock" Plans: Contracts can provide both current income based upon the equivalent of ownership of stock and also future payment for equity which would be equal to the amount to which stock might have appreciated.

[ ]I   (7)   Education: Any company employee can receive tax-free, under many circumstances, education which is related to the business and designed to improve existing skills or to qualify a person for an existing job even though these expenses are all paid for and deducted by the employer company.

[ ]I   (8)   Professional and Business Club Dues: Like education, if these are really related to the business, they may be received tax-free by an individual and can be deducted by the corporation. However, greater scrutiny is being directed at such benefits.

[ ]I   (9)   Death Benefits: Some large companies also have practices of making payments that may be considered gifts to the employees. However, the IRS frequently does not quietly accept the concept of seeing a deductible expense result in no taxable income to the employee.

[ ]I   (10) Expense Accounts: Like the private corporation, travel and entertainment expenses paid for by the employee may be reimbursed to the executive tax-free (50 percent not deductible by the corporation in some cases), to the extent that it may be shown that they are required for a company to carry out its business. More strict substantiation of such expenses has been required in recent years.

OVERVIEW OF ESTATE PLANNING — CHAPTER 1

[ ]I (11) <u>Company Lodging</u>: A long line of cases show that there may be a reasonable deduction for the corporation to provide an employee with tax-free lodging where it is in the best interests of the company that he live on the corporate premises or close to such premises. Each case must be examined on its own merits.

[ ]I (12) <u>Additional Executive "Perks" and Benefits</u>: Many other additional executive perquisites are frequently offered, including housing aid, company cars, country club dues, tickets for various performances, sabbatical leaves, and similar niceties. However, the possibility of receiving significant benefits without the recognition of income has been greatly restricted. Some benefits may well end up as a basis for income recognition by the recipients.

POTENTIAL PROBLEMS

[ ]N (1) <u>Possibility of Being Lulled into a False Sense of Security and High Spending Habits</u>: Since most of us prefer to ignore unpleasant things, many executives who have relied upon retirement based on time spent with the employer have not felt it necessary to put aside funds for retirement and often find that a change in corporate structure may cut off their plans for relying on corporate funding for retirement.

[ ]N (2) <u>Non-Diversification of Assets through Investment in Company Stock</u>: Often executives show their loyalty and find some job leverage by investing all of their available funds in stock of the employer corporations. This may be increased by the existence of an employer "stock savings plan" which invests in stock of the employer. Employees of some companies have done well with such circumstances, but many others would have done much better to diversify their asset holdings.

[ ]N (3) <u>Directing Available Cash into Tax Shelters with Little/No Real Value</u>: Where the executive feels frustrated that all of his earnings are taxable as ordinary income and that he has no "tax benefits," he often succumbs to the thought of reducing current income tax by putting his or her cash into "tax shelters." With the exception of certain investments in real property and, occasionally, oil programs on a diversified basis, most such "investments" do not produce real assets which provide security for retirement or for the family in the event of death of the executive.

Further, most tax shelters will not be effective in providing current deductions against salary income. An exception is "actively" managed real property producing losses up to $25,000. Even this exemption is phased out as the taxpayer's adjusted gross income increases from $100,000 to $150,000, at which level no rental property losses are allowed regardless of how actively the properties are managed by the taxpayer.

[ ]E (4) <u>Forced Migrancy Can Cause Asset Title Problems</u>: Company mandated moves between separate property and community property states can cause accidental gifts between spouses (generally, not taxable for federal tax purposes) and confusion with title which should be reviewed with competent tax counsel.

[ ]I (5) <u>Loss of Deduction for Unreimbursed Travel and Entertainment Expenses</u>: Substantiation of all such expenses is generally required. For the executive who plans to deduct on his own return such expenses which are not reimbursed by his employer, if he has a tax return preparer do his return, the preparer will require a written certificate from the executive that adequate records exist. Further, such deductions are permitted only to the extent that they, together with other "miscellaneous" deductions, exceed 2 percent of adjusted gross income.

[ ]I (6) <u>Recognition of Income from "Perks" and Discounts</u>: The scope of benefits that can be received tax free by the employee has been greatly restricted. Those benefits that create no additional cost for the employer, like filling empty airline seats with employees or their relatives, may continue to be tax-free (in a more scrutinized form), but those that actually cost the employer are now subjected to rules that reduce benefits usually afforded tax free to executives.

[ ]I (7) <u>"Golden Parachute" Excise Tax</u>: Where there are payments or property transfers that are contingent on a change in ownership or control of a corporation or its assets, or large payments (over certain salary limits), a 20 percent excise tax is imposed on the recipient – in addition to income tax!

THE TOOLS & TECHNIQUES OF ESTATE PLANNING

CHECKLIST FOR VARIOUS CIRCUMSTANCES

L. PERSONS PLANNING FOR RETIREMENT

AREAS OF POSSIBLE BENEFIT

[ ]N/I (1) Build Up of Assets in a Qualified Plan (Chapters 56, 57 and 59): Using the income-tax-free provisions of a qualified retirement plan permits a much more rapid buildup of assets to provide financial security for retirement than would the same amount paid out as additional current salary.

[ ]N (2) Receipt of Social Security Payments before Actual Retirement: Although the relatively vague social security eligibility rules may sometimes prevent it, some persons upon reaching age sixty-two or sixty-six have shifted their earnings to future years (e.g., to age seventy when earnings do not inhibit social security payments) by deferred compensation arrangements with employers or by shifting income to a corporation or pension plan in order to be able to draw the social security benefits for which they paid over past years.

[ ]I (3) Stretching Qualified Plan Benefits Over Retirement Period (Chapter 59): Where the plan rules permit, electing to receive plan benefits over a period of time may often provide a larger total retirement benefit by postponing the recognition of income tax until payments are received, and thus permitting a large amount of such benefits still in the plan to continue tax-free production of income for future payments to the retired employee. Generally, payment from such plans must start on the later of April 1 of the year after the participant reaches age 72 or retires.

[ ]I (4) Qualifying for "Lump Sum Averaging" for Qualified Plan Payments (Chapters 56 and 57): Some plans may require a "lump sum" distribution of plan assets. Meeting certain requirements can permit the availability of certain rules of income taxation which, for smaller and medium size plan benefits which are paid out as "lump sums," can result in lower income taxes than otherwise would result. Very strict rules must be observed.

[ ]I (5) Use of Deferred Compensation Program to Reduce Income Taxes: Where the employer makes it feasible and one's financial stability and budget permits, shifting some current compensation to future years after retirement may both reduce income tax overall and also, under some circumstances, permit an employee who does not retire at 65 to begin to receive social security payments. Local social security offices are looking more closely at such arrangements, however.

[ ]I (6) Use of Corporation to Receive Income Produced after Retirement: Many employers, particularly those with significant pension benefits, may permit an employee to "retire" and to stay on as a consultant without significant employee benefits. Using a corporation to provide such consulting services may often reduce income tax and sometimes make social security payments currently available. Social Security offices actively seek to restrict such practices.

POTENTIAL PROBLEMS

[ ]N (1) Loss of Insurance or Medical Benefits Previously Provided by Employment: Failure to review company insurance programs may result in loss of life insurance or medical coverage which might have been assumed before retirement by the employee at lower group rates not usually available to individuals.

[ ]N (2) Failure to Create Estate for Retirement: Although this problem may not be solvable in some circumstances, it can be avoided in many circumstances with good planning and will power.

[ ]N (3) <u>Stagnation of Physical and Mental Abilities</u>: Studies consistently show that continued mental abilities and physical capacities can be maintained where activity is continued as opposed to cessation of physical and mental effort upon retirement. Planning for continued activity in an area where one has the opportunity to find satisfaction will not only improve financial circumstances but also lead to a longer and fuller life.

[ ]I (4) <u>Failure to Qualify Lump Sum Retirement Plan Benefit for "Lump Sum Averaging"</u>: Failure to follow strict rules (e.g., permitting only one "averaging" after age 59½) can cause retirement benefit payments to be taxed at regular ordinary income tax rates.

[ ]I (5) <u>Requiring Sale of Company Stock Held in Retirement Plan</u>: Lack of good tax advice can lose a tax benefit to those persons who are retiring from employment which included a qualified retirement plan which, in the retiree's account, contained stock contributed by the employer or purchased by the plan. Correct treatment will permit the acquisition of such stock and taxation only at the price at which it was acquired by the plan. Sale of the stock by the plan before distribution will result in loss of the benefit.

CHECKLIST FOR VARIOUS CIRCUMSTANCES

M.   PERSONS PLANNING FOR MARRIAGE

AREAS OF POSSIBLE BENEFIT

[ ]N   (1)   <u>Entering Into Premarital Agreement Clarifying Title Holding</u>: Hindsight clearly shows the advantage to both parties of facing the question of property rights and laying out in a clear agreement any understandings with regard to change of ownership of property. Listing the property belonging to each person at the beginning of the marriage has much merit and little real detriment.

[ ]N   (2)   <u>Entering Into Premarital Agreement Clarifying Ownership of Earnings and Retirement Plan Rights</u>: Not only should the separate property or community property rights of each party in the earnings of either party be clarified before the marriage but, particularly where there may be retirement plans, the separate property aspects of such retirement rights generated before the marriage should be clarified. The increasing importance of private retirement plan rights to many people argues for maintaining them as separate property until it is certain that the new marriage will be a stable one.

[ ]N   (3)   <u>Executing New Will After or In Contemplation of Marriage</u>: By executing a will which recognizes either an impending marriage or one that has just occurred, the new spouse will not be in the position of being a "pretermitted heir" and thus the testamentary scheme will not be disrupted by the laws of intestacy which favor such "pretermitted heirs."

[ ]N   (4)   <u>Use of Trust to Avoid Probate as to Prenuptial Agreement Assets</u>: Where a spouse-to-be has been given certain rights (e.g., a life estate in specific assets in place of other marital rights), it may serve the purposes of both avoiding probate and avoiding future creditors of the donor by placing that asset or set of assets into an irrevocable trust.

[ ]E   (5)   <u>Ability to Defer Estate Tax With Marital Deduction</u> (Chapter 27): The existence of a formal marriage permits the deferral of estate tax by an arrangement which benefits the new spouse at least during his or her lifetime. A QTIP trust will permit the assets to avoid taxation at the death of the owning spouse as long as the income is paid to the new spouse. At the new spouse's death, the assets can thereafter go to the children of the prior marriage or to anyone else. This may often permit a business, which could not currently provide the funds for estate tax without causing its collapse, to mature and be in a position where cash reserves may be developed for payment of estate tax at the death of the second spouse and thus preserving the asset for the children of the first marriage.

Obviously, for the presently single person who wants to provide a benefit for a "live-in partner," marriage can provide a totally estate tax-free transition at his or her death.

[ ]E   (6)   <u>The Ability to Make Tax-Free Gifts by Deferral Until Marriage</u>: Gifts in large amounts that would produce a gift tax if given to a "friend" or "live-in partner" can be transferred totally free of gift tax if given to a person with whom there has been a formal marriage.

[ ]E   (7)   <u>Creating Estate Tax Deductible Liability in Place of Marital Right of Spouse</u>: In some states, the amount that would be automatically given under state laws to a spouse would not result in any deduction for estate tax purposes. Many such rights can be replaced with a clear liability which, when reduced to a proper contract, may result in a deductible liability for the estate of the deceased spouse.

OVERVIEW OF ESTATE PLANNING CHAPTER 1

[ ]E   (8) <u>Implications of Marriage Upon the Portability of the Estate Tax Applicable Exclusion Amount</u>: As discussed in Chapter 18, the law provides that a surviving spouse may inherit the unused estate tax exemption of a deceased spouse. This is accomplished through the Deceased Spousal Unused Exclusion Amount (DSUEA). However, the amount of this exemption available to the estate of the spouse is based upon the spouse's last deceased spouse. Therefore, if a spouse remarries, and then survives the new spouse; the amount of the DSUEA will be based upon the second spouse, as opposed to amount "inherited" from the first spouse.

POTENTIAL PROBLEMS

[ ]N   (1)   <u>Ineffective Termination of Prior Marriages</u>: In order for the marital deduction to be available, there must be a real marriage. The failure to properly terminate a prior marriage will prevent a subsequent marriage from being effective.

[ ]N   (2)   <u>Lack of New Estate Plan</u>: Failure to execute a will or trust which recognizes the new marriage may give the new spouse rights, as a pretermitted heir, which divert assets from the children of a prior marriage. For example, in California, half of the separate property of a wife will go to her new husband as a pretermitted heir if he is not recognized in her will, and thus the child of the wife from a former marriage will receive only half of the assets of the mother.

[ ]N   (3)   <u>Failure to Recognize the Possible Automatic Payments "to Spouse"</u>: Many company death benefits, salary continuation rights, and pension benefits may be paid automatically "to the spouse of the employee" where there has been a failure to properly designate the employee's intended objects of his bounty (e.g., his mother or his children from a former marriage).

[ ]E   (4)   <u>Making Significant Gifts before Marriage</u> (Chapter 20): The marital deduction does not apply to gifts made other than to spouses. Gifts made before marriage can use the $17,000 (as indexed in 2023) gift tax annual exclusion, but the excess is subject to gift tax.

[ ]N   (5)   <u>Failure to Deal With Rights in Retirement Plans</u>: Where either or both of the spouses have rights that have been built up in retirement plans, failure to deal with such rights by a written agreement may have a very bad result in the event of a divorce or a death.

[ ]E   (6)   <u>Automatic Right of New Spouse to Half of Retirement Plan Benefits</u>: Upon one year of marriage, the participant's spouse receives the equivalent of the right to half of the pension benefits. Without a specific manner of written approval of the new spouse, the participant cannot direct all of his plan benefit to the children of his prior marriage or to anyone else! Without the prescribed form of written approval from the new spouse, existing designation of persons other than the spouse are invalid as to the spouse's half! This is very important for persons about to marry.

CHECKLIST FOR VARIOUS CIRCUMSTANCES

N.   PERSONS PLANNING FOR SEPARATION OR DIVORCE

POSSIBLE AREAS OF BENEFIT

[ ]N   (1)   <u>Use of Alimony and/or Child Support Trust to Insure Payment</u>: Putting assets into a separate irrevocable trust, at the time of the divorce, may insure actual payment of such amounts as compared to the possible results of leaving the assets in the hands of the other spouse.

[ ]N   (2)   <u>Use of Life Insurance Trust to Insure Premium Payment</u> (Chapter 34): Life insurance may be a most important asset in many instances, and both the ability of the other spouse to cancel the policy and the failure of the other spouse to make premium payments can be avoided by placing into an irrevocable trust both the policy and assets which will produce income to make the premium payments.

[ ]I   (3)   <u>Avoiding Income Tax and Changing Beneficiary Designation on Division of Pension Plan Benefits</u> (Chapter 57): Proper planning and a tolerant employer can result in the division of retirement benefits upon divorce without the often premature recognition of income tax caused by the actual distribution of such assets.

Now, under current law, a properly drafted qualified domestic relations order (QDRO) can provide for such segregation and the ability of the divorced spouse who was not a plan participant to have a new and changed provision for beneficiary arrangements in the event of death prior to distribution of the assets from the qualified retirement plan.

[ ]I   (4)   <u>Arranging Deductibility of Some Legal Costs</u>: Certain aspects of a divorce (e.g., advice in regard to taxation) may be deductible. Identifying these amounts and limiting other areas of cost may result in significant income tax savings.

[ ]I   (5)   <u>Qualifying Alimony for Deductibility</u>: Requirements for deductibility of alimony should be reviewed and observed in arranging alimony payments so that the desired deductibility can be provided. Where there is only a single income earner, such deductibility can result in an overall larger amount available to both persons after income taxes.

[ ]I   (6)   <u>Providing for Children as Income Tax Exemptions</u>: The rules provide a definite means of shifting such exemptions in the manner the parties desire. Such rules must be observed closely in the child support agreement and they may even be drafted in such a way as to help enforce child support payments.

[ ]I   (7)   <u>Contribution to IRA Based on Alimony Receipt</u> (Chapter 56): Amounts received that qualify for alimony may be the basis for a deductible payment into an IRA.

POTENTIAL PROBLEMS

[ ]N   (1)   <u>Failure to Change Estate Plan</u>: Although divorce may effectively revoke a will as to spousal benefits, divorce does not necessarily change the effect of a will or trust in some circumstances, and estate plans should be reviewed and perhaps revised in contemplation of or promptly after any divorce or separation in order to carry out the intentions of the client.

OVERVIEW OF ESTATE PLANNING — CHAPTER 1

[ ]N   (2)   <u>Loss of Medical Plan Coverage</u>: Where one spouse's employment provides medical plan benefits for both spouses and possibly for children, most divorce or legal separation circumstances will terminate such protection for the non-employed family members where the employee works for a small company. However, COBRA requires that employers of twenty or more employees must provide, at 2 percent over cost, coverage for dependents of terminated employees where there has been a separation or divorce.

[ ]N   (3)   <u>Loss of Life Insurance Coverage</u>: As with the employer provided medical plan coverage described above, divorce or legal separation often destroys possible life insurance protection previously provided.

[ ]I   (4)   <u>Recognition of Income Tax on Retirement Plan Division</u> (Chapter 59): Division of retirement plan rights, which result in distribution of the assets to the participant or the spouse, will result in current income tax, a circumstance that may well be avoided by seeking an arrangement for division of the retirement benefits or other available means of preventing receipt and current income tax recognition. Actions that are not founded on good tax advice can result in the unnecessary recognition of gain. A properly drawn qualified domestic relations order (QDRO) can shift benefits to a non-participant spouse without forcing recognition of income tax. Even where assets are distributed from a qualified plan to the spouse of the participant, income tax may be deferred by reinvesting such distribution in an individual retirement account (IRA) within sixty days of its receipt.

CHAPTER ENDNOTES

1. FDIC, "How Are My Deposits Insured by the FDIC?" available at: www.fdic.gov/deposit/covered/categories.html.
2. Note that the 2010 Tax Relief Act amended I.R.C. §2010(c)(2) to provide that the applicable exclusion amount is the sum of the basic exclusion amount ($12,920,000 in 2023), plus the Deceased Spousal Unused Exclusion Amount (DSUEA). The rules for the DSUEA are discussed in Chapter 27.
3. Portions of this section are adapted from Hood, L. Paul, Jr., *Yours, Mine & Ours: Estate Planning for People in Blended or Step Families* (Paul Hood Services 2022).
4. See, e.g., Section 2-802, Uniform Probate Code.
5. See, e.g., *Egelhoff v. Egelhoff*, 532 U.S. 141 (2001).
6. Hesch, Jerry, "Financial Danger of Maximizing Taxable Gifts in 2012," Steve Leimberg's Estate Planning Newsletter 2035.

DATA GATHERING AND ANALYSIS AND INITIAL CLIENT INTERVIEW

CHAPTER 2

2.1 INTRODUCTION

The single most important skill of an estate or financial planner is the ability to understand who the client is, where that client stands in relation to the objectives (realized or subconscious) he may have, and what things have to be done to move the client closer to the realization of these goals. Knowledge of the client, the client's fears, hopes, dreams, the objects of the client's bounty and their fears, hopes, and dreams (often not the same as the client's), the client's property, and the relation of each to the others is essential to the estate or financial planner in utilizing this skill.

An ability to gather accurate, comprehensive, and useful information is most efficiently developed through the use of a data gathering system. Each question in the pages that follow is designed to help the attorney, the CPA, the trust officer, the financial planner, life insurance agent, or charitable planner obtain comprehensive and useful information in a logical, orderly manner.

The reason for some questions will be apparent, the justification for others will be less obvious but equally important. Not every question should be asked of every client or prospective client. Nor are the forms and questions meant to be used "as is" in every case. They are meant only as a starting place, to be adapted to suit each professional's needs and method of operation. Some will use only a few pages; others will ask almost every question and use almost every page. It is important to recognize that the data gathering and worksheet forms in this book must be used carefully and selectively, and modified to both the needs of the planner and the circumstances of the client.

Even the most opposed skeptics cannot deny that there are some parallels between what estate planners do in the initial client interview and follow-up counseling and what those in the other helping professions do. Many clients and patients have difficulty coming to grips with the issues involved in each scenario. Similar to mental and physical assessments, estate planning assessments and recommendations must be based upon accurate and complete information. Like psychologists, psychiatrists and social workers, the estate planner must often simultaneously obtain accurate information from new clients while, at the same time, convincing them that the planner possesses the requisite levels of trust, empathy and expertise to be given the very information that is required in order to do the jobs correctly. Both estate planners and helpers share the challenge of having to overcome barriers, some deliberate and some subconscious, constructed by the client/patient, third parties and estate/financial planning advisers, and sometimes all of the above.

The processes of engagement, data gathering, understanding, and assessment are in actuality parallel processes.[1]

That the estate planners have to do all of this at once, most without the benefit of formal training or education in these matters, will give the planner (and many of the clients) great anxiety. In fact, all aspects of estate planning are impacted by human processes. Therefore, why isn't there more focus on or study of, or formal education about, estate planning as a human process? It is due to a lack of focused and continuous research and, in many events, circumvented by our ethical responsibilities in the area of confidentiality.

2.2 WHY THE INITIAL INTERVIEW IS SO CRITICAL IN ESTATE PLANNING[2]

There does not seem to be much disagreement amongst estate planners that obtaining accurate, complete information is critical to fashion a proper estate plan and to keep the estate planner away from malpractice. Yet estate planners do not focus much attention to the formal knowledge of interviewing skills. Other helping professions see it a bit differently.

> *In a survey of practicing and teaching clinicians, comprehensive interviewing was ranked the highest of thirty-two skills by mental health practitioners.*[3]

Based upon the dearth of writing on the subject of interviewing and human processes as applied to estate planning, it is arguable that estate planners do not classify interviewing skills as very important. It is argued that the skill of client interviewing is just as important in estate planning as it is in the other helping professions.[4]

Is there really more to the initial estate planning client interview than having some basic social skills and a good fact-finder? Can estate planning interview skills be identified, taught and learned? Consider the following quote and accompanying commentary.

> *If interviewing only involved getting patients to answer questions, clinicians could assign the task to a computer and spend their time doing other things. But a good interviewer must know how to work with a range of different personalities and problems: to give free rein to the informative patient, to guide the rambling patient, to encourage the silent one and to mollify the hostile one. Nearly anyone can learn these skills.*[5]

The good news is that the statement above is true, that like technical estate planning skill, nearly every estate planner can learn and improve interviewing skills. If psychologists, psychiatrists and social workers can organize, study, teach and learn interviewing skills tailored to their respective helping professions, then so can estate planners. Estate planners must focus on the interview aspects of the estate planning process as well as the estate planning process itself. Estate planners can only do this by examining the client interview both from the respective human standpoints as refracted through the lens of the interviewer and interviewee.

Most of the efforts of estate planners in obtaining information tend to be focused solely on the cognitive aspects of "getting the facts" and getting them correct via a fact-finder. In fact, some fastidious estate planners constantly update their fact-finders in an attempt to keep up with the evolution of all possibly relevant information. In practice, rarely seen is a fact-finder that strays very far from the sub-specialty of the particular estate planner who utilizes that form. Unfortunately, the information that must be obtained in an estate planning interview includes information, which is both verbal and nonverbal, fact and feeling. Too often, some of the most critical information that a client (or someone else) sends to an estate planner is off of the estate planner's pre-set radar screen of the cold hard facts.

Have you ever had initial client interviews start out well, and then something was said or done (or not said verbally but perhaps communicated through body language), quite often unrelated or even only tangentially related to the issues at hand, that impacted the interview and ultimately the relationship? In the worst case, a client who has a negative experience in an estate planning initial interview may postpone doing the estate planning that the client needs to do, with potentially severe negative implications. The estate planner may lose the client as well. Thus, how the initial interview goes can inform or shape the remainder of the client/estate planner relationship.

2.3 WHAT GOES THROUGH THE MINDS OF THE PARTICIPANTS DURING AN INITIAL INTERVIEW?

What goes through the minds of an estate planning advisor and a new client during that initial encounter? As the quote below correctly observes, the relationship between interviewer and interviewee changes with each verbal and nonverbal exchange.

> *The initial psychiatric interview is a creative act. It is a study of movement and change. It is unique. The circumstances, the environment, and the people involved can never be duplicated. Even if the interviewer and interviewee wanted to replicate their own interaction, they could not; for with each sentence their interaction has subtly changed. This creativity is harnessed by two pivotal principles: (1) the patient must be powerfully engaged, and (2) a thorough and valid data base must be gathered in a limited amount of time. These two principles form the basis of the initial therapeutic encounter. They represent a complementary pair. When performed*

with sensitivity, thorough data gathering mirrors effective engagement.[6]

The same could be said about the initial estate planning interview. The potential thoughts of all participants in an initial estate planning interview vary greatly. The following is intended to cover the reasonable possibilities of thoughts that occur to the estate planner and client during an initial interview. The range of these possible thoughts covers the waterfront for each, certainly a wider range than most of us may realize.[7] There is a high potential for anxiety on the part of all participants in an initial estate planning interview, estate planner and client alike. Note that both the client and the estate planner have many common thoughts. But if these thoughts are not discussed in the proper manner and at the proper time, the estate planning process can be severely lagging, if not derailed.

2.4 THE MINDS OF THE ESTATE PLANNER AND THE CLIENT DURING THE INITIAL INTERVIEW

A Meeting of the Minds or Two Ships Passing in the Night?

The Estate Planner

Am I physically safe with this client?

Will this person make me uncomfortable?

If meeting with more than one person, either scheduled or unscheduled, is this too many people to be meeting with?

Am I being used or part of an agenda of this person other than estate planning?

Can this client pay reasonable fees to do the estate planning work that I feel he or she needs?

Will this client pay the reasonable fees for the work that I perform?

How likely is it that this client or his or her family will sue me or attempt to drag me into a fight after the client's death or during a divorce on an involuntary, non-paying basis as a witness?

Will this client be pleased with my work or with the work of any advisor?

Can I expand my services with this client into other needs, including those of companies owned by the client?

How likely is it that this client will refer me to other friends or relatives?

Will I run into a snag or complication that will cause the final cost of my services to be significantly higher than the quoted fee (or fee range)?

Can I rely on this client's representations of the facts and figures? How much "due diligence" will I have to do?

Does the client "have all of his or her marbles?" (Or at least enough to execute legally valid documents or enter into legally binding documents)?

Can I fit this client into one of the "standard forms or plans" that I have developed with a minimum of "original thought of drafting" (translated, without additional risk-taking or cost)? Will this client understand this reality, or should I go over that now and possibly alarm the client needlessly?

Will I enjoy working with this client?

Will I rue the day that I ever agreed to take on this client at the quoted rates?

What are this client's expectations regarding turnaround time and my personal availability?

Will this client permit me to allow his or her work (or at least original draft(s)) to be prepared by the person in my office with the lowest rate scale who is competent to perform the work?

With whom may I speak in the course of doing this work? With whom should I absolutely not speak?

What confidentiality issues are present with this client? Should I send mail, faxes or electronic correspondence to a particular place? Should

I call prior to sending? May I leave voice mail messages, even to say that I called?

Will I encounter problems with the client's spouse, children or significant others? How clear must I be that I do not represent or work for them?

How much "TLC" or "hand-holding" will this client expect or require? Does this client understand that this can have a bearing on fees or desirability to have them as a client?

Will this client ask or pressure me to do anything that would compromise my personal integrity or even my professional license or designation, *e.g.*, backdating documents, misleading others about effect of documents, forging signatures, not following formal execution procedures, lying or omitting material health information on a life insurance application, *etc.*?

How many other advisors before me has the client gone through? Why?

Will this client present problems that I lack the confidence or competence to handle? Would they allow me to bring in help? Should I discuss this candidly up front, or will this needlessly alert the client that they perhaps should choose another advisor?

The Client

Can this person help me (or us)?

Will I be able to work with this person?

Am I physically safe with this person?

Will this person make me feel uncomfortable?

Is this person going to be loyal to me?

Will this person take the time to talk to me, not down to me?

Can this person explain the issues and considerations to me and to my family?

Is this going to offend any of my loved ones or hurt any feelings?

Does this person understand that for me some of these decisions are going to be very trying?

Will this person be perceptive enough to pick up what I do not or cannot express clearly or directly? Will this person even make an effort in that regard?

If this person going to take advantage of me either on a fee or work basis?

What is really in it for this person?

What is this going to cost me?

How long will this take?

Will this person respect my feelings and desires, not try to take over to save me taxes?

Can I call this person whenever I want? If not, when may I call this person?

May I call this person at home? On weekends? After hours?

Will this person return my calls in timely fashion? Are our definitions of "timely" the same?

Will this person keep my affairs confidential?

Will this person give me his or her undivided attention during our meetings? Will this person take phone calls or office interruptions while we are meeting?

Where will my matter fall into this person's work priorities?

Will this person meet me at my home or other location, or will he or she meet only at his or her office?

Will this person be timely and prompt?

If we are eating a meal together, will this person charge me during the time we are eating?

How will this person handle "soft office costs," *e.g.* copies, faxes, long distance charges, *etc.*

Will I talk to this person or will I have to deal with others in the firm? If so, who else may I have to deal with?

Does this person have a "gatekeeper," i.e., someone I have to go through to get to talk to the estate planner?

From *Yours, Mine & Ours: Estate Planning for People in Blended or Step Families* (Paul Hood Services 2022):

You Are the Sum of Your Life Experiences

We are all the sum of our past experiences and feelings. I both love the quote: "Wherever you go, there you are" because it is so true. Give it some thought and you'll likely agree. What I have seen, heard, and done in the past all have a major bearing on our likes, dislikes, feelings, and opinions. So where have you been?

Where do you fall in the birth order in your family of origin? Birth order can play a significant role in how people perceive certain things in estate planning. Historically, it has not been that long since we got away from the oldest male heir taking the entire estate under the ancient doctrine of primogeniture. Today, birth order still subtly impacts estate planning through the frequent default use of the oldest child as executor or successor trustee. If you're an eldest child, this might suit you just fine. However, if you're not the oldest child, your view of selecting the oldest child as successor may be quite different.

If you're the only daughter, you may find yourself as the primary caregiver your parents turn to for assistance and help, and they may rely on you more than your brothers, while still giving the oldest the responsibility of carrying out their wishes. This can be confusing when you may know and understand their wishes better than your sibling. You may even be very sensitive about this issue. Perhaps you had a past experience with an older sibling where that sibling was favored solely because of being older than you, and you resented it.

These are important areas to consider as you begin to wonder which of your children and stepchildren you see in various roles related to your estate plan. Knowing how to include them effectively in the conversation can be very helpful, and it can shed light in learning what it is that the various members of the next generation care about and what roles they would be open to considering. Two variations of the Golden Rule come to mind here:

- *Do unto others as you would have them do unto you*. Take time to think about how you would have liked to be treated by your parents when it came to their estate planning and how you'd like that to translate into your plans for your estate.

- *Do unto others as they would have you do unto them*. We're all different and what would work for you might not work at all for some of your children or stepchildren. Taking time to get them to discuss what matters to them and what they would prefer is a great way to honor them as you go forward, and you can go a long way towards having the family stay connected and unified. This takes a great deal of skill and practice if you haven't opened up these sorts of conversations before.

What Constitutes Being Wealthy to You?

In James E. Hughes, Jr.'s book, *Family Wealth*, he describes a family's wealth as consisting "primarily of its human capital and its intellectual capital, and secondarily of its financial capital."

Do you see yourself as wealthy? What are some of the stories and beliefs you have around the term "wealth"? Some people have clearly defined wealth parameters. Others don't. Some people are ill at ease with being thought of as wealthy and do not want to be defined as such. It has been my experience that people who aren't comfortable with a definition of "wealthy" rarely do any substantial irrevocable lifetime gifting, even if estate planning advisors think that gifting is a great idea and that there's more than enough liquidity in the estate to do so with ease and without adversely impacting the overall robust nature of the estate.

Liquidity: How Quickly and Cheaply an Asset can be Converted into Cash

How did you obtain your wealth? How you obtained your wealth sometimes gives clues about how you view wealth and how you will divide it. It is not unusual for people who have inherited wealth to view that wealth differently than those who made the wealth themselves. People who made their own wealth often very much identify themselves by their property. In my experience, they are more often apt to demand to retain control of their property and they are more willing to take estate planning risks with it. They also tend to feel more confident in the realm of estate planning and in learning about all their various options. Contrast this with the person who inherits significant wealth. With inheritors, I see two approaches most often:

- Those who are much more apt to view themselves as mere stewards of the property. They usually play it more safely.

- Those who may come across as feeling entitled and that the money is theirs to do with as they choose. Often they seem to be more irresponsible and free with the spending of their wealth and less competent and able to see themselves in the role of managing, growing, and furthering the wealth for future generations.

This is an unfortunate circumstance for many inheritors who were not given the opportunity or training to be competent with their finances. They often feel a great deal of shame and embarrassment around their lack of acumen with their wealth and finances, and these emotions keep them from seeking and accessing professional training, coaching, and advising that could allow them to truly flourish in their lives, where they build their competence and confidence. This often leads to the "shirtsleeves to shirtsleeves" in three generations that is so common — lack of preparedness on the part of inheritors is one cause of the assets and wealth being gone in short order.

Your Union

How many previous partners have you had? How many previous unions has your current partner had? Estate planning can be impacted by the number of times that a person marries or takes on new partners. Fears, doubts, and even cynicism about whether a relationship will last can creep in and impact the degree of trust you have in yourself and in your partner to go the distance this time around.

Estate planning options vary in part by the quality of the current relationship. This is where I find working together as a collaborative team to be very helpful for blended families seeking sound estate planning advice. The more safety there is to honestly share the reality of your current situation, and not just the positive (or negative) imagination you may have about your relationship, the more grounded and effective your estate plan will be for both of you.

I find that it is imperative that the two of you, as a couple, be candid with your estate planner about your relationship. For example, if the couple's relationship is rocky, the estate planner may be less inclined to recommend significant lifetime estate planning. I once had a couple hire me to create a family limited partnership for their family. I didn't find out until after the plan had been implemented that they'd been legally separated for several years, and each partner had been dating other people. Had I known this pertinent information at the time the couple came to see me, I might have given some different advice or designed the partnership differently.

I used to make it a point when working with clients to ask direct and indirect questions about what they hope to accomplish. Questions I used to weave into the conversation include:

- Why does the couple think this is the best and right solution for their particular need or problem?

- What have they considered, if at all, should something happen to their union?

- Have they considered using other options, such as a Grantor Retained Annuity Trust (GRAT) or sales to intentionally defective grantor trusts (both discussed in Chapter 8), as each can accomplish the same end goal, while not having the same degree of expense and challenge in the event that the relationship ends in divorce rather than death?

A Grantor Retained Annuity Trust (GRAT) is a creature of United States tax law. In a GRAT, one creates a specially designed trust with property and retains a right to an annuity from the trust for a specified period of time.

Consider how well you communicate with your partner. The quality and frequency of communication between the two of you as partners can significantly impact estate planning advice. This is even more important in a blended family because people usually come into new relationships with their own way to do things and often a lot of their own property, as well as standing legal agreements from the dissolution of prior relationships. Generally speaking, couples who don't communicate often or very well should be represented by separate estate planners.

Indeed, some partners actually hide information, be it financial or family information, from the other partner, which can create ethical problems for the estate planners who represent both partners. This is a particularly challenging aspect to blended family estate planning, and points to the role that a communication coach can play in seeing how to bring the couple together in areas that matter a great deal to both. When a couple is already interacting with a desire to keep secrets from each other, there is likely a breakdown in trust that could be mended with some expert coaching, which could do wonders for the relationship and for the family as a whole.

Knowing how to communicate the emotions, hopes, dreams, and desires you both have will allow you to be much more fluid and fruitful in your estate planning process with your advisors.

Health Issues

How's your health? Health issues are significant in estate planning, as some people are more motivated to act on their estate planning after being beset with health issues; getting a diagnosis is often a potent wake-up call to get started when planning has been avoided. Unfortunately, once a diagnosis happens, it is often too late to take advantage of some vital estate planning opportunities. Sometimes people are motivated to initiate estate planning by the loss or sudden illness of a friend or an acquaintance.

Historical life expectancy in someone's family of origin can also have an impact on what advice an estate planner gives regarding possible estate planning techniques. Families who choose to take advantage of having their genome done in order to track hereditary issues should also bring this information to their estate planning advisors for better awareness of how to best design their particular plan.

Finances

Have you ever been involved with a bankruptcy or been sued for significant money? Do you owe on any promissory notes or do you have money loaned out to others? Do you have debts that your partner is not aware of by which he or she will be impacted at the time of your death? Are you aware of ways to protect your partner and your family members from debts and loans you may be liable for at the time of your death? Past experiences of financial issues such as a personal bankruptcy or having to defend against a large lawsuit, or being saddled with debts give people certain views on their estate planning.

Knowing the reality of your financial situation will be imperative for your advisors as they go about modeling your various options. You don't want them wasting their time and your money coming up with plans that would not apply to you given your current situation and obligations. You want your estate plan to be focused on what will make the most sense for you and your family. Knowing that, according to research from Lawrence H. Ganong and Marilyn Coleman of the University of Missouri, "just 20 percent of people discuss financial matters before they remarry." I am aware that your partner may not be fully apprised of all your financial details. Check and see what you may not have fully disclosed, and also consider how you might open the door to a more authentic conversation about what is true for both of you individually as well as goals for your shared finances in the event of one and then the other's deaths.

What Will Your Family Look Like at Your Death?

Have you ever envisioned your family at the time of your death? Does the idea of discussing your family after your death make you feel uncomfortable? These and many other questions should be faced because they can provide insight as to how things will play out, including how people will react at that time. In a blended family, this can be critical because relationships usually change after death — relations between your current partner and your children may be fine during your lifetime, but this can change dramatically after you're gone. Your children, who may be cordial and pleasant while you are alive, may ignore or become hostile towards your partner, and perhaps even their half-siblings. The fear of these scenarios becoming reality often keep people from addressing the underlying issues and concerns during their lifetimes, which more likely than not results in that which they fear coming to fruition.

Brought into public awareness through Dr. Richard Warshak's book *Divorce Poison*, "parental alienation" is a form of emotional child abuse where a custodial parent belittles or vilifies the other parent to the child.

When parental alienation has entered into the mix, your birth children may have been turned against you by your former spouse and you may find your options for a unified family going forward dramatically impacted, which may sway you and how you look at your estate planning options. For instance, birth children who think that they are entitled to a percentage of your estate may end up being written out of your will as a way of getting back at them for writing you out of their lives. This is the saddest and most painful way people approach estate planning — to communicate their pain, hurt, resentment, and anger at all the loss of relating during life.

I've also seen the reverse, where a conversation about estate planning can open a relationship that had been previously estranged and where important healing and re-establishment of trust can happen when using an approach aimed at responsibility, accountability, apologies, and amends. The overarching and long-lasting impact of parental alienation can be averted and reversed with a commitment to coaching towards a commonly shared goal. For better or worse, when there's an estate at stake, it can bring players to the table in ways that nothing else will.

Knowing how to have uncomfortable conversations about death and dying can be very helpful when addressing estate planning questions and ideas.

People rarely, if ever, face these questions, often because other family members are more uncomfortable discussing these issues than the person actually doing the hypothetical dying. Some key things to remember are to not take what your family members share with you personally. The more you can listen from a place of understanding that they are revealing themselves to you and what matters to them, the more you can be present for their concerns, even as you are sorting your own concerns.

I have seen estate planning interrupted by the objections of children who did not want to discuss anything to do with a parent's death and the aftermath on the grounds that it was morbid or was (they figured) too far into the future to worry about. I've also seen the next generation balk at opening these conversations out of fear of repercussions. They have learned to keep their thoughts to themselves because their parents may have reacted in the past with upset or judgment when they risked expressing their particular desires.

With a blended family, I always advise that the couple seriously contemplate that the family relationships may go south or end after the death of one partner. I wish it wasn't the case, but I've seen it happen far too often. I err on the side of realism over idealism. When you consider the statistic, from *Preparing Heirs* by Roy Williams and Vic Preisser, that 70 percent of the time families end up disconnected after the deaths of both of their parents, you can see the strong likelihood of that number being even greater if you're considering the added complexity in blended family situations.

Your Views on Life

Where did your views on life come from? Whether I want to admit it or not, we often obtain our views on life from our parents. This includes our views on estate planning. While we have a wide band of experiences with our parents, there is the specter of a parent remarrying, whether by reason of divorce from the other parent or of surviving the other parent. Many children disagree with their parent's decision to remarry or to take on a new partner, particularly after the death of the other parent. This can impact both the relations with that surviving parent as well as that child's views on remarriage for himself or herself.

Consider your formative experiences related to your parents' choices. Also consider how your choices may have impacted your children at their ages when the choices happened and the choices as they relate to their lives now. Obviously, in blended families, I am by definition talking about situations where one has taken on a partner who is not the parent of some or all of the children. Children have a variety of mixed feelings about their parent remarrying or taking on a new partner at whatever stage of development. In many instances, adult children can view new partners or stepparents as interlopers to their inheritance.

If their other parent is now deceased, some children view a parent's remarriage as somehow disloyal to the memory of the deceased parent, almost as if the surviving parent must remain in mourning forever. Their own conflicting feelings around loyalty to their deceased parent can create a barrier to engaging with their stepparent in an authentically loving and connected manner. (For a detailed discourse on how adult children can feel about their stepparents, read the book *Step Wars* by Grace Gabe and Jean Lipman-Blumen).

Did your parents discuss their estate planning with you? Another trait that we often get from our parents pertains to whether or not they discussed their estate planning with us. Children whose parents did not discuss their estate planning with them generally are far more likely not to discuss their estate planning with their own children. Some parents "discuss" their estate planning by telling their children and stepchildren various aspects of what they will be doing, even if this information changes or conflicts with or leaves out pertinent information that the parent might have told someone else. I have found that many parents do not discuss estate planning with a child until that child is also a parent. In my experience, the best estate planning includes input from all who are concerned, especially if everyone has a sense of safety and freedom to openly share their thoughts and desires.

Sharing information can be very important when it comes to family businesses, because parents usually look to the children to take over. If the parents don't have frank and open discussions with children and stepchildren in this situation, they run the risk of miscommunication, and the children could end up selling the business after the parents die, even though this is not what the parents would have wanted.

Sometimes it is a matter of two ships passing in the night. I recall a situation where a father lived cash poor for many years because he was paying the premiums for his life insurance policy that was to be used to redeem his shares in his family business, thereby passing control to his son, who also worked in the business, so the son could keep working in the business. The father told me that had his son expressed no interest in working for the business, he would have sold it and never bought the insurance. The father was undergoing some lean times so that his son could keep the business going.

When the father died, the son immediately took the life insurance proceeds and then sold the company. The son emotionally related to me that he had hated the business and that he had never wanted to work there. However, he felt obligated to his father to do so out of a sense of loyalty. When I asked him if he had ever expressed those sentiments to his father, he said that he had not because that would have demonstrated disloyalty to his family. This was a very sad situation because had the father and son had such a discussion, the father could have lived a lot better for a long time. Dad also could have sold the company during his lifetime for a lot more that what the son received in the sale. This illustrates costly scenarios that occur far too often due to a lack of open, effective communication related to significant decisions that have a great deal of impact on loved ones during life and after death.

Past Experiences with Estates or Trusts

What past experiences do you have with estates or trusts? Our experiences with prior estates and trusts often inform our views on our own estate planning, particularly if it involved our own parents. I once had a successful man break down in tears in my office over the fact that his parents only left him half as much as they left his siblings. He wondered if his parents only loved him half as much. This gentleman was significantly wealthier than his parents, so it was not an issue of money — it was about love. This was a situation where the parents could have saved their son a lifetime of worry and shame by simply telling him that they were giving more wealth to their other children because they knew that he did not need it, but that they loved him just as much. Nevertheless, this same gentleman was about to treat one of his children differently in his own estate plan by giving that child, also very successful, less than some of his other children. He was not going to tell that child either that he loved them all the same until I pointed out to him that what he was about to do was repeating what his parents did to him. Once he saw it, he changed his mind.

Children often are upset by what can be very effective estate-tax planning (where estate tax exists) by their parents, especially where the parents "skip" them and leave significant wealth to their children's children, (i.e., the parents' grandchildren). It's not that the children are opposed to their parents saving them estate taxes. It's that the children want to have their cake (i.e., the estate-tax benefits) and eat it too (i.e., enjoy the property). In other words, the children either want to have control over what their children receive or they want direct access to the wealth itself for personal reasons. Again, what the children want more than anything is to be somehow included in the planning so that they have awareness and understand the basis for decisions being made. This goes a long way towards averting resentment and pain that ends up looking like entitlement and greed.

I have found it somewhat curious that people often want things in their estate plans that differ from their views for the estate plans of others. For example, I have asked clients if they believe that trusts should last forever, and they say no, they shouldn't, yet they want this result in their own estate plans. Other issues include whether co-trustees are workable, or at what ages trusts should be distributed to children.

Many times, their views in general differ significantly from what they want in their own plans. Other issues that clients view differently for their own plans are whether institutional trustees are desirable, whether estate plans should reward or punish certain behavior, and how much authority or discretion should be given to trustees. Note: If this paragraph causes you some concern (or overwhelms you completely with all of the jargon) don't worry; as you utilize this book, you will learn what all these terms mean so that you can understand them fully as well as see how they apply to your family.

All in all, the human side of estate planning plays a huge role in the process. The more your advisors have an honest, reality-based understanding of your family situation, the more your estate plan will be able to reflect your values, your intentions, and get the best results for your family with regards to taxes and asset allocation.

2.5 DATA GATHERING FORMS

The paragraphs below provide a description of the various parts of most data gathering forms. Figures 2.1 and 2.2 illustrate two examples of estate planning questionnaires and data-gathering forms. Figure 2.1 is a condensed estate planning questionnaire, while Figure 2.2 illustrates a longer, more comprehensive form. The features of the form in Figure 2.2 are discussed in more detail below.

Sample Information Request Letter

Many estate planners prefer to obtain as much knowledge as possible about a potential client before their initial interview. This saves the time of all concerned. If handled properly, some basic pre-interview data gathering helps prepare both the client and the estate planner for the formal interview and involves the client in the planning process. While it is preferable to gather this type of information in advance, some prospective clients may never make it to the first meeting if they have to provide too much information in advance of that meeting. This may occur because the client wants to meet the professional before divulging this private information, or because the client is not sufficiently organized to easily provide the information. Therefore, while it is helpful to have this information, it becomes a judgment call as to the extent that it is necessary.

A good way to begin is with the sample information request letter which reiterates the "when and where" of the first meeting. A controllable atmosphere, such as the professional's office, is usually a much better location for data gathering than a client's home or office.

The client is asked to complete as much of the data gathering form as possible in advance of the first meeting and mail it back to the planner. If the client would feel more comfortable, they can bring the data gathering form to the meeting. Note that these are simple "non-threatening" questions, but they are necessary for many reasons. It may also be helpful to point out to the prospective client that if they do not want to complete the entire form, by reviewing the form in advance of the meeting, they can at least get an idea as to what to think about before the meeting and what documents would be helpful to bring to the first session.

2.6 THE COVER PAGE

There is a reason for every page and every line of the data gathering forms. A client notes immediately that his file is considered personal and confidential. The client also notes that it will probably take a number of interviews to complete the initial process and then the case will be reviewed at specified times. The use of the forms indicates to the client that the planner has an organized, systematic, and professional approach to estate planning.

Family Information

Here, the client is asked to print or type information about family members. Note that Question 7 is designed to list not only the names and addresses of children but also their spouse's names, as well as the names and ages of any grandchildren.

Supplementary pages may have to be added where the client or his children have large families. It may also be helpful, where grandchildren are no longer living with their parents, to list their addresses and, if appropriate, the names of their spouses. Whenever possible, obtain social security and telephone numbers. Many people are reluctant to provide social security numbers unless absolutely necessary. In these cases, you can defer getting it. Also, it is often helpful to obtain preferred email addresses along with cell phone numbers.

Often a client will be providing financial support for individuals outside his immediate family. Their names and relationship, as well as their addresses, are essential if the client wishes to provide for them either during or after his death. Likewise, clients will often want to provide financial assistance to a charitable organization. Formal names, addresses, web site addresses, and other vital information about such charities should be stated on this page (or on attached supplementary pages). Often, the websites for these charities will specify appropriate language for making gifts to the organization.

Stick Diagram

A simple stick diagram of the client's family, his parent's family, and spouse's parent's family is an invaluable tool when seniors, juniors, and third and fourth generation children have the same names. Such a diagram also helps to understand who's who if your client has been divorced, remarried, and has children by both marriages. It also serves to highlight important relationships. For example, a child with the same name as a parent or grandparent or uncle or aunt may be a "favorite." Also, because of the "portability" of the applicable exclusion amount, it is helpful to know about the details of a predeceased spouse, even if the client has remarried, and especially if remarriage is being contemplated.

Advisors

Here, a client is forced to think about who has been, or has to be, selected to care for both the person and the property of children (or grandchildren) who are minors. A client must also select an individual or corporate fiduciary (or more than one of each or combination of both) to serve as a personal representative after his death. Alternates for both primary guardian(s) and executor(s) are essential as backups in the event the primary is ineligible, incapacitated, or for any other reason fails to qualify or ceases to act.

It is important that each member of the estate planning team locate other members of the team and inform them of progress and problems in planning the client's estate. Cooperation and constant communication between the members of the team will help assure the client of the best possible coordination of planning. Whenever appropriate, the client should be copied on correspondence and e-mails.

Checklist of Documents

This list outlines the key documents that are of use to the estate planner. In various situations special documents such as contracts, leases, or other agreements should be added. But generally, those shown will provide adequate information for the first interview. Note that many of these documents can be obtained after the initial meeting. Therefore, if the client becomes lost trying to pull all of this together, the documents can be obtained at a later date.

Alternative Form for Community Property Residents

Here, an alternative data gathering form, which will be particularly useful to residents of community property states, can be found. Community property planners (and common law planners who have had clients move to or from community property states) should notice a number of questions in the forms pertaining to "changes of state of residence during marriage." Problems of the peripatetic client are becoming more acute every day.

Figure 2.1

CONDENSED – ESTATE PLANNING QUESTIONNAIRE					
Name				D/O/B	
Last	First	M.	a/k/a		
Address						
Phone	**Husband**	**Wife**			
Cell					
Work					
Home					
E Mail					
Children	(for each: Name/Date of Birth/ Parent - H - W- Joint)				
#1					
#2					
#3					
#4					

Figure 2.1 (cont'd)

General Questions	Circle			
Citizen	Y	N		
Marital Agreements	Y	N	If yes, get copies	
Existing Documents	Y	N	If yes, get copies	
Business Agreements	Y	N	If yes, get copies	
Assets				
	Husband	Wife	Joint w/spouse	Joint w/other than spouse
Residence #1				
Mortgage	( )	( )	( )	
Residence #2				
Mortgage	( )	( )	( )	
Residence #3				
Mortgage	( )	( )	( )	
Banks				
Investment Accounts				
Business Interests				

Figure 2.1 (cont'd)

Annuities			
Owner/ Beneficiary - Primary/Contingent			
	Owner	Bene - Primary	Bene - Contingent
#1			
#2			
#3			

Life Insurance (If ILIT - get copy)			
Owner/ Beneficiary - Primary/Contingent			
	Owner	Bene - Primary	Bene - Contingent
#1			
#2			
#3			

Figure 2.2

SAMPLE INFORMATION REQUEST LETTER

Dr. Allen A. Murphy
6061 Kathleen Drive
Bala Cynwood, PA 19010

Dear Dr. Murphy:

I'm looking forward to meeting with you and your wife on Wednesday, June 16, at 2 p.m. in my office.

As I promised on the phone, I have enclosed the first several pages of a comprehensive data form we'll be using in creating an estate conservation plan. Please complete as much as you can and mail it to me in the enclosed envelope.

Also enclosed you will find a list of documents we will need. I would appreciate if you would send me photocopies of the documents in advance of our meeting or, if you prefer, you can bring them with you on Wednesday. (We can probably save a great deal of time if I can study these papers in advance of our meeting.)

Please feel free to call me if you have any questions.

Sincerely yours,

Charles McClure

CMcC/dl
Enc.

PERSONAL AND CONFIDENTIAL FILE

of

Dr. Allen A. Murphy

Initial Interview: *8/4/2018*

Interviewer: *Jennifer Brown*

Date of subsequent interviews or review:

DATA GATHERING AND ANALYSIS AND INITIAL CLIENT INTERVIEW CHAPTER 2

PLEASE COMPLETE (print or type) AND RETURN IN THE ENCLOSED ENVELOPE:

			Birthdate	Soc. Sec. No.
1.	Full name	Dr. Allen Albert Murphy	9/11/1962	000-00-0000
2.	Nicknames	Al		
3.	Spouse's name	Stephanie Louise Murphy	1/1/1964	000-00-0000
4.	Nicknames	Stephie		

5. Home address: 6061 Kathleen Drive   Home phone: 353-5424
   Bala Cynwood
   PA 19010

6. Business address: 2700 Bryn Mawr Avenue   Bus. phone: 525-9500
   Philadelphia
   PA 19101

7. Children (and Spouses)

	Address	Phone	Birthdate
a. Kathleen	same as above	see above	7/6/1987
b. Christopher	"	"	9/1/1989
c. Charles	"	"	11/15/1991
d. Lawrence	"	"	6/2/1993

Names and Ages of Grandchildren

a.   b.   c.   d.

69

8.	Parent's Names	Address	Age	Phone Number
Yours:	a. *Deceased*			
	b. *Deceased*			
Your Spouse's	a. *William Lamont*	*872 W. Overbrook St.*	*67*	*566-1276*
	b. *Mary Lamont*	*same as above*	*66*	*566-1276*

9. Dependents (other than children)/Relationship

William Lamont/Father-in-Law	*see above*	*67*	*"*
Mary Lamont/Mother-in-Law	*see above*	*66*	*"*

10. Beneficiaries (other than those listed above):

DATA GATHERING AND ANALYSIS AND INITIAL CLIENT INTERVIEW   CHAPTER 2

11. Please sketch a family tree showing any brothers and sisters:

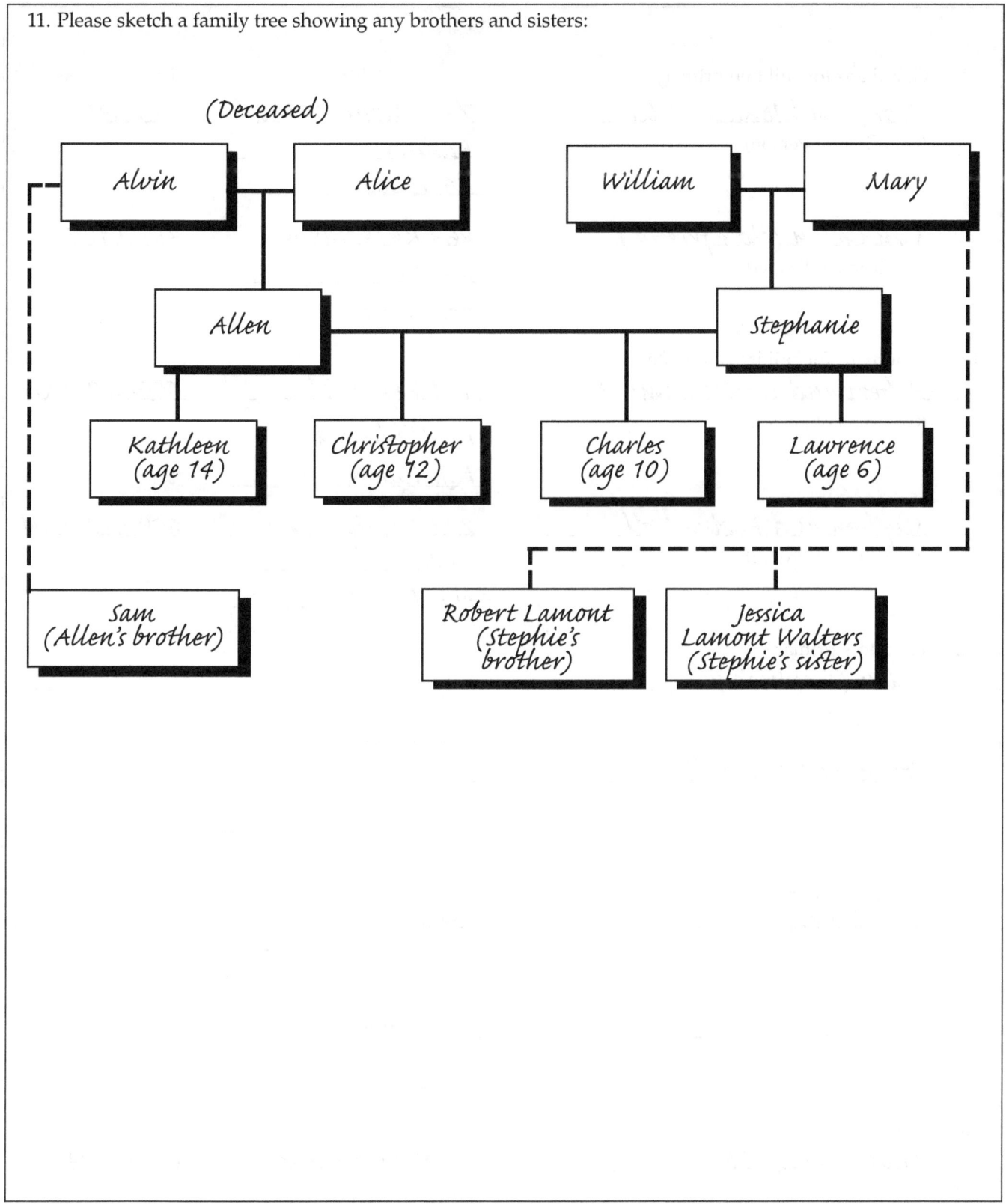

THE TOOLS & TECHNIQUES OF ESTATE PLANNING

Advisors

12. Guardians for children primary: Address   Phone Number

George and Jessica Walters   *767 Fawnhill Road*   *353-5353*
(Guardian of Person)   *Radnor*
    PA 19008

Sam Cohen (close friend)   *868 Knox Drive*   *353-5126*
(Guardian of Property)   *Radnor*
    PA 19008

13. Guardians for children alternate:

Robert and Louise Lamont   *121 Peyton Place*   *609-522-8707*
(Guardian of Person)   *N. Wildwood*
    N.J. 19808

Stephen and Evelyn Toll   *222 Fayette Lane*   *609-522-7604*
(Guardian of Property)   *Wildwood*
    N.J. 19807

14. Executors primary:
Allen (Stephie's will)

Stephie (Allen's will)

15. Executors alternate:
Sam Cohen   *see above*

Sam Cohen   *see above*

16. Accountant:
Frank Vallei, CPA   *#1 Bala Avenue*   *664-3874*
    Bala Cynwood
    PA 19010

		Address	Phone Number
17.	Attorney - personal: Robert P. Krauss	1401 Walnut Street Philadelphia PA 19102	568-5700
	Attorney - business: Robert P. Krauss	see above	"
18.	Banker/Trust Officer Allen Gart (Vice Pres. and Senior Trust Officer)	Girand Trust Co. Girand Plaza Philadelphia, PA 19101	568-4858
19.	Insurance advisor:		
20.	Investment advisor/broker: Donald Rahill/Bob Eclair	New builder & Co. 121 Rothschild Bldg. Philadelphia, PA 19010	567-6000

21. Other information not listed above:

Allen's doctor - Dr. Alton Blake

CHECKLIST OF DOCUMENTS TO BRING TO INTERVIEW

Present Wills _____

Personal Income Tax Returns: Last 3 Years (federal and state) _____

Business Tax Returns: Last 3 Years (include P&L and balance sheets) _____

Life/Health/Disability Insurance Policies _____

Employee Benefit Plan Descriptions (Pension, Profit Sharing, Group Insurance, etc.) _____

Business Buy-Sell Agreements and Employment Contracts _____

Pre or Post-Nuptial Agreements and Divorce Decrees/Property Settlements _____

Trust Documents – created by you or by others for your (or your family's) benefit _____

Gift Tax Returns _____

Homeowner's Policy and Personal Property Floaters _____

Deeds to Real Estate _____

Other documents to bring _____ _____

_____ _____

_____ _____

RALPH GANO MILLER   Client _____

INFORMATION AND DOCUMENTS
FOR ESTATE PLANNING

<u>PLEASE BRING WITH YOU COPIES OF:</u>

    Present Wills, if any

    Deeds to real property (for title purposes) and any information regarding title to property, cost and present fair market value.

    Manner of title holding of any stock (how the ownership appears on the certificates) and value of each stock.

    Last three years' income tax returns.

    Any available financial statements.

    Copies of any gift tax returns filed.

    If you feel appropriate, photos or a snapshot of yourself and spouse.

<u>IF IN BUSINESS:</u>

    Any partnership agreements.

    Any corporate minute books.

    Any buy-and-sell agreements.

    Last three years' income tax returns (partnership or corporation).

<u>FILLING OUT INFORMATION SHEETS</u>

    It is most helpful (as well as cost-saving for you) if you can fill out the attached forms and bring them with you when you come in. However, please do not delay your appointment for lack of answers to the questions, since we can often assist you with troublesome items at the conference.

THE TOOLS & TECHNIQUES OF ESTATE PLANNING

FAMILY INFORMATION

Relation	Full Legal Name	Preferred Name**	Birthdate	Birthplace	Soc. Sec. #
Husband					
Wife					
Child #1*					
Child #2					
Child #3					
Child #4					
Child #5					
Child #6					
Child #7					
Child #8					

* List children in order of birth date. Insert "PM" by that child's number if child is from a prior marriage.
** By "Preferred Name" we are asking by what name you sign checks and do business.

ADDRESSES

Relation	Street Address	City, State, Zip	Telephone
Husband			
Wife			
Child #1			
Child #2			
Child #3			
Child #4			
Child #5			
Child #6			
Child #7			
Child #8			

DATA GATHERING AND ANALYSIS AND INITIAL CLIENT INTERVIEW — CHAPTER 2

CHILDREN'S CIRCUMSTANCES

Relation	Marital Status*	No. of Children	Occupation	Spouse Name	Spouse Occupation	Estate Potential**
Child #1						
Child #2						
Child #3						
Child #4						
Child #5						
Child #6						
Child #7						
Child #8						

* Marital: (M) Married (S) Single (D) Divorced (A) Separated
** Estate Potential: Possibility of Child developing a significant estate apart from their inheritance
  (V) Very Good (G) Good (F) Fair (P) Poor

GRANDCHILDREN

Child of (Child #)	Name	Birthdate	Financial acumen (0-5 with 5 as highest)

• Attach a separate sheet for additional grandchildren.

FAMILY FINANCIAL GOALS

On a scale of 1 to 5 (5 being highest), indicate how important the following items are to you:

_____ Take care of family in the event of death   _____ Enjoy a comfortable retirement

_____ Take care of family in the event of disability   _____ Other

_____ College education for children   _____ Other

HUSBAND'S OTHER FAMILY MEMBERS

Relation	Name	Age	Spouse Name	Age	City, State	Est. Net Worth
Father						
Mother						
*						
*						
*						
*						
*						
*						

WIFE'S OTHER FAMILY MEMBERS

Relation	Name	Age	Spouse Name	Age	City, State	Est. Net Worth
Father						
Mother						
*						
*						
*						
*						
*						
*						

* Indicate brother (B), sister (S), half brother (HB), half sister (HS), step brother (SB), step sister (SS)

CURRENT MARRIAGE

Date of marriage _____ Place _____
Occupation at date of marriage Husband _____ Wife _____
Net worth at date of marriage Husband $_____ Wife $ _____

If you have changed your state of residence during the marriage, show:

State	Year of Arrival	Approx. net worth upon arrival

PRIOR MARRIAGES

H/W	Spouse Name	Termination Date	How Terminated (e.g., by death)	Children of Marriage

CITIZENSHIP

If any members of your family are not U.S. citizens, please indicate:

Name	Age	Relationship	Circumstance

ADOPTED CHILDREN/GRANDCHILDREN

Name	Relationship	Parent Name (if grandchild)

OTHER DEPENDENTS

Name	Age	Relationship	Circumstance

ADVISORS

Profession	Name	Street Address	City, State, Zip	Telephone
Attorney				
Attorney				
Accountant				
Life Insurance				
Life Insurance				
Financial Planner/ Investment Advisor				
Casualty Insurance				
Pension Admin.				
Stock Broker				

DATA GATHERING AND ANALYSIS AND INITIAL CLIENT INTERVIEW CHAPTER 2

EMPLOYMENT

Relation	Occupation	Title	Employer	Telephone
Husband				
Wife				

Previous Employment

Husband				
Husband				
Wife				
Wife				

BUSINESS ASSOCIATES

Name	Business

Do you have information on prospective purchasers of your business in the event of your death or on other aspects of disposition of the business?
❏ Yes   ❏ No
If yes, who knows the location of this information?

If you are in business, do you have any business or stock buy-and-sell agreements?
❏ Yes   ❏ No   (If yes, please furnish a copy)

MILITARY SERVICE

	Branch	Serial Number	Current Status	Disability
Husband				
Wife				

81

PLANNING INFORMATION

PRIOR DOCUMENTS

Do you have a pre- or post-nuptial agreement? ❑ Yes ❑ No (If yes, please furnish)

Do you have any continuing obligations under divorce or property settlement agreements? ❑ Yes ❑ No
(If yes, please furnish a copy of each such document.)

Trusts Which You Created (please furnish copies)

Creator	Beneficiaries	Trustee	Irrevocable?	Date Created

Trusts Created By Others Of Which You Are Beneficiary (please furnish copies)

Creator	Beneficiaries	Trustee	Irrevocable?	Date Created

GIFTS

Have you ever filed a gift tax return? ❑ Yes ❑ No (If yes, please furnish copies of all returns)

Prior Gifts Made By You

Donor (H/W/B/)	Donee	Amount		Date of Gift(s)
			❑ Outright ❑ Trust ❑ Custodial	
			❑ Outright ❑ Trust ❑ Custodial	
			❑ Outright ❑ Trust ❑ Custodial	
			❑ Outright ❑ Trust ❑ Custodial	

DATA GATHERING AND ANALYSIS AND INITIAL CLIENT INTERVIEW   CHAPTER 2

SPECIAL NEEDS

Are any family members receiving government benefits due to physical or mental disability?   ❏ Yes   ❏ No

For any family member suffering from a physical or mental disability, please indicate:

Name	Description of Disability	Current Status[1]	Projected Long Term Status[1]	Receiving Government Benefits?[2]

Do any other family members have any health concerns (e.g. heart problems, drug or alcohol problems, etc.)? If so, please specify:

Name	Description

[1] Status: SS = Self sufficient
 FD = Financially dependent but physically/mentally self sufficient
 DP = Dependent on a guardian or caretaker
 IN = Institutionalized
[2] Indicate Medi-Cal, Medicare, SSI, etc.

83

FINANCIAL ACUMEN

What is your estimate of the emotional maturity and financial acumen of your children on a scale of 1 - 10 (10 being highest)?

Names	Emotional Maturity	Financial Acumen	Comments
Child #1			
Child #2			
Child #3			
Child #4			
Child #5			
Child #6			
Child #7			
Child #8			

FUNERAL/BURIAL ARRANGEMENTS

	Religious Services	Disposition of Body	Limitation on Cost
Husband			
Wife			

Other Instructions

MISCELLANEOUS INFORMATION

Has social security status been reviewed lately? ❑ Yes ❑ No

Is there a homestead on your home? ❑ Yes ❑ No

Safe Deposit Boxes:

Number	Institution	In whose names?

HEALTH/CASUALTY INSURANCE

Do you have health insurance coverage? ❑ Yes ❑ No

If yes, maximum limits _____

Casualty Insurance

Coverage	Insurer	Liability Maximum	Replacement Maximum
Autos			
Boats			
Residence			
Liability Umbrella			

DISABILITY/LONG TERM CARE COVERAGE

Do you have disability insurance? ❑ Yes ❑ No

If yes, total amount of annual coverage on husband _____ / wife _____

Description of any long term care coverage _____
_____

ANNUAL INCOME			
Source	Husband	Wife	Dependent Children
Real Property			
Interest			
Securities			
Other Investments			
Trusts			
Pensions			
Other			
Subtotal			
Salary			
TOTAL			

2.7 ANNUAL REVIEW CHECKLIST

Below you will find a number of questions. A positive answer to any of them may indicate a need to review your estate plan. Check the appropriate boxes and return to me.

Specific Bequests
- ☐ I would like to make specific bequests to individuals not presently included in my plans - or delete the names of one or more persons (or charities) currently named.
- ☐ I would like to change the amounts of some of the bequests I have made.

Changes in Valuation
- ☐ The value of my estate has changed more than 20 percent in the last two years.

Special Provisions for Children
- ☐ My health (my spouse's or children's health) has deteriorated substantially in the last year.

Newly Born or Adopted Children
- ☐ A child (grandchild) has been born (or adopted) since our last review.

Handicapped or Incompetent Children
- ☐ A child (grandchild or other dependent) has become handicapped or seriously injured since our last review.

Status of Family Marriages
- ☐ A member of the family has become divorced or separated since our last review.

Cancellation of Loans to Children and Equalization of Inheritance
- ☐ I would like to discharge an obligation owed to me by cancelling the loan in my will.
- ☐ I would like to provide a clause to equalize any gifts made in the past (or to be made in the future) to certain children (grandchildren).

Life Insurance
- ☐ I have added (or dropped) more than $100,000 of life insurance since our last review.
- ☐ I have (or would like to) changed a beneficiary designation on an existing policy.
- ☐ I feel I may need more life insurance but I don't know how much to purchase or what type to consider.

Gifts to Minors
- ☐ I would like to make substantial gifts to minor children (grandchildren).

Gifts to Charities
- ☐ I would like to add (delete) one or more charitable beneficiaries.
- ☐ I would like to change the amount of my bequest to certain charities.

Business Interests
- ☐ I have entered into a stock (partnership) buy-sell agreement since our last review.
- ☐ My business situation has changed significantly since our last review.

Guardian, Executors and Trustees
- ☐ I would like to name a particular person as advisor to my executor and trustees.
- ☐ I would like to reconsider the designation of the guardians, executors, and trustees I have named.

Other
- ☐ I would like to review my estate plan for the following reasons.
- ☐ I'd like to know how the latest tax law affects my estate plan.

THE TOOLS & TECHNIQUES OF ESTATE PLANNING

CHECKLIST OF INFORMATION TO KEEP IN SAFE DEPOSIT BOX

The following information or materials should be kept in your safe deposit box:

- ☐ (1) Birth certificates
- ☐ (2) Marriage certificates (including artifacts or documentation from any prior marriages or divorces)
- ☐ (3) Your will (and spouse's will) and trust agreements
- ☐ (4) Listing of life insurance policies or certificates
- ☐ (5) Your Social Security numbers
- ☐ (6) Military discharge papers
- ☐ (7) Bonds, Stocks, and other securities
- ☐ (8) Real estate deeds
- ☐ (9) Business (Buy-Sell) Agreement
- ☐ (10) Automobile titles and insurance policies
- ☐ (11) Property insurance policies
- ☐ (12) Additional:

LIST number of all checking and savings accounts including bank addresses and location of safe deposit boxes:

_____   _____   _____

_____   _____   _____

LIST name, address, and phone number of fire and life insurance agent:

_____   _____   _____

_____   _____   _____

LIST name, address, and phone number of accountant:

_____   _____   _____

LIST name, address, and phone number of (current or past) employer. State date when you retired if applicable. Include employee benefits booklets:

_____   _____   _____

_____   _____   _____

LIST all debts owed to *and* owed by you:

_____   _____   _____

_____   _____   _____

LIST the names, addresses, telephone numbers and birth dates of your children and other beneficiaries (including charitable beneficiaries):

_____   _____   _____

_____   _____   _____

CHAPTER ENDNOTES

1. Shea, Shawn C., M.D. (1998), *Psychiatric Interviewing: The Art of Understanding* (2nd Ed.), Philadelphia: W.B. Saunders Co. (hereafter, "*Psychiatric Interviewing*"), p. 9.
2. Portions adapted from Hood, L. Paul, Jr., "From the School of Hard Knocks: Thoughts on the Initial Client Interview," 27 *ACTEC Journal* 297 (2002).
3. Morrison, James R., M.D. (3rd Ed. 2007), *The First Interview*, New York: The Guilford Press, p. 1 (hereafter, "*The First Interview*").
4. *In Estate of Schneider v. Finmann*, 5 N.Y.3d 306, 933 N.E.2d 718, 907 N.Y.S.2d 119 (2010), the failure to ask all of the necessary questions was the focal point of the plaintiff's contention that the holding of life insurance was unnecessarily subjected to federal estate taxation.
5. *The First Interview*, pp. 1-2.
6. *Psychiatric Interviewing*, page xi (preface to first edition).
7. Readers who have had any additional feelings not set forth there or any clients have had any feelings not listed there are asked to pass those feelings to Paul Hood by e-mail to paul@paulhoodservices.com.

HUMAN SIDE OF ESTATE PLANNING

CHAPTER 3

3.1 INTRODUCTION

In this chapter, we will address the side of estate planning that too few of us are really ever formally taught: the "human side," sometimes referred to as the "soft side" or "qualitative side,"[1] of estate planning. We usually learn these lessons in the "school of hard knocks," i.e., by making mistakes through trial and error in our everyday work with clients.

Too many estate planners still focus primarily on "the numbers" in estate planning, almost in a Jenny Craig-esque "before and after" picture way of justifying the value of their services to clients, estate planning is very much a people-oriented business.[2] We suspect that some of these estate planners simply want to distance themselves from their clients' issues in a good faith yet misguided way. Yet, the principal therapeutic value of estate planning for clients themselves is *not* the tax savings, but, rather, it is the satisfaction and peace of mind that can come with coming to grips with and completing important "unfinished business" while they are alive.[3] In our view, there is a significant difference between an estate tax technician and an "estate planner." That distinction is the acknowledgement, understanding, and ability to work with the "human side" of estate planning.

As in just about all other professional-client relationships, there usually is a very wide variance between the estate planning technical knowledge that the estate planner possesses compared to that of the client, which often creates a dependent relationship. Compounding this gulf of knowledge and the dependency that often accompanies it is the fact that, by its very nature, the process of estate planning is highly emotionally charged for most people, and that this is exacerbated in a blended family setting. Clients are forced to face some of life's most difficult questions, choices and issues regarding succession, giving up control and especially the contemplation of their own mortality.[4]

Frequently, there are actual or perceived pressures on the client from within the client's family relative to their inheritance expectations. Since many clients essentially define themselves by reference to control of their possessions, the very thought of divesting themselves of those assets – whether during lifetime or at death - is highly traumatic.[5]

Estate planners first meet clients at a certain point in their lives. We may not know exactly *where* they are in their lives when we come across them or what their life's experiences or expectations have been. In a perfect world, estate planners would know much more about their clients' backgrounds than we do. Much can be done to improve the initial client interview past the data gathering exercise.[6] For instance, clients may arrive in your office still grieving the loss of a loved relative or a dear friend. Others may be at the top of their game, while still others may be under intense work or financial pressure.

Some may even suffer from some sort of mental health issue. There is much we do not and cannot know. But we do know this: clients are the sum of their past experiences, their present physical, emotional and mental states and their future hopes, dreams and aspirations. In other words, people come into our professional world with certain belief systems and biases based upon their pasts and their perceptions of the future.

Clients also come to us with their current psychological states made up in large part from their past experiences and feelings. These experiences can run the gamut. Some may hate their parents, their own children or their siblings because of something that happened (or that they imagined had happened) in a prior estate or family squabble, and this feeling impacts their estate planning judgment and decisions. Others have been divorced in a nasty proceeding and have trouble trusting anyone, including you. Still others firmly believe that they must divide their estates among their children equally, almost as if it were some sort of unwritten but nevertheless immutable rule or "fairness" requirement. A client's feelings also may be informed by such things as:[7]

- Their birth order;

- Their personal feelings about their wealth and whether they even consider themselves as "wealthy";

- The sources of their wealth: self-made versus inherited wealth;

- Their present and past love relationships;

- Their present physical and mental health;

- Their past and present financial condition, i.e., did they grow up poor or come through a serious down economic time or even a bankruptcy in the past;

- Their thoughts and feelings about how their families will look at their deaths;

- Their views on life in general, i.e., optimism versus pessimism; and

- Past experiences with estates or trusts, including whether their parents discussed the parents' estate plans with them;

The bottom line is that clients bring their psychological "baggage" into their estate planning encounters with us, some of which can be counterproductive to their estate planning efforts and can present interesting challenges for us in working with them. Very few of us are formally trained to handle these issues, but handle them we must as best we can. However, before you simply hang all of the blame on the client, we estate planners must be aware that all too often we unwittingly bring our own "baggage" into the advisor-client relationship.

We advisors also have our good days and bad days. When the client walks through our door, we are at a certain point in our own lives too. We may be suffering through a loved one's illness or going through a divorce or nasty partnership breakup. We may be sleep-deprived from having welcomed a new addition into our family. We may be under intense work, home or financial pressure. We may not be feeling well that day or simply having a bad day. It is imperative that we advisors be aware of and have a handle on our own "baggage" before it detrimentally impacts the advisor-client relationship and our work.

Some of us are better than others at managing not only our own baggage but all of the baggage and problems that clients dump on us all day long. Some advisors handle this baggage productively through engagement in activities such as exercise or enjoying classical music, but others are not as productive and drink or engage in other self-destructive behaviors. Many psychologists are required to go through their own therapy before engaging in therapy with others to identify and get a handle on their own "issues" before they deal with the problems of others. However, there is no corollary for estate planners at present, so we must soldier on to the best of our abilities.

Many estate planners have a paternalistic view of their relationships with their clients and often believe that they know best what the client needs to do in their estate planning.[8] This is a potentially dangerous mindset as it risks disempowering the client, which we believe will retard that client's estate planning progress because the client will not feel in control of their estate planning process and will not do anything in that situation. A client should feel in charge of his or her own estate planning process. Perhaps the single best way to enable that is to listen, to carefully, openly, and honestly allow and encourage the client to voice his or her innermost fears and dreams.

3.2 FIRST, A LITTLE PSYCHOLOGY...

At this point, we're going to introduce and briefly discuss three psychological "phenomena" (for lack of a better or more descriptive term) that can be important for estate planners: transference, countertransference and triangles. We're not discussing these phenomena as an academic exercise: we're not qualified to do that. However, based upon our collective experiences as well as considerable practice experience working with clients, we have witnessed firsthand the existence of each of these phenomena in action in real life. We believe that some baseline knowledge of each of these phenomena is almost essential to the estate planner, which is why we are covering them. Simply put, we are just attempting to shorten your stay in the "school of hard knocks." Let's begin with the definition of the term "transference."

What is Transference?

The phenomenon of transference is fairly easy to illustrate in a few examples, but you should know that psychologists frequently disagree over the meaning of the term.[9] One way to define "transference" is to simply say that it is:

> a phenomenon in which people transfer feelings and attitudes, often subconsciously, from a person or situation in their past on to a present person or situation. It involves the projection of a mental representation of a previous experience or person on to the present situation or person with whom they are interacting. The recipients of the transference usually play an important role that is necessary for the projected relationship. There are subtle, usually subconscious, encouragements by the projecting individual of the recipient to take on their feelings or beliefs about the situation or person.

Let's consider a few examples of how the phenomenon of transference can occur in estate planning:[10]

> *Example 1.* Assume that you are in your office waiting for your client, who is late for his appointment. The client, who is late because of his own fault, about which he is upset because he prides himself on punctuality, snaps at you when he comes in because he also has trouble taking personal responsibility for matters for which he is to blame. You have done nothing to deserve the curtness of your client's behavior. What has happened is that the client has "transferred" his feelings of anger against himself to you, compounded by his inability to be able to admit fault or take personal responsibility.

> *Example 2.* You are meeting with a new client who is appearing extremely anxious during the meeting and checking her watch repeatedly as you talk to her. Unbeknownst to you, the client's last experience with an estate planner went badly due to a misunderstanding about the size of the estate planner's fees and the hourly rate. The client has "transferred" her anxiety caused by a bad experience with another estate planner, onto her current advisor-client relationship.

The transference can arise in many other different contexts in estate planning. For example, a client who had a bad experience with probate of a family member's estate may be hell bent on not using a will alone in her estate planning. About the best that we lay estate planners can do is to acknowledge that the projecting person's feelings are not our fault and do our best to not take on the projecting person's invitation to engage. However, what is behind and giving rise to the projected feeling may indeed be critical information for us to determine, as in the most recent example dealing with antipathy toward "probate."

In Example 1, we might simply let the curt behavior go and indicate to the client that you weren't offended and won't hold his tardiness against him. In Example 2, we can ask the client what she is anxious about and soothe her by having a frank and open discussion about both of your expectations concerning your fees and the other terms of your relationship and by following up with an "engagement letter" that confirms what you have discussed.

What is Countertransference?

Again, just like with transference, psychologists can and do differ about the definition of countertransference.[11] Indeed, there is at least one school of thought that denies the very existence of countertransference, opting to call it all transference, either belonging to the client or the therapist.[12] For our purposes, the term "countertransference" is:

> *the often subconscious response of the recipient advisor to the client's actions or perceived actions. Countertransference responses can include both the professional's conscious and unconscious feelings and associated thoughts from the advisor's past on things that the client says or does. Countertransference involves displacement and projection onto the client. Countertransference sometimes is, but need not be, harmful to the helping relationship, especially if advisor allows his or her personal feelings*

toward the client to cloud his or her professional judgment. On the other hand, if the advisor is aware of his or her countertransference feelings and is able to deal with those feelings constructively, even being able to discuss those feelings with the client where appropriate, the countertransference can be a very helpful phenomenon in the advisor-client relationship.

Recall that earlier we said that we estate planners also often bring our psychological "baggage" from our pasts into our client relationships. This "baggage" can consist of personal feelings about people, experiences or things in our pasts and often consists of unresolved issues that we personally have. This quote nicely sums up what we should look for with respect to the possibility of countertransference:

If you find yourself feeling bored, angry, or disgusted, ask yourself, "Why?" Is there someone this patient reminds you of, such as a supervisor, parent, or spouse? (When therapist's feelings toward patients are carried over from previous relationships of their own it is called countertransference.) Perhaps there are features of this patient's personality that remind you of some of your own less admirable traits. Do you have anxiety about your own health, marriage, family relationships? These feelings are ubiquitous, so even experienced therapists must take care that they do not intrude into their relationships with patients.[13]

If you find yourself getting impatient or irritated with a client, Dr. James Morrison, a noted psychiatrist, suggests the following approach, which we find very helpful:

[A]sk yourself:

Why should I be feeling so upset?

What message am I missing?

Whom does this patient remind me of?

Answers to these questions should help determine what corrective action to take.[14]

There are all sorts of possible examples of how countertransference can arise in estate planning, but we will discuss three different examples.

Example 1. Suppose your client, who is the youngest child in her family, expresses strong negative feelings about an oldest child automatically being designated as executor just because that child was the oldest child. Suppose further that the advisor is an oldest child who feels strongly that oldest children should automatically be considered for such a fiduciary position and routinely drafts wills naming the oldest child as executor where a client says nothing to the contrary. When the client states she wants a middle or youngest child to be her executor, such an advisor may view the client in a somewhat negative light, particularly since the advisor also holds his own youngest sibling in contempt for actions that the youngest sibling engaged in and was allowed to get away with just because the youngest sibling was the "baby" of the family. The advisor has allowed his decades old disdain for his youngest sibling to color his judgment about the client.

Example 2. Suppose that your client has mannerisms that remind you of someone whom you loved, like your late brother, of whom you were very protective. Because of the good feelings that you have toward your client, which are because of your late brother and not because of any action by the client, you are overly protective of the client and tolerate much more out of this particular client than just about every other client, even turning a blind eye toward some warning signs of a conflict of interest that could eventually cause you some ethical difficulties in the future.

Example 3. Your new client identifies herself as an engineer. The advisor then thinks to herself ("engineers are *always* problem clients because they ask too many questions, reduce everything to black and white and think that they know it all") and immediately gets a little defensive, condescending and short with the client about the proper estate planning process.

Countertransference also can manifest itself in biases by the advisor either in favor of or against certain estate planning techniques.[15] Additionally, estate planners can be morally opposed or outraged by their clients' behavior to the extent that it impacts the estate planner's ability to work for the client effectively.

HUMAN SIDE OF ESTATE PLANNING — CHAPTER 3

What are "Triangles"?

A triangle is a three-person relationship system. The late Murray Bowen, MD, a psychiatrist and professor of psychiatry and a pioneer in the area of family systems theory back in the 1950's, developed the triangle as part of an eight concept family systems theory.[16] Dr. Bowen was one of the first people to consider the family as an integrated relationship system and to study it. Dr. Bowen argued that the triangle is considered the base building block of larger human emotional systems because he asserted that a three-person triangle is the smallest stable human relationship system.

According to Dr. Bowen, a two-person system is unstable because it tolerates little tension before one or both participants "triangle in" a third person to reduce their anxiety that the tension between the participants caused. Dr. Bowen reasoned that a triangle can withstand much more tension than a two-person relationship because the tension can be shifted between three relationships (A-B, A-C and B-C) instead of just one, and the parties subtly shift back and forth between each other during the course of their relationship triangle. In fact, Dr. Bowen further reasoned that when even the triangle anxiety becomes unbearable to one or more of the participants, a series of "interlocking" triangles can develop. Dr. Bowen's triangles theory has since been applied past families to all human organizations.[17] At least one writer has called for a family systems approach to estate planning.[18]

Estate planning sees its fair share of triangles. Here are two possible examples:

_____

Example 1. You are meeting with a husband and wife about their estate planning, when they start to squabble over which of their children should be the successor executor. Frustrated, the wife turns to you, attempting to "triangle" you into the conversation on her side of the argument by commenting with a loaded question like "don't you think that he [the husband] is being hardheaded?"

_____

Example 2. Your clients, a husband and wife who are getting up in years, are concerned about which of their children should handle their affairs when they are no longer able to do so. They decide on one of their children to be their agent under their powers of attorney and tell all of their children of their decision. Not long after this, you receive a phone call from a child who was not selected, who expresses concern that his parents "may not be thinking clearly" in their selection of his sibling as agent, intimates his belief that his sibling has unduly influenced his parents and attempts to draw you into the conversation.

_____

Figure 3.1

PATH OF MOST RESISTANCE?

Client factors: Prior Inheritance Experience; Other Life Experiences; Attitude toward Wealth; Listening / Communication Skills; Personality Type; Mental & Physical Health; Relations With Spouse/Children/In-Laws/Descendants; Inner Child Issues; Siblings/Parents; Attitude Toward Death / Fear / Dislike of Death Talk

Flow: CLIENT → ADVISOR → ADVISOR → LOVED ONES, INTENDED BENEFICIARIES, OTHERS → GOOD ESTATE PLANNING RESULT

Client: Distrust / Fear of Advisors/; Fear of Loss of Control of Planning Process; Fear of Costs; Feelings about Taxes

Advisor: Ethical Constraints; Limitations / Teachings / Philosophy of Particular Specialty; Fear of Lawsuit

Advisor: Need for Business; "Lead Dog" Syndrome; Self Interest; Fear of Collection of Fees

Loved Ones: Fear of Loss of Person; Self Interest; Not getting whole story

3.3 WHAT IS A "GOOD ESTATE PLANNING RESULT" AND WHY IS IT SO HARD TO ACHIEVE?

All *estate planners* and clients are (or should be) united in the search for and implementation of a "good estate-planning result." What is that, you ask? To us, a "good estate-planning result" is one in which the people whom the client wants to get their possessions get them the way that the client wants them to, taxes are minimized to an acceptable level, and relationships after death are enhanced or at least not negatively affected. The tax and estate transmission parts are easy (or relatively so). It's the relationships piece that can be elusive, as Illustration 1 demonstrates. According to one study of 3,250 families, the researchers discovered that approximately 70 percent of the estate plans failed.[19]

As the illustration depicts, the client's estate planning desires and intentions have to first be filtered through past experiences, attitudes and relationships. Then the client's desires and intentions get passed through one or more estate planning advisors and their past experiences, attitudes and relationships in the same areas as those of the client, which are depicted above the arrow and which can impact and even distort the client's intentions. Then we have to negotiate the feelings of those who are impacted by the estate plan, who themselves can impact the estate plan either before or after death. Each of the "players" in the estate planning process also have unique issues, which are depicted below the arrow, which can go both forward and backward as clients sometimes progress and sometimes regress in the estate planning process.

3.4 WHAT FEARS DO OUR CLIENTS FACE IN ESTATE PLANNING?

In *Yours, Mine & Ours: Estate Planning for People in Blended or Step Families* (Paul Hood Services 2022), the author identifies 12 distinct fears that clients can encounter in estate planning, as follows:

1. Fear of contemplating their own mortality
2. Fear of not doing the right thing
3. Fear of the unknown
4. Fear of hurting someone's feelings
5. Fear of estate planners
6. Fear of the estate planning process
7. Fear of running out of money/insecurity/loss of control
8. Fear of law changes
9. Fear of facing reality
10. Fear of loss of flexibility
11. Fear of loss of privacy
12. Fear of probate

Each of these fears can be proven to either be irrational or at least partially unfounded or overstated. Nevertheless, the estate planner must acknowledge and understand that to the client, these fears are real. Therefore, the estate planner must be sensitive to these fears and do what he or she can to allay them. Unfortunately, many estate planners distance themselves from their clients' fears and fail to see that estate planning has both therapeutic and anti-therapeutic characteristics.[20] Indeed, Professor Shaffer even argued that "[l]awyers show little concern about the therapeutic counseling that goes on in an 'estate planning' client's experience."[21]

For some clients, as well as their families (who are as uncomfortable discussing death as the client and the estate planner), these fears can cause the estate planning process to either be truncated or bogged down in a form of planning paralysis. It can be vital to know which of the above fear(s) are involved in order to get past them and get the client back on track. The problem also can emanate from the client's family, which is not unusual in blended families, as both children and the new partner often jockey for the favored position in the client's estate plan.

3.5 FREQUENTLY ASKED QUESTIONS

Question – What are some of the issues for the estate planning advisor about death and dying?

Answer – We know that death is not a popular topic in our society.[22] In fact, many think that death and dying are taboo subjects. Even our society's descriptions of death and euphemisms for death include softening terms like "passed on" or "met their Maker." However, we all die.[23] What may not seem evident, however, is that the vast majority of estate planning advisors do not want to bring up death with their clients because doing so also makes the advisors feel uncomfortable.[24]

Discussions of the client's death often are awkward and punctuated by a form of "gallows humor" where the advisor and client can diminish their discomfort by making light of death with phrases like "when I kick the bucket...." Indeed, to some extent, some believe that clients actually engage in estate planning to attempt to "cheat death" and retain control of both people and property past the end of their lifetimes.[25]

The ground breaking work of Elisabeth Kübler-Ross, culminating in development of her model for the five stages of grief, has, despite some scientific criticism, significantly informed treatment of the terminally ill since it was introduced in a book back in 1969.[26] The five stages of grief as outlined in the Kübler-Ross Model are denial, anger, bargaining, depression and acceptance. For estate planners who often work with both the elderly and the terminally ill as well as those loved ones who survive them, knowledge of where a client is in the continuum of the five stages of grief can be critical in dispensing estate planning or estate or trust administration advice to that client because introducing a discussion of estate planning or administration before the client is ready can produce adverse or even explosive results.

CHAPTER ENDNOTES

1. You also see it referred to sometimes as the "holistic side" of estate planning. See, e.g., Gage, David; Gromala, John; and Kopf, Edward, "Holistic Estate Planning and Integrating Mediation in the Planning Process," 39 *Real Property, Probate & Trust Law Journal* 509 (2004) and Beach, Emily E., "Nudging Testators Toward Holistic Estate Planning: Overcoming Social Squeamishness on the Subjects of Money and Mortality," 26 *Ohio St. J. on Disp. Resol.* 701 (2011).
2. Paul Hood frequently described his estate planning practice in part as "practicing psychotherapy without a license" in which he regularly faced emotional reactions for which he was not trained to deal.
3. See, e.g., the story of Ishmael in Moby Dick, who expressed relief after signing his will this way, "After the ceremony was concluded upon the present occasion, I felt all the easier; a stone was rolled away from my heart."
4. See, e.g., Shaffer, Thomas L., *Death, Property, and Lawyers* (Dunellen Press 1970) (hereafter, "Shaffer"), p. 72. Back in 1665, in his *Reflections*, No. 26, Francois de La Rochefoucauld wrote "[N]either the sun nor death can be looked at without winking."
5. See, e.g., Sartre, Jean-Paul, *Existential Psychology* (Baines 1953), p. 132, in which Sartre wrote: "[t]he totality of my possessions reflects the totality of my being. I am what I have."
6. See, e.g., Hood, L. Paul, Jr., "From the School of Hard Knocks: Thoughts on the Initial Client Interview," 27 *ACTEC Journal* 297 (2002).
7. Hood, L. Paul, Jr., Yours, Mine & Ours: Estate Planning for People in Blended or Step Families (Paul Hood Services 2022) (hereafter, "Hood"), pp. 23-30.
8. See, e.g., Sprott, James A., "Psychological Aspects of Estate Planning," 5 *Journal of Forensic Psychology* (1973), pp. 25-39.
9. See, e.g., Marshall, Robert J. and Marshall, Simone V., *The Transference-Countertransference Matrix: The Emotional-Cognitive Dialogue in Psychotherapy, Psychoanalysis, and Supervision*, Chapter 1, which identifies at least 26 different types of transference.
10. For an extensive discussion and application of the phenomenon of transference to estate planning, see Shaffer, Chapter 7.
11. See, e.g., Wiener, Jan, *The Therapeutic Relationship: transference, countertransference and the making of meaning*, Chapter 3, which briefly describes the history of countertransference going back to Freud.
12. See, e.g., Clevans, Ethel L. Goldwater, "On Countertransference," 8 *Modern Psychoanalysis*, pp. 129-133 (1983).
13. Morrison, James R., M.D., *The First Interview (3d Ed.)* (Guilford Press 2007), pp. 198-199.
14. Id., p. 199.
15. Hamel, Louis H., Jr., JD and Davis, J. Timothy, Ph.D., "Transference and Countertransference in the Lawyer-Client Relationship: Psychoanalysis Applied in Estate Planning," 25 *Psychoanalytic Psychology*, pp. 590-601 (2008).
16. For more information on the Bowen Theory, go to www.thebowencenter.org. For another very easily accessible (and short) read on the Eight Concepts of Bowen Theory, consider Gilbert, Roberta M., M.D., *The Eight Concepts of Bowen Theory*, (Leading Systems Press 2006).
17. See, e.g., Titelman, Peter (ed.), *Triangles: Bowen Family Systems Theory Perspectives* (Haworth Press 2008); Guerin, Philip J., Jr., Fogarty, Thomas F., Fay, Leo F. and Kautto, Judith Gilbert, *Working with Relationship Triangles: The One-Two-Three of Psychotherapy* (Guildford Press 1996); and Bregman, Ona Cohn and White, Charles M. (eds.) *Bringing Systems Thinking to Life: Expanding the Horizons for Bowen Family Systems Theory* (Taylor & Francis 2011). The last book applies Bowen Theory to such diverse organizations and relationships as pastoral training and family businesses.
18. Collier, Charles W., "A 'Family Systems' Approach to the Estate Planning Process," 30 ACTEC Journal 146-149 (1994).
19. Williams, Roy and Preisser, Vic, *Preparing Heirs: Five Steps to a Successful Transition of Family Wealth and Values* (Robert D. Reed Publishers 2003), p.1.

20. See Glover, Mark, "Therapeutic Jurisprudential Framework of Estate Planning," 35 *Seattle University Law Review* 427 (2012), in which the author discusses those therapeutic and anti-therapeutic factors.
21. Shaffer, p. 72.
22. See, e.g., Hansen, Suzy, "English for Americans," Salon.com, February 3, 2003, in which Jane Walmsley, author of *Brit-Think Ameri-Think*, is interviewed and says "[t]he biggest difference between the Brits and Americans is that Americans think that death is optional."
23. Marcus Aurelius (121-180), emperor of the Roman Empire, wrote, in his *Meditations*, "[t]he act of dying is one of the acts of life."
24. See, e.g., Shaffer, p. 109.
25. Schaffer, p. 73.
26. Kübler-Ross, Elisabeth, *On Death and Dying* (Routledge 1969).

THE UNAUTHORIZED PRACTICE OF LAW

CHAPTER 4

4.1 INTRODUCTION

It is sometimes difficult to draw the boundaries of professional responsibility in an area as complex and sophisticated as estate planning. Special skills and learning are necessary prerequisites not only to the attorney but also to a CPA, CFP, ChFC, CLU, trust officer, or other individual serving a client in an advisory capacity. Yet it is clear that regardless of how knowledgeable an advisor is, the attorney is the *only* member of the estate planning team that is authorized to practice law.

The practice of law is regulated and limited for a number of reasons:

First, the public needs and deserves protection against advice by self-styled advisors who have been neither trained nor examined (nor licensed) by recognized educational or governmental authorities.

Second, many non-lawyers who are highly skilled in specific areas such as tax law may lack the broader viewpoint and depth provided by a good law school or legal experience.

Third, the lawyer-client relationship is one of confidentiality, relative objectivity, and impartiality. Even the most ethical sales person, service provider, or trust officer cannot claim complete objectivity; his job is to sell a given investment, contract, service, or the use of a particular financial institution. This does not imply that the CLU, ChFC, CFP, trust officer, or CPA does not have highly important tasks to perform as a member of the estate planning team or cannot render highly valuable advice. On the contrary, it is often that individual who motivates the client to take action – and follows through to make sure the plan is implemented. And many times it is the non-attorney who spots an issue or brings a creative suggestion to the table. So *all* of these professionals are essential members of the planning team.

Fourth, the preparation of an estate plan is always more than just pulling a form from a book. The process involves the proper coordination of how a variety of assets are to be distributed. For example, in today's world, there are many ways in which an asset may pass at death. Some assets pass under the provisions of the will, but many assets pass in accordance with a beneficiary designation, or how the assets happened to be titled. Also, some beneficiaries, such as minors, require special consideration concerning how the assets are to pass to them. Other assets require proper consideration as to the tax consequences of how the assets are to be transferred, and who will pay the taxes associated with the receipt of these assets.

Finally, the proper titling of assets has implications broader than simply estate planning. For example, how assets are titled may require considerations as to how to best protect these assets from creditors of a spouse. Also, changing the title of a house can result in the entire unpaid balance owed on a mortgage becoming immediately due. The proper treatment of these issues requires specialized training and knowledge; and this task is best coordinated through a lawyer.

Were motivation and follow-through the only responsibility and utility of those members, their positions on the "team" would be secure. But, in reality, each of those individuals can perform a function that serves as a valuable complement to the attorney's task. In fact, the attorney should not be "practicing" life insurance, providing trust services, or replacing the accountant or valuation expert.

The very idea of an estate planning team implies that each member serves the client – and complements the other members of the team – with his own special and essential skills. When *any* member of the team usurps the province of the other, it is the client who loses. Stated in a more positive manner, the client is best served if the non-attorney and attorney work together to formulate, implement, qualify, and maintain a plan that suits the client's needs and objectives.

4.2 WHAT IS THE UNAUTHORIZED PRACTICE OF LAW?

Clearly, the preparation of instruments and contracts by which legal rights are secured constitutes an invasion of the attorney's province. So, the non-attorney who drafts a will or a trust for a client is patently guilty of the unauthorized practice of law.

But what of the person who reviews a will or trust and advises clients as to the desirability in their circumstances of specific clauses or instruments? Does every discussion of a legal principle constitute unauthorized practice? Is the recognized subject matter expert excused from the proscription against unauthorized practice? What if no fee is charged for the rendering of advice? Does long-time custom and tradition offer a valid reason for practice by non-lawyers?

A working knowledge of the tax law is essential to professionals in the life insurance, trust, and accounting disciplines. Generally, the protection of the public can be achieved without hampering or unduly burdening professionals with impractical and technical restrictions that have no reasonable justification. To say that non-attorneys cannot discuss any pertinent legal principles with a client would be so unrealistic and narrow as to be absurd.

But what can be safely discussed – and what cannot? While there are few redline tests, there are some common sense guidelines. Essentially, where a statute or legal interpretation has become so well-known and settled that no further legal issue is involved, there should be no problem in suggesting its simple application on a general basis. This is known as the "general-specific" test; no violation arises from the sharing of legal knowledge that is either generally informatory or, if specific, is so obvious as to be common knowledge.

It is only when legal rules (which are general in nature) are applied to specific factual situations that the line is crossed. Providing advice involving the application of legal principles to a specific situation is clearly the "practice of law" under the "general-specific" test.

A second criterion is known as the "complexity" theory. This theory states that the non-attorney should not answer "difficult" or "complex" or "not yet resolved" questions of law. One court stated that "practicing as an attorney…is the giving of advice or the rendition of any sort of service…when the giving of such advice or the rendition of such service requires the use of any degree of legal knowledge or skill."[1]

But perhaps the court should have gone beyond the questions of difficulty or complexity of subject matter into the issue of whether legal judgment was exercised by the non-attorney and relied on by the client. When basic legal principles are applied to specific and actual facts or the resolution of controversial or uncertain questions of law is required in an actual case, the practice of law is involved.

No safety can be found in an argument that the non-lawyer is both a specialist and an acknowledged expert in the field – even one who is highly lauded. The rationale for this seemingly harsh stand is that the interest of the public is not protected by narrow specialization of a person who lacks the broad perspective and orientation of a licensed attorney. That dimension of skill and knowledge comes only from a thorough understanding of legal concepts, processes, and the interaction of all the branches of law. In other words, the *rules* may have been learned by the non-lawyer but often the full meaning and import of the rule and its components – and the impact of that rule on other seemingly unrelated rules – may not be fully understood by even a highly competent specialist who is not also a licensed attorney. For instance, a proposed arrangement might "work" in terms of its tax implications but violate ERISA or securities laws.

Charging fees for legal advice seems important only where such fees were charged. But most courts have had little trouble finding violations where clients relied on advice or were provided with legal services regardless of whether or not fees were charged. Likewise, practices of the past provide little defense in the present. ("But I've done it for years – and so have others here in River City

– and no one has ever questioned it or complained"). Recent decisions indicate that even custom and tradition long acquiesced in by the Bar does not make proscribed activities any less the practice of law.

Almost everyone agrees that the actual drafting of a will or trust or the preparation of the instruments and contracts by which legal rights are secured is the practice of law. The odds are very high that he who drafts such documents is practicing law.

Beyond this point, however, (and in the minds of some, even at this point) things become hazy. Each state has the right to decide – independently from all other states – what is meant by the "unauthorized practice of law."

Review the following fact patterns and ask, "Will this constitute the unauthorized practice of law?"

- The planner reviews a will or trust and advises a client that – in this particular circumstance – that document will (or will not) have specific legal implications or that the instrument in question is "right" or "not right" for the client.

- After analyzing client information, the planner decides on the type of trust arrangement the client should have and selects the specific provisions that should be inserted into the plan documents.

- The planner makes "bottom line recommendations" as to which trust provisions would be most suitable to a client's needs.

- The planner drafts amendments to an existing trust.

- The planner does the initial draft of a power of attorney, but submits it for review, approval, and adoption by the client's lawyers.

- The planner gives advice regarding the impact of tax and other laws on an irrevocable trust.

If these actions are the unauthorized practice of law, is the client denied the benefit of receiving advice from accountants, actuaries, CFPs, CLUs, ChFCs, or trust officers who are experts in their fields? Would prohibiting such actions by these experts amount to a questionable restraint on interdisciplinary competition? Is it not only possible, but also highly likely, that the non-attorney expert is better suited than the attorney in matters such as product choice and design? Would thwarting the non-attorney from performing these vital roles significantly increase the cost of estate planning? In some states these are still open questions. As a practical matter, practitioners should avoid most problems by working closely with the client's attorney at the earliest opportunity.

4.3 A NEW TREND TO WATCH- NON-LAWYERS OWNING INTERESTS IN LAW FIRMS

For many years, non-lawyers could not own interests in law firms, and lawyers were prohibited from splitting legal fees with non-lawyers. In 1983, the American Bar Association formally incorporated these two prohibitions in Model Rules of Professional Conduct (MRPC) Rule 5.4. In fact, until fairly recently, the District of Columbia was the only United States jurisdiction where, subject to strict restrictions, lawyers could split legal fees with non-lawyers, and where it was possible, under limited circumstances, for non-lawyers (*e.g.*, lobbyists) to own interests in law firms.

However, times seem to be changing, in part through increasing competition from diverse points ranging from CPAs to legal technology. Several states, including California, Massachusetts, Arizona, and Georgia, have begun to modify this former strict rule. These states have approached these changes quite differently. For example, in August 2020, the Arizona Bar Association eliminated its version of MRPC Rule 5.4 entirely, deciding to create a new arrangement called Alternate Business Structures ("ABS"), which provide legal services, but that may be partially owned by non-lawyers. However, every ABS, must include at least one licensed lawyer to serve as compliance counsel.

4.4 CONCLUSION

This book and our companion texts are not designed to help the non-lawyer eliminate the need for an attorney. To the contrary, it is a text designed for all the members of the estate planning team to more easily identify typical planning issues and help delineate the large number of alternative solutions to general problem areas. Definitive solutions, i.e., the choice of which specific tools or techniques to use in a given case or the decisions as to how they should be used, must be considered only by the client, together with his attorney. Likewise, the drafting or adopting of instruments needed to execute the techniques or utilize the tools discussed in this book is exclusively the province of the lawyer.

Every member of the estate planning team is obligated to be aware of these tools and techniques, to understand their limitations as well as their problem-solving potential, and to be knowledgeable enough to discuss them in general terms with clients and their other advisors.

CHAPTER ENDNOTE

1. People ex rel, *Illinois State Bar Association v. Schafer*, 404 Ill. 45, 50 (Ill. 1949).

ETHICS – A PRACTICAL GUIDELINE

CHAPTER 5

5.1 INTRODUCTION

Ethics are standards of an aspirational and inspirational nature reflecting commitments to model standards of exemplary professional conduct.[1] Every major profession[2] has adopted some form of "near law," a Code, Canon, or set of guidelines as to what the profession expects of its members.[3] This discussion is meant to provide a checklist for the practitioner in the estate planning field. It is not intended to be anything more than what its title implies, a "practical guideline," a self-monitoring device to help estate planners.

Why do professional organizations need such codes of conduct? Why do estate planners need a practical code of ethics?

First, ethics are a means of creating standards by which conduct can be measured both by the member and by the group itself. Second, ethics serve as a way to acknowledge an obligation to society, to the professional group, and to the client. Third, ethics assure the profession will be governed by high standards. Fourth, ethics are a means of examining priorities and building a tradition based on integrity.

A fifth reason for ethics is as a limitation on power. It is the "power of the experts" that ethics are meant to control: the attorney, accountant, trust officer, life insurance agent, and other members of the estate planning team all know things the client does not.[4] This special knowledge gives the professional "High Priest"-like power over a layman who must put great faith and trust in (and take great risk in the accuracy and appropriateness of) what he is told. The client cannot possibly know the full extent of the problems, possibilities, and consequences without the assistance of the planner.

The preparation of an estate plan vests in the planner enormous power for another reason: the planner is a person in whom the client places a great trust and confidence. It is this potential abuse of power that ethics are designed to prevent or limit.

5.2 WHAT ARE PRACTICAL ETHICS?

The premise upon which practical ethics must be based is that power must be exercised in the interest of those for whose benefit it was entrusted rather than abused for the self-aggrandizement of the planner. On the other hand, the limitations and restrictions on the planner must not, however, be so great as to be so unenforceable, unrealistic, and impractical as to be counter-productive. Practical ethics, therefore, must strike a balance. The questions that follow are designed to help do just that:

Honesty

Has the planner engaged in any business or professional activity that involved an act (or omission) of a dishonest, deceitful, or fraudulent nature?

Has the planner used his license, degree, or designation to attribute to himself a depth or scope of knowledge, skills, and professional capabilities he does not, in fact, possess? Has he kept up-to-date in his field? Has he kept current in related fields?[5]

Has the planner been fair and honest in dealings with the IRS and other governmental bodies and in fostering confidence in the system?[6]

Competency

Does the planner have the requisite legal knowledge, practical skill, and has he exercised thoroughness?

Has the planner undertaken a role that entails responsibilities, knowledge, or experience in addition to those inherent to the profession – and if so – is he properly trained and equipped (and willing and otherwise able) to perform them in a competent and efficient manner?[7]

Has the planner done the proper preparation? In other words, is he qualified to perform the services requested and does he know enough to perform any services required beyond those requested?

What has the planner done to understand the specific facts and circumstances of the client, the client's family, other beneficiaries, and their needs and objectives?

Does the planner keep abreast of changing economic and legislative conditions that may affect the client's plan?[8]

Representation

Has the planner established – through an engagement letter – the boundaries of his relationship so that the client knows what he/she will or will not do? Has the planner specified those limits in writing for all parties concerned? For example, has the planner made it clear who will have the responsibility to re-title assets or change beneficiary designations which are needed to implement the plan?

Has the planner – in any way – denied the client the benefit of the knowledge and skill of *another* professional who could better assist in serving the client or serve the client in a way the planner cannot?[9]

Diligence

Did the planner do what was required in a reasonably prompt manner?

If the planner is responsible for preparing IRS forms, documents, affidavits, or other papers for the client, did he do so in a timely manner?

Did the planner advise a client promptly of any noncompliance, error, or omission having to do with a state or federal tax return or other document the client was required by law to complete?

Communication

Did the planner return phone calls or answer letters or e-mails promptly? Did he keep the client (and other professionals) informed on a regular basis of economic and legal changes that may affect the client's plans?

Confidentiality

Did the planner keep client information confidential (except to the extent specifically authorized by the client in the planner-client engagement letter to disclose it)?[10] Has the planner discussed confidentiality issues when his clients are a married couple, an unmarried couple, or business associates?

Fees

Did the planner charge fees that were reasonable and fair in light of the situation?[11] Was the fee based on:

1. the amount of work performed or the number of hours it took to do the work;

2. the difficulty and judgment involved in the problems that had to be solved;

3. the importance of the problem; and

4. professional expertise, skill, and standing?

Did the planner communicate, in writing, the formula by which fees or other charges would be based?

Has the planner billed, only after performing services in a satisfactory manner?

Has the planner refunded any advance fee that has not been fully earned?

Conflict of Interest

Did the planner inform the parties he is representing of their respective rights and the pros and cons of the proposed action (or inaction) on each party?

Did the planner draft an instrument giving him or a member of his family an interest in the client's estate (assuming he is not a member of the client's family)?[12]

Has the planner written himself (or his partner) into the will as attorney for the estate and also as executor when there were family members or friends of the client who could have performed the task?

Has the planner used the special knowledge he has to the detriment of the client in any way?

Does the planner represent two or more parties who have or are likely to have conflicting interests?[13] (This problem is known as "simultaneous representation.") If so, is the planner satisfied that he can perform adequately and did he make full disclosure to, and obtain written consent from, the parties?[14]

Has the planner, in any way, allowed the pursuit of financial gain or any other personal benefit to interfere with the exercise of sound professional judgment and skills?[15]

Has the planner made full disclosure of any obvious conflicts of interest in writing to the client?

Has the planner drawn an instrument that exonerates him from liability that may be incurred in another role (such as the attorney who may also serve as executor)?[16]

Has the estate planner maintained focus upon the needs of the client? When an attorney provides estate planning services, one of the primary requirements is to maintain focus upon who is the client. If a husband and wife seek estate planning; they are both the client. If a child wants to talk to an attorney about Medicaid planning for their parent, or to prepare documents for the parent; the parent is the client, not the child. Maintaining the proper focus is essential to avoid ethical issues.

Disclosure

Has the planner (or associates, partners, or employer), in any other way, breached the duty of loyalty to the client by failing to disclose information?

Has the planner withheld information from another professional or governmental official that it is important and appropriate for that person to know?

Has the planner misrepresented the benefits, costs, or limitations of any estate planning tool or technique or failed to fully explain the advantages and disadvantages of viable alternatives?[17]

Direct Contact

Has the planner obtained information directly from the client or was it obtained second or third hand from another party or advisor acting as a conduit?[18]

Courtesy

Has the planner's courtesy extended not only to the client, but also to the other professionals who seek to serve that person?[19]

Public Regard

Has the planner followed the laws applicable to his business and professional activities?[20]

Has the planner done what he or she can to raise the level of integrity and professionalism and avoided activities that detract from the opinion the public has of his profession?

Has the planner impaired the reputation of another practitioner?

Has the planner competed unfairly?

Has the planner used his degree or designation in less than a responsible or dignified or appropriate manner?

Does the planner avoid associating with those who are not ethical?

Has the planner provided the public with useful and objective information concerning potential problems, possible solutions, and impartial advisory opinions?

Has the planner attempted – in all dealings with the public – to avoid the appearance of impropriety?

Mentoring

Has the planner helped others enter the profession? Has he helped them attain and retain competence?

Has the planner encouraged and assisted others in obtaining higher levels of professional competence?

It is not enough to NOT advocate, sanction, participate in, or carry out an unethical act. Professional ethics require more than merely NOT doing the things you should not do. It forbids condoning the unethical act of another and requires taking positive action to do the things that should be done.

Ethics are a reminder that the estate planner is more of a counselor than an advocate, more of an advisor than a scholar. Ethics reinforce the importance of the role of all the members of the estate planning team as intermediaries and protectors who look out for the overall best interests of the family and business unit in recommending a course of action.

5.3 CONCLUSION

Ethics do not demand absolute, unreasoning, and undivided loyalty to a single client nor does it demand saint-like perfection in any other area. But ethics has its (generally quite affordable) price – professional honesty, integrity, and competence compatible with the realities of modern practice. In fact, the increased pride and respect gained from others (and ourselves) is well worth the price. Can any planner afford not to pay it?

CHAPTER ENDNOTES

1. See Code of Professional Ethics of the American Institute for Chartered Property Casualty Underwriters. Available at: www.theinstitutes.org/doc/canons.pdf.
2. See "For the Long Term — Professional Ethics and The Life Underwriter," Life Association News, December 1985, for an excellent discussion on that subject. Dr. Clarence C. Walton, the author of that article, states that among the characteristics of a mature professional are:

    A. Primary commitment to the interest of the client,

    B. Possession of expert knowledge,

    C. Self-regulation, and

    D. Awareness of the long term consequences of his or her action.

    Dr. Walton provides excellent guidelines for organizations that sincerely wish to promote and enforce a code of ethics.
3. Information on the Code of conduct for your profession should be obtained by writing to the appropriate national organization to which you belong. Attorneys should refer to the ABA's Model Rules of Professional Conduct (available at: http://www.americanbar.org/groups/professional_responsibility/publications/model_rules_of_professional_conduct.html) and the applicable ethics rules for their respective jurisdictions. The ACTEC Foundation publishes the extensive *ACTEC Commentaries on the Model Rules of Professional Conduct* (5th Ed. 2016), which is a very helpful analysis of how the Model Rules of Professional Conduct apply to the trusts and estates practice. The ACTEC Commentaries are available at www.actec.org.
4. See "Estate Planners: Where Do Your Ethics Lie?," Trusts and Estates.
5. Two excellent sources of keeping current are (1) Keeping Current, series of symposiums by the Society of Financial Services Professionals, which focuses on life insurance related issues and (2) LISI – Leimberg Information Services, Inc., an almost daily e-mail estate planning newsletter, podcast, webinar and database service.
6. The duties of a professional to the IRS are spelled out in IRS circular 230 that embraces, under a uniform standard, many of the traditional ethical and professional standards common to national professional organizations. See "Regulations within the IRS," Trusts and Estates, April 1990, p. 30.
7. See "Draft Statement of Principles Comes not a Moment too Soon," Trusts and Estates, December 1988, p. 12. For instance, a competent attorney may serve in other fiduciary roles such as an executor or trustee. One competent to handle the role of attorney may not have the training or skill (or time) to serve as an executor or trustee.
8. Canon 2 of the Code of Professional Responsibility of the Society of Financial Service Professionals states, "A member shall continually improve his/her professional knowledge, skill, and competence." Furthermore, application of that rule "requires, at a minimum, meeting the applicable continuing education standards set by state licensing authorities, the Society of Financial Service Professionals, the American College, the CFP Board of Standards, and any other entity with appropriate authority over the member's license(s) or other credentials."
9. For instance, by making an unfair comparison between a person who has a license, degree, or designation, and one who does not.

    In an excellent Trusts and Estates article entitled, "ETHICS," the author, Frederic G. Corneel, poses a situation in which an insurance agent suggested to a consumer that he buy a very large amount of life insurance and adopt an estate plan including a revocable insurance trust. At the customer's request, the agent recommends a lawyer. The client tells the lawyer about his estate and the amount of insurance recommended to him. In the lawyer's opinion the amount of insurance is very much in excess of what is needed.

    What should the lawyer do? Corneel answers that the lawyer must, of course, be guided by what he believes to be in the best interest of the client. But then he adds, "The other point for the lawyer to keep in mind is that he may well be mistaken in his evaluation of how much insurance is necessary or that, this may be a question of business, personal, or investment preference which the client is just as capable of making as the lawyer himself.

    Corneel then states that "before giving his opinion to the client, however, the lawyer would be well advised to speak first with the insurance agent. The agent may have information or thought to bear on the problem that the lawyer has not considered and that might well affect his view on the matter. This is not only in the lawyer's interest, who by a simple telephone call may be kept from making a fool of himself, but it is in the interest of the client not to become the battlefield of a war among experts unless the war is unavoidable."

10. Canon 3 of the Code of Professional Responsibility of the Society of Financial Service Professionals states, "A member shall respect the confidentiality of any information entrusted to, or obtained in the course of, the member's business or professional activities."

11. An excellent guide to the factors that affect attorney's fees in estate administration can be found in "Attorney's Fees in Estate Administration," *The Chase Review*, January 1990 (Chase Private Banking Group, 1211 Avenue of the Americas, New York, New York 10036). See Rule 1.5, Model Rules of Professional Conduct, American Bar Association.

12. See "Legal Ramifications of Unethical Estate Planning Practices," Trusts and Estates, October 1985, p. 47 for court response to situations in which (a) an attorney made himself legatee or devisee, (b) the attorney named himself or his partner as executor or trustee with powers to confer upon himself many of the benefits of ownership, (c) the attorney contrived to assure himself professional employment (together with a rather generous fee arrangement) representing the fiduciary in connection with the probate of a will or the administration of a trust.

13. It is quite common for a planner to work with several members of the same family. In planning, conflicts of interests may arise over (a) the exercise of tax elections or options, (b) the interpretation of a clause in a will or trust or other document, or (c) the exercise or non-exercise of discretionary authority by a fiduciary. The attorney represents multiple clients when providing advice for both spouses, parent and child, or testator and beneficiary. An excellent discussion of these conflicts can be found in the January 1990 issue of *The Chase Review*. See also "Conflicts of Interest in Estate Planning and Administration," *Trusts and Estates*, June 1984, p. 18. For a general discussion of legal ethics rules applied to intergenerational estate planning, see, e.g., Collett, "The Ethics of Intergenerational Representation," 62 *Fordham Law Review* 1453 (1994).

14. QTIP planning presents inevitable conflicts of interest that demand full disclosure. For instance, "Is a QTIP trust contrary to the wishes or needs of a spouse who wants to obtain greater control of her spouse's property on his death?" "Is a large inter vivos intraspousal gift contrary to the interests of a wealthy spouse if some day in the future divorce occurs?"

The solution to multiple representation is, as mentioned in the body of this discussion, a "plain English" explanation of the meaning and personal impact of the planners' suggestions.

15. Code of Professional Ethics of The American Institute for Property and Liability Underwriters, Inc.

16. For instance, instruments should not include exculpatory provisions that would relieve the draftsperson of malpractice or malfeasance liability unless the instrument is reviewed by independent counsel for the instrument's creator.

17. Each professional must ask himself three questions:

   A. What are the pros and cons of the viable alternatives?

   B. Which alternatives offer the client and client's family or other intended beneficiaries the greatest financial security and the least overall cost?

   C. What if the client does nothing?

   Then these three issues must be shared with the client's other advisors and with the client.

18. Only through direct relations can a professional be sure that he has all of the relevant facts including an understanding of the client's objectives and fears and can make sure both parties fully understand each other.

19. Rule 4.2 of the Code of Professional Responsibility of the Society of Financial Service Professionals states, "A member shall establish and maintain dignified and honorable relationships with those he/she serves, with fellow practitioners, and with members of other professions."

20. Rule 6.1 of the Code of Professional Responsibility of the Society of Financial Service Professionals states, "A member has the duty to know and abide by the local, state, and national laws and regulations and all legal limitations pertaining to the member's professional activities."

MALPRACTICE IN ESTATE PLANNING

CHAPTER 6

6.1 INTRODUCTION

"You have a malpractice case if there is no reasonable explanation for a terrible result."[1]

More technically stated, when a professional breaches the duty owed to another party and the other party is injured as a result of that breach, there is malpractice.[2] Errors in estate planning and estate tax constitute an important type of legal malpractice. Reducing the risk of a malpractice suit and enhancing available defenses is the subject of this discussion.

6.2 TARGET OF OPPORTUNITY – WHY ME?

Those professionals wise enough to know that malpractice is a disease that may attack anyone will not ask the question, "Why me?" Instead, they will ask, "When?" Malpractice claims are made uncomfortably often against those who – out of ignorance, arrogance, or incompetence – thought it could not happen to them. Suits are also brought against those estate planners with fine reputations who honestly thought they had done everything right. It is a dangerous misconception to think that only those who are clearly sloppy and unethical encounter malpractice claims.[3]

Mere good faith and honest intent will not protect the practitioner who has caused a client loss. It may be true that an estate planner will not be held liable for the failure to foresee the ultimate resolution of a debatable point of law or for an error in judgment if he acts in good faith and in an honest belief that his advice and acts are well founded and in the best interest of his client.[4] But such an estate planner can still be sued and still incur most of the costs of someone who in fact is guilty of malpractice.

Who are likely "targets of opportunity"?

Deep pockets. When clients sue, they sue everyone in sight. But the bulk of the litigation effort is understandably against those from whom recovery is most likely. Your firm's prestige and appearance of success is a litigation magnet. Furthermore, "judges and juries alike may be inclined to assess the loss of the poor helpless individual against the large, seemingly impersonal institution that manages billions of dollars every day."[5] This problem is particularly evident where the defendant is a trust, insurance company, or large law firm. It is also a problem when the client is involved in a transaction which is difficult for a layperson to understand. The client is in the hands of the "professionals." When a bad result occurs, the client (or family of the client) will often attempt to assign blame for the outcome.

Insurance. Certainly one contributing factor is the common knowledge that professionals carry insurance for malpractice. Almost all professionals in the financial services field carry one or more high limit insurance coverages. Some plaintiffs feel they are not suing the professional; they are suing the insurer.

Touted experience, skill, and knowledge. In general, professionals who obtain or retain clients by holding themselves out in their marketing brochures or newspaper or magazine or radio advertisements as possessing a higher level of skill or greater experience in a field than other practitioners will be held to that higher level. If an advisor's business card says, "Estate Planner" or "Tax Specialist" or has an advanced degree or a CFP, CLU,

ChFC or otherwise advertises greater expertise or skill than an ordinary practitioner, he is expected to exercise that expertise or skill.[6]

Impersonal. It is far easier to sue a party perceived as a giant institution guided by computers rather than people than to sue a longtime advisor who has served with warmth, openness, compassion and has provided substantial personal attention in a respectful manner. This public image of banks, insurance companies, large law firms, and other institutions as impersonal money machines can best be changed from the top down by an insistence on courtesy and attention to the client from everyone in the firm – and is particularly helped by responding to phone calls and e-mails quickly and politely.

Big guy vs. little guy. There is a feeling in this country, right or wrong, that the "Big Guys" are using their weight to beat up on the "Little Guys." So when the little guy gets into the judicial system, a jury may feel sympathetic and tend to punish the big guy with an angry vengeance.

Frustration with the law(s). The potential for malpractice increases in proportion to both the complexity, speed of change, and labyrinthine interrelationship of various federal and state corporate, tax, probate, and securities laws – and clients' confusion and frustration. From the estate planner's point of view, the combination is a nightmare. If the planner feels this way, think of how angry clients must be when told that last year's law is now out of date and all the time, money, and emotional energy must be invested all over again.[7] Consider how a client feels when wrestling with Medicaid rules that continually change, with tax laws that are hair-pullingly complex, and with paperwork that is in fact never-ending.

6.3 SIMPLE VS. COMPOUND LIABILITY

One author who both sues and defends members of estate planning teams said, "There are basically two types of malpractice liability: Simple and Compound read "expensive" and "grossly expensive")."[8]

Simple liability is for simple errors in judgment or simple negligence. These mistakes are expensive but are part of the (reducible) costs of doing business. Missing a tax deadline or miscomputing a liquidity need would be examples of simple liability.

Compound liability is for gross breach of fiduciary duty, self-dealing, active concealment, fraud, oppression, and gross negligence. The author stated that "Gross negligence is usually accompanied by a fatal dose of institutional arrogance, an always fatal disease for which there is no known cure."[9] Lack of respect and common courtesy often turn what could otherwise have been a minor incident into a major, expensive legal battle.

6.4 TO WHOM IS ONE LIABLE?

This question is not always as easy to answer as it sounds. The simple answer is one is liable to those who employ you. The general rule is that a duty is only to the person with whom contracted, your client.

But one may also be liable to others as well.[10] For example, an insurance agent may have created an agency relationship with the purchaser of a life insurance policy. This would make him, or her, the agent of the insurance company for some purposes and agent of the client for others.

An advisor is not liable – even for an act of negligence – to someone to whom he owes no duty.[11] The legal term is "privity." But the defense that there is no privity, no duty to an injured party, can easily be forfeited and is currently being eroded in the courts.[12] For instance, if you advise the president of a family-owned corporation improperly about the appropriateness of a stock redemption plan and one is established because of reliance on your advice, unexpected dividend taxes upon the purchase by the corporation of its stock could be claimed by another family member shareholder.

This six-pronged test may be used to determine privity:[13]

1. To what extent is the transaction intended to benefit the third person?

2. Can harm to that third person be foreseen?

3. How likely is it that the third person will suffer real injury?

4. How close is the connection between the advisor's conduct and the injury that the third party could suffer?

5. How "morally wrong" is the advisor's action?

6. Would future harm to this or some other client be served by finding privity here?

At least one state will grant "standing" (the right to sue) to a narrow class of third party beneficiaries where it is clear that the client intended to benefit that party and the client is unable to enforce the contract.[14] Generally, for a third party to collect an award, written evidence must show that the client's intent was frustrated and the beneficiary's loss was a direct result of the planner's negligence.

6.5 WHAT CAN GET THE ADVISOR INTO TROUBLE?

If one says he knows, he'd better. Estate planning is too complex to be a sideline or part time hobby. Failure to exercise reasonable care and skill in performing duties for a person induced to rely on an advisor because of his professed skills, knowledge, or experience ("John Jones, Estate Planner") can result in liability for loss incurred.[15] Failure to exercise the degree of expertise that one professes to possess coupled with inducing reliance on that assertion to achieve a sale or sell a service creates a duty to act properly.[16] If one holds himself out as an expert and directly or indirectly promises to provide a product or service to serve a specific purpose or accomplish a particular objective, he assumes the liability for the achievement of that purpose or objective.[17] The skill, knowledge, diligence, and care used must equal or exceed that standard ordinarily exercised by others in the same profession.[18] In short, if one calls himself a professional (or by action or inaction allow others to rely on him as such), he must assume the responsibilities and duties generally associated with such a status – or be held liable for the client's loss.

Not knowing whom the client is. Interview both spouses (separately if appropriate). If there is marital discord or if this is a second marriage, consider recommending separate counsel. With families where the spouses have children from prior marriages, you may also want to have each spouse waive any conflicts which exist between them. This is important since conflicts of interest can easily arise. For example, each spouse may want to favor his or her children as opposed to the spouse's children. Also, if "the couple" is perceived as the client, both should be treated accordingly. Do not talk down to or ignore the younger, or female, or less wealthy spouse – or child – or to some other member of the family. Develop and maintain good relationships with all the members of the client's family to the extent appropriate.

There are all too many cases where the planner never, or seldom, meets with the client. For instance, assume a will was prepared for a husband and wife on the instructions of the husband. If the planner never met the wife, how can it be argued that she has been properly represented by counsel or that she understood what she signed? The situation is a "lack of informed consent" case in the making.

When a spouse chooses not to read documentation or does not want to listen to complicated tax law, that same problem exists even though caused by his or her own inaction. The solution is to commit both parties – in the engagement letter – to read documents prepared for them within a specified time and to encourage them to seek independent counsel of their choice should either feel that is appropriate. Short written summaries are helpful.

If one says he will, he'd better. An advisor should never create false expectations by making promises he has no intention of keeping or by promising results he does not know he can deliver. He may be held liable to the beneficiaries of an estate if he promises to keep them informed of significant developments and then does not.[19] He has an obligation to substantially finish the task he has begun for a client, decline the appointment, or with the client's consent, accept the employment and associate a lawyer who is competent. He must also prepare adequately for, and give appropriate attention to, the work he has accepted.

Overnight express. Clients often want insurance issued and wills drawn almost overnight – at the very time when they are about to leave on an extended vacation or business trip. This means there is insufficient time to collect, analyze, and act upon complete asset information. Deathbed planning is more of the same only worse. One should refuse to be rushed (but be prepared to work quickly).

6.6 HOW DOES ONE STAY OUT OF TROUBLE?

Hiring – and Firing – The Client

The advisor should ask why the client has chosen him. It is flattering to think that one has been selected because of one's expertise or reputation, but the reason may be because one or more other practitioners decided not to represent the client. One should obtain as much information about the client's background with other professionals as possible before agreeing to work with the client. It has been said that more money has been made from the cases which are turned down than the ones which are accepted. The first interview should be considered a primary opportunity to screen and qualify the client. Perhaps the potential client should be discarded if he seems to be a perfectionist, unrealistic, hurried, angry, overly optimistic, overly fee-conscious, or if he wants services the advisor is not positive he/she can provide cost effectively.[20] One should beware of clients who are wealthy but in constant cash flow difficulty, seem immature, refuse to accept responsibility for their own actions, or appear constantly ambivalent.[21] These personality types are likely to present a future litigation problem.

Trust your instincts. One should turn down a client who exhibits questionable ethics or requests something that is not quite right. Some of the best marketing you can do is to send problem clients down the street. If a client has outgrown the advisor's capacity, either recommend another firm or bring a specialist in to work with the client. If the advisor feels the client cannot be trusted, refuse to work with the client.

Risk-Taking Propensity

One of the biggest causes of claims is that the professional misjudges or never considers or does not re-evaluate the risk-taking propensity of the client and the client's beneficiaries as their circumstances change. The solution is constant communication and obtaining updated feedback on where the client is "now" on risk taking.

Expertise Boundaries

The advisor should do only those things he is competent (and licensed) to do – and do those things competently and in a timely manner. Should a life insurance agent review a will or trust? Should an attorney or accountant judge the adequacy or appropriateness of a client's life insurance portfolio? Should a trust company review documents? Should a financial planner serve as trustee?[22]

Document examination exposure is real. Should one disclaim any liability for review of document viability or efficacy? Incompetent, inconsistent, and informal review is a formula for disaster. If the task is undertaken, it should be done by a person with the appropriate training, expertise, and time to do the job competently and enthusiastically. "You assume an obligation to your client to undertake reasonable research in an effort to ascertain relevant legal principles and to make an informed decision as to a course of action based on an intelligent assessment of the problem."[23]

Furthermore, the estate planner has a duty to either avoid involving a client in "murky" areas of the law if there are viable alternative tools or techniques that are available or to inform the client of the risks and let the client make the decision.[24]

Lack of specialized investment knowledge on the part of the planner or fiduciary often results in investment problems. Numerous trust funds are managed by individuals who adopt a passive and simplistic approach. The need for professional investment management and the complexity of modern portfolio theory is ignored or overlooked and too little time is spent in making investment decisions or addressing overall investment policy and asset allocation.[25]

Resource Limits

The advisor should not accept engagements that will require resources beyond what can be effectively delivered. For example, if the operation does not have the backup personnel to properly service a high number of clients, the estate planner should not agree to do estate conservation for a firm's top 100 executives.

Outside Experts

An advisor should seek help before it is needed. When appropriate, recommend that another professional be used, either in the advisor's place or working together with the advisor. If the advisor makes a specific recommendation, he may be held liable for the actions of that other professional. One way to protect himself is by giving out the names of at least three qualified professionals (make sure the criteria for "qualified" extends beyond mere reputation), or stay involved with the representation.

Keeping Current

An advisor must stay up-to-date, not only with tax, ERISA, asset protection planning, and Medicaid law developments (preferably on a day-by-day basis through a service such as LISI — (Leimberg Information Services, Inc.) but also on events that can have an impact on the client's personal and business life.

6.7 PUT IT (ALL) IN WRITING

Protecting one's self means meticulous record keeping starting at the onset of the relationship. Changes in risk-taking propensity or attitude of the client or the family, comments at meetings, phone conversations, and other special instructions should be noted. The advisor's files should clearly reflect and support his recollection of events and should be dictated and transcribed as soon as possible after the occurrence (or preferably contemporaneous with the events). The more complete and organized the files, the more likely the judge, jury, or board of arbitrators will consider the advisor's word persuasive (assuming, of course, the files corroborate what he is now saying).

Many times, the preparation of the estate documents only represents part of the estate plan. It is also important to make sure that the assets are properly titled between husband and wife; and that beneficiary designations are properly completed. In order to properly complete an estate plan, it is necessary to coordinate how assets pass with the estate planning documents. Therefore, after the written documents are completed, it is important to send a letter explaining how these other issues are to be addressed.

Whenever possible, make notes that quote the client's exact words.[26] This is particularly important whenever a client – or another advisor – decides to pursue an aggressive tax policy or take an investment risk (and doubly important if one has advised against that course of action). For instance, if an attorney tells a client that the business does not need all of the life insurance the agent is suggesting, the agent should attempt to take down as accurately as possible the exact words of the attorney. The attorney should do the same.

Contemporaneous and near verbatim notes should also be taken if the client asks that the advisor not perform a service (or anything) he would normally do or if the client asks to attempt a service the advisor ordinarily would not do. For instance, if the client asks a trust officer not to review a will and trust that the bank will be handling, the trust officer should memorialize the request (and probably treat the request with suspicion). One attorney dictates, in front of the client, what he hears the client is saying, and asks the client to confirm it. Detailed notes are particularly important if the client seems uncooperative or unwilling to provide the information or documents (or access to personally interview a family member) that are necessary to do the job properly.

The Engagement Letter

The engagement letter is the first and primary step in insulating oneself from a successful malpractice suit. An engagement letter should be obtained in every client relationship at the first possible time. The letter spells out the extent and limits of the services to be performed.[27] The following are critical elements of such a letter:

- Scope of services and description of work product;
- Period of time covered;
- Responsibilities undertaken;
- Responsibilities the client is expected to assume;
- Fee arrangements—amount, terms, and frequency of billing;
- Arrangements for update and extension of service;
- List of parties represented – and exclusion of those not represented;
- Intended use and potential distribution (or restriction) of the advisor's work product;[28] and
- Client's acceptance signature and date.

Fees

Fees should not be set at levels that will require cutting corners or operating at a loss for a particular engagement. The fee must be large enough to justify internally the time that should be invested in a case — or the case should be turned down. Fees should include the costs that will be incurred to meet high ethical standards and avoid malpractice by implementation of systematic quality control and other appropriate courses of action. The fee charged should properly underwrite the risk that the estate planner is taking by accepting the engagement. For example, clients who are in a big hurry to get something done probably should be charged more for that service, since the estate planner will have to work faster than usual, which increases the likelihood of error.

A fee dispute that results in litigation with a client may trigger a malpractice case as a result. The solution is to secure a written agreement as to fees and billing procedures at the onset of the relationship with the client. One should think carefully about the wisdom of suing the client and the likelihood and expense of a malpractice lawsuit by the client. For fee disputes, consider alternative dispute resolution models like arbitration or mediation. For attorneys, if they sue a client for a fee, their malpractice policy may not cover a malpractice claim that the client brings in response to the suit for the fee. It is wise to communicate the basis or rate of fee or other method of compensation to a new client in writing before or as soon as possible after the relationship begins. The client should be billed periodically and provided detailed information of the services rendered and the time invested. Where estate planners often encounter problems on fees is where they surprise the client with a large bill, perhaps even larger than estimated. In the area of fees, there should be no surprises.

Data Forms

Many times the error or omission of the estate planner is due to an incomplete or incorrect understanding of the facts. The advisor should obtain comprehensive and accurate data by developing a data gathering system. Some planners feel they can gather data without forms or checklists but inevitably forget to ask questions such as, "Are both you and your spouse U.S. citizens?" or "Have you named yourself the custodian of a Uniform Transfers to Minors Account for gifts you made to your children?" One must be sure to confirm with the client the facts gathered – before acting upon them.

The advisor should verify property ownership and dispositive arrangements from the documents themselves. It is astounding how often otherwise competent attorneys draft wills and trusts that do not match the way property is owned. The forms should match the facts. It is necessary to check wills, divorce agreements, and retirement and employee benefit documents rather than rely on the client's memory. Simply put, one should never rely upon a client's memory of the facts. Current life insurance policy information should be confirmed by writing to the insurer.

Representation of Products

When the planner is recommending investments or insurance and, particularly if the planner is receiving a commission based on the sale, there must be a clear writing, acknowledged by the client signing, to the effect of avoiding any basis for unreasonable reliance.

With the sale of mutual funds, the warning language in the typical prospectus is worth adding to the writing to be signed by the client (e.g., that past performance is not recognized as a basis for future results, etc.).

With insurance products, there should be written recognition that all pages of the proposal have been read and understood. It would be very helpful to have the client sign the part that shows the guaranteed figures.

A significant potential problem is the rate of variable life insurance products where the return based on past performance is quite high. When or if the market turns down and the earnings evaporate, the client will only recall the high returns and will be looking for someone to blame for the disappointing results of increased premiums or lower cash value or face amount of coverage. Therefore, it is a good idea to advise clients to obtain in-force illustrations on their insurance policies every year to make sure that the policies are still performing as expected.

Some planners are reluctant to risk the possibility that the client may not go forward with the recommended action if the planner makes a point of the possible negative aspects of the transaction. However, the planner's long term reputation and success, as well as freedom from future claims, argue strongly for "getting it in writing" at the time of the decision of the client to go forward.

Label assumptions you make as such and mark them in a way that is unmistakable. Be sure assumptions (e.g. potential growth) are appropriate for the length of time under consideration. For instance, a net after-tax assumption much beyond 5 or 6 percent is aggressive – if the time frame spans many years. Mark aggressive assumptions as such and show a conservative and moderate assumption in addition to any assumption considered aggressive. Don't make conclusions (e.g. "You don't need more insurance!") you haven't quantified in writing.

6.8 LIMITS OF THE RELATIONSHIP

The client's instructions must be followed – correctly. This entails first truly understanding what those instructions are. Then it requires a written memorandum (preferably signed by the client). Meticulous records of all conversations should be made. If investments are or will be involved in the relationship, an investment policy should document agreed-upon investment objectives, risk parameters, return targets, volatility tolerance, and asset allocation ranges.

A written consent should be obtained for actions outside the scope of the relationship as contained in the engagement letter.

6.9 RECORDS AND SYSTEMS

The Really Right Write Stuff

The advisor should keep research documents that indicate decisions were made in a methodical and logical manner and that a deliberate investigation preceded and supported each suggestion. Documents that illustrate the tax law as it existed at the time tax decisions were made should be retained.[29] Memos to the file, prepared contemporaneously with conversations with a client and decision making, are highly useful in establishing the background and intent at the time an action was taken. Controversial decisions should be made only with the informed knowledge and written consent of the client. Any oral advice or telephone conversations should also be documented immediately. Refrain from giving advice at social events.

The advisor needs to develop and use a presentation system that will prove that regular discussions occurred covering all of the important areas of estate planning.[30] A checklist should be incorporated into that system in order to demonstrate that these issues have been discussed with the client and reflect the client's circumstances and objectives. It is also important to present these discussions in a manner in which the client will understand the issues being discussed. As professionals, sometimes we take for granted that that the terminology that is being used among the professionals is also understood by the client; this is a big mistake.

Trigger System

A retrieval system should be established to locate documents or plans that need updating for specific changes. For example, all estate planning clients should have been contacted to review wills and trusts drawn prior to September 13, 1981, because of the change to the unlimited marital deduction. Yet each year dozens of cases and rulings occur because the documents were never updated. Were the clients ever informed by their advisors of the need for a document review? Is there an automatic document review triggered no less often than every three years?

A checklist of follow-up procedures should be developed so time-sensitive responsibilities will be met by the appropriate parties and unreasonable delays in the preparation and implementation of the plan can be avoided. Set deadlines, establish priorities, and specify responsibilities. Create a "tickler file" (docketing system) and matrix to assign specific responsibilities to specific people and to assure that all deadlines, statutes of limitations, and filing and payment deadlines will be met. Set up a centralized follow-up system to personally remind the party responsible for action and review at given times or events. Incorporate into the system a series of client reminders (e.g., "It's been three years since your will was reviewed…" or "Major new tax law changes suggest we should review your estate plan as soon as possible"). Preferably, the estate planner should retain no continuing obligation to monitor the client's estate planning documents over time unless that service is expressly set forth in the scope of the engagement and set forth in the engagement letter.

6.10 QUALITY CONTROL

An advisor is responsible for the errors or omissions of his partners, associates, and employees. Quality control is therefore not a luxury. It is a business necessity.

Understand Ethical Issues

According to an article on malpractice, written by a Commissioner of the Texas Board of Legal Specialization, almost half the candidates who sat for the certification in Texas in Estate Planning and Probate Law demonstrated "a profound lack of knowledge of ethical problems that often lead to professional liability claims."[31] Knowledge of facts and laws is not enough! One should discuss with colleagues the danger when a breach of ethics is coupled with an angry or disgruntled client or family member.

Who Is The Quarterback?

In any operation larger than a one-person firm, it is essential that the activities of the entire staff are coordinated by a "quarterback" who accepts responsibility. This person must be sure that all staff members are kept informed and that there is a logical and automatic flow of necessary information, that no tasks have been overlooked, and that no efforts are duplicated. He must also be sure that information received by staff members is properly recorded and relayed to him and to the central file on each client. For instance, consider the lawsuit potential if the beneficiary of an estate dies within nine months of the original decedent and the same trust company serves as executor of both estates. If significant taxes could be saved by a timely disclaimer but two separate individuals are assigned to the two estates and they do not communicate with each other, the lost opportunity when the timely disclaimer period expires could turn into a lawsuit.

There should also be a quarterback for the estate planning team. All members of that team are negligent if they do not come to an agreement as to who is to do what and when each task is to be done. Liability occurs when essential tasks fall through the cracks.

Independent Review

An effective method of quality control is to have final products be reviewed by a well-qualified associate before it is shared with a client. If the estate planner doesn't have the luxury of backup, i.e., because he is a sole practitioner, we suggest letting draft documents get "old and cold" before putting them through a final review and ultimate submission to the client. We find that one-stage drafting systems don't catch all of the errors because the draftsman is too close to the document at that moment to see them all. By allowing some time to lapse between drafting and final review, the estate planner can review the draft with a fresh set of eyes.

Review Staff Competence, Experience, and Qualification

Estate planning, almost by definition, requires the input of many professionals. Most planners not only must cooperate with other planners outside their offices but must also rely on paralegal and associates within their offices. Few full-blown estate plans contain no issues other than federal or estate death taxes and quite often the planner seeks advice from others on his staff. Staff members must be currently competent, and they must be well trained in and conform to standardized office procedures, policies, and proper file management techniques. Appropriate supervision for all levels of staff should be built in. Continuing education should be part of any firm's ongoing business plan.

6.11 EXTERNAL COMMUNICATIONS

Almost every authority who speaks and every article that is written on malpractice states that many lawsuits could probably have been avoided by a simple solution: "Communicate, Communicate, Communicate!"[32]

Many, or even most, of the grievance complaints and malpractice actions can be headed off if the advisor will:

Make it clear and make it clear often. The estate planner should avoid technical jargon. He should not assume lay persons understand what he means by such terms as "a marital trust," a "durable power of attorney," or "applicable estate tax exemption. Use word pictures, graphs, flow charts, or diagrams to illustrate points – and give the clients copies to take home.[33]

Continually inform clients of all actions taken (or not taken); forward to clients copies of documents sent to other professionals; provide the client with periodic written reports even (or especially) if a particular report merely explains why no progress has been made since the last report; and confirm in writing all transactions, expenses, fees, income, or other events of importance.

Inform the client of any changes in the relationship or responsibilities of the parties; make sure reports are understandable; and use graphs, charts, and checklists to show the progress made.

Confirm through a series of scheduled meetings among the client and other advisors objectives, responsibilities, and timetables.

A newsletter is a good way to keep in touch with clients on a regular basis. E-mails, tailored to specific groups of clients, is an even more cost-effective communications tool.

Schedule regular reviews. Give special emphasis to contacting clients that have not been heard from in a given period of time; and document attempts to contact those who do not respond.

Keep copies of all correspondence and conversations with other members of the estate planning team working with the client.

Study the client's verbal and body language to be sure he/she is understood and encourage the client to call or write or e-mail after the meeting to ask questions if "I have not made myself understood."

Avoid casual or informal advice. Don't give advice at cocktail parties or other social events.[34] Liability can be imposed even though you have not charged a fee for your services if a client relies on information you have provided.

Call back – promptly. A careful advisor will return telephone calls promptly. If this is impossible, a secretary or an associate should follow up so the client does not feel ignored.

Avoid "heel cooling." A planner should not keep clients waiting on the phone or in his/her office. He should be sure he receives messages promptly – and accurately. He should not allow a phone call to interrupt a meeting with a client. It is a good idea to reward staff members for being extra polite. In short, give the client respect and common courtesy. Be sure, when on vacation, to arrange for adequate coverage of phones and e-mails.

6.12 AVOIDING (OR NEUTRALIZING) PROBLEMS

Conflicts with Clients

The duty of loyalty requires any estate planner to be extremely cautious about serving a client in more than one capacity.[35] For instance, the client of an attorney or CPA may want that person to serve as an executor or trustee – while at the same time desiring that person to continue to provide planning advice and other services to various family members. Should an attorney or CPA sell life insurance to their estate planning or business clients? Can the advice be disinterested and objective? Can the professional ethically charge fees or accept commissions for both services? Can those fees honestly be set at "arm's length"?

Corporate fiduciaries are particularly susceptible. For instance, could the banking side of an institution, as a lender, acquire and share non-public information about a borrower company with the trust department that, as an investor for its trust accounts, is considering making investments in the same company?[36] (Use of non-public information to make investment decisions might subject a corporate fiduciary to a violation of the SEC's Rule 10b-5.[37])

Although there is no legal prohibition against representing more than one client in a single transaction, estate planners should be particularly alert for situations in which there is an obvious or potential difference in their interests. For instance, in establishing a buy-sell agreement, a stock redemption plan may favor younger shareholders with lower percentages of ownership at the expense of older shareholders who own a larger percentage of the company's stock. Likewise, a defined benefit plan typically favors older, long service employees while profit-sharing and defined contribution pension plans usually are to the benefit of younger employees.

Another conflict of interest problem that often occurs where more than one person is represented is the disclosure of confidential information. Can an estate planner freely tell a wife what her husband has disclosed? (Does it provide so in the engagement letter clients have read and signed?) Can a planner share information from one shareholder with others? The planner needs to inform all parties that information may not be privileged or confidential as to other members of the group unless specific direction is given.

Some conflicts of interest are unavoidable but must be recognized. For instance, consider the family that requests estate planning advice as a unit but who, as individuals, have different needs and desires. What should be done in a marital situation where a husband calls and requests a QTIP trust as opposed to the classic general power of appointment marital trust or marital gift? What happens when there are children of a prior marriage and the client wants to make lifetime gifts to them? What if a client is ill or infirm in some way and is or becomes dependent on someone else for basic needs? How will the "undue influence issue" be handled? What are the planner's responsibilities and duties when a child, a charitable development officer, or another professional brings the case to him? What if that person also pays his fee?

Any possible conflicts of interest should be disclosed – in writing – to the client as quickly as possible or the planner should withdraw without disclosure if confidential information is involved. Recognition of disclosure and acceptance of its consequent risks should be acknowledged in any instrument signed by the client.

The planner should avoid or treat extremely carefully any financial involvement in a client's business or in a business venture.

Will acceptance of this client create a conflict for more desirable work with another client in the future?[38] It is important for the planner to train himself and his staff to recognize "red flags." A procedure for identifying problems and quickly dealing with them is essential.

Dealing with Problems

The planner must routinely review and deal with problems promptly. If a problem occurs, it is essential to call or write or e-mail the client immediately and explain the problem and the potential consequences and alternatives. If a client is angry or dissatisfied, take immediate action – talk to the client and resolve the problem. Do not assume the problem will go away or that the client will forget it.

A good idea is to create a "Problem Team" in the firm that meets immediately every time the potential for a dissatisfied client is recognized. That team should not only review the file in the case in point but also any other procedures, activities, omissions, or oversights that may trigger future problems that could develop into litigation. Use that team to develop procedures and checklists that will minimize or eliminate such problems.

The quicker an attempt is made to resolve the problem to the client's satisfaction, the less likely there will be litigation. Providing a large apology might avoid writing a small check. Writing a small check might avoid defending a large lawsuit. One litigation attorney put it this way: "The good will that can be generated by such an act and accompanying attitudes might be much cheaper and better in the long run than paying expensive attorneys for years of litigation with an uncertain outcome."[39] Sometimes, assigning a new person to speak to the client will serve to quell the objection.

6.13 ABOUT YOUR MALPRACTICE INSURANCE

Sufficient levels of coverage. The first step in evaluating your current insurance is to see if you have enough insurance to cover any likely risk. But this is only a first step. Some states require that attorneys maintain certain minimum levels of coverage.

"Claims made" policies. Most malpractice coverage is sold on a "claims made" basis. This means the policy only covers claims that are first asserted and reported to the insurer within the policy year.

"Prior acts" coverage. The cause of action alleging estate planning malpractice typically does not occur until years after the estate planning documents are signed. If the policy has a "prior acts" coverage, it covers a claim asserted during a policy year in which the negligence giving rise to the claim occurred in some prior year.[40] If a policy lacks or excludes prior acts or limits prior acts coverage, it is likely that there will be a "coverage gap." There will be no coverage under the policy in effect when the alleged negligence occurred because the claim was not made in that policy year. The current policy will not cover the alleged negligence because negligence alleged to have occurred before the present policy year is excluded or omitted from the coverage.

The tail. A tail is an extended reporting option somewhat related to prior acts coverage. If one purchases a tail, he is permitted (usually at the end of each policy year or earlier if the policy is canceled during the term) to convert "claims made" coverage to "occurrence" coverage for any negligence allegedly committed – but not yet reported – up to the end of that policy year. The extended reporting of claims option available through a tail is expensive. The premium is a multiple of the regular annual premium. Tails should be considered by retiring planners who will no longer keep their full malpractice coverage in force or by attorneys who are forced to switch malpractice insurance carriers because of a cancellation or a refusal of a carrier to renew coverage (typically due to claims made) if the new carrier refuses to provide prior acts coverage. Tails are "cut off" after some period of time unless the tail is unlimited. Under an unlimited tail, the insurer remains liable for negligence occurring before the policy period expires regardless of when the claim is asserted.

The deductible. Most estate planners opt for a higher deductible in order to reduce the premium outlay. But one should check to see if the legal costs he would incur in a malpractice suit apply against his share of the deductible. Does the deductible apply per claim or per policy year? Where there is more than one claim in a given policy year, a per claim deductible becomes a hidden cost: a second deductible must be satisfied in the event of a second claim within a year. A per year deductible means the deductible amount need be paid only once in a given year regardless of the number of claims. Because when it rains, it pours, a per claim provision might prove quite costly.

Settlement. Some policies give the insurer the right to limit its exposure through a provision entitled, "Settlement." This means the insurer can force a settlement with the plaintiff (regardless of the insured's wishes) because of the cost. Some settlement provisions state that if one does not wish to settle under specified terms, the insurer will limit its payment to the amount specified in a settlement agreement at which point all other exposure (including defense cost) becomes the insured's obligation. Why might an insured not want to settle – even though economically it might make sense? The psychological cost of admitting wrongdoing or malpractice – coupled with the loss in reputation – are strong reasons why he may want to maintain the right to say "NO" to a settlement. One should be sure that right does not expose him to a loss of coverage above the limits in the proposed settlement.

Duty to defend vs. duty to indemnify. A "duty to defend" policy requires the insurer to appoint defense counsel and pay that attorney's fees as billed. An indemnification policy allows the insured to select counsel but he must fund his defense unless he can reach an interim fee agreement.[41] The insured will not be reimbursed for defense costs until the case is concluded. Obviously, interim funding can be a problem.

Definition of damages. The way covered damages is defined is crucial. One may be exposed to fines, penalties, punitive, or even treble, damages. Check with the insurance agent to clarify how broadly or narrowly the policy construes the term "damages."

Innocent partner coverage. Does the policy provide coverage for the defalcations of another member of the firm? One is liable for his partner's embezzlement even if he has not benefited by it. The insurer will deny a claim based on your partner's fraud and/or criminal activity unless there is "innocent partner" coverage.

Other key provisions. A malpractice policy ideally will provide coverage for the defense costs if it is claimed the insured is guilty of intentional conduct (even though the policy does not indemnify the costs of the intentional conduct). Does the policy cover libel or slander or defense of RICO claims?

Insurer's stability. It is important to check the financial stability of the insurer and to be sure the insurer has a solid reputation for integrity and responsiveness. It is worth finding out if the insurer itself has been involved in litigation with its own insureds. The lowest premium will not compensate you for the aggravation and other costs of suing the carrier to get it to defend properly a malpractice case.

Handling a claim. A detailed discussion of malpractice claims procedures is beyond the scope of this chapter. However, the following steps will help in the defense of a malpractice suit:

1. Notify the insurer immediately no matter how small the suit is.

2. Once the insured has been notified formally that he is being sued, say as little as necessary to the suing client.

3. Secure all work product immediately.

4. Inform the entire staff of the problem and the action game plan.

5. Do whatever is necessary to assist in the defense of the case.

6.14 THE TOTAL COST

The frequency of malpractice actions can be expected to increase. No profession in the estate planning team will escape unscathed.[42]

Direct costs. Malpractice premiums are in the highest classification – along with corporate securities work – for a very good reason. The dollars at risk are big.

Loss of reputation. The cost of a malpractice suit cannot be measured merely in terms of the court judgment or out-of-court settlement or the cost of attorneys. The cost to a professional's reputation (win or lose) may be staggering. For instance, it would be difficult to attract new partners or new associates if one has been successfully sued for malpractice. A suit, win or lose (just or unjust), is always damaging.

Loss of standing with peers. Estate planning is a process based partially on knowledge and largely on trust. A malpractice suit calls into question competence that in turn destroys confidence, not only of current and potentially future clients but also the confidence of other members of the planning team with whom one must deal. It may also shake the confidence of other planners in your office.

The psychological trauma. An estate planner who becomes a defendant in a lawsuit must deal with the incredible pressure and emotional trauma of being sued.[43] Often, the planner (and perhaps office associates, partners, and friends) will see the action taken by the client as an attack on his professional ability, integrity, or judgment. This cannot help the practitioner's morale and will probably result in adverse fallout on other projects. This psychological strain is compounded by time; the legal process is typically long and drawn out over a period of years even if the claim is unfounded and ultimately unsuccessful.

Hidden economic costs. Colleagues from whom the practitioner received referrals and the general public may hear about the lawsuit. This will cause almost certain financial damage. The planner is required to participate in his own defense whether or not he is adequately insured. This, in turn, translates into dozens or sometimes hundreds of unbillable hours gathering facts and records and recreating the facts, giving depositions, briefing defense attorneys, and testifying at trial.

Cut and run? If it appears a matter cannot be resolved by the procedures discussed above, consider "discharging the client." Obviously, this is a last resort but it should not be overlooked in a "heads they win – tails we lose situation."

6.15 ONE LAST NOTE

Howard Zaritsky, principal author of *Tax Planning with Life Insurance*,[44] stated that "You constantly feel like you have to look over your shoulder about disgruntled clients. Yet many of the things professionals are sued for were regular or normal actions. What is wrong is the way many people practice." Some of Howard's "Eight Basic Rules of Practical Practice" may minimize risk.

Rule 1: Being right isn't enough. Most defendants had not done anything wrong. Good practice isn't enough. Even though you did nothing wrong, you can lose.

Rule 2: People don't sue their friends; they let someone else do it. But if the clients like you, they will put up with more if you own up to your mistake and address it. So return phone calls the same day. Treat your clients with respect. For instance, be on time for meetings and be prepared.

Rule 3: Restate your client's intent – in front of the client. Keep things understandable and as simple as possible. Clients who "understand" are clients less likely to sue. Get critical or difficult issues up front. The more complex things are, the easier it is for a litigator to identify an ambiguity.

Rule 4: Truth is not (necessarily) a defense. "It is what the client said they wanted me to do." Client memories are not to be relied upon. They change fast.

Rule 5: An ounce of notes is worth a pound of persuasion. The more notes you take, the better. Keep notes of *everything* but especially anything that is unusual. (If *you* do anything out of the ordinary put it in a memo. Use bold face and underline unusual items.) Send your client(s) a letter confirming your understanding. If you use numbers, be sure they are correct. Keep files "forever."

Rule 6: If a client does anything against their pecuniary interest, document it. Beneficiaries won't believe anything was not done to save tax. They (and the courts) assume taxes would always be minimized. "Dad would spend money on anything really important and if you explained it correctly he would have paid for it."

Rule 7: No Surprises. To the extent feasible and with the consent of your client, explain things to and involve beneficiaries in the estate planning process. Ask beneficiaries for their suggestions and give them a chance to have input.

Rule 8: Use Letters. For instance, use a letter of introduction about your firm. Explain the estate planning process. Provide your client with some concept of how you are paid and if you provide services by the hour, define "hourly" and whether hourly is relevant. Give advance information about conflicts of interests. Provide a letter explaining your suggested plan in simple terms. Make it clear what you – and other professionals intend to do and each person's responsibility and time line. If you have a client who is "problematic," you may want to consider a "Good bye" (disengagement) letter to the effect of: Thanks for letting us representing you. Our representation on this matter is concluded.

6.16 CONCLUSION

Creating and maintaining a successful estate planning practice requires a methodical systematic approach to risk management. Planners are vulnerable to litigation no matter how careful they are. But the risk of a claim and the potential for a successful claim can be substantially reduced through continuing a vigorous and systematized policy of internal and external positive communication, common sense courtesy, quality control, and a strong emphasis on high quality continuing education of every member of the firm.

A planner should check that he has:

- Established and improved client relationships.
- Controlled the management of client relationships.
- Improved office practices.
- Identified problem areas.
- Corrected problems before they occur.

Looking at everything in this discussion positively, the "action suggestions" described here can also be thought of not only as defensive but as the blueprint for a vigorous office quality-control organizing and client market-building campaign.

CHAPTER ENDNOTES

1. Attorney Jack Olendar of Washington, D.C. quoted in "Avoiding Malpractice Suits: Some Sound Advice," *Trusts and Estates*, April 1990, p. 18. Another good rule of thumb mentioned in this same well-written article is that "we have a true and grievous malpractice claim" where the facts and results would "surprise and dismay the average trust and estate lawyer."

2. Legal malpractice consists of three elements: (a) a duty, (b) a breach of duty, and (c) resulting damages.

3. See "Avoiding Malpractice Suits: Some Sound Advice," *Trusts and Estates*, April 1990, p. 12.

4. This is called the "best judgment" or "good faith" defense.

5. "Corporate Fiduciaries Face Special Liability Problems," *Trusts and Estates*, December 1988, p. 29.

6. *Killey Trust*, 457 Pa. 474, 326 A.2d 372 (Pa. 1974). Large corporate planners such as banks and trust companies will likely be held to a higher level of competence than others because of their access to information and expertise.

   On the other hand, the sophistication, education, and expertise of the client is not a defense. See *Blankenheim v. E.F. Hutton and Co. Inc.*, 266 Cal. Rptr. 593, 217 Cal. App. 3d 1463 (Ct. App. 1990), which held that the relationship between a stockbroker and his customer is fiduciary in nature, imposing on the former the duty to act in the highest good faith toward his customer. The court held that the plaintiff's concession that they were experts in the accounting and taxation area and any experience the plaintiff may have acquired following his investment was irrelevant to reliance on the broker's representations at the time of the sale.

7. Consider, for example, that the estate planner must consider the provisions of federal (and perhaps state) securities laws if the client holds more than 10 percent of a covered class of equity securities. Did you know that a malpractice claim might be converted into an unfair trade practice claim in order to gain the advantage of a longer statute of limitations? In one case the attorney drafted a trust that failed to qualify for the marital deduction. This action was barred by a three-year statute of limitations. So the plaintiff also sued for a violation of the state's Unfair Trade Practice Act which had a much longer statute of limitations and allowed a suit by "any person who purchases or leases goods, services, or property." The estate successfully alleged that the draftsman had engaged in an unfair and deceptive act and practice by holding himself out as an attorney reasonably skilled in the preparation and drafting of last wills and testaments and in his ability to comply with the decedent's wishes and to minimize the tax obligations of her estate.

8. "Protecting the Corporate Fiduciary's Tender Backside," *Trusts and Estates*, February 1988, p. 63.

9. Adjectives which might characterize "institutional arrogance" include unreasonable, unknowledgeable, intransigent, implacable, belligerent, and rude.

10. See "Court Decisions Reinforce the Idea that an Insurance Agent Who Holds Himself Out to Have Great Expertise will be Bound to the Exercise of It," *Trusts and Estates*, October 1988, p. 55.

11. See *Bell v. Manning*, 613 S.W.2d 335 (Tex. Civ. App. 1981) and *Simon v. Zipperstein*, 32 Ohio St. 3d 74, 512 N.E.2d 636 (1987).

12. *Lucas v. Hamm*, 56 Cal. 2d 583, 15 Cal. Rptr. 821, 364 P.2d 685 (Cal. 1961).

13. The California Supreme Court used this test in *Biakanja v. Irving*, 320 P.2d 16 (Cal. 1958). Although there is a trend toward relaxing the requirement of privity, New York, Texas and Ohio are staunch supporters of the rule. See *Victor v. Goldman*, 74 Misc. 2d 685, 344 N.Y.S.2d 672 (Sup. Ct. 1973), *Dickey v. Jansen*, 731 S.W.2d 581 (Tx. Ct. App. 1987) and *Simon v. Zipperstein*, 32 Ohio St. 3d 74, 512 N.E.2d 636 (1987).

14. Pennsylvania Supreme Court in *Guy v. Liederbach*, 501 Pa. 47, 459 A.2d 744 (1983).

15. See *Bogley v. Middletown Tavern, Inc.*, 421 A.2d 444 (1984). Of course, the knee jerk defense is, "The insurance was purchased in an arm's length transaction involving no confidential or fiduciary relationship between the insured and the agent." This tact might work if the agent never professed to be anything other than a salesperson. See *Lazovick v. Sun Life Ins. Co. of America*, 586 F. Supp. 918 (E.D. Pa. 1984).

16. See *Anderson v. Knox*, 297 F.2d 702 (9th Cir. 1961), cert. den., 370 U.S. 915 (1962); *Gediman v. Anheuser Busch, Inc.*, 299 F.2d 537 (2d Cir. 1962).

17. See *Wright Body Works v. Columbus Interstate Insurance*, 233 Ga. 268, 210 S.E. 2d 801 (1974).

18. *State Farm Life v. Fort Wayne National Bank*, 474 N.E. 2d 524 (Ind. 1985).

19. *Morales v. Field*, DeGoff, Huppert & MacGown, 160 Cal. Rptr. 239, 99 Cal. App. 3d 307 (1979).

20. See "Does This Prospect Mean Trouble?" *Practical Financial Planning*, October/November 1988, p. 23.

21. See "Reducing the Risk of Estate Planning Malpractice," BNA, *Tax Management Estates, Gifts, and Trusts Journal*, March/April 1984, p. 36.

22. See "How Not to be a Trustee," *Financial Planning*, May 1990, p. 69.

23. *Horne v. Peckham*, 158 Cal. Rptr. 714, 97 Cal. App. 3d 404 (1979).

24. Where there is reasonable doubt among well informed practitioners, there should be no liability. But this assumes a diligent quest for answers was made. Failure to research an issue or fully understand the facts will result in a denial of the "unsettled law" defense. See *Martin v. Burns*, 102 Ariz. 341, 429 P.2d 660 (1967).

25. See "Steps to Protect the Fiduciary from Liability for Investment Decisions," *Estate Planning*, July/August, 1989, p. 228.

26. As one attorney, Charles K. Plotnick of Plotnick and Ellis, was interviewing a couple, he would pause from time to time to "capsulize" their thoughts into a dictaphone. Before he did, he would remind them each time, "Be sure to stop me if this isn't exactly what you want or if I've misunderstood what you've just said."

27. For an excellent discussion of legal estate planning engagement letters, with principles that can cross disciplines, see *Engagement Letters: A Guide for Practitioners* (3rd ed. 2017), which is available at www.actec.org.

28. In "Taming the Liability Monster," *L&H Perspective*, v. 15, No. 1/1989, p. 38, the author states that "A nightmare for the professional is reliance by unknown third parties on their work product." Where might this nightmare be more real than in estate planning where a great deal of it is done specifically for others? (Of course, it is the planner's responsibility to know who those third party beneficiaries are and what circumstances and needs and desires they may have).

29. You may have to prove that, at the time you were making the decision, the available information was much different than it is at the time litigation occurs. See "How to Manage a Growing Tax Practice," *The Practical Accountant*, May 1990, p. 27.

30. See "Avoiding and Handling Malpractice Claims against Estate Planners," *Estate Planning*, September/October 1989, p. 267.

31. See "Avoiding Malpractice Suits: Some Sound Advice," *Trusts and Estates*, April 1990, p. 12.

32. See "Coping with Administrative Problems: There's More to Life and Death than Taxes," 21 *Univ. of Miami Institute on Estate Planning*, Chapter 17 (1987).

33. Some attorneys use commercially written brochures to make their points or to give clients something to take home that will help them understand more complex concepts.

34. See *Newton Estate*, TC Memo 1990-208, for an example of the damage a well-intended but offhand remark can do. The executor's reliance on the statement of an attorney as to the filing deadline did not constitute reasonable cause for the filing delay where the attorney admittedly had not been retained to render advice on federal estate tax matters, was not paid any fee for the advice, did not normally practice in that area of the law, and had advised the executor to verify any information with a tax practitioner. The "offhand remark" may not result in a malpractice case for this attorney – but it certainly would not result in a love affair with the client either.

35. Consider an index which includes data on clients and other parties to transactions with which the firm is involved. Include a procedure through which the system automatically updates the files to add the names of new family members, business associates, or others related to the client.

36. "Corporate Fiduciaries Face Special Liability Problems," *Trusts and Estates*, December 1988, p. 29.

37. The classic solution is a corporate policy that restricts or limits the information flow between the banking and the trust departments.

38. Obtain a "Waiver of Conflict" letter with respect to one-time consulting arrangements. Obtain advance written consent to future simultaneous adverse representation on any matter not substantially related to the matter undertaken for a new client.

39. "Protecting the Corporate Fiduciary's Tender Backside," *Trusts and Estates*, February 1988, p. 72.

40. See "About Your Malpractice," *Lawyer's Digest*, May 1988, p. 11.

41. "How the Accountant/Financial Planner can Reduce Exposure to Liability Claims," *The Practical Accountant*, February 1990, p. 15.

42. See "Taming the Liability Monster," *L&H Perspective*, Vol. 15/No. 1, 1989, p. 37.

43. See "Strategies to Avoid Malpractice," *Practical Financial Planning*, April/May 1989, p. 29.

44. Thomson Reuters (1995).

OWNERSHIP AND TRANSFER OF PROPERTY

CHAPTER 7

7.1 INTRODUCTION

In this chapter, we will discuss the various ways that property can be held and transferred to someone else. We will also point out how these concepts intersect with a "modern family." In order to properly plan an estate, it is necessary to know the ways in which property is owned and how property is transferred and when it is considered transferred. The way in which property can be transferred can be dependent on the form of ownership. In addition, property transfers can involve gifts, contracts such as sales or exchanges, involuntary conversion, exercise of powers of appointment, wills, intestate succession, and trusts. There may even be certain limitations on how a person can transfer property and whether an attempted transfer will be upheld. Forms of ownership and transfer of property are discussed broadly below. Gifts, powers of appointment, wills, and trusts are discussed in even greater detail in succeeding chapters.

7.2 OWNERSHIP OF PROPERTY

There are various ways in which property can be owned, as discussed in detail in the sections below. In general, property is owned:

1. outright;

2. as a legal owner only (trustee) or as an equitable owner (beneficiary) where title is in trust;

3. as a life tenant or remainderman;

4. as tenants in common;

5. as joint tenants with rights of survivorship;

6. as tenants by the entirety; or

7. as community property (most community property states allow community property to be owned with right of survivorship, but the default does not usually include a right of survivorship).

Outright Ownership

Outright ownership is often as simple as: Paul owns an automobile or an interest in a closely held entity, or Evan owns a baseball glove. Absent any transfer restrictions, Paul and Evan generally are free to do whatever they want with the property they own outright. Of course, if Paul borrowed money to purchase the interest in the entity and pledged that interest as collateral for the loan, the lender generally has the right to recovery of any outstanding loan upon a transfer of the interest. In this situation, although Paul may generally be free to enjoy the interest as he pleases, Paul can really transfer only the value of the interest in excess of the loan.

Trust

In most trusts, the beneficiary does not have any direct ownership of the assets of the trust, which generally are titled in the name of the trustee. The trustee is the legal owner but the beneficiaries are owners in equity. We include the trust here as a way that property can be held because people do own their respective trust interests, and trust beneficiaries can sell, donate or exchange them, subject to the terms of the trust instrument. For example, unless a trust instrument has a full-blown spendthrift clause that would prohibit or otherwise restrict transfer or alienation of the beneficiary's trust interest, the beneficiary is permitted to transfer interest in the trust to someone else or to encumber that interest as collateral for a loan. Spendthrift provisions can often be modified or eliminated through decanting or other form of trust amendment which may allow the sale of a trust interest.

Life Estate / Remainder

Sometimes outright ownership can be split into a life estate and a remainder interest. In this type of arrangement, ownership is divided on a temporal or "time line" basis. One person owns the property for a period of time (the life estate) and the second person owns the property after the first time period ends (the "remainder" interest). Although a term of years or for someone else's life is theoretically possible, such types of deeds or ownership are very rare. Most life estates are for the tenant's lifetime. A person with a life estate generally is free to use the property or enjoy the income from the property for life. The person with the remainder interest receives the property when the person with the life estate dies. For example, Mike owns a house. When Mike dies, his will provides that his sister, Sally, can live in the house for her lifetime, and upon her death, the house will pass to Mike's nephew, Bob. In this example, Sally has a life estate and Bob has a remainder interest after Mike dies.

When considering whether to establish this type of arrangement, it is also important to consider who pays the expenses of maintaining the house or what other conditions the client would like to establish for the arrangement. In the example, Sally would have to pay the costs of living there, which typically would include property taxes and regular maintenance. However, if the client wants to allocate a portion of the responsibilities to others, an alternative approach would be to keep the house in trust. By keeping the property in trust (as opposed to creating a life estate) the terms of the life estate can be set forth in greater detail. For example, the trust can provide that Sally's life estate terminates at such time as she ceases to use the house as her principal residence. In the context of blended family couples where there are children of prior unions, we rarely, if ever, recommend that property be divided temporally between a step-parent and the other partner's children because of the often-internecine squabbles that break out over responsibilities for maintenance (that usually fall on the life tenant) versus capital repairs (that usually fall on the remainder tenant).

Tenancy in Common

A tenancy in common probably is the preferred form of co-ownership of property. Tenants in common own an undivided right to possess property. Each tenant is generally free to transfer his interest in the property as he wishes as each is a co-owner. For this reason, we strongly believe that tenancy in common arrangements are best for blended family couples. The trustees of two different revocable living trusts, for example, can each own 50% tenancy in common interests (or any other percentage).

Joint Tenancy with Right of Survivorship

Another form of co-ownership of property is a joint tenancy with right of survivorship. Joint tenants also have an undivided right to the enjoyment of property. However, when a joint tenant dies, that person's interest in the property automatically passes outside of the probate estate to the remaining joint tenant or joint tenants. While a joint tenant is alive, a joint tenant unilaterally can sever (or divide) the joint tenancy without the consent or even knowledge of the other joint tenants or transfer his interest to another.

There is an interesting business or ethical issue with recommending severance of a joint tenancy when representing a couple jointly, especially where one partner is substantially younger than the other partner, because, from an actuarial standpoint, the younger partner stands to become the sole owner by outliving the older partner. Therefore, recommending *severance* of a joint tenancy could be viewed as being contrary to the interests of the younger partner, who also is a client. General rule: we recommend severance when a blended family couple holds property this way absent express intent to hold it as joint tenants with rights of survivorship because you really never know who will survive whom. We have been surprised many times in this regard.

There also is an interesting ethical issue when the older partner comes to you privately and asks you to assist him or her in the severance of the joint tenancy. Can you do that without telling the other partner, who also is your client? The answer will be dependent upon whether you dealt with this issue in your engagement letter. On the one hand, severance is that partner's right as he or she can do it without the other partner's knowledge or consent. However, on the other hand, you have been asked to participate in an activity that could be construed as not being in your other client-partner's best interests. When faced with this sort of scenario, we usually recommend not participating but encouraging that partner to tell the other partner what he or she intends to do. If the partner declines to do that, a red flag should go up as it signals a potential communication problem between the partners and a potential conflict of interest for the practitioner.

As noted above, most of the community property states now allow for survivorship rights to be placed upon community property. However, we reiterate that survivorship ownership may not be appropriate for blended family couples.

Example. Dad leaves a vacation home to his three children, Tom, Ann, and Rita, as joint tenants with right of survivorship. Ann dies first. The vacation home is then owned by Tom and Rita as joint tenants. Tom dies next. Rita succeeds to outright ownership of the vacation home.

Tenancy by the Entirety

Some states permit a special type of joint tenancy with right of survivorship between spouses called a tenancy by the entirety. Like joint tenancy with right of survivorship, when one spouse dies, the jointly owned property passes to the surviving spouse. However, while both spouses are alive and married to each other, unlike joint tenancy, one spouse cannot terminate a tenancy by the entirety without the consent of the other spouse. The advantage of this type of ownership is that the creditors of only one spouse cannot attach the interest in the property. This is in contrast to joint tenancy with right of survivorship where a creditor of one owner *can* attach the debtor's interest in the property. In some states, placing tenancy by the entireties property into a joint revocable living trust might destroy this valuable asset protection benefit, so consult local counsel before placing such property into trust.

Community Property

Nine states as well as Puerto Rico have a form of ownership between spouses called community property.[1] Five other states[2] offer opt-in community property arrangements primarily in trust (see the Chapter 66 on Community Property Trusts). In a community property state, the couple's earnings are community property and, therefore, each spouse owns an undivided one-half interest in property acquired with such earnings while the spouses are married.[3] Each spouse is generally free to transfer his one-half interest in the property at death as he wishes. However, while both spouses are alive and married to each other, one spouse cannot dispose of the community property without the consent of the other spouse.

Additionally, property acquired by a couple prior to moving to a community property state generally would remain noncommunity property, subject to state "quasi-community property" laws discussed below. Community property can be important even if a couple does not currently live in a community property state. Community property generally remains community property even when the spouses move to a noncommunity property state. Certain property is noncommunity property even if a couple live in a community property state:

- Property that a spouse acquired prior to marriage remains the separate property of that spouse.

- Property acquired individually by one spouse by gift or inheritance during marriage is also the separate property of that spouse.

- Property acquired by a couple prior to moving to a community property state would generally remain noncommunity property.

Spouses are generally free to make agreements regarding community property. For example, the spouses can agree that what would otherwise be community property is not community property. Generally, such agreements must be in writing. Most states have a rebuttable presumption that property acquired during the marriage is community property.[4] One big advantage of community property over tenancy in common as well as joint tenancy is that both halves of the community property generally get a new basis on the death of a spouse.[5]

A disadvantage to community property, however, is that creditors can often reach community property to satisfy debts incurred by either spouse during marriage. In some states such as Texas, the debt must be incurred for the benefit of the community in order to permit the creditor to reach community property.

Some noncommunity property states recognize community property laws of another state on the death of a spouse.[6] In fact, in California, there is a concept of "quasi-community property" whereby "all real or personal property, wherever situated, acquired before or after the operative date of this code in any of the following ways: (a) by either spouse while domiciled elsewhere which would have been community property if the spouse who acquired the property had been domiciled in this state at the time of its acquisition; and (b)In exchange for real or personal property, wherever situated, which would have been community property if the spouse who acquired the property so exchanged had been domiciled in this state at the time of its acquisition."[7] "Quasi" community property may have some of the non-tax characteristics of community property, but may not receive the "double" basis adjustment at first death described in the paragraph above.

The spouses can agree to transmute into community property what would otherwise have been one spouse's separate property. As noted above, several of the community property states allow for community property to be held with a right of survivorship feature, which may negatively impact the very purpose of community property. However, it may have a positive impact for tenancy in common or fractional interest shares in closely held entities that might otherwise receive more "discount" when valued as a 50 percent interest.

We repeat our opinion that blended family couples should rarely if ever hold property in survivorship solution because to do so often will defeat the dispositive intentions of the first spouse to die.

One aspect of community property that confuses many practitioners in other states is that whose name or names are on the title may be irrelevant. Title may be in one spouse's name only and still be community property. This is important to remember when funding irrevocable trusts, especially spousal lifetime access trusts, and it is often necessary for spouses to transmute some property into separate property in order to fund such trusts.

Totten Trust, POD, TOD

Totten trusts, Payable On Death (POD) accounts, and Transferrable On Death (TOD) accounts are available in most states. These all provide for automatic transfers of certain types of property at death to a named beneficiary, while avoiding probate.

For a *totten trust*, which is named after an old case,[8] a person can deposit money into a bank account in his own name as trustee for another person. Generally, such a transfer is revocable until such person provides otherwise (e.g., gives passbook to donee) or dies. If the person dies without having revoked the totten trust provision, the donee receives the bank account.

A *Payable on Death* (POD) account is very similar. A person deposits money into a bank account in his own name and designates that the account is payable on death to a named person. The transfer to the account is generally revocable. If the person dies without having revoked the POD provision, the donee receives the bank account.

A *Transferrable on Death* (TOD) account is similar to a POD account, except that TOD provisions are used with stocks, mutual funds, and other accounts holding securities. There is a Uniform TOD Security Registration Act passed in the vast majority of states that has sample language and abbreviations that can be used.[9]

We believe that these sorts of arrangements generally are inappropriate for blended family couples because the account holder often has intended beneficiaries other than a surviving partner. Joint tenancy and TOD/POD accounts penalize the estate of the first joint tenant/account holder by taking away the testamentary right.

7.3 LIFETIME TRANSFERS OF PROPERTY

Gift. During lifetime, a person can generally transfer interests the person owns by gift, either outright or in trust. See Chapter 8 regarding gifts.

Sale, assignment or exchange. The next way that property can be transferred during lifetime is by sale, assignment or exchange. A sale can be voluntary or involuntary, such as if someone has exercised an option to buy your property for X dollars or otherwise has a "call" right on the property. Most incorporeal goods and rights, e.g., copyrights and stock in a company, are transferred pursuant to an assignment. Virtually all property can be exchanged for other property, including other property together with cash to make up the difference in value between the exchanged properties.

Involuntary transfer. Sometimes property is confiscated via seizure or foreclosure. Other times, property must be transferred because someone else has a right, whether actual or by exercise, to acquire the property from the owner.

Exercise of power of appointment. Powers of appointment, if authorized in the instrument that granted the power, can be exercised during lifetime (although most are only exercisable at death). There are two types of powers of appointment, the general power of appointment, where the power of appointment can be exercised in favor of one's self, creditors or estate, and the limited, nongeneral or special power of appointment, which is every other type of power of appointment. We go into more detail on powers of appointment in Chapter 12. However, in brief, a power of appointment is a right to redirect property that is either being enjoyed by or destined for someone to someone else, including the power holder. In some ways, think of powers of appointment as the "magic carpet" of estate planning, because the power holder has the right to "yank" the property "carpet" out from under one or more persons and "magically" put it under others.

In blended family couples, we recommend extreme caution when granting a partner a broad power of appointment that could redirect property from the granting partner's children to others, including the receiving partner's children or other family. On the other hand, a carefully designed special power of appointment in favor of a partner that is limited to changing the sharing percentages between the granting partner's children can "encourage" the children to be cordial to their step-parent. Powers of appointment are not "all or nothing" and can be very flexible.

7.4 TRANSFERS AT DEATH

At death, property generally passes by contract, will, trust, survivorship or intestate succession.

Intestate Succession

Property passes by intestate succession when a person dies without a valid will, where parts of a will are invalid or where the will does not cover the entire estate. Each state has its own rules as to how property passes by intestate succession. For states that have adopted the Uniform Probate Code in whole or in part, the rules for intestate succession are as follows:

The intestate share of a decedent's surviving spouse is:

(1) the entire intestate estate if:

(A) no descendant or parent of the decedent survives the decedent; or (B) all of the decedent's surviving descendants are also descendants of the surviving spouse and there is no other descendant of the surviving spouse who survives the decedent;

(2) the first [$300,000], plus three-fourths of any balance of the intestate estate, if no descendant of the decedent survives the decedent, but a parent of the decedent survives the decedent;

(3) the first [$225,000], plus one-half of any balance of the intestate estate, if all of the decedent's surviving descendants are also descendants of the surviving spouse and the surviving spouse has one or more surviving descendants who are not descendants of the decedent;

(4) the first [$150,000], plus one-half of any balance of the intestate estate, if one or more of the decedent's surviving descendants are not descendants of the surviving spouse.[10]

The balance of the intestate estate under the Uniform Probate Code generally passes to relatives in a pecking order of relationship to the decedent.[11] The laws of intestacy can be particularly cruel to persons who are not legally related by blood, adoption or marriage, thereby underscoring the critical importance of unmarried partners having a full-blown estate plan. Intestacy also is particularly cruel to persons who are close to the decedent but not related by blood, adoption or marriage. This is the big risk that unmarried partners take by not having a will or full-blown estate plan that alters the law of intestacy. We cover wills in more detail in Chapter 10.

Contract. Examples of property passing by contract generally include life insurance, annuity proceeds, and retirement benefits. At the death of the insured or participant, life insurance, annuity proceeds and retirement benefits pass to the person who has been named beneficiary on the beneficiary designation form (regardless of provisions to the contrary in the person's will). If a beneficiary is not named, the property will generally pass to the owner's estate and be disposed of in the owner's will or by intestate succession. However, this is not always the case. In some retirement plans, if no beneficiary form is completed, the plan document may identify the beneficiary pursuant to its terms. This is an important concept to keep in mind since the failure to have an individual named as beneficiary of a contractual arrangement will have adverse income or other tax consequences.

The retirement plan or IRA agreement may provide that if no beneficiary designation form is completed, the assets pass to the plan participant's spouse, and if there is no spouse, to the children. Given the adverse income tax consequences in not having a beneficiary designated, it is important to check the provisions of the plan document if no beneficiary form is on file with the plan administrator. Where there is no valid beneficiary form on file and the partners are not legally married, the surviving partner will have no right to the plan benefits, irrespective of the participant's intentions.

Also, when completing a beneficiary designation form, the document can provide the opportunity to name both primary beneficiaries and contingent beneficiaries. Our "rule of two" applies here. The primary beneficiary is the person, or persons, who have the first opportunity to receive the assets. If the primary beneficiary is not living, the assets pass to the contingent beneficiary. Some beneficiary forms provide that if more than one primary beneficiary is named, all of the primary beneficiaries must die prior to the plan participant before the assets pass to the contingent beneficiary (i.e., not "per stirpes"). This type of provision can have important consequences.

Example. Mary has two children, Bob and Alice, who are named as primary beneficiaries. If Bob dies before Mary, the plan may provide that the entire balance passes to Alice as opposed to Bob's children. Since whether this result occurs depends upon the plan document, the only way to know the answer is to check the plan or beneficiary designation form itself. The beneficiary designation form may need to be modified if the objective is to have the assets pass to Bob's children.

In this case, when naming Bob and Alice as primary beneficiaries, it may be advisable to add language to the primary beneficiary designation to the effect that if "either primary beneficiary is not then living, the share of the deceased primary beneficiary shall pass to such deceased beneficiary's then living issue, per stirpes, and in default thereof, to the remaining primary beneficiary, per stirpes." It usually is critical to very carefully fashion the beneficiary designations for property that passes pursuant to contract or beneficiary designation for blended family couples and for unmarried partners, particularly where one partner wants to ensure that both the other partner and the participant-owner partner's children to share the benefits of the property.

Survivorship

Property can also be transferred at death through the manner in which it is titled. For example when property is owned jointly with right of survivorship, it passes to the survivor or survivors by operation of law when a joint tenant dies.

If the property owned by a decedent does not pass automatically by contract or form of ownership, it will pass to the decedent's estate. If the decedent has a will, the property would then pass as provided in the will. Otherwise, the property will pass as provided by state law under the rules for intestate succession.

Wills

A will is a legal instrument by which a person leaves certain instructions for after death. A will is generally used to dispose of a decedent's property. However, a will can also provide for other matters, such as the naming of an executor, or a guardian for minor children. The person creating the will is usually called a "testator."

A "legatee" is a person who receives a legacy (also sometimes referred to as a bequest or devise) from the testator. The laws of all common law jurisdictions long ago eliminated the difference between a bequest (of personal property) and a devise (of real property).

That is why people called them "last will and testament" because it was formerly customary to have two separate instruments, one for bequests of personal property (a "testament") and one for devises of real property (a "will"). When it became customary to combine the two instruments (a brilliant common sense move), the name "last will and testament" was born and is still used to this day, even though the distinction between a will and a testament went away a long time ago. Old habits are hard to break.

A will must be executed with certain formalities. A will is generally a written document and must be signed by the person creating the will at the end of the document. Each state has its own requirements for creating a will. The person creating the will is often called a testator.

The will must also generally be signed by witnesses who attest to the capacity of the testator to make a will. Two witnesses are required in most states. It may be desirable to have three witnesses. The third witness can serve as a backup witness, even if only two witnesses are required. Some states have recently begun to enact statutes regarding "electronic wills", such as a will done on a computer, tablet or iPad or even a smartphone. Check your state to see whether they have addressed this.

The legal age to make a will is eighteen in many, but not all, states. In addition to being of proper legal age, a person must have the capacity to make a will at the time that the will is executed. Capacity means that the testator must:

- be of legal age;

- understand the extent of his property;

- understand the natural objects of his bounty; and

- understand the nature of his dispositions.

To "understanding the extent of his property," the testator must know about the nature of his property in a general sense. For instance, he should know that he owns a home in Ohio and a home in Florida, two life insurance policies, retirement benefits, two bank accounts, three mutual funds, household possessions, etc.

The "natural objects of the testator's bounty" refers to the testator's knowledge of his heirs. Such knowledge might include, for example, the testator's knowledge that he has a spouse and three children.

The testator must also "understand the nature of his dispositions." For example, that his spouse Mary gets the house, his brother Tom gets $10,000, his sister Janet gets the antique ring, his estranged son Mike gets nothing, and Mary gets everything else.

A will is "ambulatory." That means it does not take effect until the testator dies. The testator is generally free to revoke or change his will up until his death. A will can provide three types of legacies:

1. a specific legacy;

2. a general legacy; and

3. a residual legacy.

A *specific legacy* disposes of a specific piece or pieces of property. For example, the will might leave "all personal and household effects to my wife, Rachel." Or the will might leave "my 1962 Corvette to my niece, Heather." If the property that is the subject of a specific bequest does not exist at the testator's death or is not owned by the testator at death, in most states, the legatee receives nothing under the principle of ademption.[12] For example, if the Corvette does not exist at the testator's death, Heather gets nothing. Also, what happens if the Corvette is destroyed in an accident? Who gets the insurance proceeds for the car? It is not clear as to who would get the proceeds. Therefore, when making these types of bequests it is advisable to gift the specific item, "and the insurance thereon" to make it clear that Heather would get the insurance proceeds. Specific legacies are paid in preference to all other types of legacies.

A *general legacy* disposes of a certain amount or value of property and is paid after specific legacies. For example, the will might leave "$10,000 to my nephew, Ralph." If there is $10,000 of property remaining after specific legacies have been satisfied, Ralph will get $10,000 even if property must be sold.

A *residual legacy* disposes of all property that has not been disposed of through specific and general legacies. In other words, a residual legacy disposes of everything that is left after all other legacies have been satisfied. One or more persons can receive a residual legacy in whatever sharing arrangements that the testator wishes to make.

Frequently, the residual legatee is a primary beneficiary. For example, the residual legatee might be the testator's spouse. The testator should take into consideration that the residual legatee may get nothing if the estate should shrink and the specific and general legacies wipe out the estate.

If a specific or general legatee is not alive at the time of the testator's death, the specific or general legacy lapses and passes to the residual legatee. However, some states provide that a specific or general legacy for certain persons related to the testator does not lapse but rather goes to descendants of the legatee under a so-called "anti-lapse" statute.[13] Do not assume that the state statute applies to revocable living trusts the same as to wills – in some states the anti-lapse statute may not apply to a trust or may apply differently. If the testator does not wish this result, the testator can provide a legacy "if he survives me," by requiring to legatee to survive the testator.[14]

The testator can provide by will which legacies are to bear the burden of death taxes. Such a provision can substantially affect the amount received by any legatee. In the absence of such a provision, most states would apportion the death taxes among all legacies including property included in the gross estate for federal estate tax purposes that is not a part of the probate estate.[15] A few states would charge the death taxes to the residuary probate estate.[16]

Note: This is a very important concept for taxable estates, because many assets pass outside of the provisions of the will (for example, assets titled joint with right of survivorship, or which pass by contract as discussed above). Since some assets pass outside of the will, it is important to plan who will pay the tax on these assets.

A will should periodically be reviewed. Questions such as the following should be asked:

- Does the testator still live in the same state or country?

- Does the testator own real estate in another state or country?

- Is the testator still married to or with the same person? Remember that while many state statutes remove an ex-spouse as beneficiary upon divorce, they may not remove the ex-spouse's family as beneficiaries!

- Does the testator wish to change any beneficiaries?

- Does the testator have any new relatives, such as a newborn child? Have any beneficiaries died?

- Has state law on wills changed? Have tax laws changed?

- How have the assets changed?

- Have any beneficiaries become incapacitated or are going through a divorce or a bankruptcy?

At the testator's death, the will must be offered for probate. The probate court will establish the validity of the will and oversee its enforcement.

For more on wills, see Chapters 10 and 11.

Limitations

There are certain limitations on how a decedent may dispose of his property at death. Under state law, a surviving spouse is generally given a right to elect to take against the will. Such a right allows the spouse to receive a statutory share of the decedent's estate, even if the decedent provided otherwise. The statutory share is often equal to the fraction of the decedent's estate that the spouse would receive under the rules for intestate succession, discussed later. Thus, a surviving spouse is usually entitled to at least a third or a half of the decedent's estate and in some cases, all of the decedent's estate.[17] However, sometimes the application of these rules can be complicated, and it is important to have an attorney calculate whether a spouse would be better off in making this election or accepting the property which the spouse may otherwise be receiving from joint assets and beneficiary designations. The share of the estate on which the elective share is computed varies from state to state.

The issue of right to an elective share can be a dicey ethical issue for the estate planner who represents the couple jointly where the spouses have not waived the elective share in a marriage contract. About the best that an estate planner can do in that situation is point out the elective share to both spouses and encourage each spouse to give the other spouse at least as much of the spouse's estate that would satisfy the elective share. There is some estate planning that can be done where the estate planner only represents one spouse to minimize the elective share or that would make the election unpalatable given the type of property that the electing spouse would receive, e.g., move to a state that does not have an "augmented estate" concept or satisfying the elective share with a minority assignee interest in an LLC.[18]

Many states have adopted the "augmented estate" concept, in which the elective share base includes not only traditional probate property[19] but adds to that the value of all non-probate transfers to both others[20] as well as the surviving spouse[21] and the net value of the surviving spouse's property.[22] The surviving spouse's elective rights grow the longer that the surviving spouse was married to the deceased spouse because the base on which the augmented estate is computed counts grows as the length of the marriage grows.[23]

The spouse's right to elect against the will can be waived by agreement during lifetime. For example, the right to elect might be waived in a marriage contract.[24] Unmarried surviving partners are not entitled to the elective share.[25]

In some states, a surviving spouse might be given a homestead right. Such a right would generally permit the surviving spouse to live in the family home during such spouse's lifetime. In some states, children might also be given homestead rights. For example, in Florida, this homestead exemption, or right, is set forth in the state constitution.

In most states, an allowance is provided to the surviving spouse and children for a period of time after the decedent's death.[26] The period might be for six months or a year. The allowance is designed to provide support for the family until the estate is administered.

In many states, exemptions are provided for certain property.[27] For example, the surviving spouse and children might be entitled to certain household furnishings or clothes.

In most states, a child born or adopted after the execution of a will is entitled to share in the estate if provision is not otherwise made for the child. In some states, a child alive at the time of the execution of the will who is omitted from the will is entitled to share in the estate unless it appears the omission was intentional.[28]

A few states provide that a will executed before marriage is revoked upon marriage. A few states provide that such a will is revoked unless other provisions are made for the new spouse. States that have adopted the pertinent section of the Uniform Probate Code[29] provide an omitted spouse who marries the decedent after the will was executed gets an intestate share of the deceased spouse's estate unless the will expressly provides otherwise. Conversely, most states provide that provisions in a will for a former spouse are revoked upon divorce. Some states have even provided for revocation of beneficiary designations upon divorce.[30] However, to the extent that this revocation would revoke a beneficiary designation on an ERISA qualified retirement plan, state law is preempted by federal law.[31]

"Mortmain" statutes that restrict the amount that may go to charity if a decedent is survived by a spouse or child[32] have just about all been repealed or declared unconstitutional.[33]

Trusts

A trust is a fiduciary relationship in which property is held by one (or more) person(s) for the benefit of one (or more) person(s). Think of the players in a trust as a three-legged stool. The "first leg" of the trust stool is the person who creates the trust, and who is generally called a settlor, trustor, or grantor. The grantor typically executes a trust document and transfers property to the person who will be responsible for administering the terms of the trust, who is called a trustee, and who forms the "second leg" of the trust stool. The person for whose benefit the trustee administers the trust is called a beneficiary, which completes the "third leg" of the three-legged trust "stool." The property held in trust is often called the trust corpus or res.

State law controls the creation, operation, and termination of a trust. Common law is generally controlling except to the extent that a state has enacted a statute dealing with a particular aspect of trusts.[34] A majority of states have now passed the Uniform Trust Code, however. The trust may generally have any terms except to the extent that a term is illegal or against public policy.[35]

Theoretically, the law of any state with which the trust has contact could apply. Such states could include the state where the grantor resided upon creation of the trust, where the trustee is located or resides, where trust property is located (especially with regard to real estate), or where the beneficiaries reside. The grantor may specify in the trust document the state whose laws are to be applied to the operation and termination of the trust. Also, the grantor may permit the trustees to "move" the trust to another state, in which case the laws of the new state will apply. This is called changing the situs of the trust.

Usually, the beneficiaries of the trust are the grantor and/or members of the grantor's family. Having a charity as a beneficiary is also very common.

A trust may provide for management of property, accumulation or distributions of income to beneficiaries, distributions of trust corpus to beneficiaries, withdrawal powers in beneficiaries, and other powers of appointment.

Trust interests are often split into an income interest and a remainder. A beneficiary with an income interest receives income from the property for a period of years or for life. The beneficiary with the remainder or principal interest receives the property when the income interest ends.

Trusts arising at death under a will (testamentary trusts) are subject to probate at the grantor's death and potentially continuing after death. Some states such as Ohio require testamentary trusts to periodically report to the probate court, which is a compelling reason why practitioners prefer to use revocable living trusts. On the other hand, trusts created during lifetime (inter vivos trusts) are generally not subject to probate.

Trusts created during lifetime are either revocable or irrevocable; a trust created at death is irrevocable. A revocable trust is a trust in which the grantor retains the right to revoke the trust; upon revocation, property in the trust would be returned to the grantor. A trust that is not revocable is irrevocable.[36] While irrevocable trusts generally cannot be changed, some states permit changes to the trust if all of the people who have an interest in the trust and the settlor agree (a.k.a. nonjudicial settlement agreement),[37] or if a court approves the change.[38] Some irrevocable trusts may be changed by someone other than the settlor, e.g., a trust protector.[39]

There are many income, gift, estate, and generation-skipping transfer tax implications to trusts (see Chapters 18 to 26, in general, regarding taxes). In fact, many of the popular trusts, such as those discussed in Chapter 27 (marital trusts and credit shelter bypass trusts), Chapter 36 (irrevocable life insurance trusts), Chapter 29 (grantor trusts), and Chapter 38 (charitable trusts and wealth replacement trusts), are designed and utilized, at least in part, to obtain favorable tax treatment.

A revocable trust is taxable to the grantor for income tax purposes.[40] The grantor is not treated as making a gift upon transfer of property to a revocable trust; however, a revocable trust is includable in the grantor's estate at death.[41] See Chapter 64 regarding revocable trusts.

The grantor of an irrevocable trust generally makes a gift upon transfer of property to an irrevocable trust.[42] Whether the grantor is taxable upon trust income or whether the irrevocable trust is includable in the grantor's estate generally depends on what interests the grantor has in the irrevocable trust.[43]

Rule Against Perpetuities

Interests of a beneficiary in a trust must generally vest within the period allowed for in the rule against perpetuities, which is a very complex animal. For example, all members of a class must generally be ascertainable immediately or within the period allowed for in the rule against perpetuities. And a beneficiary must generally be born within the period allowed for in the rule against perpetuities.

The common law version of the rule against perpetuities generally provides that interests in property must vest no later than a life in being plus twenty-one years (plus a gestation period, if necessary). Interests that did not vest within the rule against perpetuities at the creation of a trust would be void. Many states have a version of the common law rule against perpetuities (sometimes codified). Other states have adopted a "wait and see"' approach; that is, an interest is only void if the interest actually fails to vest within the perpetuities period. The Uniform Statutory Rule Against Perpetuities (1990) (some version of which is in effect in approximately 30 states)[44] provides that a nonvested interest is invalid unless:

1. as of the date of the creation of the trust, the interest is certain to vest or terminate within a period measured by a life in being plus twenty-one years (plus a gestation period, if necessary), or

2. the interest either vests or terminates within ninety years (or in some states or situations 360 years) of its creation. while many other states have significantly lengthened its vesting time.[45]

Some states have entirely eliminated the rule against perpetuities,[46] while many other states have significantly lengthened its vesting time.[47]

Trusts should be drafted so as to comply with the rule against perpetuities (if applicable). A clause may also be inserted that provides that any interest must vest within the time provided by the rule against perpetuities.

Spendthrift Provisions

In a broad sense, a spendthrift provision is a provision in a trust in which the grantor attempts to provide funds to a beneficiary while limiting the ability of the beneficiary to squander the funds or creditors of the beneficiary from reaching the funds. Spendthrift provisions might include any of the following:

- a prohibition against the beneficiary transferring the beneficiary's interest;

- forfeiture of the beneficiary's interest if the beneficiary attempts to transfer interest (more rare);

- distributions of income or principal to a beneficiary limited to support of the beneficiary (possibly, limited to distributions on behalf of beneficiary for support rather than distributions directly to beneficiary);

- distributions to a beneficiary at the trustee's discretion; or

- a prohibition against creditors reaching beneficiary's interest.

There is a considerable amount of diversity among the states as to when a creditor of a beneficiary can reach the beneficiary's trust interest. Unless the trust document or state law provides otherwise (but most do), a creditor of a beneficiary can generally reach the beneficiary's trust interest.

State laws generally attempt to restrict the ability of a grantor to prevent creditors from reaching a beneficiary's interest in one of the following ways:

1. no restriction, creditor can reach trust interest;

2. creditor can reach amount not needed by beneficiary for support;

3. creditor can reach amount above some dollar amount; or

4. creditor cannot reach trust property.

In blended family couple documents, you should give very careful thought to the spendthrift clause. Generally, it is prudent to except certain voluntary alienation from the spendthrift clause, with consent of the trustee, in order to facilitate a separation of the interests of children from a prior union from a step-parent by gift, net gift or sale of either the income interest or the principal interest.

Exercise of Power of Appointment

Property also can be transferred from one to another at death via the exercise of a testamentary power of appointment. Chapter 12 discusses powers of appointment in greater detail.

Joint Tenancy/POD Accounts

The final way in which property can be transferred from one to another at death is through holding property in Totten trusts or in accounts that have a pay-on-death feature.

CHAPTER ENDNOTES

1. Those states are Arizona, California, Idaho, Louisiana, Nevada, New Mexico, Texas, Washington, and Wisconsin.

2. Alaska, Tennessee and South Dakota. Alaska Stat. §34.77.100, Tenn. Code §35-17-101 et seq., S.D.C.L. § 55-17-1 et seq. Kentucky and Florida also now have elective community property trust statutes.

3. In Alaska, Tennessee and South Dakota, property is not community property unless the couple agrees that property acquired during marriage is the community property of the spouses.

4. See, e.g., Cal. Fam. Code §760; Ariz. Rev. Stat. §25-318(A).

5. I.R.C. §1014(b)(6).

6. See, e.g., Disposition of Community Property Rights at Death Act, which the following states have adopted: Alaska, Arkansas, Colorado, Connecticut, Florida, Hawaii, Kentucky, Michigan, Minnesota, Montana, New York, North Carolina, Oregon, Utah, Virginia and Wyoming.

7. Cal. Fam. Code §125 (divorce) and Cal. Pro. Code §§66 and 101 (death). Arizona and Texas have a similar law for divorce only. Ariz. Rev. Stat. §25-318; and Texas (*Estate of Hanau v. Hanau*, 730 S.W.2d 663 (Sup. Ct. Tx. 1987)).

    Several other states have quasi-community property for all purposes. For other states' quasi-community property probate statutes, see Cal. Prob. Code §66 and 101; Idaho Code §§15-2-201 and 203; and Wash. Rev. Code §26.16.230.

8. Matter of Totten, 179 N.Y. 112 (1904).

9. The Uniform TOD Security Registration Act can be found at www.uniformlaws.org.

10. §2-102, Uniform Probate Code. As of this time, the following states and territories have enacted all or a part of the Uniform Probate Code: Alaska, Arizona, Colorado, Hawaii, Idaho, Maine, Massachusetts, Michigan, Minnesota, Montana, Nebraska,

New Jersey, New Mexico, North Dakota, South Carolina, South Dakota, and U.S. Virgin Islands.

11. Section 2-103, Uniform Probate Code.
12. However, §2-606, Uniform Probate Code, provides for dramatically expanded rights for the specific legatee, including, without limitation, the right to receive any remaining sales proceeds from the sale of the property that was subject to the specific bequest that remains unpaid at the testator's death. The specific legatee also has the right to receive certain insurance proceeds from the destruction of the property as well as condemnation proceeds.
13. See, e.g., §2-603, Uniform Probate Code.
14. See, e.g., §§2-104 and 2-702, Uniform Probate Code.
15. See, e.g., §3, Uniform Estate Tax Apportionment Act.
16. See, e.g., Matter of the Estate of James W. Mason, 190 Ariz. 312, 947 P.2d 886 (1997).
17. See, e.g., §2-202, Uniform Probate Code.
18. See, e.g., Pennell, Jeffrey N., "Minimizing the Surviving Spouse's Elective Share," *1998 Heckling Institute on Estate Planning*, Chapter 9.
19. See, e.g., §2-204, Uniform Probate Code.
20. See, e.g., §2-205, Uniform Probate Code.
21. See, e.g., §2-206, Uniform Probate Code.
22. See, e.g., §2-207, Uniform Probate Code.
23. See, e.g., §2-203(b) (Alternative A), Uniform Probate Code.
24. See, e.g., §2-213, Uniform Probate Code.
25. See, e.g., §2-201(3), Uniform Probate Code.
26. See, e.g., §§2-402 (spousal homestead allowance) and 2-404, Uniform Probate Code.
27. See, e.g., §2-403, Uniform Probate Code.
28. See, e.g., §2-302, Uniform Probate Code.
29. See, e.g., §2-301, Uniform Probate Code.
30. Id.
31. *Egelhoff v. Egelhoff*, 532 U.S. 141 (2001).
32. See Kristine S. Knaplund, "Charity for the 'Death Tax': The Impact of Legislation on Charitable Bequests" *Gonzaga Law Review* 45:3 (2009-10), 713.
33. See, e.g., *Shriners Hospital for Crippled Children v. Zrillic*, 563 So. 2d 64 (Fla. 1990), invalidating Fla. Stat. Ann. 732.803.
34. See, e.g., Uniform Trust Code.
35. See, e.g., §105(b)(3) and 404, Uniform Trust Code.
36. See, e.g., §602, Uniform Trust Code.
37. See, e.g., §411, Uniform Trust Code.
38. See, e.g., Sections 411-416, Uniform Trust Code.
39. See, e.g., §§411(a) and 602(e), Uniform Trust Code.
40. I.R.C. §676.
41. I.R.C. §2038.
42. I.R.C. §2511.
43. I.R.C. §§671-679 and 2036-2044.
44. 8A U.L.A. 103.
45. See, e.g., Florida and Nevada.
46. For an up-to-date list of states that have enacted the rule, see "Statutory Rule Against Perpetuities," Uniform Law Commission, available at: https://www.uniformlaws.org/committees/community-home?CommunityKey=addf3263-af92-4421-a83c-2ef7bc9a1b94.
47. See, e.g., Florida and Nevada.

GIFTS

CHAPTER 8

8.1 INTRODUCTION

For gift tax purposes, a gift can be broadly defined to include a sale, exchange, or other transfer of property from one person (the donor) to another (the donee) without adequate and full consideration in money or money's worth.

In addition to an outright transfer, gifts can take other forms. For example, the forgiveness of a debt, foregone interest on an intra-family interest-free or below market loan, the assignment of the benefits of an insurance policy, or the transfer of property to a trust can also be considered gifts.[1]

Gifts are a major estate planning tool because of their potential for income as well as estate tax savings and for their nontax advantages.

The gift tax computation itself is explained in detail in Chapter 20.

8.2 WHEN IS USE OF SUCH A DEVICE INDICATED?

1. When the donor has an asset that is likely to appreciate in value over a period of time and would like to save estate taxes on the potential growth. However, when a gift is made, the potential step up in basis that beneficiaries receive if the asset were held until the donor's death is lost. With the higher estate/gift tax applicable exclusion amount of $12,920,000 (for 2023), there will be a greater incentive to retain assets until death and obtain this increased basis. But if a donor does have a taxable estate, it may still be advisable to make gifts to shift appreciation out of the estate (especially if it is to use the annual exclusion) – it depends on how low the basis is and the estimated growth from the time of gift until death It may make sense to gift a property worth $100 when the basis is $90 but not when it is only $10, but recall that many donees may be in a 0% tax bracket for long-term capital gains.

2. When a donor would like to see the donee (an individual, charity, or other organization) benefited by a gift during the donor's life for nontax motives such as the enjoyment of seeing the donee use the gift, to help the donee learn financial responsibility and property management, or to help assure and be certain of the financial security of the donee.

3. When the donor would like to reduce probate costs and estate administration expenses and protect family members from the claims of the donor's creditors. However, a gift may not be made to avoid creditors' claims of the donor if the transfer was in fraud of a known creditor.[2]

4. When giving away assets other than closely held stock will make it easier to qualify for a Code section 303 redemption of stock, a Code section 6166 installment payout of taxes attributable to a closely held business interest, and a Code section 2032A special use valuation for certain real property used for farming or closely held business purposes. (This technique generally works only if the gift is made more than three years prior to death and only applies to taxable estates.)

5. When the estate owner desires to maximize the marital deduction provisions of the federal estate and gift tax law. The estate owner could give his spouse up to an unlimited amount of property during his lifetime and pay no federal gift tax because of

135

the 100 percent gift tax marital deduction. Lifetime gifts could help even up both spouse's estates and make strategic planning easier. While it is no longer necessary to ensure that a married couple's estates are equalized for federal estate/gift tax savings (due to portability of the deceased spousal unused exclusion amount), intra-spousal gifts may still have an advantage for generation skipping transfer tax (which exemption is not portable), state estate/inheritance tax (since most states have not yet incorporated a form of portability), or potentially even income tax basis planning.

6. By giving income-producing property, the donor may be able to shift the income from being taxed at the donor's income tax bracket to the lower income tax bracket of a donee. For example, a high bracket property owner may make a gift to reduce federal income tax rate from a high of 37 percent to a bracket as low as 10 percent or even 0 percent.[3] Recall that many donees may be in a 0% tax bracket for qualified dividends and long-term capital gains (for a single taxpayer not subject to kiddie tax, up to $44,625 of taxable income in 2023, for married taxpayer filing jointly, up to $89,250 of taxable income in 2023). While shifting income to a lower tax bracket beneficiary is a good approach for most situations, sometimes the donor may wish to continue to pay the income taxes on the property transferred (with this payment of tax getting additional value out of his estate). In these situations, the gift may be made to an irrevocable grantor trust. (See Chapter 29). The payment of taxes by the donor on income flowing to the beneficiary of such a trust is not considered to be an additional gift.[4] In essence this provides a way to make an ongoing gift-tax-free gift.

All *net unearned income* of a child who has not attained age twenty-four and is a full-time student and whose earned income is less than half their support, or if under eighteen and unmarried, or if under eighteen and earned income is less than half their support, and who has at least one parent alive at the close of the taxable year will generally be taxed to the child, but not at the child's tax bracket. This applies to *all* net unearned income; the *source* of the assets creating the income, the *date* the income-producing property was transferred, and the *identity* of the transferor are *irrelevant*.

The tax payable by the child on net unearned income is essentially the additional amount of tax the parent would have had to pay if the net unearned income of the child were included in the parent's taxable income. The Tax Cuts and Jobs Act had, starting inn 2018, changed the kiddie tax to be computed at the compressed rates applicable to estates and non-grantor trusts, but this rule was changed back to using the parent's tax rates, which is generally more favorable (See Code Section 1(g) and IRS Tax Topic 553).

If parents have two or more children with unearned income to be taxed at the parent's marginal tax rate, all of the children's applicable unearned income will be added together and the tax will then be calculated. The tax is then allocated to each child based on the child's pro rata share of unearned income.

This kiddie tax is calculated in three stages (numbers below are indexed for inflation but accurate for 2023):

(1) There will be no tax on the first $1,250 (in 2023) of unearned income because of the child's standard deduction. (The standard deduction offsets *un*earned income first, up to $1,250. Any remaining standard deduction is then available to offset earned income.)

(2) The next $1,250 of unearned income will be taxed to the child at the child's bracket.

(3) Unearned income in excess of the first $2,500 will be taxed to the child at the appropriate parent's rate (for 2023).

Example. A dependent child under age twenty-four inn 2021 with $2,100 of unearned income is taxed as follows. In 2023, this would be even less due to the standard deduction increasing to $1,250:

Unearned Income	$2,100
Standard Deduction	− 1,100
Net Unearned Income	$1,000
Taxed at Child's Rate	× 10%
Tax	$100.00

GIFTS

Figure 8.1

ADVANTAGE OF INCOME SHIFTING - CHILD 24 OR OLDER				
Investment				$20,000
Rate of Return				10%
Parent's Tax Rate				39.6%
Parent's After Tax Rate of Return				6%
Child's Tax Rate				15%
Child's After Tax Rate of Return				8.5%

	Accumulated Value		Advantage
Years	Parent (6%)	Child (8.5%)	of Gift
5	$26,765	$30,073	$3,308
10	$35,817	$45,220	$9,403
15	$47,931	$67,995	$20,064
20	$64,143	$102,241	$38,098

Even for children over age twenty-four, income shifting can be advantageous, as demonstrated in Figure 8.1. For children age twenty-four or older (and often for those who are younger who are not full-time students), unearned income will be taxed to the child at his or her own tax bracket. As Figure 8.1 shows, this technique can yield tax savings for a child who is age twenty-four or older, or for younger children with incomes above $2,200 ($2500 in 2023).

Differences and advantages can be even greater considering that most returns on investment may be eligible for special qualified dividend/long-term capital gains rates, which may be 0% for lower-income donees as noted above.

8.3 WHAT ARE THE REQUIREMENTS?

1. There must be a gratuitous transfer or delivery of property.[5]

2. The property that is the subject of the gift must be accepted by the donee.[6] (Of course, when the property is of benefit to the donee, acceptance is seldom an issue.)

3. The gratuitous transfer must divest the donor of control, dominion, and title over the subject matter of the gift.[7]

Example 1. Caroline O'Gara is age fifty-five, married, and owns $20,000 of interest-paying bonds. The bonds yield $1,000 annually. Caroline is presently in a 28 percent federal income tax bracket. On the advice of her lawyer, in 2017 she gives the $20,000 of bonds to her twenty-four-year-old son, James, who is a full-time student (splitting the gift with her husband so there would be no gift tax). This will have the result of shifting the income tax liability from Caroline, who would have netted only $720 [$1,000 – (28 percent of $1,000)] from the $1,000 interest, to James, who is in a 10 percent bracket, has a personal exemption of $1,050 which would reduce the income tax payable to zero.

Example 2. Gerald Carter owns an asset that is worth $100,000 today. It is anticipated that the asset will appreciate at the rate of 10 percent per year, so that in ten years it will be worth approximately $260,000. If the property is given away now, the gift tax is computed on the $100,000 (less the annual exclusion if allowable). If the asset is not given away and it remains part of Gerald's estate (ten years from today), the estate tax is computed on approximately $260,000. Thus, a gift made currently removes future appreciation from the estate. However, as noted previously, the trade-off for this gift is the lack of a step-up in basis at Gerald's death since the asset would not be includible in his estate.

8.4 TAX IMPLICATIONS

1. A gift will remove future appreciation in the property's value from an individual's estate.

2. Gift tax may have to be paid if the value of the gift exceeds the annual exclusion and the gift tax applicable exclusion amount available to the donor.[8] The gift tax applicable exclusion amount for 2021 is $11,700,000. (The unified credits and exemption equivalents are shown below under Frequently Asked Questions.) If an individual is married and his spouse consents to split the gift, the donor spouse can effectively have the $15,000 (in 2021) annual exclusion and the gift tax applicable exclusion amount of his spouse in addition to his own.[9] A married individual can give sizable gifts to a spouse with little or no gift tax liability through the gift tax marital deduction discussed below.

3. Dividend or other income generated by the property given will be taxed to the donee rather than the donor (see the discussion above at 6 under the heading "When is Use of Such a Device Indicated?").

4. The gift tax subtracted from the tentative tax in the estate tax computation is the tax that would have been payable on post-1976 gifts if the tax rate schedule as in effect at decedent's death had been in effect at the time such gifts were made. If estate and gift tax rates at the time the gift was made and at the donor's death are the same, this deduction for gift tax payable is equivalent to a credit for the gift tax actually paid. (A credit is available for gift tax paid on pre-1977 gifts.) If estate and gift tax rates are lower at the time of the donor's death than when the gift was made, a donor may pay a larger tax than if no gift had been made. However, any lower tax rate at death should be balanced against the appreciation of the gift that was removed from the tax system.

    The top gift and estate tax rate is 40 percent in 2023.

5. The tax implications also include state gift tax (only Connecticut presently has one) where applicable, which in rare instances can be greater than the federal gift tax, because of the large credit and exemptions currently available under federal gift tax law.

6. Some states with a separate state estate/inheritance tax system will have a one- to three-year "lookback" period to prevent deathbed gifts from avoiding state estate/inheritance taxes. However, in many cases lifetime gifts can save state estate/inheritance taxes and this should go into any calculation regarding the tax effects of gifting.

Gift Tax Annual Exclusion

A donor can make gift tax free, up to $17,000 (in 2023) worth of gifts (other than future interest gifts) to any number of persons each year.[10] The total maximum excludable amount is determined by multiplying the number of persons to whom gifts are made by $17,000. Since 1997, the $10,000 amount in the tax code has been subject to an inflation adjustment, rounded to the next lowest multiple of $1,000:

Tax Year	Amount
1982-2001	$10,000
2002-2005	$11,000
2006-2008	$12,000
2009-2012	$13,000
2013-2017	$14,000
2018-2021	$15,000
2022	$16,000
2023	$17,000

If the donor is married and the donor's spouse consents (by signing the donor's gift tax return) to splitting the gift, each spouse is deemed to have given half the gift–even though one spouse in actuality made the entire gift. This has the effect of doubling the per donee exclusion to $34,000 (in 2023) per year for married couples

An annual exclusion is allowed only for present interest gifts and is denied for future interest gifts. Whether a closely held business interest is a present interest may depend on the terms of the operating agreement.[11]

A present interest gift is one in which the donee's possession or enjoyment begins at the instant that the gift is made. A future interest is any interest in which the donee's use, possession, or enjoyment will not begin until some period of time after the gift is made. In a nutshell, if there is any delay, no matter how short, or any possibility, no matter how remote, that the donee's legal right to use, possession, or enjoyment will not begin at the moment the gift is made, the annual exclusion is denied.

Future interests (which do not qualify for the annual exclusion) include:

(1) reversions,

(2) remainders,

(3) any other delayed interest. This may include gifts of LP/LLC interests, depending on the operating agreement, if it is found that the donee does not receive a substantial present economic benefit.[12]

A single transfer may actually be two gifts and for tax purposes have to be split into two parts. One may be a present interest that qualifies for the annual exclusion. The other gift may be a future interest that will not qualify for the annual exclusion.

Example. A donor put $100,000 into a trust in 2017 that provided that "all the income is to go annually to my son for ten years. The remainder is to go to my daughter at the end of that time."

The first gift, the income to the son, would be a present interest. The reason that it qualifies as a present interest is that at the moment of the gift, the son has the immediate right to the income stream for ten years. The present value of the son's right to income, according to government valuation tables, would be the gift. Assuming a Section 7520 rate of 5 percent, the value of the income interest for ten years would be $38,609 ($100,000 × .386087: which is the term-certain income factor). If the donor was married and his spouse consented to splitting the gift, the two annual exclusions would total $28,000. Therefore, only $10,609 ($38,609 − $28,000) of the income interest would be a taxable gift, split evenly for $5,304.50 from each spouse.

The second gift, the daughter's right to the remainder of the capital at the end of ten years, would be a gift of a future interest because her right to possession would be delayed. Assuming a Section 7520 rate of 5 percent, the value of the remainder interest after ten years would be $61,391 ($100,000 × .613913: the term-certain remainder factor). Each spouse's share of the remainder portion of the gift would be $30,695.50, and no annual exclusion would be allowed on this portion.

The requirements for the gift tax annual exclusion can be summarized as follows:

(1) A gift in trust is a gift to a trust's beneficiaries for purposes of determining how many annual exclusions may be allowed.

(2) The value of an income interest in a trust qualifies for the annual exclusion if the trustee is required to distribute the income annually or more frequently–even if the value of the remainder interest does not qualify.

(3) The gift of an interest that is contingent upon survivorship is a gift of a future interest. For instance, a gift, "to my son for life, then to my daughter for life, then to my brother if he survives me" is really three gifts. The first gift (to the son) is a present interest if the trustee is given no right to accumulate income and all income must be paid at least annually. The other two gifts (to the daughter and brother) are future interest gifts.

(4) A gift is a future interest gift if the donee's enjoyment depends on the exercise of a trustee's discretion. So if a trustee has the right to accumulate income, the gift is a future interest, even if the trustee never exercises the right. The nature of the gift (present or future) is ascertained as of the moment of the transfer and is not determined by whether the trustee actually accumulates or distributes the income.

(5) A gift must have an ascertainable value to qualify for the exclusion. If the donor or anyone can divert the income from the beneficiary or it is not reasonably possible at the time of the gift to value it, the exclusion may be denied.

The annual exclusion can be an extremely effective income, estate, and generation-skipping transfer tax saving device.

The illustration at Figure 8.2 multiplies the number of donees by the amount of the annual exclusion available to be split between husband and wife and then multiplies that amount by the donor's life expectancy

THE TOOLS & TECHNIQUES OF ESTATE PLANNING

Figure 8.2

ESTATE TAX OR GST TAX ADVANTAGE OF THE GIFT TAX ANNUAL EXCLUSION

Donor's Age	40
Donees' Annual After-Tax Return On Gifts	4.00%
Amount Of Unused Annual Exclusion (With Gift Splitting Between Husband And Wife)	$28,000
Number Of Donees	5
Donor's Life Expectancy (Years)	43
Total Amount Of Gifts ($28,000/Year/Donee X 5 Donees X 43 Years)	$6,020,000
Donor's Projected Estate Tax Bracket	40.00%
Potential Estate Tax Savings	$2,408,000
Projected Value Of Gifts At Life Expectancy (43 Years)	$15,401,733
Potential Estate Tax Savings If Annual Gifts Invested By Donees At Compound Interest	$6,160,693

according to the government's table in the regulations. This result is then multiplied by the federal estate tax bracket projected for the donor at death. The result is the potential federal estate tax savings if none of the annual gifts are invested by the donees.

The illustration then assumes the donees do invest the annual gifts at the specified rate of return (being conservative since this is an after-tax figure). The final result is the potential estate tax savings–the amount that might have gone to the federal government–if no gifts were made.

If a gift is made in trust, the donee is considered to be each beneficiary of the trust and not the trust itself. Therefore, there are as many annual exclusions as there are legitimate present interest beneficiaries.

Example. Robin Scott creates an irrevocable trust for his three minor children. Each child is given notice that he or she has the right to withdraw annually his or her pro-rata share of the gift to the trust not to exceed $5,000. Robin contributes $15,000 to the trust. She is considered to have made a $5,000 present interest gift to each of his three children.

The above chart does not even take into account the increases in the annual exclusion due to inflation over time. Although the annual exclusion may seem to be a small amount when considering large multi-million-dollar estates, just using annual exclusion gifting can add up to substantial amounts over time.

Qualified Transfer Exclusion

A qualified transfer means any amount paid on behalf of an individual:

(1) as tuition to an educational institution (where the check is made payable directly to the institution), or

(2) to any person who provides medical care with respect to such individual as payment for such medical care.[13]

A qualified transfer is not considered a gift for gift tax purposes, and no gift tax return is required for these transfers. It can be made to grandchildren, great-grandchildren or others who would be "skip persons" while avoiding the GST tax (see Chapter 21 on GST tax).

Split Gift

Using a split gift election, when a spouse makes a gift to a third person, the gift is treated as having been made one-half by the donor spouse and one-half by the non-donor spouse. This is true even though only one spouse actually makes the gift, provided that the non-donor spouse consents to the gift on the gift tax return.[14]

Example. A present interest gift of $114,000 (taxable gift of $100,000) made by a single individual in 2017 when the annual exclusion was $14,000 would result in a gift tax of $23,800, whereas the same $114,000 gift made by a husband and his consenting wife to a third party (such as a child) would result in each being considered to have made a $43,000 taxable gift (($114,000 / 2) – $14,000) and the gift tax would be $8,920 each ($17,840 for both). The savings would be $5,960 ($23,800 – $17,840). (These examples assume the applicable exclusion amount has already been used, but it is important to note the usage of applicable exclusion amount is important even if it does not yet cause a gift tax to be paid)

A gift tax return must be filed in order to be able to split the gift. Only individuals married to each other can consent to split a gift. The election applies to all gifts made by either spouse during the year.

In the case of community property (see below), since each spouse owns his or her one-half interest in the property, there is no need to split the gift, but each spouse would have a reporting obligation if the gift exceeds the annual exclusion amount.

Net Gifts and Net Net Gifts

A *net gift* is a gift of property subject to some obligation or encumbrance. The debt or obligation against the property may exist before the transfer or arise at the time of the gift. Typically, a net gift results when the donee agrees, as a condition of the gift, to pay gift taxes on the transfer.

Netting the gift can be an attractive means of transferring property when a donor does not have cash on hand (and does not want to sell other property to raise cash) to pay gift taxes. A net gift is also useful when a donor wants to limit the extent of the gift to its net value.

For gift tax purposes, the gross amount of the gift is reduced by the amount of the gift tax the donee must pay. In other words, the amount of the gift tax that the donee pays reduces the value of the gift and gift tax is computed on the value of the remaining (net) amount. This means that the actual gift tax liability is lowered since the gift taxes paid reduce the value of the taxable gift. In computing the donee's gift tax liability, the donor's unified credit must be used.

The formula used to compute the donee's tax is: Tentative tax ÷ (1.00 + donor's rate of tax).[15]

Note that the formula is not applicable if the gift is split between the donor and spouse, each of whom is in a different gift tax bracket because either or both have made prior taxable gifts. Quite often, however, you can determine the correct tax bracket by inspection and adjust for the bracket differential by computing the tentative tax in the correct lower bracket. In other situations, you'll have to make trial computations using first the bracket indicated by the tentative taxable gift and then later using the next lower bracket.

Net gift computations can be performed on NumberCruncher software. If you have difficulty with making the computation, you may submit your facts in a letter to the Commissioner of Internal Revenue (Actuarial Department), Washington, D.C. for assistance.

For estate tax purposes, only the net amount of the gift will be considered in the estate tax computation as an adjusted taxable gift. The gift tax paid by the donee can be credited against the donor's estate taxes.

A net gift is treated for income tax purposes as a part sale/part gift transaction to the extent the donor is relieved from paying the gift tax liability. To the extent the donor is relieved of such liability; the donor realizes an immediate economic benefit that is taxable.[16] Specifically, net gifts (made after March 4, 1981) will result in income tax to the donor to the extent the gift tax paid by the donee exceeds the donor's basis in the property. If you are considering a net gift be sure that the donor and donee sign an agreement that sets forth the agreement regarding the gift tax.

Some donees assume liability not only for the gift tax, but for the estate tax on the gift tax if the donor dies within three years of having made a taxable gift.[17] This is called a net net gift and requires some actuarial computation, i.e., how likely it is that the donor at whatever age will die within three years of having made a taxable gift. The IRS fought the net net gift, but it lost.[18]

Marital Deduction

In computing the amount of a taxable gift, a deduction is generally allowed for a gift made by a spouse to a spouse or vice versa. This deduction is unlimited if the donee spouse is a U.S. citizen; so one spouse could conceivably give an entire estate to the other spouse without adverse gift tax consequences. If the donee spouse is not a U.S. citizen, the gift tax marital deduction is not allowed; however, transfers which otherwise would qualify for the marital deduction are eligible for an increased gift tax annual exclusion (see above) of $159,000 (in 2021).

To qualify for this deduction, the donee-spouse must be given the property outright or must have at least the right to the income from the property and a general power of appointment (essentially the right to say "who gets it") over the principal.[19] (Certain so-called qualified terminable interest type property that gives the spouse only a life income may also qualify. This planning technique is discussed more thoroughly in Chapter 27 on marital deduction trusts.)

Gift Tax Unified Credit

For 2017, the gift and estate tax unified credit is $2,141,800 which is equivalent to $5,490,000 of taxable gifts. Tax reform more than doubled this applicable exclusion amount for 2018 to $11,180,000, to be adjusted for inflation based on chained-CPI through 2025, then reverting to the prior number adjusted for inflation in 2026.[20] Historically, then:

	Gift Tax Unified Credit	Exemption Equivalent
2002-2009	$345,800	$1,000,000
2010	$330,800	$1,000,000
2011	$1,730,800	$5,000,000
2012	$1,772,800	$5,120,000
2013	$2,045,800	$5,250,000
2014	$2,081,800	$5,380,000
2015	$2,117,800	$5,520,000
2016	$2,125,800	$5,450,000
2017	$2,141,800	$5,490,000
2018	$4,425,800	$11,180,000
2019	$4,505,800	$11,400,000
2020	$4,577,800	$11,580,000
2021	$4,625,800	$11,700,000
2022	$4,769,800	$12,060,000
2023	$5,113,800	$12,920,000

Example. Assume Robin Scott and her husband make a $677,000 present interest gift in 2017 to their son. The computation for *each* spouse would be as follows:

Gift (split under Section 2513)	$338,500
Annual Exclusion	14,000
Taxable Gift	324,500
Tentative Tax on Taxable Gift	96,130
Unified Credit	2,141,800 (2017)
Gift Tax Due	$ 0

If made in 2023, the annual exclusion amount would be $17,000 and the amount of unified credit $5,113,800, pursuant to the above table. To the extent that the unified credit is used during lifetime it will have the effect of reducing the unified credit available against the estate tax. Lifetime gifts will be added back into the adjusted gross estate when the federal estate tax return is prepared. This feature confuses many practitioners, since we've often heard advice to make gifts before death to save estate tax. Making a taxable gift (i.e., one above or that does not qualify for the annual exclusion or health and education exceptions) right before death, assuming the value stays the same, does not save any estate tax at all (in fact, it may cost a step up in basis).

Basis

Where property is received by gift, the donee is generally required to take over the donor's basis in the property (this is often called a substituted or carryover basis).

In addition, if gift tax is paid on the gift this can add to the carryover basis for the federal gift tax attributable to the appreciation element of the gift. Code Section 1015(d). The formula for computing this is:

$$\text{Gift Tax} \times \frac{\text{Net Amount of Appreciation}}{\text{Value of Gift}}$$

Example. Property worth $100,000 was given by Rob Sterling to his son Aaron. Rob's basis was $40,000. Gift tax paid on the gift was $18,000. Appreciation on the gift was $60,000 ($100,000 − $40,000). The donee's basis is $50,800 [$40,000 + ($60,000/$100,000 × $18,000)].

If the donee sells property at a gain, he must pay income tax on such capital gain.

For purposes of determining loss, the donee's basis is the lesser of (a) the donor's basis, or (b) the fair market value of the property at the time of the gift. Code Section 1015(a).

8.5 TYPES OF PROPERTY

The choice of property to be given away depends on the circumstances and objectives of the parties. Income-producing property can be good property to give away if the donor is in a higher income tax bracket than the donee. The advantage of this income shifting device is somewhat curtailed for children under age eighteen or even twenty-four in many circumstances. See the discussion of the kiddie tax in the When Is Use of Such a Device Indicated section of the chapter.

Property that is likely to grow substantially in value (e.g., life insurance, common stock, antiques and art, or real estate) is also prime property for giving since future appreciation can be removed from the estate and the gift can be made when the gift tax values (and therefore gift tax transfer costs) are lowest.

Property that has already appreciated should be given away if a sale of such property is contemplated and the donee is in a lower income tax bracket than the donor, although it is far better if the donee does not sell the property upon receipt. Property with relatively low gift tax value and high estate tax value (such as life insurance) makes an excellent gift.

Generally, it is not a good idea to give away loss property (property that, if sold, would result in a loss) since the donee cannot use the donor's loss. This is because the donee's basis becomes the lower of the donor's basis or the value at the time of the gift. The donor should usually sell that property, take the deduction for the loss himself, and give away the cash proceeds. However, if a donor is terminally ill and would not be able to use the capital loss on selling the property (capital losses do not pass down to heirs/beneficiaries), giving away the loss property may preserve some of the higher basis if the property later appreciates in value and it will avoid a step down in basis at death.

Although stock in a closely held corporation is often thought of as an ideal asset for gift purposes, care must be taken so that not too much stock is given away if there is a taxable estate. The retention of too little closely held stock might cause an estate to fail the various percentage tests that may qualify it for preferential treatment, e.g., Code section 303 redemptions (see Chapter 48), or Code section 6166 installment payments of the federal estate tax (see Chapter 18).

Another type of property that might be given is property owned by the donor in a state other than his own state of residence, in order to avoid facing an ancillary probate at the time of the donor's death.

Be sure to consider the age, maturity, and experience of the donee in selecting the gift.

It is extremely important to focus on the circumstances of the parties (particularly your client) before making a gift. Do not give away any asset if it will reduce the client's standard of living or financially (or psychologically) endanger his comfort level. Particularly focus on the impact of the gift on the client's income and capital needs (both present and anticipated) as well as on the client's need for liquidity.

Be aware of the effect of gifts of stock or business or farm interests on qualification for favorable tax law considerations under Code section 303 (partial stock redemptions to pay death taxes–see Chapter 48), Code section 2032A (special use valuation of closely held business and farm real property–see Chapter 70), and Code section 6166 (extension of time to pay federal estate tax attributable to closely held business interest–see Chapter 18). Also, if assets are given away that are subject to IRD, or deferred income taxes, the gift may trigger some income tax recognition. For example, a gift of a retirement account or non-qualified annuity will result in the recognition of ordinary income. Also, a gift of a promissory note issued pursuant to an installment sale may cause the unrecognized gain on the sale to become taxable. (See Chapter 41.)

Perhaps more important than *what* to give is *how* to give. Large outright gifts should be made only after a great deal of consideration. The simple fact is that property is more valuable when it is held in trust rather than outright because the trust, if properly drafted, will protect the beneficiary from creditors and other predators. A trust, custodial account, or some other form of property management arrangement is appropriate where:

(1) the beneficiary is unwilling or unable to invest, manage, or handle the responsibility of the gift;

(2) the beneficiaries are minors or are adults who lack the emotional or intellectual maturity, physical capacity, or technical training to handle large sums of money or securities;

(3) the donor does not want to significantly reduce the beneficiary's financial dependence on the donor;

(4) the property does not lend itself to fragmentation but the donor desires to spread beneficial ownership among a large number of people (e.g., real estate may be more valuable in some instances if it is not subdivided);

(5) the donor wants to limit the class of beneficiaries and prevent the donee from transferring the property to persons outside the donor's family;

(6) the donor wants to treat children or other relatives equally. A donor may own several parcels of property of equal value. If he gives each to different beneficiaries, one may go up and the other may go down in value. But if they are all placed into one trust and each beneficiary is given an equal share, they will all be treated equally.

(7) the donee may be subject to future creditors or divorce.

(8) the donor wants to engage in generation-skipping or dynasty type planning.

It is often recommended that small outright gifts be made over a period of time to allow beneficiaries to learn to handle money and other assets under the guidance of the donor. Then larger amounts can be placed into trust, again during the donor's lifetime, so that the donor can evaluate how the trustee invests and manages the property. Lifetime gifts give the donor the opportunity to see how both the trustee and the beneficiaries handle assets and make investments. The donor can then make adjustments to his will and other estate planning vehicles accordingly.

8.6 ISSUES IN COMMUNITY PROPERTY STATES

All community property states have adopted statutes that to some degree, and by different methods, grant equal powers of management and control of community property to each spouse. In many states, one spouse cannot make a gift of community property without the prior written consent of the other spouse. If one spouse makes a gift of community property to a third person without the consent of the other spouse, the gift is ordinarily voidable rather than void.

The gift can be voided only at the request of the nondonor spouse. The amount of the gift that can be declared void and brought back to the community estate is generally dependent upon whether the community circumstance is still in existence. If the spouses are still married, the entire gift is returned to the community estate. However, if the community has been terminated (e.g., divorce, death), the nondonor spouse has the right to recapture only one-half of the gift. The other half is allowed to remain with the donee. Therefore, it is advisable to obtain both spouses' consent prior to the gift transfer.

In general, gifts of community property have the same benefits as gifts of separate property where the gift is to a third party. However, since each spouse actually owns his or her one-half interest in the property, there is no need to split the gift. This provides an advantage for persons with community property since each has property and each can give an amount equal to the annual exclusion without filing a gift tax return to split gifts.

As to gifts between spouses, a marital deduction is available for the entire amount of the gift, where one spouse gives his or her community interest in property to the other, provided that the spouse is a US citizen. There is a special annual exclusion amount for gifts to non-citizen spouses under Code Section 2523(i), which is $100,000, periodically adjusted for inflation (for tax year 2022, the cap is $164,000. For 2023, it's $175,000)

Accidental gifts (i.e., taxable gifts that were not intended to be events subject to tax) can be created by transfers of title. This is particularly true in community property states where a husband and wife have acquired property in a common law state and then moved to a community property state. An example would be where a husband and wife who have acquired assets by the husband's earnings in a common law state sell their home and other real property and move to a community property state, where they invest their cash in securities in joint tenancy or community property title. The parties have always considered their property as "belonging to both of them" and frequently do not understand that purchasing joint tenancy securities resulted in a gift of one-half the value from the husband to the wife. While the unlimited marital deduction normally avoids federal gift tax on such transfers between spouses, parties should be especially careful if one of the spouses is not a US citizen.

In addition, some states (Texas, Louisiana, and Idaho) consider the income from assets with a separate property nature to be community property.[21] Others (Arizona, California, Nevada, New Mexico, and Washington) consider such income to be the separate property of the spouse who actually "owns" the property. Thus, in the latter group of states, income that comes from an asset that one spouse had before marriage or that was given to or inherited by the spouse during marriage is the separate property of that spouse.

It is important to maintain in separate accounts the proceeds of sale of one's separate property and any separate property income. Commingling these funds can transmute them into community property of both spouses and can result in a gift even though no gift was intended, by using those commingled funds to buy something in co-ownership between the spouses.

Aside from any gift tax aspects, with the increasing frequency of divorce, it may be important for ownership reasons to be able to trace separate and community property. Tracing is done by allocating withdrawals, deposits or payments between community property funds and separate property funds. The burden of proof is usually on the party attempting to rebut the community property presumption created under state law.[22]

8.7 VALUATION OF GIFTS

The gift tax is based on the fair market value of the property transferred.[23] Accordingly, it is important to obtain appraisals for non-cash gifts. This is particularly true where a gift tax return (Form 709) is filed because the adequate disclosure rules for gifts will only be satisfied if certain conditions are met; among them is proof of the value of the gift through a bona fide appraisal. If these adequate disclosure rules are not satisfied, the statute of limitations on the gift will not begin to run, and the IRS will have the ability to challenge the value of the gift at any time.[24]

For certain business interests or undivided interests in real estate and similar assets, it is permissible to take a discount for lack of control or marketability. When doing this, it is important to have a qualified appraisal from a full time independent appraiser in order to satisfy the adequate disclosure rules and substantiate the value to the IRS.

Defined Value Clause

In *Wandry v. Commissioner*,[25] the Tax Court held that a "defined value clause" is permissible. In *Wandry*, the taxpayer made a transfer of interests in an LLC, and was concerned that upon a subsequent audit, the taxpayer would face unexpected gift tax. To address this contingency, the taxpayer provided in the transfer documentation, that the transfer being made was not of a particular percentage interest in the entity, but rather a percentage interest which equaled a particular dollar amount. The documentation further provided that if, upon audit, the taxpayer's valuation is not upheld, the increase in value would be reallocated within the capital account for the entity. The court held that it was "inconsequential that the adjustment clause reallocated membership units among petitioners and the donees rather than a charitable organization, because the reallocations do not alter the transfers."[26] The IRS has issued a notice that it will not follow the decision, so this area should be watched for developments.[27]

Valuation of Life Insurance

If a life insurance policy is transferred as a gift immediately after purchase, its value for gift tax purposes is the gross premium paid by the donor.

If a person makes a gift of a previously purchased policy, and the policy is a single-premium or paid-up policy, its gift value is the single premium that the issuing company would charge currently for a comparable contract of equal face value on the life of a person who is the insured's age at the time of the gift.

If the gift is of a policy on which further premium payments are payable, its value is the interpolated terminal reserve (roughly equivalent to the cash value) and the value of any unearned portion of the last premium.[28]

A gift of group term life is measured by the value of the unearned premium at the date of the transfer, so the ideal time to make an assignment of group term life is immediately before the next premium is due.

If the insured is now uninsurable, or exceptionally ill and old, the value of the policy may be much more than the interpolated terminal reserve value, depending on health circumstances.[29]

8.8 CRUMMEY GIFTS

Typically, a gift in trust does not become immediately available to or enjoyable by beneficiaries; it is therefore a gift of a "future" rather than a present interest. Only present interest gifts qualify for the $17,000 (in 2023) annual exclusion allowed by the gift tax law.

Crummey[30] involved an irrevocable life insurance trust in which the beneficiaries were given the right to *demand*–each year–the lesser of (a) $4,000 or (b) the amount of the donor's transfer to the trust (usually an amount approximating the life insurance premiums necessary to carry the life insurance policy which is commonly held by such a trust). It was held that the beneficiaries' legal right to the immediate use and enjoyment of the contributions to the trust made the transfers present interest gifts that qualified for the gift tax annual exclusion. This *Crummey* technique is an important estate planning tool for four main reasons:

1. It enables a donor to transfer money into a trust (to enable the trustee to pay life insurance premiums) gift tax free if there are sufficient Crummey beneficiaries.

2. The donor's potential estate tax is reduced by eliminating from the estate tax base the entire amount excluded under the annual exclusion.

3. The technique is an ideal method of saving gift tax on gifts in trust to minors and works even if:

    a. the minor beneficiary's right to demand immediate distribution of the contributed corpus is specified to be within a limited period of time, such as thirty days;

    b. the beneficiary in fact does not withdraw the amount contributed to the trust and loses the right to withdraw it after the end of the year in which the gift is made or after some set time period; or

    c. the minor beneficiary does not have a formal guardian; (the parent of the minor can act as natural guardian).

4. A gift in trust that qualifies for the annual exclusion by reason of a Crummey withdrawal power will also be shielded from the GST tax if such power holder is given a separate share of the trust, which is much more restricted than the Crummey gift for gift tax purposes. However, most dynastic type trusts with a Crummey power will not qualify for the GST annual exclusion, so consider whether it is desirable to affirmatively allocate GST exemption to such trusts if they are intended to be long-term.

The effectiveness of the Crummey gift technique and the rules regarding its use have been challenged but consistently upheld for 55 years now. The donee should have a reasonable period of time (e.g., thirty days) in which to exercise the power to withdraw the funds and sufficient notice of the existence of the creation of the power.

The Crummey trust gift technique is a very important aspect of estate planning (see Chapter 36).

8.9 OTHER WEALTH SHIFTING TECHNIQUES

Beyond what has been described above, there are many other ways to shift both wealth and income and save taxes.

1. Give a Series EE U.S. Savings Bond that will not mature until after the donee-child is age eighteen. No tax will be payable until the bond is redeemed. At that time, the gain may be taxed at the child's relatively lower tax bracket. A child who already owns Series EE bonds and is reporting each year's interest accrual as income may elect to change to deferred reporting. However, once an election is made to change

from annual reporting it may not be revoked for five years.

2. Give growth stocks (or growth stock mutual funds) that pay little or no current dividends. The child will therefore pay no tax currently and can hold the stock until reaching age twenty-four when the kiddie tax no longer applies (or earlier if no longer a full-time student). Upon a sale after reaching age twenty-four, the child will be taxed at the child's bracket.

3. Give *deep discount* tax-free municipal bonds that mature on or after the child's twenty-fourth birthday. The bond interest will be tax free to the child and the discount (face less cost basis) will be taxed to the child at the child's bracket when the bond is redeemed at maturity.

4. Employ your children. Pay them a reasonable salary for work they actually perform. Remember that the standard deduction for children who are dependents is the greater of (a) $1,250 (in 2023) or (b) *earned* income plus $400; but the standard deduction cannot exceed $13,850 for single individuals. (Numbers are as indexed for inflation)

    Regardless of how much is paid to the child, the business will have a deduction at its tax bracket (or for a pass through entity, the owners' brackets), and the amount will be taxable to the child at the child's bracket. Furthermore, the child could establish an IRA to shelter income further.

5. Consider the advantages of a *term of years* charitable remainder trust for children over age twenty-four – so the income will be taxed to the child, but the grantor will receive an immediate income tax deduction.

6. In making gifts to children, consider support obligation cases such as *Braun*[31] and *Sutliff*.[32] Parents who are able to meet the support needs of even an adult college-age child may be considered obligated to provide support under certain state decisions. In *Newburgh v. Arrigo*,[33] the court held that financially capable parents should contribute to the higher education of children over age eighteen who are qualified students. If Uniform Gifts to Minors Act (UGMA) or Uniform Transfers to Minors Act (UTMA) custodial funds or Code section 2503(c) trust funds are used to send a child to college, will the parent be taxed? Do these cases mean that the custodian or the trustee violates a fiduciary duty by using such funds to pay for a college education when it is the parent's duty (thus making such funds unavailable for the very purpose for which they were intended)? The Court in *Sutliff v. Sutliff*[34] held that the parent's obligation to support minor children is independent of the minor's assets. Therefore, the UGMA funds may not be used to fulfill a parent's obligation to support minor children where the parent has sufficient means to discharge it himself. For a child over the age of eighteen, however, the support obligation does not always extend to financing a college education, and courts have held that an adult children's education may be financed from sources other than the parent, and that UGMA assets may be used.

    Assuming the support problems addressed above are not applicable, judicious use of a Code section 2503(c) trust (but not a UGMA or UTMA account) will allow significant income shifting. The trust can accumulate income while the beneficiary is under age eighteen or in some cases twenty-four, and avoid the kiddie tax. This is so because the 2503(c) trust is designed to make distributions of principal and income to meet its funding objectives.

7. Emphasis should now be placed on *convertible planning*–the use of a *value shift* followed at the appropriate time by an *income shift*. For example, a GRAT (see Chapter 29) retains for a trust grantor the right to a fixed annuity for a specified number of years. At the end of that time, all income and principal will go to the grantor's child (who by then will be twenty-four or older). None of the principal or appreciation will be in the grantor's estate if the grantor survives the trust term. (Consider a saving clause that terminates the trust in favor of the grantor if tax law is changed to provide that a completed gift does not occur until the donor's interest is terminated.)

8. Life insurance and annuity policies that stay within statutory guidelines of life insurance should be particularly attractive assuming *loading* costs are relatively low and/or backended.

This includes universal, variable, and traditional whole life of the single-, annual-, and limited-payment types. In the case of Single Premium Whole Life (SPWL), the entire single premium paid at purchase starts earning the declared interest rate immediately.

The cost of insurance and expenses are recovered by the insurer from the difference between the declared interest rate and the rate the insurer actually earns. If the policy is surrendered, any unrecovered expenses are deducted from the policy's cash values.

The owner can obtain cash values at any time by (1) surrender (gain over cost is taxable) or (2) loan (loan interest is probably nondeductible). Interest is charged at about the same rate credited on borrowed sums and is free of current tax. Earnings compound free of current taxation.

Unlike tax-free municipal bonds, there is no market risk and SPWL is highly liquid. A parent can purchase the product on his own life, which makes college education for the children more likely, and the parent does not have to give up control or make a gift. If the policy is a modified endowment contract, there could be adverse income taxes on both policy surrenders and policy loans.

9. Concentrate on gift and estate tax saving devices such as the annual exclusion. Parents should consider giving $17,000 to $34,000 (married; as indexed for inflation in 2023) a year of non-income-producing assets to a minor's trust or UTMA account; the assets could be converted into income-producing assets slowly after the child turns age twenty-four. The fund can be self-liquidating and exhaust itself by the time the child finishes college or graduate school.

10. Consider 529 plans for younger children who are likely to go to college. Recent legislation passed by the Secure 2.0 Act (effective starting in 2024) now provides an additional incentive, allowing up to $35,000 of surplus 529 plan monies that did not get used for college to be rolled into a Roth IRA tax-free.

11. The custodial parent is often the mother, who may have less income (and therefore be in a lower tax bracket) than the father. But what about the logistics of tax return disclosure where the father is filing returns and paying tax for the children? (Suppose he does not want her to know how much he has put aside for the kids, and she does not want to reveal her income or her new husband's income. Furthermore, the filing father cannot prepare the children's returns until the mother prepares her returns.) What about multiple children from multiple marriages? Split custody? Using 529 plans and trusts avoid kiddie tax complexities.

Techniques for funding a child's education are covered in greater detail in our companion book, *The Tools & Techniques of Financial Planning*.

8.10 FREQUENTLY ASKED QUESTIONS

Question – Who must file a gift tax return and when must it be filed?

Answer – The donor must file a gift tax return (Form 709) on or before April 15th following the close of the calendar year in which a gift was made exceeding the annual exclusion or a split gift was elected. (An extension of time to file the income tax return automatically extends the time for filing gift tax returns.)

Only Connecticut has a state gift tax now.

Question – When is the best time to make a gift?

Answer – Like the answer to the question "When is the best time to plant an oak tree?" the answer to this question is, "twenty years ago." The next best time could be right now! The $17,000 (in 2023) per donee annual exclusion ($34,000 when a spouse consents) discussed above is noncumulative; either use it or lose it! So long as the gift tax lifetime exemption stays high (currently $12,920,000 in 2023 adjusted for inflation through 2025), very wealthy individuals would be wise to consider large gifts of preferably high basis assets, because a gift of highly appreciated property has a basis carryover instead of the new basis at death.

Generally, stocks and other assets that fluctuate widely in value should be given away when the market value for that asset is as low as possible.

However, in any decision making as to the giving of property, the financial security of the donor, both current and long-term, should be very carefully considered. In our estimation, very few clients can financially withstand the loss of access to capital that a large gift represents.

Question – Can gifts made to a dying spouse cut estate taxes and boost up the basis of appreciated property?

Answer – The so-called reverse gift technique is still an appealing strategy where one spouse possesses most of the family wealth and the less affluent spouse is about to die. The wealthier spouse makes a gift of low basis assets to the dying spouse. This inclusion steps up the basis of the property and better utilizes the dying spouse's unified credit (while portability obviates the need for this for estate/gift tax, the GST exemption does not port and would go wasted if not used).

Note that if a decedent acquires appreciated property by gift within one year of decedent's death and that property passes directly or indirectly back to the donor (or to donor's spouse) from the decedent, the basis of such property is not stepped up. It remains the basis in the hands of the decedent immediately before the decedent's death.[35] This may also hold true if assets pass into a trust for the donor spouse, but the mechanics of this are unclear.[36] But the technique will work if the decedent lives more than one year after the transfer or the property passes from the decedent to a child (or trust therefore) or some person other than the donor or the donor's spouse.

Question – Does the purchase of property in joint names create a taxable gift?

Answer – It depends on the type of property and also the parties involved. Generally, when property is purchased with the funds of one party and the property is titled jointly, a completed gift is made. The most notable exceptions to this are the titling of property jointly between husband and wife (which because of the unlimited marital deduction is not a taxable event unless one of the spouses is not a U.S. citizen), titling of joint bank accounts and United States Savings Bonds. Any property made joint with another, and if subject to reacquisition by the donor without the permission of the donee, is not a completed gift. In the case of a joint bank account or United States Savings Bonds, a completed gift does not occur until the noncontributing joint owner draws upon the bank account or surrenders part of the bond for cash.[37]

Question – If property is sold, are there gift tax consequences?

Answer – It depends. If the property was sold for less than adequate and full consideration, there is a gift to the extent that the value of the property exceeds the value of the consideration received. An arm's length transaction among nonfamily members is generally considered to be an exchange for adequate and full consideration. An intra family exchange may not be considered arm's length and could result in a partial gift if not made for adequate and full consideration.

A bargain sale is treated as, in part, a sale and, in part, a gift. The transferee's basis in the property is equal to the sum of:

1. the greater of:

   a. the amount paid by the transferee for the property; or

   b. the transferor's adjusted basis in the property at the time of the transfer; and

2. the amount of any increase in basis for gift tax paid (see above).

However, for purpose of determining loss, the basis of the transferee cannot exceed the fair market value of the property at the time of the transfer.[21]

CHAPTER ENDNOTES

1. Treas. Reg. §25.2511-1(a); I.R.C. §7872(f)(3).
2. See the Uniform Voidable Transactions Act (UVTA), the recent update of the more common Uniform Fraudulent Transfer Act (UFTA). A handful of states still use a less common, older version of these laws called the Uniform Fraudulent Conveyances Act (UFCA).
3. I.R.C. §1.
4. Rev. Rul. 2004-64.

5. Treas. Reg. §25.2511-1(c).
6. Treas. Reg. §25.2511-1(c).
7. Treas. Reg. §25.2511-2(b).
8. I.R.C. §2503(b).
9. I.R.C. §2513.
10. I.R.C. §2503(b).
11. Treas. Reg. §25.2503-3.
12. See the cases where the annual exclusion was denied for such gifts in *Hackl v. Commissioner*, 335 F.3d 664 (7th Cir. 2003), aff'g 118 T.C. 279 (2002); *Price v. Commissioner*, T.C. Memo. 2010-2 (Jan. 4, 2010); *Fisher v. United States*, 105 AFTR 2d. 2010-1347 (S.D. Ind. Mar. 11, 2010).
13. I.R.C. §2503(e).
14. Treas. Reg. §25.2513-1.
15. Rev. Rul. 75-72.
16. See Rev. Rul. 75-72, 1975-1 CB 310, for examples of how to compute the net gift. *Diedrich v. Comm'r*, 457 U.S. 191, 82-1 USTC ¶9419, 50 AFTR2d 82-5054 (1982), aff'g 643 F.2d 499, 81-1 USTC ¶9249, 47 AFTR2d 81-977 (8th Cir. 1981), rev'g TC Memo 1979-441.
17. I.R.C. §2035(b).
18. *Steinberg v. Comm'r*, 145 T.C. No. 7 (2015). See Michael S. Arlein and William H. Frazier. "The Net, Net Gift." *Trusts & Estates* (Aug. 2008).
19. I.R.C. §2523.
20. Technically, the tax reform bill formerly referred to as the Tax Cuts and Jobs Act was passed into law with the formal title of "H.R.1 - An Act to provide for reconciliation pursuant to titles II and V of the concurrent resolution on the budget for fiscal year 2018." (Public Law 115-97). See https://www.congress.gov/bill/115th-congress/house-bill/1.
21. However, in Louisiana, a spouse can unilaterally reserve income from separate property as separate.
22. IR Manual §25.18.1.2.24 (02-15-2005), Tracing.
23. I.R.C. §2512; Treas. Reg. §25.2512-1.
24. I.R.C. §6501(c)(9).
25. *Wandry v. Comm'r*, 2012 T.C. Memo 088.
26. See LISI Estate Planning Newsletters Nos. 1941, 1945 and 1946 for a discussion of the various cases of precedential value at www.leimbergservices.com.
27. Action on Decision 2012-004, 2012-46 IRB A.
28. Treas. Reg. §25.2512-6.
29. See Rev. Proc. 2005-25.
30. *Crummey v. Comm'r*, 397 F.2d 82 (9th Cir. 1968).
31. *Braun v. Comm'r*, TC Memo 1984-285.
32. *Sutliff v. Sutliff*, 515 Pa. 393, 528 A.2d 1318 (1987). Moreover, a reading of the Superior Court opinion includes reference to consistency among many states with regard to these propositions. *Sutliff v. Sutliff*, 339 Pa. Super 523, 489 A.2d 764 (1985). See also *Shinkoskey v. Shinkoskey*, 2001 Utah App. 44, 19 P.3d 1005 (2001) and Wilson v. Wilson, 37 Kan. App.2d 564, 154 P.3d 1136 (2007) which held that there are no provisions in the Kansas UTMA prohibiting a parent custodian from using custodial property to pay expenses for a minor's benefit even when the expenses are for necessities a parent is generally obligated to provide. It also noted that the UTMA places two restrictions on disposal of UTMA property, i.e. the prudent person standard, and expenditure for the use and benefit of the minor). Accordingly, the availability of those funds to a parent is dependent on state law.
33. *Newburgh v. Arrigo*, 88 N.J. 529, 443 A.2d 1031 (1982).
34. *Sutliff v. Sutliff*, 515 Pa. 393, 528 A.2d 1318 (1987).
35. I.R.C. §1014(e).
36. I.R.C. §1014(e)(2)(B).
37. Treas. Reg. §25.2511-1(h)(4).

UNIFORM GIFTS/ TRANSFERS TO MINORS ACTS

CHAPTER 9

9.1 INTRODUCTION

The Uniform Gifts to Minors Act (UGMA) provides that during lifetime, an adult may make a gift of certain types of property, such as securities, money, or a life insurance (or annuity) contract, to a minor by (depending upon the property) registering the property in the name of, or delivering it to, a custodian for the minor. The custodian may be the donor (except in the case of unregistered securities), another adult person, or a trust company. Many states also allow gifts of real property, personal property, and intangibles, and a few states permit transfers to custodians from other sources, such as trusts and estates, as well as lifetime gifts.

The Uniform Transfers to Minors Act (UTMA) allows any kind of property, real or personal, tangible or intangible, to be the subject of a custodial gift. The UTMA also permits transfers from trusts, estates, guardianships, and from other third parties indebted to a minor who does not have a conservator. According to the Uniform Law Commission, all states have enacted the much more flexible UTMA.[1]

Under both the UGMA and the UTMA, the minor immediately acquires both legal and equitable title to the subject matter of the gift held by the custodian.

Custodial gifts reduce or avoid many of the problems and expenses of outright gifts, trusts, or guardianship arrangements for minors.

9.2 WHEN IS USE OF SUCH A DEVICE INDICATED?

1. When a person would like to give money or property for a minor's benefit without giving it to the minor outright and without having to incur the expense of drafting a trust or having a guardian of the minor's estate appointed.

2. When a person would like to shift some of the income tax burden from the donor's high tax bracket to a minor child's lower bracket (to the extent the kiddie tax does not apply. See Chapter 8).

3. When the donor wishes to use his or her gift tax annual exclusion (or twice the annual exclusion if the gift is split between spouses).

4. When a parent would like to reduce the parent's potential estate tax burden by shifting future appreciation in the value of an asset to a minor.

5. Where the donor does not object to the donee's receiving the property outright upon reaching the age specified in the relevant statute – generally eighteen or twenty-one, depending on state law and often on the nature of the transaction creating the custodianship. (In several states, the age for termination of at least certain custodianships can, within limits, be changed, often to age 25.)

6. When someone wants to leave a bequest outright at death via will or POD/TOD or other beneficiary designation to a young beneficiary, including as a beneficiary of retirement accounts and annuities. Naming a UTMA/UGMA beneficiary will avoid the requirement to appoint a guardian of the minor's estate to manage the property (if the beneficiary is under age eighteen). Most states require court oversight of any substantial inheritance, although some will allow a parent to take custody of relatively small inheritances without a guardianship under certain circumstances (e.g., usually $10,000 or less). A UTMA

custodian may typically serve until the minor reaches age twenty-one ("minor" being defined for purposes of the Act as under age twenty-one). Furthermore, an increasing number of states permit a bequest passing at death to continue to be held by a custodian in UTMA form until age twenty-five rather than age twenty-one (with at least one state allowing UTMA accounts to last until age 30).[2]

7. An alternative for some situations is a transfer to a Section 529 plan which provides taxpayers a flexible vehicle to save for qualified higher education expenses and more donor control. Contributions to these accounts constitute a gift of a present interest so that the taxpayers can utilize the gift tax annual exclusion even if the donor or someone other than the beneficiary is the owner of the account. Additionally, transfers in one year up to five times the annual exclusion amount (for 2023, up to 5 x $17,000 or $85,000) may be recognized over a five-year period. However, in order to claim this five year averaging benefit, a gift tax return must be filed.[3] Be careful, however, as designating the minor child an *owner* still presents the same problem as any outright gift, and the minor child could withdraw the entire plan at age eighteen. In most cases, the donor should remain owner and name a contingent owner other than the intended beneficiary (perhaps the contingent owner should be a spouse, or perhaps a child who is the parent a grandchild/beneficiary). Continued ownership and control (unlike other assets) does not cause estate inclusion or a loss of asset protection. A UTMA custodian may be an appropriate contingent owner of a 529 plan account in some cases.

9.3 WHAT ARE THE REQUIREMENTS?

1. Property must be transferred to a custodian who holds it as custodian for the minor under the relevant state's Gifts or Transfers to Minors Act.[4]

2. If there are two or more children to whom a parent wishes to make gifts, an account must be established for each child.[5]

3. Once made, a custodial gift is irrevocable.[6]

4. The property must be distributed to the child when the child reaches the age specified in the relevant statute – generally eighteen or twenty-one, and in some cases twenty-five.[7] (In several states, the age for termination of at least certain custodianships can, within limits, be changed.) Other options to hold funds for a minor may include a 2503(b) or (c) trust. See Chapter 28.

Example. Tony Arcangelo transfers his ten shares of IBM stock to Mrs. Arcangelo as custodian for their son, Fred, by having the stock registered as follows: "Ginny Arcangelo as custodian for Fred Arcangelo under the *Pennsylvania* Uniform Transfers to Minors Act." Such a gift is a present interest gift and would therefore qualify for the gift tax annual exclusion. The future appreciation in the value of the stock, the future dividends earned by the stock, as well as the original gift value of the stock would be out of Mr. Arcangelo's estate. Any dividend income or capital gains from sale of the stock would be taxed to Fred. (However, see "Tax Implications" below.)

9.4 TAX IMPLICATIONS

1. Income from any custodial property will be taxed to the minor whether distributed or not, except to the extent it is used to discharge a legal obligation of some other person. Where income produced by a custodial gift relieves an individual such as a parent of a legal obligation, the income is taxed to that person.[8] A parent's duty to support minor children varies among the states.

If the minor is under age eighteen or is a full-time student up to age twenty-three, all unearned income in excess of $2,100 (in 2020), although it will be taxed to the minor, will generally be taxed at the parents' tax bracket in 2020. However, as a result of recent tax reform, starting in 2021 this will be taxed under the compressed tax rates applicable to trusts and estates regardless of what the parents' tax brackets may be.[9] The first $1,050 of a child's unearned income will bear no tax because of the child's standard deduction. The next $1,050 will be taxed to the child at the child's tax bracket, and any excess will be taxed to the child at the parents' bracket (or starting in 2018 through 2025, using estate/non-grantor trust brackets). For a child twenty-four and over, all unearned income will be taxed to the child at the child's appropriate bracket. The kiddie tax can be avoided if a 529 plan is used instead.

2. The gift is one of a present interest and usually qualifies for the gift tax annual exclusion.[10] However, note that gifts of LLC/LP interests to a UTMA custodian may be subject to additional scrutiny and there are cases that have denied the annual exclusion for such gifts on the theory that the donee did not receive a substantial present interest due to various restrictions in the agreement.[11] The exclusion will be allowed even though custodial property will not be distributed to the donee until age eighteen or twenty-one (depending on the state).[12] It seems, though, that extending the custodianship beyond the donee's age twenty-one (which some states permit) may disqualify the gift for the annual exclusion.[13]

   Note that there is a growing trend in state divorce courts to assume that a financially well-off parent has a legal duty to send children to college, even if they are, under state law, adults. It is suggested that custodial income be accumulated until the child reaches college age. Income can then be paid out, semester by semester, in a series of unconditional checks. The child should deposit those checks in the child's own account and use the funds as needed. It may be that a trust, 529 plan, or a state sponsored tuition program may be better for these purposes.

3. The value of property transferred will generally be included in the estate of a donee. So if the donee dies, assets in the custodial account will be includable in the donee's estate.

4. Custodial property will be included in the estate of the donor if the donor serves as custodian and dies while serving in that capacity. Likewise, if the donor becomes successor custodian and then dies, the value of the property transferred will be includable in the donor's estate.[14] Further, the value of property, the income of which is used to satisfy a donor-parent's support obligations, could be included in the donor-parent's estate. A parent's duty to support minor children varies among the states. For donors with non-taxable estates, serving as custodian for transferred funds may actually provide a step up in basis without any estate tax cost (assuming the assets appreciate in value). However, if there is a chance that a donor would have a taxable estate (potentially including state estate/inheritance tax), the donor should name a different custodian due to the risk of estate tax inclusion.

5. Similar to the admonition above about potential estate tax inclusion when a donor serves as custodian, there may also be adverse asset protection effects. A donor serving as custodian is more likely to be pierced as a sham or alter ego of the donor.[15]

6. State gift taxes must be considered. However, as of 2023, only Connecticut has a state gift tax.

9.5 ISSUES IN COMMUNITY PROPERTY STATES

Where community property is the subject of a gift under the Uniform Gifts to Minors Act, each spouse is considered to be the donor as to one-half the value of the property given. Thus, in the example given above, if the Arcangelos lived in a community property state, Mrs. Arcangelo would not be a good choice for custodian, because if she were to die, one-half of the gift made to Fred from their community property would be included in her estate on the basis of the rules relating to powers to alter, amend, revoke, and terminate trusts.

The same problems, as discussed in Chapter 33, may arise if one spouse gives community property without the written consent of the nondonor spouse.

Typically, in community property states, a brother or sister of one of the parents may be a good choice for custodian.

9.6 FREQUENTLY ASKED QUESTIONS

Question – What types of property can be transferred to a custodian for the benefit of a minor?

Answer – In the few states that have retained the UGMA, at least money, securities (for example, stocks, bonds, evidence of indebtedness, certificates of interest or participation in an oil, gas, or mining title or lease), certain life or endowment insurance policies, and certain annuity contracts may be the subject of a custodial gift (though be aware that gifts of deferred annuities may trigger income tax). The general intention of the UTMA, on the other hand, is to allow custodial transfers of *any* interest in any kind of property from almost any source.[16] Because the laws of different states vary, it is important to check your own state's laws.

Question – Who may be a custodian?

Answer – Generally, the original custodian may be (depending on the transaction) the donor, an adult other than the donor (even someone age 18 for someone age 20 in theory), a trust company, or a bank with trust powers.[17] Because eligibility to serve as custodian is sometimes dependent upon the nature of the transaction creating the custodial property, and because the states' laws vary, it is important to check your state's statute.

Question – What use may be made of custodial property?

Answer – Under the UGMA, the custodian may use the custodial property for the support, maintenance, education, and benefit of the minor to the extent that the custodian in the custodian's discretion deems suitable and proper.

Under Section 14 of the UTMA, custodial property may be expended for the use and benefit of the minor, a more expansive use of custodial property than under the UGMA.

Question – May there be one custodial account for two or more minors?

Answer – No, a separate custodial account must be established for each beneficiary. Only one custodian can be appointed for each account.[18] However, any number of separate gifts may be made.

Question – Who receives the custodial property if a minor dies?

Answer – Custodial property passes to the administrator or executor of the minor's estate.[19]

Question – Where a life insurance policy on a minor's life is placed in a custodianship account, may the custodian be the beneficiary?

Answer – Under the UGMA, no. The beneficiary may be, depending upon the state, the minor, a member of the minor's family, or the minor's estate.[20] The situation under the UTMA is less clear. Generally a custodian can pay premiums on a custodial life insurance policy on the life of the minor only if the minor or the minor's estate is the sole beneficiary.[21] But some UTMA states let the custodian pay premiums on a custodial policy on the life of the minor even if the custodian is the beneficiary.[22] Otherwise the matter is unclear. Consult your state's statute.

Question – If a custodian dies before the minor is legally an adult, how is a successor custodian appointed?

Answer – Generally, if a custodian has designated a successor, that designee becomes the custodian. The revised UGMA seems to say that if the custodian has not picked a successor, an adult member of the minor's family, the minor's guardian, or a trust company will be appointed; if there is no guardian and the minor is at least fourteen, the minor can pick the successor – but if the minor does not pick a successor, the court (upon petition) will designate a successor; if the minor is not yet fourteen, the court (upon petition) will choose the successor.

Under the UTMA, if the custodian has not picked a successor, the minor can pick the successor if the minor is at least fourteen; if the minor does not pick a successor or is less than fourteen, the minor's guardian will be appointed; if there is no guardian, the court (upon petition) will select a successor.[23] But the relevant state law must be checked.

Question – Must the custodian under the Uniform Gifts to Minors Act file an income tax return?

Answer – No fiduciary return is required by the custodian but depending on the level of income a child (or parent/guardian) may have to file a Form 1040 to report the income. If the kiddie tax applies, see IRS Form 8615 to be filed with the child's tax return. Sometimes the parent may elect to report unearned income of the child on the parent's tax return – see IRS Form 8814 for this option. This factor, as well as the fact that no trust agreement is required, makes the custodianship perhaps the least expensive and administratively the simplest method of transferring property to a minor.

Question – If an individual (an adult) purchases a life insurance policy on the adult's life, can the adult name the custodian of a minor as beneficiary?

Answer – Yes. Under the UTMA, the owner of a life insurance policy or annuity contract can name the custodian of a minor as beneficiary.[24] Some states' versions of the UGMA permit designating the custodian as beneficiary on at least some insurance policies and annuity contracts. This provides a means for a child to be a beneficiary without appointing a guardian or creating a trust for the minor. State laws must be checked.

Question – Under either the UGMA or UTMA, can a custodian invest a minor's funds in life insurance?

Answer – Virtually all states that have a version of the UGMA or of the UTMA allow a donor to make custodial gifts of life insurance. However, not all states with versions of the UGMA specifically authorize the custodian to invest a minor's funds in life insurance. Particular state statutes must be checked.

Under the UTMA, the custodian can invest a minor's funds in life insurance. The custodian may invest in life insurance or endowment policies on:

(1) The life of the minor so long as the minor or the minor's estate is the sole beneficiary

(2) The life of another person in whom the minor has an insurable interest so long as the minor, the minor's estate, or the custodian is the irrevocable beneficiary.[25]

Question – Can someone name a UTMA custodian as beneficiary of an IRA, 401(k) or other retirement plan?

Answer – Yes, and this is an excellent option for smaller accounts where a trust may not be warranted. However, it is best to contact the IRA trustee/custodian or plan administrator to confirm that they permit this.

Question – Can a donor name themselves or gift to a UTMA account where the donor themselves is custodian?

Answer – Yes, but it's not always advisable. If the donor/custodian dies while still acting as custodian, the continued control of the funds by the decedent/custodian will cause inclusion of the UTMA funds in the estate of the donor. For 99% of the population that does not have a taxable estate, this may be a good result, due to the assets receiving a new date of death basis under Code Section 1014 without causing estate tax. However, this would obviously be a disastrous result if the decedent/custodian had a taxable estate, as it would cause up to 40% estate tax (and potentially a 40% GST tax if the minor is a skip person such as a grandchild). Those who have taxable estates who gift into UTMA accounts should avoid being custodian of such accounts, and should probably avoid naming their spouse as well (since gifts are often made from joint accounts).

CHAPTER ENDNOTES

1. See https://www.uniformlaws.org/committees/community-home?CommunityKey=4b0fd839-f40d-4021-af03-406e499ca67c.
2. See, e.g., Ohio R.C. §5814.01 et seq., specifically Ohio R.C. §5814.09. Florida, Virginia, Washington, Alaska, Ohio, Oregon, Pennsylvania and Tennessee have their version of the UTMA to permit age of majority (how long the UTMA can last) to be from age 21 to 25 (California is age 18 to 25). Wyoming has the oldest age range of any state, permitting the account termination age to be from 21 all the way up to age 30. See Wyo. Stat. § 34-13-138.
3. See I.R.C. §529(c)(2)(B).
4. E.g., Calif. Prob. Code §3909 (Cal. UTMA).
5. E.g., Calif. Prob. Code §3910.
6. E.g., Calif. Prob. Code §3911(b).
7. E.g., Calif. Prob. Code §§3920, 3920.5., and 20 Pa. C.S.A. §5321.
8. Rev. Rul. 59-357, 1959-2 CB 212; see also *Anastasio v. Comm'r*, 67 TC 814 (1977) (New York UGMA), aff'd without published opinion, 573 F.2d 1287 (2d Cir. 1978).
9. See I.R.C. §1(g) for kiddie tax and §1(j)(4) for modification for tax years 2018-2025.
10. Rev. Rul. 59-357, 1959-2 CB 212.
11. See *Hackl v. Commissioner*, 335 F.3d 664 (7th Cir. 2003), aff'g 118 T.C. 279 (2002); *Price v. Commissioner*, T.C. Memo. 2010-2 (Jan. 4, 2010); *Fisher v. United States*, 105 AFTR 2d. 2010-1347 (S.D. Ind. Mar. 11, 2010).
12. Rev. Rul. 73-287, 1973-2 CB 321.
13. See, e.g., *id.* (gifts terminating at age eighteen qualify for the annual exclusion because I.R.C. §2503(c) requires that property pass to the donee by at least age twenty-one). For this reason, some states that permit custodianship to age 25 limit it to testamentary rather than intervivos gifts.
14. Rev. Rul. 59-357, 1959-2 CB 212; Rev. Rul. 70-348, 1970-2 CB 193; *Est. of Prudowsky*, 55 TC 890 (1971), aff'd, 465 F.2d. 62 (7th Cir. 1972).
15. See, e.g., *State v. Keith*, 81 Ohio App. 3d 192, 610 N.E.2d 1017 (1991).
16. See, e.g., the Prefatory Note to the UTMA, 8B U.L.A. 497, 499 (West 1993); UTMA §1(6) and the comment thereto, 8B U.L.A. 497, 507-508 (West 1993).
17. E.g., Calif. Prob. Code §3909.
18. E.g., Calif. Prob. Code §3910.
19. E.g., Calif. Prob. Code §3920.
20. E.g., Mich. Comp. Laws Ann. §554.454(10).
21. UTMA §12(c), 8B U.L.A. 497, 536 (West 1993).
22. See, e.g., N.C. Gen. Stat. §33A-12(c).
23. See UGMA (1966) §7, 8A U.L.A. 367, 404-405 (West 1993); UTMA §18, 8B U.L.A. 497, 548-549 (West 1993).
24. See UTMA §§3, 9(a)(4), 8B U.L.A. 497, 515, 525 (West 1993).
25. UTMA §12(c), 8B U.L.A. 497, 536 (West 1993).

WILLS

CHAPTER 10

10.1 INTRODUCTION

A will is a written document which states an individual's wishes as to how property is to be disposed of at death. A will therefore, specifies "who gets what" – and in some cases – "who does not". A will is completely revocable during the individual's lifetime, but becomes irrevocable at the moment of death. Its terms are applied to whatever the situation, as it exists, at that time. Therefore, it is important to make sure that the will reflects the individual's most current objectives and names the beneficiaries (and back-ups) the client desires.

A trend in recent years in many states is to relax the strict requirements of wills, including to recognize electronic wills created on a tablet, computer or smartphone. For example, the Uniform Electronic Wills Act, as of 2023, has been passed in Colorado, the District of Columbia, Idaho, North Dakota, the US Virgin Islands, Utah and Washington, with Minnesota passing a similar act as well. Another trend in drafting is for wills to address whether or not the personal representative (executor) should have access to various digital assets of the decedent, which is addressed in the Revised Uniform Digital Assets Act (RUFADAA) which has been passed in the vast majority of states now.

10.2 WHEN IS USE OF SUCH A DEVICE INDICATED?

1. The most important reason for creating a will is to provide the testator (in some jurisdictions, "testatrix" is the feminine form; either form means the one who makes or executes the "will and testament") with an opportunity to control the passing of property and avoid "intestacy." Without a will, the decedent's assets will pass by the laws of intestate succession of the state in which the decedent is domiciled or in some cases where the property is located.

2. As described above, without a valid will, the decedent's property passes to relatives as provided by statute (or, if the decedent had no close relatives, it may even "escheat", or pass to the state government). By making a will, a person can pass property in a different manner than that provided by statute. With a will, property generally can be left to one or more relatives, of any degree, or even unrelated friends or charities to the exclusion of others. However, many states have laws that provide spousal rights through "elective shares" that allow the surviving spouse and/or children to take *some* share of the estate – *regardless* of what the will provides. Such laws grew out of a perceived need for the state to establish laws to protect spouses and children.

3. In a will, the testator can name the "personal representative" of the estate. A personal representative is also referred to as an "executor". A person or institution can be named to act as executor (in some states, "executrix" is still used as a feminine form) and be appointed to carry out the directions in the will and to dispose of the property according to the testamentary provisions.

The named personal representative may often be a relative or close friend. But, if the estate is large or complicated, the testator should consider appointing either a professional or an institution accustomed to dealing with both the assets and the sometimes complicated rules of probate either as sole or co-personal representative.

The will may provide that the executor need not be bonded, which can save money for the estate, but which costs the beneficiaries some degree of protection. If there is no valid will or if no executor is named or if the named executor for any reason fails to qualify or ceases to act, the court will appoint an "administrator" (in some states, "administratrix" is used as a feminine form) to administer the estate. The duties are essentially the same, but most state laws will require an administrator other than a bank to post bond to protect the beneficiaries.

4. A will can set out the terms of a trust in which the named trustee can manage assets on behalf of the beneficiaries for many years after the death of the testator. This may be especially appropriate in order to manage assets over a long time for the benefit of the testator's minor children. Such a trust is referred to as a "testamentary" trust since it is created through the decedent's last will and testament. The trust starts to exist at the probate of the will. This is slightly different from "pouring over" into a pre-existing revocable living trust. A revocable living trust may have a different situs (or may change situs) and avoid continuing jurisdiction by the local probate court and burdensome continual filings, whereas a testamentary trust may still retain such ties, which may be costly from both a compliance and sometimes a state income tax perspective.

   The terms of a testamentary trust are very important. Sometimes people have such trusts terminate when a child reaches age eighteen or twenty-one. Such an early lump sum distribution often results in the child's potentially squandering their inheritance. This result occurs because the child receives the assets at an age before the child has had the experience of handling large sums of money or other assets. It is important to consider the maturity levels of the beneficiaries when considering at what ages distributions from the trusts should occur. Quite often, distributions are spread out over significant periods of time or ages of the beneficiaries to give them time to learn how to handle wealth and gain economic experience and wisdom. However, it should be noted and impressed upon clients that trusts can be made very flexible and that assets usually are worth more held in trust rather than outright because of the creditor protection that the trust provides.

5. When there are minor children, the will can nominate a guardian of both the "person" and the "estate" of each child. A "guardian of the person" generally provides for the custody and care of the child. A "guardian of the estate" manages the child's assets. State laws generally require a court to give significant weight to such a nomination by a parent who has custody of a child. Without such a provision, the court names the guardian upon the death of the parent(s) based on available information and often depending on who volunteers. A testator can leave assets to a UTMA custodian for a child until the maximum age under the state statute (which is often age 21 but may be 25 or even 30).

6. A will allows the testator to make alternative provisions in case some of the heirs predecease the testator. For instance, if a child dies, the testator may want to leave that share to the child's siblings, or perhaps to the child's issue.

7. Some assets are not affected by the provisions in a will. For example, property held in joint tenancy or tenancy by the entirety pass by right of survivorship to the remaining joint tenant(s). Proceeds of life insurance, annuities, IRAs, and certain other assets pass by contract automatically according to their contractual terms to the person(s) named in beneficiary designations (unless, of course, none is named by the owner or by default in the contract).

8. Even where an individual has a living trust that holds most of the individual's assets in order to avoid probate, it is still very important to have a will which "pours over" into the previously established trust any assets that were not already transferred to the trust. Many times, the client will have failed to transfer significant assets to the trust and such a pour-over provision will be crucial to the success of the client's objectives.

9. The majority of states provide that if a child is born after the will is executed but is not named in a will that such a person is deemed to be a "pretermitted heir." Regardless of what the will says, in those states, such person will take the share of the estate that would be given to that person under the state's rules of intestacy. Thus, it is wise to mention all such persons in the will – especially if the client intends *not* to leave assets to them. Doing so helps to prevent such persons from claiming they are pretermitted heirs.

10. A will affords the testator the opportunity to minimize estate taxes (discussed below) and other transfer costs and provide who is to bear the burden of such costs.

11. A will can waive the requirement to post bond. If the personal representative is trustworthy, this can save cost and hassle. Many states will require a bond be posted for intestate estates unless the administrator is a regulated bank or trust company.

12. A will can also empower the personal representative to sell real estate without additional hearings and appraisals, which may also save costs for an estate.

10.3 INTESTATE SUCCESSION

When a decedent passes without a will, the property passes to the decedent's heirs via the rules of *intestate succession*. These rules are established by state law, but are generally similar from state to state.

The goal of intestate succession laws is to distribute the decedent's property as the government believes the decedent would have wanted had a will been executed. In some respects, it is a default will provided by the state for those who have none. The question is whether the client controls the disposition or permits probate assets to pass according to the state's intestacy laws.

Typically, in the event of intestacy, the rules for distribution of separate property are as follows:

A. Should the decedent die intestate with a spouse but no children, the spouse takes the entire estate.

B. If a spouse and children survive, each takes some portion of the estate.

C. If only the decedent's children survive, they take the entire estate.

D. If no spouse or children survive, the estate goes to the decedent's parents, and if they do not survive, then to the decedent's siblings or their heirs.

E. The next level of intestate takers is the decedent's grandparents and their heirs (the aunts, uncles, and cousins of decedent).

F. If none of the decedent's heirs survive, the next takers are the issue of the decedent's predeceased spouse.

G. If none of the above survive, the estate goes to the next of kin.

H. The state is the final taker (this rare occurrence is called an "escheat").

While the rules above are typical, the laws in a particular state may have some variation. The above rules generally apply in the nine community property states (Alaska, Arizona, California, Idaho, Louisiana, Nevada, New Mexico, South Dakota, Tennessee, Texas, Washington, and Wisconsin) as to separate property; but if the property is held as community property, even where there are children, all community property goes to the surviving spouse in the absence of a will.

Louisiana has unique rules that limit what a decedent may do with property, in some circumstances forcing the transfer of property to a certain person (known as "forced heirs") regardless of the terms of the will. Many jurisdictions outside of the United States have some kind of forced heirship as well.

Real property located in a particular state is generally subject to the rules of that state. Therefore, for example, a will dealing with oil interests or other interests in land located in Louisiana is subject to the laws of Louisiana, even though the testator is a domiciliary of New Jersey. Furthermore, absent planning, it may be necessary to have a probate – not only in the domiciliary state – but also an "ancillary" administration because of the land in a different state. This costly and aggravating procedure can be avoided through several different planning techniques that – in essence – convert the real estate to personal property (e.g., placing the property in an LLC), or using a transfer on death deed or a trust.

10.4 WHAT ARE THE REQUIREMENTS FOR A WILL?

1. The general rule is that any person eighteen or older, and who is of sound mind may make a will.[1] While this is the general rule, a few states have a different minimum age requirement.

2. The law ordinarily requires less mental capacity to make a will than to make a contract. An individual can make a will even if sick, elderly, weak, or of low mental capacity. A person can be declared legally incompetent to manage his or her affairs and *still* have sufficient capacity to execute a will. In general, in order to have capacity to make a will, most states require only that the testator know (1) the nature and extent of his property and (2) the natural objects of his bounty.

3. Except in states where a holographic will (one written entirely in the testator's handwriting) or an oral (nuncupative) will is allowed, wills must meet certain legal requirements. Typically, an attested will must be in writing, signed by the testator (or in the testator's name by some other person in the testator's presence and at his direction), and must be witnessed by at least two persons.[2] (Some states still require three witnesses while at least one, Pennsylvania, requires no witnesses at the time the will is signed.)

4. Approximately half of the states recognize a holographic or handwritten will.[3] A will which is not effective under other provisions may be effective as a holographic will, whether or not witnessed, if it is dated and the signature and the material provisions are in the handwriting of the testator.[4] In some states, having printed or typed material on the holographic will can invalidate it.

5. Less than half of the states recognize oral (nuncupative) wills. This is a will declared or dictated by the testator during the last illness, before a sufficient number of witnesses, and later reduced to writing. In some states such wills are valid only under certain circumstances. For instance, they may be valid only to transfer a limited amount of personal property.[5]

6. Technology is catching up with the law of wills. Several states have passed legislation that authorize electronic wills, e.g., a will on a cell phone. Because developments in this nascent area of law are occurring rapidly, the estate planner should stay tuned for further developments. The Uniform Law Commission has drafted proposed legislation on electronic wills, which has, as of 2023, already been enacted in seven jurisdictions, with legislation introduced in three more.[6]

10.5 HOW DOES ONE DECIDE THE TERMS OF A WILL?

Example. Jack Dickson is preparing for his retirement and has decided to "get his affairs in order." He knows that without a will, his wife Nancy and his children will each receive a portion of his estate. Since Jack's wife, Nancy, is a wealthy woman in her own right, as the recipient of the estate of her parents, Jack would rather leave his assets to the children. The children are not experienced in dealing with assets, while Nancy wife deals well with assets.

Jack and Nancy have three children. The youngest has been estranged from the family for many years. Jack makes a will leaving all of his assets in a trust for the benefit of his two other children, one-half to each. He names his eldest child as executor of the estate and the second child as the successor executor. Nancy was named as the trustee of the trust for the two older children.

Jack realizes that certain of his assets, his life insurance and his IRA account, will not pass by his will. He has named his two eldest children as equal beneficiaries of those assets. To avoid his wife and estranged child taking intestate shares as pretermitted heirs, his will names them but leaves nothing to them. However, even by doing this, a spouse is generally entitled to a share of the decedent's assets unless there was a marital agreement. Therefore, while you can attempt to exclude your spouse from receiving anything, the spouse has the right to claim a portion of the assets anyway (depending on the state and type of assets). However, the spouse must make an affirmative action to claim these assets. The rules for doing this are established by each state.

Jack has made his decisions on the basis of need and degree of positive feelings he has for each beneficiary. His exclusion of his wife does not indicate a lack of feeling for her (a fact he may wish to communicate in the will) but a recognition that she does not need his assets for her security.

By leaving the funds for the two older children in trust with his wife as trustee, he has provided good management to protect the trust assets for the children. The trust terms also provide Jack's wife with latitude as to the distribution of the assets as between the children and how and when they will receive the assets. Thus, Jack has not deprived his wife of some continuing parental control. However, many family dynamics may call for an independent corporate trustee or co-trustee.

Although some people would "always leave things equally to the children," Jack has recognized the estrangement of the one child and has made the difficult but perhaps logical decision to leave the assets to the children who are still close to the family. In making such decisions, there is simply no "right way" that can always be applied to distributing assets; the decisions must be made on the basis of what is important to each testator and the circumstances of the persons and organizations he or she wishes to benefit.

10.6 HOW IS A WILL CHANGED OR REVOKED?

A will may be changed by writing a separate document which is not intended to be a new will but which is meant to change a provision of an existing will. Such a document is called a "codicil."

A new will, to the extent that it does not state that it is revoking all prior wills, may often merely change the terms of an existing will. In other words, the unrevoked prior will(s) remain valid to the extent not inconsistent with a later will. For this reason, it is good practice to make clear in a will that it is intended to revoke all prior wills, if that is the testator's goal.

Generally, a codicil must be signed with the same formalities as a will in order to be valid. As a general rule, codicils should be avoided (especially extensive ones), in favor of simply redoing the entire will. Word processing makes it easy to reproduce a will in its entirety with minor changes. If one gets into the codicil habit, there are extra documents to keep up with. What happens, for example, if a testator made ten codicils to his will, but at the time of his death, codicil number four was missing? One can easily avoid this problem by simply reproducing the entire will as revised in the latest iteration.

Revocation of a will also may occur by destroying a will or defacing it with the intent to revoke. Sometimes the issue of the testator's intent (e.g., if the will is burned together with other papers or trash, was there an intention to revoke the will?) will result in expensive litigation. A specific statement of revocation in a new will (or writing "Revoked" across an old will and signing and dating that revocation) often may achieve the testator's goals more effectively.

Certain circumstances will cause the revocation of a will (or at least a portion of it) without any action on the part of the testator. Examples of this include revocation by marriage and revocation by divorce. Particular state law must be checked.

10.7 TAX IMPLICATIONS

Estate (Death) Tax

At death, federal estate taxes are imposed on property that is transferred to the beneficiaries. However, each U.S. resident has a unified credit that eliminates the estate tax on the first $12,920,000 in 2023 (the amount of this exemption is adjusted annually for inflation through 2025, with a potential reversion to $5 million adjusted for inflation in 2026 and beyond if the law does not change).

In a handful of states, a death tax (estate or inheritance) may be due even though there is no federal estate tax to pay. It is important to estimate the level of state death tax payable by a client's estate, since even if there is no federal estate tax, the state death tax alone can cause a serious cash liquidity drain. The personal representative or administrator may be personally liable if he or she pays beneficiaries without paying the government first![7]

If the decedent's assets are valued in excess of the applicable exclusion amount above, federal estate tax (discussed in Chapter 18) will be owed unless a deduction can be taken. The most common deductions are the marital deduction (discussed in Chapter 27) and the charitable deduction (discussed in Chapter 37).

If a married individual wishes to minimize taxes at death, the will should provide for all assets in excess of the applicable exclusion amount above to pass to his spouse or to a trust for the benefit of the spouse, so a marital deduction can be taken for those assets.

The taxable estate will thus be reduced to the value that can be "sheltered" by the decedent's applicable exclusion amount. Absent such planning, and all of the assets are left to a spouse, there could be a 100 percent marital deduction, and no assets will be available to take advantage of the unified credit (which, prior to 2010, was a "use it or lose it" benefit). However, the law currently provides that surviving spouses will be able to use the amount of the unused estate tax applicable exclusion amount that the deceased spouse did not use. This is often referred to as "portability". A personal representative should file a Form 706 estate tax return even for non-taxable estates to claim this benefit.

Generally, unless the will provides otherwise, estate taxes are apportioned among all beneficiaries of the estate (although in a few states, death taxes are paid from the residue).[8] Some states have a hybrid default rule that apportions to beneficiaries other than those receiving specific bequests. Usually spouses and charities receiving assets eligible for the marital or charitable deduction are not apportioned any tax. Tax apportionment was recently disputed among the family of writer Tom Clancy after his death. The testator can override state default rules in the will.

For example, if the will provides for taxes to be paid from the residue, and the residue passes to Susie, but Ron receives the decedent's Rolls Royce, Ron will not have to make an out of pocket payment for his share of estate taxes, providing that there are sufficient assets in the estate residue to pay such taxes.

Income Tax

For income tax purposes a probate estate is a separate taxable entity. A federal fiduciary income tax return (Form 1041), and often a state income tax return, must be filed annually during the period of administration if sufficient gross income ($600 or more for the federal return) is received during a twelve-month period, or if the trust has a beneficiary who is a non-resident alien. Estates with less than $600 of income may still want to file a Form 1041 if substantial deductions such as attorney, accountant and executor fees would be useful to flow out of the estate to beneficiaries on Forms K-1.

No income tax is recognized solely as the result of a death. In fact, there may be a tax benefit at death, since most of the assets in the decedent's gross estate receive a new income tax basis equal to the fair market value of each asset at the time of the decedent's death. Assuming the asset increased in value or is worth more than its basis in the decedent's hands during lifetime, it receives a "step-up" in basis. The taxable gain inherent in the asset disappears. Thus, an asset could be sold immediately after death and there would be no income tax to pay. However, if the asset declined in value below the decedent's adjusted basis, the new basis would step-*down* to its fair market value as of the decedent's death.

Example. Twenty years before his death, a client purchased stock for $20 per share. If it was valued in his estate at $80 per share, that $80 would become the new basis for purposes of determining gain if his beneficiary sold it. If the client had purchased the stock for $90 per shares, the basis would be stepped *down* to $80.

One exception to this basis step-up rule is any asset that would have been taxed as income had the decedent lived long enough to receive it. Unpaid fees due to a doctor or lawyer who reports his income on a cash basis, or notes resulting from the sale of property reported on the installment method would be examples of these. The most common example of this type of asset is distributions from annuities or retirement plans (for example, IRAs, 401(k)s, 403(b)s etc.) These assets are generally termed "income in respect of decedent," and they retain whatever income tax basis the testator had in them, if any.

10.8 ISSUES IN COMMUNITY PROPERTY STATES

Assets held as community property are owned equally by the spouses. At death, each spouse has testamentary power of distribution over his half of the community assets. Thus there is no certainty that the survivor will receive the decedent's one-half share of the community assets, but the absence of a will generally will produce that result.[9]

In common law (non-community property) states, the surviving spouse may sometimes be protected against disinheritance through laws of elective shares, dower, or curtesy.

In a community property state, the will of the deceased spouse may affect the survivor's half of the community property. For example, the decedent's will may purport to give all of the community property assets (the shares of both husband and wife) to a trust for the benefit of the surviving spouse and the children. If so, the survivor must elect whether to take under the will (thus assenting to the decedent's disposition of the survivor's one-half community property interest) or to take his one-half of the community property outright (denying the decedent's power to dispose of the survivor's community property interest).

10.9 FREQUENTLY ASKED QUESTIONS

Question – All of the client's assets are held in joint tenancy or in a manner in which a beneficiary is designated (e.g., IRAs). Does the client need a will?

Answer – Yes. While the assets currently owned by the client will pass to the survivors or beneficiaries without probate, at some time the client may acquire additional assets that are titled in another manner. Also, the named joint tenant(s) or beneficiary(ies) might predecease the client. A will is always valuable to prevent intestacy and to make appointments of trustees, guardians and executors.

Question – Is it difficult to change a will as circumstances change?

Answer – A will can be amended or revoked quickly and in most cases easily at any time during the lifetime of the testator. It is possible to revoke a will in full and to create a new will, or to revoke only a portion of the will and add new provisions by means of a codicil, although we discourage codicils. The will itself can provide for changing circumstances by making provisions for successor beneficiaries and/or executors in the event of the death of any named beneficiaries and/or executors. While it is easy to change a will, it is not a good idea to make a change by writing on an existing will. Changes made in this manner may be effective, but it is easy to create unintended consequences when doing this.

Question – When should a will be updated?

Answer – Generally, a will should be reviewed at regular intervals. Most specifically a will should be reviewed:

1. When there are significant changes in the value of property that is intended to be distributed.

2. Where the testator has moved from one state to another, or has purchased property in another state or out of the country.

3. Where there have been changes in family circumstances such as births, deaths, marriages, divorces.

4. Where the personal representative, guardian or trustee can no longer serve as originally expected.

5. Where federal or state tax laws change.

6. Where changes in business ventures occur.

7. Where disposition or other objectives change.

This list is not all encompassing but is representative of some of the major changes to cause a will review and possible change. Nevertheless, we encourage estate planners to remind clients to pull out and read their wills once a year (either when going onto or coming off of daylight savings time is one possibility) to ensure that the will still comports with their intentions. Obviously, if something has changed, then it behooves the client to have the will reviewed, and, if necessary, revised.

Question – Can the imposition of estate taxes at death be avoided by having assets pass outside the will?

Answer – Generally, no. The gross estate includes all assets owned by the decedent at death; or in some cases, controlled by the decedent. This includes assets held in the decedent's name, assets transferred to a revocable trust by the decedent, the decedent's interest in joint tenancy assets, proceeds of life insurance from policies owned by the decedent (or given away within three years of the insured's death), and the value of most retirement plans (IRAs, for example). Even assets outside the United States are subject to federal estate tax for a U.S. citizen or resident. Unless a will employs tax avoidance devices such as the marital or charitable deductions, the will really has no effect on the amount of estate tax that is owed. With respect to assets passing by beneficiary designation or through joint ownership, these assets will still be included with the decedent's federal gross estate for tax purposes.

However, some state death taxes are inheritance taxes, which vary the amount of deduction and tax rate based upon the relationship of the recipient to the testator. To the extent that the will provides a different distribution of property than would an intestacy, the amount of inheritance tax may be changed. The other form of death tax, called an estate tax, is a tax based in general on the total value of the assets in the estate, rather than how much is inherited by each person and the relationship of that person to the testator. Two areas where even estate taxes are affected by who is the recipient of a bequest or devise include gifts made to spouses (which may result in a marital deduction) and transfers to charities (which may qualify for a charitable deduction).

Question – Does a client with a modest estate need a will?

Answer – Yes. There are many reasons almost every adult should have a will. Certainly, any adult with minor children should have a will. Even though an estate is modest, it is important to name a guardian for both the person and the estate of the client's children. A client may have very strong feelings that a close friend is the best person to care for the children and if those wishes are not expressed, the children may end up in the custody of relatives or others who would not have been chosen to deal with the children and/or their assets. In some cases, a client may wish to leave the personal custody of a child to one person and leave the management of the child's assets to another. In some cases, a will is necessary to accomplish a person's objectives of having certain assets pass to one person rather than another – or to have no assets pass to particular persons who might receive property through intestacy.

Question – Suppose a client planned to avoid probate by putting assets in a revocable *inter vivos* trust (a living trust). Can the client change the disposition of assets in the trust by changing his will?

Answer – Generally, no. As long as the client has actually placed the assets in the *inter vivos* trust, his will does not have any effect on these assets unless the trust provides for amendment or exercise of a power of appointment to be made by a will. When a living trust is used, generally the will is only a "pour-over will" which directs to the trust any assets not already placed in the trust. The revocable trust can be changed by a written amendment in the form set out in the trust for such changes. Even where a client believes that a revocable trust is funded with all of the client's assets, it is still important to have a pour-over will because frequently there are some assets that the client forgets to retitle to the revocable trust.

In order to avoid the question of whether the trust terms are to be changed or a power of appointment exercised inadvertently by a will, the majority of planners provide that changes in a trust can be made only by an instrument in writing other than a will.

Question – Can probate be avoided through an *inter vivos* trust?

Answer – Yes, but only if the title of assets has been transferred from the client's name to that of the trustee of the trust (or pay by beneficiary designation to the trust). Failure to make the transfers will leave assets subject to a will and subject to the costs and delays of going through a probate in order to get into the trust.

Question – Is it expensive to have assets subject to probate?

Answer – Probate fees and administrative burdens vary from state to state (sometimes even county by county). In some states, they can be as high as 5 percent of all probate property – plus additional fees for "extraordinary work" (preparing tax returns, some sales of property, fighting will contests, etc.). Both the executor and the attorney for the estate are entitled to a fee for their services. However, in some states, the probate costs are not nearly that high and a revocable trust is less important. And there are important safeguards and protections afforded under the probate process that might not be available by avoiding probate. (See below).

Question – Assume a trust is desired to protect a client's children. Will it cost more to use a testamentary trust included as part of his will or more if an *"inter vivos* trust*"* is used as a separate instrument?

Answer – There are at least three cost aspects to consider. One is the cost of going through probate, which is required for a testamentary trust but which can be avoided if assets are transferred before death to an *inter vivos* trust. A different aspect is that some states require regular accounting to be made to the court by testamentary trusts, giving possibly better supervision but resulting in added attorney fees and court costs for each accounting. Lastly, the legal fees for drafting an *inter vivos* trust may be slightly more since its use requires two documents (the trust and a pour-over will) and often some documentation to transfer title of assets.

Question – Is there any benefit to having property go through probate as opposed to having assets transferred to an *inter vivos* trust prior to death?

Answer – Going through probate involves stricter supervision of the management and disposition of assets. To the extent that a client is concerned that the trustee who administers the trust may not carry out the trust terms in exactly the manner desired, the probate procedure may provide substantial benefit.

Another benefit of probate is that it often has a cut-off period for creditors that is sometimes shorter than that for revocable living trusts. As part of the probate process, a notice of the death is given to all creditors.[10] After notice, creditors have a specified period of time in which to file their claims and those creditors who do not make their claims within that time are thereafter cut off. For example, suppose a doctor were to die and a malpractice claim developed ten months after his death. That claim may well be cut off by a proper probate, but it may not be cut off with regard to any assets held in an *inter vivos* trust at his death. Those assets have not gone through the "cleansing action" of probate. Some states, such as California, have a similar termination of creditors' rights for assets held in *inter vivos* trusts. Other states may import the same cut off period, but only if a pour over trust provision is part of the will. Consult your particular state law.

Question – Under what circumstances can a will be challenged or contested when offered for probate?

Answer – A will can be contested by an interested or aggrieved party on many different grounds. Among the most common causes for contesting are:

(1) The testator lacked sufficient mental capacity.

(2) The testator was unduly influenced at the time that the will was drafted and executed.

(3) The will was not executed according to the statutory formalities.

(4) The will offered for probate has been revoked.

(5) The will offered for probate was a forgery.

Question – What things should an estate planner examine in reviewing a will?

Answer – See "How to Review a Will: A Checklist for the Estate and Financial Planner" in Chapter 11.

CHAPTER ENDNOTES

1. Uniform Probate Code §2-501.
2. Uniform Probate Code §2-502.
3. Dan E. McConaughey, *Wills*, 18 (1984).
4. Uniform Probate Code §2-502(b).
5. Dan E. McConaughey, *Wills*, 22 (1984).
6. See draft legislation, case law and other material collected by the Uniform Law Commission at: http://www.uniformlaws.org/Committee.aspx?title=Electronic%20Wills, as well as the status of legislation proposed in various states.
7. See the federal priority statute at 31 U.S.C. §3713. E.g. in *United States v. McNicol*, 829 F.3d 77 (1st Cir. 2016), *aff'g* 2014 WL 4384486, 114 A.F.T.R. 2,d 2014-5919 (D. Mass. 2014), the court found the personal representative personally liable when a widow transferred estate assets to herself before paying her late husband's income taxes.
8. Uniform Probate Code §3-916.
9. Robert J. Lynn, *Introduction to Estate Planning*, 2nd Ed., 23 (1978).
10. Known or ascertainable creditors usually receive direct notice. Unknown creditors usually are notified by publication. The United States Supreme Court has struck down as unconstitutional an Oklahoma statute that bars claims presented more than two months after notice by publication. The court held that such notice does not necessarily satisfy the requirement of due process, that if a creditor's identity is known or reasonably ascertainable, the creditor must receive actual notice. *Tulsa Prof. Collection Serv., Inc. v. Pope*, 485 U.S. 478 (1988), rev'g and remanding, 986 Okla. 72, 733 P.2d 396 (1986).

HOW TO REVIEW A WILL: A CHECKLIST FOR THE ESTATE AND FINANCIAL PLANNER[1]

CHAPTER 11

11.1 INTRODUCTION

A will is the legal document that specifies how a person wants to dispose of the real and personal property owned in his own name at the time of his death. Most mentally competent adults have the legal capacity to draw a will. But few persons are knowledgeable enough to do so properly. Only an attorney should draft a will, and even most attorneys should not attempt to draw their own.

Despite this, every member of the estate planning team, including the financial planner, should know how to review a will. This is important for several reasons.

First, it is necessary to coordinate the will properly with other dispositive documents such as employee benefit plans. For example, if the will establishes trusts for minor children, the beneficiary designation of any other dispositive document must properly direct the assets to that trust.

Second, it is impossible to know if there will be appropriate liquidity to pay taxes and other estate expenses unless the will and its various dispositive schemes are examined.

Third, wills quickly become outdated and tax laws change rapidly. For instance, a marital deduction provision in a will drafted before September 13, 1981, may not qualify for the unlimited marital deduction; the Taxpayer Relief Act of 1997[2] increased the unified credit in a series of steps and introduced a family-owned business exclusion; EGTRRA 2001[3] introduced a slow but steady increase in the unified credit, a gradual reduction in the top estate tax rates, and a repeal of the estate tax for one year in 2010, the Tax Relief Act of 2010[4] lowered rates, increased the exclusion, unified the gift and estate tax systems, and introduced "portability "of the exemption between spouses. And starting in 2013, much of what occurred in 2010 was made permanent – and still more changed. Most recently, tax reform more than doubled the exclusion again, but only for years 2018-2025.[5] The circumstances, needs, and desires of the client and his or her or their beneficiaries are always in flux. The attorney who drafted the will may have died, and it may have been many years since the will was revised or reviewed by either the client or attorney. Since wills are generally drafted to address the conditions which exist at the time of drafting, it is essential to review the will at least every two or three years and after every major tax law change or major events in the client's life to make sure it is consistent with conditions as times change.

Fourth, state laws can change with respect to the operation of estates and trusts. For example, many states have adopted all or part of the Uniform Principal and Income Act (UPIA), or its newer version, the Uniform Fiduciary Income and Principal Act (UFIPA) and the Uniform Trust Code (UTC). Both of these laws change how estates and trusts are to be administered. More recently, the vast majority of states have passed the Revised Fiduciary Access to Digital Assets Act (RUFADAA) and several states have recently passed Electronic Wills statutes, many based on the Uniform Electronic Wills Act. It is important to keep your documents up to date to address both tax and non-tax changes to the law. It's unlikely that a will drafted 10 years ago has the language necessary to authorize fiduciary access to digital assets under RUFADAA, which may be very important to many clients today.

Every professional in the estate planning team must therefore be able to examine a will and spot – in general terms at least – what's wrong.

"What's wrong" with a given will is more often a question of what has been omitted or what has changed or what are the present objectives of the client than what has been improperly drafted.

"What's wrong" is even more often the failure of the draftsman to match the facts of the case or the circumstances or desires of the parties with the provisions in the documents.

"What's wrong" may be something the accountant, for instance, knows that no other professional knows.

"What's wrong" may be that the will has not been updated for years and no longer addresses the current circumstances or client goals or latest tax law.

"What's wrong" may be that a will alone – without a trust or the use of other tools or techniques – is inadequate or does not maximize the possibility to accomplish the client's objectives with greater certainty and lesser cost.

"What's wrong" may be even be an inadequacy of cash to pay taxes or to maintain the client's survivors' lifestyle or achieve charitable objectives.

The following is a (by no means complete) checklist designed to give each member of the estate planning team the tools needed to examine a will.

11.2 INTRODUCTORY CLAUSE

Start with the introductory (exordium) clause, which should be the first paragraph in the will. The purpose of this preamble is to:

(1) identify the testator, the person disposing of property at death;

(2) establish domicile, the county that will have legal jurisdiction for purposes of determining the validity of the will and interpreting will provisions, for purposes of state inheritance taxation (technically, what is said in a will about the testator's domicile is not dispositive, but it is evidence which will usually be considered even if subordinated to proof of facts to the contrary);

(3) declare that the document in question is intended to dispose of the testator's property at death (potentially excluding assets in another country if it is more efficient to do so) and no matter how many wills have been written in the past, this is meant to be the last will; and

(4) revoke all prior wills. This is designed to nullify old and forgotten wills – and "codicils" (legally effective modifications of existing wills).

Example. "I, Morey S. Rosenbloom, a resident of and domiciled in the city of Bryn Mawr in Montgomery County, Pennsylvania, declare this to be my last will. I revoke all wills and codicils made prior to this will."

Planners should check:

(1) Is the spelling of the client's name correct? Has the client's full name been used?

(2) Is the client known by some other name, and should that name be listed?

(3) Is the domicile correct? For tax or other planning purposes, would it make sense to begin to document with a different domicile? Will the will meet all the statutory requirements of the stated domicile? If the client spends a great deal of time in more than one residence, could the address mentioned in the will trigger a "double domicile" problem (e.g., where more than one state claims the decedent was a domiciliary of the state and therefore has the right to impose a death tax)?

(4) Is there a reason prior wills and codicils should not be revoked (e.g., maybe exclude revoking a will that controls property in a foreign country)? If there is a potential for an attack on this will on the grounds of mental incompetency, fraud, or undue influence, a prior will providing a similar disposition will help prove the mental capacity of the testator and may discourage would-be contestants from attacking the current will. Thus, it is often advisable to keep the prior revoked will as further evidence (one way to thwart will contests is to have several similar wills over time requiring a contestant to attack them all in succession).

After the introductory clause, the will can take either of two directions. It can (1) describe the steps that take place in administering the testator's estate (such as payment of debts and taxes and then payment of legacies) or it can (2) dispose of legacies first and describe obligations later. We will take the former approach in formulating this checklist.

11.3 DEBTS CLAUSE

The next clause usually pertains to the payment of debts, expenses, and costs. This clause serves two purposes:

1. To state the source from which each debt will be paid. (This is an extremely important point because of the death tax implications. For instance, if a surviving spouse rather than some other beneficiary must pay debts, to that extent the marital deduction will be decreased, and taxes may be increased. Furthermore, if the burden falls on the wrong person(s), the testator's goals may not be met.)

2. To establish as debts items that might not otherwise be considered the testator's obligations.

Example. "I direct all of my *lawfully enforceable* debts (including any expenses of my last illness) and my funeral expenses be paid."

It is important to reference "lawfully enforceable debts"; because some debts may not be enforceable. For example, some debts may barred by the statute of limitations. If you direct *all* debts be paid, your executor may have to pay debts that they would not otherwise legally have to pay (or be encouraged to when they shouldn't.)

Planners should check:

(1) Does the testator have any rights to property held in the trust of another person (a so-called "power of appointment") and, if so, what effect does the debts clause have on that property? Does it expose that property to the claims of creditors? Also, do those assets get "blended" with the probate estate and became part of the probate estate, or do the trust assets pass directly from the other trust to the beneficiaries of that trust? Whether or not the assets passing from that other trust become part of the probate estate can be important if there are creditors of the testator.[6] These creditors look to the assets within the probate estate to satisfy their claims.

(2) Will the beneficiaries receive more or less than the client intended when the will was drawn because of the operation of this provision? Has the size of the debt changed since the will was drawn? What will be the federal and state death tax impact of the clause?

(3) Did the will provide detailed funeral arrangements? Most authorities feel this is inadvisable since the will may not be found or may not be accessible in sufficient time after the testator's death. Usually such provisions should be placed in a "Letter of Instructions," an informal and nonlegal list of requests, suggestions, and recommendations separate from the will. Some states permit separate directives with burial, cremation or other instructions and have forms to specifically appoint someone to make such decisions.[7]

(4) Does the client intend that "payment of debts" include the mortgage on property left to a specific individual? In many states, absent an express direction to the contrary, when specific property is left to an individual (a "specific bequest"), any debt on that property will not be paid off. In other states, such a clause will require the executor to satisfy the mortgage. Similar confusion may apply to a loan taken out to purchase or finance a business. If one child receives the business, is it the testator's intention that the loan follow the business or be paid by the child receiving the business? What about a vehicle left to a beneficiary that is still subject to a car loan and lien? Does the named beneficiary of a life insurance policy that has been pledged as the collateral for a loan have the right to have the loan paid off because of the "pay my [just] debts" clause? The planner must check state law. In at least one state, the answer depends on who the lender is. The result, absent specific direction to the contrary, is one way if the lender is the insurance company (the beneficiary takes only the net proceeds) and another (the beneficiary is entitled to have the estate pay off the debt

out of other estate assets) if the creditor is an independent lending institution.

11.4 TAX CLAUSE

The clause pertaining to the payment of death taxes can either be stated next or appear after the provisions disposing of property.

The purpose of the tax clause is to establish the source for the payment of the federal estate tax, the state inheritance and estate tax, and any federal or state GST tax.

Example. "I direct that all inheritance, estate, transfer, succession, legacy and other death taxes upon property required to be included in my taxable estate whether or not passing under this Will [except (1) transfer taxes levied pursuant to the provisions of Chapter 13 of the Internal Revenue Code of 1986, relating to "generation-skipping transfers," or any similar state law, and (2) taxes on property held in trust under the Will (or any revocable trust) of my spouse], and any interest and penalties thereon, shall be charged against and paid from my residuary estate passing under Article *FOURTH* of Part I of this my Will."

However, note that this tax clause charges the taxes on all assets which are "included in my taxable estate whether or not passing under this Will" to the residuary estate. This means that if there are joint assets, life insurance, retirement assets – or any asset that passes through a beneficiary designation; the taxes on such assets are paid from the *residuary* estate. If the residuary beneficiaries are not the same as the recipient of these other assets, then some individuals are paying taxes on assets which they are not receiving. While there are many situations where this may be appropriate, it is important to consider the ramifications of this approach.

Planners should check:

(1) State "apportionment" statutes. If there is no tax clause in the will or if it does not adequately address the payment of a particular death tax, state law will allocate the burden of taxes among the beneficiaries. There is nothing wrong with a tax clause in a will simply incorporating the state default tax apportionment statute as long as the testator and counsel know what that is. Many states require beneficiaries to pay a share of estate taxes unless the will provides otherwise. The result is often an inappropriate or unintended reduction of the shares of certain beneficiaries or adverse tax consequences. (For example, there may be a spiraling reduction of the estate tax marital deduction. The deduction is allowed only for the net amount passing to the surviving spouse. If that amount is reduced by an estate tax burden, the tax increases – further reducing the amount passing to the spouse, etc. The same thing can happen with a charitable deduction.) An "anti-apportionment" tax clause may be the solution. For instance, suppose you wanted a child to receive $100,000 of your client's $2,000,000 estate free and clear. Without special provision, that child would be forced to pay his share of taxes, or 1/20 of the total federal and state death taxes. With a special tax clause, the child will receive the entire $100,000.

(2) Does the client expect or want property passing outside the probate estate to pay its share of tax if the disposition of that non-probate asset generates tax? For instance, assume $1,000,000 of pension proceeds (or life insurance) is payable to the client's two oldest children and $1,000,000 of cash is payable to the client's two youngest children. Who is to pay the tax on the $2,000,000? What if the $1,000,000 of pension proceeds (or life insurance) is state inheritance tax exempt, but the cash is not? Unless the will provides to the contrary, estate taxes must be paid by recipients of property passing outside the will. The will should specify who pays taxes on both probate and nonprobate property.

(3) Assume a sizable amount of property will pass through a revocable living trust. Is the tax clause in that instrument coordinated with the tax clause in the will, or are they incompatible? What if assets under the will are to "pour over" into a previously funded trust that itself will generate significant estate taxes? Is there (should there be) a will provision calling upon the trust to help the estate pay taxes? Does the trust have a provision recognizing and empowering a "call" on its assets to pay the probate estate's taxes?

(4) Who is to pay the tax on a generation-skipping transfer? Absent a contrary direction, the taxes

will probably be payable from the assets of the fund subject to the tax. Some draftsmen specifically provide that such taxes are not to be imposed on the "skip person's" estate.

(5) Assume the facts indicate that very large taxable gifts have been made by the client. The taxable portion of these gifts – to the extent not included in the client's gross estate – will be considered "adjusted taxable gifts." They will increase the rate of federal estate tax payable on the taxable estate remaining. Will an unexpectedly high burden be placed on the assets remaining because of these prior gifts and should the tax clause take such gifts into account in apportioning the tax burden?

(6) Should certain beneficiaries be insulated from tax for either tax reasons or to accomplish the dispositive goals of the client or better meet the needs of the beneficiaries? For example, should a child to whom property has been given be exempted by the will from paying the estate tax on that property?

11.5 TANGIBLE PERSONAL PROPERTY CLAUSE

A clause pertaining to the disposition of tangible personal property often is next. The purposes of this clause are:

(1) to provide for who will receive personal property, and the terms under which they will receive it; and

(2) to make special dispositions among the persons and the organizations of the testator's choice.

Example 1. "I give to my daughter, Eva Grieg, all of my clothing, household furnishings, jewelry, automobiles, books, pictures, and all other articles of tangible personal property owned by me at the date of my death. If my daughter, Eva Grieg, does not survive me, I give the property mentioned above in equal shares to my grandchildren, Gretta and Gail Grieg, or the survivor who is alive at the date of my death."

Example 2. "I give the Philadelphia Museum of Art my painting of 'Helga' by Andrew Wyeth and my Douglas Mellor 'Garvey with Parachute' photograph."

Planners should check:

(1) Does (or should) the client make specific bequests of all "intimate" items such as a watch or ring? Absent such provisions, if personal property has been left to several individuals, the result is often needless expense in determining who gets what or reducing the estate to cash (not to mention the potential for bitter intrafamily fights.) If specific bequests have been made, has each item been described in enough detail so that there will be no confusion as to which diamond ring the testator meant? (Use the same description as is found in the insurance policy covering the loss or theft of the item – and by the way, any item valuable enough to require a rider on an insurance policy is valuable enough for beneficiaries to fight over). In some cases, it may make sense to take pictures of the personal property and indicate on the back of the picture how the items are to be disposed.

(2) Has provision been made in case the item specifically left to a beneficiary is not owned by the decedent at death? For instance, what if one ring is sold and the proceeds are used to purchase a second. Does the named beneficiary receive the second ring?

(3) If the item specifically bequeathed has been lost, stolen, etc. and the loss has been covered by insurance, would the client want the named beneficiary to receive the insurance? In many states, the bequest of an item of personal property does not – absent specific direction to the contrary – also pass the insurance covering the item.

(4) Does the client intend to pass – under the category of personal property – cash in a safe deposit box, travelers' checks, and cash found in his home or on his person? Does the client know that cash on deposit is typically not considered tangible personal property?

(5) If the client has property in many different places, consider allowing the executor – at the expense of the estate – to take possession of the

property "as and where is" this provision will permit the beneficiary to receive the property free of delivery costs, and protect the fiduciary and beneficiaries during administration from the risk that specific assets will be lost.

(6) The phrase "personal effects" may not encompass items of household use or even a car. Consider specific mention of items of tangible personal property.

(7) Is there a "catchall" phrase that passes the residue of tangible personal property? The phrase, "all other tangible personal property" should dispose of any residual property.

(8) Should the will confirm that certain property such as household furnishings, silverware, etc. belongs to someone else? This may be very helpful in a blended family situation.

(9) Does this clause dispose of property by referring to an instrument outside the will? This "incorporation by reference" is not recommended since it often leads to litigation.

(10) The use of the term "contents" should be avoided. Personal property should not be described by its location.

General checkup of legacies:

(1) Has property been left outright to a minor who is legally incapable of handling it, or to a person under a physical, mental, or emotional handicap who does not have the physical or intellectual capacity? This also applies to naming such individuals as beneficiaries of non-probate assets. For example, the financial institutions may require a court appointed guardian before granting access to the assets passing to a minor beneficiary. See Chapter 9 for discussion of naming UTMA custodians for minors as beneficiaries.

(2) Are all beneficiaries named alive? Are there "backup" beneficiaries (at least two) for each beneficiary? Are they the beneficiaries the client currently desires?

(3) Are any of the gifts conditioned on events or circumstances that are impossible, "against public policy," or in violation of the Constitution? For example, a bequest probably would be invalidated by the courts if it were made on the condition that the recipient first divorce their spouse.

(4) Are there gifts to "my issue" (which may unintentionally disinherit an adopted person; while states differ, in some states adopted children are considered issue, and in some states they are not)? Also, in the case of same sex couples, the children may not be "issue" of both partners.

(5) Do gifts to charities meet state law requirements? Has the charity's full legal (corporate) name and address been stated? (The popular name is often different from the full legal name). Have you checked the IRS's Exempt Organizations Select Check online[8] or obtained assurances from the charity itself, to make sure the gift to the charity will qualify for a tax deduction? Has the client named a backup charity? Check to be sure the will specifies that taxes are to be paid from the portion of the residue not passing to charity. Otherwise, what should be a tax-free bequest must bear its portion of the total taxes. That reduces the charity's share and therefore increases taxes. This in turn creates a new cycle of problems.

(6) If someone is intentionally omitted, have you checked state law to see if such an omission is permissible? Are there defamatory statements in the will concerning an heir? (At the probate of the will, such statements may become libelous and expose the client's estate to an action for damages.)

(7) Does the will make so many specific bequests of cash that the residuary estate doesn't have enough left to pay income and estate taxes (which should be paid first)? Keep in mind that the IRS can attach the assets of any beneficiary for the unpaid estate tax.

(8) Note that a tangible personal property clause should nearly always be used where the residue of the estate will be paid to a trust. Few clients want trusts involved in handling personal effects such as jewelry, or household furniture, antiques, or cars.

11.6 DEVISES OF REAL ESTATE CLAUSE

The next clause pertains to "devises," testamentary grants of real property. The purposes of the devises clause are:

(1) to specify which real estate is to be disposed of under the will and to dispose of that real estate; and

(2) to handle the problems where the property has been sold or destroyed prior to the testator's death.

Example. "I leave my residence located at 2 Red Cedar Rd, Amelia Island, Florida to my daughter, Lara Leimberg. If, at the time of my death, I am no longer using the property at 2 Red Cedar Rd, Amelia Island, Florida as my residence, then this devise is to be void and of no effect; however, if I own any other real estate which I am using as my residence at that time, then, in such an event, I devise such other real estate to my daughter, Lara Leimberg. If my daughter, Lara Leimberg, does not survive me, this devise shall lapse and such real estate shall become part of my residuary estate."

11.7 SPECIFIC BEQUESTS OF INTANGIBLES AND CASH

After disposing of tangible personal property and real estate, the will may then cover specific gifts of intangibles (property where the item itself is evidence of value) such as gifts of cash or accounts receivable.

Example 1. "I give 100 shares of Facebook stock to my niece, Danielle Green."

Example 2. "I give the sum of Five Thousand ($5,000) dollars to my sister, Sara Black, if she survives me."

Planners should check:

(1) Has provision been made in the event the primary beneficiary does not survive the decedent?

(2) Does the will spell out what gift, if any, is made if the decedent does not possess, at the time of death, the stock mentioned in the will? What if the stock had been sold but new stock was purchased with the proceeds? What if there was a stock split and only a specified number of shares were given?

(3) For cryptocurrency not held through a publicly traded fund or wallet with a beneficiary designation, does the personal representative even know of its existence or how to access it?

11.8 RESIDUARY CLAUSE

The next clause is called the "residuary clause." The purposes of the residuary clause are to:

(1) transfer all assets not disposed of up to this point;

(2) (in some cases) provide a mechanism for "pouring over" assets from the will to a previously established (*inter vivos*) trust (if a pour over is made, it is important to review the trust as carefully as the will itself); and

(3) provide for an alternative disposition in case the primary beneficiary has died or the trust to which probate assets (assets passing under a valid will or by intestacy) were to be poured over was for some reason invalid, previously revoked, or never came into existence.

Example. "All the rest, residue, and remainder of the property that I own at the date of my death, real and personal, tangible or intangible, regardless of where it is situated, I leave to my daughter, Larrissa Grieg. But if Larrissa Grieg does not survive me, then I leave the said property in equal shares to my grandchildren, Ronald Reimus and Reginald Reimus or to the survivor of them, per stirpes."

By including the reference to per stirpes, you can insure that if either Ronald or Reginald is deceased, but survived by children of their own, the bequest will pass to Ronald or Reginald's children.

Planners should check:

(1) Has a spouse been disinherited? If so, is the client aware of the elective rights (rights to a portion of the probate estate and perhaps certain other property owned by the decedent at death regardless of what the will provides) the surviving spouse has even if the will is valid? It may be possible to control the surviving spouse to some degree by inserting a provision at least as attractive as the spouse's intestate share, or by a provision reducing or eliminating the share of a person in whom the spouse is interested if he exercises his right of election. An alternative is a pre- or post-nuptial agreement, although a handful of states may still limit the ability for couples to enter into post-nuptial agreements.

(2) Has the client, inadvertently, exercised a power of appointment (a right to direct the disposition of property in a trust established by someone else)? In some states, a residuary clause automatically exercises a general power of appointment, unless the trust requires that it must be specifically referred to in order to make a valid exercise or unless the will itself states that no exercise is intended.

(3) Is there a disposition to a young adult, minor, or a person legally, mentally, or emotionally incompetent that should be made in trust? Is there provision for the executor to retain the property during the minority of such a person, or to use income or principal for that person's benefit? Has the right person been named as the custodian of a child's property, and are there backups in case that person is unwilling or unable to serve?

(4) Is there a default provision in case a trust into which the residue was to have poured is for any reason revoked or never came into existence?

(5) If a child dies, will that child's share pass to the parties desired by the client?

(6) Does the will address the possibility of the birth of a child to the client? (It's never too late!)

(7) Has the client, in lieu of leaving his residuary estate outright to his spouse, created a marital deduction formula disposition through a so-called "formula clause?"

(8) If the client was divorced, most states have statutes that automatically remove the ex-spouse, so if the testator wants a portion of their estate to go to an ex-spouse, it would be necessary to republish a new will after the divorce is finalized. Also, look out for relatives of an ex-spouse who may be named as beneficiaries, who are probably not automatically removed upon divorce. To disinherit them, a new will would usually be required.

Marital Deduction Formula Clauses

Marital deduction formula clauses are very important to review and analyze. They are often found in the wills of clients who own assets of at least the applicable exclusion amount (this amount increased from $5,490,000 in 2017 to $11,180,000 in 2018 and is adjusted annually for inflation through 2025, to revert back to $5 million adjusted for inflation in 2026). Such clauses typically divide the client's estate into two parts, one "marital" and the other "nonmarital." The marital portion passes property to the client's surviving spouse as part of the marital deduction and may contain an outright or trust disposition. The nonmarital portion is designed to set aside property exempted from federal estate tax by reason of the client's available applicable exclusion amount and passes property to persons other than the surviving spouse (or to an applicable exclusion amount "bypass trust" for the benefit of the surviving spouse that will not be included in the surviving spouse's estate on his death). While assets are passing to a "bypass trust" as opposed to the surviving spouse, this does not mean that the spouse cannot be a beneficiary of the bypass trust. In states with separate estate tax systems with lower applicable exclusion amounts than the federal, the bypass or marital trust might be further divided into a state exempt and non-state exempt trust to maximize the use of the state estate tax exemption.

NOTE: For the years beginning in 2011, surviving spouses can use the so-called "portability" provisions, which allow them to add the unused estate tax applicable exclusion amount of the spouse who died most recently to their own (known as the deceased spousal unused exclusion amount, or DSUE amount). GST exemption, however, does not "port." See Chapter 27 for more detail on bypass and marital trusts.

11.9 POWERS CLAUSE

The next clause is often one pertaining to the powers of the executor (and trustee if the will establishes a "testamentary trust," a trust created at the testator's death under the will). The purposes of the powers clause are to:

(1) give the executor (and trustee) specific power and authority over and above those provided by state law to enable the executor to conserve and manage the property, and

(2) limit, where desired and appropriate, the executor's power and authority (for instance, the client may not want the executor to make certain investments), and

(3) provide authority to continue a business (or handle other property with special management or investment problems) and the special flexibility necessary to accomplish that objective, and

(4) protect the executor against suit by other beneficiaries by specifying the powers necessary to accomplish the executor's role.

Example (abbreviated).

"I authorize my executor (as well as any substitute executor) in his, her, or its discretion, with respect to all property, real and personal, in addition to the powers conferred by law, to:

1. retain assets

2. purchase investments

3. hold cash

4. vote and grant proxies

5. sell, exchange, or dispose of assets

6. distribute in cash or in kind

7. delegate to agents (as permitted by applicable state law)

8. assign or compromise claims

9. borrow funds

10. lease, manage, develop real estate

11. abandon property

12. make certain tax elections

13. receive and use employee benefits, if such benefits are payable to the estate or trust

14. disclaim assets

15. manage and direct a business owned by the decedent's estate."

Planners should check:

(1) Are there any assets or problems for this particular client that requires special powers to fulfill the desires of the client or provide the executor with sufficient flexibility? (Beware of "boilerplate" clauses). Are there powers that should be added? Are there "standard" powers that should be removed or modified?

(2) Will any power adversely affect the estate tax marital deduction? For instance, a marital deduction trust must provide that the surviving spouse receive all income at least annually.[9] Consider the impact of a power allowing the trustee under a testamentary trust to retain non-income-producing property. Unless the will/trust also contains a provision allowing the surviving spouse to demand that the trust assets be sold or made income producing, the marital deduction may be lost.

Will such a power thwart other objectives of the testator? For instance, what if the unproductive property was stock in a family corporation? A sale of such stock would raise income, but could cause the loss of family control of the corporation.

Another problem can arise if the trust permits the trustee to withhold income distributions if those distributions would otherwise prevent the spouse from receiving Medicaid benefits. The power to withhold income for any reason is enough to disqualify the trust from qualifying for the marital deduction. If such a provision is included in the document, it cannot apply to any trust which is intended to qualify for the marital deduction. For smaller estates, the marital deduction may not be as important as maximizing the asset protection by use of a discretionary trust.

The draftsman might consider including a "savings clause" that would nullify any power, duty, or discretionary authority that might jeopardize the marital deduction if that is important.

(3) Will any of the powers granted cause a conflict of interest? For instance, if the executor is a bank, discretionary authority to invest in its own securities or common trust funds will cause a conflict that must be specifically "forgiven" by the will (assuming the client wants to do so). Is the executor a business partner or co-shareholder of the insured? What problems might they create?

(4) Is there specific authority for the executor to make distribution "in kind" (as opposed to selling estate assets and making the distribution in cash)? In some states, absent specified power to do so, the executor may have no choice: the distribution must be made in cash.

(5) Is there specific authority for the executor to make distributions in kind non-pro rata? For example, giving the valuable stock to one child and the real estate to another child, rather than dividing each 50/50. If there is no such authority under the will or under state law, dividing the assets may trigger income tax on any gain occurring between the date of death and the time of funding.[10]

11.10 APPOINTMENT OF FIDUCIARIES CLAUSE

The appointment of the executor, trustee of any testamentary trust, and guardian of any minor child often comes toward the end of the will.

The purposes of the fiduciary appointment clause are:

(1) to name the individual(s) or corporate fiduciary or combinations of individual(s) and fiduciaries who will administer the testator's estate and any trust that the will creates;

(2) to give the executor the appropriate power to act on behalf of the estate and carry out the terms of the will;

(3) to specify if and how the executor is to be compensated;

(4) state whether or not the executor is to post bond;

(5) to specify the authority of and decision-making process for co-executors; and

(6) to name guardian(s) and successor guardian(s) of any minor child of the testator.

Example. "I appoint my nephew, Farnsworth Dowlrimple III, as the executor under this will. If for any reason he fails to qualify or ceases to act, I appoint the Left Bank and Trust of Overflow, Pa. as my executor. I confer upon my executor all the powers enumerated in clause _____ above. No executor shall be required to furnish any bond or other security in any jurisdiction. I direct that my nephew, Farnsworth, shall receive no compensation for his services as Executor and that the Left Bank and Trust of Overflow, Pa. be entitled to be compensated for its services as executor in accordance with its regularly adopted schedule of compensation in effect and applicable at the time of the performance of such services."

Planners should check:

(1) Does the client trust the individual who is currently named as executor and backup executor? Is that individual or corporate fiduciary legally qualified to act as executor? Some states do not allow an out-of-state individual executor who is not an immediate relative to serve. Has the attorney who drew the will been named as executor? Typically, absent special circumstances, this potentially raises ethical questions and the specter of a conflict of interest, especially

since there could be "double-dipping" of both executor and attorney fees.

(2) Should the executor's bond be waived? Usually, yes, but thefts from trusts and estates are on the rise – perhaps if an attorney, accountant or other individual is named, a bond may not be a bad idea.

(3) Is the executor named willing to serve? How recently has the client checked?

(4) Is the guardian for minors willing to act? Is she able to act? Is that person suitable?

(5) Is a prolonged estate (or trust) administration anticipated? If so, consider giving executors (trustees) the power to appoint agents or successors by filing an instrument with the probate or other appropriate court.

11.11 TESTATOR'S SIGNING CLAUSE

The next to the last clause in a will is typically the testator's signing (or "testimonium") provision. The purposes of the testimonium clause are:

(1) to establish that the document is intended to be the testator's last will,

(2) to meet statutory requirements that require the testator's signature at the logical conclusion of the will, and

(3) to state the date on which the will was signed.

Example. "In witness of the above, I subscribe my name, this 11th day of October 2006 at Bryn Mawr, Pennsylvania to this, my last will, which consists of fourteen pages (each of which I have initialed at the bottom)."

Planners should check:

(1) Is the will signed by the testator at its logical end? Is each page numbered? Is the page count correct? Each page need not be initialed to be valid, but this may be a good idea if there is any expected challenge.

(2) Are there duplicate or triplicate signed wills in existence? If the testator was given a signed duplicate which is not found at his death, it is possible that a presumption will arise that the testator destroyed it with the intention of revoking it. The potential for litigation is therefore increased significantly. The better practice is for only one original to be executed, with copies of that signed document provided

11.12 ATTESTATION CLAUSE

The final clause in a will is the "attestation" provision. The purposes of the attestation (or "witness") clause are to:

(1) witness the testator's signing;

(2) comply with statutory requirements;

(3) underline the testamentary character of the document; and

(4) comply with state law requirements in cases where the testator signed by a mark (such as an "X") or where, at the testator's direction and on his behalf, the will was signed by someone else (as would be the case where the testator was physically incapable of signing but mentally competent).

Example. "This will was signed by Edward Grieg, the testator, and declared to be his last will in our presence. We, at his request and in his presence and in the presence of each other, state that we witnessed his signing and declaration and at his request we have signed our names as witnesses this 11th day of October 2015."

Planners should check:

(1) Are there two or three witnesses to the testator's signing? Although most states require less, three witnesses will comply with the most stringent probate requirements of any state and, as a practical matter, provide stronger evidence of the competence and testamentary intent of the testator.

(2) Were any of the witnesses beneficiaries under the will? This is generally inadvisable for at least two reasons: First, the witnesses may become incompetent to testify as to the execution or validity of the will. Second, witnesses who are also beneficiaries may be barred by state law from receiving bequests under the will (or, in some cases, be limited to what they would receive by intestacy).

(3) Are the addresses of the witnesses stated? Although addresses may not be legally required, they make it easier to locate and identify witnesses when needed.

(4) Are the names of the witnesses printed and legible? Many people's signatures are difficult if not impossible to read – if it is not possible to print the expected witnesses' names on the will, at least print the names legibly underneath the signature.

(5) Is the will "self-proving"? In some states, a notarized affidavit attached to the will signed by the witnesses (and in some states, the testator, also) that describes the circumstances of the execution of the will may permit the will to be admitted to probate without the requirement that the witnesses be found or appear before the court in the probate proceeding. This is more prevalent in some states than others.

11.13 OTHER CLAUSES

There are, of course, many other clauses that should be considered in reviewing a will. Some additional points for the planner to check are:

(1) Is the federal estate tax marital deduction important? If so, consider that the Uniform Simultaneous Death Act, which applies in most states, presumes that the testator survives in the event of a simultaneous death involving the testator and a beneficiary. This would cause a loss of the estate tax marital deduction unless the will superseded state law by providing a "common disaster" clause. This provision makes the presumption that the testator's spouse is deemed to have survived.

(2) Does the will consider the possibility that one or more beneficiaries will disclaim any interest in the estate and should it pass the same as if a beneficiary had predeceased? The default under state law is that a disclaimer causes the property to pass as if the disclaimant had predeceased the testator, but the will could provide, for example, that if the beneficiary disclaims the disclaimed property passes to charity but if the beneficiary predeceases the testator it passes to the disclaimant's issue per stirpes.

(3) Have the provisions in the will been coordinated with other dispositive instruments? For instance, is the will coordinated with all trusts, with employee benefit plans, buy-sell agreements, and life insurance beneficiary designations?

(4) Are the problems of minors, incompetents, and other beneficiaries with special needs or circumstances properly addressed in the will? In other words, is the right asset going to the right person at the right time and in the right manner?

Has the client considered the financial burden that may be placed on the guardians of minor children, and have appropriate financial provisions been made so that they can afford to raise both the client's children and their own? (Some may want to set up a special life insurance funded trust that, if necessary, can provide to the guardians needed dollars, but, if not, will go to the client's children later in life.)

(5) Is the spouse's will coordinated with the client's will? For example, we have seen couples who wish to leave, for example, $50,000 to their favorite charity or to a friend at the second death. If both spouses have such a clause in their will, is $100,000 passing ($50,000 from each), or only $50,000? It will depend on how the clauses are worded and the order of death – read such provisions closely and walk through what would happen upon simultaneous death such as a common accident as well.

(6) Is there a "spendthrift clause" to provide protection against the claims of creditors and to protect the beneficiary from improvidence (more important if there is a testamentary trust)?

(7) Has the will added clauses authorizing the personal representative to access digital assets

pursuant to the Revised Uniform Fiduciary Access to Digital Assets Act?

11.14 CONCLUSION

Although only an attorney should draft a will, every member of the estate planning team should make it a practice to review a client's will on a regular basis. The non-attorney's role in the will review process should not be thought of as a replacement for, or as a means of "second guessing," the attorney, but rather as a source of additional strength in the planning process. The estate planner can provide, in that regard, a valuable resource to ascertain how the client's total dispositive plan can most effectively and efficiently meet the current needs, circumstances, and goals of both the client and the client's beneficiaries.

CHAPTER ENDNOTES

1. A version of this article under the title "How to Review a Will" appeared in the magazine *Financial Planning* in two parts, April and May, 1988. The checklist has been updated in this book.
2. Pub. L. No. 105-34, 111 Stat. 787 (1997).
3. The Economic Growth and Tax Relief Reconciliation Act of 2001; Pub. L. No. 107–16, 115 Stat. 38 (2001).
4. The Tax Relief, Unemployment Insurance Reauthorization, and Job Creation Act of 2010; Pub. L. No. 111–312, 124 Stat. 3296 (2010).
5. The tax reform bill formerly referred to as the Tax Cuts and Jobs Act was passed into law in late 2017 with the formal title of "H.R.1 - An Act to provide for reconciliation pursuant to titles II and V of the concurrent resolution on the budget for fiscal year 2018." (Public Law 115-97). See https://www.congress.gov/bill/115th-congress/house-bill/1.
6. Generally, assets subject to a testamentary *limited* power of appointment are not subject to the power holder's creditors (or creditors of the power holder's estate). However, assets subject to a testamentary *general* power of appointment (one which allows a power holder to appoint to themselves, their estate, their creditors or creditors of their estate) may be. At common law, such appointive assets are only subject to a power holder's estate's creditors if a general power is exercised. *Restatement of Property, Second, Donative Transfers*, §13.2. However, California has changed this rule and the Uniform Power of Appointment Act seeks to change this rule among the states and make them subject to creditors regardless of exercise. Cal. Prob. Code §682(b) and *Uniform Power of Appointment Act*, §502.
7. E.g., Ohio R.C. §2108.71 to §2108.90.
8. The Exempt Organizations Select Check replaces IRS Publication 78, "Cumulative List of Organizations." It is available at: www.irs.gov/Charities-&-Non-Profits/Exempt-Organizations-Select-Check.
9. I.R.C. §2056(b).
10. Rev. Rul. 69-486.

POWERS OF APPOINTMENT

CHAPTER 12

12.1 INTRODUCTION

A power of appointment is a right given in a will, trust, or other instrument by one person (the donor) to another (the donee or powerholder) allowing the power holder to name the recipient (appointee) of the donor's property at some future time. If the power holder does not exercise the power of appointment, then the property subject to the nonexercised power of appointment will pass to persons who are named by the donor and are referred to as "takers in default,"[1] and the transfer to the takers in default is referred to as a "gift over." It is possible that a power of appointment might go unexercised; in fact, a substantial number of powers of appointment are never exercised. Therefore, it is important in drafting a power of appointment to provide where the property will go if the power of appointment is not exercised in order to account for that possibility.

Thus, it is the right to dispose of someone else's property and is, therefore, a way to give someone other than the testator or grantor a right to "complete" the provisions of the latter's will or trust.

This authority over the disposition of property can provide substantial flexibility in an estate plan, help accomplish the donor's dispositive objectives, and serve as an important tax-saving tool. However, powers of appointment can also be *dangerous* in that the power holder, if given too much latitude, can alter the donor's estate plan beyond recognition and thwart the donor's intent. This often makes powers of appointment problematic in blended family situations. In some ways, think of powers of appointment as the "magic carpet" of estate planning, because the power holder has the right to yank the property carpet use out from under one or more persons and magically put it under others.

It is also sometimes referred to as a "rewrite" power, because not only may power holders often be able to change who or what entities receive the property, but also the trust terms under which they receive it.

12.2 WHAT IS A POWER OF APPONTMENT?

For purposes of trust and tax law, there are two kinds of powers of appointment. The first type of power of appointment is the general power of appointment. A general power is "any power of appointment exercisable in favor of the power holder, his estate, his creditors, or the creditors of his estate," with some exceptions.[2] A power that can be appointed to satisfy a legal obligation of the power holder is treated as exercisable in favor of the power holder's creditors and is a general power of appointment.[3] With two exceptions, even jointly held general powers of appointment are nevertheless taxable.[4]

All other powers of appointment are called limited or special or nongeneral powers of appointment.[5] Limited, special or nongeneral powers of appointment include powers that are limited by an ascertainable standard, which is defined as a power that is only exercisable for the health, education, maintenance or support of a beneficiary (often referred to collectively as HEMS powers).[6] A power is considered a limited or special or nongeneral power of appointment if it is not exercisable by the decedent without the consent or joinder of a person having a substantial interest in the property that is subject to the power of appointment that is adverse to the exercise of the power of appointment in favor of the decedent, his estate, his creditors, or the creditors of his estate. An interest adverse to the exercise of a power

181

is considered to be substantial if its value in relation to the total value of the property subject to the power of appointment is not insignificant.[7]

However, a power of appointment, in general, is not transferable and, therefore, may be viewed as not constituting an interest in property for state law purposes.[8] You either exercise the power of appointment, or you lose it.

12.3 WHEN IS USE OF SUCH A DEVICE INDICATED?

1. When an estate owner would like someone other than himself to make decisions concerning his property. A power of appointment provides flexibility to the beneficiary of a trust to control the ultimate disposition of the property within the estate plan and to solve the problem of addressing changes in circumstances that the donor could not anticipate by giving the power holder the ability to change the trust. It is a means of providing for an interested, intelligent, and informed person who will likely be living and capable of making a wise choice of (a) who should receive trust property, (b) how much income or principal should be allocated to any given individual, and (c) when principal or income should be paid out. Often, delegation of decision-making through a power of appointment is a way to avoid family conflict or confrontation by placing the decision-making responsibility in the hands of an objective (or outside-the-family) party. However, as noted above, powers of appointment also can be dangerous if given to the wrong person or an unanticipated conflict of interest occurs. Quite often, in blended families, a general (or even broad limited) power of appointment that is given to a step-parent results in a disinheriting of the donor's children.

2. When the estate owner does not know what the future needs and circumstances of his intended beneficiaries will be–or even who or how many beneficiaries he will have. This is particularly important when a trust has many beneficiaries and the beneficiaries' needs and circumstances are likely to vary and change over time. The power of appointment makes it possible to postpone the time of decision as to the ultimate disposition of property until a date when all the relevant facts affecting that decision are known. For example, at the time of exercise of the power of appointment, the power holder might know that one of the beneficiaries has greater needs than other beneficiaries. Longer term, "dynastic" trusts almost always contain testamentary powers of appointment.

3. When the estate owner desires to qualify assets for the federal estate tax marital deduction, and would like to provide asset management through a trust and retain some right to designate who will receive the property (a gift over to third parties such as children), and, at the same time, allow the surviving spouse to retain some parental control of the assets. If the estate owner's primary objective is to be sure children or someone other than the surviving spouse receives the principal, rather than a power of appointment, he should consider a Qualifying Terminable Interest Property (QTIP) trust, a trust that provides the surviving spouse with income for life, and then passes principal to the designated remainder persons whom the estate owner designates, which we recommend over a broad general power of appointment for blended family couples where the ultimate beneficiaries usually are different. This topic is covered in more detail in Chapter 27. By using the QTIP trust and giving the surviving spouse a limited power of appointment, the donor ensures the property will pass to his intended beneficiaries, but gives the spouse the flexibility to change the amount each beneficiary receives and the manner in which it is received, to allow for changes in circumstances by being given the right to vary the sharing percentages of the children. Of course, in a blended family situation, giving a step-parent a carefully designed *special* power of appointment by will could go a long way toward "encouraging" the donor's children to be nice to their step-parent. A power of appointment can be over only a portion of trust property as well – for example, in a blended family situation where there are two children from a prior marriage and two from the current marriage, a settlor may give their spouse a testamentary power to appoint 50% of the trust to anyone they choose while keeping 50% locked into passing to the children of the first marriage.

4. When the assets in trust would otherwise be subjected to the GST tax upon a taxable termination of the trust. In these situations, it may be advisable to provide the beneficiary of the trust with a general power of appointment (which causes the assets to be taxable in the beneficiary's estate) as opposed to

a limited power of appointment (which does not cause the assets to be included in the beneficiary's estate) to help reduce the overall tax bill. The benefit of this approach has been expanded as a consequence to the increase in the amount of the estate tax applicable exclusion amount to $12,920,000 (in 2023). Even though the assets are taxed in the beneficiary's estate, (because of the general power of appointment) the assets are still sheltered from tax by the beneficiary's estate tax applicable exclusion amount.

5. When a gift to a trust for the benefit of a beneficiary would not otherwise qualify for the gift tax annual exclusion, a withdrawal right granted to the beneficiary that lapses after a specified time (e.g., thirty days) can make the gift a "present interest" that will qualify for the annual exclusion is a presently exercisable general power of appointment.[9] This is often called a "Crummey" power, named after the famous 1968 tax case that allowed an annual exclusion because the court found that the beneficiary's right to withdraw trust assets provided a sufficiently immediate and unfettered right to use, possess, or enjoy the gifted property (i.e., a present rather than future interest).

6. Whenever the donor of the power would like the remainder beneficiaries (takers in default) or eventual appointees to receive a step up in basis on the power holder's death. A testamentary general power of appointment can accomplish this. Though less certain, the exercise of a testamentary *limited* power of appointment may also cause estate inclusion (and step up in basis) if the power is exercised in such a way as to trigger the Delaware Tax Trap.[10] Such powers may be done by formula and curbed so that only assets benefitting from a step up in basis are included and that the donor's intended estate plan is not thwarted.[11]

12.4 WHAT ARE THE REQUIREMENTS?

There are no required or "magic" words or phrases for creating a power of appointment. In fact, it is possible to create such a power without even using the word *appoint*. The courts examine whether the words used in the will or trust manifest an intention to create a power. Thus, a power to invade or consume trust corpus is a power of appointment. So, too, is the power to affect the beneficial enjoyment of a trust by altering, amending, revoking, or terminating the trust.[12] In fact, a general power of appointment can be indirect. For example, if a trustee has the unlimited power to appoint trust principal, and the donor has the power to replace the trustee with anyone, including himself, the donor has a general power of appointment over the trust principal.[13] Where a trust grants a beneficiary a right to appropriate or consume trust principal, that right is a general power of appointment for tax purposes.[14]

A power holder might exercise a power by will with specific language such as:

> Under the will of my deceased husband, Alan, I have, as to certain property, a power of appointment by will; I, now, in the exercise of that power, appoint the property subject to such power as follows: (Then the exercise of the power would follow.)

Another way to exercise the power (assuming a specific reference to that power is not required for its exercise) would be for the power holder to mention powers as part of a general devise or bequest.

> I bequeath and devise all the residue of my property, real and personal, including any property over which I may have a power of appointment, to _____.

In many states, such a general reference to powers of appointment is construed as being sufficient to include that property and, in some states, the residuary clause need not even refer to powers of appointment to exercise a general power of appointment. But it is generally preferable to specifically refer to a power that one intends to exercise (e.g. "pursuant to the power granted to me in Article VII of the XYZ Trust dated xx/xx/xxxx, I hereby appoint the property subject to that power as follows:"). In many states, the residuary clause must expressly exercise the particular power of appointment (or all powers of appointment that the power holder has) in order for it to be effective.

Because of the possibility of confusion and the unintended exercise of a power by the residuary clause in the will of a power holder of a power which is exercisable by will, some draftsmen require that the power be exercised by "an instrument other than a will." In this fashion, the power holder cannot, intentionally or unintentionally, exercise the power by a will, but instead, must use a separate document. If the power can be exercised only by will, it would often be necessary to probate the will in order to exercise the power of appointment.[15] (This would not mean, however, that assets are subject to probate court administration or attendant fees). Many documents permit either. In default of more specific instructions in the trust in most states, a revocable living trust may exercise a power of appointment, even if the trust instrument says "by will."[16]

A *release* of a power is a formal statement that the power holder is giving up the power.

A *lapse* is the termination of a power without exercise. Either a release or a lapse may result in inclusion in a power holder's estate for federal estate tax purposes, under the same conditions as an exercise.

A separate categorization of powers of appointment exists with regard to federal estate tax. Regardless of whether there are other restrictions on the possible appointees of the power, the power will be termed a "general" power for purposes of federal estate tax law if it can be appointed in favor of any one or more of the group consisting of the holder of the power, his estate, his creditors, or his estate's creditors. A power that can be appointed to satisfy a legal obligation of the powerholder is treated as exercisable in favor of the power holder.[17] For tax purposes, a power of appointment includes all powers that are in substance and effect powers of appointment, regardless of what name those powers are given.[18]

The property owner must decide upon the person to whom the power is to be given (the donee or power holder). This person can be anyone who has, under local law, the legal capacity to execute the instrument that must be employed to use the power. For example, if the donor specified that the power holder must exercise the power by will, the power holder must be old enough to execute a valid will. However, the power holder need not necessarily have attained that age at the time of creation of the power.

Once a power holder has been selected, that person must follow the manner of exercising the power of appointment that the donor specified. This means that, if the donor provided the power holder with a power to be exercised during lifetime, it cannot be exercised by will (since a will takes effect after death). If the donor had not stated how the power is to be exercised, the power holder can use any normal method by which the property subject to the power could be transferred.

Therefore, real property could be appointed by deed and stock certificates by endorsement.

However, the document establishing the power of appointment will usually provide that the power of appointment be exercised through a will or other written document specifically referring to the power of appointment. In such cases, it would be acceptable to exercise the power of appointment by will, but it would be necessary to probate the will in order to exercise the power of appointment. Requiring a specific reference to the power of appointment, helps protect against an *accidental* exercise of the power.

In some states, a power of appointment will automatically be exercised–regardless of whether or not the power holder has referred to the power–by the residuary clause ("all the rest, residue, and remainder I give") in the power holder's will (unless the power holder has stated a contrary intent). If the power holder does not exercise the power, the property subject to appointment does not pass to the power holder's intestate successors (the power holder does not technically own the property for property law purposes, even if he holds a general power of appointment under federal tax law); therefore, it will pass according to the donor's desires, if they were expressed in a "gift over," also known as a provision in default of appointment. Under the Uniform Powers of Appointment Act, a residuary clause is only effective to exercise a power of appointment under very limited circumstances and requires: (a) the power holder to not express a contrary intent toward exercise; (b) the power is a general power of appointment exercisable in favor of the power holder's estate; (c) there are no validly designated takers in default; and (d) the power holder does not release or refrain from exercising the power of appointment.[19]

12.5 HOW IT IS DONE – EXAMPLES

Example 1. Alan Ferry would like to provide his wife with a power of appointment. He might do this by providing in his will language similar to the following:

Upon the death of my wife, to pay over the principal to such persons (including, but not limited to, my wife or her estate), and/or corporations, in such estates, interests, and proportions and in such manner, without any restriction or limitation whatsoever, as my said wife may, if she survives me, appoint by making specific reference to this power in and by her last will duly admitted to probate; or, in default of such appointment, then to divide the principal of the trust, as it shall then exist, into as many equal shares as I shall have children then living and deceased children of mine who shall be survived by issue then living.

This provision would give the wife a "general" power of appointment for purposes of the law of trusts. Additionally, it is a general power for estate tax purposes, since it is one in which the power holder, Alan's wife, has the power to pass on an interest to anyone including herself or her estate, her creditors, or the creditors of her estate. The example illustrates a "testamentary" power, a power exercisable only by will at the power holder's death. If Alan's wife predeceases Alan or dies without effectively exercising her power to appoint, the principal goes to the "takers in default" (of exercise), Alan's children.

Example 2. Suppose Alan wanted to be sure that his property would be kept intact within his family. He could limit the class to whom his wife could appoint by giving her a limited or "special" power. He might use language such as:

Upon my wife's death, such property shall be distributed to such of my issue [and spouses of my issue] as she shall appoint by an instrument other than a will making specific reference to this power; and if she shall make no effective appointment, then in equal shares to my children, the issue of any such child who is not then living to take their parent's share, per stirpes. Provided further, that in no event may my wife make any such appointment to herself, her estate, her creditors, or the creditors of her estate, or to satisfy any of her legal obligations.

Here, the power is a "special" (or limited) power for trust purposes, and is also not a "general power" for estate tax purposes.

However, if the wife were given the power by her husband to appoint the property to any descendants of the donor's grandfather or the spouses of such descendants, the power may be a "general" power for estate tax purposes (since, as a spouse of a descendant of the husband's grandfather, she could include herself within the group of appointees and appoint the property to herself). If this is interpreted as being able to appoint to one's estate, the power would be general. There are rulings, however, that conclude that such a power would not include appointing to one's estate, and since one cannot appoint to themselves in a testamentary power (as the power holder would be dead), such a power of appointment is *not* general.[20] Despite these positive rulings, it is best to simply avoid the issue with good drafting.

For most planning purposes, the categorization for estate and gift tax law purposes is more important, and that categorization will be used exclusively in the balance of this discussion. We will refer to a power of appointment that is not a general power as a special power of appointment for the remainder of this chapter.

The distinction between a general and a special power has very important tax ramifications that are discussed below.

12.6 TAX IMPLICATIONS

When thinking about federal income, estate, gift, and generation-skipping transfer tax consequences, the first step is to classify powers of appointment as either general or special.

General Powers of Appointment

A general power of appointment, which for federal gift, estate, and GST tax purposes grants the holder the power to appoint the assets to the powerholder, the estate of the powerholder, or creditors of either the powerholder or the powerholder's estate, or in satisfaction of the powerholder's legal obligations.

The mere existence of a general power of appointment (as considered for federal estate tax purposes) will cause property subject to it to be includable in a power holder's estate. (A power granted in a will is generally considered to be created at the testator's death.[21] A power granted in an inter vivos instrument is considered created on the date the agreement becomes effective, usually the date it is executed, but for a revocable living trust this would also not until it becomes irrevocable at death.) Code Section 2041 requires the estate of a power holder to include all property over which the power holder has at death a general power of appointment. Mere existence of the power is sufficient, even if the power holder does not know about the power or is incapable of exercising it at death (for instance, due to incapacity).[22]

If a general power is exercised or released by a disposition that, if it were a transfer of property owned by the powerholder, would be includable in the powerholder's gross estate under the lifetime transfer rules, the property subject to the power will be includable. For instance, where a beneficiary of a trust exercised a power to amend a trust by requiring mandatory payment of trust income to himself during his life instead of discretionary payments as provided by the trust, the trust property was included in his gross estate, being in the nature of a transfer of property with a retained life income interest.[23]

A release or lapse of a general power is treated the same as if the powerholder gave property he could have taken personally (or disposed of to the beneficiary of his choice) to the takers in default. For this reason, a release or lapse of a general power may be subject to gift taxation.[24] A qualified disclaimer of a general power of appointment (perhaps to avoid the tax on generation-skipping transfers) will probably also avoid the gift tax problem.

If a power of appointment is "general," the exercise, release, or lapse of the power will be considered a transfer of the property by the powerholder for gift, estate, and generation-skipping transfer tax purposes. If this occurs during life, the result is a taxable gift. If at death, the property is subject to estate tax. Such transfers could also be subject to generation-skipping transfer tax.

An exception to this rule is a de minimis power of appointment that lapses.

Example. If the powerholder has the power to appoint $14,000 from a trust each year to any person and the power lapses at the end of the year, the lapse of such a power is a taxable gift only to the extent the value of the lapsed transfer exceeds the greater of $5,000 or 5 percent of the value of the trust property. So, if the trust has assets with a net value of $1,000,000 in this example, none of the amount of each year's lapse would be considered a taxable gift [5 percent of $1,000,000 = $50,000]. (See "Five-and-Five" Powers below.)

Another exception to this rule is a power exercisable only with the consent of the creator of the power or a person who has a substantial adverse interest in the exercise of the power, generally another beneficiary who will lose something significant if the power is exercised.

Special Powers of Appointment

A special power to appoint to anyone in the world other than the powerholder, the estate of the powerholder, or creditors of either the powerholder or the powerholder's estate, or in satisfaction of a legal obligation of the powerholder. The exercise, release, or lapse of this power, as broad as it sounds, is still not a general power and will usually have no adverse tax consequences.

Neither the mere existence of a special power of appointment, nor the exercise, release or lapse of such a right, will cause inclusion in the power holder's gross estate.[25]

No gift tax is typically imposed by the exercise, release or lapse of a special power of appointment unless it is exercised during lifetime and, by so exercising, the power holder surrenders a valuable right (i.e., the income from the property).[26] A gift tax may also apply if the appointment triggers the Delaware Tax Trap, such as if the appointment is to a trust that grants a beneficiary a *Crummey*-like withdrawal power.[27]

A special power to appoint property to or for the benefit of the powerholder that is limited by so-called "ascertainable standards." These are standards relating to the Health, Education, Maintenance, or Support (HEMS) of the powerholder. The exercise, lapse, or release of this power has no tax consequences.

A power exercisable by the powerholder, acting alone, to vest corpus or income of a trust in the powerholder. This causes the powerholder to be treated as the owner of all of, or part of, the trust for federal income tax purposes.[28]

"Five-and-Five" Powers

A "five-and-five" power is a very commonly used and highly valuable technique to provide flexibility and financial security for a beneficiary with little or no tax consequence. There is a *de minimis* rule that says, in essence, that for administrative reasons the tax law will ignore lapses of small amounts subject to a general power of appointment. The law provides that property subject to a general power that lapses will be included in a powerholder-decedent's estate (or considered a taxable gift) only to the extent that the property that could have been appointed by the exercise of the power but allowed to lapse exceeds the greater of (a) $5,000 or (b) 5 percent of the total value of the fund subject to the power as valued at the time of the lapse.[29]

Stated another way, to the extent that a lapse of a general power within a calendar year exceeds the greater of (a) $5,000 or (b) 5 percent of the assets subject to the power, the *excess* is treated as a release of a general power and taxed accordingly. The excess may be treated as a gift subject to gift tax or as a transfer that may be subject to estate tax. To make certain that the limits set forth above are not breached, the right of invasion must be made noncumulative.

Example 1. Brian Gordon was the income beneficiary of a trust with assets of $200,000. The value of the trust remained constant. Brian was also given a noncumulative power (which he did not exercise and which therefore lapsed each year) to withdraw $10,000 of principal a year. On Brian's death, only the $10,000 subject to the power at the time of his death is included in his gross estate. The power that lapsed in prior years can be ignored because the amount that could be appointed each year did not exceed the greater of $5,000 or 5 percent of the corpus of $200,000.

Example 2. Jamie Gordon was the income beneficiary of a trust with assets of $80,000. She also had a noncumulative power (which she did not exercise) to withdraw $10,000 of principal a year. At the expiration of each year, Jamie is deemed to have released a general power to the extent of $5,000 (i.e., a $10,000 lapse minus the greater of $5,000 or 5 percent of $80,000).

Assume that Jamie died in the sixth year of the trust's existence and that the value of the trust assets remained constant at $80,000. Each $5,000 released by Jamie constituted one-sixteenth (5,000/80,000) of the value of the trust assets. Therefore, Jamie's gross estate would include $35,000 on account of this trust. The $35,000 consists of $10,000 on account of the power held by the decedent at the time of her death and $25,000 (i.e., five-sixteenths of the $80,000 value of trust assets equals $25,000) on account of the lapse of the power in each of the five prior years. Each year's lapse is included in the decedent's gross estate to the extent of one-sixteenth of the value of the trust assets because it had the effect of a transfer with a retained life estate.

In addition to the inclusion for estate tax purposes, the failures to exercise the power would result in gifts to the remainder persons of the trust, with the reduction each year by the then value of Jamie's life estate in the lapsed amounts. The relative value of the life estate and remainder interest can be obtained from the government valuation tables.

Income Tax Consequences

While the lapse of a five-and-five power may have no estate or gift tax consequences, the same is not true for income taxes. Code section 678(a)(2) provides that a nongrantor (e.g., a powerholder) is "treated as the owner of any portion of a trust with respect to which ... such person has previously partially released or otherwise modified such a power and after the release or modification retains such control as would, within the principles of Code sections 671 to 677, inclusive, subject a grantor of a trust to treatment as the owner thereof" (e.g., a retained income interest in the transferred interest). Thus, if a trust beneficiary has a "five-and-five" power (e.g., a Crummey withdrawal right limited to the greater of $5,000 or 5 percent of the trust corpus) and fails to exercise the power in a given year, that powerholder becomes the grantor of that portion of the trust over which the power lapsed (although if the grantor/spouse retain certain rights or powers under Code sections 671 to 677, this would override the beneficiary deemed owner status while the grantor is living and the powers are retained).[30]

As such, if the power is allowed to lapse in multiple years, the powerholder-beneficiary becomes the grantor of an ever-increasing portion of the trust assets and will be taxed on the income accordingly.[31] Although it is not entirely clear that lapses are the same as a "partial release", many private letter rulings have so held.[32]

This discrepancy between the income tax treatment of the trust and the estate and gift tax consequences of the beneficiary's lapse can, however, be useful. First, trusts reach the higher income tax rates much sooner than do individuals.[33] Therefore, taxation of the powerholder-beneficiary rather than the trust can save income taxes. In addition, if the beneficiary is treated as the owner of the entire trust for income tax purposes (e.g., all amounts contributed to the trust were subject to the income beneficiary's withdrawal power), the trust can qualify as an eligible shareholder of an S corporation under Code section 1361(c)(2)(A)(i) even if the trust is not eligible under other provisions, and qualify for many other tax benefits denied to trusts as well.[34] See the new Chapter 35 on Beneficiary Deemed Owner Trusts (BDOTs) for more information on using such presently exercisable general powers of appointment over income only.

12.7 HANGING POWERS

A hanging power creates a cumulative power in the beneficiary to appoint any lapsed property in excess of the greater of $5,000 or 5% per year in future years or by will at death.[35] The hanging power thus avoids a lapse of the excess amount by permitting the holder to exercise it in the future. If the trust is not terminated when the beneficiary dies, then the beneficiary is in possession of the power at death. Property subject to that power is therefore includable in the powerholder's estate for federal estate tax purposes. If the trust terminates before the powerholder dies, there is no adverse estate tax result (although there may be gift tax consequences if unused withdrawal powers exceed a five-and-five limitation in the year of termination).

Under this hanging power approach, the withdrawal power – up to the five-and-five limitation – lapses in any given year. The excess withdrawal power is carried over to future years. In future years the carried-over withdrawals are lapsed to the extent of the five-and-five ceiling.

The following illustrates this strategy:

Year	Gift	Withdrawal Powers	Lapses
2015	$13,000	$13,000	$5,000
2016	13,000	21,000	5,000
2017	-0-	16,000	5,000
2018	-0-	11,000	5,000
2019	-0-	6,000	5,000
2020	-0-	1,000	1,000
2021	-0-	-0-	-0-

There are a number of unresolved problems in using hanging powers. First, if the gifts continue over a number of years, the total withdrawal potential could be sizable, and a beneficiary might be tempted to make a withdrawal of the total amount available. Second, the cumulative, unused withdrawals are includable in the estate for estate tax purposes. Third, if life insurance is used, premiums are paid throughout the life of the policy, and the cumulative withdrawals may continue to increase.

Hanging powers can cause a trust that would otherwise be subject to automatic GST allocation to not be, so practitioners should be careful in relying on automatic allocation rules and affirmatively allocate GST to any such trusts that are intended to be GST exempt.[36]

Hanging powers held by a spouse may also cause an estate tax inclusion period (ETIP) that precludes allocating GST exemption until the spousal withdrawal right lapses.[37]

A private letter ruling held that the hanging power used by a taxpayer that was tied to an amount that would not cause gift tax was not valid because it was the type of adjustment clause that was "contrary to public policy."[38] While this conclusion is dubious in light of more recent case law, caution should still be used in drafting hanging powers.[39]

12.8 ISSUES IN COMMUNITY PROPERTY STATES

Since community property excludes property received by inheritance or gift, it would be very unusual for any property received (or given away by permitting a lapse) to be a community property right initially.

However, a community property agreement (some states require it to be in writing) which was all-inclusive, purporting to have both spouses hold as community property all assets they owned, can have the effect, in some states, of creating a gift, by transmuting separate property into community property, and thus resulting in a gift of one-half of the value from one spouse to the other. If the agreement can be interpreted as including rights of one spouse under a power of appointment, then the right may become community property, resulting in a gift equal to one-half the value of the right at the time of entering into the agreement. Because of the unlimited marital deduction, no federal gift tax would be triggered.

The more common problem encountered is to have the permitted appointee of the property ask to have the property transferred under the exercise of the power titled in the name of his spouse and himself, as community property, thus creating a gift to the appointee's spouse of one-half the value of the property when the spouse receives her one-half community interest in what was intended to be the sole property of the permitted appointee under the power. As was mentioned above, the unlimited marital deduction would eliminate any gift tax exposure under federal tax law. However, state gift tax law should be examined to see if any state gift tax would be caused by such an event. At present, only Connecticut has a state gift tax.

If the community property laws of a state confer upon the wife a power of testamentary disposition over property in which she does not have a vested interest she is considered as having a power of appointment.[40]

Where the holder of a "limited" or "special" power has freedom to choose among the permitted appointees of a power (e.g., where the power includes "the issue of grantor and spouses of such issue"), then the power may be exercised to give each spouse an undivided interest without any gift involvement. The property could, under these circumstances, be appointed to the spouses as community property, joint tenants, or tenants in common (each as to one-half), without any gift being recognized.

12.9 FREQUENTLY ASKED QUESTIONS

Question – How does the rule against perpetuities affect powers?

Answer – The common law rule against perpetuities states the principle that no interest in property is effective unless it *must* vest, if at all, not later than twenty-one years (plus, if applicable, a gestation period) after some life or lives in being at the time an interest is created. In other words, the measuring period under the rule against perpetuities relates back to the creation of the power. (Some states use "wait and see" rules. The interest will be valid *unless* it does not *actually* vest within the appropriate period.) In many states, if the powerholder *could*, in any fashion, make an appointment of the property under the donor's terms beyond the time period permitted by the rule, the power is void. (The test is whether the power, by its terms, *will* be exercised within the allowable time period allowed by the rule.) Note that a number of states have repealed the rule against perpetuities–either explicitly or by extending the duration to the point where the rule is essentially repealed–or permit a transferor to affirmatively opt out under certain circumstances.

However, beware of the "Delaware Tax Trap."[41] This can occur if the power of a limited appointment is exercised in a manner that creates another power of appointment which (under applicable local law) can be exercised in a way that postpones the vesting of any estate or interest in such property, or suspends the absolute ownership or power of alienation of such property, for a period ascertainable without regard to the date of the creation of the first power. In this case the limited power of appointment is treated as a general power of appointment for gift/estate tax purposes. It is a complicated area and confuses even highly experienced trust and tax attorneys. Be cautious when appointing assets to preexisting irrevocable trusts.

Question – Is a power to consume, invade, or appropriate property for the benefit of the power holder a general power for federal estate tax purposes if it is limited to an ascertainable standard relating to the health, education, support, or maintenance (HEMS) of the power holder-decedent?

Answer – No. This makes such provisions extremely useful estate planning techniques for providing financial flexibility without consequent tax burden.[42] The power over income or corpus, or both, must be reasonably measurable in terms of the power holder's needs for health, education, or support (or any combination of these needs). Maintenance and support mean the same thing, are relative terms, and are not limited to bare necessities. In other words the maintenance and support of an individual who has a $100,000 a year standard of living will be very different than someone who is accustomed to a $700,000 a year standard.

Proper wording is essential; if the holder of a power can use property for his "comfort, welfare, or happiness," the power is broad enough to be considered general and will cause the property interest to be subject to federal taxation.[43]

Question – Is property includable in a beneficiary's estate if an independent trustee has a discretionary right to make distributions to that person?

Answer – No. Where the donor gives an independent trustee discretionary authority to invade principal to meet a beneficiary's reasonable needs, that power will not cause property to be includable in the beneficiary's estate.[44] This is yet another way to provide additional security and flexibility and to meet needs not able to be anticipated at the time the trust is created - without adverse tax effects.

Question – Is property includable in a power holder-decedent's estate where there is a requirement that the power holder of a general power of appointment must give notice to the trustee before the exercise takes effect?

Answer – Yes. Whether or not the notice has been given before death and whether or not the power has actually been exercised, inclusion will result. The mere existence of a general power created after 1942 will cause inclusion of the property subject to the power.

Question – Is the creation of a special power to appoint trust property to lineal descendants of the transferor or power holder generally a good estate planning technique?

Answer – Most estate planners consider this special power to be an excellent planning technique. Since the appointees are someone other than the powerholder, his estate, creditors, etc., it is a special power, and has minimal adverse tax consequences to the powerholder. A note of caution, however – if the powerholder has an obligation to support permissible appointees, and the appointment could satisfy that support obligation, it might be classified as a general power. As a result, a lifetime power should bar the powerholder from appointing the assets to satisfy his legal obligations.

One reason such a power is so useful is that it permits someone, generally the surviving spouse, to alter the plan of ultimate distribution to take into consideration varying needs of the children and issue. If one adult child is very successful, and another is not, the appointment can be used to alter otherwise equal distributions to them. However, it is important to determine how broadly the limited power of appointment should be drafted. This becomes a client question to determine how much flexibility you want to provide. While many clients will want to limit the exercise to the descendants of the client, as previously discussed, it is permissible to allow the power holder to appoint to *anyone* other than the power holder, their estate, their creditors, or the creditors of their estate and still qualify as a limited power of appointment. Some clients will want to include charity as a potential appointee, and some will not. Some will wish to include spouses of their children as potential appointees, some will not.

An important use of this power is to permit planning for the generation-skipping transfer tax. The powerholder could "skip" generations where the property would otherwise be distributed to children, and shift it to grandchildren. If the property in question is exempt from GST tax for reasons discussed in Chapter 21, this may be very beneficial. For example, if a child has accumulated a taxable estate of his own, the power can be exercised so that assets to which the donor's (the grantor of the power) generation-skipping exemption had been allocated can pass, in trust, for that child's lifetime (thus allowing that child the use and benefit of the assets) and pass free of estate taxes to grandchildren at the child's death.

Lifetime powers of appointment can be used to shift income taxation – either to children or grandchildren in lower tax brackets, or to charity. As a result of recent tax reform, many middle-class and upper middle class taxpayers will not itemize deductions and receive no tax benefit from charitable donations. A distribution from a non-grantor trust, however, if pursuant to the terms of the trust and traceable to gross income, generally should receive a deduction that is more "above the line" under Code section 642(c).[45]

POWERS OF APPOINTMENT   CHAPTER 12

Question – Can a special (limited) power cause gift tax problems?

Answer – Yes, but the gift tax affects few taxpayers with a lifetime applicable exclusion amount of $12,920,000 (or potentially more with portability or gift-splitting). When an income beneficiary of a trust who also holds a special power of appointment exercises that power during lifetime and in doing so terminates his life interest in part, there may be a taxable gift. The amount of the gift is the present value of the income interest forfeited by the life tenant-donor. Life income beneficiaries should therefore be careful in exercising a lifetime special power because the IRS will argue that, to the extent the exercise terminates the income interest and that interest goes to someone else, a transfer subject to gift tax has been made.[46] Depending on the amount and who it is appointed to, it may qualify for the $17,000 (in 2023) annual exclusion, or even the marital or charitable deduction.

CHAPTER ENDNOTES

1. See, e.g., §102(18), Uniform Powers of Appointment Act (2013).
2. I.R.C. §2041(c)(1). Treas. Reg. §20-2041-1(c)(1). See also Section 102(6), Uniform Powers of Appointment Act (2013).
3. I.R.C. §2041; Treas. Reg. §20.2041-1(c)(1).
4. The first exception in I.R.C. §2041(b)(1)(C)(i) provides an exception to the definition of general power of appointment for those powers that a power holder could not unilaterally exercise except with the joinder or consent of the donor, i.e., the creator of the power of appointment (creator exception). Treas. Reg. §20.2041-3(c)(1). The second exception in IRC §2041(b)(1)(C)(ii) provides an exception where the power holder's exercise of the power can only be done in conjunction with someone who has a substantial interest in the property that is subject to the power that is adverse to exercise of the power in favor of the power holder ("substantial adverse interest exception"). An interest is adverse and is considered substantial if its value in relation to the total value of the property that is subject to the power is not insignificant and is valued in accordance with the actuarial principles of Treas. Reg. § 20.2031-7. A taker in default of appointment has an adverse interest. Treas. Reg. §20.2041-3(c)(2).
5. Treas. Reg. §20-2041-1(c)(1). See also §102(10), Uniform Powers of Appointment Act (2013).
6. I.R.C. §2041(c)(1)(A); Treas. Reg. §20-2041-1(c)(2).
7. Treas. Reg. §20-2041-3(c)(2).
8. See, e.g., §202, Uniform Powers of Appointment Act (2013).
9. *Crummey v. Comm'r.*, 397 F.2d 82 (9th Cir. 1968).
10. I.R.C. §2041(a)(3).
11. See Ed Morrow and The Optimal Basis Increase Trust (OBIT), LISI Estate Planning Newsletter #2080 (March 20, 2013) periodically updated via white paper titled "The Optimal Basis Increase and Income Tax Efficiency Trust" available for free download at www.ssrn.com. See also *Ed Morrow on PLR 202206008: Judicial Settlement Modification & Formula Testamentary General Powers of Appointment*, LISI Estate Planning Newsletter #2945 (March 16, 2022).
12. Treas. Reg. §20.2041-1(b)(1).
13. Treas. Reg. § 20-2041-1(b)(1).
14. Treas. Reg. §20.2041-1(b)(1).
15. Powers of appointment exercised by will (even general) should not subject an estate to additional executor or attorney for executor fees either. *In re Estate of Wylie*, 342 So.2d 996 (Fla. Dist. Ct. App. 4th Dist. Feb. 4, 1977).
16. *Restatement of Property, Third, Donative Transfers*, §19.9 – even if the document requires "by will", the default rule is to permit a revocable living trust, as long as it is still revocable at a power holder's death, to exercise a testamentary power of appointment. See also Section 304 of the Uniform Power of Appointment Act.
17. I.R.C. §2041; Treas. Reg. §20.2041-1(c)(1).
18. Treas. Reg. §20.2041-1(b)(1).
19. §302, Uniform Powers of Appointment Act (2013).
20. PLR 201229005, PLR 201231007.
21. Treas. Regs. §§20.2041-1(e), 25.2514-1(e).
22. *Est. of James C. Freeman v. Comm'r.*, 67 T.C. 202 (1976).
23. I.R.C. §2041(a)(2); Treas. Reg. §20.2041-3(d)(1). See also *Est. of Gartland v. Comm'r.*, 34 TC 867 (1960), aff'd, 293 F.2d 575 (7th Cir.), cert. den., 368 U.S. 954.
24. I.R.C. §§2514(a), 2514(b).
25. I.R.C. §2041(a)(2).
26. I.R.C. §2514(b).
27. The Delaware Tax Trap is at I.R.C. §2514(d) for gift tax purposes, and IRC §2041(a)(3) for estate tax purposes. For a discussion of this, see Les Raatz, *"Delaware Tax Trap" Opens Door to Higher Basis for Trust Assets*, 41 Est. Plan. 3 (Feb. 2014) and the white paper titled "The Optimal Basis Increase and Income Tax Efficiency Trust" by Edwin Morrow available for free download at www.ssrn.com.
28. I.R.C. §678. For discussion of how to shift income taxation in this manner without granting the power to withdraw over all of the corpus, see *Ed Morrow: IRC §678(a) and the Beneficiary Deemed Owner Trust (BDOT)*, LISI Estate Planning Newsletter #2577 (Sept 5, 2017).
29. Treas. Regs. §§20.2041-3(d)(3), 25.2514-3(c)(4).
30. Priv. Ltr. Ruls. 9625031, 9810008, 199942037.
31. PLR 9034004 describes the calculation. See also PLR 200022035 and PLR 200104005.
32. More recent PLRs include: PLRs 200022035, 200104005, 200147044, 200949012 and 201039010.
33. I.R.C. §1. As of 2018, this top marginal rate is reached at only $12,500 ($12,700 for long term capital gains).
34. See Priv. Ltr. Ruls. 9625031, 199942037 regarding S corporation eligible ownership. For more discussion on income tax advantages of such trusts, see *Ed Morrow: IRC §678(a) and the Beneficiary Deemed Owner Trust (BDOT)*, LISI Estate Planning Newsletter #2577 (Sept 5, 2017).
35. Priv. Ltr. Rul. 8229097.

36. See discussion in *Dan Griffith & Ed Morrow on Using 20/20 Hindsight for Allocating GST Exemption to 2021 Gifts to Trust*, LISI Estate Planning Newsletter #2982 (Sept. 19, 2022).
37. See I.R.C. §2642(f).
38. Priv. Ltr. Rul. 8901004.
39. Harrison, "Lapse of Crummey Power Need Not Result in Taxable Gift if Hanging Power Is Used," 17 *Est. Plan.* 140 (May/June 1990).
40. Treas. Reg. § 20.2041-1(b).
41. I.R.C. §§2041(a)(3) and 2514(d). See also PLR 201029011.
42. I.R.C. §2041(b)(1)(A).
43. Treas. Regs. §§20.2041-1(c)(2), 25.2514-1(c)(2). See also Rev. Rul. 77-60, 1977-1 CB 282.
44. *Est. of Council v. Comm'r.*, 65 TC 594 (1975).
45. I.R.C. §642(c). It is also more advantageous to avoid mandatory "all net income" provisions in trusts, so that the trust charitable income tax deduction is not limited to the amount of taxable income beyond accounting income (e.g. only income attributable to principal such as capital gains).
46. *Est. of Regester v. Comm'r.*, 83 TC 1 (1984).

DISCLAIMERS

CHAPTER 13

13.1 INTRODUCTION

A disclaimer (or renunciation) is an unqualified refusal by a potential beneficiary to accept benefits given through a testamentary or lifetime transfer of property. Most often, a disclaimer refers to the refusal by a potential beneficiary to accept a bequest under the terms of a will or trust.

The disclaimer could be of property or of a power over property, such as a power of appointment.[1] Fiduciaries also can disclaim both property and powers, but depending on state law this may require court approval.[2] Owners of jointly held property also can disclaim their survivorship interests.[3] A person may disclaim the interest or power even if its creator imposed a spendthrift provision or similar restriction on transfer or a restriction or limitation on the right to disclaim.[4] It is even possible to make a partial disclaimer, which may be expressed as a fraction, percentage, monetary amount, limitation of a power or any other interest or estate in the property.[5] It can even be by formula referencing the decedent's available applicable exclusion amount.[6]

For federal tax purposes, the disclaimant (i.e., the potential beneficiary who refuses to accept the transfer of property) is regarded as never having received the property, i.e., as if he predeceased the transferor of the property. As a result, no transfer is considered to have been made *by the disclaimant* for federal gift, estate, or Generation-Skipping Transfer (GST) tax purposes if it is qualified under Code section 2518.[7] This makes the disclaimer an extremely effective way to shift property interests without adverse tax consequences – and in some cases – affect a highly advantageous tax result which would not be possible in the absence of a disclaimer.

In some cases a disclaimer may be effective for federal tax purposes even if it is not effective under state law. However, to be fully effective for both federal and state purposes, the disclaimer must comply with federal and applicable state law and may have to meet two sets of separate and distinct rules.

It is imperative to check applicable state law because some states have a time period during which disclaimers must be made, e.g., six or nine months, although the Uniform Disclaimer of Property Interests Act and the majority of states have no time period for making a disclaimer. The disclaimant is treated for state law purposes as if he or she had predeceased the transferor of the property or the power.[8] A disclaimer *relates back* to the time of creation of the disclaimed transfer as if that transfer never existed.[9]

For federal tax purposes, the disclaimer has a different but overlapping definition than it does for state law purposes. For federal transfer tax purposes, in order to have no adverse transfer tax effects, a disclaimer must be "qualified." A disclaimer is qualified if:

1. it is unqualified and irrevocable;

2. it is in writing;

3. it is delivered to the transferor or his or her legal representative on or before:

    a. the expiration of nine months from the date that the interest was created; or

    b. the potential disclaimant's attainment of age twenty-one, whichever last occurs;

4. the potential disclaimant has not accepted the property or any of its benefits; and

5. as a result of the disclaimer, the property passes either to the decedent's spouse or to someone other than the disclaimant without any direction by the disclaimant.[10]

It is possible for a qualified disclaimer to be partial in nature, and parts measured in fractions and formulae are permitted.[11] However, the types of partial disclaimers that are qualified disclaimers are more limited than the types of partial disclaimers that state law permits. For example, a disclaimer of ten years' worth of trust income of a life income interest, which is a valid partial disclaimer under state law,[12] would not be a qualified disclaimer.[13]

Therefore, it is possible for an action to be a valid disclaimer for state law purposes but not a "qualified disclaimer" for federal transfer tax purposes. But it would be very difficult for an action to be a qualified disclaimer for federal transfer tax purposes but not for state law purposes, although the IRS interprets Code section 2518(b)(4) as requiring disclaimers to be valid under applicable state law in order to be a qualified disclaimer, and the courts have agreed.[14] About the only example of the latter would be a disclaimer in a state that had a period for disclaiming that ended earlier than nine months,[15] but it is conceivable that there could be others. An action in the form of a transfer of all of the disclaimant's interests in the subject property that is not a valid state law disclaimer and that triggers a state transfer tax but over which a qualified disclaimer is made is nevertheless still a qualified disclaimer for federal transfer tax purposes even though the disclaimant paid a state transfer tax.[16]

A disclaimer that is *not* qualified is treated for transfer tax purposes as if the disclaimant received the property and then transferred the property, which often, if not usually, results in a gift by the disclaimant.[17] Therefore, a qualified disclaimer relates back to the action that gave rise to the right, e.g., the decedent's death or gift.[18] However, once the potential disclaimant exercises a power over the property, such as a power of appointment, it is too late, and the disclaimer is not qualified, so that the disclaimant has made a transfer for transfer tax purposes.[19]

13.2 WHEN IS USE OF SUCH A DEVICE INDICATED?

1. When an individual with children and a large estate in his own right is left a bequest by another individual and this bequest would compound the recipient's potential estate tax problem, a disclaimer may be an appropriate estate planning tool. The first recipient may wish to disclaim the bequest in favor of the next recipients under the will or trust, very often his children. By making the disclaimer, the disclaimed property will not be included in the disclaimant's estate at his death.

2. Where an individual who is in a high income tax bracket is left a bequest "if he is living, otherwise to his children," and his children are in lower income tax brackets, a disclaimer can shift the income taxation attributable to the property to the children's lower tax brackets (assuming the children are age eighteen or older (or, in the case of a full time student, age twenty-four or older)) if the children are the next recipients of the bequest under the will or trust.

3. Where a beneficiary of property under a will or trust wishes to make a tax-free transfer (which does not count as a gift for tax purposes) to the person who would be the next recipient of such property under the will or trust, he or she can disclaim the property. It can be very helpful to strategically arrange estate plans of close friends and ascendants in order to be able to take advantage of the disclaimer rules.

4. When property is left to a surviving spouse who doesn't need or want it, the surviving spouse could disclaim the portion that he doesn't want and avoid a needless double taxation upon his death.

5. As a corollary to the last situation, where the value of the property left to the surviving spouse qualifies for the marital deduction, a disclaimer can be used to reduce the deceased spouse's taxable estate below the amount which is sheltered by the deceased spouse's estate tax applicable exclusion amount. In essence, a disclaimer by the surviving spouse effectively increases the deceased spouse's estate to an amount that will be fully offset by the unified credit equivalent. This also keeps the property out of the estate of the surviving spouse for estate tax purposes. Refer to the extended discussion in Chapter 27. However, two aspects of the current

estate tax laws make this strategy less important. First, the estate tax applicable exclusion amount (12,920,000 in 2023 with inflation adjustments through 2025, and reversion back to $5 million plus inflation adjustments in 2026) will make the estate tax inapplicable to all but a very small few. Second, a surviving spouse is able to use the estate tax applicable exclusion amount of the deceased spouse via portability. Portability corrects this problem by allowing the surviving spouse to use the deceased spouse applicable exclusion amount (DSUEA) under Code section 2010(c)(4). Therefore, a married couple can shelter $25,840,000 (2023) from the estate tax. These thresholds decrease the number of situations where this approach will be necessary.

6. However, most states with separate estate and inheritance taxes do not have a portability equivalent (and many have a lookback period for gifts), so residents in those states may still see a benefit in a spouse disclaiming for *state estate and inheritance tax* reasons similar to the above.

7. Where the bequest to the surviving spouse is not sufficient to take advantage of the optimum marital deduction, a disclaimer by other beneficiaries in favor of the surviving spouse may be used to qualify a transfer for the marital deduction. Refer to the discussion of marital deduction planning in Chapter 27.

8. Where there is a trust with an interest passing to charity that does not meet the requirements for a charitable deduction discussed in Chapter 37, a disclaimer by other beneficiaries may be used to qualify the trust interest for the deduction.

9. Where an error was made in the drafting of a will or trust, a disclaimer may be used to correct the error, if the circumstances permit.

10. Where there is a need or desire to avoid creditors, it may be appropriate to use a disclaimer. The desire to avoid creditors most often arises in the case of an elderly or disabled beneficiary whose receipt of assets would disqualify such beneficiary from receiving certain benefits (e.g., SSI or other medical benefits). This may be considered an "improper transfer" for Medicaid and other means tested benefits, however.[20] The majority of states would not consider a disclaimer to be a "fraudulent transfer" but a handful still have contrary law. Moreover, federal law may supersede state law if the creditor is the federal government and a disclaimer, even if not a fraudulent transfer under state law, may still have an adverse effect on qualifying a debtor for a bankruptcy discharge.[21] State and federal law should be consulted prior to making a disclaimer for the purposes of avoiding creditors.

11. Where a disclaimer can enhance or make possible an available election under the federal estate tax law.

12. Where the disclaimant wants to enhance or even create some GST tax planning. Recall that GST exemption does not "port" to the surviving spouse as the estate/gift exclusion does.

13. A disclaimer could facilitate the termination of a trust.

14. A disclaimer could allow the disclaimant to avoid some environmental liability exposure.

15. A disclaimer of an interest in an IRA may make it possible for a spouse to be able to roll over the IRA into a new IRA or enable younger beneficiaries to receive a longer "stretch."

16. A disclaimer by a surviving spouse of bank and brokerage accounts titled in joint and survivorship and/or joint revocable trust may permit the surviving spouse (or other beneficiaries taking in default) to receive an increased basis in those accounts to the extent the decedent had provided the source of funds in the account. This may be a valuable post-mortem basis increasing strategy for couples owning appreciated non-community property in such accounts.[22]

Other Factors

A disclaimer can have significant and sometimes unanticipated consequences for the disclaimant and for the others who have related interests. Some of the factors to be considered are:

1. If a disclaiming beneficiary is indebted to the estate, the instrument should specify whether the debt may be set off against the alternative takers (who might be the disclaimant's children).[23]

2. A disclaimer of a power may extinguish it; hence, it may be desirable to designate an alternative donee of the power at the drafting stage.[24]

3. A disclaimer of a legacy may result in the disclaimed legacy passing to the disclaimant's issue under an anti-lapse statute.[25]

4. A disclaimer could cause a premature closing of a class of beneficiaries.

5. It is generally desirable to express a partial disclaimer in the form of a fraction or percentage. A partial disclaimer may be valid only if it represents an "undivided portion of an interest."[26] However, the disclaimer regulations do permit a beneficiary to disclaim specific assets in a trust, if as a result of that disclaimer, the assets in question will be allocated to another trust or to beneficiaries other than the trust.

6. To guard against the possibility that the disclaimed property may not pass to someone other than the disclaimant (unless it is to a surviving spouse), an alternative taker should be provided for.

7. The instrument should indicate whether a disclaimer accelerates future interests as if the disclaimant had predeceased.

8. It is possible for a disclaimer to create a generation-skipping transfer (GST) by someone other than the disclaimant. This result can occur because, under GST tax law, a "direct skip" transfer (i.e., a transfer to or for an individual two or more generations younger than the transferor) is subject to the GST tax (if it is also subject to federal estate or gift tax). Code sections 2612(c), 2613(a). The first example under "Requirements" (below) illustrates how a disclaimer can create such a GST.

13.3 WHAT ARE THE REQUIREMENTS?

Code section 2518 lists several important requirements for making an effective disclaimer:

1. There must be an irrevocable and unqualified refusal to accept an interest in property.[27]

2. The refusal must be in writing.

3. The writing must be received by the transferor, his legal representative, or the holder of legal title to the property.

4. The refusal must be received no later than nine months after the later of (a) the date on which the transfer creating the interest in the disclaimant is made, or (b) the day on which the disclaimant attains the age of twenty-one.[28]

5. The disclaimer must be made prior to the disclaimant's acceptance of the interest or any of its benefits. A beneficiary and his counsel should exercise extreme caution in their approach to an inheritance, as seemingly inconsequential, and often unintended, actions can constitute "acceptance" of the interest, thereby precluding an effective disclaimer. This requirement that the disclaimer be made prior to acceptance is one of the major problems in implementing a disclaimer. It is essential that a beneficiary consider whether or not a disclaimer is appropriate prior to accepting or taking *any* action with respect to the assets being inherited. Compare two examples from the relevant regulations in which the IRS determined that the actions constituted acceptance that precluded a qualified disclaimer,[29] with the actions elsewhere in those regulations where living in the property[30] or paying real estate taxes on the property that was being disclaimed[31] did not rise to the level of acceptance of the benefits of the property. Taking money out of a joint account constitutes acceptance, and returning the money does not matter.[32] Exercising powers to control and manage a business entity may be deemed an acceptance of benefits.[33] Payment of a spouse's personal bills from the estate account precluded the spouse's disclaimer of estate assets.[34] Actual consideration paid to the disclaimant for the disclaimer would invalidate it.[35]

6. The interest must pass either to the spouse of the decedent or to a person other than the disclaimant without any direction on the part of the disclaimant. (A valid disclaimer by a surviving spouse may be made even though the interest passes under a will or to a trust in which the surviving spouse has an interest, but no one other than a surviving spouse can take advantage of this rule.)

7. The interest disclaimed should be an entire interest, but can be an undivided fractional part of the proposed gift. Since it is often difficult to identify within nine months the exact amount of an inheritance, the amount of a disclaimer can be calculated pursuant to the terms of a formula.

Example 1. Doug Koch, a wealthy client, has four children. Doug's aunt just died and, under the terms of her will, Doug was named as the sole beneficiary of her entire estate if he is alive. If he is deceased when she dies, Doug's four children are named equally as contingent heirs. Doug has adequate assets and income to live comfortably, and does not need additional property to compound his already high potential estate tax.

Doug should strongly consider making a qualified disclaimer. If Doug makes a qualified disclaimer, he will be deemed to have predeceased his aunt for federal transfer tax purposes. Any interest Doug had in her estate will be distributed to his children under the terms of his aunt's will without any federal gift, estate, or GST tax liability to him. However, the distribution of the property to Doug's children will constitute a direct skip from his aunt for GST tax purposes. The transfer(s) may (or may not) attract the GST tax, depending upon how much property is involved and on the extent to which the aunt's GST tax exemption ($12,920,000 for 2023) is or can be allocated to the transfers. The "predeceased child" exception that applies when a child dies does not apply to disclaimers.

Example 2. Ed Radosh specifically leaves $100,000 to his son with a gift over to his favorite charity if his son disclaims. After Ed's death, his son can decide whether to accept the bequest, donate it to charity and receive an income tax deduction on his personal income tax return, or to disclaim the property in favor of the charity and have Ed's estate receive the charitable deduction. With the increased applicable exclusion amount, the former option is likely to be more advantageous to the family, since few estates need the charitable estate tax deduction. However, if the funds were coming from a traditional IRA or qualified plan, his son would likely take the latter option to avoid taking the amount into income in the first place, essentially allowing the equivalent of a qualified charitable distribution and yielding a better result than if the funds were taken into income and the amount donated.

Example 3. Jules Einhorn thought that, at his death, his wife Carol would have ample funds and his son very little. Therefore, he left most of his property to his son, with a contingent gift to his wife if his son predeceased him. At the time of Jules's death, the son was financially well off, but the surviving spouse was in more difficult financial straits. By disclaiming his share and permitting the surviving spouse to take, the son not only allowed a better distribution of assets, but also may have qualified Jules' estate for a marital deduction due to the transfer of the assets to the surviving spouse. This could result in a substantial saving on federal or state estate taxes. The surviving spouse could then make gift tax-free transfers to her son using the gift tax annual exclusion and the applicable exclusion amount.

Example 4. The combined estates of Doug and Jody Mackle are worth approximately $2,500,000. They each intend to leave their share of the estate to the other, or if both are deceased, in trust for their minor children. Since the total value of their estates is less than the applicable exclusion amount, there is no federal estate tax consequence. However, the estate has a substantial growth potential.

The Mackles should consider the use of a disclaimer trust. This is a trust that will function only in the event the surviving spouse (or his or her estate representative) disclaims the bequest under the will or trust. The trust may be for the benefit of the surviving spouse and the children, or the children only. If, at the death of the first spouse, the combined estates of the deceased and surviving spouses would exceed the applicable exclusion amount, then the surviving spouse can disclaim into the trust to take advantage of all or part of the applicable exclusion amount of the estate of the deceased spouse. When the surviving spouse dies, the trust created by the disclaimer will bypass his or her taxable estate. However, portability also could solve the Mackle's problem. In the blended family, the use of a disclaimer trust arrangement often results in the disinheritance of the family of the first spouse to die.

State Law

State law is important because it governs property rights, and how and under what conditions and to whom property will pass. It is possible that a person could make a valid disclaimer under federal law, which would not be an effective disclaimer of property rights under state law (e.g., a disclaimer which is made within the nine-month period prescribed by federal law, but not within the shorter time period prescribed by state law). Federal law makes provision for disclaimers that fail under state law. A written transfer that otherwise meets the requirements of a qualified disclaimer for federal tax purposes will be treated as a qualified disclaimer, if the disclaimed property passes to a person or persons who would have received the property had the disclaimant made a qualified disclaimer.[36]

Conversely, someone may want to make a non-qualified disclaimer that is valid under state law, but would not qualify under Code section 2518 and therefore be a gift for federal tax law. With the lifetime gift, estate and GST tax exclusion amount currently at $12,920,000 (2023), this may not be prohibitive at all for most taxpayers. A non-qualified disclaimer may still have uses, such as to allow a trust to be terminated early in favor of the remaindermen, for example.

13.4 TAX IMPLICATIONS

1. A disclaimer of a property interest or a power is not treated as a gift by the disclaimant for gift tax purposes.[37]

2. A disclaimed interest in property is not considered to be a transfer by a disclaimant for estate tax purposes and will not be included in his estate at death.

3. If property is disclaimed by a person in favor of a surviving spouse or charity, the marital or charitable deduction will be permitted, provided the property would otherwise qualify for these deductions.[38]

4. Generally, any income attributable to disclaimed property will be chargeable to the person in whose favor the property was disclaimed (i.e., the owner of the property).

5. The gift tax regulation clearly applies for estate and GST tax purposes, but surprisingly, there is no clear statute in the income tax context. While there is no clear statute or regulation, case law and rulings suggest that disclaimers are equally effective for income tax purposes.[39]

13.5 ISSUES IN COMMUNITY PROPERTY STATES

Please refer to the background information on Community Property contained in Chapter 7. A qualified disclaimer is taken into account for purposes of the marital deduction. In either a separate property or a community property state, a disclaimer can be expected initially to qualify the estate for the marital deduction or to increase or decrease the deduction if the surviving spouse gains or loses because of the disclaimer.

The availability of the unlimited marital deduction, which applies to both separate and community property, alleviates concerns for future planning in this area. However, different rules apply to the disposition of separate and community property by will or deed in community property states and, therefore, it is still important to carefully characterize all of the property interests held by a decedent and his or her spouse to determine if under community property rules a disclaimer is desired or required.

Where the entire community property is subjected to probate (both the decedent's one-half interest and the surviving spouse's one-half interest) upon the death of only one spouse, the surviving spouse should exercise caution to disclaim only the community property interest of the decedent. A disclaimer of both halves would probably result in a taxable gift to the individual who takes as the result of the disclaimers. As mentioned in Chapter 7, several types of problems can arise when attempting to determine whether specific property is to be characterized as community, quasi-community, or separate. For instance, while Louisiana characterizes as community property that property taken by spouses under a deed (reflecting that the property is held in tenancy in common), the same property is rebuttably presumed to be separate property in California.[40]

13.6 DISCLAIMING PARTICULAR TYPES OF PROPERTY

Life Insurance Benefits

A beneficiary of a life insurance policy may disclaim his or her interest in the proceeds. The interest may be disclaimed within the earlier of nine months of the insured's death or when the claim form is submitted. However, if the beneficiary was an irrevocable beneficiary, the disclaimer most likely must be made within nine months of the beneficiary designation.

However, if a life insurance policy names a spouse but no secondary beneficiary, a disclaimer could result in the policy proceeds falling into the estate of the insured. This would expose the proceeds to creditors, additional probate fees, will provisions, and, in some states, unnecessary estate or inheritance taxes. If the disclaiming spouse is also the beneficiary under the will, a further renunciation would be necessary, because the insurance proceeds would fall into the probate estate as a result of the first disclaimer. Planners should examine beneficiary designations and coordinate life insurance (or pension plan) proceeds so that a single renunciation will accomplish the intended objectives.

Jointly Held Property

An interest in jointly held property may be disclaimed if made within nine months of the creation of the gift and before any of the property or its benefits have been accepted by the disclaimant. However, with respect to a disclaimer of joint property that passes by right of survivorship (other than bank, brokerage, and other investments accounts) the nine-month period generally starts with the date of death of the first joint tenant. This is true regardless of whether either tenant could have partitioned the property under state law while both tenants were living.[41]

The rules get more complicated when determining the amount of the interest in joint property which can be disclaimed. The answer depends upon several factors:

- what type of asset is being disclaimed
- whether each party can claim the asset without assistance from the other party
- who contributed the funds to acquire the asset.

With respect to bank, brokerage and investment accounts; and assuming either party can withdraw their own contributions to the accounts, the portion which can be disclaimed is based upon each owner's contribution. In addition, the survivor cannot disclaim the portion of the property based upon their own contribution. Therefore, if the decedent contributed all of the funds, the survivor can disclaim all of the property. By the same token, if the survivor contributed all of the funds, the survivor cannot disclaim *any* portion of the asset. With respect to real estate and other joint assets (i.e. stocks held in certificate form), the survivor can disclaim one-half of the asset and each party's contribution does not matter.

Interests Received During Minority

An individual can make a qualified disclaimer after attaining age twenty-one, if the disclaimer is made within nine months after reaching age twenty-one and if the other requirements of the law are met. However, the law does not allow a qualified disclaimer if benefits have been received from the property prior to the disclaimer.

A beneficiary who is under twenty-one years of age has until nine months after his twenty-first birthday in which to make a qualified disclaimer of his interest in property. Any actions taken with regard to an interest in property by a beneficiary or a custodian prior to the beneficiary's twenty-first birthday will not be considered an acceptance by the beneficiary of the interest. For instance, a minor who receives dividends on stock prior to the age of twenty-one will not be deemed to have made an acceptance, assuming he did not accept dividends after attaining age twenty-one.

This rule holds even with respect to a gift under the Uniform Gifts to Minors Act or the Uniform Transfers to Minors Act.[42]

Trust Benefits

A trust beneficiary may refuse or disclaim the benefits of the trust, though the trust assets are not severable.[43] Generally, this means that a beneficiary may not disclaim an interest in some trust assets and not others if it is a pot trust, for example, where the asset would still stay in the same trust if the disclaimant predeceased. If the asset would pass to a new subtrust for issue, this should be permitted.

However, a trust beneficiary may disclaim his interest in trust principal and retain his interest in trust income, since an income interest and principal interest are deemed to be separate interests. In addition, since disclaimers of an undivided portion of any separate interest in property are permitted, it is possible for a trust beneficiary to disclaim a percentage or fraction of the beneficiary's interest in the trust (e.g., 10 percent of the beneficiary's income interest).

Survivorship Benefits in Pension and Profit Sharing Plans

The IRS has ruled that disclaimers of survivorship benefits in pension and profit sharing plans are effective. This planning device can be extremely important in view of the requirements that such plans provide survivor annuities (discussed in Chapters 57 and 58).

The IRS has also ruled that it is possible to disclaim an interest in a retirement plan even if the required minimum distribution has been taken for the year of a decedent's death by the disclaimant.[44]

13.7 BLENDED FAMILY CONSIDERATIONS

It can be very important to properly plan for the possibility of disclaimers in blended family couples. In fact, creative anticipation of disclaimers of both property and powers in the form of alternate recipients or holders of powers is almost required because it is foreseeable that there well could be a disclaimer in order to settle disputes between a surviving step-parent and the children of the deceased partner. For example, if a partner is given property in a bequest, it usually is appropriate to draft so that the disclaimed property will not pass to the surviving step-parent's descendants under the anti-lapse statute under applicable state law.

13.8 FREQUENTLY ASKED QUESTIONS

Question – Can a beneficiary of a life insurance policy disclaim his interest in the proceeds? If he or she disclaims, where do the death benefits go?

Answer – Yes, such an interest may be disclaimed within the earlier of nine months of the insured's death or when the claim form is submitted. However, if the beneficiary was an irrevocable beneficiary, the disclaimer most likely must be made within nine months of the beneficiary designation. If the primary beneficiary of a life insurance policy disclaims the death proceeds, the contingent beneficiary would take, and in the absence of a named contingent beneficiary, the policy contract itself would dictate where the death benefits would go, which usually is the insured's estate.

Question – Can an interest in jointly held property be disclaimed?

Answer – Yes, if made within nine months of the creation of the gift and before any of the property or its benefits have been accepted by the disclaimant. However, with respect to a disclaimer of joint property that passes by right of survivorship, the nine month period generally starts with the date of death of the first joint tenant *regardless* of whether either tenant could have partitioned the property under state law while both tenants were living.[45] The rules get more complicated when determining the amount of the interest in joint property that can be disclaimed. The answer depends upon several factors: (i) what type of asset is being disclaimed; (ii), whether each party can claim the asset without assistance from the other party; and (iii) who contributed the funds to acquire the asset.[46]

With respect to bank, brokerage and investment accounts; and assuming either party can withdraw their own contributions to the accounts, the portion that can be disclaimed is based upon each owner's contribution.[47] In addition, the survivor cannot disclaim the portion of the property based upon their own contribution. Therefore, if the *decedent* contributed all of the funds, then the *survivor* can disclaim all of the property. By the same token, if the survivor contributed all of the funds, the survivor cannot disclaim *any* portion of the asset. With respect to real estate and other joint assets, the survivor can disclaim one-half of the asset, and each party's contribution does not matter.[48]

Question – If a testator dies leaving a trust with income payable to his wife for her lifetime and remainder payable to his child, can the child disclaim the child's remainder interest after the wife's death?

Answer – Not unless the wife died within nine months of the testator; the disclaimer must be made within nine months of the *testator's* death since this is when the gift/transfer was complete. The child would have to disclaim within this period or, if later, within nine months of the date the child reaches age twenty-one. Note that the answer here is the same even if the child must survive the wife to receive the bequest. There is an exception, however, if the wife holds a testamentary general power of appointment, in which case a new 9 month window would start at her death for the child to disclaim.

Question – Is a disclaimer valid where a surviving spouse refuses to accept all or a portion of an interest in property passing from a decedent, and, as a result of that refusal, the property passes to a trust in which that spouse has an income interest [such as the typical family (nonmarital B) trust]?

Answer – A disclaimer will be valid where a spouse refuses an interest in property even if, as a result of that disclaimer, he or she receives an income interest (as long as that income interest does not result from the surviving spouse's direction). However, the spouse must not have the power after the disclaimer, as trustee or otherwise, to direct the distribution of the trust assets to other beneficiaries, such as holding a limited power of appointment. There is an exception that permits spouses to retain a *general* power of appointment, however, which may be extremely valuable in income tax planning by permitting a shifting of tax to the spouse and/or a step up in basis at the spouse's death.[49]

This "Blank Check" postmortem marital deduction planning tool means an estate owner doesn't have to decide how much of his estate should go to a surviving spouse in trust. His will can allow that decision to be made by the survivor when more facts are known. All of the estate owner's property could be left to the surviving spouse with a provision that any part of the bequest that is disclaimed will be placed in the nonmarital (bypass) trust and/or marital trust. This planning may–in some cases–be preferable to a specific marital formula bequest. However, only a spouse can disclaim into a trust in which the disclaimant (i.e., the spouse) has retained an interest.

Question – Can the trustee of a trust disclaim powers held as a trustee, such as the power to make distributions to the trustee as a beneficiary?

Answer – Although the cases and rulings are not entirely clear on this issue, and a trustee may be able to make a qualified disclaimer, the cautious answer is that a qualified disclaimer should be made only by the beneficiary or donee, not the trustee. For example, if the trustee has the power to make distributions to himself or herself and wants to avoid the tax consequences of such a power, the trustee should disclaim the right to *receive* the distributions, not the right to make them. The trustee would then be disclaiming as a beneficiary, not as a trustee. Some states may not permit a fiduciary to disclaim, may only permit if the document expressly authorizes it or may require court permission.[50]

CHAPTER ENDNOTES

1. See, e.g., §§2-1102(3) and 2-1105(a), Uniform Probate Code.
2. See, e.g., §2-1105(b), Uniform Probate Code.
3. See, e.g., §2-1102(5), Uniform Probate Code.
4. See, e.g., §2-1105(a) and (b), Uniform Probate Code.
5. See, e.g., §2-1105(d), Uniform Probate Code.
6. Treas. Reg. §25.2518-3(d) Example (20). "A bequeathed his residuary estate to B. B disclaims a fractional share of the residuary estate. Any disclaimed property will pass to A's surviving spouse, W. The numerator of the fraction disclaimed is the smallest amount which will allow A's estate to pass free of Federal estate tax and the denominator is the value of the residuary estate. B's disclaimer is a qualified disclaimer."
7. I.R.C. §2518(a). However, it is possible for a disclaimer to create a generation-skipping transfer (GST) *by someone other than the disclaimant*. This result can occur because, under GST tax law, a "direct skip" transfer (i.e., a transfer to or for an individual two or more generations younger than the transferor) is a GST subject to the GST tax (if it is also subject to federal estate or gift tax). I.R.C. SS2612(c), 2613(a). The first example under "Requirements" illustrates how a disclaimer can create such a GST.
8. See, e.g., §2-1106(b)(3), Uniform Probate Code.
9. See, e.g., §1106, Uniform Probate Code.
10. I.R.C. §2518(b) and Treas. Reg. §25-2518-2(a).
11. I.R.C. §2518(c)(1) and Treas. Reg. §25.2518-3(c), Example 20.
12. See, e.g., §1105(d), Uniform Probate Code.
13. Treas. Reg. §25.2518-3(b).
14. *Delaune Est. v. U.S.*, 143 F.3d 995 (5th Cir. 1998).
15. See, e.g. Treas. Reg. §25.2518-1(c)(3), Example 1.
16. IRC §2518(c)(3) and Treas. Reg. §25.2518-1(c)(3), Example 3.
17. Treas. Reg. §25-2518-1(b).
18. Treas. Reg. §25.2518-1(b) and Rev. Rul. 83-26.
19. See, e.g., *Engelman Est. v. Comm'r.*, 121 T.C. 54 (2003).
20. See, e.g., Ohio's Medicaid rule at O.A.C. §§5160:1-3- 07. Health Care Financing Administration State Medicaid Manual, pt. 3, §3257(B)(3) available at https://www.cms.gov/Regulations-and-Guidance/Guidance/Manuals/Paper-Based-Manuals-Items/CMS021927.html: "For purposes of this section, the term "assets an individual or spouse is entitled to" includes assets to

which the individual is entitled or would be entitled if action had not been taken to avoid receiving the assets.

21. E.g., Fla.Stat. §739.402(2)(d) provides that a disclaimer of an interest in property is barred if "(d)   The disclaimant is insolvent when the disclaimer becomes irrevocable." However, the vast majority of states follow something akin to the rule in the Uniform Disclaimer of Property Interests Act §6, §13. Qualified disclaimers do not defeat tax liens pursuant to *U.S. v. Drye*, 528 U.S. 49 (1999).

22. See, *Ed Morrow: The "Disclaim to Gain" Strategy and the Missed Opportunities to Save Income Tax for Jointly Held Marital Accounts and Joint Trusts*, LISI Estate Planning Newsletter #2686 (November 29, 2018).

23. *Matter of Colacci*, 549 P.2d 1096 (Colo. App. 1976).

24. Schwartz, "Effective Use of Disclaimers," 19 B.C. Law Rev. 551 (1978); George M. Schain, "The Effective Disclaimer," 34 *Cath. U. L. Rev.* 19 (1985).

25. *Brannan v. Ely*, 157 Md. 100, 145 Atl. 361 (1929); *Thompson v. Thornton*, 197 Mass. 273, 83 N.E. 880 (1908).

26. Schwartz "Effective Use of Disclaimers," 19 B.C. Law Rev. 551, 567, 573 (1978).

27. It is important that there be an irrevocable relinquishment of the asset. In *Estate of Tatum v. United States*, 2011 WL 3444095 (5th Cir. Aug, 2011) reversing and remanding per curiam 2010 WL 3942738, 106 A.F.T.R. 2d 2010-6556 (S.D. Miss., 2010), the lower court had held that the disclaimer constituted a non-qualified disclaimer, and therefore a gift because the disclaimant did not also disclaim their intestate interest.

28. A special transitional rule under the 2010 Act allows disclaimers to be valid if made on or before nine months from the December 17, 2010 date of enactment.

29. See Examples 4 and 5 of Treas. Reg. §25.2518-2(d)(4).

30. Treas. Reg. §25.2518-2(c)(5), Example 10.

31. Treas. Reg. §25.2518-2(d)(4), Example 3.

32. See, e.g., PLR 9012053.

33. See, e.g., TAM 9123003.

34. See, e.g., TAM 8405003.

35. See, e.g., *Monroe Est. v. Commr.*, 104 T.C. 352 (1995), *rev'd*, 124 F.3d 699 (5th Cir. 1997).

36. I.R.C. §2518(c)(3).

37. I.R.C. §2518(a).

38. I.R.C. §§2056(d)(2), 2055(a).

39. I.R.C. §2046 (estate tax rule regarding qualified disclaimers) and I.R.C. §2654(c) (GST tax rule regarding qualified disclaimers) both reference IRC §2518. The IRS, in GCM 39858, held that it would honor any disclaimer qualified under I.R.C. 2518 for income tax purposes in the context of disclaiming retirement plans and that any qualified disclaimer would not be considered an assignment or alienation by the disclaimant. See also Rev. Rul. 2005-36.

40. Internal Revenue Manual Exhibit §25.18.1-1, Comparison of State Law Differences in Community Property States.

41. Treas. Reg. §25.2518-2(c)(4). However, if the property cannot be unilaterally severed by either party (such as with property held as tenants by the entireties); there are actually two nine-month periods. The first begins when the joint tenancy is created to the extent of the interest given to the donee; and the second relates to the survivorship period which occurs after the death of the joint owner.

42. Treas. Regs. §§25.2518-2(c)(3) and (4), 25.2518-2(d)(4), Example (11).

43. However, disclaimers of specific trust assets are permitted, if the assets are thereby removed from the trust and pass, without any direction by the disclaimant, to persons other than the disclaimant or the spouse of the decedent. Treas. Reg. §25.2518-3(a)(2).

44. In Rev. Rul. 2005-36 the IRS permitted a disclaimer of an interest in a retirement account after the decedent's required minimum for the year of death was distributed to the spouse. While the IRS approved the disclaimer, the amount of the required minimum distribution along with the income attributable to such amount, cannot be disclaimed. See also Priv. Ltr. Rul. 201125009.

45. Treas. Reg. § 25.2518-2(c)(4). However, if the property cannot be unilaterally severed by either party (such as with property held as tenants by the entireties); there are actually two nine-month periods. The first begins when the joint tenancy is created to the extent of the interest given to the donee; and the second relates to the survivorship period which occurs after the death of the joint owner.

46. Treas. Reg. 25-2518-2(c)(4).

47. Treas. Reg.§25-2518-2(c)(4)(iii).

48. Treas. Reg.§25-2518-2(c)(4)(i).

49. Treas. Reg.§25-2518-2(e)(5) Example 5 illustrates why disclaiming spouses may not retain ordinary limited powers of appointment in a bypass trust else the disclaimer be disqualified. However, Example 7 illustrates that disclaiming spouses may retain *general* powers of appointment without disqualifying the disclaimer (the "5 and 5" withdrawal power in the example is a lifetime GPOA, which is "subject to Federal estate and gift tax").

50. E.g., Ohio R.C. §5815.36(c) and (B)(2).

SELECTING THE RIGHT PEOPLE

CHAPTER 14

14.1 INTRODUCTION[1]

Selecting the people to carry out the provisions of an estate plan is one of the most important and difficult tasks involved in the estate planning process. This chapter concerns three of the most essential parties in the estate planning process: the executor, the trustee, agent under powers of attorney, and the estate planning team, which can consist of an attorney, accountant, financial planner, investments professional, life underwriter, planned giving consultant or development officer, family business consultant, family wealth coach, trust professional, and in many cases, valuation expert. This chapter discusses practical guidelines in the selection process from the point of view of the person who ultimately must make those choices: the client.

It is impossible to make a proper selection of any member of the estate planning team without understanding in general terms what each member of the team should be doing and how that person interacts with others who have important roles to fulfill. For this reason, you'll find a brief discussion of the duties of the executor, trustee, and estate's attorney before the attributes and selection criteria of each are covered.

At the outset, not only is the choice of fiduciary and the members of the client's estate planning team critical, it is even more critical that these appointments be carefully coordinated with each other. Consider the following questions. Is it wise to, in the context of a blended family, put members from both sides in the fiduciary ranks?[2] Generally, the answer is an enthusiastic "No!" This is because of the likelihood for increased costs as well as an increased prospect for dispute. Is it wise to name the same person as agent under a power of attorney and as executor without requiring the agent in the power of attorney to account to persons other than himself or herself as executor either during the principal's incapacity or at the principal's death? Again, the general answer is "No," because every fiduciary should be accountable to someone other than themselves.

Is it wise to put one side of the family, e.g., the step-parent, in as agent under the durable power of attorney, while putting someone from the other side of the family in as executor or as successor trustee under a revocable living trust, to whom the agent must ultimately account? Once again, the general answer is "No," because there needs to be coordination between these two offices so that things run smoothly and seamlessly in the transition from agent administration to post-death administration. Is it wise for one blended family partner to name someone from his or her blood family as executor or successor trustee and for the other blended family partner to do the same thing in an overall QTIP estate plan, where the two sides are going to have some interactions, particularly after the death of the surviving spouse? Again, the general answer is "No," because there needs to be cooperation in both the valuation of the QTIPed property and reimbursement of the estate taxes under Code section 2207A that are attributable to the QTIP trust's inclusion in the surviving spouse's estate under Code section 2044. Is it wise to name someone as fiduciary or as co-fiduciary of two estates or trusts where conflicts of interest in the roles are reasonably expected to occur? Same answer as above. It is very important that the client give serious consideration to the appointment of at least two backups as agent and as executor or successor trustee in case the original choice either resigns or is removed, because the chances for either to occur are much higher in a blended family.

14.2 PART I–SELECTING AN EXECUTOR (OR SUCCESSOR TRUSTEE UNDER A REVOCABLE LIVING TRUST)

Duties of the Executor

An executor is the person (and/or institution) named in a valid will to serve as the personal representative of a testator when his or her will is being probated. At one time, this person was referred to as the "executor" if male and "executrix" if female, but now is commonly referred to as the executor or personal representative regardless of gender.

In cases where the will or portions of it are invalid or incomplete or where there is no will, the personal representative is known as the estate's administrator(trix). Many people use revocable living trusts as will substitutes, so their estates are managed by the person(s) named as successor trustee. Even though our comments here apply to and reference only executors, just about all of this part also applies to successor trustees in a revocable living trust that becomes irrevocable at the decedent grantor's death.

When death occurs, the executor must locate and probate the decedent's will (prove that it was the decedent's will and that it in fact was his or her last will). At the time of appointment, the executor will take an oath before an officer in the local probate office promising to uphold the provisions of the decedent's will. The executor must then collect and safeguard the decedent's property; pay debts, taxes, and expenses; and finally distribute any remaining assets to the beneficiaries specified in the decedent's will.

An executor's responsibilities typically last from nine months to two or three years. In rare instances (such as when there is a contest of a will or the estate remains open for tax or other reasons), the executor's duties can continue for a period of years. While this focus is on the executor, it should be noted that the successor trustee of a revocable living trust usually has the same duties to perform and must possess the same skills, as well as the skills of a good trustee.

Attributes of a Good Executor

When choosing an executor, the major attributes to consider are:

1. Sensitivity;
2. Competence;
3. An understanding of the needs and appreciation of the circumstances of the beneficiaries;
4. Knowledge of the nature, value, and extent of the decedent's assets;
5. Experience in the administration of estates;
6. Business and investment experience;
7. Familiarity with the decedent's business;
8. Ability to serve;
9. Willingness to serve;
10. Geographic proximity to the estate's beneficiaries and the estate's assets;
11. Lack of any conflict of interest; and
12. Integrity and loyalty.

Sensitivity

Although the intangible attribute of "caring" both about the people involved and the performance of one's duties cannot be accurately or objectively measured, this single quality is perhaps the most important of all the factors in the selection process. It is always possible for the personal representative, if lacking knowledge in certain areas, to learn more about the subject or hire others with expertise. However, if the executor lacks empathy with the beneficiaries and for the situation, problems can result.

The highest preference should be given to the identification of an individual who is willing and able to give concerned personal attention and extra effort to the psychological as well as financial needs and individual circumstances of the beneficiaries. Often this individual will be the beneficiary with the largest share of the estate and almost always will be a close relative or friend of the decedent.

Competence

Competence encompasses both the legal ability to serve and the intellectual and emotional capacity to serve effectively.

Legal capacity entails U.S. citizenship in some jurisdictions and the satisfaction of state law requirements such as:

- age (twenty-one or eighteen in most states).

- mental competency (generally, the same required to be a testator or in some states a higher capacity, the ability to contract).

- domicile (some states require that the executor be a domiciliary of the state in which the will is probated while others allow executors from other states but may require that an out-of-state executor post a bond).

Intellectual capacity in a general sense does not require that the executor be completely aware of all the decedent's personal affairs or the intricacy of the decedent's business. What is necessary is that the person selected has the ability to analyze the situation as quickly as possible under the circumstances, determine what facets of the estate administration can be handled within the bounds of the executor's personal knowledge and capabilities, and then secure the appropriate professional assistance in these areas in which the executor knows he or she lacks experience. In other words, the executor must have the ability to organize both facts and people and understand and follow through with what must be according to state law and local probate (sometimes called Orphans' Court) rules. The executor must be able to ascertain when he or she (or even the current members of the executor's professional advisory team) does not know the answer to key questions and quickly obtain competent assistance. The executor also must know how to quickly assess whether the advice being given from the professional advisors is wise and prudent **before** acting on that advice.

Emotional capacity involves the ability to make a multitude of important decisions. Often these decisions (e.g., the selection of and negotiations with the estate's attorney and tax elections) must be made within a relatively short time span and yet may have tremendous financial significance to the estate and its beneficiaries. An intelligent individual capable of making quick, well-considered decisions will more than make up for an initial lack of experience.

Knowledge of the Beneficiaries

Personal knowledge of the beneficiaries, their ages, health conditions, income requirements, strengths, weaknesses, and eccentricities is extremely helpful to an executor. One child, for instance, may need immediate and continuing medical care, while another may be a highly successful surgeon. An elderly parent may need cash to meet the daily necessities of life or be so wealthy that a delay in the distribution of assets from a deceased child may have no adverse effect.

Knowledge of the Decedent's Assets

If an executor is familiar with the specific assets that comprise the estate, that information can be of great use in performing each of the most essential of his or her duties. For example, if one of the principal assets of the estate is a business in which the executor was active in the management, the advantage to the estate of that experience and continuity could be quickly translated into dollars.

Many individuals invest in or amass collectibles for pleasure. An executor with expertise in this area would know how to safeguard, transport, insure, have appraised, and sell such items far more readily than an executor with no particular knowledge of the subject matter. This is particularly true with respect to large collections of art, precious gems, stamps, coins, weapons, and many other similar items, although there is generally available independent expertise in the marketplace for the executor who lacks this expertise.

One of the most troublesome responsibilities of an executor is also one that must be started early in the estate administration process-the discovery and assembly of all the decedent's assets. An executor who is privy to the extent of the estate and knows the location of all of the assets or the names of those persons who can help in this key part of the estate's probate will have great advantage. This should simplify the tasks and enable the executor to realize a great deal more from those assets. Prior familiarity is of considerable benefit if the decedent's assets were varied and located in different states or overseas.

While prior familiarity as to the assets is helpful, there are steps which can be taken to help identify the assets. For example, the income tax returns can be examined to determine which financial institutions were paying dividends and interest to the decedent. Also, the decedent's checkbook can be reviewed to see if certain entries indicate the existence of additional assets. For example, there may be an entry indicating the payment of a fee for a safety deposit box rental or the payment of a property or life insurance policy premium.

Given that an increasing amount of property is accounted for in the "cloud" of the internet, it almost always is advisable and necessary for the executor to take control of the decedent's computers and to locate account passwords in order to deal with that property. It may be necessary to engage an IT security professional to assist with the computer work if the passwords are not readily available.

Estate Administration Experience

Although death is a common occurrence, few individuals have experience in being executors. Obviously, if an individual has probated at least one or two estates, he or she is an ideal candidate. Note that this criterion emphasizes one of the major strengths of a corporate fiduciary vis-à-vis an individual. Few, if any, individuals have probated as many estates as a bank or trust company specializing in estate planning and administration. In ultra large or highly complex estates this consideration should be given high priority although it may be a more costly option.

Business and Investment Experience

Intelligence and emotional maturity may not be enough to handle successfully the administration of an estate. The brightest spouse or most intelligent child may lack the business or investment experience to handle a large corporation or a sizable stock and bond portfolio. The experience-tested executor clearly will have an edge in a case where significant business or investment decisions will have to be made. Professional executors such as banks and trust companies are in the business of collecting, managing, and investing securities. They typically have separate departments to handle, analyze, and evaluate securities, supervise and sell real estate, and run businesses. To a lesser degree, professional advisors and associates (even friendly competitors in rare cases) who knew the operation of the decedent's business can provide invaluable service to the estate.

Obviously, a buy-sell agreement can incredibly simplify the task of an executor where a business interest comprises the bulk of an individual's estate. However, where there is no such agreement, the executor must-at least temporarily-assume whatever role the decedent had in the business.

Depending on the circumstances and nature of the business, it could be either continued or terminated. However, without knowledge of the details of the business or expertise in the specific area involved, the executor or administrator would obviously be working under a considerable handicap. Even a professional executor such as a bank or trust company may not have the requisite expertise if the decedent's business was in a specialized or personalized area in which particular or unique knowledge was necessary to survive in the marketplace. This often is an area where outside expertise is necessary.

Clearly, the executor who has an in-depth understanding of the inner workings of the decedent's business or profession has a tremendous edge over the neophyte. Although there is no substitute for experience, intelligent individuals who have the ability to obtain the necessary information and experience as well as the time and inclination to administer the estate can usually do a credible and often an outstanding job, if they are willing to put time and effort into the performance of their duties and have the assistance of an attorney experienced in estate administration.

Consider also that individuals or banks with strong investment or business expertise can be named as co-executors or can be hired on an hourly or annual retainer basis by the estate's executor. Certainly, any executor without extensive investment knowledge should secure the services of skilled advisors and investment personnel where appropriate. An executor who makes a mistake of omission-to the detriment of the estate's beneficiaries-is just as liable to surcharge as the executor who makes a mistake of commission. So it is essential for a nonprofessional executor to secure competent advice when dealing with an estate largely composed of securities.

Ability and Willingness to Serve

Most laypersons believe that being named the executor of an estate is a great honor. To the extent the term *executor* carries with it the ultimate in trust, this impression is justified. But with that honor, the personal representative must accept an awesome measure of responsibility and potential liability. The duties and responsibilities of an executor can amount to considerable time and effort, ranging from dozens of hours to hundreds and even thousands of hours. The duties range the entire gambit from the exciting and interesting to the arcane, tedious and mundane, even including duties such as getting up on a roof to look at a leak in the roof of the decedent's home or rental property. The decedent's heirs suffer the consequences if the designated executor is unable or unwilling to perform the necessary tasks. So it is extremely important in selecting a personal representative to consider the ability and probable willingness of the chosen person (or persons) to serve. (or oversee their performance by competent agents). Ability without willingness is meaningless, because the competent executor who is ambivalent about serving could resign and leave things in an uproar if the going gets tough during the administration of the estate or trust.

Most laymen are under the impression that to name someone the executor of an estate is to bestow upon them a great honor. To the extent that the term *executor* carries with it the ultimate in trust, this impression is justified. But with that honor, the personal representative must accept an *awesome* measure of responsibility and potential liability.

An executor is considered a *fiduciary*. This means a potential lawsuit by beneficiaries for breach of confidentiality, conflicts of interest, failure to exercise due care or diligence or prudence, failure to properly preserve or protect estate assets, failure to file timely and proper tax returns or maintain adequate records, and the breach of the duty to make all major discretionary decisions personally and not to delegate such decisions. This responsibility and potential personal liability may drastically reduce the willingness of the nominee to accept the position. For this reason, no one can be *forced* to accept the position of executor. Every will should provide at least one—and preferably more than one—backup executor in case the one named fails to qualify or ceases to act.

Geographic Proximity

Testators should consider, when selecting an executor, the physical distance the executor may have to travel and the time the executor may have to spend away from home. For example, New York state law may allow a son who lives in California to be the executor of his father's estate. But will the son be able to take the time away from his own job (not to mention his family) to serve properly – and at what cost? What expenses will be incurred out of the son's pocket or what nonreimbursable income will be lost by the son because he must be handling an estate on the opposite end of the continent? Quite often, the executor's fee or the size of the estate will be insufficient to economically justify the executor's expenditure of time. In such instances it may be preferable to appoint a local executor-perhaps a bank or a trust company-and to have the distant relative serve as an unofficial advisor to the executor or as a co-executor.

The extent to which geographic proximity for the executor is an issue may depend upon the nature of the assets within the estate. If the estate is primarily comprised of brokerage and bank accounts, it is not a problem for an executor to be located far away. However, if the estate is comprised of a closely held business or real estate which requires hands-on management, or if a primary beneficiary has special needs, it may be better to have a local executor.

In some jurisdictions certain non-resident personal representatives may have to post a bond whereas a resident would not.

Conflicts of Interest

An otherwise logical choice of a particular individual or individuals may fail to consider potential conflicts of interest. For example, an older child may well be qualified to manage her father's affairs. But will a conflict arise between the personal interest of that older child and a surviving parent or younger siblings? Such problems can easily occur when the executor makes decisions on where to take certain deductions or other tax-oriented elections. This problem can be intensified if the relatives are stepparents or stepchildren or if the decedent's intended recipients are friends rather than family. In fact, where the surviving spouse is not the other parent of the decedent's children, we generally recommend that someone *other* than the surviving spouse serve as executor because of the potential for post-death problems between a step-parent and step-children.

The problem of a potential conflict of interest is particularly acute where a business associate is named as executor. It is imperative to consider in advance of such a nomination the effect that the associate's handling of the business ("to sell or not to sell," and if so, to whom and at what price?) will have on the testator's beneficiaries – as well as on the business associate. What if the most likely purchaser is the associate himself? Wanting to pay the lowest possible price and yet obligated as executor to obtain the highest, the business associate as executor is placed in an almost certain conflict of interest. How can the beneficiaries be assured they have received a fair price for the business interest? Or how can they know the right decision was to sell rather than to retain the business? How do they know he did not pay himself an exorbitant salary (as well as an exorbitant executor's fee)? How could the business associate not resent the personal cost of "doing the right thing?" Conversely, how can the client be sure that the associate will not do financial harm to himself by going out of his way to get the best price possible for the client's heirs? The choice of a business associate as executor can easily put that person in an uncomfortable and often untenable situation. It is inevitable that doubt will linger when a partner or co-shareholder is named as executor, regardless of how careful that person is to make decisions impartially and in the best interest of the beneficiaries.

Another area in which a conflict of interest can easily occur is where a client names the attorney who drafted the will as executor. In our opinion—unless there is no choice or the parties are closely related—the will drafting attorney who unilaterally names himself or his law partner as attorney has committed a breach of ethics and has clearly acted improperly. This is arrangement is particularly troubling if it is done without the knowledge or express direction of the client.

If the attorney who drew the will is named as executor, then, technically, he or she is not an employee or agent of the beneficiaries. That means they have no power to fire him as executor if he doesn't answer phone calls or if letters requesting information about the estate go unanswered. It will be difficult for beneficiaries to challenge his/her actions or lack of action. If that person hires himself or his business partner as the estate's attorney, beneficiaries have little right to question the legality, and often little recourse save the lodging of an ethics complaint against the lawyer. Who, aside from the court upon final audit of the estate, can question the fee that such an executor pays himself as attorney? The appointment of the will drafting attorney as executor drastically reduces the checks and balances desirable in the probate of an estate and-aside from the other issues of competency, ability, and willingness to take the time away from the practice of law to do a proper job-creates inevitable conflict of interest.

As noted above, there are, of course, exceptions to the general rule that the attorney who draws the will should not be named as the estate's executor. For instance, if the attorney is a child or close relative of the testator or the natural object of his bounty, it may be proper and appropriate for that attorney to be named as executor.[3] If the attorney is the one individual most familiar with the decedent's assets, family, and business, then the attorney may be a logical choice, but in this case it may be best to name the attorney as co-executor with a family member, or, at the very least, make the attorney accountable to someone and give that person the power to remove the attorney or even a veto right over the attorney hiring his or her own law firm as attorneys for the executor or successor trustee.

Another situation where it may be appropriate to name the attorney as executor is if the client is concerned about how the beneficiaries will get along. In these situations, the attorney can act as an objective outsider to make sure that everyone is treated fairly. Even in these situations, it is still a good idea to name a family member or bank as co-executor with the attorney.

The very possibility of a conflict of interest may put the potential executor in an uncomfortable and even dangerous situation. In many cases such an individual will injure his own interest in the attempt to bend over backwards to avoid the appearance of impropriety. Nevertheless, he will always be conscious of the likelihood of second guessing by beneficiaries if they feel the apportionment of profits or proceeds was inadequate. Such an individual should, in many cases, properly and promptly refuse to serve as executor.

One possible solution to a potential conflict of interest is to name a business associate as an advisor or as co-executor with a bank and to name some third co-executor so there could not be a tie vote. In fact, wherever there is any potential for a conflict of interest a professional fiduciary should be considered. Impartiality is one of the major strengths of having a bank or trust company serve as executor.

Integrity and Loyalty

These are among the duties owed by a fiduciary to the beneficiaries of the estate.[4] However, it is as essential that the testator have absolute trust in the honesty and loyalty of the executor for reasons that go beyond the obvious legal or ethical implications; an important part of the estate planning process is the peace of mind an individual obtains in knowing that his or her affairs are in order and that the financial security he has paid for during his lifetime will serve those he loves and wants to benefit in the years beyond his lifetime. For these reasons, it is essential that the testator have absolute trust that his will shall be carried out as he intended to the best of the executor's ability.

Fees

Although fees are not among the listed attributes of a good executor, they are an important consideration in the selection process. The amount of fee a personal representative is entitled to may be determined by:

- the statutory or case law of the state where the estate is probated;

- local county rules or customs governing what the personal representative is entitled to charge to services rendered to the estate;

- in the case of professional executors such as banks or trust companies, an advertised fixed and scheduled fee (for a large estate the scheduled fee may possibly be lowered by negotiation, in which an attorney specializing in estate administration can be invaluable);

- provisions in the will; and

- separate contractual agreements between the testator and the nominated executor.

An executor is entitled to reasonable compensation for services rendered. Fees should not be determined solely on the basis of the monetary amount of the decedent's probate assets but should take into account the nature of the executor's tasks, the time spent, the complexity of the problems and decisions that have to be made, the professional background and competence of the executor, and the ultimate results and benefits obtained for the heirs.

There are valid tax and nontax reasons why an executor who is a relative or friend of the testator may or may not accept a fee. Although the selection process should encompass the likely course of action the executor will take in this regard, it is important that this factor not override or take the place of the other selection criteria.

In many cases testators expect that family members named as executors will charge no fees but that professional fiduciaries will. Although in many situations this assumption will be correct, this selection criterion should be tempered by considering the mistakes the nonprofessional may make that the professional would not and the opportunities the nonprofessional may miss that the professional would not. Additionally, most professional fiduciaries are associated with large financial institutions or trust companies that have significant assets and liability insurance to cover any mistakes that the professional fiduciary makes.

It is important to keep in mind that to the extent the executor does get paid, this payment will be taxable income to the executor.[5] Also, if it is a large estate and subject to the federal estate tax, even though the fee will be income to the executor, it will also qualify as either a deduction for federal estate tax purposes or a deduction on the estate's fiduciary income tax return.[6] Therefore, a consideration of the difference between the estate and income tax effects of the deduction will be necessary to determine if there will be an overall tax savings by having the executor take a fee (at least in the situation where the executor might not have otherwise chosen to take a fee) would otherwise receive the assets – income tax free - by virtue of being a beneficiary. If the estate is not taxable for federal estate tax purposes and if the executor also is a beneficiary, it generally makes little sense for the executor to take a fee, which is income. Generally, in such situations, it is better planning to forego the executor's fee and simply receive the legacy, which will generally be exempt from income tax.[7]

Summary

The choice of executor(s) and backups (there should always be at least one and preferably two backups) is complicated by a combination of family, personal, tax, and nontax considerations both tangible and intangible. All of these must be considered and balanced, for the executor's tasks and responsibilities are often complex and their successful and prompt completion is always-from the heirs' viewpoint-crucial.

14.3 PART II-SELECTING AGENTS UNDER POWERS OF ATTORNEY

Definitions and general rules. An "agent" under a power of attorney is appointed by the person for whom he acts, the "principal," under a document known as a "power of attorney."[8] While the deputation of the agent historically was terminated at the moment of the principal's incapacity (because the principal lost the ability to continue to approve the actions of the agent on his or her behalf), the modern view is that powers of attorney are "durable," i.e. they survive the principal's incapacity unless the power of attorney expressly provides otherwise.[9] The power of attorney is effective immediately unless it stipulates that it springs into effect at some point in the future.[10]

We advise against so-called "springing powers of attorney" because it often is impossible to determine the occurrence of the principal's incapacity with enough specificity to satisfy a third party who is asked to rely upon the agent's authority. Springing powers are impractical because they require a determination, i.e., incapacity, that has to be made from outside of the four corners of the power of attorney document.

Unless and until revoked, a durable power of attorney is extinguished by the principal's death.[11] However, a power of attorney in favor of a spouse is deemed revoked as to the spousal appointment upon the suit for dissolution of the marriage unless the power of attorney expressly provides otherwise.[12] A power of attorney does not revoke a *prior* power of attorney unless the later power of attorney specifically so provides.[13] As a result, it is essential that old powers of attorney be expressly revoked in a new power of attorney if the principal changed agents or the provisions of the power.

Powers and duties of the agent. The power of attorney document itself is the font of the agent's specific powers and duties. The agent is a fiduciary vis-à-vis the principal.[14] Applicable state law often requires that certain powers have to be expressly provided for in the power of attorney, or the agent does not have them. These express powers include (1) create, amend, revoke or terminate an *inter vivos* trust; (2) make a gift; (3) create or change rights of survivorship; (4) create or change a beneficiary designation; (5) delegate authority granted under the power of attorney; (6) waive the principal's right to be a beneficiary of a joint and survivor annuity, including a survivor benefit under a retirement plan; [or] (7) exercise fiduciary powers that the principal has authority to delegate; or (8) disclaim property, including a power of appointment.[15]

Some powers of attorney go to great lengths to spell out the powers that the agent has, while some powers of attorney simply incorporate statutory powers by reference.[16]

We prefer a "belts and suspenders" approach that carefully spells out in great detail the powers, as well as the limitations on the powers, of the agent and then also adopts the statutory powers to the extent not otherwise modified in the power of attorney. It is important that the attorney know applicable state law on powers of attorney and coordinate the power of attorney to be valid under the laws of each state in which the principal owns property.

Conclusion. In conclusion, the office of agent under a power of attorney perhaps is the hardest job to have, particularly in a blended family where the agent is on one side or the other, because the principal is still alive. The agent's job could last for a very long time, so it is important to select at least two backup agents in case the originally named agent either resigns, dies or is removed.

14.4 PART III-SELECTING A TRUSTEE

A trust is essentially an agreement where the Grantor (the person who creates the trust) asks another person (the trustee) to hold or administer assets on behalf of a beneficiary (the person who gets the assets). As such, the trustee is the person (and/or institution) named in a trust agreement to carry out the objectives and follow the terms of the trust. A trustee can be an individual (professional or nonprofessional) or a corporate fiduciary, or, in some limited circumstances, a tax-exempt charitable organization. It is also possible and common to appoint both individual and corporate trustees for reasons that will be discussed below.

Duties of the Trustee

It is useful in enumerating the duties and listing the attributes of a good trustee to consider the typical objectives that a trust is designed to accomplish. These goals include the following actions:

- Reduce or eliminate income, estate or generation-skipping transfer taxes at the federal or state level.

- Reduce or eliminate probate and administration costs.

- Provide a vehicle that will serve as a receptacle for both probate and nonprobate assets and facilitate attainment of other estate planning objectives through unified administration.

- Provide for minor children in a manner more flexible and custom-tailored to the grantor's desires than the Uniform Transfers to Minors Acts allow.

- Provide for recipients who are legally of majority age but who lack the emotional or intellectual maturity or physical capacity or technical training to handle large sums of money or an investment portfolio or a family business.

- Provide for individuals who have the capacity to handle large sums of money or an investment portfolio or a family business but choose not to make the necessary investment decisions or deal with the constant problems or devote the degree of attention required.

- Postpone full ownership of trust assets until the beneficiaries of the trust have attained ages specified by the grantor or until events specified by the grantor have occurred.

- Enable the investment of an asset that does not lend itself to fragmentation. This often occurs where the grantor desires to spread the beneficial ownership among a number of individuals. Life insurance policies and real estate are just two examples of assets that are difficult to split up or are worth substantially more if held together.

- Limit the parties who can obtain the assets and achieve particular dispositive objectives. For instance, where family control of a business or a specific asset is important, the grantor will want to limit the class of beneficiaries and prevent recipients from disposing of property to persons outside the family. A common example is the desire to protect assets from the consequence of an unsuccessful marriage or other creditor issues.

The duties of the trustee may therefore include the satisfaction of a number of tax and nontax objectives that include, but are not limited to, the investment, management, and protection of trust assets and compliance with the dispositive intentions of the grantor.

To a great extent, the selection process and decision criteria for selecting a trustee will follow the same pattern as in choosing an executor; premium will be placed on many of the same attributes. But there are several significant distinctions.

Unlike the role of the executor, which is typically concluded within a year or two, the trustee's responsibilities commonly last for at least one generation and often last beyond two or three generations. This fact should have a significant effect on the choice of trustee or on the decision to name both co-trustees and successor trustees (or to provide a mechanism for their appointment by a resigning trustee or by the beneficiaries). Usually, the trust will provide either that the last serving trustee may name his or her replacement or that a majority of the adult beneficiaries or the surviving spouse may name the replacement.

A second distinguishing factor is that the choice of trustee, unlike the selection of the executor, is tax sensitive. In other words, there will be situations in which tax consequences will vary widely (results ranging from success to tax disaster) according to whether the grantor, the grantor's spouse, the beneficiaries, the grantor's business associates, the grantor's professional advisors, or a totally independent third party is named as trustee.

The decision is further complicated by a multiplicity of personal, family, business, investment, and nontax considerations-which must all be weighed by the grantor and the attorney drafting the trust. Quite often, a trade-off between flexibility and tax-saving objectives will be required. And even with the aid of skilled counsel, some compromise may be necessary.

Attributes of a Good Trustee

When selecting a trustee, the major attributes to consider are:

1. Availability.

2. Impartiality and lack of conflict of interest.

3. Financial security.

4. Investment acumen.

5. Business sophistication.

6. Accounting and tax-planning expertise.

7. Recordkeeping and reporting ability.

8. Knowledge of and sensitivity to beneficiaries and their circumstances.

9. Fees.

10. Decision-making abilities.

11. Competence.

12. Standard to which trustee will be held.

13. Integrity.

14. Flexibility to meet changing circumstances.

15. Willingness to serve throughout the term of the trust.

16. Experience as a trustee.

17. Tax-neutral impact.

18. Neutral or positive state law impact.

Availability

This criterion has two aspects, permanency and proximity. Corporate trustees are often considered because they possess one attribute that individuals (even individuals who are professional trustees) do not possess-perpetual existence, at least in the sense that a bank (or its successor) is likely to be in business during the entire term of the trust even if it lasts for generations, whereas individuals, even professional trustees, may with unpredictable frequency retire or make a career change or die or become disabled. Although banks may take holidays, they never take vacations. So to some extent it can be said that corporate fiduciaries have the availability advantage over individuals.

This perpetual-existence theory must be considered in perspective; only change lasts forever. The real issue is whether the trustee will be able to serve effectively long enough. The briefly considered answer to this question would still seem to give unparalleled advantage to a bank, especially when the possible senility or emotional instability or physical disability of an individual trustee is considered. It is particularly difficult to protect beneficiaries against these human frailties, since there is generally no automatic retirement mechanism for superannuated or mildly incompetent trustees within the trust instrument.

However, with corporate trustees, a different type of problem can arise. If the personnel at the senior management, professional or clerical levels change over time, the beneficiaries may experience a dramatic change in the beneficiary's relationship with the institution have changed so drastically as to constitute a new entity for all practical purposes. Surely, in the time span of a trust running for two or more generations, turnover in most banks will effect a drastic, if not revolutionary, change in people dealing with and policies affecting trust beneficiaries. The bank that was so friendly and competent (perhaps because its senior management gave great priority to trust business in the years in which the trust was established) may be cold and less than satisfactory to a second generation of beneficiaries. The consolidation of the financial services industry has led to widespread mergers that can change the fiduciary landscape very rapidly.

Availability must also be considered in geographic terms. An individual trustee is likely-over a long period of time-to move from the city in which the trust or its beneficiary is located. Of course, although banks generally remain, and in fact are becoming, regional in scope, since beneficiaries often move (or perhaps did not live in the same city or state or country as the grantor to begin with), dealing with the bank selected by the grantor may no longer be convenient. Consider provisions giving beneficiaries or a trust protector the power to change from one corporate fiduciary to another. (See discussion below of removal and replacement of trustees.)

Impartiality and Absence of Conflicts of Interest

How will the trustee react when faced with a choice that favors him at the expense of other beneficiaries-or favors others at his expense? What are the intrafamily implications of those choices? For instance, will he alienate one family member by (even properly) denying a distribution, or ingratiate himself to another by being liberal in his policy of making distributions? Can he say "no" to one child and "yes" to another without causing a never-ending family feud? A trustee who is also a family member may be forced by conscience or by duty to make choices injurious to the harmony of family relationships. Can the trustee do that?

Will the trustee (such as the grantor's spouse) be subject to the influence of one or more children (or a second spouse or lover) to make distributions that may not be in the best interest of other beneficiaries? Is the family member/trustee easily persuaded or likely to show favoritism? The remarriage of a spouse or child who is named as trustee may result in less than impartial decisions-especially where the trustee has been given discretionary powers over trust income or principal-even if the new spouse is not included in the class of possible recipients.

A child/trustee may take on the role of a parent to his or her remaining parent or siblings. This may be positive, but is also may result in an attempt to control the lives of family members through the family finances as if that person were a parent rather than a child.

An independent professional trustee is not subject to such problems. Since the choice between "no" and "yes" may be one of the most important duties of a trustee, this ability of a professional trustee to be objective and impartial should be given high preference in the decision-making process. While an independent professional trustee is a good choice for this position, the combination of the professional trustee acting together with a family member can work well. On this basis the family member can help ensure that the professional trustee is aware of the personal dynamics of a situation.

Conflicts of interest can occur even where there is no issue of impartiality. For example, assume that grantor names his attorney as trustee. The attorney/trustee would most likely be objective and impartial as between the conflicting interests of family members. But consider these questions:

- Once the grantor has died, who will negotiate with the attorney to ensure that fees are reasonable?

- Who could fire the attorney (or trustee) if services were not performed properly or in a timely manner?

- Can the attorney remain impartial as a trustee if he represents the business of one of the beneficiaries?

- Is it appropriate for an accountant serving as trustee to continue in the dual capacity if he also represents a business owned by the trust?

- What if there is an argument between the attorney/trustee and the grantor (or the trust's beneficiaries) that is entirely personal or is on the attorney/client level and has nothing to do with the relationship he has as a trustee?

- Is it possible for an attorney/trustee to fairly represent the beneficiaries, the grantor, or co-trustees in a trust-related situation?

- Will the attorney or accountant be willing to allocate appropriate time to the trust or will at the same time that the person is concentrating on obtaining and servicing professional clients (especially if the fees for serving as trustee are substantially lower than that charged in the professional's practice)?

Conflict of interest problems would plague a business associate or partner who was named trustee. For instance, if the trust held stock in one or more businesses in which the trustee was an officer or shareholder, his salary, or his stock interest would be affected by his actions taken as a trustee. What if the trustee was the art dealer for the trust of an artist who trusted him and had the highest degree of respect for the dealer's integrity, judgment, and marketing expertise? Assume the trust's assets consisted mainly of the artist's paintings. The dealer/trustee would be bound to obtain the highest price possible when selling trust assets. But as a dealer, he would want to pay the lowest possible price. Would it be appropriate to continue as trustee under those circumstances? It is risky to name anyone who is likely to buy or lease assets from or sell or lease assets to the trust or have any other dealings with trust property. Typically, we recommend either a blanket prohibition of self-dealing or limit such activity in a significant way, such as giving the beneficiaries or a trust protector an approval or a veto right over self-dealing transactions.

Some of these impartiality and conflict-of-interest problems can be overcome or minimized if anticipated in advance. But in most cases, if it is foreseeable that these problems will occur, they will. Often, the problem is not that an unethical transaction has occurred or an improper decision has been made. Rather, it is that the parties are uncomfortable merely because the beneficiaries know it could happen, assume it will, and the trustee knows the beneficiaries may distrust, second-guess, or sue him/them/it merely because they suspect a conflict of interest could have occurred or might occur.

Financial Security

This refers to the security of the funds entrusted to the trustee and the "depth of the trustee's pockets" in the event of a successful malfeasance or misfeasance suit by beneficiaries. A nonprofessional trustee will not have an internal audit staff to review the acts of the person administering the trust. This lack of a system of checks and balances is one of the major shortcomings of an individual nonprofessional trustee. Conversely, banks and trust companies are audited both internally and (usually by the state or by the Office of the Comptroller of the Currency) externally. All investments made by a corporate fiduciary must be approved by a trust investment committee, and the portfolio, which is typically diversified, is reviewed frequently.

If sued, will the fiduciary be available to answer for and be able to pay damages for a wrongful act? The answer is likely to be "no" with respect to an individual trustee but "yes" with respect to a corporate fiduciary. For example, in the event of embezzlement or some other impropriety or breach of trust, the odds of a recovery from a bank or trust company are significantly higher than from an individual trustee merely because of the relative sizes of the fiduciary's own assets. Banks serving as trustees are required to meet minimum amounts of capitalization requirements, whereas individual trustees have no required minimum capitalization requirements.

An individual trustee can acquire physical security for trust assets by hiring safe deposit and other facilities. Banks and trust companies have such protection on site but of course build charges for their use into their fees.

Investment Acumen

The trustee's ability to successfully invest and reinvest trust funds is one of the more important attributes to consider in the selection process. In this regard, many professional and even nonprofessional individuals have proved more astute or competent than their corporate counterparts. In some cases, the grantor's opinion of a spouse or child as "financially inept" has proven to be an incorrect perception.

But the highly computerized and experienced investment departments of banks and professional individual fiduciaries do have an advantage over anyone who is not a professional investor. A further advantage of the professional trustee is that trust assets can be invested in a bank's common trust funds, which increases the safety of trust investments through diversity, although investing in a corporate fiduciary's proprietary funds usually represents a big conflict of interest for that fiduciary.

The ultimate decision in this category should not be made until the various track records are compared. The performance of commercial trust departments has varied considerably from bank to bank and from the investments returns of other investment managers.

Investment policy is an important consideration in the selection process. Corporate fiduciaries tend to be conservative. This may be either attractive or a drawback depending on how aggressive the grantor's own style or personal objectives are or were. However, the trustee should generally manage the trust assets in a more conservative fashion then they would manage their own assets. So it is entirely appropriate for the trust assets to be managed in a more conservative fashion.

The investment decisions of an ultraconservative trustee may not be suited to the beneficiaries' risk-taking propensities or their growth and income objectives. But this in turn may be more in keeping with the grantor's long-range goals of restraining the lifestyle of income and principal recipients. A conservative approach is also more consistent with the trustee's responsibilities.

So the ultimate decision is not between professional and nonprofessional or between individual and corporate fiduciary; it must be made on the basis of the type of investment policy the grantor of the trust desires and the particular trustee that will come closest to matching that policy. Keep in mind that in many situations, the appropriate solution is to name both individual and corporate fiduciaries.

Business Sophistication

Where one or more businesses are held in the trust, it is extremely important that the trustee have expertise in running that type of business. Even if the trustee should or intends to sell it, knowing when and how best to dispose of it is a very important skill. If the business is large or large relative to other trust assets, or if it is a specialized or personal service type of business, this may mean that a family member, business associate, professional advisor, or even a former competitor may have to be considered in spite of impartiality issues or potential conflicts of interest.

Typically, corporate fiduciaries do not continue businesses left in trust. The business is quickly sold and the proceeds are reinvested. In most cases that will be the appropriate course of action, since few banks have enough of the right type of personnel to continue the success of a growing business, and a failing business should usually be liquidated as quickly as possible. Nonprofessional individual fiduciaries rarely have the time to run a business even if they have the expertise and experience.

Accounting and Tax Planning Expertise

Corporate fiduciaries have a definite advantage over nonprofessional individual trustees when considering the myriad accounting procedures, tax compliance, and tax planning opportunities that must be handled by a trustee. The level of sophistication, expertise, and experience that should be applied over the lifetime of any trust is one that few nonprofessionals can provide. This means that most family members are incapable of fully understanding all of the problems that must be avoided and the availability and implications of the tax and property law elections that must be weighed. Even knowledgeable attorneys and accountants do not have the requisite practical day-to-day experience unless they practice solely in this field.

It is possible and in many cases appropriate for a trustee to hire agents for advice and assistance. Most trustees will communicate regularly with outside attorneys and accountants. But planning policy and decisions must be made by the trustee; these are among the duties that cannot be delegated. Thus, the trustee must have a working knowledge of the accounting laws and both federal and state tax laws (income, estate, gift, and generation-skipping). Will an untrained trustee know whom to call or if the advice received is both legally correct and practical or when that advice is wrong? Will a nonprofessional understand the interplay between tax, trust, and property law well enough to interpret provisions in the trust and adequately inform beneficiaries about the tax and other legal effects of various choices?

Recordkeeping and Reporting Ability

A trust is a long-term arrangement under which accountings must be made periodically over many years to a number of parties that may include the grantor, the beneficiaries, the appropriate federal and state taxing authorities, and the supervising court. This requires regular statements of the receipts, disbursements, and assets of the trust in an intelligible form, and careful long-term record storage. Also, some states which have adopted the Uniform Trust Code may require certain notices to be provided to the beneficiaries of a Trust including notice of changes of trustee.

Knowledge of Beneficiaries

In some cases an understanding of the family involved and their special needs or desires and how they relate to the grantor's objectives should properly take priority over many of the other objectives on this list. If the financial encouragement of a handicapped child, for example, is not provided through the trust, the trust may fail in its purpose regardless of how much tax it saves or how closely the trustee meets both the letter of the law and the terms of the trust itself. *Sensitivity* here is therefore used interchangeably with *flexibility*. If flexibility in dealings with trust beneficiaries and a high degree of personal sensitivity are primary considerations, a nonprofessional trustee is indicated, even as a co-trustee.

Fees

Corporate and other professional fiduciaries charge a fee for their services. Usually, this fee is based on a percentage of the income and principal of the trust. A distribution fee equal to a percentage of the principal disbursed from the trust is also often charged (upon termination or otherwise). Although this fee is typically set according to a standard schedule of fees, it may be possible to negotiate the fee in the case of a trust with a large amount of assets. This may be an amount agreed on or may be a flat hourly charge. Where trust assets consist solely of unfunded life insurance trusts, unimproved real estate, or closely held stock, the nonprofessional may be the best choice for a trustee, even if only over those assets. Likewise, trusts with assets of less than $500,000 in value are often discouraged from using corporate fiduciaries because of the fees. In fact, many trust companies will accept trusts only with a minimum level of assets. Depending upon the institution, these minimums can be at $1,000,000 or higher. If you are considering a corporate trustee, it will be important to find out if your situation meets the institution's minimum requirements. Many times, the institution will aggregate family members' accounts for purposes of determining if the minimum account value was attained. Also, many corporate trustees will insist on reviewing the terms of the trust prior to execution and will oftentimes request or require additional provisions to the trustees' powers.

Many individuals name their spouses or relatives, close friends or even trust beneficiaries because they will serve as a personal favor or as an accommodation and will not charge a fee to act as a trustee. This may be an economic necessity where the value of trust assets is small and payment of the minimum fees to the corporate fiduciary would significantly reduce the income and principal of the trust. However, in most cases, the fees saved by using a nonprofessional amounts to a false economy. A family member or friend who invests the time, effort, and takes the liability risk required by a trustee *should* be appropriately compensated.

There is a further aspect with respect to fees and the selection of a trustee; in selecting a relative who is also a beneficiary: Will the fees charged be understood by and acceptable to other beneficiaries, or will such fees-even if reasonable for the services performed-be resented and cause conflict? And, conversely, will the time and aggravation and liability risk assumed by an individual family member or friend trustee warrant a sizeable fee that is well deserved? Is it fair to expect that anyone – even a close family member – should put in what may be countless hours over years or decades – for no or less than a reasonable fee?

Decision-Making Ability

The trustee selected must be able to make many decisions, some of great significance, over an extended period of time. This entails the need for emotional maturity and wisdom as well as knowledge.

Competence

A trustee must have the legal capacity to contract. This precludes the appointment of a minor or an incompetent adult. In many states a nonresident individual can act as a trustee (although as a practical matter, geographical considerations often contraindicate selecting a person who lives a considerable distance from the beneficiaries of the trust). Some states bar nonresident corporations from serving as trustees.

Skill

A trustee will be held to a high degree of skill and care. Under the "prudent person" rule, a trustee must use the same degree of care and skill that a person of ordinary prudence would exercise in dealing with his own property.

The Uniform Probate Code, adopted by many states, places a higher standard on professional trustees by providing that if the trustee has greater skill than that of a person of ordinary prudence, he is under a duty to exercise such skill.

Integrity

Honesty and loyalty are the watchwords of trusts. Vast sums of money and other assets are entrusted to fiduciaries who must exercise a high degree of care over trust property and act consistently on behalf of trust beneficiaries.

Flexibility

Change in tax law and in the circumstances and goals of each of the beneficiaries is the only certainty. Since a trust is a mechanism specifically designed to meet that change, the trustee must be willing and able to change as well.

Willingness and Ability to Serve Throughout the Term of the Trust

An individual trustee could easily lose interest through the long years and even generations a trust may last. An individual could become physically, mentally, or emotionally unable to complete the many tasks of trustee. Corporate fiduciaries are more likely than individuals to continue serving for the full term.

Experience as a Trustee

This is the rarest of all characteristics. Obviously, past experience in administering a trust is invaluable. Through experience, the fiduciary is more likely to appreciate the broad and complex multiplicity of laws involved, know whom to call on for assistance, avoid many mistakes, and more efficiently administer and execute the terms of the trust.

Tax Impact of Various Types of Trustees

A revocable trust has a neutral impact on taxes at both federal and state levels. As long as the grantor has reserved the right to revoke the trust at any time, in most situations he will be treated for all federal and state tax purposes as if he had not established a trust and had remained as the outright owner of the property in the trust.[17] So, with respect to a revocable trust, it does not matter for tax purposes who is selected as trustee. For example, the grantor will be taxed on the income of a revocable trust whether he names himself, his spouse, a beneficiary, a friend, a business associate, a professional whom he employs, or an independent corporate or other professional fiduciary. However, the choice of trustee may have an impact on whether the revocable trust has to file a separate income tax return. So long as either the grantor or the grantor's spouse are at least one of the trustees, a separate return is not required for the trust, and everything will be reported on the grantor's personal income tax return.[18]

But if one of the major reasons for establishing an irrevocable trust is to save taxes (federal and state income, estate, or GST), the identity of the trustee is a very tax-sensitive decision: Inclusion of the trust's assets in income (or in the gross estate or in the GST tax base) will result if the wrong party is selected as trustee. The potential for adverse tax results increases significantly when the trustee is given discretionary powers over the income or principal of the trust if the trustee or a co-trustee is the grantor, his or her spouse, a family member (or some combination of them), or if one or more of these people becomes a trustee under a successor provision in the trust.

Consequently, the adverse tax consequences can be avoided very simply by providing that these individuals may not become a trustee or by specifying that if such a person is a trustee, he or she may not participate in a decision that will result in the to-be-avoided tax result. For example, a surviving spouse/trustee would be prohibited from exercising a broad discretionary power over principal in her own favor if the objective of the trust was to prevent inclusion of assets in her estate. However, it is obvious that favorable tax results are obtained at the cost of a loss of flexibility.

Figure 14.1 summarizes the major income and estate tax consequences of using various types of parties as trustees in irrevocable trusts. When considering the tax plication of the choice of trustee, there are four important categories:

1. Grantor
2. Adverse party
3. Nonadverse party
4. Independent party

The *grantor* is a person who provides the corpus of the trust. The Code also defines a category of parties who are "related or subordinate" to the grantor. Depending on the nature and circumstances of that person's relationship with the grantor, that definition will often encompass:

- the grantor's spouse;
- close relatives;
- a corporation in which the grantor or trust has significant holdings; or
- an employee of a corporation in which the grantor or trust has significant holdings, or in which the grantor is an executive.[19]

Adverse party is defined by Code section 672(a) as "any person having a substantial beneficial interest in the trust which would be adversely affected by the exercise or nonexercise of the power which he possesses respecting the trust. A person having a general power of appointment over the trust property shall be deemed to have a beneficial interest in the trust." Generally, a beneficiary will be considered an adverse party.[20]

A *nonadverse party* is, simply, a party that does not meet the definition of an "adverse party"[21]

An *independent trustee* is a party who is not a grantor, adverse party, or a "related or subordinate" party. Essentially, an independent trustee is unrelated to the grantor and can in no way gain any benefit from the trust (aside from the payment of reasonable fees for their services as trustee). They are often corporate trustees, such as a financial institution.[22]

Before naming the grantor or anyone with an interest in the trust as trustee, consideration must be given to these implications. In addition, while consideration is given to having the grantor be trustee of his own irrevocable trust, the potential tax consequences make it advisable to do so only as a last resort.

Through experience, the fiduciary is more likely to appreciate the broad and complex multiplicity of laws involved, know who to call on for assistance, recognize and avoid many mistakes and more efficiently administer and execute the terms of the trust.

Figure 14.1

INCOME AND ESTATE TAX CONSEQUENCES OF SELECTING VARIOUS PARTIES TO SERVE AS TRUSTEE

Part I: Powers to Affect Beneficial Enjoyment

A. Power to distribute income to the grantor or the grantor's spouse

Grantor as trustee	Nonadverse party as trustee	Adverse party as trustee
• Grantor taxed on the income of the trust since the grantor will be treated as the owner of trust assets. • Assets in the trust includable in the grantor's gross estate.	• Grantor taxed on the income of the trust. Note that the inclusion of a non-adverse party as Trustee does not affect the grantor as being treated as the owner of the Trust (and thereby having the Trust being taxed as a Grantor Trust.) • Assets in the trust not includable in the grantor's gross estate.	• Grantor not taxed on trust income. Note that the inclusion of an adverse party as Trustee removes the grantor as being treated as the owner of the Trust (absent other grantor powers). • Assets in the trust not includable in grantor's gross estate.

B. Power to distribute income to beneficiaries other than the grantor or the grantor's spouse without the restriction of an ascertainable standard

Grantor as trustee	Nonadverse party as trustee	Independent party as trustee
• Grantor taxed on the income of the trust since the grantor will be treated as the owner of the trust or transfers to the trust may be treated as incomplete gifts. • Assets in the trust includable in the gross estate of the grantor if the power can be exercised by the grantor alone or with any other party (adverse or not).	• Grantor taxed on the income of the trust since the grantor will be treated as the owner of the trust (unless the power is limited to withholding distributions temporarily during legal disability). • Assets in the trust not includable in the estate of the grantor unless the grantor has retained the right to substitute himself as trustee.	• Grantor not taxed on the income of the trust. • Assets in the trust will generally not be includable in the grantor's gross estate unless the grantor can substitute himself as beneficiary.

C. Power (subject to an ascertainable standard) to distribute income to beneficiaries other than the grantor or the grantor's spouse

Grantor as trustee	Person other than the grantor (or the grantor's spouse) as trustee
• Grantor taxed on the income of the trust since the grantor will be taxed as the owner of the trust (unless the power can be exercised only with the consent of an adverse party). • Assets in the trust will generally not be includable in the grantor's gross estate since the power can only be exercised pursuant to an ascertainable standard. However, a different result occurs if the assets can be used to discharge a legal obligation of support of the Grantor. In this case, the assets will be included in the Grantor's estate pursuant to I.R.C. §§2041(b) or 2036(a)(2).	• Grantor not taxed on the income of the trust. • Assets in the trust will generally not be includable in the grantor's estate unless the grantor can substitute himself as trustee.

Figure 14.1 (cont'd)

D. Power (subject to an ascertainable standard) to distribute principal to a beneficiary or class of beneficiaries	
Grantor as trustee	*Person other than grantor as trustee*
• Grantor not taxed on the income of the trust. Note that this section D. relates to distributions of principal; and does not address distributions of income. With respect to the power to distribute principal based upon an ascertainable standard, the grantor will not be treated as the owner of the principal of the trust (and thereby having the trust be treated as a grantor trust for the principal) because distributions are based upon an ascertainable standard. This standard will satisfy the requirement that distributions be limited to a reasonably definite standard under I.R.C. §674(b)(5). Also, for fiduciary accounting purposes, income consists of interest and dividends, but not capital gains. • Assets in the trust will generally not be included in the grantor's estate because exercise of the power is limited by an ascertainable standard.	• Assets in the trust will generally not be included in the grantor's estate because exercise of the power is limited by an ascertainable standard.

E. Power to distribute principal to a current income beneficiary	
Grantor as trustee	*Person other than grantor as trustee*
• Grantor not taxable on the income of the trust. • Assets in the trust will be includable in the grantor's estate unless the power is limited by an ascertainable standard. However, even if the power is limited by an ascertainable standard, the assets will be included in the grantor's estate if the assets can be used to discharge a legal obligation of support of the grantor. In this case, the assets will be included in the Grantor's estate pursuant to I.R.C. §2036(a)(2).	• Grantor not taxable on the income of the trust. • Assets in the trust will not be includable in the grantor's gross estate unless the grantor can substitute himself as trustee.

F. Power to distribute or accumulate income for a current income beneficiary	
Grantor as trustee	*Person other than grantor as trustee*
• Income of the trust not taxable to the grantor pursuant to §674(b)(6). • Assets in the trust will be includable in the grantor's estate unless the power can be exercised only pursuant to an ascertainable standard. However, even if the power is limited by an ascertainable standard, the assets will be included in the grantor's estate if the assets can be used to discharge a legal obligation of support of the grantor. In this case, the assets will be included in the Grantor's estate pursuant to I.R.C. §§2036(a)(2) and 2041(b).	• Income of the trust not taxable to the grantor. • Assets in the trust will not be includable in the grantor's estate unless the power can be exercised without an ascertainable standard and the grantor can substitute himself as the trustee.

THE TOOLS & TECHNIQUES OF ESTATE PLANNING

Figure 14.1 (cont'd)

G. Power to make mandatory distributions of income or principal to specified beneficiaries other than the grantor or the grantor's spouse

Grantor as trustee	*Person other than grantor as trustee*
• Income of the trust not taxable to the grantor unless trust income is used to discharge his legal obligations. • Assets in the trust will not be included in the grantor's gross estate because the grantor has retained no power to affect beneficial enjoyment of trust property.	• Income of the trust not taxable to the grantor unless trust income is used to discharge his legal obligations. • Assets in the trust not includable in the grantor's gross estate.

Part II: Administrative Powers

A. Power to allocate receipts between principal and income

Grantor as trustee	*Person other than grantor as trustee*
• Grantor not taxable on the income of the trust. • Assets of the trust will not be includable in the grantor's estate unless the power can be exercised by the grantor in a nonfiduciary capacity either alone or in conjunction with another person.	• Grantor not taxable on the income of the trust. • Assets of the trust will not be includable in the grantor's estate.

B. Power to use trust income to pay premiums on insurance insuring the life of the grantor or the grantor's spouse

Grantor as trustee	*Nonadverse party as trustee*	*Adverse party as trustee*
• Grantor is taxable on the income of the trust to extent the income is or may be used for the payment of life insurance premiums without the consent of an adverse party. • Assets of the trust will not be includable in the grantor's gross estate assuming the trust both owns and is beneficiary of the policy proceeds.	• Grantor will be taxed on the income of the trust. • Assets of the trust will not be includable in the gross estate of the grantor.	• Grantor will not be taxed on income of the trust. • Assets of the trust will not be includable in the gross estate of the grantor.

C. Power to purchase, exchange, or otherwise deal with trust assets for less than adequate consideration

Grantor as trustee	*Nonadverse party as trustee*	*Adverse party as trustee*
• Grantor will be taxed on income of the trust if he or a nonadverse party (or both) can exercise the power without the consent of an adverse party. • Assets of the trust will be includable in the gross estate of the grantor.	• Grantor will be taxable on trust income if the nonadverse party can exercise the power without the consent of an adverse party. • Assets in the trust will not be includable in the estate of the grantor unless the grantor can substitute himself as trustee.	• Grantor not taxed on the income of the trust. • Assets in the trust will not be includable in the estate of the grantor unless the grantor can substitute himself as trustee.

Figure 14.1 (cont'd)

D. Power to borrow trust income or principal without adequate interest or adequate security	
Grantor as trustee	*Person other than grantor as trustee*
• Grantor taxed on trust income if trust property can be loaned to grantor without adequate interest or security (income will not be taxed to grantor if approval of adverse party needed). • Assets in trust will be includable in grantor's gross estate.	• Grantor not taxed on trust income if person other than grantor is trustee and that person has the power to make loans to anyone. • Assets will not be included in grantor's gross estate unless he can substitute himself as trustee.

E. Power to vote the securities of a controlled corporation	
Grantor as trustee	*Person other than grantor as trustee*
• Grantor taxed on income of trust if (1) power can be exercised in a nonfiduciary capacity and (2) the stockholdings of the grantor and the trust are significant from the viewpoint of control. • Assets in the trust must be included in the grantor's gross estate.	• Grantor taxed on trust income if power to vote securities held by person with nonadverse interest in a nonfiduciary capacity without consent of person in fiduciary capacity, assuming stock holdings of grantor and trust are significant from the viewpoint of control. • Assets in the trust will not be included in the grantor's estate unless he has retained the power to substitute himself as trustee.

F. Power to reacquire trust principal by substituting property of equal value	
Grantor as trustee	*Persons other than the grantor as trustee*
• Grantor will be taxed on trust income if the power can be exercised by anyone in a nonfiduciary capacity without the consent of a person in a fiduciary capacity. • Assets in the trust will be includable in the gross estate of the grantor.	• Grantor will be taxed on trust income if the power can be exercised by anyone in a nonfiduciary capacity without the consent of a person in a fiduciary capacity. • Assets in the trust will not be includable in the grantor's gross estate unless he can substitute himself as trustee.

Part III: Powers over Principal

A. Power to revoke the trust and revest the principal in the grantor or in grantor's spouse		
Grantor as trustee	*Nonadverse party as trustee*	*Adverse party as trustee*
• Grantor taxed on trust income unless power can be exercised only with consent of adverse party. • Assets in trust includable in grantor's gross estate if power exercisable only by grantor alone or with any person whether or not adverse (unless the power can be exercised only with consent of all persons with a vested or contingent interest in the estate).	• Grantor taxed on trust income unless power can be exercised only with consent of adverse party. • Assets in trust not includable in grantor's estate unless power is exercisable by trustee and grantor can substitute himself as trustee.	• Grantor not taxed on trust income. • Assets in trust not includable in grantor's gross estate.

Figure 14.1 (cont'd)

B. Power to terminate trust and distribute principal to beneficiaries

Grantor as trustee	Adverse party as trustee	Nonadverse party as trustee	Independent Trustee
• Grantor not taxed on trust income if principal can be paid out only to income beneficiaries in same proportion as they currently receive income, or if principal can be paid out only with the approval of an adverse party. • Assets in the trust are includable in the grantor's gross estate if the grantor can exercise the power alone or with any other person whether or not adverse.	• Grantor not taxed on trust income. • Assets in trust not includable unless power exercisable by trustee and grantor can substitute himself as trustee.	• Grantor taxed on trust income unless approval of adverse party required or unless payment must be made to current income beneficiaries in proportion to income receipts. • Assets in trust not includable unless power exercisable by trustee and grantor can substitute himself as trustee.	• Grantor not taxed on trust income if half or more of trustees are independent. • Assets in trust not includable unless power exercisable by trustee and grantor can substitute himself as trustee.

A. Power to discharge support obligation

	Grantor as trustee	Persons other than grantor as trustee
Part IV: Powers to Discharge Legal Obligations	• Grantor not taxable on trust income merely because of the existence of the power unless he has the power in a nonfiduciary capacity or the power is to support his or her spouse. But the grantor will be taxed on the income to the extent it in fact is used to discharge the grantor's support obligation. • Assets in the trust will be includable in the grantor's estate if trust assets may be used to discharge the grantor's legal obligation.	• Grantor not taxable on income unless it is in fact used to discharge the grantor's legal obligation. • Assets in the trust will not be included unless the grantor could substitute himself for the trustee.

Neutral State Law impact

State trust laws must be considered in selecting a trustee. If state law trust requirements are not met, the trust will be invalid and provide none of any intended tax benefits. This is because federal laws' recognition of a trust as a separate tax entity presupposes validity of the trust under state law.

When a beneficiary is named as trustee, the Doctrine of Merger must be considered. This doctrine holds that the trust as a separate entity ceases to exist when the legal title to the property held by the trustee is identical to the beneficial interest held by the beneficiary. For instance, if the grantor's son is both the sole trustee and sole beneficiary, the trust will cease to exist. It is important to check applicable state law on this point.

14.5 CO-TRUSTEES

After considering each of the desirable characteristics of a good trustee, it will become obvious to most grantors that it is impossible to select a trustee that has all of the advantages and none of the disadvantages. Many grantors therefore attempt to obtain the strengths of both the corporate and the nonprofessional trustee by naming co-trustees. Often, one or more family members and a corporate fiduciary are selected.

Note, however, that combining the positive aspects of more than one trustee has a cost; certain drawbacks or issues must be considered. For instance, if two trustees are selected, what is the procedure if they do not agree on a given issue? If three or more are selected, will the majority rule?[23] What responsibility does a dissenting trustee have for an action (or nonaction) taken by the majority? It usually is a bad idea to take members from both sides of a blended family and make them co-trustees because they often do not have any experience working together, and each side has their own interests that they will protect.

Resignation, Removal and Succession of Trustees

As part of the selection process itself, a grantor should think long and hard about the removal of current trustees and the appointment of successor trustees (typically, at least two should be named). The trust instrument itself should provide for where a vacancy in the office of trustee opens up.[24] In fact, the trust instrument should provide for the procedure for a trustee to resign and for what happens in that event.[25] The trust instrument itself must consider issues such as the following:

- Who, if anyone, should be given the power to remove trustees?

- What is the procedure for removing a trustee? What trustees can be removed by which beneficiaries? What constitutes a "beneficiary" for this purpose?

- Should such a power be given to the grantor, the beneficiaries, the trustee(s), or an outside party such as a trust protector?

- How narrow or broad should a removal power be (i.e., under what circumstances should someone be able to remove a trustee)? Removal for cause? What constitutes "cause?" Who has the power to invoke it?

- How often may a removal power be exercised?

- How will succession be determined?

- What restrictions, if any, will be placed on the successor trustee? Does it have to be an independent trustee? Does the replacement have to be a corporate trustee? Who is eligible for appointment to the office of trustee?

- What are the various tax consequences of allowing the grantor or the beneficiaries to remove a trustee and without restriction appoint a new one?

- Should the document provide that certain persons will not be subject to the removal provisions in the document such as a spouse or other beneficiary?

In trusts that are expected to last for generations, the provision in the trust instrument that provides for removal and replacement of trustees is very important and should not simply be left to default boilerplate. In long-term trusts, where the ranks of beneficiaries could grow to be large over time, it probably is prudent for a trustee who is resigning without cause to appoint a successor trustee, rather than have to get the beneficiaries or a court involved to appoint a successor trustee to avoid an expensive and often internecine squabble over the identity of the replacement.

Summary

The selection of a trustee is a most difficult one because of the longevity of most trusts, the complexity of the tax and other laws with which the trustee must comply, and the sensitivity a trustee must have to both the grantor's objectives and the beneficiary's needs and desires. For these reasons, one or more co-trustees (almost always professionals) is indicated where the terms of the trust are complex or the estate is large or where problems between the beneficiaries can reasonably be expected, which often occurs in blended families.

14.6 PART IV—TRUST PROTECTOR

In this day and age of virtually perpetual trusts that are possible in many jurisdictions and the need to build in as much flexibility into the estate plan as possible and the need to build in as much accountability for the trustee as possible without necessarily giving the beneficiaries the power to remove a trustee, the trust protector can be a very worthwhile thing to use in all trusts that are expected to last for a while. The job duties of a trust protector can be as limited or as limitless as the imagination of the estate planner will allow. There is very little statutory guidance on trust protectors in the United States, but that is gradually changing as usage of the trust protector concept increases.

Many states have addressed the trust protector concept.[26] Trust protectors can have the following tasks, without limitation:

1. To remove any trustee, without cause, to appoint a different trustee or additional cotrustees, and to appoint successor trustees;

2. To amend the terms of the trust instrument to achieve favorable tax status, or to take account of changes in the Internal Revenue Code, state law, or any cases, rulings and/or regulations thereunder;

3. To exercise any voting rights of closely held business interests;

4. To amend the provisions of the trust instrument with regard to how the beneficiaries will benefit from the trust, and to amend the trust administrative provisions;

5. To revoke any and all powers of the grantor and/or grantor's spouse that cause the trust to be a grantor trust for income tax purposes;

6. To appoint and remove distribution committee members and investment committee members, if any:

   - To appoint successor trust protectors;
   - To terminate any trust;
   - To veto or direct trust distributions;
   - To interpret terms of the trust instrument at the request of the trustee;
   - To advise the trustee on matters concerning a beneficiary;
   - To provide direction regarding notification of qualified beneficiaries;

7. To remove all or any part of the property, or the situs of administration, of this trust or any trust established hereunder, and elect, by instrument in writing filed with the trust records, that thereafter such trust shall be construed, regulated, and governed as to its administration by the laws of such other jurisdiction; and

8. To use trust assets to hire legal counsel or other advisors to advise and defend the trust protector in connection with any matter concerning the trust.

The biggest issue in determining the scope of the trust protector role often is in deciding whether the trust protector is to be treated as a fiduciary.[27] As a general rule, trust protectors who have no investment control responsibility are not considered as fiduciaries. However, the trust instrument should expressly provide relative to that issue, as well as to the extent, if any, of the trust protector's responsibility to monitor the trustee. The trust instrument also should specify how a trust protector can resign or be removed as well as the method and sources of compensation and reimbursement of the trust protector.

There are two schools of thought on the use and role of trust protectors. The first school takes a minimalist view and gives the trust protector usually only the power to remove the trustee. The second school takes

SELECTING THE RIGHT PEOPLE CHAPTER 14

a broader view of the trust protector's role and endows the trust protector with overarching powers such as the ones that we laid out earlier. Some trust protector positions take effect immediately upon trust creation, while others "spring" into effect at some point in the future, i.e., on the occurrence of some problem or controversy. We tend to prefer the latter school, although we underscore that it is important to build in accountability for the trust protector too.

The trust instrument should expressly require the trustee to provide financing, at the trust's expense, of the trust protector's defense for any claim arising out of the trust except for claims arising out of bad faith, fraud or willful misconduct by the trust protector. The trust instrument also should permit the trust protector to release, renounce, suspend or modify to a lesser extent any or all powers and discretions conferred under this instrument by a written instrument delivered to the trustee.

The position of "Trust Protector" has evolved from its use solely for offshore asset protection trusts to common inclusion in revocable and irrevocable trusts. Many trusts are now drafted as dynasty trusts which can last for hundreds of years depending upon the rule against perpetuities in the particular jurisdiction governing the trust. The naming of a trust protector can introduce flexibility into a document which may be needed over such a long period of time.

The powers conferred on the trust protector can include the power to name a successor trustee, the power to amend the trust provisions to respond to changes in the tax law, the power to terminate the trust, the power to amend administrative provisions, or the power to change the trust situs.

One question which arises is whether the trust protector is a "fiduciary." Many states provide by statute a presumption that the trust protector is acting in a fiduciary position; however, such presumption can be overcome by language in the document which provides that he is not acting in a fiduciary position. This may be preferable to a particular client because the trust protector's duties can be greatly expanded if he or she is acting in a fiduciary position.

McLean Revocable Trust v. Patrick Davis PC,[28] is a relatively recent case dealing with trust protectors. In the document at issue in that case, the trust protector had the power to remove the trustee and appoint a successor. The trust explicitly provided that the trust protector was acting in a fiduciary capacity and the court held that "(o)ne who acts as a fiduciary assumes at least the basic duties of undivided loyalty and confidentiality." Therefore, the trust protector had a duty of care to supervise the trustees' actions. The issue in the case was whether the lower court properly granted summary judgment, and the appellate court did not rule on whether the fiduciary had violated his duty of care. However, if the trust had provided that the trust protector was acting in a non-fiduciary capacity, then the trust protector would not have owed a duty of care.[29] The *McLean* case was later cited as providing that "[u]nder Missouri law, the existence of a fiduciary relationship between the parties is an essential element of any claim for breach of fiduciary duty."[30]

14.7 PART V-SELECTING AN ATTORNEY

Duties of the Attorney

The duties of the attorney will depend on the client's stage in the estate planning cycle-accumulation, conservation, or distribution. In actuality it is sometimes difficult to know where one stage ends and another begins. Clearly, the attorney must be aware in each stage of the implications of what is done at that stage for the other two stages-and of the consequences to the client and his beneficiaries. For instance, it may be easier and less expensive in the planning stage of the cycle to draft a simple will than a series of more complex trusts. However, the client's family may have fared better in the later stages had the attorney done a more extensive estate plan.

An estate planning attorney must gather data regarding the client and his family or other potential beneficiaries and their circumstances; the client's sources of wealth, income, liabilities, and expenses; and the client's financial goals and fears. The attorney must then assemble this data and relate each of these objective facts and subjective feelings to each other and be able to ascertain the client's current position and the extent of his weaknesses in the following areas:

1. Liquidity- Will the client during his lifetime and his executor at his death be able to pay taxes and other expenses without the need for a forced sale? Is there sufficient life insurance, is it of the right type, and is it properly arranged?

2. Disposition of assets- Are they going to the right person at the right time in the right manner?

3. Adequacy of capital and income- Does the client have enough capital and income in the event of death or disability, or at retirement, or for special family needs such as the care of a handicapped child, or for charitable bequests?

4. Stability and maximization of value- Has the client first put a floor under and then maximized the value of the assets he currently owns? For instance, the value of a business without adequate liability or fire insurance or business continuation coverage has not been stabilized; the value of a partnership without a fully funded buy-sell plan has not been maximized. Absent adequate disability income coverage, a client's income floor has not been assured.

5. Excessive transfer costs- Is the client paying too much in income taxes, or will the client's estate pay an unnecessary amount of estate or other death taxes or transfer costs?

6. Special needs- Does the client have special needs or desires that must be met, such as making gifts to a charity, supporting a poor relative, or protecting a spendthrift spouse?

An estate planning attorney must not only understand these problems and their solutions but also be able to communicate them to the client in a manner that will allow the client to make informed decisions.

Often the attorney must organize and captain the entire estate planning team. Always the attorney should work with the client and the client's other professional advisors in establishing an order of priorities and responsibilities and make sure each aspect of the plan is completed in a timely manner.

Only the attorney can draft the appropriate documents. These range in complexity and length from a simple durable power of attorney, which may run nine or ten pages, to the recapitalization of the client's business and the complete restructuring of the nature of the client's estate plan, which may take hundreds of drafted pages.

Attributes of a Good Attorney

Many of the same attributes important in the selection of an executor or trustee are also of key importance in the search for an attorney. For example, an attorney with business experience who is also familiar with the client's business can be invaluable. The major attributes that should be considered in the selection of an estate planning (or administration) attorney are competence, compassion, clarity, and affordability.

Competence

The level of competence necessary depends to a great extent on the nature and extent of the client's wealth and the complexity of the client's situation. Most general practitioners are competent to draft a power of attorney or simple will. This may be all that is necessary in smaller estates where all the parties involved including the beneficiaries are self-sufficient adults and there are no unusual assets, objectives, or problems.

Compassion

The single most important distinction between a truly good estate planning attorney and the average practitioner is not a superior knowledge of the tax law, nor is it the sense of combativeness that makes winners out of litigation attorneys: it is an attitude of being counselor rather than advocate. The estate planning attorney will be keenly sensitive to the importance of the client's business, for instance, not only as figures on a ledger sheet but also as a personification of the client and as part of a goal-striving behavior. Such an attorney will be extremely conscious of the circumstances, needs, hopes, and fears of the client and of his intended beneficiaries.

Clarity

An estate planning attorney must be able to communicate. Often, the attorney will captain the estate planning team. This means he or she must be able to request information from other professionals, explain to them what each member of the estate planning team is doing and what remains to be done. The attorney must also be able to communicate clearly with nonprofessionals, such as the client or the client's family, the nature and extent of problems the client may not have known existed.

Clarity encompasses not only transferring information but also the urgency of deciding and then acting. The estate planning attorney must be able to convey the importance of the client's doing certain things (such as signing a will, obtaining adequate amounts of life or disability insurance, or establishing a buy-sell agreement) now!

Affordability

Malpractice premiums for estate planning and administration attorneys are among the highest in the profession. This is indicative of the complexity of the practice and of the potential for making expensive mistakes. The point is: selecting the right attorney is a cost-saving factor. The lowest fee may be far from the least expensive.

Most states require the attorney to send a detailed engagement letter outlining the scope and limitations of his or her duties and the fees which will be charged for the services offered.

There is one more important consideration involving the relationship of an attorney to the estate of a deceased person. In most cases the attorney who drafted a will or trust or other estate planning document should be employed to help execute it. That attorney will probably know the client and his intentions better than anyone else. However, if the personal representative of a deceased person is not satisfied with the deceased person's attorney or if the decedent gave no indication of his or her choice of attorney for the estate, the personal representative should, in practically every instance, make his or her own independent selection of an attorney qualified in the area of administering the decedent's estate.

Since the executor has the full responsibility if something goes wrong, the executor has the right and responsibility to personally select the estate's attorney-regardless of which attorney drew the decedent's will. In fact, a number of states protect that right with specific legislation.

Finding an Estate Attorney

Once the estate reaches the size at which federal estate taxes may be imposed, or if the client or any of the client's beneficiaries are under a legal, physical, mental, or emotional disability, or if there is any unusual fact pattern, or where the situation is precarious, e.g., a blended family situation, or it is best to find an attorney who specializes in estate planning and administration, and consideration should be given to the existence or competence of the attorney's paralegals since he or she can accomplish most of the administration at a much lower hourly rate than the rate charged by the attorney. The question is how do you find an attorney in the estate planning field, and then how do you ascertain his or her competence? Some of the ways to locate attorneys practicing in the estate planning field are discussed below.

1. Call the county or city estate planning council. Ask for a copy of the membership directory. This should contain lists of not only attorneys but also CPAs, CFPs, CLUs and ChFCs, trust officers, and other key members of the estate planning team. Consider also The American College of Trust and Estate Counsel ("ACTEC"), to which practitioners who are leaders in the estate planning field are subject to a nomination and screening process (www.actec.org). This list, of course, does not ensure any specific level of competence, but most estate planning councils require peer nomination for entrance, and membership fees help eliminate those who do not spend substantial time in the practice of estate planning. More important, estate planning councils make continuing education and in-depth seminars available to their members. The best attorneys active in the estate planning and administration field tend to be members of an estate planning council and often are the speakers or elected leaders.

2. Many states now certify attorneys in selective areas of practice. Texas, for example, examines an attorney through a rigorous additional state bar-administered examination in the estate planning area. Attorneys who have earned the right to specialize in estate planning through certification will usually signify that in their telephone book listing and on their business cards, V-cards, websites and stationery.

3. Trust officers are excellent sources for finding attorneys active in estate planning. Visit three or four banks with large trust offices. Ask for the names of two or three most competent attorneys. If the same name is mentioned favorably by more than one bank's trust officer, he or she might be a good choice. CLUs, ChFCs, CFPs, and CPAs are also excellent sources for the names of competent attorneys who specialize in estate planning.

4. Attorneys who specialize in estate planning often lecture at business meetings or adult education courses. After attending one or two sessions, a person should find it easy to tell if the attorney can communicate complex legal matter effectively.

5. Practicing attorneys who teach estate planning in law schools, in the tax masters' programs at business schools, and especially those who have taught the American College's estate planning courses for several years are excellent candidates.

6. Some attorneys write in professional journals such as Taxation for Accountants, the Practical Lawyer, Estate Planning Magazine, ACTEC Journal, BNA Estates Gifts and Trust Journal, The Journal of The Society of Financial Service Professionals, Trusts and Estates Magazine, The Practical Accountant, or the Journal of Accountancy. Some write regular news columns and blogs or hold radio talk shows on estate planning. Many have informative public websites. Some attorneys put instructional videos on services like Youtube. Some of the top estate planners in the country are commentators who write for LISI (Leimberg Information Services, Inc).

7. Attorneys with an LL.M. (masters) in taxation generally have higher than average expertise in the estate planning area.

8. Friends and business associates may be able to provide referrals.

9. Bar association referral services and local law schools with tax masters programs are also good sources of estate planning attorneys. Also, since many Bar associations provide continuing legal education to member attorneys, it is a good idea to visit the website of the Bar associations to see which attorneys are lecturing to the other attorneys.

Compassion. The single most important distinction between a truly good estate planning attorney and the average practitioner is not a superior knowledge of the tax law, nor is it the sense of combativeness that makes winners out of litigation attorneys: it is an attitude of being counselor rather than advocate. There is a difference between being an estate law technician and being an "estate planner," and it is knowledge of the human side of estate planning. The good estate planning attorney will be keenly sensitive to the importance of the client's business, for instance, not only as figures on a ledger sheet but also as a personification of the client and as part of a goal-striving behavior. Such an attorney will be extremely conscious of the circumstances, needs, hopes and fears of the client and of his intended beneficiaries.

Clarity. An estate planning attorney must be able to communicate clearly. Often, the attorney will captain the estate planning team. This means he or she must be able to request information from other professionals, explain to them what each member of the estate planning team is doing and what remains to be done. The attorney also must be able to communicate clearly with nonprofessionals, such as the client or the client's family, the nature and extent of problems the client may not have known existed.

Clarity encompasses not only transferring information but also the urgency of deciding and then acting. The estate planning attorney must be able to convey the importance of the client's doing certain things (such as signing a will, obtaining adequate amounts of life or disability insurance, or establishing a buy-sell agreement) now!

Clarity implies the ability to carefully listen to both the client and to the client's other advisors and assimilate and re-communicate their thoughts and concepts.

Affordability. Malpractice premiums for estate planning and administration attorneys are among the highest in the profession. This is indicative of the complexity of the practice and of the potential for making expensive mistakes. The point is, selecting the right attorney is a cost-saving factor. The lowest fee may be far from the least expensive in the long run.

Clients should demand a written and signed statement of the attorney's hourly fee or an estimate of the overall cost for planning or administering the estate-before allowing work to begin, and a competent attorney will be able to provide an engagement letter explaining the scope, responsibilities, and limitations of the relationship and an estimate of the fees and costs.

There is one more important consideration involving the relationship of an attorney to the estate of a deceased person. In most cases, the attorney who drafted a will or trust or other estate planning document should be employed to help execute it. That attorney will probably know the client and his intentions better than anyone else. But if the personal representative of a deceased person is not satisfied or for any reason is personally uncomfortable with the deceased person's attorney or if the decedent gave no indication of his or her choice of attorney for the estate, the personal representative should, in practically every instance, make his or her own independent selection of an attorney qualified in the area of administering the decedent's estate.

Since the executor has the full responsibility if something goes wrong, the executor has the right and responsibility to personally select the estate's attorney-*regardless* of which attorney drew the decedent's will. In fact, a number of states protect that right with specific legislation.

Other Members of the Estate Planning Team

Accountant. An accountant, who often is a Certified Public Accountant (CPA), is a very valuable member of the client's estate planning team because the accountant usually has an intimate knowledge of the client's personal and financial picture. Additionally, because the accountant usually has regular interaction with the client because of doing bookkeeping and tax returns for the client, the accountant usually has the most intimate relationship with the client, even more so than the lawyer for most clients, which makes the accountant a great candidate to be the quarterback of the estate planning team.

Financial planner/investments professional/life underwriter. In today's world, where the distinctions between financial products and life insurance have blurred almost beyond recognition, we group life insurance agents and investments professionals and financial planners who sell products together. Because of the sales training that most of them get, they tend to be good action motivators, usually far better than both attorneys and accountants. These professionals often are the impetus for the estate planning, so they are valued and valuable members of the estate planning team. Generally, financial planners and life insurance agents who have or who are working on a CLU, ChFC, or CFP tend to be much more knowledgeable and dedicated to professionalism than those who do not have or who are not working toward completing those designations.

Planned giving consultant. If the client is charitably inclined, it is not unusual for a planned giving consultant or even a director of planned giving at a charity to be consulted during the estate planning process.

Family business consultant/family wealth coach. Sometimes, communication between the players during the estate planning process is not optimal, particularly where there are several generations involved or where the principal asset in the estate consists of an interest in one or more family businesses. It is not unusual for forward thinking clients (or their advisors) to bring in professionals who excel in the qualitative or "soft" "people" side of estate planning.

Trust professional. It is not unusual to see a trust professional be involved in the estate planning process, whether it is the private client group at a bank or trust company or even from a family office. These professionals also can be key members of the client's estate planning team.

Valuation Professional. Quite often it is all about the value of property. Whether it is the value of property for transfer tax purposes or valuations for non-tax reasons such as for funding trusts, it is not unusual for a valuation professional to be involved in the planning and/or administration of an estate or trust. It is important that all valuation professionals be qualified by designations, education and experience to value the property in question and that they be independent of all of the fiduciaries.

Summary

The selection of an attorney who specializes in estate planning should focus primarily on identifying someone who has competence, compassion, the ability to communicate clearly with other professionals and with clients, and who is willing to work at a price that is in line with a client's means.

CHAPTER ENDNOTES

1. *Editor's Note*: This chapter was originally published as "How to Select an Executor, Trustee, and Attorney," by Stephan R. Leimberg and Charles K. Plotnick, and is reproduced with the publisher's permission from *How to Settle an Estate*, by Plotnick and Leimberg (New York: Plume Book, 2001). The authors are grateful for the significant assistance of Lawrence Brody, Esq., of Bryan, Cave in St. Louis, Missouri.

2. *In re Eiteljorg*, 951 NE 2d 565 (Ind. App. 2011), that arrangement did not work out so well.

3. See, e.g., Rule 1.8(c), Model Rules of Professional Conduct.

4. See, e.g., §3-712, Uniform Probate Code.
5. It is important that the executor waive the fee early on in the administration of the estate or trust. See, e.g., Rev. Ruls. 66-167 and 64-225. See also Rev. Rul. 56-472.
6. I.R.C. §2053(a)(2).
7. I.R.C. §102.
8. See, e.g., §102(1), Uniform Power of Attorney Act and Section 1(2), Uniform Health-Care Decisions Act.
9. See, e.g., §102(2) and 104, Uniform Power of Attorney Act; §2(b), Uniform Health-Care Decisions Act. However, with respect to health care powers of attorney, the agent's powers "spring" into existence on the principal's loss of capacity and dissolved upon the principal's regaining of capacity unless the health care power of attorney provides otherwise. See, e.g., §2(c), Uniform Health-Care Decisions Act.
10. See, e.g., §109(a), Uniform Power of Attorney Act; §2(b), Uniform Health-Care Decisions Act.
11. See, e.g., §110(a)(1), Uniform Power of Attorney Act.
12. See, e.g., §110(b)(3), Uniform Power of Attorney Act; §3(d), Uniform Health-Care Decisions Act. However, in the Uniform Health-Care Decisions Act, the power of attorney in favor of a spouse is revoked only upon rendition of the decree of divorce, dissolution or separation unless the power of attorney provides otherwise.
13. See, e.g., §110(f), Uniform Power of Attorney Act. However, with respect to a health care power of attorney, a subsequent power of attorney that is inconsistent with a prior health care power of attorney revokes the prior power of attorney. See, e.g., §3(e), Uniform Health-Care Decisions Act.
14. See, e.g., §114, Uniform Power of Attorney Act.
15. See, e.g., §201(a), Uniform Power of Attorney Act.
16. See, e.g., §§202 and 204-217, Uniform Power of Attorney Act.
17. I.R.C. §676(a); Treas. Reg. §1.676(a)-1.
18. Treas. Reg. §1.671-4(b)(2)(ii).
19. I.R.C. §672(c).
20. Treas. Reg. §1.672(a)-1.
21. I.R.C. §672(b).
22. See *Castro v. Comm'r*, T.C.M. 2001-115 (2001).
23. Absent contrary language in the trust instrument requiring unanimity, trustees generally may act by majority vote. See, e.g., §703(a), Uniform Trust Code.
24. See, e.g., §704, Uniform Trust Code.
25. See, e.g., §705, Uniform Trust Code.
26. See, e.g., South Dakota Codified Laws Chapter 55-1B.
27. See, e.g., §55-1B-1(2), South Dakota Codified Laws.
28. 283 S.W.3d 786 (Mo. Ct. App. 2009).
29. Peter B. Tiernan, "Evaluate and Draft Helpful Trust Protector Provisions," *Estate Planning Journal* (July 2011).
30. *Speaks Family Chapels, Inc. v. National Heritage Enterprises, Inc.*, 2009 WL 2391769 (W.D. Mo. 2009).

PROBATE AND TRUST ADMINISTRATION[1]

CHAPTER 15

15.1 INTRODUCTION

The administration of an estate or trust is not for the novice or the biased. This is particularly true with blended family trusts and estates, which is why we preach so hard that partners in blended family situations should – if at all possible - appoint *disinterested* third party fiduciaries. There are so many points along the way in estate and trust administration for there to be conflicts of interest and the ability to favor one side of the family over the other that giving a novice, interested fiduciary these powers is akin to giving a child the keys to the cookie jar: the temptation is all too often just too great to resist.

In this chapter, we will review the basics of probate and trust administration before zeroing in on critical elections and decisions that an executor or trustee has to make, and we will highlight the blended family interested trustee situation.

Many of the decisions that an executor or trustee has to make are dictated in the governing instrument. Therefore, drafting in advance of administration is critical, particularly for the blended family partner and especially where the client opts to appoint an interested person as a fiduciary.

The job of executor can be a thankless one. No matter what the executor does, someone is going to be unhappy.

In its most narrow sense, the term probate means to prove that the will was the decedent's, and that the will being offered to the court is the "last will" of the decedent. In its broader sense, probate refers to the entire process of administering the decedent's will, including gathering the decedent's assets, paying the decedent's taxes and debts, and distributing the remaining assets to the proper beneficiaries.

The central figure in this probate process is the personal representative, typically the estate's executor. Any legally competent adult could be an executor. But few of us would want to be if we knew the awesome, complex, and time-consuming responsibilities and potential liabilities the task entails.

15.2 GENERAL ROLE OF AN EXECUTOR OR SUCCESSOR TRUSTEE OF A REVOCABLE LIVING TRUST

When a person dies with a valid will and without having funded the property into a revocable living trust during lifetime, the law requires that his property must be collected. After debts, taxes, and expenses are paid, the remaining assets are distributed to whoever is entitled to that property. That distribution is determined by the person's will, or if there is no valid will (or to the extent a will is partially invalid), the intestate laws of the state. Many of the duties that are associated with our expansive description of "probate" fall on the successor trustee of a revocable living trust when the grantor dies; there are many similar duties, and our comments cover both the traditional probate work of the executor and the work of the successor trustee under a formerly revocable living trust.

It is the executor's or administrator's responsibility to collect and safeguard the decedent's assets, pay the death taxes, debts, and expenses of the decedent, and to make the appropriate distribution of any remaining assets. The entire process by which these tasks are accomplished (with the guidance and supervision of the court system) is called probate. The court that oversees the process is typically called the probate (or "orphans" or "surrogates") court. These types of courts usually are courts of "equity", in which courts can apply fundamental principles of fairness without having to resort to statutory law.

There are two methods of probate: independent or informal probate, where – in spite of the name - the executor is not really unsupervised[2] (although there is much greater leeway for the executor to act without constantly having to get court approval as is the case in supervised administration) and formal or supervised probate.[3] While the choice of which route of probate to travel can be dictated by the testator, or, if not so stipulated, by the executor and even by the heirs or legatees, we underscore that this decision should not be made quickly or lightly, particularly in the blended family where problems are reasonably foreseeable. There are plenty of situations where well-timed judicial guidance and supervision can circumvent a potentially costly and caustic situation.

15.3 DISTINCTION BETWEEN EXECUTOR AND ADMINISTRATOR

An executor is the person specifically named and appointed in the will of the decedent to serve as representative of the decedent's estate, even though today executors are more formally referred to in the law as "personal representatives."[4] In some jurisdictions, the person named as executor in the will has limited or no authority to act until his appointment is approved by the appropriate court.[5] If the decedent left no will, if the will is invalid for some reason, or if the named executor is unable or unwilling to serve, then either the surviving spouse or another relative of the decedent, or one or more of the persons entitled to his or her estate, may be appointed as the "personal representative" in a pecking-order priority of appointment.[6] In some jurisdictions, a creditor or any other person may be appointed if no one of higher priority is able or willing to serve. If not named in the will, the personal representative is called the "administrator" of the estate. So it is the executor or administrator (a female appointee is sometimes referred to as "executrix" or "administratrix") who will probate the decedent's will and who accepts the responsibility of carrying out the decedent's wishes with respect to the property that passes through probate, even though that person is as much the personal representative as an executor.[7] In some situations, it may be necessary to appoint a special administrator to serve prior to the appointment of a personal representative or where there is a vacancy in the personal representative position.[8] More than one personal representative may be appointed to serve simultaneously, and joint unanimous action usually is required unless the will provides otherwise, with exceptions for ministerial or delegated duties and where emergency action is necessary.[9] The executor usually will probate the decedent's will.[10]

In its most narrow sense, the term "probate" means to prove that the will was the decedent's, and that the will being offered is the "last will" of the decedent so that the will can be legally recognized and properly lodged with the court as the decedent's last will. In its broader sense, "probate" refers to the entire process of administering the will, including gathering the decedent's assets, paying the decedent's taxes and debts, and distributing the remaining assets to the proper beneficiaries. In the broader sense, the term "probate" would seem to have application to the post-death administration of a revocable living trust since many of the same duties and tasks are performed and carried out, e.g., valuation of the trust property and the preparation of federal and state death tax returns, even though administration is the more proper term.

15.4 FUNERAL ARRANGEMENTS

Typically, the funeral will take place before the executor or administrator has been appointed and funeral arrangements are generally the responsibility of the decedent's immediate family. Nevertheless, the person named in a will as personal representative often has the authority to carry out funeral arrangements prior to formal confirmation as personal representative.[11] Therefore, it is important that the decedent make sure his family is aware of what funeral and burial arrangements the person wants, as opposed to informing the executor who may or may not be a family member.

This is even more important in a blended family context where the two sides, i.e., the surviving partner and the decedent's children, may have vastly different ideas about the funeral and burial arrangements during this highly emotionally charged time. So the executor's only legal duty with respect to the funeral will be to pay the reasonable bills associated with that event. If the will contains specific instructions about the funeral and/or burial, these directions should be complied with to the extent practical and possible.

For an in-depth discussion of funeral arrangements, particularly in the context of a blended family, where funeral arrangements often are a flashpoint of emotions, see Chapter 68, infra.

15.5 APPOINTMENT OF THE PERSONAL REPRESENTATIVE

Even before the appointment of a personal representative of a decedent's estate, a determination has to be made as to where the deceased person was domiciled. Domicile should never be "assumed" and is an extremely important determination. This is because where the decedent was domiciled sets the proper location of the court that will have jurisdiction over the decedent's estate. This is either where the decedent was domiciled at death or where the decedent's property is located.[12] It is also crucial with respect to the state death tax that will be imposed.

A person's domicile is his permanent and principal home, the place to which he always intends to return. The difference between domicile and residence is that your residence is where you happen to be living. Domicile requires not only your presence, but also an *intention* to make it your permanent home.

Domicile may not always be clear because the decedent may have had more than one residence. Generally, domicile is determined by external manifestations of the decedent's intent, e.g., where the decedent was registered to vote, had a driver's license, claimed a homestead exemption for ad valorem tax purposes, the address that the decedent reflected on official documents such as personal checks, letterhead and the like, etc.

It is even possible that the decedent may have had two domiciles, in which case either domicile would be a proper venue, although it is likely in that scenario for there to be an ancillary probate in the other jurisdiction. Often, this involves a race to the courthouses to file first because the first filed action generally takes priority and venue is then transferred by the court of the second filed jurisdiction to that court of the first filed application.[13]

The will must then be recorded in the office of the local register of wills of the county in which the decedent was domiciled (often the clerk of the county court).[14] The register of wills (or the appropriate court of jurisdiction) will issue either "letters testamentary" (to an executor) or "letters of administration" (to an administrator).[15]

These letters serve as proof of the legal authority of the personal representative to collect and deal with the assets in the decedent's estate. (In some jurisdictions, to make things simpler, the register of wills gives the executor "short certificates," brief documents evidencing the fact that you are the executor or administrator of the decedent's estate.)

The executor or administrator, acting on behalf of the estate, assumes title to the decedent's property and acts on behalf of the estate.[16]

15.6 EMPLOYMENT OF THE ATTORNEY FOR THE ESTATE

An executor is entitled to use any *qualified* attorney he or she would like. The term qualified attorney is stressed because of the complexity and potential personal liability risks of handling an estate. Generally, an executor may use any attorney the executor feels is competent – even if the decedent named a different attorney in his will.

For both state law and federal tax purposes, the executor or administrator must keep informed as to exactly how the estate is being administered. He can't just shift all the responsibility to the attorney. A court could find an administratrix responsible for the actions of her attorney where she surrenders all of her duties to the attorney and exercises no effective supervision whatsoever over any of activities, because it is the personal representative's duty to properly administer the estate.[17] The court could find that she did not exercise that degree of care, prudence, circumspection, and foresight that a prudent person would employ in matters of her own. Even if the attorney is the person doing the bulk of the work, the executor or administrator is ultimately responsible for anything that goes wrong or if any harm occurs for actions that should have been taken in a timely manner but were not because the executor has fiduciary duties that are similar to those of a trustee.[18]

15.7 COLLECTING THE ASSETS

After the executor is appointed, the first thing to do is to get together with the members of the decedent's family, assuming that they are the decedent's beneficiaries, and make sure there is a clear understanding of the size and nature of the decedent's estate.

The second step, if the size, nature, and complexity of the estate warrant, is to hire competent counsel. Once appropriate counsel has been employed, the executor should act quickly to collect, safeguard, and insure the decedent's assets.[19] As assets are collected, they should also be valued. This means an appraisal must be made of the real property and of any personal property that the decedent owned, such as jewelry, clothing, automobiles, and household furniture and effects. And, of course, a value has to be placed on any business interest of the decedent.

In some jurisdictions, assets other than cash or cash equivalents must be appraised by court-appointed appraisers. In one case, the court felt that because the executor erred in calculating the value of the decedent's shares in a corporation, and thereby obtained a sales price below the value of the shares, the executor should be surcharged. It is necessary for the executor to provide certain notices within a short period of time after issuance of the letters of administration to the beneficiaries as to their interest in the estate.[20] The executor also has the duty and authority to engage one or more professional appraisers to value the decedent's property.[21]

It is extremely important that the executor take every possible measure to make certain that he has a complete inventory of all of the decedent's assets. In this regard, he should review the decedent's past income tax returns, cancelled checks, property insurance policies, employment information and mail to determine if there are any purchases, accounts, securities, or other assets or life insurance policies of which the executor is not otherwise aware.

Prior income tax returns, for example, might list interest from bank accounts or dividends from securities of which the executor has no knowledge. From this information, the executor can trace the present location of the assets and determine whether those assets were still owned by the decedent at the time of his death. In addition, the executor must try to collect all outstanding claims that the decedent had against others at his death. In one case, a court even held the executor responsible for failing to make a claim that the estate was the beneficiary of – and therefore entitled to – monies from another estate.

There is no special order in which the executor must collect the decedent's assets, but it is usually logical to file the appropriate claim form to collect the decedent's life insurance as soon as possible. This is true because the life insurance proceeds generally come fairly quickly, and it is an easy way to provide liquidity to the estate if the policies are payable to the estate. There are also forms for collecting social security and veterans' administration benefits that should be filed. Sometimes unpaid salary, as well as other fringe benefits, must be collected. Arrange to have the decedent's safe-deposit box opened and make a list of its contents.

It may also be necessary for the executor to provide certain notices to the beneficiaries as to their interest in the estate. Some states require that the executor send notices to specific individuals within a certain number of days from the date the will is probated (that is, offered to the state as the last will of the decedent).

The executor should advertise the fact that he has been appointed executor so that creditors or other persons who might have an interest in the decedent's estate will have public notice of death and thus have time to present any claims against the estate to the executor.[22] This notice is not the same as the obituary or death notice. It is an official legal notice published in local newspapers. In many jurisdictions, publication of notice in a newspaper of general circulation is required.[23]

The public notice also gives creditors warning that claims must be made before a certain date or else the claims will be barred. The executor also can send each known creditor notice by mail, preferably via certified mail with return receipt requested.[24] If notice of one's appointment as executor is advertised, and the prescribed period of time elapses from the first date of publication for barring claims, often four months,[25] then the executor pays the valid claims[26] and then files his final account with the court.[27] Only after that time elapses and the executor has accounted for what came into the estate, what went out, and what he paid to the beneficiaries, can the executor be discharged of all responsibility for handling the estate.[28]

There is no special order in which the executor must collect the decedent's assets, but it is usually logical to file the appropriate claim form to collect the decedent's life insurance as soon as possible. This is true because the life insurance proceeds are generally paid quickly, and provide an easy and efficient way to provide liquidity to the estate if the policies are payable to the estate. (Typically, the personal representative or the estate's attorney will assist the decedent's family in receiving life insurance policies that name them as beneficiary even though, technically, that is not part of the executor's duties). There also are forms for collecting social security and veterans' administration benefits that must be completed and filed by the executor. The executor must also inform the Social Security Administration that the recipient has died. Sometimes unpaid salary, as well as other fringe benefits, must be collected from the decedent's employer. Of course, the executor must also arrange to have the decedent's safe-deposit box(es) opened and is required to make a complete inventory of its contents.

It is important for the executor to immediately obtain a taxpayer identification number for the estate and then open an estate checking account and a savings account. The executor can then take all the liquid assets and pass them through the estate's checking account and savings account, if appropriate, in order to have an accurate accounting and documentation of the assets collected and bills paid.

The executor should give notice of the decedent's death to the banks where the decedent had his accounts. He should obtain from the banks letters giving the exact values of the accounts on the date of death, the dates that the accounts were opened, and the exact names on the accounts.

All securities in the decedent's name should be assembled, and the executor should maintain close contact with the decedent's broker to be certain that he has an accurate record of all the securities that the decedent owned, or had an interest in, at the time of his death. There are certain forms the executor must obtain to transfer title to stocks or bonds. The executor must also determine the value of the securities on the decedent's date of death according to the valuation method prescribed by the Internal Revenue Service.

If the decedent held real estate in his own name, the executor must be certain that the property is protected, that appropriate amounts of insurance are obtained or maintained, and that adequate safeguards are instituted to maintain the security of the property. If it is decided that the property should be sold, the executor is responsible for making sure that the sale is conducted properly and a fair price is received. Even if the executor makes a completely innocent mistake, it could cost him money. For example, one executor mistakenly obligated an estate to two real estate commissions. As a result, the court held that the executor was *personally* responsible for the amount of the overpayment.

It is also necessary for the executor to have court approval for the sale of real estate unless that power is specifically given to him in the will. In one case, the court found that even where the will gave the executor all the powers set forth in the general statutes of the state, which included the power to sell any property of the decedent without court approval, the executor still did not have the right to sell real estate without court approval, but this is a matter of applicable state law.[29] If real estate is to be sold, the title company for the buyer may have certain requirements to make sure that the executor has the authority to sell the property and that all of the death taxes have been paid, or will be paid. For this reason, it is important to have an attorney review the title report for the property as soon as possible so that all of the requirements can be addressed before the closing.

As assets are collected, they should also be valued. This means an appraisal must be made of the real property and of any personal property that the decedent owned, such as jewelry, clothing, automobiles, and household furniture and effects. And, of course, a value has to be placed on any business interest of the decedent. In some jurisdictions, all assets other than cash or cash equivalents must be appraised by court-appointed appraisers. It is possible for an executor to be personally liable for relying upon an improper appraisal report or one performed by an appraiser who was not competent to perform appraisals of the type of property involved.

15.8 HANDLING THE BUSINESS

Where the executor finds a business among the decedent's assets, particular attention must be given to the books of the business. The executor should examine prior tax returns and take whatever action is necessary to ensure that the business is being run as efficiently as possible. A determination will have to be made as to whether the business should be continued or liquidated.[30] In this regard, the executor can be guided by the decedent's instructions in his will, by the wishes of the family, or by whatever professional guidance the executor can obtain. If the decedent had any business agreements, such as a buy-sell agreement with a surviving partner, or with a surviving shareholder if the business is incorporated, or with the corporation itself, then the executor must comply with the provisions of the agreement. See the discussion of buy-sell agreements in Chapter 47.

Very serious problems can arise in trying to conserve the value of a decedent's business or real estate. If the decedent's business was a sole proprietorship, then it legally terminates at death. A partnership also terminates, in effect, unless the proper pre-death agreements have been made, such as buy-sell agreements that would enable the surviving partner or partners to continue the business. If the business is closed for any period of time following the decedent's death, its value as a going concern is greatly diminished. An interruption of the normal flow of business will result in the loss of customers and a large drop in the value for which the business might be sold. If the assets of the business are perishable, or have a time value, then the executor faces the problem of taking immediate action or having these business assets dissipated.

Unfortunately, the executor can be held personally responsible for negligence in the management of a decedent's business. In fact, the results in most cases where businesses are continued without court authorization are generally unfavorable to the personal representatives. The court in one such case held that the personal representative did not have the unqualified right to perpetuate a decedent's enterprise without approval of the court, and that any loss to the estate suffered by continuation of the business fell upon the representative.

15.9 INVESTING AND PROTECTING THE ASSETS

The executor should take steps to ascertain that the assets are properly invested, so that there will be no possibility of the executor's being held responsible for dissipating the assets or allowing their value to decrease unreasonably.[31] In investing these assets, an executor is required to exercise the same degree of judgment that a reasonable person would exercise in the management of his own estate.[32]

In investing estate assets, the executor must strike the proper balance between the appropriate level of risk in investments and the liquidity needs of the estate, including the funding of payment of death taxes, claims against the estate and legacies that are to be paid in cash. An executor can be surcharged for leaving funds in non-interest bearing accounts for too long a period of time as well as for taking an inordinate amount of risk in the investments. The safest thing for an executor to do is to immediately deposit all cash of the estate into interest-bearing accounts pending the engagement of professional investment expertise and then rely upon that expertise in making cash flow projections for the estate along an expected administration time table.[33]

Protection of assets is another responsibility of an executor, who must make certain that silverware, jewelry, and art objects are protected and insured, so that the executor will not be held responsible in the event of loss by theft, fire, or other unforeseen calamity. This caveat holds particularly true for collectibles and weapons of any kind. It is advisable that the executor maintain all policies of property and casualty insurance that the decedent owned unless the executor determines that alternate similar insurance can be obtained at a better price. If any property of the estate is not insured, then the executor should strongly consider insuring that property without delay.[34]

The executor must try to obtain a fair price if selling assets, and the executor should never sell any asset without having obtained a professional appraisal of that asset.[35] For example, the executor of the estate of a prominent painter sold paintings to an art dealer, and the dealer a few months later resold the paintings at prices ranging from six to ten times what the dealer paid the estate for them. A court might hold the executor responsible for the loss to the estate for failure to exercise prudence.

What does an executor do when property is not in the decedent's name alone, but the decedent owns it jointly with his wife, or another family member, or even a business associate? Whenever property is held in joint names, the applicable state law will determine whether the decedent's interest in the property will be included as part of the estate to be administered by the executor or whether, in fact, the property will pass directly to the remaining joint owner or owners. For example, in most states, property owned jointly by husband and wife is owned as a joint tenancy with the right of survivorship (sometimes known as "tenancy by the entirety"). The right of survivorship means that upon the death of one of these joint owners the survivor immediately and automatically owns all property rights to the exclusion of the executor.

However, property is sometimes owned by several persons as tenants in common. This is common in community property situations where each spouse is an owner of an undivided one-half of the property. In this situation, each person has an undivided right to a certain percentage of the property. Where the decedent owned a tenancy in common, the decedent's share passes under the decedent's will or by intestacy—and not automatically to the other owners. The executor will represent the decedent's interests in proportionate share of the property. In some cases, questions can be raised as to what exactly the decedent's interest is, and these cases require extreme caution on the part of the executor.

The classification of property issue can be a real problem for the interested fiduciary who is claiming ownership of property that others thought belonged to the decedent and can be a major conflict of interest for the interested fiduciary. This can happen, for example, when a surviving spouse as a fiduciary is taking the position that property that the deceased spouse's children thought was either the decedent's separate property or was community property either was her separate property or was community property.[36] There is also the problem of the responsibility for the taxes due on the decedent's interest in the share of the jointly held property.

15.10 PAYMENT OF TAXES, DEBTS, AND EXPENSES

A decedent's assets must often be converted relatively quickly into cash in order to pay expenses, debts, and taxes. Since no two decedents own exactly the same property, no two estates will be handled in an identical manner. There is very little demand for some of the personal property that people own.[37] Therefore it is hard to realize cash from many of these assets. Of course, assets such as the proceeds of life insurance, certificates of deposits, and Treasury bills may be available to take care of the estate's liabilities. Listed securities can also be quickly converted to cash, but the market value at the time that funds are needed or other circumstances might preclude or inhibit the feasibility of their sale at that time.

Assets such as real estate and business interests are not readily convertible into cash, and it might take months, or even years in the case of business interests, to realize cash from these assets. Therefore, the executor has to analyze the assets of the estate after they have been assembled, determine what amounts of cash will be needed to cover the debts, expenses, and taxes of the estate, and then develop a plan to make the necessary funds available when required. It is imperative that the executor obtain guidance from a qualified professional to assist in these determinations, which can be quite tricky and counterintuitive.

Typical debts that the decedent might have outstanding at death include outstanding loans, credit card balances, and day-to-day bills such as household bills, telephone, electric, gasoline, department store charges, and income and property taxes.

Common expenses incurred in administering the estate include probate costs, legal fees, executor's or administrator's fees, fees for appraisers, costs included in selling real estate and personal property, costs arising on account of the decedent's last illness, and the costs involved in winding up the executor's business.

Numerous categories of taxes must be paid in the process of settling an estate. In some estates, the executor must file forms for and pay two categories of death taxes – state inheritance and estate taxes, and the federal estate tax, for which the executor is personally liable.[38] In addition, the executor is also responsible for the payment of unpaid income taxes, both federal and state, and any state personal property and real estate taxes that might be due on the personal and real property in the decedent's name.

State death taxes are often paid by the executor out of the estate's assets.[39] (Technically, with respect to an inheritance tax, the person receiving the property is taxed on his right to *receive* such assets. An estate tax taxes the right to *transfer* property.) The amount of any inheritance tax, which is on the transfer itself, usually depends on the relationship of the beneficiary or receiver of the property to the decedent. There are exceptions for certain types of property held jointly by husband and wife for which no tax is due. There are also specific exemptions, such as for the proceeds of life insurance paid to a named beneficiary, for charitable bequests, and for real estate located outside of the taxing state.

It is important to keep in mind who is paying the tax with respect to a particular asset. The decedent's will usually specifies how these taxes will be allocated. If the will is silent, state law will determine the result. This is an important issue given that many assets pass by beneficiary designation or because of the asset being titled in joint names. With assets passing outside of the provisions of the will, it is possible to have one person paying the taxes on assets passing to another person. While this may be appropriate in some situations, it is important to consider the implications concerning how the taxes will have to be paid. This issue can be particularly troublesome in blended families or where the beneficiaries are estranged.

Where a decedent owns real estate located in a state different from that of his domicile at the time of death, the state in which the real estate is located has the right to tax the property. This often leads to problems, especially in those cases where two states are trying to tax the same property.

A federal estate tax return must be filed if the decedent's net assets exceed a specified amount at the time of death ($12,920,000 for 2023). It is important to remember that the decedent's estate for federal estate tax purposes may be different from the decedent's estate for state death tax purposes. See Chapter 26 for more information about state death taxes. In addition, if the surviving spouse wishes to elect portability of estate tax exemption of the deceased spouse it will be necessary to timely file a federal estate return to preserve this benefit.

Tax returns many times are accompanied with tax payments. The federal estate tax return is a long and highly complex form, requiring a great deal of time both in assembling the necessary information and in preparing the return. There are important questions that must be answered by the executor as well as available options that can result in considerable tax savings to the estate, and with which the executor must be familiar. Before listing the assets on the return, the executor must first decide on the value of the assets at the time of death. For cash or listed securities, the value of the asset is fixed. However, in determining the value of a business interest or of real estate, it is first necessary to have the properties in question appraised. Appropriate parallels should then be drawn between similar assets, so that a valuation can be arrived at that will keep taxes to a minimum, but will also be acceptable to the government as a fair representation of the market value of the properties as of the date of the decedent's death.

For estate tax purposes, the executor has the choice of using the value of property as of the date of death or selecting the alternate valuation date value. The alternate valuation date method simply means valuing the assets in the estate at a date up to six months following the decedent's death. The actual valuation date is the earlier of:

- the date the assets are sold;
- the date they are distributed; or
- six months from the date of death.

Alternate valuation would be advantageous in the event that the value of the property had fallen during that period, and this is a very important decision on the part of the executor. (Where there will be no federal estate tax because the size of the estate falls below the level of the federal applicable exclusion amount ($11,700,000 in 2021), it may be advantageous to place a higher value on the property so that the heirs receive a higher basis to reduce their gain when they later sell the property. However, caution is the order of the day because there are stiff penalties for valuation overstatements.[40]

There are also certain types of closely held business property and farm property that may qualify for specific tax advantages because of the nature of the property. The executor should be aware of these special elections, as well as other important valuation rules, and should use them to the best advantage of the estate and its beneficiaries.

Another very important tax-saving device is the marital deduction. It is possible to transfer an unlimited amount of money and/or property to a surviving spouse who is a U.S. citizen, outright or in trust, and not pay any federal estate tax. It is even possible to provide that the surviving spouse will receive only the income from that property, with the remainder passing at death to some third party, such as the couple's children. Prompt action on the part of the executor, though, is essential if this flexibility is to be secured. Still other choices and elections must be made by executors to fully maximize the almost unlimited tax-saving potential of current law.

Federal estate taxes are due nine months from the date of death. There are serious penalties if the return is not filed promptly or if an extension is not obtained within a specified time period. In certain circumstances, there are options available to an executor that will extend the time period for the payment of all or a portion of the federal estate tax. If the estate qualifies, no payment of the tax is required for four years (although interest at an extremely favorable rate is payable during this time). The executor can then pay the tax due (plus interest) in up to ten annual installments.[41] This can stretch out the payments for up to fourteen years.

The executor is responsible for knowing all of these dates and taking advantage of all options and elections. Courts have held that where the untimely filing of federal estate tax returns resulted in a loss to the estate, the executor was personally responsible. There are many cases where beneficiaries have attempted to surcharge executors for their failure to take advantage of tax saving and expense-saving opportunities.

In many cases there are other taxes to be paid and other forms to be filed. For example, income taxes have to be paid on the income that the decedent earned prior to death. Tax also has to be paid on the income generated from the assets in the estate. Options are available to the executor in regard to the timing of the estate's income tax return, because, unlike trusts, an estate can elect a fiscal year different than the calendar year,[42] and the executor should make this determination after a thorough review of the entire tax picture of the decedent, the estate, and the beneficiaries. Estates also are relieved from the obligation to make estimated federal income tax payments for the first two years of administration following the decedent's death.[43]

There is also a federal (and in Connecticut a state) gift tax, the returns for which would have been filed by the decedent in most cases. The executor should review any transfers made by the decedent prior to death and make a determination as to whether any gift taxes are due. If so, the appropriate gift tax returns should be filed. Thus an executor has to be aware of the recent changes in the gift tax laws as well as the changes in the state and income tax provisions. The executor also has the responsibility of listing the amounts reflected on any gift tax returns upon the federal estate tax return.

15.11 DISTRIBUTING REMAINING ASSETS

Once an executor has assembled the decedent's assets and paid appropriate debts, expenses, and taxes, the executor must distribute any remaining assets according to the decedent's will or under state intestacy laws.[44] In the case of a very small estate where the spouse might be the executor and sole beneficiary, distribution can be accomplished by turning the property over to the beneficiary and accepting a "receipt and release" to the executor of any liability to the beneficiary. Most legacies are to be made "in kind,"[45] which means that property of the estate other than cash is distributed, often in fractional or percentage interests. However, while this is certainly the most expedient and inexpensive way of concluding an estate, the executor may remain liable for any unpaid debts and taxes, and may be responsible for any number of other problems that might arise.

If the executor wishes to be formally discharged from his duties, responsibilities, and liabilities, then it is necessary to prepare a final account of administration with the court.[46] Unpaid creditors and beneficiaries are given notice of the filing of the account.[47] If there are charitable gifts in the will, the notice must be sent to the attorney general or other appropriate official appointed to protect the interests of the charities. On the date of the audit, those persons having any objections appear and are given the right to a further hearing, if necessary, to present their position to the court. When the court is satisfied that all of the procedures in handling the estate have been complied with, then the account is approved, a formal schedule of distribution is presented and approved, and the executor distributes the assets to the beneficiaries and is discharged from his responsibilities. When "pour-over" trusts (trusts into which the assets passing under the will "pour over" to the trust) have been established in the decedent's will, assets are transferred from the executor to the trusts so that these trusts can be immediately implemented, if assets have not already been so transferred.

Complications in making distribution often occur because the people mentioned in the decedent's will are not all available to take distribution, or assets that are supposed to pass to named beneficiaries are not in the decedent's estate at the time of his death, or are there in different form. For example, if a decedent leaves his estate equally to his two brothers, and subsequent to the writing of the will but prior to his death the two brothers die, with one leaving two children and the other survived solely by his wife, how should the executor distribute the proceeds? The answer would depend upon an interpretation of the decedent's will, or the law of the state of domicile, or perhaps a combination of both.

Further complications arise when a decedent has bequeathed specific assets that are no longer in his estate at the time of his death. For example, bequests of "all my money in my savings account at XYZ Bank to my brother" and "all of my stock certificates to my sister" would be complicated if, before his death, the decedent (or his agent under a durable power of attorney) had closed out his bank account and used part of the funds to purchase securities and part to purchase an automobile. In any event, if the executor made distribution in any contested situation without court approval, the executor could be held personally responsible if it was later determined that the distribution was improper.

Of course, the executor must make distribution promptly, unlike the tardy executrix who one court felt unreasonably and intentionally withheld distribution of the funds to her sisters, under the will of their mother, and was charged with interest at the legal rate during the period of the delay.

15.12 EXECUTOR'S PRIMARY DUTIES

An executor's duties have previously been discussed in conjunction with selecting an executor for an estate (see Chapter 11). In addition, an executor's duties with regard to probate of an estate were discussed in Chapter 14. Here, these and other duties have been summarized in a checklist of an executor's primary duties. These duties have been generally divided into estate duties, income tax duties, estate tax duties and other duties.

While it is generally useful for an executor to review the checklist after a decedent dies, it is probably also useful to review the checklist while an individual is still alive. The estate or financial planner and the individual can then address some of the issues while the individual is alive and provide some guidance to the executor. In addition, some actions might be made while the individual is alive to facilitate the availability of information or records needed after death. See also Chapter 24 on post-mortem elections.

Blended Family Issues

Ramifications of elections and exercises of duties by interested personal representative. An interested fiduciary is in a position to favor himself, often to the detriment of other beneficiaries, simply by making decisions and elections during the course of estate or trust administration. These decisions can include, without limitation, exerting indirect control over the decedent's interests in closely-held entities, funding bequests at a certain time, in a certain way and with certain assets, making or not making certain tax elections such as the QTIP election and the decision to take certain estate expenses on either the federal estate tax return or the estate fiduciary income tax return, estate tax apportionment, self-dealing, construction of the governing instrument, hiring or firing certain people, etc.

While the courts usually are the final arbiters where there is a dispute, courts generally grant a fiduciary a fair amount of leeway and do not micromanage the fiduciary on every call. In other words, while beneficiaries can (and many do) complain bitterly and often about a fiduciary's actions, courts often are reluctant to either overturn the fiduciary's decision (assuming that it was reasonable) or remove the fiduciary. Conflicts of interest of an interested fiduciary can, but do not always, result in removal of the fiduciary, despite the enthusiastic protestations of some beneficiaries. Court decisions are all over the map on what a fiduciary can do without getting removed. The only answer is that the courts consider each particular case on its merits, so that the jurisprudence, given that there are plenty of cases going both ways, is selectively "cherry-picked" to justify the court's removal decision, one way or the other.

Blended family estates present a host of potential problems where, often contrary to professional advice, the client inserts an interested fiduciary into the mix. For example, if the surviving spouse step-parent is the executor, he or she may make a QTIP election over the objections of the decedent's family, who may prefer that the estate go ahead and pay the estate tax in order to freeze the value of the estate tax liability so that it would not be a much higher number at the surviving spouse's death. What about actions concerning hiring and firing in closely held entities, where an interested fiduciary can do things such as firing the decedent's children and hiring the executor's family and cutting off the income of a surviving spouse step-parent? As noted in the previous sentence, self-dealing issues can be a real source of controversy. Estate tax apportionment issues also can be quite contentious, as can classification of property ownership by an interested fiduciary, e.g., a step-parent who claims an interest (or a larger interest than previously acknowledged) in property that the decedent's family believes belonged to the decedent.

There can be real drastic ramifications of funding bequests or shares by an interested fiduciary. For example, the fiduciary who was not given any guidance in the governing instrument may well allocate controlling interests in the decedent's closely held businesses to the fiduciary while satisfying other legacies with other assets, which often causes shifts in control of the closely-held entities, sometimes to the detriment of current employees of the entity. Whether or not to make equitable adjustments by an interested fiduciary also can cause problems. For example, where a fiduciary is given the power (but not the obligation) to adjust between income and principal, or where to charge expenses or credit income, e.g., principal or income, these decisions generally will not be overturned absent an abuse of discretion, if at all. The same thing is true where the interested fiduciary is given the discretion (but not the obligation) to distribute funds, which the fiduciary does selectively.

Importance of coordinating agent under property power of attorney, trustee and executor. For the reasons discussed above, the interested fiduciary can cause a lot of problems, but even more so in the blended family estate where there often are at least two factions who neither like nor trust each other. Even if the interested fiduciary does everything correctly, the fiduciary can be a lightning rod for controversy, even where there should be none. This is why we are so adamant in our advice to blended family couples to use disinterested third parties as fiduciaries, which is an attempt to deflate the actions that many take due to the stirring of strong emotions such as greed or hatred.

Therefore, it is critical that the client carefully coordinate the roles of agent under a property power of attorney, successor trustee under a living trust and executor. If, for example, there is friction between the appointees while the client is alive, it has been our experience that this friction will do nothing but intensify after the client's death. We have witnessed this friction firsthand and have seen it cripple administration of an estate or trust. On the other hand, there needs to be some accountability by a preceding interested fiduciary such as an agent under a property power of attorney to ensure that the interested fiduciary is not making an accounting to himself. We say that accountability and transparency are the keys to effective administration, particularly for the interested fiduciary.

Equally important is the guidance that the client gives the fiduciary in the governing instrument, which is evidence of the client's intent. In our opinion, the more guidance the better because it gives an overseeing court something to consider when a wayward interested fiduciary is operating on self-interest rather than on what the client expressly intended.

15.13 CHECKLIST OF EXECUTOR'S PRIMARY DUTIES

Estate Duties [Chapter 11]

1. Probate of will.
2. Advertise Grant of Letters.
3. Provide notice to the beneficiaries of the estate, along with immediate members of the decedent's family (to the extent required by the local rules).
4. Open estate checking and savings accounts.
5. Write to banks for date of death value.
6. Value securities.
7. Appraisal of real property and personal property.
8. Obtain three years of U.S. individual income tax returns and three years of cancelled checks.
9. Obtain five years of financial statements on business interests, together with all relevant agreements.
10. Obtain copies of all U.S. gift tax returns filed by decedent.
11. Obtain evidence of all debts of decedent and costs of administering estate.
12. File personal property tax returns – often due February 15 of each year that the estate is in administration (but check applicable state or local law).
13. Determine if the estate is subject to ancillary administration in any other jurisdiction.
14. Determine if administration expenses and losses should be claimed as an income or estate tax deduction.
15. File inventory – check local state law for requirements and due date-often this is three months following issuance of the letters of administration.[48]
16. Apply for tax waivers.
17. File account or prepare informal family settlement agreement.
18. Prepare audit notices and statement of proposed distribution / obtain waiver of accounting.
19. File schedule of distribution if applicable.

Income Tax Duties [Chapter 22]

1. File Form 56 – Notice of Fiduciary Relationship with the Internal Revenue Service.

2. Determine if any of decedent's medical expenses were unpaid at death.

3. Determine if the estate has received after death income taxable under Code Section 691.

4. Consider requesting prompt assessment of decedent's U.S. income taxes.

5. File final U.S. and state individual income tax return (IRS Form 1040) – due April 15 of the year after the year in which death occurs and gift tax returns – due by time estate tax return due [Chapter 18].

6. Apply for U.S. I.D. number if estate will file U.S. income tax returns.

7. File U.S. Fiduciary Income Tax Return (Form 1041) – choice of fiscal year.

Estate Tax Duties [Chapters 18 and 19]

1. Prepayment of state inheritance tax – check state law to determine if permissible and advantages and, if so, the applicable deadlines.

2. Obtain alternate valuation date values for federal estate tax return, if applicable. [Chapter 70].

3. Consider options for paying the estate tax, if any. Consider election of extension of time to pay U.S. estate or generation-skipping transfer tax (IRC Secs. 6161 or 6166) – must be filed on or before due date of U.S. estate tax returns including extensions [Chapters 18 and 19]. In addition, determine if tax returns should be filed in order to document the deceased spouse's unused exclusion amount. This determination relates to the portability of the estate tax exemption, and applies to estates of individuals who die after 2010.

4. Make sure that appropriate required minimum distributions from retirement assets are taken in the year of death if the decedent has not already taken such distributions.

5. Consider election to defer payment of inheritance tax on remainder interests – where permitted, determine deadline for election.

6. Consider election for special valuation of farm or business real estate under Code Section 2032A – must be made with timely filed U.S. estate tax return [Chapter 70].

7. Elect (or do not elect) to qualify certain terminable interest property for marital deduction [Chapter 27].

8. Ascertain if credit for tax on prior transfers under Code Section 2013 is allowable.

9. File state inheritance or estate tax return and federal estate tax return – federal due within nine months of death – extensions may be requested – check local state law for due date and possible extensions.

10. Consider requesting prompt assessment of U.S. estate tax return.[49]

11. Consider requesting prompt review and approval of decedent's income tax returns and release from liability for the decedent's past income taxes.[50]

12. Consider Deceased Spousal Unused Exclusion Amount election.

Other Duties

1. Inventory of safe deposit box.

2. Claim for life insurance benefits – obtain Form 712 from each life insurance company

   a. Consider mode of payment.

3. Claim for pension and profit-sharing benefits.

   a. Consider mode of payment.

   b. Obtain copies of plan, IRS approval and beneficiary designation.

4. Apply for lump sum Social Security benefits and V.A. benefits.

5. Consider redemption under Code Section 303 [Chapter 48].

15.14 POST MORTEM TAX ELECTIONS

After an estate owner dies, a number of tax elections or tax decisions must be made by the estate's personal representative. These may include income tax elections or decisions with regard to the decedent's final return, the decedent's estate or trusts or entities in which the decedent held an interest. [Chapter 18] Estate tax and GST tax elections or decisions must also be considered and made. Issues with regard to employee benefits may need to be addressed. Also, consideration should be given to the full or partial disclaimer of the decedent's property and the tax and economic implications of such an action.

The following checklist reviews a number of post mortem tax elections and tax decisions. While it is generally useful to review the checklist after a decedent dies, it is probably also useful to review the checklist while an individual is still alive. The estate or financial planner and the individual can then address the issues while the individual is alive and provide some guidance as to how the elections fit into the individual's estate plan and how the elections might be made. In addition, some actions might be made while the individual is alive to facilitate the availability of an election after death.

15.15 POST MORTEM TAX ELECTIONS CHECKLIST

Part A: Income Tax Elections

Section 1: Decedent's Final Return(s)

I. Were medical expenses of the decedent paid after death?

  A. Medical expenses incurred before death and paid by the estate during the year beginning the day after the date of death may be accrued and deducted on the decedent's income tax return for the year in which the expense was incurred.[51]

  B. In the alternative, the medical expense can be deducted as a debt of the decedent for federal estate tax purposes under Code section 2053(b).

II. Did the decedent own any U.S. Savings bonds?

  A. If the decedent had not elected to accrue and report as income interest on Series E and EE Savings bonds, the personal representative may elect to do so on the final return.[52]

  B. If this election is not made, the accrued interest is income in respect of a decedent, and a decedent's estate could elect to accrue it on the estate's income tax return.

III. Did the decedent transfer any property before death that may be replaced under the involuntary conversion rules or make an installment sale?

  A. If property of the decedent was involuntarily converted, i.e., it was destroyed by natural disaster, condemned, etc., the estate or successor to the decedent may be able to replace it and avoid any taxation of gain to decedent for income tax purposes under Code section 1033.

  B. If a decedent made an installment sale, the estate can elect out of installment reporting.[53]

IV. Filing a joint return – A joint return may be filed for decedent and surviving spouse for the year of death, unless the spouse remarries before the end of the year.[54]

Section 2: Decedent's Estate and Trusts (Chapter 22)

I. Should the estate elect a fiscal year?

II. Should the executor waive commissions?

  A. If the executor or administrator of the estate intends to waive commissions, this should be done before undertaking any duties.[55]

  B. However, it may still be possible to waive them later if no fee was deducted for any tax purpose or claimed in any probate accounting.[56]

III. Where should administrative expenses and casualty losses be deducted?

  A. These may be claimed either as estate tax deductions under Code sections 2053 or 2054 or income tax deductions under Code section 642.

B. If claimed as income tax deductions, a waiver of the right to claim them as estate tax deductions must be filed.[57]

IV. Should the decedent's revocable trust be treated as part of the estate for income tax purposes?[58]

A. If so, the election must be made both by the executor, if any, of the estate and the trustee of the revocable trust not later than the due date (including extensions) of the estate's income tax return for the first taxable year.

Section 3: Partnerships/LLCs in which Decedent Had Interests (Chapters 49 and 51)

I. Should the partnership elect to adjust the income tax basis of partnership assets?

A. If an appropriate election is made under Code sections 754 and 743(b), the basis of a deceased partner's interest in partnership assets will be adjusted to date of death or estate tax value.

B. Even if the election is not made, if within two years after death, partnership assets are distributed "in kind" to the successor of a deceased partner, the distributee may adjust basis in the same manner as provided in Code section 743(b).

Section 4: Closely Held Corporations in which Decedent Had Interests (Chapters 50-53)

I. Should the estate make or continue an S election? An estate is an eligible S corporation owner (Code Section 1361(b)(1)(B) as long as it is not unduly prolonged.

II. What are considerations in planning distributions from estates to trusts and other beneficiaries?

A. Where the executor has discretion as to funding of trusts with specific trust assets, no funding with S corporation stock should be undertaken until a determination is made as to whether the trust is a qualifying shareholder.

B. Make certain any distributee trust is a qualified trust. A revocable trust that becomes irrevocable on the death of the owner is an eligible S corporation owner for up to two years (Code Section 1361(c)(2)(A)(ii), but after this time, or after distribution to subtrusts, any trust must elect to qualify as either an electing small business trust (ESBT) or qualified subchapter S trust (QSST) or be deemed to be owned by a beneficiary, a beneficiary deemed owner trust (BDOT), in order to qualify as an S corporation shareholder.

III. Is there a buy/sell provision in place for the stock? Make sure that any procedures for a buy-out are strictly followed, otherwise the IRS may have cause to ignore the agreement for estate tax valuation purposes. See e.g., *Thomas Connelly v. United States*, No. 21-3683 (8th Cir. 2023).

Part B: Estate Tax Elections

Section 1: Alternate Valuation Elections

I. Should the estate elect to value assets at the alternate valuation date, which is:

A. Six months after the date of death, or

B. The date the asset is "disposed of" by the estate.[59]

C. However, the election is only available if it reduces the actual size of the gross estate and if the estate tax liability is reduced by the election. Code Section 2032(c).

Section 2: Special Use Valuation Elections (Chapters 18 and 70)

I. Did the decedent own land used in farming or closely held business?

II. Will the family continue the use of the property and materially participate in its operation?

Section 3: Marital Deduction Elections

I. Did the decedent employ a trust that qualifies as a QTIP?

A. QTIP elections (Chapters 18 and 27)

II. Is the surviving spouse a non-citizen? (Chapter 72)

A. Establishing qualified domestic trust (Chapters 72)

PROBATE AND TRUST ADMINISTRATION   CHAPTER 15

III. Should the Executor make an irrevocable election on the estate tax return under Code section 2010(c)(5)? Note that the first-to-die spouse's estate **must** file an estate tax return and make the election – regardless of how small the estate is – in order for the surviving spouse to obtain any of the first decedent-spouse's unused exclusion (Technically the DSUEA, Deceased Spousal Unused Exclusion Amount).

Section 4: Payment and Deferred Payment of Federal Estate Tax (Chapter 18)

I. Did the decedent own an interest in a closely held business?

II. What is its value in relation to the total estate?

III. Is the closely held business interest in a corporation?

    A. CODE Section 303 stock redemptions (Chapter 48)

Part C: Employee Benefits (Chapters 54-60 and the companion book, Tools and Techniques of Employee Benefit and Retirement Planning)

I. Is a spousal rollover available? Recall that while spousal rollovers are usually recommended, there are at least 4 situations in which it may be wise for a surviving spouse to consider delaying a rollover: 1) if the surviving spouse is under 59 ½ and may want to tap into the inherited account without penalty until then; 2) if the surviving spouse is older than the decedent spouse who was under the applicable age at the time of death (for 2023, age 73), where delaying the rollover may actually delay the required beginning date for the survivor; 3) if the surviving spouse may want to consider a qualified disclaimer of a portion of the account in favor of the contingent beneficiaries; 4) if the decedent had low basis employer stock inside a company plan that might benefit from a lump sum distribution of such stock using the net unrealized appreciation (NUA) loophole.

II. Beneficiary Elections:

A. May eligible designated beneficiaries (who are eligible to use a life expectancy payout method) elect to use the 10-year rule and should they consider it (for example, if they are older)? Prop Reg. 1.401(a)(9)-3(c)(5) permits EDBs to elect the 10-year rule if owner dies before their RBD.

B. Effective in 2024, surviving spouses (and potentially conduit trusts for surviving spouses) who inherit should strongly consider making the new election made available in Section 327 of the Secure 2.0 Act, revising Code Section 401(a)(9)(B)(iv), which may offer delayed required beginning dates and lower RMDs.

III. Should designated beneficiary changes be made?

    A. Reconfiguration of the designated beneficiary by disclaimer, cash-out, etc., is allowed if such action is taken by September 30 of the calendar year following the calendar year of the participant's death.[60]

    B. Prop. Reg. §1.401(a)(9)-4(f)(5)(iii) now allows trust modifications to be made post-mortem without adversely affecting see through trust status if done by September 30 of the calendar year following the calendar year of the participant's death as well.

IV. Should lump sum distributions and averaging be considered? Look for large amounts of employer stock inside of a decedent's qualified plan that may be eligible for special net unrealized appreciation (NUA) rule for lump sum distributions, which opportunity disappears if funds are moved into an inherited IRA.

V. If a trust is named as a beneficiary, remember that a copy of the trust (or acceptable substitute certifying the beneficiaries of the trust) MUST be given to the plan trustee/IRA custodian by October 31 of the year after death, otherwise the trust cannot qualify as a see-through trust. See Prop. Reg. §1.401(a)(9)-4(h).

Part D: Disclaimers (Chapter 13)

I. Should any beneficiaries of the estate consider refusing to accept their inheritance?

II. Should the surviving spouse consider whether or not to implement a disclaimer trust?

    A. If the surviving spouse were to disclaim assets into a disclaimer trust; this trust would essentially function like a credit shelter trust.

This means that a portion of the decedent's $12,920,000 (in 2023) estate tax applicable exclusion amount would be applied towards the assets within the disclaimer trust. The survivor's option is to disclaim nothing, and rely on the full $12,920,000 (in 2023) applicable exclusion amount that is "inherited" from the decedent by virtue of the portability of the estate tax applicable exclusion amount. While this approach works on a superficial level, there are problems associated with relying on the portability of the estate tax applicable exclusion amount. First, the growth of the assets is not protected by the amount of the DSUEA, which is frozen unless used or unless the surviving spouse remarries and survives the subsequent spouse, as these assets would be if the assets were held in a credit shelter trust. Second, the assets are not protected from the creditors of the surviving spouse as these assets would be if the assets were held in a trust. Third, the portability of the exemption does not apply to the GST tax. Fourth, the "inherited" estate tax exemption can potentially be lost if the spouse remarries. Finally, the disclaimer plan generally is not recommended in the blended family context because it usually results in the disinheritance of the deceased spouse's children.

Part E: Generation-Skipping Elections (Chapter 21)

I. How should the generation-skipping transfer tax exemption be allocated?

II. Should a reverse QTIP election be made?

III. Is the allocation mandatory or optional?

IV. Must a Form 706 be filed to reflect the allocation?

15.16 CONCLUSION

Being an executor is a serious and time-consuming task. In addition to having to understand incredibly complex state and federal tax laws, the executor must also be accountable to the decedent's family, beneficiaries if they are not members of the decedent's family, creditors, business associates, various branches of government for the myriad of taxes for which the executor is responsible, and finally to the court for the proper performance of the executor's duties. It is for these reasons that the use of a corporate fiduciary should be considered (as sole or co-executor) in many situations.

CHAPTER ENDNOTES

1. Copyright 2013 by Charles K. Plotnick and Stephan R. Leimberg.
2. See, e.g., §3-301 – 311, Uniform Probate Code.
3. See, e.g., §3-501 – 505, Uniform Probate Code.
4. See, e.g., §1-201(35), Uniform Probate Code.
5. See, e.g., §3-701, Uniform Probate Code.
6. See, e.g., §3-203, Uniform Probate Code.
7. See, e.g., §1-201(35), Uniform Probate Code.
8. See, e.g., §§3-614 – 3-618, Uniform Probate Code.
9. See, e.g., §3-717, Uniform Probate Code.
10. See, e.g., §§3-301 and 3-401, Uniform Probate Code.
11. See, e.g., §3-701, Uniform Probate Code.
12. See, e.g., §3-201, Uniform Probate Code.
13. See, e.g., §1-303(a), Uniform Probate Code.
14. See, e.g., §1-305, Uniform Probate Code.
15. See, e.g., §1-305, Uniform Probate Code.
16. See, e.g., §3-709, Uniform Probate Code.
17. See, e.g., §3-712, Uniform Probate Code.
18. See, e.g., §3-703, Uniform Probate Code.
19. See, e.g., §§3-709 and 3-711, Uniform Probate Code.
20. See, e.g., §3-705, Uniform Probate Code.
21. See, e.g., §3-707, Uniform Probate Code.
22. See, e.g., §3-801, Uniform Probate Code.
23. See, e.g., §3-801(a), Uniform Probate Code.
24. See, e.g., §3-801(b), Uniform Probate Code.
25. See, e.g., §3-801a), Uniform Probate Code.
26. See, e.g., §3-807, Uniform Probate Code.
27. See, e.g., §§3-1001 to 3-1003, Uniform Probate Code.
28. See, e.g., §3-1007, Uniform Probate Code.
29. See, e.g., §3-715(6), Uniform Probate Code.
30. See, e.g., §3-715(12) and (24), Uniform Probate Code.
31. See, e.g., §3-709, Uniform Probate Code.
32. See, e.g., §3-703(a), Uniform Probate Code.
33. See, e.g., §3-715(5), Uniform Probate Code.
34. See, e.g., §§3-703(a), 3-709 and 3-715(15), Uniform Probate Code.
35. See, e.g., §§3-715 and 3-712, Uniform Probate Code.
36. See, e.g., the cases that are collected in Kopecki, Elizabeth R., Comment: "Removing Independent Executors: Examining the Standard in Texas After the Addition of 'Material Conflict of Interest' to Section 149C of the Texas Probate Code," 44 St. Mary's Law Journal 281 (2012).
37. In many situations, the executor, after making a good faith effort to sell the tangible personal property that was not bequeathed to someone, may have to donate or otherwise abandon that property. See, e.g., Section 3-715(11), Uniform Probate Code.

38. See, e.g., Code §2002.
39. Technically, with respect to an inheritance tax, the person receiving the property is taxed on his right to receive such assets. An estate tax taxes the right to transfer property.
40. Code §6662(e)(1)(A).
41. Code §6166.
42. Code §441(a)(1).
43. Code §6654(l)(2).
44. See, e.g., §3-902, Uniform Probate Code.
45. See, e.g., §906(a), Uniform Probate Code.
46. See, e.g., §§3-1001 – 3-1003, 3-1005 and 3-1007, Uniform Probate Code.
47. See, e.g., §§3-1001 – 3-1003, Uniform Probate Code.
48. See, e.g., §3-706, Uniform Probate Code.
49. Code §2204.
50. Code §6905.
51. Code §213(a) and (c).
52. Code §454(a); Rev. Rul. 68-145.
53. Code §453; PLR 8545052.
54. Code §6013(a)(2).
55. Rev. Rul. 64-225.
56. Rev. Rul. 66-167.
57. Code §642(g); Treas. Reg Secs. §§1.642(g)-1 and 1.642(g)-2.
58. Code §645.
59. Code §2032.
60. Treas. Reg. §1.401(a)(9)-4.

EXECUTOR'S PRIMARY DUTIES

CHAPTER 16

16.1 INTRODUCTION

An executor's duties have previously been discussed in conjunction with selecting an executor for an estate (see Chapter 14). In addition, an executor's duties with regard to probate of an estate have been discussed in Chapter 15. Here, these and other duties have been summarized in a checklist of an executor's primary duties. The overall executor responsibilities have been generally divided into estate duties, income tax duties, estate tax duties, and other duties.

While it is generally useful for an executor to review the checklist after a decedent dies, it is probably also useful to review the checklist while an individual is still alive. The estate or financial planner and the individual can then address some of the issues while the individual is alive and provide some guidance to the executor. In addition, some actions might be made while the individual is alive to facilitate the availability of information or records needed after death. See also Chapter 24 on post-mortem elections.

16.2 CHECKLIST OF EXECUTOR'S PRIMARY DUTIES

Estate Duties (See Chapters 14 and 15)

1. Probate of will.

2. Advertise Grant of Letters.

3. Provide notice to the beneficiaries of the estate, along with immediate members of the decedent's family (to the extent required by the local rules).

4. Open estate checking and savings accounts.

5. Write to banks for date of death value.

6. Value securities.

7. Appraisal of real property and personal property.

8. Obtain three years of U.S. individual income tax returns and three years of cancelled checks.

9. Obtain five years financials on business interest plus all relevant agreements.

10. Obtain copies of all U.S. gift tax returns filed by decedent. If the family is not sure if returns were filed, or if they have all of the returns, copies of what was actually filed should be obtained by filing Form 4506.

11. Obtain evidence of all debts of decedent and costs of administering estate.

12. File personal property tax returns – due February 15 of each year estate in administration.[1]

13. Determine if the estate subject to ancillary administration.

14. Determine if administration expenses and losses should be claimed as an income or estate tax deduction.

15. File inventory – check local state law for requirements and due date.

16. Apply for tax waivers.

17. File account or prepare informal family agreement.

18. Prepare audit notices and statement of proposed distribution / obtain waiver of accounting.

19. File schedule of distribution if applicable.

Income Tax Duties (See Chapter 22)

1. File Form 56 – Notice of Fiduciary Relationship with the Internal Revenue Service.

2. Determine if any of decedent's medical expenses unpaid at death.

3. Determine if the estate has received after death income taxable under Code section 691.

4. Consider requesting prompt assessment of decedent's U.S. income taxes.

5. File final U.S. and state individual income tax return (IRS Form 1040) – due April 15 of the year after the year in which death occurs and gift tax returns – due by time estate tax return due (see Chapters 18 and 19).

6. Apply for U.S. I.D. number if estate will file U.S. income tax returns.

7. File U.S. Fiduciary Income Tax Return (Form 1041) – choice of fiscal year.

Estate Tax Duties (See Chapter 18)

1. Prepayment of state inheritance tax – check state law to determine if permissible and advantages and, if so, the applicable deadlines. It is also important to determine the filing requirements for each state where the decedent owned real estate.

2. Obtain alternate valuation date values for federal estate tax return, if applicable. (See Chapter 70.)

3. Consider options for paying the estate tax, if any. Consider election of extension of time to pay U.S. estate or generation-skipping transfer tax[2] – must be filed on or before due date of U.S. estate tax returns including extensions (see Chapters 18 and 19). In addition, determine if tax returns should be filed in order to document the deceased spouse's unused exclusion amount. This determination relates to the portability of the estate tax exemption.

4. Make sure that appropriate required minimum distributions from retirement assets are taken in the year of death if the decedent has not already taken such distributions.

5. Consider election to defer payment of inheritance tax on remainder interests – where permitted, determine deadline for election.

6. Consider election for special valuation of farm or business real estate under Code section 2032A – must be made with timely filed U.S. estate tax return (see Chapter 70).

7. Elect (or do not elect) to qualify certain terminable interest property for marital deduction (see Chapter 27).

8. Ascertain if credit for tax on prior transfers is allowable.

9. File state inheritance or estate tax return and federal estate tax return – federal due within nine months of death – extensions may be requested – check local state law for due date and possible extensions.

10. Consider requesting prompt assessment of U.S. estate tax return.

11. Consider requesting prompt review and approval of decedent's income tax returns.

12. Consider Deceased Spousal Unused Exclusion Amount election.

Other Duties

1. Inventory of safe deposit box.

2. Claim for life insurance benefits – obtain Form 712 from each insurance company

   a. Consider mode of payment.

3. Claim for pension and profit-sharing benefits.

a. Consider mode of payment.

b. Obtain copies of plan, IRS approval, and beneficiary designation.

4. Apply for lump sum Social Security benefits and V.A. benefits.

5. Consider stock redemption under Code section 303 (see Chapter 48).

CHAPTER ENDNOTES

1. Check applicable state law.
2. I.R.C. §§6161 and 6166.

TRUSTS IN GENERAL

CHAPTER 17

17.1 TRUST DEFINED

Technically, a trust is a *relationship*, **not** a separate entity such as a corporation (although for tax purposes a trust can and often is treated as separate from its creator). A trust is a relationship between the person who creates the trust (the **settlor or trustor or grantor**), the person who benefits from the trust (the **beneficiary**) and the person who administers the property that is placed into trust (the **trustee**). Trust property actually is legally titled and held in the name of the **trustee**, because a trust involves a separation of *legal* and *equitable* title.

A beneficiary of a trust generally has no underlying right to the *property* in trust because the trustee technically owns it. In fact, a beneficial interest in the trust is what the beneficiary *owns*. This interest can be transferred pursuant to the terms of the trust instrument. As a practical matter, if a trust instrument contains a spendthrift clause, a beneficiary is both protected from creditors and prohibited from transferring his or her beneficial interest in any way. However, if a trust does not otherwise prohibit transfer of a beneficiary's interest, i.e., if the trust instrument does not contain a full-blown spendthrift trust clause, the beneficiary is free to sell, pledge as security for a loan, give away, exchange for other property or even gamble his or her beneficial interest away-without limitation.

There are **several** different ways to classify trusts, and we will use just about every method of classifications in this chapter. We start with the simplest way to classify trusts. The first way to classify trusts - **every** type of trust, irrespective of the name of the trust - is that all trusts are either **revocable** or **irrevocable**. The second way to classify trusts is that **all** trusts - irrespective of their particular names or types - are set up either during **lifetime** and are called inter vivos trusts, or created at **death** and are called testamentary trusts. Finally, trusts can be tax-driven or not tax driven. Examples of tax-driven trusts include the grantor retained annuity trust (GRAT) and the charitable remainder trust, both of which started out as purely creatures of tax law, which state law recognized, within the parameters of the trust classifications described above. Examples of non-tax driven trusts are the revocable living trust and an irrevocable life insurance trust, even though both of these trusts may contain or involve tax *planning*.

We will begin with an anatomy of a typical trust instrument, which could be created under the terms of a will or set up as a free-standing and independent trust instrument. It is important to note that these parts are not discussed in the order that they will be included in every trust, since every trust is different. It also is important to point out that every trust might not have every one of these parts.

17.2 ANATOMY OF A TRUST

Players

One of the first parts of a trust instrument, if not at the very beginning, tells you the identities of the settlor and the trustee. This part also may, but need not, contain the identities of the beneficiaries of the trust, although they will be identified or described in the trust instrument.

Property Placed in Trust

It is not unusual very early on in the trust instrument for the initial seed property of the trust, also known as the principal, corpus or res, to be identified, often via a separate appendix or document annexed to the trust instrument. This section usually will indicate whether the trustee is authorized to accept any additional property into the trust as well as the procedure for holding that additional property, i.e., as a segregated fund, etc. Some tax-driven trusts *prohibit* additional contributions to the trust, e.g., the charitable remainder annuity trust and charitable lead annuity trust (discussed in Chapter 38) and the grantor retained annuity trust (discussed in Chapter 29).

It is customary for this section in an inter vivos irrevocable trust to affirmatively state that the settlor irrevocably parts with all dominion and control over the property contributed to the trust as well as all rights to alter or revoke the trust to both confirm a gift and keep the trust property out of the grantor's estate for federal estate tax purposes. Obviously, a testamentary trust usually will not contain information about the property placed into the trust if the trust is funded by a formula or is the residuum of the estate. However, an inter vivos trust usually will contain this information.

Office of Trustee

This section of the trust contains information about the office of the trustee. It may indicate the name(s) of the initial trustee(s) if this information was not indicated earlier in the trust instrument. This section also often specifically states who may serve as trustee, i.e., trustee qualifications, as well as who may not serve as trustee, e.g., persons who are "related or subordinate" (within the meaning of Code Section 672(c)) to the grantor, the grantor's spouse or any beneficiary of the trust. This section usually will spell out how a trustee may resign and often spells out how successor trustees are selected, although the trust instrument also may spell out the name(s) of successor trustee(s) in an order of appointment. This section also usually provides the method by which a trustee can be removed, the grounds for removal as well as the identity(ies) of the person(s) who have, individually or collectively, the power to remove a trustee and select a new trustee.

This part also often indicates the procedure by which a successor trustee is to assume authority and title to the trust assets in an orderly transfer of power and property from the previously serving trustee. Additionally, this section of the trust document will indicate the extent to which, if any, the successor trustee is liable for the acts of the predecessor trustee and how that successor trustee can minimize that liability, e.g., by giving the beneficiaries an accounting of the prior trustee's service, together with a certain period of time in which to contest the accounting or it is deemed approved by the beneficiary.

This section also usually indicates that the trustee may disclaim or renounce certain powers of the trustee as well as the procedure for so doing and what happens to those powers. It is not unusual for this section to affirmatively state that the successor by merger or purchase of a corporate trustee becomes the trustee without further action, although some trust instruments give the beneficiaries or a trust protector an opportunity to opt out on the merger or acquisition of a corporate trustee and select a different trustee. This section also generally indicates how co-trustees are to serve and act on trust business and how the co-trustees conduct trust business, e.g., by majority vote, and what happens if a trustee dissents from an action that a majority of the co-trustees vote to undertake.

Nature of the Trust

Very early on, the trust should indicate whether it is revocable or irrevocable, and if the former, the trust instrument may spell out who may revoke, the events, if any, that could give rise to revocation as well as the procedure for revocation. It is important to know applicable state law on whether a trust is revocable or irrevocable if the trust instrument is silent on this score. If the trust is testamentary, it usually will say nothing about the nature of the trust since all testamentary trusts are irrevocable. Even if the trust says that it is revocable, you have to investigate whether the holders of the power to revoke remain extant, because a revocable trust generally becomes irrevocable on the death(s) of the settlor(s).

Administration of the Trust

This section can be one separate part of the trust, or it can be separated into several parts. We discuss all of this as if it is contained in one section. If the trust is an inter vivos trust, then this section usually will spell the settlor's rights to income and/or principal, if any, as well as the frequency of payment or distribution as well as the circumstances under which the settlor either can receive or has the right to demand distributions of trust income and/or principal. This section also specifically spells out the beneficiaries' rights to receive distributions of income and/or principal, if any, e.g., the trust may only be a discretionary distribution trust, as well as the frequency of payment or distribution as well as the circumstances under which a beneficiary either can receive or has the right to demand distributions of trust income and/or principal. It is not unusual for this section to identify the initial beneficiaries as well as a method for determining who is entitled to the remaining trust property on termination of the trust and whether those rights are vested.

The trust usually will spell out any special rights, if any, of the trustee to make "sprinkling" or other unequal distributions to the beneficiaries as well as whether or not the trustee must consider other resources that may be available to a beneficiary in determining whether to make a distribution to the beneficiary. It is not unusual for this section to expressly provide that distributions to a beneficiary are not to be considered as advancements on an inheritance, as well as the grantor's intent concerning distributions to beneficiaries. If any beneficiary has a power of appointment of any kind over the trust, it usually is contained here. This section also typically provides what happens to a beneficiary's trust interest at the beneficiary's death.

The trust also may contain a section for how distributions are to be made after the grantor's death, with many, if not all, of the same considerations and provisions that are discussed in the two preceding paragraphs applying. If the trust splits for any reason into separate trusts, this section will stipulate how that is done, as well as each beneficiary's rights in the separate trusts. The same discussion above applies to each of these separate trusts, which may, but need not, be identical. This section almost always contains a "facility of payment" clause, which allows a trustee to make direct payments of a beneficiary's distributions for the beneficiary's benefit to persons other than the beneficiary, e.g., direct payments of rent to a landlord or tuition to a school. This section provides for how and when the trust is to terminate, or indeed, if the trust was established in a state that has repealed the rule against perpetuities, that the trust is essentially perpetual.

If the trustee also is a beneficiary, this section might restrict the trustee beneficiary's powers that would give the trustee a general power of appointment over the trust property, e.g., no distributions to the beneficiary trustee except as limited by an ascertainable standard and no distributions to satisfy an individual obligation of the beneficiary trustee. This section may provide for a right on the trustee's part to amend the trust in order to qualify the trust as a shareholder of an S corporation.

Generation-Skipping Provisions

Many trusts contain all of the GST tax provisions in a separate section. These sections typically allow a trustee to divide a trust into exempt and non-exempt parts (or separate trusts) and to merge trusts as well as some statement about the grantor's intent regarding these separate generation-skipping trusts. These sections usually give a beneficiary a general power of appointment over the trust property if the trust is about to incur GST taxation. Alternatively, the trust may grant a beneficiary a formula general power of appointment that only causes estate inclusion to the extent that the estate tax at the beneficiary powerholder's death would be less than the GST tax. Finally, the section usually gives the trustee express authority to amend the trust in order to comply with the GST tax provisions of law.

Grantor Trust Provisions

If the trust is inter vivos and if the grantor desires to be taxed on the trust's income, there usually is a section that spells out the rights in the grantor or in a third party, including the trustee, which make the trust "defective," i.e., a grantor trust. This section will often spell out the procedure for exercising the grantor's (or those of a third party) rights as well as any limitations on the exercise of those rights. For example, suppose that the grantor has, acting in a nonfiduciary capacity, retained a power to substitute assets of the trust for assets of equivalent value.

The trust might except property such as closely held business interests in which the grantor (or the grantor's family) own a substantial part of the business and indicate that the grantor has no power to affect the beneficial enjoyment of the beneficiaries and that the trustee must protect the beneficiary's interests in any swap to ensure that the trust receives equivalent value.[1] A well drafted intentionally defective grantor trust also should contain a provision that gives someone the power to "toggle off" grantor trust status and usually gives the trustee the discretion, but without a mandate, to reimburse the grantor for income taxes that the grantor paid on trust income. Such a discretionary power, if held by a trustee that is neither the grantor nor someone related or subordinate to the grantor, has been blessed by the IRS as not causing the trust to be included in the grantor's estate in Rev. Rul. 2004-64, provided there is no prearranged understanding and that such a power does not cause access to the trust to the grantor's creditors. A trustee power to pay a grantor's income tax bill or reimburse a grantor's income tax bill resulting from inclusion of trust income into the grantor's income is protected in most states from causing the trust to be considered a self-settled trust for debtor-creditor purposes. But not all. Check your state law on this point. If your state has passed the Uniform Trust Code, any such provision is usually found in UTC §505. The "toggle off" power can be very important, as sometimes the income tax liability for the trust becomes onerous for the grantor and even imperils the grantor's livelihood. It is doubly important if there is no trustee discretion to pay/reimburse the grantor for such liability. It is often a mistake for an irrevocable grantor trust to not provide for a "toggle off" mechanism so that the trust can become a separately recognized taxpayer before the so-called "tax burn" singes the grantor.

Trustee's Duties and Powers

This usually is a laundry list of duties and powers that the trustee holds or owes to the beneficiaries of the trust (the powers and duties may be contained in separate parts too), which usually include, without limitation:

- Investment powers, including whether the trustee must maintain a diversified portfolio as well as whether the Uniform Prudent Investor Act applies to the trust

- Retain trust property

- Acquire or dispose of trust property in any manner, whether by purchase, sale, exchange, merger or other disposal

- Lease trust property, including the authority to enter into leases of property for the trust

- Pay taxes

- Grant options

- Commingle trust property with property of other trusts

- Combining and separating trusts

- Alternate dispute resolution clause

- Adjust between income and principal

- The standard by which the trustee's discretion can be questioned

- Make loans or borrow money on behalf of the trust, including the terms on which loans can be made or borrowing done (e.g., at market interest rate and with security)

- General management authorities, including voting trust interests in entities and exercise all rights attendant to ownership of interests (although it is not unusual to see persons other than the trustee be empowered to vote closely held business interests, such that this power often is limited to voting marketable securities); mortgage or pledge trust property as collateral for a trust loan; to take all actions of an owner of real estate with respect to trust real estate; insure trust property; make non-pro rata distributions to beneficiaries; hire advisors, including, without limitation, attorneys and accountants, on behalf of the trust and terminate small trusts

- Duty to enforce claims and power to engage the trust in litigation

- Duty to keep the beneficiaries informed about the trust, including, without limitation, accountings and the frequency thereof as well as what has to be included in the trustee's report to beneficiaries, etc.

- Duties of loyalty and impartiality

If the trustee is to be compensated, this section usually will describe the method of compensation as well as how the fee is to be apportioned between income and principal beneficiaries. If the trustee is a corporate trustee, there usually will be something pertaining to the trustee's use of its proprietary funds for investment.

Trust Protectors

If the trust provides for a trust protector, there often will be a separate section that provides for the identification of the initial trust protector; how a trust protector can resign, be removed and/or replaced; whether or not the trust protector is to be treated as a fiduciary; the compensation method for the trust protector; who may or may not serve as trust protector, e.g., related or subordinate parties within the meaning of Code section

672(c); the powers of the trust protector; the duties of the trust protector; and a detailed description of the grantor's intent regarding the trust protector's role. We define and discuss trust protectors in greater detail later in this chapter.

Separate Investment and Distribution Committees

If the trust is either a directed trust (which we discuss later in this chapter) or if there are, for example, separate trustees or trust advisors for investments and distributions, the trust will specifically indicate the duties of each separate trustee, advisor or committee; who may and may not serve as a special trustee or advisor or on the committee; how the special trustees or advisors or members of each committee may be appointed, resign or be removed and who has that authority, e.g., the trust protector; and the nature of the duties of special trustee, advisor or committee, e.g., only in a fiduciary role, etc.

General Provisions

Every trust has a section of general provisions, ranging from the governing law to spendthrift trust clause and all points in between. Other significant provisions can include, without limitation, construction of terms, definitions of terms used in the trust instrument, a no contest clause, type of specificity of exercise of a power of appointment that is required to exercise a power of appointment that is contained in the trust, separate trusts clause, severability clause and a survivorship clause.

Conclusion

A trust instrument can be a lengthy and daunting document. The best way to go about reviewing a trust is to take it one part at a time. Make your own checklist of provisions that you want to review in a trust instrument and use it.

17.3 DIRECTED TRUSTS

In a directed trust, the creator of the trust (grantor or settlor), either directly or through the appointment of a trust protector or trust advisor, can direct certain duties to certain people. It involves a slicing and dicing of the component parts of the trustee's traditional duties, usually into the administrative, investment and distribution functions. This is completely different from trustee delegation regarding some function such as investments as provided for under the Uniform Prudent Investor Act and the Uniform Trust Code.

Historically, trustees could not delegate more than ministerial duties, although that standard has been relaxed to permit some delegation.[2] However, a trustee who delegates, for example, investment responsibility, still has a fiduciary duty (and the corresponding liability) as if he or she directly managed the investments themselves. In the directed trust, the trustee usually has no responsibility other than to carry out the direction when made, as well as overall responsibility for seeing that the terms of the trust are honored.[3] This is because a trustee generally must act strictly and solely in accordance with the direction and is not liable for the consequences of following such trust "orders."[4] However, under the Uniform Trust Code, the trustee must act in accordance with an exercise of the direction power unless the attempted exercise is manifestly contrary to the terms of the trust or the trustee knows the attempted exercise would constitute a serious breach of a fiduciary duty that the person holding the power owes to the beneficiaries of the trust.[5]

For example, a settlor could create a directed trust and name one individual responsible for trust administration, another responsible for investment strategy and/or decisions, and yet a third individual to make distributions. The settlor can direct that the trustee maintain a concentrated stock position, even though it may be prudent to diversify a stock portfolio. A settlor also could fund a trust with an interest in a closely held business, and then direct a named individual to continue voting the interest, or otherwise direct a specific succession plan for the business. The settlor also could give family members the power to buy, sell and/or have voting rights with respect to company stock. Obviously, this flexibility is beneficial to both the settlor and the trustee.

The trust instrument could (and probably should) clearly define the roles and responsibilities of each individual, and it must clearly delineate and define the potential liability for each party's actions. A trustee may refuse the direction only under very limited circumstances. This is a matter of applicable state law, and many states limit the liability of a so-called "excluded fiduciary" to situations involving willful misconduct in complying with the directions of the directing party, who could be the trust protector, investment advisor or distribution advisor.[6] It is important to base the directed trust on a strong state statute on the subject of excluded trustee liability in order to protect a trustee who is being directed, i.e., ordered to act in a certain way.

17.4 SELECTING A JURISDICTION

The trust laws of each state differ, sometimes dramatically, and these differences often dictate what jurisdiction in which the trust will be settled. There are a number of rankings of different aspects of the trust laws of the various states.[7] The following factors should be considered when determining the jurisdiction to form and settle a trust:

- State income and capital gains taxes for trusts

- Unlimited trust duration statute

- Existence and extent of self-settled trust/asset protection legislation, and the exceptions to protection, e.g., child support, etc.

- Treatment of third party beneficiary trust issues in asset protection (where possible discretionary trust distributions, limited powers of appointment and remainder interests are not considered property interests)

- Amount of state premium tax, if any

- State of insurance laws

- Existence of decanting, reformation and trust modification statute, as well as whether decanting can be done in non-judicial fashion

- Status of trust privacy statute

- Existence of and extent of trust protector statute

- Status of directed and delegated trust provisions that allow trustees to work with outside investment managers

It is not necessary for a grantor to create a trust only in his or her state of domicile. It often pays to "shop around" for the "right" state in which to create the trust, which depends upon the grantor's objectives and needs and the relative tax burdens and benefits as well as the creditor protection laws of the various states.

17.5 SELECTING A TRUSTEE

A trustee should possess business judgment (even if there is no business), honesty and integrity. The trustee must be able and willing to exercise a high degree of care over trust property and avoid (however tempting) investments or acts that are likely to result in losses.

A trustee must have legal capacity to contract. This precludes the appointment of a minor or incompetent adult. Geographical considerations generally contraindicate an individual who lives a considerable distance from the client or his heirs.

The type and size of assets to be placed into the trust, as well as the client's goals, are important considerations in selecting a trustee. Obviously, if the client's primary asset is a business, the trustee will have much more responsibility and must have higher and broader competence than if the trust's assets consisted mainly of cash.

Investment skill is necessary. Under the "prudent person" rule, a trustee will be liable to the beneficiary for losses unless he exercises the same care and skill that a person of ordinary prudence would exercise in dealing with his own property. But the Uniform Trust Code, now in effect in some form in many states, raises this standard for professional trustees by providing: "If the trustee has greater skill than that of a man of ordinary prudence, he is under a duty to exercise such skill."[8]

Because a trustee must examine and review the trust periodically, administrative and legal skills and knowledge are important. Accountings must be made to the client and eventually to the other beneficiaries. All parties must be advised accurately on the tax and other legal effects. Provisions in the trust must, from time to time, be interpreted. For more on what makes a good trustee, see our lengthy discussion of this subject in Chapter 14.

Family Members and Close Friends as Trustees

There are significant advantages and disadvantages to naming a family member or business associate as trustee. A nonprofessional trustee is indicated where the minimum fee charged by local professional fiduciaries is higher than it's feasible to pay, or where it is unlikely that a professional trustee would accept the trusteeship.

Is it appropriate for a family member, a close friend or a business associate to serve as trustee? The obvious advantage is that such a person may have a working knowledge of the client, the family and the finances and business. But selection of a person as trustee also must consider conflicts of interest and ethical problems. For instance, how will a trustee who also is a beneficiary react when faced with a choice that favors the beneficiary at the expense of other beneficiaries or that favors other beneficiaries at his expense? Will the trustee favor other beneficiaries at his own expense, or will the interested trustee only look out for his or her own interests? Will the fees charged by a family member or business associate as trustee be understood and accepted without resentment, or will it cause conflict? Will the trustee's "hard choices" be injurious to family relationships? Is the trustee likely to show favoritism or be easily persuaded?

Can an untrained individual deal with the legal, tax and investment functions of being a trustee? Even though a trustee is legally entitled to hire agents to serve as investment counselors, accountants and attorneys to assist on special problems, the trustee remains responsible for the ultimate decisions. Would an untrained individual know whom to call? Would the trustee know if the advice he is receiving is both legally and practically correct? Does the trustee understand that he or she is personally liable for unpaid federal estate taxes if a distribution is made to beneficiaries before the estate tax liability is fully paid (even if the trust specifically allows for immediate distributions from the trust on the grantor's death)? If a distribution is made that cannot be recovered, then the trustee will be personally liable to the extent remaining trust assets are insufficient to pay the estate's estate tax liability.

For more on this subject, see Chapter 14.

Corporate Trustees

A corporate fiduciary (with or without individuals as co-trustees) is clearly indicated where it is likely that the trust will span more than one generation. Corporate fiduciaries are also indicated where the amount placed into the trust is large and/or will require skillful and constant attention. If there is likelihood of family conflict, corporate fiduciaries can make decisions on a more objective disinterested basis than family members. In blended families, corporate trustees may cost more, but they usually are worth it, if for no other reason than to keep the animus that could be aimed at an interested trustee by the other side of the family.

State Law

The impact of state law on the selection of a trustee can be huge. A trust will be invalid if it does not meet state law requirements. Planners should be aware of two potential problems: (1) the Doctrine of Merger, and (2) The Passive Trust theory.

In some states, when the same person is both trustee and beneficiary, the trust ceases to exist as a separate entity. Legal title to the property (held by the trustee) merges with the equitable (beneficial) title (held by the beneficiary). The result is that if the sole beneficiary of the trust is also the sole trustee, the beneficiary becomes the absolute owner of the total rights in the trust assets. This is known as a "fee simple" or "fee simple absolute." The trust, as such, ceases to exist. However, in most states, the same person may be both sole trustee and a beneficiary as long as there are other contingent beneficiaries named, so it is important to check applicable state law.

A second potential problem occurs in the case of a so-called "passive trust." This is caused when a trust gives the trustee no meaningful duties to perform and gives the beneficiary unfettered enjoyment and management control of assets. The result is a merger of the legal title and the equitable title; so the trust ceases to exist. Either through operation of law or through judicial action, where the trustee's duties are purely ministerial, and all significant authority and decision making are placed in the hands of the beneficiary, the beneficiary receives total title to the property that was in the trust.

17.6 TRUST PROTECTORS

The "new kid on the block"[9] in trust planning, trust protectors, also sometimes referred to as trust advisors or special trustees, have proliferated in use in the United States in the past ten years or so, correlative with the increased use of dynasty trusts. The problem is that the position of trust protector is not well developed either professionally or in applicable state law, since very few states have statutes on trust protectors, and practices vary widely in their usage by estate planners.

Some estate planners swear by trust protectors and include them in virtually every trust, while others, notably distinguished and prolific estate planner and LISI Commentator, Alexander A. Bove, caution against their use.[10] In our opinion, there is a place for the trust protector in most estate plans, but the position must be carefully designed. If the trust protector is given broad powers, there should probably be a check-and-balance against the power of the office of trust protector, and the settlor should expressly provide whether the trust protector is to be treated as a fiduciary (state law permitting such a choice).

In this day and age of virtually perpetual trusts that are possible in many jurisdictions and the need to build in as much flexibility into the estate plan as possible as well as the need to build in as much accountability for the trustee as possible without necessarily giving the beneficiaries the power to remove a trustee, the trust protector can be a very worthwhile tool to use in all trusts that are expected to last for a significant period of time. The job duties of a trust protector can be as limited or as limitless as the imagination of the estate planner will allow. One attorney's idea of a trust protector might be merely naming a person who can fire and replace a trustee, while another attorney's idea of a trust protector may include the power make drastic changes to the trust, including to the beneficiaries of the trust. As noted above, there is very little statutory guidance on trust protectors in the United States, but that is gradually changing as usage of the trust protector concept increases.

Several states have codified the trust protector concept, including Alaska, Idaho, Missouri, South Dakota, Tennessee and Wyoming.[11] Trust protectors can have the following tasks, without limitation:

- Remove any trustee, without cause, to appoint a different trustee or additional co-trustees, and to appoint successor trustees

- Add or remove beneficiaries

- Amend the terms of the trust instrument to achieve favorable tax status, or to take account of changes in the Internal Revenue Code, state law, or any cases, rulings and/or regulations thereunder

- To exercise any voting rights of closely held business interests

- To amend the provisions of the trust instrument with regard to how the beneficiaries will benefit from the trust, and to amend the trust administrative provisions

- To revoke any and all powers of the grantor and/or grantor's spouse that cause the trust to be a grantor trust for income tax purposes (or conversely to add or add back powers to cause grantor trust status)

- To add (or remove) beneficiary powers to withdraw income (a.k.a. beneficiary deemed owner trust or BDOT provisions) to trigger Code Section 678(a) and shift income tax burden to the beneficiary

- To add, amend or remove general testamentary powers of appointment (a.k.a. optimal basis increase trust clauses) to cause estate inclusion at a beneficiary's death for basis increase purposes

- To appoint and remove distribution committee members and investment committee members, if any

- To appoint successor trust protectors

- To terminate any trust

- To veto or direct trust distributions

- To interpret terms of the trust instrument at the request of the trustee

- To advise the trustee on matters concerning a beneficiary

- To provide direction regarding notification of qualified beneficiaries

- To remove all or any part of the property, or the situs of administration, of this trust or any trust established hereunder, and elect, by instrument in writing filed with the trust records, that thereafter such trust shall be construed, regulated, and governed as to its administration by the laws of such other jurisdiction; and

- To use trust assets to hire legal counsel or other advisors to advise and defend the trust protector in connection with any matter concerning the trust.

There are two schools of thought on the use and role of trust protectors. The first school takes a minimalist view and gives the trust protector usually only the power to remove the trustee. The second school takes a broader view of the trust protector's role and endows the trust protector with overarching powers such as the ones that we laid out earlier. Some trust protector positions take effect immediately upon trust creation, while others "spring" into effect at some point in the future, i.e., on the occurrence of some problem or controversy. If the powers are broad, it is important to build in accountability for the trust protector too.

The trust instrument should expressly require the trustee to provide financing, at the trust's expense, of the trust protector's defense for any claim arising out of the trust except for claims arising out of bad faith, fraud or willful misconduct by the trust protector. The trust instrument also should permit the trust protector to release, renounce, suspend or modify to a lesser extent any or all powers and discretions conferred under this instrument by a written instrument delivered to the trustee.

Trust Protectors as Fiduciaries

The biggest issue in determining the scope of the trust protector role often is in deciding whether the trust protector is to be treated as a fiduciary.[12] This may vary based on the instrument, the powers conferred and state law. While the trend is to want to make the trust protector a non-fiduciary to lessen liability, remember that a non-fiduciary may be completely arbitrary and capricious with no duties owed to the beneficiaries. It may be desirable (if possible under state law) for a trust protector to hold some powers as a non-fiduciary (e.g. the power to eliminate a clause that causes grantor trust status, which would be hard to do as a fiduciary having duties to other beneficiaries), but hold other powers as a fiduciary, to provide some minimal level of oversight. However, the trust instrument should expressly provide relative to that issue, as well as to the extent, if any, of the trust protector's responsibility to monitor the trustee. The trust instrument also should specify how a trust protector can resign or be removed as well as the method and sources of compensation and reimbursement of the trust protector.

If the settlor's goal is to grant someone very broad amendment or termination powers as a non-fiduciary, consider whether to grant the person a broad lifetime limited power of appointment instead of using a complicated and more uncertain trust protector provision. Unlike trust protector provisions, powers of appointment have hundreds of years of common law behind them and their rules and scope are fairly well understood.

17.7 COMMON TYPES OF TRUSTS

This section reviews the highlights of the most common types of trusts that are in use today. Irrevocable life insurance trusts ("ILITs", Chapter 36) and charitable remainder and lead trusts (Chapter 38) are discussed in more detail in other chapters. Grantor retained annuity trusts and grantor retained unitrusts are discussed in Chapter 29, intentionally defective grantor trusts and beneficiary defective grantor trusts are covered in Chapters 30 and 35, and spousal lifetime access trusts are explored in Chapter 32.

Revocable Living Trust

The simplest and easiest trust to establish is the revocable living (or inter vivos) trust. An *inter vivos* (living) trust is a relationship, created during the lifetime of the grantor, in which the trustee holds property for the benefit of the beneficiary.

A living trust can be established for a limited period of time, last until the occurrence or nonoccurrence of a specific event, or it can continue after the death of the grantor. Living trusts generally are revocable unless the trust instrument provides otherwise.[13] However, this is a question of applicable state law.[14]

A revocable living trust (RLT) is one created by the grantor during lifetime, in which during his lifetime, the grantor retains the absolute and unconditional right to alter, amend or totally revoke the RLT, change its terms, and/or regain possession of the property in the RLT.[15]

An RLT becomes irrevocable when the grantor, during his or her lifetime, relinquishes title to property placed in the trust and gives up all right to alter, amend, revoke or terminate the trust, or when the grantor dies. Most of the time, the grantor's death causes the RLT to become irrevocable.

When is an RLT Indicated?

1. Where the grantor wishes someone else to accept management responsibility for all or a portion of the grantor's property and is willing to try out someone else as a manager, a form of "training wheels."

2. Where the grantor wishes to assure continuity of management and income flow of a business or other assets in the event of death or disability.

3. Where the grantor wishes to protect against the investment and asset management problems that would be brought on by his or her own physical or mental incapacity or legal incompetency, or the physical, mental or emotional incapacity or legal incompetency of beneficiaries.

4. Where the grantor desires privacy in the handling and administration of his or her assets during lifetime and at death.

5. Where the grantor wishes to minimize estate administration costs and delays at death by avoiding probate.

6. Where the client would like to see how efficient, competent and costly the RLT (and the trustee) are in operation.

7. Where the client wishes to avoid ancillary administration of assets situated in other states by placing title to those assets in the trustee of an RLT.

8. Where the client would like to reduce the potential for an election against, or a contest of, the will. However, in some states, the statutory estate that can be elected against is expanded to include RLTs.[16]

9. Where the client would like to select the state law under which the provisions of the dispositive document will be governed.

10. Where the client's financial institutions will not recognize a durable power of attorney.

When is an RLT Contra Indicated?

An RLT may not make sense if there is no specific reason to set it up other than to save probate and administration costs. The burden, costs and delays of probate will vary state by state and sometimes even county by county. The immediately payable present value cost of drafting the RLT and maintaining it may exceed the future possible savings. An RLT is not indicated where the client is not likely to follow through with the re-titling of property and the other prerequisites and operating procedures to assure the continued validity of the RLT and to assure it will be legally recognized when the client dies. Probate may be more costly and complicated if there is a partially funded trust that simply pays outright to beneficiaries. Stock in a professional corporation may not be able to be transferred to an RLT because of the prohibition against ownership by anyone other than a professional.

The deduction allowed to estates for the amount of income permanently set aside for charitable purposes is not allowed to trusts.[17] An RLT is not necessary if the client's estate is modest, the mortgage is paid off, there is no reason to keep probate proceedings private, the executor of the estate is a family member who will probably waive executor's fees, the client lives in a state where the attorney fees are modest and everything is intended to pay outright to beneficiaries. Finally, an RLT is not indicated if a less complex and less expensive durable power of attorney can satisfy the need to avoid guardianship. For instance, a broadly drawn durable power of attorney will enable the holder to do many of the same ministerial tasks (such as preparing and filing tax returns) as the trustee of an RLT.

What are the Requirements of an RLT?

In order for an RLT to exist, there must be property (also known as trust principal, res or corpus) contributed to the RLT in order for the trust to begin existence.

There must be the following parties, although in a few jurisdictions it is possible for the same individual to hold all these positions:

(a) a *grantor*, sometimes referred to as a "settlor" or "trustor" – any person who transfers property to and/or dictates the terms of a RLT;[18]

(b) a *trustee* – a party to whom property is transferred by the grantor, who receives legal title to the property placed in the RLT and who generally manages and distributes income according to the terms of a formal written agreement (called a trust instrument) between the grantor and the trustee;[19]

(c) a *beneficiary* – a party for whose benefit the RLT is created and who could receive the direct or indirect benefit of the use of income from and/or principal of the RLT property, whether vested, contingent or future, as follows:[20]

    a. *primary* (or "income") beneficiary– the beneficiary who can receive usually the "fiduciary accounting income" of the RLT or some other front end distributions from the RLT such as an annuity during the term of its existence, generally for life or for a fixed period of years or upon or until the occurrence or nonoccurrence of a particular event, who also can receive distributions of RLT principal pursuant to the terms of the trust instrument;

    b. *principal* (or "remainder")– the ultimate beneficiary of RLT property, who also can be the income beneficiary. The interests of the principal beneficiary can be vested, i.e., fixed, or not vested, i.e., subject to possible future elimination via exercise of, for example, a power of appointment.

The grantor and trustee must be legally competent. The beneficiary need not be.

Funding an RLT

Funding of an RLT can occur at the establishment of the trust or at any later date, although most states require at least a token funding at the creation of the RLT in order for it to come into existence. The holder of a durable power of attorney may be authorized to make transfers of assets or shift the title to property to a previously established RLT. In some cases, courts have allowed such transfers even where not specifically authorized by the terms of the durable power of attorney, although specific authorization is, of course, preferable. This court assistance is most likely where the dispositive terms of the RLT track closely with the terms of the client's will.

Joint Property in an RLT

For most couples, the most effective way may be to create a single RLT that has subtrusts for each of the separate property of the husband, separate property of the wife, and for community property. By having only one trust, as opposed to two trusts, it is much easier to do planning for estate tax minimization. To the extent that either spouse has separate property or an interest in property held in tenancy in common, those would be held in the subtrust for the person's separate property.

In some circumstances, it may be appropriate for each spouse to each have a separate RLT. This is what we recommend for blended family couples. It is possible for the clients to convert property to trust property by merely placing title to it in the trust. However, even though this can result in the property being controlled by the trust, in most states it is also necessary to go to the probate court in order to actually have the title of the property transferred to the trust in a way that will be accepted by title companies. The result, in this circumstance, is that a failure to actually transfer the title during lifetime results in a much more expensive legal process to have the probate court assume the responsibility to transfer the assets. It also leaves room for doubt or possible argument that is not present if there are actual recorded deeds or other indicia of title that clearly show the transfer to the trust.

Naming an RLT as a Qualified Plan Beneficiary

Naming an RLT is a beneficiary of a qualified plan has several benefits. First, naming a RLT as beneficiary of qualified pension, profit sharing plan, IRA or other retirement plan payments helps to unify the administration of the estate and achieve the client's objectives. Second, an RLT serves as a means of deferring the distribution of assets to beneficiaries who may not be ready or able to handle large sums of money. Third, an RLT enables the sprinkling of capital and the spraying of income to those beneficiaries who need or deserve it the most or who are in the lowest tax brackets. Fourth, payment of qualified plan benefits to a trustee makes it possible for the trustee to make certain advantageous tax elections on behalf of the estate.

A RLT can qualify as a "see through trust" looking through to the beneficiaries as to whether the trust will be considered a "designated beneficiary," or "eligible designated beneficiary". The latter category of beneficiaries that receive special treatment was added by the Secure Act effective in most cases for deaths after 12/31/2019 and includes: a surviving spouse, a child of the employee under age 21, someone disabled, someone chronically ill, or someone no more than 10 years younger than the employee.

See through trusts are divided into two categories – conduit trusts and accumulation trusts. See Prop. Reg §1.401(a)(9)-4(f)(1). If the beneficiaries of the trust are "designated beneficiaries" but not "eligible designated beneficiaries, the plan must be paid out by the end of the 10th year anniversary of the employee/owner's death. Only a qualifying trust for "eligible designated beneficiaries" will not be able to defer the payments from the plan over the life expectancy of the beneficiaries of the RLT. There are, however, certain requirements that must be met in order for a trust to qualify as a designated beneficiary or eligible designated beneficiary (principally that no non-individual such as a charity can receive accumulations from the plan). Also, the spouse of the participant cannot elect to be treated as the owner of plan proceeds if a trust is named beneficiary. If the trust does not qualify as a see through trust, the plan proceeds will have to be paid out either (1) over what would be the participant's remaining life expectancy if the participant died after reaching their required beginning date, or (2) no later than the end of the fifth year after the year of the participant's death if the participant died before reaching their required beginning date. Recall that Roth IRAs (and starting in 2024, other Roth accounts), have no required beginning date.

If the settlor establishes a trust for continued administration, protection and control of assets after his or her death, it makes sense to add retirement benefits to this goal by naming the trust as a beneficiary along with other assets. If, however, the goal of the trust was merely to avoid probate and the trust pays outright to beneficiaries anyway, it is cleaner and simpler (and still avoids probate) to simply name primary and contingent beneficiaries directly on the beneficiary designation form and bypass the RLT. Otherwise, there is the additional burden and hassle of retitling and transferring the retirement benefits in kind from the trust to the ultimate beneficiaries.

Effect of RLTs on Creditors

The ability of an RLT to protect assets from the claims of the client's creditors will depend on state law and the provisions of the trust instrument. As a general rule, if the grantor has retained the right to trust assets or the right to alter, amend, revoke or terminate the trust, there will be little, if any, protection from the claims of creditors. In the typical RLT, the client simply retains too many rights over the trust assets to put those assets beyond the reach of creditors. However, RLTs can provide substantial protection for the interests of beneficiaries other than the grantor. Third-party created spendthrift trusts created for others is one of the best forms of asset protection around.

When does an RLT Become Irrevocable?

An RLT becomes irrevocable upon the earlier of the death of the grantor or when the grantor gives up the right to revoke. Generally, a grantor lacks the power to revoke a trust during incompetency. It is possible to specify that as soon as the client is deemed to be incompetent, the trust becomes irrevocable. This would block a person acting under a durable power of attorney from changing the plan of disposition in the RLT unless the durable power of attorney was carefully crafted to provide that the agent has no such power, which should be a part of every durable power of attorney in a blended family where someone from one side is serving as the agent. Note that the irrevocability of a trust generally triggers adverse gift tax implications. A taxable gift is made when a client parts with dominion and control over property. But immediate gift taxation can be blocked. The client could retain a life income in the trust's assets and *possibly* delay taxation on the gift of the remainder interest (the portion going at his death to the ultimate beneficiaries of the trust) by the reservation of a *testamentary* power of appointment over that remainder interest.[21] This might work even if the grantor becomes mentally incompetent since it is assumed that he may regain competency at any time before death.

What Happens when the Client Dies?

Assuming an RLT is funded at the time of a client's death, assets can be paid directly and immediately to the named beneficiaries, and the RLT can be terminated. Alternatively, the RLT can be continued as an irrevocable trust, which is far more common. However, it should be recognized that if there is any potential estate tax due, the trustee is individually responsible for payment of any estate tax if assets have been transferred out of the RLT, and there are not sufficient assets left to pay the estate tax.[22] For this reason, in RLTs where there may be any potential estate tax due, the trustee may require the retention of a certain amount of assets to deal with any potential estate tax or any increase in estate tax on audit, particularly where the estate is comprised of a substantial concentration of interests in hard to value property such as closely-held business interests or real estate.

The trust, which is now irrevocable, can serve as a receptacle to receive assets poured over into it. It can then continue to exist until its purpose or term has been completed. A third possibility is that the assets in the trust can be consolidated with another trust, which often occurs after the death of the surviving spouse.

Assets in the RLT at the grantor's death are subject to federal estate tax that will be based, not on the value of the assets when contributed to the trust, but on the value as of the date of death.[23]

More and more in recent years, planners have been suggesting steps to reduce the value of assets for transfer tax purposes (estate tax and gift tax) of the assets held. In some cases, the family limited partnership, discussed in Chapter 49, is a tool by which the value of the assets can be significantly reduced, if it drafted and operated correctly. Additionally, a number of actuarial and charitable programs can reduce the value of assets for transfer tax purposes. However, the financial, psychological control interests of the client may preclude the use of some of these concepts since, to achieve their gift or estate tax objectives, these techniques must prohibit or limit the client's access to the principal and/or income from the assets.

Examples of RLTs

1. Russ Miller, a successful real estate broker and radio talk show host, feels that if his wife survives him, she will be able to handle the assets in his estate and properly manage them. However, he is afraid that if his spouse predeceases him, his children will be unable to properly manage the assets left to them. His estate is not subject to any estate taxes.

   Russ makes his life insurance proceeds and/or other assets payable to his wife, if she survives him. However, if Russ's wife predeceases him, those assets are payable to an RLT that Russ set up during life. This inter vivos RLT is revocable; Russ can always revoke the RLT and repossess the property or change the terms of the RLT. Often, such a trust is designed as a "contingent," or "step up," or "stand by" trust, since it will take effect only if the contingency that the grantor's wife predeceases him.

   Under different circumstances or to meet different objectives, an irrevocable living trust would be indicated. For example, if Russ were in a high income tax bracket, or would owe estate tax at his death, he might consider transferring assets to an irrevocable trust for the benefit of his wife or children. The trust could accumulate income during Russ's life or distribute that income to, or use it for the benefit of, his children (but not for Russ's own benefit). At Russ's death, the trust could provide income to his wife for life and at her death, provide income and eventually principal for his children. However, the tax rates for income retained by a trust have been substantially compressed so that in 2023 the highest federal rate of 37 percent (which applies to individuals at a level of $ 578,125of income) applies to trusts at only the $14,451 level (in 2023).[24]

2. As another example, Phil and Ilene Spector, living in a community property state, have decided to avoid the costs, delays and publicity attendant to probate and also to avoid the possibility for conservatorship by putting their assets during their lifetime into an RLT. With a medium-sized estate, they decide to use the marital deduction provisions described later in this chapter in order to have each of them be able to take advantage of both the applicable exclusion amount and the GST tax exemption, since portability does not extend to the GST tax exemption.

   The insurance on Phil's wife was arranged so that the RLT is both the owner of the policy and the beneficiary of the proceeds. Phil and Ilene each have a will that has the two major functions of (1) naming a guardian for their children and (2) "pouring over" to the RLT any assets that they neglected to place in the RLT during their lifetimes. At the death of either Phil or Ilene, the RLT becomes irrevocable and the mechanism described later in this chapter to reduce federal and state death taxes comes into play.

   As long as Phil and Ilene are competent, each has the right to be able to remove their share of community property from the RLT. In some community property states, however, both spouses will need to consent to such withdrawals. Unless the RLT provides otherwise, the law in many states is that where a trust has more than one grantor, each grantor retains a right to revoke the RLT, but it requires the consent of both grantors in order to amend the RLT.[25] Most well drafted RLTs for circumstances such as the Spectors have three "pockets" or subtrusts: one for the separate property of the husband; one for the separate property of the wife; and one for community property. In this fashion, the RLT can still maintain the beneficial ownership of the property as the clients may desire.

RLT Tax Implications

For federal income tax purposes, all income of an RLT is taxed directly to the grantor at the grantor's tax rate, since he is considered the owner of the RLT corpus.[26] As long as the grantor also is at least a co-trustee, the trust need not file a separate tax return at all, and all income can be reported on the grantor's Form 1040.[27]

No gift tax is generated by establishing or funding an RLT since the gift is not completed until the RLT becomes irrevocable.[28]

Since the grantor has not irrevocably disposed of any assets, the entire RLT corpus will be included in the grantor's estate for federal estate tax purposes.[29]

RLTs in Community Property States

In dealing with community property, the RLT would have two grantors, the husband and the wife. For an RLT, where the grantors intend to retain the beneficial ownership of the property, care must be taken to ensure that accidental gifts under state gift tax law are not made by giving either spouse ownership rights over the other spouse's half of the property. The unlimited gift tax marital deduction eliminates a federal gift tax problem on interspousal gifts.[30] Thus, if the RLT is revoked, the property should be clearly indicated as being returned to the husband and wife, as co-owners, and not to one spouse or the other.

Is the character of community property altered by a transfer to a RLT that does not have separate subtrusts for separate property of each spouse and for community property? If the transfer is simply by husband and wife to trustee, and each retains a right to revoke the RLT, and the instrument specifically provides that the character of the property remains the same as originally contributed to the RLT and also if it is withdrawn from the RLT, and state law recognizes the ability of the parties to achieve the intended result, the character of the property will remain unchanged. This means that, upon the death of the first spouse, the decedent's one-half and the surviving spouse's one-half interest in the RLT will receive a new basis equal to fair market value at death or the alternate valuation date, and only the decedent's one-half of the property in the RLT will be included in his estate.[31]

There will be no gift at the time that the RLT is created, and there will be no gift upon the death of the first spouse unless, at that time, the RLT becomes irrevocable. This is avoided by language that divides the RLT into two or three trusts upon the death of either of the donors with the formulas described later in this chapter coming into play to optimize the formerly "use it or lose it" type of effective exemption provided by the applicable exclusion amount, although portability can rescue the applicable exclusion amount of the first spouse to die by giving the "deceased spousal unused exclusion amount" to the surviving spouse (but the GST tax exemption is not portable) for use during the surviving spouse's overlife or at death. This type of RLT is used extensively in community property states, particularly, California, to deal both with community property and to deal with separate property assets of the spouses.

Much care must be taken in determining the source and nature of title holding of property before taking the position that it is community property, as one may when the property is transferred to a RLT that indicates that it is held as community property. Taxable gifts under state law may result if the property is the separate property of either spouse or is joint tenancy real property that was originally acquired with the separate property of one spouse. Although the unlimited marital deduction for federal gift tax purposes reduces the gift tax risks,[32] there still may be state gift tax implications if the client lives in Connecticut, which is the only state that has a gift tax at this time. In addition, it could well inspire litigation in the event of a divorce if there was not a clear intent between the parties that a gift take place.

Where insurance has been purchased with community property (and, therefore, belongs one-half to each spouse), care must be taken that the terms of an RLT, becoming irrevocable at the death of the insured, do not result in a taxable gift by the surviving spouse of all or part of the survivor's half interest in the insurance proceeds.[33] Such gifts are usually to the remainder person(s) of the RLT and are not protected by the marital deduction unless the surviving spouse has a QTIPable interest in the trust.

Where the clients have come to the point where the non-insured spouse does not require the financial benefit of the life insurance policy, such policies are often given to irrevocable life insurance trusts as described in Chapter 36, noting with caution that the insured spouse must live three years past the date of that gift in order for the transfer to be excluded from the non-insured spouse's estate.[34] More and more frequently now, spouses are planning for dealing with estate tax by the purchase of survivorship policies that will never be owned by their RLTs, but that would be owned from the beginning by an irrevocable trust to which they make gifts to fund the annual premiums.

Great care must be taken in drafting the provisions regarding the division of property at the death of one community property owning spouse so as to avoid unintended gifts by the surviving spouse. At times, such trusts may be intended to benefit the survivor more if he agrees to have his property also be managed and distributed according to the terms of the trust. Such "election" provisions may also result in gifts by the surviving spouse and, if used, should be drafted carefully by an experienced estate planner.

The marital deduction rules make it important that all inter vivos trusts be examined carefully and revisions considered to take advantage of the very important provisions that make it possible to have completely tax-free interspousal transfers. Chapter 18, on the federal estate tax, as well as later in Chapter 33 on inter vivos QTIP trusts, reviews this in more detail.

Community property and separate property states generally have similar rules as to how long property can be held in trust and as to other trust law matters. However, property rights are different as to separate and community property, and estate plans involving trusts must be reviewed and probably revised when one moves from a separate property state to a community property state and vice versa.

Inter Vivos QTIP trusts

A variation on the testamentary QTIP trust is to create the QTIP trust during lifetime. The inter vivos QTIP trust is a popular technique, particularly for blended family couples, where the grantor can essentially "lend" some of his or her property to the less wealthy spouse to "fill up" that spouse's applicable exclusion amount "bucket" while continuing to hold on to control over the ultimate disposition of those assets, which many find far preferable than outright spousal gifts.

As with the testamentary QTIP trust, there are a number of governing instrument requirements as well as the urgent need to timely file the grantor's gift tax return to make the QTIP election since the deadline for filing that election is statutory and cannot be extended[35] or even filed late with the first filed tax return, which is the case with the testamentary QTIP election. The spouse must be given a lifetime right to the income, even if the couple subsequently divorces. Additionally, no provision for invasions of the trust can be made for anyone other than the beneficiary spouse, or the marital deduction will be lost. Likewise, the marital deduction would be lost if there were any conditions (e.g., remarriage) or power in anyone else that could prevent the surviving spouse from receiving all the trust income for life.[36] Additionally, the surviving spouse should be given a power to require the trustee to make all of the trust assets income producing.

Advantages of Inter Vivos QTIP Trusts

The biggest advantage of the inter vivos QTIP trust is that the wealthier spouse can give the less wealthy spouse enough creditable assets to use up that spouse's applicable exclusion amount if the less wealthy spouse predeceases the wealthier spouse while still controlling the ultimate disposition of those assets at the spouse's death.[37] Moreover, the donor spouse can retain an interest in the trust that is contingent on surviving the less wealthy spouse without gift tax problem or estate tax inclusion in the donor's estate (unless the less wealthy spouse's executor elects to treat that trust as QTIP property on the federal estate tax return).[38] The inter vivos QTIP is far preferable to estate equalization done by outright gifts to the less wealthy spouse, which would then pass to persons of the spouse's choosing and would cause assets to shift out of the donor's family if the couple subsequently divorced. This plan appeals to lots of wealthier spouses who have blended families.

Disadvantages of Inter Vivos QTIP Trusts

The inter vivos QTIP trust still must give the less wealthy spouse lifetime income, even if the couple divorces, which does not appeal to many, so perhaps the inter vivos QTIP trust is effectively limited in use to couples who are in long-term stable relationships. You cannot use a "floating spouse" provision in an inter vivos QTIP trust. Moreover, even though the ex-spouse beneficiary is responsible for the income portion of the trust after divorce,[39] the grantor ex-spouse may still be responsible for tax on capital gains of the trust.

S Corporation Trusts: QSSTs, ESBTs and I.R.C. Sec. 678 Trusts

What is a QSST?

A QSST is an acronym for "qualified sub-chapter S trust." A QSST purely is a creature of tax law and is defined in Code section 1361(d) as a trust that:

1. Owns stock in one or more S corporations (and may hold other types of assets).

2. Can distribute income only to one individual (who must be a United States resident or United States citizen) at a time, so if the trust lasts longer than the lifetime of the current income beneficiary, there can be a successive current income beneficiaries.

3. Has trust terms requiring that (the governing instrument requirements are strictly mandated or the QSST election fails[40]):

    (a) there can be only one current income beneficiary at any given time;

    (b) if corpus is distributed during the term of the trust, it can be distributed only to the individual who is at that time the current income beneficiary;

    (c) if the current income beneficiary dies, the income interest itself will end at that death or upon the earlier termination of the trust; and

    (d) if the trust ends before the income beneficiary dies, all the assets of the trust must be distributed to that income beneficiary.

    (e) the QSST expressly cannot use trust income to discharge the grantor's obligation of support.[41]

4. Requires an election to be made by the income beneficiary (or the income beneficiary's legal representative) to have the QSST qualify as such.[42] Once that election is made, it is irrevocable and can be revoked only if the IRS consents.[43] That election must be made by each income beneficiary as he or she becomes one; however, as to successive income beneficiaries, i.e., beneficiaries who succeed the original current income beneficiary, they are presumed to have acceded to continuation of the QSST election unless they file an affirmative refusal to consent.[44] Separate elections must be made if the stock of more than one S corporation is held in the trust.[45]

If the requirements described above are met, the current income beneficiary of a QSST (which can be set up during the grantor's lifetime or by will) who makes the QSST election is treated as the owner of the stock.[46] The consequence is that all items of income, gains, losses, deductions and credits pass directly from the S corporation to the current income beneficiary, and the current income beneficiary is treated for purposes of Code section 678(a) as the owner of the portion of the trust that holds S corporation stock where the current income beneficiary makes the QSST election.[47]

It is okay if another person is treated as the grantor of all or any portion of the trust that does not hold S corporation stock over which a QSST was made as long as the trust instrument complies with the QSST governing instrument requirements that are discussed above.[48] However, as a general rule, if the S corporation stock is transferred to a grantor trust as to that stock, a QSST election cannot be made, although a protective QSST election can be made.[49] For purposes of determining the number of shareholders of the S corporation, since the current limit on the number of shareholders of an S corporation is one hundred, the electing current income beneficiary of the QSST is treated as the shareholder.[50] Separate and shares of the same trust under Code section 663(b) and the regulations thereunder can each be treated as separate QSSTs as long as the trust instrument complies with the QSST governing instrument requirements that are discussed above.[51]

An inter vivos QTIP trust cannot make a QSST election because the grantor is treated as the owner of the trust under Code section 677, although it can make a protective QSST election.[52] However, a testamentary QTIPable trust can be a QSST if the surviving spouse makes the QSST election.[53]

A QSST can convert into an ESBT as long as the trust and the beneficiary comply with the requirements that are set forth in the Code Section 1361 regulations, which require, inter alia, a special notice to the IRS.[54]

Advantages of a QSST

A client can make a gift of S corporation stock to a minor through the trust without incurring the disadvantages of outright ownership. (Of course, if such a gift is made to a minor, the QSST election must be made by the legal representative of the minor.) This enables an individual to split income among family members while at the same time eliminating the gift from inclusion in his or her gross estate. So both income shifting and wealth transfers are possible through the QSST.

Unlike a custodianship, a QSST can continue beyond age eighteen (or twenty-one) and can last as long as the grantor directed it to last. This means that if the current income beneficiary dies before the trust terminates, the trust can continue for the lives of a number of successive income beneficiaries and does not have to force trust assets into the estate of the deceased income beneficiary like, for example, the GST tax annual exclusion in trust rule under Code section 2642(c).

Disadvantages of a QSST

In general, the QSST is not a very flexible estate planning vehicle. The strict governing instrument and administration requirements must be maintained for the entire life of the QSST election, or it is blown Many clients do not like the "one beneficiary" rule, although, as noted above, separate and independent shares under the same trust instrument can be created. There is no way to "sprinkle" income amongst a group of beneficiaries since there can only be one current beneficiary of the trust portion that holds S corporation stock in a QSST.

Likewise, there is no way to accumulate income at the trust level; the trust instrument must require annual distribution of the trust income that is attributable to the S corporation stock, or the trustee must actually distribute all of the income at least annually, which also is not appealing to clients for many reasons, including "problem" beneficiaries. Additionally, in a trust over which a QSST election was made by the current income beneficiary where the trust will last past the lifetime of that income beneficiary, such that there will be a successive income beneficiary, there is no assurance that the successive income beneficiary will not file an affirmative refusal to consent to the QSST election, so the successive income beneficiary has some leverage when he or she becomes the current income beneficiary.

Likewise, there is a risk if an income beneficiary dies where the principal beneficiaries are different, which often is the case in a blended family situation. In this instance, because the now deceased income beneficiary does not control the ultimate disposition of the trust assets, which pass to others, there is a potential problem with respect to the deceased beneficiary's share of pre-mortem S corporation income. A good example of this is a testamentary QTIP trust or a credit shelter trust for the benefit of the surviving spouse during his or her lifetime. In exchange for consenting to make the QSST election, a shrewd beneficiary, in partial exchange for making the QSST election, should negotiate to have his or her estate receive reimbursement for the income tax on that share of pre-mortem income to be able to pay the income tax on that income. This gives the new income beneficiary some leverage over the trustee that the grantor may not want that beneficiary to have, all because the QSST election is a beneficiary, not a trustee, election.

Section 678 Trusts

The QSST and ESBT not the only alternatives to outright and UGMA or UTMA gifts. An "I.R.C. Section 678 trust"[55] can also be an eligible S corporation stock shareholder.[56] The criterion for favorable tax treatment under this type of trust is that the beneficiary must have unrestricted power "exercisable solely by himself to vest the corpus or the income therefrom in himself." In other words, the beneficiary will be taxed on the income from the S corporation held by the trust if he has the right to take both income and corpus whenever he wants. There must be no restrictions on the beneficiary's right to exercise a withdrawal power, although, and this is far more common, that unrestricted right to withdraw the trust principal can be designed to lapse in a reasonable period, e.g., thirty days, after the beneficiary receives notice of the withdrawal right.

If the beneficiary does not exercise the withdrawal right, and there always is a risk that the beneficiary will exercise that withdrawal right, the beneficiary nevertheless continues to be treated as the owner of the trust under Code section 678.[57] A trust can also be considered a section 678 trust if the beneficiary has not exercised a Crummey power to withdraw and has been given certain powers under Code sections 671 to 677 (e.g., beneficiary is a trustee who has discretionary power to distribute income, either alone or with a nonadverse party or where the beneficiary has a right, exercisable in a nonfiduciary capacity, to substitute trust assets for assets of equivalent value).

A section 678 trust can be created by a parent or grandparent who transfers S corporation stock to it for the benefit of a minor. The minor would be given an unrestricted power to withdraw income or corpus for his own benefit (or a Crummey withdrawal power that lapses, and, if desired, another power under Code sections 671 to 677, e.g., the swap right, etc.).

Advantages of Section 678 Trusts

Perhaps the biggest advantage of a section 678 trust is that the beneficiary is treated as both the shareholder of the S corporation stock as well as the owner of the trust for income tax purposes without the need to comply with the QSST stringent rules or pay the income tax price of the ESBT. This permits income shifting, subject to the "kiddie tax" issues that we discuss elsewhere in this chapter. The section 678 trust could accumulate and sprinkle income, although the person who is treated as the grantor will be responsible for all of the income tax.

Disadvantages of Section 678 Trusts

There are a couple of potential drawbacks of the section 678 trust. First, depending upon applicable state law, the beneficiary's right to withdraw the S corporation stock, even if that right has lapsed, could make the trust available to the beneficiary's creditors as a self-settled trust. The easiest way around this problem is to form the trust in a state that grants asset protection to self-settled trusts.[58] Domestic asset protection trusts are discussed in Chapter 16 in our companion book, *The Tools & Techniques of Trust Planning*.

The second drawback is that the beneficiary may be stuck with paying the income tax on the trust's share of the income without any assurance of receiving any distributions from the S corporation or from the trust. This problem can be handled with a shareholder's agreement that requires distributions to shareholders of at least some measure of the income to pay their respective income taxes and a mandated distribution to the beneficiary out of the trust of an amount that is sufficient to pay the beneficiary's share of the income tax on trust income.

Finally, grantor trust status as to a beneficiary ends at the beneficiary's death, so there has to be an exit strategy pre-drafted into the trust instrument for the post-death (actually, the former grantor trust can still be a valid S corporation shareholder for up to two years after losing grantor trust status at the beneficiary's death) period to convert the trust into an ESBT or a QSST. This is unless a new beneficiary is given a power under Code sections 671-677 that would now make that beneficiary the grantor under Code section 678, in which case grantor trust status simply shifts to another beneficiary. However, this result must be pre-drafted into the trust instrument.

Section 678 trusts also are known as beneficiary defective inheritor's/irrevocable trusts (BDITs), which are discussed in great detail in Chapter 14 of our companion book, *The Tools & Techniques of Trust Planning*.

ESBTs

An electing small business trust (ESBT) is purely a creature of the Internal Revenue Code. Unlike the QSST, the ESBT has no governing instrument requirements, and the election is made by the trustee, not the beneficiary. However, there are some requirements:

1. The trust can have only the following persons as beneficiaries:[59]

    a. Individuals (who are citizens or residents of the U.S.);

    b. Estates; and

    c. Persons that are tax-exempt under I.R.C. Sec. 170(c)(2)-(5).

    d. The trust cannot be a QSST, charitable remainder trust or any tax-exempt trust.[60]

2. No beneficiary can have acquired a trust beneficiary interest by purchase (although the trust can acquire the S corporation by purchase).[61]

3. The trustee must timely make the ESBT election.[62]

An ESBT can convert into a QSST by following the requirements that are set forth in the regulations.[63] A trustee cannot make a protective ESBT election.[64]

Beneficiaries as S Corporation Shareholders

In an ESBT, each "potential current beneficiary" is treated as a shareholder of the S corporation for all purposes, including the 100-shareholder limit.[65] A potential current beneficiary is defined as, with respect to any taxable period "any person who at any time during such period is entitled to, or at the discretion of any person may receive, a distribution from the principal or income of the trust (determined without regard to any power of appointment to the extent such power remains unexercised at the end of such period)."[66] During any period in which the ESBT has no potential current beneficiaries, the ESBT is counted as the shareholder.[67]

If the grantor is treated for income tax purposes under the grantor trust rules as the owner of the trust, that grantor also is considered to be a potential current beneficiary, in addition to the other persons who are potential current beneficiaries of the trust.[68]

A person to whom a distribution may be made during any period pursuant to a power of appointment (as described for transfer tax purposes in Code section 2041) is not a potential current beneficiary unless the power is exercised in favor of that person during that period. The nature of the power of appointment, e.g., a general power of appointment, is irrelevant.[69] A power to add beneficiaries is a presently exercisable power of appointment, such that all possible appointees would be considered to be potential current beneficiaries, but a sprinkle or spray power between current beneficiaries is not treated as a power of appointment.[70]

Advantages of an ESBT

There are several benefits of an ESBT, particularly over a QSST. For starters, an ESBT can have multiple current beneficiaries. Additionally, income can be accumulated and sprinkled in an ESBT. There are no strict governing instrument requirements to worry about. In fact, the ESBT was devised to be a better estate planning vehicle than the QSST, and the ESBT delivers. The ESBT, like the QSST, offers a strategy that lasts past the lifetime of the person who the grantor trust rules treat as the owner of the trust.

Disadvantages of an ESBT

The estate planning flexibility that the ESBT can deliver comes at a high price: the ESBT is taxed at the highest income tax rate (37 percent in 2023), utilizing the trust's compressed brackets, which reach the top 37 percent rate at a mere $14,451 in 2023, and the ESBT receives no distribution deduction for amounts distributed to beneficiaries as other complex trusts do. However, if the beneficiaries of the ESBT already are in the highest income tax bracket, the ESBT's relative cost is substantially reduced. An additional potential drawback of the ESBT is where the number of potential current beneficiaries pushes the number of shareholders close to the 100 shareholder limit for S corporations.

ESBT Income Tax Implications

The taxation of ESBTs is quite different from regular complex trusts. The trust pays tax at the trust level for all S corporation items at the highest applicable income tax rate (37 percent in 2023).[71] Also, the ESBT gets no distribution deduction for amounts of distributable net income that are actually distributed to the beneficiaries.[72]

An ESBT actually can be treated as three separate trusts for income tax purposes: the portion of the trust that is treated as a grantor trust, the portion that is attributable to the S corporation stock and the portion that is attributable to all other trust assets.[73] The grantor trust portion is taxed as a grantor trust.[74] The S corporation portion is treated as an ESBT.[75] The portion of the trust that contains assets other than S corporation stock is treated as a regular complex trust.[76]

Gift Tax Implications of QSSTs, ESBTs and I.R.C. Sec. 678 Trusts

From a gift standpoint, a contribution to any type of trust will be considered a completed gift by the grantor. Such gifts can qualify for the gift tax annual exclusion either by meeting the requirements of Code section 2503(c) or by including a Crummey withdrawal right. As a practical matter, only the current income beneficiary in a QSST can be given a Crummey withdrawal power, although if that withdrawal right converts the trust into a grantor trust as to the beneficiary, it is not a QSST for that period because it is a grantor trust.

Estate Tax Implications of ESBTs, QSSTs and I.R.C. Sec. 678 Trusts

Will the property in a QSST, ESBT or section 678 trust be includable in the estate of a beneficiary? The answer in the case of a QSST or ESBT beneficiary is that, if the beneficiary is given only income rights, assets remaining in the trust at the time of the beneficiary's death will not be includable in his estate.

In the case of a Code section 678 trust, inclusion depends on how the trust became qualified under Code section 678. If the beneficiary is given a general power of appointment (the absolute and unrestricted power of withdrawal) over all or a portion of the trust, the property that is subject to that power at the time of the beneficiary's death will be includable in his estate.[77] Also, if the beneficiary exercised or released the power and retained an interest in the trust (e.g., a life estate) such that had the beneficiary been the owner of the property, the property would have been includable in the powerholder's estate under Code sections 2035 to 2038, the property is includable in the powerholder's estate. The lapse of a Crummey withdrawal power is not treated as a release of the power if the lapse does not exceed $5,000 or 5 percent of the property subject to the power.

The QSST and the section 678 trust offer two ways to shift both business-generated income and wealth to minors at minimal gift tax cost, while the ESBT and the section 678 trust offer greater estate planning flexibility. All in all, the ESBT gives the most in the way of estate planning flexibility, followed by the section trust, with the QSST bringing up the rear. However, the QSST and the section 678 trust allows trust income tax to be paid at the beneficiary's marginal income tax rate, subject to the kiddie tax adjustments.

Therefore, there is no clear "winner" among these three trust forms, and the determination of which trust is "right" in a particular situation will be dependent upon the specific facts of the situation.

17.8 FREQUENTLY ASKED QUESTIONS

Question – What is a "contingent trust?"

Answer – A contingent trust (also known as a step up or standby trust) is one that takes over and manages and invests assets if and when the client is no longer able to do so. A contingent trust is triggered upon the occurrence of one or more specified contingencies such as the client's physical, mental or emotional incapacity. It may also be triggered by the client upon an extended trip. Such a trust works well when coordinated with a durable power of attorney (see Chapter 62) and can help avoid the need for cumbersome and expensive probate or conservatorship proceedings. The client could appoint himself as initial trustee. The trust would provide that the grantor (client) would be succeeded by a corporate fiduciary and/or another person if the grantor becomes incompetent. Typically, but not necessarily, this would be the same trustee designated to serve upon the client's death. In blended family situations, it is very important to carefully coordinate the selection of successor trustee and executor because if there is friction between the occupants of those positions, there is high likelihood of administration problems. It can be real important to build in some accountability for a successor trustee as well as agent under a property power of attorney who takes over prior to the grantor's death because pre-death shenanigans have been known to alter the grantor's estate plan beyond recognition.

Incapacity could be defined in a number of ways – as broadly or as narrowly as the client desires. Quite often, the step up trustee takes over (a) upon the decision of a third party such as a child or friend, or (b) upon the trustee's decision that incapacity has occurred but only after a determination of incompetency by one or more specified doctors, or (c) upon a decision solely by the trustee that the grantor is incompetent, or (d) upon a judicial determination of incompetency, or (e) upon the determination of an independent arbitrator.

Question – What is an "administrative" trust?

Answer – Practitioners generally use this term to refer to the RLT immediately after the death of the grantor where it is to be further divided into separate trusts, such as the marital deduction and bypass trusts discussed in Chapter 27. Since the actual funding of such separate trusts may take months or even years, most practitioners believe the RLT continues to be a separate trust entity for a period commencing with the death of the grantor and ending on the date any separate trusts are finally funded. Unfortunately, many living trust documents fail to indicate what to do with that trust during the interim period, which could have important tax consequences.

Question – If there are no federal income or estate tax savings specifically due to the creation of RLTs, why are such trusts so appealing?

Answer – There is a substantial difference in planning practice between the northeastern part of the United States, where RLTs are less popular, and the West Coast and Florida, where RLTs are fairly popular. In some of the southern states and some of the midwestern states, the RLT is gradually becoming more popular.

There are several major arguments for the use of RLTs, including the avoidance of probate, privacy and avoidance of potential conservatorship savings. In many states, the probate costs and the complexities of probate are relatively low, and the argument for the use of RLTs for avoiding probate is not as strong. However, in some states, the costs of probate can be substantial, with the fees often set by statutory formula, and the process can be complicated. It should be noted that some costs may be reduced or eliminated if a family member is involved and agrees to serve with no fee.

Whether probate is avoided or not, there will be additional costs incurred in terms of dealing with estate tax returns for larger estates and, in some cases, for dealing with income tax matters. However, the probate costs are typically the area of focus.

Another area of concern for those persons who decide to use RLTs is that, if they are unable to function, the assets maintained in their own name (as opposed to those titled originally or re-titled in the name of the trustee of the RLT) will require the appointment of a conservator or guardian by state court and a continuing proceeding and annual charges for the maintenance of the conservatorship or guardianship. By having an RLT, the potential for guardianship or conservatorship is avoided since the trustee would take over the management of the assets if the grantor is incompetent.

The other major reason for the use of the RLT is the optimum use of the various credits and deductions available under the estate tax laws. As the laws become more complicated, formulas have been developed to optimize the available applicable exclusion and marital deduction amounts.

The same RLT that is used to avoid probate and potential conservatorship, as well as to reduce estate taxes, has the separate function of protecting the assets after the death of the spouse for the benefit of the children. Thus, the RLT usually has provisions for the trust continuing on for the children at the death of both spouses.

Another important reason for opting for an RLT is the privacy that many people desire. Whereas probate is a public matter, administration of an RLT can be done in private.

Where there has been good planning, the RLT may take advantage of the rules relating to the generation-skipping transfer tax and provide for one or more generations to have the use, control and benefit of property from parents that will not be subject to estate tax at their deaths. The amount that a married couple can protect in this manner is $12,920,000 in 2023 (i.e., two times the GST tax exemption). This concept is discussed in Chapter 21 relating to generation-skipping transfers.

However, the creation of a RLT is only the beginning. It is necessary to actually *transfer* the title of assets to the trust in order to be able to avoid probate. In complicated estates, there may be more costs in the transfer of assets to the RLT than in drafting it, but that is somewhat unusual. To some extent, establishing and funding an RLT during lifetime is tantamount to "pre-paying" some of the probate costs.

As long as the grantors are the trustees or at least a co-trustee of an RLT, no separate income tax return is required to be filed for the RLT.[78] Furthermore, an RLT is a grantor trust and income is generally taxable to the grantor.[79] Thus, the RLT has little impact upon income tax planning or income taxation of the grantors until one of them dies and the RLT becomes irrevocable.

Although the RLT is recognized as a valuable estate planning tool, in many circumstances there are still many attorneys who, for various reasons, prefer to have their clients' assets go through probate. There are some situations, such as where post-death problems are reasonably foreseeable, which frequently is the case in blended families, or there are some creditor issues, or where there will be an interested fiduciary, where going through probate makes a lot of sense in order to provide some oversight by a third party, i.e., the court, which is its function.

Question – What is a "pour-over trust?"

Answer – As its name implies, a pour-over trust is one into which assets can be "poured" or funneled from the client's will, life insurance, pension or profit sharing plan or other employee benefit plan.[80] This type of RLT is set up by the client during lifetime and serves as a receptacle for any asset that the client would like to pour into it. This unification is particularly useful if the client owns property in more than one state since it may save heirs a great deal of aggravation in having to contend with ancillary probate in addition to the cost savings inherent in avoiding multiple probates, although the out-of-state property will have to be put into the trust prior to the grantor's death if the grantor desires to avoid ancillary probate. Almost all states have laws regarding the validity of pourovers to trusts established during the client's lifetime.

Question – What provisions should an RLT contain if it is designed to provide property management during the grantor's incompetency?

Answer – The RLT should:

1. provide for income distribution to or for the grantor's benefit,

2. authorize that RLT assets could be distributed to others to implement or continue a gift program (within the limits of the gift tax annual exclusion or even larger gifts if the grantor had a pattern of making larger gifts) by a duly-appointed agent,

3. specify that any pledges already made to a qualified charity be satisfied, and

4. state that the management of a business interest be delegated to certain family members.

Relatively recently, a number of states, including California, have adopted the Uniform Prudent Investor Act (UPIA). This act is based upon the idea that all trustees should be required to follow the investment concept known as the "Modern Portfolio Theory." The UPIA also requires substantial diversification and recognizes that inflation is a risk. As a result, it is no longer proper for a trustee (assuming no exculpation or specific direction to the contrary in the trust instrument) acting under the rules imposed by this law to invest solely in fixed income assets such as government bonds. The diversification rules are such that, in addition to diversifying the types of assets, it is also necessary to diversify the investments so as to benefit *both* the current income beneficiary and the possible future beneficiaries (the remainder) in order to satisfy the trustee's duty of impartiality.[81]

Thus, a trustee for a client whose trust becomes irrevocable, or for a surviving spouse, cannot really invest only for the benefit of the current beneficiary but must also invest in the stock market or some other equity investment to provide growth for future generations unless the trust instrument expressly provides otherwise because of the trustee's duties of impartiality and loyalty. Many trustees object strenuously to the rules of UPIA being imposed but, in many states, they have been imposed upon all trusts, both those in existence and those created after the date of the enactment of the law unless the trust instrument otherwise provides.

Many practitioners now are specifically providing in their trusts that the trustee is exempt from the rules of the UPIA so as to give the trustee much more flexibility to benefit the current beneficiary as opposed to having to invest so as to benefit the future beneficiaries. The law may be helpful in some circumstances and, for the first time in some state jurisdictions, may permit the shifting away from the trustee the responsibility for investments, so that an investment manager or financial planner may be engaged to manage the assets and, thus, assume responsibility for them, in the form of so-called directed trusts, which are discussed in this chapter. As people become more aware of the law, substantial new opportunities may be coming for investment managers and financial planners.

Question – Can an RLT safely hold the stock of an S corporation?

Answer – Yes. To be eligible to elect the "pass through" taxation similar to a partnership, a corporation must meet stringent requirements. There are strict limitations on the types of trusts that can hold S corporation stock. The only trusts that qualify as eligible shareholders of S corporations are:

1. Voting trusts

2. A trust receiving stock under a will (but only for the first two years after the stock is transferred to the trust)

3. Section 678 trusts (relating to trusts where a person other than the grantor is treated as the owner)

4. Grantor trusts (which includes revocable living trusts over which the grantor has retained all powers or to whom income is taxable under Code sections 671 to 677, and for two years after the grantor's death)

5. A qualified subchapter S trust (QSST)

6. An electing small business trust (ESBT)

If any other type of trust owns stock in an S corporation, the S election is automatically nullified. The result is that the corporation would be taxed as a regular corporation, and the pass through of income or deductions would be denied. See our discussion of the QSST, the section 678 trust and the ESBT later in this chapter.

Question – Are there disadvantages in putting investment real estate in an RLT?

Answer – Yes. There may be several. The impact on real property taxes and insurance must be considered. Some states have provisions for reassessment of real property for property tax purposes if it is transferred. If highly appreciated property is transferred to an RLT, this could result in a costly reassessment for property tax purposes. Many states, such as California, exempt property transferred to an RLT from reassessment. Also, it should be determined whether or not the transfer will accelerate the payment of any mortgage or deed of trust on the property under so-called "acceleration" provisions in the note or mortgage. Again, many transactions are exempt (see the Garn St. Germain Act). In some states it is also possible to have a "transfer on death deed" (in some states called a "lady-bird deed") that changes ownership to the trust at the death of the owner.

Finally, great care should be taken to determine if the real property is presently generating losses or will be expected to do so after the death of the owner. Under Code section 469, losses from various activities, including some rental real estate activities, are characterized as passive losses, not deductible except under limited circumstances. However, section 469(i) allows deduction for losses of up to $25,000 per year if the owner is actively participating in the management of the property. Section 469(i)(4) permits continued deduction of such losses for two years after the death of the owner by the owner's estate. It is generally assumed the use of the term "estate" could not be extended to cover revocable trusts unless the executor and the trustee of the RLT make the section 645 election to treat the RLT as if it was a part of the estate. The safer course is to allow such property to pass through an estate, which after two years could distribute it to the trust under pour-over provisions discussed above, or be careful to timely make the Section 645 election.

Question – What, if any, are the other downsides of an RLT?

Answer – Recent criticism has focused more on the overuse and misuse of RLTs, than on inherent problems. There has been some valid criticism of books and mass marketing presentations that emphasize the exclusive use of RLTs to avoid probate. This criticism is appropriate mainly because the marketers are providing little more than incredibly expensive one-size-fits-all cookie-cutter "trust mills" that offer little or no advice based on a careful analysis of the *client's* needs and circumstances. Likewise, all too often, the printed forms and/or web page materials that are provided for "do it yourself trusts" are, generally, not useful (and can even be harmful), since planning for clients must be individualized and based upon their particular goals, estates and circumstances. As a general rule, DIY estate planning is inviting trouble.

CHAPTER ENDNOTES

1. See, e.g., Rev. Ruls. 2008-22 and 2011-28.
2. See, e.g., Section 807, Uniform Trust Code; Section 9, Uniform Prudent Investor Act.
3. See, e.g., Section 55-1B-2, South Dakota Codified Laws, for a broad liability protection of the excluded fiduciary.
4. See, e.g., Section 55-1B-5, South Dakota Codified Laws.
5. Section 808(b), Uniform Trust Code.
6. See, e.g., Section 16.3(f), Illinois Compiled Statutes.
7. See, e.g., the annual rankings of domestic asset protection trusts and dynasty trusts at http://www.oshins.com. Other rankings are compiled by various publications.
8. See, e.g., Section 806, Uniform Trust Code.
9. For an in-depth review of trust protectors, see Ruce, Philip J., "The Trustee and the Trust Protector: A Question of Fiduciary Power. Should a Trust Protector Be Held to a Fiduciary Standard," 59 Drake Law Review 67 (2010).

10. See, e.g., Bove, Alexander, Trust Protector: Trust(y) Watchdog or Expensive Exotic Pet, Estate Planning (Aug. 2003); and The Case Against the Trust Protector, 37 ACTEC Journal 77 (Summer 2011).
11. See, e.g., South Dakota Codified Laws Chapter 55-1B.
12. See, e.g., Section 55-1B-1(2), South Dakota Codified Laws.
13. See, e.g., Section 602, Uniform Trust Code.
14. In many other states, trusts are irrevocable unless the trust instrument provides otherwise. See, e.g., Section 11.103.030, Revised Code of Washington.
15. See, e.g., Section 602, Uniform Trust Code.
16. See, e.g., Sections 201-208, Uniform Probate Code.
17. I.R.C. §642(c)(2) and Treas. Reg. §1.642(c)-2(b)(2).
18. See, e.g., Section 103(15), Uniform Trust Code.
19. See, e.g., Section 103(20), Uniform Trust Code.
20. Section 103(3), Uniform Trust Code.
21. However, see ILM 201208026, in the context of a Delaware incomplete nongrantor trust ("DING"), in which the IRS took the position that retention of a testamentary power of appointment was not effective to cause the gift to be incomplete. Moreover, the IRS took the position that the testamentary power of appointment was to be ignored for purposes of I.R.C. Sec. 2702, meaning that the gift was of the entire trust. In light of this ruling, we suggest that additional rights be retained and not just rely on a testamentary power of appointment.
22. I.R.C. §§2002 and 6018(b).
23. I.R.C. §2038.
24. Rev. Proc. 2013-15.
25. See, e.g., Section 602(b)(1), Uniform Trust Code.
26. I.R.C. §§671 and 676.
27. Treas. Reg. §1.671-4.
28. Treas. Reg. §25.2511-2(c); Burnet v. Guggenheim, 288 U.S. 280 (1933).
29. I.R.C. §2038.
30. I.R.C. §2523.
31. I.R.C. §1014(b)(6).
32. I.R.C. §2523.
33. Treas. Reg. §25.2511-1(h)(9) and Rev. Ruls. 81-166 and 94-69.
34. I.R.C. §2035(a).
35. I.R.C. §2523(f)(4)(A).
36. Treas. Reg. §25.2523(f)-1(c)(1)(i).
37. See, e.g., PLR 9731009.
38. See, e.g., I.R.C. §2523(f)(5)(A) and Treas. Reg. §25.2523(f)-1(d).
39. I.R.C. §682.
40. Treas. Reg. §1.1361-1(j)(1)(iii).
41. Treas. Reg. §§1.1361-1(j)(6)(ii)(E)(3) and (j)(2)(ii)(B).
42. I.R.C. §1361(d)(1).
43. I.R.C. §1361(d)(2)(C) and Treas. Reg. §1.1361-1(j)(11). The regulations contain the procedure for applying for revocation of the QSST election with the IRS, which must be in the form of a private letter ruling request, and the IRS expressly will not grant the revocation if the purpose of the revocation is the avoidance of taxes or after the end of a taxable year.
44. I.R.C. §1361(d)(2)(B)(ii) and Treas. Reg. §1.1361-1(j)(9).
45. I.R.C. §1361(d)(2)(B)(i) and Treas. Reg. §1.1361-1(j)(6).
46. I.R.C. §1361(d)(1)(A) and Treas. Reg. §1.1361-1(j)(7).
47. I.R.C. §1361(d)(1)(B) and Treas. Reg. §1.1361-1(j)(7).
48. Treas. Reg. §1.1361-1(j)(2)(vi).
49. Treas. Reg. §1.1361-1(j)(6)(iv).
50. I.R.C. §1361(c)(2)(A)(i) and Treas. Reg. §1.1361-1(j)(7).
51. Treas. Reg. §1.1361-1(j)(3).
52. Treas. Reg. §§1.1361-1(j)(6)(iv) and 1.1361-1(k)(1), Example 10.
53. Treas. Reg. §§1.1361-1(j)(4) and (k)(1), Example 1.
54. Treas. Reg. §1.1361-1(j)(12).
55. These also are called beneficiary defective irrevocable trusts (BDITs). For more on BDITs, see Chapter 14 of our companion book, *The Tools & Techniques of Trust Planning* (1st Ed.).
56. I.R.C. §1361(c)(2)(A)(i).
57. See, e.g., PLRs 9009010, 200011054, 9504024 and 199942037.
58. For one ranking of domestic asset protection states, consider http://oshins.com/images/DAPT_Rankings.pdf.
59. I.R.C. §1361(e)(1)(A)(i).
60. I.R.C. §1361(e)(1)(B).
61. I.R.C. §1361(e)(1)(A)(ii).
62. I.R.C. §1361(e)(1)(A)(iii).
63. Treas. Reg. §1.1361-1(m)(7).
64. Treas. Reg. §1.1361-1(m)(2)(v).
65. Treas. Reg. §1.1361(m)(4).
66. I.R.C. §1361(e)(2).
67. Treas. Reg. §1.1361-1(m)(4)(vii).
68. Treas. Reg. §1.1361-1(m)(4)(ii).
69. Treas. Reg. §1.1361-1(m)(4)(vi)(A).
70. Treas. Reg. §1.1361-1(m)(4)(vi)(A).
71. I.R.C. §641(c)(2)(A).
72. I.R.C. §641(c)(2), flush language.
73. Treas. Reg. §1.641(c)-1(b).
74. Treas. Reg. §1.641(c)-1(c).
75. Treas. Reg. §1.641(c)-1(d).
76. Treas. Reg. §1.641(c)
77. I.R.C. §2041.
78. Treas. Reg. §1.671-4(b)(2)(ii).
79. I.R.C. §676.
80. It should be noted that retirement plans payable to a trust might not permit distributions to be "stretched-out" over the lifetimes of the beneficiaries. See Treas. Reg. §1.401(a)(9)-4.
81. See, e.g., Section 803, Uniform Trust Code.

ESTATE TAX

CHAPTER 18

18.1 INTRODUCTION

The federal estate tax is a tax on the transfer of property when a person dies. It is measured by the value of the property rights that are shifted from the decedent to others; that is, it is a tax on the right to *transfer* property or an interest in property, rather than a tax on the right to *receive* property – the basic characteristic of an inheritance tax.

It is important to recognize that the estate tax is not limited to property actually transferred by the decedent at death. To thwart tax avoidance schemes, the tax is levied on certain lifetime transfers that in essence are tantamount to testamentary dispositions and on transfers over which the decedent retained certain interests or powers.

18.2 GENERAL

Basically, the federal estate tax is computed in five stages:

(1) The *gross estate* is the total value of all property in which the decedent had an interest and that is required to be included in the estate either valued at the date of death, or alternatively, under limited circumstances, for up to six months from the date of death.[1]

(2) The *adjusted gross estate* is determined by subtracting allowable funeral and administration expenses (as well as certain debts, taxes, and losses) from the gross estate. The calculation of the adjusted gross estate is primarily for the purpose of determining whether or not the Code section 303 redemption and/or Code section 6166 installment payout tests can be met. There are decisions to be made with regard to administration expenses which can either be deducted on the estate's income tax return or on the estate tax return, but not on both.

(3) The *taxable estate* is determined by subtracting from the adjusted gross estate any allowable marital deduction, charitable deduction, or state death tax deduction for state death taxes actually paid.

(4) The *federal estate tax payable before credits* (or tentative tax) is determined as follows:

   a. the *tentative tax base* (or contribution base) is calculated by adding to the taxable estate any "adjusted taxable gifts" (essentially, this means the taxable portion of post-1976 gifts that are not already included in the decedent's gross estate);

   b. the tax rate schedule is then applied to that aggregate amount to determine the tentative tax;

   c. the aggregate amount of gift tax which would have been payable with respect to gifts made by the decedent after 1976 if the tax rate schedule[2] as in effect at the decedent's death had been applicable at the time of such gift is then subtracted from the tentative tax to arrive at the estate tax payable before credits.

277

(5) To determine *federal estate tax*, the estate tax payable before credits is reduced, dollar-for-dollar, by subtracting the amount of any allowable:

   (a) unified credit

   (b) credit for pre-1977 gift tax

   (c) credit for tax paid on prior transfers (or previously taxed property credit)

   (d) credit for foreign death taxes.

(6) The portability election, which is made on a timely filed Form 706, allows the executor of the surviving spouse's estate to apply the unused exemption amount of her last deceased spouse in addition to her own. Her remarriage prior to death does not change the fact that her former spouse was her "last deceased spouse" unless her later spouse died before her, in which case, he would be her "last deceased spouse."[3]

The resulting federal estate tax is imposed on the decedent's estate and is usually payable by the decedent's executor on the due date of the return. Each stage mentioned above will now be examined in more detail. The form at Figure 18.1 may be useful in following the flow of dollars from the gross estate to the net federal estate tax payable. References to the applicable line of such form will be made throughout the text. Section references in the headings are to Internal Revenue Code sections.

Figure 18.1

	FEDERAL ESTATE TAX WORKSHEET	
1	Year of Death	
2	Gross Estate (before exclusions)	$_____
3	- Conservation Easement Exclusion	($_____)
4	Gross Estate	$_____
5	- Funeral and Administration Expenses Deduction	$_____
6	- Debts and Taxes Deduction	$_____
7	- Losses Deduction	$_____
8	- Subtotal: 5 to 7	($_____)
9	Adjusted Gross Estate	$_____
10	- Marital Deduction	$_____
11	- Charitable Deduction	$_____
12	- Other Deductions (includes state death taxes)	$_____
13	- Subtotal: 10 to 12	($_____)
14	Taxable Estate	$_____
15	+ Adjusted Taxable Gifts	$_____
16	Computation Base	$_____
17	Tax on Computation Base	$_____
18	- Gift Tax on Adjusted Taxable Gifts	($_____)
19	Tentative Tax	$_____
20	- Unified Credit	$_____
21	- State Death Tax Credit (eliminated by ATRA)	$_____
22	- Pre-1977 Gift Tax Credit	$_____
23	- Previously Taxed Property Credit	$_____
24	- Foreign Death Tax Credit	$_____
25	- Total Credits	($_____)
26	Federal Estate Tax	$_____

18.3 ASCERTAINING THE GROSS ESTATE (LINES 2-4)

The total of the value of the following items (as of the appropriate valuation date) equals the gross estate before exclusions (line 2)) for federal estate tax purposes:

(1) property owned outright;

(2) certain property transferred gratuitously within three years of death and gift taxes paid on all gifts made within three years of death;

(3) certain lifetime transfers where the decedent retained the income or control over the income from the property transferred;

(4) certain gratuitous lifetime transfers where the transferee's possession or enjoyment of the property is conditioned on surviving the decedent;

(5) gratuitous lifetime transfers over which the decedent retained the right to alter, amend, or revoke the gift;

(6) annuities or similar arrangements purchased by the decedent and payable for life to both the annuitant and to a specified survivor (joint and survivor annuities);

(7) certain jointly held property where another party will obtain the decedent's interest at death by survivorship;

(8) general powers of appointment (a power so broad that it is treated as the equivalent of actual ownership of the property subject to the power – see Chapter 12);

(9) life insurance in which the decedent possessed incidents of ownership (economic benefits in the policy) or which was payable to or for the benefit of the decedent's estate;

(10) QTIP in the estate of the surviving spouse.

The gross estate before exclusions is reduced by any qualified conservation easement exclusion (Line 3) to produce the gross estate (line 4).

(1) Property Owned Outright (Code Sec. 2033)

All property owned by an individual at the time of death valued on the applicable valuation date is includable in the computation of the gross estate. Under this section, property is includible in the decedent's gross estate if (a) it was beneficially owned by the decedent at the time of his death and (b) it was transferred at death by the decedent's will or by state intestacy laws. However, because the tax is levied on the transmission of property at death, the measure of that inclusion is the extent to which the property interest passes from the decedent to an heir, legatee, or devisee. All types of property owned by a decedent outright at death, whether real or personal property (both tangible and intangible) are includable. This means that intangible personal property such as stocks, bonds, mortgages, notes, and other amounts payable to the decedent are includable in the gross estate, as well as tangible personal property such as a decedent's jewelry and other personal effects, including such intangibles as rights to digital assets and the value of "rewards" on airlines or hotels.

It may include the value of a right to sue someone. Wrongful death claims are a bit unique, however, since most state wrongful death statutes, while typically filed by a decedent's estate, benefit the beneficiaries directly rather than the estate, and thus are excluded as an asset of the estate. Thus, if a defendant causes a death in a vehicle accident, the decedent's estate may have several causes of action – for damage to the decedent's car, pain and suffering and medical costs of a decedent prior to death, loss of consortium for the decedent's spouse and wrongful death claim. Only the first two categories would be an asset of the estate – the value of the car, medical expenses and any pain and suffering claims. The other (usually larger) claims would be an asset of the spouse and/or other beneficiaries and would not be an asset of the estate.[4]

However, the decedent must possess more than the bare legal title to property before it can be includable in the estate. For example, if under state law the decedent was the trustee of property or was a "straw man" owner and had no beneficial interest in the property, no part of such property would be includable in the estate. So, if the president of a corporation signed as owner of a life insurance policy on his life but all premiums were paid by the corporation, the policy was carried and treated as a corporate asset on its books, and the corporation was named beneficiary, there is an argument that the insurance proceeds should not be includable in his estate directly since the decedent president should be considered a mere nominal owner.[5] Of course, such an arrangement is not recommended. If the corporation is the beneficiary and premium payor, it is far preferable for the corporation to be the named owner of the policy to avoid dispute.

Furthermore, the decedent's gross estate will include the value of his share of certain property held in concert with others. For instance, if an individual holds property as a tenant in common with another person, the decedent's share will be includable as property owned at death. Similarly, the value of the decedent's share of community property will be included in his estate. These fractional interests may be subject to a valuation discount on the tax return.

It is important to note that, except for Qualified Terminable Interest Property (QTIP) includible in the estate of the surviving spouse beneficiary of the trust, there is no inclusion for property in which the decedent's interest was obtained from someone else and was limited to lifetime enjoyment; i.e., an interest that terminated at the decedent's death with no right to transmit at death. So, if Brett gives Eric the right to live in Brett's home in Miami for as long as Eric lives (and nothing more), the value of that home will not be includable in Eric's estate. On the other hand, if Brett had given Eric's wife the house in Miami for her lifetime with the remainder to Eric, and Eric dies before his wife, Eric's gross estate will include the value of his remainder interest, since it does not terminate at his death. An interest will be includable even if it is limited, contingent, or extremely remote provided it does not terminate upon the death of the decedent. (Of course, the contingency or remoteness of the interest will affect its valuation.)

The right to future income earned but not received prior to a decedent's death is a property interest that will be includable in the decedent's estate. Future income rights include bonuses, rents, dividends, interest payments, and the decedent's share of any post-death partnership profits earned but not yet paid at death. The right of a life insurance agent to receive renewal commissions is a prime example of entitlement to future income. The present value of such rights, as of the date of death or the alternate valuation date, whichever is applicable, are generally considered property owned outright and must be included in the decedent's gross estate. For income tax purposes, the receipt of such income following the death of the decedent is considered income in respect of a decedent (IRD) reportable in the gross income of the recipient. Additionally, pursuant to Code section 691, there is a special income tax deduction allowed to the recipient of the IRD to the extent of the federal estate tax attributable to its inclusion in the decedent's estate.

(2) Certain Property Transferred Gratuitously Within Three Years of Death (Code Sec. 2035)

The general rule is that gifts (defined as a transfer of property for less than full and adequate consideration in money or money's worth) made within three years of death are not, with certain exceptions, includable in a decedent's gross estate, regardless of the size of the gift or the manner in which it is made. So, an individual could (but not necessarily should) give away property worth millions, even days before his death, and it would not be included in his estate (although adjusted taxable gifts are added back into the tentative tax base).

There are two major classes of exemptions:

The first class of exceptions is a transfer of certain interests in property that would have been includible in the decedent's gross estate if the decedent had retained such interest at death. Such interests would have been includible in the decedent's gross estate under Code sections 2036, 2037, 2038, and 2042. For example, pursuant to Code section 2042, if at the time of the decedent's death, he or she possessed "incidents of ownership" with respect to a policy on the life of the decedent, the insurance proceeds are nonetheless includible in the decedent's gross estate. However, if, in an effort to remove the insurance proceeds from his or her gross estate, a decedent transfers such a life insurance policy to an irrevocable trust within three years of death, the proceeds would be includible in his or her gross estate.

Note that a bona fide purchase would not trigger Code Section 2035. Thus, if an irrevocable life insurance trust purchased an existing policy from a decedent for full and adequate consideration, this should not trigger inclusion even if done within three years of death. Note that doing this on someone's deathbed may not be advantageous, since the fair market value of the policy may far exceed its cash value but potentially be very close to the death benefit.

The second class of exceptions determine whether the estate qualifies for certain tax benefits. For example, to determine whether a decedent's estate qualifies for a

ESTATE TAX CHAPTER 18

Code section 303 stock redemption, a Code section 6166 installment payout of estate tax, or special use valuation under Code section 2032A, certain property given away within three years of death may be brought back into the gross estate. Even though, for purposes of computing the estate tax, a transfer of this type of property within three years of death would *not* be brought back for these special purposes. However, to qualify for the Code section 6166 estate tax payout, the "more than 35% of adjusted gross estate" requirement is met only if it is met with and without application of the three-year inclusion rule of Code section 2035.

(3) Gratuitous Lifetime Transfers Where the Decedent Retained the Income or Control over the Income (Code Sec. 2036)

If during life, a decedent transferred property as a gift, the value of that property will be includable in the donor's gross estate if the donor retained, for the donor's life (or for a period incapable of being determined without referring to the date of the donor's death or for a period that does not in fact end before the donor's death):

(a) a life estate;

(b) the possession, enjoyment, or right to income from the property; or

(c) the right to specify who will possess or enjoy either the property itself or the income it produces.

Example. Carolyn transfers stock in Texas Electric Company to a trust. She provides that the income from the trust is payable to herself for life and at her death, the trust corpus would pass to her daughter. Pursuant to Code section 2036, the Texas Electric Company stock would be includable in Carolyn's estate, since she has retained a life estate.

The rationale for the Code inclusion of this type of lifetime transfer is that the right to enjoy or control property or designate who will receive the property or its income is characteristic of ownership. Therefore, a decedent who transfers property but retains the right to enjoy or control ownership of such property has not really ceased to be the owner of the property. Since the donor's possession or enjoyment does not end and the donee's possession or enjoyment of the property cannot begin until the decedent's death, the donor is deemed to have died owning the property.

What is difficult about understanding Code section 2036 is that it can encompass implied understandings and agreements as well as obvious legal rights. This is the subject of much litigation discussed elsewhere in this book (see Chapters 49 and 51 on Limited Partnerships and Limited Liability Companies).

(4) Gratuitous Lifetime Transfers Conditioned On Surviving the Decedent (Code Sec. 2037)

If the decedent made a lifetime gift of property contingent on the donee surviving the decedent and the donor retained a significant (more than 5 percent chance) right to regain the property personally, referred to as a "reversionary interest" (either while living or through the right to dispose of it by will or intestacy at death), the value of the property transferred (not the value of the interest retained) will be includible in the decedent's gross estate. This is often called the "But if… back to" section. Why? Because it will not be operative unless the transferring document provides wording to the effect of: *"But if* the donee does not survive the donor, the property comes *back to* the donor." To cause inclusion, the actuarial value of the transferor's reversionary interest must be worth actuarially more than 5 percent of the property's value.

Example. During his lifetime, Stuart transferred property to his wife, Mona, for her lifetime. Upon Mona's death, the property was to return to Stuart if he was living. If he was not living, the property was to go to Stuart's daughter, Ellen. Stuart's daughter can obtain the possession or enjoyment of the property only if she survives Stuart. If not, neither she nor her heirs will receive any interest in the property. Because Stuart retained a reversionary interest, if it is worth more than five percent of the value of the property he transferred to his wife, the value of the remainder interest will be includable in Stuart's gross estate. Such a transfer is includable because it is considered to be, in substance, a substitute for disposing of the property by will.

Unlike the grantor trust provision regarding reversionary interests, this 5 percent test is calculated at the time of death rather than at the time of funding, so the calculation may change from the time of funding until death.[6]

(5) Gratuitous Lifetime Transfers in Which the Decedent Retained the Right to Alter, Amend, or Revoke the Gift (Code Sec. 2038)

If the decedent made a transfer of property during lifetime but retained a power (alone or together with others) to alter, amend, or revoke the gift, the value of property subject to that power (not the entire value of the transfer of property) will be included in the gross estate.

The courts have interpreted this provision very broadly. For example, a donor's mere power to vary the timing of when a beneficiary will receive an interest (even if the donor has no power to redirect the property to another person and the beneficiary cannot forfeit the interest) will trigger inclusion. Furthermore, if the donor has retained any of such forbidden powers, inclusion is required even if the donor only holds those powers as trustee and cannot regain the property or personally benefit from it in any way. The provision is so broad that the mere retention and possession of such power is all that is required even if the donor-decedent lacks the physical or mental capacity to use it. So, a donor trapped in a cave 6,000 miles overseas or otherwise mentally incompetent to exercise the power would nonetheless be required to include the property subject to that power in his or her gross estate.

(6) Annuities or Similar Arrangements Purchased by the Decedent and Payable for Life to Both the Annuitant and Specified Survivor (Code Sec. 2039)

Additionally, with respect to an annuity (or similar contractual payment arrangement) payable as a result of the recipient surviving the decedent that also provided the decedent with a payment (or a right to a payment) for life (or for a period which did not in fact end before death, or for a period which cannot be ascertained without referring to death), the value of that income right payable after death is includable in the decedent's gross estate. This inclusion provision applies not only to commercial joint and survivor annuities, but also to certain other types of payments made under a contract or agreement to the survivor(s) of the decedent. The value of the survivorship interest in a commercial annuity is the amount that the same insurance company would charge for a single annuity on the surviving recipient at the time of the first annuitant's death. The value of a survivorship private annuity is determined using government valuation tables. For example, Steve purchased a private annuity that would pay him $20,000 a year for life and upon his death would pay his wife, Jayne, $10,000 a year for as long as she lives. If Steve died before Jayne, the present value of future annuity payments to Jayne would be includable in Steve's gross estate (but eligible for the marital deduction). Using the government valuation tables, if Jayne were age fifty-five when Steve died and a 1.2 percent section 7520 rate was applicable, the annuity would have a present value at that time of $214,149.

This estate inclusion provision is subject to three qualifications. First, contracts (such as a life annuity) that provide payments to the decedent but end at death are not subject to this provision since there is no transferable interest and nothing is transferred from the decedent to a beneficiary at death.

Second, to the extent the survivor or anyone other than the decedent furnished part of the original purchase price of the annuity, that portion of the survivor's annuity will not be included in the decedent's gross estate. So, if the survivor beneficiary can document that she paid one-third of the initial premium for the annuity, only two-thirds of the value of survivor's income interest would be includible in the decedent's gross estate. If the decedent's employer furnished all or part of the purchase price, that contribution is treated as if it were made entirely by the decedent.

Third, death proceeds of a life insurance policy paid pursuant to a settlement option are considered life insurance proceeds, rather than an annuity, and are not taxed according to annuity rules.

(7) Jointly Held Property Where Another Party Will Obtain the Decedent's Interest at Decedent's Death by Right of Survivorship (Code Sec. 2040)

There are two rules that apply to the inclusion of property in the decedent's gross estate of property held jointly with the decedent with a right of survivorship.

The first, the "50-50 rule" provides that only 50 percent of certain property titled and held jointly by the decedent and a spouse who is a U.S. citizen, with rights of survivorship, or as tenants by the entirety, will be includable in the decedent's gross estate–regardless of the size of the decedent's contribution, even if the survivor's contribution of more than 50 percent can be proven (with an exception for jointly held real estate purchased prior to 1977).[7] Similarly, even if the decedent made 100 percent of the contribution, only 50 percent will be included in the decedent's gross estate.

Example. If Stan and his citizen wife, Shelley, purchase 100 shares of AT&T for $50,000 and hold the property as joint tenants with rights of survivorship, even if the entire contribution was made by Stan from his salary or entirely by Shelley, only 50 percent will be included in his gross estate. Thus, in either case, if at the time of Stan's death, if the stock is worth $120,000, only $60,000 will be included in his gross estate.

The new basis of the shares would be $120,000 if the property were community property even if only 50 percent is in Stan's estate. However, the basis would only be $85,000 if the stock is not community property: $25,000 carryover basis for 50 percent, and a step up to $60,000 basis for the other half included in Stan's estate. If Shelley disclaims the property, even if she receives it under Stan's will and/or trust, the amount included in Stan's estate would be $120,000 and thus the stock would have a new $120,000 basis even in a non-community property state.[8]

This 50-50 rule applies to both real and personal property, regardless of how it was acquired or when it was purchased. The rule is limited, however, to property held in a joint tenancy between spouses (and only between spouses) or a tenancy by the entirety (and if the joint interest was created after 1976).

The "percentage-of-contribution rule" (also known as the "consideration-furnished rule") is the second rule that applies to jointly held property with a right of survivorship with somebody other than the decedent's U.S. spouse. Essentially, the percentage of the value of the jointly held property with right of survivorship rights included in the decedent's gross estate is determined by multiplying the decedent's proportionate share of the purchase price of the property by the date of death value of the entire property. This rule applies to property held by non-spouses or if the surviving spouse is not a U.S. citizen.

Stated differently, there is a presumption that the entire value of jointly held property with right of survivorship is includible in the decedent's gross estate, except to the extent the survivor can prove that he or she contributed to the acquisition of the property (from funds other than those received as a gift from the decedent). So, if the survivor can prove that he or she contributed one-third of the original purchase price, only two-thirds of the value of the jointly held property will be includible in the decedent's estate. Similarly, if the survivor can prove that he or she contributed two-thirds of the original purchase price, only one-third would be includible in the decedent's gross estate. With fewer estates worried about estate tax, and more estates looking for rationale to increase inclusion to increase "step up" in basis, this presumption now works in most taxpayers' favor.

Example. Stan and his son Bill purchased 200 shares of stock for $100,000. Bill contributes $60,000 and Stan contributes $40,000 of his own funds, none of which were gifted to Stan by Bill. At Bill's death survived by Stan, 60 percent of the value of the stock at that time is includible in Bill's estate. If the stock has an estate tax value of $120,000, $72,000 (60 percent of $120,000) would be includible. On the other hand, if Stan's $40,000 original contribution was a gift from Bill, then 100 percent of the value ($120,000) would be includible in Bill's gross estate.

(8) General Powers of Appointment (Code Sec. 2041)

When a power of appointment (the right to say who is to receive property held in trust) is so extensive that it is essentially the equivalent of actual ownership of the affected property, the property subject to the power will be includible in the gross estate of the person who holds the power. Such property will be includable in a decedent's gross estate regardless of whether or not it is actually exercised and whether it could be exercised at death (i.e., by will or only during lifetime). Referred to as a general power of appointment, the power must allow the holder to appoint the property to the holder, the holder's estate, or the creditors of the holder or his or her estate. Essentially, the power to acquire property either directly by the holder or his or her estate or for the holder's benefit (i.e., to pay his or her creditors or the creditors of his or her estate is treated by the Code as being equivalent to ownership).

Inclusion of property over which a decedent held a general power of appointment in his or her gross estate will be required even if the power is "released" (formally given up) or, in some cases, if the power is allowed to "lapse" (is never exercised).

Likewise, the lifetime exercise or release of a general power of appointment is treated as if the decedent made a lifetime gift of the property subject to the power to the person who actually receives the property.

Example 1. Asher has a general power of appointment with respect to land held in a trust created by Ashley. Pursuant to the terms of the power, Asher could at any time prior to his death direct the trustee to distribute the property to him. Even if Asher dies without ever exercising the general power of appointment, the land would be includible in his gross estate.

Example 2. Assuming the same facts as the previous example, pursuant to the terms of the power, Asher could at any time prior to his death direct the trustee to distribute the property to him. In the event, Asher releases his general power of appointment (declares his intention never to use it), the property is to be transferred to John. By releasing his general power of appointment, Asher is treated as if he made a gift of the property to John (subject to potential gift tax).

(9) Life Insurance in Which the Decedent Possessed Incidents of Ownership or Which Was Payable to or for the Benefit of the Decedent's Estate (Code Sec. 2042)

If a decedent dies possessing any incidents of ownership in a life insurance policy on his life, regardless of the identity of the beneficiary, the proceeds will be includable in the decedent's gross estate. The term "incidents of ownership" refers to the right to benefit from the policy (or to decide who is to enjoy the benefit) in an economic sense. For example, if an insured had the right to name a policy beneficiary, surrender a policy, or borrow its cash value, the insured would be enjoying the economic benefits of a policy.

Almost any meaningful ownership attribute in the policy held by the decedent will cause the entire proceeds to be includable in the gross estate. This is true regardless of how the decedent obtained the ownership rights or whether the use of such powers could directly or indirectly benefit the decedent. Mere possession of any incident of ownership at death (not the capacity to utilize the power) is sufficient to cause inclusion.

A decedent's gross estate will also include insurance proceeds payable to his executor or for the benefit of the decedent's estate, regardless of whether the decedent had retained any incidents of ownership in the policy at death. Therefore, naming the insured's estate or executor either the direct or indirect beneficiary (such as naming a trustee as beneficiary and requiring the use of trust assets to satisfy estate obligations) will cause inclusion of the proceeds—even if the insured possessed none of the incidents of ownership in the policy. Naming the insured's estate as the beneficiary exposes the proceeds to the claims of creditors, whereas naming the decedent's revocable living trust as a beneficiary may provide more protection against creditors.

Corporate owned life insurance is includable in a decedent's estate if the decedent owned more than 50 percent of the corporation's stock at his death, but only to the extent it is payable to a party other than the corporation or its creditors.

Example. Blair Rothstein owned 60 percent of the BR Corporation. The corporation owned a $1,000,000 policy on Blair's life. If the $1,000,000 proceeds were payable to the corporation, it would increase the value per share of the stock included in Blair's estate (although not necessarily dollar-for-dollar). Since Blair owns only 60 percent of the BR corporation, the additional value of his stock included in his gross estate would be no more than $600,000. But if the $1,000,000 were payable to Blair's brother, the entire $1,000,000 would be includable in Blair's gross estate.

Also, the IRS would probably claim that the distribution of the policy proceeds to Blair's brother constituted either a dividend or deferred compensation to Blair potentially treated as income in respect of a decedent subject to income tax.

For more on life insurance, see our companion book, *The Tools & Techniques of Life Insurance Planning*.

(10) Assets Funding a Qualified Terminable Interest Property (QTIP) Trust Must Be Included in the Surviving Spouse's Estate (Code Sec. 2044)

If a marital deduction (either gift or estate tax) was allowed for the transfer of property in which a surviving spouse decedent had a qualifying income interest for life, such property must be included in the surviving spouse's gross estate. So if an election to have qualified terminable interest property qualify for the estate tax marital deduction (or the gift tax marital deduction) is made, the value of that property at the surviving spouse's death will be included in the estate of the surviving spouse – unless that spouse made a lifetime transfer of his or her "qualifying income interest for life" (essentially a gift subject to gift tax).

For instance, if Sam's estate was allowed a $1,000,000 deduction for property left to his wife, Sadie, at Sadie's death the value of such property at the time of her death will be included in her gross estate. On the other hand, if during her lifetime, Sadie transferred all or part of her qualifying income interest to another, such transfer would be a gift potentially subject to gift tax.

For more on QTIPs, see Chapters 27 and 33.

18.4 QUALIFIED CONSERVATION EASEMENT EXCLUSION (LINE 3)

Code section 2031(c) provides an estate tax exclusion for qualified conservation easements. The exclusion is the lesser of:

1. the applicable percentage of the value of land subject to the qualified conservation easement, reduced by the amount of any estate tax charitable deduction for the easement allowed under Code section 2055(f); or

2. the exclusion limitation.

The applicable percentage is equal to 40 percent reduced (but not below zero) by 2 percentage points for every percentage point (or fraction thereof) by which the value of the conservation easement is less than 30 percent of the value of the land (determined without regard to the easement and reduced by any development right). The exclusion limitation is capped at $500,000 which is in addition to the value of the conservation easement removed from the decedent's taxable estate.

The land subject to the conservation easement must generally (1) on the date of the decedent's death be located within the U.S. or its possessions; and (2) be owned by decedent or members of decedent's family at all times during the three year period ending at decedent's death. The 2012 American Taxpayer Relief Act removed the geographical limits on the use of the exclusions by estates containing land with conservation easements.

Surprisingly, this deduction can be obtained for a grant made after death, which enables some post-mortem tax planning opportunities.[9] This exclusion is discussed in detail in Chapter 39.

Valuation and the Alternate Valuation Date

Generally, federal estate taxes are based on the fair market value of the transferred property as of the date of the decedent's death or an "alternate valuation date," that is no more than six months after the date of the decedent's death.[10] This optional valuation date is designed to alleviate hardship of an excessive estate tax computed on the date of death value of the decedent's assets that suddenly and sharply decline in value in a relatively short time. Although the executor may use either date, the valuation cannot be piecemeal as all assets must be valued on the chosen date. The election to use the alternate valuation date must be made on a timely filed estate tax return. Generally, this means within nine months of the decedent's death subject to a filing extension.

There are, however, important exceptions to the alternate valuation date rules. First, if an alternate valuation date is elected and property is distributed, sold, exchanged or otherwise disposed of within six months after the decedent's death, the asset disposed of will be valued as of the disposition date.

Finally, there is an exception with respect to a valuation change caused by the mere passing of time.[11] For example, the present value of an annuity goes down each time a payment is made. For purposes of valuation, even if the alternate valuation date is elected, such property is valued at the date of death. The only alternate valuation date adjustments allowed must be attributable to factors other than the mere lapse of time.

The alternate valuation election is available only if the valuation as compared to a date of death valuation results in a reduction of the federal gross estate and in federal estate tax liability. This provision prevents an executor from electing the alternate valuation date as a "no cost" step-up in basis of assets included in the gross estate.

However, under certain circumstances, as the result of an alternate valuation election, there is a way to obtain an overall increase in the basis of some assets. This would occur if the value of some assets increased and some assets decreased resulting in an overall reduction of the taxable estate and federal estate tax liability. For instance, one may not care if the value of the assets in an IRA decrease by the alternate valuation date, since there would be no basis advantage to a higher fair market value.

Example. For simplicity, assume Asher's gross estate of $14,000,000 (valued at the date of death and in excess of the exemption as of 2023) is comprised of two assets. There is stock Asher had acquired for $5,000,000 with a date-of-death value of $10,000,000 and a rare painting Asher had acquired for $6,000,000 with a date-of-death value of $4,000,000. Asher's beneficiaries plan to sell the stock and keep the painting. If they do so, the basis of the stock would step up to $10,000,000, whereas, the basis of the painting would step down to $4,000,000. Six months after Asher's death, the value of Asher's stock increases to $12,000,000 while the value of the painting falls to $1,500,000. Because the value of Asher's gross estate decreased from $14,000,000 to $13,500,000 ($12,000,000 stock and $1,500,000 painting) as well as a corresponding decrease in federal estate tax liability. Asher's executor may elect the alternate valuation date. As a result, the basis of the stock will be $12,000,000 rather than $10,000,000 and the basis of the painting will be $1,500,000 rather than $4,000,000.

Although by electing the alternate valuation date, the basis of the painting would be significantly lower that the date of death basis, the basis of the stock would be significantly greater. Since Asher's beneficiaries plan to sell the stock and keep the painting, $2,000,000 of otherwise capital gain on the sale of the stock would be eliminated. Similarly, if the assets declining in value had been held in a qualified plan/IRA, the estate tax would be reduced without causing any detrimental income tax effect through decreased basis.

Valuation is discussed in detail in Chapter 70.

18.5 DETERMINING THE ADJUSTED GROSS ESTATE (LINE 9)

Once the gross estate is calculated, certain deductions are allowed in arriving at the adjusted gross estate. Allowable deductions fall into three categories:

(1) funeral and administrative expenses;

(2) debts (including certain taxes); and

(3) casualty and theft losses.

Funeral expenses, limited to a "reasonable amount" (meaning not excessively lavish), are deductible (line 5). Such expenses include internment, burial lot or vault, grave marker, perpetual care of the gravesite, and transportation of the person bringing the body to the place of burial.

Deductible administrative expenses include costs of administering property includible in the decedent's gross estate. Examples of such expenses are those incurred in the collection and preservation of probate assets, in the payment of estate debts, and in conjunction with the distribution of probate assets to estate beneficiaries. They also include court costs, accounting fees, appraisers' fees, brokerage costs, executors' commissions, and attorneys' fees. Administrative expenses vary widely from location to location, and it depends on the size of the estate as well as the complexity of the administration problems involved. Administrative expense deductions cannot exceed the amount allowed by the laws of the jurisdiction under which the estate is being administered.

Certain administration costs may be deducted as an estate tax deduction on the federal estate tax return (Form 706) or as an income tax deduction on the estate's income tax return (Form 1041). The executor may elect to take either deduction (but not both). Generally, the executor will elect to deduct attorneys' fees and executors' commissions on the return in which the tax rates are higher. Although this will result in an overall tax saving, an income tax deduction as opposed to an estate tax deduction, or vice versa, may result in favoring one beneficiary or group of beneficiaries over another. For example, if there is a "zero tax" marital deduction formula in the decedent's will, and these expenses are taken on the estate tax return, it will reduce the marital amount ultimately includible in the surviving spouse's gross estate. As a result, the income tax payable by the estate or beneficiary would be likely be higher than it would have been with the deduction.

Bona fide debts, including mortgages and other liens, that were (a) personal obligations of the decedent at the time of death (together with any interest accrued to the date of death), and (b) founded on adequate and full consideration in money or money's worth are deductible (line 6). Mortgages are deductible if the decedent was personally liable and the full value of the property was includable in the estate. But if the decedent had no personal liability for the payment of the underlying debt and the creditor's only collection option is the encumbered property ("non-recourse" debt), in lieu of a deduction, the mortgage would reduce the value of the property included in the gross estate.

If real property is held in tenancy by the entirety, the decedent's 50 percent share will pass to the surviving spouse and be includible in the estate, but offset as a deduction on Schedule M, where the marital deduction is reported. The amount of any outstanding mortgage is also reflected as a debt of the decedent, and is therefore taken as an estate tax deduction. Therefore, it is important to subtract the value of the outstanding mortgage from the value of the property passing to the spouse on Schedule M. If this amount is not subtracted, the mortgage will have been deducted twice: once as a "debt" and once as "marital property" unreduced by the mortgage resulting in an unwarranted additional marital deduction.

In the case of community property, only the decedent's personal claim and expense obligations are fully deductible. This means an allocation of claims and expenses must be made. Since only one-half of the total community property is includable, only half of any obligation attributable to community property is deductible.

Certain taxes unpaid at the time of the decedent's death are considered debts. Three common deductible taxes are:

(1) income taxes unpaid but reportable for some tax period prior to the decedent's death;

(2) gift taxes that were not paid on gifts the decedent made sometime prior to death; and

(3) property taxes that accrued but remained unpaid at the time of the decedent's death.

Casualty and theft losses incurred by the estate are deductible if the loss arose from fire, storm, shipwreck (or other casualty), or theft (line 7). To be deductible, the loss must have occurred during the time the estate was being settled prior to it being closed. Such deductions are limited in two respects: the deduction is reduced (1) to the extent that insurance or any other compensation is available to offset the loss, and (2) to the extent that a loss is reflected in the alternate valuation. In other words, if the loss is reflected in the alternate valuation elected by the executor, no casualty or theft loss deduction is allowed. Otherwise, such loss would be effectively deducted twice.

Similar to administrative expenses, the executor may elect to deduct losses as an estate tax or income tax deduction. Typically, they will be taken on the return that reduces the most tax. Note, however, that for 2018-2025, Congress severely limited many individual itemized deductions, including casualty losses, and only a small minority of such losses will be deductible.[12]

18.6 DETERMINATION OF TAXABLE ESTATE (LINE 14)

The adjusted gross estate is reduced by:

1. a marital deduction for property that is:

    a. included in the decedent's gross estate; and

    b. passes at the decedent's death to a surviving spouse "in a qualifying manner;"

2. a charitable deduction; and

3. a state death tax deduction.

For a marital deduction the property must pass in a "qualified manner," which is defined as a manner that gives the surviving spouse control and enjoyment essentially tantamount to outright ownership or that meets the requirements of Qualified Terminable Interest Property ("QTIP," defined below).

The maximum amount allowable as a marital deduction for federal estate tax purposes is the net value of the property passing to the surviving spouse in a qualifying manner. Otherwise, the marital deduction is unlimited. For this reason, an individual could transfer his entire estate to his spouse estate tax-free.

Generally, "terminable interests" (where the surviving spouse's interest would cease upon the occurrence or nonoccurrence of a particular event and the children or some other party would receive the marital property) do not qualify for the marital deduction unless it is "qualifying terminable interest." A qualifying terminable interest (QTIP):

1. passes from the decedent;

2. provides the surviving spouse income for life payable at least annually; and

3. by an irrevocable election by the decedent's executor made on the estate tax return by listing the property funding the QTIP on Schedule M (the marital deduction schedule).

The quid pro quo of allowing a QTIP marital deduction from the decedent spouse's adjusted gross estate is the requirement that upon the death of the surviving spouse, the property remaining in the QTIP must be included in the surviving spouse's gross estate. Additionally, a QTIP allows the decedent to provide a lifetime income source to the surviving spouse with the flexibility of leaving the remainder interest to other beneficiaries, such as children. Although the inclusion of the remainder interest in the gross estate of the surviving spouse could trigger an estate tax liability, his or her executor is entitled to reimbursement of such tax from the person or persons who receive the remainder interest.[13] In spite of this right of reimbursement, the surviving spouse may waive this right in his or her will.

The marital deduction is discussed in more detail in Chapter 27.

An unlimited charitable deduction (line 11) is allowed for the net value of any type of property gifted to a "qualified charity" at a decedent's death to the extent such property is includible in the decedent's gross estate. In other words, a decedent could conceivably zero out his or her taxable estate by gifting all property to charity.

Finally, a deduction for state death taxes paid (line 12, other deductions) is allowed.

18.7 ESTATE TAX PAYABLE BEFORE CREDITS (LINE 19)

Once the taxable estate (line 14) is computed, the aggregate amount of adjusted taxable gifts (line 15) are added to arrive at the tentative tax base (or computation base, line 16). Adjusted taxable gifts are defined as the taxable portion of all post-1976 gifts. A gift is taxable to the extent it exceeds the sum of any allowable:

- gift tax annual exclusion

- gift tax exclusion for qualified transfers for educational or medical expenses

- gift tax marital deduction (similar to the estate tax marital deduction but for lifetime gifts to a spouse)

- gift tax charitable deduction

Any gifts made in conjunction with a retained interest that are includible have already been taken into account in the computation of the taxable estate, and, thus are not considered adjusted taxable gifts.

Adding adjusted taxable gifts to the taxable estate makes the computation of gift and estate transfers a unified transfer tax calculation. In other words, the net effect of adding in adjusted taxable gifts to the adjusted taxable estate (line 16) is to apply the unified gift and estate tax rates to the cumulative transfers by gift and at death. Thus, making lifetime gifts beyond annual exclusion gifts and charitable donations does not by itself save any estate tax – it is only by receiving fractional interest discounts, paying tax on income from gifted assets (if given to a grantor trust) and escaping estate tax on post-gift growth that any true savings is achieved.

Next, the tax on the sum of the adjusted taxable estate and adjusted taxable gifts (line 17) is computed by applying the appropriate rates (see the Gift and Estate Tax Rate Schedules) to the computation base (line 16). Different tax rate schedules may apply depending on the year of death (line 1).

Calculating the tax on computational base (line 17), transfers exceeding $500,000 but not over $750,000 are taxed at 37 percent; transfers exceeding $750,000 but not over $1,000,000 are taxed at 39 percent, and transfers exceeding $1,000,000 are taxed at 40 percent. Therefore, taking into account the tax on transfers between $0 and $500,000 and the tax on transfers over $500,000 and $1,000,000, the tax on a transfer exceeding $1,000,000 is $345,800 plus 40 percent of the excess over $1,000,000. Therefore, the $12,920,000 exclusion applicable for 2023 will shield $5,113,800 in tax ("applicable credit"), and these numbers will adjust upwards with inflation over time depending on the year of death.

18.8 DETERMINING THE FEDERAL ESTATE TAX PAYABLE

Certain tax credits are allowed as a dollar-for-dollar reduction of the estate tax. These credits are:

- the unified credit (line 20)
- the credit for pre-1977 gift tax (line 22)
- the credit for taxes on prior transfers (line 23)
- the credit for foreign death taxes (line 24)

The state death tax credit (line 21) has been replaced by a state death tax deduction. The credit for pre-1977 gift tax is rarely used, though the issue is always worth double checking. The other credits are examined in detail below.

Unified Credit

As mentioned above, the unified credit (or "applicable credit") is $5,113,800 for 2023, and increases annually with inflation with a reversion in 2026 absent further Congressional meddling.[14] (See the Applicable Credit Amount tables.) The term "unified credit" describes how the credit is applied as an offset against gift as well as estate taxes. However, to the extent the unified credit has been used as an offset of gift taxes, the remaining credit available to offset estate tax is, in effect, lowered. In the event that the unified credit exceeds the aggregate amount of estate and gift tax, there is no refund.

The required computation process has the effect of reducing the credit by requiring the "add back" of adjusted taxable gifts. In other words, although the unified credit in the example below does not appear to be reduced by $87,800 (the tax on a $300,000 gift was not paid because the decedent used $87,800 of the credit), the effect is the same because by adding back the $300,000 adjusted taxable gifts, the unified credit is essentially reapplied to the sum of the taxable estate ($600,000) plus the adjusted taxable gifts. Stated another way, adding back $87,800 of adjusted taxable gifts into the computation "restores" the previously used $87,800 of unified credit.

Example. Assume a widow died in 2021 with a $12,000,000 taxable estate. In 2009 she made only one taxable gift of $300,000 (after utilizing the annual exclusion). The widow paid no gift tax because $87,800 of her unified credit was applied to offset the $87,800 gift tax liability. These facts resulted in the following estate tax liability (ignoring other tax credits.

Taxable Estate	$12,000,000
Adjusted taxable gifts	300,000
Total	$12,300,000
Tax on $12,300,000	4,865,800
Less: gift taxes paid on lifetime transfers	-0-
Less: unified credit	4,625,800
Tax due	$ 240,000

Credit for Taxes on Prior Transfers

Code section 2013 provides another credit available where a prior decedent (the transferor) transferred property (subject to estate tax at death) to the decedent that is presumed to be includible in the decedent's estate. To qualify for the credit, the decedent must have received the property prior to death. In addition, the transferor must have died within ten years prior to or two years after the death of the decedent. Interestingly enough, the law arbitrarily assumes that property includible in the transferor's estate that was transferred to the latter decedent who died within a short period of time before

Figure 18.2

	FEDERAL ESTATE TAX WORKSHEET		
1	Year of Death		2021
2	Gross Estate (before exclusions)		$13,000,000
3	- Conservation Easement Exclusion		$0
4	Gross Estate		$13,000,000
5	- Funeral and Administration Expenses Deduction	$35,000	
6	- Debts and Taxes Deduction	$45,000	
7	- Losses Deduction	$0	
8	- Subtotal: 5 to 7		($80,000)
9	Adjusted Gross Estate		$12,920,000
10	- Marital Deduction	$0	
11	- Charitable Deduction	$0	
12	- Other Deductions (State Death Taxes)	$532,800	
13	- Subtotal: 10 to 12		$ 532,800
14	Taxable Estate		$12,387,200
15	+ Adjusted Taxable Gifts		$ 300,000
16	Computation Base		$12,687,800
17	Tax on Computation Base		$4,900,680
18	- Gift Tax on Adjusted Taxable Gifts		$0
19	Tentative Tax		$4,900,680
20	- Unified Credit	$4,625,800	
21	- State Death Tax Credit	N/A	
22	- Pre-1977 Gift Tax Credit	$0	
23	- Previously Taxed Property Credit	$0	
24	- Foreign Death Tax Credit	$0	
25	- Total Credits		($4,625,800)
26	Federal Estate Tax		$ 274,880

Computations Courtesy – NumberCruncher Software: http://Leimberg.com

or after the transferor is subject to double taxation (and is therefore entitled to the credit).

As long as the property was includable in the transferor's estate and passed from the transferor to the decedent, the method of transfer is irrelevant. In other words, it may have passed by will, intestacy, by electing against the will, by lifetime gift, as life insurance proceeds, or as joint property with right of survivorship.

In valuing the property subject to the credit, the transferred property must be valued in the decedent's estate at the same amount at which the property was included in the transferor's gross estate. In addition, that value must be reduced by any death tax payable out of the property, the amount of any liability on the property and the amount of any marital deduction the transferor's estate received as a result of the transfer.

The credit is subject to two limitations:

- The first limitation is the federal estate tax attributable to the transferred property in the transferor's estate computed pursuant to a pro rata method; and

- The second limitation is the amount of estate tax attributable to the inclusion of the property in the decedent's gross estate.

As is relevant to the second limitation, according to the 2013 treasury regulations, there is no requirement that the property be identified or in existence at the time of the decedent's death. For purposes of the second limitation, the property is presumed to be included in the gross estate even if is not. Thus, in essence, the decedent may receive an estate tax credit for property that was not actually included in his or her gross estate with respect to which no estate tax was imposed.

If the transferor and decedent died within two years of each other, the credit is 100 percent. For every two-year increment of the time of deaths, the credit is reduced by 20 percent. For example, between years two and four only 80 percent of the credit is allowable.

Thus, practitioners should always ask the family of a decedent if the decedent had inherited any significant assets within the last ten years. If the estate of the benefactor had paid estate taxes, this may be used to reduce the decedent's estate.

Foreign Death Taxes

A credit for foreign death taxes prevents double taxation on the same assets by two different jurisdictions. The credit is the amount of death taxes paid to a foreign country or a United States possession on property that is:

1. included in the decedent's gross estate for U.S. estate tax purposes; and

2. situated (and subject to tax) in that other country or U.S. possession.

The credit is available only to United States citizens or resident aliens.

Example. Mary Green died in 2019 with a gross estate of $13,000,000. During her lifetime, she made one $300,000 taxable gift and the gift tax was offset by the unified credit. Her estate had funeral and administration expenses of $35,000, debts of $45,000, and state death taxes of $532,800. Figure 18.2 illustrates calculation of her federal estate tax.

For examples of estate tax planning calculations with marital trusts and bypass trusts, see Chapter 27.

18.9 PORTABILITY

The Tax Relief Act of 2010 created the concept of "portability" of the estate tax exemption between spouses. Under these rules, a surviving spouse can increase the amount of their applicable exclusion amount by the amount of the "deceased spouse unused exclusion" (DSUE). Portability was extended and made permanent by the American Taxpayer Relief Act of 2012.

This means the previously deceased spouse's unused exclusion amount (DSUE) can be used by the surviving spouse. However, this amount may disappear and/or be replaced should the surviving spouse remarry and be widowed again – in such case the second deceased spouse's DSUE, if any, would replace the first. This may be a terrible or beneficial result, depending on the estate size and disposition of the second-to-die spouse's estate.

The DSUE is a fixed amount that does not increase during the survivor's lifetime. This is in contrast to a bypass trust, which shelters the post-death appreciation of the assets from the first spouse's estate. Importantly, the only way to preserve the right to use the DSUE is to file a federal estate tax return on the death of the first spouse to die, even if the estate is not subject to estate tax. The practitioner should weigh the expenses of filing an estate tax return against the probability that the surviving spouse will have a taxable estate and advise the surviving spouse of same.

On the other hand, executors who file an estate tax return only to elect "portability" do not have to value property eligible for the marital or charitable deductions. The value of those assets are to be estimated and included in the gross estate. This "special rule" does not apply to assets whose value is required for alternate valuation purposes, special use valuation purposes, or if a reverse QTIP election is being made or if there is a request for deferral of estate tax under Code section 6166. The instructions to the Form 706 will provide a "Table of Estimated Values" which is a range of value for the assets in the estate subject to the special rule, and, by signing the return under penalties of perjury; the executor certifies that the estimate falls within the identified range of values. For example if the total of the assets qualifying for the special rule is between $1,000,000 and $1,250,000, then $1,250,000 must be included on the return.

Lastly, while the estate tax exemption is portable, the GST exemption is not. Therefore, if a person wants to implement some generation skipping tax planning, then trusts should be used.

While the portability of the estate tax exemption will simplify planning for many people, it does not eliminate the need for creating a conventional bypass trust, since such a trust provides better protection from creditors, enables income tax shifting, shields appreciation in the trust from the federal and potentially state estate tax, and provides management assistance for the surviving spouse.

18.10 FILING A RETURN AND PAYMENT OF THE ESTATE TAX

As mentioned above, the estate tax is due on or before the date the estate tax return is due, nine months after the decedent's death. An estate tax return (generally IRS Form 706) must be filed if the gross estate exceeds the "exemption equivalent" (applicable exemption) provided by the estate tax unified credit ($12,920,000 in 2023; see the Estate Tax Unified Credit table). This threshold amount is lowered by the total of any adjusted taxable gifts (which have not been included in the gross estate). Therefore, with respect to decedents who made a significant amount of lifetime taxable gifts, filing a return will be required even if the taxable estate is far less than the exemption equivalent. As discussed above, an estate tax return must be filed in order to take advantage of the portability of the estate tax exemption between spouses.

"Reasonable Cause" Extension

As stated previously, the estate tax is due nine months from the date of the decedent's death. However, an executor or administrator can request an extension of time for paying the tax–up to twelve months from the due date of the payment–if there is reasonable cause. Furthermore, upon the executor's showing of reasonable cause, the IRS has the discretion to grant a series of extensions which–in total–could run as long as ten years from the due date of the original return. The term "reasonable cause" is not defined in the Internal Revenue Code or regulations. However, the regulations give illustrative examples of situations of reasonable cause:

(a) a substantial portion of the estate consists of rights to receive future payments such as annuities, accounts receivable, or renewal commissions and the estate cannot borrow against these assets as a source of funds to pay the estate tax without incurring substantial loss;

(b) the gross estate is unascertainable at the time the estate tax is due, because the estate has a substantial claim that cannot be collected without litigation; or

(c) an estate does not have sufficient funds to pay claims against the estate (including estate taxes when due) and at the same time provide a reasonable allowance during the period of administration for decedent's surviving spouse and dependent children, because the executor, despite reasonable efforts, cannot convert estate assets into cash.

Closely Held Business Interest Extension

Under Code section 6166, an executor may elect to pay estate tax attributable to a closely held business in fourteen annual installments if the interest in the closely held business exceeds 35 percent of the adjusted gross estate.

See Chapter 19 on Extensions of Time to Pay Estate Tax for more detail.

18.11 ISSUES IN COMMUNITY PROPERTY STATES

In community property states, a married decedent will generally have community property, and may have separate property as well. Since only one-half of the community property will be includable in the decedent's estate, many practitioners will list the full value of the community asset on the return, followed by a line item showing "Less surviving spouse's one-half interest." That way, the community assets are distinguished from the decedent's separate property assets, and the value of the property's new tax basis (equal to the value of both halves of the community property) is established.

Similarly, only one-half of community property debts, such as the mortgage on community real property, may be deducted for federal estate tax purposes.

Upon the death of one of the spouses in a Community Property state, the total fair market value (FMV) of the community property, including the part that belongs to the surviving spouse, generally becomes the basis of the entire property.[15] For this rule to apply, at least half the value of the community property interest must be includible in the decedent spouse's gross estate, whether or not the estate must file a return.

Example. Bob and Ann owned community property with a basis of $80,000. When Bob died, his and Ann's community property had an FMV of $100,000. One-half of the FMV of the community property was includible in Bob's estate. As a result of Bob's death, Ann's basis in her half of the property is stepped-up to $50,000 (half of the date of death FMV of $100,000. The basis of Bob's half of the property (whether devised to Ann or some other beneficiary) is also stepped-up to $50,000. Note, however, that fractional interest discounts may apply to certain property.[16]

CHAPTER ENDNOTES

1. I.R.C. §2032(a). The alternate valuation rule provides that value of property which is "distributed, sold, exchanged, or otherwise disposed of" shall be the value of the property upon the date of such event.
2. I.R.C. §2001(c).
3. Treas. Reg. §20.2010-1T(d)(4); See also Treas. Regs. §§ 20.2010-2T and 20.2010-3T.
4. Rev. Rul. 69-8; Rev. Rul. 75-126; Lang v. United States, 356 F. Supp. 546 (S.D. Iowa 1973).
5. *Estate of Rodriguez v. Commissioner*, T.C. Memo 1989-13 (T.C. 1989) – in this case the court found the decedent owner was a mere nominee owner of an insurance policy, but strangely did not discuss IRC §2042 and whether the decedent retained "incidents of ownership" over the policy.
6. See I.R.C. §673 for the grantor trust income tax provision. See Rev. Rul. 76-178 for instructions on valuations using IRC §7520 tables. A trust may appear to be excluded from estate tax upon creation, but a change in §7520 rates or other events could cause §2037 to be triggered at death.
7. *M. Gallenstein*, 975 F.2d 286 (6th Cir. 1992), see also *T. Hahn*, 110 TC 140, acq. IRB 2001-42 (note that the IRS acquiesced. Thus, for such property the I.R.C. 2040(b) rule does not apply and a consideration furnished rule applies – if, e.g., H provided $300,000 consideration for a property and placed W on title as joint tenant in 1976, and then dies with property worth $1.5 million in 2017, the inclusion and new basis may be $1.5 million, not $750,000.
8. Treas. Reg. §25.2518-2(c)(5), Example (12).
9. I.R.C. §2031(c)(9).
10. The alternate valuation date is outlined in I.R.C. §2032.
11. I.R.C. §2032(a)(3).
12. Individual taxpayers may continue to deduct personal casualty losses, but only to the extent they are attributable to federally declared disasters, so two similarly situated homeowners hit by weather disasters may have completely different tax ramifications. See I.R.C. § 165(h)(5)(A).
13. I.R.C. §2207A.
14. Every year the IRS releases a Rev. Proc. with inflation adjusted numbers. For 2017's applicable exclusion increase to $5,490,000, see Rev. Proc. 2016-55, §3.35. For 2018 adjustments, see Rev. Proc. 2018-18, §3.35.
15. I.R.C. §1014(b)(6).
16. *Propstra v. United States*, 680 F.2d 1248 (9th Cir. Ariz. 1982), *Estate of Lee v. Commissioner*, 1978 U.S. Tax Ct. LEXIS 165 (T.C. 1978), *Estate of Bright v. United States*, 658 F.2d 999 (5th Cir. Tex. 1981).

EXTENSIONS OF TIME TO PAY ESTATE TAX

CHAPTER 19

19.1 INTRODUCTION

Generally, the federal estate tax is payable in full within nine months of the date of death. However, the Internal Revenue Code does provide relief under certain circumstances by allowing an executor to pay the federal estate taxes attributable to the decedent's business over a period of years.[1]

Code section 6166 permits a four year deferral of tax followed by a maximum ten year payout of the tax. If the requirements of Code Section 6166 are met, the executor in his discretion has the *right* to elect to pay the federal estate tax (and generation-skipping transfer tax) attributable to the decedent's interest in a closely held business in installments over a period of up to fourteen years.[2] During the first five years the executor pays only interest on the unpaid tax.[3] Then, in equal annual increments over as many as ten additional years, the executor pays off the principal of the unpaid tax (together with interest on the unpaid balance). Deferral interest is payable at 2 percent on the tax generated by the first $1,590,000 (as indexed for inflation in 2021) of business value and at 45 percent of the regular underpayment rate on the balance.[4]

If the estate does not qualify for the section 6166 extension, subject to discretionary approval by the IRS, it may be possible to pay the federal estate tax in installments under Code sections 6161, 6159 and 6163.

Under section 6161, the IRS may extend the period for payment of tax for a period of up to ten years beyond the due date of the estate tax return if the IRS finds that there is "reasonable cause" to grant such an extension.[5]

In addition, under Code section 6159, the IRS may permit the installment payment of taxes where the IRS believes doing so will facilitate payment of such taxes.

Finally, under Code section 6163, estate tax attributable to reversionary and remainder interests in property can be deferred until six months after preceding interests in the property terminate.[6]

Closely related to the issue of delaying estate tax payments, note that the ramifications of another option, borrowing to pay estate tax, has recently changed for the 21st Edition. See below for updates on *Graegin* loans.

19.2 WHEN IS USE OF SUCH A DEVICE INDICATED?

1. Where the estate has insufficient liquidity to pay the estate taxes when due without selling assets at a substantial loss.

2. Where the estate can earn a greater after-tax rate of return on its money or other investments than it spends in interest for the deferral payment privilege.

3. Where future profits or cash flow from the decedent's business is expected to pay all or part of the deferred tax.

19.3 WHAT ARE THE REQUIREMENTS?

Section 6166

1. The decedent must be a U.S. citizen or resident at the time of death.[7]

2. The gross estate must include an interest classified as a closely held business, the value of which *exceeds*

35 percent of the adjusted gross estate. In the case of an estate in which the decedent made a gift of property within three years of death, the estate is treated as meeting the more than 35 percent requirement only if the estate meets such requirement both with and without the application of the three-year inclusion rule of Code section 2035 (see Chapter 18 regarding the estate tax).[8]

a. Aggregation of various business interests of the decedent is allowed for purposes of meeting the percentage requirement, provided the decedent owned at least 20 percent of the total value of each business, and each activity otherwise qualifies as a closely held trade or business.[9]

b. To qualify as an interest in a closely held business, the interest can be in a sole proprietorship, a partnership, or a corporation. A partnership interest will qualify if 20 percent or more of the total capital interest in the partnership is included in the gross estate, or if the partnership has forty-five or fewer partners.[10] Stock in a corporation qualifies if 20 percent or more in value of the voting stock is included in determining the gross estate of the decedent, or the corporation has forty-five or fewer shareholders.[11]

For purposes of the forty-five or fewer owners test, a partnership interest or corporate stock held by another partnership or corporation or by an estate or trust will be treated as if owned proportionately by shareholders, partners, or beneficiaries (the rule also applies to trusts provided a beneficiary has a present interest in the trust).[12] A partnership interest or stock held by a member of the decedent's family is considered to be owned by the decedent for purposes of the "forty-five or fewer owners" test.

c. According to the IRS, the business must also be actively carried on and require a "management" function, rather than being a passive investment. A passive investment is one in which the taxpayer merely supervises his investment (such as an apartment house), and the investment is the actual capital producing factor.[13]

d. In addition, only *active* business assets can be considered in determining the value of the business interest that qualifies for the deferral. For example, a business owning stock in another corporation cannot count the value of that stock in determining if it meets the 35 percent test because the stock it owns in the other corporation is not used in carrying out a trade or business.[14] This active asset rule, which denies installment payment for passive assets, applies to all corporations and partnerships. (It does not apply, however, for purposes of determining whether or not an acceleration of the tax will be required.)

3. The amount of federal estate or generation-skipping transfer tax that may be deferred (i.e., paid in installments) is only that amount of tax attributable to the value of the closely held trade or business. The balance of the estate tax or GST tax must be paid at the regular payment due date.[15]

4. Generally, if the estate qualifies under section 6166 and an election is made, the first installment of principal is due not later than five years and nine months from the date of death. (This deferral period is not available to certain lending and finance businesses that qualify for installment payments under Code section 6166(b)(10)). Each succeeding installment must be paid within one year after the previous installment.

With the exception of lending and finance businesses and holding companies, which are limited to installment payments stretched out over only five years,[16] the maximum number of principal installments which may be paid under this provision is ten, thus generally allowing for payment over a fourteen-year period (four years of interest only plus up to an additional ten years of principal and interest payments).

During the four-year period immediately following death, interest only payments are to be made, with interest being at a beneficial 2 percent rate in relation to the tax on the first $1,590,000 (for decedents dying in 2021) in value of the closely held business (see "How It Is Done," below) and at 45 percent of the regular underpayment rate on the balance.[17] The underpayment rate varies quarterly.[18] Interest calculated using these special rates is *not* deductible for estate or income tax purposes.

5. The IRS may demand a bond of up to twice the value of the deferred estate tax. This bond is difficult (some say impossible) to obtain and relatively

expensive.[19] In certain situations, the executor can seek a special lien in lieu of the bond.[20] In *Estate of Roski v. Commissioner*, the Tax Court held that the IRS could not universally require estates electing to defer tax payments under Code section 6166 to post bond and that such a requirement must be determined on a case-by-case basis depending on whether the estate is likely to fail to make payments after the expiration of the automatic federal estate tax lien under Code section 6324(a).[21] After *Roski*, the IRS published Notice 2007-90 announcing that it had changed its policy and would begin making case-by-case determinations as to whether an estate will be required to provide a bond if it elects to pay the estate tax in installments under section 6166.[22]

6. It should be noted that pursuant to Treasury Regulations section 301.9100-3 (which provides relief in the case of a late election where the Commissioner establishes that the taxpayer acted reasonably and in good faith), an estate may not seek relief for an untimely Section 6166 election because such an election is statutory, not regulatory.[23] Also, Chief Counsel Advice 200848004 held that an estate could not make a section 6166 election by attaching the statement to an extension request since the election can only be made by attaching the election notice to a timely-filed estate tax return.

Section 6161

1. If a business interest does not qualify for deferral under section 6166, upon a showing of reasonable cause for the granting of the extension, pursuant to Code section 6161, the IRS may, in its discretion, grant an extension of the time for payment of the tax shown on the return for a period of up to ten years beyond the due date of the return.[24]

2. Reasonable cause for the extension is not expressly defined in the statute.[25] Each case is examined on an independent factual basis. However, Treasury Regulations contain certain guidelines used to establish the presence of reasonable cause.[26] These include:

   a. inability of the estate to marshal assets to pay the estate tax when otherwise due;[27]

   b. an estate comprised in substantial part of assets consisting of rights to receive payments in the future, with the estate having insufficient present cash to pay the estate tax and an inability to borrow against these assets except on unreasonable terms;[28]

   c. when the assets cannot be collected without litigation;[29] or

   d. there are insufficient funds available, after the exercise of due diligence, with which to pay the tax in a timely fashion.[30]

3. Interest on the deferred taxes computed at the regular tax underpayment rate.[31]

Section 6159

Section 6159 authorizes the IRS to enter into written agreements with taxpayers to pay taxes in installments where the IRS determines that such an agreement will facilitate full or partial collection of such taxes. The IRS can modify or terminate the agreement if:

1. information provided by the taxpayer was inaccurate or incomplete;[32]

2. the IRS believes that collection of such tax is in jeopardy;[33]

3. the IRS determines that the financial condition of the taxpayer has changed (in which case thirty days' notice to the taxpayer is required, including the reason for such change);[34]

4. the taxpayer fails to make a timely installment payment (or to timely pay any other tax);[35] or

5. the taxpayer fails to provide a financial update as requested by the IRS.

Interest is payable on such installments at the regular underpayment rate.[36] The IRS may terminate the agreement if the conditions in (1) or (2) exist; or the IRS may alter, modify or terminate the agreement if the other conditions occur. For purposes of an IRS determination of whether or not to enter into an installment plan, if the taxpayer has filed all returns, is current in payment of other taxes, the tax, interest and penalties is no more than $10,000 and the amount of the proposed payment meets a prescribed minimum, then the IRS agent is to offer an installment plan.[37]

Section 6163

If a reversionary or remainder interest in property is includable in the gross estate, the executor may elect to defer payment of the estate tax attributable to the reversionary or remainder interest until six months after the termination of any precedent interests in the property.[38] In addition, the IRS may extend the payment of such tax for a reasonable period of up to an additional three years for reasonable cause.[39] In Revenue Ruling 73-311,[40] the Service ruled that there is no reversionary or remainder interest unless there is an intervening property interest. Thus, a surviving spouse was denied relief where she was receiving payments under her deceased spouse's deferred compensation agreement, and there were eight payments remaining at her death which passed to her children.

Graegin Loans

Historically, the interest associated with funds borrowed to pay estate tax where an estate is illiquid could be deductible as an administrative expense under Code section 2053 if three conditions were met:

1. the loan is bona fide;

2. the loan is "actually and necessarily incurred"; and

3. the amount of interest to be paid is ascertainable with reasonable certainty.

It should be noted that a typical loan is not subject to a prepayment penalty, meaning that the amount of interest cannot accurately be calculated, but loans could add this feature. The issue becomes whether the interest associated with the loan to pay the estate tax will qualify for an estate tax deduction. If so, the entire amount of the interest to be paid over the course of the loan could be taken as an estate tax deduction. Surprisingly, this deduction for amounts to paid many years in the future did not have to be discounted to present value – the entire amount of the interest to be paid could be deducted. At least, that was until Treasury issued proposed regulations under Code section 2053 on June 28, 2022 that would require a present value calculation of the future interest payments to reduce the value of the deduction to more accurately reflect the true economic cost of the interest payments. First, here's a bit of background on *Graegin* loans and why the IRS found them (rightfully so) to be abusive before we summarize the proposed regulations.

In order to qualify for the full deduction, there is (or "was," assuming the proposed regulation becomes final) the option of a so-called *Graegin* loan, named after a successful court case.[41] Under this approach, the estate borrows money to pay the estate tax obligation from a third party lender. The estate is permitted to deduct all of the interest to be paid over the course of the loan on the federal estate tax return. Because the interest must be ascertainable, a "*Graegin* loan" must forbid prepayment of the amount borrowed. By including this provision, the aggregate interest payable can be determined.

However, in order for this approach to be respected, the loan must be *necessary* to pay the estate's obligations. Therefore, where stock in a closely held entity could be liquidated or redeemed to meet the estate's obligations, it is not clear whether a *Graegin* loan would work. Also, if a sale of assets could cure the estate's liquidity problem, the *Graegin* technique may be deemed to be unnecessary so that the estate could not take advantage of the interest deduction.

For example, in *Estate of Duncan v. Commissioner*,[42] the decedent's revocable trust borrowed funds from his irrevocable trust to cover the estate's shortfall in being able to pay taxes and debts. The estate claimed a deduction for the interest that would be payable at the end of the (non-prepayable) note. The IRS denied any deduction for the interest. The Tax Court, however, determined that the interest was fully deductible because the loan was a bona fide debt, was actually and reasonably necessary, and the revocable trust could not meet its obligations without selling its illiquid assets at reduced price. On the other hand, in a 2009 case *Black v. Commissioner*,[43] the interest deduction for a *Graegin* loan from a family limited partnership was denied because the court found that the loan was not necessary to avoid selling the company stock (the court held that the loan structure arrived at by the estate constituted an indirect use of the stock to pay the debts of the estate and "accomplished nothing more than a direct use of that stock for the same purpose"). Likewise in *Stick v Commissioner*,[44] the interest deduction was denied because the court found that the estate had enough liquid assets to pay the taxes without borrowing. In *Estate of Koons*, the court also denied the deduction where the estate owned an LLC comprised of $200 million of highly liquid assets.[45]

The estate can borrow from a bank as well as a family member or related family business, and it is possible this will look less abusive than loans from family LLC/LPs.[46]

An irrevocable life insurance trust (ILIT) would be an excellent source of liquidity and courts have approved the deduction of interest from *Graegin* loans payable to ILITs.[47] If interest is paid to family members or related family businesses, realize that the interest payments will be ordinary taxable income, tax on which may be even higher than the federal estate rate (up to 40.8 percent plus state, depending on the bracket of the lending parties, under current law). However, a *Graegin* loan would still be advantageous because of the timing of the savings of estate tax (nine months from date of death) versus the timing of the interest payments for income tax (which could be ten-twenty years).[48]

The Treasury Department put this topic on its 2017-2018 Priority Guidance Plan,[49] but did not issue proposed regulations until June 28, 2022. Assuming they become final, they will put the kibosh on the most abusive (or beneficial, depending on your perspective) aspect of *Graegin* loans – the ability to deduct many years of future interest expense upfront. The proposed regulations (REG-130975-08) probably went farther than they needed to to curb the abuse, going beyond simply incorporating present value concepts, but that is the main takeaway concerning Graegin loans.

Prop. Reg. §20.2053-1(d)(6)(i)(B), captioned "General Rule," states:

> The present value of each post-grace-period payment is calculated by discounting it from the payment date or expected date of payment to the decedent's date of death. The applicable discount rate is the applicable Federal rate determined under section 1274(d) for the month in which the decedent's death occurs, compounded annually. The length of time from the decedent's date of death to the date of payment or expected date of payment will determine whether the Federal rate applicable to that payment is the Federal mid-term rate or the Federal long-term rate.

Prop. Reg. §20.2053-1(d)(6)(ii), captioned "Calculating present value of amounts paid or payable," then provides that any post-grace period payment is determined as the

> Amount of future payment × $[1 \div (1 + i)]^t$
>
> Where t is the amount of time (expressed in years and fractions of years) from the day after the decedent's date of death to the payment date or expected date of payment; and i is the applicable discount rate.

While there will always be a need for estates to borrow cash to meet estate tax, specific bequests and other liquidity needs, it is doubtful that we will see many *Graegin*-style loans in the future due to the proposed regulations that not only limit the deduction to a present-value of future payments calculation but have other hurdles as well. If not for the additional estate tax savings, no one wants the additional cost and risk of a loan with a huge pre-payment penalty, and lenders typically charge more for fixed rate loans, so if the main estate tax benefit is now lost, estates and trusts will likely revert to more standard loans as needed, and take the future interest expense as an income tax deduction that would offset up to 40.8% income tax (37% plus 3.8% NIIT or higher when the TCJA cuts expire in 2026) plus state income tax, on an annual basis as paid.

Remember to factor in any state estate tax savings from a *Graegin* style loan and factor in any state income tax rates applicable in the decision to make any portion of the loan a *Graegin* loan, and review any final regulations that may be published soon under Code section 2053 that may affect the analysis.

19.4 HOW IT IS DONE – AN EXAMPLE OF SECTION 6166

Andrea Apter died in 2013 when the value of her wholly-owned, closely held business, a computer center, was $3,600,000. Her gross estate was $8,000,000. Administrative costs, debts, and expenses totaled $300,000. Federal estate taxes totaled $980,000 (the applicable exclusion amount was $5,250,000). Qualification for section 6166 is determined as follows.

Section 6166 (up to 14 year) Installment Payout

(1)	Estate Tax Value of closely held business included in gross estate	$3,600,000
(2)	Adjusted Gross Estate	$7,700,000
(3)	35% x Adjusted Gross Estate	$2,695,000

Line 1 exceeds Line 3; estate qualifies

Since the estate qualifies for section 6166 deferral, the executor can elect to pay that portion of estate taxes attributable to the inclusion of the business in installments over up to fourteen years (first four years, no tax due, only interest–up to next ten years equal annual installments of tax and declining interest on unpaid balance).

The deferral amount would be computed according to the following formula: (Assume the net estate and GST tax payable after credits is $980,000).

Computing Section 6166 Deferral Limitation

$$\text{Net Estate and GST Tax (after credits)} \times \frac{\text{Value of Includable Closely Held Business Interest}}{\text{Adjusted Gross Estate}}$$

$$\$980,000 \times \frac{\$3,600,000}{\$7,700,000} = \$458,181.82$$

The estate can defer $458,182 (rounded) of the tax, but must pay the balance of the tax not attributable to the closely held business immediately. Therefore, $521,818 of tax ($980,000 − $458,182) must be paid by the nine month deadline.

Code section 6601(j) places an overall limitation on the portion of the tax deferred under Section 6166 that qualifies for the 2 percent interest rate.

If the tax deferred exceeds this amount, the balance of the tax would be deferrable at 45 percent of the regular underpayment rate. Unlike *Graegin* or traditional loan interest, the interest under Code section 6166 is not deductible for estate or income tax purposes.

19.5 TAX IMPLICATIONS

1. Interest is payable on the tax which is not paid by the due date of the return.[50] Tax under Code sections 6159, 6161, or 6163 is deferred at the regular underpayment rate. The regular underpayment rate is redetermined quarterly so as to be three percentage points over the short-term federal rate.[51] The interest owed is compounded daily.

Under section 6166, a special 2 percent interest rate is allowed. This rate is limited to the estate tax attributable to the first $1.75 million (in 2023, this

Figure 19.1

SECTION 6166 PROJECTED PAYMENT SCHEDULE*

Year	Principal 2%	Interest 2%	Principal 4.50%	Interest 4.50%	Total Interest	Total Payment
1	$458,182	$9,256	$0	$0	$9,256	$9,256
2	458,182	9,256	0	0	9,256	9,256
3	458,182	9,256	0	0	9,256	9,256
4	458,182	9,256	0	0	9,256	9,256
5	412,364	9,256	0	0	9,256	55,074
6	366,546	8,330	0	0	8,330	54,148
7	320,727	7,405	0	0	7,405	53,223
8	274,909	6,479	0	0	6,479	52,297
9	229,091	5,553	0	0	5,553	51,371
10	183,273	4,628	0	0	4,628	50,446
11	137,455	3,702	0	0	3,702	49,520
12	91,636	2,777	0	0	2,777	48,595
13	45,818	1,851	0	0	1,851	47,669
14	0	926	0	0	926	46,744
Totals		$87,931		$0	$87,931	$546,111

* Interest is compounded daily. The underpayment interest rate changes quarterly, which controls any interest above the 2% amount, discussed below.

EXTENSIONS OF TIME TO PAY ESTATE TAX

adjusts for inflation) of farm or other closely held business property; see How It Is Done, above).[52] Amounts of estate tax attributable to value in excess of those amounts bear interest at 45 percent of the regular underpayment rate.

2. Interest for tax deferred under Section 6166 using the special 2 percent and 45 percent of the regular underpayment rate rates cannot be deducted for estate or income tax purposes (unlike interest payments on a *Graegin* loan to a third party as discussed above).

3. The IRS frequently requires the estate post a bond of as much as twice the amount of the estate tax to be deferred.[53] This may make the use of Section 6166 difficult and much more expensive.

19.6 ISSUES IN COMMUNITY PROPERTY STATES

In general, for purposes of the definition of an interest in a closely held trade or business under Section 6166, in regard to the forty-five owner test of the allowable number of shareholders or partners, the husband and wife are treated as one partner or shareholder if the interest is owned as community property. This also applies if the form of ownership is as joint tenants, tenants by the entireties, or tenants in common.

19.7 FREQUENTLY ASKED QUESTIONS

Question – When will the IRS require a bond of the executor to use Section 6166 deferral?

Answer – The IRS must evaluate the requirement to post bond on a case by case basis and will consider all relevant facts and circumstances, but identified three main non-exclusive factors in Notice 2007-90:

1. The duration and stability of the business;
2. The ability to pay the installments of tax and interest timely;
3. The business' tax compliance history.

Consult the above notice for more detail on the above factors.

Question – Is there an alternative to the requirement that the executor post bond?

Answer – The executor can make an election–under section 6166–to accept an IRS lien in lieu of the executor's personal liability or bond.[54]

The requirements of the lien (which serves to discharge the executor from personal liability and eliminate the requirement of a bond) are:

(1) The executor–and all parties who have an interest in the property subject to the lien–must file an agreement consenting to the lien.

(2) A person must be designated as agent for the persons who consented to the lien and the estate's beneficiaries.[55]

(3) The IRS may require additional lien property if the value of the original property is–or falls below–the total of (a) unpaid taxes and (b) aggregate interest owed.

Question – Once the installment payout period begins, can the IRS terminate it?

Answer – Yes, in certain circumstances. The deferred tax is accelerated (i.e., becomes due immediately) in three situations:

(1) when all of, or a significant portion of, the business is disposed of or liquidated;

(2) when interest or installment payments are not made within six months of the due date; or

(3) if the estate has undistributed net income (there may be an acceleration to the extent of such income).

Question – Why shouldn't an advisor recommend a client plan to rely on using a Code section 6166 installment payout instead of purchasing life insurance?

Answer – First, Code section 6166 cannot be relied upon for any number of reasons. The business interest may fail the mathematical percentage test or the business may be considered an unqualified business. The executor may not be able to post the required bond or may determine the cost of such a bond is exorbitant or unaffordable by the estate. The alternative to a bond is a lien, which itself may be impractical or unacceptable to the estate or the beneficiaries and may hamper business financing.

Second, Code section 6166 is merely the provision that allows the estate to spread out the payment of the estate tax through installment payments. It does not create assets with which to pay the tax. In addition, interest *added* to the tax may substantially increase the total cost.

Moreover, the business must generate sufficient income likely in the form of a dividend to pay tax on the income as well as the interest payable with respect to the installment payments. In any event, *the dollars to make the deferred payments have to come from somewhere–and they will be after-tax (expensive) dollars.*

Third, only a portion of the federal taxes can be deferred in most cases.

The executor will still need the cash to pay:

(a) administrative expenses

(b) debts

(c) the remaining portion of federal estate taxes

(d) state death taxes

(e) income taxes

(f) pecuniary bequests

Fourth, with certain exceptions, successors in interest cannot dispose of the business–or a major portion of it–without triggering an acceleration of the tax (pay it now). If successors do not want to keep and run the family business, a deferral will not be helpful.

Fifth, the executor may remain personally liable for unpaid taxes during the entire deferral period (alternately, the successors-in-interest must submit to a special tax lien to assure the IRS that payment will be made).

Sixth, final distribution to beneficiaries may be delayed over an extended period of time. Most beneficiaries will not want to wait for fourteen years to receive their full share of the inheritance.

Seventh, since all beneficiaries must sign the elective agreement to submit to a lien and discharge the executor from personal liability, guardians may have to be appointed for minors and otherwise incompetent beneficiaries. Those guardians may refuse to sign such an exoneration.

Lastly, as discussed in the *Graegin* loan section, ILIT proceeds are a natural source of funds to lend to an estate, and any interest payable, even if over many years, can be deducted on the estate tax return immediately.

Question – Is there any danger of losing the right to have an extension of time to pay if the estate, as it appears on the estate tax return as filed, qualifies for an extension?

Answer – Yes. The values of the various assets in the estate can be changed upon audit by IRS. Because it is the values ultimately determined that will control, if the IRS increases the value of assets other than the decedent's business, it is possible that the estate will not meet the section 6166 requirements. Audits are quite common when elections are made under these sections. As a result, it is advisable to make a protective election under section 6161 in case an election under section 6166 is disqualified for any reason.

Question – How is the election made under Code section 6166?

Answer – Notice of election under Code section 6166 must be filed on or before the due date (including any extensions) of the U.S. Estate Tax Return[56] (Form 706). No special form of notice is required and a letter addressed to the IRS setting forth the identity of the taxpayer, the amount of tax to be deferred, the identity of the closely held business and the computation of qualification under the applicable section will suffice.

Question – What if, based upon the value set forth on the U.S. Estate Tax Return, the decedent's interest in the closely held business does not qualify under Code section 6166, but it is possible that after examination by the IRS such interest will qualify?

Answer – If the estate does not qualify for a payout of federal estate taxes on the values returned or if the estate does qualify, but no tax is due on the values returned, the executor can file a "protective election." The protective election would set forth the information required under Revenue Ruling 74-499.[57]

Question – In determining the "at least 20 percent" requirement of Code section 6166 for the aggregation of two or more closely held businesses, or whether 20 percent or more of the value of a closely held business is included in the gross estate, can the executor elect to have interests of family members considered as owned by the decedent?

Answer – Yes. The interests of family members can, if elected by the executor, be considered as owned by the decedent in determining the "at least 20 percent" requirement for qualification under section 6166.[58] This election is applicable only to a capital interest in a partnership and to stock that is "not readily tradable."

Question – Can holding company stock qualify for installment payout of estate taxes under section 6166?

Answer – "Yes, but." Only the portion of stock of a holding company (not that of operating subsidiaries) that directly or indirectly owns stock in a closely held active trade or business (so called business company) will be treated as stock in the active company and may therefore qualify.[59] To qualify, the "forty-five or fewer shareholders" or the "20 percent or more" test and the "more than 35 percent" test must be met.

The ability to pay out federal estate taxes attributable to holding company stock may come at some cost. The executor must agree to forego both the deferral of principal payments and the special 2 percent interest rate (and the holding company is only entitled to make installment payments over five years rather than ten years). This adds to the cost of the payout in two important ways: first, the time value of money works against the estate since much more money (the principal of the unpaid estate tax) must be paid much more quickly. Second, the special 2 percent rate is not available.

Question – Can rental activities ever be classified as active businesses to meet the requirements of Section 6166?

Answer – Although the estate will face an uphill battle on this issue, the IRS has ruled that the decedent's rental activities may be classified as closely held businesses for purposes of Code section 6166. These rulings only apply where the decedent took an active role in managing the rental properties, and generally involve such activities as negotiating leases, supervising repairs and maintenance, and dealing directly with tenants.[60]

CHAPTER ENDNOTES

1. I.R.C. §§6151(a), 6075(a), 6166.
2. I.R.C. §§6166(a)(3), 6151(a), 6075(a).
3. I.R.C. §6166(f)(1).
4. I.R.C. §§6601(j)(3), 6621. For 2017 inflation adjustment, see Rev. Proc. 2016-55, §3.45. For 2018 inflation adjustment, increasing amount for estate of decedent dying in year 2018 to $1,520,000, see Rev. Proc 2017-58, §3.45.
5. I.R.C. §6161(a)(2).
6. I.R.C. §6163(a); Treas. Reg. §20.6163-1. This deferral does not apply to future interests created by testamentary act. Treas. Reg. §20.6163-1(a)(1).
7. I.R.C. §6166(a)(1).
8. I.R.C. §2035(d)(4).
9. I.R.C. §6166(c). Property held as community property, joint tenancy, tenancy by the entirety, or tenancy in common, by decedent and decedent's spouse, is included in decedent's estate for purposes of determining the 20 percent ownership requirement.
10. I.R.C. §6166(b)(1); P.L. 107-16, §901.
11. *Id.*
12. I.R.C. §6166(b)(2)(C).
13. Treas. Reg. §20.6166-2(c); Rev. Rul. 75-365, 1975-2 CB 471; Rev. Rul. 75-366, 1975-2 CB 472; Rev. Rul. 75-367, 1975-2 CB 472.
14. I.R.C. §6166(b)(9).
15. I.R.C. §6166(a)(2).
16. I.R.C. §6166(b)(10).
17. I.R.C. §6601(j).
18. I.R.C. §6621(b).
19. I.R.C. §6165; Treas. Reg. §20.2204-1(b).
20. I.R.C. §6324A.
21. *Estate of Roski v. Commissioner*, 128 T.C. 113 (2007).
22. IRS Notice 2007-90, 2007-46 I.R.B. 1003
23. PLR 200721006.
24. I.R.C. §6161.
25. I.R.C. §6161(a)(2).
26. Treas. Reg. §20.6161-1(a)(1).
27. Treas. Reg. §20.6161-1(a)(1), Ex. (1).
28. Treas. Reg. §20.6161-1(a)(1), Ex. (2).
29. Treas. Reg. §20.6161-1(a)(1), Ex. (3).
30. Treas. Reg. §20.6161-1(a)(1), Ex. (4).

31. I.R.C. §6601(a). The regular underpayment rate is determined using the Federal short term rate plus 3 percent. I.R.C. §6621.
32. I.R.C. §6159(b)(2).
33. I.R.C. §6159(b)(2).
34. I.R.C. §§6159(b)(3), (b)(5).
35. I.R.C. §§6159(b)(4), (b)(5).
36. I.R.C. §§6159(b)(4), (b)(5). The regular underpayment rate is determined using the Federal short term rate plus 3 percent. I.R.C. §6621.
37. See RIA Analysis Estate Planning 87,424 "Agreements for payment of tax in installments."
38. I.R.C. §6163(a); Treas. Reg. §20.6163-1.
39. I.R.C. §6163(b).
40. 73-2 CB 405.
41. *Estate of Graegin v Comm'r.*, T.C. Memo 1988-477.
42. Estate of *Duncan v. Comm'r.*, T.C. Memo 2011-255.
43. Estate of *Black v. Comm'r.*, 133 T.C. 340 (2009).
44. *Stick v Comm'r.*, T.C. Memo 2010-192.
45. *Estate of Koons*, T.C. Memo. 2013-94, aff'd (11th Cir. 4/27/2017)
46. PLR 1999-52039 (Sept. 30, 1999), PLR 1999-03-038 (Oct. 2, 1998) and PLR 2000-20011 (Feb. 15, 2000) involved commercial loans.
47. *Estate of Thompson v. Commissioner*, T.C. Memo 1998-325.
48. *Estate of Duncan v. Comm'r*, T.C. Memo. 2011-255 (15 year note approved), *Estate of Murphy v. U.S.*, 104 AFTR 2d 2009-7703 (W.D. Ark. October 2, 2009) (nine year note approved); *Keller v. U.S.*, 104 AFTR 2d 2009-6015 (S.D. Tex. August 20, 2009) (nine year note approved).
49. 2017-2018 Priority Guidance Plan on October 20, 2017, Part 4: "Guidance under §2053 regarding personal guarantees and the application of present value concepts in determining the deductible amount of expenses and claims against the estate."
50. I.R.C. §§6601(a), 6621.
51. I.R.C. §6621(a)(2).
52. I.R.C. §6166(a)(2).
53. I.R.C. §6165. See also, Treas. Reg. §20.6165-1(a) and IRS Notice 2007-90, 2007-46 I.R.B. 1003 issued in response to the Roski case discussed above. Office of Chief Counsel Internal Revenue Service Memorandum CC:PA: BO#: LUD POSTS-113182-07 (February 25, 2009) available online at
54. I.R.C. §6324A.
55. I.R.C. §6324A(c).
56. Rev. Rul. 74-499, 1974-2 CB 397.
57. 74-2 CB 397; see also Rev. Rul. 76-51, 76-1 CB 382.
58. I.R.C. §§6166(b)(1)(B)(i), 6166(b)(7), 6166(b)(8), 6166(b)(9), 6166(g)(1), 6166(g)(2).
59. I.R.C. §6166(b)(8).
60. Priv. Ltr. Rul. 200114005.

GIFT TAX

CHAPTER 20

20.1 INTRODUCTION — THE PURPOSE, NATURE, AND SCOPE OF GIFT TAX LAW

Purpose

If an individual could give away his entire estate during lifetime without the imposition of any tax, a rational person would arrange affairs so that at death nothing would be subject to the federal estate tax. Likewise, if a person could, freely and without tax cost, give income-producing securities or other property to members of his family, the burden of income taxes could be shifted back and forth at will to individuals in lower brackets, and income taxes would be saved.

The federal gift tax was designed to discourage taxpayers from making such *inter vivos* (lifetime) transfers and, to the extent that this objective was not met, to compensate the government for the loss of estate and income tax revenues. Because the gift tax is effectively eliminated for many taxpayers due to the increase to $12,920,000 (2023) of lifetime gift tax exclusion ($25,840,000 for spouses with portability), practitioners should consider gifting techniques that take advantage of this change of paradigm to reduce income tax.

Nature

The gift tax is an excise tax, a tax levied not directly on the subject of the gift itself or on the right to receive the property, but rather on the right of an individual to transfer money or other property to another. The tax is imposed only on transfers by individuals, but transfers by corporations, partnerships or other entities are treated as indirect transfers by the owners.[1]

The gift tax is based on the value of the property transferred.

The gift tax is computed on a progressive schedule based on cumulative lifetime gifts. In other words, the tax rates are applied to total lifetime taxable gifts (all gifts less the exclusions and deductions described in the section on Computing the Tax on Gifts) rather than only to taxable gifts made in the current calendar year. The unified credit is applied to offset the gift tax owing. However, once the annual exclusion and unified credit is exhausted, all additional gifts are taxed at a 40 percent rate, or whatever the rate may be in the year of gift.

Scope

The regulations summarize the comprehensive scope of the gift tax law by stating that "all transactions whereby property or interests are gratuitously passed or conferred upon another, regardless of the means or device employed; constitute gifts subject to tax."[2] Almost any transfer or shifting of property or an interest in property can subject the donor (the person transferring the property or shifting the interest) to potential gift tax liability to the extent that the donor does not receive adequate and full consideration in money or money's worth in exchange for the transferred property, i.e., to the extent that the transfer is gratuitous.

Direct and indirect gifts, gifts made outright and gifts in trust (of both real and personal property), can be the subject of a taxable gift. The gift tax is imposed on the shifting of property rights, regardless of whether the property is tangible or intangible. It can be applied even if the property transferred (such as a municipal bond) is exempt from federal income or other taxes.

The broad definition includes transfers of life insurance, partnership interests, royalty rights, and gifts of checks or notes of third parties. Even forgiveness of a note or cancellation of a debt may constitute a gift. There may be some uncertainty in the law, however, where a donor pays for or provides the use of expensive private jets, yachts and exclusive accommodations for a donee, as has recently been in the news with billionaire Harlan Crow's generosity towards Justice Clarence Thomas.

Almost any party can be the donee (recipient) of a gift subject to tax. The donee can be an individual, partnership, corporation, foundation, trust, or other person. A gift to a corporation or other business entity is typically considered a gift to the other shareholders in proportion to their proprietary interests. Similarly, a gift to a trust is usually considered to be a gift to the beneficiary(ies) in proportion to their interest(s).[3]

In fact, a gift can be subject to the tax (assuming the gift is complete) even if the identity of the donee is not known or ascertainable on the date of the transfer.

20.2 ADVANTAGES OF LIFETIME GIFTS

Nontax-Oriented Advantages

Individuals give property away during their lifetimes for many reasons. Although a detailed discussion of the nontax motivations for lifetime giving is beyond the scope of this chapter, some of the reasons include:

- privacy that would be more difficult to obtain through a testamentary gift;
- potential reduction of probate and administrative costs and delays;
- protection from the claims of the donor's creditors;
- the vicarious enjoyment of seeing the donee use and enjoy the gift;
- the corresponding opportunity for the donor to see how well, or how poorly, the donee manages the business or other property and provide a person of a younger generation practice with saving and investing small amounts of money; and
- provision for the health, education, support, and/or financial well-being of the donee.

Tax-Oriented Advantages

The unification of the estate and gift tax systems was intended to impose the same tax burden on transfers made during life as at death. The disparity of treatment between lifetime and "deathtime" transfers was minimized through the adoption of a cumulative single unified estate and gift tax rate schedule where such death time transfers are stacked on top of lifetime gifts to effectively push up the tax rate for death time transfers.

The American Taxpayer Relief Act of 2012 changed the top rate for gifts to 40 percent for gifts made after 2012. Transfers over $500,000 up to $750,000 are taxed at 37 percent; transfers over $750,000 up to $1,000,000 are taxed at 39 percent and transfers over $1,000,000 are taxed at 40 percent.

These changes can work to the advantage of gifts that are greater than the amount protected by the gift tax unified credit in some circumstances. For example, it may make sense to make a gift and pay gift tax in one year if the tax rate would be higher if the gift were made in a later year. However, if the estate tax is reduced or eliminated by a further increased estate tax unified credit, reduced estate tax rates, or repeal of the estate tax in the year of death, then incurring gift tax could be a mistake.

Regardless, there are still some significant advantages for making gifts.

First, an individual can give up to $17,000 (in 2023, adjusted annually for inflation) gift tax-free every year ("annual exclusion") to each of an unlimited number of donees. This means that a person who desires to gift $17,000 to each of his four children and four grandchildren could give a total of $136,000 each year (periodically increasing with inflation) without gift tax liability. (This gift tax annual exclusion is described in greater detail later in the chapter.)

The annual exclusion gifts of an individual's spouse can be aggregated with the annual exclusion gifts of the other spouse. Thus, every year, a married couple can transfer gift tax free up to $34,000 (2023) of money or other property, multiplied by an unlimited number of donees. In the example above, the donor and spouse together could combine their annual exclusion gifts to give up to $272,000 annually on a gift tax-free basis. In fact, if the other spouse consents, one spouse can make the entire combined annual exclusion gift ($34,000) to be treated as if both spouses each made a $17,000 annual exclusion gift. This is known as gift splitting. Split-gift provisions are also covered later in the chapter in the section on Computing the Tax on Gifts.

Gift tax-free transfers can translate into significant federal estate tax savings. Consider the estate tax savings potential if the amount given to the donees over the life expectancy of the donor is invested (in life insurance, annuities, mutual funds, etc.). Figure 20.1 illustrates the potential estate or generation-skipping transfer tax savings possible if a forty-year-old donor split gifts to five donees over his life expectancy. This is a very conservative number, because it does not even account for the inflation increase from $14,000 to $15,000 in 2018, or more recent or future periodic inflation increases.

A second tax incentive for making an *inter vivos* as opposed to testamentary (deathtime) gift is that if a gift is made more than three years prior to a decedent's death, the amount of any gift tax paid on the transfer is not brought back into the computation of the gross estate. In the case of a sizable gift, avoidance of the "gross up rule" can result in meaningful tax savings. Gross up rule means that all gift tax payable on taxable gifts made within three years of death are included in calculating the value of the gross estate even if the gift itself is not added back. For example, if after exhausting the unified credit, an individual makes a $2 million taxable gift (beyond the annual exclusion), the $800,000 gift tax payable on that transfer (40 percent of $2,000,000) will not be brought back into the estate tax computation if the gift was made more than three years before the donor's death. By contrast, if the gift had not been made (all other things being equal and ignoring growth), and the $2,800,000 had remained in the individual's estate, the estate tax would have been $1,120,000 (40 percent of $2,800,000). This is a net tax savings of $320,000 for using an extremely simple and straightforward technique (ignoring income tax basis ramifications which will depend on the asset gifted and growth after the gift).

Third, any appreciation accruing between the time of the gift and the date of the donor's death escapes estate taxation. This may result in a considerable estate tax (as well as probate and any state estate or inheritance tax) saving. If a father makes a taxable gift of stock to his daughter (above the annual exclusion amount) with a value of $100,000 and it grows to $600,000 by the date of the father's death, only the $100,000 value of the taxable gift enters into the final estate tax computation. The $500,000 of post gift appreciation does not enter into the computation of an adjusted taxable gift, totally avoiding taxation with no push up of the decedent's marginal estate tax bracket.

An excellent way of making use of this advantage is a gift by an insured beneficiary of a life insurance policy more than three years prior to his death to an adult beneficiary or to an irrevocable trust for adult or minor beneficiaries. For example, a $1,000,000 death benefit could be removed from a donor's estate at the

Figure 20.1

ESTATE TAX OR GST TAX ADVANTAGE OF THE GIFT TAX ANNUAL EXCLUSION	
Donor's Age	40
Donees' Annual After-Tax Return On Gifts	4.00%
Amount Of Unused Annual Exclusion (with gift splitting between husband and wife)	$28,000
Number Of Donees	5
Donor's Life Expectancy (YEARS)	43
Total Amount Of Gifts ($28,000/year/donee x 5 donees x 43 years)	$6,020,000
Donor's Projected Estate Tax Bracket	40.00%
Potential Estate Tax Savings	$2,408,000
Projected Value Of Gifts At Life Expectancy (43 years)	$15,401,7330
Potential Estate Tax Savings If Annual Gifts Invested By Donees At Compound Interest	$6,160,693
*Computations Courtesy – NumberCruncher Software: http://Leimberg.com	

Figure 20.2

ADVANTAGE OF INCOME SHIFTING - CHILD 21 OR OLDER				
Investment				$100,000
Rate of Return				10%
Parent's Tax Rate				33%
Parent's After Tax Rate of Return				6.7%
Child's Tax Rate				15%
Child's After Tax Rate of Return				8.5%

	Accumulated Value		Advantage
Years	Parent (6.7%)	Child (8.5%)	of Gift
5	$138,300	$150,366	$12,066
10	$191,269	$226,098	$34,829
15	$264,525	$339,974	$75,449
20	$365,838	$511,205	$145,367

cost of only the gift tax on the value of the policy at the time of the transfer (in the case of a whole life policy, usually roughly equivalent to the policy cash value plus unearned premiums at the date of the gift). If the insured lives for more than three years after the transfer and the premium payments made by the insured (also considered to be gifts to the beneficiaries of the trust) qualify for the annual exclusion, there would be no additional gift tax and none of the appreciation (the difference between the death benefit payable and the adjusted taxable gift if any at the time the policy was transferred) would be included in the insured's estate.

Fourth, there are often strong income tax incentives for making an *inter vivos* gift such as shifting taxable income from a high-bracket donor to a lower-bracket donee (due to the "kiddie tax", however, the savings from the shift may be limited if the donee is under age twenty-four and still a student). For example, shifting $10,000 of annual income generated by income-producing securities, real estate, or other property gifted by a taxpayer in the 40 percent federal and state combined income bracket to a donee in a combined 20 percent bracket would save $2,000 of income tax each year. Actually, since the property, and not just income from the property, is transferred, the income tax savings can be even greater after compounding. As illustrated by Figure 20.2, the year-in year-out income tax savings may far exceed the estate tax savings. The $12,920,000 (2023) lifetime exemption equivalent may be large enough to enable taxpayers to make multiple gifts to and from family members in order to take advantage of the income tax savings.

Fifth, gifts of the proper type of assets made more than three years prior to death may enable a decedent's estate to meet the mathematical tests for a Code section 303 stock redemption, Code section 6166 installment payout of taxes, or the Code section 2032A special-use valuation of farms and certain other business real property.

Sixth, no gift taxes have to be paid until the transferor makes *taxable* gifts in excess of the gift tax unified credit exemption equivalent or applicable exemption amount. Only taxable gifts in excess of a donor's unused exemption equivalent will require the donor to make an out of pocket payment of gift taxes.

20.3 TECHNICAL DEFINITION OF A GIFT

Elements of a Gift

Under common law, a gift is defined simply as a voluntary transfer of property for no consideration. But for tax law purposes, neither the statutes nor the regulations specifically define the term "gift." However, the regulations dealing with the valuation of gifts provide that

$$\frac{\text{Value of property transferred} - \text{Consideration received}}{\text{Gift}}$$

in cases where property is transferred for less than adequate and full consideration in money or money's worth.

Note that this definition focuses on whether the property was transferred for adequate and full consideration in money or the equivalent of money, rather than on whether the transferor intended to make a gift. This is because Congress did not want the IRS to have to prove something as intangible and subjective as the state of mind of the transferor. This does not completely negate the importance of donative intent, but, instead of probing the transferor's actual state of mind, an examination is made of the objective facts of the transfer and the circumstances in which it was made.

Certain factors are considered by courts to determine if there was the "intent" to make a gift:

(1) Was the donor competent to make a gift?

(2) Was the donee capable of accepting the gift?

(3) Was there a clear and unmistakable intention on the part of the donor to absolutely, irrevocably, and currently divest himself of dominion and control over the gift property?

Assuming that these three objective criteria are met, three other elements must be present. There must be

(1) an irrevocable transfer of the present legal title to the donee so that the donor no longer has dominion and control over the property in question;

(2) a delivery to the donee of the subject matter of the gift (or the most effective way to command dominion and control of the gift); and

(3) acceptance of the gift by the donee.

Although all these requirements must be met before a gift is subject to tax, the essence of these tests can be distilled into the following factors (with reference to state law to determine the presence or absence of these elements):

(1) There must be an intention by the donor to make a gift.

(2) The donor must deliver the subject matter of the gift.

(3) The donee must accept the gift.

Adequate And Full Consideration in Money or Money's Worth Defined

Sufficiency of Consideration Test

Since the measure of a gift is the difference between the value of the property transferred and the consideration received by the transferor, a $100,000 building that is transferred from a mother to her daughter for $100,000 in cash clearly does not constitute a gift. However, the mere fact that consideration has been given does not mean there is no gift; to be exempt from the tax the consideration received by the transferor must be equal in value to the property transferred. This is known as the "sufficiency of consideration test." If the daughter in the example above had paid $60,000, the difference between the value of the building and the consideration paid, $40,000, would be considered to be a gift.

Effect of Moral, Past, or Nonbeneficial Consideration

Consideration is not "in money or money's worth" when the consideration is moral consideration, past consideration, or consideration in the form of a detriment to the transferee that does not benefit the transferor.[4] The classic example is a man who transferred $100,000 to a widow in exchange for a promise to marry him. Upon remarriage she would forfeit a $100,000 interest in a trust established for her by her deceased husband; the $100,000 from her fiancé was to compensate her for the loss. The Supreme Court held that the widow's promise to marry her fiancé was not sufficient consideration because it was incapable of being valued in money or money's worth. Nor was her forfeiture of $100,000 in the trust sufficient consideration, because in spite of giving up something of value, it was of no benefit to the fiancé/transferor.

Consideration in Marital Rights and Support Rights Situations

Two issues often arise in connection with the consideration question: Does the relinquishment of marital rights and/or support rights constitute consideration in money or money's worth?

Code section 2516 specifically addresses the gift tax treatment of certain marital property settlements.[5] To that point, transfers of property or property interests made under the terms of a written agreement between spouses in settlement of marital or property rights are deemed to be for an adequate and full consideration. Such transfers are therefore exempt from the gift tax, whether or not the agreement is supported by a divorce decree, if the spouses enter into a final decree of divorce within two years after entering the agreement. So, for example, if a husband agrees to give his wife $10,000 as a lump-sum settlement on divorce in exchange for her release of all marital rights in his estate, the $10,000 transfer is not subject to the gift tax if the stated requirements above are met. But even where the two-year requirement was not met, a taxpayer successfully argued that the transfer was not voluntary and was therefore not a gift.

A spouse's relinquishment of the right to support constitutes consideration that can be measured in money or money's worth. Likewise, a transfer in satisfaction of the transferor's minor children's right to support is made for money's worth. But most transfers to (or for the benefit of) adult children are generally treated as gifts unless, for some reason, state law requires the transferor to support that child.

PLR 201707007 highlights a very creative trust solution to divorce settlement for a closely held business owner that exploited this gift tax exception (names added to PLR for clarity):

Example. Sam, a business owner, established a trust for his wife, Claire, with half his stock, granting Claire income annually from it for life. The trustee has the discretion to make distributions of principal to Claire, but is prohibited from distributing ABC Company shares to Claire or from selling ABC Company shares in order to make such principal distributions. In addition, when the trust holds assets other than ABC Company stock, Claire will have the right to withdraw the greater amount of a or b percent of the principal for the trust each year. The trust does not grant Claire any powers to appoint trust property either during her life or upon death. In exchange, Claire will relinquish all marital rights and property claims that she might have acquired while married to Sam. Upon Claire's death, the remaining trust principal will revert to Sam or Sam's estate if Sam predeceases Claire.

The IRS agreed to four rulings:

1. The IRS ruled that the transfer was not a "sale or exchange" because IRC 1041(a) provides that no gain or loss is recognized on a transfer of property from an individual to (or in trust for the benefit of) (1) a spouse, or (2) a former spouse, if the transfer is incident to a divorce.

2. No gift tax on Claire's share - no need to comply with marital deduction trust rules. The trust was not intended, and did not need to follow, rules for *inter vivos* QTIP or GPOA marital trusts under Code section 2523. The reason there is no gift of Claire's interest is because of her quid pro quo (giving up her spousal property rights), which is deemed to be full and adequate consideration and not to be a taxable gift if pursuant to divorce under Code section 2516. No marital deduction is needed!

3. No gift tax on Sam's retained reversion, and no Chapter 14 application. As noted above, the interest granted to Claire is not a gift because it is incident to property division in divorce. Had the trust named children as beneficiaries upon Claire's death, there would have been a taxable gift. But here, there was no taxable gift at all - Sam retained all the rest of the interest in the trust via reversion to him or his estate, so Chapter 14 did not apply.

4. Not all of the trust is included in Sam's estate if he dies first, only the value of his reversionary interest. The fair market value of the trust property on Sam's date of death (or the alternate valuation date) would be reduced by the fair market value of Claire's outstanding income interest (determined in accordance with the valuation tables of Treasury Regulation Section 20.2031-7), causing inclusion in Sam's gross estate upon his death under Code sections 2036(a)(1) and 2036(a)(2).

This PLR highlights a useful and creative solution whenever a richer divorcing spouse has wealth tied up in family business – in this case the husband probably had most of his wealth tied up in the family business, and wanted some controls over the stock and was probably willing to give up more income/support if some controls over disposition of the stock could be obtained, which the solution in this PLR accomplished.

GIFT TAX

Transfers Pursuant to Compromises or Court Orders

Consideration is an important factor where a transfer is made pursuant to compromises of bona fide disputes or court orders. Such transfers are not considered taxable gifts because they are deemed to be made for adequate and full consideration. For example, if a mother and daughter are in litigation, a compromise payment by the mother to the daughter is not a gift. However, if a court is not convinced that an intrafamily dispute was resolved in a bona fide arm's length adversary proceeding, a gift tax will be imposed. For example, a settlement payment to a son who threatened to contest his father's will was considered a taxable gift.

Likewise, if there is no adversary proceeding, a gift may occur with respect to a transfer made pursuant to (or approved by) a court decree. For instance, if an incompetent person's property were transferred to his mother, the transfer would be a gift even though it was approved by court decree (assuming the incompetent had no legal duty to care for the parent).

Types of Gifts

Direct Gifts

Most gifts are transfers of cash or tangible personal property. Generally, delivery of the property itself consummates the gift. In the case of corporate stock, a gift occurs when endorsed certificates are delivered to the donee or his agent or the change in ownership is delivered to the corporation or its transfer agent. Gifts of real property are typically completed by the delivery of an executed deed (not necessarily the later filing with the county recorder).

If a person purchases a U.S. savings bond registered in someone else's name and delivered to that person, a gift has been made. If the bonds are titled jointly between the purchaser and another, no gift occurs until the other person has cashed in the bond or has the bond reissued in his name only. See, "Requirements for a Completed Gift," later in this chapter.

Income that will be earned in the future can constitute a gift presently subject to tax. For example, an author can give his right to future royalties to his daughter. Such a gift is valued according to the present value of the future income rather than as a series of year-by-year gifts valued as the income is paid. Current valuation is made even if, for some reason, the payments are reduced substantially or even cease. No adjustment of the value of the gift is required or allowed if the actual income paid to the donee is more or less than the valuation.

Forgiving a debt in nonbusiness situations is more likely to be a gift. For example, if a father lends his son $100,000 and later cancels the note, the forgiving of the loan is the equivalent of a $100,000 gift. On the other hand, if the father lends his son $100,000 and the initial agreement is that the loan is repayable immediately upon the father's demand (assuming an arm's length transaction), no gift is made. However, if the father simply forgives annual exclusion amounts of principal a year, this will likely be treated as a de facto gift of the $100,000 in year one.[6]

Some forgiveness of indebtedness, however, results in taxable income to the debtor. If a creditor tore up a debtor's note in return for services rendered by the debtor, the result is equivalent to the creditor compensating the debtor in cash for those services in the amount of the discharged debt that the debtor used to satisfy the debt. In that case, the debt forgiveness results in taxable compensation to the debtor rather than a gift. There are some exceptions to this "discharge of indebtedness" income.[7]

Payments in excess of one's legal obligations may constitute a gift. Clearly paying one's bills is not a gift. Similarly, paying bills or purchasing food for a spouse or minor children is not a gift. Courts have allowed considerable latitude with regard to these types of payments. But if a father gives his minor daughter a $50,000 ring, the IRS may claim the transfer goes beyond his obligation of support. Payments made on behalf of adult children such as paying an adult son's living expenses or mortgage payments, or provides a monthly allowance are considered gifts.

In another situation, pursuant to an agreement incorporated in a divorce decree, the taxpayer created two trusts funded with a substantial amount of money for the support of his minor children. According to the terms of the trust, the children were to receive the trust corpus at age twenty-one. The court determined the economic value of the father's support obligation and held that the excess of the trust corpus over that value was a taxable gift. Only the portion of the transfer required to support the children during their minority was not considered to be a gift.

311

Indirect Gifts

Indirect gifts, such as the payment of someone else's expenses, are gifts. For instance, making an adult son's car payments or premium payments on a life insurance policy insuring the parent's life owned by a daughter are gifts. There is an exception for paying another's medical and educational tuition expenses directly to the provider.[8]

Simply shifting of property rights alone may trigger gift tax consequences. In one case, an employee who gave up his vested rights to employer contributions in a profit-sharing plan was deemed to have made a gift to the remaining participants in the plan. Similarly, an employee with a vested right to an annuity who irrevocably opts to take a lesser annuity coupled with an agreement that payments will be continued to be made to a designated beneficiary has made a gift to that beneficiary. No gift occurs until the time the employee's selection of the survivor annuity becomes irrevocable.

A third-party transfer may also result in a taxable gift. For example, if a father gives his son $100,000 in consideration of his son's promise to provide a lifetime income to the father's sister, the father has made an indirect gift to his sister. Furthermore, if the cost of providing a lifetime annuity for the sister is less than $100,000, the father also has made a gift to his son.

The creation of a family partnership may involve an indirect gift. The mere creation or existence of a family partnership (which is often useful in shifting and spreading income among family members and in reducing estate taxes) does not, per se, mean a gift has been made. But if the value of the services of some family member partners is nil or minimal and earnings are primarily due to assets other than those contributed by the partners in question, the creation of the partnership (or the contribution by another partner of assets) may constitute a gift.

At the other extreme, in cases where new partners are to contribute valuable services in exchange for their share of the partnership's earnings and where the business does not contain a significant amount of capital assets, the formation of a family partnership does not constitute a gift.

Transfers by and to corporations are often forms of indirect gifts. Technically, the gift tax is not imposed upon corporations. But transfers by or to a corporation are considered to be made by or to corporate stockholders. The regulations state that if a corporation makes a transfer to an individual for inadequate consideration, the difference between the value of the money or other property transferred and the consideration paid is a gift to the transferee from the corporation's other shareholders. For example, a gratuitous transfer of property by a family-owned corporation to the father of the shareholders of a corporation could be treated as a gift from the children to their father.

Generally, a transfer to a corporation for inadequate consideration is treated as a gift from the transferor to the corporation's other shareholders.[9] For example, a transfer of $120,000 by a father to a corporation owned equally by him and his three children is treated as a gift of $30,000 from the father to each of the three children. (The amount of such a gift is computed after subtracting the percentage of the gift equal to the percentage of the transferor's ownership.)

A double danger lies in corporate gift situations. For example, if a family-owned C corporation sold property with a fair market value of $450,000 for $350,000 to the son of its shareholders, the IRS may argue that (1) the corporation has essentially made a taxable dividend distribution to its shareholders and (2) that the shareholders in turn made a gift to the recipient of the transfer. In other words, since any distribution from a corporation to a shareholder generally constitutes a dividend to the extent of corporate earnings and profits, the IRS could claim that a transfer was first a constructive dividend to the shareholders and then a constructive gift by them to the donee. Based on this analysis, the transaction could be considered to be a $100,000 constructive dividend to the shareholder-parents (the amount the son "underpaid" the corporation for the property), followed by a $100,000 constructive gift of that dividend to their son.

Life insurance or life insurance premiums can constitute an indirect gift in three types of situations: (1) the purchase of a policy for another person's benefit, (2) the assignment of an existing policy, and (3) payment of premiums. (The first two of these three situations are discussed directly below. Premium payments are discussed in the property valuation section later in the chapter.)

If an insured purchases a policy on his life and

(1) names a beneficiary(ies) other than his estate, and

(2) does not retain the right to regain the policy or the proceeds or revests the economic benefits of the policy (i.e., retains no reversionary interest in himself or his estate); and

(3) does not retain the power to change the beneficiaries or their proportionate interests (i.e., makes the beneficiary designation irrevocable),

the insured has made a gift measurable by the cost of the policy (provided all three requirements have been met).

If an insured makes an absolute assignment of a policy or in some other way relinquishes all his rights and powers in a previously issued policy, there is a gift measured by the replacement cost (in the case of a whole life policy generally equal to the interpolated terminal reserve plus unearned premium at the date of the gift).

This scenario may lead to an insidious tax trap known as the "Goodman Triangle."[10] Assume a wife owns a policy on the life of her husband that names her children as revocable beneficiaries. At the death of the husband, the IRS would argue that the wife has made a constructive gift to the children. In this example, the gift is equal to the entire amount of the death proceeds as if she received the proceeds and then gave the funds to her children. The result would be the same if the owner were a revocable trust for the benefit of the children that became irrevocable upon the insured's death.

Does the right to use property (such as money) at no charge constitute a gift of property? Yes, interest-free and below market rate loans between family members and friends are treated as taxable gifts. A gift tax is imposed on the value of the right to use the borrowed money, the so-called "foregone interest" (see Chapter 40), generally a statutory minimum rate of interest the money could earn in the given situation. (By this reasoning, a gift of the use of real estate or other property, such as a vacation home or car, at little or no rent would seem to be a gift, but the IRS has been focusing on property interest transfers rather than permitted-use cases.)

20.4 GRATUITOUS ARRANGEMENTS THAT ARE NOT TAXABLE GIFTS

A number of common gratuitous arrangements are not considered gifts in the tax sense. These arrangements fall into three basic categories:

1. where property or an interest in property has not been transferred;

2. certain transfers in the ordinary course of business; and

3. sham gifts.

The Requirement That Property or an Interest in Property be Transferred

Gratuitous Services Rendered

The gift tax is imposed only on the transfer of property or an interest in property. Although the term property is given the broadest possible meaning, it does not include services that are rendered gratuitously. Regardless of how valuable the services one person renders for the benefit of another person, those services do not constitute the transfer of property rights and do not, therefore, fall within the scope of the gift tax.

Difficult questions often arise in this area. For example, if an executor performs the multiplicity of services required in the course of the administration of a large and complex estate, the services are clearly of economic benefit to the estate's beneficiaries. Yet, since services are just that, they do not constitute a transfer of property rights. If the executor formally waives the fee (within six months of appointment as executor) or fails to claim the fees or commissions by the time of filing and indicates through action (or inaction) that he intends to serve without charge, no property has been transferred.

Conversely, once fees are taken (or if the fees are deducted on an estate, inheritance, or income tax return), the executor has received taxable income. If he then chooses not to (or neglects to) actually receive that money and it goes to the estate's beneficiaries, he is making an indirect (and possibly taxable) gift to those individuals.

Disclaimers (Renunciations)

In some cases an intended donee may decide (for whatever reason) that he or she does not want or does not need a gift another person intends to make. For example, a trust may provide him or her with a remainder interest in trust corpus. On the other hand, if the intended donor disclaims the right to the gift (refuses to take it), it will usually go to someone else as the result of that renunciation.

By disclaiming, the intended transferee is in effect making a gift transfer of the intended property interest to the new recipient subject to the gift tax unless the disclaimer is a "qualified disclaimer." By making a qualified disclaimer, the property interest is treated as being transferred directly from the original transferor to the person who actually receives it. In other words, the person who makes a qualified disclaimer is not treated as the donor of a taxable gift to the person to whom the property interest passes. This makes the qualified disclaimer an important estate-planning tool.

Disclaimers are discussed in detail in Chapter 13.

Promise to Make a Gift

Although income that will be earned in the future can be the subject of a gift, the promise to make a gift in the future is not considered a taxable gift if the promise is unenforceable. This is because a mere promise to make a transfer in the future is not itself a transfer. On the other hand, if the promise is legally enforceable under state law, the IRS will not consider it to be a taxable gift as long as it cannot be valued. When it does become capable of valuation, the IRS may take the position that the promising party has made a taxable gift.

At the end of calendar year 2012, there was a lot of interest in this technique as a way to utilize the estate tax exemption in the event the exemption was to be later reduced. Arguably, if the promise is enforceable under local law, and is made for less than full and adequate consideration in money or money's worth, it should be treated as a taxable gift. There is significant disagreement between commentators with regard to the success of this technique or whether it would receive the blessing of the IRS, a debate which may be revived in 2025 with the potential drastic reduction in the applicable exclusion amount scheduled after December 31, 2025.[11]

Transfers in the Ordinary Course of Business

Compensation for Personal Services

Situations often arise in business settings that purport to be gifts from corporate employers to individuals. The tax code presumes that such transfers are, in fact, taxable compensation for personal services rather than income tax-free gifts.[12] As a result, the employee would receive taxable income and the corporate employer (or its owners) would not be deemed to have made a taxable gift.

To this point, the applicable regulations state that "the gift tax is *not* applicable to...ordinary business transactions."[13] An ordinary business transaction, defined as a sale, exchange, or other transfer of property (a transaction which is bona fide, at arm's length, and free from donative intent) made in the ordinary course of business, will be considered as if made for an adequate and full consideration in money or money's worth.

A transfer "free from donative intent" will be considered an ordinary business transaction. This means that donative intent becomes quite important as the taxpayer-recipient would prefer the treatment of the transfer as an income tax-free gift. On the hand, the IRS may prefer the transfer to be treated as taxable compensation.

When will a payment be considered an income tax-free gift to the recipient (potentially subject to gift tax owning by the donor) rather than taxable income? In the ordinary course of business, the transferor has made a gift if the dominant reason for making the transfer was detached and disinterested generosity. For example, flood relief payments made by an employer to his employees because of a feeling of affection, charity, or similar impulses has made a gift to those employees rather than consideration for past, present, or future services.

Conversely a transfer by an employer to an employee is not a gift if the primary impetus for the payment is (a) the constraining force of any legal or moral duty, or (b) anticipated benefit of an economic nature.

Among the factors typically studied in examining the donor's intent are:

(1) the duration and value of the employee's services;

(2) the manner in which the employer determined the amount of the reputed gift; and

(3) the way the employer treated the payments in corporate books and on tax returns, i.e., was the payment deducted as a business expense? (The corporation's characterization of payment is

often persuasive where the corporation makes a payment or series of payments to the widow of a deceased employee. The employer generally prefers to have such payments treated as taxable compensation (for the employee's past services) so that the corporation can take a corresponding deduction.

In one case, a business friend gave the taxpayer who furnished him is the names of potential customers a car. The impetus for the transfer was payment for past services as well as an inducement for the taxpayer to supply additional names in the future. For that reason, the transfer of the car was not a gift.[14] In another case, an employer had made a $20,000 payment to a retiring executive. After examining the employer's esteem and kindliness, and the appreciation of the retiring officer, the court found the transfer to be a gift rather than taxable income to the officer. In a similar case, the Supreme Court came to the same conclusion when it found payments were made "from generosity or charity rather than from the incentive of anticipated economic benefit."[15]

Whether a transfer is a gift or compensation is settled on a case-by-case basis after an analysis of the circumstances evidencing motive or intent. Generally, an intrafamily transfer will be considered a gift, even if the recipient rendered past services. On the other hands, transfers to persons outside the family will usually be considered compensation.

Bad Bargains

A bad bargain is another ordinary course of business transaction, i.e., a sale, exchange, or other property transfer made in the ordinary course of business that is treated as being made in return for adequate and full consideration in money or money's worth. This assumes the transaction is (a) bona fide, (b) at arm's length, and (c) not donative in intent.

There are a number of cases in which a bad bargain was not treated as a gift from the taxpayer who was on the short side of the bargain. In one case,[16] certain senior executive shareholders sold stock to junior executives at less than fair market value pursuant to a plan arranged to give the younger executives a larger stake in business profits. Although the transfers were for less than adequate consideration, the Tax Court stated that "the pertinent inquiry for gift tax purposes is whether the transaction is a genuine business transaction, as distinguished, for example, from the marital or family type of transaction." Bad bargains, sales for less than adequate money's worth occur every day in the business world for one reason or another; but no one would think for a minute that any gift is involved, even in the broadest sense of the term gift.[17]

But the ordinary course of business exception does not apply where the transferor's motive was to pass on the family fortune to the following generation. In one case, a father transferred property to his children at a price below the fair market value. In return, he received noninterest-bearing notes, rather than cash, and he continued to make certain payments with respect to the property on the children's behalf. Based on these facts, the court concluded that the father was not dealing with his children at arm's length. It is possible that the same result could occur if the father employed the son at a wage of $50,000 a year, but the son rendered services worth only $20,000 a year. The IRS could claim that the $30,000 difference constituted a gift.

Sham Gifts

If the taxpayer's goal is to shift the burden of income taxes from a high- to a relatively lower-bracket relative age eighteen or older, it would be advantageous to characterize the transfer of the property necessary to generate such income as a gift. But if the transfer has no real economic significance other than the hoped-for tax savings, the courts and the IRS will recognize that fact and will therefore not allow the shift the burden of income taxation contemplated by the parties. For example, a well-known golfer contracted with a motion picture company to make a series of pictures depicting his form and golf style. In return, the golfer was to receive a lump sum of $120,000 plus a 50 percent royalty on the earnings of the picture. But before any pictures were made, he sold his father the right to his services for $1. The father, in turn, transferred the rights to the contract to a trust for his son's three children. The court held that the entire series of transactions lacked any tax effect and that the income was completely taxable to the golfer.

These types of transactions may subject to the "step transaction" doctrine. Under this doctrine, the IRS can combine a series of actions which – individually - may technically comply with the tax code, but when viewed together serve no economic purpose other than to obtain tax savings. When the doctrine applies, the IRS will view the purely tax-motivated series of steps as a single integrated event and tax it accordingly. That said, the Sixth Circuit recently rebuffed the IRS for its broad use of the step transaction doctrine.[18]

Assignments of Income

Assignment of income questions are among the most common, and also confusing, in the tax law, because the property, gift, and income tax results are often inconsistent. For example, a person enters an agreement to give his son one-half of every dollar he earned in the following year. Although the agreement may be legally enforceable and effective for property law purposes, it would like be treated as a gift from the father to his son in the amount of the present value of a father's future income. Yet, for income tax purposes, the father would remain taxable on the earnings because a taxpayer who earns income cannot relieve himself of his obligation to pay the corresponding tax by assigning the right to that income to another person.

Similarly, a general agent for a life insurance company assigned renewal commissions to his wife who then had a property law right to the commissions. The present value of the assigned renewals was treated as a gift. Yet, under assignment of income principles, the general agent was taxable on the commissions as they were paid. In a similar case, a doctor transferred the right to accounts receivable from his practice to a trust for his daughter. Again, the court held that as the trustee received payments from the doctor's patients, those sums were taxable income to the doctor even though he had made an irrevocable and taxable gift to his daughter through the trust.

Gifts of income from property meet a similar fate. For example, if a person assigns the right to next year's rent from a building to her daughter or next year's dividends from specified stock to her grandson, the transfers will be effective for property law purposes and be treated as a taxable gift potentially subject to gift tax. On the other hand, all income will be taxable to the donor.

Gifts of property, however, produce a more satisfactory result to the donors; by analogy, if the tree (property) is given away, the fruit (income) it bears will be taxable to the tree's new owner. Thus, if instead of giving the donee the right to the income from the building or the stock (the fruit), the donor had given away the actual building and the stock (the tree); there would have been a taxable gift equal to the value of those properties. Subsequently, post-transfer, because the daughter and grandson now own the property (the tree); they are taxed on the income produced by those assets (the fruit). The tax moral of this example is that in order to shift the burden of taxation with regard to the fruit, the donor must gift away the tree.

One exception to this, however, may be the use of incomplete gift, non-grantor trusts (a.k.a. INGs).[19] After a series of taxpayer-friendly private letter rulings, however, the IRS has stopped issuing PLRs and placed INGs on its "no ruling" list in Rev. Proc. 2021-3, Section 5.01.

20.5 EXEMPT GIFTS

A few types of gratuitous transfers are specifically exempted in the Code from the gift tax. Examples include property transferred to an alternative beneficiary through a qualified disclaimer as well as certain transfers of property between spouses in divorce and separation agreements.

Tuition paid directly to an educational institution for the education or training of an individual is exempt from the gift tax regardless of the amount paid or the relationship of the parties.[20] This means parents, grandparents, or even friends can pay private school or college tuition directly to the educational institution for an individual without fear of incurring a gift tax.

Still another exempt transfer is the direct payment of medical care. Any donor can pay for another's medical care without making a taxable gift potentially subject to gift tax.[21] This allows children or other relatives or friends to pay the medical expenses of needy individuals (or anyone else) without worrying about incurring a gift tax.

The amount of the medical and tuition exclusion is unlimited, and may include prepayment as long as the amounts are non-refundable.[22]

20.6 REQUIREMENTS FOR A COMPLETED GIFT

A transfer subject to potential gift tax must be complete. The phrase "completed transfer" implies that the subject of the gift is now beyond the donor's reach, i.e., that he has irrevocably parted with dominion and control over the gift. Thus, there is no completed gift if the donor retains the power to change the disposition of the gift and thus alter the identity of the donee(s) or amount of the gift. More technically stated, if the donor can (alone or in conjunction with a party who does not have a substantial amount to lose by the revocation) revoke the gift, it is not complete.

Parting with dominion and control is a good test of completeness, but in a number of cases it is difficult to ascertain just when that event occurs. Some of the more common problem areas are (a) incomplete delivery, (b) cancellation of notes, and (c) incomplete transfers to trusts.

When Delivery is Complete

Incomplete delivery involves transfers where certain technical details have been omitted or a stage in the process has been completed. For example, a transfer of personal check or note is not a completed gift until it is paid (or certified or accepted) by the drawee or it is negotiated for value to a third person. For instance, if a check is mailed in December, received in late December, but not cashed until January of the following year, no gift is made until that later year. This is because, typically, the maker of a check can cancel the check and is under no legal obligation to honor the check until it is cashed (presented for payment or negotiated to a third person for value). Likewise, a gift of a negotiable note is not complete until it is paid. For this reason, terminally ill donors or those gifting at the end of the year who have taxable estates and want to use their annual exclusion for the year should gift cash, cashier's checks or use electronic transfers to avoid this issue.

An individual on his deathbed will sometimes make a gift *causa mortis* (in anticipation of his imminent death) and then quite unexpectedly recover. Assuming that the facts indicate (1) the transfer was made in anticipation of death from a specific illness and that (2) the gift was contingent on the occurrence of the donor's death, neither the original conveyance nor the return of the property to the donor is subject to the gift tax if the transferor recovers and the transferee returns the property. A gift *causa mortis* is therefore incomplete as long as the donor is alive, but becomes complete at the donor's death.

A gift of stock is completed on the date the stock was transferred or the date endorsed certificates are delivered to the donee (or his agent) or to the corporation (or its transfer agent).

Transfer of U.S. government bonds is governed by federal law, rather than by state law. Even if state law requirements for a valid gift are met, for tax purposes no completed gift has been made until the registration is changed in accordance with federal regulations. For example, if a grandmother purchases a U.S. savings bond that is registered as payable to her and to her two children as co-owners, no gift is made to the grandchildren until one of them surrenders the bond for cash.

The creation of a joint bank account (checking or savings) constitutes a common example of an incomplete transfer. Typically, the person making a deposit can withdraw all of the funds or any portion of them. Therefore, the donor has retained a power to revoke the gift and it is not complete. When the donee makes a withdrawal of funds from the account (and thereby eliminates the donor's dominion and control), a gift of the funds occurs.

A similar situation occurs in the case of a joint brokerage account; the creation and contribution to a joint brokerage account held in "street name" is not a gift until the non-contributing joint owner makes a withdrawal for his personal benefit. At that time, the donee acquires indefeasible rights and the donor parts irrevocably with the funds. Conversely, if a person calls her broker and says, "Buy one hundred shares of Texas Oil and Gas and title them in joint names, mine and my husband's, with rights of survivorship," the purchase constitutes a gift to her husband. He has acquired rights that he did not have before to a portion of the stock. (No gift tax would be due in this case, due to the unlimited gift tax marital deduction described below.)

Totten trusts (bank savings accounts where the donor makes a deposit for the donee (Joanne Q. Donor in trust for James P. Donee) and retains possession of the savings book) are, typically, revocable transfers. Many states have specific "payable on death" (POD) statutes governing such accounts. Here again, because the donor can recover the entire amount deposited, no gift occurs until the donee makes a withdrawal of funds.

Some property cannot conveniently be delivered to the intended donee; farm property is a good example. Where it would be difficult or impossible to make physical delivery of the gift, a gift will usually be considered completed where the delivery is as complete as possible. In one case, a father owned cattle he wished to give his minor children. The court held that the gift was complete when he branded the livestock with each child's initials, even though he kept the cattle with others he owned. The court held that the father was acting as the natural guardian of the children and had done everything necessary to make a completed gift.

Real estate is transferred by executing a deed in favor of the donee. But if the donor retains the deed, does not record it, makes no attempt to inform the donee of the transfer, and continues to treat the property as his own, no transfer occurs.

Cancellation of Notes

In many cases, property is transferred pursuant to an installment sale in which the transferee executes notes payable to the transferor. Although the transaction will be treated as a sale for income tax purposes, if the transferor forgives the notes, the discharge could result in a taxable gift subject to potential gift tax.

Cancellation of notes is a frequently used as a gifting technique for two reasons. First, it provides a simple means of giving gifts to a number of donees of property that is not readily divisible. Second, by forgiving the notes over a period of years, the donor could maximize the use of the annual exclusion and increasing applicable exclusion amount. A good example is a situation where the donor deeds real estate to her sons and takes back notes payable serially on an annual basis. Each son is required to pay his mother $15,000 per year. But when the notes become due, the donor marks the note "cancelled by gift." The gift would occur in the year each note was cancelled, provided there is no preestablished and predetermined plan for the donor to forgive notes on a systematic basis in future years (however, the IRS can certainly argue this, so it is generally best to avoid such arrangements).

Although, in the example above, the annual exclusion would eliminate the gift tax consequences, each note cancellation would trigger taxable income to the donor since she is actually selling the real estate to her sons. Under the installment reporting rules, in spite of the fact that the donor forgives each note, the amount of gain the donor would recognize with respect to each note must nonetheless be included in her gross income for income tax purposes.[23] Stated differently, it is as if each of her sons paid her the $15,000 as each note became due (with respect to which she would have income) and, in turn, she gifted the $15,000 back to them.

Incomplete Gifts in Trust

Donors will sometimes transfer property to a trust, but retain the right to revoke the transfer. For that reason, property transferred to a revocable trust is not a completed gift. Only when the donor relinquishes all his retained control over the transferred property (i.e., when the trust becomes irrevocable) is a completed gift made.

The amount of the gift tax is based on the value of the property or property interest at the moment the gift becomes complete, rather than the time of the transfer. For example, if the donor retains the power to alter the interests of the trust beneficiaries, even if he cannot exercise any powers for his own benefit, the transfer is not complete. This can have harsh gift tax consequences particularly if the value of the transferred property substantially appreciates subsequent to the transfer.

For example, assume a donor transfers stock to a trust for his two children and three grandchildren. Income is payable to the donor's children for life, with the remainder to be distributed to his grandchildren or their estates. If the donor retains the power to vary the amount of income his children will receive or to reach into corpus to enhance their security, the gift is incomplete. However, if and when the donor relinquishes this control, the gift will be complete. If this occurs when the stock has substantially increased in value, as is often the case, the gift tax payable by the donor would potentially be much greater than it would have been had the gift been completed when it had been initially transferred into the trust.

Grantor Retained Annuity Trusts (GRATs) and to a lesser extent Grantor Retained Unitrusts (GRUTs) are attractive gifting vehicles because the amount of the gift is determined by the value of property interest at the time the gift is complete. By making a gift to an irrevocable nonreversionary trust, but reserving an annuity or unitrust interest for a specified period of years, the grantor/donor reduces the taxable value of the gift (this is because the value of the property retained by the grantor is not considered part of the gift). The gift is the difference between the value of the transferred asset and the actuarial value of the interest retained by the grantor. (See Chapter 29 regarding GRATs and GRUTs.)

When many years after the grantor created the trust, the property is ultimately distributed from the trust to the intended beneficiaries, it may have appreciated significantly. Because appreciation occurring after the gift is completed is not considered part of the gift, none of it is subject to gift tax. So when the gift was initially completed any gift payable was offset by the unified credit and that was the end of it. In essence, this "leverages" the unified credit, because a much smaller amount of the credit was used to offset the gift when its value was significantly less.

20.6 VALUATION OF PROPERTY FOR GIFT TAX PURPOSES

Valuation is the first step in the gift tax computation process. Only after the property is valued can the annual exclusion and various deductions be applied in arriving at the amount of the taxable gift and the ultimate gift tax. (See Chapter 70 regarding "Valuation Planning.")

The value of the property on the date the gift becomes complete is the amount of the gift. Value, for gift tax purposes, is defined as "the price at which the property would change hands between a willing buyer and a willing seller, neither being under any compulsion to buy or to sell, and both having reasonable knowledge of relevant facts."[24]

Although the valuation of gifts is similar to the valuation of estate property valuations, gifts are valued on the date of the gift with no alternate valuation date.

The following variables make certain gift valuations problematic:

- indebtedness with respect to transferred property
- restrictions on the use or disposition of property
- transfers of large blocks of stock
- valuation of mutual fund shares
- valuation of life insurance and annuity contracts.

Indebtedness with Respect to Transferred Property

Generally, when gifted property is encumbered or otherwise subject to an obligation, only the net value of the gift, the value of the property less the amount of the obligation, is subject to the gift tax. This result assumes the donor is *not* personally liable for the debt so the amount of the gift is the donor's equity in the property.

However, if the donor is personally liable for the secured indebtedness on the gift property, a different result occurs. Assuming the donor remains personally liable with respect to the debt, the amount of the gift may be the entire value of the property, unreduced by the debt. The reason for the difference is that where a solvent donor makes a gift subject to a debt and the creditor proceeds against the pledged property, the donee is, in effect, paying the donor's personal debt. In some cases, this makes the donee a creditor of the donor. If the donee can then collect from the donor the amount he has paid to the donor's creditor, the donee has received the entire value of the gift, rather than merely the equity.

Example. Assume the donor transfers a $100,000 building subject to a $40,000 mortgage on which he is personally liable. If the donor's creditors collect the $40,000 by proceeding against the pledged building and the donee is subrogated to that creditor's rights against the donor-debtor (i.e., the donee now stands in the shoes of the creditor), the donee can collect an additional $40,000 from the donor. As a result, the gift would be the entire value of the building (unreduced by the debt).

A third possibility is that the donor-debtor is personally liable for the indebtedness secured by a mortgage on the gifted property, but the donee has no right to step into the creditor's shoes and recover the debt from the donor. In this case, the amount of the gift is merely the amount of the donor's equity in the property. In the example above, that amount would be $60,000 ($100,000 fair market value minus $40,000 of indebtedness).

Where the donee has no right to proceed against the donor and recover the debt, actual facts must determine the result. If the donor, in fact, pays off the liability after transferring the mortgaged property to the donee, he is making an additional gift. But if the donee pays off the liability (or if the mortgagee forecloses), the gift was only the donor's equity.

Among the obligations that could be imposed upon a donee is a requirement that the donee pay the gift tax. This is called a "net gift." Although the donor has primary liability to pay the gift tax, and the donee is secondarily liable. The donor could expressly, or by implication, require the donee to pay the donor's gift tax liability. If the donee is required to pay the gift tax imposed on the transfer (or if the tax is payable out of the transferred property), the value of the donated property must be reduced by the amount of the gift tax. But the gift tax computation is based on the value of the property transferred. Obviously, the two figures, the net amount transferred and the tax payable on the transfer, are interdependent. Fortunately, there is a revenue ruling formula for making the computation.

An example of the net gift calculation[25] follows.

TRUE TAX ON NET GIFT

Year	2017
Tentative Taxable Gift	$6,000,000
Gift Tax on $6,000,000	$2,345,800
Unified Credit	$2,117,800
Tentative Tax [$2,345,800 – 2,117,800]	$228,000
Tax Rate	40%
True Tax [$228,000 ÷ (1 + .40)]	$162,857
Net Gift [$6,000,000 – 162,157]	$5,837,843

It is important to note that, for income tax purposes, the Supreme Court has held that if the donee pays the gift tax or where the payment is made from gifted property, the donor must recognize any income taxable gain. The amount of gain recognized is the difference between the gift tax paid and the donor's basis for the property.[26] It is as if the donor sold the property for an amount equal to the gift tax, realized a gain, and then gave the remaining value of the gift property to the donee. Thus, unless the donee is a grantor trust, be careful to examine the potential for this effect when someone gifts low basis property using a net gift agreement.

Restrictions on the Use or Disposition of Property

The value of property received by gift is affected by restrictions placed on the donee's use of, or ability to dispose of such property. Although as a general rule, the most restrictive agreements do not fix the value of such property, they often have a persuasive effect on price. For example, a donor gives stock to his daughter subject to an agreement between the corporation and its shareholders. Under that agreement, the corporation is entitled to purchase those shares at their book value, $30 per share, upon the retirement or death of the shareholder.

As set forth in the above example, does a restrictive agreement fix the value of the shares at book value? Obviously, no buyer would pay more than $30 a share as long as that restriction was in effect. But if there is value to the stock other than sale values (for example, if the stock paid dividends of $10 a year) it may have a fair market value in excess of $30. On the one hand, the corporation's option right to purchase the stock at $30 a share limits the fair market value, but on the other hand the right to receive dividends increases the fair market value. How much the dividend flow increases the fair market value of the stock is largely dependent on how much time may pass before the corporation is able to exercise its option and on the probability that the corporation would in fact exercise it.

In the example above, a court would probably hold that the existence of a restrictive agreement would not fix the purchase price, since at the time of the transfer the donor was alive and not yet retired. But the existence of the agreement itself is likely to have a depressing effect on the market value of the stock and should result in a discounted gift tax value. (However, see discussion of Code section 2703 in Chapter 47 and Code section 2704 in Chapter 70 regarding restrictions that may be disregarded when valuing property.)

Transfers of Large Blocks of Stock

Another principle that applies, to some degree, to both lifetime and deathtime gifts is the so-called blockage rule. The blockage rule is not based on forced sale value. Instead, it attempts to value gifts of large blocks of stock based on the price the property would bring if the stock were liquidated in a reasonable time in some way outside the usual marketing channels. The marketability (and therefore the value) of a massive number of shares of stock may have a lower value than the current per share market value of the same stock, because of the depressive effect a block of stock would have on the market if sold all at one time. The utility of blockage evaluation is diminished, and may be inapplicable, when a large block is divided among a number of donees or when gifts are spread over a number of tax years.

Valuation of Mutual Fund Shares

Mutual fund shares are valued at their net asset value, the price of the fund net of any load charge.

Valuation of Life Insurance and Annuity Contracts

When a life insurance policy is gifted to an individual or a trust, the value is the policy's replacement value: the cost of similar or comparable policies issued by the same company. If the policy is transferred immediately (within the first year) after its purchase, the gift is equal in value to the gross premium paid to the insurer.

If the policy is paid up at the time it is assigned (or is a single-premium policy), the amount of the gift is the amount of premium the issuing company would charge for the same type of single-premium policy of equal face amount on the insured's life, based on the insured's age at the transfer date. Although impaired health of the insured is not considered by the regulations, it is possible that the IRS would argue that the adverse health of the insured at the time of the gift may affect valuation.

If the policy is in a premium-paying stage at the time it is transferred, the value of the gift is generally equal to the sum of (a) the interpolated terminal reserve, plus (b) unearned premiums on the date of the gift.

Except in the early years of most contracts, the interpolated terminal reserve is roughly equivalent to the policy's cash value. In special conditions, such as where the interpolated terminal reserve does not approximate the policy's true value (for example, if the insured donor was terminally ill and had only one or two months to live), the value of a premium-paying policy may be more than the sum of the interpolated terminal reserve plus unearned premiums as of the date of the gift. (Unearned premiums are defined as the proportionate part of the last premium paid that is attributable to the remainder of the period for which the premium was paid.)

For example, Mr. Martin owned an ordinary life policy on his partner's life to fund a cross-purchase agreement. The policy was nine years and four months old at the time of Mr. Martin's death. The gross annual premium was $2,800, and Mr. Martin died four months after the most recent "premium due" date. Assuming no accrued dividends or policy loans, the policy would be valued as follows:

Terminal reserve at end of 10th year	$14,601
Terminal reserve at end of 9th year	12,965
Increase (10th year)	$ 1,636

Portion of year between death of Mr. Martin and last preceding premium due date is 4/12 (1/3) of a year. 1/3 of increase in reserve (1/3 of $1,636)	$ 545
+	
Terminal reserve – end of 9th year	12,965
=	
Interpolated terminal reserve at date of Martin's death	13,510
+	
2/3 of gross premium	1,867
Total value of insurance policy	$15,377

The interpolated reserve method will be allowed as long as the contract is not an unusual contract and this method does not develop an amount that varies greatly from the true value of the contract.

Premiums paid by (or on behalf of) the donor after the transfers are also gifts. Therefore, when an owner of a life insurance policy irrevocably assigns that policy to another person or a trust, each premium he pays subsequent to the transfer is considered a gift to the new policy owner (or the beneficial owner[s] of the trust's assets).

Usually, the premium payor and the donor are the same. However, the IRS has stated that if an employee assigns his group life insurance policy to an irrevocable trust he had established for his family, a cash premium paid by the employer is deemed to be a gift of the amount of the premium. The deemed gift is from the employee to the beneficiaries of the trust. But (in a rather poorly considered and not widely accepted ruling) the assignment of the group term coverage itself was held not to be a taxable gift because the coverage had no ascertainable value.

In a split-dollar arrangement, an interest in a life insurance policy is often assigned to a trust. See Chapter 34, on life insurance, regarding the valuation of such interests.

20.7 COMPUTING THE TAX ON GIFTS

Gift tax rates are applied to a net figure, taxable gifts. Before the tax on a transfer is computed, certain reductions are allowed. These reductions may include:

(1) annual exclusion (including gift splitting)

(2) a marital deduction

(3) a charitable deduction

The Annual Exclusion

Purpose of and Effect of the Annual Exclusion

Generally, the annual exclusion allows the donor to make, tax free, up to $17,000 (in 2023) worth of gifts (other than "future-interest gifts" as they are defined below) to any number of persons each year. In one respect, it is a *de minimis* rule for gift giving. The purpose of *de minimis* rule is to avoid the necessity of administrative record keeping for relatively small items. The gift tax annual exclusion is a classic example as it was instituted to eliminate the need for a taxpayer to keep an account of or report numerous small gifts. Congress intended that the amount of the annual exclusion be set large enough so that no reporting would be required in the case of wedding gifts or other occasional gifts of relatively small amounts.

Significantly, annual exclusion gifts do not count against the unified credit. Thus, a donor can make as many gifts as he or she desires without using any of the applicable exclusion amount so long as none of the gifts exceed the annual exclusion amount.

Example. In a single calendar year (2021), Asher makes $15,000 gifts to each of his five children and four grandchildren, or a total amount of $135,000. To date, Asher has not used any of his applicable exclusion amount ($11,700,000 in 2021) to offset any taxable gifts. In this instance, since none of Asher's gifts exceed the annual exclusion amount, none of them need to be offset by the applicable exclusion amount. As a result, Asher's entire exclusion amount remains intact. Conversely, if Asher had gifted $20,000 to each of his children and grandchildren, each gift would have been $5,000 over the exclusion. Thus, Asher's applicable lifetime exclusion amount would be reduced by $45,000 ($5,000 for each of the nine donees) to $11,655,000 ($11,700,000 minus $45,000).

Effect of Gift Splitting Coupled with Exclusion

Gift splitting, which applies only to gifts by a married donor to a third party and only with respect to non-community property, was introduced into the tax law to equate the tax treatment of common-law taxpayers with that of community-property residents. When one spouse earns a dollar in a community-property state, fifty cents is deemed to be owned by the other spouse automatically and immediately. Therefore, if the couple gave that dollar to their daughter, each spouse would be treated as having given only fifty cents.

If an individual is married and his or her spouse consents to splitting a gift, each spouse is deemed to have made one-half of the gift. This means that both spouses can combine their individual annual exclusions to make larger gifts without using any of the applicable exclusion amounts. It does not matter how much each spouse contributes to the gift or whether one spouse makes the entire gift. The privilege of gift splitting is available only with regard to gifts made while the couple is married. Therefore, gifts the couple makes before they are married may not be split, even if they are later married during the same calendar year. Likewise, gifts made after the spouses are legally divorced or one spouse dies may not be split. But gifts made before one spouse dies may be split; even if that spouse dies before signing the appropriate consent or election, the deceased spouse's executor can make the appropriate election or consent. If the spouses elect to split gifts to third parties, all gifts made by either spouse during that reporting period must be split.

Example. In 2021 (when the annual exclusion was $15,000), Asher made the following gifts: $20,000 to his brother, $28,000 to his father and $18,000 to his son, or a total of $66,000. Asher is married to Ashley and she consents to splitting the gifts. As illustrated in Figure 20.3, even though each gift exceeds Asher $15,000 annual exclusion by some amount, when combined with Ashley's $15,000 annual exclusion, there are no taxable gifts as well as no reduction of either or their applicable exclusion amounts (assuming Ashley did not make significant gifts to the same people).

GIFT TAX   CHAPTER 20

Figure 20.3

Donee	Amount of Gift to Donee	Treated as if Donor Asher Gave	Exclusion	Subject to Tax	Treated as if Nondonor Ashley Gave	Exclusion	Subject to Tax
Brother	$ 20,000	$ 10,000	$ 10,000	—	$ 10,000	$ 10,000	—
Father	$ 28,000	$ 14,000	$ 14,000	—	$ 14,000	$ 14,000	—
Son	$ 18,000	$ 9,000	$ 9,000	—	$ 9,000	$ 9,000	—
Totals	$ 66,000	$ 33,000	$ 33,000	—	$ 33,000	$ 33,000	—

Present versus Future Interest

As significant as the annual exclusion is, it only applies to "present-interest gifts." This means any "future-interest gift" regardless of the amount is a taxable gift and must be offset by the donor's applicable exclusion amount. A present interest is one in which the donee's possession or enjoyment begins at the time the gift is made. Conversely, with respect to a future interest, the donee's possession or enjoyment will not commence, if at all, until sometime in the future. Examples of a "future interest" and includes reversions, remainders, and other interests or estates, whether vested or contingent, and whether or not supported by a particular interest or estate, which are limited to commence in use, possession, or enjoyment at some future date or time.

An easy way to distinguish between a present interest (which qualifies for the gift tax annual exclusion) and a future interest (which does not qualify for the gift tax exclusion) is to ascertain:

> At the moment of the gift, did the donee have an immediate, unfettered, and actuarially ascertainable legal right to use, possess, or enjoy the property in question?

If the answer is "Yes," the gift is a present interest. If the answer is "No," the gift is a future interest gift.

Clearly, the outright and unrestricted gift of property to a donee (even a minor) that passes legal and equitable title is a present-interest gift.

A single gift can be split into two parts: one a present interest that qualifies for the annual exclusion and the other a future interest that does not.

Example 1. In 2021, a widowed donor transfers income-producing property in a newly created trust. The income is payable annually to the donor's son for life. At the son's death, the remainder is to be distributed to the donor's grandson. The gift of an annual income interest to the son is a present-interest gift, since he has unrestricted right to its immediate use, possession, or enjoyment (the right to annual income commencing immediately). Assuming a 5.0 percent section 7520 rate, if the son is thirty years old at the time of the gift and $100,000 is placed into the trust, the present value of that gift would be worth $87,677 ($100,000 times .87677, the present value of the stream of income produced by $100,000 of capital and payable annually over the life expectancy of a thirty-year-old, according to tables in government regulations). Of the gifted $87,677, $15,000 would be sheltered by the annual exclusion in 2021. The balance, $72,677 would be a taxable gift offset by an equivalent amount of the donor's applicable exclusion amount.

On the other hand, the gift of the remainder interest to the grandson is a future interest gift because his enjoyment of the gift will not occur until the death of his father. For that reason, none of it would be eligible for the annual exclusion. So regardless of its value, the full amount of the future interest gift would be a taxable gift.

Example 2. A donor and his spouse create a trust that provides their son income for ten years after which the principal is to be distributed to their grandson. Assuming a 5.0 percent section 7520 rate, if the donor had placed only $1,000 in the trust, the exclusion for the gift of the income interest would be $386 ($1,000 times 0.386087, the term certain income interest valuation factor). Due to the relatively small amount of the present interest gift as compared to a much larger annual exclusion, gift splitting would probably not be necessary unless they intended to make additional gifts to the same donee.

As to the gift of the future interest (remainder) that passes to the grandson at the end of ten years, the annual exclusion is not available even though he has an interest that cannot be forfeited. For that reason, regardless of its value, all of it will count against the donor's applicable exclusion amounts (one-half to each spouse).

Importantly, if instead of an income interest for life or a term of years, the trustee had been given the power or discretion to accumulate the income, rather than distribute it, it would not be a present interest gift for the lack of the unfettered and immediate use of the income. For that reason, no annual exclusion would be allowed. Similarly, if a trustee is required by the trust agreement to accumulate income for a time (or until the occurrence of a specified event), the income interest is a future interest.

Crummey trusts, discussed in Chapter 34 on Life Insurance Trusts, are a common solution to the issues in these two examples.

Summary of Rules for Ascertaining the Amount and Availability of the Gift Tax Annual Exclusion

These rules regarding the annual exclusion can be summarized as follows:

(1) In determining the number of annual exclusions to which a donor is entitled, a gift in trust is a gift to a trust's beneficiaries, and not to the trust.

(2) If the trustee is required to distribute trust income at least annually, the value of an income interest in a trust qualifies for the exclusion even if the value of the remainder interest does not.

(3) The gift of an interest that is contingent upon survivorship is a gift of a future interest. (For example, if a trust provides income to the grantor's son for life, then income to the grantor's daughter for life, the son's gift is a present interest gift, but the daughter's gift is a future interest gift).

(4) A gift is a future interest if enjoyment depends on the exercise of a trustee's discretion. (The nature of the interest must be present as of the date of the gift, not determined by what the trustee may subsequently do, or not do, in the exercise of a discretionary power.)

(5) A gift must have an ascertainable value to qualify for the exclusion. (The exclusion will be denied if the donor or anyone else can divert the income from the beneficiary.)

Identity of Donees

A gift made to a trust is considered a gift to the beneficiaries of the trust (not the trust itself). For instance, if there are three life income beneficiaries, there are three potential annual exclusions. Conversely, if a donor created five trusts for the same beneficiary, only one exclusion is allowed. Technically, the actuarial value of each gift in the five trusts to that beneficiary would be totaled. That total would be added to any direct gifts the donor made to that beneficiary for purposes of computing to what extent the annual exclusion would be available to shelter those gifts.

A transfer to a corporation is treated as a gift to its shareholders. However, the gift is one of a future interest.[27]

Transfers to two or more persons as joint tenants with right of survivorship, tenants by the entireties, or tenants in common are considered multiple gifts. Each tenant is deemed to receive an amount equal to the actuarial value of his interest in the tenancy. If, for example, one person has a one-half interest in a tenancy in common, a cash gift of $6,000 to the tenancy would be treated as a $3,000 gift to that person. This would be added to other gifts made directly by the same donor to determine how much of the exclusion is available. Similarly, gifts to partnerships should follow the same rules: a gift to a partnership should be treated as if made to each partner in proportion to his partnership interest.

Note that a joint gift, in which neither party can sever his or her interest without the other's consent, will be considered a future interest gift and will not qualify for the annual exclusion. For instance, if Herb gives his daughters Diana and Laura joint ownership in a policy on his life, and if the insurer will not allow either Diana or Laura to sever her interest without the other's consent, Herb has made a future interest gift to each daughter.

Gifts to Minors

Outright gifts to minors pose no particular qualification problem. In Revenue Ruling 54-400,[28] the IRS ruled that "an unqualified and unrestricted gift to a minor, with or without the appointment of a guardian, is a gift of a present interest." But there are, of course, practical problems involved, especially with larger gifts. Although minors can buy, sell, and deal with some limited types of property, such as U.S. savings bonds, gifts of other types of property create difficulties. For example, some states do not give minors the legal capacity to purchase their own property, care for it, or sell or transfer it. Some states forbid the registration of securities in a minor's name, and a broker may be reluctant to deal in securities titled in a minor's name. In many states, a minor has the legal ability to disaffirm a sale of stock sold at a low price that later rises in value. Furthermore, a buyer receives no assurance of permanent title when a minor signs a real estate deed.

Legal guardianship of the minor is not a viable answer in many situations. Since guardianship laws are rigid, a guardian must generally post bond, and periodic and expensive court accounting is often required. A parent who is a natural guardian of a child usually does not automatically become a guardian of a child's estate (assets) without a court hearing and appointment. Most importantly, a parent may not want to give a legal minor control over a large amount of cash or other property.

To minimize these and other practical problems involved with most large gifts to minors, such transfers are generally made in trust or to a UTMA custodian. An incredible amount of litigation developed over whether such gifts qualified for the annual exclusion. Code section 2503 provides clear and precise methods of qualifying gifts to minors for the exclusion. There are three basic means (aside from Crummey trusts discussed elsewhere) of qualifying gifts to minors under section 2503:

1. a section 2503(b) trust (a.k.a. mandatory income trust);

2. a section 2503(c) trust; or

3. a custodian under the state Uniform Transfers to Minors Act.

Section 2503(b) Trust. To obtain an annual exclusion for gifts to a trust, an individual can establish a trust that requires that income *must* be distributed at least annually to or for use of the minor beneficiary. The trust agreement would state how income is to be used, and would give the trustee no discretion as to its use. The minor would receive possession of the trust principal whenever the trust agreement specifies. A distribution does not have to be made by age twenty-one; corpus may be held for as long as the beneficiary lives, or for any shorter period of time. In fact, the principal can actually bypass the income beneficiary and go directly to the individuals whom the grantor, or even the named beneficiary, has specified. The trust agreement can also control the dispositive scheme if the minor dies before receiving trust corpus. Trust assets do not have to be paid to the minor's estate or appointees.

Mandatory payment of income to (or on behalf of) beneficiaries seems onerous, especially while the beneficiary is a minor. But such income could be deposited in a custodial account and used for the minor's benefit, or left to accumulate in a custodial account until the minor reaches majority (at which time the unexpended amount would be turned over to the beneficiary).

Although the entire amount of property placed in a Section 2503(b) trust would be considered a gift, for exclusion purposes it would be split into two parts: income and principal. The value of the income, measured by multiplying the amount of the gift by a factor that considers both the duration over which the income interest will be paid and the discounted worth of $1 payable over the appropriate number of years, would be eligible for the annual exclusion. The balance of the gift would not qualify for the annual exclusion.

Example. Assume a donor places $10,000 into a Section 2503(b) trust that is required to pay his ten-year-old daughter all income until she reaches age twenty-five. Assume a 5.0 percent

Section 7520 rate. The present value of the income the daughter would receive over those fifteen years is $5,190 ($10,000 × .518983, see term certain valuation tables). If the income were payable for her entire life, the present value would jump to $9,417 ($10,000 × .94171, see single life valuation tables).

It is important to note that, according to at least one revenue ruling, the annual exclusion would be denied for a Section 2503(b) trust that permits principal to be invested in non-income-producing securities, non-income-producing real estate, or life insurance policies (since they do not produce taxable income).

Section 2503(c) Trust. The section 2503(b) trust described above has the advantage of not requiring distribution of principal at the minor's reaching age twenty-one, but it does require a current (annual) distribution of income. The section 2503(c) trust requires the distribution of income and principal when the minor reaches age twenty-one. But it does not require the trustee to distribute income currently.

Certain requirements make it possible for a donor to obtain the exclusion by a gift to a minor under section 2503(c): the trust must provide:

1. the income and principal may be expended by or on behalf of the beneficiary; and

    a. to the extent not so expended income and principal will pass to the beneficiary at age twenty-one; or

    b. if the beneficiary dies prior to that time, income and principal will go to the beneficiary's estate or appointees under a general power of appointment.

The annual exclusion will not be lost merely because local law prevents a minor from exercising a general power of appointment. Typically, the age to execute a power of appointment would be eighteen.

A substantial amount of flexibility can be built into the Section 2503(c) trust. Income that has been accumulated in the trust, as well as any principal, can be paid over to the donee when he reaches age twenty-one. This may be indicated if the sums involved are not substantial. But the donor may want the trust to continue to age twenty-five or some other age. It is possible to provide continued management of the trust assets and, at the same time, avoid forfeiting the annual exclusion by giving the donee, at age twenty-one, a right for a limited but reasonable period to require immediate distribution by giving written notice to the trustee. If the beneficiary fails to give written notice, the trust can continue automatically for whatever period the donor provided when he established the trust. Some states have lowered the age of majority from twenty-one to age eighteen or some in between age. A trust can provide that the distribution can be made between the age of majority and age twenty-one without jeopardizing the Section 2503(c) exclusion. (The rule is that age twenty-one is the maximum, rather than the minimum, age at which the right to trust assets must be made.)

A Section 2503(c) trust has a number of advantages over the type of custodianship found in the Uniform Gifts to Minors Act or Uniform Transfers to Minors Act arrangements, as shown in Figure 20.4.

Uniform Gifts (Transfers) to Minors Act. The Uniform Gifts to Minors Act or the Uniform Transfers to Minors Act (reference to either Act herein is simply to the Uniform Act; see Chapter 9 for background) provides an alternative to the section 2503(c) trust. The Uniform Act is frequently utilized for smaller gifts because of its simplicity and because it offers the benefits of management, income and estate tax shifting, and the investment characteristics of a trust, with little or none of the setup costs.

The Uniform Act is also indicated over a trust if the gift consists of stock in an S corporation. That's because, generally speaking, a trust (other than a voting, electing small business trust, QSST, or grantor trust) cannot hold S corporation stock without causing a loss of the election privilege. The result might be double taxation of corporate profits and forfeiture of the privilege of passing through profits (and losses) to shareholders. (See the discussion of QSSTs and Code section 678 Trusts in Chapter 53.)

By way of example, in Pennsylvania, a state that has a variation of the Uniform Transfers to Minors Act, a custodianship gift may be made as follows:

20 Pa C.S. §5309. Manner of creating custodial property and effecting transfer

   (a) Creation of custodial property.–Custodial property is created and a transfer is made whenever:

Figure 20.4

Factor	Trust	UGMA	UTMA
Type of property	Donor can make gifts of almost any type of property	Type of property must be permitted by appropriate statute. Gift of real estate may not be permitted	Donor can make gifts of almost any type of property
Dispositive provisions	Donor can provide for disposition of trust assets if donee dies without having made disposition	Disposition must follow statutory guideline	Disposition must follow statutory guideline
Investment powers	Trustee may be given broad virtually unlimited investment powers	Custodian limited to investment powers specified by statute	Custodian limited to investment powers specified by statute
Time of distribution of assets	Trust can continue automatically even after beneficiary reaches age 21. Trustee can make distribution between state law age of majority and age 21	Custodial assets must be paid to beneficiary upon reaching statutory age	Custodial assets must be paid to beneficiary upon reaching statutory age, however, many states now permit extending UTMA age to 25 rather than 21

(1) An uncertificated security or a certificated security in registered form is either:

    (i) registered in the name of the transferor, an adult other than the transferor or a trust company, followed in substance by the words: "as custodian for (name of minor) under the Pennsylvania Uniform Transfers to Minors Act"; or

    (ii) delivered if in certificated form, or any document necessary for the transfer of an uncertificated security is delivered, together with any necessary endorsement to an adult other than the transferor or to a trust company as custodian, accompanied by an instrument in substantially the form set forth in subsection (b).

(2) Money is paid or delivered to a broker or financial institution for credit to an account in the name of the transferor, an adult other than the transferor or a trust company, followed in substance by the words: "as custodian for (name of minor) under the Pennsylvania Uniform Transfers to Minors Act."

(3) The ownership of a life or endowment insurance policy or annuity contract is either:

    (i) registered with the issuer in the name of the transferor, an adult other than the transferor or a trust company followed in substance by the words: "as custodian for (name of minor) under the Pennsylvania Uniform Transfers to Minors Act"; or

    (ii) assigned in a writing delivered to an adult other than the transferor or to a trust company whose name in the assignment is followed in substance by the words: "as custodian for (name of minor) under the Pennsylvania Uniform Transfers to Minors Act."

(4) An irrevocable exercise of a power of appointment or an irrevocable present right to future payment under a contract is the subject of a written notification delivered to the payor, issuer or other obligor that the right is transferred to the transferor, an adult other than the transferor or a trust company, whose name in the notification is followed in substance by the words: "as custodian for (name of minor) under the Pennsylvania Uniform Transfers to Minors Act."

(5) An interest in real property is recorded in the name of the transferor, an adult other than the

transferor or a trust company, followed in substance by the words: "as custodian for (name of minor) under the Pennsylvania Uniform Transfers to Minors Act."

(6) A certificate of title issued by a state or the Federal Government which evidences title to tangible personal property is either:

(i) issued in the name of the transferor, an adult other than the transferor or a trust company, followed in substance by the words: "as custodian for (name of minor) under the Pennsylvania Uniform Transfers to Minors Act"; or

(ii) delivered to an adult other than the transferor or to a trust company, endorsed to that person followed in substance by the words: "as custodian for (name of minor) under the Pennsylvania Uniform Transfers to Minors Act."

(7) An interest in any property not described in paragraphs (1) through (6) is transferred to an adult other than the transferor or to a trust company by a written instrument in substantially the form set forth in subsection (b).

(b) Form.–An instrument in the following form satisfies the requirements of subsection (a)(1)(ii) and (7):

TRANSFER UNDER THE PENNSYLVANIA UNIFORM TRANSFERS TO MINORS ACT

I, (name of transferor or name and representative capacity if a fiduciary), hereby transfer to (name of custodian), as custodian for (name of minor) under the Pennsylvania Uniform Transfers to Minors Act, the following: (insert a description of the custodial property sufficient to identify it).

Dated: _____

_____
(Signature)

(name of custodian) acknowledges receipt of the property described above as custodian for the minor named above under the Pennsylvania Uniform Transfers to Minors Act.

Dated: _____

_____
(Signature of custodian)

(c) Control of Custodial Property.–A transferor shall place the custodian in control of the custodial property as soon as practicable.

The Effect of Type of Asset

The type of asset given and restrictions placed on that asset may prevent the donor from obtaining the annual exclusion.

An outright no strings attached gift of life insurance will qualify for the annual exclusion. Life insurance policies (and annuity policies) are subject to the same basic test as any other type of property in ascertaining whether the interest created is "present or future," even though the ultimate obligation under a life insurance policy, payment of the death benefit, is to be discharged in the future. A policy does not have to have cash value at the time of the gift to make the transfer one of a present interest. But the annual exclusion would be lost if the donor prevented the donee from surrendering the policy or borrowing its cash value or limited the donee's right to policy cash values in any way.

When a life insurance policy is transferred or otherwise assigned to a trust, will the transfer of policy cash values constitute a present interest? The answer depends on the terms of the trust. Generally, the gift will be one of a future interest, since beneficiaries are not usually given an immediate right to possession or enjoyment of the policy values or other items constituting trust corpus. For example, a trust will typically provide no payments to beneficiaries unless they survive the insured. Furthermore, there is generally no actuarially sound method of making an allocation between the value of a present interest and future interest. Unless the given beneficiary's present interest can be ascertained, no exclusion is allowed. (A related attack used by the IRS is that insurance is non-income-producing property. This concept is discussed further below.)

Premium payments will usually be considered present- or future-interest gifts depending on the classification of the policy itself; if the assignment of the policy was considered a present interest, premiums paid by the donor after the transfer will qualify for the annual exclusion. For instance, if a person makes an absolute assignment of a policy on his life to his daughter but continues to pay premiums, premiums paid subsequent to the transfer would be present-interest gifts. Conversely, if the gift of the policy was a future interest, premium payments made by the donor after the transfer may also be considered future-interest gifts.

A gift in trust of a life insurance policy or of premiums can be made a present interest by inserting a *Crummey* power (named after the major case in this area). A *Crummey* power gives the named individual(s) an immediate, unfettered, and actuarially ascertainable right; in short, the absolute right to withdraw a specified amount or portion of the assets contributed to the trust. This withdrawal right (essentially, a general power of appointment over a specified amount or portion of each year's contribution to the trust) makes the gift in trust of a life insurance policy or of premiums qualify for the gift tax annual exclusion. The holder of the Crummey power must be made aware of any contribution to the trust and the limited time period within which he or she has the right to withdraw the contribution. Obviously, the person who made the gift does not want the child withdrawing the gift (or the donor would have made an outright gift in the first place).

Clearly, an outright gift of non-income-producing property will qualify for the gift tax exclusion. Will the same property qualify if placed in a trust? The IRS uses three arguments to disallow annual exclusions:

1. the right to income (which is the only current right given to a life beneficiary) from a gift of non-income-producing property is a future interest, since its worth is contingent upon the trustee's converting it to income-producing property;

2. it is impossible to ascertain the value of an income interest in property that is not income-producing at the time of the gift; and

3. if a gift tax exclusion is allowable, the exclusion must be limited to the actual income produced by the property (or expected to be produced) for the number of years over which the income beneficiary is expected to receive the income, discounted to its present value.

Non-dividend-paying stock is a good example of property that may not qualify for the gift tax exclusion when it is placed into a trust. The IRS has been successful in a number of cases in disallowing an exclusion for gifts in trust of stock in closely held corporations paying no dividends. More recently, the IRS has made successful attacks against gifts of LP/LLC interests.[29]

Gifts in trust of life insurance policies pose the same problem: a mother assigns policies on her life to a trust created to provide financial protection for her daughter. Upon the mother's death, the policy proceeds will be reinvested and the daughter will receive the net income of the trust for life. Will the mother be allowed the exclusion for the present value of her daughter's income interest? The regulations answer in the negative, since the daughter will not receive income payments until her mother dies.

But even these last two types of property can qualify for the annual exclusion if the beneficiary is given the power to require the trustee to make assets in the trust income-producing. Consider, however, the potential adverse implications of that power if the beneficiary chooses to exercise it.

Gift Tax Marital Deduction

An individual who transfers property to a spouse is allowed an unlimited deduction (subject to certain conditions) known as the gift tax marital deduction.

The purpose of the gift tax marital deduction is to treat spouses as a single economic unit.

Requirements to Qualify for Gift Tax Marital Deduction

For a gift to qualify for the gift tax marital deduction, the following conditions must be satisfied:

1. The donor's spouse must be a United States citizen at the time the gift is made. (While the marital deduction is not available for gifts to noncitizen spouses, a form of the gift tax annual exclusion is allowed. This adjusts with inflation and is for up to $175,000 in 2023 if they would otherwise qualify for the marital deduction.)[30]

2. The recipient of the gift must be the spouse of the donor at the time the gift is made.

3. The property transferred to the donee-spouse must not be a terminable interest that will disqualify the gift for the marital deduction.

Most of the qualifications above are self-explanatory. The terminable interest rule for marital deduction gifts is similar to the rule employed for estate tax purposes. Essentially, no marital deduction will be allowed where (a) the donee-spouse's interest in the transferred property will terminate upon the lapse of time or at the occurrence or failure of a specified contingency, (b) where the donee-spouse's interest will then pass to another person who received his interest in the property from the donor-spouse, and (c) that person did not pay the donor full and adequate consideration for that interest.

The exception to the terminable interest rule is a Qualifying Terminable Interest Property (QTIP). If a donor spouse gives a donee spouse a qualifying income interest for life, and makes a timely election on Form 709, it will qualify for a gift (or estate) tax marital deduction. To qualify:

(1) the surviving spouse must be entitled to all the income from the property (and it must be payable annually or more frequently);

(2) no person can have a power to appoint any part of the property to any person other than the surviving spouse; and

(3) the property must be includible in the donee-spouse's gross estate (in the case of a bequest, the first decedent's executor makes an irrevocable election that the property remaining in the QTIP at the surviving spouse's death is includible in her gross estate).

Also, as another exception to the terminable interest rule is a life estate created for the surviving spouse in which he or she has a general power of appointment with respect to the underlying property qualifies for the marital deduction. Marital deduction trusts are discussed in detail in Chapter 27 and Intervivos QTIP trusts in Chapter 33.

Gift Tax Charitable Deduction

A donor making a transfer of property to a qualified charity may receive a charitable deduction equal to the value of the gift. The net effect of the charitable deduction is that all gifts to charity are exempt from gift tax. Thus, there is no limit on the amount that can be passed, gift tax free, to a qualified charity.

The gift tax deduction is allowed for all gifts made during the calendar year by U.S. citizens or residents if the gift is to a qualified charity. A qualified charity is defined as:

- A governmental entity, including the United States, a state, territory, or any political subdivision or the District of Columbia if the gift is to be used exclusively for public purposes;

- certain religious, scientific, or charitable organizations;

- certain fraternal societies, orders, or associations; and

- certain veterans' associations, organizations, or societies.

Technically, although all charitable gifts are exempt from gift tax, the charitable deduction is limited. A charitable deduction is allowed only to the extent that each gift exceeds the annual exclusion.

Example. In 2021, a single client makes total gifts of $60,000: $30,000 to his daughter and $30,000 to The American College. After taking annual exclusions, gifts qualifying for the charitable deduction would amount to $15,000 (the $30,000 gift to The American College less the $15,000 annual exclusion). Therefore the client's charitable gift tax deduction would be limited to $15,000.

In certain cases a donor will transfer a remainder interest to a qualified charity. A non-charitable beneficiary will be given all or part of the income interest in the transferred property, and the charity will receive the remainder at the termination of the income interest. Where a charitable remainder interest is given to a qualified charity, a gift tax deduction is allowable for the present value of that remainder interest only if at least one of the following conditions is satisfied:

(1) the transferred property was either a personal residence or a farm; or

(2) the transfer was made to a charitable remainder annuity trust; or

(3) the transfer was made to a charitable remainder unitrust; or

(4) the transfer was made to a pooled income fund.

The terms Charitable Remainder Annuity Trust (CRAT), Charitable Remainder Unitrust (CRUT), and Pooled Income Fund (PIF) are defined in essentially

Calculating Gift Tax Payable

The process of computing the gift tax payable begins with ascertaining the amount of taxable gifts in the current reporting calendar year. In order to find the amount of taxable gifts, it is first necessary to value all gifts made. If appropriate, the gift is then split. Annual exclusions and marital and charitable deductions are then applied. An example computation will illustrate the process.

Example 1. A single donor in the last month of 2021 (when the annual exclusion was $15,000) makes certain outright gifts: $160,000 to his son (full $15,000 annual exclusion), $125,000 to his daughter (full $15,000 annual exclusion), $8,000 to his grandson (only $8,000 annual exclusion due to amount of the gift), and $25,000 to The College for Financial Planning (a charity) (full $15,000 annual exclusion) for a total of $318,000).

Computing Taxable Gifts

Step 1	*List* total gifts for year		$318,000
Step 2	*Subtract* one-half of gift deemed to be made by donor's spouse (split gifts)	$ 0	
	Gifts deemed to be made by donor		$318,000
Step 3	*Subtract* annual exclusion(s)	$ 53,000	
	Gifts after subtracting exclusion(s)		$265,000
Step 4	*Subtract* marital deduction	$ 0	
Step 5	*Subtract* charitable deduction	$ 11,000	
	Taxable gifts		$257,000

Note that, although there were four donees, the annual exclusion was $53,000 [(3 x $14,000) + $8,000] and did not total four times $15,000, or $60,000. This is because the annual exclusion is the lower of (a) $15,000 (in 2021) or (b) the actual net value of the property transferred. In this example the gift to the grandson was only $8,000, which limits the annual exclusion for that gift to $8,000.

Example 2. Assume the fact pattern above will illustrate the computation where the donor is married and his spouse consented to split their gifts to third parties. In this case, only half the gifts made by the donor would be taxable to the donor (half the gifts made by the donor's spouse to third parties would also be included in computing the donor's total gifts).

A separate (and essentially identical) computation is made for the donor's spouse. That computation would show (a) the other half of the husband's gifts to third parties plus (b) half of the wife's actual gifts to third parties (since all gifts must be split if any gifts are split).

Computing Taxable Gifts

Step 1	*List* total gifts for year		$318,000
Step 2	*Subtract* one-half of gift deemed to be made by donor's spouse (split gifts)	$159,000	
	Gifts deemed to be made by donor		$159,000
Step 3	*Subtract* annual exclusion(s)	$47,500	
	Gifts after subtracting exclusion(s)		$111,500
Step 4	*Subtract* marital deduction	$0	
Step 5	*Subtract* charitable deduction	$0	
	Taxable gifts		$111,500

(The calculation on the wife's return would parallel this return.)

Note that in this example the annual exclusions were computed *after* the split. Because after the split, each donor's portion of the gift was in excess of the annual exclusion (with the exception of the gift to the grandson and charity), each donor was able to use the full annual exclusion for that split gift. Thus, each donor's exclusions would be:

(a)	Gift to son	$15,000
(b)	Gift to daughter	15,000
(c)	Gift to grandson	4,000
(d)	Gift to The College for Financial Planning	12,500
		$46,500

The charitable deduction for each spouse would be $0 [($25,000 ÷ 2) – $15,000 ($15,000 limited to the amount of the gift)].

Example 3. If the married donor in Example 2 had also made an outright gift of $200,000 to his wife, the computation would be as follows:

Computing Taxable Gifts

Step 1	*List* total gifts for year		$518,000
Step 2	*Subtract* one-half of gift deemed to be made by donor's spouse (split gifts)	$159,000	
	Gifts deemed to be made by donor		$359,000
Step 3	*Subtract* annual exclusion(s) (which includes an annual exclusion for the spouse)	$62,500	
	Gifts after subtracting exclusion(s)		$296,500
Step 4	*Subtract* marital deduction	$185,000	
Step 5	*Subtract* charitable deduction	$0	
	Taxable gifts		$111,500

When the total value of taxable gifts for the reporting period is found, the actual tax payable is computed using the following method:

Computing Gift Tax Payable

Step 1	Compute gift tax on all *taxable* gifts regardless of when made (use gift tax rate schedule)	$_____
Step 2	Compute gift tax on all *taxable* gifts made prior to the present year's gift(s) (use gift tax rate schedule)	$_____
Step 3	Subtract Step 2 result from Step 1 result	$_____
Step 4	Enter gift tax credit remaining	$_____
Step 5	Subtract Step 4 result from Step 3 result to obtain *gift tax payable*	$_____

For instance, a widow gives $1,400,000 to her daughter and $100,000 to The College for Financial Planning in 2021 when the annual exclusion was $15,000. Both transfers are present-interest gifts. If she had made no previous taxable gifts in the current or prior years or quarters, the computation would be as follows:

Computing Taxable Gifts

Step 1	*List* total gifts for year		$1,500,000
Step 2	*Subtract* one-half of gift deemed to be made by donor's spouse (split gifts)	$0	
	Gifts deemed to be made by donor		$1,500,000
Step 3	*Subtract* annual exclusion(s)	$30,000	
	Gifts after subtracting exclusion(s)		$1,470,000
Step 4	*Subtract* marital deduction	$0	
Step 5	*Subtract* charitable deduction	$85,000	
	Taxable gifts		$1,385,000

Credits

A unified credit can be applied against the tax on gifts made either during lifetime or at death or part can be applied against each. The gift tax credit, which provides a dollar-for-dollar reduction of the tax otherwise payable, is as follows:

Historically, then:

	Gift Tax Unified Credit	Exemption Equivalent
2002-2009	$345,800	$1,000,000
2010	$330,800	$1,000,000
2011	$1,730,800	$5,000,000
2012	$1,772,800	$5,120,000
2013	$2,045,800	$5,250,000
2014	$2,081,800	$5,340,000
2015	$2,117,800	$5,430,000
2016	$2,125,800	$5,450,000
2017	$2,141,800	$5,490,000
2018	$4,425,800	$11,180,000
2019	$4,505,800	$11,400,000
2020	$4,577,800	$11,580,000
2021	$4,625,800	$11,700,000
2022	$4,769,800	$12,060,000
2023	$5,113,800	$12,920,000

20.8 REPORTING OF GIFTS AND PAYMENT OF THE TAX

Split-Gifts

A return must be filed with respect to any year in which a married couple elects to split gifts; however the return may be filed late if the only reason for filing the return is to show that the couple split gifts. However, if a spouse dies in the year of the gift, the return can also be filed up to the due date of the Federal estate tax return for such spouse.

Future-Interest Gifts

A gift tax return is required for a gift of a future interest, regardless of the amount of the gift. For example, if an individual transfers $100,000 to an irrevocable trust, income payable to the grantor's wife for life and remainder to the grantor's son, the son's remainder interest would be a future interest gift. Therefore, a gift tax return would be required regardless of the value of the son's remainder interest.

The term "future interest" is defined the same as for annual exclusion purposes: a gift in which the donee does not have the unrestricted right to the immediate use, possession, or enjoyment of the property or the income from the property.

Present-Interest Gifts

No gift tax return is due (if gifts are not split and no future interest gifts are made) until present-interest gifts made to one individual for the year exceed the annual exclusion ($15,000 in 2021). When present-interest gifts made to one individual for the year exceed that limit, a return must be filed for such year, even if no gift tax would be due (e.g., if gift splitting provisions eliminated the tax). For example, if a married woman gave $18,000 to her son and split the gift, the transfer would be tax free. However, a gift tax return would be required because the gift exceeded the annual exclusion limit (and because the gift was split).

A gift tax return must be filed and the gift tax due, if any, on reported gifts must be paid by April 15 of the year following the year in which the taxable gifts were made. When an extension is granted for income tax return filing, the time limit for gift tax return filing is automatically extended.

Gifts to Charities

No return must be filed and no reporting is required for charitable contributions of the annual exclusion or less in value unless a noncharitable taxable gift is also made. In that case, the charitable transfer must be reported at the same time the noncharitable gift is noted on a gift tax return. This requirement can easily be overlooked. If the value of the charitable transfer exceeds the annual exclusion, the general rule is that the transfer must be reported on a gift tax return for that year unless the transfer is of the donor's entire interest in the property.

If a split-interest gift is made to a charity (where there are charitable and noncharitable donees of the same gift), the donor will not be able to claim a charitable deduction for the entire value of the transfer. In this case, the donor must file and report the transfer subject to the filing requirements discussed above. For example, if an individual establishes a charitable remainder trust with payments to his daughter for life and the remainder payable to charity at her death, a gift tax return would have to be filed.

Liability for Payment – Net Gift

The donor of the gift is primarily liable for the gift tax. However, if the donor for any reason fails to pay the tax when it falls due, the donee becomes liable to the extent of the value of the gift. This liability begins as soon as the donor fails to pay the tax when due.

If a donor makes a gift and the donee decides, voluntarily, to pay the gift tax out of the property just received, the gift tax value of the gift is the entire fair market value of the property. In other words, if the donee is not obligated by the terms of the gift to pay the gift tax but chooses to pay it anyway, the donee must pay a tax based on the full fair market value of the property received based on the donor's gift tax bracket.

Conversely, if the terms of the gift obligate the donee to pay the gift tax, the value of the gift (and therefore the amount of the gift tax liability) is reduced. If a gift is made subject to an express or implied condition at the time of transfer that the gift tax is to be paid by the donee or out of the property transferred, the donor is deemed to have received consideration (potentially taxable as income) in the amount of the gift tax to be paid by the donee.

The value of the net gift is measured by the fair market value of the property passing from the donor less the amount of any gift tax paid by the donee. In computing the donee's gift tax liability, the donor's unified credit must be used.

The formula used to compute the donee's tax is:

$$\frac{\text{tentative tax}}{(1 + \text{donor's gift tax rate})}$$

Example. A retired, sixty-six years old, single donor living almost entirely from the income of $4,000,000 worth of tax-free municipal bonds who made no prior gifts made a gift of property worth $6,114,000 in 2017. The gift was made to his niece on the condition that she pay the federal gift taxes. As the calculation below illustrates, the tentative tax on a tentative taxable gift of $6,100,000 ($6,114,000 - $14,000 annual exclusion) is $268,000. But the gift tax actually payable is $162,857 a difference of $105,143. The gift tax is the same as if the donor had made a taxable gift of $ 5,937,143 and paid the gift tax himself.

TRUE TAX ON NET GIFT

Year..	2017
Tentative Taxable Gift...........................	$6,100,000
Gift Tax on $6,100,000...........................	$2,385,800
Unified Credit.......................................	$2,117,800
Tentative Tax [$2,385,800-2,117,800]	$216,000
Tax Rate..	40%
True Tax [$216,000 ÷ (1 + .40)]	$154,256
Net Gift [$6,100,000 - $162,857].............	$5,945,714

Due Date of Tax

Generally, the gift tax must be paid at the same time the return is filed. However, reasonable extensions of time for payment of the tax can be granted by the IRS, but only upon a showing of undue hardship. This means more than inconvenience. It must appear that the party liable to pay the tax will suffer a "substantial financial loss" unless an extension is granted. (A forced sale of property at a sacrifice price would be an example of a substantial financial loss.)

20.9 DETERMINATION OF THE BASIS OF GIFT PROPERTY

When property is transferred from a donor to a donee and the donee later disposes of the property through a sale or other taxable disposition, gain depends on the donee's basis. In return, the donee's basis is carried over from the donor; i.e., the donor's cost basis for the gift property immediately prior to the gift becomes the donee's cost basis for that property.

Example. If an individual paid $5 a share for stock and transfers it when it is worth $25, and the donee sells it when it is worth $35, the donee's cost basis for that property is the donor's $5 cost basis. The gain, therefore, is the difference between the amount realized by the donee, $35, and the donee's adjusted basis, $5, or $30.

An addition to basis is allowed for a portion of any gift tax paid on the transfer from the donor to the donee. The basis addition is for that portion of the tax attributable to the appreciation in the gift property from the time it was acquired by the donor until the date of the gift (the excess of the property's gift tax value over the donor's adjusted basis determined immediately before the gift). This increase in basis may be added to the donee's carryover basis for the property.

Stated as a formula, the basis of gifted property is the donor's basis increased as follows:

$$\frac{\text{Net Appreciation In Value Of Gift}}{\text{Amount Of Gift}} \times \text{Gift Tax Paid}$$

This means the basis carried over from the donor is increased by only the gift tax on the net appreciation in the value of the gift. For example, an individual bought stock worth $40,000 and gave it to his daughter when it was worth $100,000. If the donor paid $18,000 in gift taxes at the time of the gift, the daughter's basis would be $50,800.

a. Donor's basis $40,000

Plus

b. Gift tax on "net appreciation in value" (here, the difference between the $100,000 value of the gift at the time of transfer and the donor's cost, $40,000)

$$\frac{\$60,000}{\$100,000} \times \$18,000 = \underline{10,800}$$

equals

c. Daughter's basis $50,800

However, for purpose of determining loss, if the basis of the gifted property is lower than the fair market value of the property at the time of the gift, the basis is equal to such fair market value.

Example. In 2010, Asher acquired land for $100,000. In 2020, Asher gifts the property then worth $60,000 to his cousin, Ashley. In 2021, Ashley sells the land for its then fair market value of $50,000. Obviously, the property was sold at a loss. However, because at the time of the gift, the fair market value of Asher's property was $60,000 and his basis was $100,000, in computing loss, Ashley must use the lower of the property's date of gift fair market value. So, in 2021, Ashley would recognize a $10,000 loss (the difference between the $60,000 basis and the amount realized of $50,000). On the other hand, had Asher not gifted the property and sold it for $50,000, he would have recognized a $50,000 loss (the difference between his $100,000 basis and the amount realized of $50,000). If Ashley had sold the land for $60,000-$100,000, she would incur neither gain nor loss.[31]

The reason for the rule is to prevent a donor to shift a built-in tax loss to a donee. For example, if at the time of the gift, Ashley had a large capital gain, being able to use Asher's $100,000 basis would have generated a capital loss she could use to offset capital gain. In order to prevent this type of tax manipulation, Ashley's basis is limited to the date of gift fair market value for calculating losses. Obviously, if the value of the property further depreciates (as it did in this example), that post-gift loss would be recognized by her.

20.10 RELATIONSHIP OF THE GIFT TAX SYSTEM TO THE ESTATE TAX SYSTEM

Going forward, the estate and gift tax system were fully unified in 2011. The unification correlates the estate and gift tax laws in three essential ways:

(1) Lifetime gifts and testamentary transfers are taxed by using the same tax rates, rather than separate and different rates. The exemption for 2023 is now $12,920,000 in 2023), and the top rate is 40 percent.

(2) The unified credit can be applied to both lifetime and post-death gifts (estate).

(3) The estate tax imposed at death is computed by adding the taxable portion of gifts made during lifetime (after 1976) to the taxable estate to arrive at the tentative tax base (gift tax calculated on post-1976 taxable gifts can be subtracted to arrive at the estate tax liability).

In spite of the correlations of the two tax systems, gift tax law is not always consistent with estate tax law. When a gift is made, certain issues must be considered. For example, will property transferred during a decedent's life be included in addition to his or her other assets in his or her gross estate? Will certain property transferred by a donor during life subject to gift tax be later included in the donor's gross estate? For example, a donor who gifts a life insurance policy on his life to his son subject to potential gift tax who dies within three years of making the gift must include the life insurance policy in his or her gross estate.

Likewise, if the donor transfers property but retains a life interest, both gift and estate taxes will be payable. Although the gift tax paid may generally be subtracted in arriving at the estate tax liability, because of the time value of money (i.e., the donor's loss of the use of gift taxes paid), the net result is less favorable than a mere washout (i.e., it is in essence a prepayment of the death tax).

20.11 FACTORS TO CONSIDER IN SELECTING APPROPRIATE GIFT PROPERTY

Gift tax strategy must be part of a well-planned and carefully coordinated estate-planning effort. This in turn requires careful consideration as to the type of property to give. There are a number of strategies and factors that must be examined in selecting the types of property that are appropriate for gifts. The dramatically increased applicable exclusion amount (at least tentatively for 2018-2025) moots estate/gift tax concerns for many, but not the income tax aspects.

Some of the general considerations in selecting property to gift include:

(1) Is the property likely to appreciate in value? Other things being equal, planners generally try to pick property that will appreciate substantially in value from the time of the transfer (at least for taxable estates). The removal from the donor's estate of the appreciation in the property (as well as the income from the property) should save a meaningful amount of estate and income taxes.

The best type of property will have a low gift tax value and a high estate tax value. Life insurance, for example, is property with a low present value, but a high appreciation potential. If held until the date the insured dies, its appreciation in value is guaranteed and estate-tax free.

(2) Is the donee in a lower income tax bracket than the donor? Income splitting between the donor and a donee age eighteen or older can be accomplished by transferring high income-producing property to a family member in a lower bracket. Examples include high-dividend participating preferred stock in a closely held business or stock in a successful S corporation.

Conversely, if the donor is in a lower bracket than the donee (for instance, if the parent who is retired makes a gift to a financially successful middle-aged child), the use of low-yield growth-type property may be indicated. Typically, gifts to children under age twenty-four should emphasize growth.

(3) Is the property subject to indebtedness? A gift of property subject to indebtedness that is greater than its cost to the donor may result in a taxable gain. In other words, if by transferring the property by gift relieves the donor of the indebtedness (effectively shifting it to the donee), it is as if the done purchased the property for the amount of the outstanding indebtedness. A gift of such property causes the donor to realize capital gain on the excess of the debt over basis. For example, the donor gifts a building that cost her $10,000 subject to a $70,000 mortgage. At the time of the gift, the fair market value of the building is $100,000. Treating the transaction as a part-sale part-gift, the donor would recognize a gain of $60,000 (the difference between the shifted debt $70,000 and the donor's basis $10,000). The difference between the fair market value of the building of $100,000 and the debt of $70,000 (that the donee essentially paid to the donor by taking on that liability) would be a taxable gift.

(4) Is the gift property's cost basis above, below, or approximately the same as the property's fair market value? As illustrated above, a pre-gift loss in gifted property cannot be passed along to the donee of the gifted property. However, the higher basis may still get used if the property

appreciates in later years after the gift, whereas dying with such property would cause a step down in basis that cannot be recovered. Furthermore, if the gift property's cost basis exceeds the date of gift fair market value, there will be no gift tax addition to basis because that addition is in proportion to the pre-gift appreciation (of which there is obviously none). Thus, in absence of appreciation, no gift tax addition would be allowed.

Conversely, if the donor's cost basis for income tax purposes is very low relative to the fair market value of the property, it might be advantageous to retain the property until death because of the stepped-up basis at death rules. (This is especially true if inclusion of the property will generate little or no gift tax because it will pass to a surviving spouse and qualify for a marital deduction, or if the donor's estate is below the applicable exemption amount.) Due to a stepped-up basis provision, the capital gain the decedent would have recognized if he or she had sold the property during his or her lifetime would be avoided in the event the property is later sold by the estate or heir. But if the property must be sold during life, it may be prudent to gift it to a low-bracket age twenty-four or over family member by gift; that individual could then sell it and realize a lower tax.

A third possibility is that the donor's cost basis is approximately the same or only slightly below fair market value. In this instance, the rules providing for a gift tax addition to basis are of little help. The addition to basis is limited to gift tax allocable to appreciation in the property at the time of the gift. One further factor that should be considered is the likelihood that the donee will want or need to sell the property in the foreseeable future. If this is not likely, the income tax basis (except for depreciable property) will be relatively meaningless.

CHAPTER ENDNOTES

1. Treas. Reg. §25.2511-1(h)(1), see also PLR 9114023.
2. Treas. Reg. §25.2511-1(c).
3. Treas. Reg. §25.2511-1(h)(1), see also PLR 9114023.
4. Treas. Reg. §25.2512-8.
5. IRC §2516.
6. *Miller v. Commissioner*, T.C. Memo 1996-3; Rev. Rul. 77-299.
7. IRC §108.
8. IRC §2503(e).
9. Treas. Reg. §25.2511-1(h)(1), see also PLR 9114023.
10. *Goodman v. Commissioner*, 56 F.2d 218 (2d Cir. 1946).
11. To read the differing opinions on donative promises, See LISI Estate Planning Newsletter No. 2033 (Dec. 3, 2012 and LISI Estate Planning Newsletter No. 2022, 12/3/2012 at www.leimbergservices.com.
12. I.R.C. §102(c).
13. Treas. Reg. §1.2511-1(g)(1).
14. *Duberstein v. Comm'r.*, 363 U.S. 278 (1960).
15. *U.S. v. Kaiser*, 363 U.S. 299 (1960).
16. *Estate of Anderson v. Comm'r.*, 8 T.C. 706 (1947).
17. Another example of a no-gift situation would be where a group of businessmen convey real estate to an unrelated business corporation with the expectation of doing business with that corporation sometime in the future.
18. See *Michael Geeraerts, Paul Vecchione & Jim Magner on Summa Holdings v. Commissioner: IRS Often Argues Substance-Over-Form, But Sometimes Form Is Substance*, LISI Employee Benefits and Retirement Planning Newsletter #670 (March 16, 2017) and *Ed Morrow on Summa Holdings Inc. v. Commissioner: 6th Circuit Properly Rejects IRS and Tax Court Substance Over Form Attack on IRAs Owning IC-DISCs, But the IRS Missed the Prohibited Transactions*, LISI Employee Benefits and Retirement Planning Newsletter #672 (March 23, 2017).
19. For a discussion of this type of trust and how it may be used for tax shifting, see *Eliminate State Tax on Trust Income: A Comprehensive Update on Planning With Incomplete Gift Non-Grantor Trusts*, by Kevin Ghassomian, ACTEC Law Journal Winter 2013 For a shorter summary see *Incomplete Gift, Non Grantor Trusts (aka DINGs, NINGs)*, by Edwin Morrow, Wealth Counsel Quarterly, Vol. 9, #3 2015 and for the more comprehensive discussion of tax shifting strategies see *Incomplete Gift, Non-Grantor Trusts: Not Just for State Tax Avoidance*, by Ed Morrow, material available at www.ultimateestateplanner.com.
20. IRC §2503(e).
21. IRC §2503(e).
22. PLR 199941013.
23. I.R.C. §453B.
24. Treas. Reg. §25.2512-1
25. This computation can be performed on NumberCruncher Software at www.leimberg.com.
26. *Diedrich v. Comm'r.*, 457 U.S. 191 (1982).
27. Rev. Rul. 71-443
28. 1954-2 C.B. 319.
29. *Hackl v. Commissioner*, 335 F.3d 664 (7th Cir. 2003), aff'g 118 T.C. 279 (2002), *Price v. Commissioner*, T.C. Memo. 2010-2 (Jan. 4, 2010), *Fisher v. United States*, 105 AFTR 2d. 2010-1347 (S.D. Ind. Mar. 11, 2010).
30. For 2018 inflation adjustment from $149,000 in 2017 to $152,000 in 2018, see Rev. Proc. 2017-58, §3.37.
31. IRC §1015(a).

GENERATION-SKIPPING TRANSFER TAX

CHAPTER 21

21.1 INTRODUCTION

This chapter discusses the generation-skipping transfer tax and planning with generation-skipping transfers, including the use of generation-skipping trusts (a.k.a. dynasty trusts).

A Generation-Skipping Transfer (GST) is any transfer of property by gift or at death, to any person who, under federal tax law, is assigned to a generation that is two or more generations below that of the transferor (i.e., one or more generations below the transferor is skipped). In the case of family members, this means, for example, that transferor's grandchildren and great nieces and nephews would be assigned two generations below the transferor. Such persons who are two or more generations below that of the transferor are defined as "skip" persons.

The GST tax applies to generation-skipping transfers and is in addition to gift and estate tax. Similar to gift tax, there is an annual GST tax exclusion ($17,000 in 2023) and an exclusion for certain transfers for educational or medical purposes is available that reduces the amount of a GST. Similar to the applicable exclusion amount with respect to gift and estate tax, a transferor has a GST tax exemption ($12,920,000 in 2023) that can be allocated to generation-skipping transfers to offset the GST tax. Also, similar to gift and estate tax, the annual exclusion and the GST tax exemption are adjusted annually for inflation. To apply the GST tax exemption, an inclusion ratio is calculated based on allocations of GST tax exemption to generation-skipping transfers. The GST tax is calculated by multiplying the GST tax rate (40 percent) by the value of the GST tax transfer property and the inclusion ratio for such property. For GST exemptions and tax rates applicable in other years, see Figure 21.1.

21.2 WHEN IS USE OF SUCH A DEVICE INDICATED?

Prior to the enactment of the GST tax, a GST was often used as a device to save federal gift and estate tax by keeping property out of the taxable estates of the members of the intermediate generation with substantial estates – in essence skipping over a generation. For example, both Asher and his daughter Ashley have substantial estates. Ashley's son, Samuel has a relatively small estate. If Asher leaves his entire estate to Ashley, upon Ashley's death, the stacking of Asher's estate on her estate would likely be subject to an extraordinary high estate tax. To avoid this result, Asher "skips over" Ashley's estate and leaves his all his property to Samuel. By doing so, before reaching Samuel, Asher's estate would be taxed only once as the estate tax generated by its inclusion in Ashley's estate would be eliminated. Such a generation skipping transfer was traditionally used by many of the country's wealthiest families such as the Rockefellers and duPonts, as a device to save federal gift and estate tax by artfully keeping property out of the taxable estates of the members of an intermediate generation. Skipping generations to avoid federal estate tax in a way that provided the benefit of great wealth without triggering estate tax became so popular and such a frequently used device by ultra-rich families that Congress targeted and taxed this technique.[1]

Significantly, in the above example, it is possible and would be more common for Asher to transfer all of some of his property into a trust for the benefit of Ashley and still avoid its inclusion in her gross estate. During Ashley's lifetime, the trust could require the mandatory or discretionary distributions of income and allow the trustee to invade the principal for Ashley's (and potentially Samuel's) health, education, maintenance and support with the remainder to be distributed to Samuel. Upon her death, provided she did not have a general power of appointment (i.e., the power to appoint the property to her or her estate, or creditors of either, or to satisfy her obligations), none of the trust principal would be includible in her gross estate. So, in the second scenario, Ashley would be able to benefit from Asher's estate at no additional estate tax cost. In fact, this latter scenario may be much more tax-efficient than completely skipping Ashley as a beneficiary, because the trust can be designed to shift the income tax burden to Ashley as a Beneficiary Deemed Owner Trust (BDOT) – see Chapter 35.

Thus, the GST tax was enacted to eliminate the loss of tax revenue such techniques would have allowed (although the currently high GST exemption still provides a substantial loophole). With the use of the GST tax exemption and some planning, it is possible to achieve significant overall tax savings. To this point, there are three scenarios in which generation-skipping transfer techniques are useful.

First, similar to the above example, a parent with substantial estate who has a child who also has a substantial estate can effectively save GST tax and provide asset protection for the child. By creating a GST trust for the benefit of the child, the trust property would be protected from his or her creditors, divorce courts, or bankruptcy. By the effective use of the GST exemption, in addition to none of the trust property being included in the child's gross estate, there would be little or no GST tax generated by the transfer. Any gift and estate tax that may also apply to such a transfer would be offset to the extent of the parent's applicable exclusion amount.

Second, the primary purpose of a GST trust may be to protect the property from a spendthrift child, or from being depleted through a child's divorce or bankruptcy for the life of the child and to preserve the principal for subsequent distribution to grandchildren. Subject only to the applicable state law limitation on the maximum life of a trust, the trust could continue to provide similar protection through the grandchildren's lives (and for great-grandchildren as well), avoiding transfer tax in each generation. In many estates, however, the generation skip occurs as a result of the death of a member of the intermediate generation before such member receives full ownership of the gift or inheritance, as when a trust is provided for a child until he attains age thirty, and that child dies before attaining age thirty leaving surviving grandchildren.

Finally, rather than creating a trust, an individual may prefer to make direct transfers to a grandchild or other skip person for the beneficiary's support or enjoyment and/or to avoid tax in the estate of the intervening generation. Similar to regular gifts, present interest gifts to grandchildren will not be subject to the GST tax unless they exceed the GST tax annual exclusion, which tracks the estate/gift tax annual exclusion. Even if it does exceed the annual exclusion, the GST tax on such transfers could be offset by the available GST tax exemption.

21.3 WHAT ARE THE REQUIREMENTS?

There is no special form of GST transfer. It could simply be a gift or bequest to a skip person, or the establishment of a trust in which distributions will or may be made to a skip person. Any gift or transfer of property that will or may benefit a skip person is potentially subject to GST tax.

21.4 HOW IT IS DONE

A GST trust can be created as part of an individual's will or revocable trust, so that it comes into being only upon the transferor's death. If the transferor intends to make *inter vivos* gifts to a GST trust, the trust will be created in a separate document. In that case, the GST trust may also serve as a receptacle for assets passing from the transferor at his death.

The trust instrument would typically provide for two trusts. The "exempt" trust would be funded with assets that will ultimately pass to skip persons to which the transferor's GST tax exemption has or will be allocated so as to avoid GST tax. Conversely, the "nonexempt" trust would be funded with assets that will ultimately pass to non-skip persons not subject to GST tax (or be included in their estate), or would otherwise be subject to GST tax. Obviously, for that reason, no part of the GST tax exemption would be allocated to the "nonexempt" trust.

For optimal results, the exempt trust should be funded with assets with the greatest growth potential (e.g., have the Roth accounts pass to the GST exempt trust and the traditional retirement accounts pass to the GST non-exempt trust). As a result, a maximum appreciation of value in the transferred assets would pass to future generations without GST tax because, once the exemption is allocated to the trust, the appreciation is also exempt.

The exempt and nonexempt trusts are established so that they have GST tax inclusion ratios of zero and one respectively (i.e., no trust is partially exempt and partially nonexempt). This is more efficient than having one trust that is partially exempt, because the distributions needed can come from the GST non-exempt trust first. When the exempt trust is established with an inclusion ration of zero that trust generally maintains its 100 percent immunity from GST tax provided there are no later additions of property.

For estate tax purposes, assuming the spouses have made no lifetime gifts, in a family *inter vivos* trust with distributions to the survivor's trusts, i.e., a bypass trust and a QTIP trust, to take advantage of the entire unified credit of the first spouse to die, the bypass trust is typically funded with an amount equal to the unified credit equivalent (the applicable exclusion). Additionally, the person (usually the executor) making the GST tax exemption allocation would typically allocate the $12,920,000 (in 2023) exemption of the first grantor to die to the bypass trust to make it GST tax exempt (and potentially to a QTIP trust as well). However, if during the grantor's lifetime, some of the applicable exemption was already used (i.e., for lifetime gifts) and the entire GST tax exemption remains intact, the two exemptions will not be equal.

Example. If at the time of death (in 2021 when the applicable exclusion amount was $11,700,000), there remains $4,000,000 of applicable estate/gift tax exclusion amount and the entire GST tax exemption, the bypass trust would be funded with $4,000,000, leaving $7,700,000 of unused GST exemption to be potentially wasted ($11,700,000 minus $4,000,000). In this situation, the amount in excess of the applicable exemption would likely be transferred into an exempt QTIP trust to with respect to which the executor of the decedent spouse would make a "reverse QTIP election." By making that election, the property transferred to the exempt QTIP would be treated as being transferred from the first spouse to die for GST purposes after the surviving spouse's death even though the QTIP would be included in the surviving spouse's estate. In other words, for the sole purpose of the GST tax, the first spouse to die would be considered the "transferor" of this amount as if none of that amount was to be transferred into a QTIP. By virtue of this "fiction," the remaining GST exemption of the first donor spouse to die would be used without incurring any gift or estate tax at the first death.

Further, the trust instrument would also require that any distributions of principal to the surviving spouse be first made from the nonexempt trust. This is because there is no GST tax on distributions to nonskip persons such as the surviving spouse. For the same reason, upon the death of the surviving spouse, the trust would require any taxes attributable to the QTIP trusts to be paid first from the nonexempt QTIP. Finally, to totally maximize both spouses' GST exemptions, upon the death of the surviving spouse, the executor would allocate the spouse's unused GST exemption to other trust property included in his or her estate not already exempted by virtue of the first spouse's exemption.

In summary, following the death of both spouses, subject to the applicable rule against perpetuities, in addition to the assets in the GST tax exempt bypass and QTIP trusts, the surviving spouse's unused GST tax exemption could be allocated to his or her other assets to be held in trust successively for the lives of the spouses' children, grandchildren and great grandchildren. Significantly, upon the death of each successive generation, there would be no further imposition of estate of GST tax.

As to a "children's" trust, for GST tax purposes, the principal would be divided and maintained in exempt and nonexempt trusts. Typically, children receive the income generated from both the exempt and nonexempt trusts. However, many exempt trusts allow income to be "sprinkled" among the child and issue of the child, or even permit income to be accumulated to allow the exempt trust to grow in value. Also, the children are usually given a nongeneral power of appointment over the assets of the exempt trust. Such a power provides the children with the flexibility to appoint the principal of the trust in different proportions either to anyone or only to persons in a specified class of beneficiaries, usually their own children or perhaps as a life estate to the spouse. Since it is not a general power of appointment, the property is not included in their estates. In addition, since the original donor's GST tax exemption was allocated to the exempt trust, the exempt trust passes from one generation to another free from estate and GST tax.

As to the nonexempt trust, the trust instrument typically grants the children a general power of appointment over the principal so that it will be purposely included in their estates for estate tax purposes. This avoids the GST tax that would otherwise be imposed at the 40 percent tax rate (because the nonexempt trust will usually pass to skip persons at the child's death). For estate tax purposes, with the inclusion of the property in the child's estate, it is possible to take advantage of the child's estate tax unified credit and graduated tax rates. Also, to take advantage of the gift tax annual exclusion, the nonexempt trust can include provisions allowing the child to make gifts to the child's issue (or others), including for health and tuition expenses that would not count as a gift or generation skipping transfer.

A testamentary power of appointment over the GST non-exempt trust might also be drafted using a formula that results in the lowest overall state and federal estate and GST tax – in some circumstances, such as when a state estate tax but not a state GST tax applies, it may be less costly to incur a 40% GST tax than a 40% plus up to 16% state estate tax.

The same exempt/nonexempt structure would continue to apply to the trusts as they pass to the grantor's grandchildren, great-grandchildren, and so on, the object being to preserve the exempt trust from transfer tax at each generation level.

Finally, a limited power of appointment is often given to some nonbeneficiary (sometimes through a trust protector, who might have similar powers) to be able to alter the trust to deal with changes in tax law or other circumstances. For example, what if the settlor's child has no children or they pass away and the child wants to appoint to their siblings at their death? In such case, the trust protector (or independent trustee) may want to modify the child's general testamentary power of appointment over the GST non-exempt trust that unnecessarily causes estate tax when no GST tax would otherwise apply.

21.5 TAX IMPLICATIONS

Every GST transfer in excess of the GST tax exemption is subject to a flat rate tax equal to the highest estate tax rate (40 percent recently; see Figure 21.1).[2] Generally, the GST tax applies to transfers to grandchildren or others in the grandchildren's or younger generations. The tax applies to outright transfers and transfers in trust or arrangements having substantially the same effect as a trust, such as transfers involving life estates and remainders, estates for years, and insurance and annuity contracts.[3]

Every individual is allowed to make aggregate transfers during lifetime or at death in the aggregate amount of the GST tax exemption without the imposition of GST tax.[4]

Essentially, the GST tax rate is equal to the maximum estate tax rate at the time a *taxable distribution*, *taxable termination*, or *direct skip* is made.[5] Technically, as described below, the *applicable rate* is the maximum federal estate tax rate multiplied by a fraction called an *inclusion ratio*.

The *taxable amount*, which is the amount to be multiplied by the applicable rate mentioned in the preceding paragraph, depends on whether the transfer is considered a taxable distribution, a taxable termination, or a direct skip.

Generation Assignment

For GST tax purposes, all persons are assigned to a generation. In the case of related persons, the assignment is made by reference to the ancestral chain beginning with the grandparents of the transferor, except a transferor's spouse or descendent is always assigned to the same generation as the transferor or descendant, respectively. Unrelated persons not more than 12½ years younger than the transferor are assigned to the transferor's generation, otherwise unrelated persons are assigned to succeeding generations on the basis of twenty-five years for each generation (i.e., first younger generation – 12½ to 37½ years younger than transferor). Where the transferee is an entity (i.e., estate, trust, partnership, or corporation), individuals who own beneficial interests in the entity are assigned to generations based on the age differential between them and the transferor.[6]

In some instances, persons who are initially assigned to one generation may be reassigned to another generation. For example, each transfer to succeeding generations of skip persons, such as grandchildren and great-grandchildren is subject to GST tax. However, upon each successive transfer, i.e., from grandchild to grandchild, the transferor is assigned to a lower

Figure 21.1

GENERATION-SKIPPING TRANSFER TAX		
Year	Exemption	Rate
2005	$1,500,000	47%
2006	$2,000,000	46%
2007	$2,000,000	45%
2008	$2,000,000	45%
2009	$3,500,000	45%
2010	$5,000,000	0%
2011	$5,000,000	35%
2012	$5,120,000	35%
2013	$5,250,000	40%
2014	$5,340,000	40%
2015	$5,430,000	40%
2016	$5,450,000	40%
2017	$5,490,000	40%
2018	$11,118,000	40%
2019	$11,400,000	40%
2020	$11,580,000	40%
2021	$11,700,000	40%
2022	$12,060,000	40%
2023	$12,920,000	40%

generation. This is to prevent the imposition of the GST tax twice on transfers to persons in the same generation.[7]

If an individual's parent who is a lineal descendant of the transferor or transferor's spouse is deceased at the time of a transfer from which the individual's interest is derived, the individual and all succeeding generations move up one generation. Qualified disclaimers do not cause a child to be considered deceased for this purpose.

Example. Asher makes a direct gift to his grandson, Samuel. At the time of the gift, Samuel's mother and Asher's daughter Ashley, is deceased. Even though Samuel would be considered a skip person (subjecting the gift to potential GST tax), at the time of the transfer, his mother was deceased. Thus, Samuel generation assignment moves up to the children level (only one generation below the transferor). Because gifts to children (the next generation) are not subject to GST tax, Samuel's gift would be exempt from GST tax. This predeceased parent rule also applies to collateral relatives (e.g., nephews and nieces) if at the time of the transfer, the transferee had no living lineal descendants.[8]

Skip Persons

A person assigned two or more generations below the transferor is a skip person. A trust is considered to be a skip person if all beneficiaries holding interests in the trust are skip persons, or if no person holds an interest in the trust, no distributions could be made to nonskip persons.[9] For instance, a trust created by a grandfather for the benefit of grandchildren and great grandchildren (all skip persons) would be considered a skip person. After the GST to the trust and the assessment of tax, there is a reassignment of generations so that the great grandchildren remain skip persons, but the grandchildren move up a generation and are no longer considered to be skip persons.

Solely for GST tax purposes, a person holds an interest in a trust or trust equivalent if the person is entitled to receive current nondiscretionary distributions of income or corpus, or is a permissible current recipient of income or corpus and is not a qualified charity.[10]

Taxable Distribution

A taxable distribution is any distribution of income or corpus from a trust to a skip person that is not otherwise subject to estate or gift tax.[11] For example, a transfer to a trust is considered a gift at the time the property is transferred to the trust. A subsequent distribution to the beneficiary is not considered a gift. So, a distribution from a trust to a grandson of the grantor would be to a transfer to a skip person subject to potential GST tax (but not gift tax). Similarly, if a trust created by a mother permits discretionary distributions of income or principal to her daughter or granddaughter, a distribution to the granddaughter would be a taxable distribution. A distribution from one trust to a second trust would be considered a transfer to a skip person if all interests in the second trust were held by skip persons.

In the case of a taxable distribution, the taxable amount is the net value of the property received by the distributee less any consideration paid by the distributee. In other words, the amount received by the distributee reduced by (1) any expenses incurred by the distributee in connection with the determination, collection, or refund of the GST tax, and (2) any consideration paid for the distribution. The transferee is obligated to pay the GST tax in a taxable distribution so if the trust pays the tax, the payment is treated as an additional taxable distribution.[12]

The tax levied upon a taxable distribution is *tax inclusive* meaning the amount subject to tax includes (1) the property *and* (2) the GST tax itself.

Example. If in 2021, a trustee makes a taxable distribution of $10,000 of trust income to a grandchild subject to a $4,000 GST tax paid by the grandchild. Therefore, with respect to a $10,000 taxable distribution, the grandchild will net only $6,000.

Taxable Termination

A taxable termination is essentially the termination by death, lapse of time, release of a power, or otherwise of an interest in property held in a trust resulting in skip persons holding all the interests in the trust. For instance, if Alan creates a trust with income to his son, Sam for live, with a remainder to his granddaughter, Gina, Sam's death terminates his life interest in trust property that then passes to Gina, a skip person. So, in this example, a taxable termination occurs on the date of the son's death. On the other hand, a taxable termination cannot occur as long as at least one nonskip person has a present interest in the property. However, nominal interests are disregarded in determining whether a person has an interest in a trust if a significant purpose for their creation is to postpone or avoid a GST tax.[13] Furthermore, there is no taxable termination if an estate or gift tax is imposed on the nonskip individual (the son in this example) at termination.

Example. Assume that in the above example, Sam has a general power of appointment. Pursuant to the trust document, if Sam fails to exercise such power, the remainder passes to Alan's granddaughter. In spite of the property passing to Alan's granddaughter (a skip person), the general power of appointment (even though unexercised) causes the remainder be included in Sam's (a nonskip person) gross estate. For that reason, at Sam's death, there would be no taxable termination.

In the case of a taxable termination, the taxable amount is the value of all property less (1) a deduction for any expenses, debts, and taxes (other than the GST tax) generated by the property, and (2) any consideration paid by the transferee. If one or more taxable terminations with respect to the same trust occur at the same time as a result of the death of an individual, the executor may elect to value all the taxable termination property under federal estate tax alternate valuation rules. The trustee (broadly defined to mean the person in actual or constructive possession of the GST property) is responsible for the payment of the tax generated by a taxable termination.

The tax payable upon a taxable termination is *tax inclusive* because, as with a taxable distribution, the property subject to the transfer includes the GST tax itself.

Direct Skips

A direct skip is a transfer to a skip person that is also subject to an estate or gift tax.

For example, a gift from an individual to a grandchild is a direct skip. Also, a direct skip is a transfer to a trust in which all the beneficiaries are skip persons. Therefore, a transfer of property into an irrevocable trust for the benefit of the transferor's grandchildren would be considered a direct skip.

For a direct skip, the taxable amount is the value of the property or interest in property (including the current right to receive income or corpus or power of appointment) received by the transferee, reduced by any consideration paid by the transferee. The transferor (the decedent in the case of a death time transfer or the donor in the case of a lifetime transfer) is responsible for payment of the GST tax.

The tax in a direct skip is *tax exclusive* meaning the tax is paid by the transferor or the estate and the taxable amount does not include the amount of GST tax.

Example. A grandfather makes a lifetime gift of $1 million to his granddaughter. Assume there is no GST tax exemption available and the inclusion ratio is one. The GST tax of $400,000 must be paid by the grandfather (not by the granddaughter transferee or out of the gift). Therefore, the grandchild will net the full amount of the $1 million gift.

Exemptions and Exclusions

As stated above, the GST exemption amount is $11,700,000 in 2021, rising to $12,920,000 in 2023 (see Figure 21.1, above). For married couples, each spouse has a GST tax exemption. For GST tax purposes, a gift split by the spouses will be treated as having been made half by each spouse, and each spouse can use some (or all) of his or her GST tax exemption to offset the GST tax.[14]

Certain transfers excluded from the definition of the term generation-skipping transfer include:

- certain transfers that, if made by gift would be gift tax free direct payments of the donee's educational or medical expenses.[15]

- transfers that would be gift tax free under the annual exclusion rules. Transfers in trust will not qualify for this exclusion unless (1) no portion of the trust's income or principal can be distributed to or used for the benefit of anyone other than the grandchild as long as the grandchild is alive, and (2) if the grandchild dies prior to the termination of the trust, the assets of the trust must be includable in the grandchild's estate. Thus, most transfers to dynastic-style trusts will *not* qualify for the GST annual exclusion even if there are *Crummey* powers added.[16]

- certain transfers that have already been subjected to the GST tax in which the transferee was in the same or lower generation as the present transferee.[17]

Unless the governing instrument directs otherwise (by specific reference to the GST tax), the GST tax is charged to the property constituting the transfer.[18]

Property subject to the GST tax must be valued as of the time of the GST. However, where the tax involves a direct skip (for example, from grandparent to grandchild), if the property is included in the transferor's estate, its value for GST tax purposes is the same as its value for federal estate tax purposes, including elections for the alternate valuation date or special-use valuation.

Computing the Tax

A GST tax exemption (see Figure 21.1) is allowed as a credit against the compute tax. Because married individuals making a lifetime transfer can elect to treat the transfer as if made one-half by each, the exemption can be doubled. To understand how this exemption works and how the tax is calculated, it is first necessary to determine the "inclusion ratio."

The inclusion ratio procedure is in two parts. Compute the *applicable fraction* as follows:

1. State the amount of the GST exemption allocated to the trust or direct skip. $_____
2. (a) State the value of the property transferred to the trust (or involved in the direct skip). $_____

(b) State the total of any federal estate or state death tax actually recovered from the trust attributable to such property. $_____
(c) State the amount of any charitable deduction allowed under estate or gift tax law with respect to the property. $_____
(d) Add (b) and (c). $_____
3. Subtract (d) from (a). $_____
4. Divide the line 1 exemption by line 3. This is the "applicable fraction." $_____

The inclusion ratio is 1 minus the applicable fraction (line 4).

An exception to the above computation is for a charitable lead annuity trust (CLAT). The computation for transfers to such a trust after October 13, 1987 is as follows:

GST exemption allocated to the transfer, increased by the interest rate used in computing the lead interest for the number of years of the term
―――――――――――――――――――――――
Actual value of property after the lead interest terminates

If a person allocates GST exemption equal to the remainder interest and if the trust performs as expected based on the IRS valuation tables, the numerator and denominator in the above fraction would be the same – 1/1. However, because it obviously impossible to predict how the trust will perform, the allocation of the GST exemption for a charitable lead annuity trust is a guessing game.

After computing the inclusion ratio, that number is multiplied by the maximum federal estate tax rate (see Figure 21.1) to arrive at the applicable rate. The total GST tax due is taxable amount multiplied by the applicable rate.[19]

The blank worksheet in Figure 21.2 and example worksheet in Figure 21.3 illustrate the entire process.

Liability for Payment of GST Tax

If the transfer is a taxable distribution, the transferee is obligated to pay the GST tax. The GST tax computed on the amount received by the transferee, less expenses relating to the determination of the GST tax. If the transfer is a taxable termination or partial termination, the trustee is obligated to pay the GST tax out of the amount to be distributed. The GST tax is computed on the value of the property in which the interest terminates, less expenses attributable to the property. In the case of direct skips (other than a direct skip from a trust), the transferor pays the GST tax. The GST tax is computed on the value of the property received.[20]

Special Provisions

There are special GST tax provisions that apply to the following:

- QTIP property (see below)

- taxation of multiple skips

- basis adjustments (In general, basis is increased by an amount equal to the portion of the GST tax attributable to the appreciation of the property transferred similar to the basis increase for gift tax paid discussed in the Chapter 20.[21])

- disclaimers (A disclaimer that results in property passing to a person at least two generations below that of the original transferor is subject to GST tax. For instance, assume a daughter disclaimed a bequest from her mother. As a result of that disclaimer, certain property passes to the mother's granddaughter. The GST tax would be imposed on the transfer – in addition to the federal estate tax.)

- administration

- return requirements (The GST tax return must be filed by the person liable for the payment of the GST tax. In the case of a direct skip other than a direct skip from a trust, the return must be filed on or before the due date of the applicable gift or estate tax return. In other cases, the GST tax return must be filed on or before the fifteenth day of the fourth month after the close of the taxable year in which the transfer occurs.)

If a trust has multiple generation skips, each skip would be taxed. For example, the beneficiaries of a trust could include a child, a grandchild, and a

GENERATION-SKIPPING TRANSFER TAX — CHAPTER 21

Figure 21.2

GENERATION-SKIPPING TRANSFER (GST) TAX WORKSHEET

Part A – Use to calculate GST tax for direct skips.
Part B – Use to calculate the new inclusion ratio for a trust whenever a transfer is made to the trust or GST exemption is allocated to the trust. It is generally preferable to keep the inclusion ratio for a trust at either one (no protection from GST tax) or zero (fully protected from GST tax). Apply ETIP and CLAT rules, if appropriate.
Part C – Use to calculate GST tax for taxable distributions and taxable terminations. Generally, use the inclusion ratio from Part B. If there were no other transfers to the trust and no other allocations of GST exemption to the trust, the inclusion ratio from Part A could be used for the trust.

Part A – GST Direct Skip

1. Transfer _____
2. Federal Estate or State Death Taxes Borne by Transfer _____
3. Federal Gift or Estate Tax Charitable Deduction _____
4. Nontaxable Gift Portion (GST Exclusions) _____
5. Total Reductions [(2) + (3) + (4)] _____
6. Net Transfer (Denominator) [(1) – (5)] _____
7. GST Exemption Allocated (Numerator) _____
8. Applicable Fraction [(7) / (6)] _____
9. Inclusion Ratio [1 – (8)] _____
10. Maximum Tax Rate _____
11. Effective Maximum Tax Rate _____ *
12. Applicable Rate [(9) × (11)] _____
13. GST Tax [(6) × (12)] _____

* If lifetime transfer, or GST tax is borne by other property, enter (10); otherwise, use formula [(10) / (1 + (10))]

Part B – GST Inclusion Ratio for Trust

1. Prior Applicable Fraction _____ *
2. Prior Value of Trust _____ *
3. Nontax Portion [(1) × (2)] _____ *
4. Current Transfer
5. Federal Estate or State Death Taxes Borne by Transfer _____
6. Federal Gift or Estate Tax Charitable Deduction _____
7. Nontaxable Gift Portion (if transfer is direct skip) _____
8. Total Reductions [(5) + (6) + (7)] _____
9. Net Transfer [(4) – (8)] _____
10. Current GST Exemption Allocation _____
11. Numerator [(3) + (10)] _____
12. Denominator [(2) + (9)] _____
13. New Applicable Fraction [(11) / (12)] _____
14. New Inclusion Ratio [1 – (13)] _____

* If no prior transfers have been made to this trust, enter 0

Part C – GST Taxable Termination/Distribution

1. Transfer _____
2. Inclusion Ratio _____
3. Maximum Tax Rate _____
4. Applicable Rate [(2) × (3)] _____
5. Gross Up Rate _____ *
6. Grossed Up Transfer [(1) × (1 + (5))] _____
7. GST Tax [(6) × (4)] _____

* If transfer is taxable distribution and donee pays GST tax, use formula [1 / (1 – (4)) – 1]; otherwise enter 0%

Figure 21.3

GENERATION-SKIPPING TRANSFER (GST) TAX WORKSHEET

Part A – Use to calculate GST tax for direct skips.
Part B – Use to calculate the new inclusion ratio for a trust whenever a transfer is made to the trust or GST exemption is allocated to the trust. It is generally preferable to keep the inclusion ratio for a trust at either one (no protection from GST tax) or zero (fully protected from GST tax). Apply ETIP and CLAT rules, if appropriate.
Part C – Use to calculate GST tax for taxable distributions and taxable terminations. Generally, use the inclusion ratio from Part B. If there were no other transfers to the trust and no other allocations of GST exemption to the trust, the inclusion ratio from Part A could be used for the trust.

Part A – GST Direct Skip

1	Transfer		8,000,000
2	Federal Estate or State Death Taxes Borne by Transfer	0	
3	Federal Gift or Estate Tax Charitable Deduction	0	
4	Nontaxable Gift Portion (GST Exclusions)	0	
5	Total Reductions [(2) + (3) + (4)]		0
6	Net Transfer (Denominator) [(1) – (5)]		8,000,000
7	GST Exemption Allocated (Numerator)		2,000,000
8	Applicable Fraction [(7) / (6)]		0.250
9	Inclusion Ratio [1 – (8)]		0.750
10	Maximum Tax Rate		40% *
11	Effective Maximum Tax Rate		0.40%
12	Applicable Rate [(9) × (11)]		0.30
13	GST Tax [(6) × (12)]		2,400,000

* If lifetime transfer, or GST tax is borne by other property, enter (10); otherwise, use formula [(10) / (1 + (10))]

Part B – GST Inclusion Ratio for Trust

1	Prior Applicable Fraction		0.250*
2	Prior Value of Trust		6,000,000*
3	Nontax Portion [(1) × (2)]		1,500,000*
4	Current Transfer		3,000,000
5	Federal Estate or State Death Taxes Borne by Transfer	0	
6	Federal Gift or Estate Tax Charitable Deduction	0	
7	Nontaxable Gift Portion (if transfer is direct skip)	0	
8	Total Reductions [(5) + (6) + (7)]		0
9	Net Transfer [(4) – (8)]		3,000,000
10	Current GST Exemption Allocation		1,000,000
11	Numerator [(3) + (10)]		2,500,000
12	Denominator [(2) + (9)]		9,000,000
13	New Applicable Fraction [(11) / (12)]		0.278
14	New Inclusion Ratio [1 – (13)]		0.722

* If no prior transfers have been made to this trust, enter 0

Part C – GST Taxable Termination/Distribution

1	Transfer	100,000
2	Inclusion Ratio	0.722
3	Maximum Tax Rate	40.0%
4	Applicable Rate [(2) × (3)]	0.289
5	Gross Up Rate	0.0%*
6	Grossed Up Transfer [(1) × (1 + (5))]	100,000
7	GST Tax [(6) × (4)]	28,900

* If transfer is taxable distribution and donee pays GST tax, use formula [1 / (1 – (4)) – 1]; otherwise enter 0%

Notes. Lifetime direct skip of $8,000,000 to trust in 2013, with GST exemption remaining to allocate of $2,000,000 (see Part A). Lifetime direct skip of $3,000,000 in 2013, with GST exemption remaining to allocate of $1,000,000, when trust is worth $6,000,000 (see Part B). [Tax on second direct skip not shown here.] Later, taxable distribution of $100,000 in 2013 (see Part C).

great-grandchild. A taxable termination would occur at the death of the child and at the death of the grandchild. But if a direct skip is directly to a great grandchild, there would be no further GST tax imposed.

Code section 303 can be used to make protected redemptions of stock to pay a GST tax.

Code section 6166, which allows for installment payments of federal estate tax also allows deferral of the GST tax generated by testamentary direct skips.

21.6 PLANNING FOR GST TAX

The GST tax is *in addition to* any estate or gift tax that may be due because of the transfer. To make matters worse, Code section 2515 adds the amount of the GST Tax paid on such gift to the amount subject to gift tax! For this reason, in many cases, the total cost of making a property transfer can exceed or approach the value of the gift.

Example. Assume, in 2021, a grandfather in the 40 percent gift tax bracket makes a $2,000,000 gift to a trust for his grandchild or to grandchild directly. Assume he has no further GST exemption to allocate to the transfer, and no applicable exclusion amount remaining. The GST tax is $800,000 ($2,000,000 × .40), paid by the grandfather. For gift tax purposes, the amount of the gift to the grandson is $2,800,000 ($2,000,000 + $800,000 pursuant to Code section 2515) with a gift tax of $1,120,000 ($2,800,000 × .40), also paid by the grandfather (unless there is a net gift agreement). Ouch!

Trust distributions are subject to GST tax whether they are made from income or from corpus. Recipients of income subject to the GST tax may take an income tax deduction (similar to the IRD deduction for estate tax under Code section 691) for the GST tax imposed on the distribution.

Allocation of the GST Tax Exemption

Given the potential severity of the GST tax, probably the most important planning decision is how to allocate the GST tax exemption. This is because the growth in value of any assets protected by the exemption is beyond the scope of the GST tax. Therefore, it would be prudent to include life insurance on the grantor's life among these assets. In selecting assets to be protected by the GST tax exemption, assets most likely to appreciate should be used. If asset values are rapidly increasing, the more quickly the allocation is made, the better.

The extent all or a portion of a GST tax exemption is allocated to a GST in computing the applicable fraction has an effect on the extent future appreciation on the property transferred would be exempt from the GST tax. For example, assume a divorced man transfers $1 million in trust for his children and grandchildren. To eliminate the GST tax, he allocates $1 million of GST tax exemption to the trust. No matter how the trust appreciates, no additional GST tax will ever be imposed.

Alternatively, if only $500,000 of the GST exemption had been allocated to the transfer, one-half of all future trust distributions to his grandchildren would be subject to GST tax as taxable distributions, and one-half of the value of the assets remaining in the trust would be subject to the GST tax upon the death of his children as taxable terminations.

Even if donor does nothing, the GST exemption will be automatically allocated to an *inter vivos* direct skip unless the donor elects otherwise. The GST exemption may be allocated by the donor (or the executor) among any property that is transferred. Once made, the election is irrevocable. Regulations specifically permit allocations of the exemption to be made by formula without requiring taxpayers to specify a dollar amount on the gift or estate tax return.[22]

For this purpose, a generation-skipping trust is generally any trust from which a generation-skipping transfer with respect to the transferor could be made unless the trust has certain provisions for nonskip persons. Such provisions include:

1. more than 25 percent of the trust must be distributed to, or withdrawn by, nonskip persons prior to reaching age forty-six (or a date or event prior to such birthday);

2. more than 25 percent of the trust must be distributed to, or withdrawn by, nonskip persons if they are living on the date of death of an individual named in the trust who is more than ten years older than such skip persons;

3. if a nonskip person dies before a date or event described in (1) or (2), more than 25 percent of

the trust must be distributed to such person's estate or subject to a general power of appointment by such individual;

4. the trust would be includable in the gross estate of a nonskip person (other than the transferor) if the person died immediately after the transfer; or

5. the trust is a CLAT, CLUT, CRAT, or CRUT with a nonskip remainder person.

As a general rule, the allocation of the exemption will be based on the fair market value of the property on the effective date of allocation. During the transferor's lifetime, the effective date of allocation for direct skips is the date of transfer. If a gift tax return is timely filed, the effective date of allocation even for GSTs other than direct skips is generally the date of transfer to which the Form 709 relates. Requests for an extension to make a timely allocation of GST tax exemption are permitted and the IRS has been quite lenient in granting such extensions.

Pursuant to EGTRRA 2001, certain retroactive allocations are permitted upon the death of certain nonskip beneficiaries. Also, for late allocations made during life, the transferor may, solely for purposes of determining the fair market value, elect to treat the allocation as having been made on the first day of the month during which the late allocation is made. However, if the insured has died, such an election is not effective with respect to life insurance.[23] For property held in trust, the allocation applies to the entire trust, rather than to specific trust assets.[24]

With respect to the allocation of the GST tax exemption to gifts of premium payments to an irrevocable life insurance trust, some practitioners suggest deliberately filing "late" so that the allocation will apply to the then reduced value of the policy rather than to the full amount of the premium. Obviously, this involves the risk of the insured dying and requiring the exemption to be allocated on the basis of the face amount of its policy. It may also require filing a gift tax return to elect out of automatic allocation.

As discussed above, taxable distributions and taxable terminations are *tax inclusive*, whereas direct skips are *tax exclusive*. Thus, it is more beneficial to use the GST tax exemption to minimize the tax on taxable distributions and terminations. Perhaps more importantly, many direct skips are gifts made directly to grandchildren,

so the exemption shelters only that transfer. If the exemption is allocated to a properly drafted trust, it may eliminate transfer tax at the death of two or more generations.

If at the transferor's death, the executor or some other person fails to allocate the exemption, it is allocated automatically according to a statutory formula. The statute allocates any unused exemption first to direct skips occurring at the individual's death on a pro rata basis, and then to any trusts from which a taxable distribution or termination could occur after the transferor's death.[25] Thus, the statutory order of allocation tends to be a less-than-optimal allocation of the GST tax exemption.

Split-Gifts and the Reverse QTIP Election

If pursuant to Code section 2513, spouses elect to split a gift, each spouse is deemed to be the transferor of one-half of the gift.[26] Since each spouse has a GST exemption to allocate, this can be extremely important in planning transfers potentially subject to GST tax.

If there is a difference between the available amount of GST tax exemption and the available amount of the applicable exclusion for estate tax purposes, so that decedent's bypass trust is funded with an amount less than the remaining GST tax exemption, the form of the marital bequest makes a difference. If the transfer is to a QTIP trust, even though the full marital deduction has been claimed, a reverse QTIP election solely for GST tax purposes can be made to treat the QTIP property as if no QTIP election had been made on the date of gift or death.[27] In other words, it is as if the QTIP was not funded, so for purposes of the GST tax, the property passed directly from the first spouse to die. For that reason, his or her unused GST tax exemption can be allocated to that amount. This is an "all or nothing election," i.e., the election must apply to all QTIP qualifying property in the trust. If the total value of the property in the QTIP trust could potentially exceed the available GST tax exemption, the will or trust should provide for division of the single QTIP trust into two trusts to take advantage of the reverse QTIP election as well as the unused GST tax exemption of the surviving spouse.

Example. In 2021, wife's taxable estate is valued at $12 million. Her estate plan creates three trusts – a bypass trust to offset her remaining estate unified credit equivalent (or applicable exclusion amount, of which she has $4,000,000 remaining), a reverse QTIP trust equal in value to any unused GST tax exemption not otherwise applied by her executor, and a second QTIP trust for the balance of her estate. Assuming the executor allocates $4,000,000 of the $11,700,000 (in 2021) GST tax exemption to the bypass trust and $7,700,000 of the remaining GST tax exemption allocated to the first QTIP trust. This will leave a second QTIP trust of $300,000 potentially subject to GST tax on subsequent distributions or termination. Upon the death of the husband, however, the executor could allocate his unused GST exemption to the second QTIP trust that would be included in his gross estate.

Grantor Retained Income, Annuity, and Unitrust ETIP

The GST tax may be applicable to transfers of remainder interests in property to a skip person in which the transferor retains the income, use of, or payment from a trust for a term of years In such a trust, it is possible to make such a transfer that is complete for gift tax purposes that is nonetheless includable in the transferor's gross estate. Perfect examples are a grantor retained income trust, grantor retained annuity trust, or grantor retained unitrust. These trusts are covered extensively in Chapter 29. Here, the issue is the GST tax consequences of the transfer of such remainder interests to skip persons. For GST tax purposes, the question is whether transfer is considered to be the date of gift or the date of the transferor's death.

With respect to these trusts, if the transferor were to die immediately after the transfer and the transferred property would be includable in the transferor's taxable estate under any statute other than Code section 2035, the allocation of the transferor's GST tax exemption will be postponed during the estate tax inclusion period (ETIP), running until the earlier of:

1. the date the property would no longer be included in the taxable estate;

2. the date there is an actual GST, or

3. if neither event occurs during the transferor's lifetime, the death of the transferor.

If the transfer is a direct skip, allocation is deemed to occur at the end of the ETIP. Importantly, the postponement period is operative solely for purpose of determining the inclusion ratio, and does not affect other rules (e.g., there is no step-up in generation for a child whose parent was alive when the transfer was made, even if the parent dies before the end of ETIP).

Multi-Generational Planning

Each successive taxable transfer to skip persons (i.e., grandchildren and great-grandchildren) is subject to GST tax. For example, where a trust provides for distributions to children for life, then grandchildren for life, remainder to great-grandchildren, it is possible to have three taxable events, – at the time the trust is created (estate or gift tax), when a child dies (taxable termination), and when the last surviving grandchild dies (taxable termination). However, a direct transfer to a person more than two generations below the transferor is subject to only one GST tax. For this reason, it may be advisable to create multi-generational trusts that permit distributions at least two generations below the transferor. Allowing distributions directly to great-grandchildren while the child is alive eliminates one level of tax. Also, direct transfers to grandchildren after a child is dead eliminate one level of tax, since the grandchildren move up a generation.

To take advantage of the GST tax exemptions of a married couple, a common approach to multi-generational planning is to create a dynasty trust intended to continue through succeeding generations as long as state law will permit. The actual distribution of these trust assets will be postponed as long as possible, to avoid estate tax as long as possible. Such trusts could last many years, limited only by the possible application of the rule against perpetuities, which prohibits the establishment of trusts that last indefinitely. For instance, if a trust with a present value of $2,000,000 is existence for at least seventy-five years, and grows at an annual rate of only 4 percent will be worth over $37,000,000. This kind of planning may appeal to clients who have a desire to preserve family wealth through succeeding generations.

Example. Tom and Pam Monson have an estate of $30,000,000, which is titled $16,000,000 in Tom's name and $14,000,000 in Pam's name. Many years ago, the Monsons decided to use life insurance and leveraging to maximize the utilization of their GST tax exemptions for the benefit of their five children and their issue. The Monsons made annual gifts to the trust to pay the life insurance premiums. Due to the annual exclusion ($15,000 in 2021), they are gift-tax free and are GST tax-free due to allocations of GST tax exemption (remember that the annual exclusion rules for GST tax purposes are far more restrictive than the annual exclusion rules for gift tax purposes). The premiums are $25,000 per year for sixteen years, for a total of $400,000 of premiums (assume $200,000 given by each spouse). The insurance is the "survivorship" type that only pays when the survivor dies. The Monsons have also each made taxable lifetime gifts of $5,000,000 (to which no GST tax exemption allocations were made), so they each have $6,700,000 of their applicable exclusion amount ($11,700,000 – $5,000,000) remaining and $11,500,000 of remaining GST tax exemption ($11,700,000-$200,000 GST exemption allocated to ILIT).

In this situation, although only $400,000 of GST tax exemption was allocated to the life insurance trust premiums, the entire $2,000,000 of insurance proceeds paid at the second spouse's death will be sheltered from GST tax and can be excluded from the children'. Therefore, they each have $11,500,000 of GST tax exemption remaining after deducting the allocations of GST tax exemption to the premiums.

At Tom's death in 2021, his $16,000,000 estate is divided $6,700,000 (the remaining applicable exclusion amount in 2021) to the bypass trust and $9,300,000 to the QTIP trust. However, the QTIP Trust is further divided into two QTIP Trusts. The first QTIP Trust, known as the non-exempt QTIP Trust, is funded with $4,500,000 ($11,500,000 – $4,800,000, and the second QTIP Trust, referred to as the exempt QTIP Trust, is funded with $4,800,000 ($11,500,000 – $6,700,000, the GST exemption already allocated to the bypass trust). Tom's executor allocates $6,700,000 of GST tax exemption to the bypass trust, $4,800,000 of GST tax exemption to the exempt QTIP Trust,.

At Pam's subsequent death (still assuming 2021 numbers), Pam's executor allocates $11,500,000 of her remaining GST tax exemption to her trusts and if any exemption is left over, to the GST non-exempt QTIP trust left to her by Tom.

If the assets were to grow in value after the allocations of exemptions, the amounts growing in the GST tax exempt trusts for the children would be even greater. Furthermore, as the trust continues to benefit subsequent generations, the value of the assets in the trust avoiding GST tax and estate tax may compound even further.

Planning to Pay Estate Tax Rather than GST Tax

Almost the reverse of multi-generational planning is planning transfers to trigger federal estate tax in the estates of each succeeding generation. Any transfer from a trust other than a direct skip that is subject to estate or gift tax with respect to a person in the first generation below the grantor is exempt from GST tax. In many situations, since the GST tax is computed at the highest possible federal estate tax rate, it would be preferable that property in a nonexempt trust pass through the taxable estates of children to grandchildren. In many cases, because the federal estate tax cannot exceed the GST tax, the latter tax will be substantially less. This could be accomplished by granting a child a general power of appointment over the trust property, at least up to the amount needed to increase the child's taxable estate to the highest estate tax bracket. While this may result in tax saving, there is always a danger the child will exercise the power and cause the property to pass to someone other than the grandchildren. Since the power to appoint to the creditors of the holder's estate (only) is considered a general power of appointment, limiting such power is a possible solution to this potential problem. Consider the effect that state estate tax (and less likely, state GST tax) may have on this comparison.

Exclusion for Nontaxable Gifts

Gift-tax free annual exclusion gifts are also exempt from GST tax. The inclusion ratio for nontaxable gifts is zero. This includes all gift-tax free gifts under Code sections 2503(b) and 2503(e), and by inference, 2503(c). In addition, nontaxable gifts to trusts would not have a zero inclusion unless:

1. No portion of the trust could be distributed to a person other than a single beneficiary, and

2. If that beneficiary dies before the trust terminates, the trust assets will be included in his estate.

Therefore, for purposes of the GST tax, the annual exclusion is not available for Crummey withdrawal powers (see Chapters 8 and 36).

To Skip or Not to Skip?

When estate planning contemplates skipping generations, the GST tax cost must be compared to the estate or gift tax cost of transferring the property to the first generation (children), who would then transfer it to the second generation (grandchildren). In making this determination, the relative tax cost on a tax inclusive basis should be considered.

1. Since the gift tax is exclusive of the gift, a 40 percent gift tax rate amounts to a tax inclusive rate of 28.57 percent [40% ÷ (1 + 40%)].

2. The estate tax inclusive rate is 40 percent, since the tax is included in the tax base, i.e., the taxable estate.

3. The GST tax on taxable distributions and terminations is tax inclusive, since it is imposed on the transferee, and the tax inclusive rate is 40 percent.

4. Similar to gift tax, the GST tax on direct skips is tax exclusive, resulting in a 28.57 percent tax inclusive rate.

5. However, the GST tax on lifetime gifts is also considered to be a taxable gift, and a gift tax will be paid on the GST tax. The total gift and GST tax could equal 96 percent [40% × (1 + (1 +.40))] of the value of the gift [but see (7) below].

6. Also, if a direct skip is made at death, the GST tax will have to be paid from assets that were also subject to the federal estate tax; but the estate tax and the GST tax reduce the GST. The total estate and GST tax could equal 57.14 percent [(40% × 1) + (28.57% × (1 − .40))] of the value of the transfer.

7. On the other hand, if a lifetime direct skip gift is made, both the gift tax and GST tax paid will reduce the taxable estate of the donor (in the case of the gift tax, assuming the donor lives at least three years after the transfer). For example, the gift in (5) above would remove the gift plus the taxes on the gift from his estate.

Other Planning Considerations

As a general rule, the GST tax applies to transfers after October 22, 1986. However, lifetime transfers that were made after September 25, 1985 and were subject to gift tax are also subject to the GST tax. GST tax does not apply to any transfer from a trust that was irrevocable on September 25, 1985, provided no additions are made after that date. Even if a trust is grandfathered for GST purposes, the trust may become tainted to the extent that there are either actual or constructive additions.

A constructive addition will occur where a general power of appointment is exercised or released, or lapses over a portion of the grandfathered trust. However a constructive addition will not occur where a nongeneral power of appointment is exercised if the exercise will not postpone or suspend the vesting, absolute ownership, or power of alienation of the interest for a period longer than allowed by the rule against perpetuities from the date of the creation of the trust. However, the exercise of a power of appointment that validly postpones or suspends the vesting, absolute ownership, or power of alienation of an interest in property for a term of years that will not exceed ninety years (measured from the date of creation of the trust) is not considered an exercise that will extend beyond the perpetuities period.[28]

These rules create the opportunity to change the distribution of grandfathered trusts via exercise of nongeneral powers of appointment without adversely affecting its grandfathered (exempt from GST tax) status.

Since irrevocable trusts created before September 26, 1985, are completely exempt from the GST tax system (but only to the extent no additions are made to the trust from that date), it is important not to taint such trusts by adding new property to them. Not only would this create a tax where none existed, but it would also create an administrative nightmare tracking and allocating pre- and post- September 26 assets and appreciation.

Whenever possible, transfer some assets from a rich spouse to a less wealthy spouse (or, see Chapter 33 on Intervivos QTIP Trusts). Similar to the rationale for making transfers to a spouse in order to achieve the full benefit of both spouses' unified credits, it should be noted that GST equalization is more important than the unified credit equalization since GST exemption is not subject to portability. So a transfer of property to a less wealthy spouse can double the advantage of the GST exemption, since both spouses can take advantage of it.

Greater emphasis should now be placed on protecting irrevocable life insurance trusts from the GST tax by advising clients to consider allocating a portion of the GST exemption to each transfer made to the trust. Significantly, allocating a portion of the GST exemption to shield twenty $50,000 annual premium gifts to an irrevocable life insurance trust protects not only that $1,000,000 of total gifts, but also the future trust corpus generated by the death benefit that ultimately passes to the trust. Leveraging the GST exemption this way (for as long as this technique is valid) may be the single most effective long term means of preserving wealth within the family.

Remember that GST can be allocated late while the settlor is still living, which in some circumstances may be even be superior to making timely allocations.[29]

21.7 ISSUES IN COMMUNITY PROPERTY STATES

In community property states, gift splitting or transferring property from one spouse to the other may not be necessary to enable both spouses to fully use their respective GST exemptions.

21.8 FREQUENTLY ASKED QUESTIONS

Question – The will of a client provides for a family trust that authorizes the trustee to make distributions from the trust to the spouse, children, and grandchildren of client. On the death of the spouse, the trust will be distributed to the then surviving children. However, if no children then survive, the share of such a deceased child will pass to the child's issue. Under what circumstances will trust distributions be subject to GST tax?

Answer – Distributions of trust income or principal to the spouse and children will not be subject to GST tax. The spouse is assigned to the same generation as the client, and the children to the first generation below. Thus, none of these beneficiaries are skip persons. However, any income or principal distributions to grandchildren will be subject to GST tax, since they are skip persons (unless the client's GST exemption allocated to the trust was sufficient to give the trust a zero inclusion ratio).

When the spouse dies, distributions of shares of the trust to children will not be subject to GST tax, since the children are not skip persons. However, any distribution of a share of the trust to the issue of a deceased child of the client will be a taxable termination subject to GST tax, since the grandchildren are skip persons.

Question – Client's will directs that his estate be distributed to a trust that will be divided into separate shares, one for each of his children living at his death, and one for the issue of any child who predeceased the client. Under what circumstances will distributions from this trust be subject to GST tax?

Answer – Under the GST rules, separate shares in a single trust are treated as separate trusts. Distributions to children from the trusts created for them are not subject to GST tax, since they are not skip persons. Distributions from the shares set aside for the issue of a child who predeceased the client are also not subject to GST tax. The reason is that when a transfer is made to grandchildren of the transferor whose parents are predeceased, those grandchildren move up a generation. As a result, the grandchildren of a predeceased parent are no longer skip persons, and distributions to them should not trigger a GST tax.

Question – Under the terms of an irrevocable trust, the trustee is directed to accumulate income until the beneficiary attains age twenty-one, and cannot make corpus distributions to the beneficiary until that time. For GST purposes, does the beneficiary have an "interest" in the trust?

Answer – The beneficiary has no interest in the trust until attaining age twenty-one. This is because the beneficiary is not entitled to receive any present distributions of trust income or principal. If that person is the only beneficiary, there is no person with an interest in the trust. If the beneficiary is a skip person, the transfer to trust would be a direct skip.

Question – A Transferor creates a trust providing for an annuity payable to his granddaughter for life, remainder to charity. Assume this is a qualified charitable remainder trust (see Chapter 38). Who is treated as having an interest in the trust?

Answer – Both the granddaughter and the charity have interests in the trust, and the future interest of the charity becomes a present interest for GST tax purposes. This is a special rule that only applies to charities. The transfer to the trust cannot be a direct skip since the charity, which is assigned to the transferor's generation, has an interest. However, distributions to the granddaughter will be taxable distributions to a skip person.

Question – A family trust created under a will is a pot trust for lineal descendants, which will terminate and be distributed to then living lineal descendants when the youngest grandchild attains age sixty-five. Assuming all children of the testator die before the youngest grandchild attains age sixty-five, what are the GST tax consequences?

Answer – Upon the death of the last child, there is a taxable termination, since the only remaining beneficiaries of the trust, grandchildren and possibly their descendants, are skip persons. Immediately after the taxable termination, the transferor is treated as being one generation above the grandchildren, so that subsequent distributions to the grandchildren will not be taxed again. But distributions to their descendants will be subject to GST tax.

Question – At the date of death, the estate value of assets in decedent's estate is $2 million. The will provides that the executor is to allocate $1 million in assets to a trust based on date of death value. However, the actual value of the assets transferred to the trust at date of allocation has increased from $1 million to $1.3 million. For purposes of computing the exclusion ratio, is the denominator of the fraction $1,000,000 or $1,300,000?

Answer – The denominator of the fraction is the pecuniary amount ($1 million in this example) only if the pecuniary payment of property must be satisfied on a basis that fairly reflects net appreciation or depreciation (between the valuation date and the date of distribution) in all of the assets from which the distribution could have been made. Otherwise the denominator of the fraction would have to be the date of distribution value ($1.3 million in this example). However, if the estate has additional GST exemption, likely in this example, it may be allocated.[30]

Question – Transferor conveyed property worth $500,000 to a generation-skipping trust in 2016 and allocated $300,000 of her exemption to it. In 2021, when that property was worth $700,000, she transferred $100,000 cash to the trust, and claimed a $100,000 exemption. What is the inclusion ratio?

Answer – The inclusion ratio is:

$$1 - \frac{\$100,000 + (.600 \times \$700,000)}{\$100,000 + \$700,000} =$$

$$1 - \frac{\$520,000}{\$800,000} = .350$$

The .600 represents the nontax portion of the trust before the second transfer, $300,000/$500,000.[31]

Question – Where a preexisting life insurance trust is grandfathered as a pre-September 25, 1985 trust, can gifts to cover premium payments continue without the trust being subject to GST tax?

Answer – No, additional transfers to pay life insurance premiums would be considered additions to the trust. The additions to the trust will result in inclusion of part of the trust for GST tax purposes, unless the lifetime exemption is allocated to cover the portion of the trust that is not grandfathered.

CHAPTER ENDNOTES

1. Congress first enacted a GST tax in 1976. That tax was repealed in 1986 and replaced by the current GST tax.
2. I.R.C. §§2601, 2602.
3. I.R.C. §2652(b).
4. I.R.C. §2631.
5. I.R.C. §2641.
6. I.R.C. §2651.
7. I.R.C. §2653(a).
8. I.R.C. §2651(e).
9. I.R.C. §2613.
10. I.R.C. §2652(c).
11. I.R.C. §2612(b).
12. I.R.C. §2621.
13. I.R.C. §2652(c)(2); Treas. Reg. §26.2612-1(e)(2)(ii).
14. I.R.C. §2652(a)(2).
15. I.R.C. §2611(b).
16. I.R.C. §2642(c).
17. I.R.C. §2611(b).
18. I.R.C. §2603(b).

19. I.R.C. §2641, 2642.
20. I.R.C. §2603.
21. I.R.C. §2654(a).
22. Treas. Reg. §26.2632-1(d).
23. Treas. Reg. §26.2642-2(a)(2).
24. Treas. Reg. §26.2632-1.
25. I.R.C. §2632(c).
26. I.R.C. §2652(a)(2).
27. I.R.C. §2652(a)(3).
28. Treas. Reg. §26.2601-1(b)(1)(v)(B)(2).
29. See *Dan Griffith & Ed Morrow on Using 20/20 Hindsight for Allocating GST Exemption to 2021 Gifts to Trust*, LISI Estate Planning Newsletter #2982 (Sept. 19, 2022).
30. Treas. Reg. §26.2642-2(b).
31. I.R.C. §2642(d).

ized accounting to understand the

FEDERAL INCOME TAX ISSUES

CHAPTER 22

22.1 INTRODUCTION

The estate or financial planner must attain a degree of familiarity with the income taxation of estates and trusts or the so-called fiduciary income taxation, in order to be able to spot issues and to properly service clients. This should include familiarity with Income in Respect of a Decedent (IRD). This chapter is merely an introduction to this complex subject and is intended to provide you with a working knowledge of fiduciary income taxation; it will not make you an expert.[1] Only through a working knowledge of the income tax ramifications of various trust arrangements will a member of the estate planning team be able to properly advise clients. Additionally, the estate or financial planner must also be familiar with the rules for income tax basis, especially for property transferred by gift or at death, and this chapter discusses those basis issues as well. Further, there is a supplement to our discussion in Chapter 30 concerning grantor trusts. Finally, we also include in this chapter an introductory discussion of so-called equitable adjustments.

With the exception of grantor trusts (see below), trusts and estates are treated in the tax law as separate taxpayers that are required to file annual federal income tax returns. Income to the trust is either retained or distributed to beneficiaries. Generally, the trust or estate reports and pays tax on the income it *retains*, while beneficiaries report *distributions* received from the trust or estate as income on their own returns.

22.2 FIDUCIARY ACCOUNTING BASICS

You might be wondering why you need to know anything about fiduciary accounting to understand the income taxation of trusts and estates. The answer is that the definition of fiduciary accounting income, which the fiduciary must maintain since that differs from the definition of "distributable net income" that we discuss below, nevertheless has a material effect on distributable net income. This requires a fiduciary to maintain (at least) two sets of books: one for tax purposes and one for purposes of fiduciary accounting. Fiduciary accounting income is important because it is the starting point for determining income for income tax purposes.[2] Applicable local law and the governing instrument, be it a will or a trust, can dictate, within limits, what constitutes "fiduciary accounting income." There is a uniform act, the Uniform Principal and Income Act (UPIA), which many states have adopted. We will not discuss the UPIA in-depth, but we will introduce the UPIA because it can have a material bearing on the taxation of the trust or estate.

Under the UPIA, items of income and expense are allocated to the income share of the estate or trust, the principal share, or allocated between the income and principal shares. Generally, items such as rents,[3] dividends[4] and interest[5] are apportioned to the income share of the estate or trust, and capital gains are apportioned to the principal share.[6] However, the governing instrument can provide for another allocation result. The IRS will respect the provisions of the governing instrument with respect to the allocation of items of income and expense between the income and principal shares, within reason.

However, the IRS usually will not recognize trust provisions that depart fundamentally from traditional principles of income and principal, presumably, standards similar to those that are in the UPIA are what the IRS contemplates as "traditional principles."[7] For example, if a trust instrument allocated interest, rents

357

and dividends to corpus that was never distributed, that allocation would not be given tax effect.

The types of items that are allocated to varying degrees between income and principal include deferred compensation, annuities and similar arrangements;[8] items that are liquidating assets, including leasehold, patent, copyright, royalty right and right to receive payments during a period of more than one year under an arrangement that does not provide for the payment of interest on the unpaid balance;[9] mineral and water or other natural resource assets;[10] and timber.[11]

Through a fairly recent amendment to the UPIA, one that was spurred by the increasing popularity of investing for total return and the advent of Total Return UniTrusts (TRUs),[12] a fiduciary now has the power under the UPIA, subject to some limitations, to adjust between income and principal "as necessary" in order to invest as a "prudent investor" who seeks to maximize total return rather than simply aiming to maximize either growth or income. In its decision, a trustee must consider a variety of factors that are layered over the duty of impartiality to all of the beneficiaries, which applies unless the trust instrument clearly alters that duty and expressly requires the trustee to favor a beneficiary or a class of beneficiaries.[13]

These factors include:

(1) the nature, purpose and expected duration of the trust or estate;

(2) the testator's or settlor's intent;

(3) the circumstances of the beneficiaries;

(4) the liquidity needs, the need for regularity of income and the importance of preservation and appreciation of the principal;

(5) the type of assets held in the trust or estate; the extent to which they consist of financial assets, interests in closely held enterprises, tangible and intangible personal property or real property; the extent to which an asset is used by a beneficiary; and whether an asset was purchased by the fiduciary or received from the settlor or testator;

(6) the net amount allocated to income under the other sections of the UPIA and the increase or decrease in the value of the principal assets, which the fiduciary may estimate as to assets for which market values are not readily available;

(7) whether and to what extent the terms of the instrument give the fiduciary the power to invade principal or accumulate income or prohibit the fiduciary from invading principal or accumulating income, and the extent to which the fiduciary has exercised a power from time to time to invade principal or accumulate income;

(8) the actual and anticipated effect of economic conditions on principal and income and effects of inflation and deflation; and

(9) the anticipated tax consequences of an adjustment.[14]

Despite this power, a fiduciary has no power to adjust if:

(1) the adjustment diminishes the income interest in a trust that requires all of the income to be paid at least annually to a spouse and for which an estate tax or gift tax marital deduction would be allowed, in whole or in part, if the trustee did not have the power to make the adjustment;

(2) the adjustment reduces the actuarial value of the income interest in a trust to which a person transfers property with the intent to qualify for a gift tax exclusion;

(3) the adjustment changes the amount that is payable to a beneficiary either as a fixed annuity or a fixed fraction of the value of the trust assets;

(4) the adjustment involves any amount that is permanently set aside for charitable purposes under a will or the terms of a trust unless both income and principal are so set aside;

(5) possession or exercise the power to make an adjustment causes an individual to be treated as the owner of all or part of the trust for income tax purposes, and the individual would not be treated as the owner if the trustee did not possess the power to make an adjustment;

(6) possession or exercise of the power to make an adjustment causes all or part of the trust assets to be included for estate tax purposes in the estate of an individual who has the power to remove a trustee or appoint a trustee, or both,

and the assets would not be included in the estate of the individual if the trustee did not possess the power to make an adjustment;

(7) the trustee is a beneficiary of the trust; or

(8) the trustee is not a beneficiary, but the adjustment would benefit the trustee directly or indirectly.[15]

Example. Here is an example of an adjustment between income and principal. Assume that $1,000,000 is held in trust, and there is an income beneficiary and a separate principal beneficiary. Assume further that the trust instrument expressly authorizes the trustee to make adjustments between principal and income and that the trustee is not a beneficiary and is authorized to invest for total return. The trustee determined that investing for the maximum return for this particular trust means investing in a portfolio of growth stocks that pay no dividends. The trustee determines that the S&P 500 average dividend rate is 2.5 percent. The trustee adjusts an amount of principal into income with respect to 2.5 percent of the current value of the trust, and the trustee distributes that amount to the income beneficiary.

The fiduciary also has the express authority under the UPIA to make various equitable adjustments between income and principal.[16] These adjustments generally involve apportionment of income to principal and are for items such as depreciation,[17] certain primarily real estate items[18] and tax items such as elections that are available to the fiduciary.[19] For example, the executor usually has the discretion of how and when to charge so-called "swing items," i.e., deductions that can be taken either on the estate tax return or the fiduciary income tax return, but not in both places, and whether and how to make equitable adjustments to income and principal for this purpose.

The concept of so-called equitable adjustments arises to a great extent from a conflict between the various duties that fiduciaries simultaneously owe to all of the beneficiaries. Some of these duties include:

(1) duty of impartiality;

(2) duty of loyalty and to refrain from self-dealing;

(3) duty to prudently manage the assets under the fiduciary's control;

(4) duty to conserve the estate or trust;

(5) duty to minimize or save taxes;

(6) duty to properly account for the assets, income and expenses of the estate or trust; and

(7) duty to follow the applicable law, including the tax law.

An inherent potential for conflict exists among the fiduciary's duties. For example, the duties to conserve the estate or trust and minimize taxes may cause the fiduciary to consider violating the duty of impartiality to the various beneficiaries of the estate, particularly where the beneficiaries of income and principal are different. The duty to conserve an estate or trust may conflict with the fiduciary's duty to properly account for fiduciary income and principal according to fiduciary accounting principles. The need for equitable adjustments arises when some of these fiduciary duties conflict and cause the fiduciary to be unable to avoid breaching one of those duties by honoring another.

As noted above, an equitable adjustment can arise for any number of possible reasons. We have identified at least one type of commonly made equitable adjustments, which actually has a name that it received from Warms, a 1955 New York surrogate court decision.[20] The so-called Warms adjustment often is made when the executor of an estate can elect to deduct estate administration expenses as *either* estate tax deductions or income tax deductions and makes the choice one way or the other. If deducted on the estate tax return, the tax benefit of the deduction typically inures to the estate's principal beneficiaries. An election to deduct the expenses on one or more of the fiduciary income tax returns transfers the tax savings of that deduction to the estate's income beneficiaries. Estate administration expenses generally are paid out of principal rather than income. Pursuant to the applicable rules of fiduciary accounting, an election to deduct the expenses on the fiduciary income tax returns shifts the benefit of the deduction away from the recipients of estate principal, who bear the fiduciary accounting actual cost of the expense. An equitable adjustment can restore principal by reallocating estate income to principal. Conversely, if the executor elects to take the deduction on the fiduciary income tax return, which frequently happens, particularly where the estate has no estate tax liability due to a marital deduction, the income beneficiaries arguably are harmed because the loss of the income tax deduction increases the amount of income tax that either the estate or the income recipients will have to pay. However, because those expenses are properly borne by the principal beneficiaries, no adjustment is necessary.

22.3 INCOME TAXATION OF TRUSTS AND ESTATES

General Scheme of Taxation

Even though trusts and estates are not treated as legal persons for purposes of state law since they act solely through the trustee or executor, trusts and estates are treated by the tax law as separate taxpayers that are required to file annual federal income tax returns.[21] The problem that Congress faced in taxing the income of trusts or estates was trying to decide how to tax trusts and estates, and, specifically, whether to tax trusts and estates in a manner similar to corporations or partnerships or to tax them in some hybrid form.

If a trust or estate were to be taxed like a corporation, then there would be a double taxation–the trust or estate would be taxed on its income for the year, and the beneficiaries would be taxed a second time on the distribution received. Beneficiaries would be treated like shareholders who receive taxable dividends even though the corporation's taxable income includes the same dollars that were used to make the dividend distribution. Such double taxation, especially for small estates or trusts, coupled with the high income rates that presently imposed on trusts and estates in very compressed income tax brackets, would make this approach highly unfavorable to taxpayers. Therefore, Congress rejected this approach.

If a trust or estate were to be taxed as a partnership, then the trust or federal estate income tax return would merely be informational like that of a partnership. All of the income of the trust or estate would be taxed to the individual beneficiaries, just as partners in a partnership must report their proportionate shares of the taxable income of the partnership on their own individual returns. This method would be particularly harsh in cases where the trustee has discretion to either accumulate or distribute income and chose to accumulate it, or in an estate where an executor generally has no duty to distribute income until the termination of the estate. If this approach had been adopted, then a beneficiary could be paying tax on amounts not yet received, which would have been inequitable, so it too was rejected by Congress.

Therefore, Congress chose to adopt a hybrid approach for estates and trusts that is known as the "sharing" concept. The general rule is that the trust or estate will pay income tax on the amount that the fiduciary (trustee or executor) retains. Beneficiaries generally will pay the tax on the income of the trust or estate that is actually distributed to them. The mechanics of obtaining this result are obtained through the utilization of a somewhat simple yet sometimes deceptively complex concept known as "distributable net income" (DNI), which is defined as the taxable income of an estate or trust, but modified as follows:

(1) no deduction for amounts that were distributed to the beneficiaries;

(2) no personal exemption;

(3) exclusion of capital gains that allocable to trust or estate corpus and not paid, credited or required to be paid out in the taxable year to a beneficiary;

(4) capital losses are excluded to the extent that such losses are taken into account in determining the amount of gains from the sale or exchange of capital assets that are paid, credited or required to be distributed to any beneficiary during the taxable year; and

(5) tax-exempt income is added.[22] Thus, income is taxed only once, either to the beneficiary or to the estate or trust.

Distributable Net Income (DNI)

The DNI concept is utilized to achieve three main results. First, it ensures that the trust or estate receives a deduction for amounts distributed, but, as will be demonstrated in the next paragraph, DNI also provides a limit for that distribution deduction. For example, assume that a trust earns $25,000 in income and distributes $15,000 of that income to the sole beneficiary. The trust would be taxed on the amount that it retains, $10,000, and the trustee would have a special distribution deduction of $15,000 for the amounts that the trustee distributed to the beneficiary.[23] Thus, the $15,000 that the trustee actually distributed to the beneficiary would be taxed only once, and then to the beneficiary. As a result, all $25,000 of trust income is taxed only once, and this is DNI in operation.

Second, DNI limits the portion of distributions that is taxable to beneficiaries. Sometimes, fiduciaries distribute principal and amounts that exceed the fiduciary's taxable income for a year. If the trust in the above example had distributed $50,000 to the beneficiary instead of just $15,000, then the trust would be allowed to only deduct $25,000 (i.e., the amount of fiduciary income in that year), and the trust would have no fiduciary income tax liability (because the $25,000 distribution deduction that it receives wipes out the $25,000 of income that it recognized). This is DNI in operation to limit a distribution deduction. The beneficiary would be taxed on only $25,000 of the $50,000 that the beneficiary received since only that amount was attributable to the fiduciary income for that year, with the other $25,000 being treated as a tax-free distribution of trust principal.

To reiterate: The first $25,000 is deemed to have come from income; and the balance, $25,000, is considered a tax-free distribution of trust corpus. In this case, for tax purposes, the characterization of the $50,000 and its breakdown into income and corpus are not left to the trustee to decide as the fiduciary income tax rules do that for the fiduciary. As you might expect, the first distribution is treated all as income to the extent of trust DNI. Under the so-called "income first" rule, the trustee's classification of a distribution as "income" or "corpus" is ignored; instead, all amounts distributed are deemed to be income to the extent of DNI[24]. For example, assume that a trust had interest income of $75,000 that a trustee decided to accumulate for the future benefit of the trust beneficiaries. In that same year, the trustee decided to distribute $50,000 of trust corpus (or principal) to one of the beneficiaries. If the trustee made this distribution, then the beneficiary would be deemed to have received $50,000 in income, even though in actuality the trustee might have been distributing an amount from corpus, all because of the "income first" rule. Because the fiduciary income, and, thus, the DNI, exceeded the amount of the principal distribution, *all* of the distribution will be taxed as income, for which the trustee would receive a distribution deduction on the trust fiduciary income tax return (Form 1041). As you can well imagine, beneficiaries often do not like the income first rule, since it favors the IRS. It also requires additional work for the fiduciary to square the fiduciary accounting implications of such a distribution with the fiduciary income tax results.

The third and final function of DNI is to ensure that the character of distributions to a beneficiary remains the same as in the hands of a trust or estate. For example, tax-exempt interest received by a trust and distributed to a beneficiary retains its character as tax-exempt interest excluded from the gross income of the distribute beneficiary or heirs.[25] This is known as the "conduit" theory, and is particularly important when calculating the Net Investment Income Tax (see below). Generally, the different types of income that are included in DNI retain their characterizations and are proportionally distributed to beneficiaries or heirs.[26] Likewise, what enters the trust or estate as ordinary income (or capital gains) remains ordinary income (or capital gains) when the fiduciary distributes it to the beneficiaries or heirs.

Example. A trust receives $30,000 in ordinary income and $10,000 in tax-exempt interest income for the year. All of the income is distributed evenly between two beneficiaries. Regardless of the actual accounting used by the trust, each beneficiary will be deemed to have received $15,000 in ordinary income and $5,000 in tax-exempt interest income.

Income Taxation of Trusts

As noted above, a trust is treated as a tax-paying entity and must pay tax on its income.[27] The taxable income of a trust (or an estate) is computed in basically the same manner as that of an individual, but with some significant modifications.[28] However, the tax brackets for trusts (and estates) are much more compact and progressive (though they are the same tax rates) than those for individuals. In other words, given the same amount of income, a trust or estate will pay a *much* higher tax for income that the fiduciary retains than an individual would pay. This has the practical effect of sometimes forcing fiduciaries to make some tough decisions based upon available options that present a Hobson's choice: either (1) distribute more to the beneficiary than the fiduciary believes that the beneficiary can handle or will spend providently in order to minimize the tax consequences to the estate or trust or (2) retain the income in order to protect the beneficiary and pay more income tax than the beneficiary would have been required to pay had the fiduciary distributed that income to the beneficiary. Either way, a fiduciary is susceptible to being second guessed on these hard decisions in the future by Monday morning quarterbacks in the form of fiduciary litigation plaintiff lawyers who are representing the beneficiary or heir at some point down the road.

In computing tax liability, multiple trusts are treated as one trust and their incomes are aggregated if the trusts have substantially the same grantor or grantors and substantially the same primary beneficiary or beneficiaries and if a principal purpose for the existence of the trusts is the avoidance of federal income tax.[29] You cannot reduce income taxes by creating "cookie-cutter" replica trusts for the same beneficiaries.

Generally, for tax purposes, trusts are treated as separate entities from the grantor, the trustee and the beneficiary. The basic question in the income taxation of trusts is "Who will be taxed on trust income—the trust, the beneficiary or the grantor?" Generally, the burden of taxation falls on either the trust itself or the beneficiary unless the trust is treated as a completely grantor trust for income tax purposes. But it is possible for the income of the trust to be taxed to the grantor in a so-called "grantor trust" situation where, for income tax purposes, the trust is essentially deemed to be the alter ego of the grantor. In fact, transactions between the grantor and a grantor trust are ignored for income tax purposes.[30]

Trusts are categorized for income tax purposes as either "simple" or "complex" trusts. Either type of trust also may be a "grantor" trust.

The 2023 income tax rates for trusts and estates are as follows:

2023 Tax Rates for Trusts and Estates

Taxable Income

From:	But Not Over:	Tax Rate:
$0	$2,900	10.0%
$2,901	$10,550	$290 + 24% of whatever is over $2,900
$10,551	$14,450	$2,126 + 35% of the amount over $10,450
$14,451		$3,491 + 37% of the amount over $14,550

Simple v. Complex Trusts

A "simple" trust has the following characteristics:[31]

- The trust agreement requires that all trust income be distributed currently to the beneficiaries.

- The trust may not make distributions from amounts other than current income;

- Principal may not be distributed; and

- No charitable gifts can be made.

A simple trust is treated as a separate tax entity. As such, it has the same deductions that an individual has, subject to certain exceptions. In that event, it also has a special distribution deduction for income that is distributable to its beneficiaries. The net result is that a simple trust would not pay tax on income that it pays out. The beneficiary of a simple trust will report the income that the beneficiary receives or that is receivable by the beneficiary. In other words, a simple trust acts like a funnel–a true and complete conduit for passing the trust income from the grantor to the beneficiaries.

A second type of trust is known as the "complex" trust. A complex trust is any trust which is not a simple trust, that is, a complex trust is one in which the trustee either must—or may—accumulate income. The trustee of a complex trust, unlike the trustee of a simple trust, can distribute corpus (principal) and also can make gifts to charities.

A complex trust, like a simple trust, is a separate tax entity. It is allowed a special deduction for actual distributions of income. But a complex trust pays tax on any income that it does not distribute. Generally, the same rules that govern complex trusts apply also to the income taxation of a decedent's estate, as estates are taxed as complex trusts.

A trust is not allowed a standard deduction. Further, the personal exemption is limited to $300 for a simple trust and $100 for a complex trust. (If a trust is required to distribute its income to a beneficiary, then it will not lose the $300 exemption even if it distributes corpus or makes a charitable contribution in a given year and, thus, is considered complex for all other purposes for that taxable year.)

In some cases, the trust itself is disregarded as a taxable entity. This means the grantor (not the beneficiaries) would be taxed on trust income, for example, is either a simple or complex trust in which the trust is disregarded as a taxable entity. Generally, in the case of either a simple or a complex trust, the trust or its beneficiary will be taxable on the income of the trust. However, in some cases, the grantor is taxed on the trust income whether or not the grantor actually receives the income. This actually is a popular estate planning technique wherein a trust in which the grantor has no retained interest is set up to purposely be a grantor trust so that the grantor will be liable for the income tax. In essence, the grantor's payment of the trust's income tax effectively is a transfer for the benefit of the trust beneficiaries, who are relieved from the income tax burden at either the trust or personal level, which is not treated as a gift because the grantor is legally liable for paying the income tax on trust income.

If the grantor of a trust possesses any of the powers set forth in Code Sections 671 to 678 (discussed below), are known as the "grantor will be taxed on-trust" rules. An understanding of these rules is essential for the trust tax planner.

Code Section 671 – Substantial Owner Rules

When the grantor of a trust is treated as the owner of a portion of the trust corpus for income tax purposes, those items of income, gain, loss, deduction and credit that are attributable to that power. Importantly, for estate tax purposes, portion of the trust are deemed to be those of the grantor. Accordingly, the grantor of the trust is deemed to be the recipient of trust income and is allowed a deduction or credit to the extent that there are trust expenses and/or credits. Note, however, that the grantor is owner only for income tax purposes under this rule. Possible estate tax inclusion or exclusion must be tested under the estate tax rules, which are different rules that are applied to determine whether from the income tax grantor trust corpus is included in the rules. (This applies to all of the grantor's gross estate. Code Sections covered below.)

Using DNI to Characterize the Beneficiary's Income

Section 673 – Reversionary Interest Rules

For income tax purposes (subject to a limited exemption for reversionary interests taking effect on the death of a minor lineal descendant under age twenty-one),[32] the grantor is treated as the owner of that portion of a trust in which the grantor or the grantor's spouse has a reversionary interest in either the corpus or the income if, as of the date of inception of that trust or at the time of an addition to that trust, the value of the reversionary interest exceeds 5 percent of the value of the property in which the reversion is retained.[33] For instance, arbitrarily assuming a 6.0 percent Section 7520 rate, the value of the reversionary interest exceeds 5 percent of the value of a term trust if the trust runs for any period of time less than approximately fifty-two years. It's actually over ninety-nine years whenever the AFR is below 2 percent.

Section 674 – Beneficial Interest Rules

In general, where a grantor of a trust, a non-adverse party, or both can control the beneficial enjoyment of a trust, the grantor is taxed as the owner of the trust for income tax purposes.[34] However, if the grantor or non-adverse party needs the consent of an adverse party to change the beneficiary's enjoyment of the trust, the trust, is not a grantor trust.[35] Additionally, a power exercisable only by will or a power to distribute corpus or income limited to an ascertainable standard will not cause the trust to be treated as a grantor trust.[36] There are several key exceptions to Code Section 674, which really eclipse the general rule under this section.

Section 675 – Administrative Powers Rules

The retention of any of the following administrative powers exercisable by the grantor in the grantor's favor, or a non-adverse party, will cause the trust to be treated as a grantor trust:

1. Power to purchase, exchange, or otherwise deal with or dispose of the corpus or income of the trust for less than adequate consideration in money or money's worth;[37]

2. Powers to borrow trust corpus or income without adequate interest or security;[38] Additionally, if the grantor borrows from the trust and fails to repay the loan by the end of the year or does not pay adequate interest or security with respect to the loan, the trust will be treated as a grantor trust.[39]

3. Powers of administration exercisable by any person in a non-fiduciary capacity without the approval or consent of a person acting in a fiduciary capacity. These powers include the power to vote stock of a corporation in which the grantor and the trust has a significant voting interest, the power to control investment of the trust fund or the power to reacquire the trust corpus by substituting other property of an equivalent value.[40]

Section 676 – Power to Revoke Rules

If the grantor or a non-adverse party has the power to revest all or any portion of the trust corpus back to the grantor, the grantor is treated as the owner (and the taxpayer) with respect to any income generated by the portion of the property subject to the power. The grantor is treated for income tax purposes as the owner of any portion of a trust for income tax purposes if the grantor can revoke the trust either acting alone or with a non-adverse party (unless the power is as remote as that permitted under the Code Section 673 reversionary interest rules).

Section 677 – Income for Benefit of Grantor Rules

The grantor of a trust is taxed on the income of the trust. If at the discretion of the grantor or a nonadverse party, or both—the income may be distributed to the grantor or the grantor's spouse, held or accumulated for future distribution to the grantor or grantor's spouse, or applied to the payment of life insurance premiums on the life of the grantor or the grantor's spouse.[41]

Section 678 – Person Other than Grantor Rules

Finally, if a person other than the grantor has the power, exercisable solely by himself or herself, to vest the corpus or income of such trust to himself or herself (such as a general power of appointment), such person is treated as the owner of the corpus so that trust income will be taxable to that person (unless the trust income is otherwise taxable to the grantor).

22.4 INCOME TAXATION OF ESTATES

Decedent's Final Return

An executor or administrator is required to file two different types of income tax returns for a decedent, i.e., the decedent's final individual income tax return and an estate's (or revocable trust's) income tax return. The decedent-taxpayer's last tax year ends on the date of death.

Example. If Stephanie dies on March 30, an income tax return must be filed for the short tax year of January 1 to March 30.

Regardless of the decedent's date of death, the return must be filed on the regular income tax return due date, April 15th, of the following year.[42] However, for the tax year of death, if the decedent is married, the surviving spouse may file a joint return with the decedent because they are treated as being married for the entire calendar year. Although in most cases a joint return will usually result in less overall income tax, the accountant should compute the tax under both methods (filing separately and jointly) to determine the best tax result.

The amount of income and deductible expenses that must be reported depends on the deceased taxpayer's regular method of accounting. For cash-basis taxpayers, only income actually or constructively received prior to the date of death must be reported. Similarly, deductions are allowed only for expenses actually paid. On the other hand, if the decedent is an accrual method taxpayer, the final income tax return must report all income and deductions that accrued through the date of death.[43]

Income in Respect of a Decedent (IRD)

Assuming (as is the case with most taxpayers), the decedent is a cash basis taxpayer, the final income tax return would not include income earned but not actually or constructively received as of the date of death.[44] So, if a taxpayer received the last paycheck the day before death, it would be reported on the final income tax return. On the other hand, if the decedent was an insurance agent, renewal commissions paid a week after death would not be reported on the last income tax return.

However, in order to tax income a decedent would have included in gross income if he or she had lived to receive it, such income is characterized as Income in Respect of a Decedent (IRD). Thus, the insurance agent's renewal commissions in the above example or an installment payment received with respect to a sale of property received after the decedent's death are examples of IRD. Generally, IRD is taxed to recipient of the payments when they are actually received. In other words, the estate or the beneficiary who actually receives the IRD a week after the decedent's death must include it in gross income in the taxable year in which it is received. Moreover, the character of the income is the same in the hands of the recipient as it would have been in the hands of the decedent. Therefore, the renewal commissions would be ordinary income and the reportable gain with respect to the installment sale would likely be taxed as capital gain to the recipient estate or beneficiary.[45] Similarly, amounts considered to be a tax-free return of capital to the decedent remains tax free when received by the estate or beneficiary.

Example. Prior to his death, Asher sold a parcel of land he originally purchased ten years earlier for $2,000. The purchase price of $10,000 was to be paid in five annual $2,000 installments plus interest. Under the installment method of reporting, Asher's aggregate profit of $8,000 ($10,000 minus $2,000 basis) capital gain would be reported ratably by Asher. Each payment would include $1,600 of capital gain, $400 of tax-free basis recovery and interest income. As of Asher's death, he had received only one installment payment. Ashley, Asher's daughter and sole beneficiary of his estate receives the final four installment payments. Similar to Asher, as Ashley receives each $2,000 payment plus interest, she would report $1,600 of taxable capital gain, $400 of tax-free basis recovery and taxable interest income. Even though the installment notes are "property," there is no step-up in basis at death (discussed below) for IRD.[46]

If the decedent had accrued unpaid interest on U.S. savings bonds, the executor may elect to include the unpaid interest on the decedent's final income tax return of the decedent, or report the interest earned up to the date of death when received as IRD (not reported on the decedent's final return).[47]

For estate tax purposes, the decedent's right to receive money or property, i.e., IRD, is included in the taxable estate potentially subject to estate tax. Thus, a decedent's last paycheck not received as of the date of death would be subject to income tax to the recipient and estate tax to the estate. For that reason, the recipient of IRD is entitled to a corresponding deduction for the amount of estate tax attributable to the inclusion of that item of IRD in the decedent's taxable estate.[48] For example, if $450,000 of estate tax is attributable to inclusion of a $1,000,000 IRA in a decedent's estate, the estate tax is ratably deducted as distributions from the IRA (IRD) are received by the beneficiary year to year and included in the gross income.

Significantly, the deduction is a miscellaneous itemized deduction meaning it is a below the line deduction and deductible only to the extent that the amount exceeds 2 percent of the recipient's adjusted gross income and itemizes. Thus, the actual tax benefit of the deduction may be substantially diminished.

Income Taxation of the Estate

As a taxable entity, an estate must pay tax on its income[49] usually consisting of dividends from stock and interest from bonds, rental income, royalty income, income from the sale or exchange of property, or income from a business carried on by the executor or administrator.

As a separate tax entity, in addition to income, an estate also is allowed to claim deductions. An estate may deduct reasonable amounts paid for administration costs including executor's fees, legal fees in connection with the administration of the estate, and expenses of preparing the income tax return of the estate.[50] If the estate manages a business, it will be entitled to deduct ordinary and necessary business expenses.

Some of these expenses, such as administration expenses, may be taken on either the income tax return of the estate or as deductions from the gross estate for estate tax purposes but not both.[51] In these cases, the executor should consider which deduction (income or estate) would be more advantageous. For example, claiming an estate tax deduction may have an effect on the size of the marital share particularly an estate divided between a marital share and a credit shelter trust. If claimed as an estate tax deduction, the size of the marital share would be reduced and the size of the credit shelter trust would be increased. Consequently, the taxable income of the estate would also be increased to the extent of the deduction claimed for estate tax purposes.

On the other hand, if the deduction is claimed on the estate income tax return, the estate's taxable income would be decreased. This may be significant considering the high estate income tax rates applicable to a relatively small amount of taxable income. Thus, an executor should probably opt to claim an income tax deduction with respect to an estate not subject to estate tax because it does exceed the applicable exemption amount ($12,920,000 in 2023).

As discussed above, an estate is taxed in a manner similar to a complex trust. For that reason, an estate is entitled to take a distribution deduction.[52] To the extent, an estate retains income (does not distribute it), the estate is subject to income tax. Also, similar to a complex trust, a beneficiary who receives a distribution must include it gross income to the extent of DNI.

Notably, a beneficiary who is to receive a bequest of a specific property or a specific sum of money is not required to include any of it in gross income regardless of the amount of DNI (treated as a tax-free bequest). However, with respect to a bequest of a specific sum of money, it must be payable all at once or in not more than three installments. If it is payable in more than three installments, each distribution will be treated as an income distribution taxable to the extent of DNI.[53] Also, any specific bequest required under the terms of the will to be paid out of income will be taxed to the beneficiary as any other distribution (included in gross income to the extent it does not exceed DNI). Beneficiaries also will be taxed on any specific bequests that are required to be paid out of income.[54]

Example 1. Leslie Little's will leaves "$5,000 to my favorite nephew, Al, and all the rest, residue, and remainder to my cousin, Jeffrey Little." During the first year of the administration of the estate, assets held by the executor generate $16,000 of income. The executor distributes $5,000 to Al and $11,000 to Jeffrey. Since the $5,000 distribution to Al (payable in full) is a specific bequest from the estate, it is income tax-free to him.

On the other hand, as the residuary beneficiary, the $11,000 distributed to Jeffrey is not a specific bequest. Thus, the entire $11,000 distribution (the lesser of the amount of the distribution or DNI - $16,000) would be taxable to him. In this case, Jeffrey would be taxed on the $11,000 he received, and the estate would be taxed on the remaining $5,000 of income (deducting the amount of Jeffrey's distribution from gross income).

Example 2. The result would be different if Leslie's will stated that the $5,000 bequest to Al was to be paid in five equal annual installments. If in the first year, Al received $1,000 he would be taxed in the same way as any other beneficiary including in gross income the lesser of DNI or the amount of the distribution.

Similarly, the estate would be entitled to a $1,000 distribution deduction. As previously discussed, the "income first" rule requires that all distributions are deemed to be paid out of income first, even if the executor, administrator, or trustee in fact distributes principal in the form of cash or property. Thus, if in the previous example the distribution to Jeffrey consisted solely of stock, he would still be deemed to have received income (i.e., as if he received cash).

22.5 APPLICATION OF NIIT TO TRUSTS AND ESTATES

Similar to individuals, unless otherwise specifically excluded, all trusts and estates that are subject to the provisions Subchapter J of the Internal Revenue Code are also subject to NIIT.[55] The impact of NIIT on trusts and estates cannot be understated. Because trusts tend to remain in existence far longer than estates, the overall tax consequences of this surtax on trusts is likely to be even more profound, and the following discussion will focus mainly on trusts.

In operation, the 3.8 percent NIIT surtax is imposed on trusts and estates on the lesser of:

- "undistributed net investment income"; or

- the excess of adjusted gross income over the amount of the highest regular income tax bracket in effect for the year.[56]

In simple terms, "undistributed net investment income" is any net investment income that is retained by a trust or an estate.[57] An in-depth calculation of net investment income is beyond the scope of this chapter, but generally net investment income includes items that are specifically enumerated by the Internal Revenue Code, as well as other items that arise from a taxpayer's business activities or ownership of interests in corporate entities. Code section 1411(c)(1)(A)(i) specifically enumerates what most would consider the "traditional" types of investment income: interest, dividends, annuities, royalties and rents.

Like other ways in which income can be characterized, distributions retain their characterization as net investment income when distributed to a beneficiary (See "DNI" above). If the trust has net investment income that is distributed to a beneficiary, it will be considered net investment income for beneficiary (as opposed to regular income).[58]

Compared to the thresholds for individual taxpayers that are based on adjusted gross income, the threshold for trusts and estates is based on the highest tax bracket of those entities. Though the threshold for trusts and estates is indexed for inflation (unlike the thresholds for individual taxpayers), that is of little comfort to fiduciaries and beneficiaries. The highest regular income tax bracket for trusts and estates (above which the NIIT surtax is imposed) begins at an amount that is significantly lower than the NIIT thresholds for individuals.[59]

For example, for tax year 2023, the highest regular income tax bracket for trusts and estates (37 percent) begins with taxable income in excess of $14,450. The unindexed thresholds for individual taxpayers (e.g. $250,000 for married taxpayers who are filing jointly) are much higher. Moreover, by their nature, most trusts and estates are likely to have *only* net investment income. This means that trusts and estates with relatively small amounts of net investment income may nonetheless be in the highest income tax bracket and be subject to the 3.8 percent NIIT.

The following example from the regulations[60] demonstrates how to compute net investment income for a complex trust, including calculations of DNI.

Example: Assume that in 2023 the trustee of this complex trust makes a discretionary FAI distribution of $10,000 to Beneficiary A.

Trust Income 2023	
Dividend Income	$15,000
Interest Income	$10,000
Capital Gain	$5,000
IRA Distribution	$75,000
Total Trust Income	$105,000

Step 1: Determine the DNI of the trust. Code section 643(a) provides that the DNI of a trust is tentative taxable income ($105,000) minus capital gain. Excluding the $5,000 of capital gain, the DNI of the trust is $100,000.

Step 2: Determine the trust's distribution deduction. According to Code section 661(a), the distribution deduction of a complex trust is equal to the lesser of the trust's DNI ($100,000) or its total distributions for the year ($10,000). Here the distribution deduction is $10,000).

Step 3: Determine the extent to which the amount distributed is deemed to be net investment income. Code section 661(b) provides that the character of the amount distributed to the beneficiary "shall be treated as consisting of the same proportion of each class of income entering into the computation of distributable net income." In this example, the distribution of $10,000 is equal to 10 percent of DNI. Thus, the beneficiary is deemed to have received 10 percent of each type of income included in DNI.

	Income in DNI	
	Retained by Trust (90%)	Distributed to Beneficiary (10%)
Dividend Income	$13,500	$1,500
Interest Income	$9,000	$1,000
IRA Distribution	$67,500	$7,500
Total	$90,000	$10,000

Step 4: Determine the amount of net investment income in DNI that is retained by the trust. In this case, most of the retained income is net investment income. The only exception is the IRA distribution. (Pursuant to Code section 1411(c)(5), distributions from IRAs are excluded from net investment income.)

	Income Retained by Trust	Trust Net Investment Income
Dividend Income	$13,500	$13,500
Interest Income	$9,000	$9,000
IRA Distribution	$67,500	$0
Total	$90,000	$22,500

Step 5: Determine the total amount of net investment income retained by the trust. This should include the portion of the DNI retained by the trust that qualifies as investment income (here, $22,500) plus any undistributed item of net investment income not included in DNI. In this example, the $5,000 of capital gain excluded from DNI (clearly net investment income) is added to the $22,500 of net investment income retained by the trust. Thus, the total amount of undistributed net investment income is $27,500.

Step 6 – Compute the NIIT. The 3.8 percent NIIT surtax is imposed on the lesser of:

- undistributed Net Investment Income ($27,500): or

- $91,950, which is the excess of the adjusted gross income ($105,000) over the amount of the highest regular income tax bracket ($13,050).

In this example $27,500 is less than $91,950, so the NIIT would be 3.8 percent of $27,500, or $1,045.

22.6 BASIS

Basis is a necessary component in the computation of the gain (or loss) realized upon a sale or exchange of property. If the proceeds of the sale exceed the basis, the taxpayer realizes a gain. If the property sells for less than its basis, the taxpayer reports a loss. Therefore, the higher the basis, the lower the amount of realized gain on a sale of an asset.

Basis is also the starting point for determining the allowable depreciation deduction with respect to buildings and other business or investment assets that wear out over time. Again, a high basis is advantageous since depreciation (i.e., the recovery of capital over a given useful life through annual deductions) or amortization (i.e., the recovery of cost in equal annual increments) depends directly on how much capital — that is, how much investment — the taxpayer has made in the depreciable property. So the higher the basis, the greater the overall depreciation deductions that may be claimed over the recovery period.

Generally, basis is amount the taxpayer paid for property. For instance, the basis of property acquired by purchase is its cost. Basis can be adjusted upward for capital improvements or downward as depreciation deductions are taken over the recovery period. This is often referred to as "adjusted basis."

Basis at Death

Regardless of a decedent's basis in property he or she owned at death, those assets receive a new income tax basis equal to the date of death fair market value.[61] If the fair market value of the asset is higher than decedent's pre-death basis, the basis is "stepped-up" to the fair market value. Thus, if a mother bought real estate for $100,000 and it was valued at $250,000 for federal estate tax purposes when she died, and she left it to her daughter, the daughter (or the mother's estate) might have to pay an estate tax, but the daughter could then sell the real estate for its $250,000 value without having to pay any income tax. This is because the $100,000 basis is "stepped-up" to $250,000. Using the formula above, when the new adjusted basis of $250,000 is subtracted from the amount realized on the sale, $250,000, there is no gain. This concept is particularly important in buy-sell agreements where stock is purchased at a shareholder's death at a pre-arranged price or under a pre-arranged formula.

Example. A father purchased a farm for $5,000 many years prior to his death. If the farm was worth $50,000 on the date of his death, his beneficiary son's basis in the land would be stepped-up to $50,000. So, even though the land may be subject to estate tax (depending on the size of the father's estate), if the son were to sell the land for its date of death fair market value, there would be no income taxable gain because subtracting the $50,000 basis the amount realized on the sale, $50,000, there is no gain.

A step down in basis in assets is also possible if the value of the property decreases between the time of acquisition and date of death. By virtue of a basis "step-down," inherent income tax loss in the property disappears at death. Thus, the beneficiary's basis in the decedent's property would be the lower fair market value basis as compared to the decedent's higher acquisition basis.

Property Acquired by Gift within One Year of Death

When a gift is made, the recipient of the gift "inherits" the donor's basis in the property (see Chapter 8). This rule gave rise to an opportunity for a tax-free step-up in basis. Under prior law, some owners of appreciated property transferred that property to a dying individual and then received a step-up in basis when the property was left to them under the decedent's will or by intestacy.

Current law contains a provision intended to prevent the avoidance of income taxes on appreciated property by such transfers to dying donees. The law currently provides that the step up in basis at death described in the section above does not apply if:

1. the decedent had received appreciated property by gift during the one-year period ending on the date of death; and

2. that property was acquired from the decedent by (or passes from the decedent to) the donor of that property (or to the donor's spouse)

If those circumstances, the basis of the property in the donor's hands (or in the hands of the donor's spouse) is the adjusted basis of the property in the hands of the decedent immediately before death.[62]

Example. Assume a daughter transferred property with a $10,000 cost and $100,000 fair market value to her mother within one year of the mother's death who in her will left the property to her daughter. Instead of receiving a fair market value step-up in basis ($100,000), the basis would be the same as the mother's lifetime basis ($10,000).

There are ways around this rule. For example, if the donee-decedent lives for more than one year after receiving the gift, or if the gift is left to anyone other than the donor or the donor's spouse, the property will receive a stepped-up basis. So if in the above example, mother gave the property to her \grandchildren, the basis would step-up to $100,000 basis. However, such a gift may be subject to generation-skipping tax if the amount of the gift exceeded the applicable generation-skipping exemption (see Chapter 8).

Effect of New Fair Market Value Basis Rules on Stock Redemptions and Cross Purchase Agreements

As noted in Chapter 48 discussing Section 303 Stock Redemptions, under certain circumstances, gain realized from the redemption of stock to pay death taxes is not recognized (included in gross income).

In a closely held business, cross purchase agreements are common. A cross purchase agreement is a contract between the owners of the business requiring surviving owner(s) to purchase the stock of a deceased owner from his or her estate. Typically, the agreement establishes a purchase price for such stock that if negotiated at arm's length should approximate its fair market value. Although the deceased owner's stock would be included in his or her estate subject to potential estate tax, the basis of the stock would adjust to the date of death fair market value (assuming the value of the stock had appreciated). So if the new basis approximates the cross purchase price (as it should), there should be no taxable gain upon the sale of the stock from the estate to the surviving owner's. Therefore, the burden of a potentially high estate tax would be offset by an income tax-free sale of the stock. Stock that is includable in the decedent's estate receives a new basis equal to its fair market value at death (or the alternate valuation date if elected). This usually is close to the redemption value, particularly if the stock redemption is promptly carried out after death, such as right after the life insurance proceeds are received that will be used to redeem the interest. Typically, no (or little) gain is recognized by the estate or other seller of the stock upon the redemption.

Overall Effect

The new basis at death rule has an effect on all tax planning that relates to the sale of assets after death or assets that might be held until death. There is an incentive for the owner of property with a very low income tax basis, in relation to its market value, to hold the property until death so that the estate can sell it without any income tax on the appreciation in value.

If, however, inflation is a significant factor in planning, the wise estate planner will take into consideration the probable future increase in value, with possible concurrent increase in death taxes (consider the implications of both the applicable estate tax credit and the unlimited marital deduction), and balance this against a current sale. In other words, holding an asset until death in order to receive a basis step-up comes with a price. Although a fair market value basis step-up would likely eliminate a substantial amount of income tax capital gain, the retention of the asset would also increase the size of the taxable estate. Thus, the estate planner must weigh the tax advantages of a decrease in income tax as compared to the potential increase in estate tax. If such a tradeoff is not advantageous, a lifetime gift of the asset to remove it from the estate (particularly if rapid appreciation is likely), may be a better choice. This is particularly appropriate to consider where the sale would be by a person who would eventually receive the property upon the owner's death.

When asset values are down, however, an owner may be tempted to make a lifetime gift of an asset with a basis in excess of current fair market value so the high basis carries over to the done. Doing so would avoid a potential date of death fair market value basis step-down if the gift were made at death. There is a down side to this strategy, however, if the donee were to sell the asset. This is because for purposes of computing a taxable loss, the donee of depreciated property (basis exceeds fair market value) must use the lower fair market value as the basis. So in this case, the basis would be the same whether the property was gifted during life or at death. Clients should be urged to begin keeping accurate records now with regard to the cost of assets, including purchase price, improvements, depreciation, etc. EGTRRA 2001 added penalties for failure to file basis information returns with the IRS under the modified carryover rules for transfers at death in excess of $1,300,000, and for any appreciated property acquired by the decedent as a gift, or for less than adequate consideration, within three years prior to the decedent's death. Similar information was also required with gift tax returns for 2010.

Both the decedent's and the surviving spouse's share of community property will be treated as owned by the decedent under the modified carryover rules. Therefore, each spouse's share will be eligible for an increase in basis (up to the maximum allowable amount).

The 2010 Act repealed the modified carryover basis rules for 2011 and 2012 and further years. They apply only to decedents who died in 2010 and even in that case they apply only if the executor does not elect to subject the estate to the post 2010 estate tax rules. However, the concept of carryover basis at death continues to resurface, and we believe that it is prudent to plan as if it eventually will be enacted.

Example. Several years ago, Asher purchased a parcel of land for $30,000. Recently, when the land had depreciated in value to $20,000, Asher gifts the property to his daughter Ashley. Because at the time of the gift, the fair market value of the property is less than Asher's basis, for purposes of computing a taxable loss, Ashley must use fair market value as her basis. So, if Ashley sells the land for $15,000, she would recognize a taxable loss of $5,000 ($20,000 date of gift fair market value and basis minus $15,000 sales price).[63] On the other hand, if Asher had died leaving the land to Ashley, the basis in the land would step-down to the $20,000 date of death fair market value. So in either case, Ashley's basis in the land for purposes of computing a loss would be the lower fair market value of the property rather than Asher's basis.

22.7 ISSUES IN COMMUNITY PROPERTY STATES

In the case of a married couple, the extent to which the basis steps-up depends on the manner in which title is held by the spouses. In a community property state, the separate property owned by a spouse receives a fair market value basis at the death of the owner spouse. If the property is held as community property, only one-half of the property is included in the estate of the first spouse to die, however, even the surviving spouse's portion of the property receives a fair market value date of death basis. Therefore, similar to the first scenario, the basis of the entire property receives a fair market value basis at the death of either spouse.[64]

When property is held in fractional interests the valuation of those interests are discounted. Community property is property held as two separate but undivided 50 percent interests. This raises a valuation issue, i.e., whether the property should be valued as a whole or should valuation discounts for fractional shares be added to the equation. The entire property can go to the surviving spouse under the marital deduction rules and will not be subject to tax. Thus, the entire property will get a new, often stepped-up basis even though it may escape estate tax entirely at that generational level.

Over time, the IRS has changed its position regarding minority interest discounts, particularly with respect to partial ownership interests in closely held businesses held by family members. For example, in Revenue Ruling 81-253[65] the IRS declared that no minority shareholder discount was allowed with respect to gifts of shares of stock between family members if, based upon a composite of the family members' interests at the time of the transfer, control (either majority voting control or de facto control through family relationships) of the corporation existed in the family unit.

Then, in *Propstra v. United States*[66] the Ninth Circuit repudiated the IRS position. In that case, the court held that property held in fractional interests were subject to discount. The IRS subsequently revoked Revenue Ruling 81-253 and indicated that it would follow *Propstra,* holding that, "If a donor transfers shares in a corporation to each of the donor's children, the factor of corporate control in the family is not considered in valuing each transferred interest for purposes of C Section 2512."[67]

Consequently, a minority discount will not be disallowed solely because a transferred interest, when

FEDERAL INCOME TAX ISSUES

CHAPTER 22

aggregated with interests held by family members, would be a part of a controlling interest. This would be the case whether the donor held 100 percent or some lesser percentage of the stock immediately before the gift.

It is therefore important to distinguish between property held by the decedent as separate property, and property held by the decedent and spouse as community property. Although in both cases, the basis of the entire property will receive a step-up (or step-down) to the date of death fair market value, the overall value of community property would be less than if was held as separate property. This is because each spouse is deemed to own fifty percent of the property. For example, a house wholly owned by the decedent spouse with a basis of $10,000 and a fair market value of $100,000 would receive a new stepped-up basis of $100,000 as compared to only a $80,000-90,000 stepped-up basis if the property was held as community property. This is because consistent with holding in *Propstra*, the fractional interest of community property would be subject to a 10 to 20 percent discount for lack of marketability and lack of control.

However, this step-up in basis of the entire property does not occur with respect to property held in joint-tenancy or tenancy-in-common. For example, husband and wife purchase property costing $1,000 with funds earned while residents of a community property state. They want the property to be held in some form of co-ownership. Assume that at the date-of-death of the first spouse to die, the property is worth $10,000.

There four different forms of in co-ownership of the property:

1. As joint-tenants (or tenants by the entirety);
2. As tenants in common;
3. As community property; or
4. As community property with right of survivorship (only available in certain states).

Note the significant difference in income tax basis in Situation II, Figure 22.1.

Figure 22.1

	#1 Tenants by Entirety	#2 Tenants in Common	#3 Community Property
SITUATION I – PROPERTY SOLD FOR $10,000 PRIOR TO DEATH OF EITHER SPOUSE			
Plan:			
Sales price of property	$10,000	$10,000	$10,000
Tax basis of spouses:			
Husband's half	$500	$500	$500
Wife's half	500	500	500
Total Basis	$1,000	$1,000	$1,000
	$9,000	$9,000	$9,000
SITUATION II – PROPERTY SOLD FOR $10,000 AFTER DEATH OF HUSBAND			
Plan:			
Sales price of property	$10,000	$10,000	$10,000
Tax basis of spouses:			
Husband's half	$5,000	$5,000	$5,000
Wife's half	500	500	500
Total Basis	5,500	5,500	10,000
Taxable gain on sale	$4,500	$4,500	$-0-

Thus, as evidenced by the above chart, only jointly owned community property is subject to a full fair market value step-up in basis upon the death of the first spouse to die.

With the new basis at death rule, where property has been paid for with community property earnings or if the contribution to the acquisition was otherwise equal, it again affords a significant advantage as to federal income tax to hold such property in community property (with or without a right of survivorship) as opposed to either joint-tenancy (known as tenancy by the entirety in some states as applied to spouses) or tenancy-in-common. In those states that allow community property with right of survivorship, the benefits of joint tenancy and community property are combined. This can be particularly beneficial for smaller estates.[68]

As to state income tax, one must look to the basic rules of the particular community property state to determine the basis of property for that state's income tax. For example, California follows the federal rule—that the income tax basis of community property will adjust to fair market value on the death of either spouse, but only a decedent's one-half interest in joint tenancy property will be so adjusted.[69]

Federal income tax is generally much more important than state income tax for most returns and, therefore, the double step-up in federal income tax basis of property held as community property will continue to be a very important tax planning consideration.

22.8 BLENDED FAMILY IMPLICATIONS

The trustee or executor often has a lot of leeway when it comes to making distributions from a trust or estate, particularly with respect to the timing and amount of distributions. When a blended family is involved, this flexibility can be viewed by various heirs as advantageous or disadvantageous since the trustee's discretionary decisions can materially affect how those distributions are taxed. The fiduciary also has a fair amount of control over a number of other decisions that can materially affect a beneficiary's interest. For example, the fiduciary has control over how to apportion income and expense between income and principal. The fiduciary also often has the duty or right to make or forego equitable adjustments between income and principal that arguably could be made for any number of reasons, including adjustments for timing differences as well as for differences between the treatment of an item for tax purposes and its treatment for fiduciary accounting purposes, even when such adjustments run counter to fiduciary accounting principles. The issue is even more difficult and the potential for a conflict of interest is even greater when the fiduciary also is a beneficiary.

In blended families, the exercise or non-exercise of the fiduciary's discretion can be particularly problematic, particularly where a beneficiary also is the fiduciary. We usually remind such fiduciaries that they are in fact fiduciaries and owe duties to all of the beneficiaries, including those on the other side, and particularly, the duty of impartiality, a duty that is easier stated then met.

22.9 FREQUENTLY ASKED QUESTIONS

Question – Does property receive a new income tax basis equal to fair market value when it is gifted during one's lifetime?

Answer – No. In general, the donee retains the donor's basis, increased by the amount of gift tax (or a part thereof) paid with respect to the gift (see Chapter 19). However, if such basis is greater than the fair market value of the property at the time of the gift, then for purposes of determining loss, upon the donee's sale of the property, the basis is such fair market value.[70] Where property is transferred between spouses or between former spouses if the transfer is incident to the divorce, the transferee's basis is the same as the transferor's basis.[71]

Gifted property that for some reason is brought back into the donor's estate for death tax purposes will receive a new basis equal to the fair market value at the time of death. Thus, having a gift brought back into the estate may be good for the donee (who gets a new basis) but bad for the estate (which may be subject to estate taxes on a larger estate).[72]

Question – Is it possible to change a trust's status from grantor trust status to non-grantor trust status?

Answer – Yes, it is possible to have certain individuals relinquish certain powers and "toggle" off the grantor trust status. In Notice 2007-73, the

FEDERAL INCOME TAX ISSUES CHAPTER 22

IRS described one such technique as a reportable "transaction of interest." Although beyond the scope of this chapter, a transactions of interest are transactions that are potentially executed for tax avoidance or evasion purposes. Under certain circumstances, the tax avoidance goal occurs as a result of the purposeful creation of a grantor trust coupled with the termination of such trust in order to achieve a favorable tax consequence that could not be achieved otherwise. Such transactions must be reported to the IRS. Obviously, sham transactions are subject to IRS attack and disallowance.

Question – If a property is sold with the seller taking back a note and the installment basis of recognizing gain is elected, does the note receive a new basis if the seller dies owning the note?

Answer – No. The gain inherent in the note is an example of IRD.[73] This is because the decedent sold the underlying property during his or her lifetime. Any installment note unpaid at death would be recognized by the estate or beneficiary who ultimately receives payment.

Question – If, instead of selling an asset such as stock, the shareholder enters into a buy-sell agreement, does the stock receive a stepped-up basis?

Answer – Yes. Unlike a lifetime sale consummated during the decedent's lifetime, the sale of stock pursuant to a buy-sell agreement is triggered by the death of the decedent shareholder. Moreover, the stock is sold by the estate to the surviving shareholders. Thus, upon the death of the decedent shareholder, the basis of the stock he or she owned during life would be stepped-up or stepped down to date of death fair market value.

Question – If an attorney (or other taxpayer) reporting on the cash basis for income tax purposes dies with unpaid accounts receivable for fees owed by clients, do these accounts receivable receive a stepped-up basis?

Answer – No. Such amounts represent amounts earned but not paid as of the decedent's death. For that reason, such accounts receivable would be considered IRD. Items of IRD do not receive a basis adjustment upon the death of the decedent.[74] Therefore, as the fees are paid, the decedent's estate or beneficiary (depending on who collects) would report the income.

Question – Does the recipient of IRD who must include it in gross income receive a deduction for the estate tax paid on such amounts included in the estate?

Answer – Yes. A taxpayer who includes IRD in gross income is entitled to a miscellaneous itemized deduction for the portion of the estate tax attributable to the inclusion of the IRD (the right to income) in the decedent's gross estate.[75]

Question – If an estate is so small that no estate tax is payable, or if no tax is payable because of the unlimited estate tax marital deduction, does the property still receive a stepped-up basis?

Answer – Yes. All property included in the decedent's gross estate (whether or not it generates an estate tax) receives a stepped-up or stepped-down date of death fair market value basis. However, even if an estate tax is not owing, it may be prudent to file an estate tax return setting forth the fair market value of the property to foreclose an IRS challenge to the basis of such property. In other words, once the statute of limitations on challenging the estate tax return on which the fair market value was reported, the IRS may no longer challenge the validity of the corresponding basis.

Question – Is an estate entitled to a personal exemption when filing its income tax return?

Answer – Yes, but it is only $600.[76]

Question – If a personal representative or executor elects to use the alternate valuation date (six months after death) for valuing property for estate tax purposes, does that affect the stepped-up basis rule?

Answer – Yes. If the alternate valuation date is elected for federal estate tax purposes,[77] the fair market value of the property on that six-months-after-death date will be the new income tax basis of the property.[78] In order to be able to elect alternate valuation, the gross estate and the sum of federal estate tax and direct skip generation skipping taxes must decrease as a result of that election. The alternate value may be even more important if capital gains rates stay so much lower than estate tax rates.

Question – How is basis adjusted in a generation-skipping transfer?

373

Answer – Very similarly to the basis adjustment allowed when a gift tax is paid on a transfer. The transferee's basis is increased—but not beyond the fair market value of the property transferred—by an amount equal to that portion of the GST tax imposed on the transfer generated by the potential gain in the property immediately prior to the transfer.

Basis Adjustments for Taxable Distributions or Direct Skips

Fair market value of transferred property...	$1,000,000
Adjusted basis before GST transfer..............	$600,000
GST tax imposed on transfer (40%)..............	$400,000
Net appreciation [$1,000,000 – $600,000].....	$400,000
Basis increase [$400,000 × ($400,000 ÷ 1,000,000)]............................	$160,000
Transferee's basis [$600,000 + $160,000].......	$760,000

If the GST tax is imposed because of a taxable termination that occurs at the same time as, and as the result of, an individual's death, the property's basis is stepped up similar to the normal step-up in basis of property at death (with certain limitations).

CHAPTER ENDNOTES

1. For two detailed treatises on fiduciary income taxation, see F. Ladson Boyle, and Jonathan Blattmachr, Blattmachr on Income Taxation of Estates and Trusts (Practicing Law Institute 2018) and Howard Zaritsky, Robert T. Danforth, and Norman Lane Income Taxation of Estates & Trusts (Thompson Reuters 2022).
2. I.R.C. §643(b); Treas. Reg. §1.643(b)-1.
3. UPIA §405.
4. UPIA §401(b).
5. UPIA §406(a).
6. UPIA §404(2).
7. Treas. Reg. §1.643(b)-1.
8. UPIA §409.
9. UPIA § 410.
10. UPIA §411.
11. UPIA §412.
12. UPIA §104(a).
13. UPIA §104(b).
14. UPIA §104(c).
15. UPIA §§503-506.
16. UPIA §503.
17. UPIA §504.
18. UPIA §506.
19. *In re Estate of Warms*, 140 N.Y.S.2d 169 (Sur. Ct. 1955).
20. I.R.C. §6012(a)(4)(trusts) and (5) (estates) provide the tax return requirements for fiduciary income tax return filing.
21. I.R.C. §643(a).
22. I.R.C. §§651 and 661.
23. I.R.C. §662; Treas. Reg. §1.662(a)-2(a).
24. I.R.C. §662(b); Treas. Regs. §1.662(b)-1, -2.
25. I.R.C. §662(b); Treas. Reg. §§1.662(b)-1 and 1.662(b)-2.
26. I.R.C. §641(a).
27. I.R.C. §641(b).
28. I.R.C. §643(f).
29. Rev. Rul. 85-13.
30. I.R.C. §651; Treas. Reg. §1.651(a)-1 – 1.651(a)-2.
31. I.R.C. §673(b)(2).
32. I.R.C. §673(a).
33. I.R.C. §674(a).
34. *Id.*
35. I.R.C. §674(b) – (d).
36. I.R.C. §675(a)(1).
37. I.R.C. §675(a)(2).
38. I.R.C. §675(3).
39. I.R.C. §675(a)(4).
40. I.R.C. §677(a).
41. I.R.C. §§6012; 6072(a); Treas. Reg. §1.6072-1(b).
42. I.R.C. §451.
43. I.R.C. §451(a).
44. I.R.C. §691(a)(3).
45. I.R.C. §1014(c).
46. See IRS Publication 550.
47. I.R.C. §691(c).
48. I.R.C. §6012(a).
49. I.R.C. §67(e).
50. I.R.C. §642(g); Treas. Reg. §1.642(g)-1.
51. I.R.C. §661.
52. I.R.C. §663(a)(1); Treas. Reg. §1.663(a)-1(a).
53. I.R.C. §§643(b) and 663(a)(1).
54. Treas. Reg. §1.1411-3.
55. I.R.C. §1411(a)(2)(B)(ii).
56. Treas. Reg. §1.1411-3(a)(1). Subchapter J deals exclusively with the taxation of trusts and estates and their beneficiaries. Treas. Reg. §1.1411-3(b)(1) lists the types of trusts and estates specifically excluded from NIIT.
57. I.R.C. §§652(b) and 662(b).
58. The threshold for trusts and estates is indexed because the regular tax income tax brackets for trusts and estates are indexed for inflation.
59. Treas. Reg. §1.1411-3(e)(5), Example 2.
60. I.R.C. §1014.
61. I.R.C. §1014(e).
62. I.R.C. §1015(a)(d).
63. I.R.C. §1014(b)(6).

64. Rev. Rul. 81-253, 1981-1 CB 187.
65. *Propstra v. United States*, 680 F.2d 1248 (9th Cir. 1982).
66. Rev. Rul. 93-12, 1993-1 CB 202.
67. Where property is held as community property with right of survivorship, no discounts apply at the first death as the surviving spouse automatically receives the entire property.
68. CA Rev & Tax C. § 18031.
69. I.R.C. §1015(a), (d).
70. I.R.C. §1015(e).
71. I.R.C. §§1014(b)(2), (3), (9).
72. I.R.C. §691(a)(4).
73. I.R.C. §§1014(c), 691.
74. I.R.C. §691(c).
75. I.R.C. §642.
76. I.R.C. §2032.
77. I.R.C. §1014(a)(2).

QUALIFIED BUSINESS INCOME DEDUCTION[1]

CHAPTER 23

23.1 INTRODUCTION

On December 22, 2017, President Trump signed into law the Tax Cuts and Jobs Act (TCJA). One of the key provisions in the Act is a 20 percent deduction for the qualified business income (QBI) of non-corporate taxpayers under new code section 199A. This section is effective for tax years after 2017 and, unless lawmakers act, it sunsets on December 31, 2025. Although the Chapter and Code section primarily income tax rather than estate planning, certain planning decisions overlap, such as whether and how much to convert to a Roth IRA, or how much to gift to or how to design trusts to hold pass through entities and obtain the optimal tax benefits. Counterintuitively, there are situations in which a Roth conversion actually enables a higher Section 199A tax deduction (if the taxpayer's 199A deduction is limited by the amount of ordinary income cap).

Rationale

The most important goal of the TCJA was to reduce the tax rates on C corporations to make them more competitive in world markets. Reducing the top C corporation rate from 35 percent to 21 percent, however, put pass-through businesses at a disadvantage relative to C corporations. Thus, the 20 percent deduction was added to the Act to give pass-through entities a comparable tax break. The 20 percent deduction, in theory, reduces the tax rate from a maximum of 37 percent to a maximum of 29.6 percent.

Eligible Taxpayers

The deduction applies to non-corporate taxpayers, including sole proprietorships, partnerships, LLCs,[2] S corporations, trusts, estates, qualified cooperatives and real estate investment trusts (REITs).[3] It is calculated on an annual basis and will be reported as a line item on Form 1040. For partnerships or S corporations, the deduction applies at the partner or shareholder level, and each partner or shareholder takes into account his or her allocable share of the deduction.[4] The section 199A deduction is not available to C corporations that own pass-through businesses.[5]

Application of the Deduction

The 20 percent deduction applies only for income tax purposes and does not reduce the net investment income tax, Medicare tax or the self-employment tax.[6] The deduction is not allowed in computing adjusted gross income (AGI), but rather is applied against **taxable** income.[7] Although it is an itemized deduction, it is not subject to any of the limitations on such deductions.[8]

23.2 MECHANICS OF THE DEDUCTION

The statute begins with a basic, relatively straightforward computation of the deduction. It is complicated, however by two important limitations, a W-2 wage/unadjusted basis limitation and a specified service trade or business (SSTB) limitation.

Basic Calculation

The statute gives eligible taxpayers a deduction equal to the lesser of:

- 20 percent of the combined qualified business income (QBI) of the taxpayer; or

- 20 percent of taxable ordinary income[9]

For purposes of this calculation, combined qualified business income is (1) the ordinary income from each qualified trade or business[10] plus (2) 20 percent of the qualified real estate investment trust (REIT) dividends and qualified publicly traded partnership (QPTP) income.[11]

Example 1. Larry, a single taxpayer, is the sole proprietor of an ice cream parlor. The store building is leased. Larry's profit from the store is $90,000 and he has no capital gains, REIT, QPTP or other income. Larry claims the new $12,000 standard deduction,[12] making his taxable income $78,000. Larry's section 199A deduction is the lesser of:

(1) 20 percent of his business income from the store (.2 × $90,000 = $18,000); or

(2) 20 percent of his taxable ordinary income (.2 × $78,000 = $15,600).

Because Larry's tentative deduction ($18,000) exceeds 20 percent of his taxable income ($15,600), his deduction is limited to $15,600, reducing his taxable income from $78,000 to $62,400. Because Larry is in the 22 percent marginal income tax bracket, he saves $3,432 in taxes (.22 × $15,600).

Example 2. Cindy is an architect with income of $280,000 from the business. She has no other income. Cindy's husband, Ned, is a student with no income. Cindy and Ned claim the $24,000 standard deduction for married taxpayers filing jointly, giving them $256,000 of taxable income. Cindy's tentative section 199A deduction is $56,000 (.2 × $280,000). However, her deduction cannot exceed 20 percent of taxable income over net capital gains. 20 percent of Cindy's taxable income is $51,200 (.2 × $256,000), so her section 199A deduction is reduced from $56,000 to $51,200.

23.3 W-2/UNADJUSTED BASIS LIMITATION

Under this limitation, the portion of the deduction attributable to the taxpayer's QBI from the trade or business[13] cannot exceed the greater of

- 50 percent of the taxpayer's allocable share of the wages paid by the business with respect to QBI; or

- 25 percent of the taxpayer's allocable share of wages plus 2.5 percent of the unadjusted basis of qualified property owned by the business.[14]

The W-2 wage/unadjusted basis limitation does not begin to apply until taxable income reaches $315,000 for married taxpayers filing jointly and $157,500 for all other eligible taxpayers. The phase-in is complete for married taxpayers filing jointly (MFJ) at $415,000 and for all other taxpayers at $207,500.[15] These numbers will adjust for inflation. The following chart shows how the limitation applies to taxpayers based on filing status and level of taxable income, with inflation-adjusted numbers for 2023 immediately below:

	MFJ	ALL OTHERS
No limitation	$0 - $315,000	$0 - $157,500
Phase-In	$315,000 - $415,000	$157,500 - $207,500
Full Limitation	$415,000+	$207,500+

For 2023, there is no limitation for up to $364,000 (MFJ) and half that, $182,000 for all others. The phase-in starts from there up to $464,200 (MFJ) and up to $232,100 for all others. The examples below, however, will still use the original numbers from the chart above for illustration.

The examples below illustrate how the Code section 199A deduction is calculated for taxpayers subject to the full limitation.

Example 3. Jake, a married taxpayer filing jointly with his wife, Julie, runs a restaurant that produces $110,000 of pass-through income. Julie is a teacher who earns $64,000. The couple claims the standard deduction of $24,000, making their taxable income $150,000 ($174,000 − $24,000). Because Jake and Julie have taxable income of less than $315,000, the W-2 wage/unadjusted basis limitation does not apply. The 20 percent of taxable income over capital gains limitation does not apply either because the tentative QBI deduction (.2 × $110,000 = $22,000) is less than 20 percent of taxable income (.2 × $150,000 = $30,000). Thus, they receive the full 20 percent section 199A deduction (.2 × $110,000 = $22,000).

Example 4. Curtis and Shannon own a restaurant that produces $500,000 of taxable income. The restaurant building is leased. The couple has another $100,000 of taxable income from investments and claims the standard deduction of $24,000. Curtis and Shannon perform most of the work at the restaurant and pay $80,000 of W-2 wages to part-time help. Because their taxable income exceeds $415,000, the W-2/unadjusted basis limitation applies in full. The QBI deduction for Curtis and Shannon is:

(1) the lesser of 20 percent of pass-through income (.2 × $500,000 = $100,000);

OR

(2) the greater of 50 percent of W-2 wages (.5 × $80,000 = $40,000) or 25 percent of Curtis and Shannon's allocable share of W-2 wages ($20,000) + 2.5 percent of the unadjusted basis in the restaurant building ($0) = $20,000.

Thus, the deduction is the lesser of $100,000 or $40,000 = $40,000.

This $40,000 deduction is substantially less than 20 percent of the couple's taxable income (.2 × $576,000 = $115,200) so the taxable income limitation does not apply.

Example 5. Assume the same facts as in Example 4, except that Curtis and Shannon buy the restaurant building for $1,000,000. Their deduction is now:

(1) the lesser of 20 percent of QBI (.2 × $500,000 = $100,000);

OR

(2) the greater of 50 percent of wages (.5 × $80,000 = $40,000), or 25 percent of wages ($20,000) + 2.5 percent of unadjusted basis ($25,000) = $45,000.

The taxable income limitation does not apply because 20 percent of their taxable income ($115,200) exceeds 20 percent of QBI ($100,000) so their deduction is increased from $40,000 to $45,000.[16]

Example 6. Grandpa Mark and Grandma Linda own an apartment building that was purchased for $500,000 and hasn't been fully depreciated. The building generates $100,000 of pass-through income, producing a tentative section 199A deduction of $20,000 (.2 × $100,000). They pay a company to manage and maintain the building. Their section 199A deduction is:

(1) the lesser of 20 percent of pass-through income (.2 × $100,000 = $20,000);

OR

(2) the greater of 50 percent of W-2 wages (.5 × $0 = $0), or 25 percent of Grandpa Mark and Grandma Linda's allocable share of W-2 wages ($0) + 2.5 percent of unadjusted basis (.025 × $500,000) = $12,500.

Thus, Grandpa Mark and Grandma Linda get a deduction of $12,500.

Example 7. Assume the same facts as in Example 6 except that Grandpa Mark and Grandma Linda hire Charles to manage the building and pay him a salary of $45,000 a year. Their section 199A deduction is now:

(1) the lesser of 20 percent of pass-through income (.2 × $100,000 = $20,000);

OR

(2) the greater of 50 percent of W-2 wages (.5 × $45,000 = $22,500), or 25 percent of Grandpa Mark and Grandma Linda's allocable share of W-2 wages ($11,250) + 2.5 percent of unadjusted basis ($12,500) = $23,750

Grandpa Mark and Grandma Linda can now claim the full $20,000 section 199A deduction each year.

Phase-in of the W-2 Wage/Unadjusted Basis Limitation

As taxable income rises from $315,000 to $415,000 for married taxpayers filing jointly and from $157,500 to $207,500 for all other taxpayers, the W-2 wages/unadjusted basis limitation is gradually phased in as illustrated in the following examples.

Example 8. Lisa is the sole proprietor of a profitable candy store who files a joint return with her husband, Chuck. The store produces $375,000 of business income. It paid wages of $120,000 and has no depreciable property. Lisa and Chuck's taxable income is $395,000. The QBI deduction is calculated as follows.

Tentative QBI (.2 × $375,000)	$75,000
W-2/unadjusted basis limitation (.5 × $120,000)	$60,000
Tentative deduction minus full W-2 limitation amount ($75,000 – $60,000)	$15,000
Phase-in % [($395,000 – $315,000)/$100,000]	= 80%
Phase-in amount (.8 × $15,000)	$12,000
Tentative deduction minus phase-in amount ($75,000 – $12,000)	$63,000
20% of taxable income (.2 × $395,000)	$79,000
Section 199A deduction	$63,000[17]

Example 9. Herb, a single taxpayer, is the sole proprietor of a profitable flower store. The store produces $160,000 of business income. It paid wages of $40,000 and had no depreciable property. Herb's taxable income is $177,500. His QBI deduction is calculated as follows.

Tentative QBI (.2 × $160,000)	$32,000
W-2/unadjusted basis limitation (.5 × $40,000)	$20,000
Tentative deduction minus W-2 limitation amount ($32,000 – $20,000)	$12,000
Phase-out % [($177,500 – $157,500)/$50,000]	= 40%
Phase-out amount (.4 × $12,000)	$4,800
Tentative deduction minus phase-out amount ($32,000 – $4,800)	$27,200
20% of taxable income (.2 × $177,500)	$35,500
Section 199A deduction	$27,200

Specified Service Trade or Business (SSTB) Limitation

Under the general rule, the section 199A deduction does not apply to specified service businesses.[18] These businesses include any business involving the performance of services in the fields of health, law, accounting, actuarial science, performing arts, consulting, athletics, financial services, brokerage services, or any trade or business where the principal asset of the trade or business is the reputation or skill of one or more owners or employees.[19] Also included are businesses that involve the performance of services that consist of investing and investment management, trading, or dealing in securities.[20]

Phase-out of the Deduction

However, taxpayers in these businesses can still claim a 20 percent deduction if their income is below certain threshold levels. For married taxpayers filing jointly, the threshold level is $315,000 and for all other taxpayers, $157,500.[21] As income rises above these levels, the deduction is gradually phased out. For married taxpayers filing jointly, the phase-out is complete at income of $415,000 and for all other taxpayers at income of $207,500.

Example 10. Brad is a married lawyer with a solo practice that generates $450,000 of pass-through income. Because taxable income exceeds $415,000, the section 199A deduction is completely phased out and Brad gets no 20 percent deduction.

Example 11. Jim is a single taxpayer and the sole owner of an accounting business. His income from the business is $189,500 and he has no other income. Jim claims a $12,000 standard deduction, making his taxable income $177,500. Jim's tentative Code section 199A deduction is $37,900 (.2 × $189,500). Because his taxable income exceeds $157,500, this deduction is phased out.

Jim's $177,500 of taxable income is 40 percent of the way through the phase-out range ($20,000/$50,000) so he loses 40 percent of the QBI deduction. Thus, Jim's deduction is reduced by $15,160 (.4 × $37,900). This leaves him with a $22,740 QBI deduction ($37,900 tentative deduction – $15,160 phase-out amount). The taxable income limitation does not apply because 20 percent of taxable income (.2 × 177,500 = $35,500) exceeds $22,740.

Note that for every increase of $5,000 in taxable income for specified service businesses above $157,500 for single taxpayers and every increase of $10,000 in taxable income above $315,000 for married taxpayers, the QBI deduction is reduced by 10 percent. In other words, each 10 percent increase in income above the threshold amount produces a 10 percent reduction in the QBI deduction. Thus, for example, for married taxpayers filing jointly the taxpayers keep 90 percent of the deduction at $325,000 of taxable income, 80 percent of the deduction at $335,000 of taxable income and so on.

23.4 DEFINITIONS

To perform the calculations shown above, it is necessary to understand the terms in the calculation formula. These terms include:

- Qualified business income (QBI)
- Qualified trade or business
- Specified service trade or business (SSTB)
- W-2 wages
- Qualified property
- Unadjusted tax basis
- Taxable income
- REIT dividends
- Qualified publicly traded partnership (QPTP) income

Most of the terms are adequately defined in the statute, but the scope of others is uncertain and further guidance will be required.

Qualified Business Income (QBI)

The term "qualified business income" means, for any taxable year, the net amount of qualified items of income, gain, deduction, and loss with respect to any qualified trade or business of the taxpayer.[22] It refers to the taxpayer's net income after payment of wages, business expenses and other deductions for the business and includes rental income.

Example 12. A qualified business has $100 of ordinary income from inventory sales, and makes a $25 expenditure that must be capitalized and amortized over five years. The business income is $95 ($100 minus $5 current-year ordinary amortization deduction).[23]

The income must be effectively connected with the conduct of a U.S. trade or business within the meaning of Code section 864(c) and must be included or allowed in determining taxable income for the tax year.[24] The term "trade or business" is discussed in the next section.

QBI does *not* include:

- Any qualified REIT dividends, qualified cooperative dividends, or qualified publicly traded partnership income[25]

- Reasonable compensation paid to the taxpayer by any qualified trade or business for services rendered with respect to the trade or business[26]

- Any guaranteed payment to a partner for services to the business under Code section 707(c)[27]

- Any payment to a partner for services rendered with respect to the trade or business[28]

- Capital gains and losses[29]

- Dividends or dividend equivalents[30]

- Any interest income other than interest income properly allocable to a trade or business[31]

- Certain foreign personal holding company income[32]

- Any amount received from an annuity which is not received in connection with the trade or business[33]

- Any item of deduction or loss properly allocable to an amount described in any of the preceding clauses[34]

Note that the statute favors business owners and self-employed individuals over wage earners. To obtain a deduction, employees must either become independent contractors or own or invest in a business.

Example 13. Mabel has $90,000 of wages, $25,000 of capital gains and $20,000 of interest income. None of the income is QBI, so Mabel gets no deduction.

Example 14. Assume the same facts as in the previous example except that Mabel also tutors high school students in mathematics, earning an additional $10,000/year. Mabel can now claim a Code section 199A deduction of $2,000 (.2 × $10,000).

Income from sources within Puerto Rico is included in the calculation of QBI if all such income is taxable under Code section 1.[35] It is not clear whether amounts treated as ordinary income under Code section 751 (unrealized receivables and inventory items are included in QBI). Finally, there is no requirement that qualified business income must be "active" income.

Section 1231 Gain

It is not clear whether Code section 1231 gain is qualified business income. Code section 1231 gain is generally gain on real property used in the trade or business or depreciable personal property used in the trade or business.[36] Certain property is excluded from the definition, however. Excluded items include:

1. inventory;[37]

2. property primarily held for sale to customers in the ordinary course of business;[38]

3. copyrights, literary works, musical or artistic compositions, letter memorandums or similar property;[39]

4. timber, coal, or domestic iron ore with respect to which Code section 631 applies;

5. certain livestock;[40] and

6. unharvested crops sold in conjunction with a sale of land that qualifies as Code section 1231 property.[41]

Code section 199A(c)(3)(B) provides that no deduction is allowed for short-term capital gains, long-term capital gains, short-term capital losses or long-term capital losses. Code section 1221 provides that depreciable property or real property used in the trade or business (i.e., Code section 1231 property) is excluded from the definition of a capital asset.[42] Thus, it would appear to follow, that gain on the sale of section 1231 assets should qualify as QBI. On the other hand, Code section 1231(a)(1) states that if the section 1231 gains for any taxable year exceed the section 1231 losses for the year, such gains and losses shall be treated as long-term capital gains or long-term capital losses, as the case may be.[43] Thus, the IRS will have to issue guidance on whether section 1231 income qualifies as QBI.

S Corporations and Reasonable Compensation

S corporation profits qualify as QBI, but salaries paid to shareholders who perform services for the

S corporation don't qualify. To increase the 199A deduction, S corporations may reduce the salaries of shareholders who perform services for the company and make a corresponding increase in profits. If the IRS believes the shareholder is not being paid reasonable compensation, however, it may re-characterize a portion of a profits distribution as compensation,[44] possibly reducing the 199A deduction.

Partnerships and LLCs and Reasonable Compensation

The Committee Report states that *"qualified business income does not include any amount paid by an S corporation as reasonable compensation of the taxpayer."* It says nothing about reasonable compensation paid to a sole proprietor, partner or LLC member, though. The reason for excluding only reasonable compensation paid to an S corporation shareholder is presumably that compensation paid to an S corporation shareholder is treated as W-2 wages subject to self-employment taxes. By converting reasonable compensation into pass-through income, S corporations can avoid self-employment tax and the IRS has long tried to prevent this by imposing a reasonable compensation requirement. Other pass-through entities cannot pay W-2 wages to their owners, so there was no reason for the IRS to try to re-characterize income passed through to owners of these businesses as compensation.

Following enactment of Code section 199A, however, pass-through income will be taxed more favorably than compensation income for all pass-through entities. Unlike, the Committee Report, Code section 199A(c)(4) does not limit application of the reasonable compensation restriction to S corporations, stating that *"Qualified business income shall not include reasonable compensation paid to the taxpayer by any qualified trade or business of the taxpayer for services rendered with respect to the trade or business."* Thus, the IRS might take the position based on the Code section that the pass-through income of sole proprietorships, partnerships and LLCs should be reduced by a reasonable amount of compensation for the owners just like the income of an S corporation.

If the IRS did this, it would create an important advantage for S corporations over other pass-through entities, however. Under current law, S corporations are subject to the reasonable compensation requirement, but this disadvantage is offset by the S corporation's ability to use wages paid to owners in calculating the W-2/unadjusted basis limitation. If the reasonable compensation requirement was extended to sole proprietorships, partnerships and LLCs, it would seem only fair that these entities should also be able to count salaries paid to owners as W-2 income for purposes of the W-2/unadjusted basis limitation.[45]

Note that although guaranteed payments are excluded from QBI, there is no requirement to make guaranteed payments to partners like there is for paying reasonable compensation to an S corporation shareholder. Thus, partnerships and LLCs could effectively convert what would ordinarily be non-qualified guaranteed payments into pass-through income by reducing or eliminating guaranteed payments and treating these amounts as pass-through income qualifying as QBI. Nothing would be lost under Code section 199A by doing so because guaranteed payments don't count as W-2 wages for purposes of the W-2 wage/unadjusted basis limitation. If a partnership interest is received by gift, however, Code section 704(e) requires that the partnership must provide an allowance of reasonable compensation for the services of the donor partner.[46] The IRS may argue that the allocation of compensation to the donor partner is unreasonably low and convert what would otherwise be QBI into salary income.

23.5 QUALIFIED TRADE OR BUSINESS

A *qualified* trade or business is any trade or business other than (1) a specified service trade or business, or (2) the trade or business of performing services as an employee.[47] Although the phrase "trade or business" appears in over fifty Code sections and 800 subsections, neither the Code nor the regulations has ever provided an all-purpose definition. Thus, the definition has been left to the courts. The case law could be summarized as follows.

- Determining whether an individual is carrying on a trade or business requires an examination of the facts involved in each case.[48]

- To be engaged in a trade or business, an individual must be involved in an activity with continuity and regularity, and the primary purpose for engaging in the activity must be to produce income or profit.[49]

- A sporadic activity, a hobby, or an amusement diversion does not qualify.[50]

- Expenses incident to caring for one's own investments, even on a large enough scale to require an office and staff, are not deductible as paid or incurred in carrying on a trade or business.[51]

- Holding one's self out to others as engaged in the selling of goods or services is not required.[52]

Rental Real Estate

Determining whether an activity rises to the level of a trade or business is particularly important in the context of rental real estate. Renting or managing rental property could be either a business activity or as an investment activity depending on the facts of the case.

The Tax Court has repeatedly held that the rental of even a single piece of real property can constitute a trade or business.[53] According to the IRS, ownership and management of real property does not constitute a trade or business as a matter of law, however.[54] The question of whether there is a trade or business is ultimately one of fact and depends on the scope of ownership and management activities. Owning rental property qualifies as a business if it is engaged in to earn a profit and the activity is sufficiently systematic and continuous.[55] If not, rental ownership will be treated as an investment rather than as a trade or business.[56]

Grouping Trades or Businesses

The computation of the Code section 199A deduction is done separately for each qualified trade or business[57] but, as noted above, the statute does not explain what is meant by a trade or business. Thus, it is unclear whether activities of separate entities can be grouped together for purposes of doing the calculations. Regulations under Code section 469, dealing with identifying and grouping activities for purposes of the passive loss rules might be used as a starting point for determining when two or more trades or businesses could be grouped together.[58] Regulations under Code section 448(d), might also be helpful.[59] These regulations address when trades or businesses are separate and distinct and, thus, eligible to use different accounting methods for the businesses.

Specified Service Trade or Business (SSTB)

A specified service trade or business is (1) any trade or business listed in Code section 1202(e)(3)(A) other than engineering or architecture,[60] and (2) any business which involves the performance of services that consist of investing and investment management, trading, or dealing in securities, partnership interests, or commodities.[61] The trades or businesses listed in Code section 1202(e)(3)(A) are trades or businesses involving performance of services in the fields of:

- Health
- Law
- Accounting
- Actuarial science
- Performing arts
- Consulting
- Athletics
- Financial services
- Brokerage services
- Any trade or business where the principal asset of the trade or business is the reputation or skill of one of its employees[62]

Section 1202 Guidance

For purposes of section 199A, the last category applies to the reputation or skill of business owners as well as to the reputation or skill of one or more employees.[63] This category may be very difficult to define because, arguably, most successful small businesses owe much of their success to the reputation or skill of their owners and/or employees. It remains to be seen how broadly this category will be defined.[64] One possible way for the IRS to address this issue would be to formulate a list of safe harbor businesses.

Example 15. Amy is a nationally known pastry chef who owns a bakery. Although the bakery produces products rather than services, the reputation or skill category may apply.

Note that although Code section 199A uses Code section 1202(e)(3) to identify service businesses, it does not mention the businesses listed in Code sections 1202(e)(3)(B), 1202(e)(3)(C), and 1202(e)(3)(D). These include:

- Any banking, insurance, financing, leasing, investing or similar business[65]

- Any farming business (including the business of raising or harvesting trees)[66]

- Any business involving the production or extraction of products of a character with respect to which a deduction is allowable under section 613 or 613(A).[67]

Inclusion of the businesses listed in Code section 1202(e)(3)(A) but not the businesses listed in the other sections of 1202(e)(3), would seem to indicate that Congress intended to exclude these businesses from the definition of specified service business. An argument might be made that these businesses might still be treated as specified service trades or businesses under the catch-all category relating to the reputation or skill of one or more owners or employees. This appears to be unlikely, however, at least for mining and most farming businesses, because they produce undifferentiated commodities.

Until recently, qualifying as a small business corporation under Code section 1202 produced little tax benefit.[68] The lack of interest in the exclusion and the difficulty of defining the term qualified trade or business, deterred the IRS from issuing regulations and taxpayers from seeking rulings. As a result, there is very little law on the scope of service businesses under section 1202. The only guidance appears to be two private letter rulings on the health care category.[69]

It is not clear how to treat an entity that combines a specified service trade or business and a qualified business. For example, there is no guidance on whether the specified service trade or business taints the qualified business, causing the entire entity to be treated as an SSTB.

Fortunately, as noted in the Committee Report, additional guidance is available on some of the categories under Code section 448(d)(2). This section prohibits use of the cash method of accounting for most C corporations, but allows an exception for personal service corporations.[70] Thus, guidance under section 448(d)(2) may be helpful in determining the scope of some of the service businesses listed under Code section 1202(e)(1)(A).

W-2 Wages

The term "W-2 wages" means, with respect to any person for any taxable year of such person, the amounts described in paragraphs (3) and (8) of section 6051(a) paid by such person with respect to employment of employees by such person during the calendar year ending during such taxable year.[71] Thus, it includes:

- wages paid to an employee as defined in Code section 3401(a);

- elective deferrals (within the meaning of Code section 402(g)(3);

- deferred compensation under Code section 457; and

- Roth IRA contributions as defined in Code section 402A.

These amounts only count, however, if they are properly allocable to QBI.[72] They are also excluded if they aren't properly included in a return filed with the Social Security Administration on or before the sixtieth day after the due date (including extensions) for such return.[73] Elective deferrals include elective contributions made to SIMPLE IRAs, 401(k) plans, SARSEPs, and 403(b) plans.[74]

The term W-2 wages does not include payments to independent contractors or management fees.[75] Note that an S corporation can pay W-2 wages to the entity's owners but partnerships and LLCs cannot.[76] This might be an important advantage for S corporations that pay most of the wages to the business owners.

Code section 199A does not address the question of whether amounts paid to leased employees from a professional employer organization (PEO)[77] are W-2 wages for purposes of the QBI and W-2 wage/unadjusted basis limitation. It appears, however, that whether amounts paid to leased employees or clients of PEOs would be W-2 wages would depend on who the worker's employer was under the common law.[78]

Under common law rules, a worker is an employee if the employer has the right to control what work will be done and how it will be done. This is true even if the employee is given freedom of action. What counts is that the employer has the right to control not that the employer actually exerts control. The IRS has listed twenty factors that can be used in determining whether a worker is a common law employee.[79]

Qualified Property

The 2.5 percent of the unadjusted basis component of the W-2 wages/capital limitation applies to any property that is:

- tangible;
- depreciable;
- held by, and available for use in, the qualified business at the close of the year;
- used at any time during the taxable year for production of QBI; and
- for which the depreciable period hasn't ended before the end of the taxable year.[80]

The depreciable period for the property cannot end prior to the last day of the year for which the deduction is claimed. For this purpose, the end of the depreciable period is the later of ten years after the property was placed in service or the last day of the last full year in the asset's regular depreciation period under Code section 168 (not the period under the alternative depreciation system (ADS)).[81]

Example 16. In 2018, Tom acquires machinery for use in his business. The depreciation period for the machinery is five years. The unadjusted basis of the machinery can be counted for the longer of five or ten years. Thus, its basis can be used for the W-2 wage/unadjusted basis calculation from 2018 through 2027.

The basis of property generally cannot be counted for the W-2/unadjusted basis limitation if it was fully depreciated before 2018. It appears, however, that property placed in service after 2008 might still be counted under the ten-year rule even if its normal depreciation period has expired.[82]

An S corporation shareholder or partner's portion of an entity's unadjusted basis is allocated based on the shareholder or partner's share of the entity's unadjusted basis immediately after acquisition of the qualified property.[83] It is not clear how these percentages change if a new owner joins the entity. Nor is it clear how improvements to tangible property are treated under the unadjusted basis rules.

Example 17. Carol and Karen are equal partners in the CK Partnership. Depreciation expense is allocated 40 percent to Carol and 60 percent to Karen. CK partnership owns depreciable property with an unadjusted basis of $100,000. Carol can use $40,000 for her W-2 wages/unadjusted basis limitation and Karen can use $60,000.

Code section 199A(h) directs the IRS to prescribe rules similar to those under Code section 179(d)(2) to prevent manipulation of the depreciable period of qualified property using transactions between related parties.[84]

Code section 199A(h) also directs the IRS to prescribe rules for determining the unadjusted basis immediately after acquisition of qualified property acquired in like-kind exchanges or involuntary conversions.[85] This guidance may also apply to sale-leaseback transactions.[86]

The Committee Report does not address the acquisition date of property acquired from a decedent. It appears that the acquisition date should be the date of death. Thus, it may be possible to increase the unadjusted basis by the amount of the step-up under Code section 1014 or, in the case of a partnership, with a Code section 754 basis step-up. Using the date of death as the acquisition date would also extend the depreciable period for the property. These questions may be covered in the anti-abuse guidance to be provided pursuant to Code section 199A(h).

Unadjusted Tax Basis

The "unadjusted basis" in qualified property is the property's basis immediately after acquisition, unreduced by any depreciation deductions.[87]

Taxable Income

Taxable income is computed in the usual manner, without regard to the 20 percent 199A deduction.[88]

Qualified REIT Dividend

A qualified REIT dividend is any dividend received from a real estate investment trust that is not (1) a capital asset, or (2) qualified dividend income subject to tax at long term capital gain rates.[89]

Qualified Publicly Traded Partnership Income

Qualified publicly traded partnership income means, with respect to any qualified trade or business of the taxpayer, the sum of:

1. The net amount of the taxpayer's allocable share of each item of qualified item of income, gain, deduction or loss from a publicly traded partnership not treated as a corporation; and

2. Any gain recognized by such taxpayer upon disposition of its interest in such partnership to the extent such gain is treated as an amount realized from the sale or exchange of property other than a capital asset under Code section 751(a) (i.e., gain on the sale of hot assets).[90]

23.6 SPECIAL RULES AND UNANSWERED QUESTIONS

Code section 199A includes a number of special rules. These include rules on:

- The application of Code section 199A to partnerships and S corporations

- The application of Code section 199A to trusts and estates

- The coordination of Code section 199A with the alternative minimum tax (AMT)

- The carryover of losses

- The treatment of NOLs under Code section 199A

- The effect of the Code section 199A deduction on tax basis

- The extension of the accuracy related penalty to taxpayers who claim the deduction

These issues are discussed in detail below.

Application to Partnerships and S Corporations

In the case of a partnership or S corporation, Code section 199A is applied at the partner or shareholder level.[91] The following rules apply for purposes of calculating the 20 percent deduction:

1. Each partner or shareholder takes into account such person's allocable share of each qualified item of income, gain, deduction, and loss

2. Each partner or shareholder is treated as having W-2 wages and unadjusted basis in an amount equal to such person's allocable share immediately after acquisition of qualified property for the taxable year in an amount equal to such person's allocable share of the W-2 wages and the unadjusted basis immediately after acquisition of qualified property of the partnership or S corporation for the taxable year (as determined under regulations prescribed by the Secretary)

3. For purposes of (2) above, a partner's or shareholder's allocable share of W-2 wages shall be determined in the same manner as the partner's or shareholder's allocable share of wage expenses

4. For purposes of (2) above, a partner's or shareholder's allocable share of the unadjusted basis immediately after acquisition of qualified property shall be determined in the same manner as the partner's or shareholder's allocable share of depreciation

5. In the case of an S corporation, an allocable share shall be the shareholder's pro rata share of an item[92]

Calculating an S corporation shareholder's allocable share of an item should be relatively straightforward. Each shareholder's pro rata share of any item would be determined by assigning an equal portion of such item to each day of the taxable year and then dividing that portion pro rata among the shares outstanding on such day.[93]

Example 18. On January 6, 2021, X incorporates as a calendar year corporation, issues 100 shares of common stock to each of A and B, and files an election to be an S corporation. On July 24, 2021, B sells 25 shares of X stock to C. Thus, in 2021, A owned 50 percent of the outstanding shares of X on each day of X's 2021 year, B owned 50 percent on each day from January 6, 2021 to July 24, 2021 (200 days), and 25 percent from July 25, 2021 to December 31, 2021 (160 days), and C owned 25 percent from July 25, 2021 to December 31, 2021. During its 2017 taxable year, X pays $720,000 of wages.

For each day in X's 2021 taxable year, the shareholders' pro rata shares are as follows.

A $720,000/360 days × 50% ownership = $1,000/day

B   first 200 days $720,000/360 days × 50% ownership = $1,000/day

last 160 days $720,000/360 days × 25% ownership = $500/day

C $720,000/360 days × 25% ownership = $500/day

The allocation of wages then looks like this:

A $1,000/day × $360/day = $360,000

B   ($1,000/day × 200 days) + ($500/day × 160 days) = $280,000

C $500/day × 160 days = $80,000[94]

Determining a partner's allocable share might be much more difficult, particularly if there are special allocations. The determination would presumably be made under Code section 704 and the section 704 regulations. Regulations issued under former Code section 199 might be helpful in this regard. Prior to its repeal by the TCJA, this section provided a deduction for income attributable to domestic production activities.[95] Like the new section 199A, former section 199 limited the deduction to 50 percent of wages paid and allocated wages at the partner or shareholder level.[96] Apparently acknowledging this complexity in this area, Code section 199A(f)(4) provides that the IRS will issue regulations on the allocation of items of wages and on applying Code section 199A to tiered entities.

Example 19. Partner X has a 40 percent ownership interest in non-service Partnership XYZ. In Year 1, the partnership had $2,500,000 of ordinary income, $900,000 of wage expense and held depreciable property with a basis of $250,000. There are no special allocations, so X is allocated 40 percent of all partnership items. Thus, X's allocable share of each item in the QBI calculation is as follows.

Income	$1,000,000
W-2 wages	$360,000
Unadjusted basis	$100,000

X's section 199A deduction is then

The lesser of

1. 20% of X's allocable share of flow-through income ($200,000)

Or the greater of

2. 50% of X's allocable share of W-2 wages ($180,000); or

3. 25% of X's allocable share of W-2 wages ($90,000) + 2.5% of X's allocable share of basis ($2,500) = $92,500

Thus, the deduction is the lesser of $200,000 or $180,000 = $180,000.

Because the taxable income limitation is applied at the partner or shareholder level, some owners might benefit more from the 20 percent deduction than others. Thus, it may be possible to maximize deductions by making special allocations of W-2 wages and depreciation deductions.

Application to Trusts and Estates

The Committee Report makes it clear that trusts and estates are eligible for the 20 percent QBI deduction.[97]

Rules similar to the rules under section 199(d)(1)(B)(i) (as in effect on December 1, 2017) apply to the apportionment of W-2 wages and the apportionment of unadjusted basis immediately after acquisition of qualified property under this section.

> *Example 20.* In the ABC Trust, 75 percent of the DNI is distributed to the beneficiaries and 25 percent is retained in the trust. It appears that the beneficiaries will get 75 percent of the QBI deduction and the trust will get 25 percent.

Coordination with the AMT

The alternative minimum tax (AMT) was designed to make sure high income taxpayers who could reduce regular income tax to very low levels by taking advantage of certain deductions and tax benefit items still paid a significant amount of tax. The AMT accomplishes this by adding to regular taxable income the amount of tax preference items in Code section 57 and making certain adjustments to income under Code sections 56 and 58. There are also some special rules under Code section 59. The AMT income is generally taxed at a rate of 26 or 28 percent.[98] For purposes of determining qualified business income under Code section 199A, the adjustments under Code sections 56 to 59 are ignored.[99]

Carryover of Losses

If the net amount of qualified income, gain, deduction, and loss of a qualified trade or business of the taxpayer is less than zero for any tax year, the amount is carried over as a loss from a qualified trade or business in the next tax year.[100]

> *Example 21.* Cathy has qualified business income of $30,000 from qualified business A and a business loss of $50,000 from qualified business B in Year 1. Cathy does not get a section 199A deduction for Year 1 and has a carryover qualified business loss of $20,000 to Year 2. Assume that in Year 2 she has qualified business income of $30,000 from qualified business A and qualified business income of $40,000 from qualified business B. To determine the deduction for Year 2, Cathy reduces the 20 percent deductible amount determined for the qualified business income of $70,000 from qualified businesses A and B by 20 percent of the $20,000 carryover qualified business loss. Thus, the Year 2 deduction is $10,000 (.2 × $50,000).[101]

Treatment of Net Operating Losses (NOLs)

The section 199A deduction cannot be used to create an NOL. It must be removed from the NOL calculation.[102]

Effect of the Deduction on the Tax Basis of an S Corporation Shareholder

An S corporation shareholder's basis in stock of the corporation is increased by the shareholder's share of the entity's income.[103] Although the TCJA does not address how this rule applies when a shareholder's S corporation income is reduced by the 20 percent section 199A deduction, it appears that the deduction shouldn't be taken into account in calculating a partner's basis increase.

> *Example 22.* Ray is a shareholder in the ABC S corporation with a basis of $15,000 in his stock. ABC was never a C corporation and has no earnings and profits. Ray's share of S corporation income for 2018 is $100,000 and he qualifies for the full 20 percent deduction under Code section 199A, reducing his taxable income to $80,000. ABC distributes $100,000 to Ray. If Ray's basis of $15,000 was increased only by the $80,000 of taxable income, he would recognize $5,000 of income on the distribution ($100,000 distribution - $95,000 basis).[104] If this was the correct result, it would seem to eliminate part of the benefit of the section 199A deduction. Thus, it appears that Ray's basis in his S corporation stock should be increased by $100,000.

Extension of Accuracy-related Penalties

Prior to enactment of the TCJA, there was a substantial understatement of income tax for purposes of imposing the 20 percent accuracy-related penalty if the amount of an understatement exceeded the greater of 10 percent of the tax required to be shown or $5,000.[105]

Apparently expecting taxpayers to aggressively claim deductions under Code section 199A, Congress reduced the threshold amount for application of the penalty to the greater of 5 percent of the correct tax or $5,000.[106]

It is important to note that the lower threshold does not just apply to understatements arising out of the Code section 199A deduction. Instead, it applies to any taxpayer who claims the section 199A deduction on a return regardless of whether the understatement resulted from an excess deduction under section 199A or because of understatements resulted from any other reporting error. It also applies regardless of the amount of the Code section 199A deduction claimed.

The term understatement for purposes of the substantial understatement penalty means the excess of:

- The amount of tax required to be shown on the return, over

- The amount of tax imposed which is actually shown on the return[107]

To the extent that a taxpayer (1) has substantial authority for the reported tax treatment of a position, or (2) has a reasonable basis for the position and makes adequate disclosure, the amount of the understatement is reduced.[108]

Example 23. In 2021, Jane, a calendar year taxpayer files a return for 2020 which shows tax payable of $64,000. Subsequent adjustments on audit increase Jane's tax liability to $70,000. There is a substantial understatement of tax if the $6,000 underpayment exceeds the greater of (1) 10 percent of the correct tax ($7,000), or (2) $5,000. Since $6,000 does not exceed $7,000, there is no substantial understatement.

Example 24. Assume the same facts as in Example 23 except that the return is filed in 2019 for the 2018 tax year and the new 5 percent rule has gone into effect. Also assume that Jane has claimed a QBI deduction under Code section 199A. Now there is a substantial understatement of tax if the underpayment ($6,000) exceeds the greater of 5 percent of the correct tax ($3,500) or $5,000. Since $6,000 exceeds $5,000, there is a substantial understatement.

Example 25. Assume the same facts as in Example 24 except that Jane had substantial authority for an item resulting in an adjustment that increased her tax liability by $2,000. The item is not a tax shelter.[109] The amount of tax treated as shown on Jane's return is increased by this $2,000 amount to $66,000. This reduces the underpayment to $4,000. Since this amount is less than the greater of $3,300 or $5,000, there is no substantial understatement of tax.[110]

23.7 UNANSWERED QUESTIONS

Code section 199A and the Committee Report left a number of important questions unanswered. In a letter to the Department of the Treasury, the AICPA requested guidance on the following issues:[111]

- The meaning of specified service trade or business.

- The calculation of QBI when flowing through multiple tiered entities.

- The netting computation of losses from one business against gains from another business.

- The effect of an existing grouping of trades or businesses (e.g., under section 469) for purposes of the limitations based on W-2 wages, adjusted basis of assets and specified service business. If grouping is allowed, will taxpayers have an opportunity to regroup their trades or businesses to take advantage of the deduction?

- Whether wages are determined in a manner similar to the concepts provided in Reg. section 1.199-2(a)(2). In other words, by considering the wages of common law employees regardless of who is responsible for paying the wages.

- Whether a trade or business is defined as an activity within an entity. For example, what if an entity has two clearly separate trades or businesses?

- Whether all similar qualified businesses are aggregated for purposes of the calculation or if each business is evaluated separately.

For taxpayers with non-qualified business activities, there is a *de minimis* percentage at which the activity is not excluded. Does the taxpayer make separate computations for the personal service activity versus the non-personal service activity?

- Whether the taxpayer may consider a management company an integral part of the operating trade or business (and thus, not a specified business activity) if substantially all of the management company's income is from that other trade or business.

- The qualification of real property rental income as qualified business income (or loss).

- If grouping is allowed, whether taxpayers may treat the rental of real estate to their related C corporation (e.g., a self-rental) as trade or business income.

- The determination of items effectively connected with a business, e.g., section 1245 gains and losses, retirement plan contributions of partners and sole proprietors, the section 162(l) deduction and one-half of self-employment tax.

- The unadjusted basis of assets expensed under section 179 or subject to bonus depreciation.

- The unadjusted basis of assets held as of January 1, 2018.

- The unadjusted basis of property subject to 743(b) basis adjustments.

- The effect, if any, of the 20 percent deduction on net investment income tax calculations.

23.8 TAX PLANNING UNDER SECTION 199A

Tax planning under Code section 199A involves the following topics.

1. Managing limitation amounts by Increasing or decreasing W-2 wages, increasing unadjusted basis, reducing taxable income to avoid limitation amounts, or increasing ordinary income to avoid the 20 percent of net income over capital gains limitation

2. Employee vs. independent contractor status

3. Planning for marital status

4. Promoting employees to partner status

5. Choice of entity decision, including choosing between a pass-through entity vs. C corporation and a sole proprietorship vs. partnership/LLC vs. S corporation

6. Tax planning for service businesses

Managing Limitation Amounts

The limitations on the QBI deduction can be managed by:

- increasing or decreasing W-2 wages

- increasing adjusted basis

- reducing taxable income to avoid the W-2 wage/unadjusted basis and SSTB limitations

- increasing ordinary income to avoid the 20 percent of net income over capital gains limitation.

Increasing or Decreasing W-2 Wages

Depending on the facts of the case, either increasing or decreasing W-2 wages may increase the Code section 199A deduction. Disregarding unadjusted basis for the time being, if 20 percent of QBI exceeds 50 percent of W-2 wages it may be possible to increase the limitation amount by increasing wages. The following examples illustrate various ways in which this might be done.

Example 26. John and his wife, Melissa, have taxable income of $415,000. They own a small coffee roasting business. The business:

- Is structured as a sole proprietorship

- Generates $100,000 of QBI

- Has no employees

- Has no qualified property because it leases its space and equipment

A sole proprietorship cannot pay W-2 wages to its owners. This means that John and Melissa's 199A deduction is the lesser of:

(1) 20 percent of QBI ($20,000), or

(2) the greater of 50 percent of W-2 wages ($0) or unadjusted basis in qualified property ($0).

Thus, John and Melissa have a section 199A deduction of $0.

Example 27. Assume the same facts as in Example 26, except that John & Melissa convert the business to a partnership and pay Melissa a guaranteed payment of $50,000/year. The section 199A deduction would still be zero because guaranteed payments aren't W-2 wages.[112] To create W-2 wages the business would have to pay wages to employees.

Example 28. Assume the same facts as in Example 27 except that John and Melissa convert the business to an S corporation. An S corporation can pay W-2 wages to its owners as well as to employees. If the business pays Melissa $50,000 in W-2 wages, the Code section 199A deduction is the lesser of:

(1) 20 percent of QBI (.2 × $50,000 = $10,000);[113] or

(2) 50 percent of W-2 wages (.5 × $50,000) = $25,000.

Thus, the section 199A deduction is $10,000.

Note that the optimal amount of income to be paid is achieved by setting 50 percent of wages equal to 20 percent of QBI. This is illustrated in the next example.

Example 29. Assume the same facts as in Example 28 except that John and Melissa realize that their section 199A deduction might be larger if Melissa was paid less because W-2 wages don't count as QBI. They determine that the optimal deduction would be achieved if Melissa was paid 28.5714 percent of the pass-through income ($28,571.40) and the remaining $71,428.60 was treated as QBI.[114] Note that 28.5714 percent equals 2/7 of the income. The amount of the QBI deduction would be the lesser of:

(1) 20 percent of QBI (.2 × $71,428.60 = $14,285.70); or

(2) 50 percent of wages (.5 × $28,571.40 = $14,285.70).

Note that if Melissa is paid either more or less than this amount, the deduction will go down.[115]

Unfortunately, if the business does not pay Melissa reasonable compensation for the work she does, the IRS will re-characterize a portion of the profits interest passing through to her as wages.[116] If $50,000 was reasonable compensation for running the coffee roasting business in the previous example and Melissa's pay was reduced to $28,571.40, the IRS might try to re-characterize some or all of the income as wages.

Wages can also be increased by converting independent contractors to employees.

Example 30. Ted, a single taxpayer, is the sole proprietor of the TR trucking company. He pays his two drivers $50,000/year each, but they work as independent contractors so there are no W-2 wages. Ted has no depreciable property because the trucks are leased. His pass-through income from the business is $225,000 per year and his taxable income is $250,000. Ted's section 199A deduction is the lesser of.

(1) QBI (.2 × $225,000 = $45,000); or

(2) the greater of W-2 wages or unadjusted basis, both of which are $0.

Thus, Ted gets no section 199A deduction.

Suppose, however, that he converts the drivers into employees. His section 199A deduction would then be the lesser of $45,000 or 50% × $100,000 of W-2 wages = $50,000. Thus, the conversion would increase Ted's QBI deduction to $45,000. The downside would be that the drivers would each lose a $10,000 QBI deduction (.2 × $50,000) because, while independent contractors qualify for the section 199A deduction, employees don't.[117]

Finally, the section 199A deduction can be increased by simply paying employees higher wages.

Example 31. Linda, a single taxpayer, is the sole proprietor of a bakery. Linda's net income from the bakery is $130,000/year and her taxable income is $240,000. Linda has one part-time employee, Marge, who Linda pays $20,000/year. The bakery has no depreciable property.

Linda's section 199A deduction is the lesser of (1) .2 × $130,000 QBI = $26,000 or (2) .5 × $20,000 W-2 wages = $10,000. Marge has been doing excellent work and Linda has been thinking of giving her a substantial raise. If Linda increases Marge's salary to $30,000 (reducing net income to $120,000), she can increase her section 199A deduction to $15,000. This is the lesser of (1) .2 × $120,000 = $24,000 or, (2) .5 × $30,000 = $15,000. Decreasing QBI does not reduce the section 199A deduction because 20 percent of QBI still exceeds the 50 percent of W-2 wages limitation. Because Linda is in the 24 percent marginal tax bracket, the additional $5,000 deduction is worth $1,200 (.24 × $5,000). In effect, the Treasury pays for part of Marge's raise.

Decreasing W-2 Wages

In the previous examples, 20 percent of QBI exceeded 50 percent of W-2 wages so it was advantageous to increase W-2 wages.[118] If, on the other hand, 20 percent of QBI is less than the 50 percent W-2 wage limitation, it may be advantageous to reduce wages. Because wages aren't included in QBI, this will increase pass-through income and the amount of QBI.

Example 32. Tim and his wife, Dora, are the sole owners of an S corporation. The business produces $150,000 of profit and pays Dora a salary of $120,000 for operating the business. The business owns no depreciable property. If Tim and Dora do no planning, their section 199A is the lesser of:

(1) 20 percent of QBI ($30,000);

OR

(2) the greater of 50 percent of W-2 wages ($60,000) or unadjusted basis ($0).

This makes the section 199A deduction $30,000. To increase the deduction, they decide to reduce Dora's W-2 wages by $40,000. This increases QBI by $40,000 and increases their section 199A deduction to the lesser of:

(1) 20 percent of QBI ($200,000);

OR

(2) the greater of 50 percent of W-2 wages ($40,000) or unadjusted basis, both of which are $0.

By reducing Dora's wages by $40,000, the section 199A deduction is increased by $8,000 to $38,000. This is a good result, but the deduction could be made slightly higher by paying Dora 2/7 of the sum of Dora's wages + company profit. This amount would be 2/7 × $270,000 = $77,142.86, leaving the $192,857.14 of pass-through income ($270,000 - $77,142.86). Then, the section 199A deduction would be the lesser of:

(1) 20 percent of QBI ($38,571);

OR

(2) the greater of 50 percent of W-2 wages ($77,143) or unadjusted basis ($0).

Again, the IRS might question whether the business was paying reasonable compensation.

Increasing Unadjusted Basis

Up to this point we have been assuming that unadjusted basis was zero and showing how changes in W-2 wages could increase the section 199A deduction. We now turn to the unadjusted basis component of the W-2 wage/unadjusted basis limitation. Unadjusted basis can be increased by either acquiring depreciable property or by owning property instead of leasing it.

Example 33. Bill and Kelly own a small unincorporated widget manufacturing business that produces $1,000,000 of net income per year. Bill and Kelly do all the work so there are no W-2 wages. They rent a building and lease the machinery used to make the widgets. If Bill and Kelly do no planning, their section 199A deduction will be $0, the lesser of:

(1) 20 percent of QBI ($200,000);

OR

(2) the greater of 50 percent of W-2 wages or unadjusted basis, both of which are $0.

Now suppose that instead of leasing, Bill and Kelly decide to buy the building for $1,000,000. Their section 199A deduction amount is now the lesser of:

(1) 20 percent of QBI ($200,000);

OR

(2) the greater of 50 percent of W-2 wages ($0) or 25 percent of wages plus 2.5 percent of basis ($0 + $25,000).

Example 34. Beth owns a trucking company with $800,000 of QBI so her tentative QBI deduction is $160,000. Beth's taxable income is $700,000 so the W-2/unadjusted basis limitation applies in full. All the company's trucks are leased, the company owns no depreciable real property and the drivers are all independent contractors so the W-2/unadjusted basis limitation is $0 and Beth gets no section 199A deduction.

Example 35. Assume the same facts as in Example 34 except that the company buys the trucks for $1,000,000. This increases the W-2 wage/unadjusted basis limitation to $25,000, giving Beth a $25,000 deduction.

Reducing Taxable Income to Avoid the W-2 Wage/Unadjusted Basis and SSTB Limitations

In 2021 the W-2 wage and SSTB limitations are phased in as taxable income increases from $164,900 to $214,900 for single taxpayers and from $329,800 to $429,800 for married taxpayers filing jointly. It may be possible to avoid, or at least diminish the effect of these limitations by decreasing taxable income.

Charitable Deductions and Qualified Plan Contributions

Two easy ways to reduce taxable income to avoid or minimize application of the W-2 wage/unadjusted basis and SSTB limitations are making charitable contributions and making contributions to qualified plans.

Example 36. Tom, a married man, is a lawyer with a solo practice. He pays $80,000 in wages to his employees. The building that houses the practice is leased. The law practice generates $500,000 of QBI and Tom's taxable income in 2021 will be $360,000. Without planning, his tentative QBI deduction is 20 percent of $500,000 = $100,000. Because the law practice is a service business and Tom's taxable income exceeds $3298000, however, part of the deduction is phased out. Tom's income is 40 percent of the way through the phase-out range ($40,000/$100,000) so he loses 40 percent of the deduction (.4 × $100,000 = $40,000). This leaves Tom with a section 199A deduction of $60,000.

Example 37. Assume the same facts as in Example 36 except that Tom makes a $40,000 charitable contribution to the American Cancer Society. This reduces his taxable income to $329,800 and eliminates any phase-out. Thus, Tom gets the full $80,000 deduction.

Gifts of Business Interests

Taxpayers might also consider gifting shares of a business to family members. This would spread income from the business among several taxpayers, making it easier to stay below the phase-in or phase-out threshold amounts.

Example 38. Al and Paula are married taxpayers filing jointly with $400,000 of QBI from AP Partnership and taxable income of $500,000. The AP Partnership pays no wages. Because Al and Paula have taxable income over $429,800, the W-2 wage limitation applies in full and they get no Code section 199A deduction.

Al and Paula have two children, Ted and Susan, both married taxpayers in their late twenties, each with taxable MFJ income of $100,000. Al and Paula gift a 25 percent interest in AP to Ted and a 25 percent interest in AP to Susan, shifting $100,000 of qualified business income to each of them. Following the transfer, Al and Paula have taxable income of $300,000 and Ted and Susan have taxable income of $200,000 each. Thus, all of them qualify for the full 20 percent deduction on AP income.

Avoiding the 20 Percent of Taxable Income Over Capital Gain Limitation—Increasing Taxable Income

Even if QBI is not limited by the W-2 wages/unadjusted basis limitation, it may be limited by the 20 percent of taxable income over capital gains limitation. In this situation, an owner of a non-service business may wish to earn additional income outside the pass-through business.

Example 39. Gary is a single farmer with income of $100,000 and no capital gains. Gary claims $15,000 of itemized deductions, reducing his taxable income to $85,000. Although his tentative QBI deduction is $20,000 (.2 × $100,000), the deduction is limited to $17,500 (.2 × $85,000) because of the taxable income limitation (20 percent of taxable income over capital gains). During the winter, Gary works at a store in a nearby town and earns $15,000 of additional income. This increases his taxable income over capital gain to $100,000 and his 20 percent of taxable income limitation to $20,000, so he can use the full amount of his tentative QBI. If Gary had instead sold a small parcel of land and recognized a gain of $15,000, this income wouldn't have increased his limitation amount.

Employee vs. Independent Contractor Status

Classification of a worker as an independent contractor or as an employee makes a big difference both for workers and for employers under Code section 199A. Payments for work done by an independent contractor are QBI and can qualify for the 20 percent QBI deduction, but payments for similar work done by an employee cannot.[119] Thus, workers receive more favorable tax treatment if they are treated as independent contractors. On the other hand, payments to employees for work done count as W-2 wages for an employer, enabling the employer to increase its W-2 wage/unadjusted basis limitation amount but payments to independent contractors don't. Thus, employers and workers have conflicting objectives under Code section 199A. Workers want to be treated as independent contractors, but employers would rather treat them as employees.

This oversimplifies the decision for two reasons, however. First, an employer cannot just decide that a worker will be treated as an employee and a worker cannot just decide that he wants to be treated as an independent contractor. The worker actually has to qualify for the desired status. The IRS takes the position that in determining whether a worker is an employee or an independent contractor it is necessary to consider all evidence of the degree of control and independence in the work relationship. The facts that provide this evidence fall into three categories: Behavioral Control, Financial Control, and Relationship of the Parties.

Behavioral Control covers facts that show if the business has a right to direct and control what work is accomplished and how the work is done, through instructions, training, or other means.

Financial Control covers facts that show if the business has a right to direct or control the financial and business aspects of the worker's job. This includes:

- The extent to which the worker has unreimbursed business expense

- The extent of the worker's investment in the facilities or tools used in performing services

- The extent to which the worker makes his or her services available to the relevant market

- How the business pays the worker

- The extent to which the worker can realize a profit or incur a loss

Relationship of the Parties covers facts that show the type of relationship the parties have. This includes:

- Written contracts describing the relationship the parties intended to create

- Whether the business provides the worker with employee-type benefits, such as insurance, a pension plan, vacation pay, or sick pay

- The permanency of the relationship

- The extent to which services performed by the worker are a key aspect of the regular business of the company[120]

In addition, even if the worker qualifies for the desired status, there may be important trade-offs. If workers are treated as employees, the employer would have to pay payroll taxes, comply with wage and hour requirements, reimburse workers for business expenses, cover the employees under worker's compensation insurance and perhaps provide other benefits. There are also downsides for workers who choose to be independent contractors. They would have to pay both halves of the Medicare and Social Security taxes up to the Social Security wage base ($142,800 in 2021) and might give up important fringe benefits like health insurance.

Increasing QBI

One way to increase QBI would be to convert guaranteed payments in a partnership into pass-through income. While guaranteed payments don't count as QBI, distributive shares are included. Unlike S corporations, partnerships aren't required to pay reasonable compensation.

Example 40. Paul and his brother Al, single taxpayers, are 50 percent partners in a non-service business that owns no depreciable property. The net income of the business is $600,000, of which $300,000 is distributed to the partners in the form of guaranteed payments. Paul and Al both have income in excess of $214,900 so the W-2/unadjusted basis limitation applies in full. The business has no depreciable property, but pays $400,000 in wages to its employees.

The total section 199A deduction, split evenly between the partners is the lesser of:

(1) 20 percent of QBI ($60,000);

OR

(2) the greater of 50 percent of W-2 wages ($200,000) or unadjusted basis ($100,000).

Since 20 percent of QBI ($60,000) is less than the partners' W-2 wage/unadjusted basis limitation amount ($200,000), their section 199A deduction could be augmented by increasing QBI.

Suppose that Paul and Al each reduces his guaranteed payment by $100,000. This would increase total QBI by $200,000 to $500,000. The amount of the QBI deduction would be the lesser of:

(1) 20 percent of QBI ($100,000);

OR

(2) the greater of 50 percent of W-2 wages ($200,000) or unadjusted basis ($100,000).

This would increase the brothers total section 199A deduction from $60,000 to $100,000.

Business income could also be increased by purchasing leased equipment and real estate. This would also increase the unadjusted basis component of the W-2/unadjusted basis limitation.

Planning for Marital Status

Getting married could either improve the tax consequences under Code section 199A or make them worse.

Example 41. Dawn is a single doctor making $282,000 per year. Her boyfriend, Sam, makes $52,000 per year as a teacher. Neither Dawn nor Sam qualifies for any section 199A deduction, Dawn because she works in an SSTB and Sam because he is an employee. Both of them claim a $12,000 standard deduction. If they get married, their taxable income will be $310,000 ($334,000 − $24,000 standard deduction). Because their income is below the $329,800 threshold amount, they will get a deduction for the full amount of their QBI (.2 × $282,000 = $56,400).

Example 42. Larry and his girlfriend, Robin, are both consultants. Larry's annual pay is $500,000/year and Robin's annual pay is $150,000. Larry currently receives no deduction under section 199A because his income exceeds the $214,900 threshold amount. On the other hand, Dawn receives the full 20 percent QBI deduction because her income is below $157,500. This deduction will be $30,000 (.2 × $150,000). If they get married and file joint returns, their income will be $650,000. Because this amount exceeds $429,800, they would receive no section 199A deduction. It appears, however, that Robin could retain her deduction if the spouses filed separately. The threshold amount for the phase-out of the deduction is $164,900 for all taxpayers other than married taxpayers filing jointly,[121] so it appears that Robin could still get $30,000 deduction if she filed a separate return.

Promoting Partnership Employees to Partner Status

Partners can qualify for the section 199A deduction, but employees of the partnership cannot. In a close case, this might tip the scales in favor of promoting a given employee.[122]

23.9 CHOICE OF ENTITY DECISION

The enactment of Code section 199A may cause taxpayers to re-evaluate the choice of entity decisions: (1) the choice between a C corporation and a pass-through entity, and (2) the choice among the various types of pass-through entities (sole proprietorships, partnerships, LLCs and S corporations).

Choice of Entity—C Corporation vs. Pass-Through Entity

Historically, pass-through entities generally had more favorable tax consequences for closely-held businesses than C corporations. The top initial tax rates on operating income were similar: 35 percent for corporations and 39.6 percent for pass-through entities.

However, when the income was distributed to owners or the business was sold, there was a second level of tax for C corporations but not for pass-through entities. Dividends were generally subject to a second level of tax at 23.8 percent. This was the 20 percent capital gains rate on qualified dividends[123] plus an additional 3.8 percent net investment income tax (NIIT).[124] The same rate applied to sales of the C corporation stock.[125] This brought the effective tax rate on C corporation income up to 50.47 percent [(.35) + (.65 × .238) = .35 + .1547 = 50.47%].

By contrast, distributions from S corporations are tax-free to shareholders unless the distribution exceeds the shareholder's basis in the stock[126] or the S corporation is a former C corporation and the distribution exceeds the S corporation's accumulated adjustment account (AAA).[127] Moreover, S corporation shareholders increase the basis of their stock by their share of corporate income, in effect eliminating the second level of tax when the stock is sold.[128] Thus, the difference in rates between C corporations and pass-through entities was generally 10.87 percentage points for taxpayers in the highest tax bracket (50.47% − 39.6%).

There are several reasons why this calculation may have overstated the tax advantage of the pass-through entities, however. First, the second level of tax may not be paid for a long time after the income is earned because it is deferred until the income is distributed as a dividend or until the stock is sold.[129] Second, there may never be a second level of tax at all. If dividends aren't paid and the shareholder dies with the stock, the heirs will receive a step-up in basis, eliminating the increase in the stock's value due to the retained earnings. Third, C corporations can deduct shareholder distributions made in the form of wages, fringe benefits and deferred compensation.[130]

Changed Tax Rates–Nominal

The most important goal of the TCJA was to lower C corporation tax rates to make American corporations more competitive. This was accomplished by reducing the corporate tax rate from 35 percent to 21 percent. If this had been the only rate change, however, it would have made C corporations far more favorable relative to S corporations, partnerships, LLCs and sole proprietorships. This presumably would have led to mass conversion of these latter businesses into C corporations. To prevent this, the TCJA made a comparable reduction in the tax rate for pass through entities by enacting the 20 percent 199A deduction. The following chart shows how the two changes left the spread between the top tax rates for C corporations and S corporations nearly the same when the second level of tax on C corporation income is taken into account.

	BEFORE TCJA	AFTER TCJA
C Corporation total tax rate	50.47%[131]	39.80%[132]
S Corporation tax rate	39.60%	29.60%[133]
Spread	10.87%	10.20%

This chart oversimplifies the difference between the C corporation and the S corporation tax rates, however. As a practical matter, the actual C corporation rate will often be significantly lower and the actual S corporation rate will often be significantly higher.

Effective C Corporation Rate

The highest initial C corporation tax rate on operating income is far lower than the S corporation rate (21 percent vs. 37 percent) and the initial C corporation rate continues to be lower than the top tax rate on pass-through income even if the owner of the pass-through entity can claim the full 20 percent Code section 199A deduction (21 percent vs. 29.6 percent). The effective C corporation rate only becomes higher when the second level of tax is taken into account. Dividends are generally taxed at 23.8 percent for affluent shareholders and the same rate applies to sales of the C corporation stock.[134] This brings the effective tax rate on C corporation income up to 39.8 percent (.21 + [.79 × .238]) following enactment of the TCJA.

But, as noted above, the second level of tax is not payable until the income is distributed as a dividend or until the stock is sold. If the shareholders don't need the income, payment of dividends could be substantially deferred, reducing the present value of the second level of tax.[135] If dividends were never paid at all, the retained income would stay in the company and increase the value of the shareholders' stock. This increase in the value of the stock wouldn't be taxed until the shares were sold, again producing tax deferral. In fact, if dividends weren't paid and the shareholders died with the stock, their heirs would receive a stepped-up basis and there would never be a second level of tax. In that case, the maximum tax rate on C corporation stock would be 21 percent compared with a top rate of tax of 29.6 percent on the income from pass-through entities.

C corporations may also be able to claim larger deductions for state and local taxes. The TCJA limits the deduction for state and local taxes to $10,000 for individuals ($5,000 for married individuals filing separately).[136] Thus, state or local taxes paid by an individual on income received from a pass-through entity are subject to the $10,000 limitation. The $10,000 limitation does not apply to C corporations so the state and local taxes paid by a C corporation are fully deductible, reducing the effective tax rate on C corporation income. In high tax states, this might be a significant advantage for C corporations relative to pass-through entities.

Effective Pass-Through Rate

In many cases, owners of pass-through entities will not receive the full benefit of the 20 percent section 199A deduction because of the phase-in and phase-out rules. Some entities will lack the W-2 wages or basis in property necessary to provide a significant benefit from the new deduction for their owners. Others will be specified service businesses. These limitations might substantially increase the rate of tax paid on pass-through income, perhaps to as high as 37 percent.

As the preceding discussion suggests, the effect of section 199A on entity choice will depend on the facts for a given business. The key variables will be the extent to which the entity could mitigate the second level of tax if it is a C corporation and the extent to which it could take advantage of the 20 percent section 199A deduction if it is a pass-through entity. Of course, all the relevant pre-TCJA choice of entity factors would also have to be taken into account.

Sunset Provision

Another factor that must be considered is that while the change in the C corporation rate is permanent, the 20 percent Code section 199A deduction is scheduled to be eliminated at the end of 2025. This may make C corporation owners reluctant to convert their business to a pass-through entity. On the other hand, some businesses might wish to start as a pass-through entity to take advantage of the deduction through 2025 and then convert to a C corporation to take advantage of the low 21 percent rate if the 199A deduction sunsets.

Finally, even if a conversion would produce somewhat better tax consequences, it might not be worth the trouble. This is particularly true if gain would have to be recognized on the conversion.[137]

Entity Choice and Qualified Small Business Stock (Code section 1202)

By converting a partnership or LLC to a C corporation, taxpayers may be able to get the low 21 percent corporate tax rate without a second level of tax. Under Code section 1202, non-corporate taxpayers can exclude 100 percent of the gain realized on the sale of qualified small business stock.[138] Qualified small business stock is stock in a C corporation that meets the following requirements.[139]

1. The stock was issued after August 10, 1993[140]

2. The issuer of the stock was a "qualified small business" when the stock was issued[141]

3. The taxpayer acquired the stock at original issue in exchange for money or property other than stock or as compensation for services to the corporation (other than as underwriter of the stock)[142]

4. The corporation met an active business requirement and was a C corporation during substantially all of the taxpayer's holding period for the stock[143]

5. The value of the corporation's aggregate gross assets does not exceed $50 million[144]

Finally, to qualify for the exclusion, the qualified small business stock must be held for at least five years.[145]

On the surface, it might appear that the conversion of a partnership or LLC to a C corporation would fail to meet the original issuance requirement because the stock would first be issued to the partnership or LLC before being distributed to the individual owners. However, under a special rule, a partner (or LLC member) who receives stock from a partnership or LLC is treated as receiving the stock at its original issuance.[146] Finally, note that only the gain accruing after the conversion date is eligible for the exclusion.[147]

The IRS provided guidance on how to convert a partnership to a corporation in Revenue Ruling 84-111.[148] The ruling allows taxpayers to use any of three methods.

One potential downside of making the conversion is that buyers generally prefer to buy assets rather than stock so they can amortize or depreciate the purchase price. As a result, they are willing to pay more for assets than for stock. While an asset sale is possible with a pass-through entity, Code section 1202 only applies to a sale of stock.

Sole Proprietorship vs. S Corporation vs. Partnership/LLC

The new Code section 199A deduction also affects the sole proprietorship, S corporation, partnership/LLC decision. It appears that S corporations may be more favorable for higher income entities while sole proprietorships and partnerships/LLCs may be more favorable for lower income entities for purposes of the Code section 199A deduction. This is illustrated in the following examples.

Example 43. Assume that a business could operate as a sole proprietorship, S corporation or partnership. The owner is a married taxpayer filing jointly with no other taxable income. His share of operating income is $800,000 and, in the case of an S corporation or partnership, he receives $200,000 as W-2 wages or as a guaranteed payment. None of the entities pays any wages to non-owner employees or has any depreciable property. The following chart shows that with relatively high income (above the applicable W-2/unadjusted basis threshold amount), the S corporation is more favorable than the sole proprietorship or partnership because of its ability to pay W-2 wages.

	Sole Proprietorship	S Corp	Partnership
Business income	$800,000	$800,000	$800,000
W-2 wages	N/A[149]	$200,000	N/A[150]
Guaranteed payments	N/A	N/A	$200,000
Net income	$800,000	$600,000	$600,000
QBI	$800,000	$600,000	$600,000

Tentative deduction	$160,000	$120,000	$120,000
50% of W-2 wages	$0	$100,000	$0
Final 199A deduction	$0	$100,000	$0

Example 44. Assume the same facts as in Example 43, except that the business has only $250,000 of operating income. The relative tax benefits of the different entities are now reversed. The payment of W-2 wages becomes a disadvantage for the S corporation because it reduces QBI without producing any offsetting benefit. There is no advantage to paying the W-2 wages because the W-2/unadjusted basis limitation does not begin to apply until taxable income reaches $329,800 for married taxpayers filing jointly. Thus, the QBI deduction for the S corporation is reduced by 20 percent of the $100,000 paid in wages and there is no corresponding reduction for the other entities, giving the sole proprietorship or partnership a QBI deduction $20,000 greater than the QBI deduction for the S corporation.

	Sole Proprietorship	S Corp	Partnership
Business income	$250,000	$250,000	$250,000
W-2 wages	N/A	$100,000[151]	N/A
Guaranteed payments	N/A	N/A	$0[152]
Net income	$250,000	$150,000	$250,000
QBI	$250,000	$150,000	$250,000
Tentative deduction	$50,000	$30,000	$50,000
50% of W-2 wages	N/A	N/A	N/A
Final deduction	$50,000	$30,000	$50,000

The best choice of entity decision will vary depending on a number of variables. Thus, extensive modeling will be necessary to determine the best option based on the client's particular fact situation.[153]

Figure 23.1

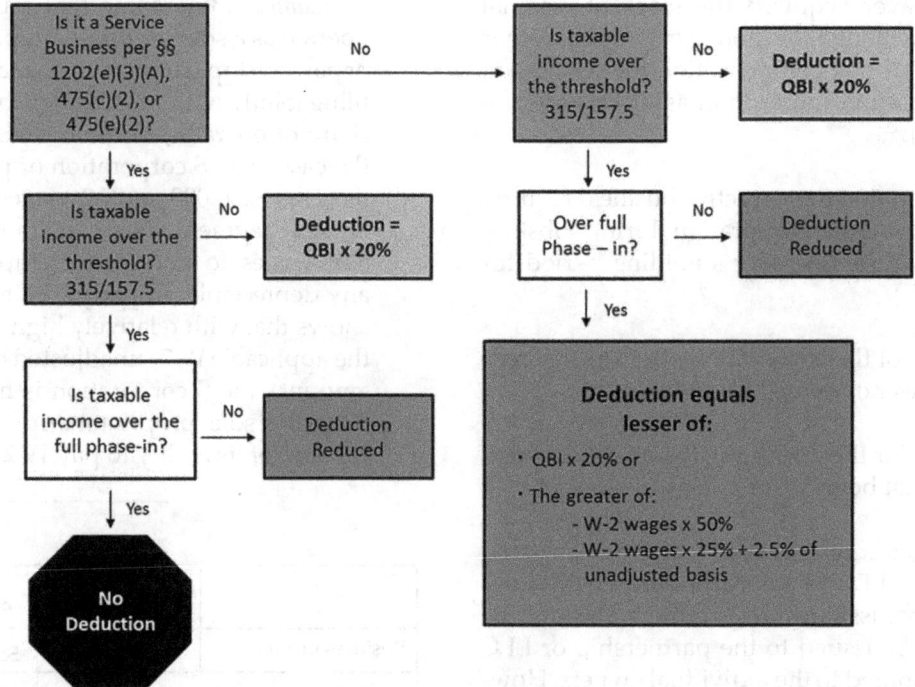

CHAPTER ENDNOTES

1. This chapter is excerpted from the *Qualified Business Income Deduction* book by Bob Keebler and Peter Melcher, available online through Leimberg Information Services (LISI) at https://leimbergservices.com/wdev/bkbooks.cfm.

2. Includes single member LLCs and any other LLC that does not elect to be taxed as a corporation.

3. A REIT is a company that invests in property or property loans and sells shares in those investments in a manner similar to mutual funds. They must pass on to shareholders at least 90% of their income.
4. I.R.C. §199A(f).
5. I.R.C. §199A(a).
6. I.R.C. §199A(f)(3).
7. New I.R.C. §62(a), as added, by Act Sec. 11011(b).
8. I.R.C. §section 62(a) and 63(b).
9. I.R.C. §199A(a).
10. Capital gains aren't included because they are already subject to a reduced rate of tax.
11. I.R.C. §199A(b).
12. Note that personal exemptions were eliminated by the TCJA.
13. Note that the REIT and QPTP portion of combined QBI is not subject to this limitation. Combined QBI is still subject to the 20 percent of taxable income limitation, however.
14. I.R.C. §199A(b).
15. I.R.C. §199A(b)(3).
16. Note that 25 percent of W-2 wages + 2.5 percent of unadjusted basis will exceed 50% of wages whenever the unadjusted basis of qualified property exceeds 10 times W-2 wages. Here, unadjusted basis ($1,000,000) is more than 10 × wages (10 × 80,000 = $800,000), so 2.5 percent of unadjusted basis will be greater than 50% of wages.
17. I.R.C. §199A(b)(3). Note that the calculation phases in the W-2 wage/unadjusted basis limitation amount.
18. I.R.C. §199A(d)(2).
19. I.R.C. §199A(d)(2)(A) and 1202(e)(3)(A). Note that under I.R.C. §1202(e)(3)(A), the reputation or skill category applies only to employees and not to owners. Thus, I.R.C. §199A expands the scope of this category.
20. I.R.C. §199A(d)(2)(B); 475(c)(2); 475(e)(2).
21. These threshold amounts will be indexed for inflation in taxable years beginning after 2018 (I.R.C. §199A(e)(2)(B)).
22. I.R.C. §199A(c)(1)(A).
23. Joint Conference Committee Explanation.
24. I.R.C. §199A(c)(3)(A)(i). Qualification is determined by substituting "qualified trade or business" (within the meaning of section 199A) for "non-resident alien individual" or a foreign corporation every place it appears.
25. I.R.C. §199A(c)(1).
26. I.R.C. §199A(c)(4)(A).
27. I.R.C. §199A(c)(4)(B).
28. I.R.C. §199A(c)(3)(C).
29. I.R.C. §199A(c)(3)(B)(i).
30. I.R.C. §199A(c)(3)(B)(ii).
31. I.R.C. §199A(c)(3)(B)(iii). This would include, for example, bank accounts.
32. I.R.C. §199A(c)(3)(B)(iv) and I.R.C. §199A(c)(3)(B)(v).
33. I.R.C. §199A(c)(3)(B)(vi).
34. I.R.C. §199A(c)(3)(vii).
35. I.R.C. §199A(f)(1)(C).
36. I.R.C. §1231(b)(1).
37. I.R.C. §1231(b)(1)(A).
38. I.R.C. §1231(b)(1)(B).
39. I.R.C. §1231(b)(1)(C).
40. I.R.C. §1231(b)(3).
41. I.R.C. §1231(b)(4).
42. I.R.C. §1221(a)(2).
43. I.R.C. §1231(a)(1).
44. See, for example, *Radke v. U.S.*, 895 F.2d 1196 (7th Cir. 1990); *Grey v. Comm'r*, 119 TC 121 (2002), aff'd, 93 AFTR 2d 2004-1626 (3d Cir. 2004).
45. This would be consistent with Congress's intention in enacting I.R.C. §199A of not favoring one type of entity over others.
46. I.R.C. §704(e)(2).
47. I.R.C. §199A(d).
48. *Higgins v. Commissioner*, 312 U.S. 212 (1941).
49. *Commissioner v. Groetzinger*, 480 U.S. 23 (1987).
50. *Id*.
51. *Commissioner v. Groetzinger*, 480 U.S. 23 (1987).
52. *Id*. For example, gambling could be a trade or business.
53. *Fegan v. Commissioner*, 71 T.C. 791, 814 (1979); *Elek v. Commissioner*, 30 T.C. 731 (1958), acq. 1958-2 C.B. 5; *Lagreide v. Commissioner*, 23 T.C. 508 (1954); *Hazard v. Commissioner*, 7 T.C. 372 (1946), acq. 1946-2 C.B.
54. The IRS recently reiterated this point in the preamble to final regulations for I.R.C. §1411.
55. *Alvary v. United States*, 302 F.2d 790 (2d Cir. 1962); *Curphey v. Commissioner*, 73 T.C. 766 (1980). *Fackler v. Commissioner*, 133 F.2d 509 (6th Cir. 1943), aff'g, 45 B.T.A. 708 (1941); *Bauer v. United States*, 144 Ct. Cl. 308, (1958); *Curphey v. Commissioner*, 73 T.C. 766 (1980).
56. *Curphey v. Commissioner*, 73 T.C. 766 (1980).
57. I.R.C. §199A(b)(1)(A).
58. Reg. §1.469-4. It remains to be seen what approach the IRS will take, however.
59. Reg. §1.446-1(d).
60. I.R.C. §199(d)(2)(A). I.R.C. §1202 provides an exclusion on the gain of qualified small business stock, which is generally stock in a corporation that operates a business other than a service business. Thus, the statute defines what is meant by a service business.
61. I.R.C. §199A(d)(2)(B).
62. It is not clear whether engineering and architecture are automatically excluded from the definition of specified service business or if they could be included as trades or businesses in which the principal asset of the trade or business is the reputation or skill of one of its employees. In some cases, it appears that the skill or reputation of an owner or employee would clearly be the principal assets of a business (e.g., an architecture business owned by Frank Lloyd Wright).
63. I.R.C. §199(d)(2)(A).
64. Some businesses would clearly fall into this category, like self-employed artists, sculptors or authors. At the other extreme would be a business that produces commodity type products that are very basic and undifferentiated.
65. I.R.C. §1202(e)(3)(B).
66. I.R.C. §1202(e)(3)(C).

67. I.R.C. §1202(e)(3)(D). I.R.C. §613 applies to percentage depletion on mines and certain other natural deposits. I.R.C. §613A applies to percentage depletion on oil and gas.

68. For qualified small business stock purchased before February 18, 2009, the I.R.C. §1202 gain exclusion was only 50 percent and the remaining portion was taxed at capital gains rates. Moreover, a portion of the excluded gain was an unfavorable adjustment in computing the AMT. The exclusion rate was briefly increased to 75 percent and then to 100% in 2010.

69. In PLR 201717010, the IRS ruled that a company providing laboratory reports to health care professionals was a qualified small business under I.R.C. §1202. In PLR 201436001, the IRS ruled that a pharmaceutical company that specialized in commercialization of experimental drugs was engaged in a qualified trade or business under I.R.C. §1202 despite the proximity of its business activities to the field of health. These activities included (1) research on drug formulation effectiveness, (2) pre-commercial testing procedures such as clinical testing, and (3) manufacturing of drugs. In addition, the company worked with clients to solve problems in the pharmaceutical industry, such as developing successful drug manufacturing processes.

70. I.R.C. §448(d)(2)(A).

71. I.R.C. §199A.

72. I.R.C. §199A(b)(4)(A).

73. I.R.C. §199A(b)(4)(B).

74. 402(g)(3).

75. I.R.C. §3401.

76. Revenue Ruling 69-184.

77. PEOs are used by small businesses to outsource employee management functions.

78. This was the result under repealed I.R.C. §199, which used a similar definition of W-2 wages. *U.S. v. Total Employment Co, Inc.*, 93 AFTR 2d 2004-1036 (D.C. Fla. 2004); Chief Counsel Advice 200415008; PLR 20134702; *U.S. v. Garami, Imre*, 95-2 USTC ¶50520 (D.C. Fla. 1995).

79. Revenue Ruling 87-41. See also Rev. Proc. 2006-22.

80. I.R.C. §199A(b)(6)(A).

81. I.R.C. §199A.

82. I.R.C. §199A(b)(6). This may have to be clarified in IRS guidance.

83. I.R.C. §199A(f)(1)(A)(iii).

84. I.R.C. §199(h)(1). I.R.C. §179 allows taxpayers to elect to expense certain depreciable business assets. I.R.C. §179(d)(1) provides that the expensing election applies to property acquired by purchase for use in the active conduct of a trade or business. I.R.C. §179(d)(2) then states that the term "purchase" applies to an acquisition of property only if: (1) The property is not acquired from a related party within the meaning of I.R.C. §267(b) or 707(a), (2) the property is not acquired by one component member of a controlled group from another component member of the same controlled group, and (3) the basis of the property in the hands of the person acquiring it is not determined in whole or in part by reference to the adjusted basis in the hands of the person from whom it was acquired or under I.R.C. §1014 (basis of property received from a decedent).

85. I.R.C. §199(h)(2).

86. Joint Explanatory Statement of the Conference Committee.

87. This would generally be the taxpayer's original cost basis under I.R.C. §1011(a).

88. I.R.C. §199A(e)(1).

89. I.R.C. §199A(e)(3).

90. I.R.C. §199A(e)(5).

91. I.R.C. §199A(f)(1).

92. I.R.C. §199A(f)(2).

93. I.R.C. §1377(a)(1).

94. Reg. §1.1377-1(c), Example 1.

95. The Domestic Production Activities Deduction, or DPAD.

96. I.R.C. §199(b) and Reg. §1.199-5(b).

97. Joint Explanatory Statement of the Committee of Conference at page 48. See also, I.R.C. §199A stating that the deduction applies to all taxpayers other than C corporations and I.R.C. §199(A)(f)(1)(B), providing a reference to I.R.C. §199(f)(1)(B) for rules for apportioning W-2 wages and unadjusted basis to trusts and estates.

98. I.R.C. §55.

99. I.R.C. §199(f)(2).

100. I.R.C. §199A(c)(2).

101. Joint Conference Committee Explanation.

102. I.R.C. §172(d)(8).

103. I.R.C. §1367(a)(1)(A).

104. I.R.C. §1368(b)(2).

105. I.R.C. §6662(d)(1)(A).

106. New I.R.C. §6662(d)(1)(C).

107. I.R.C. §6662(d)(2).

108. I.R.C. §6662(d)(2)(B). A taxpayer is generally considered to have a reasonable basis for a position if the chance of prevailing on the merits is at least 20 percent. Substantial authority is defined as a probability of success that is more than a reasonable basis but less than more likely than not. Thus, it is generally thought of as a probability of success of approximately 35 percent [(.2 + .5)/2)].

109. The substantial basis/reasonable basis + disclosure reduction does not apply to any item attributable to a tax shelter (I.R.C. §6662(d)(2)(C)).

110. Reg. section 1.6662-4(b)(6).

111. Request for Immediate Guidance Regarding Section 199A, February 21, 2018, section 14.

112. A partnership can't pay W-2 wages to a partner (Revenue Ruling 69-184).

113. Recall that wages don't count as QBI, reducing QBI to $50,000.

114. Let X = optimal wage payment. Assume income of $100,000.
- .5X = .2($100,000 -X)
- .5X = $20,000 -.2x
- X = $40,000 -.4X
- 1.4X = $40,000
- X = $40,000/1.4 = $28,571.40

115. For example, if Melissa is paid $40,000, the deduction would be $12,000 (the lesser of .2 × $60,000 QBI = $12,000 or .5 × $40,000 = $20,000). If Melissa was paid $20,000, the deduction would be $10,000 (the lesser of .2 × $80,000 QBI = $16,000 or .5 × $20,000 = $10,000).

116. This is done to prevent avoidance of self-employment tax.

117. See the section later in this Chapter on the tradeoffs between employee status and independent contractor status.

118. With the caveat that wages paid to S corporation owners reduce the section 199A deduction when wage payments exceed 2/7 of QBI.
119. I.R.C. §199A(d)(1)(B).
120. IRS Topic #762.
121. I.R.C. §199(e)(2)(A).
122. Of course many other factors would be involved in making the decision.
123. I.R.C. §1(h)(11)(A). Qualified dividend income means dividends received during the tax year from domestic corporations and qualified foreign corporations.
124. See I.R.C. §1411.
125. H. Rep. No. 108-94 (P.L. 108-27) p. 31.
126. I.R.C. §1368(b). The excess amount is treated as a dividend to the extent of earnings and profits.
127. I.R.C. §§1368(c) and 1368(e).
128. I.R.C. §1367(a)(1).
129. Note that many closely-held C corporations never pay dividends.
130. The IRS may try to re-characterize these payments as dividends under I.R.C. §316.
131. 35 percent corporate level tax + 28 percent tax at individual level on qualified dividends, corporate liquidation or sale of the stock by the shareholder. Then, .35 + (.238 × .65) = .5047 = 50.47%.
132. .21 + (.238 × .79) = .398 = 39.8%.
133. 37% top rate × .8 = 29.6%.
134. H. Rep. No. 108-94 (P.L. 108-27) p. 31.
135. The benefit of this tax deferral would be that the shareholder could obtain a return on the money that would otherwise be used to pay the tax for the period during which the tax was deferred.
136. New I.R.C. §164(b)(6)(B).
137. For example, when a C corporation is converted into an LLC, the transaction is treated as a liquidation of the corporation under I.R.C. §section 336 and 331, followed by a liquidating distribution of the net proceeds to the shareholders. I.R.C. §336 provides that gain or loss is recognized on a liquidating distribution of property as if the property was sold to the distributee at its fair market value.
138. I.R.C. §1202(a). Note that this 100% exclusion applied only to qualified small business stock acquired after September 27, 2010. For stock acquired between February 17, 2009 and before September 28, 2010, the exclusion rate is 75%. For stock acquired before February 17, 2009, the exclusion rate is 50 percent.
139. I.R.C. §1202(c)(1).
140. I.R.C. §1202(c)(1).
141. I.R.C. §1202(c)(1)(A).
142. I.R.C. §1202(c)(1)(B).
143. I.R.C. §1202(c)(2)(A).
144. I.R.C. §1202(d)(1)(A).
145. I.R.C. §1202(a)(1). When a taxpayer receives stock in an I.R.C. §351 exchange, the taxpayer's holding period in the stock generally includes the holding period for the property exchanged for the stock (I.R.C. §1223(1)). Notwithstanding this general rule, however, the five-year holding period requirement for the I.R.C. §1202 gain exclusion begins on the date of incorporation (I.R.C. §1202(i)(1)(A)). Thus, taxpayers must wait at least five years after the date of the conversion before selling the stock.
146. I.R.C. §§1202(g) and 1202(h).
147. I.R.C. §1202(i)(1)(B).
148. 1984-2 C.B. 88.
149. A sole proprietorship can't pay W-2 wages to its owner.
150. A partnership can't pay W-2 wages to partners (PLR 69-184).
151. An S corporation must pay reasonable compensation to its shareholders. See, for example, *Radke v. U.S.*, 895 F.2d 1196 (7th Cir. 1990); *Grey v. Comm'r*, 119 TC 121 (2002), aff'd, 93 AFTR 2nd 2004-1626 (3d Cir. 2004).
152. A partnership has no obligation to make guaranteed payments.
153. Concept and charts adapted from Nitti, T., *Tax Geek Tuesday: Making Sense of the New 20% Qualified Business Income Deduction, Forbes*, Dec. 26, 2017.

POST MORTEM TAX ELECTIONS

CHAPTER 24

24.1 INTRODUCTION

Upon the death of a decedent, the personal representative or executor may be faced with a number of potential tax elections or tax decisions that must be made. This list may include income tax elections, including decisions affecting the decedent's final return, the decedent's estate or trusts, or entities in which the decedent held an interest. Additionally, there may be essential estate and generation-skipping transfer tax elections or decisions to be made. Other issues include: (1) making decisions related to the decedent's employee benefits; and (2) whether certain beneficiaries of the decedent's estate should consider making a full or partial disclaimer of the decedent's property. In making these elections and decisions, the tax and economic implications must be factored into the equation.

The following checklist sets forth a number of potential post mortem tax elections and tax decisions facing the decedent's personal representative or executor. Although a post mortem review of the checklist at death is certainly necessary, a lifetime review may be helpful in rounding out a decedent's estate plan. Such a review would provide the decedent's executor or financial planner with some guidance as to how post mortem elections fit into the plan as well as how to facilitate the availability of an election after death.

24.2 POST MORTEM TAX ELECTIONS CHECKLIST

Part A: Income Tax Elections

Section 1: Decedent's Final Return(s)

I. Were medical expenses of the decedent paid after death?

A. Medical expenses incurred before death and paid by the estate during the year beginning the day after the date of death may be accrued and deducted on the decedent's last income tax return for the year in which the expense was incurred.[1]

B. In the alternative, the medical expenses can be deducted as a debt of the decedent for federal estate tax purposes under Code section 2053(b).

Why is this important? For income tax purposes, medical expenses are deductible as an itemized deduction only to the extent they exceed 10 percent of adjusted gross income for all taxpayers.[2] Even if the decedent had significant medical expenses, the deductibility of a large amount of those expenses for income tax purposes may be lost. Moreover, because medical expenses are itemized deductions, to determine total deductibility, the amount of the decedent's other itemized deductions must be taken into account. Additionally, the decedent's taxable income in the year of death will need to be considered. For example, if the decedent died relatively early in the year, he or she may have a minimal amount of taxable income. In that case, claiming deductions, regardless of the amount, may save little or no taxes.

On the other hand, if the decedent has a taxable estate and a substantial amount of medical expenses, claiming those expenses as an estate tax deduction could save a significant amount of estate tax.

Example. At Asher's death, his unpaid medical expenses were $200,000. By virtue of having a large estate, his estate is subject to a 40 percent estate tax rate. If Asher's executor claims his medical expenses as an estate tax deduction,

405

the estate would save $80,000 (40 percent of $200,000).

II. Did the decedent own any U.S. Savings bonds?

A. If prior to death, the decedent had not elected to report the accrued interest income on Series E and EE Savings bonds, the personal representative (executor) may elect to do so on the decedent's final return.[3]

B. If this election isn't made, the accrued interest is income in respect of a decedent meaning the ultimate recipient of the interest would be required to report it on the income tax return in the year it was received. Alternatively, the decedent's estate could elect to report all the accrued interest on the estate's income tax return.

Why is this important? A cash basis taxpayer can either defer reporting accrued interest on U.S. Savings bonds until the year of redemption or elect to report the interest income as it accrues. If prior to death, a decedent had not made such an election, pursuant to Code section 454(a), the executor may elect to report all interest accruing up to the date of death on the decedent's final income tax return. So if in the year of death, considering all the decedent's income (including the accrued interest), the decedent would be in a relatively low income tax bracket, such an election may be advantageous. Similarly, a decedent with significant income and a substantial amount of deductions may owe little or no income tax.

Otherwise, if the executor does not make the election, the interest would be considered income in respect of a decedent (or "IRD," see Chapter 22) includible in gross income of the ultimate recipient (the estate or a beneficiary) in the year in which the bond is redeemed. In that event and assuming the decedent left a taxable estate, Code section 691(c) provides a deduction for the estate tax attributable to the inclusion of the deferred interest (an item of IRD) in the gross estate. However, the Code section 691(c) deduction is an itemized deduction, so if the recipient does not itemize or have a substantial amount of itemized deductions, the actual tax savings may not be significant.

Finally, the estate could make the election to report all the accrued interest on its income tax return. In the absence of deductions to offset such income, however, such inclusion may result in a large tax liability. This is because the estate tax income tax brackets are condensed with the highest tax rate of 37 percent triggered at taxable income in excess of $14,450 (for 2023), as well as the 3.8 percent net investment income tax applicable at that point.

III. Did the decedent lose any property prior to death that may be replaced under the involuntary conversion rules or sell property reportable under the installment sale rules?

A. If property of the decedent was involuntarily converted, i.e., destroyed by natural disaster, condemned, etc., the estate or successor to the decedent may be able to replace it income tax-free pursuant to Code section 1033.

Why is this important? Pursuant to Code section 1033, no gain is recognized with respect to proceeds received as a result of the involuntary or compulsory conversion of property provided such proceeds are reinvested in property similar in service or use. Generally, in order to take advantage of this nonrecognition treatment, the reinvestment must occur within two years of the year in which the gain is realized. If these conditions are met, no gain is recognized and the basis of the replacement property is the same as the basis of the converted property.

Example. During his lifetime, Asher owned a warehouse used in his guitar manufacturing business acquired ten years prior to his death. Three months prior to his death in 2022, the warehouse was destroyed by fire. As a consequence of the fire, the insurance company paid Asher $500,000. At that time, Asher's basis in the warehouse was $100,000. Thus, in 2022, Asher realized a gain of $400,000. In that same year, Asher died without reinvesting the proceeds into another warehouse.

Due to Asher's failure to reinvest the proceeds in a new warehouse prior to his death, it would appear that he must recognize the gain on his final income tax return. Alternatively, if Asher's executor were to reinvest the proceeds within the replacement period, the issue is whether retroactive nonrecognition treatment would apply.

There is a split of authority on this issue. According to the IRS, nonrecognition treatment is available only if the decedent acquired the replacement property during lifetime.[4] Thus, in the above example, Asher would recognize the realized gain on his last income tax return. Conversely, several courts have held that nonrecognition treatment is available to the decedent if his or her personal representative reinvests the proceeds within the replacement period.[5]

Whether the basis of the replacement property should be the same as that of the converted property or step-up to fair market value remains an open question. In *Morris v. Commissioner*,[6] the Tax Court declined to address this issue because it was not before it to decide. On the other hand, based on the rationale of relating the nonrecognition treatment back to the decedent during life, there would appear to be no reason to preclude a date of death fair market value basis step-up of the replacement property.

    B. If in the year of death, the decedent sold property reportable under the installment sale rules, the estate can elect out of installment reporting.[7]

Why is this important? The recognized gain with respect to an installment sale of property is reported ratably over the term of the arrangement.

Example. In the year of his death, Asher sells a parcel of land with a basis to him of $2,000 for $10,000. Over a five-year period, Asher is to receive five annual installment payments of $2,000 (plus interest). Asher has realized gain of $8,000 ($10,000 minus $2,000) is recognized ratably with the payment of each note ($1,600 × 5). Conversely, if Asher elects out of installment reporting, the entire gain of $8,000 would be recognized in the year of sale.

At death, assuming Asher did not elect out of installment reporting, each unpaid installment note would be considered IRD, reported in the gross income of the recipient. However, if Asher's executor elects out of installment reporting, all IRD would be eliminated and the entire gain would be recognized by Asher on his last income tax return. Assuming Asher is in a relatively low tax bracket, it may be advantageous to elect out of installment reporting so as to flush out the gain at a relatively low tax cost.

Additionally, assuming Asher is below the adjusted gross income threshold for the imposition of the net investment income tax, accelerating the gain would potentially shelter its inclusion in the gross income of subsequent recipient beneficiaries who may be subject to such tax.

IV. Filing a joint return – A joint return may be filed for decedent and surviving spouse for the year of death, unless the spouse remarries before the end of the year.[8]

Why is this important? Generally, a married couple would owe less overall tax filing a joint return than they would filing separate returns. If the decedent spouse has unused capital loss carryovers or a net operating loss carryover, by filing jointly, the surviving spouse may use those carryovers to offset his/her capital gains and/or other income. Moreover, it may be prudent for the surviving spouse to accelerate capital gains into the year of death to take full advantage of offsetting such losses. Otherwise, the tax benefit of a decedent's carryovers would be lost as they are not deductible by the surviving spouse beyond the year of the decedent's death.[9]

Section 2: Decedent's Estate and Trusts

I. Should the estate elect a fiscal year?

Why is this important? Unlike an individual, an estate may elect any fiscal year instead of a calendar year without the consent of the IRS. The fiscal year must end on the last day of the month and cannot exceed twelve months in length. Because the executor has flexibility in choosing the fiscal year ending date, he or she may strategically time the year end so the length of the first taxable year is of the greatest income tax advantage to the estate.

For example, the executor may anticipate the receipt of a substantial amount of IRD over the first few months of the estate. By strategically electing a fiscal year that ends in the middle of that distribution period, the IRD could be spread over two tax years with corresponding tax savings.

Additionally, by electing a fiscal year, the estate can manage tax rates more efficiently. For example, if tax rates are lower in one calendar year than the next, a decedent dying in the earlier calendar year can benefit by electing a fiscal year ending on November 30 of the following year because the lower tax rate from the prior calendar year will apply. This type of tax planning may be important for decedents dying in 2025, before income tax rates are scheduled to increase on January 1, 2026, under the TCJA of 2017.

II. Should the executor waive commissions?

   A. If the executor or administrator of the estate intends to waive commissions, this should be done before undertaking any duties.[10] This is probably true for successor trustees of revocable living trusts as well.

Why is this important? The receipt of fees or commissions are includible in the gross income of the executor or administrator. On the other hand, the receipt of a bequest is generally income tax-free. So, from an income tax perspective, if such person is also a beneficiary of the estate (particularly the sole beneficiary), it may be better to waive taxable commissions so that all amounts paid from the estate would be tax-free bequests. By waiving the right to commissions prior to assuming estate administration duties establishes the executor/administrator's intent to serve for free - thus eliminating any commission income. On the other hand, such a waiver of commissions would also deprive the estate of an income tax deduction, or an estate tax deduction if there is a taxable estate.

   B. However, it may still be possible for the executor or administrator to waive commissions or fees after assuming administration duties if the executor/administrator made no attempt to collect them and they were not claimed as a deduction on the estate's tax returns.[11]

Pursuant to Revenue Ruling 66-167, under the circumstances described in B. above, an intent to waive commissions can be established where the executor/administrator does not claim fees or commissions at the time the usual estate accounting are filed.

III. Have all available deductions been accounted for?

To avoid double deductions (an estate tax and income tax deduction), if expenses are claimed as income tax deductions, the executor/administrator must file a waiver of the right to claim them as estate tax deductions.[12]

Expenses related to administering the estate (including executor's commissions, attorney's fees, and miscellaneous expenses) are deductible for estate tax purposes under Code section 2053. Deductions for casualty losses are deductible for estate tax purposes under Code section 2054. Under the TCJA, many income tax deductions were eliminated or modified significantly (note these changes are scheduled to expire on December 31, 2025). For example, under the new law, personal casualty losses are disallowed except in the case of a federally declared disaster. In light of these changes, the executor should assess which of those two options would provide the greatest overall tax benefit.

IV. Should the executor or administrator file an election to treat the decedent's revocable trust as part of the estate for income tax purposes?

   A. If so, the election must be made both by the executor, if any, of the estate and the trustee of the revocable trust not later than the due date (including extensions) of the estate's income tax return for the first taxable year.[13]

Why is this important? During the decedent's lifetime, a revocable trust is treated as a grantor trust so that all income and expenses of such trust are taxable to the grantor (in essence the trust is a disregarded entity). Upon the decedent's death, the trust becomes irrevocable, i.e., an entity disassociated with the decedent, then required to report income and expenses on its own return. However, unlike an estate, a trust is required to use a calendar year as its taxable year. By making a Code section 645 election, for income tax purposes, the trust becomes part of the estate. Consequently, its income and expenses are reported with those of estate in accordance with the estate's fiscal tax year. This may allow for income reporting and taxation to occur in a later year. Additionally, if the trust owns S corporation stock, it is only permitted to hold the S corporation stock for a period of two years. By making a Code section 645 election, the estate may be able to own the S corporation stock for longer.

In some situations, there may be a state income tax difference between which states can tax an estate versus a trust and there may be some circumstances when this could be a factor in the decision to make a Section 645 election. For example, a decedent's state of residence may tax the income from an estate whereas it may not tax the income from a non-grantor trust settled by a decedent if the trustee and beneficiaries reside outside of the state.

Section 3: Partnerships in which Decedent Had Interests

I. Should the partnership (including LLCs/LPs taxed as partnerships) elect to adjust the income tax basis of partnership assets?

    A. If an appropriate election is made under Code sections 754 and 743(b), the basis of a deceased partner's interest in partnership assets ("inside basis") will be adjusted to date of death or estate tax value.

    B. Even if the election is not made, if within two years after death partnership assets are distributed "in kind" to the successor of a deceased partner, the distributee may elect to adjust the basis of those assets in the same manner as provided in Code section 743(b).

Why is this important? Upon the death of a decedent, the basis of his or her interest in a partnership ("outside basis") steps-up or steps-down to its date of death (or on rare occasions, an alternate valuation date) fair market value, pursuant to Code section 1014. However, this basis adjustment has no effect on the basis of the decedent's partner's pro rata share of partnership assets. Therefore, if a partnership sells an asset for a gain, the partner's estate or beneficiary would recognize the deceased pro rata share of such gain.

Example. Asher and Ashley are equal partners in the A & A partnership. The partnership holds two parcels of land each with a basis to the partnership ("inside basis") of $50,000 and each with a fair market value of $100,000. Asher and Ashley each have an outside basis of $50,000 in their partnership interests and a capital account balance of $100,000. In 2021, Ashley dies and her outside basis is stepped-up to $100,000. Subsequently, the partnership sells one of the parcels for $100,000 with the $50,000 gain allocated $25,000 to each partner. Thus, in spite of the basis step-up of Ashley's outside basis in the partnership, her estate would recognize $25,000 of gain.

However, if the partnership were to make a Section 754 election, Ashley's share of the inside basis of the partnership property would also step-up to the date of death fair market value. Therefore, Ashley's deemed inside basis in each parcel of land would step-up from $25,000 (one half of the $50,000 inside bases of both properties) to $50,000. With the making of a section 754 election, Ashley's estate would not recognize any gain on the sale of the parcel because her allocable share of the proceeds, $50,000, would be equal to her allocable share of the now stepped-up inside basis, $50,000. As to Asher, the section 754 election has no effect on his allocable share of inside basis. Consequently, Asher would include $25,000 in gross income.

Section 4: Closely Held Corporations in which Decedent Had Interests

I. Should the estate make or continue an S election?

II. What are considerations in planning distributions from estates to trusts and other beneficiaries?

    A. Where the executor has discretion as to funding of trusts with specific trust assets, no funding with S corporation stock should be undertaken until a determination is made as to whether the trust is a qualifying shareholder.

    B. Make certain any distributee trust is a qualified trust.

    C. If the distribution of the S Corporation stock is to a qualifying trust, a Qualified Subchapter S Trust (QSST) or Electing Small Business Trust (ESBT) election must be filed with the Internal Revenue Service. See Chapter 53.

Why is this important? Often, a decedent may be a Subchapter S corporation shareholder. Because the class of permissible S Corporation shareholders is limited, as the executor transitions ownership to others, the executor must be careful not to distribute Subchapter S corporation stock to a disqualified person (e.g. a non-resident alien) or entity that may jeopardize the S corporation status of the entity.

III. Is there a buy/sell provision in place for the stock? How will the stock be valued?

A buy-sell plan is a legally binding contract which provides for the transfer of ownership upon a triggering event, such as the death, disability, or retirement of an owner. Buy-sell plans, which can be structured in several ways, help to avoid a fire sale of business interests by ensuring there is a predetermined buyer for a deceased shareholder's interest. A buy-sell plan sets a fair selling price and helps to maintain family harmony because there is no uncertainty about how the transition of the business will occur. Buy-sell plans are often funded with life insurance to ensure obligations under the agreement can be carried out; without life insurance, the business and/or surviving owners may not have sufficient liquidity to buy out the estate.

The terms of the buy-sell arrangement often will specify how to value the stock. Valuation methodologies include book value, capitalization of earnings, by a formula incorporating several factors (e.g., book value and capitalization of earnings), a predetermined specific price (although this may not reflect current fair market value), and valuation by an independent appraiser (usually the most accurate).

The executor of the deceased shareholder's estate should coordinate with the other business owners to identify if there is a valid buy-sell plan in place. If so, the executor can help to facilitate the deceased owner's obligation under the terms of the buy-sell agreement.

Part B: Estate Tax Elections

Section 1: Alternate Valuation Date

I. Should the estate elect to value assets at the alternate valuation date, which is:

   A. Six months after the date of death, or

   B. If earlier, the date the asset is "disposed of" by the estate.[14]

   C. However, the election is only available if both the value of the gross estate and estate tax liability are reduced.[15]

Why is this important? The computation of the taxable estate begins with a valuation of all assets that comprise the decedent's gross estate. The TCJA temporarily increased the applicable exemption amount from $5,000,000 (indexed for inflation) to $10,000,000 (indexed for inflation). This amount is scheduled to revert to a $5,000,000 exemption after December 31, 2025 (adjusting for inflation). In 2023, the applicable exemption amount is $12,920,000, meaning the majority of estates will not be subject to estate tax. However, valuation is also important to determine the income tax basis of property acquired from the decedent. Basis is determined by fair market value, meaning the higher the value, the higher the basis. A higher tax basis has many tax advantages including the lesser recognition of gain and potentially higher recognition of loss and/or depreciation deductions.

Generally, basis is the date of death fair market value unless the executor elects the alternate valuation date, i.e., the date six months after the date of death or, if earlier, the date the asset is disposed of the estate. Such option, however, is not unconditional. In order to qualify, the overall value of the gross estate as well as the ensuing estate tax liability must be less than it would have been based on the date of death valuation. This means that any estate that is not taxable (because its date of death value is below the estate tax exemption amount) may not elect the alternate valuation date.

Consequently, the election is only available to taxable estates. The rationale for making such an election would be to take advantage of the up and down post death increases and decreases in the value of various estate assets. If there are sufficient increases in the value of assets that are likely to sold or depreciated and decreases in the value of assets that are likely not be sold or are nondepreciable, it may be prudent to make such an election provided the overall value of the gross estate and ensuing estate tax liability are less.

Section 2: Special Use Valuation Elections

I. Did the decedent own land used in farming or closely held business?

II. Will the family continue the use of the property and materially participate in its operation?

III. Are discounts or control premiums applicable to the valuation of the business interest?

IV. If an audit will increase the real estate values, consider a protective special use valuation election.

Why is this important? Generally, for valuation purposes, the date of death fair market value of an asset is based on the highest and best use of the underlying property. There is, however, relief available for real property used in closely-held business or for farming. Subject to a number of rules, a special valuation election under Code section 2032A allows for a valuation based on the current qualified purpose in which the real property is being used. The purpose is to allow such businesses to pass from one generation to the other without a crippling estate tax that may require the business to be sold just to pay the tax. Since the special valuation would obviously be less than fair market value, the election would only be made if a valuation based on the highest and best use of the property would result in a taxable estate. Otherwise, if the estate would not be taxable, a higher valuation would achieve a higher stepped-up basis; and, thus, provide the beneficiaries of the estate with greater income tax benefits.

A protective special use valuation election is a nothing to lose option so that an estate would be valued via special valuation if by IRS audit or examination, it is ultimately determined that the estate is taxable (based on the property's highest and best use). The protective election is made on the Form 706 estate tax return.

Section 3: Marital Deduction Elections

I. Did the decedent create a trust that qualifies as a QTIP?

   A. QTIP elections (See Chapter 27).

Why is this important? According to the estate plan of many married couples, all the property of the first spouse to die passes to the surviving spouse. In addition to providing financial support for the surviving spouse, the unlimited marital deduction eliminates any estate tax at the first death. However, with respect to second marriages, the decedent spouse with children from a prior marriage may want to ensure that those children are provided for. Similarly, if the spouse later remarries, the decedent may want to prohibit a new spouse or children from the later marriage inheriting over the decedent's children. Use of a QTIP trust can potentially provide the decedent spouse with the best result: full use of the unlimited marital deduction, ensuring the surviving spouse is provided for, and control over the ultimate disposition of trust assets. A QTIP trust also allows the GST tax exemption to be fully utilized (the GST tax exemption is not portable). With a QTIP trust, the surviving spouse is the primary beneficiary of the trust and is entitled to receive all trust income at least annually, but the remainder of trust assets will be distributed to the decedent spouse's other beneficiaries. To treat the trust as a QTIP trust eligible for the marital deduction, an election must be made on the decedent spouse's estate tax return.

   B. Is there the need for a "Reverse QTIP election"? (See Chapter 21).

Why is this important? Unlike the applicable exclusion for estate and gift tax, there is no portability of the generation-skipping transfer tax exemption between spouses. Thus, the unused generation-skipping transfer tax exemption of the first spouse to die would be wasted. If, pursuant to Code section 2652(a)(1), a reverse QTIP election is made with respect to a funded QTIP trust, the decedent spouse is treated as the transferor for generation-skipping transfer tax purposes. As a result, the unused exemption of the first spouse to die can be allocated to the QTIP to shelter potential generation-skipping tax. The election to implement a reverse QTIP is made on Form 706.

II. Is the surviving spouse a noncitizen?

   A. Establishing qualified domestic trusts (See Chapters 27 and 72).

Why is this important? The unlimited marital deduction is not allowed with respect to noncitizen spouses. As a result, only the decedent spouse's applicable exemption amount can shield bequests to a surviving noncitizen spouse from estate tax. In order to shield amounts in excess of decedent spouse's applicable exclusion amount from immediate estate tax, a qualified domestic trust ("QDOT") must be established. Thus, the estate tax is deferred until the death of the surviving noncitizen spouse.

III. Should the Executor make an irrevocable portability election on the estate tax return of the first to die spouse? Note portability of the deceased spouse's unused exclusion amount is only available if the first-to-die spouse's estate files an estate tax return to make the election – even if the estate is not taxable.

Why is this important? A portability election allows a surviving spouse to use a deceased spouse's unused exemption and, assuming certain formalities are followed, is a simple way to ensure that both spouses' exemptions are fully utilized.

With the estate tax exemption doubled under the TCJA through 2025, the vast majority of estates will not be subject to estate tax under current law. Because many of these estates will not be subject to estate tax and will not be required to file an estate tax return, the ability to make a portability election may be lost if the executor is unaware of the portability rule. Although at the time of the first spouse to die, in many cases it may seem unlikely that the surviving spouse's estate would be sufficiently large so as to benefit from the first decedent spouse's unused applicable exclusion, there is nothing to lose (aside from the cost of filing the estate tax return) by making the election. In most cases it is prudent to file an estate tax return to make the portability election to ensure that if circumstances change (e.g., tax laws change, surviving spouse's financial circumstances change, etc.) the additional exclusion would be available to the surviving spouse.

Planning Note: Although portability is a simple way to ensure both exemptions are fully utilized, a traditional credit shelter trust is still a viable planning tool in many cases. For example, a credit shelter trust not only ensures any remaining estate tax exemption is preserved, but also preserves remaining GST tax exemption, which is not portable. A credit shelter trust also freezes any future appreciation on the assets owned in the trust outside of the estate and provides the first-to-die spouse with greater control over distribution of trust assets. Taxpayers should work with their estate planning attorney to determine the most beneficial approach based upon their particular circumstances.

Section 4: Payment and Deferred Payment of Federal Estate Tax

I. Did the decedent own an interest in a closely held business?

II. What is its value in relation to the total estate? Consider stock held by related parties.

III. Does the estate have enough cash to pay the estate tax due?

Planning Note: Particularly for estates which are largely comprised of illiquid assets such as business interests, life insurance is often purchased at the outset of the planning process to provide the estate with an immediate infusion of cash to pay estate taxes and other costs related to estate administration.

IV. Consider whether the estate qualifies under Code section 6166 to pay the estate tax in installments.

Why is this important? Code section 6166 allows for the deferral of the payment of estate tax attributable to the assets of a closely-held business. To qualify for the installment election under 6166, the value of the interest in the closely held business must account for at least 35 percent of the adjusted gross estate. The election can defer payment of taxes for up to five years, payable in ten equal installments after the deferral (in effect deferring total payment of tax for a period of up to fourteen years[16]). If an estate lacks the cash to pay the estate tax by the normal due date, a 6166 election may be the only way to be able to pay the estate tax without liquidating assets that may be necessary to continue the business.

V. Consider a protective election under section 6166 if the closely held business is revalued upon audit.

Why is this important? Qualifying for the relief under section 6166 may turn on a final determination of value (i.e., as the result of an IRS audit or examination). Accordingly, the executor should make a protective election.

VI. Is the closely held business interest in a corporation?

  A. Code section 303 stock redemptions (See Chapter 48).

Why is this important? Many estates lack the liquidity to pay estate tax, administrative expenses and burial costs. A Code section 303 stock redemption allows the corporation to redeem stock from a deceased owner's estate to pay for transfer taxes (estate and GST taxes), funeral costs, and administration. Special rules apply, including a requirement that at least 35 percent of the value of the decedent owner's estate is comprised if the business interest. Under a section 303 redemption, any gain is taxable as capital gain rather than as ordinary income (i.e., a dividend). By allowing a corporation to redeem its stock owned by the decedent, the funds received by the estate can provide the requisite liquidity to pay those expenses. If treated as a dividend, there would be no reduction for the stock's basis. Because of the date of death basis step-up and the sale being treated as a redemption, there should be little or no capital gain. The Executor should determine if the decedent qualifies for a section 303 redemption and if so, help to facilitate the redemption of the stock.

VII. Consider notice of election under Code section 6163 for deferral of payment of tax attributable to a remainder interest.

Why is it important? On occasion, a reversionary or remainder interest that has not yet matured is included in a decedent's gross estate. If the value of such interest is substantial, it may result in a large amount of estate tax. Since the preceding interest has not yet terminated, none of the actual value of the decedent's interest is liquid. By making a Code section 6163 election, payment of the estate tax is deferred for six months following the date the preceding interest is terminated. If undue hardship can be shown, the deferral can be extended for a period not exceeding three years.

Part C: Employee Benefits

I. Is a spousal rollover available? If the surviving spouse is the primary beneficiary, spousal rollovers are usually recommended, but there are at least 4 situations in which it may be wise for a surviving spouse to consider delaying a rollover: 1) if the surviving spouse is under 59 ½ and may want to tap into the inherited account without penalty until then; 2) if the surviving spouse is older than the decedent spouse who was under the applicable age at the time of death (for 2023, age 73), where delaying the rollover may actually delay the required beginning date for the survivor; 3) if the surviving spouse may want to consider a qualified disclaimer of a portion of the account in favor of the contingent beneficiaries; 4) if the decedent had low basis employer stock inside a company plan that might benefit from a lump sum distribution of such stock using the net unrealized appreciation (NUA) loophole.

II. Beneficiary Elections:

   A. May eligible designated beneficiaries (who are eligible to use a life expectancy payout method) elect to use the 10-year rule and should they consider it (for example, if they are older)? Prop Reg. 1.401(a)(9)-3(c)(5) permits EDBs to elect the 10-year rule if owner dies before their RBD.

   B. Effective in 2024, surviving spouses (and potentially conduit trusts for surviving spouses) who inherit should strongly consider making the new election made available in Section 327 of the Secure 2.0 Act, revising Code Section 401(a)(9)(B)(iv), which may offer delayed required beginning dates and lower RMDs.

III. Should designated beneficiary changes be made?

   A. Beneficiaries can sometimes affect who will be considered the designated beneficiary by a qualified disclaimer, cash-out, etc., if such action is taken by September 30 of the calendar year following the calendar year of the participant's death.[17]

   B. Prop. Reg. § 1.401(a)(9)-4(f)(5)(iii) now allows trust modifications to be made post-mortem without adversely affecting see through trust status if done by September 30 of the calendar year following the calendar year of the participant's death as well.

IV. Should lump sum distributions and averaging be considered? Look for large amounts of employer stock inside of a decedent's qualified plan that may be eligible for special net unrealized appreciation (NUA) rule for lump sum distributions, which opportunity disappears if funds are moved into an inherited IRA.

V. If a trust is named as a beneficiary, remember that a copy of the trust (or acceptable substitute certifying the beneficiaries of the trust) MUST be given to the plan trustee/IRA custodian by October 31 of the year after death, otherwise the trust cannot qualify as a see-through trust. See Prop. Reg. § 1.401(a)(9)-4(h).

Part D: Disclaimers

I. Should any beneficiaries of the estate consider refusing to accept their inheritance?

There are several valid reasons why a beneficiary may wish to disclaim an inheritance. Common reasons for a disclaimer include beneficiary creditor issues, disclaimers to maintain eligibility for certain government benefits, to correct estate planning errors or for other tax reasons (e.g., the next taker is in a lower tax bracket), for equitable reasons (e.g., one beneficiary is significantly better off than the others), or when the inherited property is more of a burden than a benefit. In such a case, the beneficiary may disclaim his or her interest to the property by making a qualified disclaimer under the requirements of Code section 2518.

For a disclaimer to be valid, it must be: (1) in writing; (2) received by the transferor of the interest no later than nine months after the date of the transfer creating the interest (or nine months after the day such person turned twenty-one); (3) the disclaimant must not have accepted the interest or any of its benefits; and (4) as a result of the refusal, the interest passes without any direction on the part of the person making the disclaimer and passes to either the spouse of the decedent or to a person other than the person making the disclaimer.[18] There may be additional requirements and formalities to consider for the disclaimer to be effective under state law.

II. Consider who will receive the property if the beneficiary disclaims.

For a disclaimer to be valid under Code section 2518, the disclaimant may not have any control over who will receive the disclaimed property. When a valid disclaimer has been made, the Executor must distribute the property to the successor beneficiary as directed under the decedent's estate plan.

III. If the beneficiary is disclaiming due to debt, lawsuit or divorce, seek knowledgeable counsel prior to disclaiming.

While the majority of states do not consider a qualified disclaimer to be a voidable fraudulent transfer, there may be a few states that do. Moreover, the Supreme Court in *Drye v. United States*, 528 U.S. 49 (1999) held that federal tax liens may not be defeated by a qualified disclaimer. There may be special issues for other federal debt (such as an SBA loan) or state tax debt and a disclaimer may adversely affect the ability of a debtor to receive a discharge in bankruptcy.

While inheritances are generally considered a beneficiary's separate property in the event of a divorce, local domestic relations courts may not view disclaimers fondly, particularly if a disclaimant's ability to make child support payments may be threatened.

IV. the surviving spouse consider whether or not to implement a disclaimer trust?

If the surviving spouse were to disclaim assets into a disclaimer trust; this trust would essentially function like a credit shelter trust. This means that a portion of the decedent's $12,920,000 (in 2023) estate tax applicable exclusion amount would be applied towards the assets within the disclaimer trust.

Alternatively, the surviving spouse may opt to disclaim nothing, and then upon his or her death rely on the full exemption "inherited" from the decedent by virtue of portability. While this approach works on a superficial level and the ultimate non-spousal beneficiaries would enjoy the surviving spouse's fair market value date of death basis step-up, there are problems associated with relying on the portability of the estate tax exemption:

- If the growth of the assets exceeds the amount of the exemption available at the death of the surviving spouse, the excess would be subject to estate tax. On the other hand, the assets passing out of the disclaimer trust would not be subject to estate tax regardless of their value.

- The assets are not protected from the creditors of the surviving spouse as these assets would be if the assets were held in a trust.

- The portability of the exemption does not apply to the generation skipping transfer (GST) tax.

- The "inherited" estate tax exemption can potentially be lost if the spouse remarries.

Part E: Generation-Skipping Elections (Chapter 21)

I. How should the generation-skipping transfer tax exemption be allocated?

II. Determine the amount of the available remaining exemption.

This is done by taking into consideration allocations of this exemption made on the federal gift tax return (Form 709) during lifetime or by virtue of the automatic allocations which occurred since 2001.

III. Consider making late allocation of GST tax exemption for transfers made during lifetime.

IV. Consider whether trusts should be severed into exempt and non-exempt portions.

V. Should a reverse QTIP election be made?

VI. Is the allocation mandatory or optional?

VII. Must a Form 706 be filed to reflect the allocation of the GST tax exemption?

Part F: Gift Tax Return Issues (Chapter 20)

I. Gather past federal Gift (and Generation-Skipping Transfer) Tax Returns. See IRS Form 4506-T to obtain a transcript of prior filings, and Form 4506 to receive actual copies (the former is free, the latter is currently $43 per return.

II. Ascertain whether any taxable gifts were made in the year of death.

III. Consider whether there were gifts made within three years of death.

Under Code section 2035, gifts made within three years of death will be brought back into the estate for estate tax purposes if: the Grantor retained a life estate; the transfer takes effect at death; the transfer was revocable; or if the Grantor disposed of a retained interest(s) in transferred property within the three years prior to death.

Additionally, the value of a life insurance policy transferred within three years of death is includible in the gross estate.[19] These gifts then are reported on Schedule G of the Federal Estate Tax Return.

Planning Note: An exception to the "three-year look back" rule for life insurance policies transferred within three years of death are policies exists for any "bona fide sale" for "adequate and full consideration." While there is no definitive answer to what constitutes "adequate and fair consideration," a transfer made in contemplation of death will not avoid the three year look back.[20]

CHAPTER ENDNOTES

1. I.R.C. §§213(a), 213(c).
2. T.J.C.A. Sec. 11027.
3. I.R.C. §454(a); Rev. Rul. 68-145, 1968-1 CB 203.
4. Rev. Rul. 64-161, 1964-1 C.B. (Part 1) 298.
5. *Estate of Goodman v. Comm'r.*, 199 F.2d 895 (3d Cir. 1952); *Morris v. Comm'r.*, 55 T.C. 636 (1971); *Gregg v. Comm'r.*, 69 T.C. 468 (1977).
6. 55 T.C, 636 (1971).
7. I.R.C. §453; Priv. Ltr. Rul. 8545052.
8. I.R.C. §6013(a)(2).
9. Rev. Rul. 74-175, 1974-1 C.B. 52.
10. Rev. Rul. 64-225, 1964-2 CB 15.
11. Rev. Rul. 66-167, 1966-1 CB 20.
12. I.R.C. §642(g); Treas. Regs. §§1.642(g)-1, 1.642(g)-2.
13. See I.R.C. §645.
14. I.R.C. §2032.
15. I.R.C. §2032(c).
16. The first installment payment is required to be paid before the end of the 5th year after the 6166 election is made. After the first payment, subsequent payments must be made from the estate each year for up to 9 years (10 installments total). Accordingly, the maximum possible payment period is fourteen years (not fifteen). See I.R.C. §6166(a)(3) and (f).
17. Treas. Reg. §1.401(a)(9)-4.
18. I.R.C. §2518.
19. I.R.C. §2035.
20. *Estate of Pritchard v. Comm'r.*, 4 T.C. 204 (T.C. 1944); *United States v. Allen*, 293 F.2d 916 (10th Cir. 1961).

DEATH TAX APPORTIONMENT AND ESTATE TAX REIMBURSEMENT

CHAPTER 25

25.1 INTRODUCTION

Death tax apportionment involves the allocation of death taxes as well as responsibility for estate debts and administration expenses between the recipients of the estate. Apportionment of (i.e., division of the obligation to pay) state and federal death taxes between the recipients of the assets of an estate, including a direction of how deductions and credits are to be apportioned, is a critical area, particularly in the blended family context where the beneficiaries of each partner may be different. This is because responsibility for death taxes that are apportioned between beneficiaries often is at the absolute discretion of the executor.

For example, if the decedent permitted the entire applicable exclusion amount to be apportioned to the legacies or asset receipts of one side of the family, e.g., the decedent's own children, the entire estate tax will be borne by the other side of the blended family. The key thing to remember is this: Apportionment goes beyond the primary question of what a beneficiary of an estate is to *receive*; it is a key determinate of what a beneficiary gets to *keep*! In fact, it is not unusual in some situations for a beneficiary, particularly a residuary legatee, to have to bear so much of the death tax burden that it completely exhausts what the beneficiary was supposed to receive! Yet this is an area that many estate planners avoid or simply treat almost as unnecessary "boilerplate."[1]

There is both federal and state law to consider in death tax apportionment, as well as what the governing instrument, i.e., will or revocable living trust, provides since the instrument can override federal and state law in this area. Sometimes, even unintentionally and without the client or the planners being aware of the implications of what has been drafted.

We will begin by analyzing the applicable federal law. We will follow that with an analysis of the Uniform Estate Tax Apportionment Act that was finalized in 2003 (replacing the 1964 version of that uniform act) as a surrogate for state law. Nevertheless, it is imperative that the estate planner be intimately familiar with the apportionment default rules under applicable state law.

The easiest way to demonstrate the importance of clear and proper death tax apportionment is with an example of how different interpretations can result in vastly different bottom lines for the beneficiaries. Consider the following situation in the context of a blended family.

Example: Art Duvall dies in 2017 with a probate estate worth $2,500,000. Art dies domiciled in a state that has an "equitable apportionment" statute that takes effect in instances where the decedent does not otherwise clearly and unambiguously provide for death tax apportionment in the governing instrument. In his will, Art made a $500,000 specific pre-residuary bequest to his oldest child, Al. He exempted Al from all death tax liability, and divided his remaining estate outright and equally between his wife, Mary Alice (who is not the mother of his children), and his three children, Al, Betty and Chuck. Art named Al and Mary Alice as co-executors of his estate. Art also had an IRA that was worth $1,500,000 at his death. He made the proceeds of the IRA payable to his wife, Mary Alice. $3,000,000 of life insurance that he owned at death was paid to two of his three children, Betty and Chuck. Art also died with a revocable trust that contained assets worth $3,000,000. The beneficiaries of that trust are his wife as income beneficiary of part and the three children and their descendants as principal beneficiaries. Art named Betty and Mary Alice as co-trustees of that trust. That trust was set up to divide the property at Art's death into a credit shelter trust of the applicable exclusion amount for the sole benefit of Al and a QTIP-able trust for the benefit of Mary Alice as lifetime income beneficiary and his three children and their descendants, equally by roots, as principal beneficiaries. Art's will expressly apportions all of the death tax to the residue of the estate, while his revocable living trust, which was settled after the execution of his will, has an equitable apportionment death tax apportionment provision. Art died while domiciled in a state that has no estate tax. Assume that the amount of deductible expenses for administration of Art's estate is $50,000.

What follows below are a series of questions in **bold** that must be answered, many of which have multiple possible answers, and some of which may have no answer. Do not fret if you do not know any of the answers to these questions yet. We discuss these issues and provide some answers in the section of this chapter entitled How It Is Done. The purpose of the questions at this juncture is to get you thinking about how the issues present themselves in real life while you are reading this chapter. Our purpose in this exercise is to further emphasize that death tax apportionment can be a *huge* issue – particularly with respect to blended families – and one that often is not well addressed in the estate planning documents. It also is an area that creates an inordinate amount of litigation and some malpractice exposure. As usual, the devil is in the details.

Q. **What is the total amount of estate tax without a QTIP election?**

A. $1,156,000.

Q. **What would the amount of the death tax be if a QTIP election *is* made?**

A. $0.

Q. **Who decides whether a QTIP election will be made?**

A. The co-executors? The successor co-trustees of the revocable living trust?

Q. **What if the co-executors or co-trustees cannot agree?**

Q. **What is the effect of a QTIP election in Mary Alice's estate?**

Q. **Where does the death tax come from?**

Q. **What about the fact that Al is specifically given an amount that is equal to the "applicable exclusion amount" in the revocable living trust?**

Q. **Who determines how much that Al's share of the trust should be?**

Q. **Does anyone who is making this determination have a conflict of interest here?**

Q. **Who is personally responsible for payment of the death taxes?**

Q. **How should the death tax on the life insurance that Art owned at his death be apportioned?**

Q. **How should death tax be apportioned to the revocable trust?**

Q. **If any of the death tax is apportionable to the revocable trust, is there any right under the Act or the Internal Revenue Code that would allow the co-executors to pursue a reimbursement claim against the co-trustees of the revocable trust?**

Q. **How should the applicable exclusion amount allocated between the various taxable transfers? Does it all go to Al because of the language in the revocable trust? Who makes that determination? Does anyone have a conflict of interest here?**

Q. **How should the $50,000 estate administrative expense deduction be allocated? Should the non-probate assets be charged with any of the administrative expenses? Who decides that issue? The co-executors? The co-trustees? A court?**

A. The will and revocable living trust conflict on the apportionment of death taxes, which is a problem, with the will apportioning all death tax to the residue of the probate estate, while the revocable living trust provides for equitable apportionment covering both probate and non-probate property.

Q. What happens then? What document controls? The will? The last signed document?

Q. Who decides how to apportion the death tax? The decedent's co-executors? The successor co-trustees of the revocable living trust? Does anyone have a conflict of interest here?

Q. What if either the co-executors or co-trustees cannot agree? Do the parties have to resort to a court to decide apportionment?

This chapter discusses these issues. In the How It Is Done section of this chapter, we offer an attempt at the answers to most of these questions, including some possible additional questions and possible answers to those additional questions. However, some of these questions have more than one possible answer, which is why these issues are so often and hotly litigated in so many estates, many of which involve blended families, because the answers affect the bottom line of what each beneficiary gets to keep.

25.2 DEATH TAX APPORTIONMENT

What It Is

As noted above, death tax apportionment involves the allocation of death taxes as well as responsibility for estate debts and administration expenses between the recipients of the estate. You might think that all of the persons who are interested in the estate simply share these items in accordance with their respective shares of the "estate." Unfortunately, (or by intent), that is not necessarily the case. For example, a legatee of real estate usually takes that property subject to the debt that encumbers the property – unless the testator *expressly* provides otherwise. One of the problems is that the term "estate" has multiple meanings. A decedent has a "probate estate" for state law purposes, an "augmented estate" for purposes of state spousal election laws and a "gross estate" for federal estate tax purposes. And each of these terms have different meanings. Yet they all are important and are somewhat interdependent of each other. Also of vital importance is that the sharing ratios of the various recipients often differ by property. Furthermore, that same property can be in the hands of or under the control of different people, many of whose personal financial interests will be directly and significantly affected by the decisions of the fiduciaries – who may or who may not be "on their side" of the blended family.

Questions such as "who is responsible for the payment of federal estate tax on life insurance that is included in the gross estate under Code section 2042 but paid to a beneficiary other than the estate?" can be perplexing, especially for the executor, where the death proceeds are paid to a beneficiary who is outside of the control of the executor. That question might prompt another question: "who is responsible for the payment of federal estate taxes?" There is an easy answer to the second question; it is the executor.[2] In fact, it actually gets worse for the executor as Code section 2205 gives a right of reimbursement *against* the executor for estate taxes that are paid by someone other than the executor. The U.S. Supreme Court held long ago that Code section 2205 adopts a scheme of apportionment of the federal estate tax to the residue of the probate estate but applies that rule *only* if the decedent's will does not express a contrary direction, and state law does not direct some form of tax apportionment.[3] In that case, the U.S. Supreme Court upheld the state of New York's estate tax apportionment law that it had adopted in 1930, which was the first such law that any state adopted. The U.S. Supreme Court specifically held that the predecessor to Code section 2205 did not preempt state laws of estate tax apportionment. Subsequent to that U.S. Supreme Court decision, Congress enacted some estate tax reimbursement provisions that some state courts have held *do* preempt state estate tax apportionment laws.

However, there could be lots of other property that is not a part of the decedent's *probate estate*, i.e., outside of the executor's control and ability to sell to assist in the payment of the federal estate tax, but that is includible in the decedent's *gross estate* for federal estate tax purposes. In fact, there is only one provision in the Internal Revenue Code, Code section 2033, which covers the decedent's probate estate, i.e., property that generally is under the control of the executor. In the "old days," this sort of arrangement, i.e., where the executor is responsible for the payment of the decedent's federal estate tax, made sense because the bulk of what people transferred was from their traditional probate estate that passes to others by will or the laws of intestacy. However, it is no longer that simple now. People today have all sorts of property and ownership options that transmit property at death by means other than by will or the laws of intestacy. Life insurance and retirement plans, which pass by contract, are good examples. We discuss other non-probate transfer options such as pay-on-death accounts, joint tenancy with rights of survivorship and transfer-on-death accounts in Chapter 7.

That is why, at present, the Internal Revenue Code contains nine provisions that specifically include non-probate property in a decedent's gross estate for federal estate tax purposes.[4] Therefore, of the ten federal estate tax inclusion provisions, only one is necessary to cover the probate estate. Conversely, it takes nine provisions to cover the inclusion of non-probate property and items that are fictitiously includible in the gross estate. It is not unusual to see people passing on the bulk of their wealth at death as non-probate property, e.g., life insurance, real estate held in joint tenancy with rights of survivorship, transfer-on-death accounts[5] and retirement plans/IRAs. So suffice it to say that estate tax apportionment with respect to those items often is filled with intrigue, uncertainty and challenge.

The above discussion may have prompted thoughts such as "is this system fair?" and "who would want to serve as executor with all of that liability for taxes on property over which you have no control?" If you had these thoughts, you would not be alone. In fact, both federal and state legislators have addressed these issues long ago with various laws virtually from the inception of the federal and state death taxes. Only a handful of states do not have an estate tax apportionment law. We will examine the various legislative responses to issues of death tax apportionment, beginning with federal laws in the Internal Revenue Code, before turning to an analysis of the Uniform Estate Tax Apportionment Act as a proxy for state law since we cannot survey the laws of every state on death tax apportionment in this book. However, you should know that the laws can differ quite a bit from state to state. The other important thing to remember is that the decedent has some say in these matters, as these laws can be overridden if the decedent specifically provides otherwise in a will or trust.

At the outset, we need to distinguish between the two types of death tax apportionment. First, there is "inside" apportionment. Second, there is "outside" apportionment. Inside apportionment refers to the apportionment of death taxes within (inside) and between the heirs of the *probate* estate. Every taker under the will or by virtue of the laws of intestacy bears a share of the death taxes payable to the extent that inside apportionment is dictated (by virtue of either state law or a direction in the decedent's will), regardless of the priority or class of disposition, and regardless of the type of property that is received. This is to be distinguished from outside apportionment, which concerns the apportionment of death taxes between the takers of *probate* property (either with or without inside apportionment), on the one hand, and the takers of *non-probate* property that is included in the decedent's taxable estate, on the other.

A person can stipulate in a governing instrument such as a will or revocable living trust whether and how both inside apportionment and outside apportionment are to apply. However, in the absence of a clear, unambiguous direction, the federal law that is discussed next and applicable state law fill in the gaps. But there remain a lot of gray areas that require interpretation by the executor or trustee or, in a worst case, eventually by a court. We begin our analysis with a consideration of applicable federal law.

Additionally, we should distinguish the two basic types of death tax apportionment schemes that the states have: the so-called "equitable apportionment" scheme and the so-called "burden-on-the residue scheme." The overwhelming majority of states employ the equitable apportionment model. In equitable apportionment, all death taxable shares of an estate share the death tax liability ratably based upon their respective interests in the taxable estate. This is to be contrasted with the burden-on-the-residue model, which is the older, common law model that most states have discarded in favor of equitable apportionment. In this outmoded (but still present in some states) model, *all* of the death tax is borne by the residuary legatees.

Federal Law of Death Tax Apportionment

In order to alleviate some of the unfairness in holding the executor primarily liable for payment of the federal estate tax, Congress enacted a number of provisions that give federal rights to the executor to be reimbursed for the estate tax that is attributable to the inclusion of some types of non-probate property as well as property that is fictitiously includible in the decedent's gross estate for federal estate tax purposes. Note that *none* of these provisions allow the executor to be exonerated from paying the estate tax; the executor remains *personally* liable for payment of the federal estate tax. However, as you will see, there are some significant differences between the patch work of these provisions, and there is not a reimbursement provision to match with every non-probate property inclusion provision.

The following chart matches up each non-probate inclusion provision with the executor's reimbursement right where a section that provides a federal reimbursement right exists (all of the citations below are to sections of the Internal Revenue Code):

Inclusion Provision[6]	Reimbursement Provision
2035(a)[7]	None
2035(b)[8]	None
2036[9]	2207B
2037[10]	None
2038[11]	None
2039[12]	None
2040[13]	None
2041[14]	2207
2042[15]	2206
2044[16]	2207A

As you can see, not every non-probate property inclusion provision has a corresponding federal right of reimbursement for the executor. Do not be concerned about this because, as we will demonstrate below, state law also comes to the executor's aid. However, the IRS has some powerful tools in its arsenal for collecting transfer tax that the executor either cannot or does not pay for *any* reason from recipients of property that is included in a decedent's estate and taxed as part of the estate. The first of these is a concept known as "transferee liability." Transferee liability means what it says: A recipient of property that is included in a decedent's estate is liable for the estate tax on that property, up to the value of the property received.[17] The second tool at the disposal of the IRS is the secret lien that automatically attaches to a decedent's probate property at death; the IRS does not have to file *anything* to have this lien (indeed, the IRS does not even have to know that the decedent is dead).[18] There also is a non-Internal Revenue Code provision that can hold persons in possession of property liable where there is an unpaid debt to the United States.[19]

The general rule is that state law governs the apportionment of death taxes.[20] However, a number, but not all, of state courts have held the federal laws such as the ones that are discussed below preempt state laws on the subject.[21] As noted above, the decedent can vary the apportionment and reimbursement rights in a governing instrument, be it a will, revocable living trust or some other instrument. It is critical for the client who has multiple dispositive instruments to carefully coordinate the death tax apportionment so that there is not any ambiguity.[22]

Code Section 2206

This section pertains to life insurance proceeds that are includible in a gross estate but paid to someone other than the executor. It gives the executor a federal right of reimbursement against the recipient of the policy proceeds for the federal estate taxes that are attributable to inclusion of the death proceeds in the insured's gross estate. The executor has the right to be reimbursed and to recover from such beneficiary that portion of the total federal estate tax paid as the proceeds of such policies bear to the taxable estate. Therefore, this reimbursement right is based upon the *average* federal estate tax rate for the decedent's estate, not the top marginal estate tax rate that the estate paid.

This provision has the effect of giving the recipient of the insurance proceeds a ratable share of the decedent's remaining applicable exclusion amount as well as the benefit of the graduated estate tax rates that apply at present to included amounts up to $500,000, since the maximum federal estate tax rate (40 percent in 2023) kicks in at the $500,001 mark. Unfortunately, it is very easy for a decedent insured to waive this reimbursement right by will without having to reference this particular reimbursement right; a general waiver of reimbursement in the will is sufficient. However, this waiver of the right of reimbursement can *only* be made by will; it cannot be waived in a revocable living trust or other dispositive instrument. As you will see, a decedent must be more explicit to waive other federal rights of reimbursement.

Code Section 2207

This provision grants to the executor a federal right of reimbursement for the estate tax that is attributable to the inclusion of property over which the decedent held a general power of appointment. This provision operates similarly to Code section 2206 in that it allows reimbursement based upon the *average* federal estate tax rate that the executor paid, i.e., not at the marginal estate tax rate, which often is higher, and it also gives the recipient of the property the benefit of the decedent's remaining applicable exclusion amount as well as the lower federal estate tax rates that apply up to $500,000. Also like Code section 2206, it is very easy for a testator to waive reimbursement rights by a general waiver of reimbursement, which often is included as boilerplate in a will. However, like Code section 2206, this reimbursement right can *only* be waived in a will.

Code Section 2207A

This section applies to property subject to estate tax in the estate of a surviving spouse by a fictitious inclusion under Code section 2044 of the value of property over which a QTIP election marital deduction over that property on the estate tax return of the first spouse to die. This federal reimbursement right is used often, particularly in blended families, where the tax liability is borne by the heirs of one spouse but the property in the QTIP trust passes to the heirs of the first spouse to die.[23] However, Code section 2207A is quite different in its operation than either Code sections 2206 or 2207. Unlike those provisions, this federal reimbursement right applies at the *highest* marginal estate tax rate as it treats the QTIP property as being stacked on top of the estate and being taxed at the highest rate.

This means that the recipients of the QTIP property do *not* get the benefit of either a share of the deceased surviving spouse's remaining applicable exclusion amount or the graduated federal estate tax rates that apply up to $500,000. Unlike Code sections 2206 and 2207, a person can waive the right of reimbursement by any dispositive instrument, be it a will, revocable living trust or other dispositive instrument. Also unlike Code sections 2206 and 2207, the reimbursement right under Code section 2207A also extends to interest and penalties on the tax that is attributable to the inclusion of the property in the surviving spouse's estate under Code section 2044.[24] Code section 2207A also applies to gift tax that is attributable to the federal gift tax on a lifetime transfer of the surviving spouse's rights in the QTIP property under Code section 2519.[25] In fact, if the surviving spouse waives his or her right to collect the gift tax under this provision, the IRS will treat the event as another taxable gift.[26]

In response to some judicial decisions holding that a decedent spouse's general waiver of the right of reimbursement included the reimbursement right under Code section 2207A,[27] in 1997, Congress amended Code section 2207A to require express reference of intent "under this subchapter" to waive the right of reimbursement under Code section 2207A. Therefore, this amendment took care of lots of arguments where the heirs of the first spouse to die, i.e., the beneficiaries of the QTIP trust, argued that general waiver of reimbursement language in a governing instrument was sufficient for the surviving spouse testator to waive the right of reimbursement under Code section 2207A. Where the children are the children of the couple, this often is not an issue. However, for blended family couples where the heirs of each spouse often are different, as a practical matter, it is doubtful that a surviving spouse wishes to extend such a benefit to step-children by waiving the right of a spouse's own family to collect the estate taxes occasioned by the inclusion of the value of the assets over which a QTIP election was made in the estate of the first spouse to die.

Given that the current high federal transfer tax applicable exclusion amount has eliminated the vast majority of estates from having to worry about the federal estate tax, the death tax apportionment issue quite often will apply only to state death taxes. The question is "does Code section 2207A govern the apportionment of decoupled state death taxes?" At least one court has held that it does,[28] while other courts have disagreed and have ruled that state law governs the apportionment of state death taxes.[29]

Code Section 2207B

This provision applies to reimbursement for federal estate taxes that are attributable to inclusion under Code section 2036 as well as to gift taxes on the transfer of such property during the decedent's lifetime. This provision is unique in that it possesses a bit of Code sections 2206 and 2207 on the one hand, and Code section 2207A on the other. Like Code sections 2206 and 2207, this reimbursement right also is based upon the *average* estate tax rate that the executor paid, so that the recipient shares the effect of the applicable exclusion amount and the effect of the graduated estate tax rates that apply up to $500,000. However, like Code section 2207A, express reference "to this subchapter" is required to waive the right of reimbursement under Code section 2207B, and this reimbursement right can be waived in any type of dispositive instrument.

State Law

We will now discuss the Uniform Estate Tax Apportionment Act (Act).[30] At present, approximately ten states have adopted the Act. The Act replaces prior acts that the Uniform Law Commissioners had previously adopted in 1958 and 1964, which many states adopted in full or in large part. The Act represents a refinement in death tax apportionment, particularly in the area of apportioning death taxes to the recipients of non-probate property. As a general rule, the Act adopts equitable apportionment, which means that each recipient generally is required to pay the share of death tax that is attributable to the property that he or she received.

The first issue is the identity of the taxes that the Act covers. The Act covers "a federal, state or foreign tax imposed because of the death of an individual and interest and penalties associated with the tax. The term does *not* include an inheritance tax, income tax or generation-skipping transfer tax other than a generation-skipping transfer tax incurred on a direct skip taking effect at death."[31] Inheritance taxes are not covered because those taxes are assessed directly on (and technically payable by) each *recipient* instead of on the estate and are based upon the recipient's relationship to the decedent. The estate that is subject to the Act is "all interests in property subject to the tax."[32] As a general rule, the estate that is apportionable under the Act is

> "the value of the gross estate for the tax to be apportioned as finally determined for tax purposes, reduced by
>
> (a) allowable deductions, whether taken as deductions on the death tax return or on a fiduciary income tax return,
>
> (b) the value of any property that is subject to either a marital or charitable deduction since there is no tax on that property,
>
> (c) any property that is exempt from the subject death tax or that the decedent provides is exempt from estate tax apportionment as well as
>
> (d) any amount of gift tax under Code section 2035(b) that is added back to the gross estate."[33]

The practical effect of these reductions in the apportionable estate is that these items are shared ratably by all persons who received property from the decedent's taxable estate in accordance with their respective interests.

Compliance with the Act is – in a sense – elective as it does not apply where the decedent opts *not* to have it apportion the death taxes. The decedent is free to deliberately modify the death tax apportionment in an "express and unambiguous" manner by will.[34] To the extent that the decedent's will is silent on apportionment of every applicable death tax, the decedent's revocable trust is to be examined for intent concerning death tax apportionment.[35] The same "express and unambiguous" standard is required for a revocable trust to alter the general rule of equitable apportionment under the Act. In the absence of any express and unambiguous intent in either a will or revocable living trust, resort can be had to examining any other dispositive instrument looking for express and unambiguous intent to alter the effect of the Act as to the property that is covered by that instrument.[36]

As noted above, where the Act governs death tax apportionment, i.e., in the absence of an express and unambiguous intent to alter the Act's effects, the general rule is equitable apportionment, so that each recipient is charged with a ratable share of any death tax.[37] However, there are exceptions to the general rule of equitable apportionment. The first exception is for Generation Skipping Transfer Tax incurred by a direct skip that takes effect at the decedent's death. Here, the tax burden is solely apportioned to the recipient of that property.[38] The second exception is for property that is included under Code section 2044, i.e., property over which a QTIP election was made in the estate of the first spouse to die, which is apportioned pursuant to rules that are identical to the rule under Code section 2207A discussed above, i.e., based upon the marginal death tax rate on the value of the included property. This tax is apportioned ratably among the beneficiaries of the QTIP trust.[39] Death taxes that are attributable to life interests are apportioned to the principal of the property.[40]

With respect to apportionment of estate tax credits, the Act only provides partial express guidance. For example, the Act expressly provides that the credit for tax on property that was previously taxed provided by Code section 2013 is apportioned "ratably to the benefit of all persons to which the estate tax is apportioned,"[41] i.e., shared equally by those who bear the estate tax burden. A similar rule is provided for the credit for foreign death taxes paid under Code section 2014, except that if the death tax is imposed on and paid by a beneficiary, the credit inures to that beneficiary's benefit to prevent double taxation.[42]

However, and quite curiously, the Act is silent as to the "grand daddy" of all transfer tax credits: the applicable credit amount (often referred to as the unified credit) under Code section 2010 (and 2505 for gift tax purposes). Presumably, the Act apportions this credit ratably amongst those who bear the estate tax burden. However, this may not be what the client wants because the client often wants to insulate the interests of some beneficiaries from the death tax by exempting their shares from those taxes. This is particularly true in blended family situations where the client wants to ensure that a substantial share passing to their children from a prior relationship is sheltered from death tax. Clients also often want to favor one class of beneficiaries over another. If death tax is deferred pursuant to, for example, Code section 6166, the deferral inures to the benefit of those to whom that death tax is apportioned.[43] A similar rule applies for interest on the death tax deferral.

With respect to death tax on so-called "time-limited interests" such as interests in defined benefit plans or outside of the control of the executor and a U.S. court such as, for example, an interest in an offshore trust that is included in the decedent's gross estate, the Act essentially requires those recipients of other property in the apportionable estate to front the death tax on the time-limited interests. That tax will be repaid as the funds are received or when they return to the jurisdiction of a U.S. court so that a reimbursement claim can be brought against the holder of such a fund.[44] Where there is a death tax benefit that is attributable to a special election on certain property, such as an election under Code sections 2031(c) or 2032A, the estate tax has to be computed both with and without the election, and the benefit of the election apportioned among those who received the property.[45] If the benefit reduces the recipient's share of the death tax to zero, then the overage is apportioned among the other recipients of the apportionable estate. If there is any recapture of those tax benefits, then they are specifically apportioned to those who are liable for the recapture tax.[46]

The Act gives some significant powers to the fiduciary who is holding property for the benefit of the beneficiaries of an estate. For example, the fiduciary can delay distribution to the beneficiary until the fiduciary is satisfied that adequate provision for the death tax has been achieved.[47] Moreover, the fiduciary can both withhold a beneficiary's share of the death tax[48] as well as require a beneficiary to post a bond or other security to ensure payment of the death tax.[49] In addition to these powers, the Act gives a fiduciary the right to seek reimbursement of a beneficiary's share of the death tax from the beneficiary.[50] For the death tax that a fiduciary is unable to collect, the fiduciary has the right to seek contribution from the other persons who are interested in the apportionable estate in the following priority:

(1) any person having an interest in the apportionable estate that is not exonerated from the death tax;

(2) any other person having an interest in the apportionable estate; and

(3) any person having an interest in the gross estate.[51]

The fiduciary also has the right to seek reimbursement from other fiduciaries.[52] However, in no event is the fiduciary authorized to collect *more* than the total death tax that is due by the decedent's estate.[53]

A person who pays more than his or her share of the death tax is entitled to seek reimbursement from a beneficiary who has not paid his or her share of the death tax[54] as well as a right to seek reimbursement from persons who paid their own death tax but who have not paid his or her share of any death tax that other persons have been called on to pay.[55] A fiduciary has the right to seek reimbursement on behalf of a beneficiary and must take reasonable steps to do so upon a beneficiary's request.[56] Finally, a fiduciary, beneficiary or transferee of the decedent's gross estate has the right to go to court to seek a declaratory judgment in order to enforce the Act.[57]

25.3 HOW IT IS DONE

As we indicated earlier, we are going to address each of the questions that we raised in an earlier section.

Q. Who decides whether a QTIP election will be made? The co-executors? The successor co-trustees of the revocable living trust? What if the co-executors or co-trustees cannot agree?

A. The co-executors of Art's estate are the ones who make the decision of whether or not to make a QTIP election.[58] This is so even though the revocable trust has more assets in it than Art's probate estate because Art named executors. Given that one of Art's children, Al, and his surviving spouse, Mary Alice, are the co-executors, it could very well be that the QTIP election is not made if either co-executor disagrees, since co-executors generally have to unanimously agree to all actions. It's highly likely that Mary Alice would want to make a QTIP election because it would preserve the maximum amount for her lifetime use and enjoyment. However, for Art's child who is co-executor, Al, the decision may not be so easy. The day of reckoning on the estate tax simply is deferred by the QTIP election until Mary Alice's death; the QTIP election often does not "save death tax." If Al believes that the value of the revocable trust is expected to highly appreciate in the future, he may opine that foregoing some current benefit will save some estate tax down the road, especially if it hurts his step-mother, with whom he really does not get along now after his father's death. Of course, if Mary Alice does not have much of an estate and is not expected to have a taxable estate in any event, Al might be inclined to go along with the QTIP election although, as we discuss below, Al probably will claim that the QTIP portion never gets funded because the entire trust goes to him as "applicable exclusion amount."

Q. **What is the effect of a QTIP election in Mary Alice's estate?**

A. A QTIP election assures that the value of that property at the time of her will be included in Mary Alice's estate,[59] and it is unlikely that Mary Alice will waive her estate's right to seek reimbursement from the beneficiaries of the QTIP trust, who are her step-children, at that time, especially if she has her own set of heirs.

Q. **Where will the death tax come from?**

A. The problem is that the will, which requires apportionment to the residue of the estate, conflicts with the revocable trust's adoption of equitable apportionment. If the will governs, then the residuary bequests to Mary Alice and the three children will be reduced by pro rata shares of the death tax, although the pre-residuary bequest to Al is not burdened by death tax, shifting that liability over to the residuary legatees. Mary Alice may try to argue that she should not have to bear any of the death tax because spousal legacies are deductible. However, she probably would lose this argument in light of the plan dictates of the will that the death tax be borne by the residuary bequests. Reduction of her legacy will, in turn, reduce the marital deduction, which will cause an increase in the federal estate tax in a circular computation.[60] Of course, the co-executors may attempt to get reimbursement of the federal estate tax from the non-probate property. Clearly, Code section 2206 could give the executors the right to be reimbursed for the estate tax that is attributable to the inclusion of the $3,000,000 of life insurance proceeds in Art's estate. However, the direction of death tax apportionment toward the residue of the estate as the source of payment of the estate tax presents probably an insurmountable obstacle to that argument since that arguably is enough to waive that reimbursement right. However, given that neither executor received any of the life insurance proceeds and each would suffer a reduction in the amount of the residue from the probate estate that each would receive by virtue of apportionment of the death tax to the residue, it is very conceivable that they would attempt to make the Code section 2206 argument for reimbursement.

Nevertheless, it appears likely that the recipients of the life insurance proceeds will get off without having to contribute to the payment of the federal estate tax, despite that the insurance proceeds constituted over 30 percent of the taxable estate, and even a lot more than that when you take the IRA out of that mix given the applicability of the marital deduction to that asset. It seems fairly clear that Mary Alice's beneficial interest in Art's IRA should bear no share of the death tax since it did not generate any federal estate tax due to the marital deduction as well as that it is not part of the residue of the probate estate.

Q. **What about the fact that Al is specifically given an amount that is equal to the "applicable exclusion amount" in the revocable trust? Who determines how much that Al's share of "applicable exclusion amount" should be? Does anyone have a conflict of interest here?**

A. This is a very interesting problem, because one interpretation of the trust instrument language as applied to the facts would give the entire $3,000,000 to Al since the "applicable exclusion amount" is greater than the amount that is in the trust, which would leave nothing to fund the QTIP trust, which Mary Alice, a co-trustee, will not like very much. However, Mary Alice has a clear conflict of interest in this determination because it is in her personal best interests to maximize the size of the QTIP trust, so she may well want to treat the $2,000,000 that passes to the children in the probate estate and the $3,000,000 in life insurance proceeds first before determining how much remaining applicable exclusion amount to allocate to Al's share of the trust, which would leave only $490,000 applicable exclusion amount remaining for Al, who would probably vociferously object to such an interpretation, and he is a co-executor.

On the other hand, the executors of Art's estate, of which Al is one, may take the position that the residuary legacies to the children in the will actually consume $1,500,000 of the applicable exclusion amount since it would protect the $1,000,000 of the probate estate that passes to Al pursuant to the will from death tax. Then the fact that Betty is a co-trustee of the revocable trust has a clear conflict of interest in interpreting the meaning of "applicable exclusion amount" in that she probably would want to include her $1,500,000 of life insurance proceeds in the "applicable exclusion amount" in order to shelter that amount from death tax. Of course, Mary Alice may well agree with Betty that the life insurance should be considered first because that helps maximize the size of the QTIP trust, so she has a clear conflict of interest. Another possible position presents a middle ground, and it is apportionment of the applicable exclusion amount ratably amongst all of the recipients of the apportionable estate, which is what the Act arguably would do had Art's will not negated its applicability by a clear, unambiguous expression. It is doubtful that this issue will be resolved by anyone other than a court, which will have to construe Art's entire estate plan in order to ascertain the intent and meaning of "applicable exclusion amount." The fact that the revocable trust was executed after the date on which the will was executed may well be important to a court construing the entire estate plan because it is the last expression of Art's intent.

Q. Who is personally responsible for payment of the death taxes?

A. The co-executors are *personally* liable for the death tax.[61] This is so despite the fact that over 75 percent of Art's taxable estate consisted of non-probate property and is outside of the co-executors' reach. We have noted several times that such a concentration of non-probate property is not that unusual today. However, as we have discussed earlier and will discuss again shortly, the co-executors do have some avenues for seeking reimbursement of the death tax.

Q. What about the death tax on the life insurance that Art owned at his death?

As we discussed earlier, it may well be that the recipients of the life insurance proceeds, Betty and Chuck, will have absolutely no death tax liability because Art arguably apportioned all of the death tax to the residue of the probate estate in his will. However, since neither recipient of the insurance proceeds is a co-executor, the co-executors, who also are responsible for preparing the federal estate tax return, may construe Art's will as only apportioning federal estate tax as to the probate estate, and that the equitable apportionment clause in the revocable trust gives them enough of an argument that Code section 2206 applies to allow them to proceed on a claim for reimbursement of the insurance recipients' shares of the death tax. There also is an argument that, under some of the state court decisions that we cited earlier in this chapter, Code section 2206 trumps state law, although the will arguably waived the executor's right of reimbursement, which would negate the applicability of Code section 2206. The co-executors also might have a right to reimbursement under the Act. But, again, that seems unlikely since Art clearly and unambiguously apportioned the death tax to the residue of the probate estate. If the co-executors do have a reimbursement right and if equitable apportionment somehow applies, then the co-executors would be entitled to collect approximately $306,030 (3,000,000/$9,950,000 x $1,015,000) in federal estate tax from Betty and Chuck. It seems that a court will have the final say on this issue because of the blatant conflicts of interest that all of the fiduciaries have.

Q. How should death tax be apportioned to the revocable trust? If any of the death tax is apportionable to the revocable trust, is there any right under the Act or the Internal Revenue Code that would allow the co-executors to pursue a reimbursement claim against the co-trustees of the revocable trust?

A. The beneficiaries will no doubt argue that no death tax should be apportioned to the revocable trust. Their grounds would be that Art clearly intended that the assets in that trust be covered either by the applicable exclusion amount or by a marital deduction by virtue of the QTIP election. Therefore, the co-executors must exonerate them from tax because of their duties of loyalty and impartiality to all of the heirs. However, as we discussed earlier, the co-executors must agree to make the QTIP election, and if they do not make that election, it seems highly likely that a substantial portion of the revocable trust will be subject to death tax. However, since Al is a co-executor of Art's estate and the recipient of the "applicable exclusion amount" portion of the trust, he could be inclined to agree to make the QTIP election to reduce the amount of death tax. But, as we noted above, there is ambiguity as to the size of his share of the revocable trust. Al will probably argue that his share should be the entire trust. The co-trustees, each of whom has interests that would be adversely affected by that position, will no doubt think otherwise. They are likely to argue that Art's intent was to split the trust into parts and that he clearly contemplated at least a portion of the trust would be allocated to the QTIP trust, which would imply some allocation of applicable exclusion amount to the other includible items. If death tax is properly apportioned to the revocable trust, then the Internal Revenue Code arguably gives the co-executors no federal right of reimbursement against the co-trustees of the revocable trust because revocable trusts are includible in a decedent's gross estate under Code section 2038. As we illustrated earlier in this chapter, *that* section has no corresponding reimbursement right provision - unless the co-executors were successful in asserting that the revocable trust also is includible pursuant to Code section 2036(a)(1), in which case Code section 2207B would give the co-executors the right to seek reimbursement from the co-trustees of the revocable trust since that provision requires express reference to that provision in order to properly waive its application. However, assuming that Code section 2207B does not apply, Sec. 9(a) of the Act gives the co-executors the right to pursue the co-trustees of the revocable trust for its allocable share of the death tax. Moreover, since the beneficiaries of the revocable trust also are recipients of Art's probate estate, Sec. 8(a) allows the co-executors to defer each heir's right to receive from the estate until the co-executors are satisfied that the death tax is paid or accounted for. Moreover, Sec. 8(b) of the Act arguably gives the co-executors the right to offset each heir's right to a share of the probate estate by that heir's apportionable share of the death tax, at least up to the value of that heir's interest in the probate estate. Sec. 8(c) of the Act also would permit the co-executors to require each heir to post a bond or other security for that heir's apportionable share of the death tax.

Q. **How should the $50,000 estate administrative expense deduction be allocated? Should the non-probate assets be charged with any of the administrative expenses? Who decides that issue? The co-executors? The co-trustees?**

A. This is yet another series of questions where at least some of them potentially have multiple answers. Taking the questions concerning who would make this decision first, it seems clear that the co-executors make this decision under both state and tax law. With respect to the allocation of the administrative expense deduction, if the will's burden-on-the-residue schema is adopted, then the residuary legatees should be allocated their respective shares of all of that deduction to the exclusion of all others who are interested in the estate. This is because they are the ones who have to pay the death tax. However, if for any reason, equitable apportionment applies, whether because of the revocable trust's dictates or that of applicable state law, then each person who has an interest in the apportionable estate should be allocated his or her respective share of that deduction.

Q. **Conflict between the dispositive documents. The will and revocable living trust conflict on the apportionment of death taxes, with the will apportioning all death tax to the residue of the probate estate, while the revocable living trust provides for equitable apportionment covering both probate and non-probate property. What happens then? What document controls? The will? The last signed document?**

A. Under Sec. 3(a)(1) of the Act, the will would govern since it is not silent on the subject of death tax apportionment and clearly and unambiguously apportions the death tax to the residue of the probate estate.[62] This apparently is the case under the Act even if the revocable trust was signed or amended after the date on which the will was executed since the revocable trust version only applies to the extent that the will is silent, which was not the case in this example. These types of conflicts are not unusual because such provisions often are buried in the boilerplate, and it is an easy area to overlook. However, as we hope that we have demonstrated in this exercise, the subject of death tax apportionment is critical, too much so to leave to chance or mindless boilerplate. It seems imperative to discuss these issues with the client before the documents are even drafted so that they can be crafted to comport with the client's expressed intent.

Q. Who decides how to apportion the death tax? The decedent's co-executors? The successor co-trustees of the revocable living trust? Does anyone have a conflict of interest here? What if either the co-executors or co-trustees cannot agree? A court?

A. It seems that the co-executors will have the first say about how the death tax is to be apportioned amongst the recipients of the apportionable estate. However, in this case, it seems highly unlikely that they will have the final say since, depending upon how they apportion the death tax amongst the recipients of the apportionable estate, someone is likely to object. Therefore, it seems highly likely that a court will have to make this determination.

Conclusion. As you should have been able to easily see, the issue of proper death tax apportionment can be murky and susceptible of multiple interpretations, particularly where there are substantial amounts of both probate and non-probate property that is included in the decedent's taxable estate. It also can be a source of division and litigation among the beneficiaries, often pitting those who feel that their oxen were gored by an erroneous apportionment and those who were favored by the apportionment. Unfortunately, these actions also often culminate in malpractice claims against the estate planning lawyer who drafted the documents.[63] These types of claims arise far more often in the context of blended family estate planning because of the possibility that the assets are allocated one way and responsibility for the death tax in the other direction. Therefore, it is very important to proceed both cautiously and at the client's express direction. Clearly, Art intended to give his children by a prior relationship a significant portion of his estate. It is not unusual for a parent to divide an estate between his or her children and a partner, but this can have the effect of increasing the amount of death tax, especially where the couple is married, since legacies to a spouse usually are deductible in full.

However, this sort of dispositive scheme can trigger questions after the client's death as to the client's intent, with the question usually being "did dad really intend to increase his death tax by doing it the way that he did?" Where the estate planner has carefully documented the client's intent before death in this regard, including preferably getting the client to sign an acknowledgment of the possibility of increased death tax as a result of the chosen dispositive scheme and/or death tax apportionment, the estate planner's exposure to being second guessed after the heirs receive their tax bills is greatly reduced.

Consider an example of this division phenomenon. Suppose that Seymour, a big fan of simplicity, wants to divide his estate "straight down the middle." Seymour dies in 2017 with a $50 million estate in a state with no death tax and an estate tax rate of 40 percent (the top estate tax rate in the year of death). He left half of his estate to his surviving spouse, Beatrice, and the other half to his children by a prior relationship. Assume that Seymour's estate administrative expenses are $100,000. Leaving aside the effect of the applicable exclusion amount, which, in 2017, sheltered $5,490,000 of assets from estate tax, **if taxes come off the top**, i.e., divided equally between the two bequests, Beatrice and Seymour's children will each take $20,102,500, and $9,695,000 will go to estate taxes. If, instead, death taxes come out of the **children's share** only because Bernice's share qualifies for the federal estate tax marital deduction, which is the result that equitable apportionment of death tax would provide, Beatrice will take $25 million, Seymour's children will take $17,164,000, and $7,736,000 will go to estate taxes. In this example, then, there is a **negative swing** of $4,897,500 in what Beatrice takes, a **positive swing** of $2,938,500 in what Seymour's children take, and an **additional** $1,959,000 in **estate taxes** paid, **just depending upon how the estate taxes are apportioned!** (Computations performed by NumberCruncher Software at **http://www.leimberg.com**) Tom Clancy's recent estate tax apportionment case in Maryland involved facts very similar to these.[64]

In our example, there is a *significant* multi-million-dollar swing in what the spouse and children receive just because of how the death tax apportionment clause is drafted. The children and spouse will likely both fight each other and the fiduciaries and pursue the estate planner's E&O carrier for that kind of change! In large estates such as this one, the use of examples with *real numbers* in the estate planning documents themselves (as well as in the explanations of those documents) can be very helpful and can provide ample cover for the estate planner after the client's death of the client's clear intentions in this regard. It is essential to perform a hypothetical probate to compute the client's projected death tax as well as the apportionment of that tax pursuant to the documents as presently drafted while the client is still *alive*. Too many death tax apportionment issues are counterintuitive or not readily apparent and do not become visible until the tax numbers are generated. Unfortunately, at that point, it is usually too late the fix the problem and is all too often not what the client intended or wanted. We cannot overemphasize the importance of documenting the client's intent in this regard.

25.4 WHEN IS THE USE OF SUCH A DEVICE INDICATED?

1. Whenever the client expects to owe any death tax whatsoever, including state death tax since that will comprise the bulk of death tax for the overwhelming majority of decedents who have taxable estates.

2. Whenever the client wants to alter the otherwise applicable default rules of death tax apportionment.

25.5 WHAT ARE THE REQUIREMENTS?

The client should be walked through the effect of death tax apportionment on his or her estate plan by assuming a death today with the estate planning documents that presently are in place. If the client is satisfied with those results, which could come either from the default state law rules that we discussed above or via election out of those rules in his or her estate planning documents, then nothing further need be done. However, it is always wise to confirm, preferably in writing, the client's understanding of the numerical results of those choices. If the client does not like the presently applicable results, then the onus is on the client to take affirmative steps to alter those results either by changing his or her current estate planning documents or by affirmatively providing for a different result in clear and unambiguous language in those documents.

Every client's situation is *unique* in this regard. The estate planner must obtain sufficient information from the client to know not only the client's intentions regarding death tax apportionment, but where the client may have greater exposure to surprise results in death tax apportionment due to the client's unique situation. Areas of heightened concern come from a number of possible areas, including:

- Having made large taxable gifts during the last three years;

- Leaving a retirement plan or IRA or personally owned life insurance to someone other than a spouse;

- Where the applicable state law or the dispositive document itself applies a burden-on-the-residue rule;

- Where the spousal or charitable bequest is of the residue;

- Where the client has a blended family and is going to divide his or her estate between a spouse and the children from a prior relationship;

- Where the client has significant portions of their estates that will be includible in the gross estate under some provision other than Code section 2033, e.g., Code sections 2036 (retention of a life interest), 2038 (retained power to alter, amend, revoke or terminate) or 2042 (life insurance payable to the estate or client has retained an incident of ownership);

- Where the client has property in more than one state; and

- Where the client desires to exempt some bequest from death tax.

25.6 ISSUES AND IMPLICATIONS IN COMMUNITY PROPERTY STATES

There are no community property implications in the area of death tax apportionment.

25.7 ESTATE TAX REIMBURSEMENT ACTIONS BY TRUSTEE OF QTIP UNDER IRC SEC. 2207A

What It Is

Generally. Code section 2207A provides for reimbursement to the estate in QTIP situations. Specifically, it provides that, if any part of the gross estate consists of property the value of which is includible in the gross estate by reason of Code section 2044 (relating to certain property for which marital deduction was previously allowed), the decedent's estate is entitled to recover from the person receiving the property the amount by which the total estate tax that has been paid exceeds the total estate tax that would have been payable if the value of such property had not been included in the gross estate. Unlike some other apportionment reimbursement provisions, the reimbursement under Code section 2207A is the *incremental* difference, i.e., at the highest effective rate, unless the decedent surviving spouse indicated a different intent with respect to the amount of reimbursement.[65] This statute provides a federal right of action for reimbursement.

The only exception to this right is where the surviving spouse waives the right of reimbursement with respect to any property to the extent that the decedent in a will (or a revocable trust) specifically indicates an intent to waive any right of recovery under Subchapter 11 with respect to such property.[66] Therefore, the battle usually is over whether the decedent surviving spouse said enough in a will or revocable living trust to waive the right of reimbursement.

What typically happens in a case for reimbursement is this: The executor of the surviving spouse's estate usually first asks the recipients of the QTIP'd property for voluntary reimbursement. If this is refused, the executor will typically follow with a demand for reimbursement. As a last resort, the executor may commence a lawsuit. Reimbursement actions often involve blended families and usually pit the descendants of the surviving spouse against the descendants of the first spouse to die. These people often have had little reason to interact with each other and usually lack any real family connection, especially after the deaths of the spouse step-parents.

We will review the facts of several of these cases to give you a flavor of how they go. We will conclude the chapter with a discussion of whether the trustee of a QTIP trust has any duty to take steps to minimize the pending death tax liability by proactively planning while the surviving spouse is still alive.

Review of cases and rulings. The first example is PLR 200452010. This private letter ruling involved a request by the personal representative of the surviving spouse's estate for a ruling about whether the surviving spouse waived her right of reimbursement under Code section 2207A. In the facts of that ruling, the personal representative of Taxpayer's estate was in communication with the trustee of the QTIP trusts. The purpose of the communication was to determine the correct value of the QTIP Trusts' assets that were includible in decedent surviving spouse's estate under Code section 2044 so that the assets could be accurately reported on decedent surviving spouse's federal estate tax return. In addition, the personal representative sought to recover from the QTIP trusts, pursuant to Code section 2207A, the estate taxes attributable to the inclusion of the QTIP trusts' assets in the taxpayer's estate.

The personal representative was advised and had proceeded on the basis that the federal estate tax attributable to the inclusion in decedent surviving spouse's gross estate of the value of the QTIP trusts would be borne by the QTIP trusts pursuant to the right of recovery granted to the decedent surviving spouse's estate under Code section 2207A. However, two business days before the due date for filing decedent surviving spouse's federal estate tax return, the trustee of the QTIP trusts notified the personal representative of the decedent surviving spouse's estate that it would not reimburse the estate for the estate taxes attributable to the inclusion of the QTIP trusts in decedent surviving spouse's gross estate. The trustee's rationale was that it believed that under Item 1 of decedent surviving spouse's last will and testament the estate's right of recovery under Code section 2207A was waived by the decedent surviving spouse.

The subject language in the decedent surviving spouse's will was as follows:

> *direct that all estate, inheritance, succession, death or similar taxes (except generation-skipping transfer taxes) assessed with respect to my estate herein disposed of, or any part thereof, or on any bequest or devise contained in this my Last Will (which term wherever used herein shall include any Codicil hereto), or on any insurance upon my life or on any property held jointly by me with another or on any transfer made by me during my lifetime or on any other property or interests in property included in my estate for such tax purposes be paid out*

of my residuary estate and shall not be charged to or against any recipient, beneficiary, transferee or owner of any such property or interests in property included in my estate for such tax purposes.

The IRS quoted the following legislative history to the 1997 amendment to Code section 2207A:

The bill provides that the right of recovery with respect to QTIP is waived only to the extent that language in the decedent's will or revocable trust specifically so indicates (e.g., by specific reference to QTIP, the QTIP trust, section 2044, or section 2207A). Thus, a general provision specifying that all taxes be paid by the estate is no longer sufficient to waive the right of recovery.

Accordingly, the IRS ruled that the decedent surviving spouse's will language was insufficient for a waiver of the right of reimbursement under Code section 2207A.

The second example is *Maurice F. Jones Trust v. Barnett Banks*.[67] In that case, which pitted the trustee for the heirs of the childless predeceased spouse against the trustee for the daughter of the decedent surviving spouse, involved the following tax clause:

I direct that all estate, inheritance, succession and other death taxes of any nature, together with any interest and penalties thereon, which may be levied or assessed by reason of my death, by the laws of any State or the United States, with respect to property passing under this Will or any other property, shall be considered a cost of administration of my estate, and that such taxes, together with all debts which I am legally obligated to pay at the time of my death, my last illness and funeral expenses and costs of administration of my estate, (including the cost of a suitable monument at my grave), shall be paid out of my residuary estate without apportionment... .

The trial court granted summary judgment in favor of the trustee of the decedent surviving spouse's estate against the trustee of the predeceased spouse, and the trustee appealed. On appeal, the focus was on the meaning of the words "which I am legally obligated to pay." The appellate court agreed with the trial court that the subject language did not rise to the level of sufficient waiver under Code section 2207A.

The final example is *In Re Probate of Lee*.[68] That case pitted two charitable beneficiaries of the QTIP trust against the beneficiaries of the decedent surviving spouse's estate. In this matter, the charitable beneficiaries sought an order that the QTIP trusts should be distributed to them without any withholding of the estate tax that was attributable to the inclusion of the QTIP'd property in the decedent surviving spouse's estate. The subject tax clause read as follows:

(b) I direct that all estate, inheritance, transfer, legacy or succession taxes, including state and federal, which may be assessed or imposed upon the transfer of any property under this Will, or upon property which may be part of my taxable estate for the purpose of any said tax shall, in the event my husband, SAMUEL LEE, survives me, be paid out of the Family Part of my residuary estate, as hereinafter defined in Article THIRD, it being my intention that the Spouse's Part and any other property passing to my husband which is not included in my estate for federal estate tax purposes be exonerated to the greatest extent possible from payment of all said state or federal taxes. In the event my said husband, SAMUEL, does not survive me, said taxes shall be paid out of my residuary estate. Notwithstanding the foregoing, if any tax shall be payable at, after or with respect to my death, pursuant to Internal Revenue Code Section 2036 (as permitted under 2207B), Section 2041 or Section 2044 or Chapter 13 of the Internal Revenue Code of 1986, as amended, or corresponding provision under state law, no part of such tax shall be paid from my estate.

The trial court found no effective waiver of the right of reimbursement. The appellate court agreed.

Based upon the case law, it seems clear to us that the legislative history to Code section 2207A means what it says: it requires a specific reference to QTIP, the QTIP trust, Code section 2044 or Code section 2207A in order to constitute an effective waiver.

Finally, there have been actions trying to claim on the part of the QTIP trustee a failure to do whatever planning that the QTIP trustee could to reduce that eventual liability. In *In the Matter of the Janice Galloway T. Galloway Nonexempt Marital Trust created by the Herbert Galloway R. Galloway Revocable Trust dated February 18, 1988*,[69] the court answered that question in the negative, i.e., there was no duty on the part of the QTIP trustee to form a family limited partnership to put the approximately $17,500,000 worth of marketable securities into in order to reduce the amount of federal estate tax due.[70] The court expressly noted the risk of the family limited partnership with marketable securities strategy.

Takeaways. In this chapter, we discussed reimbursement actions under Code section 2207A. Code section 2207A gives a federal right of reimbursement to the executor of the estate of the decedent surviving spouse against the takers of the QTIP'd property. The principal issue almost always is whether there was a valid waiver of the right of reimbursement. The principal takeaway should be that waiver has to be very specific and must refer either to the QTIP'd property or Code sections 2207A or 2044. In a blended family, the chances are very slim that a step-parent will burden his or her estate with tax liability that is properly borne by the family of the first spouse to die, so it has been our experience that waivers of the right of reimbursement of death taxes on QTIP'd property in blended families are few and far between.

25.8 FREQUENTLY ASKED QUESTIONS

Question – If the decedent did not provide otherwise, what rules of death tax apportionment apply?

Answer – To the extent that the decedent did not provide with respect to death tax apportionment in the estate planning documents, applicable state death tax apportionment law as well as the estate tax reimbursement provisions of the Internal Revenue Code apply. There can be some significant differences between the laws of the various states. Almost all states have adopted equitable apportionment laws. Those few that have not still apply the burden-on-the-residue rule.

Question – What happens if there is a conflict between the death tax apportionment provisions in a decedent's will and those provisions in a revocable living trust or other dispositive document?

Answer – The answer to this question might be dependent upon judicial interpretation. However, if the Act applies, then Act Sec. 3(a)(1) applies to provide that the death tax apportionment provisions in the will prevail over those either in a revocable living trust or any other dispositive document.[71] However, it is always possible for a court to determine that the will does not clearly and unambiguously opt out of the default rule that the state's death tax apportionment laws apply. In this case, the Act provides that the court is then to examine first the revocable living trust, followed by any other dispositive instrument and, finally, if there is no clear and unambiguous expression in any document, applicable state death tax apportionment law applies, which usually is equitable apportionment.

Some courts go to great lengths to read the documents to not have clear and unambiguous expressions so that the court can apply default state law of death tax apportionment, particularly when the death tax apportionment result under the will or other dispositive instrument conflicts with the court's view of what is equitable. However, other courts take more of a literalist reading of the dispositive instruments and honor the intentions of the decedent as expressed in the dispositive instruments to the fullest extent. It is impossible to harmonize the court decisions in this area, as they are all over the board. It is important to know the judge and what that judge's expressed tendencies are in matters of this sort in advance. This is particularly true in a case where the death tax is being apportioned to a legacy in such a way that either wipes out the legacy altogether or costs the decedent's estate a marital or charitable deduction due to apportionment of death tax, which calls the decedent's intent into question. Courts have been known to be inconsistent in this regard, ranging from not rewriting the decedent's will to save the legacy where the result was clearly not what the decedent wanted[72] to tortured construction of a document to reach a result that the court deems to be equitable.[73]

Question – What do the terms "equitable apportionment" and "burden-on-the-residue" mean? What does the term "residue" mean? Have the majority of state courts expressed a strong public policy in favor of equitable apportionment where the decedent did not clearly and unambiguously provide otherwise?

Answer – Equitable apportionment means that each holder of an interest in the apportionable estate is responsible for a share of the death tax that is in accordance with that holder's interest. It is called "equitable" because it is perceived, rightly or wrongly, to be fairer than the "burden-on-the-residue" rule. Courts have found that state legislatures, by enacting statutes that provide for equitable apportionment, have expressed a strong public policy in favor of equitable apportionment.[74] However, it should be noted that even equitable apportionment is not absolute and has exceptions, does not always work a fairer result and often conflicts with the decedent's intentions concerning death tax apportionment, particularly where courts contort and disregard a dispositive instrument to reach equitable apportionment where the decedent clearly intended otherwise. As we intimated previously, the testator, by directing so clearly and unambiguously, can deviate from the state's rule of equitable apportionment. However, the election out of equitable apportionment does not mean that the burden-on-the-residue rule applies. It is not a matter of "either-or." The testator can craft a set of unique death tax apportionment rules that apply to his or her specific situation. Another such exception relates to the apportionment of death tax to the value of a term-limited interest such as a life estate or income only interest in trust. The rule in just about every jurisdiction is that death tax that is apportionable to a term-limited interest is payable out of the remainder interest, i.e. the corpus or principal. This is what the Act also provides.[75]

Note that the term "apportionable estate" does not necessarily mean the decedent's taxable estate. (this will be further explained in a subsequent question). And not all death taxes are apportionable under the Act.

The term "residue" is defined as the property that is bequeathed to the residuary legatees under the will, e.g., "I give the rest, residue and remainder to…." The "burden-on-the-residue" rule of death tax apportionment is the old common law rule that provides a clear, bright line rule; it apportions all death tax to the residue of the estate, including the death tax on non-probate property as well as the value of property that is fictitiously included in the decedent's gross estate. The effect of this rule can wipe out the interests of the residuary legatees, which is why the vast majority of states have adopted equitable apportionment of death tax as the general rule, because of a belief that the decedent actually intended that the residuary legatees receive the bulk of his or her estate. Almost all states have enacted equitable apportionment either by positive legislation or by judicial decree.

Question – What does the term "apportionable estate" mean? Does it have the same meaning as "gross estate" for federal estate tax purposes?

Answer – No. The terms "apportionable estate" under the Act and "gross estate" for federal estate tax purposes are not synonymous. The gross estate contains all of the interests in property that the federal estate tax includes in the decedent's estate. The apportionable estate begins with the gross estate for federal estate tax purposes, at the values that are finally determined, and then makes several adjustments that remove items to reach the apportionable estate.[76] The first such item is any claim or expense that is allowable as a deduction, whether or not taken as a deduction on the federal estate tax return.[77] Recall that some items of expense, so-called "swing items," may be claimed as deductions either on the estate tax return or on the estate's fiduciary income tax return, but not on both returns.[78] The second reduction is for the value of any property that qualifies for marital or charitable deduction or is exempt.[79] This reduction is consistent with the Act's theme of equitable apportionment because property that qualifies for either a marital or charitable deduction causes or creates no federal estate tax. The final reduction from the gross estate is for the gift tax that was paid within three years of death and, therefore, includible pursuant to Code section 2035(b).[80] The effect of this reduction is to spread the increased estate tax liability that is attributable to this inclusion ratably amongst all recipients of the estate.

Question – Can a testator provide for either inside apportionment, outside apportionment, both or either one alone? What happens if the decedent does not clearly and unambiguously adopt inside and/or outside apportionment?

Answer – It is possible for both inside and outside apportionment to apply or only one of them to apply. Most states that have adopted equitable apportionment, including the Act, specifically provide for both inside as well as outside apportionment. However, states that have not adopted equitable apportionment, i.e., have the common law burden-on-the-residue rule, have no outside apportionment and, with respect to inside apportionment, generally apportion the death tax totally to the residue.

Generally, if a testator does not expressly provide with respect to death tax apportionment, it depends upon whether or not the testator is domiciled in a state that provides for equitable apportionment. If the testator's state provides for equitable apportionment, then the death tax will be apportioned pursuant to both inside and outside apportionment unless the will or other dispositive instrument clearly and unambiguously provides otherwise. If the testator is domiciled in a state that uses the burden-on-the-residue rule, then there will be neither inside nor outside apportionment unless the testator expressly provides otherwise.

Question – What happens where a decedent owns property in a state that employs the burden-on-the-residue rule as well as property that is in a state that has an equitable apportionment rule? Which rule governs?

Answer – Generally, the *situs* (where the property is located) of the property governs descent and distribution of real property that is located in a state. However, the death tax apportionment determination will depend upon where the decedent was domiciled and what the will or other dispositive instrument provided because the state of domicile probably governs apportionment of death tax. If the decedent's state of domicile applies the rule of equitable apportionment and the decedent did not clearly and unambiguously opt out of equitable apportionment, then equitable apportionment probably will apply to the federal estate tax. The only possible exception to that result would be for the state death tax in the state where the property is situated that is attributable to the property that is in the state that has the burden-on-the-residue rule. However, to the extent that the decedent clearly and unambiguously opted out of both the burden-on-the-residue rule as well as equitable apportionment, the provision that is in the dispositive instrument will govern death tax apportionment.

Figure 25.1

NAME-BURDEN ON THE RESIDUE						
	AL	MARY ALICE	BETTY	CHUCK		
IRA		1,500,000				1,500,000
Life insurance			1,500,000	1,500,000		3,000,000
Pre-residuary legacy-estate tax free	500,000					500,000
Residuary legacy	500,000	500,000	500,000	500,000		2,000,000
Revocable trust	3,000,000					3,000,000
Less: share of admin exp.	−5,000	−15,000	−15,000	−15,000		−50,000
Less: share of FET*	−289,000	−289,000	−289,000	−289,000	−1,156,000	1,156,000
Less: state death tax	0	0	0	0		0
Distributable estate	3,706,000	1,696,000	1,696,000	1,696,000	8,794,000	8,894,000
NAME-EQUITABLE APPORTIONMENT						
IRA		1,500,000				1,500,000
Life insurance			1,500,000	1,500,000		3,000,000
Pre-residuary legacy-estate tax free	500,000					500,000
Residuary legacy	500,000	500,000	500,000	500,000	2,000,000	
Revocable trust	3,000,000					3,000,000
Less: share of admin exp.	−20,000	−10,000	−10,000	−10,000		−50,000
Less: share of FET**	−478,000	0	−239,000	−239,000	−956,000	−956,000
Less: state death tax	0	0	0	0	0	0
Distributable estate	3,502,000	1,990,000	1,751,000	1,751,000	8,994,000	8,994,000

* Estate tax just burdens residue.
** This is pure equitable apportionment. Al will still argue that his revocable trust legacy should have the benefit of the applicable exclusion amount, and, as thus, be tax-free.

Conclusion: As you can see, Al, the recipients of the non-probate property and Mary Alice have vastly different results, just depending upon how the death tax is apportioned and the applicable exclusion amount is apportioned. Therefore, death tax apportionment can be a critical part of an estate planning document.

Question – Can you provide some examples, with numbers, of apportionment?

Answer – Absolutely. We return to our facts concerning Art's estate. We will assume that no QTIP election is made in Art's estate, which results in $956,000 in federal estate tax with equitable apportionment and $1,156,000 with apportionment of the federal estate tax to the residue (which results in higher federal estate tax due to the circular computation. Remember that these results are subject to debate, as we discussed earlier.

CHAPTER ENDNOTES

1. See the many contributions of Professor Jeffrey N. Pennell on this subject. See, e.g., Pennell, Transfer Tax Payment and Apportionment, 834-2d Estates, Gifts and Trusts Portfolios (Tax Mgmt. 2011).
2. I.R.C. §2002.
3. *Riggs v. del Drago*, 317 U.S. 95 (1942).
4. I.R.C. §§ 2035-2042 and 2044.
5. For a case where the Wisconsin Supreme Court held that the estate, not the recipient, owed federal and Wisconsin death tax on an approximately $3,000,000 transfer-on-death account, see *Estate of Sheppard v. Schleis*, 782 N.W.2d 85 (Wis. 2010).
6. And these technically are not the only sections of the Internal Revenue Code that cause property to be included in a decedent's gross estate for federal estate tax purposes. Other sections include I.R.C. Section 2701(d), which applies to estate planning that involves certain recapitalizations of the equity interests in corporations and partnerships, and if I.R.C. Section 2701 created a "qualified payment" obligation that was not met, the suspense account value that is attributable to the missed required payments are includible in the decedent's gross estate under I.R.C. Section 2701(d). This does not add to or represent wealth that exists in the decedent's estate, yet it is included in the decedent's taxable estate. Under I.R.C. Section 2703, the mere failure of a buy-sell agreement to qualify under the safe harbor of I.R.C. Section 2703, namely, providing for a sales price between family members that is less than fair market value, could create a situation in which the interest in a closely held entity is sold for a price that is less than the amount includible in the decedent's gross estate due to the fair market value valuation. Another section that can present difficulty is I.R.C. Section 529, specifically I.R.C. Section 529(c)(4)(C), which pertains to a situation where a donor front loads some qualified tuition gifts but dies before the end of a five year period from the date of the transfer suffers inclusion of the value of the annual exclusion gifts deemed made by an election for periods after the decedent's death, even though this property is not a part of the probate estate and outside of the executor's control.
7. This provision covers property that would have been includable in the decedent's gross estate under either I.R.C. Sections 2036, 2037, 2038 or 2042 had the decedent not either transferred that property or surrendered all rights in it where the decedent dies within three years of the transfer or surrender.
8. This provision includes gift taxes on taxable gifts that the decedent made within three years of death. For an interesting case that deals with whether the gift tax included in the decedent's gross estate is even apportionable under applicable state death tax apportionment law, see *Sommers Est. v. Comm'r.*, T.C. Memo 2013-8, where the Tax Court determined that any determination on this issue was premature. Act Section 1(C) removes this item from the definition of "apportionable estate," which has the effect of apportioning that liability pursuant to the general rule of equitable apportionment under the Act absent a clear, unambiguous expression of intent to the contrary.
9. This provision includes the value of property that a decedent transferred but retained either the lifetime use or enjoyment of the property or the lifetime right to control who received the use or enjoyment of that property.
10. This provision includes the value of property transfers made that take effect at the decedent's death.
11. This provision includes the value of property that a decedent transferred but retained the lifetime right to alter, amend or revoke the transfer.
12. This provision includes the value of certain annuities and retirement plan benefits in the decedent's gross estate.
13. This provision includes the value of property that was transferred at death due to joint tenancy laws.
14. This provision includes the value of property over which the decedent held a general power of appointment at death, irrespective of whether that power lapsed, was exercised or relinquished.
15. This provision includes the value of life insurance that a decedent owned at death, was payable to or for the benefit of the decedent's estate or transferred where the decedent retained the incidence of ownership over the policy.
16. This provision includes the value of property in a surviving spouse's estate over which a QTIP election was made in the estate of the first spouse to die.
17. I.R.C. §6901.
18. I.R.C. §6324.
19. 31 U.S.C. §3713.
20. See, e.g., *Riggs v. del Drago*, 317 U.S. 95 (1942). However, for an example of where a state court punted on deciding who bore the estate tax in a blended family situation, see *Collier v. First National Bank*, 417 S.E. 2d 653 (Ga. 1992).
21. See, e.g., *In re Klarner*, 113 P. 3d 150 (Co. 2005); *In re Blauhorn Revocable Trust*, 746 N.W. 2d 136 (Neb. 2008); *In re Stark*, Docket No. A-3913-09T4 (N.J. App. 2011 unpub. op.).
22. See, e.g., *Lurie Est. v. Comm'r.*, 425 F.3d 1021 (7th Cir. 2005).
23. See, e.g., *In re Klarner*, 113 P.3d 150 (Colo. 2005).
24. I.R.C. §2207A(d).
25. I.R.C. §2207A(b).
26. Treas. Reg. §20.2207A-1(a)(2).
27. See, e.g., *In re Estate of Miller*, 595 N.E.2d 630 (Ill. App. 1992).
28. See, e.g., *In re Klarner*, 113 P.3d 150 (Co. 2005).
29. See, e.g., *Cleveland v. Compass Bank*, 652 So.2d 1134 (Ala. 1994); and *Hollis v. Forrester*, 914 So.2d 855 (Ala. 2005).
30. Adopted by the National Conference of Commissioners on Uniform State Laws adopted and endorsed for enactment by the states in 2003.

31. Act §2(2).
32. Act §2(3).
33. Act §2(1).
34. Act §3(a)(1).
35. Act §3(a)(2).
36. Act §3(3).
37. Act §4(1).
38. Act §4(2).
39. Act §4(3).
40. Act §4(4).
41. Act §5(1).
42. Act §5(2).
43. Act §5(3).
44. Act §6.
45. Act §7(b).
46. Act §7(c).
47. Act §8(a).
48. Act. §8(b).
49. Act §8(c).
50. Act §9(a).
51. Act §9(b).
52. Act §9(c).
53. Act §9(d).
54. Act §10(a).
55. Id.
56. Act § 10(b).
57. Act §11.
58. Treas. Reg. §20.2203-1.
59. I.R.C. §2044.
60. See, e.g., Treas. Reg. §20.2056(b)-4(c)(4). See, e.g., *Roberts Est. v. Comm'r.*, T.C. Memo 1983-167.
61. I.R.C. §2002.
62. For a different rule, see New York Estate Powers & Trusts Law, 2-1.8(d).
63. See, e.g., *Creighton University v. Kleinfeld*, 919 F. Supp. 1421 (E.D. Cal. 1995).
64. *Bandy v. Clancy*, 144 A.3d 802, 449 Md. 577 (2016); In the Matter of the Estate of Thomas L. Clancy, Jr., Estate Number 101962 (Orphans' Court for the City of Baltimore), August 21, 2015. For a discussion of this case, see Hood, L. Paul, Jr., "The Intersection of Estate Tax Apportionment and Blended Families, A Legal Thriller!," Steve Leimberg's Estate Planning Newsletter No. 2512 (Feb. 2, 2017).
65. See, e.g., *Eisenbach v. Schneider*, 166 P.3d 858 (Wash. Ct. App. 2007), where the court found that the decedent surviving spouse clearly intended proportional, rather than incremental, reimbursement.
66. I.R.C. §2207A(a)(2).
67. 637 N.E.2d 1301 (Ind. Ct. App. 1994).
68. 910 A.2d 634 (N.J. Ct. App. 2006).
69. Second Judicial District, District Court, County of Ramsey, Minnesota, Court File No. C5-04-200042, Apr. 23, 2007.
70. See, e.g., Louis A. Mezzullo, Steve Leimberg's Estate Planning Newsletter No. 1144 (2007).
71. Note that this is not the law in every state. For example, New York's law allows a non-testamentary document direction concerning apportionment of death tax to prime that of an earlier executed will. New York Estate Powers & Trusts Law, 2-1.8(d).
72. See, e.g., *Lurie Est. v. Comm'r.*, 425 F. 3d 1021 (7th Cir. 2005), where inclusion of the value of trusts over which the decedent had exercised a power of appointment shortly before death caused the loss of a marital deduction in a residuary marital legacy where the death tax was apportioned to the marital share, resulting in a circular computation that caused approximately $47,000,000 in death tax in a zeroed out estate tax liability on the federal estate tax return.
73. See, e.g., *Gordon v. Posner*, 790 A.2d 675 (Md. App. 2002); *Brunetti Est. v. Comm'r.*, T.C. Memo 1988-517.
74. See, e.g., *Stevenson v. Hall*, 473 P.2d 581(Wyo. 1970).
75. See Act §6(b).
76. Act §2(1).
77. Act §2(1)(A).
78. I.R.C. §642(g).
79. Act §2(1)(B).
80. Act §2(1)(C).

STATE DEATH TAXES

CHAPTER 26

26.1 WHAT IT IS

In light of the current high federal transfer tax applicable exclusion amount ($12,920,000 in 2023), very few people have to worry about the federal estate, gift or GST tax. However, many more people have to be concerned about a state death tax. At this time, thirty-three states[1] have either repealed their death taxes outright, or those taxes are tied to the former credit for state death taxes paid under now effectively repealed Code section 2011.[2] That provision effectively served as a revenue sharing device between the federal government and the state governments until its replacement with a deduction for state death taxes paid.[3] States that only had the so-called "soak up tax" in the amount of the credit for state death tax saw their tax revenues eliminated without new replacement tax legislation.

At this time, eighteen states (including the District of Columbia) still have either a state or local inheritance tax or state estate tax,[4] while one of those states has *both* an inheritance tax and estate tax.[5] Many of these states have "decoupled" their death tax schemes, i.e., separated themselves from the former credit for state death tax under effectively repealed Code section 2011.[6] Of the states that still have a state death tax, five states only have an inheritance tax,[7] while the rest of those states have an estate tax except for the state that has both types of death tax. There has been a trend of late that states are repealing their death taxes.[8] Whether that trend will continue is unknown in light of state budget deficits. The principal reasons why states have repealed their death taxes include overall tax reduction and an attempt to attract or retain more retirees to or for the state. Only Connecticut presently has a gift tax.[9]

26.2 DIFFERENCES BETWEEN AN ESTATE TAX AND AN INHERITANCE TAX

At the outset, it is important to note that the estate tax and the inheritance tax are *different* types of taxes and operate quite differently. An *estate tax* is an excise tax on the *transfer* of property by a decedent at death. The estate tax is assessed against the property in the estate (and certain types of property that pass to recipients effective at the decedent's death as well as certain transfers that are deemed to be gifts in contemplation of death within a short period of time, e.g., less than one year prior to death). The state estate tax is paid by the executor of the estate. Unlike the present federal transfer tax, state death taxes almost all are "progressive." That means the tax rates increase as the amount in the estate or amount inherited increases.

An *inheritance tax* is an excise tax on the value of property that a specific heir *inherits*. This differs slightly from an estate tax in that an estate tax is a tax on an entire estate *prior* to the division of assets among heirs. Inheritance tax rates and exemptions vary with the heir's legal relationship with the decedent. Inheritance tax statutes typically divide heirs into categories or "classes" based on their relationships to the decedent. The closest relatives (spouses and lineal relatives, such as children and grandchildren) generally are considered Class A; collateral relatives (siblings, nieces and nephews) as Class B; and more remote relatives and nonrelatives, as Class C. In an inheritance tax, the tax rate is *lowest* and exemption is *highest* for the closest legal relatives of the decedent, i.e., Class A relatives.

The inheritance tax exemption usually *decreases* and the tax rate usually *increases* the farther away the recipient gets from a close legal relationship with the decedent. Therefore, transfers to unrelated persons, who sometimes are referred to in statutes as "strangers," usually have the lowest exemption, if there even is one, as well as the highest tax rate, irrespective of the *actual* relationship between the recipient and the decedent. This can mean the tax impact on unmarried partners and step-children/descendants is *particularly* high. In some circumstances where a client wants to significantly favor a step-child or partner, the client should consider adopting the step-child and/or marrying the partner if saving state death tax is very important to the client.

26.3 HOW DOES IT WORK?

State Estate Taxes Generally: Tax Base and Rates

The details of state estate taxes vary somewhat from state to state. But they tend to follow the pattern of equaling the amount of the repealed federal credit for state death taxes under effectively repealed Code section 2011 with varying exemption amounts. Five states have estate taxes with state-defined exemption amounts and rate schedules, i.e., rate schedules that vary from the former federal credit schedule under effectively repealed Code section 2011. The tax base for the state estate taxes (aside from the exemption amounts) generally parallels that of the federal estate tax, and most states use the old credit for state death taxes paid rates under effectively repealed Code section 2011 as their tax rates.[10] Four states, Connecticut (which, beginning in 2023, has a flat rate of 12 percent), Hawaii (which has rates that range from 10-20 percent), Maine (which has rates ranging from 8-12 percent) and Washington (which has rates ranging from 10-20 percent), deviate from the top rate under effectively repealed Code section 2011 credit for state death taxes of 16 percent (taxed at estate levels that equal or exceed $10,100,000).

Several states have totally "decoupled" from the former Code section 2011 rates and impose a set of free standing estate tax rates.

There is an anomaly in the eleven states that employ the table of Code section 2011 credit rates (.8-16 percent) that usually results in higher *effective* marginal state estate tax rates for estate values that only slightly exceed that of the next bracket threshold. This is due to the way that the former credit for state death tax under effectively repealed Code section 2011 was computed. That credit was equal to the *lesser* of the table credit amount or the amount of total federal estate tax due, which, for most, but not all, states, is based upon pre-2001 federal estate tax rates.

As a result, the marginal tax estate rate for a state that has, e.g., a $1,000,000 exemption, e.g., Oregon, is high on values of an estate just over $1,000,000 until the full state death tax credit amount is reached for that size estate, which can result in a substantial amount of additional state estate tax due. For states that have estate tax exemptions of at least $2,000,000, the marginal estate tax rates will be higher or lower, depending upon which version of federal tax computation that state uses for the limitation—the 2001 version or the 2011 version, because the applicable federal estate tax rates for those versions differ. For example, the rates under the 2001 estate tax tables effectively ranged from 37-55 percent, while the 2010 Tax Act's rate was 35 percent. However, Maryland has limited its estate tax so that the marginal rates do not exceed the top 16 percent top estate tax credit rate, unless the federal death tax credit actually applies. State-defined estate taxes[11] that have completely decoupled and that do not use the former Code section 2011 table rates should not have this issue.

State estate tax exemption amounts set forth below vary (Nebraska's inheritance tax is local). Some are flat amounts, but most are adjusted for inflation, albeit on different bases and vastly different inflation indices (. Presently, only Connecticut has an exemption amount that is tied to the federal estate tax applicable exclusion amount.

DC	$4,528,800*
HI	5,490,000***
ME	$6,410,000*
NY	$6,580,000##
IL	$4,000,000#
MD	$5,000,000#
VT	$5,000,000#
CT	12,920,000**
MN	$3,000,000#
WA	$2,193,000@
RI	$1,733,264###
MA, OR	$1,000,000#

STATE DEATH TAXES CHAPTER 26

*: 2023 amount, per statute, $5,600,000, adjusted for inflation for decedents dying on and after January 1, 2018

**: 2023 amount, tied to the federal estate tax applicable exclusion amount.

***Ambiguous and possibly wrong. On April 21, 2022, the governor signed SB 3143, which conformed Hawaii's estate and GST tax laws to the laws of the Internal Revenue Code beginning for tax years after December 31, 2021. Yet, the instructions to Hawaii's Form M-6, Hawaii Estate Tax Return, confirm that the Hawaii exclusion amount remains at $5,490,000 for 2023.

Per statute, not indexed.

Federal estate tax applicable exclusion amount prior to the 2017 Tax Act which is $5,000,000 adjusted for inflation.

$1,500,000 indexed for inflation in 2015.

@ On December 18, 2018, the Department of Revenue sent an email stating that pursuant to Revised Code of Washington (RCW) 83.100, the Department must adjust the Washington applicable estate tax exclusion amount annually using the Seattle-Tacoma-Bremerton metropolitan area October consumer price index (Seattle CPI). As of January 1, 2018, the US Bureau of Labor and Statistics (USBLS) no longer calculates the consumer price index for the Seattle-Tacoma-Bremerton metropolitan area. Instead, the USBLS will calculate the consumer price index for the Seattle-Tacoma-Bellevue Core Based Statistical Area for the Puget Sound region. As a result of these changes, the definition of "consumer price index" in RCW 83.100.020(1)(b) does not match with the current CPI measure calculated by the USBLS. The Department is using the last CPI figure for the Seattle CPI. This resulted in no increase in the applicable exclusion amount for 2019 and subsequent years.

See the discussion below about the taxation of gifts in contemplation of death.

State Estate Tax QTIP Elections

States also differ quite a bit with respect to the availability of a QTIP marital deduction for transfers for the benefit of a surviving spouse. Three states, i.e., the District of Columbia, New York, and Vermont, do not allow *any* state estate tax QTIP election. However, a number of states do allow a QTIP election to be made at the state estate tax level. The following states permit a full QTIP election by statute: Connecticut, Illinois, Maine (allows a state QTIP that differs from the federal election, but only if no federal QTIP election is made), Maryland, Massachusetts, New Jersey, New York (only permitted for estates that do not file a federal estate tax return), Oregon, Pennsylvania and Washington. Hawaii, Kentucky, Massachusetts, Minnesota, and Rhode Island permit a state estate tax QTIP election by administrative pronouncement.

State Inheritance Taxes Generally; Tax Rates; Tax Base

There is a wide variance in the inheritance tax states regarding all aspects of their respective inheritance tax schemes. However, as a general rule, surviving spouses and lineal descendants are favored both from the standpoint of higher exemptions (and, in some cases, wholesale exemptions) as well as lower tax rates. As noted earlier, other more remote legal relatives are usually given a smaller exemption and are taxed at higher rates. Finally, unrelated heirs are treated the worst from the standpoint of exemptions and tax rates. For example, the exemptions for surviving spouses and lineal heirs (typically, parents, children and grandchildren of the decedent) in four states (Iowa, Kentucky, Maryland and New Jersey) eliminate tax liability altogether for what are usually the heirs. This exemption can dramatically reduce the burden of the inheritance tax. However, Maryland also has an estate tax that can apply.

What follows are the rules for the states that have an inheritance tax:

> **Iowa:** wholly exempts class A heirs from the inheritance tax, taxes class B heirs at rates from 5-10 percent with no exemption and class C heirs at rates from 10-15 percent with no exemption.
>
> **Kentucky:** wholly exempts transfers to class A heirs, but taxes class B heirs at rates from 4-16 percent after a $1,000 exemption and class C heirs at rates from 6-16 percent after a $500 exemption.
>
> **Maryland:** as noted above, also has an estate tax, wholly exempts lineal heirs from tax but taxes all other heirs at 10 percent with no exemption.
>
> **Nebraska:** collected at the county level, Nebraska taxes "immediate relatives" at

439

1 percent after a $40,000 exemption, "remote relatives" at 13 percent after a $15,000 exemption and all others at 18 percent after a $10,000 exemption.

New Jersey: used to have four classes of heirs, ranging from A-D. Class B was eliminated, so the remaining classes of heirs are A, C and D. Class A heirs are wholly exempt, class C heirs are taxed at rates from 11-16 percent after a $25,000 exemption and class D heirs are taxed at rates from 15-16 percent after a $500 exemption. However, New Jersey's inheritance tax only applies to estates of $1,000,000 or more.

Pennsylvania: taxes lineal heirs at 4.5 percent after a $3,500 exemption, siblings at 12 percent with no exemption and all others at 15 percent with no exemption.

State Inheritance Tax QTIP Elections

The following states allow a QTIP marital deduction against the inheritance tax by statute: Pennsylvania and Tennessee. Kentucky permits a QTIP marital deduction against the inheritance tax by administrative pronouncement.

Taxation of Gifts in Contemplation of Death

At this time, nine states attempt to include gifts in contemplation of death in their estate or inheritance tax base.[12] The time periods for these attempted inclusions vary. The rules for each state are as follows:

Iowa (inheritance tax): Transfers above the federal gift tax annual exclusion that are made within three years of death, other than bona fide sales, are taxable.

Kentucky (inheritance tax): Transfers of a material part of an estate that are made within three years of death are construed prima facie to have been made in contemplation of death.

Maryland (estate and inheritance taxes): Gifts made within two years of the date of death are taxable under the inheritance tax.

Massachusetts (estate tax): Transfers (including exercises of powers of appointment) that are made within three years of the decedent's death are included in the gross estate.

Nebraska (inheritance tax): Gifts that are made within three years of the date of death are subject to inheritance taxation.

New Jersey (inheritance tax): Transfers within three years of death are deemed to have been made in contemplation of death, absent proof to the contrary.

Pennsylvania (inheritance tax): Transfers greater than $3,000 made within one year of date of death are taxable.

State Generation Skipping Transfer (GST) Taxes

In addition to the federal GST tax, three states, Illinois, Nebraska, and Vermont assess and collect a GST tax. All other states that had state GST taxes that were tied to the credit for state GST tax under effectively repealed Code Section 2604 lost their GST tax revenue when Code Section 2604 was effectively repealed for deaths occurring after December 31, 2004.

Portability and State Death Taxes

As of this time, only Hawaii and Maryland recognize portability for state death tax purposes.

Importance of Determination of Domicile

Decedents may have contacts, e.g., homes, etc., in multiple states or countries, but a decedent almost always will be considered by one or more states as *domiciled* in a state. The problem is that *more* than one state may claim that the decedent was domiciled in their state and attempt to assess a state estate or inheritance tax on the decedent's *entire* estate instead of just on the decedent's real estate located in that state. It does not take much of an estate to trigger significant amounts of state estate or inheritance tax in a state that has a death tax. The mobility of individuals in today's society, as well as the divide between states that do not have a death tax and states that do have a death tax, increases the likelihood that upon a decedent's death, more than one state will claim the decedent as a "domiciliary," and it more often than not is a state that has a death tax. This can be of particular concern when a decedent allegedly moved from a state that has a death tax to a state that has no death tax, e.g., from New York to Florida, but retained a home, earned income or spent substantial time in the state where the decedent formerly resided on a permanent basis, e.g., New York.

Status as a "domiciliary" is a crucial determinant when it is time for a state to assess a death tax. For this purpose, certain tangible personal property and almost all real estate usually are taxed in the state in which that property is located, *regardless* of the owner's "domicile." However, for *intangible* property—such as stocks, bonds and bank accounts, death taxes are assessed by the state of the decedent's "domicile." However, a number of states, including Maine, Minnesota and New York, will tax intangible property such as entities or trusts that hold real estate that is situated in the state. Generally, the term "domicile" refers to the place that an individual *intends* to be his or her permanent home, or the place to which he or she intends to return after an absence.

This is distinguished from the term "residence," because many individuals have multiple homes that are located in different states. While a decedent may simultaneously have residences in many states, from a theoretical standpoint, a decedent *should* only have one state of domicile, although sometimes one could make a compelling argument that a decedent actually possessed two domiciles. The problem in estate tax domicile cases is that the decedent is no longer around, and the estate has to live or die in the domicile determination based upon the facts and documentation of the decedent's actions while alive.

Under the laws of most states, an individual's domicile may be changed *only* by relocating to a new state with the bona fide *intention* of making a *fixed and permanent* home there, i.e., a new domicile. Unfortunately, the domicile determination often is not clear cut, and, in many cases, is absolutely unclear. For example, suppose the children of an elderly resident of New York move their parent from a nursing home in New York to a nursing home in Florida. However, the parent dies owning a home in New York, registered to vote in New York (the parent never registered to vote in Florida) and still has mail addressed to New York but forwarded from New York to Florida. But the parent also owned a home in Florida. Did the parent do enough to affirmatively change his or her domicile to Florida at death? Let's muddle the facts a little more. Assume that the parent lacked legal capacity to understand the implications of the move, and the children moved the parent under the auspices of a power of attorney. Same result? Suppose that the power of attorney *expressly* authorizes the agent to change the decedent's domicile. Same result? You should get the picture that domicile determinations often come in many shades of grey.

The problems in these domicile determination cases are two-fold. First, the executor of the decedent's estate usually bears the burden of proof that the decedent possessed the requisite necessary intention to change domicile from one state to another. Complicating matters is that many states have a *rebuttable* presumption that the decedent did not intend to change his or her domicile. States that have a death tax are notoriously aggressive when it comes to fighting domicile cases because of the revenue implications, which often are significant.

The actual legal definition of domicile often varies from one state to state, and the question of domicile depends *entirely* upon the peculiar facts of each case. Domicile cases are among the *most* fact-intensive in probate and tax law. Unfortunately, different states can view the same set of facts differently and take conflicting positions on whether a decedent was domiciled in a particular state, resulting in inconsistent determinations, with each state sometimes claiming that the decedent was domiciled in their state. If the states involved have passed part or all of the old Uniform Interstate Compromise of Death Taxes Act (1943), the states may work out a compromise between themselves as to how the decedent's state death taxes will be apportioned and, if applicable, divided. However, the estate may well pay death taxes at the rates of the highest state and could end up paying full death taxes to each state or at least fighting double taxation in each state – with the consequent expense and aggravation.

The domicile determination is based upon a consideration of the totality of the circumstances. The following is a list of the affirmative steps that a client who desires to evince an intention to change domicile can take:

- **Voter registration and political involvement:** It always is helpful to the argument that the decedent took the *affirmative* steps required to obtain voter registration in the new state of domicile, and *actually* voted there (and, just as important, *stopped* voting in the former state of domicile). If that change also brought a change in the decedent's political involvement, campaign contributions and volunteer involvement, to matters of the new state of domicile, so much the better;

- **Principal business/personal activities:** To the extent possible, the decedent should have relocated the hub of his or her business activities, e.g., banking, safety deposit, professional, e.g., doctors, lawyers and accountants, and investment relationships, to the new state of domicile, although this is not always determinative due to the prevalence of interstate national banking and financial institutions as well as the increasing incidence of on-line accounts;

- **Multiple residences:** People often are going to have multiple residences in several states, but it usually is best that the decedent's *nicest* home be located in the new state of domicile;

- **Time spent in the state/physical presence:** This factor is critical! The *actual* amount of time that the decedent spent in each state often plays a pivotal role in the domicile determination. The *more* time that the decedent spent in the new state of domicile, the better, and the decedent's calendars can be critical in this determination;

- **Principal center of social affairs:** The question often comes up as to where the decedent belonged to a synagogue, church or mosque or social and/or civic organizations, and the more concentrated the most current social, religious and civic involvement there is in the new state of domicile, the better;

- **Mail and deliveries:** The place where the decedent got the bulk of his or her regular mail and deliveries often plays an important role in divining intention with respect to domicile issues, particularly where there is evidence of the decedent taking affirmative steps to change his or her address with all third parties;

- **Taxes:** The state in which the decedent actually filed as a *resident* on federal and state income tax returns also is an important piece of evidence since that is wholly within the decedent's control to act as per his or her domicile intentions as well as that tax returns are signed under penalties of perjury. So if a decedent consistently filed in state X as a non-resident as to his or her income sited to that state and then changed tax status to that of a resident, then that is strong evidence of domiciliary intent as to that state;

- **Wills and other legal documents:** The state in which the decedent executed important legal documents such as wills, entity formation and annual reporting documents and marriage contracts, in which he or she had to affirmatively state a state of domicile can be very important. However, note that the state in which the last will or trust was drafted often is not determinative without looking at other pieces of evidence of domiciliary intent because people often do not execute new wills, for example, every time that they relocate to a new state;

- **Consistency:** Where the decedent was the most *consistent* in his or her domiciliary claims often plays a vital role in spelling out that decedent's intentions in that regard because consistency is strong evidence of actual intent, and, just as important, inconsistent behavior can give rise to a failure to rebut the presumption of change of domicile;

- **Homestead exemption:** A decedent should have claimed a homestead exemption in only *one* state. That fact is not necessarily determinative by itself. But planners should note the implications of surrendering homestead, i.e. it usually costs the decedent money to become a non-resident of that state, i.e., rent control, and other rights associated with property in the former state of domicile;

- **Affidavits of domicile change and domicile registration:** It always is helpful if the decedent took affirmative steps to *both* divorce himself or herself from the former state of domicile and to register in the new state of domicile by filing affidavits of domicile change in *both* places;

- **Judicial claims and actions:** If the decedent was actively involved either as a plaintiff or defendant in legal proceedings, then the claimed state of domicile in those proceedings is another piece of evidence of domiciliary intent since these representations often are made under penalties of perjury;

- **Other factors:** Sometimes, other facts such as the place where the decedent was buried, if the decedent selected and paid for the funeral and burial services, where the decedent's children went to school, where the decedent's family primarily resides as well as a whole host of possible other facts can loom large in the contested domicile case.

Blended family situations can present some unusual domicile situations, particularly where the couple was separately domiciled in different states before getting together. Where is the domicile of the relationship? The answer to that question can be very important in the domicile determination in a close case.

CHAPTER ENDNOTES

1. The states that have no death tax at this time are Alabama, Alaska, Arizona, Arkansas, California, Colorado, Delaware, Florida, Georgia, Idaho, Indiana, Kansas, Louisiana, Michigan, Mississippi, Missouri, Montana, Nevada, New Hampshire, New Mexico, North Carolina, North Dakota, Ohio, Oklahoma, South Carolina, South Dakota, Tennessee, Texas, Utah, Virginia, West Virginia, Wisconsin and Wyoming.
2. I.R.C. § 2011(f) terminated the credit for state death tax for deaths occurring after December 31, 2004.
3. I.R.C. § 2058.
4. The states are Connecticut, District of Columbia, Hawaii, Illinois, Iowa, Kentucky, Maine, Maryland, Massachusetts, Minnesota, Nebraska, New Jersey, New York, Oregon, Pennsylvania, Rhode Island, Vermont and Washington.
5. The state that has both an estate tax and an inheritance tax is Maryland. However, those taxes are not duplicative of one another, and the estate tax allows a deduction for the amount of state inheritance tax paid.
6. These states are Connecticut, Oregon and Washington.
7. Iowa, Kentucky, Nebraska, and Pennsylvania.
8. Tennessee repealed its death tax (effective for deaths after December 31, 2015, with an increasing exemption until then). Tennessee also increases the exemption amounts each year, decreasing the number of bequests that are subject to tax until the tax fully phased out in 2016. Additionally, Ohio's repeal of its death tax went into effect for deaths after December 31, 2012. The latest trend is that more states are adopting exemptions more in line with the federal estate tax applicable exclusion amount.
9. Connecticut. The gift tax exemption in Connecticut is $2,000,000, and the tax rate is 12 percent. However, Connecticut imposed a $20,000,000 cap per person on the amount of gift and estate tax that can be collected, although legislation has been enacted to reduce the cap to $15,000,000.
10. Those rates begin at 0 for estates of $100,000 or less and gradually rise, e.g., 8 percent between $2,100,000 and $2,600,000, until hitting the top 16 percent rate for estates that exceed $10,100,000.
11. Connecticut, Hawaii, Maine, Oregon and Washington.
12. Connecticut taxes all lifetime gifts. The other states attempt to include gifts that are made in contemplation of death or made within a short period prior to death.

MARITAL DEDUCTION AND BYPASS TRUSTS

CHAPTER 27

27.1 INTRODUCTION

The marital/nonmarital trust (also commonly referred to as the "A-B trust" or more currently sometimes the "A-B-Q" trust) is an arrangement designed to give the surviving spouse almost total use of the family's economic wealth, while at the same time minimizing, to the extent possible, the total federal estate tax payable at the deaths of both spouses.

Married couples can usually eliminate federal estate taxes entirely at the death of the first spouse to die through a carefully considered plan capitalizing on the combination of the unlimited marital deduction and the unified credit. The marital deduction is a deduction for gift or estate tax purposes for property passing to (or in a qualifying trust for) a spouse. The unified credit is a credit provided to each U.S citizen or resident, which can be used against either gift taxes or estate taxes. The use of the unified credit to reduce gift taxes correspondingly reduces the amount available to reduce estate taxes. The estate tax unified credit applies as follows:

	Unified Credit	Applicable Exclusion Amount
2004-2005	555,800	1,500,000
2006-2008	780,800	2,000,000
2009	1,455,800	3,500,000
2010	1,730,800	5,000,000
2011	1,730,800	5,000,000
2012	1,772,800	5,120,000
2013	2,045,800	5,250,000
2014	2,081,800	5,340,000
2015	2,117,800	5,430,000
2016	2,125,800	5,450,000
2017	2,141,800	5,490,000
2018	4,417,800	11,180,000
2019	11,400,000	4,505,800
2020	4,577,800	11,580,000
2021	4,625,800	11,700,000
2022	4,769,800	12,060,000
2023	5,113,800	12,920,000

Current Planning Techniques

The most common arrangement for a marital/bypass trust is to fund the bypass trust with an amount equal to the estate tax unified credit applicable exclusion (the 2023 unified credit equates to exempting $12,920,000 of assets), because the tax on those assets will be eliminated by the unified credit. The assets in the bypass trust are not taxed at the surviving spouse's death because the trust is specifically designed so that the surviving spouse has no rights sufficient to cause inclusion. The balance of the decedent's assets will go to the marital trust tax-free – because of the unlimited marital deduction. However, assets in the marital trust will be subject to estate tax at the death of the surviving spouse because of the broad powers the survivor is given in the trust.

Some couples may prefer to pay some tax at the death of the first spouse to die (since some of the taxed portion will be taxed at the lowest federal estate tax rates instead of being shifted to the surviving spouse's estate and added "on top" of the assets the survivor already owns). However, it will be rare when the payment of an "up front" tax will be advantageous and rarer still when the parties have the willingness and ability to pay any tax before its time. One reason that paying a tax at the first death rarely makes sense is that the surviving spouse often will use up the additional assets received

445

or gift them to others. The vast majority of "younger" couples may decide to accept the possibility of paying more estate tax at the second death to avoid the imposition of any tax at the death of the first spouse to die. This is obviously an important decision to review with the spouses at length by the estate planner.

Generally, the marital deduction applies to property passing outright to a surviving spouse, or in a manner that is tantamount to outright – such as in a qualifying marital trust for the spouse. One type of trust, the general power of appointment trust, gives the surviving spouse a right to the trust's income for life coupled with a power to appoint the trust property during lifetime or at death to *anyone* the surviving spouse wishes. In a second type of marital deduction trust, an estate trust, the surviving spouse receives income only, with only a testamentary right to name the recipient of the remaining property in the will. In a third type of marital deduction trust, a qualifying terminable interest property (QTIP) trust, the spouse receives income for life, but need not be given a testamentary power of appointment over the property. Typically, the spouse creating the trust specifies the identity of the remainderman. Thus, with a QTIP trust, the first (original property owning) spouse to die can control the disposition of the trust property following the death of the surviving spouse. This is particularly appealing in second and late-life marriages.

Many decedents want to ensure that at least some of the marital deduction property passes to chosen beneficiaries at the surviving spouse's death. In such a case, use of a QTIP trust is often beneficial. The balance of the marital deduction property would fund a separate trust (often called "Trust A") that the surviving spouse would be in control of its ultimate disposition via a power of appointment.

Thus, a formula will often determine the funding of the "B" trust (also known as a "family trust" or a "credit shelter trust") with the amount of the estate tax applicable exemption ($12,920,000 in 2023) at the death of the first spouse. This trust can provide income to the surviving spouse (and if desirable, give the surviving spouse some limited power of disposition to other people and/or the power to take out each year the greater of $5,000 or 5 percent of the trust principal). Despite these benefits provided to the surviving spouse, the remainder of the "B" trust will generally escape taxation at the surviving spouse's death.

If the goal is to have no estate tax at the first death, and if the decedent desires that either *all* marital deduction property or *no* marital deduction property should be subject to the surviving spouse's power of appointment, only one marital deduction or "A" Trust would be required, because the same rules will pertain to all property.

However, if the goal is to give the surviving spouse a power of disposition over only a *portion* of the assets, then the portion subject to the power can fund the typical marital or "A" trust, with the balance funding a QTIP or "Q" trust. Both trusts will qualify for the marital deduction with the remainder to be included in the survivor's estate at death. Either or both of these trusts can provide for invasion of principal for the benefit of the survivor, but only the "A" trust will be subject to a power of disposition (i.e., a power of appointment), at the survivor's death.

In some cases, the goal may be to restrict the power of appointment held by the surviving spouse so that some portion of the trust assets may only be appointed to and among family members of the grantor-spouse. While this is the typical way to structure the power, the power may be drafted more broadly. For example, the broadest power that a surviving spouse can hold and yet keep the property subject to this power out of the estate is the power to appoint the property to anyone other than the spouse, creditors, or the estate, and the creditors of the estate.[1]

Often a "pourover will" is used in conjunction with a revocable trust, meaning the grantor's will provides that the grantor's residuary estate (the amount remaining after debts, expenses, taxes, and specific bequests have been paid) is to be "poured over" into the revocable trust. The trust instrument provides the residuary estate property will then divide into two (or three) parts: a portion will fund the marital or "A" trust, a portion will fund the family or "B" trust, and if appropriate, a portion will fund the QTIP trust. The QTIP trust portion will qualify for the marital deduction to be distributed at the survivor's death to beneficiaries named by the grantor in the trust instrument (e.g., to the grantor's children).

The revocable A-B or A-B-QTIP trust may also take the form of a life insurance trust coupled with a "pourover will." In such a case, the corpus of the trust is a life insurance policy(ies) on the grantor's life and the trust is named as the beneficiary of the life insurance policy(ies). Upon the grantor's death, the grantor's residuary estate will be "poured over" into the revocable trust. The residuary estate and the life insurance proceeds will then split to fund the A-B or the A-B-QTIP trusts depending on the terms of the trust.

Whether to use a revocable trust to hold non-insurance assets to avoid probate depends on whether the other assets may be subjected to the costs, delays, and publicity that usually accompany probate.

27.2 WHEN IS USE OF SUCH A DEVICE INDICATED?

1. When the goal is (1) to ensure the survivor has complete economic benefit of, and control over, the family's wealth, (2) reduce or eliminate the aggregate death taxes of both spouses at their respective deaths, and (3) a portability election may not be sufficient to achieve all planning goals.

   If one spouse leaves all property to the other spouse, the unlimited marital deduction will result in no estate tax being due. However, this can result the estate underutilizing the unified credit and unnecessarily increasing the total estate tax due at the second death. With the permanence of portability, however, a surviving spouse can use the unused exclusion of the predeceased spouse, or the Deceased Spouse's Unused Exemption (DSUE). Under current law, a portability election can allow a married couple to shelter $25,840,000 in 2023, making portability a viable planning option for couples without substantial estates.

   While portability can simplify estate planning, it is not without some negative aspects. First, assets passing in trust for the benefit of the surviving spouse are protected from that spouse's creditors. Although some states protect assets that are held jointly from the reach of one spouse's creditors, the trust structure often provides more comprehensive protection. Second, marital trust planning can help to ensure that assets, including any appreciation between the deaths of the spouses, are not subject to estate tax upon the death of the surviving spouse. In contrast, relying upon the portability provisions, the amount of assets shielded from the estate tax remains fixed, and any appreciation in excess of the exclusion amount available at the death of the surviving spouse will be subject to estate tax. Moreover, if the surviving spouse remarries, assets held in a credit shelter trust (as opposed to assets that passed outright to the surviving spouse) will presumably pass to the children of the deceased spouse rather than to the new spouse. If the surviving spouse remarries, remarriage resets the portability amount to the DSUE of the new spouse, which may be lower than the DSUE of the first spouse, resulting in a loss of the first spouse's exemption.[2] Finally, portability provisions do not apply to the generation skipping transfer tax exemption.

   Therefore, there are many factors to consider when deciding whether or not to rely on the portability provisions or to implement a traditional marital deduction and bypass trust. A traditional A-B or A-B-QTIP trust arrangement allows for the B trust assets to pass to the named beneficiaries estate tax free at the surviving spouse's death and defers the payment of estate tax on the marital deduction trusts (i.e. the A trust or the QTIP trust) until the surviving spouse's death. This may result in no estate tax being due at the first spouse's death.

2. If the estate plan includes creating generation-skipping trusts (see Chapter 21), the generation-skipping transfer tax exemption of the first spouse to die can be lost if the property passes outright to the surviving spouse, or in any marital deduction trust other than QTIP.

3. If the goal is to achieve favorable state death tax treatment, in some states it would be prudent to distribute property to a marital trust (even if it grants the surviving with a general power of appointment over the assets) instead of outright to a spouse. In some states, property subject to a decedent's general power of appointment is not subject to state death tax. For example, in Pennsylvania, even though a surviving spouse could exercise the general power of appointment for his or her own benefit, it may be possible to structure the trust so that any property remaining in the marital trust would not be subject to state inheritance tax at the death of such spouse. Thus, in states such as Pennsylvania, in lieu of an outright bequest to the surviving spouse, it may be preferable to bequeath those assets in a marital trust coupled with a general power of appointment over such assets.

   On the other hand, although a majority of states provide for tax-free inter-spousal transfers, similar to the federal estate tax rules, the remainder of a marital trust is subject to state death tax at the death of the surviving spouse.

4. If the management of trust property for the benefit of the surviving spouse or other trust beneficiaries is desired or needed.

5. If the goal is to avoid the expense and delay of probate, consideration should be given to transferring title of assets to a revocable *inter vivos* trust containing death tax minimization provisions. If the property is transferred prior to the decedent's death, probate proceedings with respect to such property is not required.

6. If one spouse is a non-U.S. citizen. (See "Planning for Non-U.S. Persons," Chapter 72.)

7. If the goal of the first spouse to die is to benefit the survivor spouse but leave the remainder to the first spouse's children (or some other beneficiary) rather than the new spouse or other beneficiary of the surviving spouse.

8. If the goal is to defer making the decision of whether to pay some estate tax at the first spouse's death (thus lowering the estate tax due at the surviving spouse's death).

27.3 WHAT ARE THE REQUIREMENTS FOR MARITAL DEDUCTION TRUSTS?

There are three types of trusts that will qualify for the marital deduction–the "power of appointment" trust, the "estate" trust, and the QTIP trust, with the latter being the most popular.

1. *Power of Appointment Trust – Requirements*

    (a) The surviving spouse must be entitled to all of the income produced by the assets of the trust (note that the law states "all of the income" not "all of the net income").[3]

    (b) The income produced by the trust must be payable at least annually.

    (c) The surviving spouse must be given a general power of appointment (during lifetime, at death, or both) exercisable in favor of the spouse or the spouse's estate, or the creditors of the spouse or the spouse's estate. The spouse does not have to be given the power to withdraw the principal during lifetime (i.e., an *inter vivos* power of appointment).[4]

    (d) The power must be exercisable by the surviving spouse in all events.

    (e) No person may have any power to appoint any part of the trust assets to any person other than the surviving spouse.[5]

    A decedent can provide a power of appointment over trust assets but require that to exercise the power the donee's will (or a different instrument) must make specific reference to such power. This is important because, in some states, if the donee's will contains a residuary clause (leaving all property not otherwise bequeathed) such clause is deemed to exercise a general power of appointment automatically absent a specific stated intention not to exercise it. In other words, in certain states, unless the provision in a decedent's will or trust requiring the donee of a power to specifically refer to the power, the donee is deemed to have exercised the power in favor of the recipient(s) of the residuary estate.

2. *Estate Trust – Requirements*[6]

    (a) The trust must provide for income to the surviving spouse for life (payable to, or accumulated for, the surviving spouse's benefit).

    (b) The remainder of the trust (both principal and any accumulated income) must be payable to the surviving spouse's estate at the surviving spouse's death.

    An estate trust falls outside the terminable interest rules (that if applicable would preclude a marital deduction) because no interest passes to anyone other than the spouse and the spouse's estate.[7] This type of trust provides the trustee with the flexibility to accumulate income or invest trust assets in non-income-producing property. However, accumulations of income will be considered as additional corpus includible in the surviving spouse's estate at the surviving spouse's death.

    The estate marital trust is indicated where (i) there is a need or desire to invest in non-income-producing property, (ii) the survivor will not need trust assets or income during the survivor's lifetime, and (iii) the property placed into the trust is not likely to appreciate substantially in value.

3. *Qualified Terminable Interest Property (QTIP) Trust – Requirements*

The marital deduction is generally unavailable for a "terminable" interest, i.e., an interest in property that terminates due to the passage of time, the occurrence of a particular event, or the failure of an event to occur. However, a surviving spouse's interest can terminate at his or her death and still qualify for the marital deduction as long as the interest is a "qualified" terminable interest property (QTIP) trust meeting certain requirements:

(a) That the surviving spouse be entitled to all income for the spouse's entire life, payable at least annually, and not subject to any contingencies.

(b) However, there is no requirement to grant the surviving spouse a power of appointment of any kind, either limited or general.

(c) During the surviving spouse's lifetime, there must be no power to direct any trust property to anyone other than the surviving spouse.

(d) The spouse must have the power to require the trustee to produce income from the trust assets.

(e) Assuming all the QTIP requirements are met, the executor must irrevocably elect to have the trust treated as a QTIP trust by listing the trust and its value on Schedule M of the estate tax return.

With this type of trust, because there is no requirement to grant the surviving spouse a power of appointment, at the death of the survivor, the grantor spouse is assured that the remainder of the trust will go to the children or wherever the grantor decides (and not to the survivor's new spouse if he or she remarries, which may be the case with the power of appointment trust or the estate trust). As with the other marital trusts, at the surviving spouse's death, the remaining corpus must be included in the estate.

4. *Other General Requirements*

Assets in the marital trust must pass to or be held for the benefit of the decedent's surviving spouse–the person who is married to the decedent at the decedent's death.[8] Although this requirement appears simple to determine, it has been the cause of extensive litigation because of the increasing frequency of divorce and persons living together without formal marriage that is now prevalent in our society.

Furthermore, the decedent's spouse must survive the decedent. In the event of a common accident (such as a plane or car crash) when it is impossible to ascertain who dies first, the Uniform Simultaneous Death Act (the law in most states) would raise a presumption that neither spouse survived the other and therefore, would defeat the marital deduction. The application of such Act can be overcome by inserting into the documents creating the marital trust (e.g., the revocable trust) a survivorship clause that creates a presumption that, for purposes of the marital deduction, the spouse is deemed to survive if it is not possible to establish the order of deaths.[9]

27.4 HOW ARE BYPASS AND MARITAL TRUSTS CREATED AND FUNDED

Although there are a number of ways to accomplish the same objective, the life insurance trust/pourover will combination is a popular technique. In this arrangement, an individual creates an inter vivos trust and names the trust as beneficiary of a life insurance policy(ies) (the grantor is the insured). Upon the grantor's death, the death benefit is paid directly to the trust. The grantor's other probate assets are "poured over" by will into the trust. The trust is then split into two (or three) parts creating; the "A" or appointment trust, a "B" or family (also called nonmarital or bypass) trust, and, in some cases, the "Q" or QTIP trust. If the inter vivos trust was controlled by the insured grantor (or he or she retained incidents of ownership), the death benefit is included in the insured's estate for estate tax purposes. Alternatively, if the trust is structured as an irrevocable life insurance trust and the grantor-insured never had any incidents of ownership over the insurance and he or she did not transfer an existing policy to the trust within three years of death, the death benefits are not included in his or her gross estate.

A – The Survivor's Property Trust or Power of Appointment Trust

The A trust, or power of appointment trust, is the primary vehicle for receiving the marital deduction assets -unless the very popular QTIP trust is used. If the QTIP is funded with the marital deduction assets, the A trust often will hold the surviving spouse's own property, particularly in community property states, in order to provide unified management of the assets.

The A trust distributes all trust income to the surviving spouse for life. If the A trust is funded with marital deduction assets, the pourover trust would likely implement a funding formula to ensure that the A trust, together with any QTIP trust, would receive just enough property to reduce the federal estate tax at the death of the first spouse to die to zero.

With respect to the A trust, the surviving spouse will be granted a power of appointment exercisable by will or other written instrument to designate who will receive the corpus of the marital trust upon his or her death (including the surviving spouse's estate). Additionally, the surviving spouse may be given the right to withdraw any part of the corpus during his or her lifetime. Finally, the provision granting the surviving spouse the general power of appointment usually provides that if the surviving spouse fails to exercise the power of appointment, the remaining corpus in the appointment trust will pass to beneficiaries designated by the grantor.

B – The Bypass Trust

The second trust, often called the "B," bypass, nonmarital, or family trust, is funded with property not allocated to the power of appointment trust, the estate trust, or the QTIP trust. That amount is usually equal to the applicable estate tax exclusion ($12,920,000 in 2023 – assuming no taxable lifetime gifts were made). Because the surviving spouse's interest in the trust terminates at his or her death and he or she does not hold a general power of appointment over the trust property, none of the remaining trust corpus will be includible in the surviving spouse's gross estate and subject to estate tax at the survivor's death.[10] Thus, this trust "bypasses" the survivor's taxable estate and is, therefore, often called a Credit Equivalent Bypass Trust (CEBT) because it is funded with an amount equal to the exclusion equivalent of the unified credit.

To enhance the financial security of the surviving spouse without causing later estate taxation, the B trust may grant the surviving spouse a "limited" or "special" power of appointment under this family trust. For example, such a limited power of appointment may allow the surviving spouse with the testamentary right to appoint, all or any part of the B trust assets to a limited class of beneficiaries,[11] such as the children of the grantor. Although such a power would be limited to specified children, the surviving spouse is allowed to appoint the trust assets in any proportion or amounts as he or she desired. Such a power differs from a general power of appointment (which would cause the trust corpus to be included in the surviving spouse's gross estate) because the power cannot be exercised in favor of the surviving spouse, his or her creditors, his or her estate or creditors of his or her estate.

The B trust can also provide the surviving spouse with a noncumulative limited right of withdrawal without causing the trust corpus to be included in his or her gross estate. Typically, this provision states that if the A and Q trusts are depleted, the surviving spouse has the right to demand limited withdrawals from the B trust. Usually, each year, the noncumulative (use it or lose it) right to withdraw is the greater of (a) 5 percent of the corpus of the trust or (b) $5,000.[12] Although this five-or-five power will not cause the entire corpus to be included in the surviving spouse's gross estate, if the amount withdrawn is not spent by the surviving spouse, it would be included in the surviving spouse's gross estate (along with his or her other property).

At the death of the surviving spouse, the B trust can continue to function for the benefit of the grantor's family, generally his children, or the trust can be terminated, and the appropriate amounts paid out to trust beneficiaries. In many instances, the trust corpus is divided into separate equal shares to be distributed outright to the grantor's children or in separate trust for the benefit of the grantor's children, who will receive the net income currently with the right to demand distributions from principal at stated ages. Another popular approach is to keep the amounts passing to the children in a "common pot" until the children reach a certain age, such as when college is usually completed (e.g., age twenty-three). This way, the children who require larger amounts to pay for college will have the additional costs paid out of this common fund. When the youngest child reaches the designated age, separate shares are usually set up for each child. As an additional option usually applicable to large estates, the trust may continue for the lifetime of the children. Such trusts are known as "dynasty" or generation-skipping transfer tax (GST) trusts. In a dynasty trust, the trust assets can pass to the grandchildren and even lower generations with no inclusion in any of the descendants' gross estates.

Treatment of the B Trust's Net Income

The B trust may provide for (1) the distribution of net income to the surviving spouse for life; (2) for income to be "sprayed" in the trustee's discretion among the surviving spouse and other trust beneficiaries; (3) for income to be distributed to other beneficiaries so as to reduce the overall income tax burden on the family; or (4) for income to be accumulated inside of the trust.

1. *Distribute net income to the surviving spouse for life.*

2. *"Spraying" or "sprinkling" net income in the trustee's discretion.*

   Often, as an alternative to providing the surviving spouse income for life, the B trust may contain a "spraying" or "sprinkle" distribution clause. Such a clause authorizes the trustee (other than a trustee who is a beneficiary) in his or her discretion, to spray or sprinkle the net income of the B trust among the surviving spouse and the grantor's children or other issue (and sometimes spouses of issue) in any way the trustee determines. This type of language allows the trustee to apportion the trust's income among the beneficiaries based on need or other circumstances. Before considering this route, relevant state inheritance or estate taxes should be reviewed to determine whether a sprinkle provision would create adverse state death tax consequences.

3. *Apportion net income among the trust and beneficiaries.*

   Another option for trust income is to give the trustee the right to apportion the net income among the trust and the trust beneficiaries, after taking into consideration their relative tax brackets. The net income of a trust is determined in accordance with the same rules applicable to individuals, with certain important differences. Although the taxable income of the trust is subject to the federal income tax, to prevent double taxation (i.e., the trust and the beneficiaries pay tax on the same income), the trust receives a deduction for distributions made or required to be made to beneficiaries during its taxable year.[13] By deflecting income to beneficiaries with little or no personal income, the overall income tax for the family can be reduced. Note, for tax years 2018 through 2025, the unearned income of a child under age nineteen (or under twenty-four in the case of a child still in school), is taxed according to the brackets applicable to trusts and estates (i.e., a top rate of 37 percent for income over $14,450).

4. *Accumulate income inside of the trust.*

   In addition to income tax savings, the estate tax at the survivor's death may be reduced by use of an accumulation provision. Instead of the nonmarital income generated by the B trust being paid to the surviving spouse, it may be accumulated in the B trust and pass, estate tax-free, at the surviving spouse's death. Meanwhile, if the surviving spouse is permitted to invade the A trust (or the QTIP trust, if one exists) and consume some of the principal of those trusts (instead of using the income which has been accumulated in the B trust), the remainder of the A trust, and any QTIP trust would be reduced so the amount included in the surviving spouse's gross estate would be reduced and, thus, subject to less estate tax. The downside of tapping into marital trust assets (assets that will be taxed at the surviving spouse's death) and building up nonmarital trust assets that will pass estate tax-free at the surviving spouse's death is that the accumulation of large amounts of income in the nonmarital trust may result in adverse income taxation. This is because the top federal income tax rate of 37 percent—which generally does not apply to individuals until income exceeds $ 578,125 for single taxpayers—kicks in for taxable income in excess of only $14,450 for trusts (in 2023).

   The "sprinkle," "spray," or "accumulation" clauses are not appropriate if the B trust will be a recipient of stock in an S corporation. Only certain types of trusts are permitted to own S corporation stock, and a major requirement of such trusts is that the trust have a single individual beneficiary required to receive all trust income annually.[14]

   Another alternative, becoming more common in this era of divorce and remarriage, is to use the B trust as a means of benefiting persons other than the present spouse (e.g., children of a prior marriage). The trust can arrange for continued management of the trust assets for nonspousal beneficiaries, with delayed distribution, or provide for outright distribution.

   If the goal is to pass some property generation-skipping transfer tax-free, the B trust would continue to exist during the lives of children (usually giving them some "nongeneral" powers of appointment as well as income rights) so that the property in the trust can qualify as an "exempt" trust and avoid taxation at the death of the children or grandchildren. To achieve this result, the filed federal estate tax return should include an election to allocate a portion of the grantor's generation skipping transfer tax exemption to the B trust.

Q – The QTIP Trust

If the goal is to generate a marital deduction for the amount of the estate in excess of the estate tax exclusion but not be subject to the surviving spouse's control (e.g., a general power of appointment), creating a QTIP trust may be appropriate. Funding a trust that meets the requirements of a QTIP can result in zero estate tax at the death of the first spouse to die to the extent that the trustee or executor makes a QTIP election with respect to such trust.

The requirements of a QTIP are as follows: All income must be paid, at least annually, to the surviving spouse for the duration of his or her life. No provision for invasions of the trust can be made for anyone other than the surviving spouse or any condition (e.g., remarriage) or power in anyone else that could prevent the surviving spouse from receiving the trust income for life. Additionally, the surviving spouse should be given a power to require the trustee to produce income from the trust assets. Although, it is permissible to allow for the invasion of principal for the benefit of the surviving spouse, the trust terms typically require that all or part of the principal of the A trust be invaded before allowing for the invasion of the A trust.

To the extent that the trustee has elected to treat the assets funding the trust (usually 100 percent) as a QTIP, the remainder of the QTIP (Q) trust will be included in the gross estate of the surviving spouse.[15] Thus, using the Q trust merely defers estate tax on trust assets in this trust that are not used up by the surviving spouse during his or her lifetime.

Any assets remaining in this trust at the survivor's death will be distributed as the grantor has directed via the trust terms. Often a QTIP trust give the surviving spouse a limited power of appointment exercisable only in favor of the grantor spouse's issue. Accordingly, a QTIP trust is a very attractive planning tool for second marriages and to give the grantor spouse peace of mind that his or her issue will receive an inheritance if the surviving spouse remarries.

If the goal includes generation-skipping transfer tax planning and if some of the grantor-decedent's generation skipping transfer tax exemption is still available, the Q trust may be divided into two trusts: trust Q-E, funded with property to which some of the GST exemption will be allocated; and trust Q-N, not exempt from the GST tax and often subject to different terms than trust Q-E. Use of this GST split-trust planning in this manner is sometimes referred to as a "reverse QTIP election," discussed later in this chapter.

27.5 HOW DO THE MECHANICS OF THE A-B OR A-B-Q TRUST PLAN WORK?

Most marital trust planning is through an *inter vivos* (living) trust instrument. Pursuant to the terms of the trust agreement, different trusts are created – (the A or power of appointment trust, the B or bypass (family) trust and, when desired, the Q or QTIP trust.) Although the terms of the trust are determined during the grantor's lifetime, they do not become operative until the trusts are funded at the grantor's death (or prior to death to avoid probate of the trust assets).[16]

The trust is revocable because the grantor possesses the power to alter, amend, or revoke the trust until his death. Most states allow a grantor to name the trustee as beneficiary of his life insurance proceeds which obviates the need to transfer any other property to the trust during his lifetime.[17] But, if insurance is for some reason unavailable, many states recognize a trust funded with a nominal corpus such as $100, or even less.

Either as a means of shifting assets (through probate) to the trust, or as a backup provision to fund the trust with any assets unintentionally not transferred to the revocable trust during lifetime, the grantor's will often provide for the pour over of his or her probate property, after payment of settlement costs and any specific bequests or devises to the trust. In the event that the estate lacks sufficient liquid assets to pay administration expenses, the *inter vivos* trust often contains a provision allowing the trustee to provide the executor with cash through loans to the estate or the purchase of estate assets.

The essential provision in the A-B or A-B-Q trust is the marital deduction formula. All property included in the decedent's probate estate or funding the *inter vivos* trust will be divided in accordance with the formula clause set forth in the trust agreement. Such a clause might provide that the A trust, B trust and/or Q trust is to be funded in an amount equal to the amount necessary to reduce the federal estate tax payable to zero, or any other specified portion of the estate. The division of the marital deduction assets between the "A" trust and the "Q" trust could be whatever the grantor desires (e.g., half of the separate property funding the "A" trust, and the other half funding the "Q" trust). In any event, the funding clause would also provide that the amount of any marital portion be reduced by any property includable in the grantor's gross estate that passes directly to the surviving spouse because of the grantor's death (e.g., specific gifts, life insurance proceeds, or jointly owned property).

The net balance of the trust corpus remaining after allocation of the marital deduction amount and payment of settlement costs, is then allocated to the B trust.[18] Thus, the A-B/A-B-Q trust is really two or three trusts in one, administered under one trust agreement by the same trustee(s).

In some multi-marriage situations, the grantor-decedent may be unwilling to defer the inheritance to children of a prior marriage or other persons until after the death of the present spouse. In that event, the formula may provide for the payment of some estate tax at the grantor-decedent's death so that assets subject to estate tax may pass to these other beneficiaries at that time. Insurance proceeds payable at the death of the grantor is typically the most efficient and effective way to be assured that cash is available to pay the required tax when it is due.

Why is the A-B/A-B-Q trust arrangement such an important estate planning tool? To fully appreciate the implications and tax savings potential, it is necessary to examine a typical estate.

A common and often unfortunate arrangement is one where the testator leaves all property to the spouse (either by will, by jointly owning all assets with the spouse, or a combination of the two), potentially wasting the estate tax exclusion available at the death of the first spouse to die. Even with the availability of portability, the aggregate amount of federal estate tax on both estates may be higher than if a B trust was used. As illustrated below, this is particularly true in instances in which the estate appreciates to amount in excess of the sum of the surviving spouse's estate tax exclusion plus the predeceased spouse's DSUE. Moreover, the exemption from generation-skipping transfer taxes is not portable, which may result in a lost opportunity to shift wealth on a multi-generational basis.

Example. Philip Martin dies in 2022 leaving his entire $25,000,000 estate to his wife, Kaye, if living, otherwise to their son, Michael. Philip's primary objectives are to retain control of the estate during his lifetime, to provide an adequate income for his wife after his death, and to minimize his estate settlement costs. Kaye leaves her entire estate to Michael. Assuming Kaye dies in 2030 without consuming any of the principal of the estate that increased in value by 7 percent from the time of Philip's death to the time of Kaye's death, Figure 27.1 shows each estate's federal estate tax liability as well as the after tax amount that would pass to Michael upon Kaye's death.

A Typical A-B or A-B-Q Trust to Reduce the Tax at the First Death to Zero

If Philip had wished to be certain that no federal estate tax was owed at his death, regardless of the size of his estate, he should have created a B trust funded with an amount equal to his estate tax exclusion with the balance to pass to Kaye to be totally sheltered from estate tax by virtue of the unlimited marital deduction - resulting in a federal estate tax of zero. This is called the "zero tax marital deduction." In that event, Figure 27.2 shows each estate's federal estate tax liability as well as the after tax amount that would pass to Michael upon Kaye's death.

Comparison of Plans

Although pursuant to either estate plan, Philip's estate tax liability is zero, the use of the B trust results in significant estate tax savings upon Kaye's death. By funding the B trust with the estate applicable exclusion amount, none of the 7 percent of post death appreciation is subject to estate tax. Conversely, by leaving his entire estate directly to Kaye, all post death appreciation is subject to estate tax. Since the post death appreciation exceeded the aggregate amount of Kaye's estate tax exemption as well as Philip's DSUE, it was all subject to 40 percent estate tax at Kaye's death. So, in comparing the two plans, Michael nets $40,144,537 pursuant to the A-B plan versus $37,554,722, pursuant to the marital deduction plan, or a difference of $2,589,815.

THE TOOLS & TECHNIQUES OF ESTATE PLANNING

Figure 27.1

ESTATE MARITAL PLANNER All To Spouse Plan		
	Estate of Philip	**Estate of Kaye**
Adjusted Gross Estate (Year: 2023)	$25,000,000	$0
Year of Death	2023	2030*
Adjusted Gross Estate (Growth Rate: 7%)	$25,000,000	$40,144,537
Marital Deduction	– $25,000,000	– $0
Taxable Estate	$0	$40,144,53700
Adjusted Taxable Gifts	+ $0	+ $0
Computation Base	$0	$40,144,537
Tentative Federal Estate Tax	$0	$16,003,615
Gift Tax on Adj. Tax. Gifts	– $0	– $0
Unified Credit (unused)	– $r5,113,800	– $13,413,800*
Federal Estate Tax	$0	$2,5896,815
Value of QTIP trust at Death	$19,397,840	
Value of Net Estate at Kaye's Death		$37,554,722
Net Total to By-Pass trust at Kaye's death	$20,746,697	
Total Estate Tax	$0	2,589,815

* Two exemptions because second spouse may use the deceased spouse's unused exemption amount (DSUEA), and, for ease of mathematical speculation, it was assumed that the current, i.e., 2023 level applicable exclusion amount would continue to be indexed without adjustment to the base applicable exclusion amount up to 2030, which is not presently the law, although it is a reasonably foreseeable political result.

Figure 27.2

ESTATE MARITAL PLANNER Credit Shelter/Marital Deduction Plan		
	Estate of Philip	**Estate of Kaye**
Adjusted Gross Estate (Year: 2023)	$25,000,000	$0
Year of Death	2023	20301
Adjusted Gross Estate (Growth Rate 7%)	$25,000,000	$40,144,537
Marital Deduction (plus growth rate of 7%)	– $12,080,000	– $0
Taxable Estate	$12,920,0000	$40,144,537
Adjusted Taxable Gifts	+ $0	+ $0
Computation Base	$12,920,0000	$40,144,537
Tentative Federal Estate Tax	$0	$16,003,615
Gift Tax on Adj. Tax. Gifts	– $0	– $0
Unified Credit	– $0	– $5,113,800
Federal Estate Tax	$0	$16,003,615
Net Estate at Death	$19,397,840	$37,554,722
B Trust (plus growth rate of 7%)	$20,746,697	
Net Available	$40,144,537	
Total Tax	$70,960	

454

Significantly, the estate tax savings of the A-B plan would be offset by the increased income recognized on the sale of B trust assets. Pursuant to the marital deduction plan, the assets passing from Kaye to Michael would receive a full fair market value basis, which often is a step-up in basis. On the other hand, pursuant to the A-B plan, none of the assets passing from the B trust to Michael would be subject to a fair market value basis adjustment. So, if Michael subsequently sold those B trust assets, the capital gain could be as high as 20 percent and depending of his other income subject to the 3.8 percent net investment income surtax.

27.6 IMPACT OF THE REVERSE QTIP ELECTION

The generation-skipping transfer (GST) tax, discussed in Chapter 21, has an impact on how QTIP trusts are designed today. Although the GST exemption is the same amount as the estate tax exemption ($12,920,000 in 2023), it is not portable between spouses. Thus, for an estate plan looking to maximize the use of the GST exemption, it is generally recommended to fund a B trust at the death of the first spouse, allocating the unused GST exemption and estate tax exemption to the B trust.

However, even with equal GST and estate tax exemptions, it is quite possible that the GST exemption and estate tax exemption available may differ at time of death. For example, if a person makes a large lifetime taxable gift to his daughter, the amount available to fund the B trust will be less than his available GST exemption. Because the B trust is always funded up to the amount of the available estate tax exemption, in this example, the difference between the estate tax exemption available and the higher GST tax exemption available will be lost without proper planning.

In such cases, the question arises of how to fully use the decedent's excess GST exemption. The most effective solution is to allocate the excess GST exemption to a QTIP trust by making a "reverse QTIP election." Under this election, *for estate tax purposes*, the assets funding the QTIP qualify for the marital deduction for estate tax purposes, but for *GST tax purposes*, the executor can elect to treat the trust as if the assets were included in the decedent's taxable estate. Thus, the GST exemption can be allocated to the trust and will be sheltered from any future GST tax (see Chapter 21).

However, the reverse QTIP election can only be made as to a "separate" QTIP trust. This means that if the total amount to be allocated to the QTIP trust for marital deduction purposes exceeds the GST exemption available, it will be necessary to create two QTIP trusts, one to offset the remaining GST exemption, and the other to take advantage of the remaining marital deduction.

Example. Assume that in 2023, the decedent's year of death, the total value of the decedent's taxable estate per his Form 706 is $15,000,000, and the decedent made a previous taxable gift of $500,000, offset by a portion of the decedent's applicable exclusion amount, to which the decedent allocated $500,000 of his GST exemption. An amount equal to the remaining $12,4200,000 ($12,920,000 – $500,000) of his applicable exclusion amount will fund a B trust; $2,580,000 ($1,5000,000 – $11,420,000) to a QTIP trust. If the executor chooses to allocate all of the $11,420,000 of the $12,420,000 remaining GST exemption to the B trust, therefore, all of the QTIP in the amount of $2,580,000 is exposed, i.e., notexempt from the GST tax. According to private rulings, these trusts may have identical terms. However, the drafting must contemplate the possibility that the decedent's remaining GST exemption can cover some, but not all, of the QTIP trust, so that the QTIP trust can be divided into two parts, i.e., an exempt part, and a non-exempt part.

To implement this plan, most wills and trusts contain specific provisions for dividing one QTIP trust into two shares, frequently based on a formula to reflect the amount of GST exemption the executor elects to allocate to the QTIP.

27.7 TAX IMPLICATIONS

1. For a typical revocable *inter vivos* trust, no gift tax is payable upon creation of the trust because the grantor who has retained the right to terminate the trust and take the property back has not made a completed gift.[19]

2. After death, the assets that qualify for the marital deduction (the assets funding the A trust and/or the Q trust) are includable in the decedent's gross estate for federal estate tax purposes. Because they

qualify for the marital deduction, they are not subject to federal estate tax.[20] In many situations, the assets of these trusts will be minimal since the amount funding the B trust will reduce the amount funding the marital trusts and property passing outside the will may be sufficient to satisfy any marital deduction remaining.

Example. If, in 2023, the decedent's adjusted gross estate is $15,000,000, the optimum marital deduction is $3,080,000 ($15,000,000 less the effective applicable exclusion amount of $11,920,000). If the decedent's life insurance paid $1,000,000 in death benefits (includable in the adjusted gross estate) to his wife, she would already have received more than the maximum optimum marital deduction.

The marital deduction portion of the estate is established by formula and can be given outright to the surviving spouse instead of in trust. However, in that instance, the surviving spouse would have full control over the assets and can spend the assets freely, including sharing the funds with a future spouse. The decedent spouse may prefer the trust structure for enhanced control.

3. Assets that do not fund the marital deduction trusts (A and/or Q) are, by formula, placed into the B trust. Although the value of these assets are includible in the grantor's gross estate, the estate tax exemption will offset any estate tax. Further, since the surviving spouse receives only income (and perhaps some principal by exercise of certain limited powers of appointment) from the B trust, the B trust assets should not be included in the surviving spouse's gross estate for estate tax purposes.[21]

4. During the grantor's lifetime, income produced by any of the assets transferred to a revocable *inter vivos* trust are taxed to the grantor who is treated as the owner of trust assets and income for both estate and income tax purposes. At the grantor's death, the trust becomes irrevocable, and the income produced by trust assets will be taxable to the trust or to the income beneficiary depending on whether the income is accumulated by the trust or paid out to the income beneficiary.[22]

5. In California and other states that have placed limits on real property tax increases, certain transfers of the real property will cause the loss of such limits. However, transfers to revocable trusts where the owner-grantor still has the beneficial ownership and control of the property will not cause the loss of those limits. It is at the owner-grantor's death, when the trust becomes irrevocable, that there may be an increase in property tax, a circumstance that must be anticipated and that sometimes can be avoided.

27.8 ISSUES IN COMMUNITY PROPERTY STATES

Where the draftsman is dealing with community property, it should be noted that one-half of the property already belongs to the surviving spouse, and it will not be subject to the "pourover" provisions of the will of the first spouse to die, unless the first spouse specifically indicates his desire to effect distribution of both halves of the community, *and* the surviving spouse acquiesces freely in that distribution.

To the extent the surviving spouse elects to retain his or her community half of the property outside the trust, then a problem of split ownership and management arises, with the survivor owning one-half of the assets, and the trustee of the trust owning the other half. If the surviving spouse does allow his half of the community property to pass to the trust, it would typically go into the A trust, so the survivor retains control over how the assets are distributed during life or at death.

Community property laws may not apply to an item of community income that the taxpayer received but did not treat as community income. The taxpayer is responsible for reporting all of that income item if: (1) he or she treated the item as if only he or she were entitled to the income, and (2) the taxpayer did not notify his or her spouse of the nature and amount of the income by the due date for filing the income tax return (including extensions).[23]

The marital deduction rules apply to community property as well as separate property states, so community property state couples may also elect to defer the payment of any federal estate tax until the survivor's death.

Where a marital deduction is used, it will reduce the estate tax liability at the first spouse's death but may increase the tax at the second death if the surviving spouse does not use up the marital deduction portion during his or her lifetime, resulting in higher overall taxes for both estates. However, most couples would prefer to minimize the tax liability at the first spouse's death in order to leave more assets available for the survivor's support and take the risk of having slightly higher overall taxes.

In both community and common law states, holding property in joint tenancy (tenancy by the entirety) with right of survivorship between spouses will result in the property going outright to the surviving spouse, regardless of the provisions of the decedent's will. The marital deduction provisions may be drafted to reduce the marital deduction by the value of the assets passing outside the trust and thus still result in the optimum marital deduction amount passing to the spouse, so long as the assets passing outside the will do not exceed the optimum marital deduction amount. However, holding large amounts of property in joint tenancy can defeat the trust planning to a very significant degree since such holdings can be more than the optimum marital deduction and reduce the first to die spouse's estate to less than the estate tax exemption amount (thus resulting in the wasting of a portion of the estate tax exemption).

In many instances, a couple living in a community property state may have separate property as well as community property, and both kinds of property must be considered in determining the amount that will be optimum for the marital deduction.

The laws in Louisiana are unique and particular care should be taken to obtain counsel knowledgeable in Louisiana law and general tax law if a couple settles in or has community property located in Louisiana.

In any event, it is very important for persons who have an estate plan drafted with only separate property in mind to have the plan reviewed and most probably redrafted upon becoming a resident of a community property state.

27.9 FREQUENTLY ASKED QUESTIONS

Question – What are the disadvantages of an A-B/A-B-Q trust?

Answer – First, if the trust is an *inter vivos* trust and is currently "funded" (properties placed in the trust during the lifetime of the grantor), there may be significant trustee's fees. This fee can often be minimized or avoided if the grantor serves as trustee, which is permissible in some jurisdictions, or if the grantor reserves the right and obligation to administer trust assets during lifetime (unless incapacitated).

Second, after the death of the grantor, the surviving spouse cannot have unlimited control of, or unlimited access to, the assets that have been placed in the B trust without causing inclusion in the surviving spouse's estate. However, it is possible to grant the surviving spouse the right to invade principal, at such spouse's own discretion, to the extent of a noncumulative right to withdraw up to 5 percent of the corpus or $5,000 annually, whichever is greater without causing the balance of the B trust assets to be included in his or her estate (the greater of 5 percent or $5,000 will be includable in the surviving spouse's estate to the extent it is not spent down during life).[24] Additionally, the surviving spouse can be granted a "HEMS" power, i.e., the right to invade principal for health, education, maintenance, and support. HEMS is an ascertainable standard that prevents the inclusion of the B trust assets in his or her gross estate.[25] Furthermore, the trustee (assuming the trustee was an independent party) may be given a power in its sole and absolute discretion to distribute principal to the surviving spouse for any reason satisfactory to the trustee. Another power that can be given to the surviving spouse is the right to appoint during lifetime or at death to and among a specified class of individuals (but this class must exclude the spouse, his estate, his creditors, and the creditors of his estate).[26] For example, the grantor could grant his or her spouse the authority to appoint by will to and among the grantor's issue, parents, or siblings.

Question – What functions does the trustee have in the A-B/A-B-Q trust?

Answer – The trustee will hold the assets placed in the trust during the lifetime of the grantor(s) and is the recipient of life insurance proceeds payable to the trust, as well as property "poured over" from the decedent's will. The trustee will be the legal owner of the assets of both trusts and manage the trusts in accordance with the provisions of the trust agreement. The trust agreement can be either extremely flexible or severely restrictive, depending on the objectives of the grantor.

The trustee's primary duties are two-fold: (1) to manage and invest the trust corpus in such a manner as to generate income for the beneficiaries; and (2) to preserve the corpus. The Uniform Prudent Investor's Act, adopted by many states, contains guidelines (and requirements) for investments by a trustee. The trust instrument may in some cases modify the rules under which the trustee will make investments.

In many instances, a corporate fiduciary may be indicated, either as a sole or co-trustee, if the trust corpus is sizable or if conflicts of interest are likely to arise between individual trustees.

Question – What are the different ways to write provisions that qualify for the maximum or optimum marital deduction?

Answer – The first is a provision leaving a specific dollar amount bequest; however, this technique is not recommended since it is impossible, in most cases, to arrive at a dollar amount that will exactly equal the desired marital deduction at the time of the grantor's death with any degree of accuracy.

The second way is use of a funding formula that is geared to the marital deduction provisions of the Internal Revenue Code. Either a pecuniary formula bequest or a fractional share bequest is the formula clause to use. A pecuniary formula bequest is used where the testator wants the spouse to receive a fixed dollar amount (a general legacy). An example of such a clause follows:

"If my wife, Deborah, survives me, I give, devise, and bequeath to my trustees (in trust "A" or trust "Q") an amount exactly sufficient – and no larger – to reduce the federal estate tax due at my death to the lowest possible amount, after taking into consideration all other property passing to my wife or which has passed to my wife and which qualifies for the marital deduction and after allowance of all applicable credits."[27]

Under this clause, the property qualifying for the marital deduction funds the marital ("A" and/or "Q") trusts. The remainder of the property, after satisfying the marital deduction, is bequeathed to the B trust.

Instead of a fixed amount, the testator may want to give the spouse a fractional share of the estate. Here, the sum that goes to the spouse may fluctuate after the decedent's death and, in essence, the spouse receives a share in the residue. In this case, the clause (the fractional share bequest) should read as follows:

"If my wife, Deborah, survives me, I give, devise, and bequeath to my trustees (in trust A or trust Q) the following fractional share of my residuary estate (before such estate is diminished by the payment therefrom of estate, inheritance, or death taxes):

(a) The numerator of the fraction shall be exactly sufficient – and no larger – to reduce to the lowest possible amount the federal estate tax due at my death, after taking into consideration all other property passing to my wife or which has passed to my wife and which qualifies for the marital deduction and after allowance of all applicable credits.

(b) The denominator of the fraction shall be the value of my residuary estate, before it is diminished by the payment therefrom of estate, inheritance, or death taxes."

IT IS IMPORTANT TO NOTE THAT MANY OTHER PROVISIONS ARE REQUIRED, IN ADDITION TO THE FUNDING FORMULA, IN ORDER TO OBTAIN THE MARITAL DEDUCTION.

Question – Which type of funding formula is preferable?

Answer – This depends upon the circumstances. The most important factor is the type of assets the grantor owns.

If there is a high probability of a substantial increase in value during the period of settlement of the trust or estate, then the pecuniary formula clause may have some benefit if it gives the residual amount (after the marital deduction) to the B trust. Under these circumstances, any increase in the size of the estate can be shifted to the B trust and thus reduce taxation at the survivor's death.

If there is a possibility that the estate may drop in value, then it may be wise to use a pecuniary formula clause that specifies the exact amount to fund the B trust with the residue to fund the marital deduction trust.

In any use of a pecuniary formula clause, it is possible to recognize an income tax where assets that have increased in value since the date of death are used to satisfy distribution to a trust. In these circumstances, a gain can be recognized and taxed.

A fractional share clause avoids the problem of any recognition of income tax gain triggered by the transfer of assets to a trust to fund a bequest. Additionally, it shifts any increase or decrease proportionately to both the marital deduction trust and the B trust.

Question – What are some of the advantages of a B trust over an A trust?

Answer – With respect to a B trust, it is not necessary that income be distributed to the surviving spouse. Instead, income can be accumulated and remain in the trust. Where there is concern for use of income and a great deal of income available, a B trust may provide more protection for the survivor. (Note, however, if the income is accumulated in the trust, the income may be taxed at higher rates than for individual taxpayers because the top rate of 37 percent is applicable for income over $14,450 (in 2023) for trusts and estates.)

Additionally, because of the flexibility of a B trust in terms of distributions of income, it may be easier to retain assets that are not income producing.

Question – What are the advantages of having the marital deduction fund a QTIP trust?

Answer – Many advantages exist. One important one is giving the trustee the power to determine by election on the estate tax return as to the amount of trust assets are to be taxed at the death of the first spouse to die. So, if there is the expectation that the value of the trust assets will increase substantially between the deaths of the spouses, it may be prudent not to elect QTIP treatment and to have the trust treated as B trust subject to estate tax (offset by the estate tax exemption) so the post death appreciation is not subject to estate tax at the death of the surviving spouse.

A second important benefit of a QTIP trust is the grantor ability to control the distribution of the trust assets following the death of the surviving spouse to beneficiaries of his or her choice rather than the surviving spouse's new friend, new spouse, or new spouse's children (as would be possible with respect to an A trust where the surviving spouse must be given a power to appoint the property at the survivor's death).

Where it is desirable to give the surviving spouse some control over the disposition of assets, e.g., among the mutual issue of the decedent and survivor, a QTIP trust may grant the surviving spouse a limited power of appointment to direct disposition of the trust principal among a specific group of beneficiaries.

Finally, a QTIP trust is the only optimum marital arrangement by which the grantor's full GST exemption can be preserved for the next generation, with the trust property benefiting the surviving spouse during his or her lifetime with no estate tax due at the grantor's death.

Question – Can an A-B/A-B-Q trust be set up in an individual's will?

Answer – Yes. This is called a testamentary trust (as contrasted to an *inter vivos* trust). Rather than have a separate trust instrument and a separate will, the two are combined into the will document. The provisions of the testamentary trust are generally the same as the *inter vivos* trust provisions.

Question – Are there any drawbacks to setting up the A-B/A-B-Q trust in the will rather than as an *inter vivos* document?

Answer – Use of a testamentary trust will *require* a probate at the grantor's death. Often there is a delay in probating a will. If the trust were part of the will, it could not function until the will was probated. Thus, if life insurance were payable to a testamentary trust, there could be a delay in funding that trust.

In some states, life insurance proceeds payable to a testamentary trust is subject to inheritance tax purposes whereas they would not be subject to inheritance tax if payable to an *inter vivos* trust.

Question – In a marital deduction trust, what constitutes income that must be paid to the surviving spouse?

Answer – Traditionally, income is generally monies earned by the trust assets, such as dividends, interest, and rental income from real property, and did not include increases in capital. However, many states have adopted the Revised Uniform Principal and Income Act (UPIA) that allows a trustee to invest for "total return." For example, a trustee might invest in a fund that focuses on growth and yields less income than might otherwise be realized. Under the Revised Uniform Principal and Income Act, the trustee could then allocate some of that appreciation to income to make up for the smaller yield, subject to the trustee's fiduciary duty to treat the income beneficiary and the remainderpersons fairly.

Question – Can a B trust own life insurance on the surviving spouse's life?

Answer – Yes, a B trust may be permitted to purchase life insurance on the surviving spouse's life. Especially in a case where the surviving spouse does not need income, it may be possible for the trust assets to be leveraged with life insurance. At the death of the surviving spouse, the B trust will not only distribute the remaining trust principal to beneficiaries, but also the life insurance proceeds, potentially increasing the total amount left to heirs. This can be a particularly effective strategy when the B trust is funded with low basis assets, because the life insurance proceeds can act as the equivalent to a step-up in basis.

However, if a B trust owns life insurance on the surviving spouse, additional considerations must be taken to ensure that the trust assets will not be includable in the surviving spouse's estate. First, the spouse may not serve as trustee (if already serving as trustee, he or she must resign before the policy is purchased). Additionally, the insured/spouse must not hold a limited power of appointment. The surviving spouse's legal counsel will also need to determine if a spouse's income right (particularly a mandatory income right) will constitute an incident of ownership.[28]

Question – Are there any special planning opportunities or considerations in light of the Tax Cuts and Jobs Act of 2017?

Answer – The Tax Cuts and Jobs Act of 2017 temporarily increased the applicable exclusion amount from estate, gift and GST taxes from $5,000,000 (indexed for inflation) to $10,000,000 million (indexed for inflation), resulting in an $12,920,000 exemption in 2023. However, this increase is scheduled to expire at the end of 2025. For deaths occurring after January 1, 2026, the exemption is scheduled to revert to $5,000,000 (taking into account inflation).

For high net worth taxpayers, there is a unique and limited window of opportunity to accomplish significant wealth transfer through lifetime gifting. One way to do so is by funding an irrevocable trust or "lifetime credit shelter trust" using the increase in exemption. Special language, such as spousal access provisions, can be added to the trust to increase access, control and flexibility during the grantor's life while enabling the grantor to take advantage of increased exemptions and freezing the growth of the assets outside of the grantor's estate. If a high net worth taxpayer waits until his or her death to fund a credit shelter trust or relies on a portability election, if he or she dies after the exemption amounts are reduced, the opportunity will be lost.

Moreover, in light of current law, older estate plans should be reviewed to ensure that the plan takes into account higher applicable exclusion amounts. For example, consider a client with a $10,000,000 estate in 2023. Under the terms of his revocable trust drafted in 2014, upon his death, his remaining applicable exclusion amount will be left in a B trust for the benefit of his grantor's children, and the remainder will fund an A or Q trust for his surviving spouse. If the grantor dies today, the full $10,000,000 will fund the B trust, leaving the surviving spouse with nothing.

For smaller estates, doing away with the marital trust structure altogether may make the most sense from both an estate and income tax perspective, as well as for ease of administration. For example, a married couple with a $5,000,000 estate may be better off electing portability, thus receiving a new fair market value basis on assets and allowing beneficiaries to sell assets without having to recognize capital gains tax. Clients will need to work with their legal counsel to determine what planning technique works best for them in light of current law.

CHAPTER ENDNOTES

1. I.R.C. §2041(b)(1).
2. See LISI Estate Planning Newsletter 2062 (Feb. 7, 2013) at http://www.LeimbergServices.com which includes charts illustrating which utilize growth rates based on an historic Standard and Poors' rate to conclude that relying upon portability where the surviving spouse lives for a long period after the death of his or her spouse can have led to catastrophic tax results.
3. The trust should provide that the spouse has the right to demand that the trust be made income producing.
4. Treas. Reg. §20.2056(b)-5(a)(4).
5. Treas. Reg. §20.2056(b)-5.
6. Rev. Rul. 68-554.
7. *Comm'r. v. Ellis*, 252 F.2d 109 (3d Cir. 1958), rev'g in part, 26 TC 694.
8. Treas. Reg. §20.2056(a)-1.
9. For special rules that apply when one spouse is a non-U.S. citizen, see Chapter 72.
10. Rev. Rul. 66-86, 1966-1 CB 216.
11. Treas. Reg. §20.2041-1(c).
12. I.R.C. §2041(b)(2); Treas. Reg. §20.2041-3(d)(3).
13. The deduction is limited to the extent such distributions do not exceed "distributable net income," as that term is defined. I.R.C. §§651, 661.
14. Additional requirements must be met in order for a trust to be a qualified subchapter S trust, as outlined in I.R.C. §1361(d).
15. I.R.C. §2044. The property in the trust includable in the surviving spouse's estate under Section 2044 is considered property acquired from a decedent, and thus in the hands of the one to whom the property passes from the surviving spouse has a basis equal to the fair market value of the property at the date of the surviving spouse's death or alternate valuation date (see the discussion of basis in Chapter 22). I.R.C. §§1014(b)(10), 2044(c).
16. Alternatively, this same plan can be executed in a testamentary trust (i.e., one contained in the decedent's will and which will require the assets to be subject to probate).
17. It is extremely important to check the applicable state law to be sure that merely naming a trust as life insurance beneficiary will serve as adequate corpus.
18. See Rev. Proc. 64-19, 1964-1 CB 682.
19. Treas. Regs. §§25.2511-2(b), 25.2511-2(c).
20. I.R.C. §2056.
21. *Est. of Milner v. Comm'r.*, 6 TC 874 (1946).
22. I.R.C. §§641, 652, 662.
23. IRS Pub. 555 (Rev. March 2020), Community Property, p. 7.
24. I.R.C. §2041(b)(2); Treas. Reg. §20.2041-3(d)(3).
25. Treas. Reg. §20.2041-1(c)(2).
26. Treas. Reg. §20.2041-1(c)(1).
27. Certain additional provisions must be added to this "funding" formula in order to guarantee the marital deduction. See, e.g., Rev. Proc. 64-19, 1964-1 CB 682.
28. I.R.C. §2042.

SECTION 2503(B) AND 2503(C) TRUSTS

CHAPTER 28

28.1 INTRODUCTION

For a gift to qualify as an annual exclusion gift, there must be a transfer of a "present interest" in the property. A transfer is of a "present interest" if there is an unrestricted right to the immediate use, possession enjoyment of property, or the income from property.[1] Because a minor lacks the legal capacity to manage property, the issues arises of whether gifts to a minor are gifts of a future interest, because the minor, in effect, does not receive the property until reaching the age of majority. Gifts made to a guardian for the benefit of the child or to custodian under a Uniform Transfers to Minors' Act (UTMA) or Uniform Gifts to Minors Act (UGMA) custodianship qualify as present interest gifts.

Moreover, a transfer to a Code section 2503(c) trust enables a grantor to make a gift to a minor in trust that will be treated as a present interest gift qualifying for the annual gift tax exclusion. The use of this irrevocable funded trust for gifts to minors eliminates many of the following practical objections to outright gifts:

1. Brokers are reluctant to deal in securities owned by minors since minors may legally disaffirm either a purchase of stock that subsequently falls in value or a sale of stock that later rises in value.

2. Property titled in a minor's name is, to a large extent, frozen. It is difficult to sell or exchange that property since a minor's signature on a real estate deed gives the buyer no assurance of permanent title.

3. Guardianship must be used to avoid many of the objections of an outright transfer to a minor, but a guardian must generally post bond and account periodically to a local probate (sometimes called Surrogate's or Orphans') Court.

Similarly, a gift to a Code section 2503(b) trust for a minor may also be treated as a present interest gift subject to the gift tax annual exclusion. This trust is discussed in more detail below.

28.2 WHEN IS USE OF SUCH A DEVICE INDICATED?

When a client wishes to make a gift to a minor child and:

1. The client's income tax bracket is high and the minor's income tax bracket is relatively low. Significant income shifting (resulting in significant income tax savings) is possible once the child reaches age eighteen.

2. The client owns an asset that is likely to appreciate substantially over a period of time, does not want the appreciation includable in his gross estate, and wants to shift wealth and growth to family members.

3. The use of the gift tax annual exclusion is desirable. Also, a gift to a section 2503(c) trust would apparently have a zero inclusion ratio for generation skipping tax purposes due to requirement (3) below.

Example. Jeff Mandell transfers shares of stock in his closely held corporation to three trusts for his three minor sons. Assuming the trusts qualify under Code section 2503(c), the annual irrevocable transfers of stock will be considered gifts of a present interest. This will allow Jeff to use the $17,000 (in 2023) gift tax annual exclusion with respect to each gift without being subject to gift tax or using up any portion of his unified credit.

Additionally, to the extent they qualify for the annual exclusion (without taking gift splitting into account), the stock transfers reduce the value of Jeff's estate and the income from any dividends paid on the stock is taxed currently to the trusts, if accumulated, or to the children, if distributed.

Economically, such trusts could be used to fund a life insurance program for the children by providing the trusts with sufficient cash each year to pay premiums for the insurance on the boys' lives. Alternatively, trust income could be used to purchase non-necessaries or be accumulated and used to help provide nonnecessaries when the children reach college age.

28.3 CODE SECTION 2503(C) TRUSTS

1. A gift to a minor through a Code section 2503(c) trust will be considered a gift of a present interest (so the gift will qualify for the gift tax annual exclusion) if the income and principal is available for distribution to or on behalf of the beneficiary at any time prior to the time the beneficiary reaches age twenty-one. (Regardless of when a person becomes an adult under state law, the magic age is still twenty-one for section 2503(c) purposes). Undistributed income and principal can be accumulated in the trust until the child turns twenty-one.

2. Undistributed income and principal must be distributable to the beneficiary when that individual reaches age twenty-one.

3. If the beneficiary dies before age twenty-one, accumulated trust income and corpus must go to the minor's estate or to another person as the minor may appoint pursuant to a general power of appointment.[2]

4. Even if an underage minor is legally unable to exercise a power of appointment or execute a will, it will not cause the transfer to fail to satisfy the above conditions. Furthermore, the trust may continue beyond the donee's twenty-first birthday provided that upon reaching age twenty-one, the donee can withdraw the property from the trust if desired. Thus, as long at the donee has the right to withdraw the property, the trust property does not have to be distributed to a trust beneficiary upon reaching age twenty-one.[3]

28.4 DISADVANTAGES

1. Expenses entailed in drafting and administering the trust.

2. Expenses involved in filing tax returns and estimated quarterly payments (cost depends on complexity of returns and time entailed).

3. A Code section 2503(c) trust can have only one beneficiary; meaning the benefits of the trust property cannot be transferred from a child who "goes astray" to a child who "has seen the light" or to a child who needs financial assistance more than others.

4. The assets in a Code section 2503(c) trust must be distributed (or made available for distribution) to the beneficiary at age twenty-one.

5. Because the Code section 2503(c) trust is irrevocable; the grantor must relinquish total control to obtain the tax benefits.

Planning Note: Given these disadvantages, use of a 2503(c) trust as a planning device may not be as common as in the past. If parents are not concerned about the child's ability to receive income at the age of majority, a custodianship under a UTMA/UGMA account offers simplicity and is much less expensive to set up and maintain. Alternatively, if the trust structure and availability of annual exclusion gifts is of desire, using a traditional Crummey trust can accomplish many of the same goals set forth in a 2503(c) trust but without some of the limiting restrictions (namely, the one beneficiary requirement and the requirement that trust assets be distributed at age twenty-one). See the Frequently Asked Questions section for more information.

28.5 TAX IMPLICATIONS

1. If the income of the trust is distributed (or required to be distributed) each year, it is taxable to the beneficiary-child. In prior years, distributions of unearned income may have triggered the "kiddie tax," resulting in taxation at the parents' income tax levels. Under the Tax Cuts and Jobs Act of 2017, the kiddie tax was simplified, so that a child beneficiary's net unearned income is calculated using the tax brackets applicable to trusts and estates (in 2023, a top rate of 37 percent on income over $14,450; the 3.8 percent net investment income tax may also apply).[4] Otherwise, to the extent income is accumulated, it will be taxed to the trust.[5] (Because the rates for trusts and estates are the same as the rates for a minor child, the income tax impact of an income distribution to a child versus accumulation in the trust should be neutral.)

2. Gifts to the trust constitute a present interest. Therefore, the gift tax annual exclusion of $17,000 (in 2023) applies as long as the conditions discussed above are met.

3. Transfers that exceed or otherwise do not qualify for the gift tax annual exclusion are treated as a taxable gift (no gift tax will be due if the donor has lifetime exemption available). At the donor's death, the taxable portion of any lifetime gift is added back into the decedent's gross estate as an adjusted taxable gift (with an offset against estate tax for gift tax which would have been payable on the transfer). However, the amount brought back into the decedent's gross estate is the date of gift value rather than the date of death value. Therefore, any post gift appreciation of the property in trust would not be included in the gross estate. Thus, if there was a large amount of appreciation, the tax savings may be significant. If not, there may be little or no estate tax savings.

Example. If a single individual gives his son $217,000 worth of stock in 2023, assuming no other present interest gifts and subtracting the annual exclusion ($17,000), there would be a taxable gift of $200,000. Upon the donor's death, the adjusted taxable gift of $200,000 (date of gift value of the stock) would be added into his gross estate. Thus, even if the date of death value of the stock increased to $300,000, the appreciation in value, $100,000 ($300,000 − $200,000) is not factored into the estate tax computation.

4. Finally, the entire value of the Section 2503(c) trust will be includable in the grantor's estate if the grantor is the trustee at the time of his death.[6] It may also be includable if the income from the trust is used to satisfy the grantor-parent's duty to support the beneficiary.

28.6 HOLDING S CORPORATION STOCK

In general, a Section 2503(c) trust is not an eligible shareholder of S corporation stock unless it also qualifies as a Qualified Subchapter S Trust (QSST), ESBT, or a grantor trust under Code section 678.

QSST

A QSST is defined in Code section 1361(d) as a trust that:

1. Owns stock in one or more S corporations (and may hold other types of assets).

2. Can distribute income only to one individual (who must be a United States resident or citizen).

3. Has trust terms requiring that

   a. allows only one beneficiary at any given time;

   b. if corpus is distributed during the term of the trust, it can be distributed only to the individual who is at that time is the current income beneficiary;

   c. if an income beneficiary dies, the income interest itself will end at that death or upon the earlier termination of the trust; and

d. if the trust ends before the income beneficiary dies, all the assets of the trust must be distributed to that income beneficiary.

4. Requires an election for QSST status to be made by the income beneficiary (or the income beneficiary's legal representative). Once that election is made, it is irrevocable and can be revoked only with the consent of the IRS. The election must be made by each income beneficiary as he or she becomes one. Separate elections must be made if the stock of more than one S corporation is held in the trust.

If the requirements described above are met, the income beneficiary of a QSST (which can be set up during the grantor's lifetime or by will) is treated as the owner of the stock. The consequence is that the pro rata share of income, gains, losses, deductions, and credits pass directly from the S corporation to the minor beneficiary.

What are the advantages of a QSST? A gift of S corporation stock can be made to a minor through the trust without incurring the disadvantages of outright ownership. (Of course, if such a gift is made to a minor, the QSST election must be made by the legal representative of the minor.) This enables an individual to split income among family members while at the same time eliminating the gift from inclusion in his gross estate. So both income shifting and wealth transfers are possible through the QSST.

Unlike a custodianship, a QSST can continue beyond age eighteen (or twenty-one) and can last for the duration of the trust as set forth in the trust document. This means that if the minor dies before the trust terminates, the trust can continue for the lives of a number of successive income beneficiaries and is not required to distribute the trust assets to the estate of the deceased income beneficiary.

Section 678 Trust

The QSST is not the only alternative to outright and UGMA or UTMA gifts. A Code section 678 trust (a trust that essentially becomes the grantor trust of the beneficiary) can also be an eligible S corporation stock shareholder.

The criterion for favorable tax treatment under this type of trust is that the beneficiary must have unrestricted power "exercisable solely by himself to vest the corpus or the income therefrom in himself." In other words, the beneficiary will be taxed on the income from the S corporation held by the trust if the beneficiary has the right to take both income and corpus at anytime. There must be no restrictions on the beneficiary's right to exercise this withdrawal power.

A trust can also be considered a section 678 trust if the beneficiary has not exercised a Crummey power to withdraw and has retained certain grantor trust type powers under Code sections 671 through 677 (e.g., beneficiary is a trustee who has discretionary power to distribute income, either alone or with a nonadverse party).

A section 678 trust can be created by a parent or grandparent who transfers S corporation stock to the trust for the benefit of a minor. The minor would be given an unrestricted power to withdraw income or corpus for his own benefit (or a Crummey withdrawal power and another grantor trust type power under Code sections 671 through 677).

Note, however, a section 678 trust and other trust designs that fall under the purview of section 678 (including Steve and Richard Oshins' Beneficiary Defective Inheritor's Trust (BDIT) and Ed Morrow's Beneficiary Deemed Owner Trust (BDOT)), are highly sophisticated, complex planning techniques with many potential pitfalls and concerns. These techniques are largely untested and an unfavorable ruling could leave a client with significant unintended consequences. It is important to engage legal counsel with experience drafting these trusts to help mitigate these concerns.

Gift and Estate Tax Implications

How are gifts to QSSTs and section 678 trusts taxed for gift tax purposes? From a gift perspective, a contribution to either type of trust will be considered a completed gift. Such gifts can qualify for the gift tax annual exclusion either by meeting the requirements of section 2503(c) or by including a Crummey withdrawal power.

Will the property in a QSST or section 678 trust be includable in the estate of a beneficiary? The answer in the case of a QSST beneficiary is that, if the beneficiary is given only lifetime income rights, assets remaining in the trust at the time of the beneficiary's death will not be includable in his estate.

In the case of a section 678 trust, inclusion depends on how the trust became qualified under section 678. If the beneficiary was given a general power of appointment (the absolute and unrestricted power of withdrawal) over all or a portion of the trust, the property subject to that power at the time of the beneficiary's death will be includable in the estate. Also, if the beneficiary exercised or released the power and retained an interest in the trust (e.g., a life estate) such that had the beneficiary been the owner of the property the property would have been includable in the powerholder's estate under Code sections 2035 through 2038, the property is includable in the powerholder's estate. However, the lapse of a Crummey withdrawal power is not treated as a release of the power if the amount subject to the power does not exceed $5,000 or 5 percent of the property subject to the power.

28.7 SECTION 2503(B) TRUSTS

A Section 2503(b) trust for the benefit of a minor requires a mandatory distribution of income to the trust beneficiary on an annual or more frequent basis. Gifts to such trusts will qualify as gifts of a present interest and thus are eligible for the gift tax annual exclusion.

Example. Assuming a 5.0 percent section 7520 interest rate, if a section 2503(b) trust provides income for life to the donee (age eleven) to be distributed at least annually, then based on the IRS valuation tables, the amount of the gift considered to be of a present interest if $10,000 was put into a Section 2503(b) trust would be $9,390 (the actuarial value of the lifetime right of an eleven-year old to the annual income produced by $10,000).

In some respects, a section 2503(b) trust is more flexible than either a section 2503(c) trust or a custodianship account because a section 2503(b) trust is not required to distribute principal and/or unexpended income at age twenty-one or sooner. Furthermore, a section 2503(b) trust can last for the lifetime of the beneficiary or for any lesser period of time.

Also, unlike the case with a section 2503(c) trust or a custodianship, under a section 2503(b) trust, the principal is never required to be paid over to the income beneficiary. Trust principal can go to a different donee specified by the grantor of the trust or can go to a person specified by the income beneficiary.

Distributions and Tax Implications

As income is earned by a section 2503(b) trust, it must be distributed to the trust beneficiary. However, the income can be deposited in an UGMA/UTMA custodial account and used for the benefit of the minor or left to accumulate in the custodial account until the minor reaches majority. At that time, the accumulated income must be distributed to the beneficiary.

Each year, as it is earned, the income of the trust is taxed to the minor-beneficiary, except to the extent it has been used to discharge a support or other legal obligation of the minor's grantor-parent (in which case it would definitely be taxed to the parent). Under the Tax Cuts and Jobs Act of 2017, a child beneficiary's net unearned income is calculated using the tax brackets applicable to trusts and estates (in 2023, a top rate of 37 percent on income over $14,450; the 3.8 percent net investment income tax may also apply).[7]

For gift tax purposes, the entire amount placed into such a trust is treated as a gift. The gift is divided into two portions: an income portion and a principal (remainder) portion. The income portion will qualify for the $17,000 (in 2023) annual exclusion while the balance is considered a future interest gift and will not qualify for the exclusion.[8] To protect the annual exclusion for the income portion, the trust instrument should specifically deny the power of the trustee to invest in non-income producing property.[9]

28.8 ISSUES IN COMMUNITY PROPERTY STATES

Where community property is the subject of a gift into a section 2503(c) trust, each spouse is considered as being the grantor of one-half, by reason of the community ownership, under which each spouse has a 50 percent interest in the community property regardless of which spouse earned the community property income or acquired the community property asset.[10] For that reason, it is important that neither spouse be named as the trustee or successor trustee of the trust in order to avoid the trust property being included in the grantors' estates (see second question and answer below). In some states, if one spouse transfers community real or personal property to a trust for the benefit of a third party, such spouse must obtain the written consent of the nondonor spouse prior to such transfer or the gift could be entirely set aside.

28.9 FREQUENTLY ASKED QUESTIONS

Question – Would a Section 2503(c) trust be an effective gift tax savings technique if it is a relatively modest amount of marketable securities and likely to be the only gift the grantor will ever make?

Answer – No. Generally, the complexities and expenses of creating such a trust do not make it a cost effective gift. Under these circumstances, the use of a Uniform Gifts to Minors Act (UGMA) or a Uniform Transfers to Minors Act (UTMA) custodianship or a section 529 plan for the minor's education expenses may be a better alternative. On the other hand, if it is likely that additional gifts will be made in future years, and a substantial amount of valuable property will ultimately be transferred to the minor, the use of a section 2503(c) trust may be appropriate.

An additional consideration in deciding whether to use a trust is the type of property in question. For example, stock in an S corporation may be held on behalf of a minor by a custodian under the Uniform Gifts to Minors Act.[11] On the other hand, if a gift of S corporation stock is made to a section 2503(c) trust, the corporation's subchapter S election may be automatically terminated, because a trust is generally not a permissible shareholder of an S corporation. Certain exceptions apply only if:

a. the grantor or other individual is treated for income tax purposes as the owner of the trust property under Code sections 671 through 678 (a so-called grantor trust);

b. such a grantor trust continues after the grantor's death (limited to a period of two years after death);

c. the trust receives the stock under a will (a testamentary trust that holds S corporation stock only up to a maximum of two years after the stock is transferred to the trust);

d. the trust was created primarily to vote stock (a voting trust);

e. the trust is a Qualified Subchapter S Trust (QSST) (see last question and answer); or

f. the trust is an Electing Small Business Trust (ESBT).[12]

Another reason why a section 2503(c) trust may be used instead of the Uniform Gifts to Minors Act is a limitation in custodianship; UGMA provides that only one person may be custodian and specifies how a successor custodian may be named. But if a trust is created, the grantor may designate a line of succession of trustees and may provide for two or even more trustees to act together.

Question – Are there any adverse tax consequences if the grantor acts as the trustee of a section 2503(c) trust?

Answer – Yes. As noted above, if at the grantor's death, he or she is the trustee, the assets remaining in the trust will be includable in the grantor's estate (the same result occurs if the donor appoints himself as custodian under the Uniform Gifts to Minors Act or the Uniform Transfers to Minors Act and dies while serving in that capacity before the custodianship ends). A similar result may occur if the grantor (or donor) dies while serving as successor trustee (or custodian).

For example, if the grantor is appointed successor trustee upon the death of the first trustee and has the power to advance principal to the beneficiaries from time to time in his discretion as trustee or the power to terminate the trust, the corpus would be included in his or her gross estate as a power to "alter, amend, revoke or terminate" the trust.[13]

Question – If a parent places dividend-bearing securities into a section 2503(c) trust for his minor child using an independent bank as trustee, what types of expenditures of income would cause the income to be taxed to the parent?

Answer – If the income is or may be used to pay premiums on a life insurance policy on the life of either the grantor or the grantor's spouse, or if it is used for the support of a minor whom the grantor is legally obligated to support, then such income will be taxed to the grantor (father).[14] Note that the use of capital to pay premiums would not cause the grantor to be subject to income tax on trust income.

Further, if the minor is under age nineteen, or in certain cases under twenty-four, unearned income will be taxed to the minor at the rates applicable to trusts and estates (i.e. a top rate of 37 percent for income over $14,450 in 2023).

Question – In addition to giving the beneficiary the continuing right to compel distribution upon reaching twenty-one is there any other arrangement that can avoid a mandatory distribution of principal and income to the beneficiary at age twenty-one?

Answer – Yes. The beneficiary can be given a right for a *limited period* of time (i.e., thirty to sixty days), starting on his twenty-first birthday, to compel immediate distribution of the trust corpus by giving written notice to the trustee which, if not exercised, will permit the trust to continue under its own terms. Keep in mind that a beneficiary's power to compel distribution will cause the beneficiary to be treated as the owner of the trust for income tax purposes.[15]

Question – Is it possible to make a gift into a trust that can retain the property for a child past age twenty-one and still have the entire gift qualify for the annual exclusion?

Answer – Yes; based on the *Crummey*[16] case, if the donee has an immediate, unfettered, and ascertainable legal right at the time the gift is made to take out the amount put into the trust, then the gift will be considered a present interest gift and qualify for the gift tax annual exclusion. The Crummey beneficiary must be made aware of the right to withdraw the amount. This can be done by an annual letter which informs the beneficiary of right and offers the opportunity to sign a waiver to withdraw the contribution.

Ordinarily, failing to exercise a power to take property out of a trust (where the trust goes on under some circumstances to someone else) is a gift by the donee to the extent of the value that goes to someone else. However, there is a specific exception that ignores the gift consequence to the donee where the power is to appoint (i.e., to give) to oneself no more than the greater of $5,000 or 5 percent of the trust corpus.[17] To come within this "five-or-five" rule, this type of trust gives the beneficiary the right to remove only this five-or-five amount each year (on a noncumulative basis). However, the $5,000 limit is less than the amount of the annual exclusion.

There may be other persons (e.g., grandparents, uncles, aunts, etc.) who would like to make gifts to the trust. It is most probable that Crummey trusts can deal with these large gift potentials, while still avoiding a gift when the donee does not exercise his power, by giving the donee a power to appoint the trust at his death to anyone other than himself (or his estate, creditors or estate creditors).[18] This will bring the non-appointment trust assets into the donee's taxable estate, but because the size of the estate is not likely to be subject to estate tax, that is not usually an unacceptable condition.

Note that gifts to grandchildren may be subject to generation-skipping transfer tax. See Chapter 21.

CHAPTER ENDNOTES

1. Treas. Reg. §25.2503-3(b).
2. Treas. Reg. §25.2503-4.
3. Rev. Rul. 74-43, 1974-1 CB 285.
4. I.R.C. §§652, 662.
5. I.R.C. §641; Treas. Reg. §1.641(a)-2.
6. I.R.C. §2036.
7. I.R.C. §§652, 662.
8. Treas. Reg. §25.2503-3(b); *Herr v. Comm'r.*, 35 TC 732 (1961), aff'd, 303 F.2d 780 (3rd Cir. 1962), acq. 1968-2 CB 2. See also *Pettus v. Comm'r.*, 54 TC 112 (1970); *Est. of Levine v. Comm'r.*, 526 F.2d 717 (2nd Cir. 1976), rev'g 63 TC 136.
9. See *Stark v. U.S.*, 345 F. Supp. 1263 (W.D. Mo. 1972), aff'd, 477 F.2d 131 (8th Cir. 1973), cert den.
10. Internal Revenue Manual §25.18.1.2.8 (02-15-2005), Forms of Ownership and Characteristics.
11. Treas. Reg. §1.1361-1(e)(1).
12. I.R.C. §§1361(b)(1)(B), 1361(c)(2), 1361(d), 1361(e).
13. I.R.C. §§2036, 2038; *Est. of O'Connor v. Comm'r.*, 54 TC 969 (1970).
14. I.R.C. §677.
15. Rev. Rul. 74-43, 1974-1 CB 285.
16. *Crummey v. Comm'r.*, 397 F.2d 82 (9th Cir. 1968). See Chapter 31 on Crummey trusts.
17. I.R.C. §2514.
18. Priv. Ltr. Ruls. 8545076, 8517052.

GRANTOR RETAINED INTEREST TRUSTS (GRIT, GRAT, GRUT, QPRT)

CHAPTER 29

29.1 INTRODUCTION

A grantor retained interest trust is an irrevocable trust to which a grantor transfers assets such as a personal residence, closely held business interests, or other assets that generate income and have substantial appreciation potential, while retaining an interest for a period of years. Principal, at the end of the specified period of years, will pass to a noncharitable beneficiary, such as a child or grandchild of the grantor or a trust for their benefit. The main objective of a grantor retained interest trust is to reduce federal estate taxes. Three types of grantor retained interest trusts that can be especially useful are: Grantor Retained Income Trusts (GRIT), Grantor Retained Annuity Trusts (GRAT), and Grantor Retained Unitrusts (GRUT).

A GRIT, which was commonly used for income property before the enactment of Code section 2702, is now generally limited to transfers of a personal residence or certain tangible property, such as artwork, in situations where the grantor retains the use of the property during the term of the trust. In the case of the personal residence GRIT, the trust will usually be a Qualified Personal Residence Trust (QPRT) as defined below.

In a GRAT, the grantor retains a right to receive an annuity from the trust for a fixed period of years.

In a GRUT, the grantor retains a right to payment of a fixed percentage of the value of the trust property (determined annually) for a period of years.

In each of these types of trusts, the grantor is essentially making a current gift of a *future* interest in the trust assets to the remainder beneficiary. If the grantor survives the term selected, and depending on the value of the trust property remaining at the end of the term, significant tax savings may be realized with the GRAT, GRUT, and QPRT. For example, with a GRAT, the annuity payments can be structured to equal the required section 7520 interest rate, meaning the grantor will receive back all of the assets transferred into the trust via the annuity payments. Because the grantor can receive back the assets, the value of the gift to the beneficiaries will be zero (or close to zero). In this case, the GRAT is "zeroed-out" and the gift tax cost is low or zero. The advantage to the technique is that after the expiration of the trust term, any appreciation on the assets is removed from the estate and is not subject to gift or estate tax.

However, under Code section 2702, with respect to most GRITs, a grantor will now be treated as making a gift of the *entire* property transferred to trust (rather than a gift of the discounted value of the remainder) if certain family members are designated as the remainder beneficiaries. A GRIT holding a personal residence (such as a QPRT) is a notable exception to this rule.

29.2 WHEN IS USE OF SUCH A DEVICE INDICATED?

1. When the client is single and has a substantial estate upon which federal estate taxes are likely to be paid. Wealthy widows or widowers, divorced individuals, or other unmarried persons can use such a trust as a "marital deduction substitute."

2. When a married couple has an estate in excess of the couple's combined unified credit equivalent amount. The Tax Cuts and Jobs Act (TCJA) of 2017 temporarily increased this amount to $10,000,000 per taxpayer, indexed for inflation ($12,920,000 in

2023 $25,840,000 for a married couple). This amount is scheduled to revert to a $5,000,000 exemption ($10,000,000 for a married couple) in 2026. For estates which are larger than the current threshold, expected to become larger than this amount, or may exceed the reduced threshold for years 2026 and beyond, it may be worth considering these techniques. Typically, these techniques may be appropriate if a business or investment is expected to grow or generate significant cash flow relative to the value of the asset. Generally, the larger and more rapidly appreciating these estates are, the more effective such a trust may be.

3. When income producing property is located in more than one state and unification and probate savings are desired. The GRAT, GRUT, or QPRT would serve to transfer ownership of such property in a manner that would avoid ancillary administration.

4. When the client desires protection from will contests, public scrutiny, or an election against the will if the grantor survives the trust term.

5. When the remainder interest of the GRIT passes to someone other than those family members listed in Code section 2702, such as a niece, nephew, or unrelated friend.[1]

6. When the client wishes to use an alternative to (or be used in conjunction with) a recapitalization or other freezing technique that has the added advantages of gift tax leverage and possible estate tax savings.

7. When there is a high probability that the client will outlive the trust term that will result in a low present value gift to the remainder beneficiary.

8. When the client has assets so substantial that a significant portion can be committed to a remainder beneficiary without compromising his or her own personal financial security.

9. When the client has a high tolerance for complexity and a strong incentive to achieve gift and estate tax savings (rather than taking the direct but potentially more tax costly approach of making an immediate gift).

10. When interest rates are low, a GRAT is attractive since a successful GRAT requires that the asset outperform the Applicable Federal Rate of interest that must be used in valuing the gift. Also, the GRAT should be considered if interest rates are expected to rise during the term of the GRAT. However, while low interest rates are favorable to a GRAT, a different analysis applies with respect to a QPRT. In the case of a QPRT, if interest rates are low, the value of what the Grantor retains is mathematically less, which means that the value of the taxable gift is higher. Therefore, QPRTs work best when interest rates are high. That said, a QPRT is a viable option in a depressed real estate market.

29.3 WHAT ARE THE REQUIREMENTS?

In order to be effective, a GRAT or GRUT must comply with the requirements of Code section 2702 discussed in detail below.

1. A GRAT or GRUT must be an irrevocable trust in which the grantor retains the right to annual annuity or unitrust payments for a specified number of years (there is no limit to how few or how many years. Although in recent years there has been some discussion about setting a minimum GRAT term, therefore making it impossible to "zero out" the remainder interest, these proposals have not been implemented).). As noted below, the longer the specified term of the trust, the greater the value of the retained interest and therefore the lower the taxable gift the grantor is making to the ultimate beneficiaries.

2. The value of any qualified retained interest is determined under Code section 7520 (i.e., the "7520 rate"). Payment of the greater of an annuity or unitrust amount is permissible.

3. Evidence should be obtained of the value of the assets placed in the GRAT or GRUT. It is recommended that one or more qualified appraisers value the property at the time of transfer to the trustee of the trust.

4. The grantor's annuity or unitrust interest should be mandatory. The trust should specifically provide that the trustee has no discretion to withhold payments from the grantor (or possession of the trust property from the remainder beneficiary). Payments should be made annually or more frequently.

5. The grantor should be given only the annuity or unitrust interest (or possibly a noncontingent reversion). There is no requirement that the fixed annuity amount be the same for each year. The only requirement is that the annuity paid in a given year not exceed 120 percent of the amount paid the prior year.[2] The trustee generally should be specifically prohibited from making distributions in excess of the annuity or unitrust amounts. While a GRAT or GRUT can provide for payment of income in excess of the annuity or unitrust amount to the grantor, the value of the gift of a remainder interest is not reduced by the value of such an excess income provision.

6. In the case of a QPRT, a written lease may be entered into after the specified term expires. That lease should require the grantor to pay a fair market rental to the remainder beneficiary. Terms of the lease should be strictly enforced by the remainder beneficiary.[3]

7. After the grantor's retained interest has ended, neither the grantor nor any other donor to the trust should act as trustee. Retention of an interest as a trustee could lead to estate tax exposure.[4] If the grantor's spouse acts as trustee, consider the potential income tax consequences (see Chapter 30 on Intentionally Defective Trusts). Given these considerations, it is often inadvisable to name the grantor's spouse trustee.

29.4 ADVANTAGES

1. GRATs, GRUTs, and QPRTs work so well because they are based on two basic principles:

   a. Gift taxes are based on the value of the gift to the donee and a gift (and therefore the gift tax) must be "discounted" by the cost of the delay in the donee's enjoyment and possession of the property in the trust. The longer the donee must wait, the lower the value of the gift and therefore the lower the tax cost of making the gift. With IRS discount rates (the section 7520 rate) that fluctuate from month to month, there can be wide swings in gift tax cost. For instance, if the section 7520 rate is 6.0 percent, the taxable gift in the example below would be $167,518 [$300,000 − (0.441605 × $300,000)]. At a 4.0 percent rate it would be $202,669 [$300,000 − (0.324436 × $300,000)]. (These calculations can easily be made through *NumberCruncher Software*.)

   b. The federal estate tax does not reach a property interest unless the decedent owned it at death or unless he or she held a "string," i.e., a property right strong enough to cause it to be pulled back into the decedent's estate.[5] In a GRAT, GRUT, or QPRT, once the grantor lives *longer* than the specified term, the grantor neither owns the property in the trust nor has any rights to it or the income it produces. Absent some other inclusion factor, the property is then completely out of the grantor's estate and should escape estate taxation.

2. GRATs, GRUTs, and QPRTs are the closest thing to a "no lose" situation; it is an almost "what have we got to lose?" technique.

   a. If the client does not use a GRAT, GRUT, or QPRT and retains property in the client's sole name, the property plus any appreciation on the property will be includible in the estate.

   b. If the client who sets up a GRAT, GRUT, or QPRT dies during the specified term, the amount included in the grantor's gross estate depends on the type of trust. For example, under regulations finalized in 2011, under Code section 2036 if the grantor dies during the term of a GRAT, the amount included in the estate is limited to an amount necessary to produce the annuity based on IRS interest rates at the time of death.

   For a GRUT, the calculation is somewhat more complicated. It involves calculating the trust's "equivalent income interest rate," and dividing that by the section 7520 interest rate at death to determine the percentage (not in excess of 100 percent) of the trust corpus to include in the gross estate. Regulations were issued in 2011 which provide more guidance as to the amount includible in the grantor's gross estate.[6] The Regulations provide this example:

   Example. Assume the decedent transferred $100,000 to a GRAT with an annuity of $12,000 per year for ten years or until the grantor's earlier death, and the decedent dies before the termination of the term. At the time of the decedent's death, the value of the trust is $300,000 and the section 7520 rate is 6.0 percent. The amount includible in decedent's estate is the amount of corpus necessary to yield the annual annuity payment. The formula is the Annual Annuity (adjusted for monthly payments under Table K) divided by the section 7520 interest rate. In this example, at a 6.0 percent interest rate, $205,440 was includible in the decedent's gross estate because that is the amount which is needed to fund the required annuity payment.

29.5 DISADVANTAGES

The downside risks, costs, or disadvantages of a GRAT, GRUT, and QPRT include:

1. Attorney fees and the other transaction costs, such as appraisal fees and property titling costs of establishing the trust.

2. Lost opportunity cost. The GRAT, GRUT, or QPRT is an irrevocable trust, so, once assets are placed into the trust, the grantor is precluded from taking other planning measures. If the grantor has used up a sizable part of the lifetime gift credit to offset the gift of the remainder interest in the GRAT, GRUT, or QPRT, then the grantor is not in a position to make large gifts of other assets that may substantially appreciate in value. If the grantor dies during the term, the gamble will have been lost. The current estate and gift tax exemptions in 2023 are $12,920,000, however this amount is scheduled to revert to a $5,000,000 exemption (indexed for inflation) after December 31, 2025 per the Tax Cuts and Jobs Act of 2017.

3. If the grantor dies during the specified trust term, the trust property will be included in the grantor's estate for estate tax purposes. – but the property itself might not be available to pay that tax. (Solutions to this issue are discussed further below.)

4. The recipient of the property carries over the transferor's basis and therefore does not receive a new basis, which often is a "step up" in basis, at the transferor's death. This may significantly increase gain on a later sale or reduce depreciation deductions.

5. The GRAT must be administered properly. It must comply with the annual payment regulations during the donor's lifetime in the appropriate amount. If the assets in the GRAT do not appreciate, it could constitute a "failed" GRAT. It is also essential that the assets transferred to the GRAT be properly valued and that the adequate disclosure rules are complied with.

6. In the case of a QPRT, the grantor must pay rent to live in the house after the specified term has expired. This concept may be unsettling to some people.

7. With a QPRT, after the retained income period ends, there may be adverse consequences, such as the property being reassessed for property tax purposes. Moreover, certain states have state-specific benefits available for primary residences which may be lost after the retained income period ends (e.g., a Florida homeowner may lose homestead status for creditor protection and property tax purposes).

29.6 HOW IT IS DONE

Example. Assume a widow in a 40 percent gift tax bracket, and the section 7520 rate is 1.4 percent. She places her $3,000,000 personal residence into an irrevocable trust. The trust provides that she will live in the personal residence for a ten-year term. At the end of that time, the personal residence will pass to her children.

The present value of her right to live in the personal residence for ten years is $389,391 (0.12980 × $3,000,000). (See Appendix B for valuation tables.) Because the entire value of the personal residence placed in trust is $3,000,000 and the income interest retained by the grantor is $389,391 the value of the future interest gift being made at that point to the remainder beneficiary is the difference, $2,610,609. This entire $2,610,609 amount is a taxable gift, because the gift tax annual exclusion is allowed only for gifts of a *present* interest. Of course, this amount can be sheltered by the gift tax unified credit equivalent of $12,920,000 in 2023 which means that the widow will pay no gift tax - unless the widow has totally used her credit against the gift tax, in which case at a 40 percent gift tax rate, the gift tax would be $1,044,244.

If the $3,000,000 property appreciates at an after-tax rate of 3 percent, the property will be worth $4,031,749 by the end of the ten-year term. If, however, the property appreciated at 5 percent, the property would be worth $4,886,684, a potential death tax savings of $910,430.

Should the widow die before the term expires, her personal residence would be included in her estate at its date of death value and there would be no federal death tax savings.

Notice how things change if the 7520 rate is higher. At a 3 percent 7520 rate, the term certain factor is 0.255906. This makes the value of the nontaxable interest retained by the grantor $767,718 – reducing the taxable gift to only $2,232,282. At a 5 percent after tax growth, the property would be worth $4,886,684 after ten years. The potential death tax savings is over $1,061,761.

If the estate tax were discounted to reflect that it would be payable ten years later than the gift tax, then the savings, on a time value of money basis, would be less than that shown. On the other hand, because the property would not pass through probate, probate costs on the asset would be avoided.

GRATs and GRUTs can provide similar gift, estate, and generation-skipping transfer tax discounts. A married couple could each establish GRATs and GRUTs (or split gifts – see Chapter 8) so as to utilize both spouse's credits and marginal gift and estate tax brackets. However, with increased exemptions and the availability of portability between spouses (discussed in Chapter 27) the creation of a GRAT or GRUT by each spouse may become less important for tax savings.

29.7 TAX IMPLICATIONS

1. Absent other factors, if the grantor outlives the specified term, none of the trust's assets should be included in the grantor's estate. This is because the grantor has retained no interest in trust assets at death. Code section 2036 (retained life estates) applies only if the grantor retained the right to possess or enjoy the property or the income it produces:

    a. for life;

    b. for a period not ascertainable without reference to the grantor's death; or

    c. for any period which does not, in fact, end before the grantor's death.

2. The gift to the remainder beneficiary is a gift of a future interest. It therefore cannot qualify for the gift tax annual exclusion.

3. Because a GRIT is a grantor trust, the grantor will be liable for income tax on ordinary income earned by the trust.[7]

4. If the grantor lives beyond the specified term, there should be no further gift tax because the gift was complete upon the funding of the trust.

5. The taxable portion of gifts made after 1976 is considered an "adjusted taxable gift," because the entire present value of the gift to the remainder beneficiary is taxable.

    However, using a GRAT can transfer a rapidly growing asset at an extremely low transfer tax cost. This results in a significant "leveraging of the unified credit."

    Perhaps more importantly, 100 percent of appreciation in the property's value occurring after the term ending date escapes estate and gift tax. This makes a GRAT, GRUT, or QPRT an excellent "estate freezing" device with respect to post-transfer appreciation.

6. When the grantor survives the specified term of the trust, no step-up in basis for the property will be allowed. This is because the property was not acquired from a decedent. The property was acquired by gift when the trust was created, so the basis of the donee/remainder beneficiary is generally the same as in the hands of the grantor/donor (i.e., carryover basis). However, the donee's basis is increased by gift tax attributable to the gift in the proportion that the net appreciation at the time of the gift (fair market value of gift – basis) bears to the value of the gift.[8]

7. If the grantor dies before the specified term of the trust expires, the date of death value of the property or the value of the corpus necessary to

produce the annuity or unitrust if less, will be included in the grantor's gross estate.[9] If there were an estate tax inclusion, (a) there would be no adjusted taxable gift,[10] and (b) the unified credit utilized in making the gift would be restored to the estate. Note that if the spouse of the grantor "split the gift," the unified credit of the nongrantor spouse would not be restored. The simple solution to this problem is to have each spouse create a separate GRAT or GRUT, thereby making each a grantor of one trust.

One way to help mitigate the risk of the grantor dying during the trust term, known as the "mortality risk" is by creating a series of short-term, "rolling" or "laddered" GRATs. Under this technique, a series of GRATs are created with each GRAT being funded by the previous GRAT's annuity payments. In addition to mitigating the risk of the grantor's early death, rolling GRATs can be an efficient way to increase flexibility and reduce the negative impact of poor performance of the trust assets.

Another effective way to help protect against the mortality risk of a GRAT is incorporating a life insurance component to the plan. It may be appropriate for a beneficiary (or an ILIT) to purchase insurance in the amount of the potential federal estate tax savings on the life of the grantor and carry that life insurance during the trust term in which the grantor's death would cause estate tax inclusion. Assuming the grantor does not retain incidents of ownership, the insurance proceeds, received estate tax free, could then be used to purchase assets from the grantor's estate and thereby provide the estate with the liquidity to pay the estate tax. This technique in essence "bullet-proofs" the estate tax savings potential of the transaction.

8. If appreciated property is transferred to a GRAT, GRUT, or QPRT, the tax on any gain will eventually be paid by (a) the grantor (so long as the trust is a grantor trust), or (b) the trust (when the trust ceases to be a grantor trust), or (c) the beneficiaries (if the property is distributed outright to them on termination of the trust). Having taxes paid by the grantor may not, however, be a disadvantage, because the purpose of the trust is to "defund" the grantor's estate and shift as much wealth as possible to the remainder beneficiary with minimal gift taxes.

9. GRITs, GRATs, and GRUTS are generally subject to Code section 2702.

Section 2702

In valuing a transfer in trust to or for the benefit of a member of the transferor's family, Code section 2702(a) provides that all retained interests in trusts that are not "*qualified* interests" are valued at zero. The amount of any gift is then determined by subtracting from the value of the property the value of the retained interest.[11] Obviously, if no credit is given for what is retained, the value of the gift will be equal to 100 percent of the value of the property in question.

Section 2702 specifically does not apply to:

1. incomplete gifts (determined without regard to whether there is consideration);

2. personal residence trusts (see heading below);

3. charitable remainder annuity trusts and pooled income funds;

4. charitable lead trusts (if the only interest other than the remainder or a qualified annuity or unitrust interest is the charitable lead interest); and

5. certain charitable remainder unitrusts.[12]

Section 2702 also does not apply to assignment of remainder interests in trusts if the only retained interest is distribution of income in the sole discretion of an independent trustee, as defined in Code section 674(c), and certain property settlement agreements.[13]

The following definitions apply under section 2702:

1. In determining whether a remainder beneficiary is a "member of the transferor's family," such term includes such individual's spouse, any ancestor or lineal descendant of such individual or such individual's spouse, any brother or sister of the individual, and any spouse of any such individual.[14]

2. An interest is retained by the transferor if it is payable to the transferor or transferor's spouse, an ancestor of the transferor or the transferor's spouse, or the spouse of any such ancestor.[15]

3. A transfer in trust includes a transfer to a new trust or an existing trust or an assignment of an interest in an existing trust, but not a transfer

resulting from exercise of a power of appointment that would not constitute a taxable gift (e.g., lapse of a "Crummey" power which does not exceed the "5 or 5" limitation); or a disclaimer.[16]

4. A retained interest is one held by the same individual both before and after the transfer to the trust.[17]

Qualified interests are valued under Code section 7520, which requires the interest be valued at approximately 120 percent of the applicable federal midterm interest rate under Code section 1274(d)(1) for the month into which the valuation falls.

A qualified interest is:

1. a qualified annuity interest,

2. a qualified unitrust interest, or

3. a qualified remainder interest.[18]

Qualified Annuity Interests (GRATs)

A qualified annuity interest is an irrevocable right to receive a fixed amount at least annually, payable to or for the benefit of the holder of the term interest (i.e., the transferor or an applicable family member). A withdrawal right, whether or not cumulative, does not qualify, and neither does the issuance of a note or other debt instrument.[19]

The annuity payment can be a fixed dollar amount or a fixed percentage of the initial value of the trust.[20] Income in excess of the fixed amount can be distributable to the transferor, but is not considered in valuing the retained interest.[21] Subsequent contributions are prohibited. If the annuity is based on a percentage of the value of the trust, there must be a provision to adjust for incorrect valuation similar to the rules of Treasury Regulation section 1.664-2(a)(1)(iii).[22] Payment can be made after the close of the taxable year of the trust if made by the filing date for the trust income tax returns, determined without regard to extensions[23]. The annuity can be based on a fixed dollar amount or percentage of the value of the trust, and cannot vary except to the extent the amount (or percentage) in any year does not exceed 120 percent of the amount (or percentage) from the preceding year.[24]

P.J. Melcher, in his article "Are short term GRATs really better than long-term GRATs?" sets forth very clearly the disadvantages and advantages of short-term GRATs, summarized below.

Short-term GRATs

Advantages	Disadvantages
• minimize the extent years with poor returns offset years with favorable returns to reduce overall GRAT performance	• cannot lock in a low 7520 rate
• minimize mortality risk	• high payout rates may necessitate making transfers in kind which reduces the benefit of valuation discounts
• get wealth to beneficiaries sooner	• cost of appraisals each year for possible distribution in kind
• wealth transfers can be cut off at any time the donor believes beneficiaries have received enough	• using a 20% increasing payout feature provides less benefit over the short term
	• administrative costs of creating multiple GRATs

Longer term GRATs are beneficial when Section 7520 rates are low –and, favorable interest rates can be locked in.[25] However, in light of the TCJA, short-term and/or rolling GRATs with terms that end before the increased exemption is scheduled to expire at the end of 2025 may be an effective planning strategy.

Qualified Unitrust Interests (GRUTs)

A qualified unitrust interest is an irrevocable right to an annual payment of a fixed percentage of the net fair market value of the trust assets, to be determined annually.[26] Rules similar to those applicable to annuity trusts also apply here. Combinations of annuity and unitrust payments are not permitted. However, the trust may permit payment of the greater of an annuity or unitrust amount, to be valued at the higher of the two values.[27]

As to both annuity and unitrust transfers, any payments to other persons are prohibited; the term of the trust must be stated either as a period of years or the term holder's life, or the shorter of the two; successive term interests for the same individual are permitted;

and there must be no provision for commutation of any interest.[28] The transferor can retain a reversionary interest in either the GRAT or GRUT, contingent upon death during the trust term, but the reversion is valued at zero for gift tax purposes.

Qualified Remainder Interests

A qualified remainder interest is the right to receive all or a fractional share of the trust property on termination of all or a fractional share of the trust, and includes a reversion.[29] It must be noncontingent, i.e., payable to the beneficiary or the beneficiary's estate in all events. All interests in the trust (other than the noncontingent remainder interests) must be qualified annuity interests or qualified unitrust interests.[30] Payment of income is not permitted in excess of the annuity or unitrust amount to the holder of the qualified annuity or unitrust interest.[31] The right to receive a pecuniary amount or the original value of the corpus does not qualify.[32]

The retention of a remainder interest is a relatively rare estate planning technique, because any increase in the value of the transferred property is included in the transferor's taxable estate, and unless the remainder (reversion) is valued at less than 5 percent of the value of the transferred property, the grantor will be taxed on the income in any case.[33]

Personal Residence Trusts (PRTs)

A grantor retained income trust can still be utilized effectively where the transferor transfers an interest in a personal residence to a trust and the transferor retains the right to use the property for residential purposes for a term of years. Section 2702 carves out an exception for a personal residence trust. The regulations require such a trust to be limited to holding a single residence, or a fractional interest in a residence – in no case can the term holder hold interests in trust in more than two residences.[34]

The residence may not be occupied by any person other than the grantor, a spouse, or dependent; must be available at all times for such use; and cannot be sold or used for any other purposes.[35] However, merely because the grantor allows a friend to reside there with the grantor occasionally, allows house guests to use the residence rent-free, or leases a portion of the property to an unrelated third party will not result in disqualification, as long as it remains the grantor's personal residence. Under Code section 280A(d), if the grantor uses the residence (or portion of it) for personal purposes for a number of days which exceeds the greater of fourteen days or 10 percent of the number of days during the year for which the residence is rented at a fair rental, it qualifies as a personal residence.

The residence may include appurtenant structures and adjacent land reasonably appropriate for residential purposes, may be subject to a mortgage, but does not include any personal property, such as furnishings.[36] Residential use includes activities described in Code sections 280A(c)(1) or 280A(c)(4) (i.e., limited use for business or day care if only secondary); and excludes providing transient lodging and substantial services (i.e., a hotel or bed and breakfast).[37]

Interests owned by spouses in a residence, including community interests, can be transferred to the same trust so long as only the spouses hold the term interest.[38] If there is an involuntary conversion, such as destruction of the residence by fire, or its condemnation, the trust can hold the proceeds of such a conversion, such as insurance proceeds or a condemnation award, so long as there is a qualified replacement under Code Section 1033.[39] However, both the proceeds of the involuntary conversion and any income from those proceeds must be invested in a new residence within two years of when the proceeds were received.[40]

Qualified Personal Residence Trust (QPRTs)

The Treasury Regulations carve out a safe harbor called a qualified personal residence trust (QPRT).[41] A QPRT should contain provisions substantially the same as those required for personal residence trusts, but it may be more flexible in certain situations. For example, while the regulations seem to require that no assets other than an interest in a personal residence (or the proceeds of an involuntary conversion) can ever be held in a personal residence trust, and the interest in the residence cannot be sold during the term of the trust, the qualified personal residence trust permits both under limited circumstances. It is conceivable this trust could have income. If it does, it must be distributed to the term holder; no distributions can be made to any other person.

The qualified personal residence trust must prohibit the holding of any property other than the personal residence, and contain the following provisions:

1. No distributions to other persons are permitted.[42]

2. Cash can be held for the initial purchase of the residence within three months, or purchase of a replacement residence within three months of the date the cash is added to the trust.[43]

3. Cash can also be held for up to six months for payment of trust expenses, including mortgage payments, and for improvements.[44]

4. If the property is sold or insurance proceeds are received, a two year replacement period is permitted.[45] Excess cash must be distributed at least quarterly or at the termination of the trust to the term holder.[46]

5. If the property is no longer used as a personal residence, the trust must terminate and its assets must be distributed to the term holder within thirty days, unless it is converted into a qualified annuity trust.[47]

In the case of a qualified personal residence trust, it is possible to sell a residence, reinvest only part of the proceeds in a new residence, and convert the rest to an annuity. The governing instrument must prohibit the commutation (prepayment) of the term interest.[48]

The IRS has issued a sample qualified personal residence trust document.[49] However, many practitioners feel the form is lacking, particularly since it does not provide for the retention of a reversion right in the event the grantor dies before the end of the term.

If the Grantor is married, and his wife is willing to enter into a QPRT as well, a possible strategy would be to retitle the residence into tenancies in common and have each spouse contribute his or her one-half share to his or her own *separate* QPRT. A valuation discount would be based upon each trust only owning a partial interest in the property.

Subsequent Transfers of Retained Interests

A reduction of taxable gifts or adjusted taxable gifts is permitted if the individual subsequently transfers an interest in a trust that was valued under Code section 2702. The amount of the reduction is the lesser of the increase in taxable gifts resulting from the application of section 2702, or the increase in the transferor's subsequent taxable gifts, or taxable estate, which results from the subsequent transfer.[50] The rule applies to testamentary transfers only if a term interest in the trust is included in the transferor's taxable estate solely by reason of the operation of Code section 2033, or a remainder interest is included in the transferor's taxable estate, and such interest was valued under section 2702. Where spouses have split gifts, the adjustment is allocated one-half to each spouse, but one spouse may assign this adjustment to the other.

29.8 ISSUES IN COMMUNITY PROPERTY STATES

If a husband and wife transfer community property to a GRAT or GRUT, each may reserve the right to the payment for the trust term as to his or her respective community interest. It would apparently be possible for them to retain a joint payment for the term. If either dies during the term, the value of his or her community interest in the trust would be included in his or her taxable estate, either in whole or in part. To avoid this problem, most planners transmute community property to the separate property of each spouse and create a separate GRAT (or QPRT) for each spouse. If either or both spouses survive the term, his or her community interest in the trust should not be included in his or her estate. Note that in the case of the personal residence trust and qualified personal residence trust, the spouses can transfer community interests in one or two personal residences to the trust and retain the right to live in the residence for its term.

29.9 FREQUENTLY ASKED QUESTIONS

Question – Assume a husband makes a large transfer to a GRAT, GRUT, or QPRT. To reduce the potential gift tax on the value of the remainder beneficiary's interest, his wife consents to "split" the gift and use her credit against the gift tax to reduce or eliminate the tax. If the husband dies before the specified term expires, will the wife's credit be restored?

Answer – No. Although the husband's unified credit is restored if he dies within the specified term, his wife's unified credit is not restored. A potential solution to this inequity is for the husband to make a gift to his wife. She then could make her own actual contribution to the GRAT, GRUT, and QPRT. (Obviously, the IRS could consider this a step transaction, but this logic presumes that the gift to the wife (assuming the facts indicate it was an outright and unconditional gift) was per se a transfer to an agent of the husband. This presumption is at odds with the trend of constitutional and even tax law, which recognizes a spouse as an independent person and the trend of antipathy to sexual bias.)

Question – What are the best assets to place into a GRAT, GRUT or QPRT?

Answer – Assets that possess substantial appreciation potential are the best assets to place into a GRAT or GRUT.

Moreover, the transferor's basis in the assets transferred to a GRAT, GRUT or QPRT is carried over to the trust and does not receive any adjustment in basis. This may significantly increase gain on a later sale. Especially in light of the high lifetime exemption under current tax law, low basis assets may not be ideal to transfer to a GRAT, GRUT, or QPRT. Before entering into a transaction, the taxpayer's legal and tax advisors must consider not only the estate and gift tax benefits of the transaction, but any potential income tax consequences as well.

Question – Can the IRS revalue a transfer to a GRAT, GRUT, or QPRT many years after the GRAT, GRUT, or QPRT is funded?

Answer – A gift made after August 5, 1997, cannot be revalued for estate or gift tax purposes if the gift was adequately disclosed on a gift tax return and the gift tax statute of limitations (generally, three years) has passed.[51] Therefore, a gift tax return with an adequate disclosure of valuation should be filed with respect to a transfer to a GRAT, GRUT, or QPRT to start the statute of limitations with respect to valuation of the gift. In this regard, an appraisal of the property to be transferred should be performed, and a copy should be attached to the gift tax return which will be filed. The appraisal is necessary in order to satisfy the adequate disclosure rules with respect to reporting gifts. In addition, a copy of the GRAT, GRUT or QPRT document must also be attached to the gift tax return.

Question – Is there an "escape mechanism" that could redirect the remainder interest if the grantor dies during the term? For instance, is there a way to provide that if the grantor's estate has to include GRAT, GRUT, or QPRT assets, funds in the trust return to the grantor's estate rather than going to the remainder beneficiary?

Answer – A reversion to the grantor (or better yet to a revocable trust the grantor established during lifetime to avoid probate), conditioned on the grantor's death within the specified term, could be used. This actuarial assumption is easily calculated by a software product such as *NumberCruncher*. However, the value of a contingent reversion will not reduce the value of the taxable gift to the remainder person in the case of a GRAT or GRUT subject to Code section 2702.

Question – Is there a cutoff age after which the GRAT, GRUT, or QPRT no longer is mathematically logical?

Answer – Because the GRAT, GRUT, and QPRT are "little to lose – a lot to gain" tools, even clients in their eighties or nineties may want to use such a trust. For instance, assuming a section 7520 rate of 2.4 percent, the value of the income interest retained in a five-year QPRT is 0.111822 of the principal. Some clients, especially those who are in very good health, may want to gamble with a GRAT, GRUT, or QPRT. For example, if the eighty-year-old client opted for a ten-year term, the value of the income interest jumps to 0.211139 of the funds placed in the QPRT (and therefore the taxable gift to the remainder person drops accordingly).

For clients with a slightly lower risk tolerance, consider staggered terms. For instance, an eighty-year-old client could transfer some property into a two-year GRAT or GRUT and other property into a three- year GRAT or GRUT. Naturally, there are greater administrative costs with regard to multiple trusts.

Question – Are there problems with using closely held stock with a GRAT or GRUT?

Answer – The major problem with transferring closely held stock or other similarly hard-to-value assets into a GRAT or GRUT concerns valuation. If the asset is not properly valued and/or not properly disclosed to the IRS, there is a risk of having to pay additional gift tax, penalties, and interest, or of using up more of the lifetime credit against gift tax. In addition, clients should consider how closely held stock will be controlled or voted after termination of the GRAT or GRUT, particularly to avoid negative estate tax consequences once the asset has been transferred. Moreover, if the GRAT fails to generate the income necessary to satisfy the payments, then the stock must be transferred back to the Grantor as the "annuity." This defeats one of the main purposes of the GRAT. S.S. Eastland,[52] in the article "Optimize Contributions to a Grantor Retained Annuity Trust," sets forth an interesting way to structure a GRAT through the use of leverage. First, the taxpayer's financial assets would be contributed to a family limited partnership. Then 10 percent of the partnership interest would be contributed to a single-member LLC and 90 percent of the assets would be sold to the LLC for a note. Later, the client contributes non-managing membership interests in the LLC to a GRAT. The author recommends that the remainder beneficiary be a grantor trust with the spouse as a beneficiary coupled with a limited power of appointment. If leverage is used, more wealth is transferred to the remaindermen of the GRAT. Moreover, if, during the term of the GRAT, the assets have appreciated, and the grantor is worried that the assets may decline in value in the future, the grantor can utilize a power to substitute other assets that are less likely to fluctuate. In this way, the GRAT's appreciation is, as the author notes, "locked in." There is some fear that this power of substitution resembles additional contributions by the Grantor. Additional contributions are not permitted. However, there are several private letter rulings approving GRAT's that contain a power of substitution.[53]

Question – Are there special provisions that should be inserted into a GRAT, GRUT, or QPRT?

Answer – Yes. The trust instrument should carefully track the requirements of Code section 2702 and the accompanying regulations.

It also is extremely important to document the "completeness" of the transfer at the date the trust is funded. Specifically, the trust must provide that the donor has given up all dominion and control over the property.

The grantor must specifically give up any power to revoke the gift of the remainder. The trust should also forbid the grantor to change any beneficial interests in the remainder. Therefore, the grantor can retain no power of appointment (other than, possibly, a power contingent on the grantor dying during the trust term).

The grantor should not be named as trustee after the grantor's retained interest ends. An unrelated, independent trustee or another family member (depending on the terms of any continuing trusts) could be selected.

The trust should specifically deny the grantor any control over the manner or time in which the beneficiaries will enjoy the trust corpus (otherwise, that corpus will be pulled back into the grantor's estate under Code section 2038).

Question – How should clients be advised who are concerned that if they transfer their personal residence into a trust for a term, and still want to live there at the end of the term, they will be unable to do so?

Answer – This is a concern to many clients, and there are planning ideas to help. A PRT or QPRT must prohibit the grantor or the grantor's spouse from repurchasing the personal residence from the trust.[54] However, one method to accomplish this goal is for the grantor to lease the residence from either the trust or the remainder beneficiary after the initial term of the PRT or QPRT. The IRS has privately ruled that if the residence is leased at fair market value, the grantor would not retain any economic benefit in the property. The IRS concluded that if the grantor survived the initial term of the trust and continued to live in the residence until death, leasing the residence for fair market value rent, the interest in the property transferred to the trust would not be includible in the grantor's gross estate under Code section 2036.[55]

Question – Can the QPRT be effectively used for a vacation home?

Answer – Possibly the most popular use of the QPRT is for a second or vacation home. Under the facts of one ruling,[56] grantor and spouse jointly own two vacation homes that could be successfully transferred to a QPRT. They intend to retitle them so that each spouse owns one property; then each will transfer his or her vacation home to a QPRT until the death of that grantor or a term of ten years. Income, if any, will be distributed to each grantor, and each will have the right to live in his or her residence. If the residences are sold, an annuity will be paid during the remainder of the term. If a grantor survives, the property will remain in trust until the surviving grantor dies. However, income will be accumulated until the death of the surviving spouse and then distributed to children. There is a reversion if the grantor dies during the trust term.

Question – Can stock in an S corporation be placed into a GRAT or GRUT?

Answer – Under usual circumstances, a GRAT or GRUT does not qualify to hold S stock because not all of the trust income is payable to the beneficiary. See Chapter 53. However, because any trust as to which the grantor is treated as the owner for income tax purposes can hold S corporation stock, the solution has been to make the GRAT or GRUT "defective" for income tax purposes (i.e., taxable under the grantor trust rules). See Chapter 30. There are many examples of this technique in private letter rulings.[57]

Question – Should GST exemption be allocated to a GRAT?

Answer – A transfer to a GRAT is not a direct skip because the grantor who is not a skip person has an interest in the GRAT during its term. So, even if grandchildren are the ultimate beneficiaries, the transfer to the GRAT itself is not a direct skip. However, the termination of the Grantor's interest *will* constitute a taxable termination. The amount subject to the tax will be the entire value of the GRAT at that time. Therefore, the only way to have an inclusion ratio of zero is if the Grantor allocates GST exemption equal to the entire value of the property. However, that wastes exemption because there will be annuity payments coming back to the Grantor. Therefore, in many cases the Grantor will opt out of automatic allocation on the gift tax return for the year that the GRAT was created.[58] Although generally speaking, a GRAT is not an effective way to use GST exemption because much of the exemption will be wasted in the form of returned annuity payments, with the increased GST exemption under the TCJA, in some cases, clients may have extra GST exemption available to allocate before the law is scheduled to sunset after 2025. In these cases where GST exemption would otherwise be unused, it may make sense to make an allocation to the GRAT.

What of a GRAT whose remainder passes to grandchildren with parents who were living at the inception of the GRAT? The flaw in allocating GST to this GRAT is that the transfer to a GRAT can, again, never be a direct skip. The transfer is not to the remainder beneficiaries; it is to the GRAT itself.

Question – Assume a sixty-year-old grantor established a GRAT for a term of fifteen years, but with a provision that should she die before the end of the term, it will terminate at her death. The value of the property placed in the trust is $500,000, the annuity payout rate is 6 percent, and the section 7520 rate is 2.4 percent. What is the amount of the gift? What would the amount be if the gift was for a fifteen-year term certain?

Answer – See Figures 29.1 and 29.2.

Figure 29.1

GRANTOR RETAINED ANNUITY TRUST (Term With Reversion - Table 2000CM)				
Transfer to Trust:		$500,000	Annuity Payment	$30,000
Age:		60	Term of Years:	15
Frequency of Payments:		Annual	Payments:	End of Period
Section 7520 Interest Rate:		2.4%		
Check Exhaustion of Trust Fund				
Ann. Factor (15 years, 2.4%):		12.4729	Adj. Factor (Annual, 2.4%)	1.0000
Annuity Test Value:		$374,187	Special Factors	Not Required
Valuation				
Ann. Factor (60, 15, 2.4%):		11.1878	Adj. Factor (Annual, 2.4%):	1.0000
Annuity Value:		$335,634	Remainder Value	$164,366

Figure 29.2

GRANTOR RETAINED ANNUITY TRUST (Term Certain)				
Transfer to Trust:	$500,000	Annuity Payment:		$30,000
Term of Years:	15	Frequency of Payments:		Annual
Payments:	End of Period	Section 7520 Interest Rate		2.4%
Check Exhaustion of Trust Fund				
Ann. Factor (15 years, 2.4%):	12.4729	Adj. Factor (Annual, 2.4%):		1.0000
Annuity Test Value:	$374,187	Special Factors:		Not Required
Valuation				
Ann. Factor (15 years, 2.4%):	12.4729	Adj. Factor (Annual, 2.4%):		1.0000
Annuity Value:	$374,187	Remainder Value:		$125,813

CHAPTER ENDNOTES

1. I.R.C. §2702 effectively eliminates GRITs where the remainder interest passes to a member of the grantor's family, including the grantor's spouse, ancestors and lineal descendants of the grantor and the grantor's spouse, brothers or sisters of the grantor, or any spouses of the above. I.R.C. §2702 (e).
2. Treas. Reg. §25.2702-3(b)(1)(ii)(A)-(B).
3. *Est. of Barlow v. Comm'r.*, 55 TC 666 (1971), acq. 1972 CB 1.
4. I.R.C. §2038.
5. I.R.C. §§2036, 2038.
6. Treas. Reg. §20.2036-1.
7. I.R.C. §677(a)(1).
8. I.R.C. §1015(d)(6).
9. I.R.C. §§2036(a)(1), Final Regulations under Treas. Reg. §20.2036-1(c).
10. I.R.C. §2001(b); Treas. Reg. §25.2702-6(a).
11. Treas. Reg. §25.2702-1(b).
12. If the CRUT provides for simple unitrust payments. In the case of a CRUT with a lesser of trust income or the unitrust amount provision, the grantor and/or the grantor's spouse are the only noncharitable beneficiaries.
13. Treas. Reg. §25.2702-1(c).
14. I.R.C. §§2702(e), 2704(c)(2).
15. I.R.C. §§2702(a)(1), 2701(e)(2).
16. Treas. Reg. §25.2702-2(a)(2).
17. Treas. Reg. §25.2702-2(a)(3).
18. I.R.C. §2702(b); Treas. Reg. §25.2702-2(a)(6).
19. Treas. Reg. §25.2702-3(b)(1)(i).
20. Treas. Reg. §25.2702-3(b)(1)(ii).
21. Treas. Reg. §25.2702-3(b)(1)(iii).
22. Treas. Reg. §25.2702-3(b)(2).
23. Treas. Reg. §25.2702-3(b)(4).
24. Treas. Reg. §25.2702-3(b)(1)(ii).
25. Melcher, P.J., "Are short term GRATs really better than long-term GRATs?," 36 *Estate Planning* 3, 23 (March 2009).
26. Treas. Reg. §25.2702-3(c)(1). The trust assets are to be valued in accordance with Treas. Reg. §25.2522(c)-3(c)(2)(vii).
27. Treas. Reg. §25.2702-3(d).
28. Treas. Reg. §25.2702-3(d)(3)(4).
29. Treas. Reg. §25.2702-3(f)(2).
30. Treas. Reg. §25.2702(f)(1)(iv).
31. *Id.*
32. Treas. Reg. §25.2702-3(f).
33. I.R.C. §673.
34. Treas. Reg. §§25.2702-5(a), 25.2702-5(b).
35. Treas. Reg. §25.2702-5(b)(1).
36. Treas. Reg. §25.2702-5(b)(2)(C)(ii).
37. Treas. Reg. §25.2702-5(b)(2)(C)(iii).
38. Treas. Reg. §25.2702-5(b)(2)(C)(iv).
39. Treas. Reg. §25.2702-5(b)(3).
40. I.R.C. §1033(a)(B).
41. Treas. Reg. §25.2702-5(c).
42. Treas. Reg. §25.2702-5(c)(4).
43. Treas. Reg. §25.2702-5(c)(5).
44. *Id.*
45. Treas. Reg. §25.2702-5(c)(7).
46. Treas. Reg. §25.2702-5(c)(5)(A)(2).
47. Treas. Reg. §25.2702-5(c)(8).
48. Treas. Reg. §25.2702-5(c)(6).
49. Rev. Proc. 2003-42, 2003-23 IRB 998.
50. Treas. Reg. §25.2702-6(a).
51. I.R.C. §2001(f).
52. Eastland, S.S., "Optimize Contributions to a Grantor Retained Annuity Trust," 39 *Estate Planning*, No. 4, 3 (April 2012).
53. For example, Priv. Ltr. Rul. 200846001.
54. Treas. Regs. §§25.2702-5(b)(1), 25.2702-5(c)(9).
55. Priv. Ltr. Ruls. 9433016, 9735012, 9723030.
56. Priv. Ltr. Rul. 9441039.
57. Priv. Ltr. Ruls. 9416009, 9444033.
58. See "Generation-Skipping Transfer Tax Consequences of GRATs: Finding the Answers," *Journal of Taxation*, May 2011.

INTENTIONALLY "DEFECTIVE" TRUST

CHAPTER 30

30.1 INTRODUCTION

An intentionally "defective" trust is an irrevocable trust designed to have the following characteristics:

1. Transfers of property to the trust arepleted gifts for federal gift tax purposes.

2. The trust assets will *not* be included in the taxable estate of the grantor or grantors.

3. The income of the trust is taxed to the grantor, who is treated as the "owner" of the trust for federal income tax purposes.

Such a trust is created by intentionally drafting the trust to fall within the provisions of one or more of the grantor trust rules found in Code sections 671 through 677. Under Code section 671, trust income or deductions will be attributed to the grantor of the trust if the grantor is treated as the owner of the trust under the provisions of Code sections 672 through 677. These rules are discussed in Chapter 22 in connection with the Income Taxation of Trusts and Estates.

The grantor trust rules were enacted by Congress to prevent taxpayers from using trusts to shift income tax liabilities to a lower bracket taxpayer while retaining control or beneficial enjoyment of the trust property. Thus, falling within the reach of the grantor trust rules was traditionally viewed negatively in that the grantor of the trust was, for income tax purposes, the owner of the trust assets, and was personally responsible for all items of income (ordinary income and capital gains) attributable to the trust assets. This personal responsibility existed whether or not the income and/or principal was actually distributed to the grantor. Accordingly, the trust may be viewed as being "defective," in that it will not avoid and in fact is subject to the grantor trust rules. This terminology is a holdover from a time when the desire was to *avoid* grantor trust status. Now, there are good reasons to deliberately draft trusts so that grantor trust status is invoked. Therefore, these trusts are sometimes referred to as "intentionally defective grantor trusts."

The use of Intentionally Defective Grantor Trusts (IDGTs) has become increasingly popular as an estate planning technique. Since the estate tax inclusion rules are applied separately from and independently of the income tax rules, unique opportunities are available to shift assets to a succeeding generation at little or no transfer or income tax cost and to otherwise reduce the grantor's estate, and in the right circumstances, increase creditor protection.

It is important to note that the benefits touted for IDGTs are not supported by any statute. The prospect of positive results is based solely on practitioners' interpretations of IRS rulings and case law. Because these favorable benefits may be eliminated by an act of Congress or a change in IRS position, they should be considered only for clients who are not risk adverse and used only after a thorough explanation of the potential downsides and costs.

30.2 WHEN IS USE OF SUCH A DEVICE INDICATED?

Defective trusts are particularly useful when the grantor wishes to remove an appreciating asset from the estate without making a taxable gift. A gift may be undesirable for many reasons – e.g., the grantor's gift tax applicable exclusion amount may be insufficient to cover the value of the gift, the client may wish to retain the exemption for other gifts, or the grantor may desire to retain a stream of income, etc.

When interest rates are low, it is an excellent time to consider selling assets to an IDGT in exchange for an installment note, because the success of a sale to an IDGT is contingent upon the assets growing or producing income at a rate higher than the Applicable Federal Rate (AFR). The client may couple the sale with a gift to the trust to provide security, allowing the trust to borrow from the Grantor to buy even more assets.[1] If a non-controlling interest in a family business is transferred to the IDGT, a discount in value may be appropriate. It is important to have a business appraiser value the discount.

By using a defective trust, appreciating assets can be sold to the trust in exchange for an installment note without a gift made.[2] Additionally, the grantor's payment of income taxes on behalf of the trust is not considered a gift.[3] Moreover, the grantor will not recognize any taxable gain on the sale of the appreciating asset to the trust because the grantor and the trust are treated as one tax unit (i.e. they are alter egos) for income tax purposes.[4] For example, if a grantor sells a capital asset worth $2,000,000 with a basis of $1,000,000 to his grantor trust, the grantor does not have to recognize gain on the sale because the grantor and his grantor trust are deemed to be one in the same for income tax purposes. The sale, in effect, is ignored for income tax purposes because the grantor cannot sell an asset to himself. Moreover, if the trust purchases the asset in exchange for a promissory note, interest payments to the grantor on the note are also disregarded for income tax purposes.

Another key benefit of a grantor trust is that the payment of income taxes by the grantor allows trust assets to grow more rapidly. Because the grantor pays the income taxes incurred by the trust out of his or her own funds, trust assets are not depleted to pay for income taxes, allowing the trust assets to compound more quickly and grow, in essence, tax free. Additionally, by paying the income tax on the income that will pass to the beneficiaries, the grantor is reducing the estate though what is in essence a tax-free gift to the beneficiary.

Taxing income to the grantor rather than the trust will almost always result in substantial income tax savings because of the compressed tax rates applied to trusts. Consider the following income tax rates for estates and trusts in 2023:

Taxable income	
Not over $2,900	10% > $0
Over $2,900 but not over $10,550	290 + 24% > 2,900
Over $10,550 but not over $14,450	2126 + 35% > 10,550
Over $14,450	3,491 + 37% > 14,450

Conversely, if the grantor is in a higher income tax bracket than the trust beneficiary, the grantor would pay higher income taxes than if the trust income was taxed to the beneficiary. Of course, if the grantor's estate is reduced by the grantor's tax payment, the estate tax savings may justify this technique. Obviously, a comparative analysis should be made.

Grantor trusts can also be used to hold stock in an S corporation. In this case, it is particularly important that the grantor be treated as the owner of both the income and corpus of the entire trust. This is often more favorable than making an election for the trust to be treated as a qualified subchapter S Trust (QSST). It is important to note that sometimes the election to be treated as an Electing Small Business Trust might be more beneficial than qualification as a QSST because a QSST cannot be used to benefit multiple beneficiaries or allow income to accumulate. (See Chapter 53.)

Other types of grantor trusts are grantor retained annuity trusts (GRATs), grantor retained unitrusts (GRUTs), or qualified personal residence trusts (QPRTs; see Chapter 29). In the case of a personal residence trust, if the grantor is treated as the owner and the residence is sold by the trust, Code section 121 would apply to exclude gain from the sale (the $250,000 gain exclusion, $500,000 married taxpayers). Note that the trust must be defective (i.e., treated as a grantor trust) as to both income and corpus to qualify for the section 121 exclusion.

Where a GRAT or GRUT is involved, it is possible that the trust may not generate sufficient income or cash flow to make the annuity or unitrust payments. In such an instance, the GRAT or GRUT distribution would be "in kind" (i.e., of the trust assets) without any income tax consequences to the trust.

Another asset that may be desirable to transfer to IDGT is an installment note with respect to a sale of property by the grantor to a third party (other than the trust). Generally, the transfer of an installment note (by gift or otherwise) triggers the deferred gain. Because the grantor and the trust are treated as a single taxpayer, the transfer of an installment note to an IDGT will not accelerate the gain.[5] Additionally, interest payments to the grantor with respect to an installment sale to the trust is not taxable to the grantor.[6] This technique may be used to set up an income tax deduction for transfers to charitable lead trusts.[7]

Leveraging a sale to a grantor trust with life insurance can be a highly effective way to increase the total amount left to heirs in a tax-efficient manner. When trust assets will be used to pay for life insurance premiums, the assets sold to the trust ideally should be income producing, such as commercial real estate, limited partnership interests, S-corporation stock, or securities or other income-generating assets. If a residence is owned by a defective grantor trust, payments of rent by the grantor may not be taxable gifts, because the trust is considered the tax alter ego of the grantor (who can't make gifts to himself).

30.3 WHAT ARE THE REQUIREMENTS?

The trust must be irrevocable. Either the grantor or a trustee that does not have an adverse interest to the grantor retains certain powers. One common nonfiduciary power a grantor can hold to cause a trust to be grantor trust is the power to remove trust assets from the trust and substitute other assets of equal value.[8] This apparently has no adverse estate tax consequences to the grantor. Note that the IRS has refused to rule on this in all cases, because it is a question of fact whether or not the grantor is acting in a nonfiduciary capacity.

A nonadverse party, acting in a fiduciary capacity, can also be granted certain powers. One power which triggers the grantor trust rules of Code section 674 is the power to add beneficiaries other than after born or after adopted children.[9] In one private ruling,[10] a trust provided that the trustee could, in its discretion, add as beneficiaries persons who were lineal descendants of the parents of the grantor. This brought the trust under the provisions of Code section 674, making it a grantor trust and therefore eligible to hold S corporation stock.

In the case of an installment sale to an intentionally defective grantor trust, it is important that the assets that are the subject of the sale not be the sole source of the payments on the installment note. This is necessary to avoid an argument by the IRS that the grantor retained an interest in the asset that is includable in the grantor's estate under Code section 2036. If a trust must rely only on the income generated by the asset to repay the grantor, the IRS may argue that the transaction is not a bona fide sale, but rather a retained interest. This is based on the theory that most individuals would not enter into a sale arrangement with another person who has no means to pay for the asset. Thus, prior to the sale, the grantor should make a "seed" gift to the trust of cash or assets to provide the trust with economic substance and have the transaction be treated as a legitimate sale. Alternatively, some commentators have suggested that the seed capital requirement could be met by partial guarantees by beneficiaries. Some practitioners have posited that the value of the seed gift be at least 10 to 20 percent of the value of the asset being sold.[11] Citing solid United States Supreme Court jurisprudence under the "reality of sale doctrine," other commentators disagree.[12]

If the grantor would like to create a multigenerational trust that is a generation-skipping or dynasty trust, the grantor should allocate some of the generation-skipping exemption to this initial seed gift so that the purchased asset will not be treated as a gift, and, thus be excluded from the beneficiary's estate. Some commentators suggest that the taxpayer file a gift tax return disclosing the sale to the trust and taking the position that there is no gift incorporated in the transaction, but this is far from certain, and it belies the reality of the situation, i.e., there was no reportable gift, calling the return's necessity and validity into question. In the past, the IRS has disregarded returns it has deemed unnecessary.[13]

The trust beneficiary should *not* have any Crummey withdrawal right over the initial gift, so as to avoid any argument that the beneficiary, rather than the grantor, is the owner of the assets for income tax purposes.[14] However, in recent years, some practitioners have become more comfortable that a grantor will be treated as such even though Crummey powers exist with respect to the beneficiaries.[15]

It is also important that "adequate" (at least AFR) interest be charged by the trust on the installment note, so as to avoid any gift component. If the asset is sold at fair market value and the applicable federal rate (AFR) of interest is used, no gift should be deemed to have been made.

"Toggling" Grantor Trust Status

It might be beneficial to be able to "toggle" and turn off the grantor trust status. The grantor, after all, may grow dissatisfied with paying the income tax. This may also occur if the client changes residence from a low income tax state to a higher income tax state or if tax laws change.[16] Turning off grantor trust status may be accomplished by releasing the power that caused grantor trust status in the first place or by changing trustees.[17]

Alternatively, a trust which was not a grantor trust may be converted to one through, for example, changing trustees or actual borrowing of assets from the trust without giving adequate security or adequate interest.[18] Of course, one could also pursue a court modification.

If grant or trust status is toggled off, and the trust holds S-corporation stock, then an immediate QSST or ESBT election should be made. The grantor should be wary of toggling "on" and "off" grantor trust status so that he can take advantage of a loss or avoid income recognition. Such actions may draw the attention of the Internal Revenue Service. Notice 2007-73 of the IRS identifies such actions as "transactions of interest" and was essentially a notice to be aware that the IRS and the Treasury Department know that certain taxpayers are terminating grantor trust status and then re-establishing such status for the purpose of "allowing the grantor to claim a tax loss greater than any actual economic loss sustained by the taxpayer or to avoid inappropriately the recognition of gain."[19]

30.4 POWERS COMMONLY USED TO EFFECTUATE GOALS

In creating intentionally defective trusts, the following are powers most frequently granted to a trustee who is someone other than the grantor, but who is a nonadverse party:

1. Powers to control beneficial enjoyment of the trust under Code section 674(a), (but note the exceptions for certain powers under section 674(b), and the exception for powers of an independent trustee under section 674(c)). Therefore, the grantor could grant a nonadverse party who is not a trustee a presently exercisable special power of appointment over both principal and income of the trust, whether an external standard exists or not.[20]

2. Certain administrative powers under Code section 675, including:

    (a) the power to deal with the trust for less than full consideration;

    (b) the power to borrow from the trust under certain circumstances;

    (c) the power, in a nonfiduciary capacity, to vote or control investments where the trust includes stock where voting control held by the grantor and trust is significant;

    (d) and the power to remove assets and substitute assets of equal value.

    Note that if the grantor retains the power in a nonfiduciary capacity to remove assets and replace them with assets of equal value, the grantor is treated as the owner for income tax purposes but should not be for gift or estate tax purposes.

3. The power to revoke the trust in favor of the grantor under Code section 676, or to distribute income to the grantor under Code section 677. However, since this may subject the trust to the grantor's creditors, it is not recommended.

4. The power to apply income to the payment of premiums on life insurance on the grantor or grantor's spouse under Code section 677(a)(3).

As a best practice, two or more of the above "grantor trust" powers are often included in the trust document.

There is a legal distinction between powers that apply to income and those that apply to corpus transactions (such as sales or other capital gain events). If the power applies only as to the trust's income, the grantor will be income taxed on the income, but gains on sales or exchanges or other events of a principal nature will be taxed to the trust as would be the case with any non-grantor trust. Such a trust would not fully accomplish the dual objectives of shifting all lifetime taxation to the grantor while keeping the trust's assets out of the grantor's estate. Moreover, due to the condensed tax rates applicable to trusts (short-term capital gain taxed as ordinary income) and the likely imposition of the net investment income tax on capital gain recognized by the trust, the tax liability of the trust may be greater than it would have been taxed to the grantor.

Also, the IRS will not necessarily recognize the validity of certain powers as causing the trust to be treated as a grantor trust, particularly the power to substitute property of equal value, where the power is not likely to be used, particularly if the power holder does not have enough net worth to exercise it in whole. Therefore, it is often helpful to use more than one defective power.

30.5 HOW IT IS DONE

Example 1. Duncan Osborne owns all of the stock in a corporation that is electing to be taxed under Subchapter S of the Internal Revenue Code. He would like to make a gift of several shares of nonvoting common stock in trust for his children, but he also wants to retain a substantial part of the income stream from that stock for a period of years. It is explained to him about the possible use of a grantor retained annuity trust (GRAT) for a term of years. However, a GRAT is not a qualified shareholder in an S corporation since there is no guarantee that all of the trust income would be paid to the grantor (the annuity might be more, or less, than the income).

It is proposed that the trust contain a provision that grants Duncan the power, at any time during the term of the trust, to remove the trust assets and substitute other assets of equal value. Under Code section 675(4), if this power is exercisable in a nonfiduciary capacity, the trust will be classified as a grantor trust. Since S corporation stock can be held in a grantor trust, the S election will not be lost during the grantor's lifetime. Further, if the grantor does elect to swap trust assets, or repurchase assets from the trust at fair market value, such a swap or purchase will have no income tax consequences to either the trust or to Duncan.

Example 2. George establishes an intentionally defective grantor trust for the benefit of his children, Sam and Dorothy. George owns a business that he expects will significantly increase in value over the next ten years. He desires to sell this business to the defective trust in order to remove the anticipated increase in value from his estate, but he does not wish to incur any income tax consequences on the sale.

George obtains an appraisal of the business and, thereafter, makes a gift of 20 percent of this value to the trust to serve as seed money for the anticipated purchase. George then sells the business, at its appraised fair market value, to the defective trust in exchange for a twenty-year promissory note. Depending upon George's need (or desire) for income, the note can be structured to be interest-only (at the current AFR) with a balloon payment at the end of the term, or principal and interest can be amortized over the twenty-year term. The income produced by the initial gift and the purchased business will be used to make the note payments. Depending on the level of income the asset produces, the trustee may decide to purchase a life insurance policy on George's life. The income tax-free death benefit may potentially increase the total amount left in the trust for the benefit of George's heirs.

During the term of the note, George receives a stream of income that is not taxable to him. This is income he may need and want. At the end of the term, neither the business (at its increased value) nor the paid off promissory note will be included in George's estate. If, however, George dies before the note is paid, the value of the promissory note at the time of his death will be included in the estate.

Moreover, a husband and wife can create IDGTs for one another. These IDGTs can be dynasty trusts which will avoid estate tax down through the generations as well as providing for protection from marital claims which might arise against their children during their lifetimes.

A problem does arise when the grantors of the IDGTs divorce. The terms of the IDGT can address this issue by incorporating specific language into the trust document that defines the spouse as the individual is married to and living with at the time of distribution. Or, as another option, the grantor can give someone else a limited power of appointment to direct the assets back to someone other than the grantor's ex-spouse or even the grantor.[21]

However, if each spouse creates a trust for the other, there is a concern that the IRS may conclude that the "reciprocal trust doctrine" applies. This doctrine examines whether the spouses are in the same economic position they would have been if they had created trusts for themselves. If that is the case, each spouse is presumed to be the beneficiary of his or her own trust (rather than the beneficiary of the other spouse's trust). While there are not clear rules as to how to avoid the application of this doctrine, one approach is to provide for a significant lapse of time between the creation of the trusts.[22]

Another approach, subject to the admonitions of the United States Supreme Court in its seminal *United States v. Estate of Grace*[23] decision, is to have the trusts contain substantively different provisions (e.g., differing provisions regarding current or final distributions, beneficiary powers, or rights of collateral beneficiaries). Some of these differences may include:

- one trust gives the spouse a significant amount of control by virtue of lifetime and testamentary powers of appointment;

- one trust can give the spouse the ability to remove and replace trustees;

- one trust can provide that distributions can be made under a broader standard than HEMS;

- one trust can give the spouse Crummey powers of withdrawal (demand rights when additions to the trust are made);

- one trust can provide sprinkle provisions for descendants; or

- one trust can provide that there can be no distributions to the spouse for a period of years.

30.6 TAX IMPLICATIONS

Income Tax

The following is a summary of the income tax rules pertaining to grantor trusts:

1. Code section 672 contains important definitions relating to adverse and nonadverse parties, and related and subordinate parties. Under the remaining sections, whether the grantor is treated as the owner of the trust may depend on whether certain powers are conferred on persons fitting these definitions.

2. Code section 673 imposes the grantor trust rules where the grantor retains a reversionary interest in the trust, that is, a right to some future benefits.

3. Code section 674 covers the retention of control over the enjoyment of the trust by the grantor or certain other persons. It is one of the most complex provisions of the Internal Revenue Code.

4. Code section 675 treats the grantor as the owner of the trust if the grantor retains certain administrative powers over it. It is the provision most used in defective trust planning.

5. Code section 676 provides that the grantor is treated as the owner of the trust if the grantor can revoke it.

6. Code section 677 imposes the grantor trust rules where the grantor or grantor's spouse retains beneficial enjoyment of the trust, or its income is used to pay premiums on life insurance on the grantor or the grantor's spouse.

Note that the grantor could be the owner of only a portion of the trust, all or part of the trust income, or all or part of the trust corpus. Also, note that as a general rule, the grantor trust provisions apply if certain powers are retained by the spouse of the grantor.

However, many powers can be granted to a nonadverse party *other* than the grantor (including a spouse, but generally that is *not* recommended) that will cause the grantor to be treated as the owner of the trust for income tax purposes. A nonadverse party is someone other than an adverse party, defined as a person with a substantial interest in the trust that would be adversely affected by the exercise or non-exercise of the power.[24]

There are special rules for related or subordinate parties, who are presumed subservient to the wishes of the grantor. Related or subordinate parties are the grantor's spouse, mother, father, issue, brother, sister, an employee of the grantor, an employee of a corporation where the stock of the grantor and the trust is significant from the standpoint of voting control, or a subordinate employee of a corporation in which the grantor is an executive.[25]

Under Code section 674(c), certain powers granted to an independent trustee who is nonadverse do not trigger these rules. An independent trustee consists of

INTENTIONALLY "DEFECTIVE" TRUST

a trustee or trustees, none of whom are the grantor or grantor's spouse, and no more than half of whom are related or subordinate and subservient to the grantor.

Grantor trust status may be terminated by a number of actions, including renunciation of the power by which the grantor is treated as the owner, the death of the grantor, etc. Termination of grantor trust status *may* also result in the recognition of gain by the grantor.[26]

In an installment sale situation, upon the grantor's death, the value of the promissory note will generally be included in the grantor's estate. Promissory notes do not receive a step up in basis upon the grantor's death.

Estate Tax

Many grantor retained powers that cause the grantor to be treated as the owner for income tax purposes will *also* cause the trust to be included in the grantor's taxable estate, which should be avoided. For example, the trust will be included in the grantor's taxable estate if:

1. The grantor retains a reversionary interest that is valued at more than 5 percent of the trust corpus.[27] However, even where the reversionary interest is valued at over 5 percent of the value of the trust, determined at date of death, Code section 2037 will not apply if beneficiaries could have received distribution of trust assets without surviving the grantor.

2. The grantor personally retains control over the enjoyment of the trust.[28]

3. The grantor retains certain administrative powers, such as the power to vote stock transferred to the trust.[29]

4. The grantor retains the income.[30]

Use of Grantor Trusts under the Tax Cuts and Jobs Act of 2017

The Tax Cuts and Jobs Act of 2017, temporarily increased the estate tax exemption to $10,000,000 (indexed for inflation). This amount is scheduled to revert to a $5,000,000 exemption ($12,920,000 indexed for inflation in 2023) in 2026. While many individuals may not face a federal estate tax under the new laws, they may find themselves back in a taxable position in 2026. Now is an excellent time for these individuals to take advantage of higher exemptions and shift wealth out of their estates to ILITs and dynasty trusts via gifting. For those who may be reluctant to make large, irrevocable gifts a private loan arrangement, private split dollar arrangement, or sale to an intentionally defective grantor trust may be an attractive way to initiate planning while taking a "wait-and-see" approach. When leveraged with life insurance, the trust can increase the total amount left to heirs while allowing the grantor to maintain a degree of flexibility and control.

Example. In 2018, Bill Brown enters into a private loan arrangement with his grantor trust whereby B lends a large sum of money to the trust. In return, Bill receives a promissory note from the trust structured as a lump sum, eight-year loan using the mid-term AFR. The trust uses the borrowed funds to pay insurance premiums on a life insurance policy purchased by the trustee on B's life. Any excess funds will be invested. At the end of the note term, B has the flexibility to forgive the note, thus making a gift, using his increased lifetime exemption before the law is scheduled to sunset at the end of 2025. In this case, the trust will retain both the gifted assets in addition to receiving the life insurance death benefit at Bill's death. Alternatively, the trust can repay the debt owed to B by using trust funds and the death benefit and any trust assets above the loan principal will remain in trust for Bill's heirs.

Now is also an important time to consider swapping or purchasing low-basis assets from a grantor trust. If possible, a grantor should consider swapping cash for low-basis assets inside of the grantor trust, allowing the low-basis assets to receive a step-up in basis at the grantor's death. If the grantor does not have cash or high-basis assets available to swap, he or she may consider taking a loan from a third-party lender to purchase low-basis assets from the trust and using trust assets to repay the loan.

30.7 ISSUES IN COMMUNITY PROPERTY STATES

Where assets transferred to defective trusts are community assets, the planner should be aware of the fact that the "grantor" of such a trust will be each spouse as to his or her community interest. For example, if a nonadverse trustee is used, be certain that person is nonadverse as to both spouses. If the grantor retains the power to remove and replace assets, consider the fact that if only one spouse has that power, the grantor trust rule might not apply to the other spouse as to his or her community interest.

Additionally, if the spouse of the grantor will be included as a beneficiary of the trust, it is critical that the grantor does not contribute any community property to the trust. A spouse-beneficiary's community property interest in property contributed to the trust will cause inclusion in the spouse's estate as a retained interest.

In general, the grantor trust rules apply to powers retained by either spouse, and this may not be a serious problem. However, it would be wise to consider this aspect, and also the potential impact of a divorce on the defective trust plan.

As noted previously, grantor trust status is normally terminated by death. In the case of community property, however, grantor trust status will continue with respect to the portion of the trust contributed by the surviving spouse. As noted in Chapter 29 with reference to GRATs, it is usually better to either establish separate trusts for each spouse with separate funds, or to transmute community property to separate property before funding a trust.

30.8 FREQUENTLY ASKED QUESTIONS

Question – Does the payment of the trust's income taxes by the grantor constitute a gift?

Answer – The payment of income tax by the grantor that arises from the trust's income is not a gift by the grantor (because as the taxpayer, the grantor is obligated to pay the ensuing tax). Also, no portion of the IDGT will be included in the gross estate of the grantor under Code section 2036 if the grantor is not entitled to reimbursement from the trust. Grantors of a properly-structured IDGT are encouraged to pay the income tax arising from the trust and may achieve significant gift tax savings and income shifting for the benefit of their children, grandchildren, or other loved ones. This is because by paying the income tax, the income remaining in the trust is essentially income tax-free to the beneficiaries. Nevertheless, IDGTs should be considered aggressive planning tools and must be attempted with the utmost in care and by only the most competent of practitioners.[31]

Question – What are the implications if an IDGT requires the trust to pay back the grantor for any income tax liability generated by the trust?

Answer – The mandatory requirement that the trust reimburse the grantor for the trust's income tax liability would be treated as a grantor retained interest under Code section 2036 resulting in an inclusion in the grantor's gross estate. Mandatory payment obligations could arise under the terms of the trust or state law. The IDGT, therefore, should expressly *prohibit* such payments while it is an intentionally defective grantor trust. Inclusion may also result if the independent trustee has discretion to reimburse the grantor for income taxes and there was a pre-existing agreement to reimburse. This suggests a facts and circumstances analysis on a case-by-case basis. Even with an independent trustee, some may find the approach under which the trustee has discretion to reimburse the grantor for income taxes arising on income received by the trust to be too risky an approach given the large estate tax savings potential with an IDGT.[32]

Question – What are some of the ways a client can stop paying income tax on trust-generated income?

Answer – Consider including a provision in the trust authorizing a termination of the defective trust character of the trust that will cause it to be taxed as a non-grantor trust, so that the trust will thereafter pay its own income tax. Advise the client that these trusts are best suited for individuals who have sufficient income and wealth that the potential for payment of income tax is not a concern. Finally, rather than creating an IDGT, wait until a parent dies and construct a direct sale by the surviving parent to the loved ones when the gifted property has received a step-up in basis. This will minimize or eliminate the need for an IDGT from the standpoint of recognition avoidance on sale because – due to the step-up-in-basis - there will be little or no gain. If a trust is used in this arrangement, it could be structured as a standard trust. This strategy benefits the younger generation when the cash flow on the asset sold is greater than the payment required on the promissory note, while enabling the grantor/seller to not have to pay income tax on income that others receive.

INTENTIONALLY "DEFECTIVE" TRUST   CHAPTER 30

Question – Can the defective trust be used in connection with irrevocable life insurance trusts where trust income is to be used to pay insurance premiums?

Answer – Under Code section 677, the use or even possible use of trust income to pay life insurance premiums on the life of the grantor or grantor's spouse should cause the grantor trust rules to apply to the trust. This enables the client to transfer income-producing property to the irrevocable life insurance trust, which then acquires a life insurance policy and uses the income from the property to pay the insurance premiums. Since the payment of the premiums is not deductible, the effect is that the income will be taxed to the grantor. If properly planned, this will remove both the life insurance proceeds and the income-producing property from the grantor's estate. Note that the IRS will not presently rule on the income tax consequences of this technique. If the intention is to trigger grantor-trust status, it is typically recommended to add two or more grantor trust powers in the trust document.

Question – What is a Reverse IDIT and can this concept be used to shift income tax of trust income to beneficiaries?

Answer – For an excellent article on Reverse IDIT's, see *Trusts and Estates*, October 2012, Clay R. Stevens, "The Reverse Defective Grantor Trust." According to the author, the reverse IDIT works as follows: An irrevocable grantor trust is established. The beneficiaries can be the children, grandchildren and a dynasty trust can be created. Assets are irrevocably gifted to the trust. This gift can utilize the taxpayer's entire exemption amount. Then, the grantor purchases some of the assets in the grantor trust in exchange for a promissory note. Therefore, unlike a traditional IDGT, the buyer and seller are reversed. The note could be secured by the assets which are purchased from the trust. Moreover, the interest payments paid to the trust remove value from the grantor's estate. The interest rate on the note could be higher than the AFR based upon certain factors, such as the grantor's credit-worthiness. If the note is outstanding at death, it will arguably be a valid claim against the grantor's estate, and the assets which were purchased will receive a step-up in basis. It is advisable to separate the gift and sale over a period of time in order to reduce the risk that IRS will argue that it fails the step transaction test. It is best to gift non-appreciated property to this trust since gain would need to be recognized on repayment of the notes following the Grantor's death. The author further recommends that it is best not to accrue interest since income tax could be imposed on accrued but unpaid interest following the grantor's death.

Question – Can the defective trust concept be used to shift the income taxation of trust income to beneficiaries?

Answer – Possibly. There are two techniques which may successfully shift income taxation to a beneficiary. The first, a "beneficiary defective inheritor's trust" (BDIT), coined by Richard and Steve Oshins, relies on giving a trust beneficiary a Crummey power to withdrawal all of the contributions to the trust.[33] The withdrawal right is likely to constitute a general power of appointment under Code section 678, which under section 678(a)(2) causes the beneficiary to be taxed on trust income whether they exercise the power or not.[34] Because the withdrawal right applies to *all* contributions to the trust, only smaller gifts within the "5 or 5" power are typically contributed to avoid partial inclusion in the beneficiary's estate.

An alternative to the BDIT approach is Ed Morrow's "beneficiary deemed owner trust" (BDOT) design. With a BDOT, the beneficiary does not have a right to withdraw contributions to the trust, but instead is given the right to all of the trust's income each year, effectively giving the beneficiary a right of withdrawal over the taxable income and causing the beneficiary to be the owner for income tax purposes under section 678(a)(1).[35] The BDOT design is attractive because gifts of any size can be made to the trust. Case law and a Private Letter Ruling give support to the notion that a power to withdraw all taxable income of a trust without the power to withdraw principal causes the powerholder to be taxable on trust income.[36]

BDITs and BDOTs are highly sophisticated, complex planning techniques with many potential pitfalls and concerns. These techniques are largely untested and an unfavorable ruling could leave a client with significant unintended consequences. It is important to engage legal counsel with experience drafting these trusts to help mitigate these concerns.

Question – Why might a power of substitution be used with an IDGT?

Answer – Assuming the IRS does not challenge the validity of the power (in terms of the grantor's financial wherewithal to make a substitution), one popular technique of making an irrevocable trust intentionally defective for income tax purposes is to include a retained power to substitute property of equivalent value. This will not cause the trust property to be included in the grantor's gross estate under Code sections 2033, 2036, 2038, or 2039. Nor will it constitute a gift to the trust by the grantor, for federal gift tax purposes. Furthermore, such a trust is a grantor trust under Code section 671 in its entirety with respect to the grantor. Also, neither the grantor nor the trust will recognize any income or loss by reason of the grantor's exercise of the power of substitution.[37] An effective way to use this power of substitution is by having the grantor swap high-basis assets owned personally for low-basis assets owned in the trust to preserve the step-up in basis at the grantor's death.

CHAPTER ENDNOTES

1. See "IDGTS on Steroids: Current Conditions Strengthen Benefits," *Estate Planning Journal*, July 2011.
2. It is extremely important that the fair market value be accurately determined so as to avoid any argument that a gift was made.
3. The IRS has determined that the transfer of assets between a grantor and his grantor trust will not be treated as a "sale" for income tax purposes. See Rev. Rul. 85-13.
4. I.R.C. §§674, 675, 677; Rev. Rul. 85-13, 1985-1 CB 184.
5. Rev. Rul. 74-613, 1974-2 CB 153.
6. I.R.C. §§674, 675, 677; Rev. Rule 85-13, 1985-1 CB 184.
7. I.R.C. §170(f)(2)(B).
8. I.R.C. §675(4).
9. I.R.C. §674(c).
10. Priv. Ltr. Rul. 9301020.
11. Byrle M. Abbin, "[S]he Loves Me, [S]he Loves Me Not – Responding to Succession Planning Needs Through a Three-Dimensional Analysis of Considerations to Be Applied In Selecting From the Cafeteria of Techniques," 31 *U. of Miami Inst. On Est. Plan.*, Ch. 13 (1997) (setting forth IRS's informal representation that assets equal to 10 percent of purchase price should provide adequate security for the payment of the acquisition indebtedness). Some practitioners feel that 20 percent will provide a better defense. Some feel less than 10 percent is adequate and some practitioners are comfortable with little or no gift but use loan guarantees by the beneficiary or a third party.
12. Jerry Hesch, Dick Oshins and Jim Magner, "Note Sales, Economic Substance and "The 10% Myth," *Steve Leimberg's Estate Planning Email Newsletter* Message 2412 (May 9, 2016).
13. E.g., Rev. Proc. 2001-38.
14. I.R.C. §678(a)(1).
15. See I.R.C. §678(b), Priv. Ltr. Ruls. 200942020, 200022035 and 9034004.
16. See Howard M. Zaritsky, "Toggling Made Easy – Modifying a Trust to Create a Grantor Trust," 36 *Estate Planning* 48 (2009).
17. See I.R.C. §675(3) and Treasury Reg. §1.675-1(a) which provides that if the grantor has a power to permit an amendment causing the grantor to be treated as the owner of a portion of the trust under Section 675, the grantor will be treated as the owner from the trust's inception.
18. See I.R.C. §675(3) if the loan is not repaid before the beginning of the next tax year.
19. Steve Leimberg's *Estate Planning Newsletter* 1161 (8/14/07).
20. Akers, Blattmachr and Boyle, "Creating Intentional Grantor Trusts," 44 *Real Property, Trust and Estate Law Journal* 207, et seq.
21. See Dedon and Ingersoll, "Traps and Concerns in Using Intentionally Defective Grantor Trusts," *Practical Tax Strategies*, August 2012.
22. See, e.g., L. Paul Hood, Jr., "Reciprocal Trust Doctrine and Joint SLATS: Future IRS Happy Hunting Ground?," 34 *Probate Practice Reporter* No. 11 (Nov. 2022) pp. 1-6.
23. 395 U.S. 316 (1969).
24. I.R.C. §672.
25. I.R.C. §672(c).
26. See Treas. Reg. §1.1001-2(c), Example 5; *Madorin v. Comm.*, 84 TC 667 (1985).
27. I.R.C. §§673, 2037(a)(2).
28. I.R.C. §§674, 2036, 2038.
29. I.R.C. §§675, 2036(b).
30. I.R.C. §§677, 2036(a).
31. Rev. Rul. 2004-64, 2004-2 CB 7.
32. Rev. Rul. 2004-64, 2004-2 CB 7.
33. See Richard A. Oshins, "The Beneficiary Defective Inheritor's Trust ("BDIT"): Finessing the Pipe Dream," CCH Practical Strategies, November 2008.
34. I.R.C. §678(a).
35. See Ed Morrow, "IRC 678(a)(1) and the "Beneficiary Deemed Owner Trust" (BDOT)," Leimberg Estate Planning Newsletter #2516, September 2017.
36. *Campbell v. Commissioner*, T.C. Memo 1979-495; Priv. Ltr. Rul. 201633021.
37. Let. Rul. 200603040. The letter ruling generally addressed these issues relative to powers of substitutions. However, the ruling only mentions that income is payable to the spouse under IRC Section 677(a) as a reason for the trust being fully taxable to the grantor.

TAX BASIS IRREVOCABLE TRUST

CHAPTER 31

31.1 INTRODUCTION

Basically, the tax basis irrevocable trust is a living trust structured to achieve a step-up of the income tax basis of appreciated property (to date of death fair market value) owned by either spouse on the death of either spouse. This is accomplished by using a general power of appointment in tandem with a marital deduction and/or credit shelter trust so that all of the property owned by the spouses will qualify for the basis step-up by virtue of passing through the taxable estate of the first spouse to die. Ideally, the end result will be a stepped-up basis that would reduce or eliminate capital gain with little or no estate consequences.

The tax basis trust is a fairly recent development and was previously thought to require establishing a trust that would be revocable until the death of the first spouse to die. Unfortunately, pertinent IRS rulings on this subject indicate that in a non-community property state, only the basis of assets of the deceased spouse would be stepped-up to date of death fair market value.[1] This chapter explores how the goal may perhaps be achieved by creating an irrevocable trust.

31.2 WHEN IS USE OF SUCH A DEVICE INDICATED?

This device may be considered in a variety of scenarios where one or both spouses own appreciated property. By virtue of the inclusion of all the spouses' assets in the estate of the first spouse to die, the ultimate goal of a basis step-up of all appreciated assets of both spouses to the date of death (of the first spouse to die) fair market can be achieved. Thus, as a consequence of a basis step-up on all assets, potential capital gain on the sale of any of the marital assets (including those of the surviving spouse) would be reduced and possibly eliminated. Obviously, it is most advantageous when this basis step-up is accomplished with no estate tax consequences when the combined assets included in the estate of the first spouse to die is less than the available estate tax exemption (a combined total for both spouses of $25,840,000 in 2023). It will also be most advantageous when the surviving spouse owns considerably more appreciated property than the decedent spouse.

31.3 WHAT ARE THE REQUIREMENTS?

This technique starts with the transfer of appreciated property to either a single irrevocable trust created by both spouses, or two separate irrevocable trusts created by each spouse. Assuming a separate trust, to avoid making a completed gift of the property transferred to the trust, the grantor spouse(s) would retain a limited right to appoint the property. Because the appreciated property transferred to the trust is an incomplete gift, if the grantor spouse is first to die, the appreciated property will be included in his or her estate. As a result, pursuant to Code section 1014(a), the basis of the appreciated property included in a decedent's estate will step-up to its date of death fair market value.[2]

Additionally, the trust would provide the nongrantor spouse with a general power of appointment with respect to the appreciated property. So if the nongrantor spouse dies first, the property in trust would be included in such spouse's gross estate with a resulting basis step-up to its date of death fair market value.[3] This is because granting the nongrantor spouse a general power of appointment is the equivalent of making a completed gift of the underlying

495

property. However, to receive a basis step-up, the gift, i.e., transfer of the property to the trust with the general power of appointment must have occurred at least one year prior to the nongrantor spouse's death. Pursuant to section 1014I, there is no step-up in basis with respect to property acquired by the decedent from the donor (in this case the grantor spouse) within one year of the decedent grantor spouse's death. By inference, proponents of this technique argue that, as long as the nongrantor spouse was granted the general power of appointment at least one year prior to his or her death, section 1014(e) would not apply so the basis of the appreciated property in the trust should be stepped-up to its date of death fair market value.[4]

In drafting a trust into which the assets of the irrevocable trust are to be transferred following the death of the first spouse, the provisions relating to the surviving spouse should permit the property transferred to the trust to qualify for the marital deduction with respect to the estate of the decedent spouse[5] or to fund a credit shelter trust. To do so, the trust should be drafted in a way that would qualify it as qualified terminable interest property (QTIP) trust if elected to be treated as such by the executor on the first spouse to die estate tax return, or as a credit shelter trust if no election (or a partial QTIP election) is made.

An obvious drawback to this arrangement, in addition to the possibility that the IRS may deny the basis step-up, is the potential exercise of the power of appointment by the nongrantor spouse in a way that is detrimental to the ultimate goal of the grantor spouse. For this reason, this technique should be limited to spouses in very stable marriages. Some proponents of the technique attempt to minimize this drawback by limiting the nongrantor spouse's general power of appointment to creditors (rather than the broader power to appoint to anyone). Further, the general power of appointment may be limited to a testamentary power, i.e., a power only exercisable by a will or other document at death. Finally, the impact of the power may be further limited by restricting it to only those assets that would benefit most from a basis step-up, generally those assets that either have or are most likely to appreciate in value.

Example. James and Martha Edwards, husband and wife, who live in a common law state, create a joint irrevocable trust. To avoid making a completed gift upon the transfer of assets into the trust, each spouse retains a limited power to appoint the assets he or she contributes to the property. Upon the death of a spouse, the deceased spouse has a testamentary general power to direct the payment of any of his or her debts and taxes from the assets contributed to the trust by the surviving spouse.

Assume the only transfers to the trust are separate assets of James worth $500,000, with an income tax basis of $100,000. Martha dies more than one year after the transfer. Since she has a general power of appointment over the trust, i.e., a power to appoint to her creditors, the property in the trust will be included in her taxable estate and presumably its income tax basis will be adjusted to its fair market value, $500,000.

Will the property also be included in James' taxable estate upon his subsequent death? That depends on the terms of the trust. For example, if the remaining assets (those assets not used to pay Martha's creditors) were to be transferred to a trust that would qualify as a QTIP trust for the benefit of James (see Chapter 27) if so elected by Martha's executor, the property would be included in James' taxable estate. So, in that instance, upon James' death, the basis in the trust assets would be stepped-up to date of death fair market value. In the alternative, if those assets were used to fund a credit shelter trust for James, they would not be included in his taxable estate, and, thus, the basis of those assets would not be stepped-up to fair market value.

Assuming, in this case, upon James' subsequent death, if he has no other substantial assets, there may be little or no estate tax owing whether or not the property is included in his gross estate. If there is, assuming James can disclaim (see below), he could make a qualified disclaimer to prevent those assets from being included in his estate. In the alternative, to avoid inclusion in James' estate with respect to a transfer of property from the original trust to a trust what would qualify as a QTIP trust, by the executor of Martha's estate making no QTIP election or a partial QTIP election upon Martha's death. Because such trust would essentially be a bypass trust, none of the trust assets would be included in James' estate upon death.

31.4 TAX IMPLICATIONS

As discussed above, this device is entirely tax motivated and requires that the trust or trusts grant the nongrantor spouse a general power of appointment over the property that will result in its inclusion in the estate of the nongrantor spouse if the first spouse to die. What if the grantor spouse is the first to die? Because the granting of a general power of appointment to the nongrantor spouse would be a completed gift, none of the property would be included in the estate of the grantor spouse. To solve this problem, the trust could provide for the payment of income to the grantor spouse during his or her life. Thus, as a transfer of property subject to a retained interest, pursuant to Code section 2036(a). By the inclusion of the trust assets in the grantor spouse's estate, upon death, the basis of the trust property would first step-up to the date of death fair market value.

As to the surviving nongrantor spouse, the terms of the trust can provide him or her with a general power of appointment over the property, or allow a QTIP election to qualify it for the marital deduction if necessary to eliminate estate tax at the first death.[6] However, in that case, the property will be included in the estate of the surviving nongrantor spouse possibly subject to estate tax.

As a way to avoid inclusion in the surviving spouse's estate potentially subject to estate tax, the trust could be drafted to qualify as QTIP trust so that a partial QTIP election could be made with respect to a portion of the trust assets, or the surviving spouse could make a qualified disclaimer, discussed in Chapter 13.

The disclaimer should be considered as an option to be exercised upon the death of either spouse. For example, assume the nongrantor spouse dies first, and does not exercise a general power of appointment so that the property would return to the grantor spouse. By disclaiming, the grantor spouse may be able to disclaim enough of the property to be absorbed estate tax-free by the nongrantor spouse's available estate tax exemption equivalent (as much as $12,920,000 in 2023). As a consequence of a disclaimer, all property of the estate could pass either directly to children or other family members or to a trust (e.g., a credit shelter trust) for the benefit of the family without being subject to estate taxation.

To the author's knowledge, the IRS has not ruled on whether or not the disclaimer would be effective in the foregoing situation. In effect, it could be argued that the grantor spouse is disclaiming an interest in property already owned, not generally permitted under the disclaimer rules. However, since the IRS has conceded, in a number of private letter rulings that the property passes first through the taxable estate of the nongrantor spouse, the surviving owner spouse should have a disclaimer power.

The other use of the disclaimer here is in the event the owner spouse is the first to die. If the surviving nonowner spouse has a general power of appointment over the trust, it would all pass through his or her taxable estate. The surviving nonowner spouse may disclaim a sufficient part of the property to take advantage of the available estate exemption of the predeceased spouse, avoiding estate taxation to that extent. Again, the disclaimed property could pass to children, other family members, or in trust.

Another trust that can be created for a spouse without including the transferred property in the transferor spouse's estate is a SLAT – a spousal lifetime access trust. A SLAT is essentially a lifetime funded credit shelter trust which one spouse establishes for the benefit of the other spouse. However, one concern with a SLAT is that the recipient spouse can use the funds for support. Treasury Regulations section 20.2036-1(b)(2) is problematic because it requires the inclusion of the trust assets in the grantor spouse's estate if those assets are used to discharge grantor spouse's support obligation towards the recipient spouse. To avoid this result, language can be included that prohibit the use of trust funds to satisfy support obligations. See *Upjohn v. U.S.*,[7] which suggests that the trust should include a "savings" clause preventing the trustee from distributing funds in a way that would discharge the grantor's obligation of support. Also, the trust can include language that requires the trustee to look to a beneficiary's other resources prior to making a trust distribution. Finally, it is important to consider the prudence of using an independent trustee.[8]

31.5 ISSUES IN COMMUNITY PROPERTY STATES

Pursuant to Code section 1014(b)(6), upon the death of either spouse, the basis of all of the community property owned by the spouses is stepped-up to the first to die date of death fair market value. Therefore, for community property, the tax basis trust is not necessary. In fact, the purpose of the tax basis trust is to achieve the same tax basis with respect to separate property that would result if the property were community property. In a community property scenario, such a trust could, however, is used to fully fund the credit shelter trust at the first spouse's death if the decedent spouse's one-half interest in the community estate is less than the applicable estate tax exemption amount. This can be particularly useful if the community property estate held by the surviving spouse is expected to increase.

Where either spouse owns separate property in a community property state, the tax basis trust may be created to achieve the same income tax basis step-up to the separate property as applies to community property upon the death of either spouse. Depending on state law, the same result could be achieved by converting the separate property to community property conferring equal ownership of all property to both spouses.

31.6 FREQUENTLY ASKED QUESTIONS

Question – For what reason would the IRS deny the basis step-up of both grantors' assets (including the grantor spouse's assets) upon the death of a grantor spouse with respect to tax basis joint revocable trusts?

Answer – Because it can be reclaimed by the grantor at any time, property transferred to a revocable trust is not a completed gift. So, if a nongrantor spouse held a general power of appointment executable upon death, the gift became complete (meaning at that time the grantor spouse could no longer reclaim the property) at the time of death. In several private letter rulings, relying on Code section 1014(e), the IRS denied the stepped up basis in the grantor spouse's trust assets upon the death of the nongrantor spouse holding a general power of appointment with respect to those assets. Pursuant to section 1014(e), the basis of appreciated property acquired by gift by a decedent during the one year period prior to the date of death that passes from the decedent back to the donor of such property does not step-up to date of death fair market value. In Private Letter Ruling 200101021, the IRS applied section 1014(e) very broadly to include "any Trust property includible in the deceased Donor's gross estate that is attributable to the surviving donor's contribution . . . and that is acquired by the surviving Donor . . . pursuant to the deceased Donor's exercise, or failure to exercise, the general power of appointment over the Trust property." So because the completed gift occurred simultaneously to death, the gift occurred within one year of death; and, thus, there is no basis step-up with respect to the grantor spouse's property. Because that assertion appears only in a private letter ruling, however, it merely reflects the IRS' position subject to challenge in potential litigation.

Question – Based upon the answer to the question above, is the IRS likely deny the basis step-up of a grantor spouse's assets with respect to a tax basis irrevocable trust?

Answer – To date, although the IRS has not taken a position, section 1014(e) should not apply. In the case of an irrevocable trust, the granting of a general power of appointment to the nongrantor spouse is a complete gift. This is because, unlike a revocable trust, the grantor spouse has no right to reclaim the property. For that reason, assuming the nongrantor spouse survives for more than one year following the grant of the general power of appointment, the basis of the nongrantor spouse's property includible in his or her estate should step-up to fair market value would and have no control over the trust.

Question – Will the disclaimer by a grantor spouse with respect to property that passes through the nongrantor spouse's estate be honored by the IRS?

Answer – As noted above, there may be some question as to the availability of a disclaimer by the grantor spouse following the death of the nongrantor spouse, on the theory that one cannot disclaim property already owned.

However, since that property passes first through the estate of another person, the disclaimer should be honored. By analogy, it should be noted that the IRS concedes that where an individual places property in joint tenancy with another person, either joint tenant could have partitioned the property at will while both tenants were alive, and the other person is the first to die, the transferor can disclaim the survivorship interest in the transferee's half of the joint tenancy.

CHAPTER ENDNOTES

1. Priv. Ltr. Ruls. 200210051, 2002101021.
2. But see CCA 201208026 indicating that retaining a mere testamentary limited power of appointment may not be sufficient to avoid a completed gift.
3. I.R.C. §2041(a)(2).
4. I.R.C. §1014(a).
5. I.R.C. §2056.
6. I.R.C. §2056(b).
7. 1972 WL 3200 (W.D. Mich. 1972), 30 AFTR 2d 72-5918.
8. See LISI (Leimberg Information Services, Inc.) Estate Planning Newsletter No. 1379 (12/2/2008).

SPOUSAL LIFETIME ACCESS TRUST (SLAT)

CHAPTER 32

32.1 INTRODUCTION

A Spousal Lifetime Access Trust (SLAT) is an irrevocable trust created under applicable state law during the donor's lifetime for the benefit of his or her spouse. The spouse ("donor spouse") makes a gift to the SLAT using part or all of his or her current (in 2023) $12,920,000 gift tax applicable exclusion amount. The other spouse ("beneficiary spouse") is a beneficiary of the SLAT.

The SLAT looks a lot like a lifetime credit shelter trust. Many view the SLAT favorably as an estate planning technique that essentially allows the donor spouse to "have his or her cake," i.e., achieve estate and gift tax planning advantages, and "eat it too," i.e., retaining some, albeit indirect, access to the SLAT assets and income via his or her beneficiary spouse.

The SLAT provides for the beneficiary spouse, as a trust beneficiary during lifetime (other current beneficiaries, such as the donor spouse's descendants, also can be included). The beneficiary spouse may serve as trustee, provided the power to make distributions to himself or herself is limited by an ascertainable standard (e.g., health, education, maintenance, and support).

32.2 WHAT IS A SLAT?

The SLAT is an inter vivos irrevocable trust created under applicable state law by a spouse for the benefit of the other spouse and/or other beneficiaries, such as children, grandchildren, or other remote family members. A SLAT offers significant flexibility and can be structured to meet the unique needs of each family. As distinguished from an inter vivos QTIP trust, the donor spouse uses up to his or her gift tax applicable exclusion amount ($12,920,000 in 2023) to transfer assets to the SLAT.

In the usual case, the donor spouse designates his or her spouse as a lifetime beneficiary, although, unlike the inter vivos QTIP trust, in which the beneficiary spouse must have an indefeasible lifetime right to all of the trust income, the donor spouse can provide that the SLAT is wholly discretionary (if the beneficiary spouse is not the distribution trustee) as to all beneficiaries, including the beneficiary spouse, and for the automatic loss of the beneficiary spouse's rights in the SLAT on the filing of a petition for separation or divorce. Indeed, unlike an inter vivos QTIP trust, in a SLAT, the donor spouse can safely employ a "floating spouse" provision, provision whereby the definition of the "grantor's spouse" is defined as the individual to whom the grantor is married at any given time.

The key benefit of a SLAT is that, by naming his or her spouse as a lifetime beneficiary, the grantor spouse retains indirect access to the trust assets, at least as long as they're happily married. Technically, a SLAT is designed to remove trust assets from both the grantor spouse's and beneficiary spouse's estates.

The SLAT can be structured to allow only the beneficiary spouse access to the funds during his or her lifetime, although, much more commonly, a SLAT benefits both the beneficiary spouse and other family members of the donor spouse either during life or after the beneficiary spouse's death. A SLAT can be formed in a state that has significantly extended or even abrogated the Rule Against Perpetuities, which allows it to be a "Dynasty SLAT."

32.3 ADVANTAGES

The SLAT offers several advantages, including:

- Protects against reduction in the gift tax applicable exclusion amount by using it now.

- If properly established, a SLAT provides protection from the creditors of the donor spouse and beneficiary spouse, while retaining access to the SLAT.

- In a second marriage situation, the donor spouse's descendants cannot be disinherited by the beneficiary spouse with respect to the SLAT assets.

- As the spouse of the beneficiary spouse, the donor spouse would have indirect access to the trust through the beneficiary spouse, at least while they're happily married.

- There should be no estate tax inclusion (in either spouse's estate) of future appreciation in the assets funding the SLAT.

- If the SLAT holds cash value accumulation life insurance, the SLAT could accumulate cash on a tax-advantaged basis, and, if properly formed or transferred, excluded from the gross estates of either spouse.

- The donor spouse can be a trustee (but must be limited to HEMS and not if the SLAT is wholly discretionary.

- Can use a "floating spouse" provision, which, instead of specifically naming the beneficiary spouse as a SLAT beneficiary, the SLAT would name the "donor spouse's spouse" as a beneficiary and expressly define that term as the spouse to whom the donor spouse is presently married, until separation or divorce, at which point, the current beneficiary spouse would cease to be a beneficiary, but a subsequent spouse of the donor spouse would become a beneficiary of the SLAT on the date of marriage to the donor spouse.

- A SLAT can reduce state death tax if formed during lifetime (unless formed in the one United States jurisdiction that still has a gift tax (Connecticut)).

32.4 DISADVANTAGES

Unfortunately, all that glitters around the SLAT is not golden. The SLAT has several disadvantages, including:

- Limited in utility to married persons, and only during the existence of a marriage.

- Loss of direct access by the donor spouse to the capital represented by the SLAT gift, which is an advantage that must be justified in advance before advising or assisting a client with parting with irrevocable access to significant wealth.

- Only the property of the donor spouse can be used to fund the SLAT, or there will be adverse federal estate tax ramifications to the beneficiary spouse. If the beneficiary spouse makes a gift to the donor spouse shortly before the donor spouse funds the SLAT, there is the potential for significant step transaction/indirect gift risk.[1] And the same risk applies if the SLAT is funded with community property; there must be transmutation of community property into separate property before contribution to a SLAT.

- As we learned late in 2012, the gift tax applicable exclusion amount might not go down, but actually could go even higher, or the federal estate tax could be repealed altogether.

- Loss of new basis opportunities at the beneficiary spouse's death, although there are some ways around this through the use of distribution options, asset swaps and specially crafted general powers of appointment.

- Unless properly drafted, the donor spouse loses the indirect benefit at the earlier of the beneficiary spouse's death or divorce, and, thus, could be "pressured" into getting married to resume indirect access to the SLAT assets/income.

- If two SLATs are formed, one by each spouse, for the benefit of the other, the author believes that there is a significant risk that the IRS will be successful in applying the reciprocal trust doctrine to uncross the SLATs and include them in each spouse's estate even with different terms if they were formed pursuant to a single coordinated plan.[2]

32.5 POTENTIAL USES

Prudent Lock-in of Applicable Exclusion Amount. For complete gift SLATs, the SLAT provides a flexible way to use the current high level of applicable exclusion amount before the law reduces it, while hedging bets by retaining indirect access via a spouse.

Creditor protection. SLATs do provide excellent creditor protection.

Life insurance trust. A SLAT can be an excellent funded life insurance trust.

Blended families. SLATs also can be used to provide foe blended family situations, with step-parent spouse beneficiaries, and the separate descendants of the grantor spouse.

32.6 HOW IT WORKS

In this section, we'll examine various evaluation criteria relating to the SLAT.

Types of SLAT Transfers: While most people view the SLAT as a technique that involves a completed, irrevocable gift, that's not always the case. In addition to the traditional completed gift approach, a SLAT also can be arranged as an incomplete transfer through the donor spouse's retention of both lifetime and testamentary special power of appointment[3] as well as a veto power over SLAT distributions.

With a complete gift SLAT, a donor spouse can transfer post-gift appreciation on and income from SLAT assets and simultaneously achieve significant creditor protection even through indirect retention of benefits via the beneficiary spouse. But the price for these benefits is significant and includes not only loss of direct, unfettered access to the capital represented by the SLAT donation, but control over the enjoyment of those assets.

There are several ways that assets in a complete gift SLAT could benefit the donor spouse, including:

- Distribution to the beneficiary spouse.
- Distribution to a descendant of the donor spouse.
- An authorized loan to the donor spouse.
- The beneficiary spouse exercises a special power of appointment in favor of the donor spouse.

Conversely, utilizing an incomplete gift SLAT achieves much creditor protection, but achieves no transfer tax planning benefit.

Assets best suited for the SLAT: High basis assets that throw off income or that can easily be converted into income-producing property are best used in a SLAT.

Assets generally not well suited for the SLAT: As a general rule, low basis assets and those that aren't easily convertible to income-producing property usually make poor candidates to fund a SLAT.

Need for independent valuation in a SLAT: It depends upon the type of assets contributed to a SLAT and could range from no appraisals needed to multi-level appraisals required, e.g., where real estate is funded into an entity and entity interests are put into the SLAT.

Cost and importance of implementation and ongoing administration for a SLAT: Relatively speaking, a SLAT shouldn't involve significant cost of implementation unless appraisals are required. There shouldn't be a need for a separate income tax return since the SLAT generally should be a grantor trust for income tax purposes. A SLAT presents a strong need for ongoing maintenance of separateness of SLAT, so fees must be incurred for that advice.

Cash flow requirements of assets used in the SLAT: None.

Cash flow requirements of client and client's spouse and family if the SLAT is used: Relatively little.

SLAT Estate tax risks and consequences: If the beneficiary spouse is deemed to have put any property into the SLAT, there is significant risk of inclusion in the beneficiary spouse's estate. If dual SLATs are created, one for each spouse, there is a significant risk of application of the reciprocal trust doctrine, even if the trusts aren't actually reciprocal, if they are interrelated, i.e., formed within a short period of time or pursuant to a single integrated plan.[4]

SLAT Gift tax risks and consequences: Shouldn't be much for a SLAT unless you get the valuation wrong because SLATs generally are funded through using the available gift tax applicable exclusion amount. If subjectively valued assets are contributed to a SLAT, then the estate planner should consider using a defined value gift clause.

SLAT Income tax risks and consequences: Generally, a SLAT is set up to be a grantor trust while the couple is married and, thereafter, could be either a simple or complex trust for income tax purposes, depending on how the is drafted. The grantor spouse may grow to be unwilling or unable to pay the income tax on SLAT income and may have no way out. Consequently, the SLAT grantor trust powers should have safety valves in place to permit grantor trust status to be toggled off.

Clients for whom the SLAT generally works best: Spouses where there is a long-term, solid, stable marriage are best for a SLAT. The prudent estate planner will lay out the risks to the donor spouse's access on divorce or the death of the beneficiary spouse.

Clients for whom the SLAT generally may not work: Folks with unstable marriages, and currently unmarried persons, unless the future donor spouse names a generic floating spouse as beneficiary spouse and plans on marrying or remarrying.

Whether the SLAT is "age, interest rate or health sensitive:" Not particularly, although this is probably not a tool for older couples or where the beneficiary spouse is much older than the grantor spouse or in poor health.

Best recipients of the transfer made by the SLAT: Beneficiary spouse in a solid, stable, long-term marriage and the descendants of the donor spouse. A SLAT also can be an important estate planning technique for single wealthy individuals who may want to benefit a future spouse.

Asset protection, if any, offered by the SLAT: Excellent creditor protection for both the donor spouse and the beneficiary spouse.

32.7 SELECTED PLANNING POINTERS

In this section, we'll cover several important planning pointers in the design, funding and administration of a SLAT, particularly as they relate to possibly being able to direct SLAT funds to the donor spouse, just in case the donor spouse needs said SLAT funds (although this begs the question of the prudence in the donor spouse's original parting with access to the capital that the SLAT funds represent).

Power to Add Donor Spouse as Beneficiary in the Future: Consideration also could be given to granting an independent trust protector or other third party a power to add the donor spouse as a beneficiary in the future. Prudence dictates caution in conditioning the powerholder's exercise of any power to add the grantor spouse as a SLAT beneficiary only to a SLAT formed or then being administered in and/or subject to the governing law of a DAPT jurisdiction, and then only upon the occurrence of a specified future event, such as a divorce or where the grantor spouse's net worth and earnings are insufficient to support the grantor spouse's lifestyle, or if the grantor spouse's net worth drops below a specified dollar level, i.e., . an act that trust law would consider an "event of independent significance."[5]

Power to Make Loans to the Donor Spouse: Prudent SLAT scriveners could give someone, who might be called a "loan director," although other names are routinely employed, a power, exercisable in a non-fiduciary capacity, to loan trust assets to the donor spouse. A loan director can be given the discretion of whether to make loans of SLAT assets to the donor spouse with or without adequate security for the loan, but the loan director might be forced to charge interest at the applicable federal rate in order to avoid gift tax issues, even if the SLAT is a grantor trust for income tax purposes.

Power to Add Charitable Beneficiaries: A SLAT scrivener also can give someone, who might be called a "charity director," although other names are routinely employed, exercisable in a non-fiduciary capacity, the power to add charitable beneficiaries. The exercise of such a power effectively provides the donor spouse an indirect means of "access" to the SLAT assets by making a charitable out of SLAT funds instead of the funds of the donor spouse. However, the SLAT that is intentionally designed as a non-grantor trust for income tax purposes should not pay a charitable pledge of the grantor.[6]

Form SLAT in a DAPT Jurisdiction: Consider organizing a SLAT in a so-called domestic asset protection trust (DAPT) jurisdiction (jurisdictions that permit a settlor to protect assets in a self-settled trust, which is an exception to the traditional common law rule that a settlor cannot achieve protection from creditors via a self-settled trust) if it's at all conceivable (which will be the case in virtually every circumstance) that the SLAT instrument. If the spouses get divorced or if the beneficiary spouse dies, the SLAT instrument could permit an independent trust protector or other third party to add the donor spouse as a discretionary beneficiary. If this option is included in the SLAT, care will need to be taken to ensure the donor is merely one of many beneficiaries, and the SLAT will need to be placed in a jurisdiction that authorizes self-settled asset protection trusts.

Can or Should the Beneficiary Spouse be a Trustee of a SLAT?: Subject to the caveats discussed below, the beneficiary spouse also can be named the sole trustee or a co-trustee of a SLAT, and the assets of the SLAT should not be subject to the beneficiary spouse's creditors and, provided that the beneficiary spouse trustee who also is a beneficiary is limited to HEMS distribution powers, not included in the beneficiary spouse's estate. However, all other things being equal, it generally isn't prudent to name the beneficiary spouse as a trustee of a SLAT unless he or she can be removed on separation or divorce.

SLAT as Grantor Trust for Income Tax Purposes: If the beneficiary spouse is a SLAT beneficiary, then the SLAT generally will be a grantor trust as to the grantor spouse for income tax purposes, unless distributions to the beneficiary spouse require the approval of an adverse party exception to grantor trust status applies if any and all distributions to the beneficiary spouse must be approved by an "adverse party" (a party with a substantial economic interest in the SLAT that would be adversely affected distributions to the beneficiary spouse), and the beneficiary spouse is not a trustee of the SLAT, and the beneficiary spouse resigns from being a trustee.[7]

In that case, the SLAT may not be considered as owned by the grantor spouse for income tax purposes unless the grantor spouse has another "grantor trust power" over the SLAT, such as the right to reacquire SLAT assets in exchange for assets of equivalent value.[8]

Post Beneficiary Spouse's Death Income Tax Basis Planning: It's not unusual to give the Trust Protector a power to create a tightly crafted general power of appointment under conditions described below for the beneficiary spouse via a right to direct SLAT assets to creditors of his or her estate, which causes inclusion of the SLAT assets covered by the general power of appointment in the beneficiary spouse's taxable estate for federal estate tax purposes, which gives those assets a new income tax basis.[9]

But an unbridled general power of appointment is inadvisable and should be subject to the following limitations: (1) the inclusion should not create an estate tax liability, i.e., it must be limited to the beneficiary spouse's remaining unused applicable exclusion amount, after considering the other probate and includible non-probate assets in the beneficiary spouse's gross estate, all as finally determined for federal estate tax purposes; and (2) the general power of appointment grant must be limited to assets that have a date-of-death (or alternate valuation date value) fair market value that exceeds the SLAT's adjusted income tax basis at the beneficiary spouse's death.[10]

This is because Code Section 1014 adjusts basis to applicable death fair market value, i.e., date-of-death value, or, if applicable, the alternate valuation date fair market value, two possible ways, i.e., it can produce a stepped-up basis (where the asset's applicable fair market value at death exceeds the asset's adjusted basis the instant prior to death) or a stepped-down basis (where the asset's adjusted basis the instant prior to death exceeds the asset's applicable fair market value at death).[11]

32.8 RECIPROCAL TRUST DOCTRINE AND JOINT SLATS

Introduction to Joint SLATs: SLATs have become ubiquitous in estate planning, perhaps too ubiquitous in light of the risks of the reciprocal trust doctrine. Consequently, a donor spouse often wants to set up a SLAT for his or her beneficiary spouse. Sometimes, the spouses each want to establish a SLAT for the other spouse at the same time, which often are referred to as "joint SLATs." However, in situations where spouses each want to set up some sort of trust, as an alternative to joint SLATs, some cautious planners have one spouse create a SLAT where a spouse is a beneficiary with the couple's descendants and/or others and have the other spouse create a separate trust solely for the benefit of the spouses' descendants (where neither spouse is a current beneficiary (but with a power given to a trust protector to add either or both spouses as beneficiaries in the future).

Unfortunately, joint SLATs generally are significantly problematic due to the specter of the reciprocal trust doctrine. The author believes this practice exposes the estate planning lawyer to a malpractice claim if the IRS subsequently successfully prevails on the reciprocal trust doctrine. In this section, the author explores application of the reciprocal trust doctrine to joint SLATs and the only way in the author's opinion that they may be done safely.

The Reciprocal Trust Doctrine: Just as unfortunately, many estate planning commentators and thought leaders haven't been clear enough about the significant risks of application of the reciprocal trust doctrine to joint SLATs.[12] In the author's opinion, some of these commentators have misled estate planners into believing that the reciprocal trust doctrine will not apply if the joint SLATs that are formed at virtually the same time by the same lawyer who represents the spouses jointly pursuant to the same integrated estate plan but aren't *identical* trust instruments, but instead contain some *significantly different terms*, in reliance in part on a Tax Court Memorandum decision in Estate of Herbert Levy v. Comr., T.C. Memo. 1983-453 (1983). However, in the author's opinion, that conclusion flies in the face of the leading United States Supreme Court pronouncement on the reciprocal trust doctrine in United States v. Estate of Grace.[13]

In *Estate of Grace*, the United States Supreme Court, in pertinent part, stated:

> We agree that "the taxability of a trust corpus . . . does not hinge on a settlor's motives, but depends on the nature and operative effect of the trust transfer." Id., at 705. See also Commissioner v. Estate of Church, supra.
>
> We think these observations have particular weight when applied to the reciprocal trust situation. First, inquiries into subjective intent, especially in intrafamily transfers, are particularly perilous. The present case illustrates that it is, practically speaking, impossible to determine after the death of the parties what they had in mind in creating trusts over 30 years earlier. Second, there is a high probability that such a trust arrangement was indeed created for tax-avoidance purposes. And, even if there was no estate-tax-avoidance motive, the settlor in a very real and objective sense did retain an economic interest while purporting to give away his property. Finally, it is unrealistic to assume that the settlors of the trusts, usually members of one family unit, will have created their trusts as a bargained-for exchange for the other trust. "Consideration," in the traditional legal sense, simply does not normally enter into such intrafamily transfers.
>
> For these reasons, we hold that application of the reciprocal trust doctrine is not dependent upon a finding that each trust was created as a quid pro quo for the other. Such a "consideration" requirement necessarily involves a difficult inquiry into the subjective intent of the settlors. Nor do we think it necessary to prove the existence of a tax-avoidance motive. As we have said above, standards of this sort, which rely on subjective factors, are rarely workable under the federal estate tax laws. **Rather, we hold that application of the reciprocal trust doctrine requires only that the trusts be <u>interrelated</u>, and that the arrangement, to the extent of mutual value, <u>leaves the settlors in approximately the same economic position as they would have been in had they created trusts naming themselves as life beneficiaries</u>.**
>
> Applying this test to the present case, we think it clear that the value of the Janet Grace trust fund must be included in decedent's estate for federal estate tax purposes. **It is undisputed that the two trusts are interrelated.** They are **substantially identical in terms and were created at approximately the same time**. Indeed, they were **part of a single transaction designed and carried out by decedent**. It is also clear that the transfers in trust left each party, to the extent of mutual value, in the same objective economic position as before. Indeed, it appears, as would be expected in transfers between husband and wife, that the effective position of each party vis-à-vis the property did not change at all. It is no answer that the transferred properties were different in character. For purposes of the estate tax, we think that economic value is the only workable criterion. Joseph Grace's estate remained undiminished to the extent of the value of his wife's trust and the value of his estate must accordingly be increased by the value of that trust.[14] [emphasis added]

In *Estate of Levy*, a Tax Court Memorandum decision, i.e., a decision that was not reviewed by the entire Tax Court, Judge Shields stated:

> Thus, to determine whether the Herbert Levy Trust and Ilse Levy Trust are interrelated, we will consider their terms, corpus, trustees, and beneficiaries, as well as their date of creation and their relation, if any, to a prearranged plan.
>
> Respondent insists that the trusts are interrelated because: (1) they were **created on the same date** pursuant to **joint consultations with the same attorneys**; (2) they each contained twelve and one-half shares of Wel-Fit; (3) Ilse Levy and Herbert Levy were each the trustee of the other's trust; and (4) the residuary beneficiary of both trusts was Lawrence Levy, the son of Herbert and Ilse Levy.
>
> Petitioner does not dispute these facts. He argues, however, that the trusts are not interrelated because their terms are not identical. In particular, he points out that the Herbert Levy Trust gave Ilse Levy a special power of appointment which permitted her to appoint the income and corpus of the trust created by Herbert Levy to anyone except herself, her estate, her creditors, and the creditors of her estate. The Ilse Levy trust did not confer a similar power of appointment upon Herbert Levy. Thus,

petitioner asserts that the Herbert Levy Trust and the Ilse Levy Trust had very different legal consequences and were not interrelated for purposes of applying the reciprocal trust doctrine. We agree.[15]

With all due respect to Judge Shields, he essentially read the clear United States Supreme Court authority out of the law through what can fairly be characterized as a confused and strained interpretation of the "interrelated" prong of the United States Supreme Court's reciprocal trust analysis. The Supreme Court's holding and test in *Estate of Grace* was:

*Rather, we hold that application of the reciprocal trust doctrine requires only that the trusts be **interrelated**, and that the arrangement, to the extent of mutual value, leaves the settlors in approximately the **same economic position as they would have been in had they created trusts naming themselves as life beneficiaries**.*[16] [emphasis added]

In the author's opinion, the *Estate of Levy* decision is wrong and aberrational, and it shouldn't be relied upon going forward. As Judge Shields acknowledged, the subject trusts were created on the same date pursuant to joint consultation with the same lawyers and funded with related property.

But Judge Shields erroneously added the slight difference between the trust instruments to the "interrelated" analysis instead of considering it as part of the second "same economic position" prong, saying:

Petitioner does not dispute these facts. He argues, however, that the trusts are not interrelated because their terms are not identical.[17]

The Supreme Court "interrelated" prong never required perfectly identical instruments. In fact, the subject instruments in *Estate of Grace* were not identical, which the Supreme Court expressly pointed out, noting:

*They are **substantially identical** in terms, and were created at approximately the same time. Indeed, they were **part of a single transaction designed and carried out by decedent**.*[18] [emphasis added]

By so doing, Judge Shields determined that the trusts weren't interrelated, obviating the need for him to even consider the second "same economic position as they would have been in had they created trusts naming themselves as life beneficiaries" prong.

Judge Shields went on to consider whether

*During her life, and prior to the death of Herbert Levy, Ilse Levy could appoint the income and the corpus of the Herbert Levy Trust when and as she pleased except to herself, her creditors or her estate. In contrast, Herbert Levy had no power of appointment over the income or the corpus of the Ilse Levy Trust. He was merely its trustee. As a result, decedent and his wife had markedly different interests in, and control over, the trusts created by each other. The reciprocal trust doctrine does not purport to reach transfers in trust which create different interests and which change "the effective position of each party vis a vis the [transferred] property * * *." United States v. Estate of Grace, supra at 325.*

This arguably is grossly inaccurate and fails to carefully appreciate the analysis of the United States Supreme Court in the holding in *Estate of Grace*, which was:

*Rather, we hold that application of the reciprocal trust doctrine requires only that the trusts be **interrelated**, and that the arrangement, to the extent of mutual value, leaves the settlors in approximately the **same economic position as they would have been in had they created trusts naming themselves as life beneficiaries**.*[19]

In their April 2012 article in *Trusts & Estates*,[20] Marty Shenkman and Bruce Steiner posited some differences that should ensure that joint SLATs won't be caught by the snares of the reciprocal trust doctrine, including:

- Drafting the trusts pursuant to different plans.

- Refraining from putting a husband and wife in the same economic position following the establishment of the two trusts.

- Using different distribution standards in each trust.

- Using different trustees or co-trustees.

- Giving one spouse a non-cumulative "5 and 5" power, but not the other.

- Giving one spouse has power of appointment and the other spouse does not.

- Giving one beneficiary spouse the broadest possible special power of appointment and the other beneficiary spouse a special power of appointment exercisable only in favor of a narrower class of permissible appointees, such as issue or issue and their spouses.

- Giving one spouse a special power of appointment exercisable both during lifetime and by will and the other spouse a testamentary special power of appointment only.

- In the case of insurance trusts, including a marital deduction savings clause in one trust, but not the other.

- Create different vesting provisions for each trust.

- Instead of mandating distributions, give the beneficiaries control, or a different degree of control, at different ages.

- Vary the beneficiaries.

- Create the trusts at different times.

- Contribute different assets to each trust, either as to the nature or the value of the assets.

That these differences are **intentionally** built-in certainly arguably is potentially problematic as such exalts form over substance, especially if the joint SLATs are drafted by the same lawyers and/or pursuant to the same integrated plan. While reasonable minds certainly can differ, it's at least arguable that some of these suggested built-in "differences" don't actually materially alter the economic interests of the grantor spouse **as an income beneficiary** if the SLATs were uncrossed in a classic application of the reciprocal trust doctrine, rendering them ineffective in the author's opinion as shields against application of the reciprocal trust doctrine.

The Only Safe Way to Create "Joint" SLATs: In the author's opinion, the only safe way that both spouses can form SLATs is to be separately represented by unrelated lawyers in different firms without any communication or coordination between the lawyers.

32.9 CONCLUSION

The SLAT can be an effective way to ensure locking in the current high level of applicable exclusion amount while retaining indirect access to the assets via a spouse. The author suspects that the SLAT has been used to coerce clients who really can't afford to irrevocably part with access to the capital contributed to the SLAT. And the author, who predicted successfully back in the early 1990's that the IRS would be able to successfully challenge many family limited partnership arrangements on Code Section 2036 grounds, which came to pass, predicts that the IRS will enjoy equal levels of success with challenging joint SLAT's on the reciprocal trust doctrine using the *Estate of Grace* decision.[21]

32.10 FREQUENTLY ASKED QUESTIONS

What is a SLAT? The SLAT is an inter vivos irrevocable trust created by a spouse ("donor spouse") for the benefit of the other spouse ("beneficiary spouse") and/or other beneficiaries, such as children, grandchildren, or other remote family members. A SLAT offers significant flexibility and can be structured to meet the unique needs of each family. As distinguished from an inter vivos QTIP trust, the donor spouse uses his or her gift tax applicable exclusion amount ($12,920,000 in 2023) to transfer assets to the SLAT.

In the usual case, the donor spouse designates his or her spouse as a lifetime beneficiary, although, unlike the inter vivos QTIP trust, in which the beneficiary spouse must have an irrevocable lifetime right to all of the SLAT income, the donor spouse can provide for the automatic loss of the beneficiary spouse's rights in the SLAT on the filing of a petition for separation or divorce. Indeed, unlike an inter vivos QTIP trust, the donor spouse can safely employ a

The key benefit of a SLAT is that, by naming his or her spouse as a lifetime beneficiary, the grantor spouse retains indirect access to the trust assets. Technically, a SLAT is designed to remove trust assets from the gross estates of the grantor spouse and the beneficiary spouse.

The SLAT can be structured to allow only the beneficiary spouse access to the funds during his or her lifetime or it can benefit both the beneficiary spouse and other family members either during life or after the beneficiary spouse's death. When the SLAT continues in perpetuity, it is known as a "Dynasty SLAT." In other words, a Dynasty Trust in an unlimited duration state, such as South Dakota, can endure for the longest possible time and circumvent additional death taxes on the trust assets at each generation.

SPOUSAL LIFETIME ACCESS TRUST (SLAT)

How does a SLAT differ from an Inter Vivos QTIP Trust?

An inter vivos QTIP trust requires naming the beneficiary spouse as mandatory lifetime income beneficiary and prohibits distributions to any beneficiary other than the beneficiary spouse during the beneficiary spouse's lifetime, even if the couple subsequently divorces.

On the other hand, a grantor spouse can establish a SLAT using a "floating spouse" provision, which a QTIP trust can't use, and a beneficiary spouse can be displaced both as a beneficiary and as trustee on divorce. Moreover, a SLAT can provide immediate benefits to beneficiaries other than be limited to the beneficiary spouse, like a QTIP trust. Both the inter vivos QTIP trust and the SLAT can be drafted to provide future benefits to the grantor spouse under certain conditions.

Finally, an inter vivos QTIP trust is deductible, while the complete gift SLAT intentionally use the applicable exclusion amount.

CHAPTER ENDNOTES

1. See, *e.g.*, *Smaldino v. Comr.*, T.C. Memo 2021-127, 122 T.C.M. (CCH) 298.
2. *Grace Est. v. Comr.*, 395 U.S. 316 (1969).
3. While Treas. Reg. §25.2511-2(b) states, in pertinent part, "if a donor transfers property to another in trust to pay the income to the donor or accumulate it in the discretion of the trustee, and the donor retains a testamentary power to appoint the remainder among his descendants, no portion of the transfer is a completed gift[,]" the IRS Nation Office nevertheless concluded in CCM 201208026 that mere retention of a testamentary special power of appointment without more didn't render a transfer a completed gift. Commentators have questioned the correctness of CCM 201208026. See, e.g., Chuck Rubin, "Chuck Rubin & CCM 201208026: Using Testamentary Powers of Appointment to Create Incomplete Gifts-The IRS Throws Down the Gauntlet," *Steve Leimberg's Estate Planning Newsletter* No. 1959 (May 8, 2012).
4. *Grace Est. v. Comr., supra*. But see *Estate of Herbert Levy v. Comr.*, T.C. Memo 1983-453, 46 T.C.M. 910 (CCH) (1983).
5. See, *e.g.*, Uniform Probate Code §2-512.
6. I.R.C. §674(b)(4);
7. I.R.C. §677(a)(1) and (2).
8. I.R.C. §675(4)(C).
9. I.R.C. §§2041 and 1014.
10. This is due to the blind income tax basis adjustment of I.R.C. §1014 to date of death fair market value, irrespective of whether the adjusted basis of each cover asset is higher or lower than the asset's adjusted income tax basis at the decedent's death.
11. Metaphysically, there actually is a third conceivable possibility, i.e., that the asset's adjusted basis at death is exactly equal to the applicable death fair market value. While there technically is an adjustment to applicable death fair market value, the amount of the adjustment is zero.
12. See, e.g., Bruce D. Steiner and Martin M. Shenkman, "Beware of the Reciprocal Trust Doctrine," *Trusts & Estates* (Apr. 2012).
13. 395 U.S. 316, 324.
14. 395 U.S. at 322-325.
15. 46 T.C.M. 910, 912.
16. 395 U.S. 316, 324
17. 46 T.C.M. 910, 913.
18. 395 U.S. 316, 325.
19. 395 U.S. 316, 324.
20. See Endnote 12, supra.
21. For more information, see L. Paul Hood, Jr., "Reciprocal Trust Doctrine and Joint SLATS: Future IRS Happy Hunting Ground?," 34 *Probate Practice Reporter* No. 11, pp. 1-6 (Nov. 2022).

INTER VIVOS QTIP TRUSTS

CHAPTER 33

33.1 INTRODUCTION

Clients often want to fund and establish trusts for spouses during their lifetime (which may include children or other beneficiaries). Depending on the trust design, these trusts can accomplish numerous non-tax goals, such as providing security and asset protection for the spouse (and secondarily and indirectly the settlor as well), and numerous tax goals, such as state and federal estate and GST tax savings, address planning concerns for non-citizen spouses, and even achieve state and federal income tax savings.

In light of the uncertainty as to the permanence of the transfer (estate, gift, GST) and income tax code, clients welcome the tremendous amount of "look back" and flexible solutions that such irrevocable trusts can provide to adapt to potential changes in the tax code, yet provide more creditor protection and tax advantages than the standard revocable living trust.

Spousal trusts can be designed as completed gifts, or incomplete gifts. They can be designed either as marital deduction trusts, trusts that do not qualify for the marital deduction, or even trusts that can evolve into either with a later election. These trusts can be income tax neutral (grantor trusts), or even designed to be separate taxpayers (non-grantor trusts), to attain various federal, and especially state, income tax advantages. They can be designed to leverage the estate exclusion, or the reverse, affirmatively causing estate tax exclusion for increased basis.

This chapter will focus on irrevocable completed gift trusts for spouses designed to qualify for the marital deduction if so elected, known as *inter vivos* QTIP trusts.

33.2 CONTRASTING *INTER VIVOS* QTIPS WITH OTHER MARITAL TRUSTS

There are other marital trusts that can qualify for the martial deduction: a life estate with general power of appointment and an estate trust.

A life estate with general power of appointment trust has the same requirements as an *inter vivos* QTIP trust during lifetime, but it is rarely used because it must give the donee spouse a general power to appoint the assets during lifetime or at h death. Unlike other general powers of appointment, it must be exercisable "alone and in all events" (e.g., not with the consent of any other party), and cannot be limited to only creditors or creditors of the estate.[1] This means the spouse can effectively thwart whatever default disposition the settlor had established in the trust. It may also mean that the estate is subject to the donee spouse's creditors and/or creditors of his or her estate under state law.

The estate trust is even rarer. It must pay to the donee spouse's estate and cannot even establish a default disposition.[2] Neither one has been commonly used since the advent of the QTIP trust, because of the inherit asset protection disadvantages, not to mention the potential estate tax disadvantages that will be discussed further herein. Thus, this chapter will focus only on *inter vivos* QTIP trusts as the preferred form of *inter vivos* marital deduction trust.

511

33.3 ADVANTAGES OF *INTER VIVOS* QTIP TRUSTS

Nontax-Oriented Advantages

Individuals give property to their spouses in trust during their lifetimes for many reasons. Although a detailed discussion of the nontax motivations for lifetime giving is beyond the scope of this chapter, some of the reasons include:

- comply with a pre or postnuptial agreement

- potentially by providing for spouse in a QTIP, may allow children from a prior marriage to receive all other assets so that the probate of the donor's estate need not involve the spouse at all, causing much less chance for friction, litigation and delay

- may satisfy a state's spousal elective share, depending on the state[3]

- protection from the claims of the donor and donee's creditors during lifetime

- in many states, exceptions to self-settled trusts exist such that there is protection from a donor's creditors even if assets come back to the donor in trust upon the death of the donee spouse[4]

- the vicarious enjoyment of seeing the donee spouse use and enjoy the gift

- creating more financial certainty for the donee spouse and peace of mind

- as pre-divorce planning, transferring closely held business or unique assets that a donor spouse may fear losing outright in a divorce or may wish the spouse to have the income or use from

- the corresponding opportunity for the donor to see how well, or how poorly, the spouse manages the property during the donor's lifetime for the donee spouse, if the spouse is trustee or advisor

- the corresponding opportunity for the donor to see how well or poorly the trustee or co-trustee and donee spouse get along, if there are multiple parties involved

Tax-Oriented Advantages

- permits the donee spouse to be considered the transferor for estate and GST tax at the donee spouse's death, which ensures the applicable exclusion amount for gift and estate purposes (currently $25.84 million as of 2023) of the donee spouse is used, without the uncertainty of relying on the deceased spousal unused exclusion amount, which may be missed if the Form 706 is not filed properly, or may be later eliminated, if the surviving spouse permits gift splitting with a new spouse, or the new spouse dies[5]

- permits the donor spouse to receive the property in trust if the donee spouse dies first, with specific regulations safeguarding Code Sections 2036/2038 from including the assets in the donor's estate.[6] While there is some uncertainty around potential application of Code section 2041, many states have self-settled asset protection statutes or other statutory fixes to prevent this, as noted in footnote 2.[7]

- permits the donee spouse to be considered the transferor for gift tax purposes if the donee spouse releases or makes a non-qualified disclaimer during lifetime, enabling use of donee spouse's applicable exclusion amount[8]

- Ensures the use of generation skipping transfer (GST) tax exemption of the donee spouse, which could go completely unused if the donee spouse died first, since portability and the deceased spousal unused exclusion amount (DSUE) only applies to estate/gift tax, not GST tax.

- May act as a receptacle for any excess value cause by a revaluation of a formula gift, following various court cases, including circuit level cases, which have permitted similar charitable pourover clauses.[9]

- Allows a 9½ -21½ month lookback period for the donor to decide whether to use any applicable exclusion amount for a gift or not (or partial), since the donor typically has from the time of gift until October 15 of the following year, provided an extension of time to file an income or gift tax return is filed. This is much more advantageous in times of uncertainty about the gift and estate tax law.

- Probably allows the donor to divert the gift for that same time period (9½ – 21½ months), if the trust has a different disposition for the "B" portion than the "A" marital portion, sometimes known as a Clayton QTIP election.[10]

- Even if one did not want to use a trust with two sets of distribution provisions as in Clayton, the technique could be combined with a disclaimer for up to nine months from the gift, permitting further flexibility for up to nine months (or longer, if the spouse is under age twenty-one)

- Specific treasury regulations permit a formula election to zero out a gift by electing QTIP over that amount which is necessary to reduce the federal gift tax to zero (some other number could be used as well).[11]

- Permits the trust to continue as a grantor trust as to the donor spouse after the death of the donee spouse, unlike typical bypass trusts.[12] This permits a greater freeze of the donor spouse's estate and enables "swap" powers and disregarded sales to irrevocable grantor trusts.

- Enables fractional interest discounts for tenancy in common (TIC) interest in real estate or artwork or interests in closely held LP/LLP/LLC/corporations, without any aggregation for valuation purposes of any share held by the donee spouse outright.[13]

- Can participate in formations of such entities with other family members.[14]

- If established as a fully grantor trust, the settlor can swap or sell/purchase assets of equivalent value, even on installment sale, as with other irrevocable grantor trusts

- If established as a partial grantor trust as to income, partial non-grantor trust as to corpus/principal, may enable savings of state income tax on any accumulations of taxable income or gains in excess of accounting income, depending on the state of the settlor and spouse's residency.

- May permit avoidance of the one year rule of Code section 1014(e) if the donee spouse dies within one year of the gift, enabling QTIP assets to receive a step up in basis.

33.4 CREATING AN *INTER VIVOS* QTIP TRUST

Creating an *inter vivos* QTIP trust that is a completed gift is rather simple. Let's summarize the code and regulations that outline the basic rules.[15] For a gift to a trust to qualify for the *inter vivos* QTIP marital deduction it must:

1. Be funded by donor spouse

2. Grant the donee spouse a "qualifying income interest for life"

3. The donee spouse must be a United States citizen at the time the gift is made[16] and

4. Be subject to an irrevocable QTIP election on a timely filed Form 709 gift tax return.[17]

The "qualifying income interest for life" requires explaining a bit further, but readers are no doubt well familiar with these rules since this requirement is essentially the same as the more ubiquitous testamentary QTIP trust funded at the settlor's death. It requires either that all the net income to be paid annually, or for the spouse to withdrawal all the net income annually – no trustee or party can have the discretion to accumulate this income without the spouse's consent. "Income" for these purposes is not taxable income, it is trust accounting income.[18] An exclusive and unrestricted right to use a residence for life qualifies for QTIP treatment.[19]

No party can have a lifetime power of appointment or power to make distributions to anyone other than the donee spouse during the donee spouse's lifetime.[20] A "floating spouse" provision that removes an income interest upon divorce would disqualify a trust from making the QTIP election, similar to the requirement for a testamentary QTIP that an income interest cannot be removed if the spouse remarries.[21] While it is permissible to fund, retain or purchase assets unproductive of income in the trust, the spouse must have the ability to make non-income producing property productive of income or convert it within a reasonable time.[22]

It is important to note that certain rights and powers are very common and *permitted* in QTIP trusts, but are not *required*. These include such common provisions as:

- a spendthrift clause, so long as it merely prohibits alienation and assignment – a spendthrift clause that removes a mandatory income right would disqualify a QTIP;

- the ability for the trustee or any other party to distribute more than the net income (i.e. principal) to the donee spouse (under ascertainable or discretionary standards),[23]

- a provision that removes the spouse's potential access to additional distributions of principal upon remarriage;

- the ability for the donee spouse to hold a testamentary power of appointment, or a reversionary interest in the donor spouse upon the death of the donee spouse (which may even split between a bypass/QTIP trust).[24]

Estate Tax Effect

As mentioned in the bullet points above, the general effect for estate tax purposes is to include the assets in the donee spouse's estate and use the donee spouse's applicable exclusion amount and potentially GST exclusion. Thus, it has commonly been known as a technique in which a richer spouse funds a trust for a poorer spouse. However, it does not have to be. Spouses may establish *inter vivos* QTIPs for each other for the asset protection as well as the additional benefit that such trusts can provide after the death of a donee spouse over a bypass trust, as noted herein, due to grantor trust status being retainable.

GST Tax and Reverse-QTIPs over *Inter vivos* QTIPs

The donor spouse can make a "reverse QTIP election" over an *inter vivos* QTIP and allocate GST exemption.[25] This election means that for GST purposes it can be treated as if the QTIP election had not been made and the donor-spouse is considered the donor for GST purposes. With an ordinary QTIP without the reverse QTIP election, the *donee spouse* would be considered the transferor for GST purposes at the donee spouse's death.[26]

Whether one should make the reverse QTIP election depends on several factors – primarily, is the trust likely to accumulate income and grow, which may indicate making a reverse QTIP in order to leverage GST exemption over a trust likely to grow, or is it anticipated that significant withdrawals would be made? QTIPs are inherently "leaky" due to the requirement to pay out all net income annually. Thus, often this GST exemption would be put to better use for a trust that would not be as leaky. However, while it may not be used often, particularly when the settlor and spouse might see the trust as a short term solution, it is good to keep this option on the table.

Income Taxation during Life: An *Inter vivos* QTIP is usually a Wholly Grantor Trust

Most *inter vivos* QTIPs are going to be wholly grantor trusts as to the settlor. Usually the trust grants the ability to distribute more than the net income of the trust (e.g. either at the trustee's discretion or for health and support), or grantors the ability to use income to purchase insurance on the settlor or spouse, or the donee spouse may retain a testamentary power to appoint to the settlor, all of which triggers Code section 677. In addition, other administrative provisions may also trigger grantor trust status. Usually this is desirable. All income, including all capital gains, are reported on the settlor's Form 1040 (although a Form 1041 may be filed showing grantor trust status). This is often desirable for middle-class clients in light of non-grantor trusts reaching the top marginal income tax bracket at only $14,450 (as of 2023).

However, there may be specific cases when it would not be desirable to be a wholly grantor trust, such as when the settlor/spouse are already in the top tax bracket, and it would prefer a way to avoid state income tax on the gains inside the trust. Those in New York may consider this as a method of getting around the state's legislation that had closed the loophole regarding incomplete gift non-grantor trusts, since this method creates a *completed gift* non-grantor trust. Other states may be able to use this technique as well. The complexities of creating an *inter vivos* QTIP is beyond the scope of this chapter.

Unique S Corporation Issues and Opportunities

As discussed previously herein, most *inter vivos* QTIPs will be 100 percent grantor trusts, and therefore qualify to be an S corporation owner without the need of a special filing or election.[27] After the grantor's death, the trust might continue to be a grantor trust as to the settlor spouse, depending on the terms of the trust. If so, no additional election need be made. In the event that any trust after the donee's death does not still qualify as a grantor trust (such as if the settlor spouse is dead), then the beneficiaries would typically make the Qualified Subchapter S Trust (QSST) election for the QTIP to remain an owner.[28] The second most common method to ensure subchapter S qualification for a non-grantor trust is for the trustee to make an Electing Small Business Trust (ESBT) election. The majority of trusts probably use the QSST election, because it forces ongoing income to be fully taxed directly to the beneficiary.[29]

While QSSTs are more tax efficient for the 99 percent of the population who are not in the highest tax bracket, there still remains a minority for whom the ESBT is more advantageous – those in the highest tax bracket who reside in a state with a separate income tax, those fearing creditor/divorce access to forced distributions, those who are passive owners otherwise paying 3.8% surtax who might be able to avoid the tax by choosing an active co-trustee of an ESBT.

Avoiding the One-Year Rule of Code Sec. 1014(e) with *Inter vivos* QTIP Trusts

If a healthy spouse makes a completed gift to an *inter vivos* QTIP trust for a terminally ill spouse near death, can all the assets in the QTIP receive a new basis at the donee spouse's death soon thereafter? Surprisingly, the answer is probably "yes." Code section 1014(e) does have a one year rule denying a step up (but permitting a step down) in basis if:

> "A) appreciated property was acquired by the decedent by gift during the one-year period ending on the date of the decedent's death, **and**
>
> (B) such property is acquired from the decedent by (or passes from the decedent to) the donor of such property (or the spouse of such donor)."[30]

However, with the *inter vivos* QTIP, Code section 1014(e) would not apply for several reasons. First and foremost, unlike in standard outright gift situations, the donee spouse of an *inter vivos* QTIP does not "acquire" the property at all. At most, it's an income interest in the property. It's certainly not a donee spouse's property under any state law. An *inter vivos* QTIP trust is not even considered the donee spouse's property for income tax purposes under the grantor trust rules. As discussed herein, it's considered to be owned by the settlor spouse for income tax purposes unless we make the trust a partially non-grantor trust. It's not even possible to make an *inter vivos* QTIP trust a beneficiary deemed owner trust as to the spouse. Thus, for both state law and federal income tax law, the assets in an *inter vivos* QTIP trust are **not** the donee's spouse's assets and if the donee spouse dies, the prerequisite of Code section 1014(e)(1)(A) quote above does not apply. While Code sections 1014(b) and 1014(b)(10) deem receipt from a QTIP trust to be acquired from a decedent "for purposes of paragraph a", it specifically excludes any reference to paragraph e – it does not say, for example "for purposes of this section", or "for purposes of paragraphs a and e." It's extraordinarily common for such definitional or deeming rules to apply to an entire section or to several paragraphs – we're entitled to rely on express language and plain meaning. In fact, it's questionable if a regulation could even interpret it otherwise, but of course there is no such regulation.[31] Secondly, a couple in such a situation could simply use the fully grantor trust variant of a QTIP trust. The donor spouse can gift cash or non-appreciated assets to the trust, then swap or purchase the lower basis assets desired to be stepped up for equivalent value. Thus, in such a case, paragraph A would fail to apply for a second reason – that *no appreciated* assets were *ever gifted* into the trust, only cash or non-appreciated assets were gifted, and any highly appreciated assets later transferred to the trust would have been acquired by exchange or purchase for full and adequate consideration. Lastly, even if these arguments somehow failed, the disposition of the QTIP may not even revert back to the donor spouse – it may pass to the children in trust who have a lifetime power to appoint back to the spouse, or it may pass to a trust for the donor spouse. Code section 1014(e) has a later provision that addresses estate and trusts, but with little clarity and copious loopholes:[32]

> "(B) Treatment of certain property sold by estate
>
> In the case of any appreciated property described in subparagraph (A) of paragraph (1) sold by the estate of the decedent or by a trust of which the decedent was the grantor, rules similar to the rules of paragraph (1) shall apply to the extent the donor of such property (or the spouse of such donor) is entitled to the proceeds from such sale."

Again, this begs several questions and again there are several reasons why this paragraph does not apply to our situation. First, it only addresses a trust of which the decedent was a grantor! So, in an *inter vivos* QTIP trust the donor spouse is the grantor. If the donee spouse dies, the donor spouse clearly remains the grantor for income tax purposes, despite the donee spouse being deemed a transferor for estate tax purposes (and potentially for GST tax purposes, depending on whether a reverse QTIP election is made, as discussed herein).[33]

As if all of these reasons were not clear enough, it is clear (though bizarre) that the denial of basis increase only occurs if the property is "sold." Thus, there is no rationale for denying the basis increase for depreciation purposes. Moreover, even if the property were sold, the denial of step up in basis is only to the extent the donor spouse would be "entitled to the proceeds from such sale." While it may be common in an estate, it will be rare that a trust beneficiary is going to be entitled to the entire proceeds from the sale of trust property.

In short, there is very little statutory authority within Code Section 1014 to deny the use of an *inter vivos* QTIP trust for pre-mortem planning when a spouse may die within one year of death. In fact, that Congress spoke with such specific limitations argues that more amorphous "substance over form" type arguments would be inappropriate.[34] The IRS is welcome to argue that Congress didn't mean what it said, but this lack of authority for their position would likely get shot down in court, similar to the *Summa Holdings* case.

Perhaps all this is why the IRS did not bother to make the argument that §1014(e) applied in a recent high value high profile case on even more egregious facts than contemplated above. In *Estate of Kite v. Commissioner*, Mrs. Kite funded a QTIP trust for her husband, who died *only one week later*. The assets in the trust came back to her in trust (for which a QTIP election was again made) and the tax court noted *without discussion* that "All of the underlying trust assets, including the OG&E stock transferred to Mr. Kite [via QTIP trust seven days before he died] in 1995, received a step-up in basis under Code section 1014."[35] Thus, while we don't have a court case explicitly approving of this technique in the face of an IRS argument, we do have a court case noting the incredible result without the slightest questioning comment from the court and a deafening silence from the IRS when many would think they would have attacked it with vigor.

Floating Spouses, Sinking Settlors – Divorce Issues with *Inter vivos* QTIP Trusts

The prospect of divorce is a touchy subject to bring up, and especially difficult when practitioners represent both spouses. This is true with any trust, some more so than *inter vivos* QTIPs, but a few cautions are still merited. First, if there is no marital deduction sought, there is no estate or gift tax reason that the trust cannot define the beneficiary of the trust as "spouse" such that any divorce automatically removes the spouse as a beneficiary, so so-called "floating spouse" provisions can't be used in inter vivos QTIP trusts. By contrast, any clause, whether automatic or discretionary through some trust protector or other power, that may remove a spouse as beneficiary upon divorce or any other event disqualifies a marital deduction for a QTIP trust.[36]

Depending on the jurisdiction, the gift to the QTIP trust might convert the settlor spouse's gift to the donee spouse through the QTIP from separate to marital property, which might affect any division upon divorce. The potential effect may vary depending on the state and assets in question.

Exit Strategies (Other Than Death)

The surviving spouse's interest in an *inter vivos* QTIP can be terminated or vested outright through a qualified disclaimer, non-qualified disclaimer or release of interest in the trust, or the trustee or other power holders may distribute or appoint the assets to them outright.

A qualified disclaimer would have to be done within nine months of the gift, unless the spouse is under age twenty-one, in which case the spouse would have until nine months after reaching age twenty-one.[37] Remember, even though we think that the effect of a disclaimer must be the same as the effect if the disclaimant had predeceased, it does not have to be. The terms of the trust may provide for diverging dispositions between the two events – at death the proceeds may stay in trust for children and upon disclaimer the trust could even by its terms go back to the settlor.[38]

A non-qualified disclaimer or release would cause a taxable gift but could still be accomplished, even with a spendthrift provision.[39] If a non-qualified disclaimer or release were made over a trust in which a QTIP election were made, the gift would be valued as a gift of the entire trust, not just the income interest.[40]

Beware of granting any additional trust protector or amendment clauses in the trust if by any stretch they could be used in a way to disqualify a marital trust. The mere ability to amend would thwart qualification.[41] Decanting for such trusts should be limited in the document with an appropriate savings clause to preserve the eligibility for the election.[42] The ability to terminate by distributing all the assets outright to the surviving spouse would not offend the QTIP requirements, however.

Effect of Potential Estate Tax Repeal on *Inter vivos* QTIP

The exit strategies noted above can be important because if we do see the repeal of the estate tax, while keeping the gift tax intact, as proposed, this could mean the end of the step up in basis for QTIP trust on the death of the donee spouse.[43] The estate tax system and the adjustment of basis at death are sometimes, but not always, *in pari materia*. If the estate tax goes away completely, Code section 1014 would still create an adjustment in basis for assets passing under will or revocable trust of a decedent, or even under an exercised testamentary general power of appointment, but *not* (absent clarifying legislation) for a QTIP trust, which requires *estate tax inclusion* for triggering basis.[44] For those in community property states, the issue is similar for the surviving spouse's half of the community assets.[45]

33.5 CONCLUSION

Inter vivos QTIPs are a More Reliable Assurance of Using DSUE/GST

The estate tax affects fewer and fewer taxpayers, and it may even disappear altogether soon along with the GST tax, but Congress and voters are fickle and we cannot count on this result for long, if at all. *Inter vivos* QTIPs are more assured to use the donee spouse's applicable exclusion and GST exclusion amounts. Moreover, they have an important asset protection and psychological benefit for the settlor and the surviving spouse and can be an important component of any postnuptial agreement (or pre-nuptial agreement, as long as the trust is not funded until after the marriage). For wealthier clients, the ability for the trust to continue as a grantor trust even after the donee spouse dies is an important advantage over typical bypass trust planning. Lastly, for married couples with significant appreciated assets, while it may seem unseemly to consider income tax planning in light of an impending death, most families would like to seize any silver lining they can out of the situation.

CHAPTER ENDNOTES

1. I.R.C. §2523(e), I.R.C. §2056(b)(5), Treas. Reg. §20.2056(b)(5)(g).
2. See Rev. Rul. 68-554; Treas. Reg. §20.2056(c)-2(b)(1).
3. For an example, see Uniform Probate Code §2-201 – 2-214.
4. States with specific statutes protecting QTIP trusts in such a situation are: Arizona (Ariz. Rev. Stat. 14-10505(E)), Arkansas (Ark. Code Ann. §28-73-505(c)), Michigan (MCL §700.7506(4)), Virginia (Va. Code 55-545.05(B)), Ohio (Ohio R.C. §5805.06(B)(3)(b)), Delaware (12 Del Code §3536(c)(2), Florida (Fla Stat. §736.0505(3)) , Texas (Tex. Prop. Code §112.035(g)), South Carolina (S.C. Code Ann. §62-7-505(b)(2)), Kentucky (Ky. Rev. Stat. Ann. § 381.180(8)(a)), Maryland (Md. Est. & Tr. Code Ann. §14-116(a)(1)-(2)), Oregon (Or. Rev. Stat. §130.315(4)), Wyoming (Wyo. Stat. Ann. § 4-10-506(e)), North Carolina (N.C. Gen Stat. § 36C-5-505(c)), New Hampshire (N.H. Rev. Stat. Ann. §564-B:5-505(a)(2)(d)); Tennessee (Tenn. Code Ann. §35-15-505(d)); Wisconsin (Wis. Stat. §701.0505(2)(e)).
5. I.R.C. §2044(c), Treas. Reg. §20.2044-1(b).
6. Treas. Reg. §25.2523(f)-1(f), Examples 10 and 11.
7. It is arguable these savings statutes are not even needed, at least not to prevent application of I.R.C. §2041 from causing estate inclusion, since I.R.C. §2041(b)(1)(C) and §2514(c)(3)(A) exclude any power of appointment exercisable only in conjunction with the creator of the power. The settlor's indirect access to funds in a trust that is not protected by creditors would be a de facto presently exercisable general power of appointment (if not for the likely application of I.R.C. §2514(c)(3)(A). Thus, do not give up the argument if your client lives in a state that has self-settled trust statute nor a statute similar to those listed in footnote 2.
8. Treas. Reg. §25.2519-1(a).
9. E.g. *Estate of Petter v. Comm.*, 653 F.3d 1012 (9th Cir. 2011).
10. *Estate of Clayton*, 976 F.2d 1486 (5th Cir. 1992). The IRS later issued Treas. Reg. §20.2056(b)(7)(d)(3) in response to their loss in *Clayton*, but never did issue a parallel treasury regulation for gift tax purposes.
11. Treas. Reg. §20.2056(b)-7(h), Example 8.
12. Treas. Reg. §1.671-2(e)(5).
13. *Estate of Bonner v. United States*, 84 F.3d 196 (5th Cir. Tex. 1996), *Estate of Ethel S. Nowell v. Comm'r.*, T.C.M. 1999-15 (1999), *Estate of Ambrosina Blanche Lopes v. Comm'r.*, 78 T.C.M. 46 (1999) (non-aggregation for valuation at death, QTIP valued separately), *Mellinger v. Comm.*, 112 T.C. 26 (1999) (QTIP valued separately), IRS Action on Decision 1999-006. For a recent case approving discounts for fractional interest in artwork distributed in part to a SLAT and in part to a QTIP (which could have just as easily been done through partial QTIP election), see *Estate of Elkins*, 767 F.3d 443 (5th Cir. 2014)
14. IRS FSA 1999-20016 permitted QTIP trust to form FLP with spouse/beneficiary's daughter and grandchildren.
15. I.R.C. §2523(f) and Treas. Reg. §25.2523(f)-1 are the main provisions, but these in turn will reference I.R.C. §2056 and Treas. Reg. §20.2056(b)-7(d)(1) and Treas. Reg. §25.2523(e)-1(f) for further defining of a "qualifying income interest for life"
16. I.R.C. §2523(i). While the marital deduction is not available for gifts to noncitizen spouses, a form of the gift tax annual exclusion is allowed for up to $149,000 (adjusted for inflation, per Rev. Proc 2016-55, §3.37) if they would otherwise qualify for the marital deduction.

17. I.R.C. §2523(f)(4)(A) and Treas. Reg. §25.2523(f)-1(b)(4) provide that the gift tax QTIP election must be made "on or before the date prescribed by I.R.C. §6075(b) for filing a gift tax return with respect to the transfer (determined without regard to I.R.C. §6019(2)) and shall be made in such manner as the Secretary shall by regulations prescribe." An extension of time to file income tax returns can extend the deadline for filing the gift tax return. I.R.C. §6075(b). However, don't expect 9100 relief if your client misses that deadline as well – the IRS has taken the position that it cannot extend this and that even 9100 relief is unavailable (similar to how the IRS will not grant 9100 relief to missed portability elections if the Form 706 was required by statute to be filed) - see PLR 2011-09012, which had revoked an earlier PLR that had allowed a sixty-day extension. Also see Estate of Nielsen, 319 F.3d 1222 (10th Cir. 2003), in which an estate's attempt to claim there was no donative intent and void a gift after the inter vivos QTIP election was missed was rejected. Moreover, neither Rev. Proc. 2001-38 nor its successor Rev. Proc. 2016-49, which in some circumstances permit a taxpayer to undo an unnecessary testamentary QTIP election, permit a taxpayer to undo an unnecessary inter vivos QTIP election.

18. Usually determined under a state's version of the Uniform Principal and Income Act, if not otherwise addressed in the trust instrument, see I.R.C. §643(b) and Treas. Reg. §25.2523(e)-1(f), that references its definition.

19. Treas. Reg. §20.2056(b)-7(h), Example 1.

20. Treas. Reg. §25.2523(e)-1(f)(7).

21. Treas. Reg. §25.2523(f)-1(f), Example 5.

22. Treas. Reg. §25.2523(e)-1(f)(4).

23. Treas. Reg. §20.2056(b)-7(d)(6), I.R.C. §2056(b)(7)(B)(ii).

24. I.R.C. §2523(f)(5), Treas. Reg. §25.2523(f)-1(d).

25. I.R.C. §2652(a)(3).

26. Treas. Reg. §26.2652-2(d), Example 3.

27. I.R.C. §1361(c)(2).

28. I.R.C. §1361(c).

29. I.R.C. §1361(d)(1).

30. I.R.C. §1014(e)(1).

31. There are many regulations under I.R.C. §1014, Treas. Reg. §1.1014-1 to §1.1014-9, none of which add any insight to I.R.C. §1014(e).

32. I.R.C. §1014(e)(2)(B). For more discussion on I.R.C. §1014(e) and its loopholes and lack of clarity, see the Optimal Basis Increase Trust white paper.

33. Treas. Reg. §1.671-2(e):

    (1) For purposes of part I of subchapter J, chapter 1 of the Internal Revenue Code, a grantor includes any person to the extent such person either creates a trust, or directly or indirectly makes a gratuitous transfer (within the meaning of paragraph (e)(2) of this section) of property to a trust. ********

    (2) (i) A gratuitous transfer is any transfer other than a transfer for fair market value.

    ****

    (5) If a trust makes a gratuitous transfer of property to another trust, the grantor of the transferor trust generally will be treated as the grantor of the transferee trust. However, if a person with a general power of appointment over the transferor trust exercises that power in favor of another trust, then such person will be treated as the grantor of the transferee trust, even if the grantor of the transferor trust is treated as the owner of the transferor trust under subpart E of part I, subchapter J, chapter 1 of the Internal Revenue Code.

34. For a recent scathing rebuke of the IRS using substance over form to recast transactions specifically authorized by the law, see *Summa Holdings, Inc. v. Comm'r*, 2017 U.S. App. LEXIS 2713 (6th Cir. Feb. 16, 2017).

35. *Estate of Kite v. Comm'r*, T.C. Memo 2013-43, fn 9.

36. Treas. Reg. §25.2523(f)-1(c)(1)(i); Treas. Reg. §2523(f)-1(f), Example 5.

37. I.R.C. §2518(b).

38. Some readers may wonder whether this could create a reversion at common law and for §673 purposes. The spouse's disclaimer would be an "act of independent significance" in many areas of the law, such as the possibility of adding children as beneficiaries through procreation or adoption not triggering I.R.C. §§2036/2038 (Rev. Rul. 80-255), or the possibility of divorce (which allows the floating spouse absent QTIP, *Estate of Tully*, 528 F.2d 1401 (1976); PLR 9141027). However, such an alternative disposition upon disclaimer sounds a bit like a reversion under a broad definition, it's just that the chance of it occurring is remote and temporary (nine months if the disclaimant is over 21). So even if it might be ignored for I.R.C. §2037 estate tax purposes, it is not crystal clear that it is for I.R.C. §673 grantor trust purposes, especially in light of PLR 2016-42019, discussed above. The question would be, under I.R.C. §673(c), would a disclaimant be exercising an "exercise of discretion", as PLR 2016-42019 so deemed the distribution committee's potential for resigning? Ultimately, the two actions/powers are meaningfully different. Unlike a distribution committee's power, a disclaimer is not an "exercise of discretion" (defined as "n. the power of a judge, public official or a private party (under authority given by contract, trust or will) to make decisions on various matters based on his/her opinion within general legal guidelines). It is refusing to accept property. You can't be sued for exercising a disclaimer in bad faith, there are no guidelines granted in a trust document to a disclaimant to act within. If the IRS were to deem disclaimers to be acts of discretion it would lead to absurd results not intended by Congress, since there is always the possibility that all beneficiaries of any irrevocable trust disclaim, creating a resulting trust that reverts to the settlor. Such an absurd interpretation would mean all irrevocable trusts are grantor trusts under I.R.C. §673 for at least nine months. Ergo, disclaimers are not in the same category as acts of discretion, and such a remote possibility of a reversion would not trigger I.R.C. §673(c).

39. See Restatement 3d, Trusts §58 comment.

40. Technically the gift would be valued in two parts – I.R.C. §2511 would deem the spouse's income interest to be a gift and I.R.C. §2519 would deem the rest of the trust property to be a gift. Sometimes this bifurcation can make a difference for annual exclusion qualification and gift tax apportionment beyond the scope of this article.

41. See TAM 9525002 for a cautionary tale of good intentions gone awry where the trust allowed "either the trustee or any beneficiary to apply to a court of competent jurisdiction to amend this Agreement if the purposes of this Agreement may be defeated or hindered because of change in circumstance or change in law. The court may amend the terms of this

Agreement and restrict or remove any of the powers, duties, rights and privileges of the Trustee, the beneficiaries, or any other person." The government held that the power to amend disqualified the trust for marital deduction treatment notwithstanding a general provision that "the grantor intends that the Marital Trust . . . shall be available for the federal estate tax marital deduction." The IRS rejected reasonable arguments that the power to amend "adds nothing to the power already held by any court having jurisdiction over the trust" and that the power to amend was limited by the statement of intent to qualify for the marital deduction.

42. "It is my intent that my contribution to this trust shall qualify for the federal gift tax marital deduction under I.R.C. §2523 and no power or discretion shall be exercised or exercisable except in a manner consistent with this intent."

43. Ed Morrow on the Introduction of the "Death Tax Repeal Acts of 2017" - How the Proposed Bills Differ, in their Attack on INGs of All Things, and Threats to CRTs, LISI Estate Planning Newsletter #2516 (Feb. 10, 2017).

44. I.R.C. §1014(b)(1), (2), (4) and (10).

45. I.R.C. §1014(b).

LIFE INSURANCE

CHAPTER 34

34.1 INTRODUCTION

Life insurance is a contract under which for a stipulated consideration (a premium), one party (the insurer) agrees to pay the other (the insured), or his or her beneficiary, a defined amount upon the occurrence of death or some other specified event. In essence, life insurance is a contract under which economic protection is provided against the risk of cessation of income due to the insured's death. This definition of life insurance includes accidental death benefits under health insurance policies, whole life, endowment, universal, variable, and term life insurance policies. It encompasses both personally-owned and business-owned policies and includes group coverage as well as individually purchased plans. (For more extensive treatment of this most important topic, see our companion text, *The Tools & Techniques of Life Insurance Planning*, 9th edition.)

34.2 WHEN IS USE OF SUCH A DEVICE INDICATED?

1. Life insurance is an important estate planning tool to provide cash for the payment of federal and state estate and inheritance taxes, debts, administrative costs, and other estate expenses.

2. Life insurance will provide an income for family expenses.

3. Life insurance can be used for special needs such as the payment of college expenses, mortgage balances, or other large capital needs.

4. Life insurance is often used as a credit-building tool; lending institutions and other creditors often use life insurance on a debtor's life as security. It may even be a requirement for Small Business Association (SBA) loans or other loans when the services of a key person are integral to the business.[1]

5. Life insurance provides a way to pay federal estate taxes at a "discount." For example, if an individual purchases a $1,000,000 policy and dies within the first year of a contract (after having paid $15,000 in premiums), $1,000,000 worth of federal or state taxes can be paid at a cost of only $15,000. Furthermore, properly arranged life insurance owned by a third party who is also named beneficiary can be used to pay estate settlement costs with no probate cost, no inheritance or other state death taxes, no income taxes, no transfer fees, and no federal estate taxes. This may include a trust, see Chapter 36 on Irrevocable Life Insurance Trusts. It is an exceptionally efficient and effective means of both creating and transferring wealth.

6. Life insurance can be used as the "funding" mechanism for business continuation and Buy-Sell agreements.

7. Life insurance can be used by a corporation to finance certain corporate obligations such as non-qualified deferred compensation or salary continuation, as well as be used as key person insurance to indemnify the corporation for the lost services of a key person.

8. Life insurance can be used to fund a charitable gift. (See Chapter 38.)

9. Life insurance can be used to supplement an individual's retirement program.

34.3 WHAT ARE THE VARIOUS TYPES OF LIFE INSURANCE?

Term Insurance

Under this type of insurance the insured must die before the term expires for which benefits are to be paid. If the insured survives to the expiration of the "term," the insurance protection terminates. Initially, the cash outlay for insurance protection is relatively low so that the policy-owner receives the maximum short term protection for the minimum cash outlay.

There are basically five types of term insurance:

1. *Annual renewable term.* This type of policy is renewable each year (regardless of the insured's physical condition) at an increasing premium.

2. *Convertible term.* This type of policy may be exchanged without evidence of insurability, i.e., without the insured proving that he is physically and otherwise in a standard class of risks, for a whole life, universal life, variable life, or endowment type of policy.

3. *Decreasing term.* A familiar kind of decreasing term is often called "mortgage" insurance. The death benefit decreases over the specified period of time, but the premium generally remains level.

4. *Level term.* Here the death benefit remains the same for the entire term of the policy. Generally the premium also remains level. Common term periods are five, ten, fifteen, twenty, and thirty years.

5. *Re-entry term.* This type of policy provides a guaranteed term premium for an initial premium but allows the insured to re-qualify or re-enter after the initial period, if his or her health remains good. Re-entry can occur typically after a five- or ten-year period. If the insured does not re-qualify, the rates remain at the guaranteed rates, which are much higher than the re-entry rates.

Even these basic term policies may have riders (additional optional contract terms available for an additional charge), such as additional coverage for a critical illness or accidental death, for example.

Whole Life Insurance

The major characteristics of whole life insurance are: (a) the premium for a whole life insurance contract is guaranteed to remain level throughout the life of the contract; and (b) because of the "reserve" the insurance company needs to maintain a level premium when the insured reaches older ages, "cash value" builds up within the contract (this cash value increases annually and can be borrowed by the policy-owner or taken as surrender proceeds).

There are basically two types of whole life insurance. The first type is known as straight whole life, while the second is known as limited payment life. The difference is basically that under a limited payment life policy, premiums are "compressed," i.e., they are payable over a shorter period of time, whereas in a straight whole life policy, premiums are payable for the lifetime of the insured. For example, if a male age thirty-five purchased a $100,000 straight life policy, the "face amount" (death benefit) would be $100,000. If he purchased a $100,000 twenty-payment life policy at the same age, the death benefit would be the same and the protection would be provided for as long as the policy-owner wanted to keep the policy in force, i.e., it could be kept in force for the insured's life. But because premiums would be compressed into a much smaller period of time (twenty annual payments), they would be considerably higher under the limited payment type of plan.

There is another variety of whole life—modified life. A modified life insurance policy typically provides a given amount of insurance at unusually low premium rates for an initial period (e.g., five years) after issue and then the premium is correspondingly higher for the remainder of the premium period. Modified plans generally have a lower initial cash value than a corresponding face amount of typical straight life would have.

Riders, benefits in addition to the policy's death benefit, such as waiver of premium (waives and returns premium if the insured is disabled for a period of at least six months) and accidental death and dismemberment (doubles the death benefit if death is by accidental means), may be added to the basic contract.

Endowment Insurance

The primary characteristic of endowment insurance is that such a plan pays the face amount (e.g., $100,000) at the sooner of the time of "endowment" (the maturity of the contract, e.g., age sixty-five) or at the insured's death. Endowment policies are basically purchased as a means of forced savings because the protection element is relatively minimal. Various types of endowment policies are often found in pension plans or personal savings programs. Generally speaking, as a result of changes to the tax code in 1984, endowment contracts no longer qualify as life insurance. This is different from life insurance policies that are "modified endowment contracts" ("MECs") discussed later in this chapter.

Universal Life Insurance

A universal life policy is interest sensitive life insurance in which the investment, expense, and mortality elements are separately and specifically defined. A contract owner selects a death benefit level. The death benefit may be one that increases over time, coinciding with the increased cash value of the policy (death benefit option II), or, alternatively, the death benefit can remain level regardless of the underlying value changes (death benefit option I). From the premium that is paid, the insurer then deducts a "load" for contractually defined expenses. The remaining premium is then credited toward the contract owner's cash values. Mortality charges are deducted. Interest earned on the remaining cash is then credited at rates based on current investment earnings. (Specific design features will vary from company to company depending on marketing policies and product objectives.) Under this configuration, increased interest rates result in higher cash value levels while increased expense loads and increased mortality charges result in lower cash values. Typically, there is a minimum contractual guarantee as to the interest credited, such as 4 or 4.5 percent. Mortality costs also have a guarantee through a maximum premium charge for the "pure" cost of the death benefit; however, most companies charge rates lower than the contractually allowed maximum.

There is no such thing as a predetermined "standard" universal life plan; each contract owner selects the level of premium and death benefit desired as well as the length of premium paying period. Significant flexibility in premium payments is possible. Usually a stated minimum premium must be paid the first policy year. But after that the contract owner can vary the amount, the payment date, or frequency of subsequent premiums. (Depending on the amount of the initial premium, additional premiums or premium increases may be limited to stated minimum or maximum levels.) "Stop and go" features allow the discontinuance as well as subsequent resumption of premium payments at any time. As long as there is enough cash value to pay the expense (loading) charges and mortality costs, the policy will remain in force. If the cash value falls below that level, the policy will terminate.

Gross premiums are reduced by specified expense charges (as well as mortality costs) to determine the universal life policy's cash value. Expense loads run between 5 and 10 percent of the gross premium and are charged year after year. Additionally, because of greater first year acquisition costs, an extra first year expense may be levied. (This may be factored into the policy as a "per policy" amount, an amount per $1,000 of death benefits, or as a percentage of first year mortality charges.) Some companies may spread out the additional first year expenses by increasing the annual percentage of gross premium charges on some minimum amount of cumulative premium and set a lower percentage charge on premiums in excess of that stated minimum amount. Alternatively, rather than increasing expense charges, many insurers are recovering expense and surrender costs through "surrender charges." Upon surrender, the contract owner receives an amount reduced by a surrender charge, generally a percentage of the cash (or accumulated) value. Generally, the longer the policy is held, the less is taken out. Most surrender charges are applicable for fifteen years or less.

Similar to traditional policies, riders such as waiver of premium or accidental death and dismemberment may be added to the basic contract.

Also similar to traditional life insurance, loans can be taken against cash values subject to an interest charge. Unlike most traditional whole life policies, there is the ability to make partial withdrawals of cash values while the insured is alive. Since withdrawals are not loans, no interest charges are incurred.

Equity Indexed Universal Life Insurance

An increasingly popular version of universal life insurance is equity-indexed universal life insurance (EIUL). EIUL allows the policyholder to allocate the cash value to a fixed-rate account or an equity-indexed account that tracks a stock index, such as the S&P 500 or NASDAQ 100, but with some limits to the upside and downside risk. Like other universal life policies, EIUL also offers flexibility in premium payments, level of protection, and death benefit. EIUL is a complex product that combines elements of universal life and variable life insurance. Although the cash value in the policy performs like securities, EIULs are not considered investment securities.

Variable Life Insurance

A variable life insurance policy resembles a traditional whole life policy with two major distinctions. Neither the death benefit nor the surrender value payable during life are guaranteed, but either or both can increase or decrease depending upon the investment performance of the assets underlying the policy. The death benefit, however, generally, cannot decrease below the initial face amount of the policy, as long as all required premiums have been paid. With variable life, the cash surrender value guarantee is traded for the potential of investment growth by directing the overall strategy of the policy's investment program.

The policy-owner, not the insurance company, allocates the premium, after certain deductions are made, to sub-accounts held by the insurance company. Among the types of sub-accounts that may be offered and selected by the policy-owner are a money market type account, a growth stock account, a bond account, a balanced fund account, and a real estate account. And, depending on the insurance company, the policy-owner may re-allocate money going into the account several times a year. The cash value will be adjusted on a daily basis. Premiums are fixed and always remain the same. Because both the surrender value and death benefit can vary, the product is known as variable life.

Among the charges that are deducted from the premium before any investment is made in a sub-account are administrative and sales expenses, any state premium taxes, and the cost for the mortality element.

Variable life enjoys the same favorable income tax treatment as other life insurance policies. Earnings from the investments are currently income tax deferred. In other words, there is no income tax on the internal buildup of cash values until such values are realized by way of surrender, and then only if the surrender value exceeds the policyholder's cost basis, unless the policy is classified as a modified endowment contract (see question below). Death benefits, regardless of growth, pass income tax free, unless one of the rare exceptions such as "transfer for value" discussed later in this chapter, applies.

Should a policyholder wish to have access to cash values and not surrender the policy, the policyholder can borrow up to a designated percentage of the cash value (e.g., 90 percent). Interest, typically, is charged on these loans.

Similar to traditional policies, riders such as waiver of premium or accidental death and dismemberment may be added to the basic contract.

Unlike some other types of insurance, the sale of a variable life insurance product must be accompanied by or preceded by a prospectus approved by the Securities and Exchange Commission, as variable life is treated as a security. It can be sold by only agents registered as broker-dealers with the National Association of Securities Dealers (NASD).

Variable Universal Life Insurance

Variable universal life is a combination of universal life insurance and variable life insurance. It is like universal life with flexible premiums, adjustable death benefits, policy loan, and partial withdrawal privileges. However, unlike universal life and like variable life, the owner of the life contract and not the insurer decides where the premiums are invested. The alternative accounts where the premiums can be invested are similar to those in the variable life product described above.

Like variable life, variable universal life is a product subject to the rules of the Securities and Exchange Commission and, therefore, requires a prospectus be given to a prospective client before a sale can be made.

Survivorship Life Insurance

Survivorship life insurance, sometimes called joint and survivor life or second-to-die life, is a type of life insurance policy that insures two or more people. The policy may be either a whole life, term, universal, or variable type of policy. The death benefit under a survivorship policy is not realized until the last of two or more insured individuals dies. At that time the full death benefit is payable to the named beneficiary. Although there are several variations of this type of insurance, some of the policies that are of the whole life variety insure two individuals and provide for an increase in cash values upon the "first death," and, if the policies are participating (dividend paying), also provide for increased dividends. Depending upon the company, the premiums may continue until the survivor's subsequent death or, through a special option, the policy may be paid up at the "first death" and no further premiums would be required.

The policy can insure any two insureds as long as there is an insurable interest. Its use is typically confined to husband-wife, parent-child, or two related business people, such as business owners or key employees. The policy may be owned by any party that could own any of the other traditional types of life insurance policy, including an irrevocable trust. There is no requirement that there be joint owners, despite the fact that there are two insured individuals. Such insurance is particularly useful in the estate tax arena since typically the estate tax will arise only upon the death of the second spouse.

First-to-Die Life Insurance

First-to-die insurance is a life insurance policy that insures two or more people. The policy may be a whole life, term, universal, or variable life type of policy. The death benefit is realized when the first of any of the insureds dies, at which time the death benefit is payable to the named beneficiary. Some policies, through a rider, allow the survivor to continue coverage if he or she desires after the first insured dies.

The policy can be used in either business or personal planning, where there is a need for coverage only until the death of one of the two insured parties. Using a single first-to-die policy to insure multiple parties usually costs less in premiums than the purchase of two separate policies.

Single Premium Whole Life Insurance

Single premium whole life insurance is a type of limited pay life insurance policy. Unlike traditional whole life policies, however, where premiums are due generally until age ninety or one hundred, a single premium whole life policy, as the name implies, requires only one premium.

The policyholder purchases a paid-up policy with just one payment rather than paying premiums year after year. For example, a $250,000 single premium might buy a fifty-five-year-old man $750,000 worth of insurance coverage.

Single premium life offers some of the traditional tax advantages that regular whole life policies afford:

1. The money contributed to the policy builds up tax deferred through policy cash values.

2. The policyholder can borrow those cash values from the policy. Such a loan may trigger income tax consequences if the policy is classified as a modified endowment contract as it typically would be.

3. The proceeds from the policy (the face value, as distinct from the cash surrender value) at the death of the insured go to the beneficiaries completely income tax free and without probate; assuming that the insured's estate was not the named beneficiary. They may also be estate tax free, depending on the ownership (see Chapter 36 on Irrevocable Life Insurance Trusts).

4. One of the main characteristics of this type of insurance is that the policy develops immediate cash values. Interest is generally credited based upon some type of "new money" approach, and may be tied into short- or long-term investments of the particular insurance company. The values that the policy develops can be availed of either through a surrender of the policy or through a policy loan. Some companies allow the policyholder to borrow these values at no interest cost or at a nominal interest cost to the policyholder. For example, if a policyholder borrows $10,000, the insurance company might charge him 8 percent interest, but that is not his true cost. The company would credit his cash value account with the 8 percent interest he paid or 7 percent or 6 percent depending upon the company. Thus, the true interest cost to borrow would be anywhere from 0 percent to 2 percent. The policyholder need never pay back the loan. However, if the contract is classified as a modified endowment contract, borrowing from the policy will likely result in income tax consequences. Outstanding loans will reduce the death benefit, and interest on the loan is generally not income tax deductible.

34.4 WHAT ARE THE VARIOUS FEATURES OF A LIFE INSURANCE POLICY?

The professional should be familiar with the particular life insurance policy's ownership provisions, dividend provisions, and various additional benefits such as the accidental death benefit, disability waiver of premium, and guaranteed insurability, which is often called insurance of insurability.

The basic ownership rights are the right to name and change the beneficiary, the right to cash in a policy, the right to receive dividends, the right to borrow against policy cash values or to make partial withdrawals, and the right to dispose of some or all of the policy ownership rights mentioned above. An unconditional sale or gift of all ownership rights in a life insurance policy is known as an "absolute" assignment. When a policy is pledged as collateral for a loan, the assignment is known as a "collateral" assignment.

Dividend provisions are particularly important in those contracts offered by mutual insurance companies. Basically, a dividend is a refund of part of the premiums that the insured has paid to a mutual life insurance company and is the result of the insured's participation in the business fortunes of the policy class to which he or she belongs. The size of the dividend is based on the relative amount of favorable mortality, interest, and "loading" (business cost) experience of the insurance company.

The policy owner can:

1. take dividends in the form of cash;

2. use dividends to reduce premiums;

3. buy paid-up additional insurance (each dividend buys a small single premium policy in addition to the basic plan; no physical examination is required; and this additional insurance is purchased without sales charges or other costs);

4. leave the dividend with the company to earn (taxable) interest;

5. purchase one-year term insurance equal to the cash value of the policy;

6. use dividends to "vanish the premiums" on the policy at an earlier than expected date;

7. use some combination of the above dividend options.

Dividends are generally not available on universal or variable policies.

A number of additional benefits can be added (usually by paying additional money in return for a "rider") to a life insurance policy. For example, an accidental death benefit, for a small extra premium, will be paid in addition to the basic death benefit if death occurs in an accident before a specified age. (Typically, the basic death benefit is doubled.)

A second additional benefit that can be added is known as "disability waiver of premium." Under this useful benefit, premiums are waived (taken over by the insurance company) after the insured is totally disabled for a period of six months. Generally, once the six month period is met, most companies will also refund any premiums paid during that first six months of disability. Cash values on a whole life policy will continue to grow and the death benefits will be the same amount as if premiums were paid by the policyowner - regardless of how long the insured is disabled after qualification.

A third additional benefit that can be added and may be advisable when the insured is young is known as "guaranteed insurability" or "insurance of insurability." This benefit allows the insured to purchase additional life insurance at certain specified future dates without evidence of insurability. On the option dates, regardless of the insured's health at those times, the insured can exercise all, part, or none of the option to purchase additional insurance; but the options are non-cumulative. The rates for the new insurance are those applicable for the age in the year during which the option is exercised. In other words, if an insured waits until he is thirty-five to exercise an option, he pays the most favorable rates for males age thirty-five.

34.5 TAX IMPLICATIONS

Taxation of Death Benefits

Generally, proceeds payable by reason of the insured's death are exempt from income tax.[2] The exclusion applies regardless of how large the death benefit is and will be income tax free even if payable to the insured's estate, trust, or business. Such death benefit payments are, therefore, excludable without limit from the gross income of the beneficiary.

Proceeds from company owned life insurance on the lives of employees and certain owners may be taxable under Code section 101(j) if purchased after August 17, 2006 and notice is not given to the employee. Also IRS Form 8925 must be attached to the company tax return, see Notice 2009-48.

Where death proceeds are held by the insurance company and the beneficiary receives only the interest (this is known as an "interest only" option), the principal amount, when received, is exempt from income taxes. However, the annual interest earnings are taxable at ordinary income rates to the beneficiary.[3]

When the beneficiary chooses to receive death proceeds under a life income or under another settlement option under which payments will be made in installments, the annual interest produced by the death proceeds is taxable to the beneficiary. The balance is recoverable income tax free.[4]

As mentioned, generally insurance proceeds paid by reason of the insured's death are excludable from the recipient's gross income. However, where, prior to death a policy or an interest in a policy had been sold or otherwise transferred for valuable consideration, the death proceeds will be exempt only to the extent of the sum of:

- the consideration paid by the transferee;
- the net premiums paid by the transferee after the transfer; and
- for contracts issued after June 8, 1997, interest paid or accrued by the transferee on indebtedness with respect to a contract if the interest is not allowable as a deduction under Code section 264(a)(4).

The balance of the death proceeds is taxed at ordinary income rates. This is known as the "transfer for value" rule.[5]

Example. Rod Ross purchases a $250,000 policy on his own life. He pays four $5,000 annual premiums. Then he sells the policy to his son for $20,000. His son now owns a $250,000 policy on Rod's life for which he paid $20,000. Assume that Rod's son pays six additional $5,000 annual premiums ($30,000) and then Rod dies. At the time of Rod's death, his son would have paid a total of $50,000 for the policy ($20,000 for the policy itself plus $30,000 in premiums). When he receives the $250,000 of proceeds, only his cost, $50,000, will be excludable from income. The remaining $200,000 will be entirely subject to income tax at ordinary rates. Perhaps Rod's son could have loaned his father the money to pay the additional premiums, enabling him to avoid sale/transfer for value and eventually receive the funds income tax-free?

There are, however, safe harbors from the transfer for value rule. The "transfer for value" rule does not apply if the sale or transfer is to:

1. the insured (or a grantor trust which has the insured as the grantor)[6]
2. a partner of the insured;
3. a partnership in which the insured is a partner;
4. a corporation in which the insured is a stockholder or officer; or
5. if the transferee's basis is determined in whole or in part by the transferor's basis; slightly oversimplified, if the transfer does not result in a tax basis change.

Note that under (1) above, if a trust is classified as a grantor trust, then it is a grantor trust in its entirety with respect to the taxpayer. Therefore, a transfer of a life insurance policy to a grantor trust is treated as being transferred to the insured directly (thereby qualifying for this exception). This result occurs notwithstanding any withdrawal rights held by the beneficiaries that would otherwise make them owners under Code section 678(a) because the other grantor trust rules trump Code section 678(a) pursuant to Code section 678(b).

For example, where a policy owned by a partnership is transferred along with other assets to a newly-formed corporation as part of a tax-free incorporation or where one corporation transfers a policy to another corporation pursuant to a tax-free merger or reorganization, the policy does not become subject to the transfer for value rule.[7]

Transfers between spouses made after July 18, 1984 (or December 31, 1983, if the spouses elect) or incident to a divorce, even if for value, come within an exception to the transfer for value rule.[8]

The proceeds of a life insurance policy are generally subject to the federal estate tax. Life insurance on the life of a decedent will be includible in the decedent's gross estate under several circumstances:

- if the proceeds are payable to or for the benefit of his or her estate;
- if, at the time of death, the insured possessed any incidents of ownership in the policy (such as the right to change the beneficiary, the right to surrender the policy, or the right to obtain a policy loan);[9] or

- where the policy is transferred as a gift by the decedent within three years of his death.[10]

Also, the fair market value of a policy (generally the sum of the cash value plus unearned premiums) owned at death on another person's life is includible in the owner's gross estate.[11]

Gifts of life insurance policies or gifts of premium payments may be subject to the federal gift tax. The value of the gift is based on the fair market value of the insurance policy at the time of the gift or, in the case where one person pays premiums on behalf of another, the cash amount of the premiums paid.[12] The gift tax value of a policy can generally be obtained from the insurance company and is measured differently depending upon the type of policy, i.e., term, whole life, etc.[13]

Terminally or Chronically Ill Persons

A *viatical settlement* is the sale of a life insurance policy by a terminally ill person to a business that specializes in these transactions (viatical settlement companies). People with limited life expectancies oftentimes face financial difficulties. Viatical settlements allow these people to sell their life insurance policies and use the proceeds to help improve their financial or medical situation.

The proceeds from a viatical settlement will generally be treated as an amount paid under the life insurance contract by reason of the insured's death and will not be includable in income.[14]

However, amounts paid to a chronically ill individual are subject to the same limitations that apply to long-term care benefits, which were added to the Internal Revenue Code in section 7702B(d). Generally, in 2021, this is a $400 (adjusted for inflation) per day limitation.[15] Accelerated death benefits paid to terminally ill individuals are not subject to this limit.[16]

There are several special rules that apply to chronically ill insureds. Generally, the tax treatment outlined above will not apply to any payment received for any period unless the payment is for costs incurred by the payee (who has not been compensated by insurance or otherwise) for qualified long-term care services provided to the insured for the period. Additionally, the terms of the contract under which the payments are made must comply with several other requirements.

A terminally ill individual is a person who has been certified by a physician as having an illness or physical condition that can reasonably be expected to result in death within twenty-four months following the certification. A chronically ill individual is a person who is not terminally ill and who has been certified as being unable to perform, without substantial assistance, at least two activities of daily living for at least ninety days or a person with a similar level of disability. Further, a person may be considered chronically ill if he requires substantial supervision to protect himself from threats to his health and safety due to severe cognitive impairment and this condition has been certified by a health care practitioner within the previous twelve months.

The rules outlined above do not apply to any amount paid to any taxpayer other than the insured if the taxpayer has an insurable interest in the life of the insured because the insured is a director, officer or employee of the taxpayer or if the insured is financially interested in any trade or business of the taxpayer.[17]

Taxation of Premiums and Dividends

Premiums for personally owned life insurance are not deductible for income tax purposes. They are considered nondeductible personal expenses unless (a) premiums constitute alimony payments, under certain circumstances[18] (keeping in mind tax reform elimination of alimony deductions starting in 2019) or (b) premiums are paid on a policy irrevocably assigned to and owned by a charity and the insured reserves no rights in the policy.[19]

Life insurance companies generally allow a discount if the premiums are paid one or more years in advance of the due date. The yearly interest increment earned on these prepaid premiums is currently taxable to the policy-owner.[20]

Dividends paid on participating policies are not taxable income (unless they exceed the policy-owner's cost basis in the contract).[21] This is consistent with the definition discussed above, i.e., life insurance policy dividends are generally considered to be a partial return of premiums. However, if dividends are left on deposit with the insurance company and accumulate interest, any interest on the accumulated dividends is taxable to the policy-owner at ordinary income rates.[22] Dividends that are used to purchase paid-up additional insurance or one-year term insurance create no income tax liability. They are considered as if they were dividends paid in cash (a return of capital) and then used to buy single premium insurance.

Taxation of Living Benefits

Where the policy-owner receives a lump sum cash settlement in excess of the cost of the contract, the difference is considered ordinary income and is taxable in the year the contract matures or is surrendered.[23] The "cost" of the contract is measured by the total premiums paid (excluding premiums paid for accidental death benefits or waiver of premium).[24] The dividend option selected will affect the actual cost or total premiums. For example, if dividends are accumulated or applied to purchase paid-up additional insurance, then the cost of the contract would be the gross premiums paid by the policy-owner. However, if dividends are not accumulated or not used to purchase paid-up additional insurance, then the net premiums (gross premiums less dividends received in cash or applied to reduce policy premiums) paid determine the cost of the contract.

Settlement Options

Often, rather than taking a lump sum, a policy-owner will choose to take living benefits of a policy under a "settlement option." Proceeds placed under settlement options (other than the interest option) are taxed under the "annuity rules" of section 72 of the Internal Revenue Code. Basically, these rules are designed so that the annuitant will not be taxed on the portion of the annuity income that is considered to be a return of premium payments.

The portion of the annuity income that is considered to be gain is taxable; therefore, each payment is divided into two parts: (1) a nontaxable return of cost, and (2) taxable income.

To determine which portion of each payment is excludable from gross income and which portion is taxable income, an exclusion ratio or percentage is found.[25] The exclusion ratio is the ratio that the total investment in the contract bears to the total expected return; to find the percentage of each annual payment that is income tax free, divide the investment in the contract (cost) by the expected return.[26] The expected return is the annual payment multiplied by the recipient's life expectancy. (See Table V in Figure 33.1 for multiples representing life expectancy.) The exclusion ratio is then multiplied by each year's total annuity payments to yield the tax-free portion of total payments received during the year. The balance of the payments is taxable as ordinary income.

Force-outs

Provided the policy is not classified as a modified endowment contract, only cash distributions and not policy loans can cause current income taxation to the recipient. Where a policyholder reduces the death benefit of a universal life policy, either by switching from an Option II death benefit (increasing death benefit) to an Option I death benefit (level death benefit), or by making a partial surrender, which reduces the face amount of the policy, a new calculation of the policy for the definitional test of life insurance must occur. If the policy has too much cash (after the death benefit reduction), above the maximum allowable under the definitional rules of Code section 7702, the excess must be "forced out" as a distribution.

If the force-out of the cash occurs in years one through five, the policy (after the reduction in the face amount) must meet the guideline premium limitation/cash value corridor test to avoid the forced out distribution from being currently taxed as income to the extent there is a built-in gain in the policy at that time. If the policy after the reduction in face amount meets this test, the cash distributed would be considered a return of basis under the FIFO taxation rules (first in, first out). Only if the amount received exceeded the policyholder's basis would the gain be taxable to the recipient.

If the distribution occurs in policy years six through fifteen, the policy after reduction must meet the corridor percentage limits of Code section 7702. To the extent the cash value exceeds the required amount under this test and is forced out, it is taxable as income to the policyholder to the extent there is a gain in the policy.

For years after the fifteenth year, the policyholder is taxed on a FIFO basis (no income tax until basis is exceeded).

Provided the policy is not a modified endowment contract, in any year that a cash withdrawal is made and the definitional tests are still met after the withdrawal, any cash withdrawn is taxable only to the extent the amount received in that year and in all previous years exceeds the premiums paid into the contract, i.e., to the extent there is a gain in the contract.[27]

Cash Withdrawals and Loans from Modified Endowment Contracts

How are distributions such as cash withdrawals or policy loans taxable to the recipient if the policy is classified as a modified endowment contract? A modified endowment contract is one which meets the requirements of Code section 7702 (regarding what is a life insurance contract), was entered into on or after June 22, 1988 and fails to meet the seven pay test of section 7702A(b). If a policy falls into this category, lifetime distributions from the policy will be taxed less favorably than if the "seven pay test" is met.

Figure 33.1

TABLE V — ORDINARY LIFE ANNUITIES
ONE LIFE — EXPECTED RETURN MULTIPLES

Age	Multiple	Age	Multiple	Age	Multiple
5	76.6	42	40.6	79	10.0
6	75.6	43	39.6	80	9.5
7	74.7	44	38.7	81	8.9
8	73.7	45	37.7	82	8.4
9	72.7	46	36.8	83	7.9
10	71.7	47	35.9	84	7.4
11	70.7	48	34.9	85	6.9
12	69.7	49	34.0	86	6.5
13	68.8	50	33.1	87	6.1
14	67.8	51	32.2	88	5.7
15	66.8	52	31.3	89	5.3
16	65.8	53	30.4	90	5.0
17	64.8	54	29.5	91	4.7
18	63.9	55	28.6	92	4.4
19	62.9	56	27.7	93	4.1
20	61.9	57	26.8	94	3.9
21	60.9	58	25.9	95	3.7
22	59.9	59	25.0	96	3.4
23	59.0	60	24.2	97	3.2
24	58.0	61	23.3	98	3.0
25	57.0	62	22.5	99	2.8
26	56.0	63	21.6	100	2.7
27	55.1	64	20.8	101	2.5
28	54.1	65	20.0	102	2.3
29	53.1	66	19.2	103	2.1
30	52.2	67	18.4	104	1.9
31	51.2	68	17.6	105	1.8
32	50.2	69	16.8	106	1.6
33	49.3	70	16.0	107	1.4
34	48.3	71	15.3	108	1.3
35	47.3	72	14.6	109	1.1
36	46.4	73	13.9	110	1.0
37	45.4	74	13.2	111	.9
38	44.4	75	12.5	112	.8
39	43.5	76	11.9	113	.7
40	42.5	77	11.2	114	.6
41	41.5	78	10.6	115	.5

A policy fails the seven pay test if the cumulative amount paid at any time during the first seven years of the contract exceeds the net level premiums that would have been paid during the first seven years if the contract provided for paid-up future benefits. If a material change in the policy's benefits occurs, a new seven year period for testing must begin.

Distributions, including policy loans, from modified endowment contracts are taxed as income first at the time received to the extent that the cash value of the contract immediately before the payment exceeds the investment in the contract, and recovery of basis second, much like distributions from annuity contracts are taxed. Additionally, a penalty tax of 10 percent applies to distribution amounts included in income unless the taxpayer has become disabled or reached age 59½ or the distribution is part of a series of substantially equal payments made over the taxpayer's life.

With some exceptions, life insurance policies issued on or before June 21, 1988 are grandfathered and not required to comply with the seven pay test. Life insurance companies should assist in evaluating when a policy may be in danger of becoming a MEC – but if lifetime distributions are not contemplated, becoming a MEC may not be a big deal.

Surrendering Ownership

To the extent that one transfers away all of the incidents of ownership (such as to a life insurance trust) and the policy is not payable directly or indirectly to his estate, then the policy will not be included in his estate for federal estate tax purposes. However, to achieve estate tax exclusion, the policy must be transferred more than three years before the insured's death (or, it may be sold if the transfer for value exceptions are met, which may avoid the three-year rule).

Although a gift of insurance made more than three years before death can be effective in reducing the insured's estate for estate tax purposes, it also reduces the control and ownership rights of an insured during his lifetime, as many insureds have found upon dissolution of a marriage. Furthermore, with the very large federal estate tax exemption ($12,920,000 in 2023), in many cases clients will not need to transfer life insurance and can retain control safely without fear of generating federal estate tax.

Transfer of insurance is subject to gift tax and, therefore, one must also consider the value of the policy when making a gift. An alternative to a gift would be to have a life insurance trust purchase the policy from the insured. If the trust is a grantor trust, there will be no income tax consequences. The difficulty lies in the proper valuation of the policy.

Insurance Protection

Until recently, the question of whether the cost of insurance protection should be subtracted or not from the premiums paid was unsettled. A commonly held view was that the cost of insurance protection should *not* be subtracted from the premiums paid (thus decreasing the amount of taxable gain), and this view was supported by case law. See the section titled "Pre-Revenue Ruling 2009-13," below. Conversely, in 2005 guidance the IRS had indicated that on a sale of a life insurance policy, it would consider the basis of the contract to be the premiums paid *minus* the cost of insurance protection—thus, increasing the amount of taxable gain.[28]

Revenue Ruling 2009-13 provides definitive guidance to policyholders who surrender or sell their life insurance contracts in life settlement transactions.[29] Essentially, the basis is *not* adjusted for the cost of insurance protection when a policy is surrendered (Situation 1, below), but the cost of insurance protection *is* subtracted from the premiums paid when the policy is sold (Situations 2 and 3, below).

The ruling explains how to calculate the amount and character of gain upon the surrender or sale of a life insurance policy by the insured.[30] The examples below illustrate:

- the surrender of a cash value policy (Situation 1);
- the sale of a cash value life insurance policy (Situation 2); and
- the sale of a term life insurance policy (Situation 3).

Situation 1: Surrender of Cash Value Policy

Facts: On January 1, 2001, John Smith bought a cash value life insurance policy on his life. The named beneficiary was a member of John's family. John had the right to change the beneficiary, take out a policy loan, or surrender the policy for its cash surrender value. John surrendered the policy on June 15, 2008 for its $78,000 cash surrender value, including a $10,000 reduction for the cost of insurance protection provided by the insurer (for the period ending on or before June 15, 2008). Through that date, John paid policy premiums totaling $64,000, and did not receive any distributions from or loans against the policy's cash surrender value. John was not terminally or chronically ill on the surrender date.

Amount of income recognized. The IRS determined that the "cost recovery" exception[31] (to the "income first" rule[32]) applied to the non-annuity amount received by John.[33] Under that exception, a non-annuity amount received under a life insurance contract (other than a MEC) is includable in gross income to the extent it exceeds the "investment in the contract." For this purpose, "investment in the contract" means the aggregate premiums (or other consideration paid for the contract before that date) *minus* the aggregate amount received under the contract before that date that was excludable from gross income. The IRS ruled that John must recognize $14,000 income [$78,000 (which includes a $10,000 reduction for cost of insurance) *minus* $64,000 (premiums paid)].

Character of income recognized: The IRS concluded that $14,000 was ordinary income, not capital gain. The IRS determined that the life insurance contract was a "capital asset" described in section 1221(a). However, relying on earlier guidance, the IRS reiterated that the surrender of a life insurance contract does *not* produce a capital gain,[34] and further determined that Code section 1234A (which applies to gains from certain terminations of capital assets) does not change this result.

Situation 2: Sale of Cash Value Policy

In Situation 2, the IRS takes the position that the cost of insurance protection must be *subtracted* from the premiums paid.

Facts: The facts are the same as in Situation 1, above, except that on June 15, 2008, John sold the cash value policy for $80,000 to B, a "person" unrelated to John and who would suffer no economic loss upon John's death.

Amount of income recognized. The IRS first stated the general rule that gain realized from the sale or other disposition of property is considered to be the excess of the amount realized over the adjusted basis for determining gain.[35] The IRS determined that the amount John realized from the sale of the life insurance policy was $80,000.[36]

The adjusted basis for determining gain or loss is generally the cost of the property minus expenditures, receipts, losses, or other items properly chargeable to capital account.[37] The IRS specifically pointed out that section 72, which involves the taxation of certain proceeds of life insurance contracts, has no bearing on the determination of the basis of a life insurance policy that is sold because that section applies only to amounts received *under* the policy—which was not the case in this situation.

Next, the IRS noted the Internal Revenue Code's and the courts' acknowledgment that a life insurance policy—while only a single asset—may have both investment and insurance characteristics.[38]

The IRS then stated that in order to measure a taxpayer's gain upon the sale of a life insurance policy, the basis must be *reduced* by the portion of the premium paid for the policy that has been expended for the provision of insurance before the sale.[39]

Against that backdrop, the Service determined that John had paid premiums totaling $64,000 through the date of sale, and that $10,000 would have to be subtracted from the policy's cash surrender value as cost of insurance charges. Thus, John's adjusted basis in the policy as of the date of sale was $54,000 ($64,000 premiums paid - $10,000 expended as the cost of insurance). Accordingly, the IRS ruled that John would have to recognize $26,000 of income upon the sale of the life insurance policy, which is the excess of the amount realized on the sale ($80,000) over John's adjusted basis in the contract ($54,000).

Character of income recognized. The "substitute for ordinary income" doctrine (which essentially holds that ordinary income that has been earned, but not recognized by a taxpayer, cannot be converted into capital gain by a sale or exchange) was held by the IRS to be inapplicable in this situation. The IRS stated the doctrine is limited to the amount of income that would be recognized if a policy were *surrendered* (i.e., to the inside build-up under the policy). Thus, if the income recognized on a *sale* (or exchange) of a policy exceeds the "inside build-up" under the policy, the excess may qualify as gain from the sale or exchange of a capital asset.[40]

In Situation 2, because the "inside build-up" in John's life insurance policy was $14,000 ($78,000 cash surrender value - $64,000 aggregate premiums paid), the IRS concluded that amount would constitute ordinary income under the doctrine. But because the policy was a capital asset (under Code section 1221), and had been held by John for more than one year, the remaining $12,000 of income represented long-term capital gain.[41]

Effective date: The IRS has declared that the holding in Situation 2 will not be applied adversely to sales occurring before August 26, 2009.[42]

Situation 3: Sale of Term Policy

In Situation 3, the IRS takes the position that the cost of insurance protection must be *subtracted* from the premiums paid.

Facts: The facts in Situation 3 are the same as stated in Situation 2, above, except that the policy was a fifteen-year level premium term life insurance policy with a $500 monthly premium. John paid $45,000 total premiums through June 15, 2008, and then sold the policy for $20,000 on the same date to B (a person unrelated to John, and who would suffer no economic loss upon John's death).

Amount and character of income recognized: The IRS stated that absent other proof, the cost of the insurance provided to John each month was presumed to equal the monthly premium under the policy ($500). Consequently, the cost of insurance protection provided to John during the 89.5 month period was $44,750 ($500 monthly premium times 89.5 months). Thus, John's adjusted basis in the policy on the date of sale to B was $250 ($45,000 total premiums paid - $44,750 cost of insurance protection). The IRS concluded that John was required to recognize $19,750 long-term capital gain upon the sale of the term life policy ($20,000 amount realized - $250 adjusted basis).[43]

Effective date: The IRS has declared that the holding in Situation 3 will not be applied adversely to sales occurring before August 26, 2009.[44]

Gain up to the amount of the contract's cash surrender value should be taxed to the seller as ordinary income. According to the decided cases, the amount of taxable gain is determined in the same way as upon surrender of a contract. In other words, gain is determined by subtracting the net premium cost (i.e., gross premiums less dividends to the extent excludable from income) from the sale price.[45] (Therefore, under the decided cases the cost of insurance protection is *not* deducted from the premiums paid.) However, later guidance indicated that on a sale of a life insurance policy, the IRS considered the basis of the contract to be the premiums paid *minus* the cost of insurance protection.[46]

Before Revenue Ruling 2009-13, the issue of whether gain in excess of the contract's cash surrender value (such as in a life settlement) is ordinary income or capital gain was also unsettled. Some argued that the entire gain should be ordinary income. But others contended that gain in excess of the contract's cash surrender value should receive capital gain treatment. In support of the argument that a portion of a life settlement should be treated as a capital gain, proponents pointed to a footnote in the *Phillips* case where the IRS conceded that in certain situations the sale of a life insurance contract might result in capital gain treatment.[47] However, in a technical advice memorandum, the IRS pointed out that even if a life insurance contract is treated as a capital asset, the entire gain from the sale of a contract should be treated as ordinary income.[48]

The Tax Court held that settlement proceeds ($500,000) received by the taxpayer (a former corporate executive) with respect to a life insurance policy represented an extinguishment of his claim to ownership of the policy, as opposed to a sale or exchange of a capital asset. Accordingly, the proceeds were taxable as ordinary income.[49]

Miscellaneous Issues

Losses. Normally there will be no loss when a life insurance policy is sold for its cash surrender value.

Loans. If the contract sold is subject to a nonrecourse loan, the transferor's obligation under the loan is discharged and the amount of the loan is considered an amount received on the transfer.[50]

Interest Paid to Acquire Life Insurance

The general rule is that a deduction is not allowed for interest paid on indebtedness incurred to purchase or carry life insurance if the insurance is purchased pursuant to a plan that contemplates the systematic direct or indirect borrowing of part or all of the increase in the cash surrender value of such contract. There are four exceptions to this general rule:

1. *Trade or business exception*–If the indebtedness is incurred in connection with the taxpayer's trade or business, the interest deduction will not be denied.

2. *$100 a year exception*–The interest deduction will be allowed if the interest on the loan is less than $100 a year.

3. *The seven-year exception*–An interest deduction will be allowed in spite of the general rule where at least four of the annual premiums due during the first seven years of the contract are paid by means other than direct or indirect borrowing. Therefore, if a policyholder pays *any* four full years' premiums out of the first seven years' premiums due, the interest deduction on policy loans, including interest on loans made during the first seven years, will be allowed.

4. *The unforeseen event exception*–An interest deduction will be allowed if the indebtedness is incurred as the result of an unforeseen substantial loss of income or unforeseen substantial increase in the taxpayer's financial obligations.[51]

However, even if a personally owned policy comes within one of the four just mentioned exceptions to the general rule, none of the interest has been allowed as a deduction of personal interest since 1990.

For insurance loans on policies owned by a taxpayer (corporation or other entity) carrying on any trade or business, a deduction will not be allowed for interest on any indebtedness with respect to one or more life insurance policies covering the life of any individual who is a "key person" (an officer or 20 percent owner of the business), in any trade or business carried on by the taxpayer, to the extent the loans aggregate more than $50,000 per insured. If the person insured is not a "key employee", interest is not deductible for policy loans even if less than $50,000. However, for a policy owned by a taxpayer purchased on or before June 20, 1986, if the policy otherwise qualifies for an income tax deduction by coming within one of the four exceptions, interest will continue to be fully tax deductible.[52]

Several changes were made by both the 1996 and 1997 tax Acts regarding the deductibility of policy loan interest for company owned life policies. The general rule of Code section 264 states that no deduction will be allowed for interest paid or accrued on any indebtedness with respect to one or more life insurance policies owned by the taxpayer covering the life of any individual. For interest in policy loans for "key employees" however, there is an exception from the general disallowance rule and there can be an allowable deduction if the general rules regarding policy interest deductibility are met.

Furthermore, the Taxpayer Relief Act of 1997 added a new section 264(f) that generally provides that no deduction will be allowed for the part of the taxpayer's interest expense that is "allocable to unborrowed policy cash values." The portion which is "allocable to unborrowed policy cash values" is an amount that bears the same ratio to the interest expense as the taxpayer's average unborrowed policy cash values of life insurance policies and annuity and endowment contracts issued after June 8, 1997 bears to the sum of:

1. in the case of assets that are life policies or annuity or endowment contracts, the average unborrowed policy cash values; and

2. in the case of assets of the taxpayer that do not fall into this category, the average adjusted bases of such assets.

"Unborrowed policy cash value" is defined as the excess of the cash surrender value of a policy or contract (determined without regard to surrender charges) over the amount of the loan with respect to the policy or contract.

34.6 ISSUES IN COMMUNITY PROPERTY STATES

Where community property funds are used to purchase an insurance policy and there has been no agreement otherwise affecting the ownership of the policy, the policy will be owned by the community–and therefore belongs one-half to each spouse.

Thus, if a policy on the husband is community property and the beneficiary is someone other than the wife, a transfer subject to gift tax will occur when the insured dies and the proceeds are payable to that third person. The amount of the gift will be one-half of the proceeds, which represents the wife's one-half community interest in the policy.

For this reason, careful estate planners note the ownership and beneficiary designations of insurance policies to be able to consider any gift tax problems that may exist. Even payment to a trust of which the surviving spouse is the income beneficiary can result in a gift if the surviving spouse does not have a power under the trust to determine to whom the remainder interest is payable at his or her death. The amount of the gift would be the actuarial value (per IRS regulations in cases of normal health circumstances of the life tenant) of the remainder interest at the time of the transfer to trust, in the surviving spouse's community one-half of the insurance proceeds.

Policies as Separate Property

The main problem in *acquiring* an insurance policy as the separate property of the non-insured spouse is the presumption in most community property states that property acquired during marriage is community property unless proven otherwise. This means that sufficient documentation of the separate property status of the policy must exist so as to overcome the community property presumption. The first step to indicate that an insurance policy is the separate property of one spouse is to name that spouse as the sole owner of the policy. However, more evidence is usually necessary to overcome the presumption, and this requirement varies from state to state.

After the initial acquisition of a new policy as the separate property of one of the spouses or after the conversion of an existing policy into the separate property of one spouse, the question arises as to what must be done in the future to retain the separate property status of the policy. The answer depends on state law and the type of policy. Generally, community property states follow either the "premium tracing" doctrine (also known as the "apportionment" theory) or the "inception of title" doctrine with respect to whole life or other cash value life insurance policies and follow the "risk payment" doctrine with respect to term life insurance.

The "Premium Tracing" Doctrine

Under the "premium tracing" doctrine, the classification of a whole life or other cash value life insurance policy as separate or community property depends on the source of funds used to make the premium payments. Ownership of the policy is apportioned between the separate and community interests of the spouses based on separate and community contributions to the premium payments. If, for example, the policy is initially acquired as the husband's separate property and 10 percent of the premiums are thereafter paid with community funds, then, absent any documentation or action taken to preserve the separate property status of the policy, 90 percent of the proceeds would be the husband's separate property and the other 10 percent would be community property. Therefore, the husband would be treated as owning 95 percent of the proceeds and the wife would be treated as owning 5 percent.

The "Inception of Title" Doctrine

Under the "inception of title" doctrine, the ownership of a whole life or other cash value life insurance policy does not vary depending on whether premiums are paid with separate or community funds. If the policy is purchased with separate funds, the policy is characterized as separate property and, if the policy is purchased with community funds, the policy is characterized as community property. Where community funds are used to pay premiums on a separate property policy, in the absence of documentation to the contrary, the non-owner spouse generally will have a right to reimbursement on the death of the insured to the extent of one-half of the community funds used to pay the premiums. The proceeds includable in the insured's estate will be reduced by the amount subject to this right of reimbursement.

The inception of title rule is followed by most community property states. Under the rule, property is deemed acquired on the date that the right to interest, title and possession arises.[53] As a result, the date that property is physically received is not relevant in determining its character as separate or community property.[54]

Using Written Waivers and Agreements

In determining the characterization of a term life insurance policy, community property states generally employ the "risk payment" doctrine. Under this doctrine, the source of the last premium payment made determines whether the policy is separate or community property. Accordingly, if the last premium made comes from community funds, the policy is characterized as community property.

Therefore, when an insured in a community property state wants to transfer his or her ownership in life insurance policies to his or her spouse, in addition to the transfer by written notification to the insurance company, it is wise to also sign a written waiver waiving any further community interest in the policy.

To affect such a waiver of interest, presently and for the future, it is generally advisable to use the form of "Community Property Waiver" or similar form provided by the insurance company. If no such form is available, a policyholder may consider using the type of form illustrated at Figure 33.2. It is recommended that such a written waiver contain the following minimum information:

- a clear identification of the life insurance policy(ies) involved;

- a statement indicating the parties' intent that the policy(ies) be held as separate property of one spouse;

- a clear relinquishment by the other spouse of any community property interest in the policy;

- a statement that the payment of any future premiums with community funds shall be treated as a gift of the non-owner-spouse's community interest in those funds to the owner-spouse; and

- any other information, provisions, or declarations required under applicable state law to validly effect a waiver of the spouse's community interest in the policy.

In most cases, even though the insured may be shown on the policy as "Owner" or otherwise indicated as owning the policy, the policy will be considered as community property of the two spouses in the absence of any evidence that there was an agreement between the spouses that it would be separate property.

A prenuptial or postnuptial marital agreement can be effective in most states to overcome presumptions of community property and to provide that future premium payments from community property funds will not vest in the community any ownership in the policies on the life of the insured. In view of the increasing frequency of divorce and remarriage, the use of prenuptial and marital agreements is encouraged by most estate planners to avoid subsequent confusion and possible lawsuits related to the ownership of insurance policies.

NSLI and SGLI Policies

One type of insurance policy that remains the separate property of the insured, in spite of having premiums paid with community property earnings, is National Service Life Insurance (NSLI) and Servicemen's Group Life Insurance (SGLI). These policies, made available by the federal government for persons in the military, have been determined to be incapable of transfer of ownership away from the insured on the basis of federal policy. In some cases, however, the courts of California in divorce and dissolution cases have frustrated the announced federal intent by awarding community property of equal value to the non-insured spouse. Federal policy generally prevents the transfer of such NSLI and SGLI policies for purposes of planning for reduction of federal estate taxes. In some cases federal law can supersede state property law, as with plans governed by the Employee Retirement Income Security Act of 1974 (ERISA).

Figure 33.2

WAIVER OF COMMUNITY PROPERTY RIGHTS

The undersigned hereby declares that __he intends to transfer to h_____ spouse, _____, certain policies of life insurance, and that upon said transfer, all rights, privileges and incidents of ownership under any policies so transferred shall be the separate property of said spouse and the undersigned hereby waives any and all community property interest to which __he may, but for this waiver, hereafter be entitled under the community property laws of any state, province or country.

The undersigned consents to the use of community property funds by h_____self and h_____ spouse for the payment of any or all premiums and does further agree and declare that any future premium payments on the policies made with community funds shall constitute a gift from the undersigned to h_____ said spouse to the extent of h_____ interest in the community funds so applied.

Any interest the undersigned may have, now or in the future, as a designated payee of the policies is not affected by this waiver.

This instrument is executed in consideration of natural love and affection and shall be binding upon the undersigned's heirs, executors, administrators and assigns, and is executed with the intent and knowledge that any interested parties may hence forth act in reliance thereon.

Dated _____

_____
Signature

WITNESSED BY:

_____

34.7 SPLIT DOLLAR LIFE INSURANCE

Split dollar life insurance is an arrangement, typically between an employer and an employee (it can also be used between relatives such as a parent and child or grandparent and grandchild), under which the cash values, death benefits, and cost (premiums) may be split between the parties. It can also be used between a grantor and an irrevocable life insurance trust. In fact there are no limitations on the identity of the parties who can "split" a policy. Any two parties can split premiums, cash values, and proceeds in any way they choose. It is even possible to "split" a term insurance policy (although this is seldom done).

Under the classical arrangement, the employer pays that part of the annual premium that equals the current year's increase in the cash surrender value of the policy. The employee pays the balance, if any, of the premium. Under another version of split dollar, known as an "employer pay all" plan, the corporation pays the entire premium and the employee pays no portion of the premium. This provides an incentive to key employees, a way by which an employer can reward key individuals on a selective basis, and a means to provide stockholder-employees with substantial insurance at a minimal outlay.

In the event of the insured employee's death the corporation typically gets back the cash value or premiums paid by the corporation as a death benefit and the insured employee's beneficiary receives the balance of the proceeds. The result of the arrangement is for the employer to have an increasing death benefit and for the employee's beneficiary to have a decreasing death benefit. To maintain the insured-employee's death benefit on a level basis, dividends can be used to purchase an amount of term insurance equal to the cash surrender value of the contract; or, if a universal life policy is used, the death benefit can be increasing.

Furthermore, intra-family split dollar would enable a child to purchase insurance on his life that he otherwise might not be able to afford. This way, additional financial security can be provided for the child's family.

Split dollar can also be used between a corporation and its employee-stockholders. The corporation could split the premium dollars in such a way that the employee-stockholders could be able to afford sizable policies on each other's' lives.

Split dollar thus provides an attractive incentive plan. It can be entirely selective. No Internal Revenue Service approval is necessary, although there is some income tax cost to the employee (see below). The split dollar arrangement used creatively can solve a number of estate and business planning problems.

A split dollar plan of insurance can be established as either a collateral assignment type or as an endorsement type arrangement. The collateral assignment method involves either the insured or a third party as the original owner of the contract. The owner then collaterally assigns the policy to the corporation to secure the corporation's interest in the policy.

The endorsement method involves the corporation as the owner of the contract and accordingly it has all policy rights including the right to borrow against the policy. Under this method, the employer endorses out or gives to the insured the right to designate the beneficiary of the pure term insurance protection.

It is possible that a split dollar plan can be arranged so that the death benefit passing to the beneficiary of a majority shareholder will be estate tax free. If the shareholder's spouse–or an irrevocable trust for the benefit of his beneficiaries or any third party–purchases a policy on his life, and then enters into a split dollar agreement with the corporation that prohibits the corporation from taking any action with respect to the policy that might endanger the policy-owner's interest, the death benefit can be excludable. Chances of success in keeping the net amount at risk out of a controlling shareholder's estate are significantly increased if the corporation has no rights to policy values except at the insured's death. The corporation's right at that time should be limited to a recovery of the death proceeds equal to its contributions. The collateral assignment method of split dollar should be used to further evidence the limitation of the corporation's rights.[55]

IRS Regulations

Because of abuse, the IRS issued Notice 2001-10— which was then revoked by Notice 2002-8—as well as regulations effective for split dollar plans entered into after September 17, 2003 or for existing plans that are "materially modified" after that date.[56]

The final regulations create two mutually exclusive tax regimes for split dollar life insurance plans based on who is named as policy-owner of the life insurance contract: the "economic benefit" regime (for endorsement arrangements, under which the employer is the owner of the insurance policy), and the "loan" regime (for collateral assignment arrangements under which the employee is the owner of the insurance policy).

Under the economic benefit regime, if the employer is the owner, the employer's premium payments will be considered as providing taxable economic benefits to the non-owner (typically an employee), which include the value of the current life insurance protection, the amount of cash value to which the employee has "current access," and the value of any other economic benefits.

The measure of the life insurance protection for new plans is currently determined by using a published premium table[57] that the IRS provided in Notice 2001-10 (see Figure 33.3) that result in a higher taxable income to the non-owner than was the case in the past. Note that for plans entered into prior to September 18th 2003, use of the old methods for reporting the economic benefit to the employee – the lesser of PS 58 or the insurer's lowest published term rates are generally allowed, except that for plans entered into after January 28th 2002 and before September 18th 2003, the insurer's lowest term rates would have to meet certain criteria, i.e., the insurer makes those rates generally available as sold through its normal distribution channel.

Figure 33.3

TABLE 2001
(generally for use after 2000)

INTERIM TABLE OF ONE-YEAR TERM PREMIUMS FOR $1,000 OF LIFE INSURANCE PROTECTION

Attained Age	Section 79 Extended and Interpolated Annual Rates	Attained Age	Section 79 Extended and Interpolated Annual Rates	Attained Age	Section 79 Extended and Interpolated Annual Rates
0	$0.70	34	$0.98	67	$15.20
1	0.41	35	0.99	68	16.92
2	0.27	36	1.01	69	18.70
3	0.19	37	1.04	70	20.62
4	0.13	38	1.06	71	22.72
5	0.13	39	1.07	72	25.07
6	0.14	40	1.10	73	27.57
7	0.15	41	1.13	74	30.18
8	0.16	42	1.20	75	33.05
9	0.16	43	1.29	76	36.33
10	0.16	44	1.40	77	40.17
11	0.19	45	1.53	78	44.33
12	0.24	46	1.67	79	49.23
13	0.28	47	1.83	80	54.56
14	0.33	48	1.98	81	60.51
15	0.38	49	2.13	82	66.74
16	0.52	50	2.30	83	73.07
17	0.57	51	2.52	84	80.35
18	0.59	52	2.81	85	88.76
19	0.61	53	3.20	86	99.16
20	0.62	54	3.65	87	110.40
21	0.62	55	4.15	88	121.85
22	0.64	56	4.68	89	133.40
23	0.66	57	5.20	90	144.30
24	0.68	58	5.66	91	155.80
25	0.71	59	6.06	92	168.75
26	0.73	60	6.51	93	186.44
27	0.76	61	7.11	94	206.70
28	0.80	62	7.96	95	228.35
29	0.83	63	9.08	96	250.01
30	0.87	64	10.41	97	265.09
31	0.90	65	11.90	98	270.11
32	0.93	66	13.51	99	281.05
33	0.96				

Where the employee is a non-owner of the policy, he must also report as income any cash value to which he has current or future access (to the extent that the amount was not taken into account in a prior year). This means a non-owner will be taxed on the annual increasing cash value to which he has current access.

The other regime for taxing split dollar is the loan method. Under the loan regime the employee is the owner of the life insurance policy (a collateral assignment plan). The employer's premium payments are treated as a series of loans from the employer to the employee, which, unless the employee is required to pay the employer a market rate of interest on the loan, will be treated under the below market loan rules. Under these rules the employer is deemed to have paid the employee an amount equal to the "forgone interest" which is taxable to the employee, and the employee is deemed to have repaid a like amount to the employer as interest. Whether interest is sufficient or not is made by reference to the applicable federal rate. The consequences of having a below market loan depend on whether the loan is a demand loan or a term loan. (For more information on below market loans see Chapter 43.)

Three recent Tax Court decisions should be consulted for any intergenerational split-dollar (IGSD) arrangements, in which the child of the donor is typically the insured and taxpayers take, based on independent appraisals, significant discounts in valuing the decedent's interest.[58] One recent article warned that "It might not be advisable to create a new economic benefit IGSD plan until the final Cahill and Morrissette decisions are issued because of the doubt about being able to discount the donor's repayment rights, if the potential estate tax discount is a key part of the transaction. It is possible that these recent decisions may not affect loan split-dollar transactions, although practitioners should endeavor to better corroborate business purposes for such transactions in the wake of Cahill and Morrissette."[59]

34.8 BUSINESS USES OF LIFE INSURANCE

Key Person Insurance

A *key person* life insurance policy is a policy owned by a business that insures the life of a particularly valuable employee for the benefit of a business. It is a good business planning tool because it provides protection to offset financial loss to a business occurring by reason of the premature death of a valuable employee. Therefore, an employer might want to insure a key person and thereby achieve a key estate planning goal, i.e. stabilize and maximize the value of the business interest. Even more common is the situation where the business owner is the key to the success of the business. If the business is to be continued, it should consider insuring the business owner's life. A lender might even insist on insuring the owners or key employees.

The business should be the premium payor, owner, and beneficiary of the policy. Proceeds, when received, could be used to offset reduced profits and help pay for the replacement of the key individual.

Premiums paid on key employee coverage are not deductible by a corporation or other business entity. Proceeds, when received, will be free of income tax[60] with the possible exception of a corporate level alternative minimum tax for tax years ending before December 31, 2017 (corporate AMT being eliminated thereafter). But beware: In the case of insurance owned by and payable to an employer, written notice of the coverage must be given to the insured (even owners) and consent must be obtained prior to the issuance of coverage. The failure to comply with these EOLI (Employer Owned Life Insurance) rules will make the proceeds subject to ordinary income tax.[61]

For federal estate tax purposes, if the insured is a stockholder, the death proceeds will be considered in determining the value of the decedent's stock interest.[62] Even where the insured is the controlling stockholder, as long as the corporation is the beneficiary, or the proceeds are paid for the benefit of the corporation (for example, to a corporate creditor), the insurance proceeds will not be separately taxable (as insurance) in the insured's estate.[63] So if the business owner controls only 60 percent of the business, only 60 percent of the insurance–enhanced value of the corporate stock will be includable in his estate for federal estate tax purposes. Note that if the death proceeds are payable to a personal beneficiary of an insured controlling shareholder (one who owns more than 50 percent of the corporation's stock) the proceeds will be fully includible as life insurance in his estate.

Group Life Insurance

Group life insurance is a life insurance benefit provided by an employer for the benefit of its employees. Likewise, it is extremely useful in planning the estate of an executive or other common law employee. The primary objective of group life insurance is to provide financial security for the employee's family.

Generally, the premium payor is the business, although many plans are contributory, where the employee pays a portion of the premium. The insured or a third party is given a certificate evidencing the insurance. The beneficiary can be anyone (including a trust) designated by the covered employee.

For estate tax purposes, the proceeds of a group life insurance policy are includible in the gross estate of the employee. However, these proceeds can usually be removed from the insured's estate with little or no gift tax cost by an absolute assignment of all incidents of ownership. If a policy is assigned within three years of the insured's death, the entire proceeds will be includable in the gross estate.[64]

The annual gift where a policy has been assigned by the employee to a third party is apparently equal to the lesser of premium payments made by the employer or the value measured by the government Table I, below. However, the higher of premiums paid or the Table I rates is used for key employees in a discriminatory plan.[65]

Group life insurance premiums paid by the corporation are fully deductible as business expenses, subject to the limitation that they are reasonable compensation after considering all other compensation paid that employee.[66] Furthermore, employer-paid premiums are not considered taxable income to the covered employees to the extent the death benefit does not exceed $50,000 (this amount may be lower in some states).[67]

The exception to this rule is that if a plan discriminates in favor of key employees, those employees must include in income the cost of their full coverage, including the first $50,000 of coverage. The cost of the coverage is the higher of the actual cost or the Table I rates shown below.

The cost of any coverage that exceeds $50,000 of protection is taxable income to the employee. The value of this additional income is measured by the government table shown below.[68] If the employee contributes toward the cost of the insurance, his contribution can be used to offset his tax liability. When the proceeds of group life insurance are received by the insured employee's family, they are not subject to income taxation.[69]

Employer group life insurance plans are typically governed by ERISA, where federal law will often supersede state law. Thus, state laws that revoke beneficiary designations upon divorce for non-ERISA governed policies may not apply to such contracts.[70]

Coverage for Spouse and Dependents - The cost of employer-provided group-term life insurance on the life of an employee's spouse or dependent, paid by the employer, is not taxable to the employee if the face amount of the coverage does not exceed $2,000. This coverage is excluded as a de minimis fringe benefit.[71]

"TABLE I" RATES FOR GROUP TERM INSURANCE

5-year age bracket	Cost per $1,000 of insurance for 1-month period
Under 25	$ .05
25 to 29	.06
30 to 34	.08
35 to 39	.09
40 to 44	.10
45 to 49	.15
50 to 54	.23
55 to 59	.43
60 to 64	.66
65 to 69	1.27
70 and above	2.06

NOTE: Age of the employee is attained age on the last day of the employee's taxable year.

Salary Increase Plan

A salary increase pension plan (or "Section 162" plan) is a plan in which the corporation pays the premiums on a whole life, universal life, or variable life type policy insuring the selected employee. That employee is named as owner of the policy and designates his own personal beneficiary. Salary increase plans are an excellent way to:

- provide benefits where group insurance is either unavailable or inadequate;

- supplement the benefits of a qualified corporate pension or profit-sharing plan;

- reward and hold key personnel;

- provide estate liquidity for corporate executives; and

- replace part or all of group term life insurance in excess of $50,000.

For estate tax purposes, since the policy is owned by the employee who has the right to name the beneficiary, the proceeds will be includable in the employee's gross estate.

The business is able to deduct premiums paid under a "salary increase" pension plan since the premiums are considered additional compensation. The employee must report as ordinary income the amount of premiums paid by the employer under such a plan. When the death proceeds are paid to the insured's personal beneficiary, under this type of plan, they are not subject to income tax.

Advantages of a salary increase plan using life insurance include:

1. Internal Revenue Service approval is not required.

2. The plan is simple and may be established by the mere signing of an application, acceptance by the insurer of evidence of insurability, and payment of the appropriate premium.

3. The employer is free to choose the employees to include in the plan and no minimum or maximum number of lives must be covered.

4. The employer can decide how much coverage to provide.

5. The cost of the plan is deductible by the employer.

6. The employee owns and has all rights to the insurance policy.

7. Dividends can be used to reduce the premium outlay or to offset the tax cost of the plan.

8. Cash values of the policy may be used without disqualifying the plan or incurring any tax penalties, provided that the policy is not classified as a modified endowment contract. (Interest will be charged on any policy loans.)

9. The plan may be discontinued at any time.

34.9 FREQUENTLY ASKED QUESTIONS

Question – Are the annual increases in cash values for permanent insurance policies subject to income taxation?

Answer – No. The annual increases in cash values for permanent insurance policies are not subject to income taxation.

Question – If a policy has an accidental death and dismemberment (double indemnity) rider providing for a doubling of the death benefit in the event of an accidental death, are the proceeds subject to income tax?

Answer – No. They are generally considered proceeds payable by reason of an insured's death and, under Code section 101, the proceeds are received income tax free.

Question – What are the reasons life insurance is purchased by the trustee of a pension and/or profit-sharing plan?

Answer – There are a number of reasons why life insurance might be advantageously purchased inside a pension or profit sharing plan. Among others, the premium (including any additional rating charge) becomes deductible (as part of the corporation's contribution). Second, regardless of the rating imposed on a policy on the life of an insured with ill health, the Table I cost is levied at standard rates. Third, the dividend structure of a policy within a pension or profit-sharing plan is generally more favorable than dividends paid on policies owned outside the plan. Fourth, the death benefit in excess of policy cash value is income tax free, and is, generally exempt from the claims of creditors. And fifth, with some of the newer type policies, such as universal or variable life, very favorable returns may also be achieved.

Question – Can life insurance be purchased by a self-directed IRA?

Answer – No. IRAs may not own life insurance pursuant to Code section 408(a)(3).

Question – If an individual exchanges one life insurance policy for another life insurance policy (e.g., whole life to universal life), are there income tax consequences?

Answer – Section 1035 of the Internal Revenue Code provides that an exchange of one life insurance policy for another life insurance policy, whether with the same company or a different company, is a nontaxable exchange *if* both policies are on the same insured's life. If no cash or other property is received on the exchange, gain is not recognized. If there is an outstanding loan on the original policy that is not paid off, the amount of any loan assumed by the other party is treated as "boot," i.e., money received on the exchange. Such boot will be taxable to the extent the original policy is in a taxable gain position unless the new policy is subject to the same indebtedness as the old.[72]

Question – Is the interest earned on a prepaid premium deposit account taxable as ordinary income to the policyholder?

Answer – Yes. The increase in value of a prepaid deposit account is taxable as income in the year it is applied to the payment of premiums or is made available for withdrawal, whichever occurs first. The amount of income is reportable to the IRS by the insurance company. Any amount reported will increase the basis of the contract.[73]

Question – How can I determine the financial strength of a life insurance company?

Answer – In addition to looking at the annual financial reports of each company, there are a number of independent rating services that rate the insurance companies. These ratings can be obtained from the particular rating services. Among the companies who provide ratings are: (1) A.M. Best Company; (2) Standard & Poor's Corporation; (3) Moody's Investors Services; (4) Fitch, Inc. (formed by the merger of Fitch IBCA and Duff & Phelps); and (5) Weiss Research.

Rating services look at the underlying essentials of companies, such as surplus, mortality experience, investments, and expenses. They then assign a letter rating to the company. The top two ratings assigned by the above-mentioned rating services are: A.M. Best Company – A++ and A+; Standard & Poor's – AAA and AA+; Moody's Investors Services – Aaa and Aa1; Fitch, Inc. – AAA and AA; and Weiss Research – A+ and A.

Question – What is a Life Settlement?

Answer – A life settlement, also known as a senior settlement, is the sale to a third-party purchaser of an in-force life insurance policy for its "fair market value," an amount typically in excess of the contract's cash surrender value but less than its death benefit. The purchaser, also known as a "funder", pays a cash amount to the policy-owner/seller who is not restricted in use of the proceeds. The settlement company acquires policy ownership, names itself the beneficiary, and is solely responsible for future premium payments.[74]

Question – What is a STOLI arrangement?

Answer – STOLI stands for Stranger Owned Life Insurance. In a STOLI arrangement, an investor group of strangers initiate the insured's application for life insurance to acquire an interest in the policy. In its basic sense, STOLI is purely an investment vehicle. Be aware that such arrangements often fail to meet the "insurable interest" requirements of the various states. Different states have differing laws relating to such arrangements. Some courts have held that the arrangement is valid if the insured buys the policy without having a prearranged investor. Other courts have looked at whether there was an expectation upon purchase that the policy would be assigned to a person who had no insurable interest. Therefore the question becomes why the policy is being purchased. There have been years of complicated cases and articles on STOLI.[75]

CHAPTER ENDNOTES

1. See U.S. Small Business Association Insurance Requirements for SBA Loans at: https://www.sba.gov/sites/default/files/Insurance_Presentation_general_public_draft.pdf. The SBA website has this guidance: "Life or disability insurance: Life insurance and/or disability insurance is not required for all loans, but the Lender should require life or disability insurance where there is a concern over whether the business could survive in the absence of an individual or small group of individuals that provide the management for the small business concern. When life or disability insurance is deemed prudent, the Lender may accept a COLLATERAL ASSIGNMENT of an existing or new decreasing term or universal life insurance policy. LENDER SHOULD NOT BE NAMED AS A BENEFICIARY." https://www.sba.gov/offices/headquarters/oca/resources/4950.
2. I.R.C. §101(a).
3. I.R.C. §101(c).
4. I.R.C. §101(d)(1)(A), Treas. Reg. §1.101-4(a)(1)(i).
5. I.R.C. §101(a)(2).
6. See PLR 201235006 in which the IRS ruled that where the grantor holds a power of administration in a non-fiduciary capacity, the grantor will be treated as the owner of the trust under I.R.C. §675(4). Rev. Rul. 85-13 generally ignores grantor trusts for income tax purposes.
7. I.R.C. §101(a)(2).
8. I.R.C. §1041.
9. I.R.C. §2042.
10. I.R.C. §2035.
11. I.R.C. §2033.
12. Treas. Reg. §25.2512-6.

13. See Leimberg, "Policies for Valuation of Life Insurance", 139 Trusts & Estates 46 (March 2000).
14. I.R.C. §101(g).
15. For 2018 inflation adjustment, see Rev. Proc. 2017-58, § 3.55.
16. See Rev. Proc. 2009-50, 2009-450 IRB 61.
17. I.R.C. §101(g).
18. *Carmichael*; 14 TC 1356 (1950), *Est. of Hart*, 11 TC 16 (1948).
19. See *Hunton*, 1 TC 821 (1943); *Behrend*, 23 BTA 1037 (1931), acq. X-2 CB 5.
20. Rev. Rul. 65-199, 1965-2 CB 20.
21. I.R.C. §72(e)(1)(B); Treas. Reg. §1.72-11(b)(1).
22. Treas. Reg. §1.61-7(d).
23. I.R.C. §72(e); Treas. Reg. §1.72-11(d).
24. I.R.C. §72(c)(1); Rev. Rul. 55-349, 1955-1 CB 232.
25. This computation can be performed on Financial Analyzer II Software (www.leimberg.com).
26. See Treas. Reg. §1.72-4.
27. I.R.C. §§7702(e), 7702(f).
28. ILM 200504001.
29. Rev. Rul. 2009-13, 2009-21 IRB 1029.
30. Rev. Rul. 2009-13, 2009-21 IRB 1029.
31. I.R.C. §72(e)(5).
32. I.R.C. §72(e)(2).
33. I.R.C. §72(e)(5).
34. Rev. Rul. 64-51, 1964-1 CB 322.
35. I.R.C. §§1001(a), 1011.
36. I.R.C. §1001(b).
37. I.R.C. §§1011, 1012, 1016.
38. I.R.C. §7702. See also *Century Wood Preserving Co. v. Comm'r.*, 69 F.2d 967 (3rd Cir. 1934); *London Shoe Co. v. Comm'r.*, 80 F.2d 231 (2nd Cir. 1935).
39. *Century Wood Preserving Co. v. Comm'r.*, 69 F.2d 967 (3rd Cir. 1934); *London Shoe Co. v. Comm'r.*, 80 F.2d 231 (2nd Cir. 1935); *Keystone Consolidated Publishing Co. v. Comm'r.*, 26 BTA 1210, 12 (1932). See also Treas. Reg. §1.1016-2(a). But compare Rev. Rul. 2009-14, 2009-21 IRB 1031, Q 23.
40. See, e.g., *Comm'r. v. Phillips*, 275 F.2d 33, 36, n.3 (4th Cir 1960)
41. I.R.C. §1222(3).
42. Rev. Rul. 2009-13, 2009-21 IRB 1029.
43. I.R.C. §1222(3).
44. Rev. Rul. 2009-13, 2009-21 IRB 1029.
45. *Gallun v. Comm'r.*, 327 F.2d 809 (7th Cir. 1964); *Comm'r. v. Phillips*, 275 F.2d 33 (4th Cir. 1960); *Est. of Crocker v. Comm'r.*, 37 TC 605 (1962); *Neese v. Comm'r.*, TC Memo 1964-288; see also *Cohen v. Comm'r.*, 39 TC 1055 (1963).
46. ILM 200504001.
47. *Comm'r. v. Phillips*, 275 F.2d 33, fn.3 (4th Cir. 1960).
48. TAM 200452033.
49. *Eckersley v. Comm'r.*, TC Memo 2007-282.
50. Rev. Rul. 2009-13, 2009-21 IRB 1029.
51. I.R.C. §264.
52. I.R.C. §264.
53. See, e.g., *Estate of Cavenaugh v. Commissioner*, 51 F.3d 597 (5th Cir. 1995).
54. Internal Revenue Manual § 25.18.1.2.13 (02-15-2005), Community Property: When the Character of Property Is Determined.
55. Rev Rul. 82-145, 1982-2 CB 213; Rev. Rul. 76-274, 1976-2 CB 278.
56. TD 9092; Rev. Rul. 2003-105, 2003-40 IRB. 696.
57. Table 2001, which replaces the old "PS 58" Table.
58. *Estate of Clara Morrissette*, 146 T.C. 171 (2016); *Estate of Richard Cahill*, T.C. Memo. 2018-84; *Estate of Marion Levine*, Docket No. 9345-15, Order and Decision, July 13, 2016.
59. Lee Slavutin, Richard Harris & Martin Shenkman - Intergenerational Split Dollar - Recent Adverse Decisions in Morrissette and Cahill, Where Do We Go from Here? LISI Estate Planning Newsletter #2651 (July 17, 2018).
60. I.R.C. §101.
61. I.R.C. §101(j).
62. Treas. Reg. §20.2031-2(f).
63. Treas. Reg. §20.2042-1(c)(6).
64. I.R.C. §2035; Rev. Rul. 69-54, 1969-1 CB 221 as modified by Rev. Rul. 72-307, 1972-1 CB 307 and Rev. Rul. 84-031, 1984-2 CB 194.
65. See Rev. Rul. 84-147, 1984-2 CB 201.
66. I.R.C. §162(a); Treas. Reg. §1.264-1.
67. I.R.C. §79.
68. Treas. Reg. §1.79-3.
69. I.R.C. §101.
70. *Egelhoff v. Egelhoff*, 532 U.S. 141 (2001).
71. See IRS Notice 89-110 for more information on such fringe benefits.
72. I.R.C. §1035(a).
73. See Rev. Rul. 65-199, 1965-2 CB 20, and Rev. Rul. 66-120, 1966-1 CB 14.
74. S. Leimberg, R. Weber, L. Colosimo and E. R. Whitelaw, "Life Settlements: Risk Management Guidance for Professional Advisors and Fiduciaries".
75. See LISI Estate Planning Newsletter No. 1943 (April 2, 2012), PHL *Variable v. Sheldon Hathaway Family Insurance Trust and Windsor Securities: Another STOLI Scheme Bites the Dust*, LISI Estate Planning Newsletter #2174 (December 11, 2013). For an analysis of four cases, see *Howard Zaritsky: STOLI Cases Continue to Yield Inconsistent Results*, **LISI** Estate Planning Newsletter #2534 (April 14, 2017). More recently, see also *Steve Leimberg: Jackson National Life v. Crum - STOLI Case*, LISI Estate Planning Newsletter #2793 (Apr. 30, 2020).

BENEFICIARY DEEMED OWNER TRUSTS (BDOTS)

CHAPTER 35

35.1 INTRODUCTION

A beneficiary deemed owner trust (BDOT) is a trust deemed to be owned by an individual beneficiary or beneficiaries (or a trust or entity) other than the grantor for income tax purposes due to a current power to withdraw all income (but not necessarily corpus beyond this) under IRC §678.[1] The settlor is either dead or possesses no powers over the trust that would cause grantor trust status as to the settlor under other Code section in Subpart E of Subchapter J of the Code (primarily, Code sections 673-677). Any such powers would trump a power under Code section 678.[2] Sometimes the term refers to any trust deemed to be owned by a beneficiary for income tax purposes under I.R.C. §678, including powers over corpus or lapsed powers over either income or corpus, but the term BDOT usually refers to trust that contain a current power of a beneficiary to withdraw only income. The power must be clearly defined to include income allocable to corpus (principal) and not simply accounting income in order to shift the entire income tax burden to the beneficiary.[3]

This technique is similar to, but contrasts with, a beneficiary defective inheritor's trust (BDIT), which is deemed to be owned by a beneficiary other than the settlor for income tax purposes due to a lapsed power to withdrawal all of the *corpus* of a trust under IRC §678, and usually involves extremely small initial corpus ($5,000) and extremely large amounts of leverage (lending). The IRS, in Rev. Proc. 2017-3 and annual thereafter, added BDITs using large amounts of leverage to their "no ruling" list of topics on which they will no longer issue private letter rulings.[4]

35.2 ADVANTAGES

BDOTs offer many advantages in many different contexts. Primarily, they allow the shifting of the income tax burden to the powerholder without having to make any distribution. If a beneficiary has the right to withdraw $90,000 of income and they only take $30,000, they are still taxed on $90,000. This shifting of the income tax burden can avoid the compressed tax brackets of non-grantor trusts if the powerholder is not in the top tax bracket (for 2023, this is at $693,750.00 for married couples filing jointly but starts at $14,450 for non-grantor trusts, and there are similarly large differences for 20% long-term capital gains and qualified dividend tax rates and 3.8% net investment income tax thresholds).[5] The beneficiary may also pay less state income tax than the trust. This difference can be huge!

The above differential is especially important when clients have large traditional retirement benefits payable to trusts, which, after the SECURE Act, are likely to force income out within 10 years.

Usually, the powerholder is an individual, but the powerholder may also be another non-grantor trust or other entity. It may be desirable to shift income between trusts for the same beneficiary, for example, if they have different characteristics for state income tax and/or GST exempt status.

If an individual taxpayer is deemed to be the owner for federal income tax purposes, this permits many other income tax advantages that are denied to non-grantor trusts – it may be better for avoiding Section 199A caps, qualifying for the Section 121 capital gains tax exclusion for sale of a residence if the powerholder

545

resides in a home owned by the trust, qualifying for the Section 179 expensing of over $1 million if the trust owns a business that purchases such property (Section 179(d) disallows this to non-grantor trusts), allowing trust capital losses to be used to offset against non-trust capital gains, qualifying for IRC 469(i) $25,000 rental real estate offset and other advantages. Individual taxpayers do not have to trace charitable contributions to gross income, nor do they have the deduction limited or denied if traceable to pass through business income, and they may carry forward charitable tax deductions to future years, advantages denied to non-grantor trusts. For business owners, the denial of the Code section 179 expensing to non-grantor trust is huge and often overlooked. For 2023, this inflation-adjusted deduction is up to $1,160,000 – taxpayers don't like to lose that!

BDOTs qualify as S corporation owners without the various restrictions and disadvantages involved with ESBT or QSST status, provided that there is one owner. Thus, joint revocable trusts or joint IGTs should be avoided, as well as BDOTs with more than one beneficiary/powerholder that is not divided into separate trusts, unless an ESBT election is also made that would still qualify the trust under Code section 1361(c)(2)(A)(v).

The fact that distributions to not have to be made in order to achieve the same tax shifting makes BDOTs ideal in the GST planning arena – powerholders can take funds from the GST-non-exempt trusts to live on and pay tax bills before taking anything from the GST exempt trust, permitting the GST exempt trusts to grow at a much faster clip. Like irrevocable grantor trusts, the tax burden shifting to the owner allows the trust to grow income tax free, since the deemed owner is paying the tax, and this payment of the trust's tax bill (really, the deemed owner's tax bill) is not deemed to be a taxable gift to the trust or its beneficiaries pursuant to Rev. Rul. 2004-64.

This feature also dramatically improves the asset protection for the powerholder over time – the powerholder can pay their annual tax bill from exposed non-trust assets and leave assets in the protective cocoon of the trust to grow tax-free (and possibly estate/GST tax free if GST was allocated to the trust), gradually increasing the assets protected from creditors more than a non-grantor trust would. Non-grantor trusts put most trustees/beneficiaries in a bind – either accumulate the income and pay a much higher tax rate in most cases, or distribute the income and lose the asset protection!

The BDOT avoids this dilemma and permits the best of both worlds, with a few caveats noted below.

35.3 DISADVANTAGES

The BDOT design granting a beneficiary a power to withdraw income would not work well for immature adult beneficiaries for whom the settlor would prefer they take less than the annual income. It would certainly be inadvisable to grant to a disabled special needs beneficiary who may apply for government means-tested aid. That said, a clause in the trust might change the distribution/withdrawal terms if a beneficiary becomes disabled, and a trust protector or independent trustee might have powers to restrict or remove withdrawal powers in future years if the beneficiary's situation merits further protection.

Because of the withdrawal right, the amount of income currently withdrawable would be exposed to a beneficiary's creditors under most state laws (other than perhaps a DAPT state) and bankruptcy law. For this reason, a clause that removes the withdraw right (referred to as a cessor or forfeiture clause) in the event of certain triggering events is often used. Such an automatic triggering event might be the appointment of a receiver, the filing of bankruptcy, divorce or even events preceding the attachment of a federal tax lien. A trust protector can also change or remove the withdrawal right under various criteria.

Non-grantor trusts can sometimes receive the equivalent of an "above the line" charitable tax deduction under IRC 642(c) which is sometimes better than an individual charitable tax deduction that would be afforded an individual through a grantor trust– there are a few more hoops to jump through, however.

Non-grantor trusts receive better deductions than individuals for certain expenses specific to trust administration under Code section 67(e), especially for years 2018-2025 when many miscellaneous itemized deductions are eliminated for individuals. This might be tax preparation, attorney, accounting and a portion of any professional trustee fee attributable to administration rather than investment management.

Individuals (at least for 2018-2025) are capped at $10,000 state and local income tax (SALT) deductions – keeping funds and income inside a non-grantor trust might get another $10,000 deduction if the trust has that much in state and local tax payments.

Taxpayers are sometimes capped at the amount of capital gains tax exclusion granted on the sale of qualified small business stock under Code section 1202 ($10 million) – keeping such assets in a non-grantor trust might keep more gain by the individual beneficiary excluded if the stock is sold and gains might exceed this.

In some cases, such as if the beneficiary is in the highest federal tax bracket and would pay state income tax but the trust would *not* pay state income tax, it may be better to be a non-grantor trust for state income tax purposes and trap income in trust, perhaps by using an EBST structure that prevents distributions from carrying out DNI. This will vary state by state and trust by trust and beneficiary by beneficiary.

Accounting and financial firms are less familiar with BDOTs, so may initially be confused with the various grantor trust income tax reporting options (e.g., the ability to use a deemed owner's social security number or get an EIN, the ability to file a Form 1041 return checking "grantor trust" or simply giving the deemed owner a list of income and deductions to report on their own Form 1040).

While the initial withdrawal right is just as easy to understand and administer as a common distribution provision, practitioners usually add a "hanging power" in case the amount of income not withdrawn by a beneficiary in a given year exceeds their 5% lapse protection under Code section 2514(e), which adds some additional complexity.

Assets or Powers Best Suited for the Tool

Business property (S corporations, LLC/LPs taxed as partnership or S corporations) may be well suited to BDOTs due to the passing through of the Section 179 deduction denied to non-grantor trusts.

Residences used by beneficiaries may be well suited to BDOTs, due to the Section 121 exclusion.

BDOTs are better suited to GST exempt trusts – since the income tax burden can shift without having to make a distribution depleting the trust.

Situations Generally Not Well Suited for BDOTs

Where it is anticipated that the trust will pay out significant amounts of gross income, but not any principal to charity, a non-grantor trust may work better than a BDOT, due to slightly better charitable tax deductions if made from gross non-business income.

Where a beneficiary has special needs and may apply for means-tested benefits such as Medicaid, a traditional discretionary non-grantor trust is better suited to the situation than a BDOT.

Cash flow requirements and investment concerns:

Because the income accessible through a withdrawal power is taxable to the beneficiary regardless of what they take, this can generate "phantom income", similar to when one receives less in distributions from a partnership (LLC) or S corporation than the income that is reported on a Form K-1. Thus, beneficiaries will usually take at least 40% just to cover their state and federal tax bill.

The access to cash flow (income) for the beneficiaries may be different and may require a more unique conversation with the investment advisor/trustee than with traditional trusts. For example, a Roth IRA distribution and municipal bond interest payment may not be withdrawable by a beneficiary of a BDOT as taxable income, whereas it may have been paid out from a traditional "all net income" trust or unitrust (note that a BDOT seeking to qualify as a QTIP, however, must grant the power over the greater of the two). Sometimes the amount of taxable income withdrawable may be more than accounting income, sometimes it may be less. The settlor can always establish a floor or grant an alternative ability of the trustee to distributed more in such cases.

Gift/Estate/GST tax risks and consequences:

Any currently withdrawable power causes estate inclusion to the extent of the power held at death. For example, if a $5 million trust has $100,000 of taxable dividends up to July of a given year when a powerholder having the right to withdraw that amount dies, then $100,000 is in the powerholder's estate. Whether this causes an estate tax, of course, depends on the other assets and deductions in the powerholder's estate. Methods to mitigate this inclusion include taking some funds out during the year or making the power to withdraw only exercisable during the last week of the year, for example.

If there is no hanging power included, any lapse of a withdrawal right that exceeds the greater of $5,000 or 5% of the trust corpus may be deemed to be a release and a new contribution of such amount to the trust, which may cause such portion to be included in the powerholder's estate and/or cause the powerholder to be a new transferor of such amount for GST tax purposes. For example, if a $10 million trust had $700,000 of taxable income in a given year, and the powerholder only withdrew $150,000 of that income, and the trust provided that the power to withdraw the remaining $550,000 amount lapsed, then $500,000 (5% of the trust corpus, assuming this was the only trust that the powerholder had such a power over) would be protected from being considered a gift/transfer, but $50,000 would be considered a gift/transfer back to the trust and its beneficiaries.

If, instead, the power to withdraw $50,000 in the above example does not lapse but "hangs" into the following year and the powerholder dies, the $50,000 still "hanging" would be included in the powerholder's estate. However, this is much less than would be included, for example, than if the trust had made a distribution of $700,000!

If a BDOT powerholder uses their withdraw power to gift to children, grandchildren or others, it does not shift the income tax burden to them, but would be considered a gift just as if the powerholder had gifted their own assets.

Income tax risks and consequences:

The authority behind the basic principles of a BDOT is not just statutory, but predates the enactment of Code section 678 and can be traced to Supreme Court precedent holding that the taxpayer who has full unfettered control and access to income should be the one taxed on it. That said, there are still some unanswered questions and a lack of rulings and case law on various nuances. For example, can two BDOTs (or the beneficiary, or other grantor trusts as to the beneficiary) enter into a transaction that will be respected for income tax purposes, or does Rev. Rul. 85-13 and all the subsequent rulings on this apply to ignore such transactions for income tax purposes? How is phantom income from pass-through entities considered? If there is any fear that a portion of the trust may still be considered a non-grantor trust, filing a Form 1041 as a grantor trust should at least start the statute of limitation on any such arguments applying.

Clients for whom the tool generally works best

BDOTs are well-suited for settlors with responsible adult beneficiaries (including spouses and QTIP trusts) for whom the settlor wants to grant significant control and access over the income, yet provide the asset protection and tax-sheltering benefits of a trust. It works well for GST exempt trusts because it affords better options to exploit the GST exemption.

BDOTs are well-suited for settlors who want to keep things simpler for their beneficiaries, due to the decreased tax reporting burden associated with grantor trusts over non-grantor trusts. They are especially well-suited when beneficiaries will not be in the top tax bracket ($693,750.00 for married couples filing jointly in 2023).

Clients for whom the tool generally may not work

Settlors requiring a special needs trust for a disabled beneficiary, or settlors having beneficiaries for whom they would want a "tight leash", such as irresponsible, spendthrift or substance-abusing beneficiaries. Settlors with beneficiaries in the top tax bracket who can escape state income tax by leaving assets into a non-grantor trust that would not pay state income tax that the beneficiaries would pay if they were deemed the owners of it. Settlors whose beneficiaries would want to be able to spray income among lower bracket beneficiaries (e.g., child as trustee or powerholder distributing DNI via Form K-1 to grandchildren).

Upstream planning:

There is no reason a BDOT power cannot be "upstream" – shifting the income tax burden to a wealthier older relative by giving them a withdrawal right. This concept is similar to the upstream basis planning discussed in Chapter 44 on Optimal Basis Increase Trusts. If that relative has a taxable estate, this may gradually reduce their estate over time without using any applicable exclusion amount, since their payment of the income tax burden would not be considered a gift pursuant to Rev. Rul. 2004-64 and any lapse of under 5% would not be considered a gift under Code section 2514(e). However, keep in mind that any unlapsed current power of withdrawal would add to such older powerholder's estate.

Asset Protection Planning Opportunities, Concerns and Nuances of BDOTs

As mentioned previously, in the short term and at first glance, a BDOT power to withdraw income seems to *reduce* the asset protection of the trust, since any currently held power is accessible under most states' laws and the bankruptcy code. Most states protect any lapsed power, however. ACTEC maintains a 50 state chart on this issue, available by searching the publicly available portion of the www.actec.org website and searching for "Morrow state creditor protection statutes chart re PEG powers and lapses" or downloading the longer white paper on BDOTs available at www.ssrn.com.

However, there are ways to mitigate this drawback, and over time, the asset protection advantages of a BDOT structure are tremendously more powerful than other traditional trust structures, because there is less requirement or pressure to make distributions from the trust to carry out DNI to lower the income tax burden, and the protected trust can grow tax-free due to the beneficiary's payment of the income tax burden while the beneficiary's exposed assets are greater depleted. Even if, as would be common, the beneficiary withdraws at least 40% of the income to pay their tax bill, this is still superior for asset protection purposes than if they took it all, or the trust distributed it all or most of it. In short, the BDOT is a better asset protection planning vehicle for the same reason that an IGT is a better asset protection vehicle than a traditional non-grantor trust – by enabling the tax burden to be paid from non-protected assets and allowing the protected trust assets to grow tax-free, an increasing percentage of the accessible family wealth is better protected in trust.

CHAPTER ENDNOTES

1. I.R.C. §678(a) provides: "(a)General rule.

   A person other than the grantor shall be treated as the owner of any portion of a trust with respect to which:

   (1) such person has a power exercisable solely by himself to vest the corpus **or the income** therefrom in himself, or

2. IRC §678(b) provides that: "(b)Exception where grantor is taxable.

   Subsection (a) shall not apply with respect to a power over income, as originally granted or thereafter modified, if the grantor of the trust or a transferor (to whom section 679 applies) is otherwise treated as the owner under the provisions of this subpart other than this section."

3. For further discussion of the concept, see *IRC Section 678(a)(1) and the "Beneficiary Deemed Owner Trust" (BDOT)*, LISI Estate Planning Newsletter #2587 (Sept. 5, 2017), and the updated white paper with more extensive discussion downloadable for free from www.ssrn.com: Morrow, Edwin P., *IRC Section 678 and the Beneficiary Deemed Owner Trust (BDOT)* (April 19, 2018). Available at SSRN: https://ssrn.com/abstract=3165592.

4. Rev. Proc. 2017-3, 2017-1 I.R.B. 130, §4.01(43). Similar, Rev. Proc. 2020-3, §4.01(43).

5. I.R.C. §1, but the brackets are all modified annually for inflation adjustments. For the one issued in late 2022 effective for tax year 2023, see Rev. Proc. 2022-38.

IRREVOCABLE LIFE INSURANCE TRUST

CHAPTER 36

36.1 INTRODUCTION

An irrevocable life insurance trust (ILIT) is, as the name implies, a vehicle for holding life insurance policies. The primary goal of such a trust is to assure the policy proceeds will not be subject to federal (or state) death taxation at the death of the insured and/or his spouse and to provide for or enhance the financial security of the beneficiaries of the trust. The proceeds of the life insurance policy, when paid to the trust at the insured's death, provide the family with a pool of cash that can be used to loan money to or purchase assets from the grantor-insured's estate. Because all incidents of ownership over the policy are held by the trustee of the trust, the proceeds of the policy are not subject to estate tax, but still provide a source of liquidity in the decedent's estate. Thus, the event that creates the need for cash creates the cash to satisfy the need – and if properly arranged - without increasing the need.

This same result can also be achieved by making gifts of existing or newly purchased life insurance (or gifts of cash to purchase policies on the client's life) outright to responsible adult children or a later generation. However, a major benefit of using a trust is that a trustee can be chosen who understands the importance of providing liquidity for payment of taxes, debts, and other estate related needs, and it provides greater assurance that the proceeds will be used for the intended purpose. An ILIT also provides superior asset protection and estate/GST tax leverage rather than outright ownership.

Where the life insurance continues to require payment of premiums after the gift, a typical irrevocable life insurance trust plan will call for the insured to make annual gifts to the trust to cover the premium payments. In order to make each gift qualify as a "present interest gift" and therefore come within the annual exclusion under Code section 2503(b) ($17,000 in 2023) from gift tax, the trust often will provide a so-called "Crummey"[1] withdrawal power to the beneficiaries (usually the grantor's children) and later descendants. A married couple can "split" the gift and give each donee $34,000 in 2023.

With a Crummey withdrawal power, each time a contribution is made to the trust, the beneficiary has a temporary, but unconditional, right to demand a withdrawal from the trust of a specified amount. If the demand right is not exercised within the withdrawal period, the annual transfer for that year remains in the trust for management by the trustee or can be used in whole or in part to pay life insurance premiums. If the demand is made, the trustee must deliver the funds to the beneficiary. However, the beneficiary generally will recognize that such a withdrawal may affect the grantor's decision as to future transfers to that trust (or other future transfers) and the beneficiary will therefore likely not make a demand. Once the withdrawal right lapses, the trustee is then free to use the monies that were contributed to pay the premiums on the life insurance policies on the grantor (and/or grantor's spouse's) life.

36.2 WHEN IS USE OF SUCH A DEVICE INDICATED?

An irrevocable life insurance trust can be used to good advantage whenever an individual (or a couple) faces a federal (or possibly even state) estate tax, and wishes to provide liquidity for payment of those taxes with existing life insurance, or insurance to be purchased, without subjecting the proceeds themselves to death taxes and compounding the estate tax problems. Even if the grantor/insured would not face a significant (or any) estate tax, it may be used to provide liquidity for equalizing division of property in an illiquid estate – an irrevocable trust is less likely to be contested than an estate and provides asset protection for the policy during the insured's lifetime as well as after death potentially.

An irrevocable life insurance trust also allows the insured to "leverage" annual exclusion gifts, lifetime credit against the gift tax, and the insured's generation-skipping transfer (GST) tax exemption by making gifts of policies that have a low current gift value in relation to their value at the insured's death. For example, gifts of life insurance generally are valued for gift tax purposes at the "interpolated terminal reserve value" (plus unearned premiums), which in the case of a reasonably healthy individual roughly approximates the policy's cash surrender value. The face value of the policy is typically many times greater than this gift tax value.

Specifically, a trust should be used where the donor does not have confidence that the recipients of the gifts will cooperate in retaining the policies or their proceeds and making them available to the donor's estate for payment of taxes, or where the gifts are made to minor or other beneficiaries, who do not have the capacity or judgment to manage the policies/proceeds.

36.3 WHAT ARE THE REQUIREMENTS?

Requirements for Life Insurance Gift Trust

1. The grantor(s) must create a trust which will receive the gift of the insurance policy (or receive cash with which to purchase a new policy). The terms of the trust should be consistent with the grantor's estate planning goals, both with respect to the availability of funds with which to pay taxes as well as appropriate terms for investing and managing the assets for the beneficiaries both before and after the insured's death, and should authorize the trustee to hold and invest in insurance on the life of the grantor.

2. The grantor(s) must then actually transfer the policy to the trust by signing an irrevocable assignment of the policy to the trustee of the trust, or (preferably) by making a cash gift to the trust to enable the trustee to purchase a new policy. If the grantor himself transfers the policy into the trust, it will be includible in his estate if he does not outlive the three year period after the transfer.[2]

3. As mentioned above, the grantor should make a cash gift to a bank account which is titled in the name of the Trustees and carries the trust's tax identification number. Some commentators believe that the direct payment of premiums by the Grantor does not cause a problem since they are "indirect" gifts to the trust. This may only be true where there are assets or cash value in the trust because then there would be something to support the withdrawal right. That said, the court in *Turner v. Commissioner*[3] held that the insured's direct payment of the insurance premiums equaled indirect gifts to the trust but still constituted gifts of a present interest because the trust by its plain terms gave beneficiaries withdrawal rights after direct or indirect transfers. Conceivably, surrender charges could affect this in early years when there are no other assets in the trust. If the grantor/insured pays $25,000 directly to an insurance company (not to ILIT trustee and/or bank account), the policy may shortly thereafter only be worth $22,500, for example, factoring in typical early year expenses and surrender charges. Even if the trustee could surrender the policy for cash or the beneficiary has the right to demand the policy in kind, the value of the present interest available to the beneficiary may only be $22,500 (the current value of the policy if surrendered) rather than $25,000 (the amount of the gift). This issue disappears when there are additional assets in trust or additional cash value in the policy such that the trustee could easily withdraw or surrender sufficient funds to meet any hypothetical demand resulting from the gift.

4. Remember, there is no prohibition against the trust owning other assets – in fact there may be several advantages. For example, if stock or family LLC interests are also transferred to the trust, the income from those assets may later be used to pay premiums, and may serve as an additional source of liquidity to satisfy any (largely hypothetical) demand request.

Requirements for Crummey Withdrawal Power

1. Each time a contribution is made to a Crummey trust, the beneficiary must have a legal right to demand withdrawal of an amount equal to the value of the gift (immediately, not starting upon

receipt of notice). Frequently, the withdrawal right may be dependent upon the donor also specifying that the withdrawal right will apply to the gift, e.g., "This gift is made subject to the terms of the right of withdrawal provided in...."

In order to qualify for the gift tax annual exclusion under Code section 2503(b), the beneficiary's withdrawal right cannot be illusory. Implicit in every Crummey trust is the notion that the beneficiary will not exercise the right to withdraw and the gifts to the trust will remain in the trust until termination. However, the legal right to withdraw must be real and legally possible.

Notably, an individual donee need not be an adult or legally competent for the gift to qualify for the gift tax annual exclusion. For example, the annual exclusion is available for a gift in trust in which the beneficiary who is given the right (through a guardian) to withdraw is an infant.

2. For an adult beneficiary to have an effective demand right, the beneficiary must receive timely and effective notice of the demand right.[4] The IRS rulings have emphasized the importance of giving effective adequate notice of the annual trust contributions that are subject to withdrawal, at least to adult beneficiaries. In several cases, the IRS has implied that notice may be necessary even for minor beneficiaries.[5] Although this notice is typically (and preferably) made in writing to create evidence that the timely and effective notice requirement was met, it seems that even oral notice may be adequate.

It is the safest course of action to give written notice of each transfer subject to the withdrawal power. According to the IRS, a "once only" notice will not be considered sufficient.

3. In order for the demand right to be effective, an adequate amount of time must be allowed for the exercise of the power of withdrawal, especially if the exercise of the power would require a step such as appointing a guardian for a minor beneficiary. Neither the IRS nor the courts have drawn a clear distinction between reasonable and unreasonable time limits. However, the IRS has disapproved a three-day period as not being a sufficient duration,[6] but Crummey withdrawal periods of as little as thirty days after an addition to the trust have been deemed effective.[7] In many cases, a shorter withdrawal period can simplify the administration of the trust.

4. An important feature of a Crummey trust is that it allows the grantor to make gifts that qualify for the annual exclusion from gift tax under Code section 2503(b). In order to qualify for the annual exclusion, a gift must be one of a "present interest." (A beneficiary must receive the immediate, unfettered, and ascertainable right to use, possess, or enjoy the money or other property placed into the trust for that year.) A gift of a "future interest" does not qualify for the annual exclusion; if the beneficiary must wait to have absolute rights to the gift for even a short period, the annual exclusion is not available. When a trust has no provisions for a current withdrawal of the gift, at least a portion of each gift is a future interest. It is the absolute and immediate right of the beneficiary to withdraw the specified amount (or the transferred asset itself) that meets the requirement to make the gift eligible for the annual exclusion. Note, however, that annual exclusions are of less importance since the applicable exclusion amount has so dramatically increased ($12,920,000 in 2023).

It is important to note that a gift which qualifies for the gift tax annual exclusion under section 2503(b) does *not* automatically qualify for the GST tax annual exclusion under Code section 2642(c). For a dynastic trust it may be advantageous to allocate the GST exclusion to the trusts even if the gifts qualify for the annual exclusion. This is done by filing a Form 709 gift tax return.

5. The beneficiary of a Crummey trust must be able to actually receive property if the beneficiary exercises a demand right. The gift will be eligible for the annual exclusion only to the extent the trust has assets sufficient to satisfy the beneficiary's demand rights.[8] As mentioned above, this may be important to acknowledge for the early years of a policy where the policy's surrender charges may hamper access to cash to satisfy any demand right and there are no other trust assets.

6. Where a beneficiary is a minor, and is therefore unable to make an effective withdrawal, the minor will be deemed to have a present interest in the gift if the minor's guardian can make a legally effective demand on the minor's behalf.

7. The IRS has taken the position that the annual exclusion is available only where the beneficiary is a "primary" beneficiary with a substantial interest in the trust other than the withdrawal

power. However, the Tax Court has held that invasion powers held by grandchildren were eligible for the annual exclusion where a trust was created for children and the only other interests held by the grandchildren were contingent on the death of their parents before the trust was distributed.[9] Other cases have included spouses of children as well.

In the most recent IRS attack, *Mikel v. Commissioner*, the IRS did not even contest a large number of contingent beneficiaries.[10] Thus, $1,440,000 of gifted property valued at $3,262,000 qualified for the gift tax annual exclusion, based on 60 beneficiaries having withdrawal rights of $24,000 each (the annual exclusion was $12,000 per year per donor at the time of gift). The Court ruled in favor of the Mikels despite the fact that the property was apparently illiquid and many of the beneficiaries were either minors or spouses of the immediate family. The trust contained an ambiguous forfeiture clause, and included a complicated provisions for a religious arbitration panel (the IRS had contested the effect of the latter two provisions).[11]

This decision continues a long line of defeats suffered by the IRS in this area. It gives encouragement to practitioners to maximize the use of Crummey trusts, not only for taxpayers with taxable estates, but also for those with non-taxable estates who can use such trusts for income tax and asset protection reasons.

While this case is merely a memorandum rather than a full Tax Court opinion, this merely indicates that the Tax Court considered any legal issues to be well-established and well-settled. After fifty years of unsuccessfully attacking Crummey provisions, one would hope that the IRS will finally take the hint.

Despite *Mikel*, the IRS will continue to attack "naked" Crummey powers, paper powers given to persons who have little or no interest in the trust other than the Crummey powers and who are given the powers merely to artificially increase the number of annual exclusions.

Example. Harry and Donna Bradley would like to make gifts that will qualify for the annual exclusion to each of their two children and four grandchildren. Their annual exclusion amount for gifts to these donees would be $204,000 per year. The husband and wife can collectively give $34,000 to each beneficiary annually if they elect to split the gifts on a gift tax return. However, the Bradleys' would prefer not to make outright gifts, especially not to their grandchildren.

The Bradleys' would instead prefer to have a trust that would continue until their youngest child reaches the age of thirty-five. At that time, the trust would be distributed equally to the children and kept in trust for grandchildren. They decide that the trust will not make any distributions of current income.

An irrevocable life insurance trust would meet all the Bradleys' requirements. The trust they create can have all the desired investment and management terms and provide Crummey powers of withdrawal to all of their descendants. Separate shares however, are required if the trust is to be exempt from generation-skipping tax using only the GST tax annual exclusion. Otherwise, the Bradleys' would need to allocate a portion of their GST tax exemption to their transfers to the trust. With $12,920,000 of current GST exemption per donor, this may not be an issue.

There is an important "tax trap" to keep in mind when transferring an existing policy to a trust which includes GST planning. If the Bradleys' split the gift of their insurance policy into the trust, and the insured (i.e. Mr. Bradley) should die within three years of the transfer; then under Code section 2035, all of the insurance proceeds will be included within the Mr. Bradley's estate. If the Bradley's had both allocated some of their GST exemption to the transferred policy (either on the gift tax return or pursuant to the deemed allocation rules), the GST exemption used by Mrs. Bradley is not restored even though the entire death benefit is included within Mr. Bradley's estate. In effect, Mrs. Bradley will have wasted her GST exemption.

36.4 ISSUES IN COMMUNITY PROPERTY STATES

A couple owning community property can give $34,000 in 2023 per recipient without any need for gift splitting because each spouse owns half the community property. Because of the nature of community property (the fact that each spouse owns a one-half interest in each community asset), it is unusual in a community property state for a Crummey irrevocable insurance trust that benefits the surviving spouse as to the entire trust to be created.

In a separate property jurisdiction, the typical terms of such a trust might provide that at the death of the insured spouse (e.g., the husband) the proceeds of an insurance policy (purchased with funds given by the husband) will benefit the wife in the form of a life interest in the proceeds. After her death, the proceeds would be available to be lent to her estate (or to purchase assets from her estate) to provide funds to pay estate taxes then due.

In a community property state, on the other hand, the wife usually is the grantor as to one-half of the gifts used to pay the insurance premium, and it would not be appropriate to give the wife a life interest in the entire policy proceeds, for that would be a transfer with a retained interest, includible in the wife's estate as to the one-half purchased with her share of the community property gift. For this reason, ILITs established for spouses in community property states are often preceded by a marital property or transmutation agreement that establishes a source of funds to be separate property of the grantor spouse.

Even in a community property state, one spouse may have separate property already, or a "split" of community property can be achieved to produce separate property. With a trust funded by such separate property gifts, the other spouse can have a life estate in all of the policy proceeds without making them subject to estate tax in her estate. Such planning must, however, be carefully undertaken.

If a trust is created, it is recommended that the trustee retain the insurance policy/policies and all endorsements with other trust documents, and that all premium notices be sent directly to the trustee who will then forward copies to the grantor/insured party.

36.5 TAX IMPLICATIONS

The gift of a life insurance policy is subject to gift tax, usually based primarily on the policy's "interpolated terminal reserve" value, an amount which typically approximates the contract's cash surrender value. However, where the insured is terminally ill at the date of the gift, the IRS is likely to claim that the value of the gift is closer to the policy's face amount. The interpolated terminal reserve value for a policy can be obtained from the life insurance company.

For the grantor/donor, a Crummey withdrawal power is an effective way to make a gift that qualifies for the section 2503(b) annual exclusion from gift tax while avoiding the potential problems of outright transfers of property. The Crummey withdrawal power can enable both cash gifts and gifts of policies transferred by the grantor to the trust to qualify for the annual exclusion.

The lapse of a beneficiary's right to withdraw trust property pursuant to a Crummey power may have gift tax implications. If the holder of a right to make a current withdrawal from the trust allows the amount to instead stay inside the trust, the holder has made a gift to the trust that would not qualify for the gift tax annual exclusion. This gift would be deemed made to the beneficiaries of the trust, which may include the powerholder (and not be a gift), but would also include any remaindermen (which would be). Under Code section 2514, the lapse of a Crummey power of withdrawal is taxable to the extent that the amount of the release exceeds $5,000 or 5 percent of the trust corpus. If, however, the lapse of a Crummey power falls within this so-called "five-and-five" exception, the lapse is not taxable.

In such a case, the beneficiary could have inadvertently used a portion of his or her lifetime credit against the gift tax or be subject to actual tax liability in the unlikely event their applicable exclusion amount had already been used. Moreover, it also could be that the property subject to the lapsed power would be included in the beneficiary's estate for estate tax purposes as a gift transfer in which an interest has been retained.[12] In many states, a lapse in excess of the "five and five" power may cause the powerholder to be deemed a settlor for amounts in excess of the lapse protection (and thus, since the powerholder is a beneficiary, causing a self-settled trust), impairing the asset protection of the trust.[13]

The gift and estate tax problem (and potentially, the asset protection issue) resulting from the lapse of a power relating to trust property in excess of $5,000 or 5 percent of the trust corpus can be resolved through good tax planning and careful drafting. One alternative is to draft the trust to include "hanging" powers of withdrawal so that the beneficiary's withdrawal right lapses each year only to the extent of the section 2514(e) "five and five" rule. The remaining withdrawal right is carried forward to future years and lapses when it would not create a gift tax problem. This may create a problem if the gift to the trust is so large that it will continue to "hang" around and will be includible in the beneficiary's estate at his or her death. Another alternative (although not a perfect solution) is for the terms of the trust to reserve in the beneficiary a power that keeps the lapse from being a completed gift (e.g., the power to direct where the trust property will go upon lapse of the withdrawal power), no gift tax is due. However, the estate tax problem is not avoided and the technically incomplete gift is included in the beneficiary's taxable estate. Because most Crummey trusts are intended to be paid out during the beneficiary's lifetime, and many beneficiary-Crummey powerholder's estates are well below the estate tax unified credit applicable exclusion amount, this may not be a significant issue for all clients.

Regardless of how much of the gift is within or in excess of the "five and five" rule, as mentioned above, the portion of the trust over which the beneficiary has a right of withdrawal at his death (e.g., the amount subject to the Crummey withdrawal where the withdrawal period had not lapsed) is included in the beneficiary's estate for estate tax purposes. This is because the beneficiary had the power to appoint (or transfer out) the property to himself and thus had a "general power of appointment" as described in Code sections 2514/2041. If the beneficiary survives the period for withdrawal, then the property that was subject to the withdrawal power can no longer be taken from the trust, and thus may escape taxation in the beneficiary's estate.

When creating the trust, especially with transfers of existing policies that may implicate the three year rule of Code section 2035, consider including contingent marital deduction planning if the grantor is married. In this way, if there is unintended inclusion in the grantor's estate, qualifying the trust for the marital deduction will avoid any estate taxation of the policy. This may be especially helpful if existing insurance policies are transferred to the trust and the grantor dies within three years.

Generation Skipping Transfer Tax

As noted above, the gift tax annual exclusion is available for transfers to the trust if the beneficiaries have Crummey powers of withdrawal, but this does not qualify the transfers for the GST tax annual exclusion. A transfer qualifies for the GST tax annual exclusion only if (1) during the life of the beneficiary no portion of the trust (or separate share) corpus or income may be distributed to or for the benefit of any other person, and (2) the trust (or separate share) would be included in the beneficiary's estate if such individual were to die before the trust terminated.[14]

These restrictions, of course, preclude the use of a true dynastic trust that is able to avoid transfer tax at each generation, or typical lifetime powers of appointment or spray powers that enable more flexible distributions and tax shifting from the trust once it becomes liquid. As a simpler alternative, an irrevocable life insurance trust would not be subject to GST tax if upon making a gift the donor allocates sufficient GST exemption to the gift such that the trust has a zero inclusion ratio.

If transfers to an irrevocable life insurance trust do not qualify for the GST tax annual exclusion and the donor does not allocate GST tax exemption to the gifts, then the "automatic allocation" rules of Code section 2632(c) may apply to allocate a portion (or all) of the donor's unused GST tax exemption to the gifts.[15] Because this analysis can sometimes be complicated (especially if there are hanging powers) or lead to an undesired default either way, clients may consider permanently opting in or out of the application of these rules on an attachment to Form 709 Gift/GST Tax Return, depending on the terms of the trust at issue. Practitioners should review how the default rules would apply and whether they would prefer to allocate GST exemption to the trust or not. For example, it may be a waste of exemption if there is automatic allocation, and the client's child is likely to receive the entire proceeds, or if coverage is likely temporary and may lapse. By contrast, there may not be much to lose by allocating a small amount of GST exemption to a trust that may be much larger at the date of death, as insurance policies often cause a large increase in value. This is even more true for families that may rely on portability, since the GST exemption does not port to a surviving spouse as the estate and gift tax exclusion does.

36.6 DEALING WITH OLDER TRUSTS

What should be done with an older irrevocable life insurance trust that has terms no longer consistent with the grantor's estate planning objectives? Many practitioners are looking for ways to abandon such older trusts. In some cases, the terms of the trust or applicable state law would allow the assets to be distributed to the beneficiaries and the trust terminated. For example, many trusts have an uneconomical trust termination provision, and many states have statutes that permit the same, some for as high a corpus as $200,000.[16] The grantor then could create a new trust with updated terms and use that trust to facilitate his or her estate planning.

In some other cases, grantors are buying the insurance policy from the trust, and making a gift of those policies to a new trust with terms more consistent with the grantor's current interest. Alternatively, the grantor could establish and fund a new irrevocable trust that is a grantor trust for income tax purposes, which then purchases the life insurance policy from the old trust. Because the transfer is considered a purchase of the policy by the grantor-insured (a grantor trust is, by definition, the income tax alter ego of its grantor), for income tax purposes it is as if the policy was transferred to the insured, thus falling within one of the exceptions to the transfer for value rule. A transfer from one grantor trust to another grantor trust is a non-event for income tax purposes; it is as if the insured took the policy from one pocket and transferred it to another pocket. The old trust then could be terminated by its terms, under state law, or administered with the proceeds from the sale of the insurance policy. However, the discussion in Chapter 30 relating to grantor trust status where a beneficiary has a Crummey power is relevant to this discussion. In PLR 201235006, the IRS approved the transfer of a policy from one trust to another trust since the receiving trust was a grantor trust. This avoided the application of the transfer for value rule.[17] This rule would result in the death benefit being treated as ordinary income. See also Rev. Rul. 2007-13 which provided that a transfer from a non-grantor trust to a wholly grantor trust qualifies as a transfer to the insured so that the transfer avoids the transfer for value rule.

From a trust administration perspective, it is important to note that the IRS in the past few years has refused to assign tax identification numbers to trusts which bear the same name even though they bear a different date. Therefore, the attorney should call the second trust "The John Jones Trust II," dated _____ when applying for a tax identification number.

Practitioners are also increasingly using decanting, non-judicial settlement agreements and other state law provided methods of amending irrevocable trusts.[18] The efficacy of these strategies of course, would depend on state law and the extent of the desired amendment. Similarly, some newer trusts have "trust protectors" or other persons appointed who may have the authority to amend the trust.

36.7 SELECTION OF TRUSTEES

The IRS takes the position that a grantor's retention of the power to remove a trustee without cause and arbitrarily replace that trustee with another trustee is tantamount to the grantor's retention of the trustee's powers, even though the grantor could not name himself as trustee.[19] Therefore, if the trustee had powers or ownership rights over the trust property which, if held by the grantor would cause the property to be includible in the grantor's estate, the trust property will be includible in the grantor's estate. For purposes of Code sections 2036 (retained life estates) and 2038 (revocable transfers), but not section 2042 (life insurance), the IRS states that it will not include property in a grantor's estate because of the retained power to replace a trustee with an independent trustee.[20] A later ruling determined that the right to replace a trustee for cause with someone other than the insured/grantor was not an incident of ownership.[21]

In certain very restricted circumstances it is possible to have the donor act as trustee where there is no life insurance on the donor-trustee's life. However, this requires a severe restriction of powers of the trustee. It is far better to have both no opportunity for the IRS to attack the transfer as being one that is included in the donor's estate and also to avoid subjecting property to management under very restricted circumstances. The more flexibility that can be given to a competent trustee, the better the trustee can manage the property.

A spouse may be an appropriate trustee of an ILIT, unless the policy to be purchased or transferred is a second to die policy that also insures the spouse. Corporate trustees are often appropriate, especially for larger policies or when other assets will also be transferred to the trust, and they may charge a discounted fee if there is an insurance advisor appointed in the trust to make decisions regarding the policy (this is sometimes referred to as a directed trust).

36.8 FREQUENTLY ASKED QUESTIONS

Question – Is there a simple yet effective way to transfer an existing life insurance policy currently owned by the insured and still avoid the transfers within three years of death rule?

Answer – There is really no simple way that is both totally tax safe and still effective. Some estate planners recommend that the insured give cash to an irrevocable life insurance trust, and then the trustee use those funds to purchase the policy from the insured. This transfer of the policy in return for consideration triggers the "transfer for value" rule under Code section 101(a)(2). If the transaction does not qualify for certain safe harbors, the policy proceeds will be taxed as ordinary income to the extent that they exceed the sum of the purchase price of the policy and any premiums paid by the trust after the transfer. However, if the trust and the insured are legitimate partners in a partnership or the trust is considered a grantor trust of the insured, (which is almost always the case with an irrevocable life insurance trust), the sale may qualify for one of the safe harbor exceptions to the transfer for value rule; although the IRS may have other grounds to challenge such a transaction. If there is real concern about the three-year rule, a much simpler solution is to purchase an additional term insurance rider lasting three years and equal to the potential estate tax that would be attributable to the policy proceeds.

Question – How does one avoid the three-year rule and still give an insurance policy as a gift?

Answer – Where the donor is still insurable, the best approach is to give cash to the trust, and allow the trustee to buy a new policy on the donor's life and name itself as beneficiary. In certain situations, buying a new policy can be advantageous, because some newer policies offer a higher effective rate of return. As long as the trustee is not *required* to purchase insurance with the funds contributed by the grantor and there is no other basis to recharacterize the grantor's gift of cash as a gift of an insurance policy, the Code section 2035 transfer within three years of death rule should not apply to the new insurance policy.

Question – If a person wants to cash in an insurance policy and buy a new one, are there any income tax aspects to the transaction?

Answer – Yes, to the extent that the transaction results in receiving more dollars than had been paid in net premiums, the "cashing in" of the policy can result in any gain being taxed as ordinary income to the owner of the policy. See Chapter 34.

Question – If a beneficiary of a Crummey trust does not exercise the withdrawal power, the beneficiary is considered to have made a gift to the trust. How is it determined what is subject to gift tax and what is not?

Answer – In this circumstance, under Code section 2514, any amounts subject to the Crummey withdrawal power in excess of $5,000 or 5 percent of the trust corpus (and not withdrawn) will potentially be taxable.

Question – What are the basic requirements for a Crummey Power?

Answer – The basic requirement is that actual notice must be made in a timely manner. In order to show compliance, it is best to give written notice to all beneficiaries (and to the natural guardian of any minor) at least thirty days before the end of the applicable withdrawal period (which is typically December 31). The letter should be sent return receipt requested, or other verifiable means of delivery, so the grantor has documentary evidence that the letter was received in sufficient time for a withdrawal of the transferred funds to have been made. While written notices are the best approach, the critical element is that notice be given. Printing out email reply confirmations may also be sufficient evidence. If the clients provided oral notice to the beneficiaries or the beneficiaries were aware of their rights, then it may be advisable to have the Trustee sign an affidavit that the beneficiaries were made aware of their Crummey rights in another more informal way. The IRS does sometimes ask for Crummey notices during an audit.

Question – Is it sufficient if the beneficiaries are just given notice at the time the trust is created, not for every premium payment?

Answer – Not according to the IRS. As noted above, it appears that a "once only" notice will not be considered adequate by the Service – even if the notice clearly indicates that later contributions will give rise to additional withdrawal rights in future years.

Question – Can a beneficiary of a Crummey trust have multiple demand rights, no one of which exceeds the greater of $5,000 or 5 percent of trust principal, and avoid the gift tax problems and estate tax problems when such powers lapse?

Answer – No. A donee is allowed only a single $5,000 or 5 percent limitation for lapsed withdrawal rights

IRREVOCABLE LIFE INSURANCE TRUST

during a calendar year. Thus, where a donor made a $5,000 gift to each of two Crummey Trusts, the donee was required to aggregate the two gifts (as if they were made to the same trust) for purposes of the $5,000 or 5 percent limitation.[22] In fact, this may also be the case if there were multiple donors (even if completely unrelated).

Question – Would it ever be wise planning to have a life insurance trust without a Crummey withdrawal power?

Answer – Yes. Donors may be using their annual exclusion for other outright gifts and have plenty of lifetime exclusion or not want beneficiaries to have knowledge of the trust. This might be helpful in family situations where there is not complete confidence the beneficiary will not exercise their withdrawal right, the beneficiary is receiving needs based government benefits, is embroiled in a pending divorce, or where the gift is so large that the lapsing portion will continue to be subject to the "hanging powers" for an extended period of time. More recently, the large increases in the applicable exclusion amount may lead many to avoid the Crummey power hassle as well.

In the same way that gifts of life insurance can effectively "leverage" the benefits of the donor's credit against the gift tax, such gifts can "leverage" the benefits of the GST tax exemption because the donor need allocate only enough exemption to cover the "gift" value of the policy (or the cash transferred for premium payments) as opposed to the face value of the policy.

Question – What impact did recent tax law changes have on irrevocable life insurance trusts?

Answer – None directly, but there were several changes that have a potentially significant impact on planning with irrevocable life insurance trusts.

The federal estate tax exemption and GST exemption have significantly increased and most estates will not incur a federal estate tax. But ultra-wealthy individuals' estates will be facing an estate tax and a large number of estates will be liable for a significant state death tax. For those estates, irrevocable life insurance trusts will still be needed in order to provide liquidity to pay the tax due and to meet the many other objectives trusts satisfy.

Question – How much can be transferred to an irrevocable life insurance trust using the gift tax annual exclusion?

Answer – In 2023, the section 2503(b) annual exclusion is $17,000 per donee, (or $34,000 if a married couple elects to split the gifts on a gift tax return).

Since 1998, the annual exclusion for gifts has been indexed annually for inflation, rounded down to the next lowest multiple of $1,000. Inflation increases should be used, when available, to help donors make slightly larger gifts under the gift tax annual exclusion. If possible, Crummey withdrawal powers should be drafted by referring to "the maximum amount allowable for the year as an exclusion under section 2503(b)" rather than to a fixed amount. This allows the donor and beneficiary to take advantage of inflation increases.

This indexing may eventually enable the payment of larger life insurance premiums without the need to pay gift tax on transfers to the irrevocable life insurance trust.

There is no maximum number of donees. The *Mikel* case discussed above had sixty beneficiaries and sixty annual exclusions. If a billionaire couple wanted to benefit their hometown and gift $34,000 each to 50,000 beneficiaries they could gift $1.7 billion gift tax free.

Question – What type of life insurance is best to put into an irrevocable life insurance trust?

Answer – The best type of product to put in such a trust is one that matches the objectives and circumstances of the parties involved. Because the main purpose of many, if not most, life insurance trusts is to provide for estate liquidity to help pay estate taxes and other death related expenses, or to replace assets used to pay taxes and expenses, some form of permanent insurance is usually preferable. Among the types of permanent insurance that can be placed in trust are whole life, universal life, or variable life insurance. Policies can be on the life of a single insured or can be survivorship policies, where two parties, typically husband and wife, are co-insureds, and the policy pays the death benefit only after both parties die. This will be best if the proceeds are meant to be used to pay the death taxes due upon the death of the second spouse.

For those circumstances where it can be accurately predicted how long the need will be, and that the coverage won't run out or become very expensive, before the need for insurance does, term insurance can be appropriate. Term insurance may be a way to acquire coverage for a short period at lower cost.

CHAPTER ENDNOTES

1. The name "Crummey trust" comes for the case *Crummey v. Comm'r.*, 397 F.2d 82 (9th Cir. 1968).
2. I.R.C. §2035.
3. *Estate of Clyde W. Turner*, TC Memo 2011-209.
4. Rev. Rul. 81-7, 1981-1 CB 474; Priv Ltr. Ruls. 7946007, 7947066.
5. Priv. Ltr. Rul. 8019038.
6. Rev. Rul. 81-7, 1981-1 CB 474.
7. Priv. Ltr. Ruls. 8103074, 8006048, 8004172.
8. Priv. Ltr. Rul. 8103074.
9. TAMs 8727003, 914008; *Est. of Cristofani v. Comm'r.*, 97 TC 74 (1991), acq. in result 1992-2 CB 1.
10. Mikel v. Commissioner, T.C. Memo 2015-64.
11. See discussion at *Ed Morrow and Alan Gassman on Mikel v. Commissioner: Tax Court approves the mother of all Crummey trusts with 60 beneficiaries*, LISI Estate Planning Newsletter.
12. I.R.C. §2036.
13. See, e.g., Uniform Trust Code §505(b). For a fifty state chart outlining the asset protection ramifications of a lapse of a withdrawal power in each state, see *Ed Morrow - IRC §678(a)(1) and the "Beneficiary Deemed Owner Trust" (BDOT)*, LISI Estate Planning Newsletter #2577 (September 5, 2017).
14. I.R.C. §2642(c)(2).
15. I.R.C. §2632.
16. See Uniform Trust Code §414 originally pegged this amount at $50,000. However, states often increase the particular dollar threshold. Ohio, for instance, increased the amount to $100,000 at Ohio R.C. §5804.14, Utah §75-7-414 ($100,000), Nebraska ($100,000), Massachusetts ($200,000), Kansas §58a-414 ($100,000), South Dakota SDCL §55-3-27 ($150,000). Some states are silent as to the guideline amount that is "uneconomical": 20 Pa. CS § 7740.4.
17. I.R.C. §101(a)(2).
18. E.g., see the Uniform Trust Decanting Act at www.uniformlaws.org, or a list and description of state decanting statutes at http://www.actec.org/assets/1/6/Bart-State-Decanting-Statutes.pdf. For various methods of amending irrevocable trusts pursuant to the Uniform Trust Code, see §§411-417, at www.uniformlaws.org.
19. TAM 8922003.
20. Rev. Rul. 95-58, 1955-2 CB 191.
21. Let. Rul. 9832039.
22. Rev. Rul. 85-88, 1985-2 CB 201.

CHARITABLE CONTRIBUTIONS

CHAPTER 37

37.1 INTRODUCTION

A charitable contribution is a gratuitous transfer of property to a charitable, religious, scientific, educational, or other specified organization. If the donee (recipient) of the gift falls within one of the categories designated in the Internal Revenue Code, a charitable deduction may be taken for income, gift, or estate tax purposes.

Charitable contributions have tax value; therefore, because they can result in a current income tax deduction, may reduce federal estate taxes, and can be made free of gift tax. From the charity's point of view, charitable contributions are also tax favored – the charity itself pays no tax upon receipt of either a lifetime gift or a bequest and, generally, no income tax is paid by the qualified charity on income earned by the charity on donated property.

Taxpayers who are age 70½ or older can make tax-free distributions to a charity directly from an Individual Retirement Account of up to $100,000. These qualified charitable distributions are not subject to the charitable contribution percentage limits since they are neither included in gross income nor claimed as a deduction on the taxpayer's return.[1] They also count as a part of the donor's required minimum distribution for the year.

37.2 WHEN IS USE OF SUCH A DEVICE INDICATED?

1. When the donor wishes, for non-tax reasons, to benefit one or more charities.

2. When the donor wishes to reduce income or estate taxes by taking advantage of the deductions allowed for such gifts.

3. When the donor would like to achieve certain personal objectives. These are discussed below.

37.3 WHAT ARE THE REQUIREMENTS?

1. Charitable contributions are deductible only if they are made to organizations that are "qualified." Examples of "qualified" organizations include nonprofit schools and hospitals, churches and synagogues, the United Way, Community Chest, United Cerebral Palsy, YMCA, YMHA, The American Red Cross, the Boy Scouts, Campfire Boys and Girls, and the American Heart Association.

   A donee will be considered qualified only if it meets all three of these conditions:

   (1) It must be operated exclusively for religious, charitable, scientific, literary, or educational purposes; or to foster national or international amateur sports competition, or to prevent cruelty to children or animals;[2]

   (2) No part of the organization's earnings can benefit any private shareholder or similar individual;

   (3) The organization cannot be one disqualified for tax exemption because it attempts to influence legislation or participates in, publishes or distributes statements for, or intervenes in, any political campaign on behalf of any candidate seeking public office.[3]

561

Generally, an income tax deduction is available for contributions to churches, educational organizations, hospitals and medical research organizations, governmental units, and various support organizations described in Code section 170(c). To the extent that the donor receives some benefit in exchange for the contribution, only the amount in excess of the benefit received by the donor is deductible.[4]

It is important to note that the statutory descriptions of qualified charities for federal income tax purposes are not exactly the same as the descriptions of qualified charities for federal estate or gift tax purposes. One basic distinction is that except where a tax treaty says otherwise for income tax purposes the donee must be a domestic organization, whereas the donee for estate tax charitable deduction purposes can be a foreign *or* a domestic charity. (Be certain to check the rules under all applicable Code sections.)[5] The client or practitioner should ascertain whether a potential donee is qualified under the Code. If it is not listed with the IRS,[6] it is wise to request a copy of a determination letter from the IRS indicating that the charity does (or does not) qualify.

If you are making a bequest to a charity in a will, and you are not sure if it will qualify for the deduction, it may be advisable to include a provision in the Will that to the extent the organization does not qualify for the charitable deduction, the bequest will be paid to an alternate qualified charity. Of course, this is only necessary if the size of the estate is large enough where the charitable deduction is necessary.

2. The second requirement necessary for a charitable contribution deduction is that *property* must be the subject of the gift. Therefore, the value of a taxpayer's time or services, even if contributed to a qualified charity, is not deductible.[7] For example, if a carpenter spent ten hours building chairs for his church, he could not deduct his normal hourly wage as a charitable contribution. However, he could deduct the cost of materials he purchased and used in producing the finished product. To view this from a conceptual perspective, since the carpenter never recognized the income associated with the ten hours building chairs, he cannot deduct the value of his services. The cost of the materials purchased can be deducted since the carpenter spent money that had previously been taxed to purchase the donated materials.[8]

Likewise, a taxpayer who donates the *use* of his property to a charity has not made a contribution of property. So the rent-free use of an office, or even an office building, no matter how valuable the rent-free use of the facility might be, will not be considered a charitable contribution any more than a contribution of personal services.

3. A third requirement for a charitable contribution deduction is that there must be a contribution to the charity in excess of the value received by the donor. In some cases, the donor will receive a benefit in conjunction with his charitable gift. Such a contribution is deductible only to the extent that the value of the contributed property exceeds any consideration or benefit to the donor.[9] For example, the individual might donate cash to a charity. The charity in turn might pay the donor (and perhaps his survivors) an annuity income for life. Only the difference between the contribution made and the value of the annuity would be deductible (see Chapter 38). What the donor receives in return must be both incidental *and* insubstantial in relation to the gift made. It is very important that the facts demonstrate the individual's intent to make a charitable gift rather than engage in an exchange or obtain a bargain, regardless of how favorable that exchange or bargain is to the charity. Charitable intent is a *sine qua non* (i.e., an indispensable condition) to deductibility.

4. The fourth requirement that must be met for a deduction to be allowed is that the gift to charity must actually be paid in cash or other property before the close of the tax year in question. Typically, therefore, even an accrual basis taxpayer must actually pay cash or contribute other property before the close of the tax year in order to receive a deduction.[10]

5. A charitable contribution at death will be deductible regardless of whether it is made by will, by the terms of a life insurance policy, or by gift during the decedent's lifetime in such a manner that the gift will be includable in his gross estate. But in order to be deductible by the decedent, he or she must make the gift, as distinguished from a transfer made by his estate or beneficiaries. Therefore, a deduction would not be allowed for a bequest to charity if the bequest requires the approval of a third party.

6. Where the lifetime transfer or bequest to charity is a gift of a "partial interest" (i.e., where the gift will be split between non-charitable and charitable beneficiaries), the general rule is that no deduction will be allowed – unless the strict rules in the statutory

exceptions are met. Generally, if a charity's interest in the transfer of property is a remainder interest (i.e., the charity receives what remains after the non-charitable income beneficiaries have received income for a specified time), a transfer in trust will qualify *only* if it is an annuity trust, unitrust, or a pooled income fund as these terms are defined by the Code. (See Chapter 38.)

A qualified appraisal (as required by IRS Form 8283)[11] must accompany a tax return showing donations of property valued at over $5,000. Who can be an appraiser? Anyone who attempts to appraise property valued at over $5,000 must be a qualified appraiser as defined in the Treasury Regulations.[12] An individual is qualified to be an appraiser for tax purposes only if the individual:

a. has earned an appraisal designation from a generally recognized professional appraiser organization or demonstrated competency in valuing the type of property being appraised or met certain minimum education and two year experience requirements;

b. regularly prepares appraisals for which they are paid;

c. demonstrates verifiable education and experience in valuing the type of property being appraised; and

d. has not been prohibited from practicing before the IRS.[13]

The appraiser must also understand that an overstatement of value may lead to the imposition of penalties, including at least one penalty against the appraiser.[14] Under recently issued Treasury Regulations, a qualified appraiser has to sign a certification that the Treasury Regulations provide.[15] The appraisal may not be made by the donor, the organization receiving the contribution, any person from whom the property was acquired, or certain related individuals or entities. Generally, a separate appraisal must be made for each item of property unless similar items are donated in the same year. Partnerships donating property valued at over $5,000 must provide a copy of the appraisal to every partner who receives a proportionate share of the deduction.

The appraisal must also meet the requirements of Treasury Regulations section 1.170A-17. In general, the appraisal must be signed, certified and dated by the appraiser. In addition, the appraisal must:

a. be made no earlier than sixty days prior to the date of contribution and no later than the due date of the tax return on which the charitable contribution was first claimed;

b. be prepared, signed and dated by a qualified appraiser;

c. include certain required information; and

d. not involve a prohibited fee.[16]

7. In addition, in the case of charitable contributions of art valued at more than $50,000, the taxpayer may request a "Statement of Value" from the IRS to substantiate the gift for income tax purposes. The request must be accompanied by a copy of the appraisal, a completed appraisal summary, and the user fee ($7,500 for the first three pieces of art, and $400 for each additional piece of art).[17]

While the appraisal requirement does not apply to gifts of publicly traded securities, it does apply to non-publicly traded securities worth more than $10,000. Note there are severe penalties for overvaluation of charitable gifts.[18]

In the case of all contributions, including cash, a charitable deduction is not allowed for any contribution of $250 or more unless the donor also obtains contemporaneous written acknowledgement that includes:

a. the amount of money, or a description of the property contributed;

b. whether the organization gave any goods or services to the taxpayer in return for the contribution;

c. a description and good faith estimate of the value of the goods and services; and

d. a statement that the goods and services provided consisted solely of intangible religious benefits.[19]

Canceled checks, alone, are not sufficient in such cases.

In addition, no charitable deduction is allowed for a non-cash contribution in excess of $500 unless the taxpayer attaches Form 8283 to his tax return showing the required information (on Part A). If you are donating clothing or household items worth more than $500, you must get an appraisal unless the property is in good condition or better. If the property is not in good condition or better, you can still claim the deduction so long as you get the item appraised.

Special rules also apply when donating automobile vehicles to charity.[20] If the motor vehicle is worth more than $500, you must attach to your tax return an acknowledgement from the organization to which you donated the vehicle. With certain exceptions, the amount of the deduction is equal to the smaller of the vehicle's fair market value on the date of the contribution or the gross proceeds received from the sale of the vehicle. The second limitation, relating to the sales proceeds, does not apply if the charitable organization improves the vehicle, uses the vehicle, or gives/sells the vehicle to someone below fair market value in furtherance of the organizations purpose of helping out the poor.

All donors must keep canceled checks, receipts, or other reliable written records. These documents must show the name of the donee, the date of the contribution, and the amount of the gift.[21] The safest approach is to make the records at the same time that the gift is made and have the recipient charity sign a receipt.

37.4 HOW IT IS DONE

A direct gift to charity is probably one of the simplest estate planning techniques. During lifetime, such a gift can be accomplished merely by writing a check, assigning stock, transferring life insurance policies, signing a deed to real estate, or conveying property to charity in any other standard outright manner.

Likewise, at death, gifts to charity can be made by will, by life insurance contract, by employee benefit contract (i.e., the death benefits from a pension plan, IRA, 401(k) plan, or nonqualified deferred compensation plan can be paid to charity), or by trust. Generally, lifetime gifts to charity yield both higher tax and non-tax rewards.

37.5 TAX IMPLICATIONS

1. A charitable contribution to a qualified charity may reduce current income taxes (assuming the donor itemizes deductions).

2. No federal gift tax is payable on a gift to a qualified charity regardless of the size of the gift.

3. Gifts to qualified charities can reduce the federal estate tax, with the amount of the deduction limited only by the value of the gift (i.e., the donor's entire estate can be left to charity and a deduction will be allowed for the entire gift).

4. The charity itself will pay no tax upon the receipt of either a lifetime gift or a bequest.

5. Generally, no income tax will be payable by a qualified charity on income earned by donated property.

6. If an otherwise deductible charitable contribution to a college or university entitles the donor to purchase tickets for athletic events, 80 percent of the contribution will be deductible.

7. For federal income tax purposes, there are percentage limitations on the amount that can be claimed as a charitable contribution deduction; these depend on, among other things, the type of property transferred. (The percentage limitations are discussed, below, in the "Frequently Asked Questions" section, and are also displayed in Figure 35.1.)

For tax purposes, potential charitable donees generally will be classified either as a private foundation or a public charity. The percentage limitations discussed below are those generally applicable to public charities. There are stricter percentage limitations on deductions for contributions to most private foundations.

Any organization that is classified as a charity under Code section 501(c)(3) is deemed a private foundation *unless* it is: a church; an educational organization with a regular curriculum, faculty, and student body; a hospital; a governmental unit; or certain other publicly supported institutions and support organizations.

In view of the importance of the income tax charitable contribution deduction and the percentage limitations, it is important for the advisor to determine not only whether the charitable recipient is a qualified charity, but also whether it is a private foundation – and if so, what type of private foundation.

Calculating the Deduction

The amount of a charitable contribution deduction that will be allowed for income tax purposes depends on the five following factors, which will be discussed in detail below:

1. *The type of property given away:*

    (a) Rent-free occupancy;

    (b) Cash;

    (c) Long-term capital gain property;

    (d) Ordinary income property;

    (e) Tangible personal property where the use of that property by the donee is *related* to the exempt functions of the donee; and tangible personal property where the use of that property is *unrelated* to the exempt purposes of the donee;

    (f) Future interests in property. (The various types of property listed above will be discussed in detail below.)

2. *The identity of the donee.* Generally, contributions to publicly supported domestic organizations – so-called "public charities" – are more favorably treated than contributions to foreign organizations or to most private foundations. Cash contributions to public charities, for example, are fully deductible up to 50 percent of a donor's contribution base (i.e., adjusted gross income computed without regard to any net operating loss carryback to the taxable year).[22]

    The deduction for an individual's contributions to most nonpublic (private) charities, regardless of the type of property given away, is limited to the lesser of (a) 30 percent of the taxpayer's contribution base, or (b) 50 percent of his contribution base minus the amount of charitable contribution deductions allowed for contributions to the public-type charities.[23] For example, if a wealthy individual donates property worth 40 percent of his contribution base (AGI) to a public charity such as the Boy Scouts, his contributions to "30 percent charities" (private charities) are deductible up to only 10 percent of his contribution base.[24] The limitation for gifts of capital gain property to private foundations is the lesser of 20 percent *or* the unused portion of the 30 percent limitation.

    Donations to individuals or to foreign charities (except where allowed by treaty) are not deductible for income tax purposes.

3. *The identity of the donor.* Deductions for contributions made by individuals are limited to specified percentages of their contribution base. An individual must itemize deductions in order to claim an income tax charitable contribution deduction. A corporation is limited to a deduction based on a percentage of its taxable income.[25]

4. *The amount of property given away.* Both individuals and corporations can carry over excess contributions (i.e., contributions above their deductible limit) for up to five years. If an individual dies during the carryover period, the excess deductions are lost.[26]

5. *The place where the contribution is to be used.* As mentioned above, gifts made to United States charities are treated more favorably than gifts to most foreign charities.

Types of Property

Generally, a charitable contribution of less than a donor's entire interest in property is not deductible. Gifts of a partial (a.k.a "split") interest in property are deductible only in four very narrowly defined situations:

1. The first is a gift of an undivided portion of the donor's entire interest in property.[27] For example, if Jesse Torelli, a successful businesswoman, gave her original Ramlo sculpture to the Philadelphia Museum of Art, but agreed with the museum that she could keep it in her home as long as she or her husband Wayne lived. No current deduction would be allowed. However, if Jesse gave an undivided one-half interest in the sculpture (i.e., if she gave the museum an immediate, absolute, and complete right of ownership, for display purposes or otherwise, for one-half of each year), she would likely be successful in obtaining a current deduction.[28]

2. The second situation involves a gift of a remainder interest in a personal residence or farm.[29] If Robin

Lynn Kay gives her home or her farm to a qualified organization with the stipulation that she may live there for life, she may take a current income tax deduction for the value of the future gift. This assumes, of course, that the gift is irrevocable.

3. The third circumstance in which a charitable contribution of less than the donor's entire interest could generate a deduction is where the donor makes a gift to a qualified charitable organization of a remainder interest in real property granted solely for conservation purposes.[30]

4. Finally, a gift of a partial interest would be deductible if transferred in trust. This exception allows a charitable deduction for transfers of property in trust even if the taxpayer transfers less than his entire interest. The deduction is allowed to the same extent that a deduction would be allowed had the same property been transferred directly to the charitable organization rather than in trust.

However, where there is a gift of a partial interest in tangible personal property to charity, it is necessary for the portion of the interest retained by the donor to be gifted within ten years of the initial contribution (or the date of death of the donor if the donor dies within the ten years). Failure to do so will result in a recapture of the tax benefits, plus interest and a ten percent penalty.[31]

Figure 37.1 and the discussion that follows illustrate how each type of property influences the limitation on the deduction for an individual who itemizes deductions.

Figure 37.1

CHARITABLE CONTRIBUTION DEDUCTION LIMITATIONS

PERCENTAGE LIMITATION

	Type of Property (1)	Donee† (2)	INDIVIDUAL AS DONOR Adjusted Gross Income** (3)	CORP. AS DONOR Taxable Income (4)	Individual Carryover (5)	Corporation Carryover (6)	TAX TREATMENT (7)
(A)	Rent-Free Occupancy or Services	—	—	—	—	—	No Deduction
(B)	Cash	Public	60%	10%	5 yrs.	5 yrs.	Full Deduction
(C)	Long-Term Capital Gain Property (except for tangible personal property)	Public	30%*	10%	5 yrs.	5 yrs.	Full Deduction for Fair Market Value
(D)	Ordinary Income Property	Public	50%	10%	5 yrs.	5 yrs.	Deduction Limited to Basis††
(E)	Tangible Personal Property (L.T.C.G. Property)						
	(1) Use-Related	Public	30%*	10%	5 yrs.	5 yrs.	Full Deduction for Fair Market Value
	(2) Use-Unrelated to Exempt Purposes of Donee	Public	50%	10%	5 yrs.	5 yrs.	Deduction Limited to Adjusted Basis
(F)	Future Interests in Property*						

* See detailed discussion in text.
** With certain adjustments.
† Regardless of the type of property given, the deduction for an individual's contributions to private charities is limited to the lesser of (a) 30 percent of the taxpayer's "contribution base" (roughly the same as adjusted gross income) or (b) 50 percent of the contribution base less any charitable contribution deduction allowed for contributions to public-type charities.
†† There is an important exception. The deduction for corporate donors (other than S corporations) has a higher limit, basis plus one-half of appreciation in value, where the property is to be used by the donee solely for the care of the ill, the needy, or infants. (See the text below).

CHARITABLE CONTRIBUTIONS CHAPTER 37

Rent-Free Occupancy

Contributions of a mere right to use property (such as a rent-free lease of meeting space in a building owned by an individual to the Boy Scouts) are not deductible.[32] This is because contributions must be made in cash or other property. The mere right to use property is considered neither cash nor other property. The IRS considers a contribution of the right to use property as a contribution of less than the donor's entire interest in the property.

Cash

Where the property is cash (as in a gift of any other type of property), it is necessary to ask, "Who is the donee?" If the donee is a publicly supported charity, the deduction ceiling (column 3) is 50 percent of the individual taxpayer's contribution base (generally, adjusted gross income).[33]

A corporation's deduction is limited to 10 percent of its taxable income (with certain adjustments).[34] Regardless of the type of property given, a corporation can always take a current deduction of up to 10 percent of its taxable income (column 4). Likewise, regardless of the identity of the donee, a corporation may carry over excess contributions for up to five years (column 6).

Contributions by individuals to "public" charities in excess of the deductible limit for the taxable year may also be carried over (column 5) for a period of up to five years.[35] In other words, excess contributions are not wasted and can be used as itemized deductions in future years. However, if the donor dies before using up all of the excess deduction, it is forever lost. For example, if Scott Jeffries contributed $50,000 in cash in 2023 to a synagogue, but his contribution base was only $36,000, he could currently deduct only 50 percent of his contribution base, $18,000. He could, however, carry over the $32,000 excess ($50,000 contribution minus $18,000) to the following year. (A five-year carryover is also provided for excess contributions to private foundations.)

A full deduction, up to 50 percent of the contribution base of individuals who itemize deductions, or 10 percent of taxable income for corporations, is allowed for gifts of cash (column 7).[36]

Long-Term Capital Gain Property

"Long-term capital gain property" is property that would have produced a long-term capital gain (held for more than one year) on the date of the gift had it been sold rather than donated to charity.

Long-term capital gain property can be divided into two types:

(1) The first type consists of intangible personal property and all real property. A gift of Xerox stock purchased eleven years ago at $100 a share, now worth $400 a share, would be considered intangible personal long-term capital gain property. Appreciated land held the requisite "long-term" period would be an example of real property that is properly classified as long-term capital gain property.

(2) The second type of long-term capital gain property is tangible personal property, such as a car, a painting, sculpture, an antique, or jewelry. Tangible personal property will be discussed below.

Where intangible long-term capital gain property, such as stock held for the requisite period, is given to a "public" donee (column 2), an individual's deduction may not exceed 30 percent of his contribution base (column 3).[37] If his gift exceeds this percentage limitation, he may carry over the disallowed portion of the deduction for up to five succeeding years (column 5). The full fair market value of the gift is deductible (column 7).[38]

Example. Suppose Nick Catrini donates stock worth $25,000 to the United Way. The stock cost $12,000 when he purchased it four years ago. If his adjusted gross income is $50,000, his maximum deduction for the contribution is $15,000 (30 percent of $50,000). He will be able to carry over the $10,000 balance and apply that as a 30 percent-type deduction against future years' income.

The deduction for contributions of long-term capital gain property is doubly advantageous. First, a person saves the taxes on his potential profit; in the above example, Nick saves the tax on a $13,000 long-term capital gain. Second, he gets a deduction for the full fair market value of the gift; here it will be $25,000.

Contributions of certain publicly traded stock to private foundations share the same advantages as similar gifts to public charities. Generally, a gift of publicly traded stock (which, if sold, would result in a long-term capital gain) made to a private foundation is deductible at its full fair market value, provided that the amount of stock does not exceed 10 percent in value of all the outstanding stock of the corporation.[39]

There is an election that the taxpayer may want to make in certain situations. The 30 percent limitation can be increased to 50 percent if the donor is willing to reduce the value of his gift by the amount of his potential gain.[40] The election can be extremely important for a taxpayer whose income fluctuates widely from year to year. It is of particular value when the amount of appreciation is small. For example, the value of a gift of long-term capital gain property with a basis of $980 and a fair market value of $1,000 would be reduced by only $20. In this way, the taxpayer could qualify for the higher 50 percent limitation at the expense of losing only a very small portion of his deduction.

Ordinary Income Property

"Ordinary income property" is an asset that would have generated ordinary income (rather than capital gain) on the date of contribution had it been sold at its fair market value rather than contributed.[41] Ordinary income property includes:

- capital assets held less than the requisite long-term period at the time contributed;

- Section 306 stock (i.e., stock acquired in a nontaxable corporate transaction that is treated as ordinary income if sold);

- works of art, books, letters, and musical compositions, but only if given by the person who created or prepared them or for whom they were prepared; and

- a taxpayer's stock in trade and inventory (which would result in ordinary income if sold).[42]

Ordinary income property given to a public charity (column 2) by an individual is deductible subject to a 50 percent of contribution base ceiling. However, a taxpayer's deduction is generally limited to his basis (cost) for the property (column 7).[43] For example, if a famous painter donated one of his paintings worth $25,000 to an art museum, his deduction would be limited to his cost for producing the painting. This means that only the cost for canvas, paint, etc., would be deductible. No deduction would be allowed for the value of his time and talent.

Example. A similar situation occurs in the case of Tony Molino, who owned his National Motors stock for 4 months (i.e., a sale would have resulted in short-term capital gain). He purchased the stock at a cost of $12,000 and gave it to Villanova Law School when it was worth $25,000. Therefore, since the property is considered ordinary income property, only his cost (basis) is deductible. Tony will be limited to a charitable deduction of $12,000, even though the property had a fair market value of $25,000 at the time of the gift. Had Tony waited until the sale of the stock would have generated long term capital gain; he would be entitled to the deduction for the full fair market value of the stock.

An exception to this rule is provided for certain ordinary income property, such as inventory, given by a corporation to a public charity, or a private operating foundation for use in its exempt purpose for the care of the ill, the needy, or infants (e.g., a contribution of medical supplies to the Red Cross).[44] In situations where this requirement can be met, the allowable deduction for contributions of appreciated ordinary income property is limited to (a) the donor's basis plus (b) one-half the potential gain in the property (but in no event can this deduction exceed twice the basis).[45]

Example. Assume a pharmaceutical corporation donates $11,000 worth of medicine (inventory) to a charity that performs services for ill and infirm individuals. If the basis to the corporation was $5,000, it may deduct $8,000 – its $5,000 basis plus one-half of the $6,000 potential gain.

Gifts of substantially appreciated ordinary income property should be avoided if possible. Capital assets should be held for the requisite long-term period if that will make it long-term capital gain property (i.e., deductible at full fair market value), or left to charity by will so that a full estate tax deduction can be obtained. Alternatively, ordinary income property could be left to the donor's children by will. The stepped-up basis the children would receive in the property after the donor's death would enable them to obtain a larger income tax deduction then if they were to give the property to charity.

Tangible Personal Property

Tangible personal property (which would have produced capital gain if sold) includes cars, jewelry, sculpture, art works, books, etc., but only if created or produced by a person other than the donor.[46] With respect to this type of property, a distinction must be made between (a) gifts that will be used by the donee charity in such a manner that the use of the gift is related to the exempt purposes of the donee ("use related" gifts), and (b) gifts that will not be used by the charity in a manner related to the exempt purposes of the donee ("use unrelated" gifts).

An example might be the contribution of a stamp collection to an educational institution. If the stamp collection is placed in the donee organization's library for display and study by students, the use of the donated property is related to the educational purposes constituting the basis of the charitable organization's tax exemption. However, if the stamps were sold, even if the proceeds were used by the organization for educational purposes, the use of the property would be an unrelated use.

Example. Elwood Chester has a $10,000 contribution base. He contributes a collection of whaling harpoons to the Cape May County Historical Museum for display purposes. The collection cost him $2,000, but on the date of contribution it was worth $10,000. The type of property contributed is tangible personal property. The donee is a public charity and the gift is "use related" to the exempt purposes of the Museum. Therefore, for the year of contribution, he can deduct up to 30 percent of his contribution base (AGI), $10,000. This figure is $3,000. In addition, because the full $10,000 contribution is deductible, he will be able to carry over the remaining $7,000 for up to five years (subject to the 30 percent rule each year).

If the gift is "use unrelated" (i.e., made to a donee whose direct use of the asset is unrelated to the charitable function of the donee), the deductible amount is limited to the donor's basis in the property. This is true for corporations as well as individuals.[47]

Future Interests in Property

A "future interest" is any interest or right that will vest in possession or enjoyment at some time in the future. The term "future interest" includes situations where a donor purports to give tangible personal property to a charitable organization, but has made a written or oral agreement with the organization reserving to a non-charitable beneficiary (himself or a member of his immediate family) the right to use, possess, or enjoy the property. For example, suppose Robin Lynn donates a genuine Douglas W. Mellor photograph to an art museum, but arranges with the museum to keep the photograph in her home as long as she lives. The museum has a future interest in the photograph.

One of the basic general rules governing charitable deductions is that contributions must be:

- actually paid;
- paid in cash or other property; and
- paid before the close of the tax year.

Furthermore, generally no deductions are allowed for an outright contribution of less than the donor's entire interest in property.

Since the benefit to the museum – and consequently to the public – was deferred in the gift of the D. W. Mellor photograph, no current tax deduction would be allowed. The implication is that a deduction will not be allowed until the charity receives actual possession or enjoyment of the work of art. The gift of tangible personal property must be complete in the sense that all interests and rights to the possession and enjoyment of the property must "vest" in the charity. This means that a transfer of a future interest in property to a charity is not deductible until all intervening interests in and rights to possession held by the donor or certain related persons or organizations have expired, or unless the gift is in the form of a future interest in trust that meets the requirements discussed in Chapter 38.

Charitable remainder interests are a form of future interest in which an income interest is either retained by the donor or is given by the donor to another person. At the death of the income beneficiary, the principal goes to a designated charity. An example would be a gift to X for life where the "remainder" (i.e., the principal at the death of X) goes to charity (the "remainder person") upon the death of X (the income beneficiary). A gift "to X for life, remainder to Villanova School of Law" would be considered a gift of a future interest to the law school. Charitable remainder trusts are discussed in more depth in Chapter 38.

37.6 BARGAIN SALES

The bargain sale is a device used to minimize the out-of-pocket cost of a charitable gift. At one time, an individual could sell appreciated property to a charity at his cost. The donor would receive an amount equal to his investment. In addition, he would obtain a charitable deduction for the appreciation in the property with no tax on his portion. That's no longer possible.

Under current law, a taxpayer may have to recognize a taxable gain on the bargain sale because he must allocate his cost basis between the part of the property he sold to the charity and the part he donated.[48] This means the donor pays tax on his pro rata share of the appreciation. In other words, he's treated as if he engaged in two transactions – one a sale to the charity, and the other a gift. He'll be required to pay income tax on any gain realized in the "sale" portion of the transaction, but he will receive a deduction for the portion considered to be his charitable gift.

Example. Suppose a donor sells property he has owned for several years to his favorite charity. On the date of the sale the property was worth $10,000. The sale price is the same as the donor's cost, $4,000. So four-tenths of the transaction is the sale portion. The gift portion amounts to the remaining 6/10 (60 percent) of the property, so he is deemed to have made a gift to the charity equal to 60 percent of his $4,000 cost basis, $2,400. This leaves the donor only the difference, $1,600 of cost basis, to apply against the $4,000 he is deemed to have realized in the "sale." His long-term capital gain is therefore $2,400 ($4,000 amount realized - $1,600 basis).

The $6,000 gift ($10,000 – $4,000) saves the donor $2,100 in taxes if he is in a 35 percent marginal tax bracket. He also has recovered his $4,000 investment, so his total "recovery" is $6,100 ($2,100 + $4,000). Since the maximum capital gain rate for capital assets held more than twelve months is 15 percent, his tax will be $360, 15 percent of his capital gain, $2,400. His net return, $5,740 ($6,100 – $360), is the sum of (a) his tax savings plus (b) the amount he realized in the sale less (c) the tax he had to pay on the sale, and the charity is enriched by $6,000. It is important to keep in mind that the documentation requirements still apply in the case of bargain sale gifts. With a bargain sale, the donor is receiving some type of benefit in exchange for the contribution. The requirements associated with gifts of property apply to these benefits received by the donor. One court disallowed a deduction because the taxpayer failed to disclose consideration received by the donor in exchange for the contribution.[49]

37.7 ISSUES IN COMMUNITY PROPERTY STATES

Because of the equal ownership aspect of community property between a husband and wife, care must be exercised in the creation of a charitable trust, since a taxable transfer may occur.

Example. If community property is used to fund a trust that benefits only one of the spouses, there has been a gift by the other spouse. Conversely, if the separate property of one of the spouses is used to fund a trust that provides for a lifetime benefit for both spouses, there is a recognized gift to the non-contributing spouse. The availability of the unlimited marital deduction for federal gift tax purposes eliminates prior concerns as to the federal gift tax (see Chapter 20). Connecticut is the only state now with a gift tax. However, if community property is used to fund a trust that provides a lifetime benefit for *both* spouses, there will be no gift tax consequences.

It is possible for community property to be "split," creating separate interests for each spouse, which could then be used to fund separate charitable trusts, each involving life interests of only the spouse making the gift. Or, one spouse can make a gift with her half of the "split" funds, and the other spouse can use the funds for his own purposes or to pay their joint income tax liability. In order for community property to be "split," an agreement between the parties must be made to that effect. A "split" is essentially a transmutation of community property to separate property; such transmutations must be in writing in some states (e.g., California).

If there is no written agreement requiring a particular division of the property in the community estate, the law generally requires the estate to be divided equally between the spouses.

As a general rule, no consideration is necessary to support a transmutation agreement between the spouses, and such agreements may be entered into both before and during marriage.[50]

Under the community property laws in many states, a valid contribution of community property cannot be made to a charity by one spouse without the consent of the other spouse. This consent should be obtained before the close of the tax year for which the deduction will be claimed; otherwise, the IRS may argue the contribution was not complete and is not deductible.

Generally, the same income, estate and gift tax advantages that are available for gifts of separate property will be available in situations where community property is the subject of a charitable contribution.

37.8 USING LIFE INSURANCE

Life insurance, like any other type of property, can be, and often is, the subject of a gift. In fact, life insurance is a favored means of making charitable contributions for many reasons.[51]

First, the death benefit going to charity is guaranteed as long as premiums are paid. This means that the charity will receive an amount that is fixed in value and not subject to the potential downside risks of securities.

Second, life insurance provides an "amplified" gift that can be purchased on the installment plan. Through a relatively small annual cost (premium), a large benefit can be provided for the charity. A large gift can be made without impairing or diluting the control of a family business interest or other investments. Assets earmarked for the donor-insured's family can thus be kept intact.

Third, life insurance is a self-completing gift. If the donor lives, cash values, which can be used by the charity currently, grow constantly from year to year. If the donor becomes disabled and the policy contains a waiver-of-premium feature, the policy will remain in full force, guaranteeing the ultimate death benefit to the charity as well as the same cash values and dividend build-up that would have been earned had the insured not become disabled. Even if death occurs after only one deposit, the charity is assured of its full gift.

Fourth, the death proceeds can be received by the designated charity free of federal income and estate taxes, probate and administrative costs and delays, brokerage fees, and other transfer costs. Thus, the charity, in fact, receives "one hundred cent" dollars. This prompt cash payment should be compared with the payment of a gift to a selected charity under the terms of an individual's will. In that case, probate delays of up to several years are not uncommon.

Fifth, because of the contractual nature of the life insurance policy, large gifts to charity are not subject to attack by disgruntled heirs.

Finally, a substantial gift may be made with no attendant publicity (i.e., confidentially) because the life insurance proceeds to be paid to charity can be arranged so that they will not be part of the decedent's probate estate. Of course, publicity may be given if desired.

Warning: In Private Letter Ruling 9110016, the Service denied a charitable deduction for premiums paid on a life insurance policy assigned to a charity on the grounds that since the charity had no insurable interest (under New York law) in the insured, payment of the proceeds to the charity could violate state law. If so, it was determined that the proceeds would be included in the insured's estate and, thus, subject to federal estate tax. Subsequent to the Service's treatment of the matter, New York amended its insurable interest statute to give charities an insurable interest in donors' lives. The Service responded to New York's amendment by issuing Letter Ruling 9147040, which revoked Letter Ruling 9110016.

Most states now have insurable interest statutes giving charities an insurable interest in the lives of their contributors. Some states require the charity to be the owner and irrevocable beneficiary while others allow the insured to be the initial owner if a subsequent transfer to the charity is made. A complete list of every state's insurable interest law with respect to charities is available at http://www.leimbergservices.com.

Valuing Life Insurance

Since the bundle of rights in a life insurance policy can be considered equivalent to property, a gift of a life insurance policy is valued according to the same general tax rules as any other gift of property, i.e., willing buyer-willing seller fair market value. Life insurance companies historically have issued policy valuations on Internal Revenue Service Form 712. However, as insurance products have become much more sophisticated, the best approach is to have the policy appraised by an independent qualified appraiser.

If a life insurance policy were sold at a gain, the gain would be taxed at ordinary income rates; to the extent the cash surrender value exceeds premiums paid and capital gain for any excess value over the cash surrender value; therefore, a gift of life insurance is at least partially a gift of ordinary income property. Assuming the value of the policy (i.e., the interpolated terminal reserve plus unearned premium on the date of the sale) exceeds the policyholder's net premium payments, the deduction for a gift of a policy is generally limited to the policyholder's basis (cost) – in other words, his net premium payments (plus by capital gain if the policy was held more than one year).

Example. Suppose an individual assigns a policy on his life to the American Heart Association. His charitable contribution deduction is limited to his basis (i.e., his cost in the contract) or the value of the policy, if lower. If the individual paid net premiums of $15,000, but the policy had a value of $18,000, his charitable contribution deduction would be limited to $15,000 if the value of the policy is its cash surrender value.

If there had been no gain upon a sale of the policy, the value of the donated policy would then be equal to its replacement cost at the date of the gift. In other words, if the total net premiums paid exceed the value of the policy when the individual assigns it (i.e., the policy would not give rise to a gain if sold), the deduction would be limited to the lower of the two, its replacement cost.

The amount of the deduction is dependent on the replacement cost of the policy. This differs depending on whether the policy in question is (1) a single premium or paid-up policy, (2) a premium-paying policy, or (3) a newly issued policy. The insurance company in question will generally calculate the exact value on IRS Form 712 upon request. One concern is that a gift of an insurance policy valued in excess of $5,000 must be accompanied by an appraisal. Generally, the issuing insurance company will value the policy but there is a question as to whether it may be a qualified appraiser.

The replacement cost of a single premium or paid-up policy is the single premium the same insurer would charge for a policy of the same amount at the insured's attained age (increased by the value of any dividend credits and reduced by the amount of any loans outstanding).

The replacement cost of a premium-paying policy is the policy's interpolated terminal reserve plus any unearned premium at the date of the gift (again, taking into consideration any dividend credits and outstanding loans).

The replacement cost of a newly issued policy is the gross premium paid by the insured.

A gift of a life insurance policy to charity must, of course, satisfy local requisites of a valid gift. In most states, this means that the donor must have intended to make a present gift of the policy and that he delivered it, actually or constructively, to the charitable donee. An absolute assignment is the most straightforward way of effectuating the transfer.

Charity-owned Life Insurance

Premium payments are considered gifts of cash and are, therefore, fully and currently deductible as charitable contributions if the charity owns the policy outright.

The donor should send his check directly to the charity and have it pay the premium to the life insurance company in order to assure the most favorable tax results. The canceled check will serve as proof of (1) the fact that a gift was made to the charity, (2) the date the gift was made, and (3) the amount of the gift. It will also assure the donor of a full deduction up to 60 percent of his contribution base.[52]

When an "indirect" gift is made to a charity, the annual deduction limit is lowered to 30 percent of the taxpayer's contribution base. A gift in trust is one such example. Another example of an indirect gift is where premiums on a policy owned by a charity are remitted directly to the life insurance company instead of to the charity itself.

If the gift to the charity exceeds $250, a statement will be required from the charitable organization showing

CHARITABLE CONTRIBUTIONS CHAPTER 37

the amount of money contributed and whether the charity gave any goods or services in return for the contribution.

Life Insurance and Immediate Gifts

Life insurance can serve as a means of enabling a donor to make a large current gift. For example, assume that an individual is fifty years old, a widower, and has three children. His gross estate is about $6 million. One of his assets is a parcel of land with a basis and fair market value of about $200,000. He wants to perpetuate the memory of his late wife through a memorial scholarship fund, but at the same time he does not want to deprive his children of a significant part of his estate.

He can satisfy his overall objective through an immediate gift coupled with the purchase of life insurance to replace the gifted property. Assuming his income is taxed at a marginal combined federal and state rate of 40 percent, the arrangement would work like this:

He would contribute the $200,000 parcel of land to his favorite charity immediately. Since the gift is an outright contribution, it will be currently deductible up to 30 percent of his contribution base. (If his income is not high enough to allow him to deduct the entire $200,000 in one year, he could carry over the excess and deduct it against his next five years' income.) The $200,000 charitable contribution would result in $80,000 of tax savings, since he is in a 40 percent combined federal and state income tax bracket. He can take this $80,000 that otherwise would have been used to pay taxes and instead make annual gifts of up to $17,000 (in 2023) each to his children. They in turn could purchase a policy on his life and name themselves as owners and beneficiaries.

Split Benefits

A life insurance policy can be split into two parts, the protection element and the policy cash value. The protection element, often called the net amount at risk, is the difference between the face amount of the policy and its cash (surrender) value. By splitting the proceeds of a policy between a donor's family and a charity, a donor can provide additional protection for the benefit of his family and at the same time make a meaningful gift to charity.

Note that if a donor attempts to "split dollar" the charitable gift (i.e., to name his personal beneficiary as the recipient of the policy's pure death benefit (the amount at risk), but make the charity the owner of the cash value), the Service will disallow a deduction for the gift.[53]

Group Term Insurance

Currently, employees must include the cost of group term life insurance coverage over $50,000 in their taxable income. The tax on this economic benefit must be paid with after-tax dollars, which has the effect of reducing the spendable income of the employee.

However, by naming a charity as the beneficiary of group insurance coverage over $50,000, the employee can provide for a gift to charity and at the same time avoid the tax on the economic benefit.

Example. A sixty-three-year-old executive who is taxed at a combined federal and state marginal rate of 40 percent who had $140,000 of coverage would save 40 percent of $59.40 per month ($712.80) annually, or $285.12 annually (based on $140,000 of coverage *minus* $50,000 tax-free coverage, resulting in $90,000 taxable coverage; and 90 (per $1,000 of coverage) × .66 (cost of $1,000 of protection for a one-month period for an individual aged sixty-three) equals $59.40).

37.9 FREQUENTLY ASKED QUESTIONS

Question – How do you calculate the tax savings and after-tax cost of a charitable contribution?

Answer – The tax savings and after-tax cost can be found as follows:

Tax Savings = Amount of deductible gift × Effective tax bracket

---

Example. A $2,000 gift by a taxpayer in a 40 percent (federal and state) income tax bracket equals $800 in tax savings. Stated another way, the out-of-pocket cost of the gift equals:

Amount contributed – Tax savings

573

For instance, the $2,000 gift above less the $800 in income tax savings equals the out-of-pocket cost of the gift, $1,200.

Question – Why are stocks and bonds often used for charitable gifts?

Answer – Securities such as listed stocks, mutual funds, or bonds are often selected as the subject of a charitable gift because:

(1) They are transferable with minimal cost or delay;

(2) As mentioned above, appreciated securities can often be transferred without causing the donor to realize gain on the appreciation and still yield a current deduction measured by the fair market value of the gift;

(3) If securities selling below their cost are sold, the net proceeds can be donated; this "sale-gift" procedure can lower the donor's tax;

(4) The donor's spendable income is often increased, rather than decreased, by the contribution;

(5) A lifetime gift removes appreciating property from an individual's estate and, thus, may lower death taxes and administration expenses; and

(6) The gift is easily valued and documented.

Question – How can a gift of closely held stock be used to generate a charitable contribution deduction?

Answer – Several court decisions opened the door to another charitable contribution deduction tool: the use of closely held stock. The idea is to enable the owner of a closely-held corporation to siphon funds from his business free of income tax by making a charitable contribution of his personally owned stock, followed by an unrelated redemption of that stock by the corporation.[54] If used properly, the technique may reduce or eliminate the threat of an accumulated earnings tax problem, generate a current income tax deduction for the donor (with no loss of control), and provide cash for the donor's favorite charity with no out-of-pocket outlay.

It works like this. First, the stockholder donates some of his stock to the charitable organization. He receives a charitable deduction measured by the present value of the stock contributed. Then, at some future date, the corporation redeems (i.e., buys back) the stock from the charity. (Had the corporation redeemed the stock directly from the donor, dividend treatment would probably have resulted.)

One use of this device involved a closely held corporation whose controlling shareholder gave a school about 200 shares of his corporation's stock each year. He took an annual deduction for the present value of the gifts, about $25,000.

The terms of the gift provided that the university could not dispose of the shares without first offering them to the corporation at their book value. The corporation was not required to purchase the stock, but did have sixty days in which to purchase any stock offered to it. Within a year or two after the shares were received by the school, they were offered to the corporation, which always purchased them – even though it was not legally bound in any way to do so. The proceeds of these redemptions were then invested by the school.

It appears that the key elements to the success of this device are the fact that the gifts were, in fact, complete and irrevocable, and that there was no formal or informal agreement that the university would offer the stock for redemption or that the corporation would purchase the stock from the school. This avoided the obvious IRS attack that the corporation's redemptions from the charity were in essence indirect redemptions from the donor and, thus, should have been taxed as ordinary income to the donor.[55]

A donor's retention of substantial rights in the stock given to charity, such as voting rights, will result in disallowance of the deduction because the entire interest in the property will not have been transferred.[56] Furthermore, the stock will be included in the gross estate of the donor because of the retention for life of the right to vote the stock.

Question – Aside from tax savings, why do people make charitable contributions?

CHARITABLE CONTRIBUTIONS — CHAPTER 37

Answer – There are many reasons why, aside from tax savings, people (and their businesses) make gifts to charities. These non-tax motives include situations where there was "no one else to leave it to," the desire to "ransom the donor's reputation," a feeling that the charity's mission expressed and furthered the donor's own values, passion, and interest, and the donor wanted to help assure the continuation of that mission. Gifts to charity are also made because the donor strongly relates to the needs of others or perhaps because the donor sees giving as a moral imperative. Sometimes, charitable gifts are made because the donors want to transfer values to their children and grandchildren, and to help their children and grandchildren grow and enhance their family values (or protect them from the problems unearned wealth often creates). Charitable gifts are sometimes made as part of a donor's desire to find meaning in abundance, or to "make a mark," (i.e., to have significance and to obtain a measure of immortality). Charitable gifts bring honor to both the giver and the giver's family.

Sometimes charitable gifts fulfill a sense of debt while other cases represent the donor's desire to share good fortune, to enhance the family's image and access, or out of a sense of competitiveness. Some people give to encourage and inspire others, while many give because it is part of their religious/ethical/social/family/cultural upbringing ("It's what we do.") Yet others give to charity because they are, or desire to become, distinguished human beings, because they feel wealth is a responsibility and that they possess wealth as stewards. To some, charitable gifts are a "means of fighting back" (e.g. against cancer or bigotry or ignorance). Some see charitable giving as a way to determine the future and to assure a higher quality of life for future generations. Charitable gifts are made by others to honor the charity for its efficiency, because it "makes me happy," and as an important step in the search for meaning. In all probability, most charitable gifts are motivated for more than one reason and in many cases the donor is not fully conscious of all the reasons he or she is giving.

Question – What is a donor advised fund?

Answer – In general, a donor advised fund is a charitable plan where the donor makes a gift to a public charity or community foundation, which sets up a sub-account or fund in the donor's name. For many years, until the Pension Protection Act of 2006, there was no definition of "donor advised fund" in the Internal Revenue Code. The term is defined in Code Section 4966(d)(2). The donor, or a person appointed by the donor, then makes recommendations of grants to be paid from that fund to selected charitable beneficiaries. For charitable deduction purposes, the sponsoring organization must provide a contemporaneous, written acknowledgement substantiating the gift. One of the key benefits of the donor advised fund is that the donor obtains a current income tax deduction even though the selection of the charity to receive the donation may not happen for some time. This is accomplished by having the property contributed to the donor advised fund remain within the fund and be invested. The donor has the ability to make *suggestions to* the donor advised fund as to which charities will receive distributions. While the donor cannot require the recommendations be followed; the suggestions are typically are followed. This allows for the current charitable deduction followed by the future benefit to the charities. Donor advised funds have attracted the ire of some in Congress, who have proposed a minimum required annual distribution in the 5 percent range, which is the rule for private foundations.

Question – May a donor gift a fractional interest in tangible personal property to a charity and claim an income tax deduction?

Answer – Yes, but special rules apply under Code section 170(o). These rules typically are applied with respect to fractional gifts of artwork. In these situations, no deduction is allowed unless all interests in the property are held immediately before the contribution by the donor, or the donor and the charity. Also, the charitable deduction will be subject to recapture if the donor fails to transfer the entire property within the earlier of: ten years of the initial donation; or the donor's death. The tax that is recaptured is accompanied with a 10 percent penalty. Finally, the amount of the deduction is based upon the value at the time of the initial contribution. Therefore, the donor does not get an additional deduction if the value of the property increases.

Question – May a donor gift assets from an IRA, and is it advantageous to do so and if so, how is it done?

Answer – If a donor wishes to make a charitable gift, the most tax efficient way to do so is to donate IRA money. IRA money will be estate taxed in the estate of a decedent whose assets are valuable enough to cause tax and will be income taxed to the recipient as IRD (less the estate tax on the IRA). See Chapters 56 and 59. A direct donation at death avoids the income tax to the beneficiaries and so, is a more tax efficient way to donate to charity. A donation during lifetime not only avoids income tax on the distribution but has the effect of boosting the tax effect of the donation, especially in states that do not permit itemized deductions such as Ohio. Lifetime gifts to charity from an IRA however are limited to persons over 70½ making the donation directly from the IRA to a public charity, not including donor advised funds, supporting organizations, private foundations, charitable remainder trusts, or charitable gift annuities. The donation may be used to satisfy the donor's required minimum distribution and is limited to $100,000 annually.[57]

CHAPTER ENDNOTES

1. I.R.C. §408(d)(8).
2. I.R.C. §170(c) for definition of charitable contribution. See also IRS Publication 526, Charitable Contributions.
3. The Internal Revenue Service publishes a list of qualified charities at: www.irs.gov/Charities-&-Non-Profits/Search-for-Charities.
4. Rev. Proc. 90-12, 1990-1, CB 471.
5. I.R.C. §2055 sets forth the rules associated with claiming a charitable deduction for estate tax purposes. The amount of the deduction is limited to the value of the property included within the gross estate. See Section 2055(d). Therefore no deduction is permitted if property is directed to a charity pursuant to the exercise of a limited power of appointment. Also, if the property to be donated appreciates during the period of estate administration, the amount of the deduction is limited to the amount included within the gross estate. The amount of the estate tax charitable deduction is also limited to the extent that taxes or administrative expenses are to be paid out of the funds otherwise passing to a charity. See §2055(c) and Treas. Reg. §20.2055-3. This will often become an issue if there is a residuary bequest to a charity.
6. To check the status of a charitable organization with the IRS, go to https://www.irs.gov/charities-non-profits/exempt-organizations-select-check
7. Treas. Reg. §1.170A-1(g).
8. Ibid.
9. I.R.C. §6115.
10. Treas. Reg. §1.170A-1(a)(1).
11. Instruction for Form 8283. See also §1.170A-13(c)(5), which further clarifies the requirements. Under the Regulations, the term "qualified appraiser" means an individual (other than certain excluded parties as identified in the Regulations) who hold themselves out to the public as an appraiser or performs appraisals on a regular basis; have appropriate qualifications; and is not a disqualified person. A disqualified person is generally someone who has some type of connection with the transaction. The IRS has also issued new Form 8283, which requires additional information for donated vehicles.
12. Treas. Reg. §1.170A-17(b).
13. Treas. Reg. §1.170A-13(c)(5).
14. I.R.C. §6695A.
15. Treas. Reg. §1.170A-16(d)(4).
16. See Treas. Reg. §1.170A-17(a)(4).
17. Rev. Proc. 96-15, 199601 CB 627, 12/28/1995 sets forth the requirements for obtaining a Statement of Value from the IRS. For the latest user fee requirement, see Rev. Proc. 2023-1, or the first Revenue Procedure of each year for changes in the user fee.
18. I.R.C. §6662. There also are appraiser penalties. I.R.C. §6695A. Additionally, appraisers can be disciplined under Circular 230 and forbidden from practicing before the IRS.
19. I.R.C. §170(f)(8).
20. I.R.C. §170(f)(12).
21. I.R.C. §170(f)(8).
22. I.R.C. §170(b)(1)(A).
23. I.R.C. §170(b)(1)(B).
24. Treas. Reg. §1.170A-8(f).
25. I.R.C. §§170(b)(2), 170(d)(2)(A); Treas. Reg. §1.170A-11.
26. I.R.C. §170(b)(1)(B).
27. I.R.C. §170(f)(3)(B)(ii). See also, Rev. Rul. 58-260, 1958-1 CB 126; Treas. Reg. §1.170A-7(a).
28. Treas. Reg. §1.170A-7(b)(1).
29. I.R.C. §170(f)(3)(B)(i).
30. I.R.C. §§170(f)(3)(B)(iii), 170(h); Treas. Reg. §1.170A-7(b)(5).
31. I.R.C. §170(o)(3).
32. I.R.C. §170(f)(3)(A); Treas. Reg. §1.170A-7(a).
33. I.R.C. §170(b)(1)(A).
34. I.R.C. §§170(b)(2), 170(d)(2).
35. I.R.C. §§170(d)(1), 170(b)(1)(B), 170(b)(1)(D)(ii); Treas. Reg. §1.170A-10(a).
36. I.R.C. §§170(b)(1), 170(b)(2); Treas. Regs. §§1.170A-8(b), 1.170A-11.
37. I.R.C. §170(b)(1)(C)(i).
38. I.R.C. §170(b)(1)(C)(ii).
39. I.R.C. §170(e)(5).
40. I.R.C. §170(b)(1)(C)(iii); Treas. Reg. §1.170A-8(d)(2).
41. I.R.C. §170(e)(i).
42. I.R.C. §1221.
43. I.R.C. §170(e)(1)(A); Sen. Rep. P.L. 91-171 (12060).
44. I.R.C. §170(e)(3).
45. I.R.C. §170(e)(3)(B).
46. I.R.C. §170(e)(1)(B)(i); Treas. Reg. §1.170A-4.
47. I.R.C. §170(e)(1)(B)(i).
48. Treas. Reg. §1.1011-2.
49. *Marshall Cohan, et ux., et al. v. Comm'r.*, TC Memo 2012-8.
50. See for example California Family Code §850.
51. See S. Leimberg, "Life Insurance as a Charitable Planning Tool: Part I," *Estate Planning*, March 2002, Vol. 29, No. 3, Pg. 132; "Life Insurance as a Charitable Planning Tool: Part II," *Estate Planning*,

April 2002, Vol. 29, No. 4, Pg. 196; and *Tools and Techniques of Charitable Planning* (800 543 0874).

52. The enhanced 60 percent contribution base limitation is in effect for gifts made after December 31, 2017 and January 1, 2026, at which time it will revert to 50 percent if not otherwise amended between now and then.

53. I.R.C. §170(f)(10).

54. Note that the basic planning principle in these cases (i.e., that the redemption by a corporation of closely-held stock from a charity will not be considered a dividend to the individual who donated the stock to the charity in the absence of a prearranged plan) is still useful. *Grove v. Comm'r.*, 490 F.2d 241 (2d Cir. 1973); *Dewitt v. U.S.*, 503 F.2d 1406 (Ct. Cl. 1974); *Carrington v. Comm'r.*, 476 F.2d 704 (5th Cir. 1973). Although both *Grove* and *Carrington* were decided after 1969, they were decided on the basis of pre-1969 Tax Reform Act law. This is why the retention of a life income by the donor did not cause a loss of the charitable deduction. But under present law, a retention of the life income produced by the donated stock or by the proceeds of a sale of such stock would make the contribution a gift of "less than the donor's entire interest in the contributed property." Such a gift would not qualify for a charitable deduction. See Letter Ruling 8123069 where the Service held that appreciated securities used for the redemption of all stock held by the charity would not cause dividend consequences.

55. *Palmer v. Comm'r.*, 62 TC 684 (1974), *aff'd on other grounds*, 523 F.2d 1308 (8th Cir. 1975), *acq.* 1978-1 CB 2. *See also* TAM 8623007, reaching the same conclusion as *Palmer* on "materially identical" facts. *But see* TAM 8552009, where controlling shareholders, H and W, gave nonvoting common stock shares in a family corporation to a qualified charitable trust. The shares were subject to a stock restriction agreement that would not allow the trust to sell the stock to anyone outside the stockholder group without first offering it to the corporation and the other authorized shareholders at a value contained in the agreement. The donors claimed a fair market value for the stock on their income tax return for the year of the gift of $18 million, and later had the corporation redeem the stock from the trust for the same amount. The IRS refused to apply the rationale of the *Palmer* case, above, claiming that the fair market value of the stock at the time of the gift was $32 million and at the time of the redemption was $36 million, and that the gift and the redemption were part of the taxpayers' plan to use the trust as a conduit to make a gift to the remaining stockholders, their descendants, by increasing the value of their descendants' shares and correspondingly decreasing the value of H's and W's shares. The Service characterized the transaction as redemption by the corporation from H and W of all the ostensibly donated stock, followed by a gift of the proceeds to their descendants.

56. Rev. Rul. 81-282, 1981-2 CB 78.

57. I.R.C. §408(d)(8).

CHARITABLE SPLIT INTEREST TRUSTS

CHAPTER 38

38.1 INTRODUCTION

With the exception of pooled income funds and wealth replacement trusts, discussed below, this section deals with charitable split interest trusts that have, as the chapter title implies, split interests That is, these trusts have both charitable and non-charitable beneficiaries who have vested interests.[1]

A distinction must be made between trusts established *solely* for the benefit of charity (which are deductible without meeting the requirements below), and trusts that have both charitable and non-charitable beneficiaries. Deductions for contributions to this second type of trust are measured by the present value of the ultimate gift to charity.[2] If the charity benefits *before* the non-charitable beneficiary, i.e., it receives annuity or unitrust payments for a specified term and the corpus then goes to the donor's family or some other non-charitable beneficiary, the trust is referred to as a charitable *lead* trust, where the charity receives the lead interest (discussed in more detail below).

But if non-charitable beneficiaries receive annuity or unitrust payments for a specified period (e.g., for ten years or for life) and *afterwards* the charity receives the remaining corpus, the trust is called a charitable *remainder* trust. The charity receives what remains after the non-charitable beneficiary's interest ends, i.e. it gets the remainder interest.

Gifts of a remainder interest in trust generally are deductible only if made in one of three ways:

1. a fixed annuity trust;
2. a unitrust; or
3. a pooled income fund.[3]

These three permissible forms of trust are an outgrowth of congressional concern over potential abuses of gifts of a remainder interest in trust to charity.

Example. Mr. and Mrs. Wilson are a financially secure, but childless, couple. Mr. Wilson might leave his property to his wife in trust. Mrs. Wilson, according to the terms of the trust, would receive the income for life if she survived her husband. At her death, the principal in the trust would pass to a designated charity. Mr. Wilson would take a current charitable contribution deduction for the present value of the gift that the charity would receive at the death of his wife, the income beneficiary. To counteract inflation and provide for contingencies, a clause might be inserted in the trust agreement authorizing an invasion of principal for Mrs. Wilson's benefit.

The potential for abuse was that the trustee, by design, would invest the principal in the trust in securities that produced an extremely high income to provide the donor's spouse with as much income as possible, but at the cost (mainly to the charity) of a correspondingly high risk that the principal would be lost or diminished. This situation naturally worked to the detriment of the charitable remainder beneficiary. In addition, the ability of the trustee to make substantial invasions of the principal of the trust further increased the likelihood that little, if any, of the original contribution would be received by the charity. Too often, the result was a significant decrease in the value of the charity's remainder interest. So the trust, when created, resulted in a deduction that assumed the charity would receive $X when in reality the charity would receive far less – if anything.

For these reasons, a multiplicity of rules were imposed to prevent a taxpayer from receiving a current charitable contribution deduction for a gift to charity of a remainder interest in trust that may be substantially in excess of the amount the charity may ultimately receive (because the assumptions used in calculating the value of the remainder interest had little relation to the actual investment policies of the trust).

Pursuant to these rules, deductions are basically limited to situations where the trust specifies:

- a *fixed* (read limited) annual *amount* that is to be paid to the non-charitable income beneficiary (i.e., an annuity trust);

- the amount that the income beneficiary will receive in terms of a *fixed percentage* of the value of the trust assets ascertained each year (i.e., a unitrust); or

- property contributed by a number of donors is commingled with property transferred by other donors, and each beneficiary of an income interest will receive income determined by the rate of return earned by the trust for such year (i.e., a pooled income fund).[4]

A charitable lead annuity trust or unitrust, which is essentially the reverse of the charitable remainder trust, provides that a fixed annual payment, either in the form of an annuity or a unitrust percentage, is made to one or more qualified charities during the term of the trust. At the end of that term, the property is usually transferred either to the donor or members of the donor's family.[5]

A wealth replacement trust (discussed below) is often used in conjunction with a charitable remainder trust to help replace the loss of value to the family of the donor of the trust assets passing to a charitable remainder trust.

38.2 WHEN IS USE OF SUCH A DEVICE INDICATED?

A primary function of a charitable split interest trust is to provide either a present (remainder) or future (lead) economic benefit to the donor or other members of the family, or both, with a present or future transfer to charity which qualifies for income, estate, and gift tax charitable deductions.

However, in the case of Charitable Remainder Trusts (CRT), particularly the charitable remainder unitrust, a primary motivation for using the trust is often the transfer of substantially appreciated property by the donor, which will then be sold by the trust. A charitable remainder trust is exempt from federal income tax (unless it has unrelated business taxable income, discussed later) and, therefore, will not be taxed on the gain. The trustee will then reinvest the proceeds from the sale to generate an income yield that will be higher than if taxes had been otherwise paid on the sale. The retained annuity or unitrust interest of the donor (and/or the family of the donor) will be based on the pre-tax value of the property transferred to the trust. In other words, the donor can receive payments based on the entire value of the fund, with no reduction for tax on the built-in gain on the transferred assets. As such, it is a very good technique where someone has a highly appreciated asset, and wants to diversify this asset without paying an immediate capital gains tax.

A principal drawback to this concept is the loss of the value of the (after-estate tax) trust assets that the donor's family would have received had no charitable gift been made. This leads to the concept of the Wealth Replacement Trust (WRT), generally an irrevocable life insurance trust. The idea is that the additional income that the donor receives because of the use of the Charitable Remainder Trust (CRT) can be given by him/her to the WRT and used to pay premiums on insurance on the donor's life held in the WRT, which ultimately is distributed to the family to replace the wealth (i.e., the value of the assets in the charitable remainder trust that would have passed, had it not gone to charity, to the donor's family). It is important to keep in mind that by deferring the capital gains tax on the sale of the assets, the donor has more money available to be invested and to produce a higher rate of income. In some cases, this higher level of income can cover most of the cost of annual premiums to purchase the life insurance. The age and health of the donor will affect the cost of the insurance and the extent to which this enhanced income stream can cover the cost of the insurance. In many circumstances, the income tax savings is insufficient to cover the cost of the life insurance, so clients need to be kept aware of this possibility.

38.3 WHAT ARE THE REQUIREMENTS?

CRATs

A Charitable Remainder Annuity Trust (CRAT) is a trust designed to permit payment of a fixed amount annually to a non-charitable beneficiary with the remainder going to charity.[6]

In the basic charitable remainder annuity trust configuration, the donor transfers money or securities to a trust that pays him a fixed dollar amount (a fixed annuity) each year for life or for a term of years that can't exceed twenty years. If the actual income generated by the assets of the trust is insufficient to meet the required (promised) annual fixed payment, the shortfall is paid from capital gains or principal. If the annuity trust's actual income is greater than the amount required to be paid out to the non-charitable beneficiary in any given year, the excess income is reinvested in the trust and becomes part of the trust's corpus, eventually going to the charitable remainderman.

The donor's income tax deduction is computed in the year that funds are irrevocably placed in trust. It is measured by the present value of the charity's right to receive the trust assets upon the death of the annuity beneficiary (or at the end of the specified term of years).[7] While the trust is generally irrevocable, the IRS has approved reformations in order to qualify the trust. In addition, the Code does permit certain qualified reformations in order to correct issues with the trust.[8]

The value of the remainder interest is determined by a calculation using actuarial factors based on the beneficiary's age (or the specified term of the trust), the annual amount payable to the beneficiary, and the appropriate monthly section 7520 rate.[9]

In order to qualify for income (and estate and gift) tax deductions, a charitable remainder annuity trust must meet a number of tests.[10] The primary requirements are these:

1. A fixed amount or fixed percentage of the initial value of the trust must be payable to the non-charitable beneficiary.

2. The annuity percentage must not be less than 5 percent nor more than 50 percent of the initial fair market value of all the property transferred in trust.

3. The specified amount must be paid at least annually to the non-charitable beneficiary out of income and/or principal.

4. The trust must be irrevocable and not subject to a power by either the donor, the trustee, or the beneficiary to invade, alter, or amend the trust. However, with certain limitations, while the terms of the trust cannot be changed, the donor can retain the right to change the charitable beneficiary to one or more different qualified charities. In addition, the donor may retain the testamentary right to terminate the non-charitable interest.[11]

5. The trust must be for the benefit of one or more persons (at least one of which is not an organization described in Code section 170(c)) who must be living at the time of the transfer in trust, and their interests must consist of either a life estate or a term of years not exceeding twenty years.

6. The entire remainder must go to charity.

7. The value of the remainder must equal at least 10 percent of the initial fair market value of all assets transferred to trust. Because the donor must receive at least 5 percent per year, and at least 10 percent of the fair market value of the assets must ultimately pass to charity; it is possible that a young donor may not be able to qualify for this type of trust.[12]

If all the necessary tests are met, the donor of a charitable remainder annuity trust will be entitled to an income tax deduction equal to the value of the remainder interest (assuming his contribution base is sufficient to utilize the full amount of the deduction).

38.4 CRUTs

A Charitable Remainder Unitrust (CRUT), like a charitable remainder annuity trust, is basically designed to permit payment of a periodic sum to a non-charitable beneficiary with a remainder to charity.[13] The key distinction is in how the periodic sum is computed.

Example: A donor irrevocably transfers money or securities to a trustee. In return, the trustee agrees to pay the donor (or other beneficiary) a unitrust amount from the property for life. The donor also requires that if he predeceases his spouse, she in turn will receive a unitrust amount from the donated property for life. The donor will receive payments based on a fixed percentage of the fair market value of the assets placed in trust. The assets will be revalued each year.

In order to qualify for income, gift, and estate tax deductions, the structure of a charitable remainder unitrust must conform to guidelines set forth in the Internal Revenue Code.[14] These include:

1. A fixed percentage of the net fair market value of the principal, revalued annually, must be payable to the noncharitable beneficiary.

2. The percentage payable to the noncharitable beneficiary must not be less than 5 percent nor more than 50 percent of the annual value.

3. The unitrust may provide that the noncharitable beneficiary can receive the *lesser* of: (1) the specified fixed percentage; or (2) the trust income for the year, *plus* any excess trust income to the extent of any deficiency in the prior years (by reason of the distribution being limited to the amount of trust income in such years).

4. The noncharitable income beneficiaries must be living at the time of transfer in trust, and their interests must be for a life estate *or* a term of years not exceeding twenty years.

5. The entire remainder must go to charity.

6. The value of the remainder must equal at least 10 percent of the net fair market value of the assets transferred to trust. As with the CRAT, a young donor may not be able to qualify in creating a CRUT unless the unitrust amount is payable over a term of years (not to exceed twenty) rather than over one or more life expectancies.

An income tax deduction, if allowed at all, is permitted in the year that funds are irrevocably placed in trust. As with the charitable remainder trust, even though the trust is irrevocable, the donor may retain the testamentary right to terminate the *non*-charitable interest.[15]

The deduction is measured by the present value at the date of the gift of the charity's right to eventually receive the unitrust's assets, subject to percentage limitations (discussed in Chapter 37). The portion of the deduction disallowed generally may be carried forward for five years.

A variation of the CRUT is one in which the payment to the beneficiary is limited to the lower of the set percentage *or* the actual income of the trust. Usually, there is also a provision to "makeup" for any occasion when the income is less than the set percentage. This Net Income with Makeup CRUT (NIMCRUT) has been used a great deal for several years. Such NIMCRUTs have been used as an alternative to qualified pension plans by investing in assets that produced little or no income in the early years (while the donor's income is high), and then converting to high income investments in years after the donor's retirement.

A CRUT with a lesser of trust income or the unitrust amount provision may be subject to Code section 2702 (see Chapter 29) if:

1. the grantor retains an interest in the CRUT;

2. the CRUT has more than one noncharitable beneficiary; and

3. at least one of the noncharitable beneficiaries is other than the grantor or the grantor's U.S. citizen spouse.

However, section 2702 would not apply if there are only two consecutive noncharitable beneficiary interests and the grantor holds the second interest. If section 2702 applies, the gift to the noncharitable beneficiary by the grantor would generally be valued as equal to the value of the property transferred to the trust reduced only by the value of the charity's remainder interest; interests retained by the grantor would be valued at zero.[16]

Pooled Income Funds

A Pooled Income Fund (PIF) is a trust generally created and maintained by a public charity rather than a private donor, which meets the requirements explained below.

The basic requirements are these:

1. The donor must contribute an irrevocable, vested remainder interest to the charitable organization that maintains the fund.

2. The property transferred by each donor must be commingled with the property transferred by other donors.

3. The fund cannot invest in tax-exempt securities.

4. No donor or income beneficiary can be a trustee.

5. The donor must retain for himself (or one or more named income beneficiaries) a life income interest.

6. Each income beneficiary must be entitled to and receive a pro rata share of the income, annually, based upon the rate of return earned by the fund.

If these tests are met, the donor will generally be entitled to an income, gift, or estate tax deduction.[17]

Wealth Replacement Trusts

In order to deal with the fact that the assets in a charitable remainder trust will go to charity and not to the family, a "wealth replacement trust" is often used in conjunction with a CRT. A wealth replacement trust is usually an irrevocable life insurance trust that will benefit the remaining family members. Premium payments are usually funded at least in part by the income tax savings from the charitable deduction for creating the CRT, and the increase in income from reinvestment of the sales proceeds from the assets that were transferred to the CRT.

Because the client receives immediate tax benefits upon establishing a charitable remainder trust (through an income tax deduction), and because the client would have an increased cash flow with the trust (since the trust paid no income tax on the sale of the assets, which could be reinvested at a potentially higher yield), the funding for the premium on the life insurance policy held in irrevocable life insurance trust can, in many cases, be achieved between the tax savings and the increased cash flow without any additional outlays by the client.

Example 1. Assume a client, who is in a combined 48 percent federal and state estate tax bracket transfers $1,000,000 worth of appreciated stock to a charitable remainder annuity trust, retaining a 6 percent annuity interest for himself. After his death, the assets pass to a charity of his choice. Had he not created the trust, his heirs would have inherited $520,000 ($480,000 would have been the total federal and state estate tax). Therefore, to replace the amount his heirs would have been disinherited by, he created an irrevocable life insurance trust, which can purchase insurance on his life.

Example 2. A client has a sizeable block of stock in a company that he started and has since taken public. He is now able to sell that stock. However, the stock has an income tax basis of $100,000 and a current market value of $1,100,000. How might he use the wealth replacement trust concept? Assume a 10 percent investment return.

Depending upon the taxpayer's taxable income, under current capital gain rates for assets held for more than twelve months, the client would pay federal income tax of $150,000 ($1,100,000 − $100,000 basis = $1,000,000; $1,000,000 × 15 percent), and the client would be left with $950,000 ($1,100,000 − $150,000). If the amount of that capital gains tax were reinvested at 8 percent, he would have an annual yield of $76,000. Assume, instead, that the client transfers the stock to a charitable remainder annuity trust, in which he retains a 10 percent annual annuity. The trustee sells the stock, pays no income tax, and pays the client an annual annuity of $110,000 per year for life, which is $34,000 per year more than if the client had simply sold the stock and reinvested the proceeds.

However, the client's family will lose a potential inheritance of $1,100,000, *plus* the future growth in that investment (but *minus* the federal and state death taxes that would have to be paid on that amount). Assuming the investment would double in value by the time that the client dies (based on the client's life expectancy and an anticipated growth rate of the property), his net loss of wealth would be $1,900,000 (2 × $950,000) *minus* federal and state estate tax of $912,000 (assume a combined death tax of 48 percent × $1,900,000), or $988,000.

If the client is insurable, the client could replace this lost wealth by purchasing approximately $988,000 in life insurance, which would be owned either directly by his potential heirs or by an irrevocable trust for their benefit. If the annual premiums for such insurance were less than $15,000, the transaction would produce a net economic savings to the client.

Charitable Lead Trusts

As stated above, a Charitable Lead Trust (CLT) is essentially the reverse of a CRT. If it is a grantor CLT, it is an income tax device that enables a taxpayer to reduce the tax burden of an unusually high income year. If certain requirements are met and the CLT is a grantor trust, the taxpayer will be allowed a current income tax deduction for the value of the annuity or unitrust interest (the present value of the stream of dollars) given to a charity. Anything remaining after the trust's obligation to pay the charity's annuity ends passes to the specified non-charitable beneficiaries.

The trade-off for the large up-front current deduction is that the donor will be taxed on the income that the trust earns each year (under the grantor trust provisions—see Chapter 30). This means that the grantor *must* be treated as the owner of such interest under Code section 671 in order to obtain a current income tax deduction. Also, the charity must receive either a guaranteed annuity or a fixed percentage of the annual net fair market value of the trust assets.[18]

If for some reason the taxpayer is no longer taxed on the annual income of the trust, there will be a partial recapture of the previously allowed deduction, which must be reported by the taxpayer as income in that year. For example, if the individual contributes the income for five years but dies within three years of this contribution, recapture would be triggered. His income for the year of his death would have to include a recaptured portion of the excess deduction that he took at the time that the trust was established.[19]

An alternative income tax plan is one in which the CLT is not a grantor trust and there is no income tax charitable contribution deduction at the time of transfer to the CLT. This plan is often used where the goal is to avoid percentage limitations on gifts to charities, and to avoid the amount going to charity from the CLT each year being treated as income to the donor.

Alternatively, the transfer can be made at death, in which case there is no income tax deduction, but there is a step-up in income tax basis of the assets going into the trust.

Another use of the CLT is to permit the transfer of assets to the next generation at a very low transfer tax value (a portion of such value having been given to charity). This situation typically arises where the assets within the CLT are expected to increase in value at a rate higher than the section 7520 rate.

The CLT works like this: The donor transfers income-producing property to a trust. The trust in turn will provide the charity with a guaranteed annuity (i.e., a charitable lead annuity trust), *or* annual payments equal to a fixed percentage of the fair market value of the trust property as annually recomputed (i.e., a charitable lead unitrust). At the end of the specified period, the property would be returned to the donor, or go to a noncharitable beneficiary of the donor's choice. Since the noncharitable beneficiary is receiving the money in the future, the value of this future gift is reduced to an amount equal to the present value of that future gift. In some cases, the duration of the charitable interest can reduce the amount of this future gift to zero.

As long as the donor has a reversionary interest in the income or the principal of the trust that is greater than 5 percent, or is otherwise considered the owner of the income or principal under the grantor trust rules (see Chapter 30), he can take an immediate income tax charitable contribution deduction at the inception of the trust. The deduction is based on the present value of the charity's future rights to annuity or unitrust payments.

A lead trust structured in such a way ensures that the income from the property held in trust, while payable to the charity, is includable in the donor's income. The donor does not receive an income tax charitable contribution deduction each year of the trust for the income payable to the charity, but does receive a charitable contributions deduction in the year that the trust is funded for the present value of the payments the charity is to receive over the ensuing years. The donor would not receive this deduction unless he was considered the owner of the annuity or unitrust amount (as described in Code section 170(f)(2)(B)).

38.5 ISSUES IN COMMUNITY PROPERTY STATES

As explained previously in the chapter, split-interest trusts are essentially trusts with both charitable and non-charitable beneficiaries that have both (1) assets for which a charitable deduction was allowed for income, estate, or gift tax purposes and (2) unexpired noncharitable interests. There are two kinds of split-interest trusts: charitable remainder trusts (the most common) and charitable lead trusts.[20]

As discussed in Chapter 37 (Charitable Contributions), since community property is owned equally by the spouses, a contribution of community property to a split interest trust that benefits only one of the spouses may be treated as a gift, and it may be taxable if it does not qualify under both the federal and any state marital deduction rules.

A gift into a charitable lead trust is attributable, one-half, to each of the spouses. Therefore, each spouse would be considered a "grantor" as to the half contributed by him or her.

A gift of community property can only be validly made with the consent of both spouses.

38.6 ANNUITY TRUSTS VS. UNITRUSTS

The choice between an annuity trust and a unitrust involves a number of considerations. An annuity trust is indicated where simplicity in administration is desired since there is no need for an annual revaluation. (At least 5 percent of the initial fair market value of the trust property must be distributed in the case of an annuity trust, whereas if a unitrust is used, there must be a distribution of at least 5 percent of the trust's fair market value as re-determined *each year*.) Furthermore, depending on payout rate, and age of the annuitant, the annuity trust may yield a larger charitable contribution deduction. Generally, if the payout is greater than the current valuation table interest rate, the unitrust will produce a larger value for the remainder interest than would the annuity trust.

There are, however, a number of disadvantages of an annuity trust when compared with a unitrust. First, inflation may cause a fixed annuity to lose some of its value. Of course, the unitrust may, under adverse circumstances, also fail the income beneficiary. If investment results are poor, the life income beneficiary may experience an absolute loss of income. This will result in both an inflation loss and a diminution of the dollar amount of his annual payment. On the other hand, if the trustee of the unitrust is skillful, he may be able to enhance the value of the principal fund and, consequently, the dollar amount of the annual payment.

A second disadvantage of the annuity trust is caused by regulations providing that the governing instrument in the case of an annuity trust must prohibit any additional contributions from being made.[21] This is probably done to confine the trust to a single valuation date. It therefore becomes impossible to pour over future testamentary bequests into the trust or to have other grantors make inter vivos additions to the already created trust, rather than having to set up new trusts for the same purpose. Conversely, regulations specifically permit additional contributions to unitrusts if the governing instruments contain provisions regarding the effect of such an addition upon valuation and the unitrust amount payable.[22] If trust income is less than the required percentage payment in a unitrust, the liquidity problem could be avoided if the noncharitable beneficiary is willing to forgive all or a part of any particular year's payment, an act tantamount to a contribution to the trust.

A third disadvantage of an annuity trust is that the specified annuity must be paid each year regardless of whether there is sufficient trust income. If the corpus of the trust were real property, such as an apartment house, and if rents were to fall below the specified annuity plus expenses, the trustee would have to borrow against the property or sell it to make the required payments. However, if the trust instrument so provides, a unitrust can limit its payout to the income beneficiary to the actual trust income. In later years, if trust income exceeds the percentage regularly distributable, the deficiency could be made up by excess distributions. This is referred to as a Net Income with Makeup Unitrust (NIMCRUT).

Example 1. A client is considering transferring $100,000 to a trust that will pay him $5,200 a year for life, with a remainder to charity.

The client's deduction would depend on his age at his nearest birthday. As Figure 38.1 illustrates (arbitrarily assuming a 5.0 percent section 7520 rate), a fifty-five-year-old donor would receive a $30,354 deduction. A sixty-five-year-old would receive a $43,879 deduction for the same contribution.[23]

Example 2. Assuming the same facts, how would the result be different if the client were to transfer $100,000 to a charitable remainder unitrust, retaining an annual payment equal to 5 percent of the value of the trust each year?

The donor would receive $5,000 the first year. If the value of the trust had increased to $120,000 a year later, the donor would receive 5 percent, $6,000, and so on each year. If the income of the unitrust were insufficient in a given year to pay the stated percentage, capital gains or principal could be used (but need not be, if the trust so provides) to make up the deficit.

Example. A sixty-seven-year-old donor places $250,000 in a charitable remainder unitrust, retaining a payment equal to 9 percent of the annual value of the trust, payments to be made quarterly at the end of each period. Assuming the use of a 5.0 percent section 7520 rate, the donor's deduction would be $74,280. The computation is illustrated in Figure 38.2.

Figure 38.1

CHARITABLE REMAINDER ANNUITY TRUST
(One Life - Table 2000CM)

Transfer to Trust:	$100,000	Annuity Payment:	$5,200
Age:	55	Frequency of Payments:	Annual
Payments:	End of Period	Section 7520 Interest Rate:	5.0%
Valuation			
Ann. Factor (Age 55, 5.0%):	13.3935	Adj. Factor (Annual, 5.0%):	1.0000
Annuity Value:	$69,646	Charitable Contribution:	$30,354

Figure 38.2

CHARITABLE REMAINDER UNITRUST
(One Life - Table 2000CM)

Transfer to Trust:	$250,000
Age:	67
Months Until First Payment:	3
Unitrust Payout Rate:	9.0%
Frequency of Payments:	Quarterly
Section 7520 Interest Rate:	5.0%
Adjusted Payout Rate Factor (Quarterly, 3 months, 5.0%):	.970057
Adjusted Payout Rate [9.0% × .970057]:	8.731%
One Life Unitrust Remainder Factor (Age 67, 8.6%):	.30161
One Life Unitrust Remainder Factor (Age 67, 8.8%):	.29476
Difference [.30161 – .29476]:	.00685
Interpolation Adjustment (8.731%):	.00449
Unitrust Remainder Factor [.30161 – .00449]:	.29712
Charitable Contribution [$250,000 × .29712]:	$74,280
Unitrust Interest [$250,000 – $74,280]:	$175,720

38.7 ESTATE TAX IMPLICATIONS

The estate tax deduction created by the use of a qualified charitable remainder trust is measured by the value of the remainder interest that will pass to charity, using the same tables applied in connection with trusts created during life.

Figure 38.3 shows the federal estate tax savings possible for a sixty-seven-year-old woman, through an *inter vivos* charitable remainder trust. The "without charitable trust" column shows the results for a widow who makes no provisions for a charitable remainder trust (or outright donation). In this situation her taxable estate is $8,000,000. If the same individual created a charitable remainder trust, which is funded in January 2015, with $2,000,000 and provides for a 9 percent payout. This Charitable Remainder Unitrust (CRUT) will generate a deduction of $580,680; her taxable estate would be reduced considerably. In addition, a current income tax deduction would have been obtained for the value of the remainder interest of the property donated.

Example 1. A client, who is sixty-eight years of age, has been approached by her alma mater with a request that she make a sizeable contribution. She would like to transfer $100,000 to the university, but believes she will need the income generated by that amount to live on the rest of her life. The university maintains a pooled income fund that is producing an annual return of 6 percent. As illustrated in Figure 38.4, the client would be able to deduct $44,887.

Example 2. A client is a physician with a large annual income from her practice. She has reached the maximum limits on her qualified retirement plan, and is seeking a method to invest in such a way that she can accumulate funds tax-free for her retirement.

Here the client may want to consider what is sometimes called the net income charitable remainder unitrust. As noted in the text, this is a trust in which the annual payment is the lesser of the fixed unitrust percentage or the actual income generated by the trust.

An optional provision in such a trust is called the makeup provision. Under that provision, if the actual unitrust payment in any year based on the income is less than the unitrust percentage,

Figure 38.3

ESTATE TAX SAVINGS USING A CHARITABLE REMAINDER TRUST
(assume death occurs in 2015)

	Without Charitable Trust	With Charitable Trust
Adjusted Gross Estate	$8,000,000	$8,000,000
Charitable Contribution	———	580,680
Taxable Estate (Tentative Tax Base)	$8,000,000	$7,429,320
Estate Tax Before Unified Credit	$3,145,800	$ 2,917,528
Unified Credit	$2,045,800	2,045,800
Estate Tax after Unified Credit	$ 1,100,000	$ 871,728
Net Estate Cost of $2,000,000		
Charitable Contribution Is $1,771,728 ($2,000,000 – $228,272) In addition, there is the income tax benefit of the $580,680 income tax deduction		$228,272 Estate Tax Savings

Figure 38.4

POOLED INCOME FUND
(One Life – Table 200CM)

Transfer to Trust:	$100,000
Rate of Return:	6.0%
Age:	68
One Life Remainder Factor (Age 68, 6.0%):	.44887
Charitable Contribution ($100,000 × .44887):	$44,887

the net difference is carried over to later years, so that in any subsequent year in which the net income exceeds the unitrust percentage, the amount carried over can be paid (so long as the total does not exceed the actual income).

Assume the physician contributes $20,000 per year to such a trust, and the trustee invests in maximum growth, minimum income investments. Assume the unitrust percentage is 6 percent, and the actual income is in the range of 2 to 3 percent. The trustee would distribute only the actual income for the next several years, during which the donor will build up a substantial carryover credit. When the physician is ready to retire, the trustee changes the investments to maximum growth, and is now able to pay the entire amount of income to the donor because of the makeup provision. This plan functions much the same as a deferred annuity. In some cases, it may be helpful to have the trust purchase an annuity so that the distributions from the annuity contact will be treated as income to the trust. The IRS has approved the purchase of an annuity within a charitable remainder annuity trust.[24]

Again, life insurance may be a key element in such a plan. It can function as a wealth replacement vehicle in the manner just described. It can also be used as a hedge against the premature death of the client. In other words, since the purpose of this technique is to provide for retirement, there will be a substantial economic loss if the client dies before retirement, or early into retirement.

Charitable Lead Trusts

A charitable lead trust can be used for purposes of estate tax savings. As explained above, property is placed in the trust. A fixed amount of the income the property produces is paid annually to a charity for a specified period of time (this is the front-end or lead period). At the end of that period, full ownership of the property and the income it produces passes to non-charitable beneficiaries, such as the children or grandchildren of the trust's grantor.

When property is placed in the trust by bequest, an estate tax deduction is allowed for the actuarial value of the front-end annuity interest. As illustrated in Figure 38.5, a $747,732 estate tax deduction would be allowed (arbitrarily assuming a 5.0 percent section 7520 rate) if a client left a $1,000,000 bequest in trust to pay $60,000 a year to The American College for twenty years. Stated another way, the deduction could remove about 75 percent of the trust property from the taxable estate. Furthermore, the property would go intact to the donor's family after twenty years. And, by properly combining the annuity payout level and the duration of the annuity period, it might be possible to eliminate an even greater amount of estate tax. For example, an annuity payout of $80,000 for twenty years would result in a deduction of $996,976 (arbitrarily assuming a 5.0 percent section 7520 rate). Furthermore, those same remainder beneficiaries could be named as trustees and, therefore, control the property they someday will own. If the trust property earned a return greater than the 5.0 percent section 7520 rate which is assumed, the actual amount of funds within the trust (which will pass to the heirs) will increase.

Figure 38.5

CHARITABLE LEAD ANNUITY TRUST (Term Certain)				
Transfer to Trust:	$1,000,000	Annuity Payment:		$60,000
Age:	20	Frequency of Payments:		Annual
Payments:	End of Period	Section 7520 Interest Rate:		5.0%
Check Exhaustion of Trust Fund				
Ann. Factor (20 years, 5.0%):	12.4622	Adj. Factor (Annual, 5.0%):		1.0000
Annuity Test Value:	$747,732	Special Factors		Not Required
Valuation				
Ann. Factor (20 years, 5.0%):	12.4622	Adj. Factor (Annual, 5.0%):		1.0000
Charitable Contribution:	$747,732	Remainder Value:		$252,268

38.8 FREQUENTLY ASKED QUESTIONS

Question – If an appreciated asset is transferred to a charitable remainder trust, does the donor, the annuity or unitrust beneficiary, or the charity pay an income tax or capital gains tax if that asset is sold by the trust and the proceeds are reinvested?

Answer – None of the parties to a charitable remainder trust would have any immediate income tax liability on the sale because charitable remainder trusts are exempt from income tax (except in years when they have unrelated business income). Therefore, a charitable remainder trust can accumulate, free of income or capital gains tax, any income in excess of that needed to satisfy its annuity or unitrust obligations to the non-charitable beneficiaries.

This fact would also allow the donor to receive a greater income than he otherwise would be able to, since if he sold the asset without transferring it to the trust, he would have to pay income or capital gains taxes.

However, as distributions are received from the trust by the noncharitable annuity or unitrust beneficiary, part of each distribution may be taxed to that beneficiary as ordinary income or capital gain from sale of the asset by the trust. The method by which this is calculated is called the tier system.

CHAPTER ENDNOTES

1. For more detail on these trusts, see *The Tools & Techniques of Charitable Planning*, 3d Ed. (National Underwriter Co.).
2. I.R.C. §170(f)(3) which generally provides that no deduction will be allowed for the contribution of a partial interest in property unless the contribution if of a: (i) remainder interest in a personal residence or farm, (ii) an undivided portion of the taxpayer's entire interest in property, and (iii) a qualified conservation contribution. In *Upen G. Patel, et ux. v. Comm'r.*, 138 T.C. No. 23, (June 2012) the court denied a charitable deduction to the taxpayer for permitting a local fire company to destroy the house as part of a training exercise. The court reasoned that this was not the contribution of an undivided property interest, but was more like the grant of a license.
3. I.R.C. §§170(f)(2)(A), 664(d). But see the discussion of gifts of a partial interest in Chapter 37 for an exception.
4. I.R.C. §170(f)(2)(A).
5. I.R.C. §170(f)(2)(B).
6. I.R.C. §§664(d)(1), 2055(e)(3); Treas. Reg. §20.2055-2(a).
7. Charitable trust calculations can be performed on Number-Cruncher Software.
8. PLR 201125007. See also I.R.C. §2055(e)(2) relating to qualified reformation of trusts.
9. A complete history of Section 7520 rates can be found at http://www.leimberg.com under Free Resources.
10. I.R.C. §§170(f)(2)(A), 664(d)(1).
11. Treas. Reg. §1.664-2(a)(4).
12. Rev. Rul. 79-368, 1979-2 CB 109.
13. I.R.C. §664(d)(2).
14. I.R.C. §664(d)(2).
15. Treas. Reg. §1.664-3(a)(4).
16. Treas.Reg. §25.2702-1(c)(3).
17. I.R.C. §642(c)(5). To calculate the deduction for a contribution to a pooled income fund: (1) take the highest rate of return for the previous three years, (2) look to Valuation Table S for that rate, (3) find the proper age of the donor, (4) proceed to column 4 to find the appropriate remainder factor, and (5) multiply the factor by the amount contributed to obtain the deduction.
18. Treas. Reg. §1.170A-6(c).
19. Treas. Reg. §1.170A-6(c)(4).
20. Adapted from "Trusts: Common Law and I.R.C. 501(c)(3) and 4974" by Ward L. Thomas and Leonard J. Henzke, Jr., IRS Exempt Organizations -Technical Instructions Program for Fiscal Year 2003.
21. Treas. Reg. §1.664-2(b).
22. Treas. Reg. §1.664-3(b).
23. The computation of these amounts and all like amounts referred to involve the following steps (and of course charitable split interest trust calculations can be performed on NumberCruncher Software at http://www.leimberg.com):

    For both annuity trust and unitrust computations, age is determined as of the individual's nearest birthday. Treas. Regs. §§20.2031-7A(d)(1)(ii), 1.664-4(e)(5).

    In the case of an annuity trust, go to Valuation Table S (reproduced) to determine the value of an annuity at the given age. Arbitrarily assuming a Section 7520 rate of 5.0 percent, in the case of a person age 55 this is 13.3935. Also, the principal sum is $100,000 and the annual annuity payout is $5,200. The value of the annuity equals $69,646 ($5,200 × 13.3935). The value of the remainder is $30,354 ($100,000 – $69,646).

    In the case of the unitrust, go to IRS Publication 1458, Table U(1). The value of a remainder interest after a 5 percent unitrust payout at age 55 is .32836. This factor applied to the principal sum of $100,000 is $32,836, the deduction allowed. (The actual payout rate may require adjustment under Table F, also found in Publication 1458, to reflect the number of months by which the valuation date precedes the first payment.)

    It is interesting to note that the value of a charitable remainder interest of a residence in the hands of a noncharitable tenant may be greater for gift tax than for income tax purposes because no deduction for depreciation is required for gift tax purposes. Rev. Rul. 76-473, 1976-2 CB 306. For relevant decisions regarding the federal estate tax deduction for charitable remainders, see Rev. Rul. 76-543, 1976-2 CB 287, as amplified by Rev. Rul. 77-169, 1977-1 CB 286, and distinguished by Rev. Rul. 83-158, 1983-2 CB 159; Rev. Rul. 76-545, 1976-2 CB 289, as clarified by Rev. Rul. 82-97, 1982-1 CB 194; Rev. Rul. 76-546, 1976-2 CB 290; Rev. Rul. 77-385, 1977-2 CB 331; Rev. Rul. 87-37, 1987-1 CB 295.
24. PLR 201126007.

CONSERVATION EASEMENT EXCLUSION

CHAPTER 39

39.1 INTRODUCTION

A very special and significant incentive is provided to private U.S. landowners to preserve undeveloped land. Specifically, Code section 2031(c) provides for a federal estate tax exclusion related to the value of land that is subject to a donated qualified conservation easement.

There are actually multiple advantages to the donation of a qualified conservation easement. First, donors of conservation easements that fulfill the requirements of Code section 170(h) are entitled to an income tax deduction. The income tax deduction is equal to the value of the public easement. Second, if the gift of the public easement is made either during lifetime or at death, the donor will also be entitled to reduce the value of the land for federal estate tax purposes to take into consideration the effect of the gift on the fair market value of the property. Third, there is an estate tax exclusion under Code section 2031(c), if, in general, the requirements of section 170(h) are also met.[1]

The value of the section 2031(c) exclusion is limited to $500,000. In general, qualification for the exclusion is dependent on meeting certain geographical and ownership criteria, and on meeting specific requirements for the grant of the easement.

Within these limitations, the estate may deduct the lesser of (a) $500,000 or (b) 40 percent of the value of the land subject to a qualified conservation easement, reduced by 2 percent for every 1 percent that the easement represents less than 30 percent of the value of the land, to zero if the value is 10 percent or less of such land. The values taken into account are such values as of the date of the contribution of the qualified conservation easement.

39.2 WHEN IS USE OF SUCH A DEVICE INDICATED?

1. When the land meets the specified geographical requirements.

2. When the land has been owned by the decedent or a family member for at least three years immediately prior to decedent's death.

3. When the easement is contributed on or before the due date (including extensions) for filing an estate tax return, and no interests are retained, except as allowed.

39.3 WHAT ARE THE REQUIREMENTS?

1. As of the decedent's date of death, the land must be located in the United States or its possessions.[2]

2. The land must have been continuously owned by the decedent, or a member of the decedent's family, during the three years immediately preceding the decedent's death.[3]

3. The land must be subject to a qualified conservation easement, which is a "qualified conservation contribution of a qualified real property interest," as generally defined in section 170(h) and Treasury Regulation section 1.170A-14.[4]

4. The contribution must be made to a qualified organization and used exclusively for conservation purposes. In general, an organization is qualified to receive such a contribution if it is a federal, state, or local agency, or a charity qualifying under Code section 501(c)(3).[5] The recipient must be a qualified

591

organization with a "commitment to protect the conservation purposes of the donation and have the resources to enforce the restrictions."[6]

5. A real property interest is qualified if it is a restriction granted in perpetuity on the use which may be made of the property.[7] This requirement can be violated if the parties can revoke the interest through the consent of the parties.[8]

6. A conservation purpose includes preservation of land for public recreation or education, protection of a natural habitat of fish, wildlife, or plants, or the preservation of open space, including farmland and forestland.[9] The preservation of historically important land or certified historic structures, although referenced under section 170(h)(4), is not a conservation purpose under section 2031(c).[10] The conservation purpose must be protected in perpetuity to be treated as exclusive.[11]

7. The donor may not retain rights to develop the easement for commercial purposes (other than farming).[12] To the extent that the donor does retain any development rights, than the value of what may be taken as a deduction, can be limited. If this should occur, and the heirs desire the full deduction, the heirs can agree to waive the development rights on a post mortem basis.

8. The applicable percentage of the value of the land subject to a qualified conservation easement that may be excluded from the decedent's gross estate is equal to the lesser of (a) $500,000 or (b) 40 percent of the value of such land, reduced by 2 percent for each 1 percent (or fraction thereof) by which the value of the easement is less than 30 percent of the value of the land.[13]

9. The election to take the exclusion under section 2031(c) must be made on the decedent's estate tax return, and, once made, is irrevocable.[14]

10. The taxpayer must satisfy certain substantiation requirements in order to obtain the deduction. The taxpayer must obtain a qualified appraisal, attach an appraisal summary to the tax return, and maintain proper records.[15]

39.4 HOW IT IS DONE

Mary Peshel inherited a ranch in the backcountry located next to a national park. The ranch had been in the family for forty years. At the time of her death, the ranch was worth $1,000,000, without regard to the easement, which she donated shortly prior to her death.

Mary had conveyed a qualifying easement worth $250,000 (25 percent of the property value) for use by the Friends of the Earth organization, reducing the net value of the property to $750,000. Friends of the Earth qualifies as a publicly supported charity under Code section 501(c)(3). Mary retained the right to operate the property only for ranching and farming. She gave up and retained no development rights.

Since only 25 percent of the value was conveyed, the 40 percent exclusion percentage is reduced by 2 percent for each 1 percent that the easement is below 30 percent of the value of the entire property. The reduction equals 10 percent [(30% − 25%) × 2%)]. This results in a 30 percent exclusion (40 percent less the 10 percent reduction), and the estate benefits from an estate tax exclusion of $225,000 (30 percent of $750,000). This is less than the $500,000 exclusion limit. Thus, Mary's estate can exclude $225,000 under section 2031(c).

39.5 TAX IMPLICATIONS

1. The decedent's gross estate is reduced by the qualified conservation easement exclusion.

2. The basis in the property subject to the qualified conservation easement exclusion is not stepped-up for income tax purposes with respect to the exclusion.

39.6 ISSUES IN COMMUNITY PROPERTY STATES

Where property is held as community property, both spouses must consent to the granting of the conservation easement. Also, each spouse will be entitled to an exclusion for a qualified conservation easement as to each spouse's respective one-half of the gift.

In the case of community property, a conservation easement is a legal agreement between both spouse/community property owners and a governmental body or land trust that restricts the type and amount of development and use that may take place on the property. The restriction is a "perpetual conservation restriction" granted in perpetuity on the use which may be made of real property—including, an easement

CONSERVATION EASEMENT EXCLUSION — CHAPTER 39

or other interest in real property that under state law has attributes similar to an easement (e.g., a restrictive covenant or equitable servitude). For these purposes, the terms easement, conservation restriction, and perpetual conservation restriction have the same meaning.[16]

39.7 FREQUENTLY ASKED QUESTIONS

Question – Does it matter when the easement was donated?

Answer – Generally, no. The exclusion election is available after the qualified easement donor's death. The amount of the exclusion is calculated based on the date of transfer of the easement (although an easement donated after death must be made within a certain period after death, see below).

Question – May a married couple both use the exclusion for separate transfers of easements in the same property?

Answer – Yes. The exclusion is applied to a decedent's gross estate, without regard to the individual property, so that a married couple may exclude up to $1 million for gifts of easements in one property.

Question – May an executor or trustee donate land subject to a qualified conservation easement and make a post-mortem election under Code section 2031(c), even though the decedent made no provision during his lifetime for such transfer?

Answer – Yes. Under Code section 2031(c)(8)(A)(iii), an executor or trustee may make the necessary election and donate the easement.

Question – May an executor or trustee take remedial action after the death of the decedent to qualify an easement under Code section 2031 that would not otherwise qualify for the exclusion?

Answer – Yes. section 2031(c)(8)(A)(iii) also presents an opportunity for the executor or trustee to correct defects that might prevent an easement that was transferred *inter vivos* from qualifying for the exclusion. Thus, to the extent that an easement is not qualified, an executor or trustee may donate an interest that will qualify for the exclusion, since an executor or trustee are considered qualified persons.

Question – Will the decedent's heirs receive a full stepped-up basis in land subject to a qualified conservation easement?

Answer – No. The portion of basis equal to that fraction of the value of the land represented by the qualified conservation easement receives a carryover basis.[17] For example, using the illustration provided in the preceding section, the exclusion allowed to Mary's estate represented 30 percent of the estate tax value of the ranch. Thus, 30 percent of the basis in the ranch would be carried over to Mary's heirs, and added to 70 percent of the fair market value at death (representing the step-up), to arrive at the adjusted basis. Figure 39.1 illustrates the steps necessary to calculate the heirs' basis in Mary's ranch, assuming that at Mary's death, the property had a basis of $100,000 and a fair market value of $750,000 after the gift of the easement.

Figure 39.1

1.	Gross Value of Ranch Prior to Easement	$1,000,000
2.	Fair Market Value of Ranch After Gift of Easement	$750,000
3.	Basis of Ranch at Mary's death	$100,000
4.	Value of Exclusion to Mary's Estate	$225,000
5.	Percentage of Gross Value Represented By Exclusion Amount (line 4 divided by line 2)	30%
6.	Carryover Basis (line 3 multiplied by line 5)	$30,000
7.	Stepped-Up Basis (line 2 multiplied by 70%)	$525,000
8.	TOTAL ADJUSTED BASIS (line 6 plus line 7)	$555,000

Thus, the conservation easement excluded from the gross estate does not receive a basis stepped-up to fair market value. However, even for estates in the lowest marginal estate tax bracket, the election should be beneficial, to the extent that the capital gains tax is lower than the estate tax rate.

Question – What type of development rights would disqualify an estate under section 2031(c), should they be retained?

Answer – Code section 2031(c)(5)(D) defines a development right as "any right to use the land subject to the qualified conservation easement in which such right is retained for any commercial purpose which is not subordinate to and directly supportive of the use of such land as a farm for farming purposes (within the meaning of section 2032A(e)(5))." Thus, a donor must carefully assess whether he will, even inadvertently, retain rights to the easement that may fall under this broad definition. Counsel should use caution in drafting easements until regulations and judicial decisions become available for guidance.

Question – Will an executor or trustee be able to save the exclusion, if the decedent (or any other party) retained development rights in the easement?

Answer – Yes. Code section 2031(c)(5)(B) provides that, if those persons with an interest in the land execute an agreement to extinguish some or all development rights on or before the filing date of the estate tax return, the exclusion shall be allowed to the extent that such rights were terminated. In addition, the I.R.C. allows a donor to provide flexibility to heirs, since such an agreement need not be implemented until the earlier of (a) two years after the decedent's death, or (b) the sale of the land. Thus, where commercial development may prove more profitable than the value to the estate of the exclusion, the donor may wish to retain commercial development rights when creating the easement. If the agreement is not implemented within the proscribed period, an additional tax will be due, equal to the tax saved by the exclusion.

Question – Will recreational use of a commercial nature on the easement prevent qualification for the exclusion?

Answer – Yes, if it is more than a *de minimis* use for a commercial recreational activity. Congressional intent in this area was to prevent the nominal preservation of land that would be used for large commercial enterprises, such as golf courses or ski resorts. Committee Reports indicate that it was also intended to provide exceptions to leased use for hunting and fishing. However, in the absence of regulations, a donor should carefully consider any type of commercial use before relying on qualification for the exclusion.

Question – Does land that is subject to indebtedness qualify for the exclusion?

Answer – No. To the extent that property is debt-financed, and such debt is acquisition indebtedness, as defined under Code section 2031(c)(4), the exclusion will not apply.

Question – Can someone who has made an election under Code section 2032A sell a conservation easement?

Answer – Code section 2032A permits certain shareholder to value their real estate at its special use value. This approach allows property to be valued as it is being used, as opposed to what its highest and best use might otherwise be (which is the typical standard). A typical example of this type of property might be a farm, where its value would be much higher if the land were to be developed as opposed to being operated as a farm. However, when a taxpayer claims this special use valuation approach, the property cannot be disposed of within ten years – without a tax penalty. Should a disposal within ten years occur, the tax savings under the special use valuation approach are recaptured. If the heir wants to make an election under both section 2032A and implement a conservation easement, than the easement must be contributed (and not sold) to the charitable entity.[18]

Question – Can a conservation easement be extinguished after it is granted?

Answer – Generally no. The Regulations provide a limited opportunity to terminate the easement if "a subsequent unexpected change in the conditions surrounding the property . . . make it impossible or impractical for the continued use of the property for conservation purposes, the conservation purpose can nonetheless be treated as protected in perpetuity if the restrictions are extinguished by judicial proceeding and all of the donee's proceeds (determined under paragraph (g)(6)(ii) of this section) from a subsequent sale or exchange of the property are used by the donee organization in a manner consistent with the conservation purposes of the original contribution."[19] In one case, the court denied the deduction where the easement could be extinguished through the mutual consent of the parties.[20]

Question – Can a conservation easement be granted on a property subject to a mortgage?

Answer – Only if the mortgage is subordinate to the conservation easement. Generally, in order to obtain the deduction, the donation must be in perpetuity. If the underlying property is subject to a mortgage, a question can arise as to whether the donation is in perpetuity. The Regulations provide that the mortgage will be permitted so long as the mortgage is subordinate to the contribution.[21]

CHAPTER ENDNOTES

1. Treas. Reg. §1.170A-14 became applicable on May 1, 2009. These Regulations address how a taxpayer can obtain a deduction for a "qualified conservation contribution."
2. 2012 Tax Relief Act, §101.
3. I.R.C. §2031(c)(8)(A)(ii).
4. I.R.C. §2031(c)(8)(B).
5. I.R.C. §170(h)(3); Treas. Reg. §1.170A-14(c).
6. Treas. Reg. §1.170A-14(c)(1).
7. I.R.C. §170(h)(2); Treas. Reg. §1.170A-14(b).
8. *Kayln M. Carpenter, et al. v. Comm'r.*, TC Memo 2012-1 (01/3/2012).
9. I.R.C. §170(h)(4); Treas. Reg. §1.170A-14(d).
10. I.R.C. §2031(c)(8)(B).
11. I.R.C. §170(h)(5)(A); Treas. Reg. §1.170A-14(e).
12. I.R.C. §2031(c)(5); Treas. Reg. §1.170A-14(g).
13. I.R.C. §2031(c)(2).
14. I.R.C. §2031(c)(6).
15. Treas. Reg. §1.170A-14(i), which cross references to the substantiation requirements of Treas. Reg. §1.170A-13(c). See also, *E, B. DiDonato, et ux. V. Comm'r.*, TC Memo 2011-153 (06/29/2011) where the deduction was denied for failing to obtain a contemporaneous written acknowledgement under Treas. Reg. §1.150A-13(f)(2).
16. Treas. Reg. §1.170A-14(b)(2).
17. I.R.C. §1014(a)(4).
18. PLR 200840018.
19. Treas. Reg. §1.170A-14(g)(6).
20. *Kayln M. Carpenter, et al. v. Comm'r.*, TC Memo 2012-1 (01/3/2012).
21. Treas. Reg. §1.170A-14(g)(3). See also *Ramona L. Mitchell v. Comm'r.*, 138 T.C. No. 16 (04/3/2012) in which the deduction was denied where the mortgage was not subordinate to the easement at the time easement was granted.

INTRA-FAMILY LOANS

CHAPTER 40

40.1 INTRODUCTION

On a superficial level, an intra-family loan is simply a loan among family members. The usefulness of the technique becomes apparent as it is applied in different situations. First, where an asset is sold from one family member to another and the seller lends the buyer the money to pay the purchase price over a period of time. Second, it can come into play where money is simply loaned to another family member for whatever reason. From the lender's perspective, it essentially "freezes" the value of the asset, because all the lender can gain after the loan is made is the return of the principal plus a fixed rate of interest. In either situation, what is included within the lender's estate is the (sometimes discounted) value of the note. Any appreciation in the value of the asset which is sold, or the investment which is made with the loan proceeds, takes place outside the seller's estate. Therefore, the seller's value is "frozen" to its value at the time of the transaction and the growth in the asset occurs in the family-member buyer's hands.

Another benefit of this structure is that the payment of interest can result in income tax shifting among the family. This occurs if the loan is structured with a trust which allows the income to be spread among (and taxed to) a group of family members in lower tax brackets. If the note is with a so-called "defective grantor trust," the seller will be taxed on both the interest expense and the interest income. In these situations, the payment of the interest will be a neutral event to the seller, subject to any limitations on the seller's ability to claim the interest expense as a deduction. In essence, the seller is making a gift free of the tax he/she pays to the other family members involved in the transaction.

40.2 WHEN IS USE OF SUCH A DEVICE INDICATED?

One of the primary benefits of using this wealth-shifting technique is to allow the seller to remove an appreciating asset from the estate. In these situations, the seller can sell the asset to the seller's child, or a trust for the child's benefit. Ideally, the asset would be income producing so that the purchaser (i.e. the trust or the child) will be able to fund the payments to the seller with the income produced by the asset. This technique can also be used to transfer an interest in a business. Another benefit to the seller in retaining a promissory note is that this arrangement permits the seller with the ability to indirectly tap into the equity of an asset with the receipt of principal and/or interest payments. These payments will provide a cash flow stream to the seller, who may use these funds as a part of retirement income.

A loan can also be useful if the younger generation is going to make an investment which will likely produce a greater rate of return than the interest rate which the seller or lender must charge the borrower under IRS guidelines (i.e. Applicable Federal Rate, or AFR). Therefore, if the family were to pursue a new venture or investment, it may be advisable to lend the money to the younger generation so that they can make the investment and it can grow in their hands rather than in the senior member's estate.

Another way the device can be helpful is if the lender wants to provide the funds to the borrower; but does not want to make this a gift. By charging the AFR with respect to such loan, there is no gift liability to the lender. It can also be used if the lender wants to equalize distributions among the family.

For example, assume a father has two children and wants to treat them equally. One child wants $100,000 to purchase a house. If the father gifts the money to that child, the estate is reduced by the amount of the gift. Then, if the father dies and this reduced estate is divided equally, one child will have received more than the other. However, if the funds had been a loan rather than a gift, the father's estate is reduced by the loan. Therefore, the estate can still be distributed equally between the children, because the father's loan receivable from the one child would be attributable and credited to that child's share of the estate.

40.3 WHAT ARE THE REQUIREMENTS?

Since the parties are attempting to establish a bona fide lender – borrower relationship, it is essential to adhere to and document compliance with the formalities of this arrangement. The Tax Court has reviewed this issue and provided guidance as to how to determine if the loan is bona fide. Courts have noted that a key characteristic of a loan is the intention of the parties that the debt be repaid. In making this determination, there are certain relevant factors to help determine if this test is satisfied. The factors are non-exclusive, and no one is determinative of the issue. These factors are an indicia of a bona fide loan upon which the courts may analyze the transaction.[1]

1. *Whether the promise to repay was evidenced by a note or other instrument.* Applicable state law may not require that the debt be in writing in order for it to be enforceable. If the terms of the obligation can be established through other means, a court may still enforce the obligation. However, that is in third party enforcement cases. When trying to establish a transaction for tax purposes, it is important to have the appropriate written documents. This is especially true with intra-family transactions. These transactions receive additional scrutiny. The presumption is that the transfer between family members is a gift. However, this presumption may be rebutted by an affirmative showing that there was a real expectation of repayment and an intention to enforce the debt.[2] This is why it is some important to document the understanding.

2. *Whether interest was charged.* In a typical arms-length loan transaction, a lender would charge interest. Otherwise, if the loan is between family members, the lack of adequate interest is treated as a gift from the lender to the borrower.[3] The question then becomes, "What is the appropriate rate of interest?" The interest rate must be no lower than the Applicable Federal Rate (AFR) for the month in which the loan was entered into. The AFR rate to be applied is based upon the term of the loan. The short term rate applies to a loan of up to three years. For loans with a term of three years to nine years, the mid-term rate applies. The long term rate applies for loans with terms of more than nine years. The AFR as adjusted is issued monthly by the IRS in a Revenue Ruling, and a history of all three AFRs since 1998 is available for free at https://leimberg.com/Free-Resources/Key-Rates-Valuation.3. *Whether a fixed schedule for repayment was established.* In a bona fide loan transaction, there will be a schedule of payments which will be honored. It is important to follow the formalities of the transaction and make the payments when due. The failure to enforce a default by the borrower would be relevant in determining that it was not a real loan.

4. *Whether collateral was given to secure payment.* Again, in a typical arm's length transaction there would be collateral for a loan. To the extent that this collateral is against real estate, then a mortgage should be executed and recorded. For non-real estate related loans, it would be appropriate to have guarantees or other assets pledged to secure the arrangement. However, if other assets are pledged as collateral, it is important to respect the security interest associated with the assets being pledge. Therefore, these same assets should not be pledged for a different loan particularly one having a priority in terms of its security interest.

5. *Whether repayments were made.* While many times the loans are structured to be interest only with a balloon payment some years in the future, the loan may have more credibility if the loan payments include the amortization of principal plus interest. Because most arm's length loans are structured this way, it will help establish the legitimacy of the lender – borrower relationship.[4]

Sometimes, an intra-family loan is not structured as being between individual family members; it is instead between a family member(s) and a trust for the benefit of other family members. If the borrower of the funds is a trust, it is important that the trust have its own assets other than the loan proceeds. If there were no assets in the trust, the IRS may view the loan as illusory. Some commentators have suggested funding the trust with assets (as a separate gift) worth at least 10 percent of the value of the loan, but there is no real basis for this rule of thumb, which is mre myth than reality.[5] This initial funding will constitute a gift and utilize a portion of the transferor's lifetime applicable exclusion amount ($12,920,000 per person in 2023).

If the parties do not want to fund the trust with a gift, a beneficiary may be able to avoid a gift by the donor by providing a personal guaranty with respect to the loan, but there is no authority confirming that this will avoid a gift under the *Dickman* indirect gift principle that the United States Supreme Court enunciated therein. In fact, using the AFR does nothing but prevent application of the Balkan reconfiguration of principal into interest provisions set forth in Code sections 1274 and 7872, with potentially both income and gift tax consequences. Specifically, use of the AFR does not preclude the IRS from asserting an indirect gift, based on the difference between the interest rate actually charged, i.e., the AFR, and the interest rate that an unrelated third-party lender would charge the debtor, based on the debtor's creditworthiness, etc., but this would be a difficult case for the IRS as it would necessitate valuation evidence that the IRS would have to present qualified appraisal evidence.

40.4 HOW IT IS DONE

If the transaction involves a sale, the initial step would be to determine the asset to be sold. Ideally, it would be an asset with a good chance of appreciating. By selling the asset, all future appreciation of the asset would by-pass the seller's estate. It is also important to make sure that the arrangement will be followed. Therefore, the terms of the note should be structured so that there will be no problem in following its provisions.

Example. Bob wants to sell to his daughter, Mary, a condominium which Bob has been renting out. The tenant pays $600 per month and the property has been appraised for $100,000. If Bob sells it to Mary pursuant to a fifteen-year note charging interest at the rate of 4 percent, the monthly payments will be $739.68. If the note is for thirty years, the payments decrease to $477.42. Therefore, since the rent is $600 per month, in order for Mary to generate the cash flow necessary to service the note, the loan term must be longer than fifteen years.

Importantly, the foregoing example only considered the mortgage payment. The other property operating expenses including the condominium fee, utilities, taxes, and an allowance for maintenance should also be considered. Finally, any income tax associated with the rental is another cash flow factor.

Therefore, if cash flow is an issue, it may be necessary to charge interest below the applicable AFR resulting in a gift. This will assure that Mary, in our example, has a reasonable prospect of having the ability to service the loan and that the rental is profitable to her.

40.5 TAX IMPLICATIONS

The tax implications are broken into two parts: first, the payment of interest; and second, the payment of principal. As indicated above, the minimum interest rate which must be charged is based upon the AFR. Generally, if the interest charged is below the applicable AFR, the foregone interest is treated as a gift to the borrower who is deemed to pay that amount to the lender as interest. As a result of that deemed payment of interest, the lender must include that amount as interest income and the borrower may be entitled to an interest deduction (depending whether interest paid on such a loan, i.e., a business loan, would be deductible).[6] There are certain exceptions to this minimum interest requirement that relate to certain loans under $100,000 and $10,000. See Chapter 43.

However, if the grantor (lender) loans the funds to a grantor trust, the grantor and the trust are treated as the same taxpayer. Therefore, the grantor is treated as both paying and receiving the interest. As a result, there are no income tax consequences (i.e., interest income to be claimed or an interest deduction) to either the grantor or the trust.

With respect to the repayment of principal, the tax consequences to the seller/lender will somewhat depend. There are not income tax consequences to the lender because repayment of principal is simply a return of capital. On the other hand, if there is an installment sale of an asset involved, like any installment sale, there may be capital gains tax associated with these payments. Installment sale treatment permits the seller to recognize the capital gains as the payments are received.[7] Significantly, if the seller dies prior to end of the installment sale term, the remaining deferred gain is considered to be IRD. Therefore, to assure that that gain is recognized by the ultimate recipient of the remaining installment sale payments, there is no step up in basis.[8]

However, while the value of the note will have to be included within the estate, the value may not be equal to the face value of the note. Depending upon the terms of the note and credit worthiness of the borrower, it may be possible to have the note be valued at less than its face value. It is important to have a qualified appraiser determine the appropriate level at which to value the note.

40.6 ESTATE PLANNING LAWYER CAUTIONARY TALE

Too often, estate planners do not fully appreciate the professional risks attendant to recommending and implementing estate planning techniques like intra-family loans and/or installment sales. Unfortunately, the lawyers for the oldest generation lenders/sellers simply paper these non-gift transactions, in the form of promissory notes, loan and security/pledge agreements, and sales agreements without negotiation or even discussion of the salient terms with those who are borrowing or buying. In fact, the lawyer for the creditor/lender too often does not clarify in writing that the lawyer for the seller/lender does not represent the buyer/borrower.

Credit documents, e.g., promissory notes, loan/pledge/security agreements, etc., come in gradations of creditor v. debtor-friendly terms on a continuum from creditor bullet-proof to even-handed documents that opt toward exhaustion of extrajudicial ADR techniques before pursuit of litigation.[9]

40.7 FREQUENTLY ASKED QUESTIONS

Question – Can the terms of the note be changed after it is established?

Answer – Yes, the terms of the note can be changed. However, there are certain tax issues which should be considered. From an income tax perspective, a modification of a note can be treated as a disposition under Treasury Regulations section 1.1001-3. Under this Regulation, a significant modification is treated as a sale and exchange of the two instruments. With respect to changes in the interest rate, section 1.1001-3(e)(2) provides that if the yield changes more than the greater of: 0.25 percent (25 basis points); or 5 percent of the annual yield of the unmodified instrument (.05 x annual yield).

From a gifting perspective, if the old interest rate and the new interest rate are both within the AFR, then there should not be any gift tax consequences. However, if the debtor was not credit worthy, it would not make sense to reduce the interest rate. Therefore, the facts and circumstances may indicate whether or not the modification resulted in a gift.[10]

Question – Can a promise to make a gift be considered to be a completed gift?

Answer – Toward the end of 2012, there was a lot of concern that the estate tax exemption would be reduced to $1,000,000. One planning idea was based upon the thought of permitting a client to make use of their estate tax exemption without relinquishing the assets. In this context, a planning concept arose whereby an individual could make a legally binding *promise* to pay pursuant to a promissory note. Assuming the note was legally enforceable under state law, the thought was that this possibly constituted a completed gift.[11]

CHAPTER ENDNOTES

1. *See, e.g., Welch v. Comm'r*, 204 F.3d 1228, 1230 (9th Cir. 2000); *Kaider*, 102 T.C.M. (CCH) 77, 2011 WL 2976203, at *5.
2. *Elizabeth B. Miller et vir v. Comm'r.*, TC Memo 1996-3 (01/11/1996).
3. I.R.C. §7872(a)(1).
4. These requirements are set forth in *Frederick D. Todd, II, et ux. v. Comm'r.*, TC Memo 2011-123 (06/06/2011); however, very similar requirements are also set forth in *Elizabeth B. Miller et vir v. Comm'r.*, supra. See also Howard M. Zaritsky, "Tax Court Reviews What Constitutes a Real Loan," *Estate Planning Journal*, Vol. 38, No. 09 (September, 2011).
5. Martin M. Shenkman, "Role of Guarantees and Seed Gifts in Family Installment Sales," *Estate Planning Journal*, Vol. 37, No. 11 (November, 2010). The article discusses providing adequate

capitalization for the trust and the extent to which it is necessary to have guarantees from the beneficiaries to support the obligations.

6. I.R.C. §7872(a)(1).

7. Importantly, not all sale transactions qualify for installment sale treatment. For example, installment sale treatment does not apply to dealer disposition (I.R.C. §453(b)(2)), sales of inventories of personal property (I.R.C. §453(b)(2)), sales of depreciable property to related persons (I.R.C. §453(g)), depreciation recapture (I.R.C. §453(i)), and the sale of marketable securities (I.R.C. §453(k)(2)).

8. I.R.C. §1014(c).

9. For an article about a recent case that raises these issues, see, L. Paul Hood, Jr., "Paul Hood on *Yost v. Carroll*: Fun & Frivolity In The Northern District Of Illinois - Caution At The Intersection Of Estate Planning Intra-Family "Sales/Loans" And Divorce," *Steve Leimberg's Estate Planning Email Newsletter - Archive Message No. 3052*.

10. M. Read Moore and Lauren A. Geoffrey, "Planning for Lifetime Wealth Transfers in an Era of Lost Value – Part 2, *Estate Planning Journal*, Vol. 37, No. 2 (February 2010).

11. LISI (Leimberg Information Services, Inc.), *Estate Planning Newsletters* Nos. 2034; 2001; 2022; and 2033.

INSTALLMENT SALES AND SCINS

CHAPTER 41

41.1 INTRODUCTION

As its name implies, an installment sale is one where property is sold in return for at least two payments, rather than a lump sum, and at least one payment is made in the taxable year after the sale. The installment sale is a device for spreading out the taxable gain and thereby deferring the income tax on gain from the sale of property. The Self-Cancelling Installment Note (SCIN), is a variation of the installment sale. Specifically, it begins as an installment sale (i.e. the purchase of property in return for payments over more than one tax year) but ends upon the earlier of the expiration of the agreed-upon term or the death of the seller – no matter when that occurs. Therefore, a SCIN is a hybrid between an installment sale and a private annuity (see Chapter 42). It is not a statutory device, and its taxation is covered by interpretation of statutes by the courts, the IRS and taxpayers. When it is used, the note contains a provision under which the balance of any payments due at the date of the seller's death are automatically canceled, with language such as the following:

> "Unless sooner paid, all sums due hereunder, whether principal or interest, shall be deemed canceled and extinguished as though paid upon the death of (Seller)."

The term of the SCIN must be less than the life expectancy (actual) of the seller; otherwise, it will be taxed as a private annuity.

41.2 WHEN IS USE OF SUCH A DEVICE INDICATED?

1. An installment sale is indicated when a taxpayer wants to sell property to another individual who may not have enough capital to purchase the property outright. The installment sale provides a way, for example, for employees with minimal capital to buy out a business owner who, in return for allowing a long-term payout, may receive a higher price for his business. This device is often used to create a market for a business where none previously existed.

2. An installment sale is indicated where an individual in a high income tax bracket holds substantially appreciated real estate or securities (other than marketable securities). So rather than report the entire amount of the gain in the year of sale, all or a portion of the tax on a sale of such property can be spread over the period of installments spanning multiple tax years.[1] Thus, the seller may be able to shift most of the profit from a high income (high tax) year to a year or years in which he or she is in a lower bracket.

3. The installment sale permits more flexibility than the private annuity, an alternative. The agreement can be made to begin or end whenever the parties involved desire. This eliminates the need to follow a rigid schedule of payments such as is found in a private annuity.

4. An installment sale can be an effective estate freezing device where the sale is between family members and involves rapidly appreciating closely held stock, real estate, or other assets. Used in this manner, the installment sale may serve to freeze the size of the seller's estate subsequent to the sale and thus stabilize the value of the seller's estate for federal estate tax purposes and shift future appreciation to a younger generation. An installment sale to a grandchild at full fair market value, for example, will avoid the generation-skipping transfer tax.

5. A SCIN is appropriate in instances where the seller desires to retain a payment stream that will not continue beyond his or her death and may end at an earlier date. Unlike a private annuity, the SCIN allows the buyer to depreciate assets based on the purchase price paid and to deduct the portion of payments attributable to the interest on the note.

6. A SCIN is appropriate where the tax benefits attributable to excluding the unpaid principal from a taxable estate exceed the income tax cost that results from the buyer paying a premium for the cancellation at death feature.

41.3 WHAT ARE THE REQUIREMENTS?

1. A seller of property can defer as much or as little as desired using an installment sale and payments can be set to fit the seller's business or financial needs. The amount of payment received in the year of the sale is irrelevant. A sale for $1,000,000 can qualify even if $500,000 is paid in the year of the sale and the remaining $500,000 (plus interest on the unpaid balance) is paid over the next five years.

   Conversely, since a SCIN is a hybrid between an installment sale and private annuity, its requirements are still being determined. The IRS has stated its position as to when it will accept a SCIN.[2] Of importance is the requirement that the term of a SCIN not extend beyond the seller's life expectancy.

2. No payment has to be made in the year of the sale. The only requirement is that at least one payment must be made in a taxable year *after* the year of sale.[3] This means the owner of property can contract to have payments made at the time when it is most advantageous or least disadvantageous. For example, the parties could agree that the entire purchase price for payment of a $1,000,000 parcel of land will be paid five years after the sale.

3. No minimum sale price is required.

4. Installment sale treatment is automatic unless the taxpayer elects *not* to have installment treatment apply.[4] A SCIN is treated as a private annuity if the term extends beyond the seller's life expectancy.

5. A sale can be made on an installment basis even though the selling price is contingent.[5]

6. Installment reporting is not available for sales of marketable securities.[6]

Example 1. An individual would like to sell appreciated property she now owns. Her accountant has explained that a high tax on the inherent gain in the property could consume a substantial portion of her profit. If she receives all of the sale proceeds in the year of sale, the result is that her entire profit will be taxed in one year. So she would like to find a way to reduce or minimize the impact of taxes, or defer those taxes.

The installment sale is a possible solution to that problem. By taking advantage of the installment sale provisions of the Internal Revenue Code, she may be able to save a great deal of overall tax.[7] Under an installment sale, the title to the property passes immediately from the seller to the buyer. But the distinguishing feature of an installment sale is that the seller does *not* receive a lump sum payment outright. Instead, the seller typically receives the sale price in installments spread out over two or more tax years (although a lump sum payment in a later year will qualify for installment reporting).

Example 2. If Mrs. Murphy sold land that cost her $500,000 and received $1,000,000, she would have a $500,000 gain reportable all in the year of the sale. But if she sells it for $1,000,000 and agrees to accept $100,000 a year for ten years (plus appropriate interest on the unpaid balance), she will not have to report the $500,000 gain in the year of the sale. Instead, since her ratio of gross profit ($500,000) to contract price ($1,000,000) is 50 percent, she will report $50,000, 50 percent of each $100,000 payment she receives, as capital gain. (Interest has been ignored here for simplicity.) This approach will allow Mrs. Murphy to spread the payment of the tax over number of years during which she is receiving payments.

To compute the installment payment by a hand held financial calculator or computer program such as NumberCruncher, make the following entries:

(1) Interest rate (for semiannual divide annual rate by two);

(2) Number of periods (for semiannual multiply years by two); and

(3) Amount to be repaid.

The result will be the annual (or other payment period) payment necessary. For example, to compute the semiannual payment where property worth $100,000 is sold over a ten-year period and the interest rate is 9 percent, input 4.5 (the annual interest rate divided by two) and press the i (interest) button; input 20 (two payments a year for ten years) and press the N (number of periods) button; and input the present value of the loan, $100,000, and press the PV (present value) button. Then press PMT to compute the $7,687.61 outlay.

The rule used to compute the annual gain above is:

Income is realized on each annual payment received in the same proportion that the gross profit (selling price less seller's adjusted basis) bears to the total contract price (amount to be received by the seller).

If the sale results in a loss, the installment method may not be used. The loss deduction must be taken in the tax year of the sale.[8] More technically, for income tax purposes, there are parts to each installment payment:

1. a return of basis;
2. the gain portion; and
3. interest income.

The taxpayer must report that part of the payment that represents the gain on the sale and the interest income.

Interest is segregated from principal payments and taxed as ordinary income. The profit percentage (basically the gain, or difference between the sale price and adjusted basis, expressed as a percentage of the total contract price, exclusive of interest) is applied to each installment payment of principal in order to determine the amount of each payment that is gain. The balance is considered a tax-free return of the seller's basis. (See Figure 41.1.)

What if the agreement does not specify an interest rate or the stated interest rate is inadequate? This often occurs in intra-family transactions. These types of sales will be taxed according to what is known as the "unstated interest" rule. Under this rule, the IRS impute interests an interest element to the transaction (a legal fiction in which all the parties to the transaction are treated as if interest was paid at a statutory rate, compounded semiannually) unless the stated principal amount is at least equal to the present value of the principal and interest payments based on an AFR test rate of interest. In other words, the unstated interest rule ensures that a portion of the deferred payments will include adequate interest with respect to the buyer and the seller. For all tax purposes, from the buyer's perspective the imputed interest part of a payment does

Figure 41.1

TAXATION OF SELLER UNDER INSTALLMENT SALE	
A. Recovery of basis (cost element)	Tax free
B. Gain element	Capital gain or ordinary income
C. Interest income	Ordinary income

Computing Tax Free, Gain, and Interest Elements of an Installment Payment		
STEP 1	Segregate interest from payment principal	
STEP 2	Compute portion of principal payment which is gain	$\dfrac{\text{Total gain}}{\text{Sales price}} \times$ principal payment
STEP 3	Compute portion of principal payment which is a return of capital	Principal payment − gain (Step 2)

not increase his or her basis in the property received; however, it is potentially deductible as interest. From the seller's perspective, the imputed interest part of the payment is taxed as ordinary income rather than capital gain. For additional details, see Chapter 43.

For SCINs, a premium is required to reflect the possibility that the seller will die during the term of the SCIN. Because the unpaid principal is forgiven upon an early death, the present value of expected payments will be less than the purchase price unless an adjustment is made. The adjustment is made by increasing the payments under the SCIN so that the actuarial present value of payments equals the purchase price.

There may be some flexibility to increase SCIN payments by either raising the interest rate or principal due on the rate. If the interest rate is increased, the buyer may take greater interest expense deductions. If the principal is increased, the buyer will have a higher basis for taking depreciation deductions.

The following rules should be considered: Interest will not be deductible if it is considered personal. To make this determination, the buyer's use of the property is relevant. Generally, this means there is no interest deduction unless the debt was properly allocable to:

1. Investment purposes (if the property or stock to be purchased is investment property, the interest deduction will generally be allowed, but only to the extent of the buyer's investment income);

2. The conduct of a trade or business (other than the trade or business of performing services as an employee), in which case the interest would be deductible without limit;

3. Part of the computation of income or loss from a passive investment activity;

4. Estate or generation-skipping transfer taxes in installments under Code sections 6166 or 6161 (there is no limit on the amount of interest deduction in this case, but no deductions are allowed for interest paid in installments under section 6166 for decedents dying after 1997); or

5. A debt secured by property that at the time the interest is paid or accrued is a qualified residence (this is called qualified residence interest and is generally deductible only if the residence in question is the taxpayer's principal residence or a second residence). This deduction is limited to interest on a maximum of $1,000,000 of acquisition indebtedness and up to $100,000 of home equity indebtedness.

Imputed interest is considered only for purposes of the income tax; it does not directly affect the terms of the sale. The imputed interest rules are extremely difficult and will not be discussed at length. The following rules of thumb should be helpful in planning the interest rates that should be built into an installment sale:

1. There will be no imputed interest problem unless the installment sale contract if the stated principal amount is at least equal to the sum of the present values of all principal and interest payments due under the contract. The present value is determined under the test rate of interest, i.e., the AFR.

2. To determine the present value of principal and interest payments due under an installment contract of land between family members to the extent the sales price does not exceed $500,000, the test rate is the lesser of 6 percent, compounded semiannually, or the AFR in effect on the date of the sale.[9] On the other hand, if sales price of exceeds $500,000 the AFR is used as the test rate.

3. If an installment note is $6,734,800 or less (in 2023 and for a cash method debt instrument),[10] the minimum interest rate that can be charged is the lower of 9 percent, compounded semiannually (as adjusted for inflation) or the AFR. If the installment note exceeds that amount, the minimum interest rate is the AFR. The selling price under which either rate applies is adjusted annually for inflation.[11]

41.4 TAX IMPLICATIONS OF THE INSTALLMENT SALE

1. Many of the income tax ramifications have been mentioned above. Note also that depreciation recapture as well as any investment tax credit recapture is reportable in full in the year of the sale, even if no proceeds from the sale are received in that year.

Stock or securities that are traded on an established securities market do not qualify for installment treatment; all payments to be received are treated as received in the year of disposition.

In addition, installment treatment is generally not allowed for sales of depreciable property to a controlled entity, such as a more than 50 percent owned partnership or corporation, or trust benefiting the seller or the seller's spouse. All payments to be received are treated as received in the year of disposition.

2. An installment sale will remove the property in question from the transferor-seller's estate, but the fair market value of the note is included in the seller's estate at death. The fair market value is sometimes determined by calculating the present value of any installments due at the seller's death.[12] For instance, if at the date the seller died ten annual payments remained on an installment sale, and each payment (made at the end of the year) to the estate or its heirs were $12,000, using a 5.0 percent AFR, $92,660, the present valve of the ten-year stream of payments remaining would be includable in the seller's gross estate ($12,000 × 7.7217 term certain annuity factor for 5 percent and ten years). In family situations, the remaining principal balance on the note is often presumed the fair market value unless interest rates or the solvency of the payor have changed dramatically. However, the installment sale is still a valuable estate planning tool since it removes the future appreciation on the property from the transferor-seller's estate without any gift tax implications. For instance, at a 10 percent growth rate, property worth $500,000 when sold in exchange for ten annual payments would be worth $1,296,871 when the payout was complete.

Additionally, a great deal of the cash proceeds of the sale may be removed from the seller's estate, gift tax free, by maximizing the use of the gift tax annual exclusion. After receiving payments, the seller could then give back – at his or her whim – all or a portion of the amounts paid.

3. For federal gift tax purposes, there is a split of authority in the courts as to whether the interest rate charged on the family installment sale must be equal to the prevailing market rate, the applicable federal rate, the special rates applicable to sales of farm land under $500,000, or the 9 percent rate specified in the case of sales under $6,734,800 (in 2023 for a cash method debt instrument) that are charged for *income* tax purposes. (See the related discussion in Chapter 40.) The Tax Court has held in two separate cases that if a rate lower than the prevailing market rate is used, there will be a taxable gift measured by the difference between the fair market value of the property sold and the discounted present value of the installment note that is based on the lower interest rate used for sales of land (6 percent).[13] However, in one of these cases on appeal, the Court of Appeals for the Seventh Circuit reversed the Tax Court decision and held that the use of rates specified for income tax purposes would also control for gift tax purposes.[14] Conversely, in the other case on appeal, the Court of Appeals for the Eighth Circuit sustained the Tax Court's position on the issue and held that the income tax rate does not control for gift tax purposes.[15] The Supreme Court has refused to review the Eighth Circuit Court's decision.

It should be noted that the sales in both of the above cases arose before the adoption of applicable federal rates of interest, and it would seem that these federal rates should eliminate the gift tax problem. However, the law is unclear on what would happen if the federal rates were lower than prevailing market rates. Anecdotal evidence however is that the AFR will control for estate and gift tax purposes as well.

4. If the seller should die, the unrecognized gain with respect to the remaining payments are income in respect of a decedent. (See the Frequently Asked Questions, below.) As a result, the estate, or other testamentary beneficiary of the installments due would report the gain on such payments in the same way that the decedent would have reported them had he or she lived to receive them.[16] In other words, the allocation of the payments (return of basis, gain, or interest) is not affected by reporting on the installment basis.

Although there is no step-up in basis at death with respect to the unpaid notes; however, the testamentary beneficiary of the installment payments would be entitled to an income tax deduction in the amount of estate tax attributable to the installment sale balance that was subject to estate tax.[17]

5. Importantly, even though the payment of the full amount of the purchase price is spread out over the term of the installment agreement, the transferee-buyer's income tax basis in the property is its fair market value at the date of the sale (i.e., the

purchase price).[18] Thus, as of the date that the property is acquired, the buyer's basis is the purchase price.

By virtue of the fair market value basis in the acquired property (subject to the second disposition rules discussed in the next section), a lower bracket family member purchasing the property from another family member would likely be able to re-sell the property and reinvest the sale proceeds in more liquid or higher yielding assets and pay much less in tax on the sale than the transferor-seller would otherwise have owed.

An increased basis is of particular advantage in the case of high value, low basis property such as highly appreciated real estate. For example, if the transferor-seller bought undeveloped, non-income-producing land ten years ago for $10,000 and it is now worth $100,000, he could sell it to his son for its $100,000 fair market value. After holding the land for at least two years (see below), the son could then sell it and purchase mutual funds or other income-producing securities with the proceeds of the sale. If the son received $105,000 for the land, his gain would be only the difference between his $100,000 cost and the amount realized on the sale, $105,000 (i.e., his total gain would be $5,000). He does not have to pay tax on the $90,000 gain his father would have been subject to had he sold the land for cash. The advantage is compounded if the son is in a lower tax bracket than his father. Father's estate is also reduced by the amount of the capital gains tax he eventually pays with respect to the amounts paid to him by his son. The overall tax savings is even more dramatic if the father is in a relatively high income tax bracket at the time of the sale, but is about to retire. Since the father may be in a lower tax bracket after retirement, he would owe less tax on his profit.

6. Special rules apply to installment sales to related parties. For example, second dispositions (re-sales) by a related party purchaser to a third party within two years of the installment sale trigger recognition of the entire remaining deferred gain *by the initial seller*.

7. Generally, interest paid by the purchaser on the unpaid balance will be deductible in full only if the property is either investment property, business related property or a qualified or qualified principal residence interest.

Special Rules for Disposition of Property between Related Parties

Technically, there are three related party rules: one applicable to second dispositions of installment sale property by a purchaser related to the original seller; a second that applies only to installment sales of depreciable property between "closely related" entities; and a third applicable to forgiveness or cancellation of installment debt between related parties. The term "related party" for purposes of these rules, includes brothers and sisters, spouses, ancestors, and lineal descendants, as well as many other related entities.[19]

Second disposition rule: The rule for second dispositions of installment sale property is as follows: If a related party (defined below) disposes of the property purchased in an installment sale (in other words if a second disposition occurs) within two years of the date of the installment sale before the initial seller (the person who made the first disposition) has received all the payments he or she is due under the installment sale, then to the extent of the remaining principal balance of the original installment note(s), the amount realized on the second disposition is treated as received and includible in gross income of the initial seller.[20] This rule only applies, however, to the extent that the related party receives more in the second disposition than the initial seller has received. For example, if a mother sells appreciated land to her daughter (to be paid in installments with no down payment), and the daughter immediately resells the land, the mother must report the entire gain even though she has not received any payments under the installment agreement.

The following is a more detailed example of the application of the second disposition rules:

Assume Herb Cheezman bought land for $500,000 and sold it to his son Stephen for $600,000. Assume payment in installments of $60,000 a year for ten years. (For simplicity, interest is ignored.) In the second year Stephen sells the land to a third party for $1,000,000.

Herb, the person making the first disposition (Herb) is treated as having received the *lesser of*:

INSTALLMENT SALES AND SCINS　　　　　　　　　　　　　　CHAPTER 41

(A) (1) the total amount realized with respect to the second disposition prior the close of the tax year, ($1,000,000)
or
(2) the total contract price for the first disposition (in our example, $600,000)
exceeds the total of
(B) (1) the sum of payments actually received with respect to the first disposition (Herb received $60,000 × 2 years, or $120,000)
Plus
(2) the aggregate sum treated (under the related party – second disposition rules) as received with respect to the first disposition for prior taxable years (here $0)
So, in this example, Herb would be deemed to have received $480,000 ($600,000 minus $120,000)

So Herb would recognize the remaining $80,000 of gain ($480,000 minus $400,000, Herb's remaining unrecovered basis). Additionally, Stephen would recognize $400,000 of gain with respect to the second disposition ($1,000,000 (amount realized) minus $600,000 (Stephen's cost basis)).

Finally, since Herb's entire gain was triggered by the second disposition, the remaining installment payments he receives from Stephen will be tax-free.

There are limited exceptions to the second disposition rule. If the second disposition occurs more than two years after the date of the first sale, the rule will not apply (unless the sale was of stock or securities).[21] So, if Stephen waited two years and one month before he sold the land, Herb would not recognize any gain as a result of Stephen's disposition. This rule also will not apply if the second disposition results from the death of either party or from an involuntary conversion. Regardless of Herb's recognition or non-recognition of the gain from the original sale, Stephen would nonetheless report the $400,000 gain with respect to the second deposition.

Rule for sales of depreciable property: A sale of depreciable property between related entities may not be reported on the installment method, unless it can be shown that avoidance of income tax was not a principal purpose.[22] This rule, unlike the other two related party rules, applies only to related entities, such as a corporation and an individual who owns more than 50 percent of its outstanding stock.

In addition to this rule, there is a special rule for *all* installment sales of depreciable property, regardless of whether the buyer and seller are related. Generally, that rule (described below) requires recapture (all in the year of sale) of certain depreciation deductions claimed by the seller.

Rule for cancellation of debt: If an installment sale between related parties is canceled or payment is forgiven, the *seller* must recognize gain to the extent that the fair market value on the date of cancellation (or the face amount, if less) exceeds the seller's basis in the obligation.[23] In other words, the forgiveness of an installment payment is the equivalent of an actual payment to the seller. Related party has the same meaning for purposes of this rule as for the second disposition rule.

Special Depreciable Property Rule

The installment sale reporting method generally does not apply to the extent the seller would be required to recapture prior depreciation deductions (using accelerated depreciation) had the seller received actually received the full amount of the purchase price in the year of sale. For that reason, it does not apply to the portion of the prior depreciation deductions on residential and certain commercial real property that are depreciated under the straight-line method. Thus, recaptured depreciation must be reported by the seller in the year of the sale up to the amount of the seller's gain – even if any other gain is reported on the installment basis as payments are received.[24]

To the extent depreciation recapture is reported in the year of sale, such recapture increases seller's basis in the property. Therefore, the amount of otherwise reportable gain over the term of the installment agreement is reduced.

For example, Charles Plotnick sells equipment to Nick Martin for $70,000, payable in three instalments plus interest of 9 percent on the unpaid balance. Also assume that Charles originally paid $90,000 for the equipment, but due to total depreciation deductions of $40,000, his adjusted basis in the equipment was $50,000.

Although Charles' total depreciation deductions were $40,000, his recapture income is limited to $20,000 (the difference between the sale price of $70,000 and his adjusted basis of $50,000). Because the $20,000 of recaptured deductions is included in his gross income in the year of the sale, his basis is increased basis by $20,000 (from $50,000 to $70,000). Consequently, the purchase price and his basis would be the same ($70,000); and, thus, Charles would not recognize any gain with respect to the remaining installment payments.

609

On the other hand, if Charles sold the property for $110,000, his total realized gain would be $60,000 (the $110,000 amount realized minus his adjusted basis of $50,000). Because his gain is greater than the $40,000 previously deducted depreciation, that entire amount of recapture is included in gross income in the year of sale. Then, increasing his $50,000 basis by the $40,000 of recapture income, his basis would be $90,000. Thus, his $40,000 gain is ratable includible in gross in each of the three installment payments. So, of each of $36,667 (one-third of $110,000, not including interest), $30,000 will be a tax-free recovery of basis and $6,667 will be reportable gain.

41.5 TAX IMPLICATIONS OF THE SCIN

All of the tax rules applicable to the installment sale apply to the self-cancelling installment note. However, there are additional factors to consider.

The Tax Court has held that if an installment sale by a decedent to his children includes a provision cancelling the outstanding balance, if any, at the time of the decedent's death, the decent must include any remaining unrecognized gain on the decedent's final return.[25] On appeal, the Eighth Circuit reversed the Tax Court decision, holding that the gain would be fully taxable to the decedent's estate as income in respect of a decedent, not as income on the decedent's final income tax return.[26]

In GCM 39503, the IRS set forth the circumstances under which a SCIN will be treated as an installment note or as if it were a private annuity.

Note that for gift tax purposes, there should be no taxable gift if the seller has a reasonable expectation of repayment (based on his or her life expectancy) and the underlying SCIN has the indicia of an enforceable obligation that the seller intends to enforce in the event of default. For estate tax purposes, the Tax Court has held that since the balance of the note is canceled at the death of the seller, there is nothing to include in his or her estate.[27]

With a SCIN, there must be a "premium" in either the amount of interest or principal to be paid in exchange for the consideration provided. If the selling price is increased to take into account the risk of dying prior to receiving all the payments, but the seller does live out the term, the seller will have reported gain in excess of the amount he or she would have reported had the property been sold at fair market value (without the risk premium). An alternative to the risk premium, a higher interest rate could be used. However, this would result in a larger amount of ordinary interest income as compared to a smaller amount of capital gain.[28]

Valuation Issues With Respect to Contingent Installment Sales

Often, the price of property will be determined by some contingency. For example, if Susan Harmon sold her stock in the SH Corporation, a closely held business, to her son Mark for installment payments, rather than setting a specific dollar price, the price may be set as a percentage of the gross profits of the business for each of the next ten years. The parties may – or may not – put a maximum dollar amount on the selling price.

Installment sale treatment is available even when the actual price cannot be determined with precision. If there is a stated maximum selling price, the seller (in this example Susan) can recover basis by means of a "gross profit ratio."[29] This ratio is multiplied by the installment payment (exclusive of interest) to determine the portion of the payment that is gain.

$$\frac{\text{gross profit (realized or to be realized)}}{\text{total contract price (assume this is maximum selling price)}} \times \text{installment payment}$$

(The maximum selling price is defined as the largest price that could be paid assuming all contingencies, formulas, etc., operate in the seller's favor.) The seller then reports income on a pro rata basis (and recovers his basis over the scheduled payment period in equal annual increments) with respect to each installment payment.

Later, if it is found that the contingency will not be met (and therefore the seller will not actually receive the maximum selling price) a recomputation of the seller's income is allowed. The seller may report reduced income (not only in the adjustment year, but in all subsequent years). If as a result of the recomputation, the seller does not recover his or her entire income tax basis for the property sold, the amount of basis will be deductible as a loss.[30]

If the sale price is indefinite and no maximum selling price can be determined – but the obligation is payable over a fixed period of time – the seller's basis would be recoverable ratably over that fixed period.[31]

If neither selling price nor payment period can be ascertained with certainty in advance, the arrangement will be closely scrutinized to determine whether there has been a sale or whether the payments, in economic effect, are in essence either rent or royalty income. If it is determined that there has been a sale, the seller's basis will be recovered over fifteen years commencing with the date of sale. Any basis not recovered in that time may be carried forward to succeeding years until recovered in full.

Generally, if in any year payments received are less than the basis allocated to that year, the excess basis must be reallocated over the balance of the fifteen-year period. (A period other than fifteen years may be used or required where it is shown that a substantial and inappropriate deferral or acceleration of the recovery of the seller's basis would otherwise result.)[32]

The effect of the contingency sale price rules allowing installment reporting is that taxpayers have little justification for treating transactions as "open." (In open transactions the cost recovery method allows a taxpayer to recover his or her basis prior to reporting any gain). Only in rare and extraordinary cases in which it is impossible to ascertain the contingent price would the "cost recovery" method be allowed.

Special rules apply with respect to contingent installment payments for sales of depreciable property to a controlled entity, such as a more than 50 percent owned partnership or corporation (assuming installment reporting is allowed). The rules are:

(1) The seller's basis is recovered ratably in annual increments if (a) the installment sale is to a controlled entity, and (b) it is impossible to reasonably ascertain the fair market value.

(2) All noncontingent payments plus the fair market value of contingent payments must be reported in the year of the sale. For instance, assume Tom Miller sells depreciable property to a corporation he controls for no down payment and 10 percent of the net profits from the business for the next ten years. Assume the fair market value of the promise can be reasonably ascertained to be $200,000. Tom would have to include $200,000 in income in the year of the sale ($0 noncontingent payments plus $200,000 fair market value of contingent payments).

(3) The purchaser of the property may not increase his basis in the property by any amount before such time as the seller includes the amount in income.[33]

41.6 USING LIFE INSURANCE

From a seller's perspective, pursuant to an installment sale, he or she may often purchase insurance on the life (or lives) of the transferee(s) to protect against the potential cessation of payments at the death of the transferee(s). In doing so, the seller is the owner and beneficiary of the policy paying the premiums. This is a form of security to protect against the transferee dying before all of the installment payments are made. The agreed-upon amount of payments made by the purchaser of the property could be increased to provide enough cash to make premium payments.

From the buyer's perspective, he or she may also purchase insurance to provide the liquidity necessary to pay taxes and other death expenses with respect to the purchased asset that would be includible in his or her estate. The beneficiary of the policy could be the transferee's spouse, adult children, or the trustee of an irrevocable trust. Upon the death of the buyer, the insurance proceeds would be used to pay any estate tax owing as a result of the purchased asset being includible in the buyer's gross estate. As an additional benefit, the insurance payments could be used by the buyer's family to pay the remaining installment payments should the buyer die prior to the end of the term.

41.7 ISSUES IN COMMUNITY PROPERTY STATES

Installment sales by married individuals in community property states often involve real property. In such situations, it is important to ascertain whether the interest in real property is community property. Both spouses should join in any conveyance of community real property. If one spouse does not join in the conveyance of community real property, he or she may be able to void the sale for a specified period (e.g., one year from the date of recording of the deed in California). This statute of limitations applies only to land in the name of the transferor spouse alone. If the land is in the name of both spouses, an attempt by either spouse to transfer complete title would be void with respect to the interest of the other spouse. Certain sales made to parties, in good faith, who are not aware of the marriage relationship may be incontestable, but such controversies should be avoided.

A purchaser of personal property should also ascertain whether any community property rights are involved. California does not require the written consent of each spouse in connection with the sale of community personal property if the property is sold for "valuable consideration." However, as an exception, neither spouse can sell, convey, or encumber the furniture, furnishings, or fittings of the home or wearing apparel of the other spouse or minor children without the written consent of the other spouse.

Problems could arise as a result of cases regarding joint property rights of non-marital partners. Some courts have found implied agreements between non-married individuals to treat their property similarly to community property. Caution should be exercised if property is purchased from an individual involved in such a relationship. It may be advisable to ask the partner who may have a claim to convey title to any interest he or she may have in the property.

Another possibility to consider is the separate sale of each spouse's interest. One spouse could sell his or her interest outright and recognize all of his or her capital gain immediately, while the other spouse could sell his or her interest on the installment method and spread out his or her capital gain. This can reduce capital gain taxes while effectively allowing a greater amount of the sale price to be received in the year of the sale. Some community property states may require a partition of the spouses' interests before a separate sale of the interests can take place. For instance, in Louisiana, neither spouse can sell, mortgage or lease his/her undivided interest in the community property until it is partitioned.[34] If undivided interests are sold at a discount, the amount of capital gains will be less, thereby creating estate tax savings and lower installment payments.

41.8 FREQUENTLY ASKED QUESTIONS

Question – How can the related party rules be avoided?

Answer – For property other than marketable securities, the related purchaser could hold the property for at least a two-year period after the sale (to the extent that the special depreciable property rule does not apply). The installment obligation could be structured so that no payments need to be made until after the two-year holding period has lapsed. If the related party was going to sell the property to raise cash to make installment payments, as an alternative the related party could use the property as collateral for a loan to provide the funds needed to make installment payments. (Note, however, that the loan must be bona fide, and the debtor must continue to bear the economic risk of loss.)

A private annuity could be used instead of an installment sale to avoid all three related party rules. Since the installment sale rules do not deal with private annuity arrangements, the transferee should be free to dispose of the transferred property at any time without accelerating the recognition of gain to the transferor. Under proposed regulations issued in 2006, IRS changed the calculation of basis on a resale of property acquired using a private annuity, making it more difficult to circumvent the related party installment sale rules. Also, under the private annuity rules, if the obligations are structured as "debt instruments", then all of the gain will be accelerated into the year the transaction is entered into. To avoid this result, it is necessary that there be a maximum amount due under the notes and these payments do not extend more than twice the life expectancy of the recipient.

In any installment sale to a related party, the risk of illiquidity of the initial seller in the event of a second disposition by the new owner should be considered. How can this potential problem be overcome? Perhaps the seller might insist on an acceleration clause. This would give the seller the right to demand additional cash payments if the property subject to the installment sale is disposed of before the two-year waiting period has been met.

It probably would not be advisable to impose formal restrictions on the related purchaser's ability to dispose of the property. Likewise, it probably is not wise to give the seller a legal right to insist that the purchaser must lend him funds to pay a tax imposed on a second disposition. Such contractual restrictions or requirements could be viewed by the IRS as evidence that the entire transaction lacked economic substance.

Question – What type of security can the seller of property under an installment sale require without being taxed on his entire gain in the year of the sale?

Answer – The issue raises the question of whether "security" provided by the buyer to the seller is in essence a payment. So, if the security was deemed to be a payment, the seller would be required to report gain. A third party guarantee payment, i.e., a standby letter of credit used as security for a deferred payment sale will not be treated as a payment received on the installment obligation.[35]

But third party notes or other third party obligations that are transferable or marketable prior to default by the installment buyer will be treated as payments to the seller (and therefore trigger taxable gain in the year received).[36]

Typically, the IRS and the courts will deem funds placed in an escrow account to secure the interest of the seller to be constructively received – and, therefore, currently taxable in the year of the sale. However, this result is not certain. No presumption of tax avoidance arises merely because the seller requested an installment payout or merely because the buyer was at all times willing to pay the entire purchase price in a lump sum.

The seller is more likely to be successful in avoiding current taxation of escrowed funds if (1) the arrangement serves a legitimate business purpose, and (2) the seller continues to look to the contractual obligation of the buyer for payment. An example would be where the escrow arrangement was negotiated in a manner that provided that payments from the escrow account were contingent on the seller's continued adherence to his agreement not to compete. This type of agreement would probably not result in constructive receipt by the seller even if he could control the investment of the money in the escrow account.

Question – What are the income and estate tax implications when the holder of an installment obligation dies?

Answer – The right to receive payments under the obligation is treated as income in respect of a decedent under Code section 691. Thus, payments on the installment obligation are taxable income to the person or entity that receives those payments to the extent that they would have been taxed had the seller lived and received payment himself.

For estate tax purposes, the fair market value of the installment obligation is also includable in the decedent's gross estate. But to reduce the harshness of double taxation, a deduction from income is allowed to the recipient based on the federal estate taxes paid by the decedent's estate attributable to the inclusion of the installment obligation. This is called the section 691 (income in respect of a decedent) deduction. Although it is an itemized deduction, it is important to keep this deduction in mind since many people forget to take advantage of this deduction when it is available.

Question – Is there a problem in arranging an installment sale of property with an existing mortgage on it?

Answer – Yes. Where property subject to an existing mortgage is sold and the purchaser assumes or takes the property subject to that mortgage, any debt in excess of the seller's tax basis (cost) will be considered a payment received by the seller in the year of the sale. Any mortgage encumbering the property will be treated as assumed or taken subject to, even though title to the property does not pass in the year of sale and even though the seller remains responsible for payment of the mortgage (as in a wrap-around mortgage).[37] Also, many mortgages contain a "due on sale clause" which provides that the entire outstanding balance due on the mortgage becomes immediately due if the property is transferred. In these situations, it will be necessary to obtain the consent of the lender not to enforce this clause prior to making the transfer of the property.

Question – Does the second disposition rule mean there are no advantages to a transfer of property (which is not within the special depreciable property rule) from an individual to an irrevocable trust established for his family in return for installment payments or SCIN payments?

Answer – Many advantages still exist, including the following:

(1) Taxation on the gain can be spread over a larger number of years (assuming the trust does not dispose of the property within two years, and assuming the trust does not benefit the seller or the seller's spouse if the property is depreciable to the trust). This could lower the applicable total rate.

(2) The family of the seller is more secure from the claims of his creditors.

(3) No gift tax is incurred on the transfer if the property is sold to the trust at its fair market value.

(4) The trust may have little or no gain on the resale of the asset since it takes as its basis the full purchase price it agreed to pay. (Of course, the property may appreciate or decline in value during the two years it must be held in order to avoid accelerating the initial seller's gain.) The amount of gain to the buyer will be reduced if a SCIN having a premium on principal is used.

(5) None of the assets of the trust, or income, will be includable in the original owner's estate if the trust is irrevocable and the seller maintains no control. (The present value of future payments remaining on the note would, however, be includable if he died within the installment period. This, in turn, could cause a serious lack of liquidity. Conversely, the payments due on a SCIN are canceled at death and excluded from the seller's estate, but liquidity is needed for any income tax due at death.)

To obtain this favorable treatment, it is important that:

(1) The trustee be completely independent, and the grantor maintain no control over the trustee's actions;

(2) There be no prearrangement between the parties requiring the trustee to resell the property;

(3) The original owner not have a stake in the resale by the trust (i.e., the amount he receives cannot be dependent on the amount the trustee receives);

(4) There be a motive–other than tax savings–for the arrangement; and

(5) The "two-year holding rule" be met.

Question – Must there be any down payment in the year of sale to qualify for the installment method of reporting?

Answer – No. There is no requirement that there be any payment in the year of sale. The only requirement of this type is that at least one payment be made in a taxable year *after* the year in which the property was sold. However, some practitioners believe that if a trust created by the seller or a related party is the buyer, the buyer should have additional assets to make the payments, or a guaranty of the note should be given, so as to avoid possible inclusion of the sold asset in the seller's estate.

Question – Are there special considerations associated with structuring an installment sale with an irrevocable trust?

Answer – Many practitioners feel that it is necessary to seed the trust with cash equal to 10 percent of the value of the note in order to lend substance to the transaction. The theory being that a typical person would not enter into an installment sale with a debtor that has no assets. By funding the trust with some amount of cash or other assets, this concern is addressed. As an alternative to funding the trust with assets; it may be advisable to have a beneficiary of the trust provide a personal guaranty for the installment obligation.[38]

Question – Will a bequest of an installment obligation to the obligor avoid tax recognition of the untaxed gain by the seller?

Answer – The installment obligation rules cannot be circumvented by canceling the obligation during the seller's lifetime. Likewise, when an installment seller dies holding an installment obligation, the gain is not forgiven. Instead, gain is reportable by the seller's estate – or the recipient of the obligation – as payments are made. The amount of gain and the character of income realized are the same as the deceased seller would have reported had he or she lived. (Note that death itself does not trigger an acceleration of gain; tax is due only if payments are actually or constructively received or if the obligation is sold.)

Under prior law, it had been argued that if an installment obligation was bequeathed to the purchaser of the property, the interests of the obligor and the obligee merged. Under this theory, there would be no gain realized because the estate would never realize the unpaid balance.

Current tax law accelerates the unrealized gain when the seller makes a bequest of the obligation to the buyer or his estate cancels the debt. Gain or loss will be recognized to the extent the fair market value of the obligation exceeds the obligation holder's basis. (Where the decedent-seller and the purchaser are related, the fair market value of the obligation cannot be less than its face amount.) To avoid the recognition of gain, it may be advisable to bequeath the note to a trust for the benefit of the buyer.

If a person forgives an installment obligation in his will, the cancellation is treated as a transfer of the obligation by the decedent's estate. The estate will report the accelerated gain. If a trust or some party other than the decedent held the obligation, the cancellation will be treated as a transfer by that person immediately after the decedent's death.

An installment obligation that becomes unenforceable at the seller's death is treated as if it were canceled in favor of the obligor.

Question – What other considerations are associated with including the installment note within the seller's estate?

Answer – Since the value of the note will be included within the seller's estate, the value of this note could result in estate taxes. If the note is not satisfied at the seller's death, the estate tax attributable to the note could result in liquidity issues since the estate tax on the note will be due even though the note remains outstanding.

Question – What is the tax effect where the seller cancels a buyer's obligation to make installments?

Answer – If a seller cancels a buyer's installment obligation (or it becomes unenforceable), the cancellation will be treated as a disposition of the obligation. This means the seller must report gain (or loss). The gain (or loss) is measured by the difference between the fair market value of the obligation at the time of its disposition and its basis.

Note that if the seller and buyer are considered related persons, the fair market value of the obligation will be considered as not less than the face value. For instance, mom sells her summer home in Avalon to her daughter in an installment sale in 2023. Mom's basis in the home was $15,000. Her daughter will pay the purchase price, $85,000, in five equal annual $17,000 installments. (Interest is ignored for simplicity.) If mom immediately cancels the daughter's obligation, mom must report gain. Her gain is the difference between the value of what is owed to her, $85,000, and her $15,000 basis, or $70,000. She is also liable for any gift tax on the gift.

A solution would seem to be for mom to forgive – at her whim, and on a year-by-year basis – all or a portion of each $17,000 payment as it is paid. Her daughter should write a check for the full $17,000 to her. Then, without a prearranged or legally binding plan, mom can write her daughter, son-in-law, and each of her grandchildren, checks of $17,000, all of which would be gift tax-free as a result of the gift tax annual exclusion (and she could double the amount of each check if her husband joined in on a split gift). Mom will recognize gain of $9,600 each of the five years, rather than $48,000 in the year of sale.

Question – How soon does a taxpayer have to elect to report payments in installments?

Answer – No election is necessary. Installment sale treatment is automatic for qualifying sales unless an election is made specifying installment sale treatment is *not* to apply. Although the temporary regulations are not specific as to how such an election is to be made, reporting the entire gain in gross income for the taxable year in which the sale occurs (on or before the due date for filing the tax return – including extensions) will operate as an election that installment sale reporting is not to apply.[39] Once a valid election out of the installment method has been made, it may not be revoked except under very limited circumstances. The Service has provided guidance in the form of a revenue ruling concerning when it will grant permission to make a late election out of the installment method.[40]

Question – When might it be a good idea to forego the installment method of reporting a gain, even though a sale was made on the installment basis?

Answer – If a taxpayer has unrelated losses, he might wish to offset those losses with the gain from the installment sale. He may have unusually low income or high deductions for the year. Thus, he or she would report the full gain in the year of sale even though the sale was an installment sale. Also, if capital gain tax rates go up, paying the tax early at lower rates may make sense.

Question – When is interest payable on the unpaid balance of an installment sale deductible by the buyer?

Answer – Interest is deductible only in the period in which that interest is properly allocable. Regardless of how the parties have formed the agreement, the IRS will treat the interest as "constant" (whether the taxpayer is on the cash or accrual method). The IRS allocates the interest over the term of the contract. The net effect is that the parties must determine the effective interest on a compound interest basis and use that effective rate to compute the amount of any allowable interest deduction.

This rule limits both the interest deduction and the interest income to the amount of interest that accrues economically. The compounding period used in determining the effective rate of interest will probably be the same as that called for in the parties' agreement.

Question – When will a taxpayer be subject to the interest surcharge for installment sales in excess of $150,000?

Answer – There is a special interest surcharge imposed on certain installment obligations in which the sale price exceeds $150,000 and the aggregate deferred payments for such sales during the taxable year exceed $5,000,000. There are three exceptions to the application of the surcharge: (1) property used or produced in the trade or business of farming; (2) timeshares and residential lots; and (3) personal use property.[41]

CHAPTER ENDNOTES

1. I.R.C. §453.
2. See Rev. Rul. 86-72, 1 CB 253; GCM 39503 (5-7-86).
3. I.R.C. §453(b).
4. I.R.C. §453(d).
5. I.R.C. §453(j); Treas. Reg. §15A.453-1(c).
6. I.R.C. §453(k)(2).
7. I.R.C. §453.
8. Rev. Rul. 70-430, 1970-2 CB 51.
9. I.R.C. § 483(e)(1); I.R.C. § 483(e)(2).
10. Rev. Rul. 2016-30, 2016-52 I.R.B. 876.
11. I.R.C. §1274A; IRB 2013-48
12. I.R.C. §2033; Treas. Reg. §20.2033-1.
13. *Ballard v. Comm'r.*, TC Memo 1987-128; *Krabbenhoft v. Comm'r.*, 94 TC 887 (1990).
14. *Ballard v. Comm'r.*, 854 F.2d 185 (7th Cir. 1988).
15. *Krabbenhoft v. Comm'r.*, 939 F.2d 529 (8th Cir. 1991), *cert. denied*, 502 U.S. 1072 (1991).
16. Treas. Reg. §1.691(a)-3.
17. Treas. Reg. §1.691(c)-1.
18. *Ballard*; I.R.C. §1012.
19. See I.R.C. §§453(f)(1), 318(a), 267(b).
20. I.R.C. §453(e)(1).
21. I.R.C. §453(e)(2). Thus, if Herb sold his son Stephen *stock* instead of land, the time period for the "second disposition" rule is unlimited, and Herb will recognize gain on any subsequent disposition by Stephen, to the extent that Herb has not received all payments due on the sale.
22. I.R.C. §453(g).
23. I.R.C. §453B(f).
24. See I.R.C. §453(i).
25. *Est. of Frane v. Comm'r.*, 98 TC 341 (1992). This decision was based on Code section 453B, which provides that where an installment note is canceled or becomes unenforceable, this is treated as a taxable disposition of the note.
26. *Est. of Frane v. Comm'r.*, 998 F.2d 567 (8th Cir. 1993).
27. *Est. of Moss v. Comm'r.*, 74 TC 1239 (1980), *acq. in result*, 1981-1 CB 2.
28. GCM 39503 (5-7-86).
29. Temp. Treas. Reg. §15A.453-1(c)(2).
30. Treas. Reg. §15A.453-1(c)(2), Example (5).
31. Treas. Reg. §15A.453-1(c)(3).
32. Treas. Reg. §15A.453-1(c)(4).
33. I.R.C. §453(g)(1).
34. Community Property: What is Mine? What is Yours?, Louisiana State Bar Association.
35. Treas. Reg. §15A.453-1(b)(3).
36. Treas. Reg. §15A.453-1(e).
37. Treas. Reg. §15A.453-1(b)(3)(ii).
38. See Role of Guarantees and Seed Gifts in Family Installment Sales, Estate Planning Journal, Volume 37, Number 11, November 2010, Martin H. Shenkman, for a good discussion of the topic.
39. Treas. Reg. §15A.453-1(d)(3).
40. Rev. Rul. 90-46, 1990-1 CB 107.
41. I.R.C. §453A(b).

PRIVATE ANNUITY

CHAPTER 42

42.1 INTRODUCTION

A private annuity is an arrangement between two parties, neither of whom is an insurance company. The transferor (annuitant) conveys complete ownership of property to a transferee, the obligor who is the party obligated to make payments to the person who has sold the property. The transferee, in turn, makes a legally enforceable commitment to make periodic payments to the transferor for a specified period of time. Usually, this period of time is the transferor's life but in some cases, the annuity is set to last for the transferor's life plus the life of his or her spouse or some other designated party. There are basically two types of private annuities: (1) the single life annuity under which payments cease at the death of the annuitant; and (2) the joint and last survivor annuity, in which payments continue until the death of the last survivor, e.g., payments continue as long as either spouse is alive. Generally, since payments under this latter type of arrangement will continue for a longer period of time than payments under a single life annuity, the amount paid each year will be less than that payable under a single life annuity.

There are many reasons to set up a private annuity. The major estate planning objective of a private annuity is to remove property from a wealthy client's taxable estate. Under current regulations, the seller's entire gain is recognized at the time the transaction is executed. This significantly limits the utility of the private annuity technique because, instead of allowing gain to be reported over a period of many years, it is now all reportable in the year the transaction is consummated. However, if the gain is relatively small (e.g., where the property was inherited by the seller and had received a step-up in basis) or in situations where the seller can apply significant capital losses to offset any gain triggered by the transaction, the private annuity can be extremely appealing.[1]

42.2 WHEN IS USE OF SUCH A DEVICE INDICATED?

Advantages

1. When a client wishes to retire and shift control of a business to a family member or to a key employee.

    Example. Ed Staller is the sole shareholder of a closely held corporation. Ed has no heir other than his wife. He has two key employees in the business who are capable of managing it and interested in owning it. Ed would like to sell them the business but he is concerned about adequate income upon his retirement. Presently, his business does not provide pension, profit-sharing, or nonqualified deferred compensation benefits. The key employees tell Ed they would like to buy the business but cannot afford to pay Ed in a lump sum or in relatively few installments. Ed could sell all of his stock to the two key employees and in return they could promise to pay him an income for his life (and perhaps for his wife's life). This should yield a higher income than if he sold the business in an installment sale. The size of the annuity stream income would be based on the fair market value of the business as well as on Ed's age and the section 7520 rate (discussed below) on the date the transaction is executed.

2. When a client desires to remove a sizable asset, such as a business, from his or her estate for estate tax purposes.

    Example. Abe Marks is the sole shareholder of a closely-held real estate corporation. He has two daughters who are presently working in the business. He could sell the business to his daughters in return for their agreement to pay an annuity for life. This will result in a reduction in Abe's estate (and thus save estate taxes) because the value of the business as well as any future appreciation will not be included in his gross estate. This is because upon Abe's death, the daughters' annuity payments cease and the close corporation stock he sold to them will not be included in his estate.

The daughter's income tax basis in the stock, *after Abe's death*, will be the sum of the annuity payments paid to Abe during his lifetime. Until Abe's death, their basis will be the greater of the sum of their payments or the amount paid plus the present value of all future payments Abe will receive if he lives to his life expectancy. Initially, the transferee's basis is equal to the fair market value of the property transferred–assuming no gift is built into the transaction.

3. When a client who owns a large parcel of non-income producing property wants to convert it to income producing property.

Example. Your client is a widow whose married son is currently providing $700 a month to support her. The widow owns real estate that is currently not income producing, but because of its choice location in Wildwood, New Jersey, is increasing substantially in value. It is expected that the property might double or triple in value over the next ten years.

As a possible solution, her son could discontinue the gifts and purchase the property from his mother in exchange for a monthly lifetime income (say, $750 a month, assuming the present value of the land will support this payment). By virtue of this transaction, the property would not be included in the widow's estate; and, thus not be subject to estate tax. Moreover, the payments would provide her with financial independence. The son becomes the immediate owner of the real estate. Finally, any increase in value would inure to the benefit of the son and not further increase his mother's estate. This concept of removing the appreciation from the donor's estate is one of the primary objectives of making lifetime transfers.

4. When a client with a very large and has a major or sole heir who is a grandchild (or other individual two or more generations below that of the client). Because the private annuity is a sale and not a gift, the transfer of the property to a grandchild is not subject to generation-skipping transfer tax. This technique can be implemented by selling the property to a trust for the benefit of a grandchild(ren) to protect it from the beneficiar(ies)' creditors with no inclusion in the gross estate of the trust beneficiaries.

5. Where the family's objective is to keep certain property in the family or direct it to specified family members (or the purchaser's objective is to bar others from obtaining the property in question) and the present owners do not want it to be subject to a will contest or any statutory rights that might thwart their directive wishes.

Disadvantages

As is the case with any tool or technique, private annuities have downsides. These include:

1. The obligation to make payments cease at the transferor's death – even if only one payment had been made to that point. Although this is obviously a disadvantage to heirs of the seller-annuitant is, it is an advantage to the transferee who is required to pay the annuity. Additionally, the transferor's estate is not entitled to a deduction for the loss suffered as a result of the transferor's premature death. Life insurance, as described below, can help alleviate this problem.

2. If the transferor outlives his life expectancy, the transferee might essentially overpay for the property (and the estate of the transferee remains liable to continue to make those payments if the transferee predeceases the transferor). For example, in one celebrated case involving the DuPont family, senior family members transferred $13.5 million worth of stock to a family-owned holding company in return for a private annuity with payments of $900,000 a year. Because the annuitant lived for thirty more years, over $30,000,000 was paid for

the stock originally worth only $13.5 million. Notwithstanding this apparent overpayment, the stock was worth over half a billion dollars! However, even where the transferor outlives his or her life expectancy, the payments should be limited to no more than twice the original life expectancy at the time that the transaction was consummated.

3. If the transferor is unable to consume or give away annuity payments, his or her estate is increased, thus defeating the "intentional freeze" intended by the transaction.

4. The older the transferor, the higher the annual outlay required. Although techniques to mitigate this problem are discussed below, at a certain point, the transferee may be unable to make required payments.

5. Inflation is a factor to be considered. Over time, the purchasing power of fixed annuity payments will be greatly reduced by inflation. On the other hand, this same decline in the purchasing power of the dollar may make it easier for the transferee to make the required payments.

6. In many situations, when the income tax consequences to the purchasing family trust are taken into account, the financial detriments to the purchaser may outweigh the financial benefit to the seller of capital gain deferral.[2]

7. Perhaps the most significant disadvantage is the possibly that the IRS will deny the proration of the inclusion of taxable gain over the duration of the annuity. As discussed below, Proposed Regulations would require the seller-annuitant to recognize the entire gain on the transfer of the property to the buyer in the year the transaction is consummated.

Alternatives

One alternative to a private annuity is the installment sale. However, if the seller were to die shortly after the sale took place, the death tax results would differ significantly. Since an installment sale is often involves a series of notes, the present value of those notes would be includable in the estate of the seller. But under the private annuity arrangement where payments are only payable for the life of the seller-annuitant and cease on the annuitant's death (no matter how soon after the signing of the agreement that occurs), upon his or her death, nothing would be included in his or her gross estate; and, thus totally escaping estate tax.

Another disadvantage of an installment sale with regard to property acquired by the buyer from the seller for investment, the interest paid by the buyer is deductible only to the extent of the buyer's investment income (treated as an itemized deduction). Also, unlike a private annuity, the types of property that can be sold pursuant to the installment sale rules are limited. For example, the installment sale of appreciated publicly traded securities is recognized in year of sale regardless of the payment arrangement.

Finally unlike a private annuity, installment sales are subject to the second disposition related-party rule of section 453(e). As discussed in Chapter 41, if a related buyer (i.e., a family member of the seller) resells the property within two years of the initial installment sale, the deferred gain will be recognized in whole or in part by the original seller. Conversely, because the taxation of a private annuity is not governed by section 453, the second disposition rules do not apply. Therefore, the related-party may immediately resell the property acquired with a private annuity.

42.3 WHAT ARE THE REQUIREMENTS?

1. Legally, almost any type of property may be used. For example, it is possible to transfer a home, undeveloped real estate, stocks, or a business interest. Preferably, the property transferred will be income producing, rapidly appreciating, and the transfer will not trigger depreciation or investment credit recapture or to the seller-annuitant.

2. Importantly, prior to entering the arrangement, the transferee's wherewithal to make annuity payments should be ascertained. If the transferee (the obligor) has substantial independent income, then almost any asset can be sold. But, if the transferee has little or no other income, then the property sold should be either income producing or of a type that the transferee can easily and quickly resell or borrow against.[3]

3. Until recently, in order to be assured of that the seller-annuitant's gain on the transfer of the

property to the buyer was prorated over the term of the annuity, it was extremely important that the obligor's promise to make the annuity payments be unsecured. If the promise was secured, the transaction would be taxable immediately on the transfer[4] and the annuitant would then recognize the full amount of the gain, i.e., the difference between the amount realized (the present value of the right to the promised payments) and the transferor's adjusted basis in the property.

As noted above, the IRS issued Proposed Regulations applicable to transactions after October 18, 2006. These Regulations eliminate any gain deferral as the seller-annuitant would be treated as if he or she sold the property in a totally taxable transaction, and, then reinvested the proceeds into an annuity. Considering the tax consequences of the Proposed Regulations (if they are finalized), it may be advisable to set a maximum amount payable to the annuitant. Annuity payments cannot continue for more than twice the remaining life expectancy of the annuitant. While it may be possible to still structure the transaction to maintain the tax benefits associated with annuities, before setting up a private annuity, it would be prudent to check on the current status of the Proposed Regulations before going forward.[5]

4. To avoid being classified as a commercial annuity that under current law would be fully taxable in the year in which the sale is consummate, the transferee (obligor) should be not be a person regularly engaged in issuing private annuities.[6] Generally, the obligor would be the natural object of the transferor's (annuitant's) bounty. For example, most private annuities are made between parents and children. The device may also be useful for transfers between employers and trusted key employees. It is also a very useful device between unmarried couples and close friends because there is no law requiring that the parties to a private annuity be related.

5. The annuity amount must be determined by measuring the fair market value of the property. An appraisal by independent court-recognized appraisal experts shortly before the execution of the private annuity is suggested.

6. The ideal client is an individual with a taxable estate desiring to reduce the size of his or her estate while receiving a lifetime income.

7. An agreement with a trust or corporation that has very few other assets may be attacked by the IRS as a sham. The authors are very wary of what is referred to as the private annuity trust viewed by the IRS as being abusive.[7]

8. Payments must be completely contingent on the life (or lives) of the transferor(s). However, it may be advisable to include a "maximum payout provision" in your private annuity agreement. This type of provision will limit the maximum payment possible to the person receiving the payments (the annuitant). For example, it will provide for an annuity payable for the shorter of the life of the annuitant or a fixed term of years. This fixed term of years must not be longer than double the life expectancy of the annuitant. These provisions may allow you to avoid the application of the Proposed Regulations in this area which would otherwise require the seller of the annuity to recognize gain upon the sale of the annuity.[8]

Example. George Gargas is sixty-five years old. He owns farmland with a fair market value of $1,000,000. His basis is only $100,000. He would like to remove the land from his estate and have his son, Bill, own it. He does not, however, want to pay any gift taxes on the transfer.

A private annuity agreement would be drawn stating that the farmland was sold to Bill in return for Bill's promise to pay his father an income for the shorter of his father's life; or a period not to exceed thirty-eight years (which is less than double the annuitant's remaining life expectancy). At age sixty-five, the father's life expectancy (expected return multiple) is 19.5 years (twenty years - 0.5 frequency of payment adjustment).

Assume the annuity agreement was signed in a month when the section 7520 discount rate was 5.0 percent. The annual annuity generated by property worth $1,000,000 is $92,657. This is arrived at by dividing the fair market value of the property transferred by the present value factor for an annuity at the appropriate age (10.7925 – see single life table).

Note that the private annuity payments are significantly impacted by upward or downward changes in the Section 7520 rate, the

PRIVATE ANNUITY — CHAPTER 42

Figure 42.1

TAXATION OF SELLER UNDER PRIVATE ANNUITY

A. Recovery of Basis (cost) Element	Tax Free
B. Gain Element	Capital gain
C. Income Element	Ordinary income

General Formula for Computing Annual Payment — Tax Free, Gain and Ordinary Income Elements

STEP 1. Compute Annual Payment	$\dfrac{\text{FMV of Property Transferred}}{\text{Present Value of Annuity Factor}}$
STEP 2. Compute Exclusion Ratio	$\dfrac{\text{Seller's Cost Basis}}{\text{expected return (annual payment} \times \text{life expectancy)}}$
STEP 3. Compute Excludable Amount (until total basis recovered)	Exclusion ratio × Annual Annuity
STEP 4. Compute Gain Element (until total gain recognized)	$\dfrac{\text{Present value of annuity minus property's basis}}{\text{life expectancy of annuitant}}$
STEP 5. Compute Ordinary Income Element	Annual Payment minus sum of (a) excludable amount and (b) gain amount

federal discount rate published by the IRS once a month in a revenue ruling. The Section 7520 rate can be found at www.leimberg.com under "Free Resources."

Out of the $92,657 he receives each year, Bill's father can exclude a portion ($5,128) from income. Assuming the annuity starting date is after 1986, Bill's father could exclude $5,128 each year *only* until his basis is recovered.

The exclusion ratio is determined by dividing the father's $100,000 basis in the property by his $1,806,812 expected return ($92,657 annual payment x 19.5 expected return multiple). The excludable amount is then found by multiplying this exclusion ratio ($100,000/$1,806,812) by the $92,657 annual payment.

Total capital gain to be recognized equals $900,000 ($1,000,000 fair market value - $100,000 adjusted basis). Assuming that the Proposed Regulations apply, *all* of this gain will have to be recognized in the year of sale. If the Proposed Regulations can be avoided (by including a maximum payout provision), then, gain from each annuity payment equals $46,154 ($900,000 ÷ 19.5 expected return multiple). See Figure 40.1.

The balance of each payment, $41,375 [($92,657 − ($5,128 + $46,154)], is taxable as ordinary income.

Once the basis is recovered and the total capital gain included in income, the full amount of the annuity payment is treated as ordinary income.

IRS Valuation Tables

The IRS and the courts have indicated that the government's valuation tables may *not* be used where there is substantial evidence that the annuitant has a very short life expectancy. In general, the courts and the IRS have taken the position that the tables must be used unless death is imminent.[9] However, the courts seemed to limit this to situations where the annuitant was not expected to live over a year.[10] More recently, the IRS has sought a broader rule, and has had success in at least one case.[11]

The standard valuation tables are not to be used where an individual is terminally ill (a person with an incurable illness or other deteriorating physical condition and at least a 50 percent probability of dying within one year). However, if such an individual survives for 18 months after the transaction, the individual is presumed not to have been terminally ill at the time of the transaction unless the opposite is proved with clear and convincing evidence.[12]

As a rule of thumb, practitioners should consider a private annuity when the life expectancy of the client exceeds two years. Perhaps the best objective third party evidence of life expectancy is the acceptance of the individual as an insured by an insurance company. If an insurer will accept the risk, regardless of the rating (additional premium charged by the insurance company to place the insured in the risk category appropriate under the circumstances known to the insurer), the issuance of the policy is almost perfect documentation that individual's life expectancy at that time exceeded two years.

42.4 TAX IMPLICATIONS

Estate Tax

For federal estate tax purposes, where the annuity ceases at the death of the transferor, the value of the property sold to the transferee-obligor in return for his promise to pay the annuity is excludable from the annuitant-transferor's estate. This is because property sold by a decedent for full and adequate consideration before death is not taxable in his or her estate.[13]

Likewise, the value of the promised payment will be excludable. This is because the selling price in a private annuity arrangement is an annuity that will expire (in the case of a single life annuity) upon the annuitant's death.

Note that this is not the case with a joint and survivor annuity. In a joint and last survivor annuity, payments will continue until the death of the last survivor. So if the spouse of the transferor-annuitant is the other annuitant and the spouse survives, the present value of future payments to her will be includable in the transferor-annuitant's estate (assuming he was sole owner of the property that was transferred in return for the joint and survivor annuity payments).[14] However, because of the unlimited estate tax marital deduction, there would be no federal estate tax. This, of course, would not be the case if the survivor were someone other than the first annuitant's U.S. citizen spouse (keep in mind that the marital deduction will generally not apply to non-citizen spouses).

Income Tax

Each annuity payment made by the transferee-obligor to the transferor-annuitant is treated partially as a tax-free return of capital, partially as a capital gain and the balance as ordinary income.[15] This does, however, depend somewhat upon whether the transaction can be structured to avoid the Proposed Regulations on private annuities. Assuming that this is accomplished, if the annuity starting date is after 1986, once the transferor-annuitant has recovered his basis, the entire payment will be taxed as ordinary income. The obligor is not allowed a deduction for any payments made to the annuitant.[16]

There will be no gift if the annual payments made by the obligor to the annuitant are actuarially equal to the fair market value of the property sold. However, if the value of the promise made by the transferee-obligor is less than the value of the property transferred, the difference will constitute a gift by the annuitant-transferor.[17] (If the annuity were a joint and survivor annuity, the value of the survivor annuity would be a gift from the transferor to the survivor. Since it would be a gift of a future interest, it would not qualify for the gift tax annual exclusion.[18] If the donee were the transferor's spouse, the gift may qualify for the gift tax marital deduction.)[19]

Example. Assuming a 5.0 percent section 7520 rate, the government valuation tables indicate an annuity valuation factor of 10.5490 for a person age 65 section. If such an individual transfers property with a fair market value of $1,000,000, a fair exchange would be a life annuity of $94,796 per year ($1,000,000 divided by 10.5490). But if annuity payments were actually set at, say, $85,000 per year, which has a present value of about $899,665 ($85,000 × 10.5490), the difference, $100,335 ($1,000,000 − $899,665), would constitute a gift. Note that that entire amount, $100,335, would be treated as a gift from the transferor to the transferee made in the year the agreement was executed.

The income tax treatment of unsecured private annuities is based on the following principles:

1. Gain is equal to the difference between the present value of the annuity promised and the transferor's basis.

2. Gain should be reported ratably over a period of years measured by the life expectancy of the annuitant. (See Steps 2 through 4 in Figure 35.1, and the example in "What Are the Requirements?" above.)

3. The transferor's investment in the contract is the transferor's basis in the property.

4. A portion of each annuity payment payable to the transferor is treated as:

    a. return of basis;

    b. capital gain; and

    c. ordinary income.

Outliving Life Expectancy

If the annuitant outlives his life expectancy, the transferee must continue to make the annuity payments and such payments continue for the life of the annuitant or until the maximum payout is satisfied. This is one of the risks involved in a private annuity; the actual amount to be paid by the transferee may exceed the expected return (the annual payments multiplied by the annuitant's life expectancy).

If an annuitant outlives his life expectancy (and thus has recognized total gain), the portion previously treated as capital gain is thereafter treated as ordinary income. Also, where the annuity starting date is after 1986, Code section 72(b) provides that if an annuitant outlives his life expectancy (and thus has recovered his basis) the remaining payments will be taxed entirely as ordinary income.

Basis

In the case of a private annuity, the transferee-obligor has, as his new tax basis, the fair market value of the property, which is the actuarial value of future payments (temporary or "floating" basis).[20] This provides a means for immediately increasing the basis for depreciation or depletion and can be a very significant benefit. The same basis is used to calculate gain if the transferred property is sold by the transferee. In many cases the property can be immediately resold for its fair market value and because of the high basis, little, if any, gain will be realized.

It is because the basis is the fair market value of the property at the time the agreement is executed that the private annuity is so useful. The new owner can immediately sell the property and reinvest the proceeds in more liquid or higher yielding assets. He does not have to worry about tax on gains that the transferor-annuitant would otherwise have had to report. The basis is "stepped-up," not carried over, for purposes of determining the tax on gain if the property is sold or depreciated. This would enable a fully depreciated property (such as an apartment or office building) to receive a new (fair market value) basis for depreciation by the transferee.[21] (Be aware of potential recapture problems where accelerated depreciation has been used by the transferor.)

However, upon the transferor's death, the transferee's basis "sinks," i.e., it is adjusted to what the transferee actually paid in annuity payments. If he has retained the property, the only concern for imposition of income tax at the transferor's death would be his having depreciated the property below the basis as adjusted at such death. In that event, he would realize ordinary income to the extent of the difference between the adjusted basis at death and the basis after depreciation. On the other hand, if the transferee had sold the property at a gain based on the temporary (floating) basis amount, and if the adjusted basis at the transferor's death is less than that temporary basis, the difference between the temporary basis and the adjusted basis will be immediately taxed to the transferee.

If the annuitant dies prematurely, the transferee may have to readjust his temporary basis or report a gain. If the annuitant dies before the length of his life expectancy according to government tables, the transferee-obligor must make a downward adjustment to his basis for the property. His basis becomes the amount of payments he actually has made. However, if he had sold the property before the annuitant's death, adjustments are made to reflect the reduced basis in light of previously recognized gain or loss.[22]

Computing the Transferor's Tax Treatment

The transferor's tax treatment is computed using the following steps:

Step 1-Determine the value of the promised annuity by using the appropriate IRS annuity valuation tables.

Step 2-Compute the excludable amount. An exclusion ratio is found. This is a formula that can be applied against each annuity payment to determine the portion recoverable income tax free as basis. This is done by dividing the transferor's investment in the contract by expected return, i.e., the annual payment is multiplied by the transferor's life expectancy (expected return multiple) measured by IRS life expectancy annuity (Code section 72) tables. This exclusion ratio is applied to each payment received by the transferor to determine the income tax free portion that is recovery of basis. As noted above, once the transferor has recovered his total basis, this portion will be taxed as ordinary income.

Step 3-Determine the portion of each payment that is taxable at capital gain rates. Total gain is the difference between the value of the annuity (annual payment multiplied by the present value annuity factor) and the transferor's basis. This gain is then divided by the transferor's life expectancy to determine the portion of each payment that is capital gain. As noted above, once the transferor has recovered his total capital gain, this portion will be taxed as ordinary income.

Step 4-Determine the ordinary income portion. This is simply the difference between each payment and the sum of the portion of each payment that is tax free recovery of basis plus the portion of each payment that is capital gain. As noted above, once the transferor has recovered his total basis and recognized his total gain, the entire payment will be taxed as ordinary income.

Assuming that the Proposed Regulations are finalized, it would not matter whether the private annuity was secured or unsecured. To avoid total recognition of gain, it would be necessary to include a maximum payout provision and avoid being classified as a debt instrument. This will allow the annuity to be taxed under the installment sales rules. Otherwise, a private annuity that fails to include this provision, the transferor must immediately recognize income on the entire gain.

42.5 USING LIFE INSURANCE

The obligation of the transferee may not be made if the transferee is not alive to ensure that the payments are made. At the death of the transferee-obligor, the obligation passes to his or her estate. The question then arises as to how to eliminate or minimize the possible hardships on the transferee's family and heirs. (The estate of the transferee will still have to continue promised payments for as long as the transferor-annuitant lives.)

Looking at the same problem from another viewpoint, how does one assure the financial security of the transferor-annuitant if the transferee dies before the transferor? Perhaps the best answer is life insurance. Life insurance should be obtained on the life of the transferee-obligor. It might be owned by and payable to the obligor's spouse (or preferably an irrevocable trust for her and the children's benefit).

When the income and estate tax free insurance proceeds are received, the spouse and children will have cash to continue payments to the transferor, and/or (depending on the amount of the insurance proceeds) pay estate taxes caused by the inclusion of the property received in the private annuity transaction in the transferee's estate.[23]

Occasionally, there is another reason that life insurance may be useful in conjunction with a private annuity. Assume a widow owns a business and has two adult sons and two adult daughters. How can she transfer the business to her sons but at the same time avoid disinheriting her daughters if she does not have considerable other assets?

Life insurance can be used to equalize the inheritance. The widow would sell the business to her sons in return for a private annuity. The daughters could be named owners, premium payors, and beneficiaries of a policy (or policies) on their mother's life. Annual gifts by the widow to the daughters could be used to provide premium payments. The widow could obtain the cash to give to her daughters from the after-tax private annuity income. When the widow died, each daughter could receive–in the form of tax-free life insurance proceeds–an amount equivalent to what she would have received if the business were divided in four equal shares. (Actually, since the sons are paying their mother for the business, the amount the daughters are to receive might be considerably less than half the value of the business.)

42.6 USING TRUSTS

The use of a trust will not automatically cause the loss of the tax benefits of the private annuity, but it is likely that the IRS will treat property for annuity exchanges involving trusts as if the transaction created a grantor trust rather than a sale. Therefore, all the income of the trust would, if the IRS were successful, be taxed to the seller (grantor, according to the IRS) as owner.

However, this harsh result is neither automatic nor certain. The Ninth Circuit Court of Appeals checks to see if annuity payments are tied to the income of the trust, how payments are calculated, and what role the taxpayer takes in trust investment decisions. Case law[24] indicates that client success is most likely where:

1. payment is computed by dividing the fair market value of the property by the appropriate annuity factor determined from the government's own tables;

2. the trust is obligated to pay the annuity without regard to the value of the property held in the trust or the income produced by trust assets; and

3. the grantor holds no powers to manage the trust or control the trustee.

The Tax Court has indicated that the annuity may lack substance where the transferor-annuitant retains too much control, the trustee is not independent, and there is a tie between the annuity payments and the income produced by the transferred property.[25] In another decision,[26] the Tax Court considered the following factors:

- The relationship between the creation of the trust and the transfer of property to it.

- The relationship between the income from the property and the annuity payments.

- The degree of control the annuitant exercises over the property.

- The nature and extent of the annuitant's continuing interest in the property.

- The source of the annuity payment.

- The arm's length nature of the annuity-sale.

42.7 ISSUES IN COMMUNITY PROPERTY STATES

In a community property jurisdiction, since the property is owned one-half by each spouse, the practitioner can either arrange a private annuity sale on a joint and survivor annuity basis, or on the basis of a separate annuity contract for each community half of the husband and wife, respectively. If the joint and survivor annuity is used, the total amount payable to the husband and wife is somewhat lower at the beginning than would be the total paid under separate annuities, but the payment remains constant at the death of the first spouse to die. Under the separate annuity approach, at the death of one spouse, the payments to that spouse cease, and the survivor does not have any benefit continuing under the decedent's annuity.

Each spouse has a half interest in each item of community property. Community property is created by operation of law, so no affirmative acts are required to create community property. Each spouse has a 50 percent interest in the community property regardless of which spouse earned the community property income or acquired the community property asset.[27]

There are implications in community property states also from the standpoint of the purchaser of the property under a private annuity contract. A typical arrangement is to have a private annuity contract between the parents and a child (rather than a child and his spouse). However, it is unlikely that the property acquired by the child will generate sufficient income to make the private annuity payments. If the child uses his earnings to make up the shortfall, the child's spouse could either be acquiring a community property interest in the property purchased, or could be making a gift to the child as each annuity payment is made. Absent a prenuptial agreement, the spouse will acquire an equal interest in the purchased property. Consideration should be given to this aspect before the annuity contract is entered into.

42.8 USING PRIVATE ANNUITIES FOR NON-FAMILY MEMBERS

The private annuity can be used in situations *other* than between family members. For instance, a private annuity could be highly useful as a conveyance device between unmarried couples.

Another possible use for a private annuity involves stock redemptions. For example, assume a corporation is owned and operated by an elderly widow and her son-in-law. Each owns 50 percent of the corporation's stock. The corporation's financial health is strong. The widow would like to retire but needs the assurance of a steady income. The son-in-law is in a high income tax bracket but is personally cash poor.

The corporation could purchase the widow's stock in return for the corporation's promise to pay her an income for life. The transaction would give the son-in-law 100 percent ownership of the corporation. No gift tax would be payable assuming the amount of the annual annuity payment was derived from the appropriate government tables and as the result of an arm's length transaction.

If the son-in-law had no primary and unconditional personal obligation to purchase the stock, the use of corporate dollars to affect the redemption will not result in a dividend to him. The widow should receive "sale or exchange" treatment if the redemption completely eliminates her interest (attribution rules do not cause problems in this factual situation, but extreme care should be taken before a redemption of stock is made by any family-owned corporation).

42.9 FREQUENTLY ASKED QUESTIONS

Question – Can the property that will be the subject of the private annuity be placed in escrow as security for the private annuity?

Answer – Yes. Under the prior rules, the presence of security for the payments made a difference in the tax treatment of the transaction. Under the Proposed Regulation rules, if the payments were unsecured, a promise to pay a private annuity in return for an appreciated security or other asset did not cause the transferor-annuitant to realize an immediate gain because the value of the buyer's promise to pay was deemed to be too contingent to value. In other words, the favorable annuity rules applied because of the uncertainty as to whether or not the person agreeing to make payments will actually be able to make them. Under the Proposed Regulations, this distinction has been eliminated, and it does not matter whether the transaction is or is not secured. All the built-in gain will be taxed in the year of the transaction.

Question – In a previous example in which a sixty-five-year old individual transferred property worth $1,000,000 in return for an annuity of $92,657 per year, the annuitant's expected return in that example was $1,806,812. If the individual lived for the full 19.5-year life expectancy, how could have saved federal estate taxes by transferring property worth $1,000,000?

Answer – The property transferred is the fair market value of the property on the date of the transfer, which in this example occurs 19.5 years prior to the annuitant's death, according to life expectancy tables. Assuming that the fair market value of the property continues to increase at a net rate of 7 percent per year, on the projected date of the annuitant's death in 19.5 years, the fair market value of the property would be $3,740,965.

The entire $1,806,812 of expected return would not be included in the annuitant's estate since a portion of that amount must be used by the transferor-annuitant to pay capital gains and ordinary income taxes. Further, the annuitant could make sizable gifts to decrease the net amount of cash realized as a result of receiving the annuity payments. Finally, assuming that the annuitant would like spend the majority of his annuity payments on living expenses, those amounts would not be included in his gross estate.

The key to success is to select property that has a high probability of appreciating in value at a rate that significantly exceeds the Section 7520 rate in the month the agreement is executed.[28]

Question – In arranging a private annuity transaction, is it wise to tie the annuity payments to the income generated by the transferred property?

Answer – No. Such a connection between the income and the property could be treated as a retained interest, so that the property would be included in the transferor's estate pursuant to Code section 2036.[29] While the income cannot be contractually tied to the annuity payment, being aware of how much income the transferred property will likely generate is important since this income may in many cases be necessary to make the annuity payments.

Question – Can a joint and survivor private annuity be designed?

Answer – Yes. Since the advent of an unlimited estate tax marital deduction for transfers between spouses, the joint and survivor annuity has become a more attractive planning technique. It has the advantage of providing security for the surviving spouse with no additional federal estate tax cost at either spouse's death (but may trigger state death taxes since some states do not have an unlimited marital deduction). At the time of the exchange, the gift of the survivor annuity may qualify for the gift tax marital deduction as qualified terminable interest property.[30] A second advantage is that the amount payable by the transferee each year is less than it would be in a single life private annuity. This makes it easier for a purchaser to meet annual obligations under the private annuity.

Example. Assume a client age sixty, a spouse age sixty-two, property with a fair market value of $1,000,000, and a 5.0 percent section 7520 federal discount rate. The annual payment would be $72,133 for a joint and survivor private annuity. This is $22,663 less than the $94,796 payment for a single life annuity for a sixty-year-old client.

CHAPTER ENDNOTES

1. Prop. Treas. Reg. §§1.1001-1(j) and 1.72-6; See also "Is the Private Annuity Really Dead for Estate Planning?" *Estate Planning Journal*, Vol. 39, No. 1 (January 2012).
2. Hesch, "Intra-Family Sales Using Private Annuities: The House Wins!" *Tax Management, Estates, Gifts, and Trusts Journal*, Vol. 30, No. 1, Jan. 13, 2005.
3. Where a sale is made to children through a private annuity, they or the trustee representing them should have a source of capital or income – other than solely the income from the transferred property – from which to make required payments, otherwise the IRS could argue that the seller's income is in reality inextricably tied to the success of the enterprise. See *Lazarus v. Comm'r.*, 513 F.2d 824 (9th Cir. 1975), aff'g 58 TC 854 (1972), acq. 1973-2 CB 2.
4. *Comm'r., v. Kann*, 174 F.2d 357 (3d Cir. 1949); *Lloyd v. Comm'r.*, 33 BTA 905 (1936) acq., 1950-2 CB 3; *Est. of Bell v. Comm'r.*, 60 TC 469 (1973); *212 Corp. v. Comm'r.*, 70 TC 788 (1978).
5. S. Leimberg, K. McGrath, and H. Zaritsky, "Deferral of Gain Eliminated in Sales of Appreciated Property for a Private Annuity," Estate Planning, Feb. 2007, Vol. 34, No. 2, Pg. 3; See Proposed Reg. §1.1001-1(j) and Proposed Reg. §1.72-6(e).
6. Rev. Rul. 62-136, 1962-2 CB 12.
7. See Kevin McGrath, "Private Annuity Trusts — The Numbers Don't Support the Hype," 109 *Tax Notes* 93 (Oct. 3, 2005). The author of this well considered article states that "the private annuity trust is a questionable tax strategy from a tax perspective. It is not clear that the transaction works in the manner in which its promoters claim. Even more problematic, however, is that assuming a private annuity trust does in fact offer the tax benefits that it purports to offer, it is an economically bad transaction. In fact, economic analysis of private annuity trusts reveals that not only is a private annuity trust worse than perhaps almost every other tax minimization strategy that would be available to a taxpayer, but a private annuity trust also leaves the taxpayer in a worse economic position than the taxpayer would be in by merely selling the asset and paying the tax." See also Jerome Hesch, "Intrafamily Sales Using Private Annuities: The House Wins," 30 *Tax Management Estates, Gifts and Trusts Journal* 81 (Jan. 13, 2005) for a thorough analysis of the costs, downsides, and relative disadvantages of private annuities.
8. See Deferral of Gain Eliminated in Sales of Appreciated Property for a Private Annuity, Stephan R. Leimberg, Kevin J. McGrath, and Howard M. Zaritsky, *Estate Planning Journal*, Vol. 34, No. 2 (Feb. 2007).
9. *Est. of Fabric v. Comm'r.*, 83 TC 932 (1984); *Est. of Jennings* 10 TC 323 (1948).
10. *Est. of Fabric*, 83 TC 932 (1984).
11. *Est. of McLendon*, TC Memo 1993-459; Let. Rul. 9504004.
12. Treas. Reg. §20.7520-3(b)(3).
13. I.R.C. §2033; *Fidelity-Philadelphia Trust Co. v. Smith*, 356 U.S. 274 (1958).
14. I.R.C. §§2039(a), 2039(b).
15. I.R.C. §72; Rev. Rul. 69-74, 1969-1 CB 43.
16. *F. A. Gillespie & Sons Co. v. Comm'r.*, 154 F.2d 913 (10th Cir. 1946) (cert. den., reh. den.); *Steinbach Kresge Co. v. Sturgess*, 33 F. Supp. 897 (D.C.N.J. 1940).
17. I.R.C. §2512(b).
18. Treas. Reg. §25.2503-3(c), Example (2); Rev. Rul. 70-514, 1970-2 CB 198; Let. Rul. 8811017.
19. I.R.C. §2523(f)(6).
20. Rev. Rul. 55-119, 1955-1 CB 352.
21. Rev. Rul. 55-119, 1955-1 CB 352.
22. Rev. Rul. 55-119, 1955-1 CB 352.
23. I.R.C. §2033.
24. *LaFarge v. Comm'r.*, 689 F.2d 845 (9th Cir. 1982), aff'g in part and rev'g in part 73 TC 40 (1979); *Stern v. Comm'r.*, 84-2 USTC ¶9949 (9th Cir. 1984), rev'g and remanding, 77 TC 614 (1981); *Est. of Fabric v. Comm'r.*, 83 TC 932 (1984).

25. See, for example, *Weigl v. Comm'r.*, 84 TC 1192 (1985).
26. *Stern v. Comm'r.*, 84-2 USTC ¶9949 (9th Cir. 1984), rev'g and remanding 77 TC 614 (1981).
27. Internal Revenue Manual §25.18.1.2.8 (02-15-2005), "Forms of Ownership and Characteristics."
28. See Jerome Hesch, "Intra-family Sales Using Private Annuities: The House Wins," *Tax Management Estates, Gifts and Trusts Journal*, Vol. 30, No. 1, Jan. 13th, 2005, for a thorough analysis of the costs, downsides, and relative disadvantages of private annuities.
29. *Lazarus v. Comm'r.*, 513 F.2d 824 (9th Cir. 1975).
30. I.R.C. §2523(f)(6).

INTEREST-FREE AND BELOW MARKET RATE LOANS

CHAPTER 43

43.1 INTRODUCTION

An interest-free or below market rate loan provides the borrower with the economic value of the time value of money. In other words, by not charging adequate interest on a loan, the lender is providing the borrower with use of money at a reduced or no cost. Generally, the lender and borrower are related parties such as a corporation and non-shareholder employee or a parent and child or other family member, etc.

Although in most situations, I.R.C. Section 7872 eliminates all potential income tax savings such loans could generate, there may be other reasons that interest-free and below market rate loans are viable and in many cases very appealing planning techniques.

43.2 WHEN IS USE OF SUCH A DEVICE INDICATED?

1. To reduce the estate of the lender by shifting the future growth potential of the amount loaned to the borrower.

2. As an employment fringe benefit to enable an employee to purchase a home, provide for a child's college education, purchase stock of the employer-corporation, pay life insurance premiums, or pay medical bills.

3. To provide funds to support parents, and for children in school, or to help adult children, grandchildren, or other relatives, or even friends purchase a home or business.

43.3 HOW DOES IT WORK?

Although in most cases, the negative income tax consequences of foregone interest cannot be avoided, it is important to avoid an even worse income tax consequence - the IRS not recognizing the loan itself as a valid debt. To do so:

1. The loan must have all the indicia of a bona fide debt (preferably in writing).

2. If the parties maintain books or records of account, the debt should be entered properly.

3. There should be a provision in the debt instrument (assuming it is an interest-free loan) expressly precluding interest or, in the case of a below market rate loan, stating the interest rate to be charged.

In order to assure that a loan from a corporation to an employee is not characterized as compensation or a dividend, the loan must conform to the following requirements:

1. The loan must have all the indicia of a bona fide debt (preferably a written note containing a reasonable repayment schedule or a note payable on demand).

2. A demonstrated intent and obligation to repay must be evidenced by an agreement between the parties. This is especially important where the loan is to a majority shareholder-employee. Otherwise, the IRS could claim that the "loan" is in fact a disguised dividend.

3. The amount of the loan must be reasonable in relation to the salary of the employee.

43.4 HOW IT IS DONE

Example 1. Your client, Maxine Grayboyes, is a key singer in the industrial productions corporation called, "Off Broad Street." To enable her daughter to purchase a new home, Maxine makes an interest-free loan of $150,000 to her daughter.

Example 2. Terry Halpern is the owner of "Show Time," a magazine devoted to promoting show business and informing people who work for television, radio, theater groups, and other entertainment vehicles about news and current events. To provide Terry with the means to promote and portray a more favorable press image for herself, Sarah Fawcelips loans Terry $4,000,000 at 2 percent interest for eight years as compared to 6 percent - the best bank interest rate otherwise available to Terry.

While the lender would be imputed taxable interest income (see Tax Implications, below), the nontax advantages realized by lender by loaning the funds to the borrower are significant.

43.5 TAX IMPLICATIONS

Types of Below Market Loans

There are six types of below market loans subject to Code section 7872: gift loans, compensation-related loans, corporation-shareholder loans, tax avoidance loans, other below market loans and loans to qualified continuing care facilities. The manner in which the Section 7872 rules operate depends on whether the loan is a demand loan and a term loan.

Calculation of the Taxable Amount of Foregone Interest

Demand Loans and Gift Loans

For purposes of applying the Section 7872 rules, demand loans (loans payable on the demand of the lender) and gift loans bearing no interest or interest at a below market rate are re-characterized for tax purposes are treated in the same way. Each year the loan is outstanding, the foregone interest, i.e., the amount of interest that would have been payable had the loan charged interest at the applicable AFR less the amount of interest actually charged, is treated as if the lender transferred that amount to the borrower. In turn, the borrower is deemed to have re-transferred that amount back to the lender as interest.

Focusing on the foregone interest deemed to be transferred by the lender to the borrower, if the lender was a corporation and the borrower was a shareholder, the foregone interest would be treated as dividend income to the borrower. On the other hand, if the lender was a parent and the borrower was a child, the foregone interest would be treated as a gift from parent to child. Finally, if the lender was an employer and the borrower was an employee, the foregone interest would be treated as compensation to the employee. Although gifts are not subject to income tax, the deemed dividend and compensation would be taxable to the borrower. Finally, gifts and dividends are non-deductible. So, the lender would not be entitled to a deduction for either deemed transfer of foregone interest. On the other hand, compensation is deductible and, thus, the deemed payment of compensation would be deductible.

Example. Asher makes a $200,000 interest-free demand loan to his daughter, Ashley. Ashley intends to use the loan as operating capital in her photography business. Assuming that based on the short-term AFR (the rate that applies to demand loans), the foregone interest is $8,000. The following "phantom" transactions are deemed to have occurred.

Step 1 - Asher is deemed to have transferred (given) $8,000 to Ashley.

Step 2- Ashley is deemed to have re-transferred the $8,000 to Asher as an interest payment.

The tax consequences to Asher are as follows: The deemed transfer of $8,000 to Ashley is a present interest gift. Since it is a gift, there is no income tax deduction. The $8,000 interest payment he is deemed to have received from Ashley is includible in his gross income.

The tax consequences to Ashley are as follows: The deemed receipt of $8,000 by Ashley is an income tax-free gift.[1] The $8,000 deemed interest payment to Asher is deductible because Ashley used the loan proceeds in her business.[2]

Note that had Asher been Ashley's employer, the deemed $8,000 transfer to her would have been treated as compensation. Such deemed compensation payment would have been deductible by Asher and taxable to Ashley. As to the deemed interest payment to Asher by Ashley, the tax consequences would have been the same as described above.

Term Loans

A term loan is defined as any loan which is not a demand loan.[3] How much interest is foregone in the case of a term loan? Based on the applicable AFR,[4] the foregone interest amount is the present value of the interest that should have been charged, minus the amount from the present value of the interest that was, in fact, charged. The difference is the foregone interest. In calculating present values, the applicable AFR at the time the loan is made must be used.

More specifically, on the date the loan is consummated, the lender is treated as transferring to the borrower the amount of such foregone interest.[5] So, depending on the relationship between the borrower and the lender, the amount transferred may be deemed to be a gift, compensation, dividend, etc. Similarly, from the lender's perspective, the amount deemed to be transferred to the borrower may or may not be deductible depending on his or her relationship with the borrower.

As to the foregone interest, it is treated as original issue discount.[6] From the lender's and borrower's prospective, daily portions of original issue discount interest is deemed to accrue each day of the taxable year in which the debt is outstanding. On that basis, interest would be includible in the lender's gross income and deductible (if in fact, the interest is deductible at all) by the borrower.

Assuming the interest is deductible by the borrower, however, depending on the relationship between the lender and the borrower, there would a significant mismatch between the inclusion of the deemed transfer in the borrower's gross income and his or her interest deduction. Stated differently, although the full amount of the deemed transfer to the borrower would be includible in his or her gross income in the first year of the loan, the interest deduction would be spread out over the term of the loan.

Example. Asher makes a ten-year term loan with his employee, Ashley. Ashley intends to use the loan as operating capital in her photography business. In the year the loan is consummated, assuming that the foregone interest on the loan is $50,000, Ashley would include that full amount in gross income. As to the deductibility of the deemed payment of interest to Asher, pursuant to the original issue discount rules, Ashley's deduction would be spread out over the ten-year term.

Finally, for gift tax purposes, the foregone interest is treated as a present interest gift. So depending on the lender/donor's gift tax annual exclusion and the amount of the foregone interest, some or all of the gift may be taxable.

Exceptions

There are three important exceptions to rules governing taxability of below market loans.

De minimis rule- A loan made from one individual to another, from a corporation to an employee or independent contractor, or from a corporation to a shareholder is exempt from both gift and income tax rules described above if the outstanding balance on the total of all loans made to that person from the lender does not exceed $10,000. This is known as the "$10,000 and under" *de minimis* rule.[7]

This exception will not apply to a gift loan the proceeds of which are used in connection with income producing property. Furthermore, for term loans that are not gift loans, once the outstanding balance exceeds $10,000, the exception no longer applies, even if the outstanding balance is later reduced below $10,000.[8] Finally, if the loan is a "compensation-related" loan or a "corporate-shareholder" loan (any loan between a corporation and any shareholder), the exception will not apply if federal tax avoidance is a principal purpose for the loan.

"$100,000 and under" rule- This exception applies to gift loans made directly between individuals and the outstanding balances due on the aggregate of the loans made to that person by the lender do not exceed $100,000. In that case, the amount treated as foregone is the lower of (a) the applicable AFR or (b) the borrower's net investment income for the year. If the borrower does not earn more than $1,000 in the year, the foregone interest is zero.

The $100,000 and under exception rule applies only if federal tax avoidance is not a principal purpose of the loan.[9]

Continuing care facility- The third exception to the general rules governing interest-free and below market rate loans is for any below market loan made by a lender to a qualified continuing care facility pursuant to a continuing care contract if the lender (or his or her spouse) attains age sixty-two before the close of such year. This exception applies to the extent that the aggregate amount of the loan, added to the aggregate outstanding amount of all other previous loans between the lender (or his or her spouse) and any qualified continuing care facility, does not exceed a specified amount, which is indexed for inflation. In 2006, the amount is $163,300 as indexed.[10] Inflation adjustments after 2006 are no longer published because of changes made by TIPRA and Section425 of the Tax Relief and Health Care Act of 2006.

43.6 IMPLICATIONS AND ISSUES IN COMMUNITY PROPERTY STATES

As discussed in Chapter 8, relating to gifts (which should be reviewed in conjunction with this section), some states impose gift taxes on interspousal gifts. The following are some of the potential problem areas which can arise:

1. If the money loaned is the separate property of one spouse (e.g., that spouse having inherited the funds) a gift can occur between the lending spouse if the demand note is made in favor of both spouses. The amount of the gift would be one-half of the value of the note (presumably the face amount of the note).

2. A similar gift may be found if the money loaned is community property and the demand note received in exchange for the funds names only one spouse. It may be possible to show successfully that the named spouse was holding the note as trustee for the community and a gift avoided, but it creates the opportunity for the taxing authorities to claim that a gift was made and thus creates exposure to either gift tax, legal expense, or both, in dealing with the problem created.

3. Another unintended gift could occur if the money were loaned to one spouse and then used to purchase assets in the names of both spouses.

4. An accidental gift may also result from the repayment of the loan. If the loan is made to one spouse and is used to make investments in the name of that spouse, the liability belongs entirely to that spouse. The use of community funds or the separate property of the non-borrowing spouse to repay the loan provides the basis for a taxable gift to be recognized.

5. If the note is called by the lender and the borrower does not have the funds to repay and his spouse or the community does, then a gift can be avoided by the borrower giving to the spouse (or the community) a note for the amount of funds used to repay his obligation.

These problems can be avoided by careful attention to the source of funds for loans and the manner in which investments or repayments are made.

43.7 FREQUENTLY ASKED QUESTIONS

Question – How can a loan to a key employee be structured in order to tie that employee into the business?

Answer – By making the loan callable upon separation from service or payable in the event of the employee's pre-retirement death, the corporation can protect its interest. The employee could protect his own estate by purchasing life insurance in the amount of the loan.

Question – What are the implications of a loan that is treated as a gift?

Answer – If a loan is considered a gift, the lender is treated as if he or she made a present interest gift to the borrower in the amount of the "foregone interest." This gift may not qualify for the annual $17,000 (in 2023) gift exclusion. (See the discussion of term and demand loans below.)

Question – What are the implications if a loan is not a gift?

Answer – The tax characterization of a loan which is not a gift depends on the relationship between the parties. In any case, the IRS will treat the lender as having made a transfer to the borrower in the amount of the "foregone interest."

The IRS will generally treat foregone interest as a dividend when the borrower is solely a shareholder (nondeductible by the corporation, taxable to the shareholder (although maybe at preferred rates), as interest paid by the shareholder, and taxable to the corporation as interest income).

If the borrower is solely an employee, the lender will have interest income to the extent of the foregone interest and a corresponding deduction for compensation paid (if reasonable). The borrower will have compensation income, but a deduction for the foregone interest may be denied or limited (depending on how the borrower uses the loan proceeds).

Question – How will interest-free or below market rate loans to shareholder-employees be treated?

Answer – The foregone interest will generally be treated as a dividend.

Question – Are there transactions that will be treated as interest-free or below market rate loans even though they appear to be something else?

Answer – Yes. Congress was concerned with all transactions that in effect were tax avoidance or significant tax-shifting schemes. Therefore, many situations which do not look like loans will invoke the below market rules. For example, assume a local country club requires its members to pay a refundable, non-interest-bearing deposit as part of their membership fee. In essence, the member is paying part of the fee with the income that the club earns on the deposit. The IRS could easily apply the rules described above.

CHAPTER ENDNOTES

1. I.R.C. §102(a).
2. I.R.C. §163.
3. I.R.C. §7872(f)(6).
4. The AFR (applicable federal rate) is based on the term of the loan. For a term that is three years of less, the short-term rate applies. A term that is greater than three years but less than nine years, the mid-term rate applies. Finally, if the term is greater than nine years, the long-term rate applies. I.R.C. §1274(d).
5. I.R.C. §7872(b)(1).
6. I.R.C. §§7872(b)(2)(B).
7. I.R.C. §7872(c)(2),(3); Prop. Reg. §1.7872-8(b)(3).
8. I.R.C. §7872(f)(10).
9. I.R.C. §7872(d)(1).
10. I.R.C. §7872(g)(1),(2); Rev. Rul. 2005-75, 2005-49 IRB 1073.

USING FORMULA POWERS OF APPOINTMENT/OPTIMAL BASIS INCREASE TRUSTS (OBITS)

CHAPTER 44

44.1 INTRODUCTION

An Optimal Basis Increase Trust (OBIT) is an irrevocable trust, usually established by the settlor's death such as a bypass (credit shelter) trust or trust for children, but it could also be included in an intervivos trust, like a SLAT, that attempts to maximize the step up in basis of the trust assets at the current primary beneficiary's death through selective estate inclusion.[1] The goal is to avoid a "step down" in basis and avoid any increase in estate or GST tax yet soak up any unused applicable exclusion amount the powerholder may have that can be used to increase basis without causing estate tax in the powerholder's estate. 99.9% (or more) of the U.S. population has an estate smaller than $12,920,000, which is the applicable exclusion amount as of 2023, and could include more assets in their estate without causing estate tax.

Intentionally causing estate inclusion but avoiding a step down in basis or an estate tax is typically accomplished through one of two ways:

1) adding a testamentary general power of appointment (TGPOA) that is customized so as to exclude assets whose basis would not increase with inclusion in one's estate (cash, income in respect of a decedent, assets with basis higher than fair market value at the time of death), typically with a formula that would only apply the power to the extent that inclusion in the powerholder's estate does not cause federal estate or GST tax (and if it causes state estate tax, only to the extent that the value of the basis increase is worth causing a state estate tax); or

2) adding a testamentary limited power of appointment (TLPOA) that is affirmatively exercised by the powerholder in such a way as to trigger the Delaware Tax Trap (Code section 2041(a)(3)) to selectively cause estate inclusion over only targeted assets for the same purpose.

A general testamentary power of appointment is one in which the powerholder may appoint to themselves, their estate, their creditors or creditors of their estate.[2] It is strongly recommended when crafting such a clause to provide that an independent trustee or trust protector can amend the clause later should state or federal tax law or other circumstances change.

44.2 ADVANTAGES

Code section 1014 is one of the *most valuable loopholes in the tax code* and the applicable exclusion amount should be considered as a "basis increasing coupon." The idea of maximizing one's estate to exploit this loophole is an income tax play, but can be a very valuable one, especially if the trust was funded via gift or the primary beneficiary has outlived the settlor for many years. In many cases, the assets in an irrevocable trust have extremely low basis, yet the primary beneficiary (be it a spouse, children or others) often have nowhere near a taxable estate and could safely include a large portion if not all of the low basis trust assets in their estate without any adverse state or federal estate tax ramifications.

Basis increase is especially valuable for depreciable property such as real estate, or a farm or business, because the beneficiaries who inherit such property receive an immediate tax benefit of having a higher basis for depreciation, without having to sell the property to realize the benefit of a higher basis.

Such a power can be crafted in such a way that makes it extremely difficult if not impossible to thwart the settlor's intentions by requiring the consent of non-adverse parties (essentially, parties who are not beneficiaries of the trust. Code section 2041(b)(1)(C), in defining what constitutes a general power, provides that:

> (ii) If the power is not exercisable by the decedent except in conjunction with a person having a substantial interest in the property, subject to the power, which is **adverse to exercise of the power in favor of the decedent—such power shall not be deemed a general power of appointment**. For the purposes of this clause a person who, after the death of the decedent, may be possessed of a power of appointment (with respect to the property subject to the decedent's power) which he may exercise in his own favor shall be deemed as having an interest in the property and such interest shall be deemed adverse to such exercise of the decedent's power.

Corollary to the definition above, a power exercisable only in conjunction with a *non-adverse* party is still a general power if it otherwise meets the definition.[3] Surprisingly, even an independent bank co-trustee with duties to the beneficiaries, is not sufficiently adverse.[4] What are the odds that a bank as trustee would agree to allow a powerholder to appoint to their estate or creditors instead of the remainder beneficiaries to whom it owes a fiduciary duty to protect? Remember that a testamentary general power of appointment triggers estate inclusion by its very existence at the time of death, and it is completely irrelevant whether it is ever exercised, or even what the odds are of it ever being exercised.

Upstream "OBIT" powers can also be added to SLATs, IGTs and other trusts that grant such general powers to an older generation as well to soak up some of their basis-increasing coupon rather than have it go to waste. There is no reason whatsoever that powers of appointment can only be granted to spouses or younger beneficiaries.[5]

Powers may be added to pre-existing irrevocable trusts, but this is a more involved analysis. Is there a trust protector or a decanting power or a decanting statute that may apply? Trustees in most states probably have the power to petition the local probate court to approve an amendment if another avenue does not work. This occurred in most recent PLR where the family wanted to get a new basis step up on the death of the current beneficiary.[6]

44.3 DISADVANTAGES

Some settlors may not want to give their spouse, children or other beneficiaries any power to deviate from the distribution terms of the trust. However, it is possible to craft a testamentary power of appointment, even a general one, that can still count as such for federal tax purposes but be difficult if not practically impossible to actually exercise, by conditioning the exercise on the consent of various non-adverse parties.

A minority of states, e.g., California, may count assets subject to a testamentary general power of appointment as subject to a powerholder's estate's creditors. While this is very rarely a problem, since people with the level of wealth to have irrevocable trusts are rarely bankrupt, it is possible that a powerholder causes a wrongful death accident in excess or insurance, for example, and has an insolvent estate due to the litigation. The power might be conditioned on the powerholder's estate's solvency, however, and PLRs have approved of that concept still causing estate inclusion.[7]

The drafting of a basic testamentary power of appointment over all of a trust's assets, or over only trust assets with basis less than fair market value at death whose basis would increase under Code Section 1014, is easy to draft and administer. However, if there is a formula cap involved, tied to the largest amount that can pass in a powerholder's estate without causing estate/GST tax, this creates more complexity in drafting and in post-mortem administration should the cap ever apply. Such a cap may be quite desirable even when people think it may not be currently necessary, due to the applicable exclusion amount being cut in half in 2026 under current law and the possibility that Congress (or even a state) may change the estate tax law applicable to the powerholder.

For example, you have a client who is a widow with $5 million of her own assets and is the primary beneficiary of $10 million in a bypass trust. She currently has $12.92 million of her own basic exclusion amount (and GST exemption) and $3 million of DSUE – if she died in 2023, her applicable exclusion amount ($15.92 million) could safely absorb the entire bypass trust being included in her estate without any fear of estate tax, but in 2026 her basic exclusion amount might be cut in half (approx. $7 million), and her estate may have grown, in which case any estate inclusion of the bypass trust should be capped so as not to cause an estate *tax*. If $3 million of the bypass trust consists of IRAs, annuities, short term bonds and cash equivalents, that may still leave $7 million of asset with a basis lower than fair market value that could be stepped up, but in this latter example, the widow only has $5 million of excess applicable exclusion amount in 2026 ($7 million basis exclusion plus $3 million DSUE minus her $5 million estate).

If the formula does restrict the amount of assets over which the general power applies, how are the potentially appointive assets chosen? Can the trustee choose? Is there an ordering rule so that the power applies to the assets with the lowest percentage basis to fair market value first? To depreciable property first? Crafting the ideal ordering rule and formula can be complicated, and there may be some uncertainty involved– e.g., would the IRS respect the trustee simply choosing which assets a capped testamentary power of appointment applies to, or would they force the basis adjustment to apply to potentially appointive assets pro rata in such instance? Any formula general power of appointment should probably have a provision whereby an independent trustee or trust protector can amend the general testamentary power of appointment to adapt to any state or federal tax law changes, or changes in the use of trust assets (e.g., a changed plan to sell the family vacation home rather than hold it forever as initially expected may cause the trustee to amend the power to apply to that asset first). Don't let the perfect become the enemy of the good. Even if the trust had a general power over 5/7 of every asset in our example above (which is less than optimal, since it would be preferable to apply to lower basis assets especially depreciable property first), it is still much better than having it apply to nothing at all and receive no basis step up whatsoever.

Cost and Importance of Implementation and Ongoing Administration

The cost of drafting and additional administrative cost is usually negligible compared to the potential savings obtained from a higher basis at the powerholder's death. However, there is a cost, especially if the cap applies and the trustee has to collaborate with the powerholder's estate/executor to determine the amount of the powerholder's outside estate and remaining applicable exclusion amount. For hard to value assets, an appraisal may be required, as with any estate. That said, usually the potential basis steip up is in the millions of dollars, and the savings therefrom would often dwarf the additional costs involved.

Estate/GST Tax Risks and Consequences

The law behind Code section 2041 is largely well-settled. There are some commentators who believe, however, that if someone has a power to appoint to their creditors (and not to their estate), that the amount included under Code section 2041 by such a power is limited to the amount of debt that the powerholder has. There is no statutory, regulatory or basis in case law for this conclusion, but there are some reputable attorneys who apparently so argue. For this reason, some prefer that their powers include appointment to the estate. Since most OBIT powers are going to require consent of non-adverse parties, this is hardly a drawback.

It makes sense for Congress to have included a power to appoint to creditors as equivalent to ownership for estate tax purposes because under contract law it takes very little effort to create a binding contract and debt. First year law students learn that "consideration" for a contract can be minimal and that courts do not examine the adequacy of the equivalency of consideration on both sides. Thus, if John promises to give Joe $1 million to take a selfie with a silly hat, and Joe does so, John owes Joe and Joe is now a creditor for $1 million. This is why the non-adverse party consent is important to draft into such powers even if someone does not fear the powerholder actually appointing to creditors.

While there are many PLRs approving of formula general powers of appointment, some fear that the powerholder's ability to manipulate their net estate by leaving assets to a spouse or to charity (eligible for the marital or charitable deduction) means that the cap on the appointive assets (only so much as would not cause an estate tax) may not apply as intended, and the cap should apply to the gross estate for this reason. This may be overly conservative, but in many cases would not detract from the benefit by very much, since many beneficiaries have enough excess applicable exclusion amount, and don't leave assets to spouse or charity, that would make this consequential.

Gift/GST Tax Risks and Consequences

As noted above, there is a risk that the IRS does not honor the cap, but there is also a risk that a formula tied to the maximum amount that can pass through a powerholder's without causing estate and GST tax makes the resulting trust less tax efficient for GST purposes. This can be complicated. Should the power be limited to what does not cause tax, or to the maximum extent of GST exclusion available? Let's go back to the prior example of the widow who has $5 million of her own assets, $10 million in a bypass trust, and after 2026, $7 million of basic exclusion amount and GST exemption, plus $3 million of DSUE. The bypass trust is GST exempt due to her late husband's estate's prior GST allocation to it. Should the formula step up the most assets possible in the bypass trust ($5 million) or the most possible that can still remain GST exempt, up to her remaining GST exclusion (only $2 million, assuming she used some of her GST exclusion for her own estate). It depends on the situation and the amount of step up involved, but many families would prefer a "bird in the hand" – i.e., tax savings sooner rather than later.

Income Tax Risks and Consequences

There is a risk of a "step down" if the general power can apply to assets whose basis is greater than fair market value at the time of a powerholder's death. This is very easily drafted around by excluding any such assets from the definition of appointable assets subject to the general power (one can still have a limited power of appointment over such assets). It may not be worth bothering adding formula general powers of appointment if a trust invests conservatively in money market, short-term bonds, etc., or consistently churns investments such that the basis of the assets is relatively high and will not benefit much from a new basis.

Asset Protection, if any, Offered by the Tool

Testamentary general powers (not limited) may cause susceptibility to a powerholder's estate's creditors in a handful of states – if that is the case, using a testamentary limited power of appointment coupled with triggering the Delaware Tax Trap might be an alternative, or conditioning the power on the solvency of the powerholder's estate, as was accomplished in PLR 9110054. However, in the majority of states, this does not cause a problem when the power is not exercised.[8]

CHAPTER ENDNOTES

1. For further discussion, see *The Optimal Basis Increase Trust (OBIT)*, LISI Estate Planning Newsletter #2080 (March 20, 2013) and the follow up white paper, *The Optimal Basis Increase and Income Tax Efficiency Trust*, available for download for free on www.ssrn.com.
2. IRC §2041(b)(1).
3. See also Treas. Reg. §20.2041-3(c)(2).
4. *Estate of Vissering v. Commissioner*, 96 T.C. 749 (1971), reversed on other grounds, *Estate of Jones v. Commissioner*, 56 T.C. 35 (1971), *Miller v. United State*, 387 F.2d 866 (1968) and Treas. Reg. §20.2041-3(c)(2), Example 3.
5. See *The Upstream Crummey Optimal Basis Increase Trust*, May 2014 issue of CCH Estate Planning Review and *The Upstream Optimal Basis Increase Trust*, LISI Estate Planning Newsletter #2635 (April 17, 2018). LISI Estate Planning Newsletter #2635 (April 17, 2018) for further discussion of this type of planning. A version of the latter is also included in the white paper cited in endnote 1.
6. See discussion of the PLR in *Ed Morrow on PLR 202206008: Judicial Settlement Modification & Formula Testamentary General Powers of Appointment*, LISI Estate Planning Newsletter #2945 (March 16, 2022).
7. PLR 9110054.
8. *Restatement of Property, Second, Donative Transfers*, §13.2. Consistent with the Second Restatement is Page on the Law of Wills §45.24 (3d Ed. 1962), Scott and Fratcher, The Law on Trusts §147.3 (4th Ed. 1987), *Restatement of Property, Second, Donative Transfers*, §13.4.

SPLIT INTEREST PURCHASE OF PROPERTY (SPLIT)

CHAPTER 45

45.1 INTRODUCTION

A SPLIT is an arrangement under which two parties agree to co-purchase an asset. Rather than purchase, it in equal shares, with a SPLIT, one party (usually a parent) purchases a life estate (the right to receive the income from the property or the right to use, possess, and enjoy the property itself for as long as the life tenant lives). The second party (usually a son or daughter or grandchild of the life tenant) purchases a remainder interest (the right to the property, whatever it is worth, when the first party's interest terminates. If the first party purchased a life interest, by definition his interest terminates when he dies). Each party to the SPLIT pays the actuarial value of the interest purchased.

The adoption of Code section 2702 has considerably reduced and limited the estate tax attractiveness of SPLITs between related persons. However, SPLITs between *un*related persons, such as an unmarried couple, are *not* subject to section 2702. This may suggest the SPLIT in a number of estate planning situations involving individuals who do not fall within the reach of section 2702 and may provide unmarried couples with a very exciting planning opportunity. A SPLIT is still available for tangible personal property such as artwork, undeveloped real estate, or transfers that qualify as Qualified Personal Residence Trusts.

45.2 WHEN IS USE OF SUCH A DEVICE INDICATED?

1. When an individual would like to improve current income. If a SPLIT is used to purchase income producing investment property, the individual's lifetime income is enhanced by the return provided on the remainder person's investment.

2. When it is important to keep property within a family and provide the older generation with the lifetime use of the property or the income it generates, structuring a SPLIT may provide protection from a potential will contest or a spousal election against the will. Because SPLIT property passes by contract (upon the life tenant's death to the remainder person), it should not be included in the life tenant's probate estate. Therefore, generally, a disgruntled heir would have no right to property purchased through a SPLIT. Additionally, a SPLIT protects the underlying property from the claims of the life tenant's creditors, because the property does not pass through the life tenant's estate. Finally, because the property does not pass through probate, the parties' privacy is assured.

3. In a situation in which the property is located in a state other than the life tenant's state of residence, when it is desirable to avoid ancillary administration, upon the death of the life tenant, by contract, the remainder person automatically becomes full and complete owner of the property. This means the cost of multiple state probate preceedings would be avoided.

4. When the parties are unrelated (as defined in IRC Section 2702). For example, an unmarried same gender or even opposite gender couple should be able to create a SPLIT that is not subject to section 2702.

45.3 WHAT ARE THE REQUIREMENTS?

Ownership of the property is bifurcated into two parts: a "term" interest, which may be either the right to receive stipulated payments from the property for a term of years, or life, or in a very limited situation, the right to use the property for that period. The second part is the "remainder" interest, which will pass to the other joint owner when the term interest expires.

Both the term holder and the remainder holder pay their proportionate part of the purchase price for the property based on government valuation tables setting an actuarial value for the term interest and the remainder interest. NumberCruncher software will do these computations quickly and accurately. It is essential that the purchaser of the term interest furnish no part of the consideration used by the remainder person to purchase the remainder interest.[1]

Because the term holder and remainder holder are co-owners of the property, it cannot be sold without the consent of *both* parties. Because, under most circumstances, the term holder is limited to a fixed dollar payment from the property, the term holder will apparently have no other rights in the property. In the limited situations where the term holder can retain full possession and enjoyment of the property for the term, the term holder should have all of the legal rights of a joint tenant in the property. The exact nature of the rights of the term holder and the remainder holder is dependent on state law.

Example. An about-to-be-separated fifty-year old father wishes to invest in a painting or in some unimproved real estate. He wants his daughter to receive the painting or unimproved real estate at his death. He has used none of his annual exclusion or unified credit. He wants to begin to shift wealth to his daughter who is a financially successful women's clothing designer. If he purchases the painting or unimproved real estate in his own name, he knows that it could be lost in litigation with his about to be ex-wife or included in full in the computation of his taxable estate. He expects the painting or unimproved real estate to appreciate considerably each year.

The father purchases a life estate (or term interest) in the painting or unimproved real estate. He must pay an amount equal to the present value of what the painting or unimproved real estate could be rented for over his lifetime (or term interest).[2]

The daughter pays the balance with her own money. Upon her father's death or at the end of the term, the daughter becomes the full owner of the artwork or appreciated property. Alternatively, the father could purchase property with his daughter and retain an annuity or unitrust interest in the property for life (or for a term). Upon her father's death or at the end of the term, the daughter becomes the full owner of the artwork or appreciated property. Based on government valuation tables, the father's contribution to the purchase price would be the actuarial value of his annuity or unitrust interest and his daughter's contribution to the purchase price would pay the actuarial value of her remainder interest.

45.4 TAX IMPLICATIONS
Section 2702

For federal gift tax purposes, joint purchases of property by related parties are treated as transfers to a trust under the provisions of Code section 2702 (discussed in more detail in Chapter 29), and the person or persons who acquire term interests in the property in a transaction or series of transactions shall be treated as having acquired the entire property and then having transferred the other interests to the other persons in exchange for any consideration provided by such other persons.[3] Any term interest in property, such as a life estate or term of years, but not co-ownership, such as tenancy in common or joint tenancy, is treated as if held in trust under section 2702.[4] A leasehold is not considered a term interest - *if* made for full and adequate consideration where a good faith attempt is made to determine fair rental value.[5]

In the case of a joint purchase, the amount considered transferred by an individual to family members for this purpose will not exceed the actual consideration furnished by that individual for the property.[6]

The SPLIT purchase technique can have disastrous gift tax consequences if section 2702 applies. This is because the purchase of the property is considered a gift of the entire property from the life or term tenant to the remainder person (the retained income interest is treated as having a zero value for gift tax purposes). The amount of the gift is the fair market value of the property less any consideration (amounts paid toward the purchase price) paid by the remainder person. Thus, the amount of the gift is limited to the actual consideration paid by the term holder.

Retained Annuity or Unitrust Interests

The unfortunate results just described can be avoided if, instead of retaining the income for the term, the term holder retains a fixed annuity payment or percentage payments based on the annual valuation of the property under the same rules described in Chapter 29 for GRATs and GRUTs, which are statutory exceptions to the section 2702 rules. If the GRAT or GRUT rules are followed and the consideration paid by the term holder is exactly equal to the actuarial value of the annuity or unitrust payments, there would be no taxable gift. This is because for gift tax purposes the value of the annuity or unitrust payments *plus* the consideration paid from the remainder person are subtracted from the fair market value of the property. Assuming the sum of these two amounts equal the fair market value of the property, there would be no gift to the remainder person.

The Tangible Property Exception

As noted above, section 2702 does preserve the traditional form of SPLIT in certain limited circumstances. There is, however, the tangible property exception rule. The tangible property exception rule applies to property for which no allowance for depreciation or depletion would be allowable, and as to which the failure to exercise any rights with respect to the property will not affect its value. There is a *de minimis* rule for depreciation of certain improvements.

The nonexercise of rights under a term interest in tangible property, such as a painting or unimproved real property which does not have a substantial effect on the value of the remainder interest, is not valued at zero, but at the amount a third party would pay for the term interest (e.g., the right to possess the painting for life).[7] This means that it is possible to arrange for the SPLIT purchase of a work of art, or unimproved real estate, with the term holder acquiring the right to use the property for the term, or life, and the remainder to someone else.

However, the valuation of a term interest in tangible property is valued under a willing buyer-willing seller test, not under actuarial tables.[8] This means that to avoid a taxable gift, the term holder would have to prove that the amount paid for the term interest in the tangible property is the same as the amount an unrelated person would pay for the same interest in an arm's length transaction. The difficulties of proving this are tremendous. In most cases, comparable sales or rentals are given greater weight in valuation than appraisals.

Finally, a conversion of the term interest into some other property right (other than a qualified annuity trust) is treated as a gift transfer of the retained term interest determined at the date of original transfer. Any alteration or improvement of the property that so alters its character that it would not qualify under this rule is treated as a conversion of the property. If the property is converted, it is possible to switch to a qualified annuity trust described in Chapter 29.

Planning Implications

While the pros and cons of grantor retained interest transfers generally apply here, there is an important difference. Section 2702 is a gift tax provision, and should not apply in determining whether or not the joint purchase has estate tax consequences. If the term holder pays full and adequate consideration for the term interest, whether it is in the form of an annuity or unitrust payment, or the use of qualified tangible property, then the death of the term holder *should* have no federal estate tax consequences. Unlike a GRIT, GRAT, or GRUT, the term of a SPLIT can be for the life of the term holder. The retained interest should not result in inclusion of the value of the property in the term holder's estate because the term holder did not "transfer" the remainder interest. Therefore, Code section 2036(a), which applies to transfers in which the transferor retains income or other interests for life, should not be applicable (but see "Frequently Asked Questions," below). The joint acquisition of income producing property could be a very useful technique for certain clients.

45.5 ISSUES IN COMMUNITY PROPERTY STATES

The situation here is analogous to the transfer of community property to a grantor retained annuity trust or unitrust discussed in Chapter 29. If community funds are used to purchase the term interest, presumably the retained interest will either be paid jointly to the transferors or each will receive one-half of the required payment for the term.

45.6 JOINTLY PURCHASED PROPERTY

The personal residence trust and qualified personal residence trust, or QPRT, are discussed in Chapter 29. Some commentators have suggested that a personal residence could be acquired through a joint purchase, and then placed in a personal residence trust.

Under a typical scenario, parent and children would acquire residential property the parent would occupy as a personal residence for a term of years, and, then, at his or her death, the children would become the owners of the property. With respect to the purchase price, parent would pay an amount equal to the actuarial value of a term interest, and the children would pay an amount equal to actuarial value of a remainder interest. Under the joint purchase rule of Code section 2702, the effect would be a gift from parent to children, because the term interest would be valued at zero for federal gift tax purposes.

However, if the residence were purchased via a joint purchase trust agreement containing the requirements of a personal residence trust, pursuant to the statutory exception described above,[9] the full value of the term interest plus the amount paid for the remainder interest equal to the fair market value of the property would result in no taxable gift. Further, if the parent dies during the term, nothing should be included in the parent's gross estate under Code Section 2036(a) because the parent paid "full and adequate consideration" for the value of the term interest.

If the transaction is not structured and maintained properly, however, the entire value of the property could be included in the estate of the term holder. In a letter ruling, the IRS ruled that the entire property was brought back and included in the term holder's gross estate because the term holder furnished all the consideration with which the remainder holder purchased his interest.[10]

In addition, if jointly purchased property is sold and the joint purchase trust is converted to a GRAT, the IRS may include the value of the property back into the grantor's estate under Code section 2039. In Letter Ruling 9412036, the parties unsuccessfully attempted to create a SPLIT-purchase grantor retained unitrust that would provide one parent a unitrust for life followed by a unitrust for the other parent for life. In purchasing property to be held in trust, the parents would pay the part of the purchase price equal to their actuarial interests in the trust. There would also be a right of first refusal should any of the interest holders seek to sell their interests. The trust failed to contain required provisions relating to commutation of interests and adjustments for incorrect valuations, so it did not qualify under Code section 2702.

However, the ruling went even further and held that the property would be includable in a parent's estate under either Code sections 2036 or 2039. Under Section 2036, the amount includable would be equal to the lesser of (1) the original value of the parent's transferred share of property held in the trust reduced by the original value of the income interest attributable to transfers to the trust by others, or (2) an amount which would yield the unitrust payment at the parent's death. Under section 2039, a parent's estate would include that portion of the date of death value of the property that is proportionate to the decedent's share of all trust contributions.

45.7 FREQUENTLY ASKED QUESTIONS

Question – Should the SPLIT-purchase technique be completely abandoned?

Answer – In the right situations, the joint or SPLIT purchase may still be very useful. Unlike the GRAT or GRUT, the gift in a SPLIT in a worst-case scenario is limited to what the term holder pays for the life or term interest rather than the entire value of the property. Therefore, even if the term holder retains an income interest valued at zero under section 2702, the gift will still be limited to the actuarial value of the income interest (assuming that is what the term holder pays for the term interest). It will not be 100 percent of the value of the property, as it might in the case of a GRIT. In other cases, there could be no gift at all.

If the term holder pays full fair market value for the income interest, annuity interest, or unitrust interest, there should be nothing to include in the term holder's estate at death under Code section 2036(a), because the term holder never transferred an interest for federal estate tax purposes. However, as noted above, if the transaction is not properly structured, the IRS will apparently take the opposite position on this issue.

CHAPTER ENDNOTES

1. TAM 9206006.
2. This will require an arms-length appraisal from a qualified independent professional appraiser. Comparable market rate rental values may be extremely difficult to obtain, yet failure to do so could lead to adverse gift tax results.
3. I.R.C. §2702(c)(2).
4. Treas. Reg. §25.2702-4(a).
5. Treas. Reg. §25.2702-4(b).
6. Treas. Reg. §25.2702-4(c).
7. I.R.C. §2702(c)(4).
8. Treas. Reg. §25.2702-2(c).
9. I.R.C. §2702(a)(3)(A)(ii).
10. TAM 9206006.

SALE (GIFT) – LEASEBACK

CHAPTER 46

46.1 INTRODUCTION

A sale-leaseback involves one party selling property (or in the case of a gift-leaseback, giving property) to another party and then leasing back the same property. This type of transaction is usually intended to secure one or more of a number of income and/or estate tax advantages.

46.2 WHEN IS USE OF SUCH A DEVICE INDICATED?

1. When a client's problem is cash flow; the client's corporation is "rich" in assets, but it is "poor" in cash. The sale of a selected corporate asset and the immediate leaseback of that asset can generate cash without a loss of the use of that asset.

2. When a client earns a large amount of income and is, therefore, in a high income tax bracket. He wants to divert highly taxed income to a member of his family in a lower tax bracket. The hoped-for result is the netting of more after-tax income within the family unit.

3. When a client owns property that is rapidly appreciating and would like to shift that future wealth to a family member in order to save estate taxes on that appreciation.

4. When a client would like to find an alternative to financing business property through a mortgage. Sale-leasebacks have been called "off balance sheet" financing because the lease obligation will often appear as a footnote on the balance sheet rather than as a liability. This should have the effect of increasing the client's credit standing and ability to borrow money.

46.3 WHAT ARE THE REQUIREMENTS?

The transaction must have validity to avoid litigation and conflict with the IRS. There must actually be a completed and irrevocable sale (or gift) and a legally enforceable lease agreement. In the case where real estate is to be sold, the transaction may result in the imposition of a realty transfer tax. This type of tax is imposed by the state or local governments where the property is located. Typically, there are many exemptions, but it will still be necessary to check the applicable state rules before proceeding with the transaction.

The following factors should be considered:

- Are the lease provisions, especially payments, strictly observed?

- Does the lessee pay the entire amount of the promised rent?

- Is the rent reasonable?

- Was the sale price equivalent to the fair market value of the property?[1]

A positive answer to these questions is necessary for a successful shift of income tax burdens and the attainment of a rental deduction by the lessee. Essentially, it is important to follow the formalities of the transaction.

The terms of the transaction, and especially the amount of the lease payment, must be arrived at in an arm's length, bona fide manner. Any rent or lease amount should be reasonable and preferably developed by an independent appropriately credentialed professional. The process by which that rent amount is computed should be documented.

Sale-Leaseback

In the case of a sale, the transaction must represent a necessary business operation and not one designed solely and merely to shift income tax responsibility to a lower bracket family member. Several tests have been used by courts to ascertain if the buyer should be treated as a buyer in a sale-leaseback:

1. What is the size and extent of the purchaser's equity interest in the property? (If beneficial ownership in the property never vests in the purchaser that supports characterizing the transaction as financing.)

2. Does the useful life of the property extend beyond the term of the lease?

3. Is the lease renewal or purchase option at the end of the lease term based on a formula or price representing an arm's length fair market value of the equipment at that time?

4. Does the projected residual value of the equipment plus the cash flow generated by the rental of the equipment make it possible for investors to break even?

5. Is it likely a turnaround point will be reached when depreciation and interest deduction are less than income received from the lease?

6. Are the net tax savings for the investors less than their initial cash investment?

7. What is the reasonable potential for realizing a profit or loss on the sale or release of the equipment? (If the taxpayer's potential for realizing a profit—income in excess of its expenses—is "locked-in," at a fixed amount, this is indicative of a financing transaction.)

8. Is the agreement in question more like a lease or a conditional sale contract?

Gift-Leaseback

Where a donor transfers an office building or other income producing assets to a trust for a child and then leases it back:

1. The donor cannot retain substantially the same control over the property as the donor did before the gift was made.

2. The leaseback must be in writing and must provide for a reasonable rental (obtain an appraisal from an independent full time professional appraiser, preferably one who has expertise and specializes in the type of property to be valued).

3. The leaseback, as distinguished from the gift in trust, must have a bona fide business purpose.[2]

4. The trust must have an independent trustee unrelated to the grantor.[3]

5. Title to the property should be in the trust or the child and should be recorded.

Under the kiddie tax rules, too successfully shift taxation to a child's tax bracket, that child must generally be age eighteen or over (twenty-four in some cases).

The best types of property to use in a gift-leaseback are *tangible* assets used in the client's trade, business, or profession, such as land, depreciated buildings (beware of recapture), office equipment (such as computers, word processors, photocopiers), library, trucks and machinery, and other tangibles and office accoutrements needed in business.

A client (the grantor) *could* fund the trust with cash. The trustee could then acquire new equipment and lease it to the grantor or the grantor's corporation or purchase equipment from the grantor and then lease it back. (Note that some authorities feel the "transfer of cash" method is more vulnerable to IRS attack than the "transfer of property" method where the cash is used to buy property already owned by the grantor.)

Using a Trust

If a trustee is involved, the trustee should, in fact, be independent from the grantor of the trust. When the term of the trust is over, trust corpus should not return to the grantor. If a trust is used, these questions should be asked:

- Is the trust temporary?

- Will the property revert to the grantor at the end of a given period (reversionary interest trust)?

- Is the trust or trustee controlled by the grantor?[4]

A positive answer to any of these questions will result in taxation of income to the grantor (see "Tax Implications" below).

The following terms should be specified in the lease in order to demonstrate an equal bargaining position between the donor and the trustee:

a. Set rent at current market rates (obtain at least one independent professional appraisal expert's opinion).

b. Provide for a single year lease term that must be renegotiated each year. When renegotiating the rent, it is also advisable to obtain one independent professional appraisal as to the expert's opinion concerning the rent.

c. Place the property on the open market for lease (the higher the rental the grantor actually pays, the greater the overall tax shift). Note, however, that to the extent rents are deemed "excessive," they might be disallowed as deductions.

d. Provide that lease payments are made "as a condition to the continued use or possession of the premises."

e. Trustee should establish–and strictly enforce– a payment schedule. (Where payments were made randomly, in different amounts, at the client's convenience, and not according to a schedule determined by the trustee, it was held that the grantor failed to relinquish total control over trust property.)

Transactions between Related Parties

The danger factors noted above are particularly important where the transactions are between related parties. "Related parties" can include:

- a corporation and its stockholders;

- spouses;

- parents and children;

- grantors using relatives as trustees to create benefits for dependents;

- affiliated corporations with common stockholders;

- taxpayers and foundations created by them; and

- partnerships and their partners.

Basically, the IRS is trying to determine whether the transaction is genuine or merely structured as a sale. If the transaction is, in reality, a disguised loan, at best only part of the "rental" payments will be deductible because they will be considered payments of interest and principal. Only the interest portion can be taken as a tax deduction. Assuming the interest is considered "investment interest," it will be deductible, but only to the extent the taxpayer has investment income. Interest will be deductible without limit if it is considered "business interest." The characterization will be determined case by case, based on the facts and circumstances.

Alternatively, if the transaction is considered a sale, the seller-lessee has to pay a tax on any gain realized and recapture accelerated depreciation. If the property is leased for business purposes, the taxpayer will be able to deduct payments under the lease as rent.

The buyer-lessor also would be concerned with the distinction. In the case of a bona fide sale, the buyer-lessor may take depreciation or cost recovery deductions to the extent of the portion of the purchase price that is allocable to buildings or improvements and deduct all expenses relating to the maintenance and operation of the property. However, if the IRS treats the transaction as a loan, the buyer will not be entitled to these deductions because taxpayer would will be considered a mere mortgagee rather than as owner of the property.

If the transaction is considered a sale, the sale price must be equal to the fair market value of the property. If the sale price is less than the fair market value of the property transferred, the difference may be considered a gift. This may result in a gift tax being imposed on the seller-lessee.

An adjustment clause in the agreement may trigger an additional payment to the seller if the IRS revalues the property at a higher price. Although in the past, the IRS has challenged the defined value clauses, there have been some recent taxpayer successes in this area.

Safe Harbor

If possible, the transaction should be structured so that it falls within the following safe harbor:

1. the lessor must be a corporation other than an S corporation;

2. the lessor must have a minimum "at risk" investment of 10 percent of the adjusted basis of the property at all times;

3. the term of the lease, including extensions, must not exceed certain limits; and

4. the property must be leased within three months of its acquisition or, in the case of a sale-leaseback, it must be purchased by the lessor within three months of the lessee's acquisition for a price not in excess of the adjusted basis of the property in the hands of the lessee.

If the safe harbor test cannot be utilized, then the transaction should be based on economic reality. In this regard, all the significant burdens and benefits of ownership should be transferred to the new owner. The parties should assume their obligations as lessee and lessor, respectively. The sale price of the property should be fair and reasonable in light of current market conditions and sales of comparable properties. Financial arrangements must be reasonable. The IRS has indicated it will litigate two party gift and leaseback cases (i.e., the lessee is the donor, or an S corporation or partnership).

The transaction should not force a "buy-back." If there is a compulsory repurchase option, the seller is in virtually the same position had the property been mortgaged rather than selling it and leasing it back. If a buy-back provision is included, the terms must be arranged and the amount of the purchase price computed as a result of arm's length bargaining. (For related parties, consider Code Section 2703.)

The buyer must receive the benefit of any appreciation in value. A final factor generally examined is the application of rent toward the repurchase price. The rental price paid by the lessee should be realistic, and it is advisable to obtain documentation to support how the rent was determined. It should closely approximate rentals for comparable property and comparable facilities. If part of the rent is to be applied to a repurchase price, the IRS might claim that such payments are in reality disguised payments of interest rather than rental payments.[5]

Example. Your client, Dennis Raihall, is the president of the Son Ray Corporation. Although the business is on the verge of a break-through in its production process that could double corporate earnings, it needs money immediately to pay for expensive retooling.

In order to obtain the necessary funds, there are a number of types of assets the Son Ray Corporation could sell and then lease-back from the buyer: trucks, cars, machinery, equipment, fixtures, office buildings, apartment houses, and other types of real property. Furthermore, professional equipment such as computers, X-ray machines, etc., are all possibilities. One of the company's valuable assets is selected and sold to the LeClair Corporation for its fair market value and leased back from the LeClair Corporation for a reasonable rental price. (It is important that the shareholders of the two corporations are not the same individuals).

The after-tax proceeds of the sale will give the Son Ray Corporation additional cash and increase its working capital. The sold asset(s) are used in operation just as before the sale. The basic difference is that, instead of Son Ray carrying that particular item on its books as an asset, it now leases the property and pays fair market rent for its use. Son Ray will now have the use of a large sum of cash, the after tax proceeds of the sale, which can be used to generate additional profits.

(CAVEAT: Beware of depreciation recapture on the sale. Note that gain is both realized and recognized on the corporate level if an appreciated asset is sold.[6]) It is important to make certain that the proposed sale-leaseback is not prohibited by a loan agreement with the company's bank.

Suppose that Son Ray Corporation owned a factory that it built more than ten years ago at a cost of $200,000. The market value of the property is currently $250,000 (land $50,000, building, $200,000). The Son Ray Corporation has decided not to mortgage the property because the rate of interest it would have to pay is very high. Moreover, it would not be able to deduct the principal payments and, in any event, would be able to obtain more cash through a sale. Another reason not to mortgage the property is that such a debt would adversely

SALE (GIFT) – LEASEBACK   CHAPTER 46

affect its credit standing and ability to borrow additional funds.

The property could be sold for $250,000 and leased back for ten years with additional rental options at an annual rate of $30,000. Only the profit on the sale (net proceeds less adjusted basis) would be subject to tax. If an accelerated method of depreciation had been used, deductions taken in prior years may have to be recaptured and reported as additional income.

The leaseback arrangement is often utilized in intra-family transfers.

Example. Your client, Mary Jo Kopeznsky, a highly compensated physician, complains about the high income tax burden she faces every year. She wants to know how she can maximize her family income by minimizing her overall tax burden.

She could transfer by gift a professional office building and medical equipment she owns to the trustee (either a bank or other independent fiduciary) of an irrevocable *inter vivos* trust established for her eighteen-year-old daughter. The trust leases the building and medical equipment back to Doctor Kopeznsky at a reasonable rent so she does not have to move out of her building or lose the use of her equipment.

Pursuant to the terms of the trust, each year's net rental income could be distributed to the daughter or accumulated for later distribution to her when she reaches age twenty-one.. At that time, any undistributed income or principal might be paid outright and unconditionally to the daughter. Assuming trust income and/or principal was distributable to the daughter at age eighteen or twenty-one, and she chooses to use the funds for college and under the applicable state law, a parent is not obligated to provide a college education of a minor or an adult child, none of the income will be taxable to the high tax bracket mother. Moreover, the property in trust would be outside the reach of the doctor's creditors, an additional benefit.

46.4 TAX IMPLICATIONS

1. In the case of a sale and leaseback, the corporation that sells an asset must pay tax on any gain realized just as in the case of any other sale. Likewise, just as any partnership or corporation that rents property is allowed to take a tax deduction for the cost of the rental, when a sale-leaseback occurs, the fair rental paid by the seller for the use of its previously owned property is completely deductible as an ordinary and necessary business expense.[7]

2. In the case of a properly executed gift-leaseback, the donor would receive a double benefit. First, the donor will claim a deduction for rent payments. Then, the rent he or she pays to the trust (assuming it is a nongrantor trust) will generally be taxed to the trust (as long as it is accumulated) or to the donor's child or other trust beneficiary.[8] Ideally, the beneficiary's tax bracket will be lower than that of the donor. The tax savings could be used to establish a college education fund. Note, however, if the income is paid to a minor below age eighteen (or full time students up to the age of twenty-three), the child will be taxed, but generally at the parent's top bracket, to the extent that the payment exceeds $2,300 in 2023 as indexed for inflation. Therefore, a recipient child must generally be eighteen or older (or in some cases twenty-four or older) for the income shift to work.

3. By making an irrevocable gift of an asset (except for life insurance transferred by the insured within three years of death), future growth is removed from the client's estate at no additional estate tax cost.

4. There may be gift tax implications if there is an outright gift or if the sales price is less than the property's fair market value.

5. If property is purchased using an installment note, depreciation and interest deductions may offset a significant portion of the income from the lease. The lessee will be able to completely deduct the lease payments as an ordinary and necessary business expense. In the case of a sale-leaseback, the lessee would have to report interest income. If the lessee-user acquires the property and subsequently disposes of it, he will be subject to the recapture rules relating to depreciation deductions, just as if he had been the owner of the property all along.

6. Where the property is sold to family members, and the installment payments are closely tied into to the rental paid by the seller under the leaseback, the IRS will contend, and the courts will probably agree, that the arrangement is essentially a transfer with a retained life estate under Code Section 2036(a). This will certainly be the case where the lease is in effect for life. See *Est. of Maxwell*,[9] where a mother sold the property to a son on an installment sale, then forgave the payments on the sales price except the interest on the installment note, which was almost exactly the same as the rent she paid. She was in her eighties and had cancer when she sold the property. Although the property here was a personal residence, the same rationale could extend to business assets.

7. If property is sold to a related party using an installment note, the resale of the property within two years will cause the original seller to have to recognize the deferred gain.

Trust Income Taxable to Grantor

The grantor will be taxed on trust income if:

1. the grantor or grantor's spouse has retained a reversionary interest;

2. the grantor or grantor's spouse retains power to control beneficial enjoyment;

3. the grantor or grantor's spouse retains certain administrative powers;

4. the grantor or grantor's spouse retains the power to revoke the trust;

5. the income is used to pay support and maintenance to a person whom the grantor or spouse is legally obligated to support;

6. the income can be distributed to, or accumulated for, the grantor or his spouse without the approval of an adverse party.

Note that avoiding these situations does not per se assure a rental deduction. These situations concern only the issue of "Is there a valid trust?" and "To whom is the income taxable?" Although the two issues are concurrently operative, and are treated by the IRS as mutually exclusive.

One possible solution is to have someone other than the client or his spouse fund the trust. For instance, the client's parents could put cash into an irrevocable trust for the client's children. A loan to the trust from relatives or a third party, such as a bank, could be used to fund the purchase. The trust could use that cash to purchase assets owned solely by the client in his own name. The trust could then lease the assets to the client's corporation.

46.5 ISSUES IN COMMUNITY PROPERTY STATES

With respect to the sale-leaseback, two aspects are present. Initially, if the sale price is later found to be less than what was the then fair market value, the amount of the gift (undervaluation) is spread between both spouses if the asset was community property. However, some states' gift taxes have a much lower threshold than federal gift taxes, as to current cash tax payments, and consideration may be given to filing, in the year of the sale-leaseback, a gift tax return based on some other gift, thus possibly starting any statute of limitation periods to begin to run as to any subsequent imposition of a gift tax deficiency, including interest and penalties. The filing of a federal gift tax return should be considered to start the running of the statute of limitations if the risk of an audit is not significant.

The second concern is making sure that valid legal title has passed. The California statutory scheme, for example, grants the right to the management and control of community property to either spouse, with certain exceptions. However, in Texas, community property is either joint management property or the management property of one of the spouses. If property is classified as the "sole management" community property of a particular spouse, that spouse has the right to control or otherwise dispose of the property despite the other spouse's interest in the property. If community property is joint management property, both spouses must participate. Sole management property is the property the spouse would have owned if single. If one spouse incurs a tax liability, the IRS may have different remedies against sole management community property as opposed to joint management community property.[10]

With respect to the lease, mortgage, or transfer of real property, both spouses must join in executing the conveying instrument, and practitioners should obtain both signatures for any transfer (including the gift) of any asset.

46.6 ECONOMIC SUBSTANCE

For transactions entered into after March 30, 2010, Congress has codified the economic substance test[11] which requires that transactions, including a sale leaseback transaction, change the taxpayer's economic position in a meaningful way and have a substantial non-federal income tax purpose. Failure to meet both tests will negate the tax benefits and subject the transaction to a 20 percent penalty on the underpayment (40 percent if not adequately disclosed). The penalty may not be abated. Except for the penalty, this new rule does not really change the requirements previously imposed by court cases and rulings which state that both business purpose and economic substance are essential to tax success.

For instance, in Field Service Advice (FSA) 200011004, the Service expressed doubt that the taxpayer's leveraged lease transaction had either business purpose or economic substance. It didn't give credibility for federal income tax purposes to the purported sale and leaseback and would therefore not give basis credit and therefore reduce or disallow depreciation deductions. It would also disallow interest deductions on "debt" incurred by the taxpayer used to "purchase" the property.

Recent cases have clearly illustrated that the IRS and the courts will give credibility for tax purposes to a transaction only where it is genuine both as to form *and* substance. In other words, the taxpayer must have entered into the arrangement compelled or encouraged by a business or profit motive and with assumptions based on market-place realities. Stated differently, the transaction must be "imbued with tax-independent considerations" rather than being shaped solely by tax-avoidance features with self-serving, yet otherwise meaningless, labels.

The IRS and the courts, in ascertaining whether or not a transaction meets these criteria, look to two issues: the taxpayer's subjective business motivation and the objective economic substance of the transactions. Planners have only to ask:

1. Did the taxpayer have one or more business purposes (other than merely to avoid tax) in entering into this maneuver?

2. Was there economic substance beyond just the creation of tax benefits?

For tax purposes, the IRS and the Courts will invalidate and give no credibility to a transaction which has no economic or commercial objective and which was entered into solely for the purpose of tax reduction. So no matter how pristine or proper the outward form appears to be, the IRS and the Courts can feel free to go beyond that outer skin and look at the reality of the situation to determine the proper tax treatment each of the parties to the transaction should receive. Even a series of otherwise legitimate transactions can be disregarded if the IRS can put the pieces of the puzzle together and prove to a court that, when viewed as a whole, the transaction has no economic substance. That's exactly what occurred in FSA 200011004. The taxpayer structured a sale-leaseback that – when taken as a whole – had no reasonable business purpose aside from the possible tax savings. In fact, the only context in which this transaction could make sense was in the avoidance of income tax.

One test the courts will use is the "true owner" test. Does the taxpayer have a real stake in the risks and rewards? For instance, is the taxpayer really liable for purported debt? How likely is it that the taxpayer might suffer a loss or enjoy a gain? Will the taxpayer have a real economic loss (beyond a tax loss) if things don't go as planned? If the taxpayer can't re-lease the property at the end of the lease term, will the taxpayer suffer? Or does the taxpayer lack any real liability for the transaction financing? Is there a series of artificial games being played that eliminate either real risk or real reward – other than tax risks and rewards? Does the transaction have more than a *de minimis* economic effect on a taxpayer?

Near absolute limitations on the taxpayer's risk of loss (and opportunity to profit) deprive a transaction of meaningful economic substance. Has real risk been negated by the use of nonrecourse financing? Is the opportunity for pre-tax profit remote because the leased property is unlikely to have residual value? Here, the taxpayer's transaction was structured in a way that almost entirely eliminated the risk of loss from physical depreciation of the rail cars.

Nor could the taxpayer realize any significant upside gain because a third party was given the option of purchasing the rail cars at the end of the lease term under favorable conditions if the cars in fact had significant residual value. Even if the third party didn't exercise that option, the taxpayer was required by contract to sell the railroad cars and pay over any excess of the train cars residual value over their purchase price to the third party. The potential to profit was capped from inception, as the likelihood of loss was almost entirely limited. In arriving at a conclusion that there was no reasonable expectation of profit apart from the tax benefits of the transaction, courts will take a real world approach: For example, they will (and should) take into consideration the time value of money – and the money value of time.

Even if the form of a transaction is held to be valid, the IRS and courts might still deny deductions to the taxpayer on the basis that someone other than the taxpayer is the real owner. For instance, according to the logic above, if the taxpayer here never received the benefits and burdens of ownership of the rail cars, then the taxpayer is not entitled to the deductions and/or depreciation that property generates. Once again, the potential of gain or loss from the residual value or sale or re-lease of property is the acid test of ownership in sale-leasebacks. If the taxpayer is indirectly guaranteed to recover its costs, that is indicative of a lack of economic substance. Here, the taxpayer was assured from the start that it would receive a specified amount as a termination payment even if the rail cars lack any residual value and even if the third party didn't exercise its purchase option.

If a leaseback arrangement is challenged, courts will examine the economic substances of several aspects of the transaction, discussed below.

Establishing a Lease

There can be no lease(back) if what is really intended is something other than a lease. Courts will consider these factors:

1. Are portions of the periodic payments specifically allocated to equity to be acquired by the lessee?

2. Will the lessee acquire title upon payment of the required amount of rentals?

3. Does the total amount which the lessee is required to pay for a relatively short period of use constitute an inordinately large proportion of the total sum required to be paid to secure the transfer of title?

4. Do the rental payments materially exceed the current fair rental value? (Do the rental payments include an element other than compensation for the use of property?)

5. Can the property be acquired under a purchase option at a price which is nominal in relation to the value of the property at the time when the option may be exercised, or is relatively small when compared with the total payments made?

6. Is there a specific portion of the payments designated or identifiable as interest?

Establishing a Sale or Gift

There can be no leaseback if there was no sale (or gift). So it is important to document that there was a sale - as distinguished from a loan (where the original owner never really relinquishes ownership). Courts will consider these factors:

1. Does the assignee of property have the right to repayment? If so, this indicates that an assignment may be a loan-type investment secured by the right to future revenue (a nonrecourse secured loan).

2. Are there amounts deposited in a bank or some other place that directly or indirectly guarantee repayment? This is, of course, a characteristic of a loan.

If the court determines that (assuming that the debt is bona fide) the transaction is a secured financing and not a sale and leaseback, the result will be that the funds the taxpayer pays and characterizes as rental payments are really loans. They must be repaid to the taxpayer and so are not taxable income to the borrower, the party that receives the money – nor is it deductible by the taxpayer.

Establishing a Loan

When determining whether cash paid to one party is a bona fide loan or is taxable income, a court will ask:

1. Does a note or other evidence of indebtedness exist?

2. Is there a written loan agreement?

3. Is there a fixed schedule for repayment?

4. Has any security or collateral been required?

5. Was interest (no matter how classified) charged?

6. Was there a demand for repayment? Have there been repayments?

7. Do the facts indicate the parties intended for the transaction to be a loan?

8. Was the borrower was solvent at the time of the loan?

Establishing a Valid Debt

The question is important because, if there is no genuine debt, then the taxpayer can't use it as part of basis for depreciation purposes. Nor can interest payments be deducted if they arise from transactions that have no purpose, substance or utility apart from their anticipated tax consequences.

Factors a court will examine to determine the genuineness of debt include:

1. Does the purchaser acquire equity in the property by making payments and have an economic incentive to pay off the note? If not, debt will not be considered bona fide.

2. Is the overall transaction valid? If so, the debt will not be. Is money moving in a circle without any economic substance? Is there an "internal accounting circle" in which no meaningful cash will every really be exchanged?

Be sure the donor does not retain any control over the property once it is transferred. Carefully document each step of the transaction. The agreement for the leaseback must be in all respects an arm's length transaction, in writing, independently and professionally reasonably appraised, and have a bona fide business purpose and economic substance.

46.7 FREQUENTLY ASKED QUESTIONS

Question – What is the primary economic disadvantage to funding through a sale-leaseback rather than a mortgage?

Answer – The primary drawback to funding through a sale-leaseback is the loss of the residual value of the property at the termination of the lease. This drawback can be minimized through an arms' length repurchase option or option(s) to renew the lease over the expected life of the property.

CHAPTER ENDNOTES

1. See Rev. Rul. 55-540, 1955-2 CB 39; Rev. Proc. 75-21, 1975-1 CB 715, as modified by Rev. Proc. 79-48, 1979-2 CB 529; Est. of Franklin, 64 TC 752 (1975); *Narver v. Comm'r*, 76 TC 53 (1980); *Hager v. Comm'r*, 76 TC 759 (1981).

2. *Van Zandt v. Comm'r*, 341 F.2d 440 (5th Cir. 1965) aff'g, 40 TC 824, cert. den., 382 U.S. 814.

3. *Oakes v. Comm'r*, 44 TC 524 (1965).

4. See *Oakes v. Comm'r*, 44 TC 524 (1965); *Audano v. U.S.*, 428 F.2d 251 (5th Cir. 1970).

5. See Rev. Rul. 55-540, 1955-2 CB 39; Rev. Proc. 75-21, 1975-1 CB 715, as modified by Rev. Proc. 79-48, 1979-2 CB 529. See also AOD 1984-037.

6. I.R.C. §§1245, 1250.

7. I.R.C. §162. Can a sale-leaseback result in a deductible loss? Yes, says the Tax Court, if there is a bona fide sale and not an exchange of like-kind property. But, in the favorable case of *Leslie, Co. v. Comm'r*, 64 TC 247 (1975), the IRS has non-acquiesced. Nonacq. 1978-2 CB 1.

8. I.R.C. §§641, 652, 662.

9. 3 F.3d 591 (2d Cir. 1993), aff'g, 98 TC 584 (1992).

10. See Internal Revenue Manual §25.18.1.2.12 (02-15-2005), "Management and Control."

11. I.R.C. §§7701(o) and 6662(i); See J. F. Bresnahan, II, G. M. Fowler and A. M. Mattson, "Tax Practice Responsibilities: Codification of Economic Substance Affects All Tax Practitioners," *The Tax Adviser*, 42.8 (Aug. 2011).

BUY-SELL (BUSINESS CONTINUATION) AGREEMENTS

CHAPTER 47

47.1 INTRODUCTION

A business continuation (buy-sell) agreement is a legal contract providing terms for the disposition of a business interest in the event of the owner's death, disability, retirement, or upon withdrawal from the business at some earlier time. Business continuation agreements can take a number of forms:

(1) an agreement between the business itself and the individual owners (either a corporate stock redemption agreement or partnership liquidation agreement), frequently called an "entity" plan;

(2) an agreement between the individual owners (a cross-purchase or "criss-cross" agreement);

(3) an agreement between the individual owners and key person, family member, or outside individual (a "third-party" business buy-out agreement); or

(4) a hybrid combination of the foregoing, such as the "Wait and See" Buy-Sell[1] discussed below.

In the case of corporations, the most common types of business continuation agreements are stock redemption plans (often called stock retirement plans), or shareholder cross-purchase plans. The distinguishing feature of the redemption agreement is that the corporation itself agrees to purchase (redeem) the stock of the withdrawing or deceased shareholder. In a cross-purchase plan the individuals agree between or among themselves to purchase the interest of a withdrawing or deceased shareholder.

In the case of a partnership, an agreement similar to the corporate stock redemption plan is the partnership liquidation agreement, where the partnership in effect purchases the interest of the deceased or withdrawing partner by distributing assets in liquidation of the partner's interest, or the partners agree to a cross-purchase similar to the corporate cross-purchase plan.

47.2 WHEN IS USE OF SUCH A DEVICE INDICATED?

1. When a guaranteed market must be created for the sale of a business interest in the event of death, disability, or retirement.

2. When it is necessary or desirable to help establish the value of the business for federal and state death tax purposes.

3. When a shareholder or partner would be unable or unwilling to continue running the business with the family of a deceased co-owner.

4. When the business involves a high amount of financial risk for the family of a deceased owner and it is desirable to convert the business interest into cash at the owner's death.

5. When it is necessary or desirable to prevent all or part of the business from falling into the hands of "outsiders."

   This could include a buyout of an owner's interest in the event of a divorce, disability, or insolvency, if there is a danger a business interest would be transferred to a former spouse or creditors.

6. Where it is desirable to lend certainty to the disposition of a family closely-held business. Rather than relying on will provisions of a parent to transfer the business interest, a binding buy-sell agreement between parent and child or other relative could be used. However, under Code section 2703, this has become exceedingly difficult.

7. When state law restricts the parties who can own an interest in the entity. An example is a professional corporation or association. State law might allow only licensed practitioners in that field, doctors for instance, to own the stock. In such a case, an heir or beneficiary of one of the doctors who is not a duly licensed professional in that field could not be an owner of an interest in the firm. A buy-sell agreement between the practitioners already in the firm or with a practitioner outside the firm (perhaps a friendly competitor) would be a legal and practical necessity.

47.3 WHAT ARE THE REQUIREMENTS?

A written agreement is drawn stating the parties to the agreement, purchase price (or a formula for determining that price), terms, and funding arrangements. The agreement typically obligates the retiring (or disabled) owner (or owner's estate) to sell the business to:

1. the business itself;
2. the surviving owner(s);
3. a third party non-owner; or
4. a combination of parties.

Occasionally the agreement provides alternatives for the buyout. For example, the agreement may give the remaining owners the option to purchase the stock or partnership interest, but provide that if they fail to exercise that option, the interest must be redeemed or liquidated by the corporation (or partnership). Conversely, the agreement may provide that, if the entity cannot purchase the interest, the remaining owners have either an obligation or option to do so. Such agreements must be carefully drafted to avoid a situation in which the entity discharges an obligation of the other individual owners to purchase the interest, which could have adverse tax consequences to the other owners.

For example, if the shareholders under the agreement are personally legally obligated to buy the stock of a deceased shareholder, and the corporation redeems (buys back) the stock, the entire amount of the obligation of which the remaining shareholders are relieved could be considered a taxable dividend to them.

The buy-sell agreement specifies the event triggering the respective obligations. Generally, that event is death, disability, or retirement of the owner. However, as already indicated, it could (and usually should) include other potential events such as divorce, insolvency, or bankruptcy, and should also include such possible events as long term disability, loss of a professional license by an owner, or conviction of an owner of a state or federal crime. Valuation may be based on several factors, including book value, asset value, formula value, or some agreed amount.

"Funding" pertains to how the promises under the agreement will be financed. Generally - and preferably - in a redemption or liquidation agreement, the business will purchase, own, pay premiums, and be the beneficiary of adequate and continually reviewed amounts of life (and often disability income) insurance on each person who owns an interest in the business. In the case of a cross-purchase agreement, the prospective buyer (each business associate) purchases, owns, pays for, and is a beneficiary of a life and disability income insurance policy on the other owners. So, when an owner dies, the life insurance proceeds would provide the funds to satisfy the obligation of the surviving owner(s) to execute the buyout with the deceased owner's estate.

Example 1. Stock Redemption Plan. Herb and Steve are equal stockholders in a business valued at $5,000,000. The business purchases $2,500,000 of life insurance on stockholders.

At Herb's death, his stock passes to his estate. The life insurance proceeds paid to the business are in turn paid to Herb's estate in accordance with the amount or formula price set forth in the buy-sell agreement. In return, Herb's executor transfers the stock to the business; and, thus, Steve, the surviving owner, would then own all the outstanding stock.

Additionally, the buy-sell agreement would provide that if Herb (or Steve) became totally disabled prior to retirement, he would receive his full salary for one year. At the end of a year of total disability, Herb's (or Steve's) interest would be redeemed by the business. As a down payment of the redemption price, the business would pay at least $250,000 (10 percent of $2,500,000) to Herb (or Steve). The balance owing to Herb (or Steve) would be evidenced by a ten-year interest bearing note (secured by Herb's or Steve's stock placed in an escrow account). The interest rate would be set at the long-term applicable federal rate, i.e., the safe harbor rate required to avoid the below market interest rules. As a source of funds to be used to pay off the note, the business would secure a disability income insurance policy naming itself as the beneficiary.

In the event Herb (or Steve) retired, the business would redeem his stock. As a down payment of the redemption price, the business would pay at least $250,000 (10 percent of $2,500,000) to Herb (or Steve). The balance owing to Herb (or Steve) would be evidenced by a ten-year interest bearing note (secured by Herb's or Steve's stock placed in an escrow account). As a down payment of the redemption price, the business would pay at least $250,000 (10 percent of $2,500,000) to Herb (or Steve). The balance owing to Herb (or Steve) would be evidenced by a ten-year interest bearing note (secured by Herb's or Steve's stock placed in an escrow account). The rate would be set at the long-term applicable federal rate, i.e., the safe harbor rate required to avoid the below market interest rules. Assuming the business was the owner and beneficiary of a whole life insurance policy on Herb's (or Steve's) life, its cash value could be used to help finance the down payment. One limiting factor, in general, is that in many states, the corporation can redeem its stock only to the extent it has earned surplus.

Example 2. Cross-Purchase Agreement. Assume Herb and Steve are equal stockholders in a business valued at $5,000,000. Herb purchases a $2,500,000 life insurance policy and a disability income policy on Steve's life. Steve purchases policies in equal amounts on Herb's life.

Assuming Herb dies first; his stock passes to his estate. The insurance proceeds on Herb's life paid directly to Steve are in turn paid to Herb's estate according to the cross-purchase agreement. In return, Herb's executor transfers Herb's stock to Steve, and, thus, he becomes the sole owner of the corporation.

In the event of Herb's permanent and total disability, he receives his full salary for one year. At that time, Herb is required to sell his stock to Steve for $2,500,000. As a down payment, Steve will pay at least $250,000 (10 percent of $2,500,000) to Herb. The balance owing will be evidenced by an interesting bearing ten-year note (secured by his stock). As a down payment of the redemption price, the business would pay at least $250,000 (10 percent of $2,500,000) to Herb (or Steve). The balance owing to Herb (or Steve) would be evidenced by a ten-year interest bearing note (secured by Herb's or Steve's stock placed in an escrow account). The rate would be set at the long-term applicable federal rate, i.e., the safe harbor rate required to avoid the below market interest rules. During this period, Steve will be receiving distributions from the disability income insurance policy purchased on Herb's life that can be used to pay off the note.

Similarly, at Herb's retirement or departure from the firm prior to normal retirement, Herb will sell his stock to Steve. Steve will pay at least $250,000 (10 percent of $2,500,000) as a down payment to Herb. Steve will also give Herb a ten-year note (secured by his stock) for the balance. Steve will pay the balance owing as evidenced by an interest bearing ten-year note (secured by his stock). As a down payment of the redemption price, the business would pay at least $250,000 (10 percent of $2,500,000) to Herb (or Steve). The balance owing to Herb (or Steve) would be evidenced by a ten-year interest bearing note (secured by Herb's or Steve's stock placed in an escrow account). The rate would be set at the long-term applicable federal rate, i.e., the safe harbor rate required to avoid the below market interest rules. Assuming Steve was the owner and beneficiary of a whole life insurance policy on Herb's life, its cash value could be used to help finance the down payment.

These, of course, are merely examples. There are infinite variations on how the buy-sell can be arranged and what the terms will be. The professional's challenge is to match the forms with the facts and the objectives and circumstances of the parties.

47.4 TAX IMPLICATIONS

Stock Redemption Agreements

1. Assuming the corporation is sole owner and sole beneficiary of the policy(ies), the value of the insurance on the decedent's life will not be includable (as insurance proceeds per se) in the gross estate for federal estate tax purposes. However, the receipt of the insurance proceeds will be considered in valuing the decedent's interest in the business unless there is a valid arm's length agreement fixing the price for federal estate tax purposes and the proceeds are excluded from the purchase price under the terms of the agreement.[2]

   The buy-sell agreement will generally establish the value of the business owned by unrelated parties for federal estate tax purposes if:

   a. the estate is obligated to sell at the decedent-shareholder's death, or the estate is obligated to offer the decedent's shares at death at the agreement price;

   b. the agreement prohibits the shareholder from disposing of interest during his lifetime without first offering it to the corporation at no more than the contract price;

   c. the price was fair and adequate at the time the agreement was made and resulted from a bona fide arm's length transaction between the parties; and

   d. the price was fixed by the terms of the agreement, or, preferably, the agreement contained a formula for determining the price.[3]

   Where the shareholders or partners are related, or the "natural objects of the bounty" of each other, there are additional requirements, discussed later under the heading "Family Business Enterprises."

2. Life insurance or disability income premiums used to fund the agreement are not deductible by the corporation.[4] On the other hand, death proceeds (or disability income proceeds) received by the corporation are income tax-free regardless of amount.[5] (But see the discussion later on the corporate alternative minimum tax). Premiums paid by the corporation are not treated as dividends or other income otherwise taxable to its shareholders.

3. The biggest potential problem in a corporate stock redemption agreement is the possibility that the redemption will be treated as a dividend distribution. There is the possibility that, no matter how the parties label a transaction, a distribution of money or property in redemption of stock by a corporation will be treated as a dividend (so that the entire distribution would be taxable to the extent of the corporation's earnings and profits). Fortunately, if certain requirements are met, such dividend treatment can be avoided so that the redemption is treated as the sale of the redeemed stock taxed as a capital gain.

   For example, absent the application of the attribution rules, a redemption of *all* of a shareholder's stock (a complete termination of his interest) will not be treated as a dividend. This would be the case if Herb and Steve, unrelated parties, own all of the stock of the corporation. So, when Herb dies, the corporation redeems (buys back) Herb's stock from his estate. Because by virtue of the redemption, Herb's estate has given up all control, share of future profits, and share of future assets in the event of a sale or liquidation of the corporation, Herb's interest in the corporation that passed to his estate has *completely* terminated. So only the gain, the difference between the amount realized by the seller and the seller's basis (generally stepped up to fair market value if the stock was obtained at a shareholder's death) is taxed at capital gains rates.

   Unfortunately, this favorable sale treatment can be complicated or even thwarted by the "constructive ownership" (attribution) rules.[6] Essentially, the basic constructive ownership rules work as follows:

   a. The "estate/beneficiary" attribution rule. Under this rule, stock owned by a beneficiary of an estate is considered constructively (treated for tax purposes as if it were actually) owned by the estate.[7] So, a redemption of all stock actually owned by the estate (without a simultaneous redemption of stock owned by a beneficiary) may be considered as only partial redemption; and, thus may be taxable to the estate as a dividend. This is because the estate would still be deemed to be a stockholder by virtue of the attribution of stock owned by its beneficiary.

Example. Herb and Steve are father and son. Herb owns 75 percent of the stock while Steve owns the remaining 25 percent. Steve is a beneficiary under Herb's will. If the corporation redeems Herb's stock from his executor, it would not be treated as a complete redemption because the estate is deemed to own all Steve's stock. Therefore, before and after the redemption, the estate remains the 100 percent owner of the corporation. As a result, the redemption amount may be taxed as a dividend (to the extent of corporate earnings and profits).

To avoid the application of the above-described Code section 318 attribution rules, if, *before* the redemption takes place, the son has received all property to which he is entitled from the estate, no longer has a claim against the estate, and no liabilities of the estate can be assessed against him as a beneficiary, his stock will not be attributed to the estate because he will no longer be considered a beneficiary.)

    b. The "family/trust/corporation" attribution rule. Under this rule, an individual is considered to own the stock owned directly or indirectly by or for the individual's spouse, children, grandchildren, and parents. Depending on an individual's ownership interest in certain entities, stock owned by such entities is also attributed to and from such entities in determining whether all the stock has been redeemed.[8] These other parties include:

      (i) With certain exceptions, a trust and its beneficiaries.

      (ii) A partnership and its partners.

      (iii) A corporation and over-50-percent shareholders.

There is also the possibility of an incomplete termination as a result of the double attribution of stock ownership, first from a close family member to an estate beneficiary and then through the estate beneficiary to the estate.

Example. Herb owns 1,000 shares in a closely held corporation. His son, Steve, owns the remaining 500 shares. Herb's widow is the sole beneficiary under Herb's will. Even if the corporation immediately redeems Herb's entire 1,000 shares at death, the redemption will be treated as less than a complete redemption and therefore may become subject to dividend treatment because Steve's 500 shares are attributed to (treated as if actually owned by) his mother under the family attribution rules. Those shares are attributed a second time to Herb's estate under the estate/beneficiary attribution rules. So even though the corporation redeems all Herb's shares from his estate, the estate is still treated as the owner of 100 percent of the corporation.

There is an important exception to the family attribution rule. Under certain circumstances, it may be possible to "waive" the family attribution rule (but not the estate or entity rules) and therefore break the fictional "chain link" between family members. This "ten-year family attribution waiver rule" works as follows: In essence, the family attribution rules will not be applied if, immediately following the redemption, the redeeming shareholder retains or acquires no interest in the corporation (except as creditor) and agrees not to acquire an interest for ten years following the redemption, other than by bequest or inheritance.[9]

One of the difficulties of implementing a redemption of a family member coupled with a waiver of family attribution is the typical unwillingness of a key person, often a founder of the business, to completely disassociate from it. The cases are clear that the key person severing the link cannot safely function in the business in any capacity (other than creditor), even as a consultant.

In the example discussed above, following the redemption of Herb's stock from his estate, Herb's widow would notify the IRS of her election to waive attribution between her son, Steve, and herself. Because she has no direct stock ownership and has "waived" her right to receive any stock except by bequest or inheritance, there is no attribution from Steve to her and then from her to the estate.

Therefore, the redemption is complete and not subject to dividend treatment.

Entities such as a corporation, trust, or estate may waive the constructive ownership and break the fictional ownership linkage from a family member who actually owns stock to a beneficiary who does not (but is deemed to own it). The individual who is deemed to own stock must join in the waiver. After the redemption, neither the entity nor the beneficiary may hold an interest in the corporation. They must agree not to acquire such an interest for at least ten years. They must also agree to notify the IRS if they do acquire such an interest. There is joint and several liability in the event either the entity or the waiving family members acquires a prohibited interest within the ten-year period. The statute of limitations remains open during that time for the IRS to levy on any deficiency.

As noted above, it is important to be aware that an entity may break the fictional linkage only between family members; it may not waive "entity" attribution, the constructive ownership between a beneficiary and an entity. For example, assume 30 percent of the stock of a corporation is owned by a trust. Its beneficiaries, Michael, David, and Danny Green, own no stock personally. Debbie Green, the trust beneficiaries' mother, owns 52 percent of the corporation's stock. The remaining stock is held by unrelated employees of the corporation.

Assume the trust sells all of its stock back to the corporation. The redemption is still not complete because the trust's beneficiaries, Michael, David, and Danny, are deemed to own stock owned by their mother through the "family" attribution rule. The stock they are deemed to own is then attributed from them to the trust through the entity attribution rule. So the redemption of stock from the trust would be less than complete. But if the trust and all three brothers waive attribution and break the link connecting the mother's stock to the sons, the redemption would be complete. But what if one or more of the sons actually owned stock in the corporation? In that case the trust could break the link from Debbie Green to her children (the family attribution) but not the link between the children and itself (the entity attribution).

4. Because stock in an estate receives a "stepped-up basis," a purchase (either through stock redemption or cross-purchase) of a decedent-shareholder's interest is not likely to trigger any taxable gain. Such basis, i.e., a new "cost" in the executor's hands is equal to its value for federal estate tax purposes. Because the value of the stock as of the applicable federal estate valuation date (i.e., date of death) is likely to be the fair market value paid by a purchaser, there is no gain - the amount paid equals the basis of the stock.

Example. Initially, Herb and Steve, who are unrelated, each invested $50,000 in a corporation. Upon Herb's death, the corporation has a value of $5,000,000 (each shareholder's interest is worth $2,500,000). If the corporation redeemed Herb's stock now held by his estate for $2,500,000, there would be no gain because the basis in Herb's stock "stepped up" from $50,000 to $2,500,000. In other words, the "amount realized" ($2,500,000) is equal to the stock's basis ($2,500,000) and so there is no taxable gain.

Note that the surviving shareholder (Steve) does not receive an increase in the basis of his stock since the corporation is redeeming Herb's stock. In a cross purchase arrangement, however, in which Steve purchased Herb's stock from his estate, his basis in the stock he acquired from Herb would be equal to the purchase price. Thus, basis considerations is an important factor in deciding whether a buy-sell should be structured as a cross purchase rather than as stock redemption.

Cross-Purchase Agreements

1. The value of life insurance owned on a decedent-shareholder's life by a surviving co-shareholder (to fund the cross-purchase of shares) will not be included in the decedent's estate for federal estate tax purposes. This is because the decedent-shareholder insured has no incidents of ownership in the policy his co-shareholder owns. However, the value of life insurance the decedent owned at the time of death on the lives of surviving co-shareholders will be includable.[10] (Generally, the includable amount is equivalent to the policy's interpolated terminal reserve plus unearned premiums but may be much higher if the insured shareholder is terminally ill at the time of the owner-co-shareholder's death.)

As with the stock redemption agreement, a properly drawn cross-purchase agreement will, generally, be effective in helping to establish the value of the business for federal estate tax purposes providing:

a. the estate is obligated to sell at the decedent-shareholder's death, or the estate is obligated to offer the decedent's shares at his death at the agreement price;

b. there is a lifetime "first offer" provision prohibiting a shareholder from disposing of his stock interest without first offering it to the other shareholders at no more than the contract price;

c. the price was fair and adequate when made and resulted from a bona fide arm's length transaction; and

d. the price is fixed by the terms of the agreement or the agreement contains a formula or method for determining the price. (But where family members are involved, the requirements are much more onerous. See discussion below on Family Business Enterprises).

2. Life insurance or disability income premiums paid to fund the agreement are not deductible by the co-shareholders. The death proceeds or disability benefits will be received by the respective co-shareholders income tax free. There will be no AMT consequences regardless of the size of the policy.

3. Assuming the corporation does not directly or indirectly take over the buying shareholder's existing liability once it becomes fixed, there is no possibility that the purchases of stock by the remaining shareholders will be treated as dividends and no attribution problems because there are no redemptions and no transactions between the corporation and its shareholders in a cross-purchase agreement.

4. Under a cross-purchase agreement, if the price paid for the stock is more than its basis (cost) in the selling shareholder's hands, the difference is usually taxable at capital gain rates. Under a stock redemption, the distribution for the stock may be as a dividend to the estate if the attribution rules (discussed above) are an issue and not effectively waived.

5. Under a cross-purchase agreement, the surviving shareholder who acquires a decedent-shareholder's stock has a cost basis in such stock equal to the purchase price. So, in a subsequent sale of the acquired stock by a surviving shareholder, there may little or no gain. In a stock redemption, however, because the purchaser is the corporation, there is no basis adjustment.

6. Where more than one shareholder is involved, the implications of the transfer for value rule[11] (see Frequently Asked Questions below), must be analyzed if there are life insurance policies that could be transferred among the shareholders or from the corporation to the shareholders.

47.5 CROSS-PURCHASE VS. STOCK REDEMPTION PLANS

As alluded to above, if a corporation purchases (redeems) the stock of a withdrawing, disabled, or deceased stockholder, the surviving shareholders do not increase their basis in their stock (cost for purposes of determining gain) by the amount paid. For example, assume Steve, Roberta, and Lee each own an interest in the SRL Corporation worth $100,000. Each invested $10,000 in 1977 when the corporation was formed. If Lee dies and the corporation (pursuant to a fully funded buy-sell agreement) redeems Lee's stock from his estate for $100,000, Steve's and Roberta's basis each remain at $10,000. But if Steve and Roberta had each purchased one-half of Lee's stock for $50,000 to Lee's executor, their overall basis would have increased by that $50,000 amount. The distinction is important because, in this simplified example, the taxable gain on a future sale of Steve's stock or Roberta's stock could be as much as $50,000 less using a cross-purchase arrangement.

It is important to recognize, however, that this does not mean a cross-purchase plan will always be better than a stock redemption. In some cases, a stock redemption will be preferred:

(1) The basis increase may be higher when a stock redemption is used if:

(a) surviving shareholders intend to retain the stock they own until death, and

(b) there is high appreciation in the value of the stock.

(2) Shareholders may prefer, for both psychological and cash flow reasons, that corporate dollars be used to pay premiums.

(3) Non-deductible premium payments by a corporation may be indicated when the corporation is in a lower income tax bracket than the individual shareholders.

(4) Where there are more than three shareholders involved, administrative inconvenience and cost generally make corporate-owned life insurance preferable over the multiplicity of policies required in a cross-purchase arrangement. For example, if there were five shareholders, twenty separate policies would be required. (The formula for determining the number of policies is N x (N - 1) with N being the number of shareholders.)

Other factors to consider in deciding between a cross-purchase and stock redemption include:

(1) possibility of dividend treatment pursuant to a redemption because of constructive ownership (attribution) rules in family-owned corporations;

(2) state law restrictions on a corporation's right to purchase its own stock in the absence of sufficient surplus;

(3) transfer-for-value problems at the death of a shareholder if estate-owned life insurance policies are transferred to individuals other than the insureds;

(4) stock ownership desired after the purchase occurs;

(5) premium outlay differences due to differences in age and ownership interests between shareholders; or

(6) possible alternative minimum tax problems where life insurance is used to fund a stock redemption and the corporation is not a "small corporation" and therefore not exempt from the alternative minimum tax.

One technique that may avoid or minimize problems inherent in a buy-sell of either the cross-purchase or the stock redemption type is the "Wait and See" (also known as the option or hybrid) Buy-Sell approach. Under a Wait and See type agreement, the estate of a deceased shareholder is bound to sell at an agreed-upon price or according to a predetermined formula, but the parties *wait* a specified length of time after the death of a shareholder to *see* if – and see to what extent – a cross-purchase or stock redemption or combination (perhaps even coordinated with a Code section 303 stock redemption) should be used.

The suggested method is for the corporation to have a first option to purchase any or all a deceased shareholder's interest. Surviving shareholders have a secondary option to purchase any or all stock remaining. If, at this point, some stock still remains in the executor's hands, the corporation is *required* to purchase the entire balance.

Life insurance could be purchased by the corporation, by the surviving shareholders, or by both. (The corporation might, for example, purchase permanent life insurance while the shareholders might purchase term insurance.) If the corporation is owner and beneficiary of the insurance, the proceeds could fund the redemption or loaned to the surviving shareholders to purchase a decedent shareholder's stock. If life insurance is owned by the shareholders, they could use the proceeds to purchase the stock of the decedent shareholder or make loans or capital contributions to the corporation to fund a stock redemption.

The Wait and See approach provides an infinite variety of options and a maximum in planning flexibility.

47.6 BUSINESS CONTINUATION PLANS FOR S CORPORATIONS

Where the entity or cross-purchase plan is structured for a subchapter S corporation, there are additional issues that must be considered. The tax characteristics of S corporations are discussed in Chapter 53.

Most practitioners favor the cross-purchase buy-sell type plan for an S corporation. There is some concern that a stock redemption plan would create a second class of stock that would disqualify the corporation from being an S corporation. However, rulings and regulations indicate the IRS will rarely take this position. More practical reasons for preferring the cross-purchase plan include the fact that any non-deductible premiums paid by the corporation on life insurance used to fund a stock redemption agreement is really paid for with shareholder dollars, because the non-deductible payments are essentially taxed to the shareholders. Also, the impact of the life insurance premiums and proceeds on the income tax basis of the shareholders' stock is unclear. If the S corporation has corporate earnings and profits accumulated before the S election is made, depending on whether non-deductible premiums decrease a shareholder's stock basis, the insurance may affect the amount the corporation can distribute to shareholders without dividend consequences. The impact of life insurance on S corporation shareholders is discussed further in Chapter 53.

On the other hand, life insurance in an S corporation, no matter how large, does not trigger alternative minimum tax problems. A stock redemption decreases any of the S corporation's earnings and profits, which could someday give rise to dividends. And because most S corporations have little or no earnings and profits (unless it was previously a C corporation), all the complex dividend issues under the redemption-family attribution rules are generally not an issue, because a redemption cannot create a taxable dividend if there are no earnings and profits.

In structuring a buy-sell agreement for an S corporation, note that corporate profit and loss is allocated on a daily basis to all shareholders, including a deceased shareholder, to the date of death, or a selling shareholder to date of sale. An election can be made to actually close the tax year on the date of death or sale and allocate income or loss between two tax years. The agreement should spell out which approach is to be used. Remember that a shareholder's pro rata share of corporate profit or loss will increase or decrease the income tax basis of the shareholder's stock, which would have an impact on the gain or loss realized on the sale.

One of the purposes of a buy-sell agreement in an S corporation is to prevent the stock from falling into the hands of a disqualifying shareholder, such as a trust that cannot own S stock or a nonresident alien. The agreement should be structured so that the sale is complete before any such disqualifying transfer is made and should specifically bar sales to any disqualifying party.

47.7 BUSINESS CONTINUATION PLANS FOR PARTNERSHIPS

Partnership buyouts present several different problems and solutions. Unlike a corporation, if more than 50 percent of the total partnership capital *and* profits are sold within a twelve-month period, the partnership is dissolved under Code section 708. However, the regulations under section 708 indicate that if the interest of a partner is liquidated rather than sold, there is no dissolution even if that interest exceeds 50 percent. If the buyout does terminate the partnership, it is treated as having made a pro rata liquidating distribution of all of its assets to the partners, which are then treated as re-contributed to the partnership. Both functional transactions are generally tax free.

If a partnership buy-sell agreement involves the sale of a partnership interest to other partners (or even a third person, such as an employee), any gain or loss realized by the selling partner is treated as a gain from sale or exchange of a capital asset, except to the extent it is attributable to so-called "hot assets" as defined in Code section 741 (generally, unrealized receivables and inventory items). Note that in the case of a sale of a deceased partner's interest, the stepped-up basis at death will eliminate most of this gain, except that attributable to items of income in respect of a decedent owned by the partnership. The purchaser acquires the cost basis in the partnership interest under Code section 742, and in addition, may seek to adjust the basis of the partnership assets to reflect the purchase price under Code sections 743(b) and 754.

Consideration should always be given to the use of a liquidation plan that meets the requirements of Code section 736, so that part of the payment can take the form of a tax-deductible guaranteed payment that can be spread over a period of several years. Under that section, payments in *complete* liquidation of a retiring or deceased partner's interest are broken into two categories, 736(b) payments and 736(a) payments.

Section 736(b) payments are those made in exchange for a deceased partner's interest in partnership property, including goodwill if specified as such in the agreement, and will result in taxable gain to the selling partner only if cash received, including relief from liabilities, exceeds the basis of the partner's interest in the partnership.

Section 736(a) payments made to successors of a deceased partner are classified as guaranteed payments, or represent an interest in future partnership income. Either way, they are tax-deductible to the partnership and taxable income to the recipient as income in respect of a decedent under Code section 691. Payments for receivables are always characterized as 736(a) payments. Payments for goodwill can be 736(a) payments unless the partnership agreement specifies they are for goodwill.

In summary, liquidation plans prevent termination of the partnership because the over 50 percent sale rule will not apply, so long as there are at least two partners remaining after the liquidation is complete. Part of the liquidation payment can be made tax deductible to the remaining partners, and payments for goodwill can specifically be made tax deductible by bringing them under section 736(a).

However, the use of guaranteed payments under section 736(a) has been severely curtailed in the case of partnership agreements entered into after January 4, 1993. Section 736(b) has been amended to provide that payments for unrealized receivables and goodwill of the partnership cannot be characterized as guaranteed payments under section 736(a) unless capital is not a material income producing factor for the partnership, and the partner who is retiring or deceased is (or was) a general partner. This rule will not apply to partners retiring under an agreement that was binding on the parties on January 4, 1993. This change effectively limits the use of section 736(a) guaranteed payments to service partnerships, such as professional practices.

If life insurance is used to provide funding in the case of the liquidation plan, the insurance is owned by the partnership and used to make liquidation payments. The IRS could argue that each partner has incidents of ownership in the policy on his life because of his management rights as partner. However, the IRS has taken this position only where the insurance proceeds were payable to a party outside the partnership.[12]

Note that the receipt of the insurance proceeds increases the income tax basis of the partnership interests of all partners, including the interest owned by the decedent. It may be possible to change this result by a provision in the partnership agreement.

Where insurance on the life of each partner is owned by other partners under a cross-purchase plan, the policies can be transferred between the partnership and partners without fear of the transfer for value rule under Code section 101(a)(2)(B). This is because of an exception if the transferee is either a partnership in which the insured is a partner or a partner of the insured. If an LLC is taxed as a partnership, the same exception should apply. Partnerships are subject to the same notice requirements for life insurance on the lives of partners as discussed above under Code section 101(j) in order to prevent income taxation of the proceeds.[13]

Cross ownership should not be the basis for an IRS claim that each partner has incidents of ownership in the policy on his life owned by the other partner by reason of the agreement.[14]

47.8 SPECIAL RULES FOR FAMILY BUSINESS ENTERPRISES

Code section 2703, applicable to options or agreements created or substantially modified after October 8, 1990, raises a host of additional problems in planning business continuation agreements for family businesses. It provides that any restrictions that result from options or agreements permitting *any* person to acquire any property at less than fair market value, or any such restriction on the right to sell or use the property, are disregarded in valuing that property. However, there is an exception for options, agreements, etc., that meet the following three tests:

- They are bona fide business arrangements;

- They are not devices to transfer property to the decedent's family or the natural objects of the decedent's bounty for less than full and adequate consideration; and

- The terms are comparable to similar arrangements entered into by persons in arm's length transactions.

While the first two requirements are not really new, the third requirement, requiring that the terms and conditions of the agreement must be comparable to others entered into by unrelated persons, is very difficult to meet in most planning situations. Comparable agreements are very hard to find and are generally not available for comparison. Both the congressional committee reports and the regulations under section 2703 indicate that there are four factors in such agreements:

- the present fair market value of the property or business,

- its expected value at the date of exercise of rights under the agreement,

- adequacy of any consideration offered for the option or agreement, and

- the expected terms of the agreement.

According to the congressional committee reports, the third test is not met simply by showing isolated comparables but requires a demonstration of the general practices of unrelated parties. Expert testimony would be evidence of such practice. In unusual cases where comparables are difficult to find because the taxpayer owns a unique business, the taxpayer can use comparables from other businesses.

The Senate report also emphasizes that the law does not alter other preexisting requirements for buy-sell agreements, such as a requirement of lifetime restrictions if the agreement is to be binding at death. In other words, all the tests that must be met by unrelated parties must be met here – as well as the requirement that the terms and provisions in the buy-sell in question be comparable to the terms and provisions of buy-sells of similar businesses.

According to the regulations, the restrictive agreement will meet the requirements of the statute to control valuation if it is a binding agreement and if more than 50 percent of the value of the property or business is owned by persons who are not family members (or natural objects of the transferor's bounty).

However, the use of the term "natural objects of the transferor's bounty" is broadly defined and means that the provisions of section 2703 may apply even where the shareholders are unrelated. The final regulations do not say this, but they do say that members of the family include persons described in Code section 2701, covered in Chapter 29, and other persons who are natural objects of the transferor's bounty. The preamble to the final regulations also states that natural objects of bounty may include persons not "related by blood or marriage."

Similar arrangements among unrelated parties in the same business are generally comparable, if they consider the term of the agreement, present and anticipated fair market value of the property, and adequacy of consideration. General business practice of unrelated parties is comparable, but again, isolated comparables are insufficient, and if two or more valuation methods are generally used, the fact that the agreement falls within one of them is not sufficient.

It is important to note that the requirement of finding comparable buy-sell agreements, which is very difficult in most cases, appears to have been replaced in the regulations by a requirement of proof that unrelated persons dealing at arm's length would have entered into the same agreement. Thus, in setting the terms of a business continuation agreement where family members are involved, remember to consider the key factors – present and anticipated future value of the business, the expected term of the agreement, and consideration.

Obtain evidence and expert opinions to establish that the terms and conditions of this buy-sell agreement would be acceptable to unrelated persons. Under no circumstances should a client be allowed to arbitrarily set prices or values, such as, for example, a price based on the face value of the life insurance. Finally, consider a provision requiring periodic review and adjustment of the price, or preferably, a formula.

If a business continuation agreement was in place before the effective date of section 2703, it is not covered by the requirements of Code section 2703 - unless it is substantially modified thereafter.

The following are *not* considered substantial modifications:

- a modification required by the instrument;

- a discretionary modification containing a right or restriction that does not change the right or restriction, or results in only a *de minimis* change;

- a modification of a capitalization rate tied to a market rate; or

- a modification to a price that more adequately reflects fair market value.

The following *are* considered substantial modifications:

- failure to update an agreement that by its terms requires periodic updating; and

- the addition of a family member to the agreement, unless mandated by the terms of the agreement, or unless the new family member is assigned to a generation no lower than that of existing parties to the agreement (generation assignment is determined under the generation-skipping rules, discussed in Chapter 21).

47.9 ISSUES IN COMMUNITY PROPERTY STATES

Several problems can arise in connection with buy-sell agreements as a result of community property rights. If all or part of the stock is subject to a buy-sell agreement, careful planning is required to:

1. protect against the risk that the shareholder's spouse may predecease the seller and leave the

spouse's community property interest in the stock to third parties;

2. protect against attachment by creditors of the shareholder's spouse; and

3. protect the agreement from attachment by the stockholder's spouse if the spouse survives the stockholder and seeks to claim his or her community property interest in the stock free of the agreement.

If all or part of the stockholder's interest is quasi-community property, care should be taken to protect against the spouse's claim, if the spouse survives the stockholder, that the spouse is entitled to a community property interest in the stock free of the agreement. Appropriate written consents should be obtained in the above situations.

The impact of divorce in a community property state must be considered. If a spouse who is not active in the business should receive stock in the closely held corporation, or a partnership interest, as part of the property settlement, this may not be covered by the buy-sell agreement.

Consideration should be given to making provisions in the buy-sell agreement for such an eventuality. One solution is to grant the remaining shareholders or partners, particularly the other spouse in the divorce action, a right to purchase the interest of the soon-to-be ex-spouse. Alternatively, the corporation or partnership could have at least an option to purchase the interest. If the spouses are all made parties to such an agreement, great care must be taken to assure these provisions are fair, or else they may be unenforceable.

It is important to determine the nature of the interest held by the stockholder, not only for purposes of determining whether consents need to be obtained and wills reviewed, but also to evaluate the tax consequences. If all of the stock is community property, the community property interest of the stockholder's spouse will be included in the spouse's estate if the spouse predeceases the stockholder, and will be excluded from the stockholder's estate if the stockholder dies first. If all of the stock is the separate property of the stockholder, it will be included in the stockholder's estate only (unless the stockholder passes the stock to the spouse and then dies). If all of the stock is quasi-community property, the stockholder's spouse will have no interest if the spouse dies first, and the full value of the stock will be in the stockholder's estate for federal estate tax purposes.

The basis of property acquired from a decedent is subject to a peculiar set of rules.

Generally, the basis of property acquired from a decedent is the fair market value of the property at the date of the decedent's death. Code section 1014 defines which property is deemed "acquired from a decedent" and therefore subject to these special basis rules. Generally, section 1014 applies to all property includable in the gross estate.

The surviving spouse is deemed to have acquired his or her one-half share of the community property from the decedent spouse. This gives the surviving spouse a new basis even though his or her one-half of the community property was not included or taxed in the decedent spouse's estate. The new basis for the surviving spouse's one-half will therefore be equal to the fair market value of the property at date of death. This rule operates, however, only if the decedent's one-half is fully included in the gross estate.[15] If the property's fair market value is greater than its adjusted income tax basis, the basis will receive a "step-up." If the fair market value is less than the adjusted basis, the new basis will actually be a "step-down."

This "step-up" or "step-down" in basis for both spouses' halves of the community property does not apply to property held as joint tenancy or tenancy in common property. Even though the original nature of the property was community property (e.g., a spouse's earnings in a community property state), taking the title as joint tenants or tenants in common will change its nature so that it no longer has the attributes of community property. However, in most states with community property laws, it is possible to re-establish the property as community property by an agreement between the spouses without actually changing the recorded title to the property.

The ability of the surviving spouse to sell immediately the entire community interest of corporate stock, either under a buy-sell contract to other shareholders or to redeem some or all of it within the scope of Code section 303 (avoiding dividend treatment), can often be the most significant estate planning step taken by husband and wife shareholders in community property states.

Problems can occur when attempting to determine whether stock held by a married person in a community property state is community property. A portion of the stock can be separate property and a portion community property. A common example is an individual who owns a business prior to marriage.

Example. Assume that Tom Jones owns all of the stock in Jones Manufacturing Company, Inc. The company was incorporated prior to his marriage to Mary Jones. At the time of the marriage, the company was worth $100,000. However, during the marriage the value of the company appreciates rapidly. If Tom Jones dies, will the stock in the company, or, in the alternative, the appreciation in value of the stock, be deemed his separate property or will it be community property?

Court decisions characterizing appreciation in closely-held businesses arise in only three settings:

1. a claim by a creditor that the business should be made available for the payment of a debt;

2. divorce and the division of property pursuant to divorce; and

3. the death of one of the spouses.

Most states use some form of an "apportionment rule" to characterize the increase in value of closely-held business interests during marriage which were originally held as a spouse's separate property. Under the apportionment rule, if one of the spouses invests separate property in a business and conducts that business during the marriage, the resulting projects or increases in value of the business will be apportioned or allocated between the community estate and the spouse's separate estate according to the amount attributable to the spouse's personal efforts on the one hand (inuring to the benefit of the community), and to the capital improvement on the other (inuring to the benefit of the spouse's separate estate).

The possibility of creating such a community property interest in a corporation originally held as the separate property of one spouse can be determined only by a court in the absence of a written agreement. Thus, it is advisable for the spouses to agree, in writing, on the nature of their interests and the proportion of community and separate property.

There are other possible combinations of interest, such as combinations of community property and quasi-community property, combinations of separate property and quasi-community property, or combinations of all three types of property. In any event, the exact nature of stock ownership and their respective proportions should be identified and agreed upon in writing. In many situations it may be advisable to incorporate the property agreement into the buy-sell agreement.

In all of the community property states, appreciation in value of separate property is separate property, unless the appreciation in value is attributable to the personal services of one of the spouses or due to the application of community property funds. For example, market appreciation of publicly traded stocks held as separate property is also separate property. If, on the other hand, a house is owned as separate property, and one of the spouses is a carpenter and builds an addition with materials acquired with community property, any increase in value due to the addition is either community property or creates a right to reimbursement of the community. Community property states do vary in their treatment of these issues. For example, Idaho characterizes the appreciation in value of separate property as separate property, unless a portion is derived from community property. If so, an allocation must be made. A federal tax lien attaches to the right to reimbursement. Similarly, Arizona characterizes the appreciation as separate property if a spouse's labor or community property funds are used to acquire or improve the asset, a right to reimbursement exists, but this does not change the character of the asset.[16]

47.10 BUSINESS VALUATION TECHNIQUES

The purchase price to be paid for the stock of a shareholder may be set by a variety of methods. One method is to provide for the exact purchase price in advance with the further provision that the parties may change the price at any time upon mutual agreement.

Another method of fixing the price is to use book value based on the company's financial statements.

A third and more preferred method of valuation is a formula approach. Formula valuation methods are often used to take into account net profits and, to some degree, goodwill. An example of "a simplified place to start" would be straight capitalization of the adjusted average net profits of the business at a definite rate. For instance, as the NumberCruncher (www.Leimberg.com) illustration below shows, at a 12 percent rate, a business producing adjusted average net after-tax profits of $100,000 would be worth about $833,333 using this approach ($100,000 divided by 0.12). A 50 percent interest in such a business would be worth $416,667, half of $833,333. Combinations of these three methods can also be used as a starting place to derive a price in a buy-sell agreement. (See Chapter 70 on Valuation Planning).

CAPITALIZATION OF INCOME	
Input: Capitalization Rate...120	
Input: Adjusted Earnings................................. 100,000	
Expected Rate of Return	Value of Asset or Business
0.08	$1,250,000
0.09	$1,111,111
0.10	$1,000,000
0.11	$909,091
0.12	$833,333
0.13	$769,231
0.14	$714,286
0.15	$666,667
0.16	$625,000
0.17	$588,235

Goodwill Valuation

A closely-held business should (and often does) produce an income in excess of the amount that could be expected from the mere employment of the capital its shareholders have invested. That additional amount of income is derived from an intangible value in the business, a value in excess of the total value of the tangible assets. This is called "goodwill."

By capitalizing this "earnings attributable to intangibles," i.e., by dividing the additional profits generated by the firm's goodwill by an appropriate rate, it is possible to estimate goodwill value. If this amount is then added to book (net tangible asset) value, an estimated total business value can be found.

Some of the elements that may comprise a firm's goodwill include:

1. location of the business,

2. reputation of the business,

3. public recognition of the company's name,

4. list of customers and prospects owned by the business,

5. management effectiveness and depth,

6. sales, operations, and accounting skills,

7. employee morale,

8. position of the business relative to competitors,

9. other factors that generate income in excess of that amount which could be expected after multiplying the value of tangible assets by a reasonable rate of return.

Note that goodwill does not include the portion of profits attributable to the corporation's ownership of patents, copyrights, formulas, or trademarks, even though they are intangible, since these are all specifically identifiable.

Goodwill, as is the case with other valuation formulas and procedures, should be used only as a guideline along with other valuation methods and not as the sole determinate of value. Goodwill has minimal relevance to the valuation of most investment companies since they usually do not have large amounts of intangibles. Officially, the IRS does not give strong credibility to goodwill (although the IRS still insists that goodwill must be taken into account in the valuation process). It can still serve as a guideline. The NumberCruncher (http://www.Leimberg.com) illustration below shows the operation of this method.

GOODWILL VALUATION				
Average Annual Earnings:................................$100,000				
Estimated Capitalization Rate:............................0.2000				
Average Annual Asset Value:..........................$500,000				
Rate of Return on Tangible Assets:........ 16.000 percent				
Option	Return on Tangible Assets	Earn from Tangible Assets	Earn from Intangible Assets	Goodwill Value	Total Business Value
1	16.000%	$80,000	$20,000	$100,000	$600,000
2	17.000%	$85,000	$15,000	$75,000	$575,000
3	18.000%	$90,000	$10,000	$50,000	$550,000
4	19.000%	$95,000	$5,000	$25,000	$525,000
5	20.000%	$100,000	$0	$0	$500,000

47.11 FREQUENTLY ASKED QUESTIONS

Question – Under what situations would a business buy-out by a third party be indicated?

Answer – There are certain situations in which an owner of a business interest is either unwilling or unable to enter into a conventional stock redemption or cross-purchase agreement. Usually, such a business owner will have problems such as estate liquidity or lack of management skills or interest by members of his family, or desires the value of the business to be persuasive for federal estate tax purposes.

A typical example is where an individual is married and has three children, only one of whom he desires or expects to be able to take over the business. He or she would like to treat his children as equally as possible. One way he could do this is by entering into a buy-sell agreement with the one child expected to take over the business. If the child would acquire the business through the buy-sell agreement, the amount paid by that child could provide the surviving spouse and remaining children with funds to pay for their living needs and estate settlement costs.

Alternatively, the individual could create a trust for the other children funded by life insurance to help "equalize" the estate. Alternatively, the individual could make annual gifts to the adult financially responsible children who are not involved in the business to be used to purchase life insurance on the parent's life. At his or her death, those children would receive the death benefit as an alternative for the business interest they will not receive.

Another example is where one of two individuals in business together desires a child who presently owns no stock to come into the business at his or her death. In this instance, the agreement can be structured to require a sale to and purchase by someone who presently owns no interest in the business. In addition to a child, this could be another relative, employee, or competitor.

Question – What can be done if one of the persons involved in a business continuation agreement is uninsurable?

Answer – First, planners should remember that with modern underwriting techniques and companies that specialize in placing coverage on individuals with certain medical conditions or hazardous occupations or avocations, few individuals are truly "uninsurable". Almost all individuals, except those in "exceptionally" ill health or in an exceedingly dangerous occupation or avocation, can obtain life insurance, albeit at a rate higher than the rate the standard insured would pay. Life insurance may be used for the insurable stockholders, and for the uninsurable stockholders, a sinking fund method should be used to at least accumulate enough money for a down payment. Often an amount equivalent to the appropriate insurance premium on the uninsurable person's life (given that person's age) is deposited into some type of segregated reserve account. Such an account might be invested in bonds, mutual funds, a fixed or variable annuity, or merely left in a savings account until the death of the uninsurable.

Typically, the agreement will provide that installment payments covering the remainder of the purchase price can be spread over a relatively long period of time.

Several life insurance companies are offering guaranteed issue type contracts even on those stockholder-employees previously thought to be uninsurable as long as the stockholder-employee is actively working full time. One type of policy provides that if a death occurs during a certain initial period of time, e.g. three years, only premiums paid plus interest are payable as a death benefit. After the initial period the full death benefit is payable. A second type policy provides for a graded death benefit, i.e., one that increases over a period of time to the full death benefit.

Question – Will an agreement giving a surviving stockholder or the corporation an *option* to buy the deceased shareholder's stock usually fix the value of a business interest for federal estate tax purposes?

Answer – Yes, if there is a "first offer" provision and the price was fair and adequate when made. (A "first offer" provision requires the selling shareholder [or his executor] to offer the interest to the specified purchaser at an agreed upon price [fixed or set by formula] both during lifetime and after death before offering it to others.) Although the estate must be either obligated to sell at death or obligated to offer at death at the agreement price, the survivor(s) or the corporation need not be obligated to buy. An option in their hands would be sufficient. However, agreements involving substantially only family members may be determined not to be made at arm's length and therefore not effective in pegging the value for federal estate tax purposes. (See discussion above – Family Business Enterprises).

Question – Assume that there are three stockholders of a corporation and all stockholders have entered into a cross-purchase agreement. One of the stockholders dies and the other two stockholders purchase the decedent's stock using the life insurance proceeds under which the decedent was the insured and the remaining two stockholders were the policyowners and beneficiaries.

The decedent's personal representative now owns an insurance policy on the life of each of the surviving shareholders. They purchase their respective policies from the personal representative. Are there any potential tax problems?

Answer – No. This situation brings into play the "transfer-for-value" rule.[17] This tax trap creates an exception to the general rule that the proceeds of an insurance policy are exempt from federal income tax.

The transfer-for-value rule provides that if insurance policies are transferred for value (consideration in money or money's worth has been given for such transfer) then the owner-beneficiary of that policy will have taxable income when the insured dies. The difference between the proceeds of the policy and the sum of (a) the value paid and (b) the premiums paid by the new owner-beneficiary after receipt of the policy will be taxable as ordinary income.

There are exceptions to the transfer-for-value rule where the transfer for value is made:

(1) to the insured (as is the case here),

(2) to a corporation in which the insured is an officer or stockholder,

(3) to a partner of the insured,

(4) to a partnership in which the insured is a partner,

(5) where the new owner's basis (cost) is determined in whole or in part by reference to the transferor's basis, or

(6) where a transfer of a policy or an interest in a policy is made between spouses or between spouses incident to a divorce. For instance, if a divorce decree requires one spouse to transfer a policy to another, the transfer will be considered a nontaxable event that results in a carryover basis in the policy and avoids the transfer-for-value tax trap.

Question – Assume that there is a stock redemption agreement funded by life insurance. The amount of the life insurance on the date of the death of one of the stockholders exceeds the corporate obligation under the redemption agreement. Are there any tax consequences?

Answer – The proceeds of corporate-owned life insurance will generally not be taxable to the corporation when it receives the same (except for potential exposure of certain corporations to a corporate level alternative minimum tax). However, the earnings and profits of the corporation will be increased by the amount of the proceeds and then reduced when a portion of the proceeds is used to redeem the shares of stock.

If the entire amount of the proceeds has not been used to redeem a decedent-shareholder's interest, there will be a permanent increase in corporate earnings and profits, which means that there should be additional dollars available for the payment of dividends; because of this, the potential exists for imposition of the accumulated earnings tax penalty, as well as dividend treatment on any distribution made by the corporation to its shareholders.

Question – Assume that the parties enter into either a redemption agreement or a cross-purchase agreement. Should anything be done to protect their rights with respect to a possible transfer to third parties?

Answer – The stock certificates owned by the parties to either the redemption agreement or the cross-purchase agreement should bear a legend (stamp) indicating a restriction on the ability to transfer those shares of stock as a result of the redemption or cross-purchase agreement.

Question – If a cross-purchase agreement funded with life insurance is changed to a stock redemption agreement, and the insurance that was owned by the individuals on each other is transferred to the corporation, will there be any income tax consequences as relates to the insurance?

Answer – No. Changing insurance from a cross-purchase agreement to a stock redemption agreement will not violate the transfer-for-value rule, because policies can be transferred from a stockholder to a corporation of which the insured is a stockholder. This will qualify as an exception to the transfer-for-value rule. Note, however, that the reverse, i.e., change from a stock redemption to a cross-purchase, will be a violation of the transfer-for-value rule if insurance is transferred from the corporation to a stockholder other than the insured.

Question – Can a buy-sell agreement "peg" the value of a business interest for federal gift tax purposes?

Answer – Although a buy-sell agreement will probably not be absolutely controlling for federal gift tax purposes, it should carry strong evidentiary weight as to the business value and will be considered along with other relevant factors. An agreement will probably be successful in establishing value if:

(1) the price (or formula) is reasonable at the time the agreement is signed;

(2) the agreement is negotiated by parties knowledgeable of relevant facts and at arm's length;

(3) the price (or formula) agreed upon is as binding during lifetime as at death, i.e., the lifetime price permitted cannot be higher than the sale price at a shareholder's death; and

(4) the price is fixed by the terms of the agreement or the agreement contains a formula or method for determining price.

Where family members own at least 50 percent of the business, additional requirements will probably apply. See discussion above – Family Business Enterprises.

Question – What is the advantage of using a trustee in a buy-sell agreement?

Answer – Potential difficulty can be avoided through use of a trustee in carrying out the terms of the agreement. Prior to death of one of the parties to the agreement there are many duties to be performed. The trustee can obtain the premiums on insurance used to fund the agreement from the appropriate parties and can pay the premiums when they become due. The trustee can also serve as custodian of the policies subject to the agreement.

After death of a party to the agreement, the trustee will receive proceeds of the insurance on the life of the deceased business owner. The trustee can then act as a disinterested middleman in paying the purchase price for the decedent's business interest to the legal representative of the decedent's estate and in transferring the business interest to the purchaser.

Question – What is the potential tax trap in using a trusteed buy-sell approach?

Answer – Note that although the law is not entirely clear, the use of a trustee will probably not eliminate a transfer for value problem as to life insurance acquired by the trustee. For example, assume a corporation has three equal shareholders who enter into a cross-purchase plan. A trustee is named to act under the agreement and purchases insurance on all three shareholders to fund the agreement. After the death of the first shareholder, the agreement continues for the remaining two shareholders. The authors believe that the shift of economic interests in the insurance policies on the remaining shareholders will constitute a transfer for value. This is not a problem in a partnership buy-sell. In fact, if shareholders in a buy-sell are also partners in an unrelated business, even though there is a transfer of an interest in a policy and even if there is valuable consideration, the insurance may still be income tax free at death because of the "partnership safe harbor" to the transfer for value rules, discussed below.

Question – Is it possible to be certain the price established in a business continuation agreement involving family members will establish the estate tax value of the interest of a deceased partner or shareholder?

Answer – No. Assuring that values in a family buy-sell agreement will be accepted by the IRS and the courts has become much more difficult since the adoption of Code section 2703. Because related persons are by definition not dealing at arm's length in establishing the terms and price of their business continuation agreement, the price may not determine value for tax purposes unless it can be shown that the terms and price of the agreement could have been obtained in a fair bargain among unrelated parties in the same business dealing with each other at arm's length.[18] This standard, which is from the regulations, appears to be more demanding than the one Congress intended, which mandates a showing that the agreement could have been obtained in a hypothetical arm's length agreement.[19]

Careful planning, arms' length bargaining between the parties, and the use of an independent professional valuation expert, however, should significantly increase the likelihood that the agreement will be persuasive with respect to the federal estate tax value. . Using a formula approach, rather than a stated dollar value, has a better chance of accomplishing this goal.

Question – Four shareholders in a closely held corporation want to enter into a cross purchase plan to acquire the stock of a deceased shareholder, fully funded with life insurance. You have explained to them the problems that will occur upon the death of any shareholder under the transfer for value rule if economic interests in the insurance policies on the remaining shareholders are shifted so that the agreement may remain in effect. Can you offer any solutions to this problem?

Answer – Other than canceling existing policies and acquiring new ones, there are at least two other techniques to deal with this problem. The first is to have all of the remaining shareholders transfer their interests in policies on the other shareholder to the corporation, and substitute a stock redemption plan for the cross purchase plan. Since they are all shareholders in the corporation, the transfer of the policies to it falls within a safe harbor exception to the transfer for value rule.

Another solution, which has been the subject of a series of private letter rulings, is to consider the establishment of a partnership among all of the shareholders. As discussed above, transfers of policies among partners is one of the safe harbor exceptions to the transfer for value rule. Frequently the shareholders are involved in other business or investment activities, such as the ownership of property leased to the corporation, which could be the basis for the formation of a partnership. One private letter ruling held that the mere ownership of the life insurance policies would be a sufficient business or investment activity to justify formation of a partnership. However, cautious practitioners should not rely on this ruling, and advise the parties that they should carry out some legitimate business or investment activity in such a partnership to assure its validity.

Question – Are the costs involved in a stock redemption deductible to the corporation?

Answer – No. The costs involved in a stock redemption are non-deductible.[20] This prohibition applies even if the purchase of the interest is necessary to save the corporation's business life. The purchase of a corporation's own stock is a capital transaction and no deduction is allowed for either the purchase price or the expenses associated with the purchase.

CHAPTER ENDNOTES

1. The "Wait-and-See" Buy Sell name was coined by Stephan Leimberg and Morey S. Rosenbloom.
2. I.R.C. §2042; See *Newell v. Comm'r.*, 66 F.2d 102 (7th Cir. 1933); *Est. of Blount v. Comm'r.*, 2005-2 USTC ¶60,509 (11th Cir. 2005), rev'g TC Memo. 2004-116; *Huntsman v. Comm'r.*, 66 TC 861 (1976). However, in *Est. of Connelly v. United States*, the Eighth Circuit declined to follow the Eleventh Circuit's decision in *Est. of Blount* concerning whether life insurance held by an entity on the life of a deceased owner where the entity is legally obligated to redeem the deceased owner's interests and intends to use those proceeds to redeem those interests, irrespective of the entity is expressly obligated to use the life insurance in the redemption. It's important to note that neither the buy-sell agreements in *Est. of Blount* or *Est. of Connelly* expressly required that the life insurance proceeds be used in the redemption, which is better practice, i.e., require that the life insurance proceeds expressly be so used.
3. Treas. Reg. §20.2031-2(h); *May v. McGowan*, 194 F.2d 396 (2d Cir. 1952); *Comm'r. v. Child's Est.*, 147 F.2d 368 (3d Cir. 1945); *Est. of Mitchell*, 37 BTA 1 (1938). See also Rev. Rul. 59-60, 1959-1 CB 237.
4. I.R.C. §264(a)(1).
5. I.R.C. §101(a)(1).
6. I.R.C. §§302(c)(1), 318.
7. I.R.C. §318(a)(3).
8. I.R.C. §318(a).
9. I.R.C. §302(c)(2).

10. I.R.C. §§2042, 2033.
11. See Brody and Leimberg, "Avoiding the Tax Trap of the Transfer for Value Rule," *Estate Planning*, Vol. 32, No. 10, p. 3 and Brody and Leimberg, "Using a Transactional Analysis to Avoid the Transfer for Value Rule," *Estate Planning*, Vol. 32, No. 11, p. 3.
12. Rev. Rul. 83-147, 1983-2 CB 158.
13. See Notice 2009-48.
14. See *Est. of Infante*, TC Memo 1970-206.
15. I.R.C. §1014(b)(6).
16. IR Manual §§ 25.18.1-1, 25.18.1.2.21 (02-15-2005), "Community Property: Capital Gains from Separate Property."
17. See Brody and Leimberg, "Avoiding the Tax Trap of the Transfer for Value Rule," *Estate Planning*, Vol. 32, No. 10, p. 3 and Brody and Leimberg, "Using a Transactional Analysis to Avoid the Transfer for Value Rule," *Estate Planning*, Vol. 32, No. 11, p. 3.
18. Treas. Reg. §25.2703-1(b)(4).
19. *Explanation of Revenue Provisions for Inclusion in Fiscal Year 1991 Budget Reconciliation Package as Approved by Committee 10/13/90*, Senate Finance Committee, 101st Cong., 2nd Sess., 136 Cong. Rec. S 15679, S 15683.
20. I.R.C. §162(k).

SECTION 303 STOCK REDEMPTION

CHAPTER 48

48.1 INTRODUCTION

Internal Revenue Code section 303 allows the purchase of a portion of a decedent shareholder's stock by the shareholder's corporation to be treated as a sale or exchange rather than as a dividend. A section 303 partial redemption can provide cash and/or other property from the decedent shareholder's corporation to provide liquidity for the decedent shareholder's executor to use to pay death taxes and other death-related expenses.

48.2 WHEN IS USE OF SUCH A DEVICE INDICATED?

1. When there is a desire to keep control of a closely-held or family corporation within the decedent-shareholder's family after death.

2. When the corporation's stock is a major estate asset and a forced sale or liquidation of the business is in order to pay death taxes and other costs is a threat.

3. Where a tax-favored withdrawal of funds from the corporation at the death of the stockholder would be useful.

4. When a redemption of Code section 306 stock is desirable.

48.3 WHAT ARE THE REQUIREMENTS?

Stock to be Redeemed

The stock to be redeemed by the corporation must have been included in the decedent's gross estate for federal estate tax purposes.[1] The value for federal estate tax purposes of all stock of the corporation that is included in determining the value of the decedent's gross estate must comprise *more than* 35 percent of the excess of:

a. the value of the gross estate over

b. the sum allowable as a deduction under Code sections 2053 (estate expenses, indebtedness, and taxes) and 2054 (losses).[2]

Essentially, that means the stock includible in the gross estate must be worth more than 35 percent of the adjusted gross estate.

Example. Assume the gross estate is $12,250,000; administrative and funeral costs are $250,000, and there are no other deductible expenses. To qualify for a section 303 redemption, the value of the stock in question must *exceed* $4,200,000 (i.e., must be more than 35 percent of ($12,250,000 − $250,000)).

The corporation can redeem stock other than that held by the executor at the time of the stockholder's death subject to the limitations discussed directly above; if for any reason stock was included in the decedent-stockholder's gross estate, it can be redeemed even if in the hands of someone other than the estate's executor at the time of the redemption.[3]

Example. A mother purchased stock with her own funds and held it jointly with her daughter when she died. Here the entire value of the stock would be in the mother's estate, but the daughter would become the owner of the stock.

675

A section 303 redemption would be permissible to the extent the daughter's interest had to bear a portion of her mother's estate's taxes and estate settlement costs, which should be considered when drafting the tax clause in the documents. The corporation could purchase (redeem) the stock directly from the daughter.

Likewise (subject to the limitation discussed above regarding an obligation for taxes and expenses), where the stock transferred is considered included in the decedent's estate because of a transfer with a retained life estate, a transfer taking effect at death or a revocable transfer,[4] the corporation could purchase the stock under section 303 from the new owner. The same result occurs where the stock is placed into a revocable trust by a shareholder. Because the stock would be included in the decedent-stockholder's estate, a redemption from the trustee would be allowed (again, assuming the share of the estate going into the trust bears a direct or indirect burden to pay death taxes or administration costs or is reduced by such amounts).

Amount

The amount that can be safely redeemed under Code section 303 is limited; section 303 limits the "safe" redemption amount to the sum of

(a) all estate, inheritance, legacy, and succession taxes (including generation-skipping transfer taxes) and interest thereon imposed by reason of decedent's death; and

(b) funeral and administration expenses (whether or not claimed as a deduction on the federal estate tax return).

Any amounts in excess will be taxed under the rules of Code section 302.[5] This means any balance may be taxed as a dividend to the "seller," the estate or heir from whom the stock is being redeemed, or it may qualify for favorable tax treatment (treated as a sale of the stock so that the amount realized would be reduced by the stepped-up basis of the stock likely resulting in no gain) if the tests for sale or exchange treatment of Code section 302 are met.

A redemption under section 303 will qualify for favorable tax treatment only to the extent that the interest of a shareholder whose stock is redeemed is reduced either directly or indirectly through a binding obligation to contribute toward the payment of the decedent's death taxes and/or administration expenses.[6] See Figure 48.1 for illustrations of the Section 303 Stock Redemption qualifications and favorable tax treatments.

Figure 48.1

DETERMINATION OF WHETHER ESTATE QUALIFIES FOR SECTION 303 STOCK REDEMPTION		
Federal Estate Tax Value Of Corporate Stock In Gross Estate	(1)	$4,200,000
Gross Estate Less Allowable Deductions	(2)	$6,500,000
35% of Gross Estate Less Allowable Deductions	(3)	$2,275,000
Qualifies If (1) Is Greater Than (3)		

REDEMPTION UNDER SECTION 303 PROTECTED TO EXTENT OF	
Funeral And Administration Expenses	$90,000
Federal Estate And Generation-Skipping Taxes	$400,000
State Death Taxes	$250,000
Generation-Skipping Transfer Taxes	$0
Interest Collected As Part Of Above Taxes	$0
Maximum Allowable Section 303 Redemption	$7,440,000

Computations Courtesy – NumberCruncher Software: http://Leimberg.com

48.4 HOW IT IS DONE

The mechanics of a section 303 stock redemption are relatively simple. The corporation redeems (buys back) stock from the party who holds the stock at the death of the decedent-stockholder in question. Usually, the recipient of the decedent's stock will be the decedent-shareholder's executor or administrator. Sometimes the seller will be a direct heir, surviving spouse, or trustee of an irrevocable trust created by the decedent. The redemption is given preferential tax treatment because it is characterized as a sale of stock so that any gain would be taxed at capital gain rates.

Stock may not be redeemed from any stockholder who acquired stock by purchase or gift (if the donor was not the decedent).[7] For example, if a father devises stock by wills to his son who then sells it or gifts it to his brother, the redemption of the brother's stock would not qualify as a section 303 stock redemption. Also, section 303 does not apply to stock acquired by a shareholder from the executor in satisfaction of a specific monetary bequest.[8]

Using Life Insurance

Without adequate prior planning, a corporation may lack the funds to effect a section 303 redemption. Although the corporation could borrow funds, its ability to borrow a sufficient amount of cash in a relatively short period of time may be uncertain and the terms and conditions of the loan may be prohibitive. As an alternative method of funding, the corporation should consider purchasing an insurance policy on the life of the shareholder.

The life insurance used to fund the section 303 redemption should be a typical key person policy. The corporation should be the applicant, owner, premium payor, and beneficiary. (In the case of an uninsurable stockholder, a sinking fund can be established by using fixed or variable annuities, mutual funds, or other securities.)

Example. Assume Aaron Sterling, a widower who dies in 2023, owns 75 percent of a corporation. His son Joshua owns the remaining 25 percent. Aaron's portion of the stock is valued at $6,000,000. The value of his estate, after subtracting allowable deductions under Code sections 2053 and 2054, is $15,000,000. Assume there was little cash in Aaron's estate. Assuming Aaron's estate and inheritance taxes and other death-related expenses are projected to be about $4,000,000. The corporation would purchase $4,000,000 of life insurance on Aaron's life.

Step 1: At Aaron's death, his stock will pass to his estate.

Step 2: The corporation then receives the insurance proceeds on Aaron's life.

Step 3: The corporation uses the life insurance proceeds to pay Aaron's estate for stock qualifying for the section 303 redemption.

Step 4: The estate transfers stock with a value equal to the money it receives to the corporation.

Step 5: Aaron's estate uses the cash to pay federal and state death taxes and administrative and funeral expenses.

In order to meet the 35 percent threshold, the shareholder should consider making lifetime gifts of personally owned life insurance or other property (except the stock in question) to the surviving shareholder's family so as to increase the percentage of the estate attributable to his or her stock (but only to the extent such gifts are not made within three years of the stockholder's death. Gifts of assets within three years of death are brought back into the gross estate under Code section 2035 for purposes of section 303 35 percent test).

Alternatively, the shareholder could sell personally owned life insurance or make a capital contribution to the corporation to make qualification for a Section 303 redemption easier. Although neither transaction would significantly affect the size of the shareholder's overall estate, the relative percentage of stock interest would be increased. (This may also make it easier to qualify for a section 6166 installment arrangement to pay estate taxes attributable to the business.) Another technique to accomplish the same result is the purchase by the corporation of new key person insurance coverage. This would increase the value of the business at the insured's death relative to the value of the adjusted gross estate.

In general, if in any tax year the corporation's taxable income is retained for the purpose of paying insurance premiums (or for any other purpose) in excess of the $250,000 accumulated earnings credit ($150,000 in the case of certain personal service corporations), the corporation should be prepared to show that such excess retentions are necessary to meet the "reasonable needs of the business"; such excess retentions that are beyond reasonable business needs may be subject to the accumulated earnings tax. Where an uncommitted key individual life insurance policy (of the appropriate amount and type) is used to shift the risk of the loss of a key person's services, it will generally be considered to meet the reasonable needs of the business, and, thus not trigger the accumulated earnings tax.

Likewise, even though death proceeds do increase earnings and profits (to the extent they exceed premiums paid), they should not, per se, trigger the accumulated earnings tax. In any event, term, whole life, or a similar low cash value policy should be used. Furthermore, the redemption should be consummated, wherever possible, in the same fiscal year that death occurs.

Note: Although Code Section 537(a)(2) provides that "the reasonable needs of the business" include the "Section 303 redemption needs of the business." However, the IRS's position is that this provision applies only to amounts accumulated in the year of death and thereafter.

Consider having a third party, such as an irrevocable trust for family members, own the life insurance. At the shareholder's death, the proceeds would be paid to the policyowner trust which could then make a fully secured loan at a reasonable (market) rate of interest to the corporation. The corporation could then redeem the stock under section 303. The three advantages of this technique are:

- the insurance proceeds don't "swell" the value of the corporation for estate tax purposes;

- cash values cannot trigger an accumulated earnings tax problem; and

- neither cash values nor death proceeds can trigger an alternative minimum tax problem.

Furthermore, the interest paid by the corporation to the trust enhances the financial security of the beneficiaries of the trust.

Corporate Control

It is possible to complete a section 303 stock redemption without losing corporate control or diluting stock interest. Where there is a nonvoting class of stock outstanding, it is permissible for the corporation to redeem only the nonvoting stock.[9]

Generally, only one class of stock (common) is outstanding. There are two or perhaps three ways to accomplish the 303 redemption without creating voting or control problems. Recapitalization is the first method. If a corporation has only one class of stock outstanding, a shareholder may exchange a portion of his or her voting common stock for nonvoting preferred stock of equal value. The new preferred stock is then redeemed under section 303 with no adverse effect on the voting control of the corporation.

A second method of overcoming voting and control problems is the issuance of a preferred stock dividend prior to the death of a decedent-stockholder. A preferred stock dividend is declared on the common stock. This entails no recapitalization and, normally, the dividend is tax free. Then the preferred stock is redeemed pursuant to section 303.

A third possible means of taking money out of a closely held corporation through section 303 without a relative loss of control was suggested by a ruling that allowed the company to issue a stock dividend of nonvoting stock and to redeem the newly issued stock from the estate without creating a taxable distribution. The approval for such a stock dividend followed by a redemption should be obtained from corporate shareholders.[10]

Timing

The proceeds from the redemption must be received after the decedent's death and no later than:

- three years and ninety days from the due date of the federal estate tax return;

- sixty days after a Tax Court decision in a contest of estate tax liability has become final; or

- the time permitted for the payment of estate tax installments where the executor has elected and the estate qualifies for a deferred payment of estate taxes attributable to the business under Code Section 6166 (up to fourteen years).

However, where a distribution is made *more* than four years after the decedent's death, the amount subject to Code Section 303 is limited to the lesser of: (a) the amount of taxes, funeral, and administrative expenses remaining unpaid at that time, or (b) the taxes and expenses that are actually paid within one year of the section 303 payment to the stockholder.

Written Agreement

Generally, an agreement is unnecessary in the case where the executor will acquire the controlling interest in the corporation. However, an agreement would be advantageous to a minority stockholder. This would provide assurance that the corporation will consummate the redemption and the shareholder's estate will benefit from a section 303 redemption. (Quite often, however, a complete redemption is preferable to a partial redemption. This is particularly true in the case of the death of a minority shareholder because of the relatively weak voting control position the survivors of such a shareholder will have.) Specific permission should be granted by the stockholder in his will allowing his or her executor to effect the redemption.

48.5 TAX IMPLICATIONS

1. The amount paid to the estate should not be treated as a dividend distribution. Instead, it will be treated as the "exchange price" for the stock and will generally result in little or no gain recognized by the estate if the basis for the stock was "stepped-up" by reason of being included in the shareholder's estate. (Note: if the stock was a gift to the decedent and that gift was made within one year of his death and it then passes from the donee-decedent back to the donor or the donor's spouse, it will not receive a step up in basis!).[11] However, to the extent the price paid by the corporation to the estate exceeds the estate's basis, the estate will pay a tax at capital gains rates on any such gain.

2. The insurance premiums paid on the life of the insured stockholder are not income tax deductible by the corporation.[12]

3. The proceeds of key person life insurance paid to the corporation at the death of the stockholder are income tax-free (with the possible exception of any corporate level alternative minimum tax).[13]

4. Section 303 redemptions are specifically exempt from the "attribution" (constructive ownership) rules which artificially attribute stock actually owned by one party to another party. The application of these attribution rules often cause a redemption to be treated as a dividend rather than a sale or exchange of the underlying stock. This is significant because if the redemption was treated as a dividend and the corporation had sufficient earnings and profits, the taxable amount would not be reduced by the stock's date of death stepped-up basis. As a result, the entire redemption proceeds would be taxable. On the other hand, if the redemption is treated as a sale of the underlying stock pursuant to Code Section 303, little or none of the redemption proceeds would be taxable.

48.6 ISSUES IN COMMUNITY PROPERTY STATES

In order to qualify (aggregate) an ownership interest in two or more corporations for purposes of meeting the "more than 35 percent of adjusted gross estate" test, there must be at least 20 percent in value of each corporation included in the decedent's estate. In determining the 20 percent stock ownership by decedent, the surviving spouse's half of stock constituting community property may be included by treating it as if it had been included in determining the value of the gross estate of the decedent.

48.7 FREQUENTLY ASKED QUESTIONS

Question – Is cash the only property that may be distributed by the corporation?

Answer – No. If the need for liquidity exists, cash is generally the most practical type of property. However, section 303 does not require that the corporation make its purchase of the decedent's stock in cash. The corporation can distribute property "in kind." For instance, the corporation might distribute income-producing assets such as rental property (e.g., an apartment house, office building, or parking lot) in return for the stock it receives. Unfortunately, the corporation would recognize gain on the distribution of any appreciated property. The corporation could also have taxable income in the event of a recapture of depreciation,[14] liability in excess of basis,[15] and the excess of the fair market value distributed over the adjusted basis.[16]

The corporation can also issue notes to pay for the stock. The redemption rules are tested when the notes are delivered, not when they are paid. However, the notes should have a fairly short maturity (five years or less).

Stock of the corporation making the distribution does not qualify as "property" and therefore may not be used to buy back the decedent's stock.[17]

Question – Do the funds received in the redemption have to be used to pay estate settlement costs?

Answer – No, the funds received in the redemption do not *have* to be used directly to pay estate settlement costs. Sometimes, an estate will already have sufficient cash. The estate's settlement costs (exclusive of debts) only serve as a measure of the amount which can be redeemed. As long as the requirements for section 303 are met, the corporation can redeem the permitted number of shares regardless of whether or not the executor actually needs the cash for liquidity purposes. Similarly, money or property received by the seller does not actually have to be used to pay estate settlement costs.

Question – If there is more than one class of stock outstanding, can the aggregate value of all classes be taken into account in meeting the "more than 35 percent" test?

Answer – Yes, all classes of stock can be added together in meeting the "more than 35 percent" test regardless of which class of stock is being redeemed.[18]

Question – May stock of two or more corporations be aggregated for purposes of meeting the "more than 35 percent of adjusted gross estate" tests?

Answer – Only if 20 percent or more in value of the outstanding stock of *each* corporation is included in the decedent's gross estate.[19]

Question – Are the constructive ownership (attribution) rules a problem?

Answer – No. As noted above, to the extent that stock is redeemed under section 303, these rules can be ignored.

Question – Assume the executor needs cash quickly. Before an IRS audit, a section 303 redemption takes place. Upon an audit of the estate tax return: (a) the IRS increases the valuation on the stock; (b) the IRS decreases the valuation; or (c) for some other reason the redemption does not qualify under section 303. How can dividend treatment be avoided?

Answer – Arrange for the first contingency by providing that the purchase price and the number of shares redeemed will be adjusted so that the corporation will pay no more, and no less, than the value of the stock as finally determined for federal estate tax purposes. Alternatively, a contingency agreement that voids the purchase and sale could be arranged in the event that the "more than 35 percent" test is not met.

Question – If closely held stock is left to a specific legatee under the terms of a deceased stockholder's will, and there is a provision in the will that states that estate and inheritance taxes will be paid out of the residue of the estate, can there be a section 303 redemption?

Answer – No. There cannot be a section 303 redemption because the specific legatee will not bear any portion of paying the taxes. The redemption will qualify under section 303 only to the extent that the interest of the redeemed shareholder is reduced directly or through a binding obligation to contribute to the payment of death taxes or funeral or administration costs.

Question – Can stock of an S corporation qualify for section 303?

Answer – Yes. Stock of *any* corporation, including an S corporation, may qualify under section 303.[20] In addition, any class of stock, common, preferred, voting or non-voting may be redeemed if otherwise qualifying for a section 303 redemption.

Question – If the executor elects to take an income tax deduction on the estate's income tax return for funeral and administration expenses, rather than deduct such expenses on the estate tax return, does this have any impact on the amount qualifying for redemption under section 303?

Answer – No. The fact that the executor deducts funeral and administrative expenses on the income tax return of the estate will not reduce the amount of stock that can be redeemed.

CHAPTER ENDNOTES

1. I.R.C. §303(a).
2. I.R.C. §303(b)(2)(A).
3. Treas. Reg. §1.303-1.
4. I.R.C. §§2036-2038.
5. I.R.C. §303(a).
6. I.R.C. §303(b)(3).
7. Treas. Reg. §1.303-2(f).
8. Treas. Reg. §1.303-2(f).
9. Treas. Reg. §1.303-2(c)(1).
10. Rev. Rul. 87-132, 1987-2 CB 82.
11. Treas. Reg. §1.303-1; I.R.C. §1014(e).
12. I.R.C. §264(a)(1).
13. I.R.C. §101(a)(1).
14. I.R.C. §§1245, 1250.
15. I.R.C. §311(b)(2).
16. I.R.C. §311(b)(1)(B).
17. Rev. Rul. 65-289, 1965-2 CB 86; I.R.C. §§303(a), 317.
18. Treas. Reg. §1.303-2(c)(1).
19. I.R.C. §303(b)(2)(B).
20. Priv. Ltr. Rul. 9009041.

FAMILY LIMITED PARTNERSHIPS

CHAPTER 49

Note: A checklist of issues to consider when choosing an entity, such as a proprietorship, partnership, limited liability company (LLC), C corporation, or S corporation, appears at the end of this chapter.

49.1 INTRODUCTION

A family partnership is a partnership that exists between members of a family (defined for income tax purposes as including only an individual's spouse, ancestors, lineal descendants, and any trusts established primarily for the benefit of such persons).[1] If a partnership among family members is respected as a genuine partnership, it will be treated tax-wise the same as any other partnership and the same rules will apply.

The family partnership is a technique frequently used as a means of both shifting wealth and splitting income among a family unit. Although some family partnerships have sometimes been attacked by the IRS as being mere tax avoidance schemes that should not be recognized for tax purposes, if the rules for establishing and operating such partnerships are carefully followed, the IRS currently recognizes the validity of this income shifting device.[2] Although the IRS has asserted that a taxable gift can arise upon the contribution of capital to a family limited partnership, this argument was rejected where the partnership agreement allocated income and expenses on a pro rata basis based on the partners' contributions to the partnership. The court stated there cannot be a gift on formation where each investor's interest is proportional to the capital contributed.[3]

Two major forms of family partnerships commonly used are the general partnership and the limited partnership.

The general partnership is an entity under which all partners have a voice in management (by percentage vote) but are personally liable for all of the debts and other liabilities of the general partnership. This very negative aspect often makes the general partnership entity unsuitable for family wealth preservation and has prompted the use of the limited partnership for the majority of family activities for which a partnership is appropriate.

One benefit of a general partnership is that, in some circumstances, the partners may share in the losses generated by the partnership for income tax purposes. This is much more difficult for limited partners due to the passage of various "anti-tax shelter" laws which restrict the sharing of losses among partners in limited partnerships.

A Family Limited Partnership (FLP) is a limited liability entity created under state law. Family limited partnerships are so named because ownership of partnership interests typically is limited to members of the same family unit. Since the limited partnership form is most frequently used for the majority of family activities, this chapter will deal mainly with that form of doing business or holding assets.

Ownership rights in the FLP are governed by state law as modified by the partners' FLP agreement. Most states have adopted the Uniform Limited Partnership Act (ULPA) or some modified version thereof. Although there may be slight differences in the statutory partnership rules from one state to another, there generally is a high degree of uniformity among the states.

Upon formation, family members contribute property in return for an ownership interest in the capital and profits of the FLP. The partners designate a general partner (or general partners) who will be given management responsibility and who will assume personal liability for debts and other liabilities that are not satisfied from the assets of the FLP. The general partner(s) typically hold a small interest in the FLP (e.g., 1 or 2 percent interest) and gift the remaining limited partnership interests to the next generation over a period of time, and often at a discounted value for gift tax purposes. The general partner is typically a senior generation or may be an LLC or trust controlled by family members. The limited partners have no control or say over decisions related to management of the FLP. In return for giving up their rights of management and control, the personal liability of the limited partners generally is limited to the amount of capital that they contribute, if any. Because FLP assets are typically beyond the reach of the limited partners' creditors, an FLP can be an excellent wealth preservation and asset protection vehicle.

Although an underlying purpose of most FLPs is to manage family assets and to plan for the transfer of such assets from parents to children, many parents are not willing to part with control over their assets when the FLP is created. In some cases, the parents simply desire to continue managing their property, and in other cases, the children lack the maturity or business skills required to manage the assets. The FLP structure is attractive because the senior generation is typically the general partner, and thus in control of all decisions related to management of FLP assets. Because the next generation, as limited partners, have no control over the underlying assets, the parents are provided with the time and opportunity to educate their children about managing and investing their assets and involve them in the process and thus provide an important non-tax reason for their creation.

Although a thorough understanding of partnership law is essential to preparing an effective limited partnership agreement, the concepts underlying FLPs are not difficult to comprehend and an FLP can be easily integrated into an estate plan.

49.2 WHEN IS USE OF SUCH A DEVICE INDICATED?

Family limited partnerships are often used to fractionalize the ownership of business assets, investment assets such as marketable securities, or real estate to take advantage of gift and estate tax valuation discounts (see Chapter 70) which significantly reduces transfer taxes.

In most cases, an FLP will be used to facilitate the making of gifts of limited partner interests from parents to children and other family members without divesting control from the parents. In other cases, an FLP will be used to ensure continuous ownership of assets within the family unit for several generations.

Until most recently, FLPs were used primarily as a means of (1) shifting the income tax burden from parents to children or other family members or (2) to "freeze" the value of assets by shifting future growth in various assets to other family members. Although these uses have been somewhat curtailed by the Kiddie Tax (note, these rules were simplified under the TCJA so that a child's unearned income is taxed at the rates applicable to trusts and estates) and the special valuation rules for intrafamily transfers under Code section 2701, the many other benefits provided by the FLP have made it a valuable tool in developing a comprehensive estate plan.

With greater frequency, many practitioners are coming to recognize the many tax and non-tax benefits that an FLP can provide. An FLP would be an appropriate device in the following circumstances:

1. To reduce the value of an estate for transfer tax (e.g., estate, gift, and generation-skipping) purposes.

    Because control of the assets of an FLP is centralized in the general partner(s), a limited partner often experiences an immediate decrease in the value of interest compared to the overall value of the property contributed to the FLP. This decrease in value results because of the lack of control and highly reduced marketability that accompany ownership of assets indirectly through a limited partnership interest, as well as the inherent inability of a limited partner to unilaterally or immediately access the capital or the profits of the FLP.

    It is well accepted that value often appears and disappears in an FLP. Value can appear in the form of a control premium that attaches to the right to manage assets or to liquidate assets into cash. Value can disappear due to the giving up of management rights and exchange of assets in return for a virtually unmarketable ownership interest.

    Past cases demonstrate that the value of FLP interests typically will be reduced by valuation discounts falling within the 30 percent to 35 percent range. Under these circumstances, it is possible that a married couple with a taxable estate (before discounts) of approximately $30,000,000 in 2023 could use an FLP to reduce the value of their estate to a point where little or no estate tax is owed (taking advantage of the increased lifetime exemption amount of $12,920,000 per person in 2023 under the TCJA plus valuation discounts). Note, however, in recent years there have been proposals to limit the availability of valuation discounts to curtail what was perceived to be an abusive tax-avoidance scheme. Most recently, proposed regulations were introduced under Code section 2704 which would have significantly limited the availability of valuation discounts for FLPs. Although under the Trump Administration the Treasury Department withdrew the proposed 2704 regulations in late 2017, it is possible that similar measures may be introduced at a later date or under a new administration. Taxpayers should use caution when taking large discounts and should seek the advice of tax counsel to determine what is an appropriate valuation discount based upon their particular circumstances.

2. When it is desired to shift the income tax burden from a parent who is in a high income tax bracket to a child or other relative who is in a lower income tax bracket.

    Use of an FLP can facilitate parents' shifting of income to their children, with the income taxed at the child's lower income tax bracket. This will increase the family's cash flow.

    However, the benefit of shifting income to children under age nineteen and in some cases under age twenty-four is somewhat limited. In the past, children under age nineteen—and in some cases under age twenty-four—with unearned income in excess of $2,300 (as indexed for 2023) generally were taxed at the parent's top marginal rate under the "Kiddie Tax" rules. The Tax Cuts and Jobs Act of 2017 simplified the "Kiddie Tax" for tax years 2018 through 2025. Under the new law, a child's unearned income will be taxed at the rates applicable to trusts and estates (i.e., a top rate of 37 percent on income over $14,450). Although the rates applicable to trusts and estates are significantly compressed as compared to the individual rates, children with lower amounts of unearned income may now pay less under the new law. (*Example* 1 at the end of this chapter presents an illustration of the income shifting context in the case of a family business).

3. Where it is desirable to conduct a family business in a form other than a sole proprietorship or a corporation.

    In selecting a choice of business entity, the use of a corporation may cause tax problems that would not exist if the business were instead operated as an FLP. For example, subchapter C corporations are subject to personal holding company rules, the accumulated earnings tax, and unreasonable compensation problems, while subchapter S corporations are restricted as to who and how many persons may be shareholders. Similarly, placing a sole proprietorship business into a trust may result in the trust taxed by the IRS as a corporation, which is usually a very bad result. FLPs generally offer flexibility in income taxation compared to these other forms of businesses. (A summary of some of the differences in these business entity forms is provided at the end of this chapter.)

4. Where a parent desires to maintain control over assets that will be transferred to younger generations through gifts of limited partner interests.

    One of the major benefits of an FLP is the ability to retain control over assets or business interests without having to own a majority of the interests of the FLP. This permits parents to transfer their assets to an FLP and then give or sell a majority interest (50 percent or more) to the children while retaining control over the assets. Such control can be achieved by retaining as little as a 1 percent general partner interest in the FLP. Although the children may hold a majority interest in the FLP, the effective control over the assets remains in the hands of the general partner.

    Use of an FLP can also permit the parents to implement a succession plan for the ownership, management, and control of assets so that undesired beneficiaries do not gain access to the assets.

5. Where it is desirable to protect assets from creditors of the partners.

    If a senior family member is in a high-risk profession, such as a doctor, engineer, or builder who is vulnerable to lawsuits, an FLP may be effective to shield personal assets by placing them in the hands of other family members, away from the reach of the senior partner's future creditors. In most cases, a judgment creditor will be unable to attach partnership assets to satisfy a debt of an individual partner.

However, although the asset protection features of an FLP (discussed below) may discourage a creditor from aggressively seeking satisfaction of the debt from the partnership assets, the use of an FLP as an asset protection device may also prevent the assets from being reached by the partner since a judgment creditor has the right to attach the partner's interest in the FLP or attach any assets that are distributed by the FLP to the partner. This characteristic may cause a stalemate between the partner and creditor and encourage settlement of the debt at an amount that is favorable to both parties.

Protecting assets may also present a number of ethical issues for the practitioner since certain transfers can be attacked as fraudulent conveyances. For these reasons, extreme care and consideration should accompany the use of an FLP for any such purpose.

6. When retention of ownership of assets within the family unit is desired.

By including in the FLP agreement, a right of first refusal for transfers of partnership interests, the partners can virtually guarantee that outside persons will not acquire ownership interests in the FLP. Also, by limiting the rights of a transferee partner to that of an "assignee" (who lacks voting rights) the ability of a partner to sell his interest is likely to be severely impaired, thereby achieving the intended goal of maintaining immediate family ownership.

7. Where a parent desires to protect assets, which are to be transferred to younger generations, from being dissipated through mismanagement or divorce.

A parent who makes gifts of property to his children runs the risk that the child will cause the gift to be unwisely managed or lost to a spouse or creditor. These pitfalls can be avoided by placing the assets into an FLP instead and transferring a limited partner interest to the child. In this case, the parent may retain control over the assets until the child is mature and has achieved sufficient financial acumen to manage the property. Moreover, as discussed above, partnership assets are typically beyond the reach of an individual partner's creditors (although a creditor may receive a court order entitling the creditor to the debtor-partner's distributive share of partnership income), making the FLP an attractive vehicle if a child has creditor issues.

Similarly, because a divorce action can result in the court awarding the spouse a share of the limited partner interest, it may be worthwhile for the parent to transfer the interest to the child in trust to be held for the child's lifetime, thereby defeating the rights of the divorcing spouse.

8. Where flexibility in setting the rules for managing property is desired.

Unlike an irrevocable trust, an FLP can be amended by vote of a given percentage of partnership interests. This results in a parent being able to easily change the governing rules that apply to the partnership, if the parent maintains the necessary percentage ownership interest to amend the agreement.

9. To simplify ownership of assets.

Use of an FLP may allow for cost savings through consolidation of ownership into one entity with centralized management. Such consolidation may result in diversification of money managers and reduced investment adviser fees. By pooling family assets, the FLP may obtain advantages in terms of diversification and size of investment that cannot be achieved individually by the partners.

Further, by giving the general partner discretion to reinvest partnership profits over the long-term, the FLP can carry out an investment strategy that focuses on long-term benefits to the partners. In situations where generation-skipping trusts are used to hold FLP interests during the lifetime of a beneficiary, the death of the beneficiary will not pose a threat to the continued operation of the FLP, since the FLP provides for continuity of ownership and estate tax will not be due on the FLP interest held in a generation-skipping trust (to the extent the assets and estate tax "skip" the child).

10. To ease the distribution of assets at death among family members without having to remove the assets from the partnership.

Upon the death of a parent, assets may remain in the partnership and only partnership interests are transferred to the heirs (to the extent permitted under the Limited Partnership Agreement), thereby enabling the partnership operations to remain intact.

11. To avoid out-of-state probate costs.

    Since FLP interests are considered *personal* property, they should not be included for probate purposes in those states in which the property exists – even if it is real estate. Such interests are subject to probate only in the domiciliary state of the partner.

12. To discourage family members from fighting over FLP assets, and to provide a forum for the resolution of disputes among family members if and when such disputes arise.

    Unlike trusts, an FLP agreement may require binding arbitration of disputes among the partners for all issues relating to partnership assets. Further, the FLP agreement may be drafted so that the losing partner must pay the court fees of the prevailing party, thereby reducing the likelihood and cost of litigation among the partners.

49.3 WHAT ARE THE REQUIREMENTS?

Because state law governs the formation of partnerships, it is necessary to refer to the applicable law of the state in which the partnership is formed to determine the various procedural aspects of forming a limited partnership. In general, the following formalities will need to be met in order to create a limited partnership that will be respected for state law purposes.

1. A written agreement setting forth the rights and duties of the partners. If no written agreement exists, the terms of the partnership may be difficult to prove if claimed to be different than under applicable state law.

2. Filing a certificate of limited partnership and obtaining all necessary business licenses and registrations.

3. Obtaining a separate tax identification number for the partnership.

4. Transferring title of all contributed assets into the name of the partnership and opening new accounts in the name of the partnership.

5. Amending contracts to show the partnership as the real party in interest (e.g., adding the partnership as an additional insured on liability insurance policies).

6. Avoiding commingling of partnership assets with those assets of the individual partners or using partnership assets for personal business of the partners.

7. Filing annual state and federal income tax returns and allocating partnership income to the partners.

8. Paying annual state franchise taxes, if applicable, and making any other filings required under state law.

After the FLP is created, there are certain requirements which must be satisfied for the FLP to be valid under state law, such as the requirement that interests in the FLP be held by family members only. There are additional requirements that must be satisfied for a partner of an FLP to be recognized as a partner for income-tax purposes. These factors are discussed under "Income Tax Aspects" below.

49.4 PROVIDING MANAGEMENT AND CONTROL

Control over assets contributed to an FLP is achieved by retaining ownership of the general partner interest (or the managing partner interest in cases where the FLP has multiple general partners). In most instances, the most important decision to be made in creating an FLP is deciding whom to name as the general partners since they will exercise exclusive control over the partnership business operations and determine if, when, and how much of, the partnership income is to be distributed to the partners. The general partners must also be aware that as general partners, they will have unlimited personal liability for the debts of the FLP.

For estate planning purposes, it may be advisable for the partners to implement a succession plan for management. This may be achieved by designating a non-managing general partner who will succeed in the duties of management and control upon vacancy of the general partner's interest.

For most FLPs, possible general partners include one or both parents, either individually or as trustee of a family living trust, an S corporation or limited liability company controlled by one or more persons, or mature and financially experienced and responsible children or grandchildren (individually or using trusts for their benefit). It is not recommended that children be given management powers over their parents' assets unless the parents expressly desire to relinquish control and the child has sufficient experience and maturity in managing property.

Even though much of the value of the FLP may be given away by transferring limited partner interests to the children, the general partners maintain control of the management and investment of the assets in the FLP even though they retain only a small percentage ownership interest. For this reason, many practitioners recommend use of an FLP for parents who desire to maintain control of their assets while having transferred away most of the assets' economic benefits.

The general partner should have the necessary willingness, knowledge, and experience to do the following:

1. Manage and invest partnership assets.

2. Make decisions as to distributions of partnership income and/or assets.

3. File income tax returns on behalf of the partnership and understand the income tax law.

4. Furnish annual partnership income tax information (Schedule K-1) to the partners.

5. Make necessary filings with the state's Secretary of State.

6. Give or withhold consent to transfers of partnership interests and amendment of the FLP agreement.

49.5 ENSURING FAMILY OWNERSHIP

One requirement of an FLP is that distributions of interests must only be made to family members (i.e., the spouse, lineal descendants, ancestors, and trusts created for these individuals). Continuous family ownership of the FLP is guaranteed by restricting each partner's ability to sell or otherwise transfer his interest to non-family members. Because most FLPs are used by parents to transfer partnership interests to their children at reduced transfer tax values, the existence of rights of first refusal, buy-sell provisions, or other restrictions on transfer are of paramount concern and require considerable attention. However, much care must be exercised in drafting the partnership agreement in order to avoid the transfer tax pitfalls of Chapter 14 of the Internal Revenue Code (see Chapter 70).

In almost all instances, the FLP agreement should prohibit the partners from selling or transferring their interests in a manner that is disruptive to the continuation of the family asset arrangement plan or disruptive to family harmony. To achieve this result, the FLP agreement typically will provide the partners and/or the partnership a right of first refusal to deal with a circumstance where another partner wishes to sell, or otherwise transfer, his interest to a non-family member. In such cases, the non-selling partners will usually have the right to purchase the interest of the selling partner for cash or with an unsecured long-term promissory note which bears an interest rate favorable to the buyer (but note that the restriction should not constitute "financial detriment" to any donee partner and such restriction should also satisfy the requirements of Code sections 2703 and 2704). Only if the non-selling partners or the partnership itself fails to exercise purchase rights may the interest then be sold to the non-family member.

If the family members do not wish for the new partner to possess any voting rights, then the agreement should permit them to treat the new partner as a mere assignee, who is entitled to receive only income distributions and a proportionate share of partnership income, expenses, deductions and credits. This mechanism provides the family members with protection from the influence of undesired active partners, enhances continued family ownership, and does not disrupt good asset management.

49.6 REDUCING TRANSFER TAXES

For individuals having substantial wealth, another important benefit of implementing an FLP is the reduction of values for transfer tax purposes. As a general rule, the value of an FLP interest is worth less than direct ownership of the same percentage interest in the underlying assets of the FLP. Put another way, the sum of each of the FLP interests combined does not equal the sum of the assets themselves. This is because ownership of a limited partner interest in an FLP does not convey any rights of management or control over the underlying assets and the FLP agreement prohibits the partners from freely transferring their interests to non-family members. Accordingly, transfer tax values are reduced by the application of discounts (determined by appraisal) to reflect these restrictions.

Example: Mr. Walker transfers commercial real estate with a current fair market value of $5 million to an FLP. He retains a 2 percent interest in the FLP as its sole general partner and gifts the remaining 98 percent of the FLP as limited partnership interests in equal shares to his two adult children (49 percent each). Basic math would indicate that the value of the gift Mr. Walker has made to each child is $2,450,000 (49 percent of $5 million). But this does not reflect the *true* fair market value of the interests – i.e., the price a willing buyer would pay a willing seller for the assets. The children, as limited partners, have no control over the management of the property. Moreover, there is no ready market for fractional limited partnership interests such as these. Accordingly, Mr. Walker takes lack of control and lack of marketability discounts totaling 30 percent on the gifts. After applying a 30 percent discount, the total gift Mr. Walker has made to each child is only $1,715,000 ($3,430,000 total), for a total gift tax savings of $1,470,000. What's more, any appreciation on the property will be removed from Mr. Walker's estate.

Because FLPs may be used to transfer partnership interests to lower generation family members, reduced transfer tax values allow for (1) shifting a greater amount of partnership interests by percentage from parents to subsequent generations, and (2) lower overall estate tax liability on those interests retained by a deceased partner. For the majority of FLPs, combined discounts in the range of 25 percent to 35 percent are typically achieved – and in some cases valuation discounts are even higher. Lower discounts in the range of 5 percent to 10 percent should generally be expected when the underlying assets are themselves readily marketable. Even with a modest discount, the potential gift or estate tax savings can be considerable when compared to taking no action.

In *Keller v. U.S.*,[4] the court dealt with the question of whether securities were actually transferred upon the formation of the partnership even though the actual title was not transferred until after the death of the donor. On this basis, the Court upheld the valuation discount. The government had argued that decedent's failure to complete the formalities of the transfer or fill out Schedule A prior to her death prohibited the bonds' transfer. The prevailing argument in the case was that the transferor's intent to transfer the assets was sufficient. This is an interesting case; but it is important to note that the holding was based upon Texas law and may not be generally applicable.

Despite the reduction in value of FLP interests, the real income production and growth potential of the FLP's assets remain available to the partners since control remains within the family unit.

49.7 SECURING VALUATION DISCOUNTS

A *discount for lack of control* is routinely applied in establishing estate and gift tax values of minority limited partner interests (see Chapter 70 for a detailed discussion of discounts to FLP interests). This discount reflects the inability of a limited partner to control the operations of the FLP and to invest its assets in a manner that is of the greatest benefit to such limited partner.

Because management and investment decisions (including the decision as to when to distribute partnership income) are outside the control and influence of the limited partners, the value of a limited partner's interest is reduced to reflect such lack of control. Typical discounts for lack of control (minority interest) generally range between 20 percent and 30 percent.

A *discount for lack of marketability* is also applied to the value of privately-held limited partnership interests that do not offer a readily available market for trading. Such a discount reflects the fact that a partner who contributes assets to an FLP in return for a limited partnership interest generally will have difficulty in finding a buyer (if one exists).

Because a central purpose of most family limited partnerships is to maintain ownership of assets for the benefit of members of one or more selected families, FLP documents generally contain specific provisions to assure that ownership interests will remain within the family group. Each of these provisions, by design, reduces the marketability and therefore the value of an interest to a hypothetical buyer.

Factors that typically influence the level of the discount for lack of marketability include the nature of the FLP's asset mix (e.g., real property, securities, equipment, etc.), the availability and accuracy of information relating to the FLP and its owners, the existence of transfer restrictions against ownership interests, the willingness of the partners to accept new partners, whether income is currently distributed to the partners, and the expected date on which capital contributions will be returned to the partners.

The inclusion of rights of first refusal and other transfer restrictions in the FLP agreement reduce the marketability of an FLP interest for transfer tax valuation purposes (provided that the requirements of Code section 2703 are satisfied), further reducing values for estate tax and gift tax purposes. Based upon the number and severity of the transfer restrictions and the factors stated above, lack of marketability discounts may reach as high as 30 percent or more.

A discount for built-in capital gains tax may also apply to the value of privately-held limited partnership interests if the tax basis of the assets owned by the partnership is demonstrably lower than the current fair market value of such assets, thereby signifying future potential capital gains tax liability. To the extent that the net asset value of the partnership is subject to inherent gains tax liability, consideration should be allowed for valuation purposes.[5]

Additionally, in determining the value of an interest in an FLP, consideration should always be given as to whether the interest can be liquidated through the enforcement of withdrawal rights. If the partnership agreement or state law does not confer upon the limited partner any right to withdraw capital, then the limited partner's investment may remain in the partnership until expiration of the partnership term (often thirty-five to fifty years in length) or longer if the partners elect to amend the limited partnership agreement and continue the term of the partnership. In such case, the limited partner's interest is said to be "locked-in" to maintaining his investment in the partnership and a *lock-in discount* is appropriate.

In determining whether a lock-in discount is applicable, Code section 2704(b) must be reviewed. This section is discussed in greater detail in Chapters 49 and 70.

Planning Note: The ability to shift wealth to younger generations at a substantial discount is one of the most attractive features of an FLP. However, in recent years, there has been heightened scrutiny over the availability of valuation discounts due perceived and potential abuses. Most recently, the Treasury Department introduced proposed regulations under Code section 2704 which, had they been enacted, would have significantly hindered the ability to transfer wealth at a substantial discount using an FLP. In the fall of 2017, the Treasury Department withdrew the proposed regulatory changes to section 2704 under the Trump Administration. While this was immediate victory for individuals looking to use an FLP as a vehicle to manage and transfer family wealth, taxpayers should be aware that FLP discounting rules may come under future scrutiny under a new administration. The IRS has also been known to challenge FLPs which appear to have been created solely for tax-avoidance. To mitigate the risk of an IRS challenge, taxpayers should work with their advisors to ensure any discounts are not excessive and that other formalities of a partnership are carried-out.

49.8 PROTECTING ASSETS

Family limited partnerships provide a limited degree of asset protection to the partners since underlying assets of the FLP generally cannot be attached to satisfy personal debts of the limited partners. Under the Uniform Limited Partnership Act, the remedy of a personal creditor is to obtain a "charging order" from a court against the interest of the limited partner. The charging order entitles the creditor to receive the distributions that would normally be paid to the limited partner until the debt is fully paid.

A charging order does not give the creditor any voting rights in FLP matters and the creditor cannot be assured that the general partner will elect to pay out the FLP income to the partners (the creditor essentially acts as an "assignee" to the debtor-partner's FLP interest). Furthermore, the IRS in Revenue Ruling 77-137 has indicated that even though the general partner does not pay out any income to the creditor and other partners, the responsibility for paying the income tax attributable to the attached limited partner's interest will fall upon the creditor (essentially as "phantom income").[6] This may, or may not, prove true in a given case. However, the mere threat of tax liability without income to pay that liability is strong incentive for creditors to enter into more favorable settlement with debtor-partners.

Notwithstanding the negative aspects of a charging order, a debtor partner is not necessarily guaranteed access to FLP assets if the judgment creditor is insistent upon collecting its debt. The judgment creditor may quietly wait for the partnership to distribute assets to the debtor partner in hope of attaching the assets immediately after distribution. For this reason, the use of an FLP by itself as an asset protection device is not a guaranteed means of avoiding creditor liability. If creditor protection is a primary motivating force, tools and techniques other than FLPs should be considered.

Additionally, in view of the surge in popularity of the use of FLPs and the emphasis placed on their asset protection features, it is likely that future courts may be reluctant to continue such asset protection for partnerships in which substantially all of the interests are owned by one person or family, or the assets of the partnership are mainly liquid in nature (e.g., marketable securities, cash, etc.).

49.9 INCOME TAX ASPECTS

Code section 704(e) was enacted to prevent taxpayers from using family partnerships as a means of artificially splitting family income to circumvent the progressive tax rate structure of the federal income tax. In order for a donee-partner of an FLP to be recognized as a partner for income tax purposes, the following three factors must be satisfied:

(a) Income-producing assets must be owned by the FLP. The FLP's business must require substantial inventories or substantial investment in plant, machinery, or other equipment, as contrasted with a personal service corporation in which income is generated primarily by the personal services of one or more individuals.[7]

(b) A donee or purchaser of a capital interest in a partnership is not recognized as a partner unless such interest is acquired in a bona fide transaction (either a bona fide gift or sale), not a mere sham for tax avoidance or evasion purposes. The donee or purchaser must be the "real owner" of such interest.[8]

(c) The donee's distributive share must be included in his gross income, except to the extent that such distributive share is determined without allowance of reasonable compensation to a donor partner for services rendered to the partnership and except to the extent that the portion of such distributive share attributable to donated capital is proportionately greater than the share of the donor attributable to the donor's capital.[9]

The validity of an FLP for income tax purposes is dependent upon the donee partner's "owning" a capital interest. The Code does not specifically define what constitutes "ownership" of a capital interest. However, the regulations state that a transferee of a partnership interest must be the "real owner" of the capital interest and have dominion and control over that interest.

As provided in the IRS regulations, there are four types of retained controls (i.e., powers retained by a donor of an FLP) that are of particular importance in showing that a donee lacks true ownership of his interest. If the donee is not the real owner of his capital interest, then the income attributable to the capital interest will be taxable to the donor.

These controls include:

(a) The donor's retaining control of the distribution of income or restricting the amount of such distributions.

(b) The donor's limiting the right of a donee partner to dispose of his interest without financial detriment.

(c) The donor's retaining control of assets that are essential to the operation of the partnership's business.

(d) The donor's retaining management powers which are inconsistent with normal partnership relations.[10]

The cases that have discussed whether a donee is a real owner stress the importance of receiving current distributions of income.[11]

Because partnership agreements frequently limit the ability of a partner to transfer or liquidate his interest, it is important that the partner be able to dispose of the interest "without financial detriment." This test is aimed at determining whether the partner has control over the current benefits of the interest. The term "financial detriment" is interpreted as requiring that the partner be able to realize the fair market value of the interest. Thus, the regulations indicate that a partnership agreement that requires a partner to first offer his interest to the partnership (or partners) at the same price as that of any bona fide offer from an outside party will not be considered as imposing a financial detriment upon the interest of a donee partner.

The regulations under section 704(e) allow a donor to retain management or voting control over a family partnership if the retention is of a manner that is common in ordinary business relationships.[12] However, the donor's retention of control is directly related to the donee's ability to dispose of the interest without financial detriment. Generally, the donee will not be deemed to possess this right unless he is both independent of the donor and has sufficient maturity and understanding of his rights to exercise his right to withdraw his capital interest from the partnership. Thus, FLP interests that are transferred to minors should be held either by a guardian or in trust.

In addition to these direct controls, an examination of several indirect controls may determine if a donee partner is a real owner of his capital interest. As provided in the regulations, the following factors are to be examined:

(a) Whether the donee participates in the management of the business.

(b) Whether there have been income distributions to the donee partner.

(c) Whether the donee partner is held out to the public as a partner.

(d) Whether the partnership has complied with local laws regarding use of fictitious names and other business registration statutes.

(e) Control of business bank accounts.

(f) Whether the donee's rights in distributions of partnership property and profits have been recognized.

(g) Whether the donee's interest is recognized in insurance policies, leases, and other business contracts, and in litigation affecting business.

(h) The existence of written agreements, records, memoranda, which establish the partnership and partners' rights.

(i) Whether the partnership has filed income tax returns.[13]

Assuming that a FLP satisfies the requirements of section 704(e), a number of valuable income tax benefits may be provided to the partners. Among these benefits are the following:

1. Pass through of items of income, expense, credit, and deduction to the partners.

2. Achieving a "step-up" in income tax basis in FLP assets for interests received from a deceased partner (or upon purchase by a new partner) if an election is made by the general partner under Code section 754.

3. Withdrawal of assets without recognition of taxable gain (unlike corporate ownership).

4. Income shifting to family members.

5. No income tax gain on contribution of assets to the FLP or upon dissolution of the FLP in most cases.

These income tax benefits make FLPs extremely attractive in planning for income tax responsibilities of the partners. If properly structured, the FLP will not increase income taxes and may even reduce income taxes in some cases.

Other tax implications exist in operating an FLP. In general, the following rules will apply:

1. A reasonable allocation of partnership income must be made to any donor partner (which includes a parent who has sold a partnership interest to a family member) to recognize the value of his services to the FLP in order for the family partnership rules of section 704(e) to be satisfied.

Where interests of family members are acquired by gift and/or intra-family sale, a mandatory allocation of the FLP's profits in proportion to capital contributed, after due allowance has been made for the donor's services, must be made. For example, assume father and son are each 50 percent partners in an FLP that has a net income of $100,000. Father is paid $20,000 as reasonable compensation for his services. The remaining $80,000 would be taxed $40,000 each to father and son. The $40,000 of net income allocated and taxed to the father would be in addition to his reporting $20,000 of compensation for services he provided to the FLP.

If a contributing partner acquires capital from an independent source and not by an intra-family gift or purchase, the mandatory allocations described above will not apply and profit and loss may be allocated in a different manner.

2. Unless an election is made by the FLP to be taxed as a corporation, the partnership itself does not pay federal income taxes since it is a pass-through entity.

However, a federal income tax return (Form 1065) must be filed showing each partner's allocable share of income, expenses, deductions, and credits. Each partner must report and pay income taxes with respect to allocable share of partnership income.

3. Generally, no gain or loss is realized when property is contributed to the FLP.

However, the potential application of Code section 721(b) should be considered to ensure that the FLP is not classified as an "investment company" which triggers the recognition of gain with respect to the property contributed to the partnership if the formation causes diversification of concentrated positions. The underlying rationale is to prevent taxpayers from diversifying their investments without the recognition of gain implementing the same rules as are applicable under Code section 351 (relating to the formation of a corporation). Under these rules, an investment company exists if 80 percent or more of the entity's capital is comprised of marketable securities held for investment purposes and diversification of assets among the partners has occurred.[14] If applicable, a limited partner will be forced to recognize built-in gain on appreciated marketable securities he or she contributes. In making contributions to an FLP, the basis of the FLP in the contributed assets is the same basis the property had in the hands of the contributing partners.

Recognition of gain can occur upon receipt of distributions to the extent that the money received exceeds the limited partner's basis in his partnership interest. Marketable securities are deemed to be money unless they were contributed by the limited partner who receives the distribution. Also excluded from being considered the same as "money" are securities which were not a marketable security at the time they were acquired and distributions from an investment partnership (any partnership not engaged in a trade or business, 90 percent of whose assets consist of marketable securities).

Income recognition upon the contribution of property to the partnership may occur if the property contributed is subject to debt, and the contribution relieves the contributor of liability with respect to recognition debt. A partner who contributes property with built-in gain can trigger recognition to him or her if: the partnership sells the property for a gain; the partnership distributes the property to a partner other than the contributing partner within seven years of contribution (the gain is allocated to the contributing partner); or the property is distributed to the contributing partner within seven years which will cause recognizable gain "to the lesser of the fair market value of the distributed property in excess of the contributing partner's tax cost basis in the partnership interest or the pre-contribution gain."[15]

4. Gifts of FLP interests are subject to gift tax and will likely raise questions concerning the value of the transferred interest.

The regulations state that the same principles that apply in valuing stock in corporations apply to valuing interests in an FLP. The fair market value at the date of gift will be the value for gift tax purposes.[16]

In valuing interests in a family limited partnership, regulations set forth requirements for providing "adequate disclosure" to the IRS, in order to commence running of the gift tax statute of limitations.[17] The following is a synopsis of these requirements:

a. *Non-gift transactions*

- same information as required for adequate disclosure of a gift

- explanation describing why the transfer was not subject to the gift tax

b. *Gift transactions*

- description of the transferred property and any consideration received

- identity of and relationship between the transferor and transferee
- if property transferred in trust, the trust's tax identification number and a brief description of the terms of the trust or a copy of the trust
- detailed description of the method used to determine the FMV of the property transferred
- any restrictions on the property or discounts taken

c. *Securities*

- recitation of exchange
- CUSIP number
- mean between the highest and lowest quoted selling price on the valuation date

d. *Transfer of an interest in an entity* (e.g., FLP or LLC)

- description of any discount claimed in valuing the interest or any assets of the entity
- if the value of the entity is determined based on the net value of the assets
- a statement regarding the FMV of 100 percent of the entity without regard to any discounts in valuing the entity or assets owned by the entity
- the pro rata portion of the entity subject to transfer
- a description of how the fair market value of the transferred interest is determined
- if 100 percent of the value of the entity is not disclosed, the taxpayer bears the burden of demonstrating that the FMV of the entity is properly determined by a method other than a method based on the net value of the assets held by the entity

- if the entity owns an interest in another non-actively traded entity, the same information must be provided for that entity if the information is relevant and material in determining the value of the interest

e. *Submission of appraisals*

- prepared by an appraiser who is an individual who holds himself out as an appraiser
- the appraiser must be qualified to make appraisals of the type of property being valued
- the appraiser must not be the donor, the donee, or a member of the family or any person employed by the donor, the donee, or a member of the family

f. *Appraisal contains*

- date of the transfer
- date on which property appraised
- purpose of appraisal
- description of the property
- description of appraisal process employed
- description of assumptions, hypothetical conditions, and any limiting conditions and restrictions
- information considered in determining the appraised value
- appraisal procedures followed and reasoning that supports analyses, opinions, and conclusions
- valuation method utilized
- specific basis for the valuation

5. Increased scrutiny for estate, gift, and generation-skipping transfer tax purposes of transaction involving FLP and valuation discounts.

49.10 ESTATE TAX CONSIDERATIONS

One of the primary reasons for using an FLP is to avoid or limit the impact of transfer taxes. As discussed throughout this chapter, a valid transfer of FLP interests (either via gift or sale) removes the value of those interests, plus any future appreciation, from the donor-partner's estate, making an FLP a popular estate-freeze tool. When the transfer is done via gift, the federal annual gift tax exclusion ($17,000 per donee in 2023) can be utilized, and as discussed, valuation discounts for gift tax purposes may be available, allowing the donor-partner to transfer significant assets from the estate often at a low gift tax cost. Under 2036(a), the value of an asset transferred by an individual will be brought back into his or her taxable estate if the individual retained the possession or enjoyment of, or the right to income from, the transferred asset. The only exception is if the asset was a bona fide sale (i.e., transferred for full and adequate consideration). In recent years, the IRS has challenged use of FLPs as a mechanism to transfer wealth out of the estate, in certain cases bringing the value of the FLP interest into the taxable estate as a retained interest under Code section 2036(a).

Whether 2036(a) applies is highly fact-specific and requires evaluating a number of factors, such as whether there is a valid nontax, business-related purpose for the FLP. See the Frequently Asked Questions section below for more information on specific cases where the IRS has challenged the validity of an FLP.

49.11 ISSUES IN COMMUNITY PROPERTY STATES

In Arizona, California, Nevada, New Mexico, and Washington, the income from separate property of one spouse is separate property income. In Texas, Louisiana, Idaho, and Wisconsin, the income from the separate property of one spouse is community property income, although Louisiana permits the separate property owning spouse to unilaterally reserve the income from separate property as separate property. It is in the former group of states where the FLP may require extra vigilance if it is owned prior to marriage, is given or inherited, or is separate property of a spouse for whatever reason. In these instances, it is necessary to make a distinction between the earnings of the manager (which is probably community property) and the income received from ownership of the partnership interest (which is separate property).

Using the separate property income from the FLP to purchase items that are taken in the names of both spouses creates a taxable gift (with the exception of real property taken as joint tenants). Thus, if the partner-spouse receives $80,000 in income from an FLP that was owned prior to marriage, over and above his wages from the FLP, and if he uses the $80,000 to buy stock in both his and his spouse's names, he will have made a gift of $40,000 taxable to the spouse. This does not create a federal gift tax problem because of the unlimited marital deduction that applies to both separate property and community property (see Chapter 27). Depending upon state gift tax law, however, it may still create a gift tax problem.

The FLP should consider making an election under Code section 754 to obtain a basis adjustment under section 743 due to the death of either spouse. The election will adjust the income tax basis of the community property interest of both spouses in the FLP.

Another frequently encountered problem in an FLP in community property states is the failure to designate in the agreement whether the FLP interest is separate property or community property. This failure is a great source of comfort and fees to litigation attorneys in divorce proceedings. Particularly in view of the high rate of divorce, it is essential that the FLP agreement explicitly state whether the FLP interest is community property or not.

If an interest is held in a partnership, and income from the partnership is attributable to the efforts of either spouse, the partnership income is community property. If it is merely a passive investment in a separate property partnership, the partnership income will be characterized depending on the state involved. In some states, dividends, interest and rents from separate property are separate property. These states include Washington, Nevada, California, Arizona and New Mexico. Other states characterize interest, dividends and rents from separate property as community property. These states include Louisiana, Wisconsin and Texas (although Louisiana law permits a spouse who owns separate property to unilaterally reserve the income from separate property as separate).[18]

49.12 DETRIMENTS

As exists with the formation of any entity (or for that matter the use of any tool or technique), the use of an FLP has some costs and downsides. For example, the following issues will generally be encountered:

1. The FLP will be required to pay applicable minimum franchise tax fees in most states in which it does business.

2. The FLP must file annual income tax returns and keep separate accounting records.

3. In states with restrictions on real property tax increases, great care should be taken in contributing real property to the FLP and in transferring partnership interests so that the property tax assessment on the property is not adversely changed.

4. There will be a cost incurred on the formation of the FLP and upon transferring title of assets into the FLP.

For the most part, the detriments that accompany the use of an FLP are heavily outweighed by its benefits and the decision to implement an FLP should not be materially affected by these issues.

49.13 COMPARING FLPS WITH OTHER BUSINESS ENTITIES

The differences between FLPs and other business entities can be significant in determining which entity would best suit a particular business need. Figure 46.1 provides a brief review of the differences between an FLP, C corporation, S corporation, and a limited liability company taxed as a partnership. More detailed explanations concerning these different types of business entities are discussed elsewhere in this book. (See Chapter 50 on Incorporation Planning With C Corporations, Chapter 51 on Limited Liability Companies, and Chapter 53 on S Corporations.)

Example 1. Mark Ciarelli, a successful businessman, is married and has two children, Irv and Eric. He presently is the sole owner of an unincorporated manufacturing business (Pierz Enterprises) in which both personal services and capital are material income producing factors. The net profits from the business for last year were approximately $200,000, before Mark's salary. Mark files a joint return with his wife, Judy. His wife and children do not have an income of their own. Mark pays himself a salary of $1,000 per week. The net profit of the business after salary was actually $148,000. Because Mark is unincorporated, both the $52,000 salary and the $148,000 net profit are taxable to him.

Figure 49.1

	S Corp.	C Corp.	FLP	LLC
Limited Liability	All Owners	All Owners	Limited Partners	All Owners
Income Tax Levels	Single	Double	Single	Single
Capital Ownership Restrictions	Yes	No	No	No
Limits on Classes of Capital	Yes	No	No	No
Basis Adjustments	Outside Only	Outside Only	Outside and Inside	Outside and Inside
All Members Vote	Yes	Yes	No	Yes
Federal Tax Election Required	Yes	No	No	No
Distributions on Liquidation Taxable	Yes	Yes	No	No

Mark can minimize his income tax burden by "splitting" the income with his children through an FLP. He could transfer a 30 percent interest in the business assets directly to Irv and Eric, with each child receiving a 15 percent interest. If Irv and Eric were minors, these interests could be placed in trust for their benefit. A gift tax return would be filed and gift tax paid to the extent that Mark's (and Judy's) gift tax unified credit has been used up.

Then, an FLP agreement could be drafted and Irv and Eric could transfer their 15 percent interests to the FLP. Mark could continue to run the business and be paid a salary of $52,000 per year. However, the balance of the FLP income would be divided 70 percent to Mark, 15 percent to Irv, and 15 percent to Eric.

Pursuant to this plan, Mark would receive a distribution of $103,600 in addition to his salary and Irv and Eric would each receive and be taxed on $22,200 of annual income. The net result would be the shifting of $44,400 of income each year to his children. This income will be taxed at the children's lower income tax brackets (if they are over the age of seventeen or in some cases over twenty-three), thus generating an immediate income tax saving. Further, if the business continues to grow, the 30 percent of any future appreciation would be attributable to the interests of Irv and Eric and not to Mark, thereby reducing Mark's estate.

Example 2. John and Robin Scott are each age seventy. They have four children and six grandchildren and their estate consists of the following assets held in their family living trust:

Asset	Value
Marketable Securities	$4,500,000
Apartment Complex	$3,000,000
Other Real Estate	$4,500,000
Residence	$1,500,000
Total	$13,500,000

During the year, the Scotts meet with their attorney and agree to implement an FLP to maintain ownership of their property in the family. The securities, apartment, and other real estate (but not the residence) with a total value of $12,000,000 are contributed to an FLP.

In return for their capital contributions, Mr. and Mrs. Scott each receive a 1 percent general partner interest, and the Scott Family Trust (a revocable trust with respect to which the Scotts are co-grantors) receives a 98 percent limited partner interest. The FLP agreement gives the general partners the discretion to accumulate partnership income for future business needs and restricts the partners' ability to transfer their interests to persons outside the Scott family.

At the end of the year, from the Scott Family Trust, the Scotts each gift a 6.25 percent limited partner interest to each of their four children, thereby transferring away a total of 50 percent of the partnership and $6,000,000 of the underlying asset value. An appraiser hired by the Scotts to value the gifts of limited partner interests applies a combined 40 percent discount for lack of control, lack of marketability, and lock-in status.

After applying this discount to the proportionate value of FLP assets, Mr. and Mrs. Scott each gifted limited partner interests worth $576,000 to each child, or a total gift by each spouse of $960,000. Because the gift tax unified credit for each spouse was totally available, no cash payment of gift tax was required. At the end of the year, the ownership interests of the Scott FLP is as follows:

	General Partner	Limited Partner
John Scott	1.00%	0.00%
Robin Scott	1.00%	0.00%
Scott Family Trust	0.00%	48.00%
Child No. 1	0.00%	12.50%
Child No. 2	0.00%	12.50%
Child No. 3	0.00%	12.50%
Child No. 4	0.00%	12.50%
Totals	2.00%	98.00%

In the next year and each year thereafter, the Scotts make annual gifts from the Scott Family Trust (a revocable trust) of limited partner interests worth $17,000 to each of the four children and six grandchildren. The same 40 percent discount to value is applied to the gifts. During the next ten years, the assets in Scott FLP grow at a 5 percent annual rate.

At the end of the tenth year, John is struck with a sudden illness and dies. At that time, the underlying value of the FLP assets is $18,615,939 and ownership is as follows:

	General Partner	Limited Partner
John Scott	1.00%	0.00%
Robin Scott	1.00%	0.00%
Scott Family Trust	0.00%	18.40%
Child No. 1	0.00%	15.46%
Child No. 2	0.00%	15.46%
Child No. 3	0.00%	15.46%
Child No. 4	0.00%	15.46%
Grandchild No. 1	0.00%	2.96%
Grandchild No. 2	0.00%	2.96%
Grandchild No. 3	0.00%	2.96%
Grandchild No. 4	0.00%	2.96%
Grandchild No. 5	0.00%	2.96%
Grandchild No. 6	0.00%	2.96%
Totals	2.00%	98.00%

In determining the value of the FLP interests includable in John's estate, a 25 percent discount was applied to the general partner interest and a 40 percent discount was applied to the limited partner interest (held by the Scott Family Trust) on his estate tax return. As shown on the return, the estate tax value of Mr. Scott's interest in the FLP after adding back his $3,000,000 of gifts he made in prior years is as follows:

	Value
General Partner (1.00%)	$139,620
Limited Partner (9.20%)	$1,027,599
Total	$1,167,219
Prior Taxable Gifts	$3,000,000
Total Gifts and Interests	$4,167,219

Had the Scotts not formed an FLP and no discounts to value had been applied, the date of death fair market value of John's one-half interest in the apartments, real estate, and marketable securities would have been $9,307,971. However, the implementation of a gift program of partnership interests in an FLP, his taxable estate was reduced by $5,140,752, saving a significant amount of estate tax.

49.14 FLP SUCCESS CHECKLIST

In order to reap the benefits of an FLP, including income and estate tax benefits, certain formalities and steps must be carried out. Key questions to ask at the onset of the planning process as well as to reevaluate periodically include:

1. Were the papers necessary to set up an FLP under the appropriate state law filed in a timely manner?

2. Has the planning team carefully documented the significant non-tax benefits to the client to justify the creation and maintenance of an FLP? (i.e., Are there demonstrable bona fide business/investment purposes, beyond income or estate tax savings, in both the formation and operation, and is there real economic substance to the entity?)

3. Has the appraisal been obtained from a full time accredited, independent, and experienced (preferably court-tested) valuation professional who created a studiously crafted individual report (rather than a "fill in the blanks" quickie) based on this specific FLP's facts? (And were realistic and justifiable assumptions used in developing the valuation discounts, and did the expert document the reasons for the types and amounts of discounts?)

4. Has the client avoided co-mingling of funds? Has the client not treated the money and other assets in the FLP as his or her own money?

5. Has it been verified that there has in fact been a significant change in the administration and management of the transferred assets after the creation and funding of the FLP? Can it be proved that there was much more than merely a name change and a different wrapper around the assets?

6. Has the transfer of assets to the FLP account in a timely and business-like manner been supervised? Was the timing right? Has it been verified that the capital contribution was first credited to the senior member's (parent's) capital account and then, a discrete time later, followed by a gift of the partnership interest to the children?

7. Did the client keep passive or personal assets that are not appropriate to a business or investment enterprise out of the FLP?

8. Was the FLP set up while the client was young/healthy/competent (or was the entity formed by a very old and very ill person, on or practically on his or her deathbed, or was the client incompetent at the time the FLP was set up?)

9. Did the client retain sufficient assets to maintain his or her standard of living without the need to rely on FLP assets (or did the client place all or essentially all of his or her assets into the FLP, leaving no visible and adequate means of support other than the FLP's assets and income)?

10. Were parties advised in writing that they could have no expectation or understanding that, directly or indirectly, status prior to creation of the FLP would remain (i.e., "It's still Pop's money" or "All of this will continue to be available to pay Mom's bills and meet her financial needs and expenses.") Did Dad always get what he asked for or what he wanted or needed from the FLP? Did Mom expect that her children would provide support for her through the FLP? Were Mom and Pop's taxes (income or estate) and related expenses (or funeral bills and death taxes) paid by the FLP?

11. Were only business or investment assets placed into the FLP and personal assets, such as the family home (particularly the client's personal residence), kept out of the FLP? Was the client made aware that the client had to either vacate a residence that he/she placed into FLP or actually pay the entity (not accrue) a fair and arm's length rent? Has the client actually paid rent in a timely manner? Has documentation been retained?

12. Does this FLP really represent more than a mere change in title and more than a recycling of value? What has been done to prove it?

13. Did the FLP initially, and does it continue to, meet the appropriate state's definition of an FLP?

14. Are general partners really and actively involved in business?

15. Has investment strategy actually changed after securities were contributed?

16. Did the client give up the right to be, to replace, or to remove the general partner?

17. Did the client (and his or her spouse) give up the right (directly or indirectly) unilaterally to decide when distributions from the FLP would be made, how much would be distributed, and to whom distributions would go?

18. Does the FLP conduct formal meetings and observe business formalities?

19. Are there meaningful negotiations and bargaining between the general partners?

20. Do adult children actively represent their own interests, or did they do just what Mom and Pop tell them to do?

49.15 VALUATION QUALITY CONTROL CHECKLIST

1. Have an appropriately large number of guideline comparable companies been used in the comparison?

2. Are these comparable companies really comparable? Are they similar in fundamental ways? (Have core fundamentals been stated in the report?)

3. Have the companies used been sufficiently identified?

4. Has the valuation report justified and documented why they should be considered comparable?

5. Have cogent, realistic, defensible, and objective reasons been provided for the size of the discounts taken?

6. Has the valuation date been checked and rechecked?

7. Have full-time professional appraisers been used who have appropriate credentials, considerable experience with the type of property/entity being appraised, and court-experience?

8. Has it been verified that appraisers had full access to legal, financial, and tax documents and to information from the key people?

9. Has it been anticipated what the appraiser as a witness will have to testify to in court?

10. Has each and every assumption and position been backed up and proved or justified, in writing?

11. Has the appraiser shown, in writing, why numbers or assumptions or comparables are not arbitrary?

12. Have the arguments/assumptions/positions the other side should, and is likely to, make been examined?

49.16 FREQUENTLY ASKED QUESTIONS

Question – Can a minor hold a partnership interest directly?

Answer – Yes. A minor will be recognized as a bona fide partner if it is determined that he is competent to manage his own property and to participate in the FLP activities. This requires that the minor possess sufficient maturity and experience to assume dominion and control over the interest transferred to him. Ordinarily, however, a minor will not be deemed to possess the requisite maturity and experience. Therefore, as a practical matter, an FLP interest should not be transferred directly to a minor.

If a minor's interest is transferred to a fiduciary, such as a court-appointed guardian whose conduct is subject to judicial supervision, the minor will be recognized as a partner. Similarly, if an FLP interest is transferred in trust for the benefit of a minor to an independent trustee, this will also permit the minor to own an interest in the FLP.

Question – Parent and children create an FLP to hold and operate a farm. The parent transfers interests in the farm partnership by gift to the children, who are limited partners. The parent is the sole general partner, lives in a farm house on the property, operates the farm, and takes most of the partnership profits as salary. Is this a valid FLP for estate tax purposes?

Answer – The IRS will likely assert that the parent has retained the enjoyment of the entire farm for his life and seek to include 100 percent of the value of the farm in the parent's taxable estate under Code section 2036(a). The IRS reached this conclusion in Letter Ruling 7824005, where the parent lived on the property and received income in the form of salary although she did not manage the property. Compare Letter Ruling 9131006 where the FLP was recognized although the parent retained a great deal of control over it.

It is recommended that a person who uses assets of the FLP for non-business purposes should enter into an independently brokered arm's length lease agreement and pay a reasonable market rent for the use of the property. The payment of rent is consistent with the FLP's business purpose of owning assets for the purpose of making a profit. A failure to timely and consistently pay reasonable rental rates could be construed as a retention of the enjoyment of FLP assets and result in federal estate tax inclusion of the FLP interest.

Question – Do gifts of interests in an FLP qualify for the gift tax annual exclusion?

Answer – The IRS has ruled that such gifts do qualify where there is no substantial restriction under the FLP agreement on the rights of the donee partners to dispose of their interests in the FLP. However, if the partnership agreement attempts to prohibit assignment, for example to bolster the position that a steep valuation discount is appropriate, the IRS may disallow use of the annual exclusion.[19] In addition, advisors and practitioners should be aware that the IRS has taken the position that gifts of membership interests in a family LLC were not gifts of present interests and therefore did not qualify for the gift tax annual exclusion. This position was upheld by the Tax Court and the Seventh Circuit in *Hackl v. Comm'r*.[20] It is very important that advisors and practitioner be familiar with *Hackl*, and that gifts of FLP interests be carefully structured to qualify as present interests that qualify for the gift tax annual exclusion.

Question – When a partner dies, is there any change in the income tax basis of partnership assets?

Answer – Generally, under Code section 1014, the income tax basis of a decedent's assets is adjusted to the value of such assets for federal estate tax purposes, typically their fair market value as of the date of death. Where the estate owns an FLP interest, this basis adjustment will apply to the basis of the FLP interest. Also, if the general partner makes a timely election under Code section 754, the basis of the assets owned by the FLP will be adjusted to reflect the date of death values according to section 743(b). If assets have appreciated in value, this adjustment will be advantageous only to the interest of the deceased partner who will receive a date of death basis in the FLP assets.

Question – What are some helpful hints for operating an FLP?

Answer – Helpful hints (see the checklists above as well) include:

1. There should be a written FLP agreement setting forth the rights of the partners.

2. Accurate business records should be kept.

3. The donor (general partner) should receive reasonable compensation for his services.

4. Distributions to the donee partners should not be used to discharge parental support obligations.

5. If minors are partners and their interests are held in trust, the trustee should be an independent trustee and not subject to the direct or indirect control of the donor.

6. Assets should be transferred into the name of the partnership.

Question – Can a family partnership be funded solely by contributing marketable securities?

Answer – To date, family partnerships holding such assets have not yet been successfully attacked by the IRS. Code section 7701(a)(2) defines a partnership as including a "syndicate, group, pool, joint venture, or other unincorporated organization, through or by means of which any business, financial operation, or venture is carried on, and which is not, within the meaning of this title, a trust or estate or a corporation." Those practitioners who advocate the creation of family partnerships solely to hold marketable securities often point to this statute as partial authority for their position. However, the attempt of the IRS in promulgating Treasury Regulation section 1.704-2 and retraction of Examples (5) and (6) (the latter of which was to be used to attack certain "paper shuffling" partnerships) suggests that the IRS may attack such entities in the future. Where the transferred assets include large amounts of publicly traded securities, the investment company rules, discussed above, which could result in gain or loss on the transfer, must be met. Obviously, gift and estate tax valuation discounts based on an FLP holding mostly or totally marketable securities will be lower than an FLP holding business interests or real estate. In fact, the Tax Court has upheld the use of a FLP as a vehicle for owning primarily marketable securities. In a couple of cases, the IRS attacked the use of a FLP as a vehicle for applying valuation discounts to the interests of the decedent, but still allowed discounts.[21]

Question – How does the IRS determine whether an entity should be taxed as a partnership?

Answer – Business entities other than corporations or trusts can elect their tax classification (under the so-called "Check-the-Box" regulations). If the entity has at least two members, it can be classified either as a partnership or an association taxable as a corporation. An election will be effective on the date specified by the entity on the IRS Form 8832 or the date filed if no date is specified on the IRS Form 8832 (the effective date specified on IRS Form 8832 cannot be more that seventy-five days prior to the date on which the election is filed and cannot be more than twelve months after the date on which the election is filed). After that period, the election is effective on the date the election is made. A copy of the election must be included with the entity's first tax return. If the entity with two or more members fails to file an election, the default classification would be a partnership.[22]

Question – How does a state determine whether an entity should be taxed as a partnership for state tax purposes?

Answer – Prior to enactment of the Check-the-Box regulations noted in the preceding answer, the IRS and states determined the tax classification of an entity based upon the number of corporate characteristics it possessed. Since enactment of the federal Check-the-Box regulations, many states have conformed their state law to the new federal classification regulations. California elected to follow federal entity classification for state income tax purposes, beginning January 1, 1998.[23]

If a state does not follow the federal Check-the-Box regulations, then the state may treat a family partnership as an association taxable as a corporation for state tax purposes if three or more of the following characteristics are determined to exist in the partnership.

1. Centralized management;
2. Free transferability of interests;
3. Continuity of life; and
4. Limited liability.

The drafter of the partnership agreement in such a state should be careful in assuring that the partnership lacks at least two of the above corporate characteristics. For FLPs, the agreement is usually drafted so that free transferability of interests and continuity of life are lacking.

Question – What are guaranteed payments and are they significant in the family limited partnership?

Answer – Guaranteed payments are payments for services or the use of capital, often made to senior partners, under Code section 707(c). If these are determined without regard to partnership income, they will be treated as payments to unrelated persons, which will generally be taxable income to the recipient and deductible by the partnership if they are reasonable, ordinary, and necessary. They provide a method of making cash flow available to senior family members on a tax deductible basis. Note, however, they may be subject to the self-employment tax.

Question – What action should be taken in structuring a family limited partnership to avoid the special valuation rules of Code section 2701?

Answer – Gifts of interests in a family limited partnership may be required to be valued under the artificial valuation rules of section 2701, which are discussed in Chapters 49 and 70. Section 2701 will apply if the senior family members retain interests that are defined as "applicable retained interests." These partnership interests resemble preferred stock in that they confer preferential distribution rights, or have a fixed liquidation value.

A so-called "vertical slice" in the entity is not covered by this section. For example, if the transferor, each family member, and each applicable family member hold substantially the same interest before and after the transfer, section 2701 does not apply. Similarly, it does not apply if the interests transferred are of the same class proportionately as the interests retained. Differences only in voting rights, or in the case of partnerships, differences in management and liability, are generally considered proportionate.

The key to avoiding section 2701 is to structure the partnership so that each partner will share proportionately in capital, income, losses, and distributions. For examples, see Letter Rulings 9427023 and 9451050.

Question – Are there any problems in transferring stock in a closely held corporation to a family limited partnership?

Answer – If voting stock in a controlled corporation as defined in Code section 2036(b) is transferred to a family partnership and the transferor votes the stock as a general partner, this would appear to be an indirect retained voting power over the stock, resulting in its inclusion in the transferor's taxable estate. It would be better to limit transfers of stock to nonvoting shares. Note that control under this statute is broadly defined, and includes any corporation in which the transferor and family members own a 20 percent interest. If the stock is S corporation stock, the S election will generally be deemed revoked.

Question – Can life insurance be transferred to a family limited partnership?

Answer – The family partnership may be an excellent vehicle for holding life insurance, functioning in a manner similar to an irrevocable insurance trust as discussed in Chapter 36. However, if the *only* function of the partnership is to hold life insurance policies, there are serious questions. Under both general legal principles and tax law, a valid partnership is supposed to engage in some business or financial activity. Although one private letter ruling implies that ownership of life insurance with investment characteristics is sufficient,[24] caution indicates (and the authors strongly suggest) the partnership should be engaged in some other business or investment activity in addition to merely holding life insurance.[25]

As the table below indicates, life insurance inside an FLP is advantageous because of the increased flexibility and control the FLP affords the reduction in estate tax exposure to the policy proceeds, and the reduction in paperwork and aggravation.

Irrevocable Trust	FLP
Irrevocable	Can be changed
Entire amount includable if client is trustee	Only portion includable
Crummey notice required	No Crummey notice needed – no "5 or 5" limits

Question – What are the potential IRS attacks against FLPs?

Answer – The IRS has been aggressive in attacking FLPs. However, many of the theories underlying these IRS attacks have been rejected by the courts. In creating and administering a FLP, it is very important to be familiar with and understand the arguments the IRS has made, and is continuing to make, against FLPs and the manner in which the courts have dealt with such arguments. Below is a list of several arguments the IRS has made against particular FLPs, with citations to some of the cases in which the arguments have been litigated. It is not an exhaustive list of IRS arguments against FLPs or cases dealing with FLPs, and it should not serve as a substitute for reading the cases cited. The "FLP Success Checklist" above should eliminate or minimize most of these IRS attacks.

1. The FLP should be disregarded because it lacks a valid business purpose and/or economic substance.[26]

2. On formation of the FLP, the founding partners made a gift to the other partners of the difference between the fair market value of the assets transferred to the partnership and the discounted value of the partnership interests.[27]

3. All of the assets of the FLP should be included in the estate of a decedent under section 2036(a)(1), because the decedent retained the possession or enjoyment of, or the right to withdraw income from, such assets.[28]

4. All of the assets of the FLP should be included in the estate of the decedent under section 2036(a)(2), because the decedent retained the right, either alone or in conjunction with any person, to designate the persons who shall possess or enjoy the property or its income (e.g., the ability, either alone or in conjunction with the other partners, to dissolve the partnership).[29]

A discussion of strategies for minimizing the potential for a successful IRS attack is beyond the scope of this chapter.[30] It should be noted, with regard to family limited partnerships that most cases which resulted in a government loss relied on the parenthetical in Code section 2036(a), i.e. "The value of the gross estate shall include the value of all property to the extent of any interest therein of which the decedent has at any time made a transfer (except in case of a bona fide sale for an adequate and full consideration in money or money's worth)."

However, the case of *Estate of Kelly*,[31] was noteworthy in that it held that section 2036 does not apply to assets held in a family limited partnership without relying entirely on the bona fide sale exception. While the Court held that the bona fide sale exception did apply, the gifts of the partnership interest were not included in decedent's estate because the court concluded that there was no implied agreement of retained enjoyment under section 2036(a)(1). The government, as it has in the past, also contended that the management fee paid to the decedent was a retention of income such that the interests are includable under section 2036. The court held that the value of the transferred partnership interests should not be includable in the estate. The decedent's primary motive was to ensure effective property management and equal distributions among the children – not reduction in tax.[32]

Likewise in *Stone v. Commissioner*,[33] the Court held that the value of woodland parcels transferred during decedent's lifetime to an FLP are excludable from her gross estate under the bona fide sale for adequate consideration exception; that the transaction was motivated by the family's interest in managing the property and that decedent received partnership interests proportional to what she transferred.

A recent case where a decedent was determined to hold a retained interest in an FLP, *Estate of Powell v. Commissioner*,[34] was notable for several reasons. In *Powell*, assets were transferred into an FLP via a power of attorney in exchange for a 99 percent limited partnership interest. The decedent's two sons took a 1 percent general partnership interest in exchange for a promissory note. The decedent's attorney-in-fact (her son) transferred all of her 99 percent FLP interest into a charitable lead annuity trust, naming the decedent's private foundation as the annuitant and a trust for the benefit of her sons as the remainder beneficiaries. Decedent died seven days after the creation of the FLP. While the facts of *Powell* were decidedly "bad facts," (i.e., deathbed planning, use of a power of attorney, no obvious non-tax reason for the FLP), what was so interesting in this case was the court applied Code section 2036(a)(2) to trigger inclusion solely by the decedent's power to liquidate the FLP and control distributions. This finding is consistent with the holdings in *Estate of Strangi* and *Estate of Turner*, but unique because in *Strangi* and *Turner*, the taxpayer was a general partner; in *Powell*, the decedent-taxpayer only held a limited partnership interest.[35] Moreover, the Tax Court in *Powell* outlined the mechanics of how to value the FLP interest for estate tax inclusion. In light of *Powell*, taxpayers should work with their advisors to ensure an FLP structure is sound (i.e., has a bona fide business purpose, valuation discounts are reasonable, etc.).

CHAPTER ENDNOTES

1. I.R.C. §704(e)(3).
2. Treas. Reg. §1.704-1(e) sets forth additional requirements in order for a family partnership to be acknowledged for income tax purposes. Although the IRS's attempt at applying the scope of these regulations to estate, gift, and generation-skipping taxes has generally failed, it is likely that the IRS will continue to look for ways to challenge family partnerships that substantially reduce transfer taxes.
3. *Church v. U.S.*, 2000-1 USTC ¶60,369 (W.D. Tex. 2000).
4. *Keller v. U.S.*, 110 AFTR 2d 2012-6061 (Sept. 25, 2012).
5. *Est. of Davis v. Comm'r.*, 110 TC 530 (1998).
6. Rev. Rul. 77-137, 1977-1 CB 178.
7. I.R.C. §704(e)(1).
8. Treas. Reg. §1.704-1(e)(1)(iii).
9. I.R.C. §704(e)(2); Treas. Reg. §1.704-1(e)(1)(ii).
10. Treas. Regs. §§1.704-1(e)(2)(ii)(a), 1.704-1(e)(2)(ii)(d).
11. See, e.g. *Payton v. U.S.*, 425 F.2d 1324 (5th Cir. 1970), cert den., 400 U.S. 957 (1970); *Kuney v. U.S.*, 524 F.2d 795 (9th Cir. 1975).
12. See Treas. Reg. §1.704-1(e)(2)(ii)(d).
13. See Treas. Reg. §1.704-1(e)(2)(vi).
14. See Treas. Reg. §1.351-1(c) for rules pertaining to what constitutes diversification of investment securities.
15. See LISI Income Tax Planning Newsletter #21 (Jan. 12, 2012), at http://www.LeimbergServices.com which provides an in depth analysis.
16. See Treas. Regs. §§25.2512-2, 25.2512-3. See also Rev. Rul. 59-60, 1959-1 CB 237.
17. Treas. Reg. §301.6501(c)-1(f).
18. IR Manual §25.18.2.1 (03-04-2011), Community Property: Income Reporting Considerations of Community Property.
19. See TAMs 199944003 (present interests) and 9751003 (future interests).
20. *Hackl v. Comm'r.*, 118 TC 279 (2002), aff'd, 335 F.3d 664 (7th Cir. 2003).
21. See, e.g. *Knight v. Comm'r.*, 115 TC 506 (2000).
22. Treas. Reg. §301.7701-3.
23. Cal. Rev. & Tax. Code §23038(b)(2).
24. Rev. Rul. 9309021.
25. See Let. Rul. 200017051.
26. See, e.g., *Est. of Strangi v. Comm'r.*, 96 AFTR 2d 2005-5230, 417 F.3d 468 (5th Cir. 2005); *Knight v. Comm'r.*, 115 TC 506 (2000); *Church v. United States*, 2000-1 USTC ¶60,369 (W.D. Tex. 2000), aff'd without published opinion, 268 F.3d 1063 (5th Cir. 2001).
27. See, e.g., *Est. of Strangi v. Comm'r.*, 96 AFTR 2d 2005-5230, 417 F.3d 468 (5th Cir. 2005); *Knight v. Comm'r.*, 115 TC 506 (2000); *Estate of Kelly*, T.C. Memo 2012-73.
28. See, e.g., *Est. of Bigelow*, 503 F.3d 955 (9th Cir. 2007); *Est. of Schauerhammer v. Comm'r.*, TC Memo 1997-242; *Est. of Reichardt v. Comm'r.*, 114 TC 144 (2000); *Est. of Harper v. Comm'r.*, TC Memo 2002-121; *Est. of Thompson v. Comm'r.*, TC Memo 2002-246, aff'd, 94 AFTR2d 2004-5764; *Est. of Strangi v. Comm'r.*, 96 AFTR 2d 2005-5230, 417 F.3d 468 (5th Cir. 2005).
29. See, e.g., *Est. of Strangi v. Comm'r.*, 96 AFTR 2d 2005-5230, 417 F.3d 468 (5th Cir. 2005).
30. For a discussion of such strategies, see Blattmahr and Gans, "Avoiding the *Strangi II* Legacy for Old and New Partnership," Tax Notes, September 1, 2003 and Qualifying New FLPS for the Bona fide Sale Exception: Managing Thompson, Kimbell, Harper and Stone, Journal of Taxation, Feb. 2005, J. Joseph Korpics.
31. *Estate of Kelly*, T.C. Memo 2012-73.
32. See LISI Estate Planning Newsletter No. 1956 (April 30, 2012).
33. *Stone v. Commissioner*, TC Memo 2012-48.
34. *Est. of Nancy H. Powell v. Comm'r.*, 148 T.C. No. 18, May 18, 2017.
35. See *Est. of Strangi v. Comm'r.*, 96 AFTR 2d 2005-5230, 417 F.3d 468 (5th Cir. 2005); *Est. of Clyde W. Turner, Sr. v. Comm'r.*, T.C. Memo. 2011-209, Aug. 30, 2011.

PLANNING WITH C CORPORATIONS

CHAPTER 50

Note: This discussion deals with the general treatment of corporations. In the case of corporations that have elected special status under Subchapter S, different rules apply (see subsequent Chapter 53, Planning with S Corporations).

50.1 INTRODUCTION

For federal tax purposes a business entity with two or more owners is classified as either a corporation or partnership. A business entity such as an LLC with only one owner may often elect to be classified as a corporation or elect to be treated as a sole proprietorship. However, an organization that is incorporated under Federal or state law is treated as a corporation for tax purposes and is not eligible to elect a different classification under the so-called "Check-the-Box" rules.[1]

In addition, the "Check-the-Box" rules generally permit unincorporated organizations to elect to be treated as associations taxable as corporations for federal tax purposes without regard to the number of corporate characteristics (limited liability, continuity of life, centralized management, and free transferability of interest) they possess.

Under the regulations the term corporation means:

(1) a business entity organized under a federal or state statute, or under a statute of a federally recognized Indian tribe, if the statute describes or refers to the entity as incorporated or as a corporation, body corporate, or body politic;

(2) an association;

(3) a business entity organized under a state statute, if the statute describes or refers to the entity as a joint-stock company or joint-stock association;

(4) an insurance company;

(5) certain state-chartered business entities conducting banking activities;

(6) a business entity wholly owned by a state or a political subdivision of a state;

(7) a business entity that is taxable as a corporation under a provision of the Internal Revenue Code other than section 7701(a)(3); and

(8) certain foreign entities.

All entities included in the above list are classified as corporations for income tax purposes. An entity not on the above list with two or more owners may elect to be taxed as a corporation or as a partnership for income tax purposes. In addition, an entity not on the above list with only one owner may also elect to be taxed as a corporation or as a sole proprietorship.[2]

50.2 WHEN IS USE OF SUCH A DEVICE INDICATED?

1. When the individual owners desire limited liability. Legally, a corporation, not its individual shareholders, is responsible for corporate obligations. The limited liability protection is the primary reason

705

to operate a business in the form of a corporation. Therefore, if this protection is desired, it is important to follow the formalities of how the corporation must operate. (Note, as a practical matter, in the case of smaller corporations, the owners may be required to personally sign for corporate debts – thus negating to some extent the protection of corporate liability.)

2. When the individual owners desire a relatively simple and inexpensive means of transferring ownership. It is relatively easy to provide for a new owner's entrance and an existing owner's exit merely by endorsing shares of stock. This is especially important in making gifts, particularly to minors.

3. When the individual owners desire to take advantage of the wide range of fringe benefits that the corporation can provide. These benefits are, within limits, tax deductible by the corporation and generally not currently taxable to the employee – including shareholder-employees (which is not always true for partnerships or S corporations for certain fringe benefits). These fringe benefits may include:

    - pension/profit-sharing plans
    - 401(k) plans
    - group life insurance
    - group health insurance
    - disability income coverage
    - medical reimbursement plans
    - cafeteria plans, and
    - auto and travel costs.

4. When the applicable corporate tax rate is lower than the stockholder-employee's personal rate. For instance, assuming a corporation does not need to pay out substantial dividends, the overall tax result may be lower federal income taxes than if the enterprise were run in the form of a sole proprietorship or partnership. It might be easiest to illustrate this point by comparing partnership with corporate tax treatment. If a partnership were formed, partner owners would be taxed on all the income at their individual rates (which may be higher than the applicable corporate rate) – even if they did not actually withdraw all partnership earnings from the business. However, as stockholder-employees, they would be taxed only on salaries (assuming no dividend had to be paid). The entity would be taxed on any undistributed earnings. Thus, there would be tax savings to the extent the corporate income tax rate was less than the individual partners' income tax rate. See "Corporate vs. Individual Rates" below.

5. When an individual wants to entice family members into the business by giving them a stake in the business without giving them control or the ability to bind the corporation with their actions.

6. When privacy is desired. The transfer of stock in a closely held corporation is not generally a matter of public record. This makes it possible to shield family financial affairs from public scrutiny.

7. When continuity of operation is important. A corporation may, within limits, legally continue its business with little or no hindrance from the probate court. This makes it possible for corporate officers to make major decisions regarding property that the client has contributed to the corporation without the necessity or delay of the probate process, and with little or no publicity.

8. When gift tax savings are desired. The transfer of a minority interest in a closely held business may result in a discounted value for gift tax purposes. In other words, transfers of the underlying property held by a corporation (via its stock) can sometimes be made at discounted values for gift tax purposes. It is also possible to create "nonvoting stock" as a means of transferring a portion of the corporation's value without shifting any control.

9. When estate tax savings are desired. Transfers of stock reduce the donor's estate by (1) shifting future appreciation in value from donor to donee and (2) shifting income on stock (dividends) to the donee. Thus, by virtue of lifetime gifting, the stock ultimately included in the donor's estate may be a minority interest and due to lack of marketability be valued at a discount.

10. When the corporation may qualify for the Code section 1202 small business stock capital gains tax exclusion and/or Code section 1045 rollover,

which is only available to C corporations and not to S corporations or partnerhips, the owners may defer or avoid capital gains tax upon the sale of the business entirely. Not all types of businesses qualify for these generous tax loopholes and the Code section 1202 exclusion requires a holding period of at least five years.

50.3 DISADVANTAGES OF THE CORPORATE FORM (C CORPORATIONS)

1. There are a number of additional expenses associated with forming and maintaining a corporation (e.g., attorney fees, accounting fees, corporate supplies, state incorporation fees or annual filing fees, and the ongoing expenses of maintaining the corporate form).

2. While some types of income passed through to shareholders are taxed only once (e.g., salaries), dividends are subject to both corporate and shareholder level tax.

3. At one time, a corporation could avoid recognizing a gain upon a liquidation or sale (followed by a liquidation) of the business. There was generally only one tax at the shareholder level (except for certain recaptures, receivables, etc.).

   For example, under the *General Utilities* doctrine, if a shareholder contributed $10,000 to a corporation invested in land that was worth $100,000 after ten years, upon liquidation, the corporation would transfer the land to the shareholder in exchange for his or her stock. This would result in a shareholder level capital gain of $90,000 ($100,000 land minus $10,000 stock basis). At the corporate level, no tax was triggered.

   Today, with the *General Utilities* doctrine legislatively abolished, upon liquidation, the corporation is treated as having sold the corporate assets for fair market value resulting in a corporate level gain equal to the excess of the amount realized over the corporation's basis in the assets. So, if the corporation's basis in the land was $10,000 and its fair market value was $100,000, there would be a $90,000 corporate level gain. The after tax remainder distributed to the shareholder is taxed (to the shareholder) to the extent that the amount distributed exceeds his or her basis in his or her stock.

   Simply stated, a corporate liquidation of appreciated property triggers tax at both the corporate and the individual level.

4. Corporations demand a more complex organizational structure and may have to contend with additional tax issues (e.g., personal holding company tax, accumulated earnings tax, dividend treatment, and collapsible corporation rules).

5. Corporations must also follow their formalities of operation. For example, the shareholders and board of directors must meet at least once a year. Minutes should be kept which document the significant actions of the corporation. Each of the officers has a specific role to fulfill, although most states have "close corporation" statutes that permit a more informal structure. Most state laws permit shareholder and director actions to be taken without a meeting but regular updates should occur.

50.4 HOW IT IS DONE
Transfers to a Corporation and Code Section 351

Example. Stevens, Roberts, and Lee are engineers and plan to develop a process for manufacturing an aircraft safety component in great demand for new jet airliners.

Stevens is a sole proprietor currently engaged in producing aircraft parts. Roberts has worked for Stevens for a number of years and his sales efforts have been so successful that Stevens would like to offer him an interest in a new business venture.

Lee is a well-known and highly respected authority in the area of aircraft safety parts. Lee is quite wealthy and is interested in keeping both his money and his mind at work.

In exchange for what they can contribute to their new corporate venture, they want to participate in the control and profits of the business and a distribution of corporate assets if the corporation liquidates. In exchange for stock in the new corporation, Stevens will contribute his sole proprietor business assets, Lee will contribute cash, and Roberts will contribute his services and a small amount of cash.

When Lee contributes cash to the corporation, the stock he receives will normally have a value at the time of the exchange equal to the cash. For example, if he transfers $10,000 of cash to the corporation, he will ordinarily receive back stock with a fair market value of $10,000. Because the value of the stock he receives is no more or less than the value of the cash he transfers to the corporation, he realized neither a gain nor a loss. If he later sells his stock for $21,000, he would recognize a gain of $11,000, the difference between his basis for the stock ($10,000) and the sales price ($21,000).

Absent provisions in the tax law to the contrary, using the above fact pattern, if any of the three contributed appreciated property to the corporation in return for its stock, a taxable gain would result. But there is an important exception to that general rule under Code section 351.

The exception was designed to encourage the formation of a new corporation. It enables a taxpayer to transfer appreciated property, or even a going business, into a new corporation without the transferor recognizing income on the appreciation at the very time when other expenses – the expenses involved in the organization and operation of the corporation – are the highest. The exception provides that even if the transferor realizes a gain when he transfers appreciated property to the new corporation, he or she does not have to recognize gain for tax purposes when certain conditions are met.[3]

This non-recognition treatment applies where a person or persons transfer *property* to a corporation (a) solely in exchange for the corporation's own stock, and (b) the transferor(s) control the corporation immediately after the transfer, no gain will be recognized on the appreciated business or securities contributed to the new corporation. Control generally means ownership of 80 percent or more of the corporation's stock.[4]

As indicated above, stock received in exchange for appreciated assets does not trigger the recognition of gain. However, if the shareholder receives anything *other than* stock, such as cash, securities, or machinery, it will be treated as taxable "boot." Gain is recognized to the extent of the lesser of the amount of the realized gain inherent in the assets transferred or the amount of "boot" received. Note, however, if the contributed property is in a loss position (i.e. basis is higher than fair market value), boot will never cause the shareholder to recognize a loss on a section 351 exchange.

A section 351 tax-free exchange for stock is similar to the theory making a like-kind exchange tax free. The transferor who receives stock in exchange for his property has really maintained an interest in the original property. The form of the ownership has merely changed from actual ownership to stock ownership. This continuity of interest concept is a key to nonrecognition of the gain on the appreciated property transferred.

It is important to recognize, however, that for the purposes of corporate law, a shareholder has an undivided interest (shared with all other shareholders) in all corporate property, but that his rights in any specific corporate property—even though originally transferred by him to the corporation in a tax-free exchange)—are extremely limited.

Example. Suppose Stevens, who is now operating as a sole proprietor, decides to transfer his going business to the new corporation. If his basis for the sole proprietorship is $100,000, and the fair market value of his business is $500,000 at the time he transfers it to the new corporation, he would probably receive $500,000 worth of stock.

Under general tax rules, Stevens would realize a $400,000 gain, the difference between the basis of his business ($100,000) in exchange for stock worth $500,000. However, the nonrecognition treatment is appropriate because he received only stock by which he controls the business of the corporation (just as he previously controlled his sole proprietorship). So, there as only been a change of form as evidenced by a substitution of stock certificates for his former physical possession of the property.

This rule is logical because to realize gain there must be a taxable event that converts property from one form to another. This usually occurs when the taxpayer sells, exchanges, or otherwise disposes of property. In this example, Stevens has not disposed of his property that results in a conversion. He has merely received stock reflecting a change in the form of ownership in the original property. Nonrecognition treatment applies regardless of the number of individuals transfer property to

Figure 50.1

CHOOSING AN ENTITY — A CHECKLIST OF ISSUES TO CONSIDER

PROPRIETORSHIP

(1) One person owner
(2) Few employees
(3) Relatively low income
(4) Relatively low start up costs
(5) No double tax on business earnings
(6) Not possible to "time" or "split" income
(7) Administration of estate difficult
(8) Valuation freezing techniques not available
(9) Should not be operated as part of a trust
(10) No shield against personal liability
(11) Income reportable on owner's individual income tax return
(12) May represent self pro se in small claims or other court (unlike entities such as LLC/LP/Corp)
(13) Generally may avoid franchise tax imposed by many states on operating as a corporation
(14) Self employment (payroll) tax now equal to total of employer and employee federal payroll tax
(15) May hire minor children as employees and avoid paying employment taxes (FICA/Medicare/FUTA), saving the family employment and income taxes

PARTNERSHIP & LLC

(1) Sharing of net profits
(2) Presence of loss sharing
(3) Pass through of losses
(4) Avoidance of double taxation on profits
(5) Relatively low start up costs
(6) Relatively economical operation costs
(7) Taxable years must match those of partners or members
(8) No restrictions on who can invest or number of investors
(9) Easy to convert to another form of entity
(10) No accumulated earnings tax
(11) No personal holding company tax
(12) Unlimited personal liability unless limited partnership (LP) or LLC used to protect limited partners or members
(13) Subject to "at risk" limitations
(14) Losses not deductible in excess of basis
(15) Interest deduction limits at personal level
(16) Equity received for services creates income
(17) On contribution of encumbered property, generally, only liabilities assumed by other partners or members in excess of contributing partner's basis is taxable
(18) Income splitting – wealth shifting potential
(19) IRS can reallocate income if member of family renders services without reasonable compensation
(20) Partners who render services are treated as employees for certain fringe benefit purposes but tax law typically precludes nontaxable fringe benefits for most partners or members
(21) Separate income tax return required
(22) Unlike corporations, can often distribute appreciated property to partners without triggering gain
(23) Franchise tax imposed on partnerships or LLCs by some states

Figure 50.1 (cont'd)

CORPORATIONS – "C"
(1) Limited liability to creditors if capital is adequate and corporate amenities observed
(2) Shareholder-employees can exclude certain fringe benefits from income
(3) Income taxed at corporate level subject to tax again at shareholder level on payment of dividend or on liquidation
(4) Reasonableness of compensation an issue
(5) Accumulated earnings and alternative minimum tax liability
(6) Losses trapped at corporate level
(7) Passive loss rules avoided at corporate level (except for certain closely-held C corporations and personal service corporations) and deductions at corporate rates
(8) Flexibility in terms of numbers of shareholders
(9) Can have more than one class of stock
(10) Stock can be used as compensation
(11) Ability to form subsidiaries
(12) Must be adequately capitalized
(13) Decision making centralized through management structure
(14) Possible to retain earnings without tax at personal level but taxed at corporate level
(15) Dividends received deduction
(16) Low federal income tax rate on first $75,000 of income
(17) 21 percent flat rate on certain professional service corporations
(18) Subject to double taxation upon liquidation
(19) Separate income tax returns required
(20) Franchise tax imposed by many states
(21) Non-calendar fiscal year end may be chosen by regular corporations, permitting some shift of income from one year to next by timing of salaries – not for personal service corporations in many circumstances
(22) Possible for employees to borrow up to $50,000 from their accounts in corporate retirement plans

CORPORATION – "S" – DIFFERENCES FROM "C" CORPORATION
(1) Restrictions on who can hold stock (no IRAs, CRTs, non-resident aliens, etc.)
(2) Limits on number of investors (now 100)
(3) Only one class of stock (common) allowed
(4) Only limited subsidiaries permissible
(5) Some states do not recognize pass through of income or losses
(6) Limited liability as with "C" corporation
(7) Decision making centralized through management structure
(8) Pass through of income, losses, and credits
(9) Difficult to do estate planning since certain trusts cannot own S stock
(10) Limits on type of business an S corporation can be
(11) Potential for accidental or nonvoluntary termination of S election
(12) Limits on employee benefits for owners
(13) Ineligible for Code section 1202 small business stock exclusion or Code section 1045 rollover upon sale of stock

the corporation provided it was done collectively and those transferring property to the corporation still have both (a) control and (b) interest in the property they originally owned.

Under the facts of the original example, if Roberts were to receive stock in the new corporation in exchange for his services, the value of the stock would be currently taxable to him as compensation because services are not considered to be property. Thus, nonrecognition does not apply with respect to the transfer of stock for services. Consequently, if Roberts' stock was issued solely for services, it will not be counted in determining whether the transferors of property control the corporation after the exchange.

Finally, if the property that is contributed is subject to liabilities in excess of basis, the amount of liabilities in excess of basis is treated as boot so that gain will be recognized to the extent of such excess.

The basis in the hands of the transferee corporation of the property transferred subject to a section 351 exchange is typically the transferor's basis (i.e. carry-over basis). As such, recognition of gain or loss is postponed, not eliminated.[5]

50.5 TAX IMPLICATIONS

A corporation is taxed as an entity separate from its shareholders. Prior to 2018, there were four corporate tax rates with a top rate of 35 percent. The Tax Cuts and Jobs Act (TCJA) of 2017 replaced the existing rates with a flat 21 percent rate applicable to all corporations. While many of the provisions in the TCJA related to individual and transfer taxation are scheduled to expire at the end of 2025, the provisions related to corporations were made permanent.

Example. In 2021, a corporation with $500,000 of taxable income would pay a tax of $105,000 (21 percent flat tax rate). Corporations, like individuals, are liable for a number of other state and local taxes as well. The corporation reports its federal income tax on IRS Form 1120.

Gross income includes such items as profit from sales and receipts from services. It also includes gains on sales or exchanges, income from rent, royalties, interest, and dividends.

Personal Service Corporations

Under current law, personal service corporations are also taxed at a flat rate of 21 percent. The term "qualified personal service corporation" means one in which:

1. substantially all of the activities involve the performance of services in the fields of health, law, engineering, architecture, accounting, actuarial science, performing arts, or consulting; and

2. substantially all of the stock of which is held by employees, retirees, their estates, or persons acquiring stock due to the death of an employee or retiree (but only for a two-year period following the death).[6]

Code section 269A specifically authorizes the IRS to reallocate between an employee-owner of a personal service corporation (defined as a corporation whose principal activity is the performance of personal services, with such services substantially performed by employee-owners) and the personal service corporation all income, deductions, credits, exclusions and other allowances to the extent necessary to prevent tax avoidance or evasion or to reflect clearly the income of the personal service corporation or any of its employee-owners. The authority to reallocate applies only in the event that substantially all of the services of the personal service corporation are performed for or on behalf of one other corporation, partnership or other entity and the personal service corporation was formed for the principal purpose of avoiding or evading federal income tax by reducing the income of the employee-owner or by securing for him a significant tax benefit not otherwise available. The typical corporation affected by this law is a corporate partner in a partnership of personal service corporations.

The potential impact of section 269A has been greatly reduced by the parity created between corporate and Keogh plans, because the tax benefits of a corporate qualified plan are now available to non-corporate entities.

Personal Holding Companies

Code section 541 imposes a 20 percent tax on companies classified as personal holding companies. The tax applies to undistributed personal holding company income and is designed to discourage the use of corporations as incorporated pocketbooks wherein income from securities, real property, or personal talents is taxed at corporate rates rather than individual rates.

To be classified as a personal holding company, the corporation must meet both of the following tests:

1. at any time during the last half of the taxable year more than 50 percent of the value of its stock is owned by five or fewer individuals, and

2. at least 60 percent of its adjusted ordinary gross income is "personal holding company income."[7]

Personal holding company income consists of (1) passive income, such as rents, royalties, dividends, and interest, and (2) income from personal service contracts under which the corporation is to furnish personal services but the corporation does not have the right to select the individual who will perform the services, and the individual selected by the client owns directly or indirectly 25 percent or more of the stock in the corporation.[8]

Note, the Tax Cuts and Jobs Act of 2017 did not modify the rules related to personal holding companies. Therefore, closely-held corporations must continue to take measures to avoid triggering the personal holding company tax. If a corporation will have undistributed personal holding income, the application of the 20 percent penalty tax should be considered to determine if the corporate structure is appropriate for a new business endeavor.

For more on personal holding companies, see Chapter 52.

Deductions

A corporation is entitled to two types of deductions: ordinary deductions and special deductions.

Ordinary deductions include compensation of officers and salaries, bonuses, rent payments, charitable contributions, repair expenses, interest paid on indebtedness, casualty losses, deductions for depreciation and amortization of research and experimental costs, advertising, and corporate contributions to pension and profit-sharing plans.

Many of the ordinary deductions that were available to corporations in prior years were eliminated or modified under the TCJA, including:

- Research and experimental expenditures must be capitalized and amortized ratably over a five-year period starting after 2021.

- The repeal of the deduction for lobbying expenses.

- The repeal of the deduction for expenses related to social purposes such as entertainment, amusement, or recreation activities, and the modification of the deduction for meal expenses.

- The repeal of all deductions for transportation fringe benefits (except to the extent the deducted value is included in an employee's taxable income).

The TCJA also modified the rules related to the deduction for net operating losses. Under prior law, a corporation received a carryover deduction for a net operating loss up to 100 percent, which could be carried back two years and carried forward twenty years. The TCJA notably limits the net operating loss deduction to 80 percent of taxable income in a given year. Additionally, under the new law, net operating losses are still allowed to be carried forward, but NOLs cannot be carried back to prior years.

Example. In 2020, a corporation has a NOL of $90,000. In 2021, the corporation has taxable income of $100,000. Assuming the entire $90,000 NOL from 2020 was carried over to 2021, under the new law, the deduction in 2021 is limited to $80,000 (80 percent of $100,000). The remaining $10,000 can be carried forward indefinitely.[9]

In 2020, the CARES Act temporarily – and retroactively – changed the NOL rules again. Under the CARES Act, an NOL from a tax year beginning in 2018, 2019 or 2020 can be carried back five years. As of 2023, this five-year carryback provision is eliminated for tax years beginning in 2021.[10]

Another notable change under the TCJA is related to the section 179 expensing election. Under prior law, depreciable tangible personal property and certain real property was deductible up to $500,000, reduced dollar-for-dollar to the extent the property placed in service during the year exceeded $2 million. The TCJA increased the maximum allowed expense level to $1 million and increased the phase-out threshold to $2.5 million. This is adjusted periodically for inflation and for 2023 the maximum Section 179 expense limit is $1,160,000. The TCJA also broadened the definition of "tangible personal property" to include property used with furnishing lodging and certain expenses related to improvements made to nonresidential real property.

The TCJA also greatly accelerated the rate at which a corporation may deduct the expense of new qualified business property (i.e., "bonus depreciation") acquired and put into service after September 27, 2017. The definition of property that may generate such a deduction was also expanded. Under the new law, a 100 percent deduction of the acquisition cost of qualified property is allowed for years 2018 through 2022 (phased down gradually through 2027, with some exceptions).

Special deductions available to corporations include a domestic dividends received deduction (DRD) under Code section 243 which allows domestic corporate shareholders to deduct a portion of dividends received from domestic corporation. The DRD helps to ensure that domestic income is taxed only once too corporate shareholders (and again when distributed to individual shareholders). The TCJA modified the DRD by reducing the general DRD as follows:

1. If the recipient corporation owns less than 20 percent of the voting power and value of stock of the issuing corporation, the corporation may deduct 50 percent of the amount of the dividend (down from 70 percent in years prior to December 31, 2017).

2. If the recipient corporation holds at least 20 percent and up to 80 percent of the stock of the issuing corporation, the corporation may deduct 65 percent of the dividends received (down from 80 percent in years prior to December 31, 2017).

3. If the recipient corporation owns 80 percent or more of the stock of the issuing corporation, a 100 percent deduction may apply to dividends received (unchanged from prior law).[11]

Example. A closely held corporation holds less than 20 percent of the stock of a publicly held corporation. The closely held corporation likely be entitled to deduct 50 percent of every dollar it receives in the form of dividends on the stock it holds. It therefore will pay tax of 21 percent on 50 percent of each dividend dollar, an effective rate of only 10.5 percent.

A corporation may also deduct up to $5,000 of start-up costs and organizational expenditures. This $5,000 amount is reduced by the amount that organization expenditures exceed $50,000. The remainder of organizational expenditures may be amortized over fifteen years.[12] This would also be considered a special deduction.

Taxable income is what is left after taking ordinary and special deductions. It is the amount to which the various percentage tax rates are applied. Certain credits are then directly applied against this tax, such as corporate overpayments of tax in previous years, payments for estimated taxes (paid on a quarterly basis), and credit on certain foreign taxes paid.

Like-kind exchanges under Code section 1031 were also modified under the TCJA. Section 1031 allows for the nonrecognition of gain for qualifying exchanges of "like-kind" property held for productive use in a trade or business. Under the new law, nonrecognition of gain is limited to the exchange of real property (real estate).

Compensation

In most instances, a corporation is entitled to a deduction for salaries or any other compensation for personal services, but only if the services are actually rendered and the amount paid as compensation for those services is considered reasonable. Reasonable means only that amount which would ordinarily be paid for similar services by other corporations under similar circumstances. See "Frequently Asked Questions" below for more information on what is considered "reasonable" compensation.

This reasonableness test is imposed most frequently on closely held corporations because of the large degree of coincidence of executive and shareholder interest. It is designed to prevent the shareholders from draining off corporate profits in the disguise of tax-deductible salaries. Corporate profits are usually paid out in the form of dividends that are taxable to the shareholders, but nondeductible by the corporation. The portion of the salary considered unreasonable is usually classified as a disguised dividend and, to that extent, the corporation's deduction is disallowed. However, even though that amount may not be deducted by the corporation, it is still taxable as a dividend to the shareholder-recipient.[13] Reasonableness is a question of determining the amount that would ordinarily be paid for like services by like enterprises under similar circumstances. Generally, where an executive employee does not own or have options to purchase stock, arm's length bargaining as to the amount of salary is assumed. One element that could be considered in determining reasonableness is the fact that a given individual was not adequately compensated in prior years. Thus, if high compensation in the current year can be attributed to services rendered in prior years, the total current salary might be considered reasonable.

However, the amount of cash compensation is not the only relevant factor. Corporate contributions to pension and profit-sharing plans are considered business expenses and are allowed as deductions as long as the total amount of all forms of compensation paid on behalf of an individual does not exceed a reasonable total.

Some of the other indirect forms of compensation may be: premiums for life insurance, hospitalization, medical care, and salary continuation plans. Costs of these plans, although generally deductible by the corporation, often do not result in taxable income to the individual. Because the corporation is a separate and distinct tax entity, and because working shareholders would be considered salaried employees, they would be eligible for these forms of indirect compensations. This is true even if in addition to being employees, they are also officers, directors, and shareholders of the corporation.

One exception to the general rule of deductibility for compensation paid falls under Code section 162(m). There is a $1 million per year deduction limit for compensation paid to "covered employees" of publicly traded companies. The TCJA expanded the definition of "covered employee" to include the CFO, CEO, and the next three highest-compensated officers plus any individual who was previously a covered employee (i.e., once a covered employee, always a covered employee). Moreover, the TCJA repealed the exception for "performance-based" compensation (e.g. certain bonuses and commissions).

Fringe Benefits

The TCJA repealed or modified the deductibility of many employee fringe benefits. Under the new law, no deduction is allowed for entertainment, recreation or amusement expenses. Meals, including food and beverages provided as de minimis fringe benefits, are generally 50 percent deductible under the new law. Transportation benefits, including expenses related to commuting, are no longer deductible under the new law.

An employee may exclude from gross income the following fringe benefits:

- a no-additional-cost service (e.g., free stand-by flights to airline employees)

- qualified employee discounts (e.g., discounts on the selling price of qualified property or services of the employer)

- certain working condition fringes (e.g., employer paid subscriptions to business periodicals)

- de minimus fringes such as typing of personal letters by the company secretary or the personal use of company copying machines.[14]

In order for the no-additional-cost services and the qualified employee discounts to be excluded from income of officers, owners and highly compensated employees, they must be provided to employees on a nondiscriminatory basis.

Corporate vs. Individual Rates

Because the corporation's tax rate may be lower than the individual's tax rate, income splitting can yield a lower overall current tax. This is especially true under current law where corporations enjoy a 21 percent tax rate (in 2021, an individual hits the 22 percent individual income tax rate at income of just $40,525).

Although the new lower corporate tax rate makes the corporate form appear to be very attractive, there are multiple other factors which must be weighed to determine if incorporation is appropriate, such as the personal holdings tax and the accumulated earnings tax. Furthermore, it may be more expensive tax-wise to be a corporation when it comes down to selling the business (with a notable exception if the business qualifies for the small business stock exclusion in Code section 1202). Under the rules, there may be two taxes as a result of a corporate sale of assets (followed by liquidation) instead of one tax when the seller is a proprietorship or partnership. Thus, if the corporation has assets that are likely to appreciate, the income-splitting benefit may be more than offset by the additional taxes at liquidation.

A corporation can generally declare and pay dividends – as well as salaries – in such a manner as to avoid a "bunching" of income at the entity level in those years when personal income is highest. On the other hand, if the business were established in the partnership form, the owners would have little control over the receipt and taxation of income. This ability to "time" income is important because, if income can be timed, the ultimate taxes payable can be lowered.

Accumulated Earnings Tax

One of the easiest and most common means of financing growth is to accumulate earnings and plow them back into the corporation to purchase new machinery, buildings, and other necessary capital assets. These plowed-back earnings and profits begin to add up very quickly. Because the corporate tax rate may be lower than the rate of tax upon the incomes of individual shareholders, which is likely to be the case after the TCJA, they may attempt to use the corporation as a vehicle for reducing taxes by having the corporation retain earnings rather than make taxable distributions in the form of nondeductible dividends.

If a corporation reasonably allows earnings to accumulate in order to fund current or anticipated needs or projects that the corporation has planned, there should not be a problem. However, once earnings are allowed to accumulate beyond the reasonable needs of the business, those earnings may be subject to an additional tax, the accumulated earnings tax.[15]

The accumulated earnings tax is imposed on every corporation that is formed or used for the purpose of avoiding personal income tax with respect to its shareholders by permitting earnings and profits to accumulate instead of being distributed. The purpose of the tax is to discourage the use of a corporation as an accumulation vehicle to shelter its individual stockholders from taxation at personal income tax rates. As a regulative device, the accumulated earnings tax was designed to force the distribution of retained earnings at the point where they no longer serve a legitimate business purpose. Without such a tax on improper accumulations, stockholders could arrange to have dividends paid in years when their incomes were low or they could indefinitely accumulate earnings and profits inside the corporation until the corporation was liquidated.

An accumulated earnings credit of $250,000 ($150,000 in the case of personal service corporations) is allowed that will be presumed to be for the reasonable business needs of the corporation.[16] A controlled group of corporations is allowed one accumulated earnings credit, not one per corporation. Thus, if a corporation begins to accumulate amounts in excess of $250,000, it should be prepared to show a bona fide business reason for not distributing these earnings in the form of dividends.

The accumulated earnings tax is designed to tax only earnings retained beyond the reasonable needs of the business. The question then becomes: "What reasonable needs would a corporation have for accumulating profits?" The regulations state that working capital needs and capital for building expansion or for the replacement of plant or equipment are among the needs that would allow a business to properly accumulate earnings.[17] In addition to these needs, a sinking fund to retire corporate bonds at maturity has often been found to be a reasonable need to accumulate cash. In other cases, funds set aside to acquire minority interests or quarreling stockholders' interests were also deemed to be retained for reasonable business needs. The term reasonable needs of the business includes the Code section 303 redemption needs of the business (see Chapter 48), although specific protection from the tax (within limits) is provided only in the corporation tax year in which the stockholder dies and in subsequent years.[18] The reasonableness of accumulations in years prior to a year in which the shareholder dies is to be determined solely upon the facts and circumstances existing at the times the accumulations occur.[19]

The tax, if applicable, is imposed only on accumulated taxable income; an amount that is derived from the taxable income of the corporation for the particular year in question. Thus, the tax does not apply to all of the accumulated earnings and profits of the corporation, but only to the accumulated taxable income of the year or years as to which the tax is asserted. To the extent that the tax is applicable, it is equal to 20 percent of the accumulated taxable income.

This tax on a corporation's *accumulated taxable income* is payable in addition to the regular tax payable by the firm. "Accumulated taxable income" generally means the corporation's taxable income for the year in question with certain adjustments (such as a reduction for federal income taxes paid) minus the sum of:

1. distributions from current earnings and profits that the shareholders have reported as ordinary income (dividends paid);

2. amounts from earnings and profits that the shareholders have reported as dividends even though no actual distribution was made (disguised dividends); and

3. the accumulated earnings credit.

In determining whether or not the current year's accumulated taxable income has been retained for the reasonable needs of the business, the availability of prior years' accumulated earnings must also be considered. If past years' accumulations are sufficient to meet current needs (i.e., this year's business needs) there is no justification for accumulating current earnings.

Corporate AMT

The corporate AMT was a tax imposed in addition to the regular corporate income tax imposed on corporations with certain tax preferences. The TCJA permanently repealed the corporate AMT effective for tax years after December 31, 2017. AMT credit carryovers for tax years after that date may be used to eliminate or reduce the taxpayer's regular tax liability or to the extent the taxpayer's AMT credit carryovers exceed his or her regular tax liability, the credits may be fully refunded in 2021.

50.6 ISSUES IN COMMUNITY PROPERTY STATES

Stock purchased by an investor in a corporation will take on the character of the assets used to purchase the stock. Thus, if an individual transfers $1,000 to a corporation in return for stock and that $1,000 consists of community property earnings, the stock itself will be community property. Of course, this result could be altered by a written agreement between the spouse and the investor to treat the stock as property other than community property, or by titling the stock in some other fashion, e.g., as joint tenancy or as the separate property of one spouse.

Upon divorce or death of the stockholder, the community property interest of the spouse will become important. It will be necessary to determine what portion of the stock is community property. As discussed in Chapter 47, a common problem is the situation where a person owned all or most of the stock of a corporation prior to marriage, the person works full time for the corporation, and the value of the corporation increases significantly. A portion of the increase in value of the person's stock may be community property to the extent the increase is attributable to his or her insufficiently rewarded hard work during the marriage, and a portion will be separate property to the extent the increase is the result of the natural increase or earnings of the original stock. The method of valuation cannot be predicted with certainty.

One question that often arises in community property states is the power to manage and control the community property. Until 1975, California law provided that the husband had the management and control over the community property. Under a revision of the community property laws, both spouses now have management power and control over community property. (Similar changes have occurred in the laws of other community property states.) This has implications in connection with the management and control over a corporation. California law provides that a spouse who is operating or managing a business or an interest in a business that is community personal property has the sole management and control of the business or interest. Thus, if an individual owns all the stock in a manufacturing corporation and that individual is also the manager of the business, or a substantial participant in the management of the business, the individual's spouse will not be able to exercise equal control in regard to the management of that business. This allows people to choose business associates and manage a business without regard to the effect of community property laws.

Note that under federal regulations, an individual will not be considered the owner of an interest in a corporation that is owned by his spouse if:

1. the individual does not directly own an interest in the corporation at any time during the taxable year;

2. the individual is not a member of the board of directors, a fiduciary, or an employee of the corporation and does not participate in its management at any time during the year;

3. no more than 50 percent of the corporation's income for the year was derived from royalties, rents, dividends, interest, and annuities; and

4. the interest in the corp. is not, at any time during the year, subject to conditions which substantially restrict or limit the spouse's right to dispose of the interest and which run in favor of the individual or the individual's children who have not reached the age of twenty-one.[20]

50.7 CORPORATE BONDS

One of the key advantages of operating a business in the corporate form is that many different types of ownership interests in corporations can be created. The interests of any particular investor can be met by creating a security that fits his special needs and desires. This factor facilitates the acquisition of capital. Suppose that in order to acquire working capital and capital for long-term planning the corporation issued bonds. A corporate bond is a written obligation to repay a definite sum of money on a definite date, usually at least ten, and more often twenty-nine or more, years from the date the bond was issued.

Bonds are a favored means of raising corporate capital. One reason is the interest deduction allowed for the interest paid on the indebtedness that is not allowed for dividends paid to preferred or common stockholders. As long as a corporation can earn money at a rate higher than the corporate bond interest paid (with the cash raised by issuing the bond), corporate borrowing is a prudent way to raise capital. This is known as leverage.

Issuance of the bonds generally creates no tax liability to either the corporation or the bondholder. This is because the issuance of a bond is the equivalent of borrowing money. When the bond matures, the principal becomes payable and the bondholders are entitled to a tax-free return of their capital investment. In contrast, a shareholder who receives a corporate distribution is taxable as a dividend, unless the return can qualify as a stock redemption.

Any money bondholders receive in the form of interest, and any money they receive at the maturity of their bonds in excess of their capital investment will be taxed at ordinary income rates. Receiving money in excess of capital investment can occur when bonds are purchased at a discount but are paid off at face value.

(When bonds are *issued* at a discount by the issuing corporation, a bondholder must include a ratable portion of the discount in income each year as the bond matures. For example, if a bond with a par value of $1,000 was issued for $800 and is payable in ten years, the $200 discount would be included in the taxpayer's income at the rate of $20 a year.)

Another reason bonds are often favored over an increase in equity is that the accumulation of earnings and profits within the corporation to pay debt obligations can be justified more readily than accumulating income to redeem stock. This helps avoid an additional tax on an unreasonable income accumulation.

A final reason for lending money to the corporation as opposed to making a capital contribution concerns asset protection planning for the owners. For example, if the corporation stops operating and wants to dissolve, the corporation's creditors must be paid before the owners of the business. Therefore, if the owners of the corporation lend money to the corporation, (and to the extent of these loans) the owners will be entitled to receive a pro-rata share of the distributions which are otherwise being made to outside creditors. While attempting to treat contributions to the corporation as a loan is a good strategy, it is important that the loan obligation be properly documented. This will require a loan agreement and security agreement which contain terms that are similar to the same types of terms that would be entered into with an unrelated lender. It is also important to make sure that there is adequate capital in the corporation in order to avoid being considered thinly capitalized.

Thin Capitalization

Because the interest paid on corporate indebtedness is deductible, the cost of borrowing money through long-term corporate debt is substantially reduced. However, some shareholders attempt to overdo it – they contribute almost no equity investment and characterize almost their entire contribution as debt owed to them by the corporation. This is known as thin capitalization, because the capital investment is thin in relation to the debt, but the debt is really disguised stock.

Once the form of the debt is disregarded by the IRS and the substance is treated appropriately, corporate deductions for interest payments to shareholders are disallowed. Second, receipt of interest payments by shareholder-creditors are reclassified and treated as dividends. Third, when the corporation pays off its debt to the shareholders, the payments may be taxed as dividends. This means that instead of treating the amount received as a tax-free repayment of a debt, the shareholder-creditor must report some or all of the distribution as income. Fourth, money that the corporation purportedly was accumulating to pay off the debt may be subject to the accumulated earnings tax (which is discussed below). Finally, a debt that is reclassified as stock could cause a termination of a Subchapter S election, because a Subchapter S corporation is allowed to have only one class of stock.

To determine if a security should be classified as debt rather than equity, the courts usually examine a number of factors such as: Was there an intention by shareholders to enforce payment of the debt? Was there a debt instrument and did it give the shareholders management or voting rights (like stock)? What was the ratio of debt to equity? A general rule of thumb, subject to variation depending upon the industry, is that if the amount of debt exceeds shareholders' equity by more than four to one, the corporation is thinly capitalized. Basically, the court would examine all the factors relevant to determining if a loan by shareholders was in reality more like an ownership interest (stock) than a debtor-creditor relationship.[21]

Keep in mind that, while bonds are a tax-favored means of obtaining corporate funds, frequently a corporation does not want to become obligated to make fixed payments for interest and debt amortization. To avoid a cash flow problem, therefore, corporations often finance long-term operations or investments by the issuance and sale of common stock, which entail no obligation to pay dividends or preferred stock on which dividend payments can frequently be avoided.

Thin capitalization can also be a problem in protecting the shareholders from claims by the corporation's creditors. In order for there to be limited liability protection within a corporation, the corporation must have sufficient assets to stand behind its obligations.

50.8 FREQUENTLY ASKED QUESTIONS

Question – Will corporate-owned cash value life insurance purchased for key person, split dollar, or deferred compensation financing cause an accumulated earnings tax problem?

Answer – That depends on whether or not the insurance answers a valid corporate business need. There must also be a close correlation between the type of policy and amount of death benefit and the alleged corporate need. Generally, hedging against the loss of a key employee's service because of unexpected death is considered to be a reasonable business need.[22]

Key person life insurance is insurance that is owned by the corporation insuring the life of a key employee. The purpose of such a policy is to provide a fund at the employee's death that will compensate the corporation for the financial loss resulting from the unavailability of the employee to render services to the corporation. Often, key person insurance death proceeds are also used to help in finding and compensating a suitable replacement. Therefore, the purchase of life insurance and the earnings used to pay policy premiums should not, per se, be subject to the penalty tax. The point is that it is not the amount, but the purpose of the accumulation, that is important.

The same question often arises as to the effect of a split dollar plan. If a corporation attempts to prevent taxation of income to shareholders by accumulating its earnings rather than distributing them, the existence or nonexistence of a split dollar policy will not, by itself, deter the imposition of the tax penalty provided by the law. Conversely, the existence of a split dollar policy will not, per se, incur the accumulations tax penalty if the corporation is not, in fact, accumulating earnings beyond the reasonable needs of the business.

This provision exists to deter tax evasion and not to prevent a business from operating in a normal businesslike manner. The same principle applies in cases where the corporation has obligated itself to make pre-retirement death benefits to a key executive under a deferred compensation agreement. An accumulation of corporate earnings to meet obligations under such an agreement is generally considered a reasonable business need (just as the funds accumulated to retire an outstanding corporate bond would be considered reasonable).

A third area where this question often arises is the use of accumulated earnings to provide surplus cash for the redemption of stock. In this case, if the redemption is to be utilized to shift partial or complete control to the remaining shareholders without depleting their personal funds (as for example, where, by shareholder agreement, the corporation will retire shares on the death of a shareholder), it is doubtful that accumulations to reach this result would be found to be a reasonable need. However, if a business purpose can be found, such as an accumulation to purchase the shares of a dissenting minority, then the accumulation may be found to be reasonable.[23] The primary purpose must be a corporate, rather than an individual, benefit from the stock redemption.

In light of the TCJA, there may be a greater incentive for corporations to use corporate dollars to implement these techniques which may be an exception to the accumulated earnings tax (versus distributing excess income out to shareholders who may then be taxed at higher individual income tax rate). Moreover, the repeal of the corporate AMT removes the perceived disadvantage of corporate-owned life insurance, allowing corporations to own life insurance to fund an entity-redemption buy-sell agreement without concern of triggering AMT.

Question – Should new and existing businesses considering becoming C corporations in light of the Tax Cuts and Jobs Act of 2017?

Answer – Although the TCJA permanently reduced the corporate tax rate to 21 percent, making C corporation status appear more attractive than ever, the TCJA also enacted a new Code section 199A which allows a deduction for pass-through entities of up to 20 percent of "qualified business income" (QBI). The new "199A deduction" is subject to strict testing limitations and requirements, including a reduction for owners with income over certain thresholds and the availability of the deduction for specified service trades or businesses (e.g., health professionals, attorneys, consultants, etc.) is severely limited (unavailable over certain income thresholds). Moreover, the deduction is limited to 50 percent of an owner's pro rata share of W-2 wages paid by the business. However, for owners of pass-through entities which qualify for the deduction, the effective federal tax rate may be lower for these individuals. (Note, under current law, the 199A deduction for qualified business income is allowed for years 2018-2025 only.) Clients must work with tax counsel to determine which choice of entity is most beneficial under current law. A calculation to determine whether C corporation or pass through is more beneficial purely from a federal income tax standpoint will include weighing factors such as profitability, whether profits or losses will be retained in the business or distributed out to owners, and how distributions will be structured (e.g., as compensation or not). An additional factor arguing for C corporation status would be if the stock would qualify as Code section 1202 small business stock exclusion.

CHAPTER ENDNOTES

1. Treas. Reg. §301.7701-2(b).
2. Treas. Reg. §301.7701-3(a).
3. I.R.C. §351.
4. I.R.C. §368(c); Treas. Reg. §1.351-1(a)(1).
5. I.R.C. §§358, 362.
6. I.R.C. §448(d)(2).
7. I.R.C. §542.
8. I.R.C. §543.
9. Example is modified from the example in the *Complete Analysis of the Tax Cuts and Jobs Act – Chapter 1000, Business Deductions and Credits*, published by Thomson Reuters Checkpoint.
10. See I.R.C. §172.
11. I.R.C. §243.
12. I.R.C. §248.
13. In *Mulcahy, Pauritsch, Salvador & Co., Ltd. v. Comm'r.*, 109 AFTR 2d 2012-2140, 680 F.3d 867 (7th Cir. 2012), the Court of Appeals for the Seventh Circuit upheld a decision to recharacterize payments to entities related to the shareholders as dividends. The court noted that "whether the deduction that the corporation takes for the owner-employee's salary really is a dividend can usually be answered by comparing the corporation's reported income with that of similar corporations, the comparison being stated in terms of percentage return on equity." This approach is known as the "independent investor test" and creates a rebutable presumption. In the case at hand, an accounting firm paid "consulting fees" to entities owned by the founders of the firms. There were no services provided for these fees. The court disallowed the deductions.
14. I.R.C. §132.
15. I.R.C. §§531-2.
16. I.R.C. §535(c).
17. Treas. Reg. §1.537-2.
18. I.R.C. §§537(a)(2), 537(b)(1).
19. Treas. Reg. §1.537-1(e)(3).
20. Treas. Reg. § 1.414(c)-4(b)(5)(ii)(A).
21. I.R.C. §385.
22. *Bradford-Robinson Printing Co. v. Comm'r.*, 1 AFTR 2d 1278 (D. Colo. 1957).
23. *Gazette Publishing Co. v. Self*, 103 F. Supp. 779 (E.D. Ark. 1952).

LIMITED LIABILITY COMPANIES

CHAPTER 51

Note: A checklist of issues to consider when choosing an entity, such as a proprietorship, partnership, Limited Liability Company (LLC), C corporation, or S corporation, appears in the Chapter on Planning for C Corporations at Figure 50.1.

51.1 INTRODUCTION

The limited liability company (LLC) is a form of business organization intended to obtain for investors, called members, the same advantages of limited liability as in the corporate form of business (if not more), while at the same time avoiding corporation income tax rules. All fifty states and the District of Columbia have adopted LLC statutes, although these statutes vary widely from state to state.

As noted above, the LLC is used to obtain the advantages of limited liability for investors and participants (i.e., they cannot be liable for debts of the entity beyond their investment), while being classified as a partnership for federal income tax purposes. The result is avoidance of corporate double tax on income, and in many situations, avoidance of any tax on liquidation. The impact of double taxation of income of normal ("C") corporations is discussed in connection with the S corporation in Chapter 53. Note that it is possible for an LLC to elect to be taxed as a C or S corporation, which may be superior for asset protection purposes in some states than using the traditional corporate form.

Another significant reason for the use of the LLC is that any losses incurred by the entity will be passed through and deductible by the members under the partnership rules, provided the LLC is classified as a partnership for income tax purposes (or if there is only a single member, as a sole proprietorship). No such pass-through is permitted in the case of a C corporation. Additionally, LLCs are easier and less expensive to start up with less complex ongoing requirements than is required by the corporate form.

It is helpful to compare the LLC to the S Corporation. See Figure 51.1.

From an estate planning standpoint, a major advantage of either the partnership, or an LLC classified as a partnership, over a C or S corporation is that upon the death of a partner or member, the partnership or LLC may elect to adjust the basis of its assets to fair market value to the extent of the decedent's interest.[1]

The LLC may also be considered an alternative to the family limited partnership, discussed in Chapter 49. The transfer of family business, real estate, or other investments to a family partnership has become a major estate planning technique. It would appear the LLC would function just as well in many cases, with the advantage that no family member needs to function as a "general" partner and assume liability for debts of the entity. However, as covered in the "Frequently Asked Questions" section below, there are potential problems with the use of an LLC in this situation.

In most jurisdictions, the LLC—or its counterpart the Limited Liability Partnership (LLP)—may also be used as a form of organization for a professional practice. The advantage is that while a professional will remain liable for his own errors or omissions in the practice or business, he or she can generally avoid liability for the acts of any of the other owners. In an ordinary professional partnership, each partner may be held liable for the errors or omissions of any other partner.

Figure 51.1

COMPARING S CORPORATION TO LLC taxed as a partnership)		
	S Corporation	LLC
Avoids Double Taxation?	Yes - Pass-through of Income	Yes - Pass-through of Income
Pass-through of Losses Allowed?	Yes	Yes
Limit on Number of Owners?	100	No limit
Types of Permissible Owners	Only individuals, estates, and certain trusts are permitted to be shareholders	No limit. Any individual or entity can be a member
Limitation on Pass-Through of Losses	Generally limited to income tax basis of shareholder's stock plus any loans to corporation	Limited to the amount of basis a member has in his membership interest.
Type of Classes Permissible	Only voting and nonvoting common stock may be issued	No limit on classes of memberships

51.2 WHAT ARE THE REQUIREMENTS?

The content of LLC statutes varies widely. Most statutes borrow heavily from the Uniform Limited Partnership Act (ULPA) discussed in Chapter 49 and about half the states have now passed some form of the Revised Uniform Limited Liability Company Act.

The "Check-the-Box" rules discussed below eliminate much – but not all – of the tax classification uncertainty with respect to LLCs.

While it is impossible to generalize on the various statutes, with variations, provisions regarding the following will be found in all of them:

1. There must be articles of organization that state the purposes for which the entity is formed. Those articles should provide that the entity can generally exercise the same powers as a partnership or corporation.

2. The participants/owners are called members. Originally, there had to be at least two members, but most states now permit LLCs with only one member (in which case it will default to being taxed as a sole proprietorship but can elect C or S corporation tax status). Individuals as well as various entities such as corporations, partnerships, trusts, and estates, can be members.

3. There are provisions for capital contributions similar to partnerships.

4. An LLC will have an operating agreement, which governs management of the entity. The LLC may have officers, like a corporation, if specified in the operating agreement. The agreement should also provide that the entity may be managed either by delegation to "Managers," who are elected in somewhat the same manner as a Board of Directors, or the right to management can be retained by all of the members. Unlike partnerships, voting in an LLC is generally in proportion to capital contributions. However, it may also be based on profit participation. To the extent that the LLC is "Manager Managed," it will operate like a traditional limited partnership where the general partner operates the entity and the limited partners are passive investors.

5. Allocation of profits and losses and distributions to members is generally covered by the operating agreement. Under most, if not all, statutes it is possible to have different classes of members who participate differently in profits, losses, and distributions.

6. Assignment of interests in the LLC generally follows the pattern of the limited partnership, with some unique characteristics. A complete assignment of an interest generally means the

assignor is no longer a member. However, just as in the case of a partnership, the assignee of an LLC interest does not automatically become a member, and is only entitled to receive distributions that would otherwise be made to the member. There may be a provision for admission of an assignee as a member based on a vote of the members or member-managers.

7. The dissolution of the entity, which also has considerable tax consequences, normally will occur upon the unanimous consent of the members, or if the LLC is formed for a fixed term, upon the expiration of that term. However, under most statutes, events such as death, disability, voluntary withdrawal, expulsion, or bankruptcy of a member results in automatic dissolution, unless the business is continued either by unanimous consent or majority vote of members.

8. Many of the legal requirements can be altered under many state statutes by provisions in the operating agreement or a separate business continuation agreement.

Example. Ten unrelated investors are considering establishing a joint venture to acquire and develop mining property in a western state. This is an extremely risky operation. But if it is successful, there will be large profits. If it is not successful, the investors would experience large losses. Also, the mining operation may result in considerable liability to its owners, both for debts incurred in the operations, and potential damages to adjacent property or injuries to workers. While some insurance is available to cover these risks, it may not be sufficient to cover the potential exposure.

These investors could form an S corporation, assuming they are all qualified shareholders, and achieve limited liability and direct pass-through of profits and most losses. However, they find the S corporation structure too limiting. Under their proposed agreement, different participants would share in profits and losses unequally, and an S corporation can have only voting and nonvoting stock, with no special allocation of profits and losses. They cannot use a general partnership, because they would all be personally liable for claims and lawsuits. They cannot use a limited partnership, because no participant is willing to assume the liabilities of a general partner.

The LLC would allow all members to achieve limited liability and to participate in the venture or delegate management, would enable the creation of different classes of ownership and participation, and would allow a direct pass-through of either profits or losses.

51.3 TAX IMPLICATIONS

The key to the use of the LLC is (assuming there are at least two members), almost always, is the classification of the entity as a partnership for federal income tax purposes. In the past, great effort was made to structure the LLC so that it had no more than two of the four corporate characteristics set forth in the regulations.[2] These are limited liability, centralized management, free transferability of interests, and continuity of life. However, because of an incredible number of cases on this issue, so called "Check-the-Box" regulations were issued to eliminate much of the uncertainty. To properly classify an entity, it is necessary to ask three questions:

1. Is there an entity separate and apart from its owners? If so,

2. Is that entity a trust – or is it a business entity? If it is a business entity, then

3. Is the entity – per se – a corporation? If "no," then it can elect its classification for federal tax purposes – merely by checking a box.

The regulations state that federal tax law and not state law determines whether or not an organization will be recognized as an entity separate from its owners.[3] A joint undertaking merely to share expenses will not be sufficient to be considered a separate entity - nor will mere co-ownership of property that is maintained, kept in repair, and rented or leased. On the other hand, the co-owners of an apartment building who provide services to tenants, directly or through an agent, have a separate entity. A joint venture or other contractual arrangement may also create a separate entity for tax purposes if the participants carry on a trade, business, financial operation, or venture and divide the profits.[4] It appears that the level of activity is the key factor.

An entity will be considered a business entity if it is not a trust (a trust has no associates or business objective[5]) or is subject to a special tax regime. Once considered a business entity, it will then be treated as (a) a corporation, (b) a partnership, or (c) a sole proprietorship. "Per se" corporations, which are typically ineligible to make a partnership election, include:

1. business entities incorporated under federal or state statutes where the statute describes or refers to the entity as incorporated or as a corporation;

2. associations;

3. joint stock companies;

4. insurance companies;

5. state-chartered banks insured by the FDIC;

6. business entities owned by a state or one of its political subdivisions;

7. business entities taxed as corporations under certain provisions of the Internal Revenue Code; or

8. certain foreign entities.[6]

A partnership is a business entity that is not a corporation and that has at least two members. (A business entity that is not a corporation but which has only one member is not considered an entity separate from its owner.[7]) The following chart summarizes the Check-the-Box regulations:[8]

TYPE OF ENTITY	TREATMENT
Corporation Under State Law or Publicly Traded Entity	Always Taxed as Corporation
Two or More Members (Partnership, Limited Partnership, LLC, LLP)	Taxed as Partnership Unless it Affirmatively Elects to be Taxed as Corporation
Single Member Unincorporated Association (e.g., 1 Person LLC)	Taxed as Sole Proprietorship Unless it Affirmatively Elects to be Taxed as Corporation

These rules make it possible – without risk of being considered a corporation for federal income tax purposes – for a partnership or LLC to have officers and a board of managers, permanent life, freely transferable certificates, and even limited liability. The election to change classification from the default in the chart above is made by the eligible entity by filing Form 8832, Entity Classification Election, within the first seventy-five days after the year to which it applies.

Does a mere checking of a box eliminate all problems and uncertainty? Probably not. Nor is it clear that if the only asset in the entity is life insurance that the IRS will recognize the entity as a partnership merely because a box was checked – especially if the entity would not qualify as a partnership under state law. This is particularly important for transfer for value purposes.[9] Although a life insurance death benefit is typically received income tax free under Code section 101(a), an exception to this general rule is when a life insurance policy has been transferred for "valuable consideration." To ensure that the death benefit proceeds will still be income tax free, the transfer must fall under one of the exceptions outlined in the Code.[10] Exceptions to the "transfer-for-value" rule include a transfer to a partner of the insured or to a partnership in which the insured is a partner. However, the partnership should have a legitimate business purpose – if the partnership is established solely to own life insurance and circumvent the transfer-for-value rule, it is unclear if the exception to the rule will apply. Until the IRS rules in this area, caution is advised, especially if the LLC or partnership holds only life insurance or marketable securities. It is highly likely, however, that pooling money among two or more participants to make such investments together to make a profit and assist with another business would be a partnership for tax purposes.

While an LLC is typically used when multiple individuals want to operate a business together, it is also possible to form a one person, or "single member', LLC. A one person LLC allows an individual to operate a business and still have limited liability protection. This approach is also possible with a corporation. However, when a one person LLC is formed, unless the member elects otherwise, it is treated as a sole proprietorship for tax purposes, and provided there are no employees, will generally not need to get a separate tax identification number, or file a separate federal income tax return. Note that it may still be necessary to file a separate tax return for state income tax purposes. Note that for federal income tax purposes, grantor trusts and beneficiary deemed owner trusts are generally ignored in favor of their deemed owner, so it is possible to have multiple grantor trusts and their grantor be owners for state law purposes, yet there be only one owner for federal income tax purposes.

51.4 ISSUES IN COMMUNITY PROPERTY STATES

In a community property state, the investment in an LLC may be of cash or property which is characterized as community or marital property under state law. In such cases, the IRS has ruled that the number of members in the LLC will be determined by the spouses' characterization of the LLC, either as a disregarded entity (e.g., a single-member LLC) or a partnership.[11] Thus, if only one spouse is listed as a member, it may be characterized as a single member LLC. If both spouses are listed as members, it will be a two-member LLC.

Where the membership carries voting or management rights, this classification may be material as to the rights of the spouse of a member to participate in either a vote or management decisions. While state law may vary on this point, some states, such as Californi13a, generally restrict the voting or management to the spouse who is designated as the member. If this is not true in a particular jurisdiction, it may be necessary to make the spouses parties to the operating agreement to clear up voting and management rights.

In the event of death of either the member or non-member spouse, or a divorce, the rights in the membership may be divided to reflect the rights of the spouses under state community property laws. It would appear a nonmember spouse who is assigned an interest in the membership would not have the full rights of a member, but would be treated as an assignee of an interest as described in the foregoing discussion. However, this will again depend on the law of the particular state.

Also, upon the death of either spouse, the LLC should consider making a timely election under IRC Section 754 to adjust the income tax basis of the community property interest in the assets of the LLC to the date of death value of the community property interest.

51.5 USING AN LLC TO TRANSFER A FAMILY BUSINESS OR INVESTMENTS

In most family limited partnerships, discussed in Chapter 49, the entity is formed by parents or members of a senior generation who transfer business or investment assets to a partnership in which they retain general partnership interests. They then make gifts of limited partnership interests to children or younger generation members.

One drawback of the family limited partnership is the fact that senior generation members, by acting as general partners, assume personal liability for any debts or obligations of the venture. Using an LLC has the great advantage of allowing the senior family members to avoid personal liability. They may still retain management of the business or investments by providing in the articles or operating agreement that they will be the managing members.

A major problem with the use of the LLC in place of the family limited partnership is that unless the LLC operating agreement specifies otherwise, under some states' laws, the entity will dissolve on the death, withdrawal, etc., of any member for any reason. This would permit transferees to force a dissolution of the entity, unless there is either a unanimous or majority vote, depending on state law, of the remaining members to continue the entity. Many senior family members would not be willing to confer that power on the younger generation. In a family limited partnership, only the withdrawal of the last remaining general partner will trigger a dissolution.

As discussed in Chapter 49, one of the reasons for the use of family limited partnerships as a vehicle for gifts is the ability to claim valuation adjustments or discounts to reflect the fact that the transferred limited partnership interests are not marketable, represent minority interests, have no right to participate in control of the entity, and most important, cannot force a dissolution of the entity. In the case of the LLC, the withdrawal of a member for any reason, as noted above, may result in dissolution of the entity. This provided the IRS with a good argument that valuation discounts should be eliminated - or at least substantially reduced, since the transferee members are in a position, by withdrawing from the LLC, to realize the net asset value of their interests in the LLC. It may be possible under a state LLC statute to modify the right of transferee members to withdraw from the LLC. Prior to the Check-the-Box rules, this would create the risk of the entity being classified as a corporation for federal tax purposes, but it should not present a problem under current regulations.

However, even if there is no issue of whether the entity will be taxed as a corporation or a partnership, there is still a major problem: Under Code section

2704(b), any restriction on the rights of the members to force a liquidation of the LLC which are greater than those imposed by state law will be ignored in valuing their interests. Since the so-called "default" rule under most state LLC statutes is that the entity will dissolve if a membership interest terminates for any reason, that rule can only be modified by a contrary agreement among the members. The IRS will likely characterize this as a restriction which will be ignored under section 2704(b) for valuation purposes. It will instead value the transferred interests on the assumption that those members can force a dissolution of the LLC and reach the underlying assets, thus negating the argument that a valuation discount based on a member's inability to unilaterally reach his/her share of the underlying assets should be allowed. Only a change in underlying state law will eliminate this problem.

As of this writing, some states have begun to modify their LLC statutes to avoid the so-called "default" rules of section 2704(b). In particular, Arizona has limited the value of the interest of a family member who withdraws from an LLC, and Colorado has restricted the rights of members who withdraw to receive the full liquidation value of their interests in the LLC.

If the LLC is classified as a partnership for federal income tax purposes, it will likely be subject to the special restrictions on family partnerships under Code section 704(e) as discussed in Chapter 49. Basically, the allocation of income to transferee partners will not be recognized for federal income tax purposes if capital is not a material factor in producing the income, substantial capital interests are not transferred, or the managing transferor family members are not adequately compensated for their services. In addition, the regulations under section 704(e) provide the allocation of income to transferees will not be recognized if the transferors retain too much control over the transferred interests.

51.6 FREQUENTLY ASKED QUESTIONS

Question – Is there any way of achieving limited liability for the senior family members in the family limited partnership?

Answer – *Yes, but an LLC may be superior.* The IRS has issued several rulings, five holding that the general partner in a limited partnership could be a corporation, and in particular, an S corporation. Note that under those rulings, the corporation must have at least a one percent interest in the partnership, and should have some substantial assets. Thus, the senior family members could form a corporation which they control to act as general partner, and could generally be successful in avoiding personal liability. It seems likely they could also use an LLC as the general partner in the family limited partnership. However, when a corporation is used as a general partner, there are two tax returns which must be filed each year; one for the corporate general partner; and one for the partnership as a whole. If an LLC is used, the same objectives can be accomplished with having to file only one tax return each year.

Question – Is the LLC a better alternative for unrelated individuals entering into new ventures or investments?

Answer – With only a few exceptions, the LLC is probably now the entity of choice for a variety of new business enterprises, particularly those that involve a degree of risk, or are likely to generate losses.

Like the S corporation, the participating members in the LLC may fully participate in the management and operation of the venture without exposure to personal liability. Examples include real estate, investments in mineral rights, and oil and gas. It should be noted, however, that there is always some possible exposure to liability, as in the case of shareholders in a corporation, if the entity is undercapitalized or used in an abusive manner, or if, as is almost always the case with small businesses, the members sign as individuals on business loans or guarantee the debts of the business. However, the entity is not subject to the limitations which apply to S corporations, discussed above.

Question – Is the LLC the entity of choice for professional practices?

Answer – In the states that permit its use for professional practices, it has already become the entity of choice. Most major accounting firms have already been reformed as LLCs or LLPs, as have many major law firms. What is good for the large professional firms is probably also good for small professional practices.

Question – Can a charity form a single member LLC to avoid liability?

Answer – In Notice 2012-52, after years of neglecting to answer this question, the IRS provided guidance on this issue. Now charities and donors are assured that a contribution to a disregarded single member LLC, owned and operated by a charity, will be deductible so long as the requirements of Code section 170 are otherwise met. The particular LLC in that situation was formed to engage in an unrelated trade or business (which was not significant enough to cause the charity to lose tax-exempt status).[12] See LISI Charitable Planning Newsletter No. 190 (August 9, 2012).

Question – How are pass-through entities such as an LLC impacted by recent tax law changes?

Answer – The Tax Cuts and Jobs Act of 2017 permanently reduced the corporate tax rate to 21 percent, making the corporate form appear more attractive than ever. However, the TCJA also enacted a new Code section 199A which allows a deduction for owners of pass-through entities, including members of an LLC, to deduct up to 20 percent of "qualified business income" (QBI). The new "199A deduction" is subject to strict testing limitations and requirements, including a reduction for owners with income over certain thresholds and the availability of the deduction for specified service trades or businesses (e.g., health professionals, attorneys, consultants, etc.) is severely limited (unavailable over certain income thresholds). Moreover, the deduction is limited to 50 percent of an owner's pro rata share of W-2 wages paid by the business. However, for LLC members which qualify for the deduction, the effective federal tax rate may be lower for these individuals. (Note, under current law, the 199A deduction for qualified business income is allowed for years 2018-2025 only.) Clients must work with tax counsel to determine which choice of entity is most beneficial under current law.

CHAPTER ENDNOTES

1. I.R.C. §§743(b), 754. For a useful and detailed discussion of the LLC, see Commito, *Working with LLCs and FLPs*, National Underwriter Company (2d ed. 2000).
2. Treas. Reg. §§301.7701-1, 301.7701-2, as in effect prior to January 1, 1997.
3. Treas. Reg. §301.7701-1(a).
4. Treas. Reg. §301.7701-1(a)(2).
5. Treas. Reg. §301.7701-1(b).
6. Treas. Reg. §301.7701-2(b).
7. Treas. Reg. §301.7701-2(c)(2)(i).
8. TD 8697 and Notice 97-1, 1997-1 CB 348, which makes obsolete prior rules under I.R.C. §7701.
9. See Brody and Leimberg, "Avoiding the Tax Trap of the Transfer for Value Rule", *Estate Planning*, vol. 32, no. 10, pg. 3 and Brody and Leimberg, "Using a Transactional Analysis to Avoid the Transfer for Value Rule", *Estate Planning*, vol. 32, no. 11, pg. 3.
10. I.R.C. §101(a)(2).
11. Rev. Proc. 2002-69.
12. New York has a sales and use tax provision that imposes tax liability on a LP or LLC member solely by reason of that person's status as a limited partner or LLC member of an entity that has not paid the taxes. It imposes personal liability for unpaid entity taxes on persons who have the authority to cause the tax to be paid and have willfully failed to do so. So the liability is based solely on the person's status.

PERSONAL HOLDING COMPANY

CHAPTER 52

52.1 INTRODUCTION

The term "personal holding company" might be used in a generic sense, such as an LLC owning several single member LLCs that in turn own different parcels of real estate. This term also refers to a specific tax classification, and it often comes up after a portion or all of an active C corporation is liquidated and the proceeds used to invest in more passive investments. More specifically for corporate tax purposes, a personal holding company is a corporation that meets two particular tests (and is not specifically excluded from such status).[1] These two tests are: (1) a stock ownership test; and (2) an income test. Both tests must be met in the same taxable year so that it is possible for a corporation to attain personal holding company status in one year and not in the next.

The *stock ownership* test works like this: The corporation meets the stock ownership requirements if more than 50 percent of the value of its outstanding stock is owned directly or indirectly by or for five or fewer individuals at any time during the last half of the taxable year.[2]

The *income test* is sometimes referred to as the "60 percent test." If the stock ownership test has been met and at least 60 percent or more of the corporation's adjusted ordinary gross income is personal holding company income (generally passive income such as dividends, interest, certain royalties, rents, or amounts received in return for a certain type of personal services), the corporation will be classified as a personal holding company.[3]

If a corporation meets the definition of a personal holding company, a penalty tax (in addition to regular corporate income tax) is imposed on the undistributed personal holding company income. The Taxpayer Relief Act of 2012, increased the personal holding company tax to 20 percent.[4] The Tax Cuts and Jobs Act (TCJA) of 2017 did not modify the rules related to personal holding companies but did modify the graduated corporate tax rate system to a single, flat 21 percent corporate tax rate. Therefore, if a corporation has undistributed personal holding income, it may have a substantial total corporate tax liability of 41 percent.

For that reason, if a corporation is to be formed to hold passive assets which would constitute personal holding income and with the requisite ownership interest that would cause it to be subject to the 20 percent penalty tax, proper planning is essential. To avoid meeting the income test, property that produces personal holding company income, such as rental property, should be sold. Conversely, diversifying its activities so as to produce more active than passive income, the corporation could avoid meeting the 60 percent test.

Finally, distributions of dividends paid during the tax year in amounts sufficient to avoid the 60 percent test would be prudent. Another possible way to avoid the penalty tax is to expand the number of unrelated shareholders beyond five. Additionally, in certain instances where a corporation has undistributed personal holding income and would otherwise be subject to the penalty, a "deficiency dividend" may be issued retroactively to provide relief from the penalty.[5]

Care should be exercised in the use of personal holding companies based on the repeal of the *General Utilities* doctrine by the Tax Reform Act of 1986. If assets in the corporation appreciate, generally there will be two taxes created, one at the corporate level (upon a sale of the assets or liquidation of the corporation) and one at the shareholder level (upon a liquidation of the corporation or dividend distribution).

Assuming a personal holding company can be formed in a manner that does not invoke the penalty tax, it is important to have a business purpose when establishing the personal holding company. This technique is subject to many of the same considerations associated with the use of family limited partnerships. Therefore, it is important to follow a similar analysis in determining the appropriateness of this planning device.

52.2 WHEN IS USE OF SUCH A DEVICE INDICATED?

1. Where an individual has a large estate consisting of highly appreciated and readily marketable securities and wants to reduce federal estate taxes attributable to those assets by transferring shares to family members or other individuals, a master LP/LLC to own and transfer such assets may be warranted, but care should be taken to usually avoid Code section 542 and the "personal holding company" definition. LPs/LLCs are generally the entity of choice to hold disparate investments, but unless it is a single member disregarded LLC, such an entity cannot hold S corporation stock without terminating the S election.

52.3 WHAT ARE THE REQUIREMENTS?

A corporation is formed by an individual who owns a substantial amount of appreciated property. The individual transfers a portfolio of common stock of various companies to a newly formed closely held corporation in return for its stock. This transfer can be accomplished without recognition of any gain provided that the transferor controls 80 percent of the voting power and 80 percent of each class of stock immediately after the transfer.[6]

The individual transferring this stock will have a basis (cost for purposes of determining gain or loss) in the new stock equal to the basis in the property transferred to the corporation (i.e., "carry-over basis").[7] Likewise, the corporation will receive the portfolio stock transferred to it with the same basis this property had in the individual's hands.[8]

Example. Denise Lopez, a wealthy investor, purchased shares of Gro-Quick, a closely held corporation, many years ago. These shares are now worth ten times what she paid for them and are continuing to appreciate rapidly. If Denise retains the stock, the shares will be includable in her estate. If she gives them away, she will incur a sizable gift tax. Furthermore, some of her beneficiaries are minor children and she does not want to make outright gifts. However, she does not want to use a trust because of certain administrative problems associated with a trust.

Denise forms a corporation by transferring her Gro-Quick stock (fair market value of $1,000,000). In exchange for the stock, Denise receives non-voting common stock with a fair market value of $800,000 and voting common stock with a fair market value of $200,000. The stock Denise received is 100 percent of the new corporation's stock. (The breakdown is arbitrary and can be varied according to the particular situation.)

Since one of Denise's main objectives is to maintain control of the new corporation and limit future appreciation includible in her estate, she retains the voting stock and begins gifting the non-voting common. Over a period of years, Denise gifts the non-voting common stock (fair market value $800,000) to family members. Because Denise retained all the voting common stock, she continues to direct and control the corporation's investments. Moreover, with the high gift tax applicable exemption and the annual exclusions, there would be no gift tax owing on the gifted non-voting common stock. Since the non-voting common represents 80 percent of the financial growth of the corporation, substantial future appreciation is removed from Denise's estate. For example, if after the gifts of non-voting common stock, the corporate assets double in value, 80 percent of that appreciation is attributed to the gifted stock, and, thus is removed from Denise's estate.

Note that in the above example it has become more common to use an LLC for this purpose in recent years, but you may still see many legacy corporations previously established for this purpose. This technique is also beneficial when the gifted assets are not readily divisible, such as artwork. By transferring this type of asset to a corporation and gifting a percentage of the stock to beneficiaries, a fractional interest in the asset can be transferred while the donor retains control over the corporation. Again, however, the LLC has become the entity of choice for holding/transferring passive holdings such as this.

Beware: In the case of family corporations, the use of common and preferred stock in either capitalizing or recapitalizing the entity, followed by a transfer of shares to other family members by gift or sale, may and probably will create a gift tax valuation problem under Code section 2701 or a gift, estate, or generation-skipping transfer tax problem if restrictions on certain classes of stock lapse under Code section 2704. However, this problem will not occur in the case of an unmarried couple or a transfer between two unrelated friends since it would fall outside the scope of section 2701.

An additional benefit to transferring significant assets to a corporation is that the value of the corporate stock may be worth less than the value of the assets in the corporation. Courts have consistently allowed discounts of 10 percent and more (in one case as much as 55 percent). This is because a shareholder in a personal holding company (particularly a minority shareholder) has no control over the underlying assets. Thus, an investor would place a higher value of a direct ownership interest in stock held in a personal holding company than he or she would in a personal holding company that owned such stock.

Example. A gift of 100 shares of AT&T has greater value than a gift of 10 percent of the stock in a personal holding company owning 1,000 shares of AT&T. For example, unlike shares of personal holding company stock, shares of AT&T stock are readily tradable in the stock market. This is the primary reason for the discount from the net asset value of the underlying shares. (See Figure 52.1, which illustrates the percentage discounts allowed in a number of personal holding company cases.) Thus, in the example above, Denise's 20 percent voting common shares in the corporation holding the portfolio stock she transferred to it may be valued for estate tax purposes at considerably less than the $200,000 that the underlying portfolio stock is worth. (The value of a gift of less than a controlling interest would be further reduced because of the lack of voting control.) Again, note that the LLC has become the entity of choice for such planning in most situations now.

52.4 TAX IMPLICATIONS

1. As mentioned above, substantial estate and gift tax savings may be possible through any number of valuation discounts. (See the list of cases in Figure 52.1.) However, these discounts are subject to IRS scrutiny. In order to maintain these discounts, it is important that the business have a purpose and the formalities in operating the business are properly followed.

2. The individual forming the personal holding company who performs bona fide services is entitled to receive a salary. Assuming the salary paid is reasonable and depending on other income, he or she will be taxed at a maximum rate of 37 percent that in most cases will be fully deductible by the corporation. Any excess compensation (compensation deemed unreasonable) would be subject to tax at the corporate level (nondeductible) and then taxed at the individual level as a dividend. Operating expenses may even generate a net operating loss. (Local and state franchise taxes should be considered.)

3. The taxable income of the corporation can be lowered further by providing a working stockholder and working members of his family with various fringe benefits. These include a qualified pension or profit-sharing plan. Furthermore, some medical expenses may be deductible. These expenses must be reasonable in view of the services performed by the employee shareholder. Note, the deductibility of certain fringe benefits such as deductions for entertainment expenses, meals, and transportation were eliminated or repealed under the TCJA.

4. Under prior law, a corporation received a carryover deduction for a net operating loss up to 100 percent, which could be carried back two years and carried forward twenty years. The TCJA notably limits the net operating loss deduction to 80 percent of taxable income in a given year. Additionally, under the new law, net operating losses are still allowed to be carried forward, but NOLs cannot be carried back to prior years. The CARES Act created another temporary exception to the NOL carryback for years before 2021.

5. There is, of course, a substantial disadvantage if a personal holding company is not properly handled. As discussed throughout this chapter, undistributed personal holding income is subject to a penalty

Figure 52.1

PERSONAL HOLDING COMPANY CASES INVOLVING ESTATE TAX DISCOUNTS

Case	Company & Holdings	Shs. to be Valued	Total Shares	Discount Allowed
Celia Waterman 20 TCM 281 (1960)	Maxcell Corp. (Apt bldgs)	299	571	30.8%
Lida E. Tompkins Est. 20 TCM 1763 (1961)	H Street Building Corp. (Gen'l real estate business, building, contracting and construction)	186	650	32.8%
Drybrough v. U.S. 60 TCM 645 (W.D. Ky 1962)	(5 separate real estate holding companies)			35.0%
Harry S. Leyman 40 TC 100 (1963)	Leyman Corp. (Real estate, 2 Buick agencies, parking garages)	2,309	9,400	36.7%
Hamm v. Comm'r. 325 F.2d 934 (8th Cir. 1963)	United Properties, Inc. (Commercial real estate and 10 closely held subsidiaries)	263N	1,000	27.2%
Gregg Maxcy Est. 28 TCM 783 (1969) Rev'd on appeal, 441 F.2d 192 (5th Cir. 1971)	Maxcy Securities, Inc. (Citrus grove, restaurant, mortgages (1) and accounts receivable (2))	164 86	174 174	15.0% 25.0%
Heckscher v. Comm'r. 63 TC 485 (1975)	Anaheim Realty Co. (Undeveloped Florida real estate and securities)	2,500	108,675	48.3%
Lloyd R. Smith Est. 9 TCM 907 (1950)	Smith Investment Co. (Stock of A O Smith Corp)	408	1,860	22.1%
Bishop Tr. Co. Ltd. v. U.S. 501 USTC ¶10,764 (DC Hawaii 1950)	Henry P. Baldwin Ltd. (Stock listed on Honolulu Exchange)	1,861	15,000	32.8%
Goss v. Fitzpatrick 97 F. Supp. 765 (D.C. Conn. 1951)	Alden M. Young Co. (Marketable securities; some real estate)	1,900	13,518	42.9%
Clarence J. Grootematt, Est. 79,049 (P-H)	Greendale Land Co. (development and sale of real estate)	40	400	25.0%
Ernest A. Oberting Est. TC Memo 1984-407	Warrior Oil Co. (percent interest in Indonesian oil contracts)	45	225	65.0%
Estate of Cotchett TC Memo 1974-31	Eddy Investment Co. (cash and marketable securities)	20,692	103,621	34.0%
Estate of Hayes TC Memo 1973-236	DuQuoin Coca Cola (farm land, dairy business, soft drink bottling business)	930	5,952	25.0%

tax of 20 percent. Moreover, as in any corporation, there is the potential for double taxation (the first incident when the corporation sells securities and again when the shareholder receives the proceeds or other property as a dividend or on the liquidation of the corporation). However, the potential for double taxation can be minimized or eliminated by carefully controlling the type of investments and expenses incurred. Most now prefer LLCs (partnerships).

The other problem is the imposition of state capital stock or franchise tax on the value of the personal holding company stock or on the net income remaining in the corporation each year.

6. Although in some cases it is still desirable to use a personal holding company to achieve gift and estate tax savings for appreciated assets, the TCJA of 2017 increased the lifetime exemption to $10 million per person ($12,920,000 in 2023), meaning the majority of Americans will no longer face a federal estate tax under current law. Even when the exemption is scheduled to return to a $5,000,000 exemption (indexed for inflation) after December 31, 2025, many Americans will still never be subject to federal estate tax. For these individuals, income tax planning is particularly important. In many cases, receiving a step-up in basis at death may be more beneficial to heirs than the estate and gift tax savings (if any) which could be achieved under this technique. Moreover, as discussed earlier in this chapter, if achieving gift and estate tax savings is a top planning priority, given the potential for double taxation and the 20 percent penalty, other entities (such as an FLP or an LLC) may achieve the same goals without the added tax problems. Clients should work with their advisors to determine the most appropriate strategy based upon their particular circumstances.

52.5 HOW CAN LIFE INSURANCE ENHANCE THIS TOOL?

It is possible to transfer life insurance policies to a personal holding company, in addition to other assets. For instance, an individual could transfer existing life insurance policies (term or whole life) which may have a lower present value as compared with the policies' face amounts to the personal holding company in exchange for voting common stock. (The value of a life insurance policy when it is sold for valuable consideration is its "fair market value." Fair market value may be determined by using one or more of the following valuation approaches: unearned premium, ITR, PERC value, cash surrender value.[9] Tax/legal counsel should be consulted to determine the most appropriate valuation methodology.) Alternatively, the personal holding company could purchase insurance on the life of the holder of the voting stock. By then giving non-voting common stock in the holding company to the donee-family members (alternatively, the corporation could sell those family members stock for cash or other property), most of the eventual appreciation due to the death value of the life insurance can be transferred out of the donor-owner's estate.

Because the decedent's executor will have voting control over the personal holding company by virtue of his ownership of the personal holding company voting common stock, that individual could direct the corporation to make a section 303 stock redemption of corporate stock held by the estate, thus providing estate liquidity.

52.6 ISSUES IN COMMUNITY PROPERTY STATES

The particular form of property ownership between spouses holding an interest in a corporation classified as a personal holding company has no particular bearing on meeting the stock ownership test, by virtue of the family attribution rules.[10] That is, the ownership interest of one's spouse will be attributed to the other spouse, regardless of whether the spouse's interest is community or separate property.

However, for estate planning purposes, a community property form of ownership is advantageous, as compared to joint tenancy or tenancy in common, because of the step-up in the tax basis of both halves of the community property on the death of one spouse. Under IRC Section 542, a personal holding company is a corporation where

1. at least 60 percent of the adjusted ordinary gross income of which is personal holding company income (i.e., dividends, interest, royalties, and certain rents); and

2. more than 50 percent of the stock of which is owned by five or fewer individuals.

Of particular importance to estate planners when dealing with a personal holding company is the classification of the income produced by the enterprise, because, in order to meet the 60 percent test, a significant amount of the income must be classified as personal holding company income.

If the stock ownership is community property, then, absent an agreement to the contrary, the income will also be community property. However, as noted in Chapter 49 on Family Limited Partnerships, in some community property states, if the stock ownership is separate property, this does not necessarily mean that the income produced, or any accretion in value, will also be separate property.

As previously discussed in Chapter 46, if an increase in the value of separate property is attributable to the ability or activity of either spouse, for which the community has not been sufficiently rewarded (e.g., by an appropriate salary), at least a portion of that increase may well be determined to be community property (thereby reducing the gross estate of the original owner-spouse).

In addition, the income produced may be classified as both community and separate property. If one spouse invests separate property in a business and conducts that business during marriage, without adequate reward to the community for the spouse's efforts, the resulting profits may be community and separate property in proportion to the amounts attributable to the personal efforts and to capital investment, respectively.

In such circumstance, depending on which spouse dies first, it may be important to be able to show that the profits from, and appreciation in value of, the business are from one (or both) spouse's efforts, rather than merely a natural enhancement in value, in order to spread the increased value between the two estates, and to provide a step-up in basis for both halves of the community property at the first death. If the spouse who originally owned the business dies first, then the entire business will receive a "stepped-up" basis regardless of the amount of community property effort.

52.7 FREQUENTLY ASKED QUESTIONS

Question – How can stock be shifted to children and grandchildren without incurring gift tax costs if the children do not have cash or other property to purchase the stock?

Answer – The parent of a child can lend money directly to children or their custodian or to an irrevocable trust established for their benefit, or guarantee a loan between the child and a third party, such as a bank.[11] The child (or trust) can then purchase stock directly from the corporation for cash. The child could obtain cash to pay back the loan if the personal holding company declares dividends on the common stock. Income shifting from parent to child (to the extent the kiddie tax does not apply) – and therefore income tax savings – can potentially be achieved.

Question – Assuming that personal holding company status is – at some date – considered onerous, how can such classification be avoided?

Answer – As mentioned above, there are two tests – both of which must be met – before a corporation will be classified as a personal holding company. The first requires that five or fewer shareholders own more than 50 percent of the value of the stock at some time during the last six months of the taxable year. This test can be sidestepped by distributing ownership of shares to a sufficient number of unrelated parties or by issuing a second class of stock to a sufficient number of unrelated parties to fall outside the five or fewer shareholders test or to dilute ownership value to fall below the 50 percent of ownership threshold.

The second test requires that personal holding company income be greater than or equal to 60 percent of adjusted ordinary gross income. To avoid this test, property that produces personal holding company income, such as rental property, can be transferred out of the corporation (with potential tax consequences). Conversely, by producing more active as opposed to passive income within the corporation, the 60 percent test can be avoided.

Furthermore, expenses related to adjusted ordinary gross income can be deferred into future periods or a depreciation method can be selected to maximize adjusted ordinary gross income.

Finally, if there is a potential personal holding company liability, cash dividends can be paid out during the tax year, post year-end dividends can be paid, consent dividend procedures can be used, deficiency dividend procedures can be used and, as a final last-ditch alternative, the corporation can be liquidated. However, the lack of a capital gains deduction upon a sale or exchange or liquidation makes the liquidation alternative more expensive. In addition, gain from appreciated property that the corporation distributes will be taxed at the corporate level. If the corporation does not have any earnings and profits (or declares a dividend to eliminate any), it can elect S corporation status and avoid any personal holding company tax regardless of the level of passive income. This is because S corporations are not subject to tax under Chapter 1 of the Internal Revenue Code.[12] Such an election may bring into play the built-in gain rules.[13]

Question – Is the personal holding company technique a sure fire way to obtain an estate or gift tax valuation discount?

Answer – Not every personal holding company will result in an estate or gift tax valuation discount. In one case, the value of stock in two personal holding companies that were owned by the decedent was not reduced by a lack of marketability discount.[14] The court held that the proper estate tax value was the net asset value of the companies less the cost involved in liquidating them. Note that the result occurred because the decedent owned 100 percent of both companies and therefore had the unqualified right to liquidate them at any time. Note also that all the assets in both companies were cash or marketable securities, and that neither corporation had any significant liabilities. Planners should use this case as a "how not to do it" guideline. Another area where a discount may be available relates to a discount in the value of the stock in order to recognize the built-in capital gains tax associated with liquidation of the corporation.[15]

CHAPTER ENDNOTES

1. I.R.C. §542(c) contains ten types of business entities that are specifically excluded from personal holding company status, such as tax-exempt corporations, banks, and life insurance companies.
2. I.R.C. §542(a)(2). The ownership test pertains to value and not to the number of outstanding shares. Under constructive ownership rules an individual is deemed to own all the stock directly or indirectly owned by or for his brothers and sisters, spouse, ancestors, and lineal descendants. Likewise, stock owned directly or indirectly by or for a corporation, partnership, estate, or trust is considered as being owned proportionately by its shareholders, partners, or beneficiaries. I.R.C. §544(a).
3. I.R.C. §542(a)(1). "Adjusted ordinary gross income" is essentially gross income less gains from sales or other dispositions of capital assets and I.R.C. §1231 property, and further reduced by depreciation, certain taxes, interest, and rents attributable to income from certain rents and royalties. I.R.C. §543(b).
4. Taxpayer Relief Act of 2012, §102(c)(1).
5. I.R.C. §547.
6. I.R.C. §§351, 368(c); Treas. Reg. §1.351-1(a).
7. I.R.C. §358(a).
8. I.R.C. §362(a).
9. Rev. Rul. 2005-25.
10. I.R.C. §544(a)(2).
11. TRA '84 severely limited the utility of interest-free loans. See I.R.C. §7872. Also, note the IRS position in PLR 9113009 that a guarantee, for less than full and adequate consideration, is a completed gift for gift tax purpose. (This ruling was withdrawn by the IRS in PLR 9409018 without comment on the taxable gift issue.)
12. I.R.C. §1363.
13. I.R.C. §1374.
14. *Est. of Jephson v. Comm'r.*, 87 TC 297 (1986).
15. *Eisenberg v. Comm'r.*, 82 AFTR 2d 98-5757 (155 F.3d 50); AOD 1999-001, 2/01/1999 in which the IRS acquiesced in the concept that a discount for built in capital gains may be appropriate. The IRS concluded that there was no legal prohibition against such a discount and the amount and circumstances of such discount will depend upon the facts of each case.

PLANNING WITH S CORPORATIONS

CHAPTER 53

53.1 INTRODUCTION

An "S" corporation is a corporation (or an LLC that has elected to be taxed as a corporation) that has made an election under Subchapter S of the Internal Revenue Code to have its income, deductions, capital gains and losses, charitable contributions, and credits passed through to its shareholders. To a great extent, an S corporation is treated for tax purposes similarly to a partnership, but there are important exceptions.

Note: A checklist of issues to consider when choosing an entity, such as a proprietorship, partnership, limited liability company (LLC), C corporation, or S corporation, appears in Chapter 50 as Figure 50.1.

53.2 WHEN IS USE OF SUCH A DEVICE INDICATED?

1. When a client (currently a sole proprietor or partnership) is entering a new business and would like the legal protection against creditors offered by corporate status, but wants to be able to personally deduct losses of the business enterprise if the venture fails. (This same goal can be achieved to a limited degree through the use of Code section 1244 stock in a normal corporation.)

    An "S" election enables corporate losses (in addition to income) to be passed through the corporation and deducted on the tax returns of the individual shareholders (but only to the extent of the adjusted basis of their stock in the corporation and loans made to the corporation).[1] Thus, losses of an S corporation may be used to offset income earned outside of the business.

2. Where the business, although not inherently risky, has a period of loss during the first years of starting up, the client may elect S corporation status for the early loss years. When the business begins to make a profit, the election may be terminated and future profits taxed at separate corporate tax rates. The method and other effects of the conversion from S corporation to a regular corporation ("C corporation") should be carefully planned.

3. When the stockholder(s) desire one layer of taxation – i.e., distributions of some or all corporate income without being subject to the normal double taxation on corporate earnings and such payments could not be justified as reasonable compensation. In other words, by electing S corporation status, there is generally no tax at the corporate level. Instead, income earned by the S corporation is taxed only once, as a distribution to the individual shareholders, regardless of the amount of income or the services performed, if any, by the shareholders. S corporations are unique in that distributions made to a shareholder are not subject to employment taxes (i.e., social security and Medicare tax). Caveat: If a shareholder performs significant services for the corporation (i.e., a doctor) and does not receive "reasonable compensation," the IRS has the authority to re-characterize some or all of the S corporation income as compensation. Therefore, it is important that a shareholder who performs services for the S corporation be paid reasonable compensation.

    Double taxation has always been the consequence of the accumulation of income earned in a C corporation. Double taxation under current law is even more onerous than in the past. There are four reasons:

737

a. The corporate tax rate may exceed individual rates (although per the Tax Cuts and Jobs Act (TCJA) of 2017, the corporate tax rate was permanently reduced to a flat 21 percent tax rate).

b. A corporate liquidation of appreciated property (assets with a fair market value in excess of their tax basis) or even in kind distributions of the appreciated property itself, will trigger both corporate and shareholder level taxes.[2]

c. Corporate gains on capital assets are taxed at the same corporate rate as all other income, i.e., there is no preferential long term capital gains tax rate for C corporations.

d. The net proceeds of the gain or other corporate income already taxed at the corporate level are again taxed when distributed to shareholders.

The double taxation problem suffered by C corporations' shareholders year after year can be alleviated, or in some cases even eliminated, by an increase in shareholders' salaries (thus reducing corporate taxable income). However, as noted above, compensation is subject to social security and Medicare tax, and is in some extreme cases, can be deemed unreasonably high and denied a deduction.

But this ploy of increasing shareholder salaries in the year of liquidation when the corporation would likely be subject to a potentially huge tax may not work. First, the unusually high tax triggered in the year of liquidation may be many times the normal "double tax." Second, justifying proportionately large salaries in the year of liquidation may be hard to do. Because income averaging is not an option, the ultimate tax on a final liquidation could consume the product of years of hard work.

4. When the non-tax benefits of incorporation are desired and it is also more advantageous from a tax-perspective to have income earned by the corporation taxed directly to shareholders at their individual rate. Although the TCJA permanently reduced the corporate tax rate to 21 percent, making C corporation status appear more attractive than ever, the TCJA also enacted a new Code section 199A which allows a deduction for pass-through entities, including S corporations, of up to 20 percent of "qualified business income" (QBI). The new "199A deduction" is subject to strict testing limitations and requirements, including a reduction for owners with income over certain thresholds and the availability of the deduction for specified service trades or businesses (e.g., health professionals, attorneys, consultants, etc.) is severely limited (unavailable over certain income thresholds). Moreover, the deduction is limited to 50 percent of an owner's pro rata share of W-2 wages paid by the business. However, for S corporation shareholders which qualify for the deduction, the effective federal tax rate may be lower for these individuals. (Note, under current law, the 199A deduction for qualified business income is allowed for years 2018-2025 only.) Clients must work with tax counsel to determine which choice of entity is most beneficial under current law. A calculation to determine whether C corporation or S corporation is more beneficial purely from a federal income tax standpoint will include weighing factors such as profitability, whether profits or losses will be retained in the corporation or distributed out to shareholders, and how distributions will be structured (e.g., as compensation to shareholders). For a more detailed discussion of the QBI deduction, see Chapter 23.

5. Where it is desired to spread income among a number of family members, an S corporation is a useful device. By giving stock, the tax on corporate earnings may be shifted to a large number of relatively low tax bracket individuals and taxed at their brackets rather than at the client's bracket (to the extent the kiddie tax does not apply). Note that there are serious limitations on the ability of a partnership to shift taxation to other family members under the family limited partnership rules.

6. When avoidance of the accumulated earnings tax is desirable.

7. When owners wish to avoid Medicare and other employment taxes on a portion of their income, an S corporation may be used to pay the owner a reasonable salary as employee but retain all earnings above that or distribute some of them as S corporation distributions, which avoid such taxes (though not on income in general, which passes out similar to a partnership on a Form K-1 to its owners).

53.3 WHAT ARE THE REQUIREMENTS?

There are several formalities which an S corporation must follow, including adopting bylaws and complying with state-specific reporting and administrative requirements. Additionally, there are numerous ongoing requirements unique to the S corporation form which must be followed:

1. The corporation must be a domestic corporation that is created or organized in a U.S. state or territory.[3]

2. It must have no more than one hundred shareholders.[4] Note that a husband and wife are treated as one shareholder, and certain members of a family may elect to be treated as one shareholder.

3. Shareholders must be individuals, estates, or certain types of trusts. Many trusts, corporations, and LLCs do not qualify as S corporation shareholders. Nonresident aliens may not be shareholders.[5] An IRA or a charitable remainder trust (CRT) cannot be a shareholder. A tax-exempt organization such as a qualified retirement plan trust or a charitable organization may be a shareholder in an S corporation. The qualified tax-exempt shareholder is counted as only one shareholder for purposes of determining the number of shareholders.[6]

4. The corporation can have only one class of stock.[7] That means each share must confer equal rights to distribution and liquidation proceeds. However, it is possible to provide for differences in voting rights among shares of common stock. For instance, there can safely be a "Class A" and a "Class B" voting stock with different terms or powers, so long as both classes confer equal rights to distribution and liquidation proceeds. Similarly, bona fide buy-sell agreements, agreements restricting transferability of shares, and redemption agreements will not be held to constitute a second class of stock so long as they are not entered into to circumvent the one-class-of-stock requirement and do not establish a purchase price that is significantly in excess of or below the fair market value of the stock.

Note that a "straight debt instrument" is not considered, for these purposes, a second class of stock. A "straight debt instrument" means a written unconditional promise to pay on demand or on a specified date a sum certain in money so long as:

1. the interest rate and payment dates are not contingent on the corporate profits, the discretion of the corporation, or other similar factors;

2. the instrument is not convertible into stock; and

3. the creditor is a person, estate or trust eligible to hold S corporation stock, or a person actively and regularly engaged in the business of lending money.[8]

The interest rate may vary based upon the prime rate or a similar factor that is unrelated to the debtor corporation.

53.4 LLCS TAXED AS S CORPORATIONS

As noted earlier, LLCs can elect to be taxed as C or S corporations (provided they would otherwise qualify). This may have state law asset protection advantages over using a corporate form. For example, many state laws generally permit creditors to garnish stock but prohibit garnishment of LLC interests, permitting at most a charging order against distributions. In theory, a corporate S corp and LLC/S corp are exactly the same for federal income tax purposes. However, be careful in drafting the LLC agreement that there are not two classes of stock created, or default provisions that would provide for distributions upon termination to be according to a capital account (a partnership concept) in lieu of strictly according to ownership percentages. State law default provisions on termination may mimic partnership tax rules. If it is found that the operating agreement was not consistent with S corporation requirements, it can be corrected and the taxpayers may seek resolution without an expensive PLR, pursuant to the newly simplified procedures in Rev. Proc. 2022-19.

53.5 TAX IMPLICATIONS

S corporations and their shareholders are taxed under essentially the same rules that apply to partnerships and their partners. Generally, the S corporation does not pay federal income tax. Its income (or loss) is passed through directly to its shareholders and therefore avoids the double tax on corporate earnings.[9] Depending on the shareholders' individual circumstances (active v. passive investor), S corporation income may be subject to the Net Investment Income Tax. Allocation of profits and losses which flow through to individual S corporation shareholders is based upon the shareholder's ownership percentage.

Example. There are five equal shareholders in the ABC Corporation, taxed as a C corporation, generating profits of $100,000 per year. After subtracting the flat 21 percent corporate level rate on $100,000, equaling $21,000, the amount that could be distributed to the shareholders as a dividend is $79,000 ($100,000 − $21,000). Each shareholder's share is $15,800 ($79,000 ÷ 5). Assuming each shareholder is subject to the highest tax rate on dividends (20 percent in 2021), he or she would be subject to tax of $3,160 (20 percent of $15,800) on the dividend. So, the total shareholder level tax ($15,800) plus the corporate level tax ($21,000) would be $36,800. The 3.8% net investment income tax may also apply to the dividend.

Conversely, if the shareholders had elected to be taxed as an S corporation, the corporate profits of $100,000 would not change. However, in lieu of a corporate level tax, the $100,000 would pass directly through to the shareholders (the character of the income also is passed through). Dividing the net profit by five, each shareholder's share is $20,000. Assuming a marginal tax rate of 32 percent for each shareholder (a distribution from an S corporation retains the corporate level character and is not taxed in the same way as a C corporation dividend); the tax would be $6,400 each. Thus, the aggregate tax payable by the shareholders with respect to the $100,000 corporate level profit would be $32,000.

Taxes Before S Election	Taxes After S Election
$36,800	$32,000

The S election saves $4,800 ($36,800 − $32,000) annually in this case, but this may be greater if we consider that the NIIT may apply to the corporate dividend and the S corporation income may escape the NIIT and be eligible for a further 20% QBI deduction.

For tax years 2018-2025, depending on other factors including total income limits and the nature of the business (whether a "specified service" trade or business), a deduction for "qualified business income" under Code section 199A of up to 20 percent also is also likely to be available, further reducing the taxpayers' effective federal income tax rate.

Essentially, taxable income of an S corporation is computed as follows:

- Any income that could affect the individual tax liability of a shareholder is passed directly through the corporation to the shareholders based upon the shareholders' ownership percentage. Distributions from the S corporation to a shareholder are not subject to employment taxes. Note, however, if a shareholder performs significant services for the corporation and does not receive "reasonable compensation," the IRS has the authority to re-characterize some or all of the S corporation income as "compensation" which will be subject to employment taxes. Likewise, any loss, deduction, or credit that could affect the liability of a shareholder is passed through just as if the entity were a partnership. Even tax-exempt income such as municipal bond interest or life insurance proceeds is passed through as tax exempt income.

- Shareholders must report or deduct all these "separately treated" items in proportion to their stock ownership interests. In other words, a 10 percent shareholder would be required to report 10 percent of the corporation's income as well as 10 percent of any corporate deductions or credits.

- Typical separately treated items include (1) gains and losses from corporate sales or exchanges of capital assets, and (2) charitable contributions (the corporation's contributions are passed through to shareholders who add them to their own personal contributions in determining the charitable contribution deduction on their own personal returns).

- Under the TCJA, a new Code section 199A was enacted, allowing owners of pass-through entities, including S corporation shareholders, to deduct up to 20 percent of "qualified business income" (limited to 50 percent of an owner's pro rata share of W-2 wages paid by the business) for tax years 2018 through 2025. The "199A deduction" is subject additional strict testing limitations and requirements, including a reduction for owners with income over certain thresholds, and the availability of the deduction for specified service trades or businesses (e.g., health professionals, attorneys, consultants, etc.) is more limited (unavailable over certain income thresholds). See Chapter 23 on this topic.

Tax exempt interest received by an S corporation retains its tax-exempt character and as in the case of taxable income, increases the shareholders' basis. If the interest is subsequently distributed, as is the case with any distribution, it is not taxable but reduces the shareholders' basis.

Amounts passed through as credits are passed through on a per-share per-day basis to be claimed by the shareholders on their personal returns. Allowances for depletion with respect to oil and gas wells are separately computed for each shareholder.

Corporate level net operating loss is deductible by a shareholder as an ordinary loss in computing in the individual shareholder's adjusted gross income. The TCJA notably limits the net operating loss deduction to 80 percent of taxable income in a given year beginning after December 31, 2017. Under the new law, net operating losses are still allowed to be carried forward (apparently indefinitely), but NOLs cannot be carried back to prior years (note there are certain exceptions, including some exceptions created under the CARES Act for year 2018-2021).

The corporation's remaining (the non-separately computed) income or loss, if any, is passed through to the shareholders. Each shareholder reports on Schedule E of Form 1040 his or her pro rata share.

All this income must be reported by a shareholder in the taxable year in which, or with which, the corporation's tax year ends. (S corporations must use a calendar year for tax accounting purposes, unless a business reason is established for using a fiscal year period, so the tax year of most S corporations ends on December 31.) In the case of a deceased shareholder, pro rata shares of income attributable to the portion of the corporation's tax year up to the date of death are reportable on the decedent shareholder's final return. Income earned in the balance of the year is reported on the estate's income tax return or on the return of the beneficiary who received the stock.

The pro rata shares are determined on a day-by-day per-share basis. This "per share per day" method of prorating income liability also applies where S corporation stock is sold or given away. There is an election to "close the books" when shares are sold or transferred under Code section 1377(a)(2), but be careful of the exceptions in the regulations for grantor trusts converting to non-grantor trusts.

21 Percent Corporate Tax Rate

There are two circumstances where an S corporation may be subject to corporate level tax, currently at a flat 21 percent rate.

The first situation is where the S corporation has earnings and profits, (derived either while it was a C corporation or due to an acquisition of a C corporation), and now has passive investment income. Passive investment income includes such items as rents, royalties, dividends, and interest. The tax is based on the passive investment income for the year in excess of 25 percent of the corporation's gross receipts.[10]

The second situation occurs where a corporation converts from a C to an S corporation (see "S Corporation Election" below) and had appreciated assets at the time of the conversion. Previously, the so-called "built in" gain on such assets was taxable at the highest corporate level rate (currently a flat 21 percent) if the appreciated assets are sold or distributed within ten years of converting to an S corporation.[11] Then, the 2012 Taxpayer Relief Act temporarily reduced the recognition period to five years.[12] Finally, the Protecting Americans from Tax Hikes (PATH) Act of 2015, part of the Consolidated Appropriations Act, 2016, P.L. 114-113 permanently set the recognition period to five years. Thus, it is important to determine the value of corporate assets when an S election is made, if the corporation was previously taxed as a C corporation.

53.6 S CORPORATION ELECTION

Shareholders of a C corporation that otherwise meets the requirements of an S corporation may elect for the S corporation treatment. All shareholders on the day the election is made must consent (on IRS Form 2553 or on a separate consent document). Minors can sign the consent even without legal or natural guardians (or such individuals may consent on behalf of a minor who is unable to act). A decedent's personal representative (executor or administrator) signs on behalf of an estate holding S corporation stock.

An "S" election may be made (a) at any time during the entire taxable year prior to the election year, or (b) on or before the fifteenth day of the third month of the election year. Elections made after that date are treated as made for the next tax year.[13] For instance, for an election to be effective in 2021, a corporation must file the election sometime between January 1, 2021 and March 15, 2021.

An effective election presupposes both that all eligibility requirements are met and that the proper consent from shareholders has been obtained. It is possible to obtain an extension of time to file in certain cases even if a shareholder fails to consent in time.

Certain types of entities are not eligible to elect S corporation treatment:

- a financial institution that uses the reserve method of accounting;
- an insurance company;
- corporations that elect to have credits for certain income from non-U.S. sources; and
- a current or former domestic international sales corporation (a.k.a. DISC or IC-DISC), a type of shell company established to exploit loopholes created to encourage exports.[14]

Advantages of an S Election

Reasons an S election is advantageous include:

1. The corporate-level exclusion on gains for distributions of property at liquidation are taxed at the corporate level. Therefore, the liquidation of a regular ("C") corporation will often result in gain at the corporate level and then again at the shareholder level (because the shareholder is treated as if he or she had sold his or her stock to the corporation in exchange for the liquidating proceeds). This will seldom occur in an S corporation liquidation.

2. A flat tax rate of 21 percent is imposed on all taxable income of personal service C corporations. But corporations electing S corporation treatment are generally not subject to any tax at the corporate level, and their shareholders – even professional shareholders – remain entitled to the "run through the brackets" starting with rates as low as 10 percent.

3. As discussed throughout this chapter, the new "199A deduction" available to pass throughs, including S corporations, of up to 20 percent of qualified business income (subject to strict requirements) may make an S corporation more attractive purely from a federal income tax standpoint than a C corporation, even with a reduced, flat corporate tax rate of 21 percent. Clients must work with tax counsel to determine which choice of entity is most beneficial under current law and their particular circumstances.

Although the S election is not available for all businesses and is, likewise, not appropriate for every circumstance, a substantial number of closely held corporations can benefit from these tax advantages.

Disadvantages of an S Election

Among the drawbacks to S corporation status are that:

1. Because S corporation earnings are taxed at the shareholders' individual tax rates (whether or not the earnings are distributed), S corporations cannot accumulate earnings and profits for capital needs at lower corporate brackets;

2. An S corporation is limited in its ability to use carryovers (such as, net operating losses or investment tax credits) as they pass through to the shareholders;

3. A corporation is restricted in the fringe benefits it can offer its shareholder-employees (although the tax law does not prohibit the S corporation from offering the benefit, the benefit to the shareholder-employee is taxable and may be nondeductible by the corporation making the cost of many fringe benefits prohibitive);

4. An S Corporation is not appropriate as a holding vehicle for certain real estate or other investments;

5. At the death of a shareholder, the pro rata share of assets in the S corporation do not receive a step-up in basis, although the decedent's outside basis in the stock does get stepped-up.[15]

6. Unlike partnerships, S corporation owners do not receive additional basis for S corporation borrowing.

Additionally, shareholders of an S corporation are prohibited from borrowing from their retirement plans (and will likely have to pay back all loans from such plans before an S election becomes effective).

State Laws

Before making the decision to elect S corporation status, shareholders must consider applicable state tax laws:

- Some states do not recognize the S corporation's status for state income tax purposes. There are a number of jurisdictions that do not currently allow corporate income to be passed through directly to shareholders as it is under federal law. In those instances, this means the corporation will have to pay state tax at the corporate level.

- States tax "passed-through" income at their own rates. Therefore, the reduction of federal tax rates on individuals has not, in many cases, been carried through at the state level.

- If the federal income tax base of individuals is used at the state level for computing the state income tax and itemized deductions of a shareholder, an S election may increase the shareholder's state taxable income.

- Nonresident shareholders of S corporations typically must pay income tax to the state where the S corporation does business. But if the S corporation is "doing business" in several states, the multiple tax preparations and payments could be burdensome.

- Some states require both a federal and a separate state S corporation election. This increases costs and administrative burdens as well as the possibility for unintentional loss of S corporation status. The IRS may not recognize for federal purposes a corporation that was not recognized as such for state purposes.

Termination

An election of an S corporation will terminate under any of the following circumstances:[16]

1. Shareholders holding more than 50 percent of the corporation's stock consent to revoke the election. There is no official form; the corporation files a statement with the IRS revoking the election. The termination is effective for the entire taxable year if the revocation is filed on or before the fifteenth day of the third month of the taxable year; otherwise, the revocation is effective on the first day of the following taxable year. The entrance of a new stockholder cannot revoke an election unless that person owns more than 50 percent of the corporation's stock and that person revokes the election; if no revocation occurs, new shareholders are bound by the same rules that apply to other shareholders.

2. The corporation fails to satisfy any of the four qualification requirements discussed above under the heading "What Are the Requirements?" The involuntary termination is effective on the day the disqualifying event occurs. For instance, the election ends if the limit on the number of shareholders is exceeded or shares are transferred to an ineligible party. Therefore, a transfer of even one share of S corporation stock to a partnership, corporation, nonresident alien, or non-qualifying trust terminates an election. Likewise, if a second class of stock is issued the election would terminate.

3. Certain passive income exceeds 25 percent of the corporation's gross receipts for three consecutive tax years and the corporation has accumulated earnings and profits (either from its days as a C corporation or due to a corporate acquisition) at the end of each such year.

Upon voluntary or involuntary termination of the S corporation, the corporation will immediately be taxed as a C corporation. Once terminated, an S election cannot be made again for five years without the consent of the IRS. The IRS may waive the effect of an inadvertent termination for any period if the corporation (a) corrects the event that created the termination in a timely manner and (b) agrees, together with all its shareholders, to make such adjustments as may be required by the IRS with respect to such period.

However, Rev. Proc. 2013-30 provides relief when: (1) the entity is an eligible entity, intended to be classified as an S corporation and failed to qualify solely because the election was not timely; (2) there is reasonable cause for the failure to timely make the election; (3) the corporation and the shareholders have reported income consistent with the S corporation status for the year in which the S election should have been made and every subsequent year; (4) less than 3 years and 75 days have passed since the effective date of the election.[17]

The IRS recently issued more taxpayer-friendly guidance on inadvertent S corporation terminations with simplified procedures in Rev. Proc. 2022-19 on Oct. 11, 2022. Both of these revenue procedures should be consulted if the owners find that an event has occurred to inadvertently disqualify their S corporation status.

53.7 ISSUES IN COMMUNITY PROPERTY STATES

A husband and wife, shareholders of community property stock in an S corporation, both must give their consent to the corporation's election to have its earnings taxed to the shareholders. If retention of the S corporation election is desirable, in a situation where an individual is purchasing shares with community property funds, a contract should be entered into with both that individual and his spouse whereby they would agree not to refuse to consent to the election.

The same concern discussed in Chapter 50, dealing with earnings from a separate property investment, should also be considered.

As noted, husband and wife holding stock as community property are counted as only one shareholder. Additionally, community property stock, because half is owned by each spouse, can be more easily given within the scope of the annual exclusion without the necessity of filing a gift tax return.

The estate tax value of a deceased spouse's share of community property stock should be valued on a non-controlling basis. For example, in *Estate of Bright v. Commissioner*, the Fifth Circuit[18] ruled that a 55 percent controlling block of community property stock was properly valued as a 27.5 percent interest in the decedent's estate.

53.8 TRANSFERS OF S CORPORATION STOCK

An S corporation is an ideal vehicle to shift both wealth and income to other family members. For instance, assume a doctor, as a sideline, establishes a laboratory or dispensary. He could incorporate the business as an S corporation and give all the shares of the newly formed business to his children.

The business would pay no income taxes at the corporate level. The children would pay income taxes on their share of the company's profits (which would otherwise have been taxed at their father's income tax rate, which is assumed to be higher), although the kiddie tax could apply depending on their age and student status. If the children were transferred shares through a defective grantor trust, the grantor would pay the income tax while the beneficiaries would receive non-taxable distributions.

The best type of business for wealth and income shifting purposes is one in which the client performs no services (or the services performed by the client are only incidental). If the client performs significant services or services that generate all of the corporation's income, the IRS is likely to attribute earnings to the client and tax him accordingly. For instance, if the doctor, as a sideline, gives medical lectures for a fee, the S corporation will not be able to shift the tax on income it receives as compensation for his lectures to his children.

Conversely, if income from a passive investment (such as S corporation income from a laboratory run by a person unrelated to the doctor) is channeled to a child, income (and therefore tax) can be shifted without challenge. Note, however, the subchapter S election may be jeopardized if the S corporation has certain passive income which exceeds 25 percent of the corporation's gross receipts for three consecutive tax years and the corporation has accumulated earnings and profits (either from its days as a C corporation or due to a corporate acquisition) at the end of each such year.

It is important to follow formalities. For instance, stock-owning children or their guardians should be invited to shareholder meetings.

Transfers to Minors

An outright gift of S corporation stock to a minor makes it impossible to exercise any rights with the stock unless a court-appointed guardian is obtained. This is usually expensive, inconvenient, and typically involves a great deal of administrative inflexibility.

An alternative to an outright gift to a minor is a gift to a custodian for the child under the appropriate Uniform Gifts to Minors Act (UGMA) or Uniform Transfers to Minors Act (UTMA). Unfortunately, this device has its limitations.

First, once the minor reaches age twenty-one (but 18 in some states and up to 25 or 30 in others), shares must be distributed. Many clients feel that this age is an inappropriate time to distribute large amounts of money or securities. Most individuals are unwilling to allow a donee-child to obtain unlimited ownership and control at that time.

A second possible problem is that if the minor dies prior to the age at which the shares must be distributed under applicable local law, the likelihood is great that the shares will be returned to the donor through the operation of state intestacy statutes.

The third potential problem is that the custodian may die or become unable to act. Under the Uniform Gifts to Minors Act and Uniform Transfers to Minors Act it is possible that the custodian could name a successor. (Such a successor may be named by the donor when the UGMA/UTMA account is established or the custodian may name his or her own successor.) Lacking advance preparations, court proceedings may have to be instituted in order to name a successor custodian; a procedure that would entail costs and delays.

Gifts to a minor in trust should be considered as an alternative to custodianship. Additionally, gifts of non-voting stock should be considered if it is desired that the minor (guardian) not participate in business decisions.

53.9 TRUSTS AS SHAREHOLDERS

A trust can be a shareholder of an S corporation, but only if:

1. the grantor or other individual is treated for income tax purposes as the owner of the trust property under Code sections 671 to 678 (a so-called "grantor trust"). It is unclear whether joint trusts with more than one grantor or deemed owner qualify under this section. After the grantor's death, such a trust remains an eligible S corporation shareholder provided that:

    a. such a grantor trust continues after the grantor's death (limited to a period of two years after death); and

    b. the trust receives the stock under a will (a so-called "testamentary trust") and it holds S corporation stock only up to a maximum of two years after the stock is transferred to the trust;

2. the trust was created primarily to vote stock (a so-called "voting trust");

3. the trust is a Qualified Subchapter S Trust (QSST); or

4. the trust is an Electing Small Business Trust (ESBT).[19]

From a gift standpoint, if no inappropriate powers are retained by the trustor(s), a contribution to a trust will be considered a complete gift. Such gifts can qualify for the gift tax annual exclusion either by meeting the requirements of Code section 2503(c) or by including a Crummey withdrawal power.

Grantor Trusts

A grantor trust, one in which the grantor is treated as if he owned trust property for income tax purposes, is eligible to own stock in an S corporation. A grantor trust can hold S corporation stock regardless of whether it is revocable. In fact, such a trust can continue as an S corporation shareholder even after the death of the grantor (but only for a limited period of up to two years). Thus, revocable living trusts may own stock in an S corporation.

The disadvantage of the grantor trust as a receptacle for S corporation stock is obvious: its income will be taxed to the grantor (and therefore the ability to shift the tax on income is lost). While many may perceive this result as a disadvantage, it can actually also be viewed as an advantage in that such payment of income taxes reduces the grantor's estate without any gift tax consequences (pursuant to Rev. Rul. 2004-64). Moreover, a trust can be structured in such a way as to terminate grantor trust status if the grantor no longer wants to pay the tax. If grantor trust status is terminated, an ESBT or QSST election must be immediately filed.

A grantor trust will be includable in the grantor's gross estate if the grantor holds certain interests at death or transfers such interests within three years of death. In general, these include interests such as a retained life estate, a reversion, a revocable transfer, or certain interests in an annuity or in life insurance. Inclusion of a trust in a grantor's estate can occur whether or not the trust is treated as a grantor trust for income tax purposes.

Section 678 Trusts (BDOTs)

A Section 678 trust is another alternative to outright gifts and UGMA gifts to a minor. To be deemed the owner under Code section 678, the beneficiary must have unrestricted power "exercisable solely by himself to vest the corpus or the income therefrom in himself." In other words, the beneficiary will be taxed on the income from the S corporation held by the trust if he or she has the right to take either the income and corpus whenever desired. There must be no restrictions on the beneficiary's right to exercise a withdrawal power.

A Section 678 trust can be created by a parent or grandparent who transfers S corporation stock to it for the benefit of a minor. The minor would be given an unrestricted power to withdraw income or corpus for his own benefit.

See Chapter 35 on Beneficiary Deemed Owner Trusts.

Qualified Subchapter S Trusts

A qualified subchapter S trust (QSST) is one type of trust that is eligible to hold S corporation stock.[20] Specifically, a QSST is defined in the Internal Revenue Code as one that:

1. owns stock in one or more S corporations (and may hold other types of assets)

2. actually distributes all of its income to one individual (who must be a United States resident or United States citizen)

3. has trust terms requiring that:

    (a) there can be only one beneficiary at any given time

    (b) if corpus is distributed during the term of the trust, it can be distributed only to the individual who is at that time the current income beneficiary

    (c) if an income beneficiary dies, the income interest itself will end at that death or upon the earlier termination of the trust

    (d) if the trust ends before the income beneficiary dies, all the assets of the trust must be distributed to that income beneficiary

4. requires an election to be made by the income beneficiary (or the income beneficiary's legal representative) to have the QSST qualify as such. (Once that election is made, it is irrevocable and can be revoked only if the IRS consents.) That election must be made by each income beneficiary as he or she becomes one. Separate elections must be made if the stock of more than one S corporation is held in the trust.

If the requirements described above are met, the income beneficiary of a QSST (which can be set up during the grantor's lifetime or by will) is treated as the owner of the stock as if it had qualified under Code section 678. The consequence is that any income, as well as any gains or losses, passes directly from the S corporation to the beneficiary, not to the trust.

QSSTs can be useful when contemplating the transfer of an S corporation to children. Through the use of a QSST, a gift of S corporation stock can be made to a minor through the trust without incurring the disadvantages of outright ownership. This enables an individual to split income among family members while at the same time eliminating the gift from inclusion in his gross estate. So both income shifting and wealth transfers are possible through the QSST.

Unlike a custodianship, a QSST can continue beyond the age of majority and can last as long as the grantor directs it to last. This means that if the minor dies before the trust terminates, the trust can continue for the lives of a number of successive income beneficiaries and does not need to force trust assets into the estate of the deceased income beneficiary. If trust assets are distributed to the beneficiary at death, the trust is includable in his or her gross estate.

Electing Small Business Trusts

An electing small business trust (ESBT) is another type of trust that can hold stock in an S corporation.[21] Unlike a QSST, an ESBT may have multiple beneficiaries. The beneficiaries of an ESBT may be individuals, estates, or certain charitable organizations that are eligible to be S corporation shareholders. With an ESBT, trust income is not required to be distributed to trust beneficiaries annually. Instead, trust income may be accumulated or may be sprinkled among trust beneficiaries. Each potential current beneficiary is counted as a shareholder for purposes of the one hundred shareholder limitation. A beneficiary of an ESBT need not be given any interest that would cause the trust to be includable in the beneficiary's estate.

Trusts exempt from the income tax, QSSTs, and charitable remainder trusts may not be ESBTs. An interest in an ESBT may not be obtained by purchase. An ESBT is taxed at the highest income tax rate for individuals (in some states, for state income tax purposes as well).

An ESBT is entitled to the new 199A deduction to the extent of the portion of the ESBT that is considered to own S corporation stock.[22]

53.10 FREQUENTLY ASKED QUESTIONS

Question – What protections to Subchapter S status can be included in shareholders' agreements?

Answer – Shareholders' agreements should prevent transfers of stock to shareholders who would be ineligible to hold stock in a subchapter S corporation. A provision could be included that required consent of corporate counsel for any transfer so that there would not be an inadvertent termination.

Question – How is life insurance owned by an S corporation for key person purposes taxed?

Answer – Key person life insurance premiums are nondeductible. Death proceeds are typically received income tax free by the corporation. When life insurance is owned by a business on the life of an employee, Code section 101(j) requires certain conditions and notice and consent requirements be satisfied in order to keep the death benefit income tax free. When the proceeds are distributed to the corporation's shareholders, they will be treated in the same manner as any other distributions. If a policy is surrendered during the insured's lifetime or the policy matures, any gain is taxable directly and proportionately by ownership to the corporation's shareholders.

Most advisors recommend that insurance that is indicated be owned on a personal basis. This is because shareholders in an S corporation are currently taxed on corporate income used to purchase nondeductible items such as corporate life insurance, even if there is no actual distribution of cash to pay that tax. For instance, if a corporation pays a $10,000 premium, shareholders of an S corporation may be taxed on $10,000 of phantom income - even though they do not receive it.

The corporation could pay a deductible bonus to each shareholder, which, after tax, would be sufficient to pay premiums on the appropriate amounts of insurance.

Question – Can an S corporation set up a nonqualified deferred compensation plan?

Answer – An S corporation *can* establish a deferred compensation plan. But the tax advantage enjoyed by employee shareholders in a conventional corporation is not available. This is because shareholders are taxed directly and immediately on the current taxable income of the corporation, whether or not that income is distributed to them. Because premiums are not deductible, the outlay for life insurance that is used to finance the corporation's obligation under the deferred compensation plan is immediately taxable to the individual shareholders. For example, a corporation with a $50,000 gross income, $30,000 of deductible expenses, and which pays $5,000 in key person insurance premiums has only $15,000 available for distribution. Yet shareholders are taxed *as if* they had received $20,000.

Question – How are S corporations treated for fringe benefit purposes?

Answer – S corporations generally will be treated as partnerships for purposes of plan eligibility and taxation of "employee fringe benefits." All shareholders owning more than 2 percent of the stock will be considered partners.[23]

The result is that most shareholder-employees would not be "employees" for purposes of favorable Code section 79 group term, medical reimbursement, or other coverage. This results generally in taxation of the more-than-2 percent shareholder-employees.

Question – Do the passive loss rules affect S corporations?

Answer – If a shareholder does not materially participate in the business, losses from the business would be considered "passive." They can therefore be used only to offset passive income of the shareholder. Likewise, income received by such a shareholder from the business should be considered "passive" and should therefore offset any passive losses from other investments of the shareholder. The passive v. active participation distinction may also matter for application of the net investment income tax.

Question – Will the pro-rata allocation of income to shareholders in a family S corporation always be allowed for federal income tax purposes?

Answer – Not necessarily. Following rules based on those applicable to family partnerships, discussed in Chapter 50, the allocation of S corporation income to family members may be disregarded if the income is not derived from capital, the transferor family members are not adequately compensated for their services, or the transferor family members retain too much control over the transferred stock.[24]

Question – Are there any special estate planning considerations for S corporation shareholders?

Answer – Business owners, including S corporation shareholders, face unique estate planning considerations. Without a proper plan in place, the successful transition of ownership can be a challenge. A client's estate plan and business plan should be fully integrated to address some of the following key issues:

- *Who will be the business owner's successor?* At the owner's death, disability, or retirement, is there a known successor identified? Is the successor a family member, existing co-owners, a key employee or someone else?

- *How will ownership be transferred?* Will ownership of the business be transferred through gift or sale? And if the owner will be a trust, how will it qualify as an S corporation shareholder (grantor trust, QSST, ESBT?)

Many of the questions related to succession planning can be addressed in a formal buy-sell agreement. The buy-sell plan is a legally binding contract which provides for the transfer of ownership upon a triggering event, such as the death, disability, or retirement of an owner. Buy-sell plans, which can be structured in several ways, are often funded with life insurance to ensure obligations under the agreement can be carried out. Without life insurance, the business and/or surviving owners may not have sufficient liquidity to buy out the estate.

Example: Shareholders Andy Adams and Bob Black are each 50 percent owners of an S corporation valued at $5 million. Neither of their spouses or adult children are qualified or interested in taking over the business. They enter into a cross-purchase agreement where they each agree to buy out the other's interest upon death or another triggering event. To fund the plan, Andy purchases a life insurance policy with a $2.5 million death benefit on Bob's life and vice versa. When Bob dies in 2021, Andy receives the $2.5 million life insurance death benefit income-tax free. He uses the death benefit to purchase Bob's $2.5 million business interest from the estate. Bob's wife and children receive a liquid, cash inheritance. Andy receives cost basis equal to the purchase price in Bob's shares. Unlike partnership interests, Andy can track a separate basis for the newly purchased shares than his prior purchased shares, and if he desires, for example, to gift/sell 20% to his children, he can use the higher basis newly acquired shares. With partnerships, the basis of inherited interests must be blended with prior acquired interests.

A fully integrated estate and business plan can also help to address estate tax concerns. For many business owners, the business interest comprises a large portion of their estate. If the owner dies without a plan in place and estate taxes are due, a flash sale of the business may be required to liquidate the estate to pay for taxes. To lock-in a selling price and minimize stress to the decedent's family, the buy-sell plan can address these issues and more. A proper plan can also help to determine if other options are available, such as the ability to defer estate taxes under a Code section 6166 election.

Finally, when life insurance is integrated into the plan, the life insurance death benefit can help to equalize an estate among all beneficiaries when one beneficiary will receive business interests and others will not.

Example: Charlie Cook is a widower with three adult children. He is the 50 percent owner of an S corporation worth $1 million. His daughter, Daphne, is actively employed and engaged in the business and Charlie has full confidence that she will make an excellent successor. Charlie purchases a $2 million life insurance policy and names his other two children as 50 percent beneficiaries of the policy. Upon Charlie's death, Daphne receives 100 percent of the business interest (valued at $1 million), and her siblings each receive a $1 million cash inheritance, effectively equalizing the estate among all of Charlie's children.

CHAPTER ENDNOTES

1. I.R.C. §1366(d); Treas. Reg. §1.1363-1.
2. Under prior law, the "built-in gains" in corporate assets usually escaped taxation on the corporate level when the assets were sold or distributed in a liquidation or I.R.C. §303 distribution even if the corporation had not made an S election. This is no longer true following the repeal of the General Utilities doctrine.
3. I.R.C. §1361(b)(1).
4. I.R.C. §1361(b)(1)(A).
5. I.R.C. §§1361(b)(1)(B), 1361(b)(1)(C).
6. In *Taproot v Comm'r.*, 109 AFTR2d 2012 (CA-9), the Court held that a Roth IRA cannot be a shareholder of a subchapter S corporation. See Leimberg Information Services, Inc. (LISI) Employee Benefits and Retirement Planning Newsletter No. 506 (April 17, 2012) at www.leimbergservices.com.
7. I.R.C. §1361(b)(1)(D).
8. I.R.C. §1361(c)(5)(B).
9. I.R.C. §§1363, 1366, 1368.
10. I.R.C. §1375.
11. I.R.C. §1374. There is a special rule for 2012 and 2013 whereby this ten-year period is shortened to five years.
12. I.R.C. §1374(d)(7)(C).
13. I.R.C. §1362(b).
14. I.R.C. §1361(b)(2).
15. EGTTRA 2001 replaced a stepped-up basis with a modified carryover basis for one year for property acquired from a decedent dying in 2010. The 2010 Act reinstated the old basis step-up rules but permit an executor for decedents dying in 2010 to elect the modified carryover basis regime.
16. I.R.C. §1362(d).
17. See https://www.irs.gov/businesses/small-businesses-self-employed/late-election-relief.
18. 658 F.2d 999 (5th Cir. 1981).
19. I.R.C. §§1361(b)(1)(B), 1361(c)(2), 1361(d), 1361(e).
20. I.R.C. §1361(d).
21. I.R.C. §1361(e).
22. REG-107892-18, 83 FR 40884, August 16, 2018.
23. I.R.C. §1372.
24. I.R.C. §1366(e).

DEFERRED COMPENSATION (NONQUALIFIED)

CHAPTER 54

54.1 INTRODUCTION

Nonqualified deferred compensation is an arrangement whereby an employer promises to pay an employee in the future for services rendered currently. There is a tremendous variety of nonqualified deferred compensation plans, from severance plans to certain equity compensation arrangements, but many are established as retirement plans that provide income over a period of years after retirement or other termination of employment. These payments are referred to as "deferred" compensation because they represent compensation earned currently but which will not be paid to the person who earned that money until a future date or event. The term "nonqualified" refers to the fact that the plan does not attempt to meet the stringent coverage and contribution requirements necessary to obtain government approval and the very favorable tax treatment available only to qualified retirement (pension and profit-sharing) plans.

The top two reasons that employers sponsor these plans are to provide a competitive benefit package to recruit and retain key employees, and to help their top talent save for retirement beyond traditional 401(k) or 403(b) plan limits.

The Tax Cuts and Jobs Act of 2017 included changes to the treatment of executive compensation and indirectly impacted the economics of non-qualified deferred compensation (NQDC) plans. Dramatically decreased C corporation tax brackets for any income deferred and higher effective tax brackets for employees residing in states with high state income taxes (and state and local income tax deductions limited to $10,000) make NQDC plans even more attractive to employers and employees alike.

54.2 WHEN IS USE OF SUCH A DEVICE INDICATED?

1. When a business does not have a government approved (qualified) retirement plan to offer key employees and would like to provide those key employees with retirement benefits.

2. Where a business has a qualified retirement plan, but would like to provide additional retirement benefits for certain key people over and above those permissible under a qualified plan.

3. Where a highly paid employee or executive would like to defer the taxation on income from peak earning years to a future date when he/she might be in a lower income tax bracket (usually at retirement). With recent tax reform increasing the top individual tax brackets from starting at $418,400 (2017) to $578,125 (single in 2023) and from $470,700 (2017) to $693,750 (married filing jointly in 2023), this may increase the incentive even further.

4. When an executive or other highly paid individual would like to use an employer to, in effect, provide a forced savings program for him and to use such a savings program as a retirement plan. By providing a forced saving account that is notionally invested in company stock or otherwise tied to company performance, the plan can align the incentives of key employees and shareholders.

5. When the corporate (C corporation) rates at the top brackets are lower than individual rates at the top bracket, deferred compensation becomes more attractive and the deferral of both income to the employee and the deduction to the employer makes more sense. This delta changed dramatically

751

as a result of the Tax Cuts and Jobs Act passed in late 2017 - for tax year 2017, the difference was only 35 percent top corporate rate v. 39.6 percent top individual rate (40.5 percent if the 0.9 percent Medicare surtax is included). In 2023, the contrast is much greater - the difference being a top corporate rate of 21 percent (with no AMT) versus 37 percent top individual rate in 2021 (37.9 percent if the 0.9 percent Medicare surtax is included). For individuals in states with higher state income tax, any lowering of the top federal tax bracket may be offset by the loss of the Schedule A state and local tax deduction, which is now capped at $10,000 (married filing jointly) and will now go unused by many, pushing up the overall combined tax rate.

6. When an employer would like the ability to pick and choose who will be covered and would like to determine on a person-by-person basis the benefit levels and terms and conditions of coverage.

7. When a business wants to create an incentive to attract new talent without diverting current cashflow to compensation.

8. When a business wants to provide "golden handcuffs" to retain key employees by requiring those employees to work for a specified number of years and/or until a specified age, or by conditioning payment on the attainment of business goals (such as a successful sale of the company)

9. To permit key employees that may retire in a state without income tax (or a lower income tax rate) to shift income to retirement and avoid state income tax.[1]

54.3 ESTATE PLANNING IDEAS FOR DEFERRED COMPENSATION

In most cases, someone will cash in their deferred compensation before they die, usually after retirement but sometimes even sooner. But what happens when an employee dies before that? Deferred compensation is a unique asset for income and estate planning purposes because it is "income in respect of a decedent"(IRD), pursuant to Code section 691. This means that anyone (other than a tax-exempt entity) receiving the income after death will pay income taxes on it. This is similar to traditional retirement plans, but even worse from an income tax perspective, because there is no lifetime "stretch" for the surviving spouse or other eligible designated beneficiaries – not even the 10 years allowed to other beneficiaries!

Often deferred compensation is paid within a year. Under IRS Revenue Ruling 64-150, all amounts earned but unpaid at an employee's or former employee's death received by an estate or beneficiary of a deceased employee should be reported as non-employee compensation on a Form 1099-MISC. Large amounts of deferred compensation to a widow or other beneficiaries can drive up the tax bracket of the beneficiary so that more income tax is paid than would have been otherwise.

When you see a client with large sums in deferred compensation, examine their estate plan. Do they leave any sums or percentages of their estate to charity? If so, explore whether a charity or charitable remainder trust might be an ideal beneficiary of the deferred compensation as opposed to other assets. A charitable remainder trust (CRT) can defer the taxation over a number of years for the individual – not only allowing more to grow tax-deferred, but spreading out the income over the years of the CRT's lifetime individual beneficiary or beneficiaries, which may keep their tax bracket from jumping into higher and higher brackets. All things being equal, this estate planning technique of leaving deferred compensation to a CRT at death is even better than leaving a traditional IRA to a CRT at death, because there are greater opportunities to stretch or even rollover (if a spouse) IRAs that deferred compensation plans do not grant.

This may be an ideal situation in which to name a charity or CRT as a contingent beneficiary in the event of a qualified disclaimer by the primary beneficiary, to permit the primary beneficiary the option to defer or shift the ordinary income burden and benefit charities in a more tax efficient manner. Remember that a spouse can disclaim as a primary beneficiary and still receive a lifetime benefit through a charitable remainder trust that is a contingent beneficiary, but that qualified disclaimer rules do not permit non-spouses to do so.

54.4 WHAT ARE THE REQUIREMENTS?

In order to successfully defer income tax, an agreement should contain a contingency that may cause the employee to forfeit rights to future payments. As long as the employee's risk of forfeiture is substantial, the employee will generally not recognize income.[2]

DEFERRED COMPENSATION (NONQUALIFIED)   CHAPTER 54

Even if an employee's rights are nonforfeitable, the income can be deferred provided that the arrangement complies with the requirements of Code section 409A, which was passed in the wake of the Enron collapse and which governs nonqualified deferred compensation arrangements. The employee will generally not be in constructive receipt of income if the agreement is entered into before the employee earns the compensation in question, the plan otherwise complies with section 409A, and the employer's promise to pay is not secured in any way. This latter requirement means that the agreement cannot be formally funded (no interest in a trust or escrow fund or in a specific asset can be given to the employee) without causing the money to be immediately taxable.[3]

However, it is permissible for a corporation to finance its obligation under the agreement by purchasing a life insurance contract, annuities, mutual funds, securities, or a combination of these investment media, without adverse tax consequences to the employee. The assets that will be used to finance the employer's obligation to the employee must remain the unrestricted property of the corporation (subject to the claims of the corporation's creditors). The employee must be given no interest or specific rights in the monies that the corporation sets aside to meet its obligation under the agreement.[4]

Rabbi Trusts

The Internal Revenue Service has permitted the establishment of so-called "Rabbi Trusts" in conjunction with certain plans of deferred compensation.[5] These trusts enable an employer to transfer funds to an irrevocable grantor trust that satisfies certain criteria (most importantly the requirement that the trust assets remain subject to the claims of the employer's general creditors in the event of insolvency).[6] The Department of Labor, which has jurisdiction over ERISA plans, has ruled that Rabbi Trusts, because they are subject to the corporation's creditors, are exempted from ERISA since they are considered unfunded.[7] Although such a trust can provide some protection from loss of benefits (for example, in the event of a hostile takeover or change in management), its real benefit is more psychological, since in the event of employer insolvency or bankruptcy the assets held in trust must be available to the employer's general creditors.[8]

A recent 7th Circuit decision, *Bank of America v. Moglia*, induces a twist wherein the Rabbi Trust may ironically provide additional protection against *secured* creditors.[9] In *Moglia*, the Seventh Circuit determined that the corpus of a Rabbi Trust would not be subject to a security interest where the trust agreement reserved the assets of the trust for "general," or as the court read it, "unsecured" creditors. After filing for bankruptcy, it was discovered that the company had $14 million set aside in a Rabbi Trust. Importantly, the funds had been deposited prior to the execution of the security agreement on which Bank of America, the creditor, relied. The secured creditors sought to include the $14 million as a part of the assets of the debtor from which they could seek repayment, but the bankruptcy trustee successfully claimed that that amount was only subject to *unsecured* creditors' claims, which included claims of the executives who would benefit. Therefore, although the executives did not obtain a security interest in the corpus of the trust, the instrument provided that, upon insolvency, the assets would be subject to the company's "general creditors," and the company would not create a security interest with respect to any specific creditor. Thus, Bank of America was unable to attach an interest to the amounts held in the Rabbi Trust, as it was not deemed a "general creditor," but rather, a secured creditor, and secured creditors were specifically excluded by the terms of the trust agreement. The court determined that had these funds been deposited after that security agreement, rather than before, they would have been subject to that agreement. This suggests that a Rabbi Trust may properly hold the assets of the trust for the unsecured creditors, including executives, which may preserve some additional security and rationale for Rabbi Trusts.

(This topic is covered in more detail in our companion text, *The Tools and Techniques of Employee Benefit and Retirement Planning*.)

All agreements must now comply with the requirements of Code section 409A (see below) to achieve deferral and avoid penalties and interest.

54.5 HOW IT IS DONE

The selected employee enters into an employment contract with his employer. The contract stipulates that specific payments will be made to the employee or the employee's beneficiaries in the event of death, disability, or retirement. This creates a "legally binding right". The employer must provide the agreed upon benefits if the contractual conditions are met. In return for this promise, the selected employee agrees to provide services until a specified age or date. The agreement will

753

often obligate the covered employee to (1) refrain from engaging in any competitive business after retirement; and (2) remain available for consultation purposes after retirement. While post-retirement consulting arrangements must be structured very carefully to avoid the imposition of penalties and interest under section 409A, they can provide important flexibility in a business's succession plan.

Often, the employer will purchase life insurance (alone or in combination with other savings vehicles, such as a fixed or variable annuity or a mutual fund) to provide the required benefits, since any gains inside the policy will be tax deferred (or tax free death benefit). The business will apply for and own the policy (or other security) on the life of the employee (or sometimes, it may be on a select group of key employees). The business will pay the premiums and be named the policy beneficiary. The business will completely control and own the policy (as well as any other asset used to finance the employer's obligation under the agreement).

The purpose of the life insurance policy is to provide funds necessary to pay retirement benefits called for under the contract. Policy cash values can be used for this purpose. Alternatively, the policy can be held by the corporation until the employee's death, and the employee can be paid the agreed upon deferred compensation at the specified age or date out of other corporate assets. Should the employee die prior to retirement, the corporation will receive the life insurance and then can use it to provide death benefit payments to the employee's family.

Example. The Krauss Corporation is in the 34 percent federal and state income tax brackets (we'll stick with this in the example, but note that the TJCA changed the top federal rate to 21%). The corporation enters into a nonqualified deferred compensation agreement with its president, Robert P. Krauss, who is forty-five years old. Krauss agrees to defer a $5,000 annual salary increase. Instead of receiving the $5,000 salary increase currently, the after-tax cost of this raise ($3,300) is applied on Krauss' behalf as the annual premium for a life insurance policy on his life.

The Krauss Corporation then agrees to provide retirement and death benefits as follows: (1) if Krauss dies before retirement, a lump sum will be paid to his widow; and (2) if he remains with the corporation until retirement at age sixty-five, he will receive $10,000 a year for ten years.

Because the Krauss Corporation is in a 34 percent marginal tax bracket, each $1,000 of benefit payments made to its president (or his widow) would actually cost only $660. Retirement benefits could be paid out of current earnings and the corporation could continue the insurance policy in force until the tax-free death proceeds are received. Alternatively, the cash values of the policy could be used to finance the corporation's obligation under the contract.

Assume for this example that a premium of $3,300 would purchase approximately $185,000 of life insurance (whole life) for a male age forty-five. If Krauss died at age fifty after five years' worth of premium payments, the corporation would receive $185,000 of tax free policy proceeds[10] (in addition to dividends and perhaps interest); it would have paid $16,500 in premiums; it is obligated to pay a total of $25,000 ($5,000 a year for five years) to Bob's widow, but its after-tax cost for making such payments is only $16,500 (66 percent of $25,000). This results in a net gain to the corporation of approximately $152,000 ($185,000 insurance proceeds less $16,500 of premiums and less $16,500 of after-tax cost of such payments).

If Bob Krauss' death occurs at age seventy-five, the corporation receives over $325,000 in death proceeds and dividends; it has paid $66,000 in premiums; it has made lifetime payments of $100,000 ($10,000 a year for ten years) so its net after-tax-deduction cost for those deferred compensation payments has been $66,000 ($100,000 minus 34 percent of $100,000 percent). This results in a net gain to the corporation of approximately $193,000 ($325,000 insurance proceeds minus $66,000 premiums, minus $66,000 cost of deferred compensation payments).

Note that the Tax Cuts and Jobs Act passed in late 2017 reduces the corporate tax cost of the deferral in the above example from 34 percent C corporation tax rate to only 21 percent plus whatever state tax income tax rate applies.

54.6 ERISA

ERISA has very little impact if the plans fit into certain "safe harbors." For example, unfunded plans maintained primarily for the purpose of providing deferred compensation for a select group of management or highly compensated employees (often referred to as "top hat" plans) are exempt from almost all ERISA requirements. They are subject to easily complied with reporting requirements, and are subject to administrative and enforcement provisions–including the obligation to provide a claims procedure. (To the extent that such a deferred compensation plan is also considered an employee welfare benefit plan for ERISA purposes, it may also be subject to at least some fiduciary responsibility requirements, although this is not clear.) Thus, such plans are not subject to ERISA requirements as to participation, vesting, nondiscrimination, minimum funding, and (at least to the extent they are not employee welfare benefit plans) fiduciary responsibility rules.[11]

The employer can comply with the reporting requirement by:

1. filing—within 120 days of the adoption of the plan—a simple written statement (a letter will do) with the Secretary of Labor, including:

    a. the employer's name and address;

    b. the employer's IRS identification number;

    c. a declaration that the employer maintains a plan primarily for the purpose of providing deferred compensation to a select group of management or highly compensated employees; and

    d. a statement of the number of such plans and the number of employees in each plan; and

2. providing plan documents upon request to the Secretary of Labor.

Securities Issues

It appears that, subject to certain exceptions noted below, the SEC will require the registration of all nonqualified deferred compensation plans as "securities" if the plan involves employee contributions. The key is whether the employees making the contributions have "investment motives" (i.e., the plan involves investments in underlying securities whose return is credited to the employee) or "tax deferral" motives (i.e., primarily to save income taxes). An investment-motivated plan will be considered a security and must be registered; however, a deferral-motivated plan will not be considered a security and will not need to be registered.

If a NQDC plan is required to register as a security with the SEC, the failure to register the plan may have tax implications. A participant in a plan that has not registered with the SEC, and is required to do so, may be able to rescind the deferral of compensation; however, such a right to rescind could cause the participant to be in constructive receipt of the deferred amounts. NQDC plans provide an employer with the ability to:

1. create a retirement plan for specified individuals;

2. select who will be covered; and

3. determine the terms and conditions of that coverage.

Although many of these plans were previously financed by crediting the amounts deferred with a given interest rate, more and more frequently these plans are financed through a combination of variable life insurance (to finance a death benefit) and equities such as mutual funds or other equity-type assets. Additionally, although most NQDC plans in the past covered only a select group of high level executives or other key employees, recently plans have become much more broad based.

The key registration exemptions that would apply to most small corporation plans are for:

- Securities offered and sold only to persons resident within a single state, and where the issuer is doing business in that state. This is commonly called the "intrastate exemption."

- Small offerings. This is commonly called the "small offering" exemption.

- Nonpublic offerings. This is commonly called the "nonpublic offering" exemption.

There is a "Regulation D, Rule 505" and "506" safe harbor, which encompasses the later two exemptions and works like this:

1. Offers and sales of securities with a total offering price of $5,000,000 or less in which there are no more than thirty-five purchasers and which meet certain other rules will be protected from registration requirements.

2. Offers and sales of securities which do not involve more than thirty-five purchasers are protected from registration requirements – regardless of the dollar amount of the offering – if every purchaser who is not considered an "accredited investor" is considered capable of evaluating the merits and risks of the prospective investment.

The SEC has left businesses in a state of uncertainty on this issue, since each case will be measured on its own facts and circumstances.[12] Few companies will set up plans covering a large number of employees, and most "smaller companies" that set up plans for a dozen or so key executives will be able to fall within the safe harbor exemptions described above–and therefore avoid the cost and aggravation of SEC registration. Many plans, however, involving a very large number of covered individuals or large amounts of money, may have to register. Certainly, employers cannot ignore this issue and should obtain competent legal advice.

54.7 TAX IMPLICATIONS

Code Section 409A

In the American Jobs Creation Act of 2004, Congress created a new Code section 409A that imposes additional requirements on nonqualified deferred compensation plans. Section 409A creates strict requirements for determining whether and when participants are to be taxed on deferred compensation, it imposes new limitations on funding plans, and it imposes substantial penalties for failing to meet the requirements when deferring compensation.

Limitations on Distributions. Under Code section 409A, a participant may only receive a distribution of previously deferred compensation upon the occurrence of one of six events:[13]

- separation from service;
- the date the participant becomes disabled;
- death;
- a fixed time (or pursuant to a fixed scheduled) specified in the plan at the date of the deferral;
- a change in the ownership or effective control of the corporation or assets of the corporation, to the extent provided in regulations; or
- the occurrence of an unforeseeable emergency.

In addition, payments to key employees (as defined in Code section 416(i)) of publicly traded corporations arising upon a separation from service must be delayed until six months after separation from service (or, if earlier, the date of death of the employee)..[14]

Within the meaning of Code section 409A(a)(2)(A), "unforeseeable emergency" means "a severe financial hardship to the participant resulting from an illness or accident of the participant, the participant's spouse, or a dependent (as defined in Code section 152(a)) of the participant, loss of the participant's property due to casualty, or other similar extraordinary and unforeseeable circumstances arising as a result of events beyond the control of the participant."

Limitations on Deferral Elections. Code section 409A also imposes requirements for participants making elections to defer compensation. Participants now must generally make deferral elections prior to the end of the preceding taxable year.[15] In the first year in which a participant becomes eligible to participate in a plan, however, the participant may make an election within thirty days after the date of eligibility, but only with respect to services to be performed subsequent to the election. In the case of any performance-based compensation covering a period of at least twelve months, a participant must make an election no later than six months before the end of the covered period.[16] This election may only be made if the amount of compensation to be paid under the performance goal is not readily ascertainable.

A separate set of new election rules allows participants to elect to change the form or timing of distributions from a plan as long as the plan requires the new election to be made at least twelve months in advance of the time at which the compensation was slated to be made. Any change in the election that occurs less than twelve months prior to the time of payment will be ineffective. In addition any election to delay a distribution must delay the distribution at least five years from the date of the new election. Distributions made on account of disability, death, or an unforeseeable emergency are not subject to the five year requirement. An election related to a scheduled series of distributions made pursuant to a fixed schedule must be made at least twelve months in advance of the first such scheduled payment.[17]

Limitations on Funding. Securing or distributing deferred compensation upon the employer's falling net worth or other financial events unacceptably secures the payment of the promised benefits.[18] This includes hybrid rabbi/secular trust arrangements that distribute assets from nominal rabbi trusts to secular trusts on the occurrence of triggering events indicating the employer's financial difficulty. "Secular" trusts differ from Rabbi Trusts in that they are funded and not subject to general creditors and may be subject to ERISA and therefore receive the anti-alienation creditor protection. Secular trusts are not usually preferred by employees because, unlike Rabbi Trusts, there is no tax deferral benefit for the employee.

Setting aside assets in an offshore trust to directly or indirectly fund deferred compensation also unacceptably secures the payment of the promised benefits.[19] This limitation does not apply to assets located in a foreign jurisdiction if substantially all of the services to which the nonqualified deferred compensation relates are performed in such jurisdiction.

Penalties. Code Section 409A also includes substantial penalties for failing to meet the statutory and regulatory requirements when deferring compensation. Any violation of Code section 409A results in retroactive constructive receipt, with the deferred compensation being taxable to the participant in the first year in which it was "vested," or not subject to a substantial right of forfeiture. In addition to the normal income tax on the compensation, the participant must pay a 20 percent penalty tax, as well as interest at a rate 1 percent higher than the normal underpayment rate.[20]

Effective Date. The requirements of Code section 409A generally apply to amounts deferred after December 31, 2004. The requirements also apply to amounts deferred prior to January 1, 2005 if the plan under which the deferral is made is materially modified after October 3, 2004. There is an exception for material modifications made pursuant to IRS guidance (see below).

Initial Guidance and Treasury Regulations

Notice 2005-1. In early 2005, the IRS released Notice 2005-1, providing the first guidance on new Code section 409A.[21] Notice 2005-1 provided general guidance with respect to what arrangements are covered by Code section 409A and provided transitional guidance generally covering the calendar year 2005. In September 2005, the IRS issued proposed regulations under Code section 409A.[22] The regulations generally follow the principles outlined in Notice 2005-1, but are much more extensive. In general, the proposed regulations are to be effective January 1, 2007. Further delays were finally put to bed with final regulations issued by IRS effective January 1, 2008.

Notice 2008-113 provides some relief to correct operational failures. The relief allows taxpayers to avoid the taxes that result from plan aggregation rules but also Code section 409A penalties. To qualify for relief, taxpayers must request every type of relief they require. There are different types of relief for non-insiders than for directors or officers. So, if using this Notice, first one must determine whether someone is an insider, when the failure happened and whether the amount involved was more than the Code section 402(g) limitations. Moreover, the regulations treat each year separately. So if an employer is out of compliance for one year, it only affects that one year and the taxpayer can get back into compliance. The regulations require employees to recalculate their income tax for all deferral years and then add interest. Notice 2010-06 clarified Notice 2008-113 and then was modified by Notice 2010-80. This Notice provides an additional method for correcting the problem. Noncompliance under Code section 409A results in inclusion in income for all amounts deferred under the plan by a participant, an interest charge and an additional 20 percent tax. These latest notices encourage businesses to correct their non-compliance. However, these relief provisions only apply to inadvertent failures to comply; the failure cannot be intentional. In addition, the relief provisions cannot be used if the taxpayer is currently under audit. The relief provisions provide an opportunity to correct certain document failures without current income inclusion or additional taxes.

In Notice 2010-06, the IRS refers to the "document correction program" and encourages taxpayers to review nonqualified deferred compensation plans. It further motivates taxpayers who were intimidated in drawing attention to their plans.

On June 21, 2016, the IRS issued proposed regulations, which may be relied on, under §1.409A-1,

1.409A-2, §1.409A-3 and §1.409A-6 that clarify and modify the final regulations issued in 2007 and the proposed income inclusion regulations issued in 2008.[23] In many cases, these changes are consistent with the prior views of practitioners. In several instances, however, the proposed regulations curtail practices that many practitioners had thought to be compliant with Section 409A. In what may be a small consolation, the rules regarding payments in the event of the death of a plan participant and payments to beneficiaries (#11 below) were liberalized. These proposed regulations:

1. Clarify that the rules under section 409A apply to nonqualified deferred compensation plans separately and in addition to the rules under section 457A.

2. Modify the short-term deferral rule to permit a delay in payments to avoid violating Federal securities laws or other applicable law.

3. Clarify that a stock right that does not otherwise provide for a deferral of compensation will not be treated as providing for a deferral of compensation solely because the amount payable under the stock right upon an involuntary separation from service for cause, or the occurrence of a condition within the service provider's control, is based on a measure that is less than fair market value.

4. Modify the definition of the term "eligible issuer of service recipient stock" to provide that it includes a corporation (or other entity) for which a person is reasonably expected to begin, and actually begins, providing services within twelve months after the grant date of a stock right.

5. Clarify that certain separation pay plans that do not provide for a deferral of compensation may apply to a service provider who had no compensation from the service recipient during the year preceding the year in which a separation from service occurs.

6. Provide that a plan under which a service provider has a right to payment or reimbursement of reasonable attorneys' fees and other expenses incurred to pursue a bona fide legal claim against the service recipient with respect to the service relationship does not provide for a deferral of compensation.

7. Modify the rules regarding recurring part-year compensation.

8. Clarify that a stock purchase treated as a deemed asset sale under section 338 is not a sale or other disposition of assets for purposes of determining whether a service provider has a separation from service.

9. Clarify that a service provider who ceases providing services as an employee and begins providing services as an independent contractor is treated as having a separation from service if, at the time of the change in employment status, the level of services reasonably anticipated to be provided after the change would result in a separation from service under the rules applicable to employees.

10. Provide a rule that is generally applicable to determine when a "payment" has been made for purposes of section 409A.

11. Modify the rules applicable to amounts payable following death.

12. Clarify that the rules for transaction-based compensation apply to stock rights that do not provide for a deferral of compensation and statutory stock options.

13. Provide that the addition of the death, disability, or unforeseeable emergency of a beneficiary who has become entitled to a payment due to a service provider's death as a potentially earlier or intervening payment event will not violate the prohibition on the acceleration of payments.

14. Modify the conflict of interest exception to the prohibition on the acceleration of payments to permit the payment of all types of deferred compensation (and not only certain types of foreign earned income) to comply with bona fide foreign ethics or conflicts of interest laws.

15. Clarify the provision permitting payments upon the termination and liquidation of a plan in connection with bankruptcy.

16. Clarify other rules permitting payments in connection with the termination and liquidation of a plan.

17. Provide that a plan may accelerate the time of payment to comply with Federal debt collection laws.

18. Clarify and modify § 1.409A–4(a)(1)(ii)(B) of the proposed income inclusion regulations regarding the treatment of deferred amounts subject to a substantial risk of forfeiture for purposes of calculating the amount includible in income under section 409A(a)(1).

19. Clarify various provisions of the final regulations to recognize that a service provider can be an entity as well as an individual.

Stock Appreciation Rights. Code section 409A excludes certain nonstatutory stock options from coverage, but did not exclude stock appreciation rights (SARs) that may yield economically equivalent results. In the final regulations, the IRS exempted SARs from section 409A provided they meet similar tests governing exempt stock options. Under the exception, a SAR will not constitute a deferral of compensation if:

1. The SAR exercise price may never be less than the fair market value of the underlying stock on the date the right is granted.

2. The compensation payable under the SAR may not be more than the excess of the fair market value of the stock over the strike price times the number of SARs granted.

3. There are no additional features for the deferral of compensation (for example, a plan that provides for dividends to be paid on exercise or to reduce the exercise price would constitute an additional feature providing for the deferral of compensation).

Under the 2016 proposed regulations, a stock price in a stock appreciation rights plan will not be treated as based on a measure other than fair market value if the amount payable upon a service provider's involuntary separation from service for cause, or the occurrence of a condition that is within the control of the service provider, such as the violation of a covenant not to compete or a covenant not to disclose certain information, is based on a measure that is less than fair market value.

Change in Control Events. Code Section 409A permits payments from a deferred compensation plan upon a change in ownership, a change in the effective control, or a change in the ownership of a substantial portion of the assets of the corporation. Under IRS guidance, a change in ownership occurs when an individual or persons acting as a group acquires more than 50 percent of the total fair market value or total voting power of the corporation. Ownership under these rules is subject to attribution under Code section 318(a). A change in effective control occurs when an individual or persons acting as a group acquires 30 percent or more of the total voting power of the stock of the corporation within a twelve-month period or where there is an adversarial change in a majority of the membership of the board of directors within a twelve-month period. A change in the ownership of a substantial portion of the assets of the corporation occurs when an individual or persons acting as a group acquires assets equal to or greater than 40 percent of the total gross fair market value of assets of the corporation.

Acceleration of Payments. The regulations provide for several exceptions under which a plan may permit the acceleration of payments, some of the key ones of which are:

1. to comply with a domestic relations order,

2. to comply with a conflict-of-interest divestiture requirement (see Code section 1043),

3. to pay income taxes due upon a vesting event under a plan subject to Code section 457(f),

4. to pay the FICA tax imposed on compensation deferred under the plan ("pyramiding"), and

5. to terminate a participant's interest in a plan after separation from service where the payment is not greater than the Code section 402(g) limit governing deferrals to qualified plans. This amount is inflation indexed and currently stands at $18,000.

The 2016 proposed regulations provide that the exception for the death, disability or unforeseen emergency of a service provider (employee) also applies to the payment of deferred amounts upon the death, disability, or unforeseeable emergency of a beneficiary who has become entitled to payment due to a service provider's death. These proposed regulations also clarify that a schedule of payments (including payments treated as a single payment) that has already commenced prior to a service provider's or a beneficiary's death, disability, or unforeseeable emergency may be accelerated upon the death, disability, or unforeseeable emergency.[24]

Material Modifications. Code section 409A is effective with respect to (i) amounts deferred in taxable years beginning after December 31, 2004 and (ii) amounts deferred in taxable years beginning before January 1, 2005 if the plan under which the deferral is made is materially modified after October 3, 2004. Code section 409A is effective with respect to earnings on amounts deferred only if it is effective with respect to the amounts deferred.

A plan is materially modified if a new benefit or right is added or if a benefit or right existing as of October 3, 2004 is enhanced. According to IRS guidance, a material modification may be a formal plan amendment or may occur simply by virtue of an employer's exercise of discretion in the plan participant's favor. For example, a material modification would occur if an employer exercised discretion to accelerate vesting of a benefit under the plan to a date on or before December 31, 2004. It is not, however, a material modification to exercise discretion over the time and manner of payment of a benefit to the extent such discretion was provided under the terms of the plan as of October 3, 2004. Where a new benefit is adopted after October 3, 2004, a plan may limit application of section 409A to the new benefit by explicitly identifying the additional deferral of compensation and providing that the additional deferral to subject to Code section 409A.

It is presumed under Code section 409A that the adoption of a new arrangement or the grant of an additional benefit after October 3, 2004 is a material modification of a plan. The IRS allows that the presumption may be rebutted by demonstrating that the adoption of the arrangement or grant of the additional benefit is consistent with the employer's historical compensation practices, where, for example, an employer grants certain stock appreciation rights each year on November 1, 2004. In these cases, Code section 409A will not apply to amounts deferred on or before December 31, 2004.

Independent Contractors. Under IRS guidance, Code section 409A does not generally apply to amounts deferred under an arrangement between a service recipient and an unrelated independent contractor, if, during the contractor's taxable year in which the amount is deferred, the contractor provides significant services to each of two or more service recipients that are unrelated, both to each other and to the independent contractor. Code section 409A does, however, apply to members of the board of directors.

The regulations include a safe harbor providing that an independent contractor will be treated as providing significant services to more than one service recipient where not more than 70 percent of the total revenue of the trade or business is derived from any particular service recipient (or group of related service recipients). This rule will be important to many insurance agents who work for multiple insurance companies.

The 2016 proposed regulations provide additional guidance for those who may have dual status as employee and independent contractor and who may change status from employee to independent contractor (or vice versa).[25]

Short-Term Deferrals. According to the IRS, Code section 409A does not apply to certain "short-term deferrals." Under the guidance, a deferral of compensation does not occur when amounts are paid within 2½ months after the end of the year compensation is no longer subject to a substantial risk of forfeiture. Under this rule, many multi-year bonus arrangements that requirement payments promptly after the amounts vest will not be subject to Code section 409A.

Changes in Time and Form of Payment. Under Code section 409A and the regulations, plans may only permit an employee to make a subsequent election to delay or change the form of a payment in limited circumstances:

1. the election may not take effect until at least twelve months after the date on which the election is made;

2. the payment with respect to which the election is made must be deferred for at least five years beyond the date it was originally scheduled to be paid (except for payments made on account of death, disability, or unforeseeable emergency); and

3. the election must be made not less than twelve months prior to the date of the scheduled payment.

The regulations generally provide that each separately identified amount to which an employee is entitled to receive on a determinable date is a separate payment. Plans have flexibility to separately identify payments, but once payments have been separately identified, any subsequent aggregation must comply with the above requirements. A series of installment payments under a single plan will generally be treated as a single payment for purposes of the subsequent election rules; however, a plan may specify that a series of installment payments is to be treated as a series of separate payments.

The Employer's Tax Position

1. If life insurance is purchased, premiums paid by the employer are not tax deductible. The life insurance policy is considered an asset of the employer and is, therefore, carried on the books of the employer as such. Therefore, no tax deduction is allowed for payment of the premiums.[26] (Nor is a current deduction allowed for any other informal funding vehicle.)

2. When the executive reaches retirement age, the employer, as owner of the policy, may choose one of the settlement options available under the policy to fulfill its obligation under the plan. In this case, a portion of each installment payment received by the employer would be taxable under the annuity rules.[27] However, if the policy is surrendered and a lump sum payment is received, that portion which exceeds the employer's cost (the net premiums the employer has paid) is treated as ordinary income.[28]

3. At the employee's death, the entire policy proceeds receivable by the employer are generally income tax free.[29] (See "Tax Implications" in Chapter 50 for the possible alternative minimum tax on proceeds received by a regular C corporation that does not qualify as "small.") If the employee dies before retirement, these proceeds can be used to pay his or her family the agreed-upon benefits. If the employee lives beyond retirement and begins to receive deferred compensation, the employer, rather than surrendering the policy at this time, may choose to make benefit payments out of current or accumulated corporate earnings. Therefore, the employer can continue the policy in force until the employee dies. At that time, the death proceeds would be received by the corporation on an income tax free basis (aside from any AMT).

4. When the benefits are paid by the employer under the deferred compensation plan, either to the employee (after retiring) or to his or her family (on death before retirement), payments by the corporation are deductible, assuming that benefits constitute reasonable additional compensation.[30]

5. Deferred amounts will be considered to be wages and will be subject to social security tax in the year in which services are performed unless they are subject to a substantial risk of forfeiture, in which case the deferred amounts will be subject to social security tax when there is no longer a substantial risk of forfeiture. Similar rules apply to FUTA (the Federal Unemployment Tax).[31]

All nonqualified deferred compensation taken into account as wages for social security tax purposes is subject to the Medicare Hospital Insurance (HI) portion of the social security tax.[32] Whether such nonqualified deferred compensation will also be taxed under the Old Age, Survivors, and Disability Insurance (OASDI) portion of the social security tax will depend upon whether the participant's other earnings for the year at issue equal or exceed that year's OASDI taxable wage base ($160,200 in 2023).

The Employee's Tax Position

1. During employment, the employee is not taxed on amounts set aside by the employer to meet its financial obligation. Therefore, if a life insurance policy is purchased on the life of the employee, assuming it is part of the general assets of the employer and is not specifically earmarked for the purpose of carrying out the liabilities under the deferred compensation agreement, premiums paid by the employer will not be taxable to the employee.[33] This same principle applies to the employer's purchase of an annuity, mutual fund, or other savings vehicle to finance its obligation.

2. Benefits received from the deferred compensation plan by the employee (or his family) are taxable at ordinary income rates as received; however, the tax liability may be reduced because benefit payments typically commence at retirement. Yet, while some individuals will be in a lower income tax bracket at retirement, others will not be. Additionally, because the employee is receiving wages, the compensation may be subject to the Additional Medicare surtax.

3. The commuted (present) value of benefit payments remaining at a covered employee's death will be

included in the employee's gross estate for federal estate tax purposes. Therefore, the present value of the future income promised to the employee's spouse will be taxable in the employee's estate.[34] This is "income in respect of a decedent" (under Code section 691) and an income tax deduction will be allowed to the recipient of such income for the additional federal estate tax attributable to the inclusion of the deferred compensation.[35]

But because of the unlimited federal estate tax marital deduction, if the death benefit is payable to the employee's surviving spouse in a qualifying manner, no estate tax will be incurred when the employee dies.[36] (Therefore, no deduction for income in respect of a decedent will be allowed.)

4. As pointed out in paragraph 5 of "The Employer's Tax Position," above, deferred amounts are generally considered wages for social security tax purposes in the year in which services are performed or, if later, when they are no longer subject to a substantial risk of forfeiture.[37] Because all wages are now subject to the HI portion of the social security tax, nonqualified deferred compensation counted as wages will be taxed under at least the HI portion of the social security tax.[38] Whether nonqualified deferred compensation counted as wages will also be taxed under the OASDI portion of the social security tax will depend upon whether the participant's other earnings for the year at issue equal or exceed that year's OASDI taxable wage base.

54.8 ISSUES IN COMMUNITY PROPERTY STATES

As stated previously (see general discussion in Introduction), the earnings of a married resident are generally treated as community property in the nine community property states. This can cause some problems in the context of nonqualified deferred compensation. A spouse may enter into a deferred compensation arrangement with his or her employer. The deferred amount would be community property if paid currently. If the spouses obtain a divorce or one of the spouses dies, it may be necessary to determine the present value of the deferred amount in order to divide the community assets.

Whether, as regards forfeitable nonqualified deferred compensation rights, there is "property" subject to division in divorce or at death is a preliminary problem, although not one of as much importance now as it was previously under the former reasoning that only "vested" rights could be "property" subject to division. Under the extreme view, there was "property" only if the rights had fully matured and payments were either being presently received or there was a non-forfeitable right to immediate payment. The generally accepted current analysis establishes that there is "property" subject to division even though there is no certainty that compensation will ever be received.

IRS has determined that unfunded deferred compensation rights may constitute property within the meaning of Code section 1041 ("Transfers of property between spouses or incident to divorce"). According to the IRS, while the term "property" is not defined in section 1041, there is no indication that Congress intended "property" to have a restricted meaning under section 1041. To the contrary, Congress indicated that section 1041 should apply broadly to transfers of many types of property, including those that involve a right to receive ordinary income that has accrued in an economic sense (such as interests in trusts and annuities). Accordingly, stock options and unfunded deferred compensation rights may constitute property within the meaning of section 1041.[39]

A useful classification of nonqualified deferred compensation rights and pension rights has been suggested:

1. "vested and matured"–a nonforfeitable right to immediate payment;

2. "vested and unmatured"–a nonforfeitable right to payment at some future time, even though the right might terminate on a participant's death prior to retirement;

3. "contingent"–a nonvested accrued right and the contractual right to continue in the plan with, probably, a reasonable expectation of acquiring vested benefits within a relatively short time; and

4. "mere expectancy."

While forfeitable deferred compensation has been treated as a "mere expectancy" and thus of no value in a division of community property, at least one community property state, California, has abandoned this approach in the context of deferred compensation. California courts hold that the present value of deferred compensation can be determined. The fact that the deferred compensation obligation is unsecured and not formally funded would be a significant factor in reducing value. If the benefits are forfeitable, additional reductions in value are appropriate. In many circumstances, it may be appropriate to order a division of deferred compensation as it is paid, rather than requiring a current division. Thus, the spouse who did not earn the deferred compensation may not be paid. He or she presumably would receive a greater amount if the deferred benefit was actually paid (as opposed to 50 percent of a current value discounted for risk factors).

Another aspect commented on elsewhere in *Tools and Techniques*, which also relates to all community property planning, is the danger of signing a so-called "community property agreement," which makes all property owned by both spouses the community property of both of them.

Example. Dr. Lee Stein, an employee who worked for a national corporation while he was a resident of a separate property state, accrued a substantial deferred compensation benefit. If Lee then moves to a community property state, the deferred compensation benefit already accrued is still his separate property (specifically in some states, "quasi-community property"); if he then signs an agreement making all property of his wife, Rhonda, and himself community property, he will be making a taxable gift to Rhonda.

Because of the nature of the gift, it may be that even the $14,000 gift tax annual exclusion will not be available (since Rhonda may not be able to dispose of her newly received interest). On the other hand, the transfer should qualify for the unlimited marital deduction; however, the long range tax implications of that deduction should be fully understood (see Chapter 27).

Therefore, one should be very careful in entering into such agreements without receiving competent advice from an attorney knowledgeable in both property law and taxation.

54.9 DISABILITY BENEFITS

A plan may be set up to include a disability benefit. There are several ways of providing disability benefits:

1. A disability income policy can be purchased along with the other assets used to finance the employer's obligation under the plan.

2. A disability waiver of premium benefit attached to the life insurance policy will enable the company to cover its liability in the event that the employee becomes totally disabled.

3. A combination of these methods can be used.

The second approach works like this:

Example. If Bob Krauss, in the example above, became disabled, the money normally set aside for premium payments ($3,300 a year) would not have to be paid since premiums would be waived. The Krauss Corporation would have $5,000 to pay out to the employee since his salary continuation payments by the corporation would be deductible.

Generally, wage continuation payments and disability retirement income payments are fully includable in an employee's gross income. However, under Code section 22, an employee who is under the age of sixty-five, is retired on disability, and is considered totally and permanently disabled may be entitled to a tax credit for disability retirement income.

54.10 FREQUENTLY ASKED QUESTIONS

Question – What is the earliest date the corporation can take a deduction for unfunded deferred compensation payments?

Answer – Generally, a corporation cannot take a deduction until it actually makes payments to the employee (or a deceased employee's beneficiary), regardless of whether the corporation is on a cash or accrual basis of accounting.[40]

Question – Can directors' fees be deferred through an unfunded deferred compensation agreement?

Answer – Yes. Individual nonqualified deferred compensation agreements can be made with independent contractors, directors, and even employees of other business organizations.[41] Also, tax-exempt organizations can establish nonqualified deferred compensation plans.[42]

Question – If a corporation finances its obligation under a deferred compensation agreement with corporate owned annuity contracts, are there any current adverse tax consequences to the employee or to the employer-corporation?

Answer – There are no current tax consequences to the employee so long as the annuity remains the asset of the corporation and the employee has no interest in the annuity. However, for contributions made after February 28, 1986, to annuity contracts held by a "nonnatural person," such as a corporation, "the income on the contract" for the tax year of the policyholder is generally treated as ordinary income received by the contract owner for that year.[43]

Question – What is a secular trust?

Answer – A secular trust is an irrevocable trust used to formally fund and protect nonqualified deferred compensation. Funds placed in a secular trust are not subject to the claims of the employer's creditors. Thus, a secular trust can protect deferred compensation from an employer's bankruptcy or insolvency.

There are two principal types of secular trusts: employer-funded trusts and employee-funded trusts. The employer can make contributions to an employee-funded trust, but the arrangement is structured in such a way that the employee is considered to have constructively received the amounts before they are given to the trust.

Generally, use of a secular trust causes immediate or accelerated taxation to the employee and provides an immediate or accelerated deduction to the employer.[44] Thus, they are relatively rare. Employers may "gross up" participants to help them pay their taxes.

The secular trust became popular in the years after the Tax Reform Act of 1986 (TRA '86), when the top corporate income tax rate bracket (34 percent before OBRA '93) was higher than the top individual income tax rate bracket and the top individual rate bracket was relatively low (28 percent after TRA '86, 31 percent after the Omnibus Budget Reconciliation Act of 1990). However, the imposition in OBRA '93 of brackets of 36 percent and 39.6 percent marginal rates on individuals curtailed the use of this device, since most employees who are candidates for this planning are in their highest income tax brackets while employed, and may be in lower brackets when deferred benefits are received.

Question – What is the impact of deferred compensation plans that allow an employee to make a "phantom" investment of the deferred amounts, or that provide for interest to be credited on the deferred amounts?

Answer – Such arrangements are often considered as a hedge against inflation or to offset the erosion in the value of the deferred benefit equal to a fixed dollar amount payable at the end of several years. Both plans present problems. If the employee is permitted to make a hypothetical investment of the funds, the employer will be put to the cost of record keeping for hypothetical gains, losses, dividends, etc., and will be faced with a problem of accounting for the actual cost of the benefit.[45]

The use of hypothetical interest is more feasible. It could be based on something like a cost of living adjustment, or an average rate of inflation, such as 3 percent. Such interest or other adjustment should be treated as part of the total deferred compensation, with no deduction to the employer or taxation to the employee until paid or made available to the employee.[46]

Question – Where an employer has entered into a deferred compensation plan that provides for accrual of additional benefits based on the passage of time, could these additional amounts be deducted by the employer before they are paid or made available to the employee on the theory that they are interest?

Answer – The answer is apparently no, since the Ninth Circuit Court of Appeals reversed a 1993 decision allowing such an interest deduction and now holds that there is no deduction for such amounts until they are includable in employee income.[47]

Question – Under what circumstances is income and tax deferral not appropriate?

Answer – Although tax deferral is generally beneficial, it can be counterproductive if an employee's tax rate increases by the time the compensation is actually received. In the current environment of constantly changing tax policy, fluctuating federal and state deficits, and economic uncertainty, predicting future tax rates can be difficult if not impossible.

Therefore, the critical issue for many employees and employers who are contemplating the use of nonqualified deferred compensation arrangements is whether deferral is a sound financial tactic. That is, will employees be better off with the deferred compensation arrangement than they would be if compensation were paid currently?

Clearly, if tax rates do not rise, a highly compensated employee will almost always be better off deferring some of his or her compensation until a later date. However, if tax rates do rise, an employee will be better off deferring the compensation to a later date only if the compensation is deferred for a sufficient period of time – the break even period.

Specifically, if compensation is deferred and tax rates do rise, the employee will be taxed in a future tax year at a higher tax rate on the entire amount, including the interest credited on the account. If compensation is not deferred, he or she will pay tax at the current lower tax rate immediately and therefore have less available for investment.

The tradeoff is between: (1) the current lower tax rate, which must be paid immediately and which reduces the amount available for investment; and (2) the higher future tax rate, which must be paid later and which allows the entire before-tax amount to earn interest.

If the period of time is sufficiently long, the benefit of earning interest on the before-tax amount of deferred compensation will exceed the cost of the higher tax rate that is applied to the whole amount when it is ultimately received.

The NumberCruncher (http://www.leimberg.com) illustration that follows shows the years to break even under various assumptions.

Amount to be Deferred:	$20,000
Current Tax Rate:	35 %
Number of Years Compensation will be Deferred:	20
Assumed Future Tax Rate:	33%
Assumed Before Tax Rate of Return:	6%
Current After-Tax Value of Compensation:	$19,500

After-Tax Accumulation in 20 Years

If Tax Rate Decrease Occurs:	Early	Middle	Late
With Deferred Comp. Plan:	$64,463	$64,463	$64,463
Without Deferred Comp. Plan:	$42,892	$42,399	$41,913
Gain From Deferring Comp.:	$21,571	$22,064	$22,550
Years to Break Even:	0	0	0

Note that when the retirement tax rate is higher than the before retirement tax rate, it will take a number of years to break even by deferring compensation as this second NumberCruncher illustration demonstrates:

Amount to be Deferred:	$30,000
Current Tax Rate:	33%
Number of Years Compensation will be Deferred:	20
Assumed Future Tax Rate:	35%
Assumed Before Tax Rate of Return:	6%
Current After-Tax Value of Compensation:	$20,100

After-Tax Accumulation in 20 Years

If Tax Rate Decrease Occurs:	Early	Middle	Late
With Deferred Comp. Plan:	$62,539	$62,539	$62,539
Without Deferred Comp. Plan:	$43,202	$43,704	$44,211
Gain From Deferring Comp.:	$19,337	$18,835	$18,238
Years to Break Even:	2	2	2

Question – What methods are available to informally fund deferred compensation obligations?

Answer – In the "pay-as-you-go" approach, the employer uses working capital as needed to make any benefit payments, and there is no advance "funding."

With the "sinking fund" approach, a certain amount of assets is set aside to fund the obligations under the deferred compensation plan.

Since neither one of these approaches protects either the employer or the employee in event of a premature death, corporations will very often turn to Corporate Owned Life Insurance (COLI) to finance both the retirement and pre-retirement obligations under the plan.

Finally, a combination of the above approaches can be used.

CHAPTER ENDNOTES

1. This must be paid over at least ten years in close to equal installments, but if so federal law will trump any state law to the contrary. See 4 U.S.C. §114. If payments are over a lesser time period, individual state tax law will apply and it is possible for

1. someone to owe tax in both the state where the income was initially earned and also in the new state of residency (although an offsetting credit may apply).
2. See Treas. Regs. §§1.451-1, 1.451-2. see also Treas. Reg. 1.409A-1(b)(4), 1.409A-1(d).
3. See Rev. Rul. 60-31, 1960-1 CB 174, as modified by Rev. Rul. 70-435, 1970-2 CB 100. See also Priv. Ltr. Rul. 8439012, under which an executive's deferred compensation was placed in a trusteed bank account, but his rights were only those of an unsecured general creditor of the company. No income was recognized by the executive as a result of the company's placing the money in the trust account. See also *Oates v. Comm'r.*, 18 TC 570, aff'd, 207 F.2d 711 (7th Cir. 1953), acq., 1960-1 CB 5.
4. See, e.g., Rev. Rul. 72-25, 1972-1 CB 127; Rev. Rul. 68-99, 1968-1 CB 193.
5. Initially addressed in PLR 8113107, in which a congregation sought to establish a trust for its rabbi.
6. See Rev. Proc. 92-64, 1992-2 CB 422, including model form of the trust. Also see Rev. Proc. 92-65, 1992-2 CB 428.
7. DOL Advisory Opinion 92-13 at http://www.dol.gov/ebsa/programs/ori/advisory92/92-13a.htm (last accessed on May 1, 2017).
8. See, e.g., *Goodman v. Resolution Trust Corp.*, 7 F.3d 1123 (4th Cir. 1993).
9. *Bank of America v. Moglia*, 330 F.3d 942 (7th Cir. 2003).
10. See "Tax Implications" in Chapter 50 for possible alternative minimum tax on proceeds received by a regular C corporation.
11. See ERISA §§201(1), 201(2), 301(a)(1), 301(a)(3), 401(a)(1), 503, 4021(a), 4021(b)(6); Labor Regs. §§2520.104-23, 2520.104-24, 2560.503-1(a), 2560.503-1(b).
12. In 1995, several companies set up such plans and, to be safe, requested "no action" letters from the SEC. One such company was Merrill Lynch, whose plan covered about 2,000 brokers. The SEC responded negatively by refusing Merrill Lynch's request. Merrill Lynch then registered its plan with the SEC—and a number of other companies followed by registering their own plans. The Employee Benefits Committee of the American Bar Association Section on Taxation requested clarification from the SEC. At a 1997 meeting of the Committee, an SEC spokesperson stated that the SEC considered all NQDC plans (with certain exceptions discussed in the text above) as "registerable" and that it would be issuing a formal statement on its position.
13. I.R.C. §409A(a)(2)(A).
14. I.R.C. §409A(a)(2)(B)(i).
15. Treas. Reg. 1.409A-2(a).
16. I.R.C. §409A(a)(4)(B).
17. I.R.C. §409A(a)(4)(C).
18. I.R.C. §409A(b)(2).
19. I.R.C. §409A(b)(1).
20. I.R.C. §§409A(a)(1)(A)(i), 409A(a)(1)(B), (b)(4).
21. Notice 2005-1, 2005-2 IRB 274.
22. Treas. Reg. §§1.409A-1 through 1.409A-6.
23. Internal Revenue Bulletin: 2016-28 available at https://www.irs.gov/irb/2016-28_IRB/ar06.html (last accessed on Aug. 1, 2023).
24. Prop. Treas. Reg. §1.409A-3(j).
25. Internal Revenue Bulletin: 2016-28 available at https://www.irs.gov/irb/2016-28_IRB/ar06.html (last accessed on Aug. 1, 2023).
26. I.R.C. §264(a)(1).
27. See generally, I.R.C. §72.
28. I.R.C. §72(e); Treas. Reg. §1.72-11(d)(1).
29. I.R.C. §101(a)(1).
30. See I.R.C. §§404(a)(5), 162(a)(1), 212. Note that publicly held corporations generally cannot deduct compensation in excess of $1 million per tax year to certain top level executives. See I.R.C. §162(m).
31. I.R.C. §§3121(v)(2)(B), 3306(r)(2)(B). See also Notice 94-96, 1994-2 CB 564. Final regulations became effective January 29, 1999 and are applicable to amounts deferred and benefits paid on or after January 1, 2000. Treas. Regs. §§31.3121(v)(2)-1, 31.3306(r)(2)-1(a).
32. See I.R.C. §3121(a)(1).
33. Rev. Rul. 68-99, 1968-1 CB 193. See also Rev. Rul. 72-25, 1972-1 CB 127 (annuity contracts).
34. I.R.C. §2039(a); *Goodman v. Granger*, 243 F.2d 264 (3d Cir. 1957), cert. denied, 355 U.S. 835 (1957).
35. I.R.C. §691(c). The income tax deduction for the additional federal estate tax generated by the inclusion of the IRD is as follows:

> Federal estate tax payable (with net I.R.C. §691 income included in the gross estate)

Minus

> Federal estate tax payable (with no I.R.C. §691 income included in gross estate)

Equals

> Portion of Federal Estate Tax attributable to I.R.C. §691 items

Note the planning implication of this computation: To the extent that no estate tax is generated by IRD, no income tax deduction will be allowed. So, if deferred compensation payments are made to a surviving spouse (or to a marital trust on such spouse's behalf), to the extent that they qualify for the marital deduction, the IRC Section 691 income tax deduction is lost.

36. The federal estate tax was repealed for one year in 2010 as a result of the Economic Growth and Tax Relief Reconciliation Act of 2001. However, the 2010 Act reinstated it for decedents dying after 2009, but by election of the executor, a decedent dying in 2010 may opt out of the estate tax.
37. See note 12, above. Self-employed individuals pay social security taxes through self-employment (SECA) taxes rather than through FICA taxes. Nonqualified deferred compensation of self-employed individuals is usually counted for SECA purposes when it is includable in income for income tax purposes. See I.R.C. §1402(a); Treas. Reg. §1.1402(a)-1(c). (As with the FICA tax, there is no wage base cap for the hospital insurance portion of the SECA tax. See I.R.C. §1402(b)(1)). So, deferred compensation of self-employed individuals is generally counted for SECA purposes when paid (or constructively received, if earlier). I.R.C. §1402(a); see also Priv. Ltr. Rul. 8819012.
38. See note 13, above.
39. Rev. Rul. 2002-22, 2002-19 IRB. 849.
40. See I.R.C. §§404(a)(5), 404(d). The weight of authority even holds that an accrual basis taxpayer cannot take a current deduction for amounts credited as "interest" on unfunded deferred compensation; the deduction for such amounts must be postponed

41. See Rev. Rul. 71-419, 1971-2 CB 220.
42. See, generally, I.R.C. §457.
43. I.R.C. §72(u).
44. The full picture of the taxation of employees participating in secular trusts is much more complex than this. For the rules applicable to participants in employer-funded secular trusts, see I.R.C. §402(b); Regs. §§1.402(b)-1(a), 1.402(b)-1(b); Priv. Ltr. Ruls. 9502030, 9417013, 9302017, 9212024, 9212019, 9207010, 9206009. For the rules applicable to employees participating in employee-funded secular trusts, see Priv. Ltr. Ruls. 9450004, 9437011, 9337016, 9328007, 9322011, 9316018, 9316008, 9235044, 9031031, 8843021, 8841023. For more on the employer's deduction in the context of an employer-funded secular trust, see Treas. Reg. §1.404(a)-12(b)(1); Priv. Ltr. Ruls. 9502030, 9417013, 9302017, 9212024, 9212019, 9207010, 9206009. For more on the employer's deduction in the context of an employee-funded secular trust, see Priv. Ltr. Ruls. 9450004, 9437011, 9337016, 9328007, 9322011, 9316018, 9316008, 9235044, 9031031, 8843021, 8841023.
45. The ground rules governing employee direction of investments in nonqualified deferred compensation plans are not entirely clear. To avoid accelerated taxation, plans probably should not allow employees to control the actual investment of funds. In other words, plans allowing employee input into the actual investment of funds probably should provide that the asset holder (for example, the employer, or the trustee of a rabbi trust) need not follow the employee's wishes. Whether plans that allow participants to select hypothetical investments also should provide that the employee's investment wishes need not be followed is not clear. See generally Priv. Ltr. Ruls. 9517019, 9505012, 9504007, 9452035, 9332038, 9122019, 8952037, 8903088, 8834015, 8804057, 8804023, 8648011, 8607022, 8507028; Tax Mgmt. (BNA), U.S. Income Series, Portfolio #385-3rd (Deferred Compensation Arrangements), V.D.1; AALU *Washington Report*, Bulletins Nos. 94-107 (12/19/94) and 94-46 (May 13, 1994).

    Plans allowing employee input into the actual investment of funds may also want to limit the employee's investment choices to broad categories of investments (such as stocks, bonds, or money market instruments) rather than allowing the employee to choose more specific investments. Compare Rev. Rul. 82-54, 1982-1 CB 11 (annuity policyholders who could direct investment of annuity fund among several mutual funds representing different, broad investment strategies would not control individual investment decisions and for tax purposes would not be considered to own the mutual fund shares). Whether plans permitting employees to select hypothetical investments should similarly limit choices is not clear.
46. Treas. Reg. §1.409A-1(b)(2).
47. *Albertson's Inc. v. Comm'r.*, 42 F.3d 537, 94-2 USTC ¶50,619 (9th Cir. 1994), *vacating in part* 12 F.3d 1529 (9th Cir. 1993), *aff'g in part*, 95 TC 415 (1990) (divided court), *en banc rehearing denied* (9th Cir. 1995), *cert denied*, 516 U.S. 807 (1995); see also Notice 94-38, 1994-1 CB 350; Priv. Ltr. Rul. 9201019; TAM 8619006.

EMPLOYEE STOCK OWNERSHIP PLAN

CHAPTER 55

55.1 INTRODUCTION

An Employee Stock Ownership Plan (ESOP) is a type of qualified retirement plan that must invest its assets primarily in the employer's securities. ESOPs are essentially qualified stock bonus plans, but differ in that a stock bonus plan is not required to invest in employer securities. Additionally, an employer may lend funds or the use of its credit facilities to an ESOP, but not to a stock bonus plan, to facilitate the purchase of employer securities.[1]

A formal designation must be made to set up an ESOP, and a trust must be established. The ESOP plan trust is usually called an employer stock ownership trust (ESOT), and it may qualify as a tax-exempt employee trust.

An ESOP trust may be a shareholder of an S corporation. There are significant advantages to both the employer and the employee that can be derived from the ESOP, and it can offer significant benefits for business owners in need of an exit strategy. Favorable tax treatment has made ESOPs even more attractive for many small employers.

Congress recently enacted another encouragement to the use of ESOPs. On August 13, 2018, the bipartisan-sponsored Main Street Employee Ownership Act became law as part of the John S. McCain National Defense Authorization Act. Section 862 of the Act contains pro-employee ownership provisions to encourage the creation of ESOPs and worker cooperatives through the Small Business Administration (SBA), by supporting loan transactions and directing outreach to encourage business owners to consider employee ownership.[2] ESOPs were already technically eligible for so-called SBA 7(a) loans, but some prior program requirements were out-of-line with commercial ESOP lending practices, and were overly burdensome, uncertain or impractical. This new law should eventually lead to increased ESOP use, particularly for smaller company transactions that could be eligible for SBA assistance.

Two minor new ESOP changes were included in the Secure 2.0 Act passed in late 2022, but the effective dates for them do not incur until a few years after its passage. Below is Congress' summary of the new provisions:

Section 117 - Deferral of tax for certain sales of employer stock to employee stock ownership plans sponsored by S corporations: Deferral of tax for certain sales of employer stock to employee stock ownership plan sponsored by S corporation. Under section 1042, an individual owner of stock in a non-publicly traded C corporation that sponsors an ESOP may elect to defer the recognition of gain from the sale of such stock to the ESOP if the seller reinvests the sales proceeds into qualified replacement property, such as stock or other securities issued by a U.S. operating corporation. After the sale, the ESOP must own at least 30% of the employer corporation's stock. Section 117 expands the gain deferral provisions of Code section 1042 with a 10% limit on the deferral to sales of employer stock to S corporation ESOPs. Section 117 is effective for deferrals made after December 31, 2027.

Section 118 - Certain securities treated as publicly traded in case of employee stock ownership plans: Certain securities treated as publicly traded in case of employee stock ownership plans. Section 118 updates certain ESOP rules related to whether a security is a "publicly traded employer security" and "readily tradeable on an established securities market". In particular, Section 118 allows certain non-exchange traded securities to qualify as "publicly traded employer securities" so long as the security is subject to priced quotations by at least four dealers on an SEC-regulated interdealer quotation system; is not a penny stock and is not issued by a shell company; and has a public float of at least 10 percent of outstanding shares. For securities issued by domestic corporations, the issuer must publish annual audited financial statements. Securities issued by foreign corporations are subject to additional depository and reporting requirements. The updated definitions in Section 118 will allow highly regulated companies with liquid securities that are quoted on non-exchange markets to treat their stock as "public" for ESOP purposes, thus making it easier for these companies to offer ESOPs to their U.S. employees. Section 118 is effective for plan years beginning after December 31, 2026.

For more detailed information on ESOPs, see our companion text, *The Tools & Techniques of Employee Benefit and Retirement Planning*.

55.2 WHEN IS USE OF SUCH A DEVICE INDICATED?

1. When a shareholder who is a substantial owner of a closely-held business would like to shift his investment in that business, on a tax-deferred basis, into publicly traded securities. Tax-free rollover of the proceeds received from the sale of a business to an ESOP may be available if the proceeds are invested in U.S. businesses, enabling greater diversification. This rollover provision is intended to encourage employee stock ownership (see discussion of mechanics under Tax Implications, below).

2. When an employer would like to obtain an income tax deduction with little or no cash outlay. A current deduction is allowed (within limits) for both employer contributions of cash and for contributions of stock (including stock of the employer company) or other property contributed to the ESOP.[3] A contribution of an employer's stock generates a deduction equal to its fair market value. The sizable deduction reduces cash flow out of the corporation in profit years. In loss years, the contribution of stock to an ESOP can create a carry-back which might result in a tax refund to the corporation (but note that Congress has modified the carry-back rules several times and it may depend on whether it is pre or post 2021 – see Code section 172).[4]

3. When an employer wants to create a market for its closely-held (and therefore otherwise relatively unmarketable) stock. An ESOP may be able to purchase treasury stock or authorized but unissued stock, as well as stock owned by individual shareholders, without causing a loss of corporate control by majority shareholders. (But note that if a defined contribution plan–other than a profit sharing plan–is established by an employer whose stock is not readily tradable on an established market and employer stock constitutes more than 10 percent of the plan's assets, participating employees must be entitled to exercise voting rights of stock allocated to their account on certain major corporate matters.)

4. When a corporation faces an accumulated earnings threat. An ESOP can be used to take cash out of a corporation and thus reduce the potential for an accumulated earnings tax problem. The reduction in taxable income of the corporation due to deductible contributions lessens the pressure on a corporation to pay dividends. Certain dividends may be subject to lower income tax rates to the recipient, but they are nondeductible by the corporation.

5. When an employer is seeking a way to motivate and compensate long-service employees. Since the ultimate value of an employee's ESOP interest is directly related to the value of the employee's stock, increased productivity and corporate growth become a direct employee concern. ESOPs also provide a means for employees (including shareholder-employees) to supplement Social Security as well as other corporate-provided retirement benefits.

6. When shareholders with large amounts of corporate stock in their estate want liquidity, the stock may be sold to the ESOP in exchange for cash, thus providing the liquidity to pay state and federal death taxes and other debts.

7. When a corporation desires to make payment of premiums for life insurance on key employees from deductible contributions. In appropriate cases, life insurance payments on key employees, who are also shareholders, may be shifted to the ESOP from the corporation, and these premium payments, which are otherwise not deductible to the corporation, effectively become deductible contributions to the ESOP. The insurance policy is an investment of the ESOP and may be the source of liquidity for the ESOP to purchase the shareholder's stock at his death.

EMPLOYEE STOCK OWNERSHIP PLAN CHAPTER 55

8. When an employer is seeking a means for financing corporate growth through the use of untaxed dollars. By selling rather than contributing stock to the ESOP, an employer can obtain a large amount of cash. Conversely, if the corporation had borrowed cash from a bank to finance corporate expansion, only interest payments on the loan would be deductible. The principal would have to be repaid with "expensive" (nondeductible) dollars. On the other hand, the corporation will obtain a deduction for the dollars it then contributes to the ESOP. The ESOP receives these free of tax and uses them (without reduction for income taxes) to repay the bank loan.

9. When a minority shareholder wishes to retire or is forced to sell his or her stock, and there is no market, or when there is a dispute among shareholders. The ESOP can provide liquidity which may allow the shareholder to sell her stock. The ESOP can borrow funds to acquire a selling shareholder's stock.[5]

55.3 WHAT ARE THE REQUIREMENTS?

1. ESOPs meeting certain requirements may distribute benefits in the form of employer stock *or* cash. Participants must be given the right to receive employer stock if they so desire, unless the employer's charter or by-laws restrict the ownership of substantially all outstanding employer stock to employees and/or the ESOP. (This would be quite common, see the frequently asked questions related to S corporations later in this chapter.) If ownership is so restricted, a participant need not be given the right to receive employer stock. The participant must then be given the right to receive his benefit in cash.

   If employer stock is distributed, participants must be given a "put" option for a limited time, which allows them to sell the stock to the employer at its fair market value. The put option requirement does not apply to a bank which maintains an ESOP if the bank is prohibited by law from redeeming or buying its own stock and participants are given the right to receive their benefits in cash. It appears that an ESOP with no cash distribution option (which would not be typical) is required to give a put option to participants only with respect to employer stock acquired by the plan after December 31, 1979 or acquired with proceeds of a loan obtained from or guaranteed by a disqualified person (unless the stock is readily tradable on an established securities market).[6]

2. The plan must meet the same requirements as apply to other qualified plans, with respect to coverage, nondiscrimination in contributions, nonforfeitability on termination, rules regarding forfeitures, and rules relative to the source of contributions.[7] IRS regulations do not allow an ESOP to be integrated with Social Security.[8] However, certain ESOPs in existence on November 1, 1977 that were integrated with Social Security were "grandfathered" and may be able to continue to use those provisions. As is the case for all qualified retirement plans, an ESOP must be in writing.[9]

3. The trust must be for the exclusive benefit of the employees and their beneficiaries (e.g., the ESOP is not meant as a means of bailing out financially troubled employers).[10]

4. The trust must be a United States trust and not a foreign trust.

5. The cost of employer stock purchased by the trustee must not exceed its fair market value. An independent appraisal is required for ESOP transactions unless the securities are publicly traded on a national securities exchange.[11]

6. Participants must be entitled to vote employer stock that has been allocated to their accounts if the stock is registered under the Securities Exchange Act of 1934. If the employer's stock is not readily tradable on an established market and more than 10 percent of the plan's assets are invested in employer stock, the plan must give participants voting rights on major corporate issues (generally those involving the approval or disapproval of any corporate merger or consolidation, recapitalization, reclassification, liquidation, dissolution, sale of substantially all assets of a trade or business, or similar transactions).[12]

7. Qualifying participants who have completed ten years of participation in the ESOP and reached age fifty-five must be given the opportunity to diversify 25 percent of their account balances for the first five years and an additional 25 percent (fifty percent) in the sixth year.[13]

8. Generally, the plan must provide that, if the participant elects (and if the required spousal consent is properly given), the distribution of a participant's account balance will commence within one year after the plan year (1) in which he separates from service by reason of attainment of normal retirement age, disability, or death, or (2) which is the fifth plan year following the plan year in which he otherwise separates from service.[14]

9. The plan must ensure that, in the case of certain "qualified sales" (after October 22, 1986) of employer securities by a participant (under Code section 1042) or executor (under former Code section 2057) to the ESOP, no portion of the assets of the plan attributable to the securities purchased by the plan may accrue or be allocated during the nonallocation period for the benefit of:

   a. the taxpayer who made the election under section 1042 (or the decedent whose executor made the election under former section 2057);

   b. any individual who is a member of the family (brother, sister, spouse, ancestor, lineal descendant) of the taxpayer or decedent; or

   c. any person who owns, or is considered as owning under the attribution rules of Section 318(a), more than 25 percent (by number or value) of any class of outstanding stock of the employer or any corporation which is a member of the same controlled group of corporations as is the employer.[15]

10. An ESOP can own stock in an S corporation, so long as the plan provides that no portion of the assets of the plan attributable to the employer securities accrue to the benefit of a "disqualified person" in a "nonallocation year."[16] In basic terms, a "disqualified person" includes:

    a. an officer or director (or an individual having powers or responsibilities similar to those of an officer or director);

    b. a person who owns 10 percent or more of the stock in the employer's S corporation; and

    c. a highly compensated employee earning 10 percent or more of the yearly wages of an employer.[17]

Example 1. A corporate client has been consistently earning $200,000 per year. The corporation has no pension or profit-sharing plan. The employees are eager to see some type of deferred compensation program instituted. Because of an expansion program, the corporation periodically is in a cash-poor position. The schedule below shows the amount of the increase in corporate working capital by comparing an ESOP with a profit-sharing plan and with no deferred compensation plan.

From the comparison, it is clear that establishing an ESOP gives the greatest increase in working capital.

	No Plan	Profit Sharing Plan	ESOP
Earnings Before Tax	$200,000	$200,000	$200,000
Contributions (15% x $600,000 of compensation eligible for coverage)	$0	$90,000	$90,000
Taxable Income	$200,000	$110,000	$110,000
Tax (assume combined federal and state bracket is 40%)	$80,000	$44,000	$44,000
Net Earnings After Taxes	$120,000	$66,000	$66,000
Net Worth Increase: Net Earnings After Taxes	$120,000	$66,000	$66,000
Cash from Sale of Capital Stock to ESOP	$0	$0	$90,000
Increase in Working Capital	$120,000	$66,000	$156,000

Example 2. Another corporate client needs a new building that will cost approximately $250,000. The only available loans require an amortization of the $250,000 at the rate of $50,000 per year over five years, plus interest on the unpaid balance. Using the schedule above, if the corporation established a profit-sharing plan, only $66,000 would be left after taxes on $200,000 of earnings in order to amortize the principal debt and pay the interest. Clearly, this would not be enough money. If the corporation had no plan, sufficient monies would be available to amortize the debt and pay the interest

although the net worth increase after such payments would be rather small. If an ESOP were established, the ESOP could borrow the $250,000 from the bank (the loan usually being guaranteed by the corporation) and the ESOP would immediately purchase $250,000 of capital stock from the corporation. The corporation's net working capital would be immediately increased by $250,000. The corporation would then make contributions to the ESOP on an annual basis and the ESOP would repay the bank.

For loans made prior to August 21, 1996 for an ESOP to purchase or refinance employer securities, one-half of the interest received by a lender is exempt from income tax provided certain conditions are met.[18] Although lenders may no longer exclude such interest for post-August 20, 1996 loans, the exclusion is still available for loans made under a binding written contract prior to June 10, 1996, or for certain refinancing loans, provided the loans meet the requirements of former Code section 133.

Example 3. A majority of the stock of a closely held corporation is owned by one individual, and his wife and/or children own the balance of the stock. The stock represents a part of the individual's estate, but not more than 35 percent of his adjusted gross estate and, therefore, not enough to qualify for a redemption under section 303 of the Internal Revenue Code. Additionally, the spouse and/or the children, also shareholders, are beneficiaries of the estate and therefore a redemption of the stock by the corporation would constitute a dividend to the estate (by reason of the attribution rules of section 318 of the Code). Also, consider that the corporation may not have sufficient funds to redeem all the shares of stock and certainly any partial redemption would also constitute a dividend.

The creation of an ESOP would establish an entity that could purchase all or any portion of the stock owned by the estate and not create dividend consequences to the estate. Such a purchase would indirectly give rise to a deduction for the corporation, a deduction it could not take if the purchase were made directly from the estate. (Although such a transaction has been given approval by the Internal Revenue Service in at least one private letter ruling, it would be advisable to obtain a favorable ruling in advance of a sale.) The Internal Revenue Service has stringent requirements that must be met for an advance ruling. These requirements are updated annually.[19]

A fourth example of the use of an ESOP involves the conversion of premiums on nondeductible key individual life insurance into – what is in essence - a tax deduction.

Example 4. Assume that a corporation is owned by two or more stockholders equally and the stockholders desire to have a buy-sell agreement (either an entity or cross purchase type) funded by life insurance so that on the death of any one stockholder there will be sufficient monies to purchase or redeem the shares of stock of the decedent and permit the company to continue in business. Payments of the life insurance premiums are normally nondeductible.

If, however, the company established an ESOP and the investment committee directed the ESOP to purchase key individual insurance on the lives of all of the stockholders, then upon the death of any stockholder, the trust (as the beneficiary of the life insurance policy) would be entitled to the proceeds - income tax free. The trust would then be able to use the proceeds and negotiate with the personal representative of the deceased stockholder for the purchase of the shares of stock, at the then fair market value of those shares on the date of the decedent's death. Consideration must be given to the possibility that the ESOP would not be able to acquire the stock, which then would leave the life insurance proceeds in the plan. Final regulations prohibit an ESOP from buying life insurance with the proceeds of a loan obtained from or guaranteed by a disqualified person. In addition, a leveraged ESOP must not obligate itself to purchase stock at an indefinite future time (although it can be given an option to acquire stock).[20]

55.4 TAX IMPLICATIONS

A corporation is allowed a deduction (within limits) for contributions made to the ESOP even if it had no profits during the year the contribution was made.[21] The excess deduction might therefore generate a net operating loss carryback with a resulting tax refund.

Generally, an employer can deduct a contribution to a single ESOP of up to 25 percent of the total compensation paid or accrued to the beneficiaries.[22] If the employer contributes less than the deductible amount, the difference between the amount that was actually contributed and the amount that could have been deducted may be carried forward and used to increase the deduction limit in future years.[23]

Special deduction rules apply to C corporation plans that have incurred debt to purchase employer stock (i.e., leveraged C corporation ESOPs). An employer may contribute as much as 25 percent of covered compensation to a single ESOP where the contributions are applied to make principal payments on the loan. Additional unlimited deductions are allowed for employer contributions used to pay interest on the loan.[24] However, these provisions are not available for S corporation ESOPs.[25] In addition, limitations on allocations to employee accounts (which apply if more than one-third of contributions are allocated to certain key employees) may limit the availability of these special deduction limits in some circumstances.[26]

The employer does not have to make the contribution to the ESOP in the form of the stock of the employer. The contribution may be made in cash, any other property, or employer stock. However, a contribution of property may result in a prohibited transaction or other problems that should be carefully examined. Any one of the three contribution media, alone or in combination with the others, can create a deduction to the corporation equal to the sum of the cash and the fair market value of the assets being transferred.

If the corporation transfers assets to the ESOP that have appreciated in value, the gain will constitute income to the corporation.[27] For example, if the corporation bought stock, which grew from $3 to $8 a share, a contribution of that stock would result in a $5 per share gain. This rule applies to any transfer of property with the exception of cash and stock of the employer.

The corporation is allowed a special deduction for cash dividends paid with respect to stock held on the dividend record date by an ESOP, provided the dividends are:

1. paid directly in cash to participants or their beneficiaries;

2. paid indirectly to them through the plan within ninety days after the close of the plan year; or

3. used to make payments on a loan incurred to purchase qualifying employer securities.[28]

For shares acquired by an ESOP after August 4, 1989, a deduction is allowed under (3) only if the dividends are paid on shares purchased with the loan proceeds.

A corporation is also generally permitted a deduction for dividends paid to the plan (or paid out to participants or beneficiaries) and reinvested in qualifying employer securities, if so elected by the participants or their beneficiaries.[29]

A major income tax benefit is available to an individual who sells C Corporation (not S Corporation) stock to an ESOP and *replaces* it with within certain time limits. Under Code section 1042, recognition of gain may be deferred on the sale of closely held stock to an ESOP if all of the following apply:

1. the sale would qualify for long-term capital gain treatment;

2. after the sale the ESOP owns at least 30 percent of the total value of the employer securities;

3. within a fifteen-month period (beginning three months prior to the day of sale) "qualified replacement securities" are purchased;

4. the taxpayer held the shares for three years or longer.

5. the seller affirmatively elects non-recognition on a timely filed income tax return; and

6. the seller obtains from the company and files a statement consenting to excise taxes under Code sections 4978 and 4979A if certain post-sale conditions apply. These apply if there is a disposition of stock (for reasons other than

participants retiring or separating from service) within the three-year period after the sale to which Code section 1042 applied which causes the employer stock held by an ESOP to fall below thirty percent of the total value of all employer securities (certain reorganizations are excepted), and if allocations of qualified securities are made to related parties (discussed further below).[30]

"Qualified replacement securities" generally means stock or bonds issued by a domestic corporation which, for the taxable year of issuance, does not have passive investment income of more than 25 percent of gross receipts. If the cost of the replacement securities is less than the amount of the deferred gain, the difference is currently taxable.

A company could conceivably convert to a C corporation just before sale and the owners may still come under Code section 1042. Although it is possible for a shareholder to obtain beneficial nonrecognition of gain on the sale of stock to an ESOP, there is a pitfall to avoid. With respect to sales of securities after October 22, 1986, if there is a prohibited accrual or allocation (see paragraph (9) under "What are the Requirements," above), a penalty tax equal to 50 percent of the amount of the prohibited accrual or allocation will be levied against the employer sponsoring the plan.[31] In addition, the amount of any prohibited accrual or allocation will be treated as if distributed to the individual involved and taxed as such.[32] Up to 5 percent of the securities purchased by the ESOP in the Section 1042 transaction can be allocated to the benefit of lineal descendants of the seller without creating any adverse tax consequences.[33] Professional guidance will steer owners away from this danger.

Furthermore, if an ESOP has made an investment in stock of an S corporation, allocations to a person who directly owns 10 percent or more of the S corporation stock (or owns 20 percent or more indirectly with members of his family) may result in significant penalties. Thus, for smaller corporations, a purchase of S corporation stock must be very carefully considered.[34]

Assuming none of the penalties described above apply, employer contributions are not currently taxable to participating employees. ESOP trust assets grow tax free, even if an employee's rights become nonforfeitable. An employee pays no tax until a distribution is made to him (see the discussion of the tax treatment of distributions in Chapter 57).

Distributions to Plan Participants

If employer stock is paid to a plan participant in a lump sum distribution (as that term is defined in the Internal Revenue Code), any net unrealized appreciation (NUA) on that stock that is not attributable to deductible employee voluntary contributions will not be taxed to the participant until the participant sells the stock.[35]

This unrealized appreciation will be treated as long-term capital gain when the stock is sold. Any appreciation after distribution will be treated as long- or short-term capital gain depending on whether the participant has held the stock for the requisite holding period following the date of distribution. The cash portion and that portion of the lump sum distribution that is an amount equal to the employer contributions used to purchase stock may, under some circumstances, be taxed to the participant at the time of distribution.

Example. If the individual receives an ESOP distribution of $30,000 cash and employer stock worth $100,000 on the distribution date and if the employer had contributed an amount equal to $75,000 which was used to purchase that stock, then the $25,000 gain will not be taxed to the participant until the securities are sold. But at the date of distribution, the $105,000 ($30,000 cash plus $75,000 "basis" of the appreciated securities) will be taxed under the lump sum distribution rules in effect at the time of distribution. The employee may rollover a portion of this to an IRA to further defer income tax.

Amounts attributable to deductible employee contributions are not considered part of a lump sum distribution and are taxed as ordinary income on receipt; any net unrealized appreciation on employer securities attributable to deductible employee contributions is taxed upon distribution of the securities, whether or not they are sold.[36]

If the participant or beneficiary of a participant does not take a lump sum distribution of the cash or employer securities but instead receives the employer securities over a period in excess of one taxable year of the recipient (or beneficiary), the entire amount attributable to the employer contribution, deductible employee contributions, and any subsequent appreciation on employer stock will be taxed at the ordinary income rate in effect at the time of distribution, since this would not be a lump sum.[37]

To take advantage of the special NUA tax treatment, advisors must pay careful attention to the definitional rules of lump sum distributions, which require "distribution or payment within one taxable year of the recipient of the balance to the credit of an employee which becomes payable to the recipient—

1. on account of the employee's death;

2. after the employee attains age 59½;

3. on account of the employee's separation from service; or

4. after the employee has become disabled."[38]

If the employee has made any nondeductible contributions to the ESOP, any unrealized appreciation in the employer stock that is attributable to such contributions will escape taxation until the participant sells the securities. At that time, the gain will be taxed.[39]

Anti-abuse Rules

Treasury Regulations section 1.409(p)-1 was both highly complex and harshly punitive but it has effectively foreclosed any remaining ability of the owners of a closely held S-corporation ESOP to funnel all or most of the tax benefits from the ESOP to themselves. Generally, an ESOP is permitted to hold S corporation stock, provided that the ESOP benefits a sufficiently broad-based group of employees. But Congress has long been concerned about ownership structures involving S corporations and ESOPs that concentrate the benefits of the ESOP, directly or indirectly, in a small number of persons, particularly if those persons are the business's owners and/or its highly paid executives. To enforce its intent, the Code provides that an ESOP holding employer securities consisting of stock in an S corporation must provide that no portion of the assets of the plan may accrue or be allocated directly or indirectly for the benefit of certain disqualified persons. Treasury regulations made final December 20, 2006 provide guidance on the definition and effects of a prohibited allocation under Code section 409(p), identification of disqualified persons and determination of a non-allocation year, calculation of synthetic equity under section 409(p)(5), and standards for determining whether a transaction is an avoidance or evasion of section 409(p).[40] These regulations generally affect plan sponsors of, and participants in, ESOPs holding stock of Subchapter S corporations.

The primary purpose of the "anti-abuse" rules of Code section 409(p) was to ensure that ESOPs result in broad based employee ownership and meaningful benefits to rank and file employees. In a nutshell, section 409(p) requires that if "deemed owned" shares of S corporations that are attributable to "disqualified persons" result in a "non-allocation year," significant penalties are triggered in the form of a 50 percent excise tax. A "non-allocation year" results when "disqualified persons" are deemed to own more than 50 percent of the equity of the entity that sponsors the ESOP. The calculations that determine "deemed owned" shares include not only direct equity interests but also "synthetic equity."

Subsequent to the addition of section 409(p) to the Internal Revenue Code, which shut down abuses involving one- and two-person ESOPs, some creative promoters shifted gears and attempted to navigate around the "anti-abuse" rules by creating alternative structures involving shell companies (which were then sold at a later date to unsuspecting consumers), management companies and Nonqualified Deferred Compensation (NQDC)-related ESOP schemes. While these new variations did technically involve rank and file employees, the same abusive result occurred - the vast majority of the economic benefit ends up with a very small group of highly paid executives while rank and file employees received virtually nothing of any substance. The term the IRS created to describe the failure to deliver meaningful economic benefit to rank and file employees in these newly devised ESOP related schemes was "insubstantial benefits."

One of the most important elements of the "anti-abuse" rules is the concept of "synthetic equity." section 409(p) provides a very broad definition of "synthetic equity." Revenue Ruling 2003-6 clarified the definition of "synthetic equity" and the newly issued regulations expand the definition to include NQDC benefits (which is at the heart of the various S corporation ESOP scams), whether a management company is included or not. Whether or not a management company is involved, the result is the same – a large amount of the company's earnings are being funneled into the pockets of highly paid executives at the expense of rank and file employees.

Under the newly issued regulations, "synthetic equity" now includes Nonqualified Deferred Compensation (NQDC) plans (whether stock based or not), allocated ESOP shares, unallocated ESOP shares, restricted stock, phantom stock, stock appreciation rights, qualified stock options, non-qualified stock options, warrants and other rights to acquire stock in the S corporation that sponsors the ESOP or any related entity to that S corporation.

55.5 ISSUES IN COMMUNITY PROPERTY STATES

Benefits from qualified plans (pension/profit sharing plans, and ESOPs) and IRAs are generally:

- held to be community property to the extent contributions are made by or on behalf of a married employee who is a resident of one of the community property states (enumerated in the discussion of community property in the "Introduction") during the period of employment; and

- characterized based on the period of participation in the pension while subject to community property over the total period of participation in the pension.

That said, some applications of federal tax law regarding retirement plans are "applied without regard to community property laws."[41]

For example, a spouse works for forty years and earns a pension. For twenty years she is married and subject to community property. 50 percent of the pension is community property (20/40= 50 percent).[42]

These rules, while relatively simple to state, can present significant problems when applied to specific situations, and may vary somewhat between states, so it is important to consult the law of the applicable state or with local Counsel.

The major areas of difficulty are divorce and death of an employee.

It was unclear after the enactment of the Employee Retirement Income Security Act of 1974 (ERISA) whether community property laws continued to apply to qualified plan benefits. Some argued that ERISA "preempted" state community property laws. Others argued that award of a part of an employee's qualified plan benefits to his spouse was an assignment or alienation of benefits prohibited by ERISA. If the courts had followed these latter arguments, spouses in community property states would no longer be entitled to the 50 percent of qualified plan benefits that they had prior to ERISA. Many courts faced with the issue determined that ERISA did not supersede state community property laws. However, in a landmark 1997 case, the U.S. Supreme Court held in a five-to-four decision that a deceased spouse may not make a bequest of her community property interest in her participant spouse's undistributed qualified plan benefits.[43] Writing for the majority, Justice Kennedy upheld ERISA's prohibition on the assignment or alienation of benefits, thus preempting state community property law. Nonetheless, it is generally accepted that a non-participant spouse personally retains a valid community property interest in qualified plan benefits, as discussed in this chapter and Chapter 57.

A spouse's community property interest in his spouse's qualified plan benefits is included in his gross estate if he or she predeceased the spouse with the qualified plan benefits. Estate taxes apply even though the surviving spouse may have no immediate access to the benefit to provide funds to pay the tax. Unfortunate situations also arise where the appraised "value" of the deceased spouse's community property interest is much greater than the benefit actually received from the plan; for example, when the surviving spouse is less than 100 percent vested and terminates employment soon after his spouse's death. However, most such benefits go to the surviving spouse and thus are eligible for the marital deduction and no federal death tax is due.

However, if any employee with qualified plan benefits predeceases his spouse, and benefits are paid to a beneficiary other than the surviving spouse, the surviving spouse may be treated as making a gift of 50 percent of the benefits payable to other beneficiaries (to the extent the benefits were community property). Thus, it may be found that the surviving spouse has made a taxable gift where the participant has directed that both community property interests in the benefit be paid to other beneficiaries. However, with the significant rights given to non-participant spouses by the Retirement Equity Act of 1984, it became difficult to have significant plan proceeds distributed without the spouse's permission. Such accidental and unintended taxable gifts can be a problem for persons not aware of the possible trap.

A question arises as to whether a spouse's consent to the designation of a trust as a beneficiary of the employee's plan benefits is a transfer with a retained life estate under Section 2038 of the Internal Revenue Code. If the spouse is a lifetime beneficiary of the trust, care must be exercised to minimize the possibility that the IRS will claim that the spouse's community property share of plan benefits remaining in the trust is subject to federal estate tax at the spouse's death.

The community property states have adopted varying positions to deal with the problem of valuing qualified plan benefits for purposes of division in a divorce. Prior to 1976, for example, California courts divided only *vested* qualified plan benefits, holding that non-vested benefits were "mere expectancies." However, a 1976 decision of the California Supreme Court overruled that position and held that *non-vested* qualified plan benefits were community property assets subject to division in a divorce proceeding. The benefits can be valued using actuarial methods. The court, recognizing that unfairness may result if the benefit does not actually "vest," stated that it may be appropriate in certain situations to divide benefit payments as they are received (rather than fixing a lump sum value at the time of the divorce). Thus, each spouse would share the risk that the full benefit would fail to fully vest.

55.6 FREQUENTLY ASKED QUESTIONS

Question – Can the employees vote shares of the stock held in the ESOP?

Answer – Not while stock is in the plan. While the plan participants have the right to direct the ESOP trustee in voting their allocated shares for specific major transactions, this does not mean employees vote them directly; the ESOP trustee actually votes the shares held by the ESOP.

Question – How should employer stock be valued?

Answer – If the employer's stock is not readily tradable on an established market, an independent appraisal is necessary annually to establish the value of the stock for contribution purposes (if the corporation contributes its stock) or for purposes of determining a proper purchase price (if the ESOP purchases stock from the corporation or from any third party stockholder). This valuation is always subject to scrutiny by the Internal Revenue Service and the Department of Labor. It should therefore be performed by a qualified independent full time professional appraiser, preferably one who specializes in appraising the employer's type of company.

Question – If there are no stock purchases or stock contributions during the year, is an annual appraisal still necessary?

Answer – An annual appraisal is probably still necessary in order to meet the reporting requirements established by ERISA with respect to the current value of the plan assets and the ERISA requirement that the value of a participant's account be determined annually. This information would have to be submitted to the Department of Labor, and current value probably could not be determined without such an appraisal. If there is a purchase of employer stock by the ESOP trust, the value of the stock must be ascertained at the time of purchase. If an ESOP were to pay a price greater than the fair market value of the employer's stock, the investment would be considered improper and might result in a disqualification of the plan.

Question – Are there any provisions of ERISA that do not apply to an ESOP?

Answer – ERISA treats the ESOP as an individual account plan. An individual account plan escapes that part of the ERISA reporting provisions that requires a statement of an actuary and is also exempt from paying plan termination insurance premiums to the Pension Benefit Guaranty Corporation.

Question – Can an ESOP allow voluntary nondeductible employee contributions?

Answer – Voluntary nondeductible contributions can be made to an ESOP, as well as to qualified pension, profit-sharing, or stock bonus plans. These contributions will be deemed annual additions for maximum contribution (i.e., section 415) purposes and thus, will have the impact of reducing the maximum employer contribution. The contributions will also have to pass a special nondiscrimination test.[44]

Provisions allowing voluntary nondeductible contributions to an ESOP should be approached with caution. Voluntary contributions to an ESOP should not be invested in employer stock unless the employer has complied with applicable federal and state securities requirements.

Question – A participant in an ESOP retires. He receives a distribution of employer stock. Is he under any obligation to sell the stock to the ESOP?

Answer – The default rule is that no prearranged enforceable agreement can exist between the participants of the plan and the ESOP that requires that the participants, upon receipt of the stock distribution from the ESOP, sell those securities back to the ESOP. Regulations specifically prohibit any security acquired with the proceeds of an exempt loan from being subject to a put, call, or other option, or buy-sell or similar arrangement while held by and when distributed from a plan.[45]

There are major exceptions. An ESOP may retain a "right of first refusal" on employer stock that is not publicly traded. In other words, if the participant wants to sell the employer stock distributed to him to a third party, he must first offer it to the employer or the ESOP.[46]

In addition, if the employer sponsoring the ESOP is a closely held company whose bylaws restrict the ownership of substantially all of its stock to employees or a tax-qualified plan, the ESOP is not required to distribute stock; instead, it can distribute cash, or the employer can require the employee to sell distributed stock back to the employer.[47] This can help ensure inadvertent disqualification of S corporation status and is common for S corporations.

It is possible to have a large number of stockholders with minimal interests in a company as a result of employer-stock distributions from the ESOP. All of these "small" stockholders are entitled to certain information and have certain rights under ERISA, state corporate laws, and state and federal securities laws. This factor can be a deterrent to establishing ESOPs, because buying out these shareholders can drain cash flow from the company.

Question – Can an ESOP purchase life insurance on the life of a key employee of the corporation?

Answer – The ESOP can purchase life insurance, commonly referred to as "key person" life insurance, on the life of an important employee of the corporation. The ESOP can use monies contributed to it by the corporation to pay the premiums, provided, however, that the amount of dollars used for the purchase of such insurance is limited. This limitation is designed to ensure that the ESOP meets the requirements of investing *primarily* in qualifying employer securities.

Question – Can an ESOP purchase life insurance and make the proceeds payable to the beneficiaries of employees participating in the ESOP?

Answer – An ESOP may provide life insurance for its participants so long as the insurance is deemed "incidental." The plan will generally meet this requirement if the premiums for any participant do not exceed 25 percent of the amount allocated to his or her ESOP account.[48]

Question – If a shareholder makes a sale of "qualified securities" to the ESOP, can the replacement securities be transferred to a revocable trust or other form of grantor trust?

Answer – The IRS has ruled that such a transfer will not result in a recapture of the gain rolled over, and that any purchases of stock by the trust will be deemed purchases by the grantor.[49]

Question – Assume that there is only one key person in a corporation and that key person owns 100 percent of the stock of the corporation. Is an ESOP an appropriate estate planning tool to use if there is no one in management who wishes to, or who is capable of continuing the business?

Answer – In this situation, an ESOP may not be an appropriate estate planning tool because the obligation to continue the business would be on the trustee of the ESOP. It can be very difficult to find a trustee willing to take the responsibility for operating a business. However, this problem can be avoided by finding another company (possibly a competitor) or person who will want to acquire the corporation at the stockholder's death.

Question – Can an ESOP be used to purchase the majority of the stock of a corporation from present owners?

Answer – There is no problem with a transfer of ownership from present stockholders to employees through an ESOP purchase of the present owners' stock.

Question – Do ESOPs have similar rights and restrictions regarding spouses as other qualified plans under ERISA?

Answer – Yes. However, depending on the plan and circumstance, a spouse's rights under the Retirement Equity Act of 1984 may not kick in until one year of marriage (but caution, the plan may vest spousal rights sooner than one year).[50]

Question – A man entitled to $50,000 from an ESOP dies having designated his adult son as the beneficiary of his plan benefits. Assume the funds are community property, and that the wife did not consent to the beneficiary designation. Can the wife be deprived of her 50 percent share of the pension benefits by her husband's action? If she did consent, has she made a taxable gift to her son of $25,000?

Answer – Certain restrictions are imposed on a married participant's ability to name a beneficiary for plan death benefits other than the surviving spouse. Generally, unless the surviving spouse is designated as the sole beneficiary, a qualified plan is required to pay plan benefits in the form of a "qualified preretirement survivor annuity" for participants who die prior to reaching retirement age and in the form of a "qualified joint and survivor annuity" for married participants who die after reaching retirement age (see Chapter 57).

With respect to the community property rights, in most community property states, the wife cannot be deprived of her community property interest by her husband's unilateral action of naming their son as the sole beneficiary. Thus, she is entitled to $25,000 from the plan. If the plan has already paid the funds to the son, the plan could be liable to the wife. Thus, it is important for plans to verify the existence or nonexistence of community property rights before distributing benefits. If the wife consented to the designation of the son as beneficiary, however, she would have no claim. It may be found that the surviving spouse has made a taxable gift to the son.

Question – Can an employer make contributions in excess of the annual additions limit to pay interest on a loan obtained by an ESOP to buy employer stock?

Answer – Employer contributions applied to pay loan interest, and forfeitures of fully leveraged (loaned) employer stock owned by the ESOP are disregarded for purposes of the annual additions limit on contributions to a participant's account in the ESOP; however, this rule applies only if deductible contributions allocated to "highly compensated employees" (as defined in Code section 414(q)), are not more than one-third of the total contributions.[51] Furthermore, this applies only to C corporation ESOPs, not S corporations.[52]

Question – What types of employer stock qualify as "employer securities" for purposes of an ESOP?

Answer – An ESOP must be designed to invest primarily in "employer securities." Shares of common stock of an employer that are readily tradable on an established securities market are "employer securities." If the employer has no stock that is publicly traded, "employer securities" are shares of common stock issued by the employer with a combination of voting power and dividend rights equal or greater than the classes of common stock of the employer with the greatest voting power and dividend rights. Noncallable preferred stock can be "employer securities" if the preferred stock is convertible at any time into common stock meeting the above requirements, and the conversion price is reasonable.[53] It is best to consult with an experienced wealth manager or portfolio manager experienced in investing Section 1042 qualifying replacement securities.

Question – Can an S corporation implement an ESOP?

Answer – Yes. The Small Business Job Protection Act of 1996 (SBJPA '96) provided that certain trusts (i.e., including an ESOP trust) may be a shareholder in an S corporation in tax years beginning after 1997. Furthermore, the Taxpayer Relief Act of 1997 (TRA '97) provided that an ESOP established by an S corporation is not required to grant participants the right to receive distributions in the form of employer stock, provided that distributions will otherwise be made in cash equivalent to the fair market value of the stock.[54] The 1997 provision was enacted to prevent inadvertent termination of S corporation status where ESOP participants could demand distributions in the form of stock, thus causing the total number of shareholders to exceed the 100-shareholder limit permitted for corporations maintaining an S election, or cause disqualification if they became a non-resident alien (or if they rollover to an IRA).

Under EGTRRA 2001, provisions generally effective for plan years ending after March 14, 2001 are designed to restrict the allocations that can be made to owners in small S corporation ESOPs. Generally, an allocation under the plan to a person who owns 10 percent directly, or 20 percent indirectly (or more), of the S corporation may result in a 50 percent excise tax against the plan, an additional 50 percent excise tax on certain shares of the S corporation, and current income taxation of the allocation. These rules are intended to limit perceived abuses of the ESOP provisions by S corporations designed primarily to benefit highly compensated employees.[55]

Question – How will S corporation income be treated in the hands of an ESOP?

Answer – S corporation income is not treated as Unrelated Business Taxable Income (UBTI).[56] Prior to the legislative protection enacted by TRA '97, ESOP participants were technically subject to the unrelated business income tax on their proportionate share of items of S corporation income. This protection extends to S corporation income or loss on employer securities.

Question – In general, does an ESOP provide much in the way of tax benefits?

Answer – Yes. ESOPs are presently one of the most effective tax minimization techniques available under the Internal Revenue Code![57]

CHAPTER ENDNOTES

1. See I.R.C. §§401, 4975(e)(7); ERISA §§407(d)(1), (5) and (6); 408(e).
2. H.R. 5515, "John S. McCain National Defense Authorization Act for Fiscal Year 2019" Sec. 862. Opportunities for employee-owned business concerns through Small Business Administration loan programs.
3. See I.R.C. §§404(a)(3), 404(a)(9).
4. I.R.C. §172.
5. See ESOPs: a tax advantaged way to provide liquidity for minority shareholders, *Federal Taxes Weekly Alert Newsletter* (2/3/11).
6. I.R.C. §§4975(e)(7), 409(h)(1)(B).
7. See generally, I.R.C. §401(a).
8. Treas. Reg. §1.401(l)-1(a)(4).
9. ERISA §402(a)(1).
10. I.R.C. §401(a).
11. ERISA §§408(e); I.R.C. §401(a)(28)(C).
12. I.R.C. §401(a)(22). This rule applies to employer stock acquired after December 31, 1979.
13. I.R.C. §401(a)(28)(B). This applies only to stock acquired after December 31, 1986.
14. I.R.C. §409(o). This rule applies only with respect to distributions attributable to stock acquired after December 31, 1986.
15. I.R.C. §409(n).
16. I.R.C. §409(p).
17. See I.R.C. §4975(e)(2)(H).
18. I.R.C. §133, prior to repeal by SBJPA '96.
19. See, e.g., Rev. Proc. 2004-4, 2004-1 IRB 125. Requirements for PLRs are usually the subject of the first few Revenue Procedures of the year, e.g. Rev. Proc. 2018-4 will contain the latest guidelines for employer plan related PLRs.
20. See Treas. Regs. §§54.4975-7, 54.4975-11.
21. Treas. Reg. §1.401-1(b)(iii).
22. I.R.C. §404(a)(3)(A)(i)(I). For plan years beginning before January 1, 2002, the limit was 15 percent.
23. I.R.C. §404(a)(3)(A)(ii). Special rules apply to unused pre-1987 contribution carryforwards. See I.R.C. §404(a)(3)(A)(v).
24. I.R.C. §404(a)(9).
25. I.R.C. §404(a)(9)(C).
26. I.R.C. §415(c)(6).
27. Rev. Rul. 73-345, 1973-2 CB 11.
28. I.R.C. §404(k).
29. I.R.C. §404(k)(2)(A). This rule applies to tax years beginning after 2001.
30. I.R.C. §4978(a). I.R.C. §4979A.
31. I.R.C. §4979A.
32. I.R.C. §409(n)(2).
33. I.R.C. §409(n)(3)(A).
34. See I.R.C. §§409(p), 4979A. See the question, "Can an S corporation implement an ESOP?" under the Frequently Asked Questions, for additional information.
35. I.R.C. §402(e)(4)(B).
36. I.R.C. §402(e)(4)(A).
37. I.R.C. §402(e)(4)(A).
38. I.R.C. §402(e)(4)(D).
39. I.R.C. §402(e)(4)(A).
40. Treas. Reg. §1.409(p)-1, https://www.irs.gov/pub/irs-regs/td_9302.pdf.
41. See., e.g., I.R.C. §402(e)(4)(D)(iii), I.R.C. §408(g).
42. See, e.g. Wis. Stat. §§766.61 and 766.62; *Taggart v. Taggart*, 552 SW 2d, 422 (Tx 1977).
43. *Boggs v. Boggs*, 117 S.Ct. 1754 (1997).
44. I.R.C. §401(m).
45. Treas. Reg. §54.4975-7(b)(4).

46. Treas. Reg. §54.4975-7(b)(9).
47. I.R.C. §409(h).
48. See IRS Publication 6392 for discussion of "incidental" ownership of life insurance by qualified plans.
49. Priv. Ltr. Rul. 9141046.
50. Treas. Reg. 1.401(a)-20, Q&A 25.
51. I.R.C. §415(c)(6).
52. I.R.C. §404(a)(9)(C).
53. I.R.C. §§4975(e)(8), 409(l).
54. I.R.C. §1361(c)(6), I.R.C. §409(h)(2)(B).
55. I.R.C. §§409(p), 4979A. For ESOPs established after March 14, 2001, and ESOPs in effect on or before March 14, 2001 for which an S election was not in effect on that date, the new rules apply for plan years ending after March 14, 2001. For any other ESOPs, the amendments generally apply to plan years beginning after 2004.
56. I.R.C. §512(e)(3).
57. See Leimberg and Thon, "ESOPs Can Produce Results Not Available Through Other Planning, *Estate Planning*, March 2003, vol. 30, no. 3 (March 2003), p. 107 and Leimberg and Thon, "The Advantages and Uses of ESOPs in Estate and Business Planning", *Estate Planning*, vol. 30, no. 2 (Feb. 2003), p. 59.

INDIVIDUAL RETIREMENT PLANS (INCLUDING SEP AND SIMPLE IRAS)

CHAPTER 56

56.1 INTRODUCTION

At their most basic, individual retirement plans are an investing tool used by individuals to acquire and allocate funds for retirement savings. There are several types of IRAs: Traditional IRAs, Roth IRAs, SIMPLE IRAs and SEP IRAs. Starting in 2023, the SECURE 2.0 Act allows Roth contributions to both SEP and SIMPLE IRAs.

Traditional and Roth IRAs are established by individuals. The individual is then allowed to contribute 100 percent of compensation (self-employment income for sole proprietors and partners) up to a set maximum dollar amount to that plan. Contributions to the Traditional IRA may be tax deductible depending on the taxpayer's income, tax filing status and coverage by an employer-sponsored retirement plan. Roth IRA (or other Roth retirement account) contributions are not tax-deductible.

SEP and SIMPLE IRAs are retirement plans established by employers, and are acronyms for Savings Incentive Match Plan for Employees (SIMPLE) and *Simplified Employee Pension (SEP)*.

Withdrawals from a non-Roth IRA are taxed as ordinary income (except potentially to the extent of any basis from non-deductible contributions), even if traceable to capital gains. Since income is likely to be lower after retirement, the hope on the part of the individual is that the tax rate will be lower. Combined with potential tax savings at the time of contribution, IRAs can prove to be very valuable tax management tools for individuals. Also, depending on income, an individual may be able to fit into a lower tax bracket with tax-deductible contributions during working years while still enjoying a low tax bracket during retirement.

Roth IRAs are the exception. With a Roth IRA, there is no deduction for contributions, but distributions are usually tax-free, as long as all eligibility requirements are met.

In recent years, both the SECURE Act and the Secure 2.0 Act (passed December 29, 2022) have made sweeping changes to many of the rules surrounding retirement plans, and the law will likely change further after the publication of this edition, due to either corrective legislation, or more likely, final regulations around the Secure Act which are expected in late 2023 and/or proposed and final regulations surrounding the Secure 2.0 Act (none are yet proposed but industry groups such as the American College of Trust and Estate Counsel (ACTEC) have asked Treasury to clarify some aspects of the new legislation). So, be careful to check for any updates in this area.

56.2 WHEN IS USE OF SUCH A DEVICE INDICATED?

1. The use of a traditional IRA is indicated when the married client or spouse is covered under a qualified plan and does not make in excess of the AGI amount at which deductible contributions to an IRA are not permitted. Even if the contribution is not tax deductible under the above limits, the earnings will accumulate income tax-deferred, although in such cases, it is likely to be more beneficial to make non-deductible contributions to a Roth IRA rather than a traditional IRA (or if income is too high, possibly later convert to one). Additionally, the client should be receiving an income which is not needed by the family to maintain its current standard of living, and which could be put aside for retirement.

2. A traditional IRA is indicated where neither the client nor spouse is covered under a qualified plan, but both work. If the client and spouse are both working, each can have his or her own traditional IRA and contribute up to the maximum based on his or her respective income, assuming both otherwise qualify.

3. A traditional IRA is also indicated where the client is not covered under a plan, has earned income, is married, and has no income from employment.

4. A rollover IRA may also be indicated where an individual has received a distribution from a qualified plan, tax sheltered annuity or an eligible section 457 governmental plan and seeks to avoid current taxation on all or a part of the distribution.

5. The client may be an employer who does not have any type of qualified retirement plan and would like to establish a plan covering only himself.

6. A Roth IRA is indicated where the client would not otherwise qualify for a deduction for contributing to a traditional IRA. Alternatively, where a client anticipates a reduced need to access IRA funds during retirement, a Roth IRA may be preferred, since the mandatory distribution rules of traditional IRAs (requiring traditional IRAs to be distributed after their required beginning date over the participant's lifetime) do not apply to Roth IRAs. Thus, funds can continue to accumulate tax free in a Roth IRA through retirement, preserving more benefits for the heirs.

7. Clients anticipating that they will be in a high marginal tax bracket following retirement may benefit more from the tax-free withdrawal benefit of the Roth IRA than from the initial deduction associated with traditional IRAs. Factors to be considered include the clients' tax bracket at the time of the contribution, the length of time until anticipated distributions begin, the estimated return on invested assets, and estimated post-retirement income. State income tax may also be a factor.

56.3 WHAT ARE THE REQUIREMENTS?

1. An individual can set aside retirement savings in a variable premium annuity contract, a regular fixed rate annuity contract, or a trusteed or custodial account with a bank, savings and loan, or credit union. Many brokerage firms are eligible to act as custodian as well. Also, it is possible to split total contributions into more than one IRA. For example, a part of the permissible contribution could go into a variable premium annuity contract and the balance could be placed into a trusteed bank account.[1]

2. Three parties can make deposits to a traditional IRA. These are the employee, the employee's employer, or the employee's union.

3. Annual contributions must be made in cash. Contributions of other property are not permissible (except in the case of "rollovers"; see below).[2]

4. The plan must be established and the contribution made within the taxable year for which a deduction is allowed or before the due date (not including extensions) for filing the individual's tax returns for that taxable year. For most taxpayers, contributions to a traditional or Roth IRA must therefore be made by April 15th of the following year.

5. Traditional IRAs (including SEP and SIMPLE IRAs) must begin to pay a participant's benefit by the April 1st following the calendar year in which the participant reaches age 70½. The Secure Act changed this applicable age to age 72 and the Secure 2.0 Act changed this to age 73 in 2023, scheduled to change to age 75 in 2033. This April 1 of the year after the applicable age is called the required beginning date or RBD and is very important not only as to when RMDs start, but how RMDs are calculated for beneficiaries after death. Roth IRAs have no required beginning date and so all Roth IRA owners are deemed to die before their required beginning date for their Roth IRA account.

6. For all IRAs, including Roth IRAs, if the IRA owner dies *before* the required beginning date, there are three basic alternatives after the Secure Act.

   a) If there is an eligible designated beneficiary, payments are made over the life expectancy of the beneficiary - similar in most cases to the law prior to the Secure Act, with a newly created exception and new rule for minor children. The five categories of eligible designated beneficiaries are 1) a surviving spouse, 2) an owner's child under age 21; 3) someone disabled; 4) someone chronically ill; and 5) someone no more than 10 years younger than the owner. These categories can use the old "stretch" rules to pay out over the beneficiaries' life expectancy, but for minor children of the owner, the ten-year rule kicks in at age 21, forcing the account to be terminated by the end of the tenth year after the child turns age 21. Proposed regulations would allow an eligible designated beneficiary to elect into the 10 year rule if the plan permits. This might occur, for example, if the beneficiary would not much longer than 10 years of life expectancy anyway.

   b) If there is no designated beneficiary (such as to an estate, LLC or non-qualifying trust),

INDIVIDUAL RETIREMENT PLANS (INCLUDING SEP AND SIMPLE IRAS) CHAPTER 56

payments must be paid out by December 31 following five years after the IRA owner's death. For instance, if the owner dies on October 1, 2023, all payments must be made by December 31, 2028. Note this rule is the same as pre-Secure Act.

c) If there is a designated beneficiary that is not an eligible designated beneficiary (which would be common, such as naming an adult child or grandchild), then the Secure Act (for most cases, effective for deaths after December 31, 2019) mandates that payments be paid out by December 31 following ten years after the IRA owner's death. Very similar to the 5-year rule noted above, but twice as long. For example, if the IRA dies on October 1, 2023, all payments must be made by December 31, 2033.

If the sole beneficiary is the IRA owner's spouse, the spouse may also roll over the balance to the spouse's own IRA or elect to treat the decedent's IRA as the spouse's own. There may be circumstances when a surviving spouse may not want to do this right away, or does not do this, such as when the surviving spouse is older than the deceased, when they may further delay their required beginning date if it is a traditional IRA, or if the surviving spouse is under age 59 ½, when keeping it as an inherited IRA can avoid a 10% penalty on withdrawals should the surviving spouse need to tap the funds before that age. If the surviving spouse keeps the funds in an inherited IRA, distributions must be made over the remaining life expectancy of the spouse, recalculated annually, beginning at the later of the end of the calendar year immediately following the calendar year in which the owner died or the end of the calendar year in which the owner would have attained the applicable age (73 as of 2023, scheduled to be age 75 in 2033).

Starting in 2024, however, Section 327 of the Secure Act forces the surviving spouse to make a special election to receive this spousal benefit of a delayed RBD, However, if they do make this new election, not only do they keep the special delayed RBD in effect prior to the effective date of Secure 2.0 Act, but once their RMDs start, they can be based on the Uniform Life Table, recalculated annually, as opposed to the single life table, recalculated annually.

If the IRA owner dies *on or after* the required beginning date (which is not possible for a Roth IRA, since there is no required beginning date), there are also three alternatives that are slightly different than the rules that apply if the IRA owner dies before their RBD.

a) If there is an *eligible* designated beneficiary (spouse, owner's minor child, disabled, chronically ill, those no more than 10 years younger), payment is made over the life expectancy of the beneficiary with the age 31 limit for minor children, similar to the situation noted above. Proposed regulations under the Secure Act would allow eligible beneficiaries to elect to use the decedent's date of birth (see paragraph below) if more advantageous, such as if the eligible designated beneficiary were older than the decedent.

b) If there is no designated beneficiary, payments shall be made over the remaining life expectancy of the IRA owner immediately before death using their date of birth (aka "ghost" life expectancy).

c) If there is a designated beneficiary but not an eligible designated beneficiary, the 10-year rule applies as noted above, but the Proposed Regulations issued February 24,2022 added a twist if the owner dies after their RBD. Designated beneficiaries must take RMDs over their life expectancy using the single life table for years 1-9 after death, where it all still must be distributed by the end of the 10th year. Note that this is in contrast to the rule if the decedent died before their RBD. Numerous comments to the Treasury Department regarding the proposed regulations have asked to change this rule in the final regulations, so while it may not be likely, it is possible that this rule may change. In the meantime, the IRS has issued Notices that they will waive any penalty for failure to take an RMD in this situation, at least until they issue further guidance. See IRS Notice 2022-53.

If the sole designated beneficiary is the IRA owner's spouse, distribution can be made over the remaining life expectancy of the spouse, recalculated annually, beginning with the calendar year immediately following the calendar year in which the IRA owner died. The spouse may also roll over the balance to the spouse's

785

own IRA or elect to treat the decedent's IRA as the spouse's own IRA.[3]

No matter who the beneficiaries are, if the decedent died after his required beginning date without having taken the required minimum distribution for the year, it is important that the beneficiary or beneficiaries (not the decedent's estate) withdraw the required minimum distribution for the year of death.[4] When a decedent dies towards the end of the year, this is problematic since the deadline for taking the RMD would be December 31 of the year of death. Fortunately, Treasury has proposed regulations under section 54.4974-1(g)(3) that will now automatically waive any penalties for failure to take the decedent's RMD in the year of death so long as a beneficiary takes it by the filing date of their federal tax return for that year. For example, if a traditional IRA owner aged 76 dies on October 10, 2023 without having taken their RMD, leaving the IRA to child, child has until April 15 (or later, with extension) of 2024 to take the decedent's RMD that was not taken in 2023. If they do so, the excise tax will be waived automatically.

Generally, Roth IRAs follow the rules above for IRA owners dying before the required beginning date. Roth IRAs do not have a lifetime required beginning date.

IRAs are relatively easy to establish and tax savings could be substantial. Banks, brokerage firms and insurance companies provide prototype plans, and the IRS also provides prototype trusteed and custodial plans.[5] Once an IRA is established all that need be done is to make contributions.

> *Example.* A $5,000 annual deductible contribution to a traditional IRA by an individual in a 15 percent bracket would save $750 a year in taxes. A partner in a partnership who did not care to include any other employees in the plan could establish an IRA for himself without having to cover other employees. If the partner's tax bracket were 25 percent, a $5,000 annual deductible IRA contribution would save $1,250 a year in taxes.

Similarly, a Roth IRA can be a powerful tax saving device. The exact benefit will depend upon many factors, including whether, in the absence of establishing a Roth IRA, the client would have paid tax at ordinary income rates (such as would be the case on most distributions from traditional IRAs), or at capital gains rates (which would apply if the client had invested in an asset outside of a retirement plan which qualified for capital gains treatment).

56.4 WHAT IS A TRADITIONAL IRA?

Any individual who is not participating in a qualified private or governmental pension plan, profit-sharing plan, or tax sheltered annuity can set up a traditional individual retirement account (IRA) and take a deduction from gross income equal to the lesser of:

(1) $6,500 in 2023; (or $7,000 for taxpayers who are age fifty or older), or

(2) 100 percent of compensation includable in his gross income for the taxable year.[6]

If an individual or his spouse is actively participating in a qualified plan or tax sheltered annuity, the maximum annual contribution may be made to an IRA, subject to certain limitations. The tax deduction for this contribution to an IRA is allowed in full to the extent that the taxpayer's Adjusted Gross Income (AGI) does not exceed an applicable threshold. These thresholds vary according to the taxpayer's filing status and the tax year.[7] The thresholds are as follows:

AGI Threshold*

Tax Year	Single Returns	Joint Returns
2005	$50,000	$70,000
2006	$50,000	$75,000
2007	$50,000	$80,000
2008	$55,000	$85,000
2009	$55,000	$89,000
2010	$56,000	$89,000
2011	$56,000	$90,000
2012	$58,000	$92,000
2013	$59,000	$95,000
2014	$61,000	$98,000
2015	$61,000	$98,000
2016	$61,000	$98,000
2017	$62,000	$99,000
2018	$63,000	$101,000

INDIVIDUAL RETIREMENT PLANS (INCLUDING SEP AND SIMPLE IRAS) CHAPTER 56

2023 IRA Contribution and Deduction Limits - Effect of Modified AGI on Deductible Contributions If You ARE Covered by a Retirement Plan at Work

Tax Year	AGI Threshold* Single Returns	Joint Returns
2019	$64,000	$103,000
2020	$65,000	$104,000
2021	$66,000	$105,000
2022	$68,000	$109,000
2023	$73,000	$116,000

*covered by a workplace plan

If you're covered by a retirement plan at work, use this table to determine if your *modified AGI* affects the amount of your deduction.

If Your Filing Status Is...	And Your Modified AGI Is...	Then You Can Take...
single or **head of household**	$73,000 or less	a full deduction up to the amount of your contribution limit.
single or **head of household**	more than $73,000 but less than $83,000	a partial deduction.
single or **head of household**	$83,000 or more	no deduction.
married filing jointly or **qualifying widow(er)**	$116,000 or less	a full deduction up to the amount of your contribution limit.
married filing jointly or **qualifying widow(er)**	more than $116,000 but less than $136,000	a partial deduction.
married filing jointly or **qualifying widow(er)**	$136,000 or more	no deduction.
married filing separately	less than $10,000	a partial deduction.
married filing separately	$10,000 or more	no deduction.

Source IRS.gov, Page Last Reviewed or Updated: 26-Oct-2022

2023 IRA Contribution and Deduction Limits - Effect of Modified AGI on Deductible Contributions if You are NOT Covered by a Retirement Plan at Work

If you're not covered by a retirement plan at work, use this table to determine if your *modified AGI* affects the amount of your deduction.

If Your Filing Status Is...	And Your Modified AGI Is...	Then You Can Take...
single, head of household, or qualifying widow(er)	any amount	a full deduction up to the amount of your contribution limit.
married filing jointly or **separately** with a spouse who **is not** covered by a plan at work	any amount	a full deduction up to the amount of your contribution limit.
married filing jointly with a spouse who **is** covered by a plan at work	$218,000 or less	a full deduction up to the amount of your contribution limit.
married filing jointly with a spouse who **is** covered by a plan at work	more than $218,000 but less than $228,000	a partial deduction.
married filing jointly with a spouse who **is** covered by a plan at work	$228,000 or more	no deduction.

If Your Filing Status Is...	And Your Modified AGI Is...	Then You Can Take...
married filing separately with a spouse who **is** covered by a plan at work	less than $10,000	a partial deduction.
married filing separately with a spouse who **is** covered by a plan at work	$10,000 or more	no deduction.

If you file separately and did not live with your spouse at any time during the year, your IRA deduction is determined under the "Single" filing status.
Source: IRS.gov. Page Last Reviewed or Updated: 26-Oct-2022

The threshold remains zero for married individuals covered by a retirement plan at work and filing a separate return. For non-active participants with an active participant spouse, the deduction for the participant spouse begins to phase out when AGI exceeds $103,000 for 2019. (See chart above for AGI numbers for other years and see below for further example). For a taxpayer who exceeds these thresholds, the maximum deduction is reduced by the following formula:

$$\text{Maximum annual contribution} \times \frac{\text{AGI - AGI Threshold}}{\$10,000}$$

Example. In 2019, Sarah's AGI is $65,000. Sarah is unmarried, and is an active participant in a qualified retirement plan. The applicable threshold is $64,000. If Sarah contributes $6,000 to her IRA for taxable year 2019, her deduction is reduced by $600 [$6,000 × (($65,000 − 64,000) ÷ $10,000)]. Thus, Sarah may claim a deduction on her return for 2019 of $5,400 ($6,000 − $550).

All taxpayers may continue to make a nondeductible IRA contribution of up to the lesser of the dollar limit or 100 percent of compensation, to the extent that contributions to all IRA accounts (including Roth IRAs, discussed below) do not exceed the maximum annual limit in total.

For married individuals filing a joint return, if only one spouse is a participant in an employer-sponsored plan, the limit on deductible IRA contributions applies only to the participant spouse (see "Active Participants" below). The non-participant spouse may be eligible to make a deductible IRA contribution. However, the deductible IRA contribution limit begins to phase out for the non-participant spouse if the couple's adjusted gross income is above $193,000 (in 2019). It is eliminated at $203,000 in 2019. See above chart for 2023 numbers and check for annual inflation adjustments for future years. In other words, the threshold in the previous ratio is $193,000 and the denominator is $10,000 (the difference between the top and bottom thresholds of the phaseout).

Example 1. Jill is a participant in her employer's retirement plan, but her husband, Jack, is not. They file a joint return in 2019 showing adjusted gross income of $125,000. Jack, as a non-participant in his employer's retirement plan, can make a deductible $6,000 contribution to his IRA (because Jack and Jill's adjusted gross income is under $203,000). However, Jill cannot make a deductible contribution to her IRA because their combined adjusted gross income exceeds the threshold for 2019, $123,000 discussed above, for a deductible contribution by an active participant filing a joint return.

Example 2. The facts are the same as above, except that Jack and Jill's combined 2018 adjusted gross income is $205,000. Neither Jack nor Jill can make a deductible IRA contribution. Jack cannot make a deductible contribution, even though he does not participate in his employer's retirement plan, because Jack and Jill's 2019 adjusted gross income exceeds $203,000. Jill cannot make a deductible contribution because their income is above $123,000.

An individual may make a deductible contribution to a spousal IRA for a spouse with less taxable compensation than the individual.[8] Such an individual may deduct the lesser of: (1) the maximum annual limit; or (2) 100 percent of the spouse's compensation for the taxable year plus 100 percent of the individual's compensation for the taxable year, less any IRA deductions taken by the individual, less any nondeductible contributions made by the individual, and less any Roth IRA contributions for the individual. The effect of this is to potentially allow a couple with one non-working spouse to contribute and deduct up to twice the maximum annual limit into two traditional IRAs (for example, in 2023, $6,500 could be contributed to one IRA and another $6,500 to a spousal IRA). Simplified Employee Pensions (SEPs) and SIMPLE IRAs are discussed below in the question and answer section.

Active Participants

An individual is considered an "active participant" for a taxable year if the individual is covered by:

- a qualified pension, profit-sharing or stock bonus plan

- a qualified annuity plan

- a tax sheltered annuity plan

- a simplified employee pension (SEP) plan,

- a government-sponsored plan

- an employee only contributory plan exempt from tax under Code section 501(c)(18).[9]

The rules vary depending on whether the plan is a defined benefit pension plan or a defined contribution plan:

1. *Defined benefit pension plan* – An individual is an active participant as long as he is not excluded under the plan's eligibility provisions. Active participation exists even when the individual declines participation, fails to make mandatory contributions or fails to perform the minimum service required to accrue a benefit. The plan being in frozen status does not necessarily mean active participation does not exist.

2. *Defined contribution plan* – An individual is an active participant if employer contributions, employee contributions, or forfeitures are added to the individual's account.[10]

Investment Vehicles

IRAs can be invested in a variety of ways. It is possible to liquidate an IRA and reinvest the proceeds within sixty days in another IRA on a tax-free basis. This tax-free reinvestment of funds can occur only once each year. At one time, this rule was thought to apply to multiple IRAs separately, but this was clarified in a tax court case and follow up IRS announcement to apply a limitation to all IRAs collectively.[11] Thus, it is no longer possible to do a sixty-day rollover from the first IRA, followed by another sixty-day rollover from the second IRA one hundred days earlier or later. Thus, one should always ask an IRA owner if they have made prior sixty-day rollovers within the last year if they are initiating one. This same rule, incidentally, applies to Coverdell ESAs.

It is also possible (and preferable) to initiate a trustee-to-trustee transfer at any time without restrictions. For example, an individual may choose to move an IRA account from a bank to a brokerage or vice versa. So long as the transaction is completed between the two institutions (i.e., the check or securities are not payable to the IRA participant, but to the new firm), it will not count as a rollover, nor will any tax consequences result.

Of course, the investment vehicle itself (e.g., Certificate of Deposit, bond, stock, fund, etc.) may be liquidated within a "master" IRA account, and the funds reinvested in the same master account, without regards to either the sixty-day rollover or trustee-to-trustee rules. Such transactions are commonplace.

If an IRA acquires collectibles, the cost of such collectibles shall be regarded as a current taxable distribution to the IRA owner. A collectible is defined as any work of art, any rug or antique, any metal or gem, any stamp or coin, any alcoholic beverage, or any other tangible personal property specified by the IRS. Watch out for new-fangled assets such as nonfungible tokens (NFTs) – see recent IRS Notice 2023-27. However, an exception to this rule is permitted for IRA investments in gold or silver coins issued by the United States or any coins minted by a state. An exception is also allowed for gold, silver, platinum or palladium bullion. Certain platinum coins are also excluded.[12]

IRAs may not invest in life insurance.[13] IRAs may invest in closely held businesses, real estate or other unique assets (sometimes referred to as a "self-directed IRA"), however, the prohibited transaction rules may prevent many purchases or dealings with related parties.[14] If an IRA invests in an S corporation, even if completely unrelated, the IRA would not be an eligible owner of an S corporation and the corporation would become disqualified and thereafter taxed as a C corporation.[15]

Distributions and Loans

Distributions can begin as early as age 59½ without penalty, but do not have to be made until April 1 following the calendar year in which a client reaches age 73 (this was age 70½ before the Secure Act, was changed to age 72 and then again to age 73 by the Secure 2.0 Act, with a further change to age 75 anticipated in 2033).[16] Roth IRAs have no RMDs. IRAs are subject to minimum distribution requirements which mandate a certain amount be withdrawn each year once a client reaches the applicable age. The amounts that must be distributed are based on the client's life expectancy and can be calculated using a worksheet form the IRS.[17] Financial institutions that offer IRA accounts will automatically track minimum distribution requirements for an account holder as well (but they have no obligation to for inherited accounts)

Unlike a 401(k), for example, loans from an IRA account, or even pledging the account for a loan, are not permitted. See Code section 408(e)(4). Your client will be deemed to have received all the assets in his or her account and must pay ordinary income tax to the extent includable in income.[18] In addition, if the client is neither disabled nor 59½ years old at that time, unless another exception applies, there will also be a 10 percent nondeductible "premature distribution" tax.

56.5 WHAT IS A ROTH IRA?

TRA '97 created a new type of IRA called the "Roth IRA."[19] With a Roth IRA, contributions are not deductible. But, if certain requirements are met, the build-up and all withdrawals from a Roth IRA may be entirely tax free.

Annual contributions to a Roth IRA may be made up to the lesser of $6,500 (2023) or 100 percent of compensation includable in gross income for the taxable year, reduced by any contributions made to a traditional IRA for that year on the individual's own behalf. Additionally, taxpayers age fifty and above can make additional contributions of $1,000. (Contributions to a SIMPLE IRA or a SEP are not taken into account for the maximum annual contribution limit. Additionally, SIMPLE IRAs and SEPs, discussed later in this chapter, were not allowed to be designated as Roth IRAs until the Secure 2.0 Act changed this starting in 2023.) Distributions are not required to begin until after death, and even then may be deferred until after the surviving spouse's death if the surviving spouse rolls it over.

If the taxpayer's AGI (Adjusted Gross Income) exceeds certain limits, the maximum allowable contribution to a Roth IRA is phased-out, similar to the above charts:

	2018 Phase-out Amounts	
Single	$120,000	$135,000
MFJ	$189,000	$199,000
MFS	$0	$10,000
	2019 Phase-out Amounts	
Single	$122,000	$137,000
MFJ	$193,000	$203,000
MFS	$0	$10,000

Amount of Roth IRA Contributions That You Can Make For 2023
This table shows whether your contribution to a Roth IRA is affected by the amount of your **modified AGI** as computed for Roth IRA purpose.

If your filing status is...	And your modified AGI is...	Then you can contribute...
married filing jointly or **qualifying widow(er)**	< $218,000	up to the limit
married filing jointly or **qualifying widow(er)**	> $218,000 but < $228,000	a reduced amount
married filing jointly or **qualifying widow(er)**	> $228,000	zero
married filing separately and you lived with your spouse at any time during the year	< $10,000	a reduced amount
married filing separately and you lived with your spouse at any time during the year	> $10,000	zero

INDIVIDUAL RETIREMENT PLANS (INCLUDING SEP AND SIMPLE IRAS)   CHAPTER 56

If your filing status is...	And your modified AGI is...	Then you can contribute...
single, **head of household**, or **married filing separately** and you did not live with your spouse at any time during the year	< $138,000	up to the limit
single, **head of household**, or **married filing separately** and you did not live with your spouse at any time during the year	> $138,000 but < $153,000	a reduced amount
single, **head of household**, or **married filing separately** and you did not live with your spouse at any time during the year	> $153,000	zero

Amount of your reduced Roth IRA contribution

If the amount you can contribute must be reduced, figure your reduced contribution limit as follows.

1. Start with your modified AGI.

2. Subtract from the amount in (1):

    a. $218,000 if filing a joint return or qualifying widow(er),

    b. $-0- if married filing a separate return, and you lived with your spouse at any time during the year, or

    c. $138,000 for all other individuals.

3. Divide the result in (2) by $15,000 ($10,000 if filing a joint return, qualifying widow(er), or married filing a separate return and you lived with your spouse at any time during the year).

4. Multiply the maximum contribution limit (before reduction by this adjustment and before reduction for any contributions to traditional IRAs) by the result in (3).

5. Subtract the result in (4) from the maximum contribution limit before this reduction. The result is your reduced contribution limit.

See Publication 590-A, Contributions to Individual Retirement Accounts (IRAs), for a worksheet to figure your reduced contribution.

Source IRS.Gov. Page Last Reviewed or Updated: 26-Oct-2022

Thus, for example, single taxpayers in 2019, no contributions can be made to a Roth IRA if AGI is more than $137,000 and the amount that may be contributed is reduced proportionately if AGI is between $122,000 and $137,000. For joint filers, no contributions can be made to a Roth IRA if AGI is more than $203,000 and the amount that may be contributed is reduced proportionately if AGI is between $193,000 and $203,000. Note the severely restricted phase-out amounts for married taxpayers filing a separate return: no contributions can be made to a Roth IRA if AGI is more than $10,000 and the amount that may be contributed is reduced proportionately if AGI is between $0 and $10,000.

The rules on allowable Roth IRA contributions apply without regard to a taxpayer's active participation in a qualified retirement plan. For some clients, the permitted "rollover" (aka "conversion") of a traditional IRA to a Roth IRA (discussed further in this chapter) may be desirable.

Some taxpayers cannot contribute to a traditional deductible or Roth IRA because they earn too much money. Anyone, however, can contribute to a non-deductible IRA, a type of traditional IRA in which only earnings are taxed when withdrawals are made. A particular device has become popular and involves making a contribution to a regular non-deductible IRA and soon thereafter (within a few months) converting the regular IRA into a Roth IRA, thereby only incurring income tax on the small amount of income (if any) earned on the account since the rollover. (This is known as the "back door Roth IRA.") This is a good strategy if one has no other IRAs, but one drawback to this is the "pro rata rule." That rule says that you have to aggregate all of your IRAs to determine how much income tax you owe when you convert. If you have a $95,000 traditional IRA (all pre-tax contributions possibly because it was rolled over from a 401(k)) and you convert a separate new $5,000 nondeductible IRA, the conversion would be 95 percent taxable because the two IRAs must be aggregated for this purpose. It may be possible to roll your traditional deductible IRAs with no

791

basis into a 401(k) with your employer to avoid this - if the plan permits. However, you may lose the investment flexibility you have with your IRA.

56.6 WHAT IS A SEP?

A simplified employee pension (SEP) is a type of IRA or annuity established by an employer, to which the employer can contribute on the employees' behalf, and where contributions are only made according to a predetermined formula. The dollar limit on contributions to SEPs is the lesser of $66,000 (in 2023), or 25 percent of employee compensation without regard to the employer contribution. The employee excludes the contribution from gross income up to the same limits.

Employee elective deferrals are no longer allowed, with the exception that a SEP maintained by an employer of no more than twenty-five employees (for the year prior to the tax year in question) that allowed for elective employee salary reduction as of December 31, 1996, may qualify to continue offering elective deferrals. These are known as SARSEPs (salary reduction simplified employee pension).[20] If permitted, such employee deferrals cannot exceed $22,500 in 2023. Elective deferrals in excess of the annual limit will be included in gross income.[21]

Catch up contributions are not permitted in SEP Plans. However, catch-up contributions can be made to the IRA's that hold the SEP contributions if the plan's documents allow. The catch-up amount for employees aged fifty and older is $1,000.

Participants in simplified employee pension plans are permitted to participate in other employer qualified plans. Any contribution by an employer to a SEP must be aggregated with other contributions by that employer to other qualified plans for purposes of the overall limit on contributions or benefits. A participant can take a deduction for an IRA contribution, under the limits discussed above. Participation in a SEP is treated as active participation for purposes of the traditional IRA deduction limitations.

SEP Requirements

1. The employer (can be a corporation, partnership, or sole proprietorship) must make a contribution to the plan for each employee age twenty-one or older who has worked for the employer during at least three of the last five years. An employer need not contribute on behalf of any employee for a calendar year in which the employee's compensation was less than $$750 (as indexed in 2023).[22] In the case of elective deferral SEPs that are grandfathered (SARSEPs), the employer must have had twenty-five or fewer eligible employees during the prior taxable year, and at least 50 percent must have elected to contribute to the SEP.[23]

2. The employer's contribution cannot discriminate in favor of employees who are "highly compensated." It is possible to exclude nonparticipating union employees with respect to whom there is good faith bargaining on retirement benefits and nonresident aliens in considering whether or not contributions are discriminatory in favor of any member of the prohibited class. A special nondiscrimination test is applicable to salary reduction SEPs. Employer contributions may be made for an employee who has reached their applicable age.

3. A limited disparity between the contribution percentages applicable to compensation above and below the social security wage base is permitted (this is also referred to as "integration"). An elective deferral SEP may not be integrated. Integration is not permitted for a year in which the employer also maintains an integrated pension, profit sharing, or stock bonus plan or tax deferred annuity.

4. The employee must own the IRA account or annuity. That means 100 percent immediate vesting for all employees. The employer cannot restrict the employee's right to keep or withdraw money contributed to the SEP.

5. The SEP has to be in writing. It must spell out:

    a. what an employee has to do to "get a piece of the action"; and

    b. how the "pie is to be sliced," i.e., the manner in which the amount allocated is to be computed.

6. In general, the employer must make contributions no later than the tax filing deadline, plus extensions (unlike a traditional IRA contribution, for which an extension is irrelevant). If the employer elects a calendar year, contributions are deductible for the tax year in which the calendar year ends. In fact, the plan itself need not be established until such dates.

7. A self-employed individual may also make SEP-IRA contributions, which may be quite a bit larger than ordinary IRA contributions. However, see IRS

Publication 560 for details on calculating net income and the contribution amount.

Model SEP

To establish a SEP, there must be a written agreement. IRS has issued Form 5305 – SEP, Simplified Employee Pension – Individual Retirement Accounts Contribution Agreement for those employers wishing to have a pre-approved IRS agreement. Plans using the IRS form are called model SEPs, while plans using other agreements are called non-model SEPs. Employers who currently maintain any other qualified plan cannot use a model SEP, but, rather they must use a non-model SEP.

56.7 WHAT IS A "SIMPLE" PLAN?

A Savings Incentive Match Plan for Employees (SIMPLE) has the following major features:

- The plans are available only to employers with one hundred or fewer employees (only employees with at least $5,000 in compensation for the prior year are counted) during any two preceding years.

- The plans are available only to employers who do not sponsor another qualified plan 403(b) plan, or SEP.

- Contributions can be made to each employee's IRA or to a 401(k) account for the employee. In effect, there are thus two types of SIMPLE plans – those that include the 401(k) requirements, and those funded through IRAs.

- Employees who earned at least $5,000 from the employer in the preceding two years, and are reasonably expected to earn at least $5,000 in the current year, can contribute (through salary reductions) up to $15,500 (in 2023). Additionally, taxpayers age fifty and above will be allowed catch-up contributions of $3,500 in 2023.

The plans require an employer contribution equal to either:

1. a dollar-for-dollar match of up to three percent of the employee's compensation (the employer can elect a lower percentage, not less than one percent, in not more than two out of any five years), See Notice 98-4, or

2. a nonelective contribution of two percent of compensation for all eligible employees earning at least $5,000 (whether or not they elect salary reductions).

56.8 TAX IMPLICATIONS

1. Money set aside in a traditional IRA is currently deductible from gross income up to the limits specified.[24]

2. The earnings of the IRA account, between the time contributions are deposited and the time distributions are received, accumulate tax free.[25]

3. An individual generally must be at least 59½ years old to receive a traditional IRA payment without tax penalty. The nondeductible penalty tax on a "premature distribution" is 10 percent of the amount of the distribution that is includable in income. Under some circumstances, the total value of the assets of the account may be deemed to be distributed.[26] (An example of this would be where an individual borrows against his IRA.) So, if your client received (or is deemed to have received) a total distribution at age fifty-three and his account is worth $5,000 at that time, he must pay a $500 nondeductible tax in addition to the regular income tax on the $5,000 distribution. The 10 percent penalty tax also applies to an early taxable distribution from a Roth IRA.

The exceptions to this rule include withdrawals due to death or disability, and withdrawals taken in the form of a series of periodic payments which meet certain requirements.

In addition, the 10 percent early withdrawal penalty tax does not apply to a "qualified first-time homebuyer distribution." Distributions for this purpose cannot total more than $10,000 during the taxpayer's lifetime. A withdrawal qualifies as a first-time home buyer distribution if it is used within 120 days to pay the "qualified acquisition costs" of the "principal residence" of the first-time home buyer. Qualified acquisition costs include funds used for reasonable settlement, financing or other closing costs. The buyer can be a spouse, or any child, grandchild or ancestor of the IRA participant. A "first-time home buyer" must not have had an ownership interest in a principal residence during the two-year period ending with the date the contract of sale is entered into, or the date when construction begins. Thus, a "first-time home buyer" under these rules does not necessarily mean a person buying a home for the first time.

Furthermore, the 10 percent early distribution tax does not apply to withdrawals used to pay "qualified higher education expenses." Of course, the withdrawal will be subject to income tax under the rules applicable to traditional and Roth IRA withdrawals. These expenses include tuition at an eligible post-secondary educational institution, as well as room and board, fees, books, supplies and equipment required for enrollment or attendance. Expenses for graduate level courses are also covered. Qualifying recipients include the IRA participant, the participant's spouse, children, the spouse's children, grandchildren or spouse's grandchildren.

4. Upon distribution of the funds accumulated in a traditional IRA account, the client will be taxed at ordinary income tax rates (with potential reduction for any basis due to non-deductible contributions).[27] Lump sum distribution tax treatment is not available for distributions from IRAs.

5. A "qualified distribution" from a Roth IRA is not taxable. A distribution is a "qualified distribution" if it is not made within the five-year period starting with the first taxable year for which the individual or the individual's spouse made a contribution to a Roth IRA established for the individual, and it is made at or after age 59½ or in the event of death, disability or for first-time homebuyer expenses.[28] Since assets must be held in a Roth IRA for five tax years before they can be withdrawn in a tax-free distribution, it appears that the waiting period includes the calendar year for which the contribution is made, even if the contribution is not made until the due date of the income tax return in the following year.

Unlike traditional IRAs, there is not a requirement to begin distributions from a Roth IRA during the owner's lifetime. However, the traditional IRA minimum distribution rules apply to the beneficiary of a Roth IRA following the death of the IRA participant. Thus, a beneficiary can continue to shelter the Roth IRA earnings from income tax, subject to minimum distribution requirements.

Withdrawals from Roth IRAs that do not meet the requirements for qualified distributions are still taxed in an advantageous manner. They are includable in income only to the extent that the withdrawal (plus any earlier withdrawals) exceeds the total of contributions made to the Roth IRA. These non-qualified distributions from Roth IRAs are treated as made first from contributions other than rollover contributions, then from qualified rollover contributions and finally, from any earnings on the contributions. All of an individual's Roth IRAs are aggregated for this purpose.

56.9 ROLLOVERS

The Internal Revenue Code also allows certain individuals receiving certain distributions from a qualified plan (including pension, profit-sharing, stock bonus, or annuity plans) or a tax deferred annuity to "roll over" the distribution to an IRA without incurring income tax on the distribution. This tax-free rollover treatment is available to individuals who receive most types of distributions from a qualified plan or tax deferred annuity. Distributions of accumulated deductible employee contributions which were made to such qualified plans or tax deferred annuities may also be rolled over tax free to an IRA (or in some cases even to another qualified employer plan–if such plan permits).

EGTRRA 2001 increased the portability of retirement plan assets. Any part of the taxable portion of a distribution received after 2001 from a qualified retirement plan, tax sheltered annuity, or eligible section 457 governmental plan can be rolled over without incurring income tax to an IRA or to any of the above listed plans.[29] Also, after-tax contributions will be allowed to be rolled over into an IRA.[30] There are exceptions to this general rule allowing rollover treatment. No tax-free rollover is permitted if the distribution is a required minimum distribution, is part of a series of substantially equal payments made over the life expectancy of the plan participant or the joint life expectancies of the participant and his or her beneficiary, or over a period of ten or more years. Additionally, hardship distributions generally will not be eligible for tax-free rollover treatment.[31]

Further, any qualified plan, tax sheltered annuity, or eligible section 457 governmental plan must allow its participants to elect to have any distribution that is eligible for rollover treatment handled by means of a direct rollover, i.e., a trustee-to-trustee transfer. If this method is not elected, but rather the funds are distributed to the individual participant, a mandatory income tax withholding of 20 percent must be made. The participant cannot elect out of withholding from such a distribution. This mandatory 20 percent withholding applies even if the participant receiving the distribution rolls the funds over within sixty days.[32]

Individuals who receive a distribution which includes property can make a bona fide sale of the property and roll over, within the usual sixty-day period, all or part of the proceeds to an IRA. It is not necessary to roll over the actual property received.

The spouse of a deceased IRA holder may be able to roll over a distribution received after the deceased spouse's death to an IRA. This is discussed in the question and answer section of this chapter.

Rollovers to Roth Accounts

Any taxpayer may roll over a traditional IRA into a Roth IRA (also called a conversion).[33] The rollover must be completed within sixty days after the distribution, as with the regular rollover rules. Distributions from the traditional IRA are subject to income tax, but the 10 percent premature withdrawal penalty is waived for rollovers from traditional to Roth IRAs.

Note that if a portion of a distribution is properly allocated to a qualified rollover contribution, and such distribution is made within the five-year period beginning with the year the contribution was made, then the 10 percent penalty tax for early distributions applies as if such portion of the distribution was includable in gross income.

56.10 ISSUES IN COMMUNITY PROPERTY STATES

In most community property states, the non-participant spouse is deemed to have an interest in the participant-spouse's IRA, but the application of this principle is not well developed among the states, particularly in the situation where the non-participant spouse is the first spouse to die. In one case,[34] the heirs of the non-participant spouse were able to successfully assert a claim against the IRA upon the subsequent death of the participant. Although a distribution to the heirs of the non-participant spouse will trigger an income tax liability, PLR 8040101 provided that the recipients of the distribution (and not the participant) were liable for the tax.

If the participant names someone other than his or her spouse as the beneficiary, the *non-participant* may be deemed to have made a gift when the IRA is paid to the third party beneficiary, if the spouse does not assert their rights.

The division of community property interests in qualified plan benefits is becoming an increasingly important factor in divorce proceedings in community property states. In many situations the spouses' respective retirement benefits are their largest assets.

IRAs will undoubtedly be the subject of controversy in many divorce proceedings. To some extent, however, the division of an interest in an IRA should be less difficult than dividing an interest in a qualified corporate plan (which requires a QDRO). All benefits in an IRA must be nonforfeitable. Thus, the problems of valuing nonvested benefits will not be present.

In many cases, each spouse will have his or her own IRA. If the contributions to each IRA were similar, each spouse could agree to keep his own IRA in a divorce settlement. If only one spouse has an IRA or one IRA contains substantially more assets than the other spouse's IRA or spouses with equal IRAs or IRA subaccounts cannot agree to divide their IRA interests equally, significant problems could arise. A spouse may find he or she is obligated to divide an interest in his or her IRA with the other spouse. The obligated spouse may not have sufficient assets outside of the IRA to provide the other spouse with the value of his or her interest. Thus, the obligated spouse may (unwisely) seek a distribution from the IRA to provide funds to settle with his or her spouse. If, however, the spouse with the IRA is under age 59½ and not disabled, the spouse will incur a 10 percent "premature distribution" tax as well as be subject to ordinary income tax on the distribution he or she received (or is deemed to receive). To avoid this undesirable result, the spouses could agree to divide and transfer the IRA assets into an IRA for the spouse pursuant to a divorce decree or other agreement incident to such a divorce decree.[35] A transfer of an IRA to a spouse incident to a divorce is not a taxable transfer.[36] Thereafter, the IRA will be treated as that of the other spouse.

Figure 56.1

IRS ROLLOVER CHART*

ROLL TO

ROLL FROM	Roth IRA	Traditional IRA	SIMPLE IRA	SEP-IRA	Governmetal 457(b)	Qualified Plan[1] (pre-tax)	403(b) (pre-tax)	Designated Roth Account (401(k), 403(b) or 457(b))
Roth IRA	Yes[2]	No	No	No	No	No	No	No
Traditional IRA	Yes[3]	Yes[2]	Yes[2,7] after two years	Yes[2]	Yes[4]	Yes	Yes	No
SIMPLE IRA	Yes[3] after two years	Yes[2] after two years	Yes[2]	Yes[2] after two years	Yes[4] after two years	Yes, after two years	Yes, after two years	No
SEP-IRA	Yes[3]	Yes[2]	Yes[2,7] after two years	Yes[2]	Yes[4]	Yes	Yes	No
Gov't 457(b)	Yes[3]	Yes	Yes[7] after two years	Yes	Yes	Yes	Yes	Yes[3,5]
Qualified Plan (pre-tax)	Yes[3]	Yes	Yes[7] after two years	Yes	Yes[4]	Yes	Yes	Yes[3,5]
403(b) (pre-tax)	Yes[3]	Yes	Yes[7] after two years	Yes	Yes[4]	Yes	Yes	Yes[3,5]
Designated Roth Account (401(k), 403(b) or 457(b))	Yes	No	No	No	No	No	No	Yes[6]

[1] Qualified plans include, for example, profit-sharing, 401(k), money purchase, and defined benefit plans.
[2] Only one rollover in any 12-month period.
[3] Must include in income.
[4] Must have separate accounts.
[5] Must be an in-plan rollover.
[6] Any nontaxable amounts distributed must be rolled over by direct trustee-to-trustee transfer.
[7] Applies to rollover contributions after December 18, 2015. For more information regarding retirement plans and rollovers, visit Tax Information for Retirement Plans.

* Source: www.IRS.gov

The tax consequences above should be considered when dividing community property IRA or qualified plan interests. Courts have taken varying approaches to consideration of tax aspects in division of retirement benefits. Some are unwilling to consider tax consequences when dividing retirement benefits. Others, however, have held that tax considerations should be taken into account when dividing retirement benefits in divorce proceedings.

As indicated above, there are several kinds of individual retirement arrangements (IRAs), including traditional IRAs (including SEP-IRAs), SIMPLE IRAs, and Roth IRAs. Note that IRA rules are by federal tax law applied without regard to community property law.[37] Therefore, taxable IRA distributions are separate property for income tax purposes, even if the funds in the account would otherwise be community property. These distributions are wholly taxable to the spouse whose name is on the account, not 50/50 (which may lead to a different result if spouses file separately). That spouse is also liable for any penalties and additional taxes on the distributions.[38]

56.11 FREQUENTLY ASKED QUESTIONS

Question – A partner owning more than 10 percent of the partnership's capital was a participant in his partnership 401(k) plan. He left the partnership and received the distribution of his retirement plan monies. Can he use a "rollover" traditional IRA? Secondly, assuming he can establish a "rollover" IRA, several years later when he is employed by a corporation which has a retirement plan, can he make a contribution from the "rollover" IRA into the corporate retirement plan?

Answer – The partner can roll over the distribution into a "rollover" IRA, and he may roll over those monies from the "rollover" IRA into another qualified plan if the plan permits.[39]

Note that distributions received are subject to a mandatory 20 percent income tax withholding unless a direct rollover is used.

Question – May a divorced spouse make and deduct contributions to a spousal IRA?

Answer – A divorced or legally separated person can make an IRA contribution from taxable alimony or separation payments he or she receives during the year.

Question – May an alternate payee rollover a distribution to an IRA or a qualified plan if made pursuant to a Qualified Domestic Relations Order (QDRO)?

Answer – If an alternate payee who is the spouse or former spouse of the participant receives a distribution by reason of a Qualified Domestic Relations Order, the rollover rules apply to the alternate payee as if the alternate payee were the participant.[40] Thus, the alternate payee has sixty days in which to roll over any portion of an eligible rollover distribution without the distribution becoming includable in income.[41] Generally, such a rollover must be handled as a direct rollover to avoid a mandatory income tax withholding rate of 20 percent.[42]

Question – Are there special rules for "inherited" IRAs acquired by someone other than a surviving spouse?

Answer – Yes. Inherited IRAs acquired by someone other than a surviving spouse cannot be "rolled over" tax-free and cannot receive tax-free rollovers from other qualified plans or IRAs. No new amounts may be contributed to an inherited IRA.

Question – May a contribution be made to a traditional IRA even though it is not deductible?

Answer – Yes. Designated nondeductible contributions may be made on behalf of an individual to an IRA even though he participates in a qualified pension or profit sharing plan. These contributions are intended to provide a tax incentive for retirement savings, and the tax on the earnings on the nondeductible contributions is deferred until withdrawn. The nondeductible limit is the excess of:

(a) the lesser of the maximum annual limit or 100 percent of compensation over

(b) the amount allowable as a deduction for IRA contributions by active participants.[43]

Question – When may a surviving spouse roll over a distribution received from a qualified plan or IRA of a deceased spouse?

Answer – There is no deadline. A surviving spouse can roll over all or part of a distribution from a qualified plan or IRA of the deceased spouse to an IRA.[44] If this is done, the IRA of the deceased spouse is treated as if the surviving spouse was the original participant. Thus, the rules pertaining to rollovers discussed in this chapter are applicable. A surviving spouse may also make a rollover to another qualified plan in which the spouse is a participant if the plan permits. It is important that the surviving spouse withdraw the required minimum distribution of the deceased spouse if such spouse died after their required beginning date without having taken their RMD.

Since it is possible the surviving spouse already has an IRA, or will create one after the rollover, it is a good idea not to commingle the funds from the rollover with the separate IRA funds of the surviving spouse if one of the spouse's has any basis in their IRA.

Where the deceased spouse's IRA or qualified plan benefit is transferred to a trust in which the surviving spouse is a beneficiary, there is no right to roll over the distribution even if the spouse is the sole beneficiary of the trust.[45] However, many private letter rulings have permitted a rollover in cases in which the spouse had the right to withdrawal the assets of the trust or estate, such as with a marital trust containing a presently exercisable general power of appointment (withdrawal right).[46]

Question – Are there situations when a surviving spouse should not immediately roll over an inherited qualified plan or IRA from a deceased spouse?

Answer – Yes, in four situations. First, if the surviving spouse is under 59½, leaving the funds in an inherited IRA until that date will allow the surviving spouse to take funds out without a 10 percent penalty (whereas such a distribution would cause tax if from the widow(er)'s own IRA). If funds might be needed before then, a 100 percent rollover may be premature. Second, if the younger spouse dies first and has not reached their required beginning date, leaving the funds in an inherited IRA will allow the surviving spouse to delay required minimum distributions longer. For example, if spouses were age sixty and seventy-two and the sixty-two year old spouse died, the seventy-four-year old surviving spouse would have to start RMDs if rolled over into their own IRA, but could delay distributions another thirteen years by leaving funds in an inherited IRA, since the surviving spouse's required distributions would not start until the decedent would have reached their applicable age (73, to be increased to 75 in 2033, as amended by the Secure 2.0 Act). Note that starting in 2024, this delayed RBD requires the surviving spouse to make an election. Third, some spouses may want to disclaim a portion of the IRA in favor of children (or trusts for them) who would usually be the contingent beneficiaries and may be in lower tax brackets and receive longer tax deferral. Fourth, the decedent may have employer securities in a qualified plan that might be better to take as a lump sum distribution than as a rollover to take advantage of the net unrealized appreciation (NUA) loophole that allows infinite deferral and, upon any sale, more advantageous long-term capital gains tax rates on the gain component of the employer securities.

CHAPTER ENDNOTES

1. I.R.C. §§408(a); 408(b).
2. I.R.C. §408(a)(1).
3. For the regulations regarding required minimum distributions, see Treas. Reg. §1.408-8.
4. Treas. Reg. §1.401(a)(9)-5, Q&A4.
5. IRS Forms 5305 (trusteed IRA), Form 5305-A (custodial IRA, Form 5305-R (trusteed Roth IRA), Form 5305-RA (custodial Roth IRA), Form 5305-SEP, Form 5305-SIMPLE, all available at www.irs.gov.
6. Technically, the initials IRA have a more limited connotation but will be used here to denote any type of individual retirement savings plan.
7. I.R.C. §219(g).
8. I.R.C. §219(c).
9. I.R.C. §219(g)(5).
10. 87-16, 1987-1 CB 446.
11. *Bobrow v. Commissioner*, TC Memo 2014-21, IRS Announcement 2014-15, 2014-16 IRB.
12. I.R.C. §408(m).
13. IRC §408(a)(3).
14. IRC §4975 contains the prohibited transaction rules applicable to IRAs. For an article discussing prohibited transaction rules for IRAs investing in closely held businesses and discussion of recent cases, see *Ed Morrow on Summa Holdings Inc. v. Commissioner: 6th Circuit Properly Rejects IRS and Tax Court Substance Over Form Attack on IRAs Owning IC-DISCs, But They Missed the Prohibited Transactions*, LISI Employee Benefits and Retirement Planning Email Newsletter #672 (March 23, 2017).
15. Rev. Rul. 92-73 and *Taproot Administrative Services v. Comm'r*, 133 T.C. 9 (U.S.T.C. 2009).
16. IRC §§408(a)(6); 408(b)(3).
17. See "IRA Required Minimum Distribution Worksheet," available at: https://www.irs.gov/retirement-plans/plan-participant-employee/ira-required-minimum-distribution-worksheet.
18. I.R.C. §408(e)(3).
19. I.R.C. §408A.
20. See IRS Publication 4336 for details on SARSEPs.

21. I.R.C. §402(g).
22. I.R.C. §408(k)(2).
23. I.R.C. §408(k)(6).
24. I.R.C. §219(a).
25. I.R.C. §408(e)(1).
26. IRC §§72(t), 408(e)(2), 408(e)(3).
27. I.R.C. §408(d).
28. I.R.C. §408A(d).
29. I.R.C. §402(c)(8)(B).
30. I.R.C. §402(c)(2).
31. I.R.C. §402(c)(4).
32. I.R.C. §3405(c).
33. I.R.C. §512, TIPRA 2005, Pub. Law 109-222.
34. *Estate of MacDonald*, 794 P.2d 911 (Cal. 1990).
35. IRC §71(b)(2).
36. IRC §408(d)(6) references §72(b)(2) cited above.
37. IRC §408(g).
38. IRS Publication 555.
39. I.R.C. §408(d)(3)(A).
40. I.R.C. §402(e)(1).
41. I.R.C. §402(c)(1).
42. I.R.C. §3405(c)(1).
43. I.R.C. §408(o)(2)(A).
44. I.R.C. §402(c)(9).
45. Treas. Reg. §1.408-8, A-5.
46. E.g., PLR 201225020.

PROFIT SHARING/401(k)/PENSION PLAN

CHAPTER 57

57.1 INTRODUCTION

A profit sharing plan, as its name implies, is a retirement plan for sharing employer profits with employees. A profit sharing plan need not provide a definite, predetermined formula for determining the amount of profits to be shared. However, there must be a definite formula for allocating these profits to each participant. But absent a definite contribution formula, an employer must make recurring and substantial contributions to a profit sharing plan.[1]

A pension plan is a retirement plan established and maintained by an employer to provide a *definitely determinable benefit* for the employer's employees and their beneficiaries. The primary purpose of a pension plan must be to provide benefits for the employees upon their retirement because of age or disability.

A 401(k) plan, also known as a Cash or Deferred Arrangement (CODA), is actually a feature that is part of a profit sharing plan, stock bonus plan, and, in some cases which are beyond the scope of this book, a money purchase pension plan. CODAs provide an employee an option to choose whether his employer should pay a certain amount to him in cash or contribute that amount to a qualified profit sharing or stock bonus plan on his behalf. A plan that contains a 401(k) feature generally must include the customary provisions required of all defined contribution plans. For additional information on 401(k) plans, see the Frequently Asked Questions at the end of this chapter.

57.2 WHEN IS USE OF SUCH A DEVICE INDICATED?

1. When your client would like to be sure of a steady, adequate, and secure personal retirement income.

2. When your client would like to set aside money for retirement on a tax deductible basis.

3. When your client wants to reward long-service employees and provide for their economic welfare after retirement.

4. When your client would like to put his or her business in a better competitive position for attracting and retaining personnel.

5. When your client's C corporation is about to run into an accumulated earnings tax problem. The corporation may need to siphon off some of its earnings and profits and reduce or eliminate the threat of a penalty tax on unreasonably accumulated earnings.

6. When your client has employees who would like to defer compensation on an elective, pre-tax basis to a qualified retirement plan.

57.3 WHAT ARE THE REQUIREMENTS?

1. The plan must be for the exclusive benefit of employees or their beneficiaries.[2]

2. The primary purpose of the plan must be to offer employees a retirement benefit (or, in the case of a profit sharing plan, provide employees with a share in the company's profits).

3. The plan provisions must set forth, in writing, a description of the plan and details of the plan.[3] Furthermore, details of the plan must be communicated to employees.

801

4. The plan must be permanent. This means the plan must contain no set termination date.

5. The plan must not discriminate in favor of highly-compensated employees. Plans that are top heavy, that is, plans that provide more than 60 percent of aggregate accumulated benefits or account balances for current key employees, must meet more stringent vesting, minimum benefit, and other rules.

6. The plan must meet minimum age and service standards, minimum coverage requirements and, in the case of defined benefit plans, a minimum participation test.

7. The plan must meet minimum vesting standards and provide for benefits or contributions that do not exceed the section 415 limits.

8. Distributions generally must begin to *all* participants by the April 1 following the year of attaining age 73 (this used to be age 70 ½ but was changed to age 72 by the Secure Act and then to age 73, increasing to age 75 in 2033, by the Secure 2.0 Act). Secure 2.0 also provides that, starting in 2024, Roth employer plans won't be subject to mandatory distributions during their life. Until then Roth plans and thereafter non-Roth plans still have a unique difference in their required beginning date from IRAs. Distributions generally need not begin until April 1 of the year following the year the employee retires, if that is later than the applicable age. There are exceptions, however, for (1) employees who are not more-than-5 percent owners and (2) participants in governmental or church plans,.[4]

9. Although traditional 401(k) plans are entitled to favorable tax treatment, they must meet certain special qualification requirements in addition to the regular plan qualification requirements. These special qualification requirements are as follows:

   (a) The plan must permit the employees to elect either to have the employer make a contribution on his behalf or to receive an equivalent amount in cash.

   (b) Unlike a typical profit sharing or stock bonus plan, a 401(k) plan cannot allow employees to receive a distribution of funds held in the plan which are attributable to elective deferrals merely because of the lapse of a fixed number of years or the completion of a specified period of participation.[5]

   (c) The employee's rights to benefits derived from elective contributions, as well as from qualified matching and qualified nonelective contributions used to satisfy the Actual Deferral Percentage (ADP) test, are nonforfeitable.[6]

   (d) The employer cannot condition the availability of any other benefit (except employer matching contributions) on whether an employee elects to make elective contributions under the CODA or to receive cash in lieu thereof.[7]

   (e) The plan must meet special nondiscrimination tests with respect to the amount of elective contributions made to the plan each year. See Frequently Asked Questions for more details.

   (f) Unlike a typical profit sharing or stock bonus plan, the CODA cannot require, as a condition of participation, that an employee complete more than one year of service for the employer maintaining the plan.

   (g) The amount of the elective contributions made to the plan on behalf of a participant cannot exceed $19,000 in 2019 ($22,500 for 2023).[8] This limit is indexed for inflation. For 2023 inflation adjustments in this area, see IRS Notice 2022-55 (or for future years, look for similar IRS Notices).

   (h) Participants who have reached age fifty by the end of the plan year may make catch-up elective deferrals of up to $6,000 in 2019 ($7,500 in 2023, the number adjusts for inflation). However, the total amount of a participant's elective deferrals may not exceed 100 percent of compensation for the year.[9] The Secure 2.0 Act, Section 109, will increase these limits to the greater of $10,000 or 50 percent more than the regular catch-up amount in 2025 for individuals who have attained ages 60, 61, 62 and 63. The increased amounts are indexed for inflation after 2025. This provision is effective for taxable years beginning after December 31, 2024.

The requirements for pension and profit sharing plans listed above are not exhaustive. For example, other requirements may include meeting minimum standards on participation, coverage, and funding.[10]

Types of Plans

There are two basic types of qualified retirement plans. The first is known as a fixed or *defined benefit plan*. Here, definitely determinable retirement benefits are computed using a pre-determined benefit formula established when the plan is created. Each employee is promised a specific amount of retirement benefits. The amount of the employer's contribution to fund that benefit is based on an actuarial determination of the cost of benefits promised. In other words, contributions are based on benefits and the limits on contributions are based on the benefit they will produce.

The second—and now more common—type of plan is a defined contribution plan. In these plans, each employee's benefit is determined by how much is contributed by the employee and the employer during the life of the plan and the rate of return on the investments made by the plan.

The most common types of plans are outlined below. The comments that follow explain the basic principles of eligibility, vesting, contributions, actuarial assumptions, death benefits, retirement age, and Social Security integration for qualified plans in general. There are also special rules for "top heavy" plans; see below.

Money Purchase Pension Plan

A money purchase pension plan, which is a type of defined contribution plan, bases the retirement benefit upon an employer's commitment to make an annual contribution. Benefits are directly dependent upon the length of time an employee participates in the plan and the amount of money contributed on the employee's behalf each year (plus interest and appreciation on such funds). In a money purchase pension plan, therefore, the employer is not obligated to provide a specific amount of retirement benefits, but is required to make the specified amount of contributions.

Profit Sharing Plan

A profit sharing plan is an arrangement by which an employer shares a portion of corporate profits with employees. Contributions can be made even if there are no profits. It is a type of defined contribution plan. For all defined contribution plans, the limits on annual additions to the plans are based on the lesser of the employee's salary or a set limit ($66,000 in 2023, plus a $7,500 catch-up contribution if it is applicable). This limit is indexed for inflation.[11] There is no limit to the benefits produced by the plan.

The corporation can distribute these payments currently in the form of cash bonuses, or profits can be shared on a deferred basis through contributions to a profit sharing plan.

In deferred profit sharing, contributions are made into an irrevocable trust. Funds then accumulate and are distributed to participants, usually as a retirement benefit, at some later date. Under a profit sharing plan, participants can also receive benefits in the event of a termination other than retirement, such as death, layoff, or disability.

One important advantage of a profit sharing plan is that the employer need not make a contribution in years in which no profits are earned. (However, a substantial amount of contribution flexibility can also be made possible in a well-designed pension plan.)

401(k) Plan

A traditional 401(k) plan may stand on its own (e.g., permit only elective contributions) or it may permit other types of employer contributions and/or employee contributions. The key feature of a cash or deferred arrangement is that an employee can elect to have the employer make an elective contribution on his behalf in the form of a compensation reduction agreement under which the employee elects to reduce cash compensation. In some cases, the employer may agree to make a matching contribution based on the employee's contribution (e.g. 50 cents from the employer for every dollar put in by the employee from his or her compensation).

To the extent the employee elects to receive cash or make after-tax (Roth) contributions, the payment or contribution will be subject to all payroll taxes currently.[12] If the employee elects to make a traditional elective contribution, such contributed amount will not be subject to payroll tax withholding, but it will be subject to Social Security taxes and the Federal Unemployment Taxes Act (FUTA).[13] Of course, amounts contributed in excess of the elective deferral limit of $22,500 (in 2023), are subject to income tax as well.[14]

A 401(k) plan may also allow special catch-up contributions by participants who have reached age fifty by the close of the plan year. The elective deferral limit for such individuals is increased by the lesser of (a) an applicable dollar amount, or (b) the amount of the participant's compensation, reduced by any other elective deferrals of the participant for the year. The applicable dollar amount is $7,500 for 2023, and may be adjusted for inflation annually.[15]

Target Benefit Pension Plan

It is a retirement plan under which the required contribution is initially based upon an assumed retirement benefit for each participant, but under which the actual retirement benefit received is based upon the market value of the assets in the individual participant's account at the time of retirement.

Age-weighted Profit Sharing Plan

Under traditional profit sharing plan arrangements, employer contributions are generally allocated each year to employees either in proportion to relative compensation or in proportion to relative compensation together with integration with Social Security benefits. However, an employer may maintain a qualified profit sharing plan in which the participant's age is taken into account when allocating the employer's contribution.[16] The result is that somewhat larger allocations (as a percentage of pay) are provided to older employees than to younger employees. Nonetheless, the allocations must satisfy either a minimum allocation gateway (e.g., generally 5 percent of compensation for non-highly compensated employees or one-third of that provided to highly compensated employees) or broadly available allocation rates must be used.[17]

Thrift and Savings Plan

The major characteristic of a thrift and savings plan is that employee-participants must contribute some percentage of compensation to the plan. The employer matches contributions of employees according to some formula. For example, an employer may match each dollar of employee contribution with more or less than $1 of employer contribution. A thrift and savings plan can be tax qualified or can be informal.

A tax qualified thrift and savings plan will result in a current employer deduction for contributions to the plan and, yet, employees will not be currently taxed on employer contributions. Both employer and employee contributions will grow tax-free within the plan. When distributions from a qualified thrift and savings plan are made, they are subject to the same rules applicable to other qualified retirement plans. Typically, a thrift and savings plan will require employees to contribute a percentage of compensation in order to participate. It is important when incorporating thrift and savings features in a plan that such required contributions meet a special nondiscrimination test.[18] All contributions are counted for purposes of the annual additions limitation.

Eligibility

A qualified corporate retirement plan may not impose an age or service requirement that would exclude any full-time employee who has attained age twenty-one, or who has completed one year of service, whichever is later.[19] If there is 100 percent immediate vesting, a two-year waiting period is permitted.[20]

A plan must be nondiscriminatory in its coverage of employees. (It is permissible to favor rank and file employees.) A plan will qualify if it benefits at least 70 percent of the nonhighly compensated employees, or benefits a percentage of nonhighly compensated employees which is at least 70 percent of the percentage of highly compensated employees benefiting under the plan.[21] Alternatively, a plan will qualify if it does not discriminate in favor of highly compensated employees and the average benefit percentage for the nonhighly compensated employees is at least 70 percent of the average benefit percentage for the highly compensated employees.[22] Additionally, a defined benefit plan must cover, on each day of the plan year, the lesser of fifty employees or 40 percent or more of all employees of the employer.[23]

A plan may exclude part-time and seasonal employees (those employees who work less than 1,000 hours in a twelve-month period, but note some changes in the Secure and Secure 2.0 Act noted below).[24] Also, a collective bargaining unit may be excluded if the union prefers not to be covered under a plan and the decision is made as the result of good-faith bargaining.[25]

The Secure 2.0 Act made many small changes to encourage expansion of vesting, eligibility and establishment of qualified retirement plans and will encourage more participation among part-time workers. Section 125 of the Act improves coverage for part-time workers. The first SECURE Act had required employers to allow long-term, part-time workers to participate in the employers' 401(k) plans. The SECURE Act provision provides that – except in the case of collectively bargained plans – employers maintaining a 401(k) plan must have a dual eligibility requirement under which an employee must complete either 1 year of service (with the 1,000-hour rule) or 3 consecutive years of service (where the employee completes at least 500 hours of service). Section 125 of the Secure 2.0 Act reduces the 3 year rule to 2 years, effective for plan years beginning after December 31, 2024. This provision also extends the long-term part-time coverage rules to 403(b) plans that are subject to ERISA.

Another unique Secure 2.0 provision, Section 112 of the Act, effective in 2023, incentivizes small employers to make military spouses eligible for plan participation and matching sooner than they would otherwise have to. Military spouses often do not remain employed long enough to become eligible for their employer's retirement plan or to vest in employer contributions. The new provision provides small employers a tax credit with respect to their defined contribution plans if they (1) make military spouses immediately eligible for plan participation within two months of hire, (2) upon plan eligibility, make the military spouse eligible for any matching or nonelective contribution that they would have been eligible for otherwise at 2 years of service, and (3) make the military spouse 100 percent immediately vested in all employer contributions. The tax credit equals the sum of (1) $200 per military spouse, and (2) 100 percent of all employer contributions (up to $300) made on behalf of the military spouse, for a maximum tax credit of $500. This credit applies for 3 years with respect to each military spouse – and does not apply to highly compensated employees. An employer may rely on an employee's certification that such employee's spouse is a member of the uniformed services.

Vesting

Minimum vesting standards must be met by all plans. Vesting refers to nonforfeitability of benefits by covered employees. The general rule is that the benefits attributable to employee contributions must always be 100 percent vested.[26] Likewise, with respect to a 401(k) plan, an employee's rights to benefits derived from elective contributions, as well as from qualified matching and qualified nonelective contributions used to satisfy the Actual Deferral Percentage (ADP) test, must be 100 percent vested at all times.[27] Other types of benefits must vest under one of the schedules outlined in Figure 57.1.

A plan must take into account all years of service (generally 1,000 hours in a plan year) completed after the employee attains age eighteen for vesting purposes.

Contributions and Benefits

The law imposes certain limitations on contributions and benefits.

Figure 57.1

REQUIRED VESTING SCHEDULES								
Years of Service	1	2	3	4	5	6	7 +
401k matches, top-heavy plans, and cash balance plans*							
Three-year Schedule	0%	0%	100%				
Graduated Schedule	0%	20%	40%	60%	80%	100%	
All other plans							
Five-year Schedule	0%	0%	0%	0%	100%		
Graduated Schedule	0%	0%	20%	40%	60%	80%	100%
*Cash balance plans must vest on a three-year schedule.							

Defined Contribution Plans

Defined contribution type plans include money purchase pension plans, profit sharing plans, stock bonus plans, 401(k) plans, ESOPs, thrift plans, and target or assumed benefit plans. They are subject to an annual additions limit equal to the lesser of (a) 100 percent of compensation or (b) $66,000 (in 2023, as indexed).[28]

An employer who sponsors a profit sharing plan is permitted a maximum deduction of up to 25 percent of the total compensation of plan participants.[29]

Furthermore, elective deferrals are not counted toward the maximum deduction limit. In addition, total compensation in a 401(k) plan is determined before subtracting any elective deferrals.[30]

Employees are typically not required to contribute their own funds as a condition of plan participation but plans can provide for voluntary contributions. Thrift plans commonly do require employees to contribute and require the employer to make matching contributions.

Defined contribution plans may be integrated with Social Security based on the Social Security tax (excluding hospital premium) for the current year.

Disabled plan participants (other than a disabled employee who is highly compensated) can receive the benefit of an employer contribution to a defined contribution plan based on the annualized compensation of the employee during his last year of employment. All such contributions must be immediately 100 percent vested.[31]

Defined Benefit Plans

A defined benefit plan is a plan which provides a fixed or determinable benefit such as 40 percent of an employee's final three years average salary or 1 percent times final three years average salary times number of years of plan participation or service with the employer.

The maximum normal retirement benefit for a defined benefit plan, based on retirement no earlier than age sixty-two, is the lesser of (a) 100 percent of the highest three consecutive years of average compensation while actively participating in the plan, or (b) $265,000 (in 2023, as indexed).[32] The limitation is increased for retirement after age sixty-five and decreased for retirement before age sixty-two.[33] These limits are based on the annual payment which, with interest compounded until the retirement date of the employee, will create a fund sufficient to provide the described benefit to the employee for his actuarial life expectancy. The benefit must be reduced pro-rata if the employee has fewer than ten years of plan participation with the employer.[34]

A $10,000 minimum annual benefit may always be provided for an employee who has never been covered by a defined contribution plan maintained by the employer regardless of the rules mentioned above.[35] But this amount must be reduced pro-rata if the employee has served the employer for less than ten years at retirement.[36]

All the limits above must be actuarially reduced to reflect any post retirement death benefits except in the case of a qualified joint and survivor annuity.[37]

Further reductions must be made in the limits described above if an employee retires before age sixty-two.[38] If retirement benefits are to commence prior to age sixty-two, the limit is reduced to the actuarial equivalent of a $270,000 benefit at age sixty-two. If retirement benefits commence after age sixty-five, the limit is increased to the actuarial equivalent of a $270,000 benefit at age sixty-five. For this purpose, the interest rate assumption must be not greater than the lesser of 5 percent or the rate specified in the plan.[39]

Furthermore, the limit must be reduced if the normal form of retirement is something other than a nonrefund life annuity.[40] All of the dollar limits described above are subject to the annual cost-of-living changes.

Target or Assumed Benefit Plan

A target or assumed benefit plan is a hybrid between a defined contribution and defined benefit plan in which a "target benefit" is established under the plan for each participant, such as 50 percent of an employee's five highest years' average salary.

Once the target benefit is found, contributions necessary to attain that goal are then actuarially determined based on a conservative interest assumption, such as 5 or 6 percent, and the age of the participant. The plan then becomes a money purchase plan.

The maximum annual addition to the account of a participant in a target benefit plan cannot exceed the lesser of (a) 100 percent of salary or (b) $66,000 (in 2023, as indexed).[41]

Each participant's account is credited with any investment earnings or gains and losses. This means the actual retirement benefit of a participant under a target benefit plan can be more or less than the actual target itself.

Deduction of Contributions

In a defined benefit pension plan, an employer can contribute and deduct the amount necessary to pay for the benefits promised. Technically stated, the employer may pay and deduct the plan's "normal cost" plus any amount necessary to amortize liability for benefits earned through the past service of employees. Past service (simplified, past service is the cost of financing benefits credited for past services) liability can be amortized over as few as ten years (but no more than thirty years).[42] But the Pension Protection Act of 2006 (PPA) provides that certain amounts need to be funded over seven years. Some relief from this requirement was temporarily enacted after the economic downturn in 2008.

An employer sponsoring a profit sharing plan may contribute and deduct a maximum of 25 percent of the total compensation of plan participants (without carry-forwards). A $100,000 covered payroll would therefore yield the right to a $25,000 deductible contribution.[43]

Where the employee is utilizing both a defined contribution pension plan and a profit sharing plan, the maximum deductible contribution for both plans is the greater of 25 percent of the compensation of covered employees or the contribution required to fund the minimum funding standard. This deduction limitation does not apply to combinations of defined benefit and money purchase plans.[44] For 2008 and later plan years, if the defined benefit plan is subject to PBGC coverage then there is no combined plan contribution limit.

Prior to 1987, employees could deduct "qualified voluntary employee contributions" made to the plan up to a maximum of $2,000 per taxable year or, if less, 100 percent of compensation. The plan had to contain special provisions allowing these contributions.[45] Qualified voluntary employee contributions (made prior to 1987) must be accounted for separately, although separate investment will not be required. No loans to participants or investments in life insurance contracts should be made with plan assets attributable to deductible employee contributions or such action will be considered a distribution.[46]

Since a CODA must be part of a profit sharing or stock bonus plan, the limitation on the employer's tax-deductible contributions to such a plan is 25 percent of the participants' total compensation.[47] Furthermore, for purposes of the limitation on annual additions, elective contributions made under a qualified CODA are not considered employer contributions.[48]

Employers may also permit employees to make voluntary contributions to a separate account or annuity, referred to as a "deemed IRA." If certain requirements for a traditional or Roth IRA are met, then the account or annuity will be treated as a traditional or Roth IRA, not as a qualified plan.[49]

Actuarial Assumptions

In a defined or fixed benefit pension plan, a conservative estimate should be made as to the rate of return of funds invested in assets other than life insurance. Any actual return in excess of the amount assumed must be used to reduce the employer's future contributions.

After challenging the use of rates as low as 5 or 6 percent for a number of years, the IRS backed down on its position that such rates were too conservative. The Tax Court and several circuit courts had sided with the employers in several such cases, noting that Congress intended actuaries to be "afforded a range of latitude in establishing a mix of reasonable assumptions, and that only if such assumptions are 'substantially unreasonable' should they be challenged and changed retroactively."[50]

In a money purchase plan, the investment experience directly affects the amount a participant will have at retirement. Normally, earnings are allocated to the participant's account in proportion to his or her account balance.

In a profit sharing plan, the investment experience directly affects the amount in a participant's account. Gains and losses must be allocated proportionately to each individual. Typically, such allocations are made in proportion to the account balances of each participant. At retirement a participant may have more or less than was contributed, depending on the investment experience of the plan.

In the event an employee terminates, under a defined benefit plan the portion of a terminated participant's nonvested account is used to reduce future employer contributions.[51] However, in a profit sharing plan, the funds in a terminated participant's nonvested account (forfeitures) can be allocated among the accounts of remaining participants on the same basis as the following year's contribution, or can be used to reduce future employer contributions, depending upon what provisions have been made in the plan.[52] Generally, forfeitures under all defined contribution plans, including money purchase plans, may also be used to increase participants' account balances.[53]

Mortality is an important actuarial assumption. In a fixed benefit pension plan, if life insurance is included in the plan, the investment account is generally not used to provide the death benefit. Instead, the investment account that would have gone to the deceased employee had he or she lived is used to reduce future employer contributions to the plan. If life insurance is included in the plan, death proceeds generally go to the employee's beneficiary.

In either a money purchase pension plan or a profit sharing plan, the total funds in a participant's account are paid to a beneficiary as a death benefit. This includes the life insurance proceeds as well as any other investments.

Retirement Age

Generally, plans will make provision for normal, early, and late retirement age. Usually, normal retirement age will be age sixty-five.

Mandatory retirement is generally prohibited. Exceptions exist for certain top executives and for good faith occupational requirements.

Employers are required to accrue additional benefits or pay the actuarial equivalent of normal retirement benefits to employees who choose to work beyond normal retirement age. It is unlawful to eliminate the accrual of further benefit credits to an employee's retirement account after the employee attains normal retirement age.[54]

It is also unlawful to exclude an employee from participation in a pension plan even though his age is within five years of the age set for normal retirement. Allowance is made, however, for the extension of the normal retirement date for any such late-age-hired person.[55] Some pension plans state that the normal retirement age of participants who are over age fifty-five at the time they enter the plan is five years from the date of entering the plan.

Early retirement benefits are generally available under a defined benefit plan at an actuarially reduced amount. In a money purchase plan, the amount of a pension that can be provided with the participant's vested share is what he or she will receive at early retirement. Under a profit sharing plan, in the case of early retirement, the amount accumulated in a participant's account will be paid generally as a lump sum or as monthly income.

The IRS has challenged the use of retirement ages under age sixty-five in small defined benefit plans; however, it backed down on this issue. The Tax Court and several circuit courts had sided with the employers in litigation of some of these cases. (See the discussion above, under "Actuarial Assumptions" with regard to IRS challenges to the use of low interest rates.) However, PPA 2006 requires plans to have a normal retirement age of no less than sixty-two unless a valid reason is shown.[56]

Social Security Integration

Generally speaking, the benefit structure of Social Security can be viewed as discriminating against the higher-paid employee, which usually includes the key shareholders and highly-paid management. Social Security benefits replace, relatively speaking, a higher percentage of the lower-paid employee's pre-retirement income. In essence, the business owner is already providing a base pension through contributions to the Social Security system.

Integration of a retirement plan with Social Security allows an employer to coordinate the benefits provided by Social Security with those provided by the employer's retirement plan. Through integration, the two benefits combined produce roughly the same proportionate benefit for higher-paid employees as for lower-paid employees. (The Internal Revenue Code and the IRS refer to integration as "permitted disparity.")

Example: In the case of a money purchase or profit sharing plan, the contribution rate (percent) that applies to compensation above the taxable wage base may not exceed the contribution rate (percent) that applies to compensation below the taxable wage base by more than the *lesser of* (1) the rate applied to compensation below the wage base or (2) 5.7 percent points (or, if greater, the rate of Social Security tax attributable to old-age insurance).[57] Thus, if the plan provides for contributions of 10 percent of pay in excess of the wage base, it would be properly integrated if it provided for contributions of at least 5 percent on pay below the wage base.

It is also possible to integrate a defined benefit pension plan. But here integration is on the basis of benefits rather than contributions.

Top Heavy Plans

Plans that are considered top heavy must meet the basic qualification requirements of other qualified plans and, in addition, meet the following requirements:

1. implement one of two alternative rapid vesting schedules;

2. provide minimum nonintegrated contributions or benefits for plan participants who are non-key employees; and

3. reduce the aggregate limit on contributions and benefits for some key employees.[58]

A plan is considered top heavy when more than 60 percent of its aggregate accumulated benefits or account balances is provided to key employees. An employee's status and whether or not a plan is top heavy is determined on a year by year basis. The determination is made on the last day of the preceding plan year for existing plans and on the last day of the first plan year for new plans.[59]

A key employee is any employee-participant who, at any time during the plan year is an officer earning more than $215,000 (in 2023, as indexed), a 5 percent (or more) owner, or a 1 percent (or more) owner earning more than $150,000 a year.[60]

Special rules apply for smaller employers: If the business (or aggregated group of businesses) has fewer than 500 employees, only 10 percent will be considered officers, but if the business has fewer than thirty employees, at least three officers must be counted.

Each additional qualification requirement will be discussed below.

Vesting

A top heavy plan must meet one of two special vesting rules. The first is a three-year 100 percent vesting rule. Under this rule an employee who is at least twenty-one years old and who has completed at least three years of service with the employer (or employers) maintaining the plan must be given a nonforfeitable right to 100 percent of his accrued benefit derived from employer contributions. The second is a six-year graded vesting rule. This provides 20 percent vesting at the end of the second year of service and 20 percent in each succeeding year. Full vesting must be attained by the end of the six-year period.[61] (See Figure 57.1, above)

Contributions and Benefits

Special limitations on contributions and benefits are imposed if the plan is considered top heavy.[62] Minimum benefits under defined benefit plans must be provided to non-key employees. The benefit accrued during a top heavy year must be at least 2 percent of average pay for the highest five years for each year of service in which a top heavy plan year ends, up to a total of 20 percent of average pay.

In the case of top heavy defined contribution plans, in each year the plan is top heavy, non-key employees must receive minimum contributions of at least 3 percent of compensation. But if the plan provides the contribution rate of less than 3 percent for all participants, then instead of the 3 percent contribution rate, the highest contribution rate percentage on behalf of any key employee can be used (counting only the first $270,000 of compensation for plan years beginning in 2017).

In determining benefits under a top heavy plan, only the first $330,000 of compensation (for plan years beginning in 2023) can be counted, as is the case in non-top heavy plans.[63] The $330,000 limit is indexed for inflation. Social Security benefits or contributions cannot be counted against the required minimum benefits or contributions.

57.4 HOW IT IS DONE

There are basically three ways an employer places funds into a retirement plan. The first is known as a fully-insured plan. Here, the employer places contributions into a funding vehicle of an insurance company, such as a retirement income life insurance contract. The funds usually receive a guarantee as to principal, minimum rate of interest, and annuity purchase rate (the rate of exchange at which pension funds can be changed into lifetime payment guarantees). It is the simplest method of investing pension monies.

The second type of investment vehicle is known as the split funded plan. Here, the employer places contributions into a trust fund. The trust fund splits contributions into two parts: part of the funds are placed in fixed assets, annuities, and/or life insurance, while the remainder is invested in other investments for diversification. There are principal, interest, and annuity purchase rate guarantees for the funds invested with the insurance company. However, frequently funds invested otherwise have no guarantees of principal or interest, but they may have the advantage of appreciation if invested in equities.

The third type of funding vehicle is known as uninsured. This type of funding implies that the employer contributions are invested solely by investments including equities. Contributions are made by the employer to a trust fund. There are no guarantees as to principal or interest although funds may be applied to buy a guaranteed annuity at normal retirement age. This funding method involves the highest risk because there are no guarantees made by a third party, but in return for the extra risk, this method offers the greatest potential appreciation (or depending upon how the plan is arranged, the lowest possible employer cost).

All three arrangements have advantages and disadvantages. For example, the fully-insured plan guarantees the principal, interest, annuity purchase rates, and expenses. It is the easiest plan to install and administer. The cost and effort of compliance with the Employee Retirement Income Security Act (ERISA) is relatively minimal. A disadvantage is that the growth of dollars in the plan is fixed, and so there is no chance for an equity-type appreciation of funds.

The split funded plan combines guarantees with the possibility of appreciation. The funds invested in insurance contracts obtain guarantees on principal and interest earnings, expense costs, and annuity rates. The side fund is usually invested in growth-oriented securities. Of course, since the side fund is invested in equities, the possibility exists that depreciation in the value of the securities will result in lower benefits for employees (or higher costs for the employer).

The main advantage of a full equity funded approach is that all funds have the possibility of appreciation. If the investment manager is successful, the result will be either reduced cost for the employer or increased benefits for the employees, depending on the type of plan utilized. The disadvantage of this arrangement is that there are no guarantees applied to the funds. Also, if an insurance company is not used, the employer or the plan must pay directly for actuarial, administrative, and investment expenses. The cost of hiring private actuarial and administrative services will be higher for small employers in most cases than if an insurer's services were utilized.

57.5 TAX IMPLICATIONS

Income Tax

Within the limits mentioned above, employer contributions to these plans are fully deductible for income tax purposes,[64] and earnings on plan assets accumulate income tax free.[65]

Distributions

Distributions before the participant attains age 59½ are subject to a 10 percent penalty tax with certain exceptions (death, divorce, disability, payments made over the participant's life starting from separation from service, and medical expenses).[66] The penalty is increased to 25 percent in the case of distributions from a SIMPLE IRA during the first two years of participation in the plan.

Distributions made in the form of a lump sum distribution are included as ordinary income to the employee in the year paid. Certain amounts may still be subject to ten-year averaging (though now rare), in the case of a taxpayer who attained age fifty before January 1, 1986. In any event, special averaging cannot be used for the portion of a taxable distribution attributable to deductible employee contributions. Payment of such amounts can be distributed in a different tax year from the balance of the lump sum payment without jeopardizing any special averaging treatment that may still be available.

Before distribution is made, an employee generally does not have to include an employer's contribution in gross income, even if rights to the benefits in the plan are fully nonforfeitable. Benefits payable under a qualified retirement plan–including deductible employee contributions and earnings on those contributions–are taxed only when paid to a participant or beneficiary and are not taxed if merely "made available."[67]

However, if life insurance protection is provided under the plan, an employee is considered to have received a distribution each year (a current economic benefit) equal to the portion of the employer's contributions or trust earnings that have been applied during the year to provide pure insurance on the employee's life. This is the so-called "Table 2001 cost."[68] The employee includes this as income just as if he or she had received a bonus in that amount; however, such costs will be recovered income tax free when benefits are received under the contract. (If life insurance is purchased with deductible employee contributions, the amount spent is treated as a distribution.)[69]

When an employee first becomes eligible to receive benefits, those benefits do not have to be paid and immediately rolled over into an IRA to avoid current income taxation. If the plan allows, they can be left in the plan and are not taxed until paid (but if paid to a child or creditor of the employee, they are treated as if paid to the employee).

Deferral Limits

The plan must place some limits on this deferral of receipt of benefits. Distributions generally must begin by April 1 of the year following the year the participant reaches age 73 (see item (8) under "What are the Requirements" above). The Secure Act and Secure 2.0 Act changed this applicable age from 70 ½ to age 72, then in 2023, age 73, and will change it again in 2033 to age 75. The plan must provide that the entire interest of the participant will be distributed over one of the following permissible periods:

a. the life of the participant;

b. the lives of the participant and his or her designated beneficiary;

c. a period not extending beyond the life expectancy of the participant; or

d. a period not extending beyond the life expectancy of the participant and his or her designated beneficiary.

Note, however, that the Secure Act and Secure 2.0 Act changed the rules for payouts after the participant's death to beneficiaries (and special categories of beneficiaries called "eligible designated beneficiaries" and "designated beneficiaries") significantly. See Chapter 59 on IRAs for more detail on those rules.

Under regulations issued in 2003, a Uniform Distribution Period is used to determine the participant's lifetime distributions, regardless of who is named as the beneficiary.[70] However, the amount required to be distributed will be somewhat less if the sole designated beneficiary is the participant's spouse and the spouse is more than ten years younger than the participant (this may also apply if a conduit trust for a spouse is named as primary beneficiary).[71] A designated beneficiary is generally any individual designated by the participant to receive the balance of his or her benefits remaining at the participant's death, but may be certain qualifying trusts under see-through trust rules discussed elsewhere in this book.

Periodic Payments

An employee who retires and receives periodic payments from the retirement plan is taxed on the receipt of such payments in accordance with the annuity rules, which vary depending on the annuity starting date.

Effective for annuity starting dates that are later than November 18, 1996, a table is set forth in the Code for determining the excludable portion of each monthly payment from such an annuity (normally none is excludable, but there may be after tax or nondeductible contributions). The excludable portion of an annuity subject to this provision is determined by dividing the employee's investment in the contract by the number of anticipated payments based on the age of the annuitant, as follows:[72]

Age on annuity starting date	Number of anticipated payments
Not more than 55	360
More than 55 but not more than 60	310
More than 60 but not more than 65	260
More than 65 but not more than 70	210
More than 70	160

In the case of annuity starting dates after December 31, 1997, a separate table is provided for annuities payable over two or more lives. The excludable portion of such an annuity is determined by dividing the employee's investment in the contract by the number of anticipated payments based on the age of the annuitant, as follows:[73]

If the combined ages of the annuitants are:	Number of payments
Not more than 110	410
More than 110 but not more than 120	360
More than 120 but not more than 130	310
More than 130 but not more than 140	260
More than 140	210

For annuity starting dates beginning after July 1, 1986 and before November 19, 1996, an exclusion ratio is used to determine the taxable portion of the annuity payouts. The exclusion ratio is the ratio of the employee's "investment in the contract" (cost) to the employee's "expected return," expressed as follows:

$$\frac{\text{Investment In Contract}}{\text{Expected Return}}$$

The employee's cost or "investment in the contract" is essentially his nondeductible contributions. Where life insurance is included in the plan, it also includes the total of all one year term insurance costs that have been reported as taxable income. The "expected return" is the annual payment the employee will receive multiplied by the employee's life expectancy (see Table V, One Life-Expected Return Multiples). (Adjustments must be made for payouts made over differing time periods or where minimum payout guarantees are present.) Once the fraction is determined, it is multiplied by the annual payment. The product is the amount not subject to taxation. The balance of each payment is taxable as ordinary income.[74] A simplified safe harbor method for taxing annuity payments (see IRS Publication 575, Pension and Annuity Income) is available for individuals whose annuity starting date is after July 1, 1986.[75]

Distributions of deductible employee contributions are generally taxed under a pro-rata recovery rule.[76]

Life Insurance and Death Benefits

A beneficiary receiving death benefits from a qualified retirement plan is taxed on the amount received for income tax purposes under either the lump sum or annuity rules. However, voluntary employee contributions that were deductible are not allowed the relief granted lump-sum distributions and are includable in ordinary income.[77] In computing the amount of taxable income the beneficiary must report as a result of the distribution, if the distribution is made in a lump sum and if any portion of the distribution consists of life insurance proceeds for which the employee paid the insurance costs or reported the Table 2001 cost as taxable income on his return, then the difference between the face amount of the insurance contract and the insurance contract cash value (this difference is called the "pure insurance") passes to the beneficiary free of income tax.[78] Thus, the beneficiary treats only the cash value portion of any death benefit plus any other cash distributions from the plan as income subject to tax.

If, on the other hand, the employee did not pay the insurance cost of the life insurance contract or did not report the cost of such insurance as taxable income, the portion of the insurance proceeds consisting of pure insurance (as defined above) will be considered taxable income to the beneficiary.

Accident and Health Plans

If the plan participant suffers permanent loss or loss of use of a member or function of the body, or permanent disfigurement, it may be possible for him or her to receive benefits under a qualified plan free of income tax under Code section 105(c). In order for the payment to qualify, the plan must provide 100 percent vesting of benefits if the participant ceases employment due to total and permanent disability, and must also include statutory language from section 105(c) to establish the dual purpose of the plan (i.e., a retirement plan and an "accident and health" plan).

Code section 105 applies to amounts received under Accident and Health Plans. A minority of courts have found that a qualified plan can serve a dual function of providing retirement benefits and disability benefits. To the extent benefits are provided due to the participant's disability, they may be income tax free if the requirements of section 105(c) are satisfied. But expect vigorous IRS objection.

Section 105(c)(2) requires that the disability payment be computed by taking the nature of the injury into account in determining the benefit without regard to the period the employee is absent from work. This requirement may be difficult to satisfy in most pension plan contexts. However, a provision giving the committee discretion to determine disability benefits with reference to the nature of the injury may enable the disabled participant to overcome this hurdle.

Estate Tax

The *entire* value of a qualified plan death benefit is subject to inclusion in the decedent's gross estate for federal estate tax purposes. However, only the estates of exceptionally wealthy plan participants will actually be subject to estate tax. First, there is a substantial unified credit which can be applied which essentially eliminates estate taxes for net estates of less than $12,920,000 for 2023 (indexed for inflation).[79] In addition, the unlimited marital deduction for federal estate tax purposes defers federal estate tax on property transferred at death to a spouse in a qualifying manner until the death of the second spouse.[80] Avoiding federal estate tax can be significant if the estate is exceptionally large, the participant is single, or, for whatever reason, the participant is unwilling to pay the death benefit to the spouse. In each of these situations, the marital deduction would not be available. Also, even when the death benefit is payable to a spouse, federal estate tax is merely delayed and is not really avoided; a spouse is often about the same age as the decedent, and thus within a few years much of the property transferred to the spouse is potentially subject to federal estate tax at the surviving spouse's death.

State inheritance tax laws covering distributions from qualified pension and profit sharing plans vary, but the majority of states with estate and inheritance taxes consider these taxable similar to federal estate tax inclusion.

Other Tax Issues

Generally, there are four other taxes affecting retirement plans which have not been discussed elsewhere. The taxes are as follows:

1. A 20 percent nondeductible excise tax is imposed on the amount of any employer reversion from a qualified plan if:

    a. a significant amount of the reversion is used to fund benefits in a replacement plan;

    b. a significant amount is used to increase the benefits of participants under the terminating plan; or

    c. the employer is in bankruptcy.

    Otherwise, the tax is 50 percent.[81] Liability for this tax rests on the employer. An employer reversion is the amount of cash and the fair market value of other property received (directly or indirectly) by an employer from a qualified plan. Certain mistaken excess payments may be excluded.

2. There is a 50 percent nondeductible excise tax imposed on the participant in the event of a failure to make a minimum required distribution from the plan. The tax is equal to 50 percent of the amount by which the minimum required distribution exceeds the actual amount distributed during the taxable year. Section 302 of the Secure 2.0 Act reduced this tax rate starting in 2023, however, to only 25%. Further, if a failure to take a required minimum distribution is corrected in a timely manner, the excise tax on the failure is further reduced from 25 percent to 10 percent. The tax is imposed on the payee. A "waiver" is allowed for "reasonable error" if steps are being taken to pay out the balance due.[82]

3. An additional penalty tax applies in cases where there is an underpayment of tax due to an overstatement of pension liabilities. The amount of the penalty depends on the amount of the overstatement: 20 percent for overstatements of 200 percent or more but less than 400 percent of the correct amount of liabilities and 40 percent for overstatements of 400 percent or more.[83]

4. There is a 50 percent excise tax on prohibited allocations of employer securities acquired in a transaction involving the tax-deferred sale to an ESOP.[84]

57.6 ERISA ISSUES

Reporting Requirements

In general, every plan that is not specifically exempted must file certain reports each year. The annual report for plans with one hundred or more participants must include an audited financial statement. Annual reports of defined benefit plans must contain a certified actuarial report. If the plan terminates, additional special reports are required.

The number of participants covered by a plan has no effect on the reporting and disclosure requirements–an annual report must be filed regardless of how many or how few participants are covered. However, where a plan contains less than one hundred participants, a simplified report may be authorized.

Furthermore, certain information must be provided to plan participants and beneficiaries. They must be given a summary of the plan written in a manner understandable by the average participant or beneficiary (i.e., a Summary Plan Description). Furthermore, beneficiaries and participants can request a status report once a year showing total benefits accrued and nonforfeitable pension benefit rights. Employees who have terminated employment during the plan year must also be given a statement of their deferred vested rights in the plan. Many of these documents become public information and can be inspected.[85]

Failure to meet the reporting and disclosure requirements can result in serious civil and/or criminal penalties, which include fines and imprisonment.

Fiduciary Rules

ERISA established rules governing the conduct of fiduciaries and other persons dealing with the plan. The Department of Labor administers certain provisions that pertain to rules and remedies similar to those under traditional trust law governing the conduct of fiduciaries.

Specifically, these fiduciary responsibility rules relate to plan administration, provide general standards of conduct for fiduciaries, and cause certain transactions to be "prohibited transactions" in which plan fiduciaries may not engage.[86] Other provisions that are enforced by the Treasury Department impose an excise tax on certain persons who violate the prohibited transaction rules.[87]

Basically, ERISA requires each fiduciary of a plan to act with the care, skill, prudence, and diligence under the circumstances then prevailing that a prudent person acting in a like capacity and familiar with such matters would use in conducting an enterprise of like character and with like aims.

A fiduciary is a person who:

1. exercises any discretionary authority or discretionary control respecting management of the plan or exercises any authority or control respecting management or disposition of assets;

2. renders investment advice for a fee or other compensation, direct or indirect, with respect to any monies or other property of the plan, or has any authority or responsibility to do so; or

3. has any discretionary authority or discretionary responsibility in the administration of the plan.[88]

The term fiduciary also includes persons named by a fiduciary to carry out fiduciary responsibilities (other than trustee responsibilities) under the plan.

Furthermore, ERISA requires that a qualified retirement plan be for the exclusive benefit of the plan's employees and their beneficiaries.[89] Under the exclusive benefit umbrella:

1. the cost of plan assets must not exceed fair market value at the time of purchase;

2. assets should bring a fair return commensurate with the prevailing rate;

3. the plan should maintain sufficient liquidity to permit distributions; and

4. the safeguards and diversity that would be adhered to by a prudent investor must be present.

Protection from Creditors

ERISA provides that a pension, profit sharing, or other qualified plan will not be qualified unless it provides that benefits provided under the plan may not be assigned or alienated, voluntarily or involuntarily. An exception to this rule exists for assignments used to secure plan loans to a participant and voluntary and revocable assignments that do not exceed 10 percent of any benefit payment to a participant, unless the assignment is made for purposes of defraying plan administrative costs.[90]

It has generally been accepted in the non-bankruptcy context that the anti-alienation provision protects pension interests from the reach of creditors. In the bankruptcy context, federal bankruptcy law provides broad protection for the retirement benefits of participants against the claims of creditors, for personal bankruptcies filed on or after October 17, 2005. This protection is subject to a $1 million limit for the total of an individual's IRAs and Roth IRAs, but this limit does not apply rollover amounts transferred from qualified plans, nor to simplified employee pensions or SIMPLE IRAs, and is subject to a triennial inflation adjustment (currently $1,512,350 in 2023).[91] For earlier bankruptcies, the Supreme Court extended the reach of the federal Bankruptcy Code to shield IRA assets in a 2005 decision,[92] having resolved the issue of bankruptcy protection in 1992 with respect to qualified plan assets.[93]

Domestic Relations Orders

The creation, assignment, or recognition of a right to any benefit payable from a plan under a Qualified Domestic Relations Order (QDRO) is not treated as a prohibited assignment or alienation under ERISA or the Internal Revenue Code, thus allowing enforcement of state QDROs.[94] All qualified retirement plans are required to provide for the payment of benefits in accordance with the terms of any QDRO.

1. The term "domestic relations order" means a judgment, decree, or order (including approval of a property settlement agreement) which relates to the provision of child support, alimony payments, or marital property rights to a spouse, former spouse, child or other dependent of a participant, and is made pursuant to state domestic relations law. To be *qualified*, a domestic relations order must: create or recognize the existence of an alternate payee's right to receive all or a portion of the benefits payable with respect to a participant under a plan;

2. clearly specify certain facts (e.g., name and address of participant and alternate payee, amount of benefits to be paid and the number of payments); and

3. not alter the amount or form of benefits under a plan.

The term "alternate payee" means any spouse, former spouse, child or other dependent of a participant who is recognized by a domestic relations order as having a right to receive all, or a portion of, a participant's benefits under a plan.[95]

A QDRO can require benefits to be paid to an alternate payee at the participant's earliest retirement age under the plan without regard to whether the participant has separated from service or retired.

Plan Termination Insurance

ERISA established, within the Department of Labor, a public corporation named the Pension Benefit Guaranty Corporation (PBGC). The PBGC is a federal insurance company that provides mandatory plan termination insurance to protect the benefit rights of workers whose defined benefit pension plans go out of existence. As one of its main duties, the corporation administers plan termination insurance for defined benefit pension plans, up to specified limits.[96]

Premiums for PBGC coverage are $96 per participant (in 2023), plus an additional amount, calculated by dividing the plan's unfunded vested benefits as of the end of the preceding plan year by the number of plan participants at that time.

The Bipartisan Budget Act of 2013 increased both the per-participant and additional amount for unfunded liabilities significantly. Pursuant to the act, in 2016 the additional rate for unfunded liabilities will increase by $5 on top of the indexed rate. Thereafter, both rates will be indexed for inflation.[97] See this Pension Benefit Guarantee Corporation (a government agency) website for updated rates: https://www.pbgc.gov/prac/prem/premium-rates.

57.7 ONGOING COMPLIANCE ISSUES

Nondiscrimination Testing

In order to meet the nondiscrimination requirement, qualified 401(k) plans must either satisfy the Actual Deferral Percentage (ADP) test, adopt a safe harbor plan (see below), or adopt a SIMPLE 401(k) plan, as described below.

The ADP test is designed to limit the extent to which elective contributions made on behalf of highly compensated employees may exceed the elective contributions made on behalf of nonhighly compensated employees.[98]

The amount of elective deferrals to be credited to a participant's account for any plan year must satisfy the following tests.

If the non-highly compensated group contributes an average of:	The highly compensated group may contribute an average of:
Under 2% of compensation.	2 times the rate of the non-highly compensated group.
Between 2-8% of compensation.	2% of pay more than the non-highly compensated group.
Over 8% of compensation.	1¼ times the rate of the non-highly compensated group.

The ADP test can be performed by comparing the ADP of highly compensated employees for a plan year to the ADP of nonhighly compensated employees for either the same plan year (current year testing) *or* the preceding plan year (prior year testing).[99]

The plan may limit the amount subject to deferral and, if necessary, provide for a minimum level of nonelective employer contributions. For example, if a profit sharing plan provides for nonelective employer contributions of 2 percent of compensation, which are nonforfeitable and subject to appropriate distribution restrictions, and if eligible employees are limited to deferring an additional 2 percent of compensation, the nondiscrimination tests will be satisfied in all cases. An alternative would be to make the cash-or-deferred election irrevocable for the entire plan year. Adoption of either the safe harbor or SIMPLE 401(k) design will also assure that the plan remains in compliance with the nondiscrimination requirement.

Safe Harbor 401(k) Plan

A safe harbor 401(k) plan is one that meets the nondiscrimination requirement by satisfying an alternative safe harbor in place of the traditional ADP test. Under the safe harbor, the plan will be considered nondiscriminatory if:

1. the employer satisfies a matching contribution requirement for nonhighly compensated employees (100 percent of the employee contribution up to 3 percent of compensation, plus 50 percent from 3 percent to 5 percent of compensation) and certain design requirements, including 100 percent vesting; or

2. the employer makes a nonelective (nonmatching) contribution for all eligible nonhighly compensated employees equal to at least 3 percent of compensation.[100]

SIMPLE 401(k) Plan

A SIMPLE 401(k) plan is a cash or deferred arrangement that satisfies the nondiscrimination requirement by meeting special design requirements instead of the ADP test. Among these requirements are that:

1. the employer must have one hundred or fewer employees (only employees with at least $5,000 in compensation for the preceding year are counted) on any day in the year;

2. employees must be eligible to make elective salary reductions contributions for the year of up to $15,500 in 2023, $14,000 in 2022 and $13,500 in 2020 and 2021 (adjusted for inflation);

3. the employer is required to make a contribution equal to either (i) a dollar for dollar matching contribution up to 3 percent of the employee's compensation, or (ii) 2 percent of compensation for all eligible employees earning at least $5,000 (whether or not they elect salary reductions);

4. the employer may not maintain any other plan (e.g., qualified plan, SEP, 403(a) annuity, 403(b) tax-sheltered annuity) that covers any of the same employees as the SIMPLE 401(k) plan; and

5. all contributions to the SIMPLE 401(k) plan must be nonforfeitable. SIMPLE 401(k) plans are not subject to the top-heavy requirements, nor to separate nondiscrimination testing; however, they are subject to the other qualification, administrative and ERISA requirements that apply to a qualified Section 401(k) plan.[101]

Excess Contributions

Excess contributions are the excess of the elective contributions (including qualified nonelective and matching contributions that are treated as elective contributions) made on behalf of highly compensated employees for the plan year over the maximum amount permitted under the ADP test for such plan year.[102] A 401(k) plan will not fail the ADP test for any plan year, and thus will maintain its qualified status if:

1. the amount of excess contributions for such plan year, along with any income attributable thereto, is returned to highly compensated employees within twelve months after the close of the applicable plan year; or

2. the highly compensated employee elects to recharacterize the excess amount contributed as an after-tax voluntary contribution.[103]

A 10 percent excise tax is imposed on the employer unless the excess contributions are corrected within 2½ months after the end of the plan year for which they were made.[104] If excess contributions are not corrected before the end of the plan year following the plan year for which the excess contributions were made, the plan will fail to qualify for the plan year for which the excess contributions were made and for all subsequent plan years during which the excess contributions remain in the plan.[105]

57.8 PLAN FEATURES

Loans to Participants

Plans may make loans to participants if the loan is made in accordance with specific provisions in the plan governing such loans, a reasonable charge is made for the use of plan assets, and the loan is adequately secured. Loans must be available to all participants on a reasonably equivalent basis.[106]

Limits are imposed on tax-free participant borrowing from qualified plans, from tax sheltered annuities, and from plans (qualified and nonqualified) of federal, state, and local governments and their agencies and instrumentalities.

Certain loan transactions are treated as distributions. Special rules apply if the loan constitutes a qualified hurricane distribution.[107]

Loan transactions include: (1) the direct or indirect receipt of a loan, and (2) the assignment (or agreement to assign) or the pledging (or agreement to pledge) of any portion of an employee's interest in a plan.[108]

The following rules and exceptions apply to plan loans:

1. *Loan agreement.* The plan loan must be evidenced by a legally enforceable agreement, specifying the date, amount and term of the loan;[109]

2. *Term requirement and dollar limitation.* The term of the loan must be no longer than five years.[110] Loans which are to be repaid within five years are taxed as distributions only to the extent that the amount of the loan (together with any other outstanding loans the employee has made from plans with the same employer) exceeds the lesser of (a) $50,000 reduced by the highest outstanding loan balance during the prior twelve months, or (b) half of the employee's vested benefits under the employer plans from which he has borrowed (or $10,000, if greater).[111] If the loan exceeds the dollar limitation, a distribution of the amount in excess of the dollar limit is deemed to occur when the loan is made.[112]

3. *Loans that do not have to be repaid within five years* are fully taxable as distributions. Whether or not a loan must be repaid within five years is ascertained as of the date the loan is made.

4. *Repayment.* The loan agreement must specify the amount and terms of the loan and the repayment schedule. Failure to make a repayment of a plan loan installment when it is due will generally result in a deemed distribution, unless payment is made within specified cure (grace) periods.[113]

Some loans of five years or less may be subsequently extended. The loan balance at the time of the extension is considered a distribution at that time. If repayment under a five-year-or-less loan is not made (so at the end of five years, the participant still owes the plan money), any remaining amounts due are considered plan distributions.

More-than-five-year loans are not converted to five-year-or-less loans or in any other way favorably treated merely because they are repaid in five years or less (regardless of the reason for the early repayments).

Exception 1: *Housing loans.* A loan of more than five years generally is not treated as a distribution to the extent that it is used by the plan participant to purchase the participant's principal residence.[114]

Exception 2: *Certain mortgage loans.* Where plan trustees invest a specific percentage or amount of plan assets in residential mortgages or in other types of mortgage investments, such investments are not considered loans as long as the amount lent does not exceed the fair market value of the property the loan was used to purchase. Loans to officers, directors, or owners (or their beneficiaries) are not protected under this exception.

Hardship Distributions

A 401(k) plan must provide that amounts attributable to elective contributions may not be distributed before the occurrence of one of the following events:

1. The participant's retirement, death, disability, or other termination of service;

2. The termination of the plan without the establishment of a successor defined contribution plan;

3. The sale of the business or subsidiary;

4. The participant's attainment of age 59½, or

5. The participant's financial hardship.[115]

For a distribution to be considered as having been made on account of financial hardship it must be made due to an immediate and heavy financial need of the employee and it must be necessary to satisfy that need. The determination of the existence of the immediate and heavy financial need must be made in accordance with nondiscriminatory and objective standards set forth in the plan.

A distribution that is made due to hardship must be limited to the distributable amount. The "distributable amount" is equal to the employee's total elective contributions as of the date of distribution, reduced by the amount of previous distributions on account of hardship.

A distribution is treated as being made on account of immediate and heavy financial need if it is for:

1. The payment of expenses for medical care that were either previously incurred by, or are necessary for the medical care of, the employee or the employee's spouse or dependents;

2. The costs directly related to the purchase, excluding mortgage payments, of the employee's principal residence;

3. The payment of tuition, related educational fees and room and board for the next twelve months of post-secondary education for the employee, his spouse, children, or dependents; and

4. The payment of amounts necessary to prevent the eviction of the employee from his principal residence or to prevent foreclosure on the mortgage on the employee's principal residence.

The IRS has the authority to expand the above list of expenses found under the regulations, through the issuance of revenue rulings, notices and other documents of general applicability, rather than on an individual basis.[116]

Distributions are not treated as necessary to satisfy an immediate and heavy financial need of an employee:

1. To the extent that the amount of the distribution is in excess of the amount required to relieve the financial need. The amount of the immediate and heavy financial need may include amounts necessary to pay federal, state or local income taxes or penalties reasonably anticipated to result from the distribution; and

2. To the extent that the need may be relieved from other sources that are reasonably available to the employee, referred to as an "employee resource."

For example, a vacation home owned by the employee and his spouse is treated as an employee resource. However, property held in an irrevocable trust for the benefit of the employee's children is not treated as an employee resource.

Surviving Spouse Benefits

A participant's surviving spouse must be provided automatic survivor benefits.[117] Defined benefit plans and defined contribution plans are required to provide automatic survivor benefits (1) in the form of a qualified joint and survivor annuity, to a vested participant who receives a plan distribution for reasons other than the participant's death (i.e., termination of employment, retirement or disability); and (2) in the form of a qualified pre-retirement survivor annuity to a vested participant who dies before reaching the annuity starting date under the plan and who has a surviving spouse.

For automatic survivor coverage purposes, a vested participant means a participant who has a nonforfeitable right to any portion of the accrued benefit or account balance, whether or not the participant is still employed by the employer. The term annuity starting date means the first day of the first period for which an amount is payable as an annuity (or, in the case of a non-annuity benefit, the first day on which all events have occurred entitling the participant to the benefit).[118] The automatic survivor coverage rules do not apply to a profit sharing or stock bonus plan if:

1. the plan provides that the participant's vested account balance will be paid to his or her surviving spouse (or to a designated beneficiary if there is no surviving spouse or if the surviving spouse gives the proper consent);

2. the participant does not elect payment of benefits in the form of a life annuity; and

3. with respect to the participant, the plan is not a transferee of a plan required to provide automatic survivor benefits.[119]

A qualified joint and survivor annuity is an annuity for the life of the participant with a survivor annuity for the life of the spouse that is not less than 50 percent (and not greater than 100 percent) of the amount that is payable during the joint lives of the participant and spouse, and that is the actuarial equivalent of a single life annuity for the life of the participant.[120]

A qualified pre-retirement survivor annuity is an annuity for the life of the surviving spouse of the participant with payments to the surviving spouse which are not less than the payments that would have been made under the qualified joint and survivor annuity (or the actuarial equivalent thereof), under the rules set forth in Code section 417(c).

A qualified joint and survivor annuity and a qualified pre-retirement survivor annuity need not be provided by a plan unless the participant and the surviving spouse have been married throughout the one-year period ending on the earlier of the participant's retirement, disability or the date of the participant's death.[121]

These annuity payments automatically qualify for the gift and estate tax marital deduction so long as no payments can be made to anyone other than a spouse until the death of the surviving spouse. This is true even though there could be payments or distributions to another person after the death of both spouses.

Note that in the case of the estate tax marital deduction, the executor of the estate of the first spouse to die can elect out of the marital deduction.

Participant Election

A plan participant may elect not to receive the qualified joint and survivor annuity and/or the qualified pre-retirement survivor annuity at any time during an applicable election period and to receive benefits in another form offered under the plan. The participant is permitted to revoke any such election during the applicable election period. The applicable election period, in the case of a qualified joint and survivor annuity, is the ninety-day period ending on the annuity starting date. The applicable election, in the case of a qualified pre-retirement survivor annuity, is a period beginning on the first day of the plan year in which the participant attains age thirty-five and ending on the date of the participant's death. If the participant separates from service, the applicable election period begins not later than the date of separation.[122]

An election by the participant not to take survivor coverage is effective only if the participant's spouse consents in writing, the consent is witnessed by a plan representative or a notary public, and the spouse's consent acknowledges the effect of the election. Spousal consent is not required if it is established (to the satisfaction of a plan representative) that there is no spouse or that the spouse cannot be located.[123]

Alternate Gifts to Family Trusts

The Retirement Equity Act of 1984 generally provides that all benefits from pension and profit sharing plans, with some exceptions, must be in the form of annuities. If the participant has died, then the general provision under REA '84 is that there be an annuity for the lifetime of the survivor as to at least one-half of the property. Whether the transfer can be made to a trust in lieu of the surviving spouse is something that has been questioned by a number of practitioners. Indeed, *The REA Book* says that the requirements of the Act cannot be met by naming an irrevocable trust as sole beneficiary even though the surviving spouse is the sole beneficiary of the trust and the benefits payable under the trust meet the survivor annuity benefit requirements of the Act.[124]

If the surviving spouse dies, then it may be that REA '84 no longer applies, and any normal transfer can be made and property can go to a trust outright as opposed to being in an annuity form.

On the other hand, the Act seems to lay out clearly the rule that any transfer outside the normal REA '84 rules must be done only on the basis of a written exception being made by the participant and a particular form of written waiver by the surviving spouse of any annuity rights. There have been suggestions that payments by pension plan administrators to trusts without such a formal written request and written waiver might cause the trust to be disqualified.

This is an area of the law in which a pension law expert should be consulted on beneficiary designations involving large amounts.

The spousal consent forms illustrated in Figure 57.2 are used by Ralph Gano Miller in his California practice and contain language designed to overcome the problems inherent in the law as it presently reads. Figure 57.3 is a beneficiary designation form patterned after those suggested in Natalie Choate's book entitled, *Life and Death Planning for Retirement Benefits*. It is almost always preferable to name an individual or see through trust as a beneficiary in order to achieve the best income tax outcome, although the Secure Act and Secure 2.0 Act do provide some narrow exceptions to this.

57.9 ISSUES IN COMMUNITY PROPERTY STATES

Many community property implications and issues have been discussed in previous chapters. Some additional tax implications should also be mentioned.

Generally, for purposes of divorce, the community property laws are recognized; however, there will be a substantial difference in rights in the event of the prior death of the nonparticipant spouse. Generally, if the participant spouse is married, the required form of distribution on the death of either spouse is in the form of a survivor annuity for the surviving spouse. Where the participant spouse is the first to die, this means the surviving spouse will receive the required annuity regardless of the community nature of the qualified plan benefit.

Further, where the nonparticipant spouse is the first to die, one court[125] has held that his or her community interest in a pension plan in effect passes to the surviving participant spouse regardless of any direction of the deceased spouse, or any contrary provisions in the will of the deceased spouse. In effect, the required survivor rights supersede state community property laws.

This position was affirmed in a landmark 1997 case,[126] in which the U.S. Supreme Court held in a five-to-four decision that a deceased nonparticipant spouse could not make a testamentary transfer of her community property interest in her participant spouse's undistributed qualified plan benefits. Noting that community property laws have, in the past, been preempted in order to prevent the diversion of retirement benefits, the court said the attempted transfer conflicted with ERISA, frustrated its purpose, and was a prohibited "assignment or alienation" of benefits under Section 206(d) of the law. The Court held that ERISA therefore preempts a state law allowing a nonparticipant spouse to transfer by testamentary instrument an interest in undistributed pension plan benefits.

Note that the survivor annuity rule does not apply to distributions from IRAs, SIMPLE IRAs, or Simplified Employee Pensions, as discussed in Chapter 56, and that the survivor annuity may be waived, as discussed at the end of this chapter.

57.10 USE OF LIFE INSURANCE

In a profit sharing plan, less than 50 percent of the aggregate employer contributions and forfeitures allocated to each participant's account can be used to purchase ordinary life insurance. If insurance may be purchased only with funds that have been accumulated in the plan for two or more years, the 50 percent rule does not apply.[127] In addition to this requirement, a profit sharing plan must require the trustee at or before retirement either (a) to convert the policies into cash, or (b) to distribute the policies to the employee. A money-purchase plan has the same "less than 50 percent" rule with regard to the purchase of ordinary life insurance.

Life insurance is a permissible purchase in a defined benefit pension plan if it meets either of two tests. The first test is essentially the same as the money-purchase plan test. The alternative test is the "100 to 1" test whereby the insurance is permissible if the insurance amount does not exceed 100 times the expected monthly retirement benefit.[128] For example, if the projected monthly benefit is $1,000, the life insurance cannot exceed $100,000.

There are a number of advantages of life insurance in a qualified retirement plan. These include:

- Protection against the premature death of a participant

- Securing the right to use guaranteed annuity rates at a future retirement date

- Assurance that insurance can be purchased at original age rates when the participant retires or terminates employment

- In a profit sharing plan, providing key person insurance on the lives of corporate officers or valuable employees for the benefit of the trust and its participants.

57.11 FREQUENTLY ASKED QUESTIONS

Question – When does an employee become subject to tax on benefits accruing in a qualified plan?

Answer – An employee or beneficiary of a qualified plan will not be taxed until benefits are received from the plan. For example, even though a participant in a profit sharing plan has the unrestricted right to make withdrawals of employer or deductible employee contributions, or the earnings on nondeductible employee contributions, there will be no current tax based on constructive receipt. This increases the appeal of making contributions to qualified plans even when such contributions are nondeductible.

Figure 57.2

GENERAL CONSENT OF SPOUSE TO WAIVER OF QUALIFIED JOINT AND SURVIVOR ANNUITY PAYMENT FORM [DEFINED BENEFIT PLAN OR DEFINED CONTRIBUTION PLAN]

I am the spouse of Participant. I understand that I have a right to the Qualified Preretirement Survivor Annuity ("QPSA") benefit from the above-referenced Plan if my spouse dies before he or she begins receiving retirement benefits (or, if earlier, before the beginning of the period for which the retirement benefits are paid). I also understand that if the value of the QPSA benefit is Five Thousand Dollars ($5,000) or less, the plan will pay the benefit to me in one lump sum payment.

I agree to give up my right to One Hundred Percent (100 Percent) of the QPSA benefit and to allow my spouse to name the beneficiary(ies) so designated in the beneficiary designation to which this Consent is attached to receive that benefit. This Consent is valid only with respect to the above-referenced beneficiary designation and is not valid with respect to any future beneficiary designation by my spouse.

I understand that by signing this Consent, I may receive less money than I would have received under the special QPSA payment form and I may receive nothing from the plan after my spouse dies.

I understand that I do not have to sign this Consent. I am signing this Consent voluntarily.

I understand that if I do not sign this Consent, then I will receive the QPSA benefit from the plan if my spouse dies before he or she begins to receive retirement benefits (or, if earlier, before the beginning of the period for which the retirement benefits are paid). I also understand that if I do not sign this Consent and the value of the QPSA benefit is Five Thousand Dollars ($5,000) or less, the plan will pay the benefit to me in one lump sum payment.

DATE _____   _____
                                                              Signature of Spouse

STATE OF CALIFORNIA   )

)

COUNTY OF SAN DIEGO   )

On _____ before me, _____, a Notary Public in and for the State of California, personally appeared _____ personally known to me or proved to me on the basis of satisfactory evidence to be the person whose name is subscribed to the within instrument and acknowledged to me that _he executed the same in h__ authorized capacity, and the by h__ signature on the instrument the person, or the entity upon behalf of which the person acted, executed the instrument.

WITNESS my hand and official seal.

                                                _____
                                                              Signature

Figure 57.2 (cont'd)

GENERAL CONSENT OF SPOUSE TO WAIVER OF QUALIFIED JOINT AND SURVIVOR ANNUITY PAYMENT FORM [DEFINED BENEFIT PLAN OR DEFINED CONTRIBUTION PLAN]

I, the undersigned, am the spouse of Participant. I understand that I have the right to have the above-referenced Plan pay my spouse's retirement benefits in the special Qualified Joint and Survivor Annuity ("QJSA") payment form.

I agree to give up my right to the QJSA benefit and to allow my spouse to name the beneficiary(ies) so designated in the beneficiary designation to which this Consent if attached to receive that benefit. This consent is valid only with respect to any future beneficiary designation by my spouse.

I understand that by signing this Consent, I may receive less money than I would have received under the special QJSA payment form and I may receive nothing after my spouse dies.

I understand that I do not have to sign this Consent. I am signing this Consent voluntarily.

I understand that if I do not sign this Consent, then my spouse and I will receive payments from the plan in the special QJSA payment form.

I hereby acknowledge that my right to a QJSA can only be waived during the Applicable Election Period, as defined in Section 417(a)(6) of the Internal Revenue Code, and that I will have to re-execute this Consent during such Applicable Election Period in order for the waiver of my rights to a QJSA hereunder to be valid.

DATE _____   _____
                                                  Signature of Spouse

STATE OF CALIFORNIA   )
)
COUNTY OF SAN DIEGO   )

    On _____ before me, _____, a Notary Public in and for the State of California, personally appeared _____ personally known to me or proved to me on the basis of satisfactory evidence to be the person whose name is subscribed to the within instrument and acknowledged to me that _he executed the same in h__ authorized capacity, and the by h__ signature on the instrument the person, or the entity upon behalf of which the person acted, executed the instrument.

    WITNESS my hand and official seal.

_____
Signature

Figure 57.3

CONTINGENT BENEFICIARY DESIGNATION

FOR: SUSAN SMITH

Name or Type of Account:_____(the "Account")

Owner's Name:

Social Security No: _____

A. Distributions After My Death

1. The balance thereof shall be divided into two (2) equal, separate fractional shares, with one share for each of my children, KEN SMITH and MARY JONES and with each such share to be paid to the separate Trust created for the benefit of such child under ARTICLE X and ARTICLE XVII. C. of my Revocable Trust dated December 2, 2012, together with any future Amendments, Modifications or Restatements being collectively referred to as "Revocable Trust"). It is my intention that the above paragraph references relate to the Trusts created for my children within my Revocable Trust, and to the extent that the paragraph references within my Revocable Trust to the Trusts for my children are changed in subsequent amendments to said Revocable Trust, then the paragraph references set forth herein shall change accordingly. For purposes of this beneficiary designation, the provisions of said Revocable Trust shall be interpreted as being those provisions which exist at the time of my death, and not as such provisions may be modified through the exercise of any power of appointment which any beneficiary of said Trust may possess.

2. Each year, beginning with the year of my death, the Trustee of any Trust which is designated to receive any portion of the Account shall withdraw, at least annually, amounts equal to the amount required to be distributed under the minimum distribution rules under I.R.C. Section 401(a)(9) and the regulations thereunder, or any subsequent statute requiring minimum distributions from such retirement plans. In addition, the Trustee of such Trust shall have the right at any time to withdraw all or any part of the remaining Account allocable to such Trust or to designate a beneficiary of each said Trust to (a) receive any remaining payments directly from the custodian of such funds; and/or (b) deal directly with the custodian and make withdrawals at any time of all or any part of the remaining balance in said Account. The custodian, or any successor custodian of this Account, shall not bear the responsibility for making any distributions from the Account, and will rely on the instructions of the Trustee or Account Beneficiary in connection with any distributions.

B. Miscellaneous

1. Rights of Beneficiaries. After my death, all rights and obligations held or exercisable by me under the Account shall inure to, and be enjoyed and exercised by, the beneficiary. Benefits payable as a result of my death shall be paid in such form and manner and at such time as may be permitted by the Account or law and as the beneficiary shall elect. If there is more than one beneficiary, then each beneficiary may exercise rights and make elections with respect to that beneficiary's interest. Each beneficiary shall have the unrestricted power and right to draw down and take a distribution of all or any portion of the benefits to which he is entitled under this designation, including the unrestricted power to accelerate any installment distributions.

2. Distributions to Representatives. Any distribution payable to a beneficiary may be made to the beneficiary's legal representative, including the holder of such beneficiary's power of attorney. Distributions payable to any beneficiary who at the time of distribution is under the age of twenty-one (21) years shall be paid instead to a custodian for such beneficiary under the applicable Uniform Transfers to Minors Act as may be selected by the parent of such beneficiary who is my lineal descendant, and as identified by the legal representative of my estate, or if none is so selected, by the personal representative of my estate. Such representative or custodian shall also have the power to make any elections or designations that the beneficiary is empowered to make, to the extent otherwise consistent with the scope of the legal authority of such representative or custodian.

Dated: _____   _____

SUSAN SMITH

Adapted from Natalie Choate's, *Life and Death Planning for Retirement Benefits*, 7th Edition (ATAXPLAN Publications, 2011).

Question – Are there any restrictions on pension or profit sharing plan investments in collectibles?

Answer – Yes. Investment in collectibles by an individually directed account under a qualified plan is treated as a current taxable distribution. Collectibles are defined as

- art
- rugs or antiques
- metals or gems
- stamps or coins
- alcoholic beverages
- any other tangible personal property designated as a collectible by the Secretary of the Treasury.[133]

Question – Will a plan participant on a one-year leave of absence from work due to a maternity/paternity reason incur a break-in-service and therefore cease to participate in the plan?

Answer – No. An employee who is on a leave of absence for maternity/paternity reasons will not incur a one-year break-in-service for purposes of participation or vesting in the year in which a break would otherwise occur.[134] Maternity/paternity reasons include pregnancy, childbirth, adoption or child caring immediately after childbirth or adoption.

Question – If a distribution from a qualified plan is made to a surviving spouse on the death of the participant, can he or she roll this over into an individual retirement account (IRA)?

Answer – A spousal rollover is permitted as to all or part of such a distribution, and the distribution will not be subject to income tax to the extent it is rolled over. Spousal rollovers are discussed in Chapters 56 and 59.

CHAPTER ENDNOTES

1. Treas. Reg. §1.401-1(b)(2).
2. I.R.C. §401(a).
3. I.R.C. §402(a)(1).
4. I.R.C. §401(a)(9).
5. I.R.C. §401(k)(2)(B)(ii).
6. I.R.C. §§401(k)(2)(C), 401(k)(3)(D).
7. I.R.C. §401(k)(4)(A).
8. I.R.C. §402(g); I.R.C. §401(a)(30). See IRS Notice 2017–64 for 2018 inflation adjustment.
9. I.R.C. §414(v).
10. I.R.C. §401(a).
11. I.R.C. §415(c).
12. I.R.C. §§402A(a), 402A(e)(1).
13. I.R.C. §§402(g), 3121(v).
14. I.R.C. §402(g).
15. I.R.C. §414(v).
16. Treas. Reg. §1.401(a)(4)-2(b)(4).
17. See Treas. Reg. §1.401(a)(4)-8(b)(1).
18. I.R.C. §401(m).
19. I.R.C. §410(a)(1).
20. I.R.C. §410(a)(1)(B).
21. I.R.C. §410(b)(1).
22. I.R.C. §410(b)(2).
23. I.R.C. §401(a)(26). In years beginning before 1997, this provision applied to all qualified plans.
24. I.R.C. §410(a)(3)(A).
25. I.R.C. §410(b)(3)(A).
26. I.R.C. §411(a)(1).
27. I.R.C. §§401(k)(2)(C), 401(k)(3)(D).
28. I.R.C. §§415(c)(1), 415(d)(1).
29. I.R.C. §404(a)(3)(A).
30. I.R.C. §404(n).
31. I.R.C. §415(c)(3)(C).
32. I.R.C. §415(b)(1).
33. I.R.C. §§415(b)(2)(C), 415(b)(2)(D).
34. I.R.C. §415(b)(5)(A).
35. I.R.C. §415(b)(4).
36. I.R.C. §415(b)(5)(B).
37. I.R.C. §415(b)(2)(B).
38. I.R.C. §415(b)(2)(C).
39. I.R.C. §415(b)(2)(D).
40. I.R.C. §§415(b)(2)(B); 415(b)(2)(E)(ii).
41. I.R.C. §415(c)(1).
42. I.R.C. §404(a)(1).
43. I.R.C. §404(a)(3). Pre-1987 unused contribution carryforwards may still be available.
44. I.R.C. §404(a)(7).
45. I.R.C. §219(e).
46. I.R.C. §72(o)(3).
47. I.R.C. §404(a)(3).
48. I.R.C. §404(n).
49. I.R.C. §408(q).
50. *Vinson & Elkins v. Comm'r.*, 93-2 USTC ¶50,632 (5th Cir. 1993); *Rhoades, McKee & Boer v. U.S.*, 93-2 USTC ¶50,425 (W.D. Mich. 1993); *Wachtell, Lipton, Rosen & Katz v. Comm'r.*, TC Memo 1992-392, aff'd, 94-1 USTC ¶50,272 (2d Cir. 1994).
51. Treas. Reg. §1.401-7.

52. Treas. Reg. §1.401-4(a)(1)(iii).
53. I.R.C. §401(a)(8).
54. I.R.C. §§411(b)(1)(H), 411(b)(2).
55. I.R.C. §411(a)(8).
56. See I.R.C. §411.
57. I.R.C. §401(l).
58. I.R.C. §416.
59. I.R.C. §416(g).
60. I.R.C. §416(i)(1). For 2018 inflation adjustment see IRS Notice 2017-64.
61. I.R.C. §416(b).
62. I.R.C. §416(c).
63. I.R.C. §401(a)(17).
64. I.R.C. §§404(a)(1), 404(a)(3).
65. I.R.C. §501(a).
66. I.R.C. §72(t).
67. I.R.C. §402(a).
68. Notice 2002-8, 2002-1 CB 398; see also Notice 2001-10, 2001-1 CB 459, revoking Rev. Rul. 55-747, 1955-2 CB 228, which set forth "P.S. 58" rates; see also Treas. Reg. §1.72-16(b).
69. I.R.C. §72(o)(3).
70. I.R.C. §401(a)(9)(A); see Treas. Reg. §1.401(a)(9)-9.
71. Treas. Reg. §1.401(a)(9)-5(a)(4).
72. I.R.C. §72(d)(1)(B)(iii).
73. I.R.C. §72(d)(1)(B)(iv).
74. I.R.C. §72(b).
75. Notice 88-118, 1988-2 CB 450.
76. I.R.C. §72(e)(8).
77. I.R.C. §402(d)(4)(A), prior to repeal after 1999 by SBJPA '96.
78. See Notice 2002-8, 2002-1 CB 389; See also Notice 2001-10, 2001-1 CB 459, revoking Rev. Rul. 55-747, 1955-2 CB 228; Treas. Reg. §1.72-16(c).
79. I.R.C. §2010(c).
80. I.R.C. §§2001(c), 2010(a), 2505(a), 6018(a).
81. I.R.C. §4980.
82. I.R.C. §4974.
83. I.R.C. §6662(f).
84. I.R.C. §4979A.
85. ERISA §§101-105.
86. ERISA §406(a)(1)(D).
87. I.R.C. §4975(a).
88. ERISA §3(21)(A).
89. ERISA § 404(a)(1).
90. ERISA § 206(d).
91. See Bankruptcy Abuse Prevention and Consumer Protection Act of 2005 (BAPCPA 2005), P.L. 109-8, signed April 20, 2005. 11 U.S.C § 522(n), adjusted for inflation by Federal Register Vol. 72, No. 30 (Feb. 14, 2007), Vol. 75, No. 23 (Feb. 25, 2010), Vol. 78, No. 35 (Feb. 21, 2013). Increased from $1,245,475 to $1,283,025 effective Apr. 1, 2016 by 81 FR 8748 (Feb. 22, 2016). This amount is adjusted for inflation every three years, so a further (though as of yet unannounced) increase is expected to become effective on April 1, 2019.
92. See *Rousey v. Jacoway*, 544 U.S. 320 (2005).
93. See *Patterson v. Shumate*, 504 U.S. 753, 112 S. Ct. 2242 (1992).
94. I.R.C. §401(a)(13)(B).
95. I.R.C. §414(p).
96. ERISA §4022(b)(3); PBGC Reg. §2621.
97. See https://www.pbgc.gov/prac/prem/premium-rates.
98. I.R.C. §401(k)(3).
99. I.R.C. §401(k)(3)(A); see also Notice 98-1, 1998-1 CB 327.
100. I.R.C. §401(k)(12).
101. I.R.C. §401(k)(11).
102. I.R.C. §401(k)(8)(B).
103. I.R.C. §401(k)(8)(A).
104. I.R.C. §4979.
105. I.R.C. §401(k)(8).
106. ERISA §408(b)(1); Labor Reg. §2550.408(b)-1.
107. See I.R.C. §1400Q(c), as added by GOZA 2005; see also Notice 2005-29, 2005-52 IRB 1165. For this purpose, qualified hurricane distributions include distributions during designated periods after Hurricanes Katrina, Rita and Wilma.
108. I.R.C. §72(p)(1).
109. Treas. Reg. §1.72(p)-1, A-3 (b).
110. I.R.C. §72(p)(2)(B)(i).
111. I.R.C. §72(p)(2)(A).
112. Treas. Reg. §1.72(p)-1, A-4 (a).
113. See Treas. Regs. §§1.72(p)-1, A-3 (b), 1.72(p)-1, A-10.
114. I.R.C. §72(p)(2)(B)(ii).
115. I.R.C. §401(k)(2)(B).
116. Treas. Reg. §1.401(k)-1(d)(2)(iv).
117. I.R.C. §§401(a)(11), 417.
118. I.R.C. §417(f)(2).
119. I.R.C. §401(a)(11)(B).
120. I.R.C. §417(b).
121. I.R.C. §417(d).
122. I.R.C. §417(a)(6).
123. I.R.C. §417(a)(2).
124. Wilf, et al., *The REA Book* (REA Publishing Company: Pa., 1987), Qs I.54 and I.55. Q. I.67 also addresses the question of the surviving spouse's disclaimer of annuity benefits required under REA, pointing out that such a disclaimer may be a prohibited assignment or alienation, in which event payment pursuant to the disclaimer could subject the plan administrator to fiduciary liability and could endanger the qualified status of the plan.
125. *Ablamis v. Roper*, 937 F.2d 1450 (9th Cir. 1991).
126. *Boggs v. Boggs*, 117 S. Ct. 1754 (1997).
127. Rev. Rul. 61-164, 1961-2 CB 99; Rev. Rul. 66-143, 1966-1 CB 79.
128. See e.g., Rev. Rul. 60-83, 1960-1 CB 157.

SURVIVOR'S INCOME BENEFIT PLAN

CHAPTER 58

58.1 INTRODUCTION

A Survivor's Income Benefit (SIB) plan (often called a "Death Benefit Only" or "DBO" plan) is an agreement between a corporation and an employee. There is a similar-sounding Survivor Benefit Plan designed for military personnel (see https://militarypay.defense.gov/Benefits/Survivor-Benefit-Program/Overview/), not discussed herein. In the SIB plan, the corporation agrees that if the employee dies before retirement, it will pay a specified amount (or an amount determinable by a specified formula) to the employee's spouse or other employer-designated class of beneficiaries, such as the employee's children. Typically, the amount may be a multiple of salary, such as two, three, or five times the average base pay in the three years preceding death.[1]

Could Such a Plan Run Afoul of IRC Section 409A?

Code section 409A provides specific requirements for nonqualified deferred compensation agreements; however, the requirements are met if the plan provides that compensation deferred may not be distributed earlier than death.[2]

58.2 WHEN IS USE OF SUCH A DEVICE INDICATED?

1. When additional income is desired for the family at the death of an individual.

2. When an employer would like to provide a selected employee or employees with an impressive fringe benefit over and above that provided under a qualified retirement plan.

3. When a client covered under a split dollar arrangement is experiencing rapidly-increasing economic benefit (also known as "Table 2001") costs, has run into Sarbanes-Oxley issues, or the split-dollar arrangement has been or is about to be terminated.[3] The split dollar plan might be converted into a survivor's income benefit plan so that the security could be continued without the current income tax burden.

4. When a corporation would like to provide an immediate death benefit for the family of a young employee, which could later be coupled (by changing the SIB at retirement to a nonqualified deferred compensation plan) with a retirement benefit.

58.3 HOW IT IS DONE

The employer's promise to pay a death benefit to the specified beneficiary in return for the employee's promise to continue working has been considered to constitute a transfer by the employee of a property right. Under most circumstances, this will result in the value of the benefit being included in the employee's estate:

1. If the agreement gives the employee the right to change the beneficiary, that retention of the power to designate who will enjoy the "transfer" will result in inclusion of the present value of the stream of payments in the employee's estate.

2. If the beneficiary's right to receive the death benefit is conditioned upon surviving the employee and the employee retained a right to direct the disposition of the property (for example, where the death benefit is payable to

the employee's spouse, but if the spouse does not survive the employee, the death benefit is payable to the employee's estate), that reversionary interest may cause inclusion.

3. If the beneficiary is a revocable trust established by the employee, the right to alter, amend, or revoke the transfer by changing the terms of the trust would cause inclusion.

4. If the employee already has post-retirement annuity benefits, such as a nonqualified deferred compensation agreement that pays a retirement benefit, the IRS could claim that the pre-retirement survivor's death benefit and the post-retirement deferred salary plans should be considered as one plan. This would cause the present value of the death benefit to be treated, for estate tax purposes, as if it were a joint and survivor annuity; the present value of the death benefit would be includable in the deceased employee's estate.

5. If the death benefit is payable to a trust over which the employee had a general power of appointment, the IRS might argue that he had a power of appointment over the death proceeds.

6. If the death benefit is funded with life insurance on the employee's life and the employee owned the policy or had veto rights over any change in the beneficiary, the IRS would probably attempt to include the policy proceeds, because of the employee's incidents of ownership.

Another problem relates to an employee who is also a controlling (more than 50 percent) shareholder. Does such an individual, by virtue of his or her voting power, have the right to alter, amend, revoke, or terminate the agreement? The Tax Court has held that the answer is "yes." It appears, however, that DBOs can be safely installed in corporations owned equally by two individuals. Since neither will have the unilateral power to alter, amend, revoke, or terminate the DBO, there should be no estate tax inclusion because of corporate ownership.

Example. Nina Wasserman is a thirty-five-year-old senior executive of Ship Shape Model Corporation (SSM). In order to encourage her to give her ultimate effort for SSM, the corporation makes a legally binding promise to her that, "If Nina should die while an executive of SSM, SSM will pay her children, Ross and Michelle, a death benefit equal to three times the average annual base compensation she received for the three years prior to her death–up to a maximum of $500,000. The payments will be made in equal annual installments over a ten-year period." In this example, assume payments would be $50,000 a year. Assume also that SSM is in a 40 percent combined federal and state corporate tax bracket.

SSM could finance its obligation by purchasing a $500,000 life insurance policy on Nina's life. The policy would be owned by and payable to SSM. At Nina's death, SSM could use the cash proceeds to purchase $500,000 worth of tax-free municipal bonds. Assuming the bonds earned 8 percent, the net income from the bonds would be $40,000 a year. This means corporate cash inflow would be $40,000. Outflow, after the corporation's $20,000 tax deduction (40 percent of $50,000) would be $30,000 ($50,000 - $20,000). Its net positive inflow each year would therefore be $10,000. In ten years, the corporation could add $100,000 to its surplus. At the end of the payout period, SSM would have $500,000 worth of bonds, and would have accumulated $10,000 a year for ten years. At 8 percent, this $10,000 annual amount would grow to $156,455 by the end of the tenth year. This would probably be enough to reimburse the business for its costs, the use of its money, and any administrative expenses it may have incurred.

Voluntary Plans

If a death benefit is not made under a contract or plan but is purely voluntary on the employer's part, it will not be includable in the employee's estate.[4] An employer could adopt a program that is something less than a legally binding commitment giving rise to "hopes and expectancies, not enforceable obligations with respect to a death benefit."

Voluntary benefits are not includable in the employee's estate because neither the employee nor the employee's beneficiary possessed any right to compel the employer to pay the benefit, and therefore there was no transfer.

The problem here is a practical one. The benefit provides neither peace of mind nor financial security in an economic sense, except to the extent that the employee can rely on the willingness and ability of the employer to pay a substantial sum of money after the employee's death. Therefore, most will be includable in the decedent employee's estate.

58.4 TAX IMPLICATIONS

For the Employer

The premiums that the corporation pays on the life insurance policy covering the insured employee are not deductible,[5] but life insurance proceeds received by the corporation at the employee's death are income tax free.[6] By virtue of the Tax Cuts & Jobs Act, the alternative minimum tax (AMT) was repealed for corporate taxpayers. Payments made by the corporation to the designated beneficiaries are deductible if and to the extent that (a) such payments represent reasonable compensation for services that the employee rendered, and (b) the plan serves a valid business (as opposed to a shareholder) purpose.[7]

For the Employee

Payment of premiums by the corporate employer will not be income to the employee.

The IRS now agrees with the Tax Court that when the taxpayer and his employer enter into a DBO plan, there is no taxable gift to the beneficiary, either at the time when the plan is entered into, or upon the death of the employee.[8]

For the Beneficiary

Payments received from the corporation by beneficiaries will be treated as taxable income.

58.5 ERISA

ERISA issues have been addressed by both courts and the Department of Labor. The *Dependahl* case[9] stated that DBOs did not qualify for various exemptions from ERISA, though at first impression, it appeared that the court improperly interpreted both the facts and ERISA in its desire to assist employees who seemed to have been terminated for malicious and unjustifiable reasons. The company involved in this case sent a letter each year to the executives covered by its DBO plan. Those letters advised the participants of the annual status of "their" insurance policies. The obvious implication is that the participants could look to the policies for their families' security under the DBO plan. This fact was not contained in the Court's opinion, and may well have been the key reason the Court reached the conclusion the plan was "funded" for ERISA purposes.

Subsequent to the *Dependahl* case, the Department of Labor issued an Advisory Opinion, which states that life insurance is not considered a "plan asset" if:

- it is owned by and payable to the corporation;

- it is under the total control of the corporation;

- it is subject to the claims of the corporation's creditors;

- no participant has a preferred claim against the policies;

- the policies are not formally tied to the plan; and

- there will be no representation to any participant or beneficiary that the policies would be used solely to provide plan benefits or represent security for the payment of benefits or that plan benefits would be limited by the amount of the insurance proceeds received by the corporation.[10]

In light of *Dependahl* and the Department of Labor Advisory Opinion, the use of the phrase "to fund" (or "to informally fund") should be avoided in discussing the use of life insurance policies to support the plan in any documentation associated with the plan (e.g., corporate resolutions, plan document, SEC annual report disclosure statements). It is probably safest to purchase and own insurance (and to reflect this ownership in a corporate resolution) as key employee coverage. See the instructions on IRS Form 8925 for required employee consents to employer-owned insurance coverage on employees.

Part of the corporate resolution authorizing the plan and the purchase of the supporting policies might better read as follows:

> RESOLVED: that in order for the X-ON Corporation to support its financial obligations under the Death Benefit Only plan and to insure itself against all other financial losses which would be

incurred in the event of a pre- or postretirement death of *[Name of Executive]*, the vice-president of the Corporation is hereby authorized to enter into a contract of *[Description of Life Insurance Contract]* life insurance with *[Life Insurance Company]* for coverage of $___ insuring the life of *[Name of Key Executive]*.

58.6 ISSUES IN COMMUNITY PROPERTY STATES

In community property states, it may be necessary to determine whether the employee's spouse has any community property interest in the survivor's income benefit. This becomes important upon the divorce of the employee and the spouse.

This may also be the case upon a divorce after an employee has entered into a survivor's income benefit plan. As of the date of the divorce, the employee would have no interest which could be includable in his estate, and thus there may not be any interest to be divided in a divorce proceeding.

However, many courts and the IRS generally have found that the employer's promise to pay a death benefit to a specified beneficiary in return for the employee's promise to continue working is a transfer by the employee of a property right. Community property states typically provide that a spouse may not make a gift of community personal property or dispose of community personal property without a valuable consideration, unless he or she obtains the written consent of the other spouse. The employee's employment, by its very nature in a community property state, is generating a community property interest in the spouse through salary and other employment benefits.

In a divorce proceeding, although an employee may be performing some services in return for the employer's promise to pay a stated amount to a named beneficiary at the time of the divorce proceeding, it does not follow that there are current property interests which can be divided equally between the spouses. The employee has no current right to any benefit, nor is there any assurance that he will ever have a named beneficiary to receive a benefit. The survivor's income benefit is subject to many contingencies, among them the employee's continuing to work for the employer. Assuming the employee's spouse is the beneficiary of the survivor's income benefit plan, the spouse has obtained a benefit during the term of the marriage (i.e., if the employee were to die during the marriage, the spouse would receive the survivor's income benefit).

If the employee's spouse contends that there is an interest which can be valued and divided upon a divorce, the question of whether any value can be attributed to the survivor's income benefit may be solved differently in the various community property states. California, for example, has found that a non-vested benefit from a pension plan is not a mere expectancy, but is a contingent property right. Although we are not familiar with any case actually valuing a survivor's income benefit under this theory, it may be possible that California courts would attempt to value the survivor's income benefit and divide that value in the divorce proceedings. The value would probably be very low because of the substantial discounts for the many contingencies involved in this type of an arrangement.

As one can imagine, severe problems of valuation and the proportion of benefits to be paid to a former spouse could arise in the event that the employee were to remarry and continue working for the same employer. What portion of the survivor's income benefit is attributable to the employee's employment while married to his first spouse and what portion is attributable to the portion of his employment while married to his second spouse? With vexing problems like this, coupled with the employee's lack of any right to a benefit prior to his death, it is likely that a court will put little or no value on the survivor's income benefit plan in the event of a divorce.

In most instances, the employee's spouse will be his or her beneficiary under the survivor's income benefit plan. In this instance, upon the employee's death, there will be no controversy over the community property issue, unless the employee was previously married. In the event of a divorce, the community property issue may arise, even though the spouse is designated as the beneficiary, but the result is quite uncertain.

58.7 FREQUENTLY ASKED QUESTIONS

Question – If proceeds are payable to the employee's spouse, will they qualify for the unlimited marital deduction?

Answer – Yes. If, for any reason, the IRS successfully maintains that the SIB generated a taxable transfer (either during life or at death), there should be no adverse gift or estate tax consequence if the spouse of the employee is named an outright beneficiary. It is also possible that the employer could pay SIB payments to a QTIP (Qualified Terminable Interest Property) trust established by the employee (see Chapter 33). This would secure the marital deduction–if one were needed–and, in any case, assure that the principal would pass to the party designated by the decedent upon the surviving spouse's death.

However, if the SIB were not included in the employee's estate for tax purposes, the payment could not result in a marital deduction.

CHAPTER ENDNOTES

1. Some insurance carriers offer a coverage known as group survivors' income benefit insurance, commonly written as a supplement to group life insurance. Under this coverage, the employee has no choice of beneficiary, benefits are paid only if there is a survivor who qualifies, and a lump-sum payment of the commuted value of benefits is not available.
2. I.R.C. §409A(a)(2))(iii).
3. Current life insurance protection provided under a qualified plan may be valued by using government one-year term premium rates. The IRS has issued "Table 2001" generally for use in determining the value of life insurance protection after 2000. See Notice 2002-8. See Chapter 34.
4. *Courtney v. U.S.*, 84-2 USTC ¶13,580 (N.D. Ohio 1984).
5. I.R.C. §264(a)(1).
6. I.R.C. §101(a). But notice will have to be provided to the employee and Form 8925 attached to the company tax return per I.R.C. §101(j).
7. I.R.C. §162(a)(1).
8. See *Estate of DiMarco*, 87 TC 653 (1986), *acq. in result* 1990-2 CB 1.
9. *Dependahl v. Falstaff Brewing Corp.*, 491 F. Supp. 1188 (E.D. Mo. 1980), *aff'd* in part, 653 F.2d 1208 (8th Cir.), *cert. denied*, 454 U.S. 968 (1981); see also *Belka v. Rowe Furniture Corp.*, 571 F. Supp. 1249 (D. Md. 1983), where the court found a plan to be exempt from ERISA funding requirements where less than 5 percent of total employees were participants, and where participants' compensation averaged $55,000.
10. DOL Ad. Op. 81-11A.

PLANNING WITH IRAS AND QUALIFIED RETIREMENT PLANS

CHAPTER 59

59.1 INTRODUCTION

A comprehensive analysis of these subjects is covered in great detail in Chapters 56 (IRAs) and 57 (qualified retirement plans and 401(k) plans). In this chapter, we will simply discuss estate planning options with IRAs and qualified retirement plans. The first thing to consider is the fact that, as a general rule, retirement plan benefits (other than Roth accounts) are income in respect of a decedent (IRD) when received and do not obtain a new basis at the participant's or account holder's death.[1] Therefore, a sizeable portion of the benefits received will be diminished by income taxes. If left to a trust other than a Beneficiary Deemed Owner Trust (BDOT) (see Chapter 35), the income may be taxed at significantly higher tax rates than those applicable to an individual beneficiary. This significantly impacts the estate planning analysis and potential tools and techniques that should be brought into the strategic mix.

The second thing to consider are the complex minimum required distribution rules.[2] Some claim that the Secure Act and Secure 2.0 Act simplified these, but it is more accurate to conclude that they added another layer of complexity. These rules essentially force the account holder (while alive) and the beneficiary (after the account holder's death) to take required minimum distributions under threat of significant penalty.[3] Before 2023, this penalty was 50% of the amount not withdrawn, but the Secure 2.0 Act reduces this penalty to 25%, and even lower, to 10%, if timely corrected.

Both the SECURE Act and the Secure 2.0 Act (passed December 29, 2022) have made sweeping changes to many of the rules surrounding retirement plans, and the law will likely change further after the publication of this edition, due to either minor corrective legislation, or more likely, final regulations around the Secure Act which are expected in late 2023 and/or proposed and final regulations surrounding the Secure 2.0 Act (none are yet proposed but industry groups such as the American College of Trust and Estate Counsel (ACTEC) have asked Treasury to clarify some aspects of the new legislation). Proposed regulations around the Secure Act changes were issued in February of 2022. So, be careful to check for any updates in this area, especially the final regulations.

The biggest consideration in estate planning for qualified plans and IRAs is determining the "right" beneficiary (especially the terms of a trust). Different rules apply between qualified retirement plans and IRAs that impact an account holder's right to name a beneficiary other than a spouse. Under the Retirement Equity Act of 1984 (REA), a participant in a qualified retirement plan must obtain the written consent of the spouse in order to name a beneficiary other than the spouse.[4] This subject frequently is the subject of prenuptial agreements, and we address it in this chapter. The REA restrictions are inapplicable to IRAs because IRAs are not covered by the applicable parts of ERISA and are not included in Code Section 401(a)(11).[5]

There is a lot to estate planning for qualified plans and IRAs. Entire books are devoted to this subject.[6] The aim of this chapter is much more modest: it is to lay out the principal issues in estate planning for these benefits.

Clients tend to fall into three basic types of categories:

1. Those who need the qualified plan/IRA balances to sustain themselves and those who don't.

2. Those for whom the qualified plan/IRA forms a "substantial" part of the estate and those for

whom the qualified plan/IRA is not a substantial part of the estate. For this purpose, "substantial" is defined as a qualified plan/IRA balance equal to at least one-half (½) of the person's total estate.

3. Those who are participants (in qualified plans) or account holders (of IRA's) and those who are only beneficiaries. For all purposes herein, unless otherwise expressly noted, the terms "participant" and "account holder" shall have the same meaning.

59.2 WHEN REQUIRED MINIMUM DISTRIBUTIONS MUST BE PAID OUT AFTER THE DEATH OF THE ACCOUNT HOLDER

We will now discuss the general rules under the required minimum distribution regulations under Code Section 401(a)(9), and, specifically, the rules concerning when the required minimum distributions must be paid out. These rules apply to qualified retirement plans and IRAs equally, with a few exceptions noted. The rules are inapplicable to Roth IRAs (and starting in 2024 pursuant to Section 325 of the Secure 2.0 Act, other Roth accounts) during the lifetimes of the account holder and the account holder's spouse (if the spouse survives the account holder and is able to rollover the account).

The first task in determining the rules that apply when the account holder dies is to determine that person's "required beginning date." The required beginning date is April 1 of the year *following* the year that the account holder attains the age of 73 (this was age 70 ½, then the Secure Act changed it to 72, the Secure 2.0 Act to age 73, and eventually in 2033, age 75). There is an exception that delays the required beginning date for a participant in a company plan if the person is employed at that time and is a 5 percent owner or less, in which case it is the year in which the employee retires.[7] There are only two possibilities for the account holder from the standpoint of distribution consideration: (1) death *before* reaching the required beginning date and (2) death *on or after* reaching the required beginning date. The second consideration is whether the now deceased account holder or participant has named a "designated beneficiary of the benefits. It is possible that both apply. For example, Maya is age 75, still working and contributing to her traditional 401(k), and also has a Roth IRA and traditional IRA when she dies in 2023. She is past her required beginning date for her traditional IRA, but not her Roth IRA or traditional 401(k).

It is *very* important to understand that not all named beneficiaries will *qualify* as "designated beneficiaries" under these rules, which directly affects when the beneficiaries must be forced out of the plan or IRA. The Secure Act added a new category of beneficiaries which is a subset of designated beneficiaries, called "eligible designated "beneficiaries." Only eligible designated beneficiaries (or in some cases, trusts therefore) will now be eligible for the "stretch" over their life expectancy.

The five categories of eligible designated beneficiaries are 1) a surviving spouse, 2) an owner's child under age 21; 3) someone disabled; 4) someone chronically ill; and 5) someone no more than 10 years younger than the owner. There is also a special way to design a see through trust for one or more disabled or chronically ill EDBs, strangely referred to in the Code and Regulations as an "applicable multi-beneficiary trust" (AMBT). While a conduit trust for such EDBs can still get the "stretch," it is usually undesirable from a government benefits and management perspective, so this specialized accumulation trust is the best way to go for trust planning. In a nutshell, AMBTs require that only EDBs can be beneficiaries of the trust during their lifetime, and if that's the case, any regular designated beneficiaries can be remaindermen without blowing the stretch. The Secure 2.0 Act amended this further to even allow certain charities to be remaindermen.[8]

These five categories of EDBs can use the old "stretch" rules to pay out over the beneficiaries' life expectancy, but for minor children of the owner, there is a hybrid rule: the ten-year rule kicks in at age 21, forcing the account to be terminated by the end of the tenth year after the child turns age 21. Proposed regulations would allow an eligible designated beneficiary to elect into the 10 year rule if the plan permits. This might occur, for example, if the beneficiary would not have much longer than 10 years of life expectancy anyway.

There are now three general categories of beneficiaries: (1) the designated beneficiary who is not an eligible designated beneficiary, 2) an eligible designated beneficiary, and (3) a beneficiary that is neither, such as an estate, charity, or non-qualifying trust. Of the eligible designated beneficiaries, the surviving spouse has special unique rules that apply.

As a general rule, in order to qualify as a designated beneficiary, one must be an individual, i.e., estates, entities such as corporations and a charity will not qualify as a designated beneficiary.[9] The regulations make it clear that one cannot go beyond the beneficiary designation or the plan or IRA document, i.e., someone who obtains the benefits due to the laws of descent and distribution is not a designated beneficiary.[10]

There are special rules for trusts where certain trusts are subject to the "look through" rules whereby usually the oldest trust beneficiary is treated as the designated beneficiary (or potentially, eligible designated beneficiary).[11] These are referred to as "see through trusts" in the proposed regulations, and are further divided into two types of see through trusts: a conduit trust and an accumulation trust. Proposed regulations now provide that: "(A) The term conduit trust means a see-through trust, the terms of which provide that, with respect to the deceased employee's interest in the plan, all distributions will, upon receipt by the trustee, be paid directly to, or for the benefit of, specified beneficiaries." Accumulation trusts are trusts that still qualify as a see through trust, but allow for accumulations to accrue rather than require that all distributions be paid out to beneficiaries. In order to qualify as a see through trust, the trust must comply with the following requirements:

(1) The trust must be a valid trust under state law, or would be but for the fact that there is no corpus. This one is hard to fail.

(2) The trust is irrevocable or will, by its terms, become irrevocable upon the death of the account holder. This one is also hard to fail, but it's possible that a joint trust might be revocable by the surviving settlor and this may be an instance where a trust could fail.

(3) The beneficiaries of the trust who are beneficiaries with respect to the trust's interest in the account holder's benefit are identifiable within the meaning of Treas. Reg. Sec. 1.401(a)(9)-4, A 1 from the trust instrument (which includes contingent beneficiaries). This is more complicated than it sounds.

(4) The documentation described in Treas. Reg. Sec. 1.401(a)(9)-4, A 6 has been provided to the plan administrator by October 31 of the year after death. This required documentation includes either a copy of the trust instrument and a complete list of the trust beneficiaries.[12] This criteria is easy to comply with, but also very easy to inadvertently overlook – best practice is to get a written confirmation of receipt or send a copy of the trust with return receipt requested to prove compliance.

Death Before the Required Beginning Date

If the decedent dies *before* reaching the required beginning date (RBD), no minimum required minimum distribution need be made for the year following death of the account holder or participant *if* the designated beneficiary is the surviving spouse. If the designated beneficiary is the surviving spouse, required minimum distributions need not commence before the year in which the deceased account holder would have attained age their applicable age (73 in 2023, rising to age 75 in 2033) had he or she lived until then.[13] Section 327 of the Secure 2.0 Act changes this rule starting in 2024, however, forcing the surviving spouse to make a special election have this special delayed required beginning date, he or she will have to make a special election.[14] Of course, surviving spouses who inherit outright can later rollover the inherited account into their own IRA, but these rules are also important to remember when the surviving spouse inherits through a conduit trust that will also be considered the sole eligible designated beneficiary.

There is no delayed starting date, however, for non-spouse eligible designated beneficiaries. Such beneficiaries must commence receiving required minimum distributions on or before the end of the calendar year immediately following the calendar year in which the account holder died.[15] Designated beneficiaries who are not "eligible designated beneficiaries," however, have a new rule as a result of the Secure Act. If the decedent dies before their RBD, there is no RMD for the first nine years after death, but the entire account must be withdrawn by December 31 of the 10 year anniversary after death. This works similar to the 5 year rule that applies when there is neither a designated nor an eligible designated beneficiary, but it's twice as long of a deferral.

Eligible designated beneficiary (EDB)-If there is an eligible designated beneficiary, the beneficiary can "stretch out" receipt of minimum required distributions over the beneficiary's remaining life expectancy determined as of the *beneficiary's* age in the year following the year of the account holder's death.[16] However, if the surviving spouse is the eligible designated beneficiary,

835

then the applicable distribution period is measured by the *surviving spouse's* life expectancy using the surviving spouse's birthday for each distribution calendar year after the calendar year of the account holder's death up through the calendar year of the surviving spouse's death. This means that a surviving spouse who is the sole eligible designated beneficiary is able to recalculate life expectancy each year, something that no one else can do.[17] Section 327 of the Secure 2.0 Act, starting in 2024, sweetens this deal further for surviving spouses provided they make the proper election, and permits the use of the uniform life table rather than the single life table. Being able to recalculate life expectancy has the effect of further stretching out distribution of the benefits because the surviving spouse is in essence rewarded for having survived another year. That is because life expectancy still reaches out further in the future even for an elderly person who has continued to survive, i.e., a living person has some remaining life expectancy irrespective of age. Proposed regulations (1.401(a)(9)-3) under the Secure Act would allow an EDB to elect into the 10 year rule if the plan permits. This might be desirable, for example, if the EDB were age 83 and would not have longer than 10 years of life expectancy anyway and would prefer the greater flexibility of the 10 year rule.

No designated beneficiary -Where there is no designated beneficiary, the plan benefits must be paid out by the fifth anniversary of the account holder's death.[18] We will call this the "five year rule" in this chapter. The five year rule essentially eliminates the right to stretch out the benefits beyond five years. Neither the Secure Act nor the Secure 2.0 Act changed this rule. There are situations when the result could be even worse –many qualified plans force out a lump sum distribution and I.R.C. 408(c)(11) only permits "designated beneficiaries" to move the inherited funds to an inherited IRA (which would otherwise almost always allow the five years). Thus, a non-designated beneficiary of a plan may be stuck with a lump sum distribution from the plan.

Death on or after the Required Beginning Date

If the account holder survived *until* the required beginning date, then the following rules apply:

Eligible designated beneficiary (EDB) - If there is a eligible designated beneficiary, then it depends upon whether the surviving spouse is the designated beneficiary and whether or not the surviving spouse treated the IRA as inherited or whether the surviving spouse elected to roll over the benefits into a new IRA or plan. If the surviving spouse simply inherited the IRA and did not elect to treat the IRA as his or her own IRA, which the surviving spouse often has the right to do, then the surviving spouse must take the required minimum distribution for the year of the account holder's death based upon the *account holder's* life expectancy. However, thereafter, the minimum required distribution will be based upon the *surviving spouse's* remaining life expectancy, as recalculated for each year of the surviving spouse's overlife, or the account holder's remaining life expectancy had he or she survived, if longer.[19] Section 327 of the Secure 2.0 Act, starting in 2024, will allow a surviving spouse with an inherited IRA to use the Uniform Life Table if the appropriate election is made. If the surviving spouse rolled the account holder's benefits into his or her own IRA, then the decedent's required minimum distribution for the year of death must be taken if not taken prior to death. But, thereafter, the required minimum distributions will be based upon the surviving spouse's remaining life expectancy, as recalculated annually, pursuant to the Uniform Life Table.[20]

With respect to eligible designated beneficiaries *other than* the surviving spouse, the beneficiary must take the required minimum distribution for the year of the decedent's death if it was not taken prior to death. Thereafter, the required minimum distributions will be based upon the beneficiary's remaining life expectancy for the year following death or the account holder's remaining life expectancy had he or she survived, if longer. This life expectancy is fixed and is reduced by one year for each year of the beneficiary's overlife, or the account holder's remaining life expectancy had they survived, if longer.[21] The Code Section 401(a)(9) regulations permit a single account to be divided into separate sub-accounts, each having different required minimum distribution provisions, provided that separate accounting, including allocation of investment income, gains and losses, is established.[22] Where there are multiple beneficiaries, it always makes sense to divide the account, particularly where there is some age disparity between the beneficiaries.

There is a special rule when a participant/owner's child under age 21 is the eligible designated beneficiary. The RMDs are the same as noted above, but the account must be withdrawn by the end of the tenth year anniversary of the child turning age 21 (i.e. the end of the year when the child turns age 31).

Designated beneficiary (who is not also an eligible designated beneficiary) – Naming designated beneficiaries will be the most common scenario (such as leaving assets to adult children or grandchildren). The 10 year rule noted above under the "death before RBD" section applies, but with a twist that practitioners did not quite expect. Proposed regulations, if made final, require that RMDs be paid in each of years 1-9 before the tenth year when the decedent dies after their RBD. Because this interpretation was generally unexpected (and late), the IRS issued Notice 2022-53 indicating that it will automatically waive the 50% (now 25% as of 2023) excise tax penalty for failure to take an RMD in this situation for years 2021 and 2022. For example, if Paul dies after his RBD in 2020, leaving assets to Ringo, a designated beneficiary, the proposed regulations claim that Ringo had an RMD for 2021 and 2022 (indeed, according to the proposed regulations, he will for every year until 2030 when it must be terminated). However, the IRS in Notice 2022-53 waived the 50% excise tax applicable in 2021 and 2022. Perhaps they will issue another such notice for 2023?

Note that waiving the penalty is not the same as saying there is no RMD for those years. If a trust instrument requires the trustee to take the RMD and distribute it to a beneficiary, the trustee should probably still comply with the trust instrument unless some kind of settlement agreement is reached.

No designated beneficiary- Neither the Secure Act nor the Secure 2.0 Act changed this rule. If there is no designated beneficiary (such as when an estate is named, or non-qualifying trust), then the applicable distribution period measured by the account holder's remaining life expectancy is the life expectancy of the account holder using the age of the account holder as of the account holder's birthday in the calendar year of the account holder's death. In subsequent calendar years, the applicable distribution period is reduced by one for each calendar year that has elapsed after the calendar year of the account holder's death.[23] If the account holder names no beneficiary, which can happen even where the primary beneficiary predeceases the account holder without a contingent beneficiary, then the deceased account holder's age must continue to be used.[24]

Analysis of Possible Alternative Beneficiaries

What follows are potential beneficiaries of both qualified retirement plans and IRAs:

- Spouse
- Unmarried partner
- Child(ren)
- Bypass (credit shelter) trust
- QTIPable trust
- Estate
- A charitable organization
- Charitable remainder trust

We will lay out the effects of naming each of these alternatives as a beneficiary as well as the advantages and disadvantages of each one.

Surviving Spouse

In general, naming the surviving spouse as beneficiary (with disclaimer as an option in favor of contingent beneficiaries such as a trust that has credit shelter and QTIP provisions) is an advantageous selection for several reasons. First, it is simple and, at least in the case of a qualified retirement plan, mandated unless the spouse consents in writing pursuant to a certain required procedure to a different beneficiary. For both income tax and estate tax purposes, the selection of the surviving spouse usually provides the most tax deferral opportunities. This is because the surviving spouse, through a "rollover" or direct transfer from either a qualified plan or an IRA to a new IRA and treating that IRA as the spouse's IRA,[25] can get a "fresh start," with an effectively "new" IRA and recalculate life expectancy annually using the Uniform Life Table.[26]

A new IRA affords the spouse the opportunity to restart and "stretch out" the required minimum distributions to a (sometimes) later required beginning date (April 1 of the year following the year that the surviving spouse attained the age of 73, to increase to age 75 in 2033). This assumes that the surviving spouse is younger than the deceased spouse. The new IRA permits the surviving spouse to name eligible designated beneficiaries, who can use their own life expectancies for remaining distributions after the surviving spouse dies, or name designated beneficiaries who can at least get another ten years.

Five reasons to delay the rollover when the surviving spouse is primary beneficiary:

There are at least five situations where the surviving spouse should pause before doing a rollover of an inherited retirement account and counsel should look for these situations:

1) First, if the surviving spouse is under 59½, leaving the funds in an inherited IRA until after they reach that age will allow the surviving spouse to take funds out without a 10 percent penalty (whereas such a distribution would cause a 10% tax if from the widow(er)'s own IRA before age 59 ½ unless a special exception applies). If funds might be needed before then, a 100 percent rollover may be premature.

2) Second, if the younger spouse dies first and has not reached their required beginning date, leaving the funds in an inherited IRA will allow the surviving spouse to delay required minimum distributions longer, until December 31 of the year in which the deceased spouse would have attained the applicable age. For example, if Taylor age 63 dies in 2023 and leaves assets to her spouse Tim, age 74, Tim can keep funds in an inherited IRA and instead of having to take an RMD right away (if he rolled over), not have to take an RMD until Taylor would have reached her applicable age, which would not occur for another 12 years when she would have reached the applicable age. Note that starting in 2024, this delayed RBD requires the surviving spouse to make an election.

3) Third, some spouses may want to disclaim a portion of the IRA in favor of children to shift some of the income and benefits to them without counting as a gift. The contingent beneficiary may also be a trust for children, or perhaps an A/B or QTIPable trust for the spouse and children. This may better shelter the plan (and any accumulations) from creditors, lawsuit, divorce or state/federal estate tax.

4) Fourth, the decedent may have employer securities in a qualified plan that might be better to take as a lump sum distribution than as a rollover to take advantage of the net unrealized appreciation (NUA) loophole that allows infinite "stretch" deferral and, upon any sale, more advantageous long-term capital gains tax rates on the gain component of the employer securities.

5) Fifth, the surviving spouse may have a small non-deductible IRA with basis that would be ideal to convert to a Roth IRA and delaying the rollover would allow this to occur nearly tax-free, but the income tax on conversion would dramatically increase if the spouse rolls it over in the same year. Example: Taylor has a $50,000 IRA that was funded with $40,000 of nondeductible contributions that she has been considering converting to a Roth IRA, which would only trigger $10,000 of taxable income. Unfortunately her husband Tim dies and she inherits his $500,000 IRA. If she rolls it over, then the rules regarding the taxation of the $50,000 Roth conversion require her to consider the basis and value of ALL her IRAs when calculating the tax on conversion, meaning that most of the $50,000 is fully taxable and the conversion is much more costly and inefficient. She should delay the rollover until the following year after the Roth conversion is complete.

Despite all of the benefits of naming a surviving spouse as the beneficiary of a retirement plan or IRA, many people do not wish to do this or shouldn't do this, particularly in blended families where a large chunk of the wealth may be in the qualified plan or IRA. Reasons can include a desire on the part of the client to give those benefits to someone other than the surviving spouse, e.g., children of a prior relationship or charity, a desire to fully exhaust the account holder's applicable exclusion amount (for state estate tax purposes as well as federal) at death and a desire to not "stack" these assets into the surviving spouse's estate (not everyone wants to rely on portability and some want to use their GST exemption that doesn't port). Often, it is purely a matter of preferring their own selections of the ultimate recipients over those whom the surviving spouse may select, particularly in the blended family situation. Clients must be told about the pros and cons of naming a spouse versus a trust and let them make the call.

As noted above, a surviving spouse may elect to treat the deceased spouse's IRA as his or her own. Where the deceased spouse's IRA or qualified plan benefit is transferred to a trust in which the surviving spouse is a beneficiary, there is no right to roll over the required minimum distribution even if the spouse is the sole beneficiary of the trust.[27]

Unmarried Partner

Another option as a beneficiary is a partner to whom the account holder is not legally married. While this choice is as simple as naming a surviving spouse, this choice is not as attractive as naming a spouse because an unmarried person 1) cannot defer distributions until December 31 of the year in which the deceased account holder would have reached their applicable age had he or she survived; 2) use the uniform life tables with the special election available in 2024; 3) recalculate the RMDs annually; 4) may not even be able to use the life expectancy rule allowed for eligible designated beneficiaries unless the partner is not more than 10 years younger and finally; 5) rollover. Additionally, the plan balance will not be sheltered by the estate tax marital deduction, which could expose the benefits to double taxation, i.e., income tax and estate tax. In fact, if the unmarried surviving partner is more than 37½ years younger than the deceased account holder, the plan benefits also could be subject to the GST tax, although this will not be applicable where the partners are fairly close in age, which usually is the case.

Traditionally, only a surviving spouse could roll over the deceased spouse's qualified retirement plan or IRA into a new IRA. However, beginning with the effective date of the Pension Protection Act of 2006, a non-spouse beneficiary can at least now roll over the deceased participant's interest in a qualified retirement plan into an inherited IRA.[28]

This selection assumes that the surviving partner can manage his or her own finances and has no need for creditor protection. If this selection is made and if the plan permits withdrawal of the *entire benefit* in a lump sum, the account holder's desire to see the benefits stretched out over the partner's lifetime could be thwarted if the surviving partner takes the benefit out in a lump sum. Additionally, by naming a partner as the beneficiary, the account holder loses all dispositive control over who will receive the remaining benefit at the partner's death. For these reasons, many account holders do not want to name a surviving partner as outright beneficiary, particularly in the blended family context. Again, the size of the account often matters as well in this choice.

Children

Similar rules and considerations that are attendant to those of an unmarried partner apply. There also is the fact that if the benefit is in a qualified retirement plan and if the participant is married, selecting children can only be done with the advance written consent of the non-participant spouse. Where there is a surviving spouse or unmarried partner, that survivor will not be entitled to any of these benefits on which to live, which may not be acceptable to the account holder. The same drawbacks that are applicable to spouses and unmarried partners apply to naming children as outright beneficiaries of plan benefits, i.e., no management or creditor protection.

The Secure Act dramatically impacted how see through trusts will be designed for children or grandchildren. Prior to the Secure Act, many taxpayers and practitioners preferred to simply use the conduit trust safe harbor for children or grandchildren – after all, the RMDs for younger beneficiaries were minimal, and the trust is easy to draft, easy to understand, the remainder beneficiaries could all be ignored (even charities can be named) and no ordinary income from traditional retirement account distributions would be trapped in trust at the higher tax rates. However, now that the 10 year rule will apply (unless a child/grandchild is disabled or chronically ill), the conduit trust makes very little sense except in rare instances, since all protections of the trust would be lost in 10 years. The proposed regulation §1.401(a)(9)-4(f)(3)(ii)(B) even adds a special allowance for accumulation trusts now that, as long as they require distribution by age 31, permits the other remainder beneficiaries (even if a charity) to be ignored for purposes of identifying all the potential designated beneficiaries of the trust. This new paradigm will likely kill the use of conduit trusts for all but surviving spouses as a practical matter.

Bypass (Credit Shelter) Trust

Alternatively, to *outright* selections of individuals as designated beneficiaries of plan benefits, an account holder may choose to name a credit shelter trust as the designated beneficiary. This permits the account holder to select the ultimate beneficiaries of the plan benefits, and these beneficiaries can include not only children but a spouse or unmarried partner. Using plan benefits to fund a credit shelter trust can facilitate full usage of the account holder's applicable exclusion amount (in some states, it may be necessary to use retirement plan assets to use the *state* estate tax exemption). Traditional retirement benefits are not ideal since they are pregnant with income tax, which effectively significantly reduces the benefit of the applicable exclusion amount. Roth accounts, however, are even better than other non-retirement assets, since they can grow tax-free for another ten years, or much longer if it qualifies as a conduit trust for spouses, especially once the sweetheart deal for conduit trusts with the special election kicks in in

2024. An additional downside to naming a credit shelter trust vis-à-vis a spouse is the loss of the right to defer the required minimum distributions until such time as the account holder would have attained their applicable age for traditional accounts and for their lifetime with Roth accounts, which only a spouse rolling over into their own IRA/plan can do.

If a Bypass trust is beneficiary, the required minimum distributions would be forced to commence in the year following the account holder's death. The right to recalculate life expectancy annually also is lost since that right only exists for spouses (unless it is a conduit trust with the surviving spouse as the sole beneficiary).

The measuring life for the purpose of determining the minimum required distributions will be the remaining life expectancy of the *oldest* beneficiary of the trust if the trust is designed to qualify under the Code Section 401(a)(9) regulations, but after the Secure Act, only if all of the designated beneficiaries are *eligible* designated beneficiaries.[29] In most cases, people name a spouse and children as beneficiaries, and the latter would usually not be "eligible designated beneficiaries." Section 327 of the Secure 2.0 Act, starting in 2024, provides some additional incentives if the trust is a conduit trust for a surviving spouse – if the proper election is made, the conduit trust may be able to not only receive a delayed required beginning date in some cases, but also use the Uniform Life Table once RMDs start! This is nearly as good a deal as a rollover tax-wise – in some cases better.

Trusts permit a third party to manage and invest the trust funds. Trusts also can provide creditor protection to the trust beneficiaries. Trusts also allow the account holder to select the beneficiaries of the trust, which can come in very handy in blended family situations. Therefore, the tradeoff is loss of income tax benefits of stretch out versus asset protection and management.

QTIP-able Trust

Another alternative trust selection would be a QTIP-able trust. This choice would be limited to account holders who are married and who want to see that spouse benefit significantly from the plan benefits. Where the account holder wants to ensure that plan benefits can qualify for a QTIP election, the spouse must receive or be able to withdraw the plan's internal income for that year, in addition to meeting the regular QTIP requirements.[30] The advantage to the account holder is that the account holder, not the surviving spouse, will control the ultimate disposition of the plan benefits that remain at the surviving spouse's death. This could come in handy in a blended family scenario, while deferring the federal estate tax on the remaining benefits until the surviving spouse's death. The QTIP trust option generally forces out the retirement funds over 10 years if it is an accumulation trust, but may allow the use of the surviving spouse's age for purposes of determining the amount of the required minimum distribution if it is a conduit trust, as discussed in the above section on Bypass trusts.

The downsides to the QTIP trust are (1) complexity; (2) the fact that the plan could have to distribute an amount that could be *larger* than the required minimum distribution (if income exceeds the RMD), which accelerates income recognition and diverts those assets to persons of the surviving spouse's choosing; (3) if the benefit is in a qualified retirement plan, then the spouse's advance written consent will be required to name a QTIP-able trust as the beneficiary; (4) to the extent that the plan income *exceeds* the required minimum distribution and applicable state law apportions the benefit between income and trust principal, e.g., Section 409 of the Uniform Principal and Income Act, which apportions the income of the plan to fiduciary accounting income and the balance of the required minimum distribution to principal (except that if plan income exceeds the required minimum distribution, the trustee must allocate trust principal to income), taxable income could be *trapped* at the trust level, where the compressed fiduciary income tax brackets can adversely affect it; and (5) to the extent that all of the QTIP and plan requirements are not met, the potential loss of the estate tax marital deduction. See Chapter 35 on Beneficiary Deemed Owner Trusts for further discussion on avoiding the compressed tax rates of trusts without having to make a distribution out of the trust.

Revocable Living Trust

Another alternative to naming a beneficiary outright is to name the account holder's revocable living trust as the beneficiary of the plan benefits. This selection offers all of the advantages that trusts can offer, e.g., management and creditor protection. The revocable trust can be fashioned to include B (credit shelter) and QTIP-able trust provisions, although it will be important to utilize a *fractional* formula and *not* a pecuniary formula because of the income recognition issue on funding of a pecuniary bequest or allocation. This selection also works even if the other partner or spouse dies first. The use of a revocable living trust is not without its disadvantages. The downsides are especially apparent when compared to a payment to a surviving spouse, namely the inability to defer receipt of the minimum required distributions earlier if the account holder died before reaching his or her required beginning date as well as the loss of the right to recalculate life expectancy on an annual basis. The trust must be arranged so that it will qualify as a "look through" trust, which we discussed earlier, or the five year rule will apply. It will be very important that (1) the portion of the trust that receives the benefits not be responsible for any of the estate taxes or administration expenses; and (2) there is no non-individual beneficiary such as a charity.

Charitable Remainder Trust (CRT)

Another possible beneficiary is a charitable remainder trust (CRT). Utilizing a CRT as a beneficiary of a qualified retirement plan (assuming that if there is a spouse, that spouse grants written consent) or IRA would allow the individual trust beneficiary to receive distributions that are based upon the earnings from the entire plan, as compared with taking the benefits out in a lump sum, paying immediate income tax on those benefits and investing the net after tax. Because a CRT has a non-individual beneficiary, i.e., a charity, the trust will not qualify as a designated beneficiary under any circumstance. This means that the five year rule applies or if the decedent dies on or after their RBD, the "ghost" life expectancy rule applies.[31]

However, because the CRT is tax exempt (except for rare receipt of unrelated business taxable income), the CRT will not have to pay income tax at the time of receipt of the benefits.[32] So where a CRT is named as beneficiary, the five year rule is only important as the deadline for distribution out of the account to avoid the penalty for failure to pay the benefits out of the account. Rather, the income will be recognized with each distribution to the individual trust beneficiary.[33] This income will be in the "first tier" of distributions from the charitable remainder trust, i.e., ordinary income, so that it will be deemed distributed first, i.e., prior to capital gains or return of basis.[34]

One downside of a CRT is that the individual beneficiary will essentially receive only the income from the benefits unless the payout is set high. This will decrease the charitable deduction and could cause the trust to be disqualified for failure to meet the 10% remainder requirement. Or, if the trust is a charitable remainder annuity trust (CRAT), the "so remote as to be negligible" probability of exhaustion test under Rev. Ruls. 70-452 and 77-374 (where a less than 5 percent probability of exhaustion was the safe harbor to meet the requirement of Treas. Reg. Sec. 20.2055-2(b)) applies. Another downside is that whatever is left in the account or plan at the end of the term of the CRT will pass to charity, which may not be what the client wants.

Charity

The last possibility for a beneficiary of plan benefits is to give them outright to charity. For persons who are in a high net worth, i.e., large taxable estate, situation, charity is a very good destination for these benefits because combined state and federal income and transfer taxes could exhaust up nearly half of the benefits before the family receives a penny (except for Roth accounts, which should be left to individuals or GST exempt trusts). As noted above, the charity will not qualify as a designated beneficiary, thereby triggering the five year rule for distributions out of the account. However, this will be of no consequence to the charity since it is tax-exempt. The account holder's estate will get an estate tax charitable contribution deduction for whatever benefits are left outright to charity, even though the income tax would have otherwise reduced the net benefits available had the account holder left the benefits to family members. A beneficiary designation form can name a charity as a beneficiary of any percentage, and charities can include a donor advised fund that continues to be advised by the family.

59.3 THE SPOUSAL CONSENT RULES AND MARRIAGE CONTRACTS

With respect to ERISA qualified plans, which do not include IRAs as to these provisions,[35] spouses have certain rights that cannot be taken away without their advance written consent. Congress enacted these spousal rights in REA. The rights consist of a (1) qualified preretirement survivor annuity ("QPSA"), where the participant dies prior to separation from service to the employer, and (2) qualified joint and survivor annuity ("QJSA"), where the participant dies after separating from service and beginning to receive benefits under the plan. In essence, without the advance written consent of the non-participant spouse, any payment to the participant during lifetime must be made in the form of a QJSA, and payments prior to the participant's retirement have to be in the form of a QPSA.[36]

The QPSA is required to be funded with only one-half of the participant's account balance, leaving the remaining one-half free for the participant to give away as he or she may wish, without the need for consent.[37] A plan may, but is not required, to provide that the QPSA or QJSA, whichever is applicable, does not apply if the spouses have been married for less than one year at the participant's death.[38] If the plan does not contain this restriction, then the length of the marriage is irrelevant; even one day of marriage will be sufficient to vest the non-participant spouse.

Once it has begun, a QJSA will continue for the spouse to whom the participant was married on the date that the benefit payments began, even if the two subsequently divorce, unless a qualified domestic relations order ("QDRO") otherwise provides.[39] The QPSA/QJSA benefit does not have to be paid only if (1) the participant elects to waive the particular benefit and (2) such waiver is consented to by the participant's spouse.[40] Therefore, no action with respect to the benefits, such as a rollover to an IRA or a loan securitized by plan benefits, can be taken without a waiver and consent by the non-participant spouse. However, once rolled-over funds are in an IRA, there are no further spousal rights because REA rights do not extend to IRAs.

The consent to waiver of a QPSA or QJSA must (1) specify the specific non-spouse beneficiary to receive the benefit or, alternatively, expressly agree that the participant may name or change beneficiaries without further spousal consent, (2) acknowledge the effect of the election, and (3) be witnessed by a plan representative or notary public.[41] The QPSA may be waived only after the participant reaches the age of thirty-five. An earlier waiver may be made, but it will become ineffective at age thirty-five.[42] This anomaly causes some interesting timing issues where a younger participant, i.e., younger than thirty-five, desires that his or her spouse waive the QPSA because, in order to have effect, that waiver may have to be made twice. However, a plan may provide for a waiver (with spousal consent) by a participant who is younger than thirty-five, provided that the participant receives a written explanation of the QPSA. Such a waiver becomes invalid upon the beginning of the plan year in which the participant's thirty-fifth birthday occurs. If there is no new waiver after such date, the participant's spouse must receive the QPSA benefit upon the participant's death.[43] The QJSA may be waived only within ninety days of when benefits are scheduled to begin, and no later than when the benefits begin.[44] Therefore, even where the spouse has previously consented to a waiver of the QPSA, once the participant retires and wishes to rollover or take regular distributions from the plan (other than in a QJSA), another waiver and consent will be necessary.

The next question then becomes how does one obtain a binding waiver? The sad answer is that the parties have to negotiate the waiver in advance of the wedding for what will happen immediately after the non-participant becomes a spouse. This is because one cannot execute a valid and binding waiver as a *prospective* spouse, as well as at the key junctures along the road, i.e., upon the participant's attainment of the age of thirty-five and right before, i.e., within ninety days, beginning to receive benefits under the plan. Sadly, the participant spouse must threaten and be willing to divorce unless the spouse goes through with the waiver that he or she gave in a prenuptial agreement, i.e., before the wedding, if the participant spouse encounters any reneging or change of heart down the road. There have been many attempts to provide waivers in prenuptial agreements, but these do not work alone. Nevertheless, we believe that a waiver provision should be part of a prenuptial agreement.

Blended Family Issues in IRAs and Qualified Retirement Plans

It is not unusual in a blended family situation for a client to completely divide his or her estate so that the two sides, i.e., the partner step-parent and the client's children, would possess independent shares of the estate and not share temporal interests in any part of the estate. Such a dispositive plan can extend to non-probate property in general and qualified retirement plans and IRAs in particular.[45] If the account holder desires to make a trust the beneficiary of plan benefits and to incorporate estate tax planning, the only safe way to do maximum estate and income tax planning for plan benefits is to use a fractional formula division between the credit shelter trust and a marital deduction trust (or possibly name the bypass or QTIP trust directly rather than the main revocable trust).[46] Where there is a blended family situation, it is not unusual to see the plan benefits first allocated to the marital trust.[47] It is very important for an account holder to immediately change a beneficiary designation upon divorce, or they will have to depend upon the ex-spouse beneficiary to disclaim the interest unless a state statute divests the ex-spouse of any interest in the plan.[48]

Given the advantage of naming a spouse as beneficiary, it may be better to name the spouse as beneficiary and compensate the children with other assets. Whether this is feasible often depends on the size of the retirement plan benefit compared to the total estate. Quite often, the most simple and certain solution is to make gifts of cash to adult children who use that money to purchase life insurance on their parents' lives or to create a trust for children to own the policy and receive the life insurance proceeds.

"Short" List of Factors to Consider

Plan Documents. Obtain a copy of the qualified plan/IRA document. A Summary Plan Description is insufficient. What does the qualified plan/IRA document permit or restrict? IRAs can be made very flexible by additions to the document.

Does the document permit the beneficiary to take all of the money out of the qualified plan/IRA? If not, what are the distribution options? Some IRAs, called trusteed IRAs, may permit the owner to add restrictions on a beneficiary's right to withdraw more than the RMD.

Beneficiary Designations. What is on file? Get confirmation letter from custodian or administrator.

Who are the contingent beneficiaries? If the participant does not name any beneficiaries, what does the plan document provide? Can disclaimers be used? Should they be used? Is "per stirpes" the default if a beneficiary predeceases, or do the benefits go to the other beneficiaries?

Client's Goals and Objectives. With respect to qualified plans but not IRAs, these usually are limited where the participant is married by REA. Under REA, a non-participant spouse is entitled to a joint and survivor annuity in a qualified plan if the participant dies after retirement as well as a preretirement survivor annuity if the participant dies prior to retirement, or a spousal benefit in most defined contribution plans. Code Sections 401(a)(11), and 417. These rights may be waived only in very restricted circumstances and under strict rules.[49]

Client's Income/Cash Flow Needs. Should examine potential income sources and cash needs of the client, spouse and beneficiaries both before and after age eighty-five.

Client's Family Situation. Children of prior relationships will require more careful planning. Relationships between spouse and children and children between themselves. Status/strength of marriage. Ability of spouse and other beneficiaries to manage money.

Ages of Participant, Spouse and other Beneficiaries. Minimum Distribution Incidental Benefit Rule (MDIB), which limits, for purposes of calculating the minimum distribution, the age of any person other than the participant's spouse is limited at most to a ten (years less than the participant. Code Section 401(a)(9)(G).

Required Beginning Date (RBD). With one limited exception for participants in qualified plans who own 5 percent or less of their employer, April 1 of the year following the year that the participant or beneficiary (depending upon the circumstances) attains the age of 73 (this was 70 ½ prior to Secure Act, then 72, and will be 75 in 2033 pursuant to the Secure 2.0 Act). Code Sections 401(a)(9) (as to qualified plans) and 408(a)(6) (as to IRAs).

10 percent penalty for premature distributions. Code Sections 72(t) and 4974(c).

50 percent penalty for failure to make minimum required distribution. Code Section 4974(a).

Recalculation of life expectancy of the participant and/or the participant's spouse (but no one else). Code Section 401(a)(9)(D).

Estate Tax Considerations. Applicable exclusion amount. Unlimited marital deduction. QTIP.[50] Estate tax apportionment—Who will be responsible for the federal estate tax on the benefits still in the qualified plan/IRA? Where will those taxes come from?

Access to Capital Needs. Even though income needs may be satisfied in projected fashion, what is the chance for needed access to the plan balance? Do the plan documents and any trust set up to receive that balance permit access for such need?

Estate Tax Liquidity. Is any liquidity set aside from which to pay estate tax on the qualified plan/IRA balance?

If so, who controls it? (Hopefully, it will be controlled by the person who ultimately will owe the estate tax.)

Ethical Considerations. No ERISA or REA rights in IRA's for non-participant spouses where the participant retires and rolls over qualified plan balances into an IRA.[51] Reliance on disclaimers or on the non-participant-spouse to "do the right thing."[52]

Client's Age and Health. Are there health disparities between the participant and the participant's spouse? What is the family history of illness and life span?

When Expert Assistance Needed. Who will compute the required minimum distributions? The penalty is 25 percent of what should have been distributed but was not. Roth conversions are not for everyone, but should at least be periodically analyzed and considered:

The client should come visit you at the following times:

A. Upon becoming a participant in a qualified plan.

B. Prior to marriage while a participant in a qualified plan.

C. Upon separation from service, *e.g.*, retirement, layoff or changing jobs.

D. Upon attaining age 59½.

E. Upon the death of a named beneficiary.

F. At age seventy-two (gives you some time before the required beginning date).

Beneficiary Designation Forms

The beneficiary designation form on file with the plan administrator or custodian will govern ownership and distribution of the plan/IRA, *not* the client's will or trust. All plan administrators and IRA custodians have pre-printed beneficiary designation forms that usually must be used. However, there are three main points to consider here: First, one must compare what the provided form stipulates with the client's wishes. Often, what the form provides is different or even contrary to what the client wants. Second, those beneficiary designation forms can be modified by simply typing in "see attached" where it asks for the names of the beneficiaries and attaching beneficiary designation language that the client wants (most custodians allow this, but don't go overboard with complicated amendments). This is the *only* way to be certain as possible that the plan administrator or IRA custodian will do what the account holder wants at the right time. Finally, it is important to remember that the qualified plan administrator and IRA custodian are only thinking of their own best interests in designing these beneficiary designation forms, i.e., how to maximize the ease of administration, and most could be a lot more customer-friendly.

There is a *big* distinction between "per stirpes" and "per capita" in the law of descent and distribution. The term "per stirpes" means by root, while the term "per capita" means by heads. For example, if Steve has three children, Ed, Marty and Jay, and Steve leaves his estate to the children, what happens to Ed's share if he dies before Steve? The answer is that his share is then divided between Jay and Marty, and Ed's children get nothing. This is *not* what most clients want, yet it is the default rule under many retirement plan/IRA documents. This is impossible to easily correct even if Jay and Marty agreed, because their assignment of a portion of the IRA to Ed's children would trigger both gift and income tax and even a qualified disclaimer may not work. What most clients want is a *per stirpes* distribution, so that if Ed predeceases Steve, but is survived by two children of his own, Ed's children will inherit Ed's share, in equal portions.

You might think that major IRA custodians and qualified plan administrators would provide for per stirpes distribution as the default rule, but this is not the case. While it has become more common to see in the last two decades, it is still probably a minority of custodians who do so. Therefore, the estate planner must be familiar with the beneficiary designation form of the particular provider or administrator and potentially make the necessary changes to the form. It also is true that the beneficiary designation forms of the qualified plan administrators and IRA custodians are anything *but* standard or uniform. Therefore, one should never assume that the beneficiary designation form of, e.g., Wells Fargo, is the same as the beneficiary designation form of, e.g., Fidelity, because those forms are different, often very different.

How do the forms for some of the major IRA custodians differ? For starters, they differ significantly where the intended beneficiary predeceases the account holder. As the left column of Figure 56.1[53] indicates, none of the IRA custodians listed thereon (this is not

PLANNING WITH IRAS AND QUALIFIED RETIREMENT PLANS — CHAPTER 59

intended to be either a criticism or an endorsement of these IRA custodians, but merely an acknowledgment of the major place that these companies occupy in the IRA custodian marketplace) provide for a per stirpital distribution, meaning that if the beneficiary was one of two beneficiaries named, the surviving beneficiary would take the entire share of the predeceased beneficiary unless the account holder provided otherwise, and the descendants of the predeceased beneficiary would receive nothing. This result conflicts with the spirit of the anti-lapse statutes in the area of descent and distribution, which were enacted to prevent the disinheritance of those descendants.

However, as the left column of Figure 56.1 also reflects, these providers differ in the manner of per capita sharing by the surviving beneficiaries. As you can see, ten of these IRA custodians divide the predeceased beneficiary's share *equally* among the surviving beneficiaries, while the other three custodians provide for *pro rata* sharing, e.g., if Steve left half of his IRA to Joanne and divided the remaining half between his sons, Ed and Jay, Joanne would take 2/3 of the share of the predeceased Ed because her share (50 percent) was twice as large as Jay's share (25 percent). In the equal sharing scenario, Joanne and Jay would split Ed's 25 percent share, 12.5 percent apiece.

This is a *significant* issue, but it begs the question of whether Steve wanted Ed's children to have Ed's share. In the typical parent/children scenario, it is our experience that parents overwhelmingly want to give the share of a predeceased child who left descendants behind to those descendants, i.e., the client's grandchildren/great-grandchildren. Nevertheless, this is not how any of the listed IRA custodians arranged their beneficiary forms. Therefore, it is incumbent upon the estate planner to apprise the clients of this issue and to help them modify the beneficiary designation form so that it aligns with their wishes.

As the center column of Figure 56.1 provides, the listed IRA custodians also differ significantly in the selection of a successor beneficiary where the account holder named a beneficiary, but that beneficiary either disclaims or dies before providing who would receive the remaining benefits of the IRA at that beneficiary's death or disclaimer. At the outset, note that eleven of the IRA custodians default toward the *beneficiary's* side, while the other two IRA custodians default toward the *account holder's* side. As you can see, seven of these IRA custodians default to the *beneficiary's* estate, which is not a designated beneficiary under the RMD rules, meaning that the five year rule applies, which is not optimal in most situations. However, the rest of the IRA custodians do quite different things in this event. For example, two of the IRA custodians do default first to the *account holder's* spouse before defaulting to the account holder's estate, which gives many more options for taking out distributions, as we discussed earlier in this chapter. Four of the IRA custodians default to the *beneficiary's* spouse. Finally, one IRA custodian also includes the *account holder's* parents before defaulting to the *account holder's* estate, which could be beneficial for distribution because it could facilitate a stretch out as opposed to being stuck with the five year rule.

As the right column of Figure 56.1 reflects, the listed IRA custodians also differ sharply in what happens where none of the named beneficiaries are deemed to

Figure 56.1

	COMPARISON OF DEFAULT PROVISIONS OF VARIOUS IRA BENEFICIARY DESIGNATION FORMS		
	PRE-DECEASED BENEFICIARY	**"POST-DECEASED" BENEFICIARY**	**NO BENEFICIARY**
	O names A, B & C as beneficiaries. A dies first. O dies next without making any changes. Who gets A's share at O's death?	O names A as beneficiary. O dies first. A makes no arrangements for who succeeds to the account at A's death. A dies next. Who receives the balance at A's death?	O dies without having filed a beneficiary designation form OR O dies last of all of the beneficiaries O had named on the form. Who takes at O's death?
IRA Provider			

Figure 56.1 (cont'd)

COMPARISON OF DEFAULT PROVISIONS OF VARIOUS IRA BENEFICIARY DESIGNATION FORMS			
Ameriprise	B & C equally. (A's children receive nothing.)	A's spouse, or if none, A's probate estate.	O's spouse, or if none, O's probate estate.
Charles Schwab	B & C equally. (A's children receive nothing.)	A's probate estate.	O's probate estate.
Edward Jones	B & C equally. (A's children receive nothing.)*	A's spouse, or if none, A's descendants, per stirpes, or if none, A's probate estate.	O's spouse, or if none, O's descendants, per stirpes, or if none, O's probate estate.
Fidelity	B & C equally. (A's children receive nothing.)	A's probate estate.	O's spouse, or if none, O's probate estate.
LPL Financial	B & C equally. (A's children receive nothing.)	A's probate estate.	O's spouse, or if none, O's probate estate.
Merrill Lynch	B & C pro rata. (A's children receive nothing.)	A's probate estate.*	O's spouse, or if none, O's probate estate.
Morgan Stanley	B & C equally. (A's children receive nothing.)	O's spouse, or if none, O's probate estate.	O's spouse, or if none, O's probate estate.
Raymond James	B & C equally. (A's children receive nothing.)	A's probate estate.	O's probate estate.
Stifel Nicolaus	B & C equally. (A's children receive nothing.)	A's probate estate.	O's probate estate.
TD Ameritrade	B & C equally. (A's children receive nothing.)	O's spouse, or if none, O's children equally, or if none, O's parents equally, or if none, the probate estate of the last to die of O and O's named beneficiaries.	O's spouse, or if none, O's children equally, or if none, O's parents equally, or if none, the probate estate of the last to die of O and O's named beneficiaries.
UBS	B & C equally. (A's children receive nothing.)*	A's spouse, or if none, A's probate estate.	O's spouse, or if none, O's probate estate.
Vanguard	B & C pro rata. (A's children receive nothing.)	A's probate estate.	O's spouse, or if none, O's probate estate.
Wells Fargo	B & C pro rata. (A's children receive nothing.)	A's spouse, or if none, A's children, or if none, A's probate estate.	O's spouse, or if none, O's children, or if none, O's probate estate.

*Official documents are silent. Entry is assumed.

survive the account holder or where there is no beneficiary designation form on file with the IRA custodian. Three of the listed IRA custodians still defaults to the account holder's estate, while the majority interpose the account holder's spouse, children and/or parents as beneficiaries before winding up with the account holder's probate estate, but these are not uniform either, so caution is advised. There is no substitute for reading *and* understanding the form's default provisions so that appropriate changes can be made, and the client's beneficiary designation form can be customized to his or her desires.

The safest route is to *affirmatively* provide for the beneficiary(ies) that your client wants, and to name successor beneficiary(ies) as well as provide what happens where a beneficiary predeceases the client or desires to disclaim. This is easily done by simply typing "see attached" on the line that asks for the name(s) of the beneficiary(ies) and submitting a beneficiary designation provision that the client wants. Also note that the authors have not independently verified those custodial agreements since 2018 and they could have changed. Also be careful that some banks may have different beneficiary designation forms and defaults depending on whether you are dealing with their retail or private bank (where it may be a trusteed IRA), or brokerage arm (where it would usually be a custodial IRA).

59.4 FREQUENTLY ASKED QUESTIONS

Question – Given that a spouse cannot waive REA spousal rights prior to marriage in qualified plans, is it ever worth it to put those types of provisions in prenuptial agreements?

Answer – Yes. It is still worthwhile to include such provisions in a prenuptial agreement because it evinces a condition of the impending marriage and the participant's intent and understanding, where the participant relied upon the future spouse's agreement to execute the required waivers after the wedding and at all times thereafter. It is not unusual for the prenuptial agreement to contain all of the waivers of REA rights as well as a requirement that the spouse execute the valid waiver right after the wedding takes place, often right after the ceremony where the spouses are signing the marriage certificate/license. If the non-participant spouse decides to breach the agreement, the participant spouse could use that breach as leverage to obtain an annulment of the marriage based upon misrepresentation or fraud.

Question – Where a prospective spouse participant wants the intended spouse to execute a waiver of all rights in the retirement plan, what should the waiver include?

Answer – A waiver should be *comprehensive* and apply to all future beneficiary changes since, without that provision, the spouse's consent might again be required to change the beneficiary, i.e., the waiver could only apply to one waiver of the right to be the beneficiary. The waiver should *require* the spouse to execute any and all additional documents that either the plan administrator/account custodian might require in the future. The waiver also should include a waiver of the right to consent to a rollover of the plan benefits into an IRA.

CHAPTER ENDNOTES

1. I.R.C. §§691(a) and 1014(c).
2. I.R.C. §401(a)(9); Treas. Reg. §1.401(a)(9)-0 – 9. The minimum required distribution rules also apply to IRAs. I.R.C. §408(a)(6) and Treas. Reg. §1.408-8.
3. I.R.C. §4974(a).
4. I.R.C. §§401(a)(11) and 417.
5. I.R.C. §401(a)(11)(B).
6. See, e.g., Choate, Natalie B., *Life and Death Planning for Retirement Benefits* (7th ed. 2011), which is available at www.ataxplan.com.
7. I.R.C. §§401(a)(9)(A) and (C) and 408(a)(6).
8. For more details, see Ed Morrow & Nancy Welber: *Secure 2.0 Act Enhances Special Needs-See Through Trust Planning*, LISI Estate Planning Newsletter #3027 (Mar. 30, 2023).
9. Treas. Reg. §1.401(a)(9)-4, A 3.
10. Treas. Reg. §1.401(a)(9)-4, Q-4, A-4(c).
11. Treas. Reg. §1.401(a)(9)-4, A 5 and 6.
12. Treas. Reg. §1.401(a)(9)-4, Q-5, A-5(b).
13. Treas. Reg. §1.401(a)(9)-3, A 3(a).
14. See extension discussion of this in *Ed Morrow: Secure 2.0 Offers Longer Stretch for Conduit Trusts, but Contains Traps for Surviving Spouses*, LISI Estate Planning Newsletter #3010 (Jan. 24, 2023).
15. Treas. Reg. §1.401(a)(9)-3, A-3(b).
16. Treas. Reg. §1.401(a)(9)-5, A 5(c)(1).
17. Treas. Reg. §1.401(a)(9)-5, A-5(c)(2).
18. I.R.C. §401(a)(9)(B)(ii) and Treas. Reg. §1.401(a)(9)-3, A-4(a)(2); see, e.g., PLR 200644022.
19. Treas. Reg. §1.401(a)(9)-5, A-5.
20. Treas. Reg. §1.401(a)(9)-5, A-5(a) and (c)(2).
21. Treas. Reg. §1.401(a)(9)-5, A-5(a) and (c)(1).
22. Treas. Reg. §1.401(a)(9)-8, Q-2, A-2(a).
23. Treas. Reg. §§1.401(a)(9)-5, A-5(c)(3) and 1.401(a)(9)-4, A-3.
24. See, e.g., PLRs 200742026 and 201021038.
25. I.R.C. §§402(c)(9) and 408(d)(2)(C)(ii).
26. I.R.C. §401(a)(9)(D).
27. Treas. Reg. § 1.408-8, A-5.
28. I.R.C. §402(c)(11).
29. Treas. Reg. §1.401(a)(9)-5, A-7(a)(1).
30. Rev. Rul. 2002-2, modified by Rev. Rul. 2006-26.
31. I.R.C. §401(a)(9)(B)(ii); Treas. Reg. § 1.401(a)(9)-3, A-2.
32. See, e.g., PLR 9634019.
33. See, e.g., PLR 199901023.
34. See, e.g., PLR 9634019.

35. I.R.C. §401(a)(11)(B).
36. I.R.C. §401(a)(11).
37. See, e.g., *Nat'l Auto Dealers & Assocs. Retirement Trust vs. Arbeitman*, 89 F.3d 496 (8th Cir. 1996); *Gallagher v. Park West Bank & Trust Co.*, 921 F. Supp. 867 (D. Mass. 1996).
38. I.R.C. §§401(a)(11)(D) and 417(d)(1). However, there is an exception where the participant marries within one year of retirement and the couple is married for one year at the participant's death. I.R.C. § 417(d)(2).
39. Treas. Reg. §1.401(a)-20, A-25(b)(3).
40. I.R.C. §417(a)(2).
41. I.R.C. §417(a)(2)(A).
42. Treas. Reg. §1.401(a)-20, A-33(b).
43. Treas. Reg. §1.401(a)-20, A-33(b).
44. Treas. Reg. §1.417(e)-1(b)(3)(i).
45. See, e.g., PLRs 200248031, 200449042 and 201210045.
46. See, e.g., PLR 199931033.
47. See, e.g., PLR 201203033.
48. See, e.g., PLRs 200532060 and 200837046.
49. Treas. Reg. §1.401(a)-20, Q&A 31.
50. Rev. Rul. 89-89 and PLR 9220007.
51. DOL §2510.3-2(d); Code Sections 401(a)(11) and 417.
52. See, e.g., *Bank One Milwaukee, N.A. v. Fueger*, 201 Wis. 2d 216, 549 N.W. 2d 742 (Ct. App. 1986).
53. These IRA custodian comparison charts (Charts I, II and III) were provided by Salvatore J. LaMendola, Esq., of Giarmarco, Mullins & Horton, P.C., Troy MI. Mr. LaMendola's e-mail address is sjl@disinherit-irs.com.

PLANNING WITH ROTH RETIREMENT ACCOUNTS

CHAPTER 60

60.1 INTRODUCTION

Roth IRAs (and newer variations such as "designated Roth accounts" more simply known as Roth 401(k) or Roth 403(b) accounts and now even SEP and SIMPLE Roth IRAs), are of course a financial retirement vehicle rather than an estate planning technique.[1] Most of the rules discussed in prior Chapters, such as post-mortem RMD rules, apply to Roth accounts. However, many articles on estate planning with IRAs rarely differentiate between the planning differences, opportunities and concerns when a Roth IRA (or Roth 401(k) or other Roth account) is involved, or a large part of one's estate. Roth accounts have been consistently on the rise over the last decade or more and we will continue to see an increase in the value of various Roth Accounts due to recent incentives included in the Secure 2.0 Act and the prospect of tax increases in 2026 due to the expiration of many provisions of the Tax Cuts and Jobs Act. Thus, this edition adds a short chapter dedicated to tax and planning concerns unique to Roth accounts.

Roth accounts can be funded with non-deductible contributions, or more often for larger accounts, via conversion of a traditional retirement account to a Roth. The conversion to a Roth is an income taxable event (except in cases where the basis is equal to or greater than the fair market value at the time of conversion) and a contribution to a Roth does not generate an income tax deduction, but the assets can grow for the owner (and potentially spouse's) lifetime income tax-free.

Estate planning opportunities that involve Roths include deathbed or earlier Roth conversions and allocating the Roth account to different trusts or beneficiaries than traditional accounts. Conversions can be especially valuable for those with estates subject to state or federal estate tax. Financial planning opportunities include analyzing the appropriate mix between traditional and Roth accounts and the viability of conversion, plus examining the source of investment management fee payments. Before tackling the pros and cons of Roths, conversions thereto, and trust design, let's first summarize some of the basic characteristics and then recent tweaks to Roth Accounts included in the Secure 2.0 Act that will encourage the further growth of such accounts.

60.2 ROTH BASICS

Roth IRAs are treated the same as traditional IRAs except as specifically provided.[2] Roth IRAs have two key advantages over traditional IRAs: 1) no RMDs during lifetime[3] (and if a surviving spouse rolls over the account, none during the spouse's lifetime either), and most importantly; 2) tax-free distributions provided some minimal requirements are met.[4] There used to be a third differentiating characteristic that has now gone away: there is no maximum age for Roth IRA contributions. Until recently workers could not add to traditional IRAs after age 70 ½. However, the Secure Act changed this so that after 2020, taxpayers can now add to traditional IRAs as well as Roth IRAs after such age.

The requirements for tax-free distributions are indeed minimal and the rules are rather generous to taxpayers but are important to remember and may still come up unexpectedly. To be a "qualified distribution" (i.e., tax-free), it must be made:

After the five year period which starts January 1 of the year a taxpayer establishes a Roth IRA – this is true for any Roth IRA, and holds true even if funds are added by contribution or rollover from a Roth account within 5 years; and either:

(i) made on or after the date on which the individual attains age 59½,

(ii) made to a beneficiary (or to the estate of the individual) on or after the death of the individual,

(iii) attributable to the individual's being disabled (within the meaning of section 72(m)(7)), or

(iv) which is a qualified special purpose distribution. [first time home purchase up to $10,000][5]

The generous tax rules of Roth IRAs provide that even if a distribution is not qualified under the above rules, it still may not be taxable. This is because distributions are deemed to come from an individuals contributions (basis) first, which is not taxable.[6]

Roth IRA contributions have various limits and phase outs, but these are a bit illusory, since taxpayers can simply make non-deductible contributions to a traditional IRA and then later convert the account to a Roth, but this may not be the same if a taxpayer has other IRA accounts with no basis, since all IRAs and basis of such accounts have to be considered together in calculating the tax on conversion. Nonetheless, here are the numbers for tax year 2023 (source: IRS.gov):

This table shows whether your contribution to a Roth IRA is affected by the amount of your **modified AGI** as computed for Roth IRA purpose.

If your filing status is...	And your modified AGI is...	Then you can contribute...
married filing jointly or **qualifying widow(er)**	< $218,000	up to the limit
married filing jointly or **qualifying widow(er)**	≥ $218,000 but < $228,000	a reduced amount
married filing jointly or **qualifying widow(er)**	≥ $228,000	zero
married filing separately and you lived with your spouse at any time during the year	< $10,000	a reduced amount
married filing separately and you lived with your spouse at any time during the year	≥ $10,000	zero
single, head of household, or **married filing separately** and you did not live with your spouse at any time during the year	< $138,000	up to the limit
single, head of household, or **married filing separately** and you did not live with your spouse at any time during the year	≥ $138,000 but < $153,000	a reduced amount
single, head of household, or **married filing separately** and you did not live with your spouse at any time during the year	≥ $153,000	zero

Amount of your reduced Roth IRA contribution

If the amount you can contribute must be reduced, figure your reduced contribution limit as follows.

1. Start with your modified AGI.

2. Subtract from the amount in (1):

   a. $218,000 if filing a joint return or qualifying widow(er),

   b. $-0- if married filing a separate return, and you lived with your spouse at any time during the year, or

   c. $138,000 for all other individuals.

3. Divide the result in (2) by $15,000 ($10,000 if filing a joint return, qualifying widow(er), or married filing a separate return and you lived with your spouse at any time during the year).

4. Multiply the maximum contribution limit (before reduction by this adjustment and before reduction for any contributions to traditional IRAs) by the result in (3).

5. Subtract the result in (4) from the maximum contribution limit before this reduction. The result is your reduced contribution limit.

See Publication 590-A, Contributions to Individual Retirement Accounts (IRAs), for a worksheet to figure your reduced contribution.

60.3 SECURE 2.0 ACT CHANGES INVOLVING ROTH ACCOUNTS

The Secure 2.0 Act adds a few minor provisions that will lead to even more money flowing into Roth accounts than previously:

Section 126 of the Act adds special rules for distributions from old 529 Plans to Roth IRAs. Beneficiaries of 529 college savings accounts will be permitted to rollover up to $35,000 over the course of their lifetime from any 529 account in their name to their Roth IRA. These rollovers are also subject to Roth IRA annual contribution limits, and the 529 account must have been open for more than 15 years. Section 126 is effective with respect to distributions after December 31, 2023.

Section 127 of the Act adds a provision that allows emergency savings accounts linked to individual account plans. At separation from service, employees may take their emergency savings accounts as cash or roll it into their Roth defined contribution plan (if they have one) or IRA.

Section 325 of the Act modifies the Roth retirement plan distribution rules. Under current law, RMDs are not required to begin prior to the death of the owner of a Roth IRA. However, pre-death distributions are required in the case of the owner of a Roth designated account in an employer retirement plan (e.g., 401(k) plan). Section 325 eliminates the current pre-death distribution requirement for Roth accounts in employer plans, effective for taxable years beginning after December 31, 2023.

Section 601 of the Act modifies the provisions for SIMPLE and SEP Roth IRAs. Generally, all plans that allow pre-tax employee contributions are permitted to accept Roth contributions with one exception – SIMPLE IRAs. 401(k), 403(b), and governmental 457(b) plans are allowed to accept Roth employee contributions. Section 601 now allows SIMPLE IRAs to accept Roth contributions too. In addition, aside from grandfathered salaried reduction simplified employee pension plans, under current law, simplified employee pension plans ("SEPs") can only accept employer money and not on a Roth basis. Section 601 allows employers to offer employees the ability to treat employee and employer SEP contributions as Roth (in whole or in part). The provisions in Section 601 are effective for taxable years beginning after December 31, 2022.

Section 603 of the Act now forces some catch up contributions to be Roth. Under current law, catch-up contributions to a qualified retirement plan can be made on a pre-tax or Roth basis (if permitted by the plan sponsor). Section 603 provides all catch-up contributions to qualified retirement plans are subject to Roth tax treatment, effective for taxable years beginning after December 31, 2023. An exception is provided for employees with compensation of $145,000 or less (indexed).

Section 604 of the Act now allows optional treatment of employer matching or nonelective contributions as Roth contributions. Under prior law, plan sponsors were not permitted to provide employer matching contributions in their 401(k), 403(b), and governmental 457(b) plans on a Roth basis. Matching contributions had to be on a pre-tax basis only. Section 604 now allows defined contribution plans to provide participants with the option of receiving matching contributions on a Roth basis, effective on the date of enactment of the Act.

These are all relatively minor tweaks but taken together will mean more money flowing into Roth accounts and Roth IRAs.

60.4 ADVANTAGES

Analyzing the income tax benefit of contributing or converting large amounts of retirement plan assets to Roth accounts can be complex – it depends on a taxpayer's current and future state and federal income tax rates, not to mention the assumed investment rate of return, all of which may change. We will therefore focus on the *estate and asset protection planning* effects.

From an asset protection planning perspective, making a Roth contribution rather than a traditional one or doing a Roth conversion means that the owner pays more income tax up front, which usually comes from creditor-exposed taxable accounts, permitting the creditor-protected Roth accounts to grow more for longer (Roth IRAs have no RMDs during the owner's lifetime and other Roth accounts will not have RMDs during the owner's lifetime starting next year. This correspondingly reduces the value of creditor-exposed accounts which are used to pay the tax bill. This gradually leads to a greater percentage of the owner's assets being protected than if only traditional retirement accounts are used.

This depletion can save state estate taxes. Imagine a single taxpayer with a $5 million estate, $2 million of which is in a traditional IRA. He lives in a state with a $4 million state estate tax threshold and 12% tax beyond that. If he (or his agent under a power of attorney on his deathbed) converts the $2 million IRA to a Roth IRA, paying 40% state and federal income tax of $800,000, this would reduce the state estate tax by $800,000 times 12%, or $96,000.

The analysis of a Roth conversion's potential effect on federal estate tax is more complicated, because Code section 691(c) permits an income tax deduction for the federal (but NOT state) estate tax paid due to an IRA or other retirement plan's inclusion one's estate.[7] However, this is a miscellaneous itemized deduction (not eliminated by the Tax Cuts and Jobs Act, but minimized as a practical matter) which requires a beneficiary to itemize their deductions to get any benefit, and it can get even more complicated if the beneficiary is a trust where some of the income would pass through as distributable net income (DNI) to an individual beneficiary. Doing a Roth conversion before death allows beneficiaries of taxable estates to effectively get the equivalent of a Code section 691(c) deduction sooner, but also for state estate and inheritance taxes, and with much more certainty, without having to waste their standard deduction and worry their itemized deduction may never get used.

Converting to a Roth prior to death solves one of the main planning dilemmas when retirement plan assets are left in a trust where some of the funds may be accumulated (which, after the Secure Act's 10 year limit, will be the vast majority of trusts) and pay tax at highly compressed trust tax brackets. Income may be taxed at the highest tax rates for trusts at only $14,450, but that is not an issue if most of the funds are in a Roth, since Roth distributions are generally tax-free to any beneficiary, whether it is through a trust or not. When traditional IRA funds are left in trust, the trustee is pressured by economics and tax rate differentials to distribute more funds out that might otherwise be advisable, to avoid the compressed tax brackets of the trust (unless a Beneficiary Deemed Owner Trust (BDOT) design is used, see Chapter 35).

Roth conversions of a portion of one's retirement plan assets allow for better use of GST exempt v. non-exempt trust planning. Roth accounts are ideal assets to fund in a GST exempt trust due to their tax-free growth (in most cases after the Secure Act, for only 10 years, but perhaps longer if the trust has eligible designated beneficiaries, but even 10 years tax-free is much better than other assets). Traditional retirement accounts are better suited to GST non-exempt trusts, due to the inherent income tax drag on after-tax returns. While most taxpayers can now afford to leave everything into a GST exempt trust (with $12.92 million GST exemption as of 2023), Congress may decrease this exemption in the future, and the law already contemplates a 50% reduction in 2026 with the expiration of the doubling of the gift/estate/GST exemptions in the Tax Cuts and Jobs Act, which might make the proper placement and division of such accounts into GST exempt v. non-exempt trusts more and more important to address.

Roth conversions may see a surge in 2024-2025 due to anticipated tax increases with the expiration of many of the Tax Cuts and Jobs Act provisions at the end of 2025 (e.g., 37% → 39.6% top rate)

60.5 DISADVANTAGES

Roth IRA contributions mean a higher income tax bill than traditional contributions that would otherwise reduce one's income. Roth conversions require paying the income tax bill upfront, since they are included in income in the year of conversion. Conversions thus make more financial sense when the taxpayer has cash to pay the tax bill, or can liquidate funds without triggering gains, rather than when they have to sell assets at a capital gain to pay the tax, which would create a snowball effect of an even larger income tax bill.

If the client puts themselves in a higher tax bracket from the conversion than they would otherwise ultimately pay when receiving a traditional distribution, it makes less economic sense. Many taxpayers do indeed fall into a lower bracket in retirement than while working. Large conversions would probably not make sense for such taxpayers. Many taxpayers expect to have close to the same income and be in close to the same bracket in retirement. For them, it may make sense to convert up to an amount that would not take them into a higher tax bracket gradually over a number of years, rather than incurring a larger and more expensive tax on a large conversion. Some taxpayers may plan to move to a sunnier clime or closer to grandchildren in another state – the change to a higher or lower tax rate state (or one that has a generous deduction or credit for retirement income) can also make a difference in the analysis. Moving to a higher tax state – convert before the move. Moving to a lower tax state – hold off and convert after the move.

There is always a risk that someone's tax rates go *down* in the future rather than stay static or go up, in which case the Roth conversion will not have been advantageous and could easily be disadvantageous. No financial advisor, accountant or attorney can predict with certainty – it's just a best guess and reasonable estimates may differ. Don't be afraid to get different opinions or "split the difference" and "hedge your bets" by doing smaller partial Roth conversions over time than one large one. Or it may make sense to wait (e.g. if someone plans to retire at 65 and start collecting social security at 67, perhaps age 66 would be a good year to convert some funds to a Roth). If Congress someday moves to a lower flat tax rate or enacts a consumption tax in the future as many Republicans have proposed, this might make the large Roth conversion look foolish in hindsight, due to paying an income tax earlier at a *much* higher rate than if they had not done so at all. This may not be likely, but it is far from impossible. Having a bucket of tax-free money in a Roth, however, opens up more distribution options in the future.

Taxpayers may not realize how their tax rate might be reduced in their future retirement with high medical expense deductions either.

Taxpayers who are charitably-minded should not convert all of their traditional retirement plans so that they retain at least enough to make anticipated qualified charitable distributions (QCDs) after age 70 ½ over the years from their traditional IRA accounts – QCDs are a very efficient way to make charitable contributions and cannot be (and should not be, even if it were allowed) done from Roth IRA accounts.

Impact of Conversions on the Beneficiary Designation and Estate Plan

Clients should let their estate planning attorney know if they convert an account to a Roth IRA, and re-evaluate the beneficiary designation forms of any new accounts (e.g., if 10% of a traditional account was earmarked for charity previously and half converted to a Roth, the new Roth beneficiary designation form should probably omit the charity and the old traditional account might increase its earmark to charity to 20% to account for the reduced size of the account). And, parties should re-evaluate whether the trust as beneficiary should be modified in any way, due to the Secure and Secure 2.0 Act or otherwise.

Financial Planning: Modelling Roth Conversions and Optimizing the Payment of Investment Management and Trustee Fees

Clients should strongly consider working with a financial planner to model various Roth conversion scenarios. No financial advisor can predict future investment returns and tax rates, but they can model a range of outcomes and "worst case scenarios."

When taxpayers pay a wrap fee or trustee fee for investment management of IRA accounts (fee based not commission based), consider how and where such fees should be paid from – it may be optimal to pay fees from different sources for traditional IRA accounts than Roth IRA accounts. Taxpayers can pay such fees from the IRA itself without being considered a taxable distribution (and not counting towards an RMD).[8] Or they can pay the fee from outside funds (but be careful, one cannot pay a Roth IRA management fee or taxable account fee from a traditional IRA account – criss-crossing of such payments may create an unexpected taxable distribution or worse, a prohibited transaction).

Investment management fees for traditional IRA accounts used to qualify for a miscellaneous itemized deduction subject to the 2% floor under Code section 212, but the Tax Cuts and Jobs Act has eliminated this. Thus, many taxpayers may want to simply pay those fees from the traditional IRA account itself, using pre-tax money rather than after-tax money from their taxable accounts. While the authors lean towards usually paying such fees from the traditional IRA itself, there is still a case to be made for paying them from outside accounts, however, particularly if the client has a longer time horizon and no problem with cash flow to pay them, or if the client is concerned about asset protection (since paying from outside accounts allows more to be protected inside the IRA). Paying fees from an outside account allows the traditional IRA to grow tax-deferred and asset-protected, but it will eventually probably be taxed as ordinary income when it comes out (absent distributions to charity).

While the case for paying investment management fees for a traditional IRA is a bit of a toss-up and should probably lean towards usually paying fees from the IRA itself for convenience, the case for paying investment management fees for a Roth IRA is much clearer. Pay the investment management fees from outside taxable accounts! Paying fees from a Roth IRA uses after-tax dollars and depletes the amount growing tax-free. Paying the fees from an outside taxable account also uses after-tax dollars but allows the Roth to grow fee-free. Simply put, a Roth IRA is more valuable than a traditional IRA all things being equal, and efforts should be made to maximize its growth wherever possible.

Estate/Gift/GST Implications of Roth Conversions:

If a taxpayer has a taxable estate (federal or potentially state), Roth conversions lower one's state and federal estate by the state and federal income tax bill incurred and there is no need for beneficiaries to qualify for any I.R.C. §691(c) miscellaneous itemized deduction to receive the benefit.

Asset Protection Implications of Roth Contributions and Conversions:

As discussed above, Roth conversions reduce the creditor-exposed accounts used to pay the income tax bill and allow the creditor-protected accounts to grow tax-free without any need for depleting distributions (since Roth IRA accounts have no RMDs during life).

Quirk Allowing Inherited Qualified Plan to Inherited Roth IRA Conversions

Whether Congress meant to or not, they created a loophole that allows a designated beneficiary (including a trustee of a trust) who inherits a traditional qualified plan to move/convert the plan into an inherited IRA (of course, they would pay income tax on the value over any basis). This cannot be done with an inherited traditional IRA – inherited IRAs cannot be converted except by a spouse. These post-mortem conversions are admittedly quite rare and the number of advisors who even know this rule is even rarer. Why do this, when most beneficiaries would only get the benefit for 10 years now?

Example: John recently inherited his father's $100,000 traditional 401(k) plan. He had planned to simplify his financial affairs and simply cash it in and pay $28,000 tax, but then he found out about this rule and decided instead to move it to an inherited Roth IRA – he still pays the $28,000 tax bill, but now he has a $100,000 inherited Roth Account that can grow tax-free for 10 years! Of course, an eligible designated beneficiary can receive an even longer stretch. For example, if John inherited the same account from his brother (and is not more than 10 years younger than him), he could allow the Roth account to grow and take RMDs over his life expectancy, not limited by the 10 year rule. Not only might this be advantageous from a tax perspective, but in either situation John may have also improved his overall asset protection exposure to creditors, since the $28,000 depleted his exposed accounts and inherited IRAs are protected from creditors in about half the states.[9]

Trustees of see through trusts that inherit such funds can also make the same choice.

CHAPTER ENDNOTES

1. Roth IRAs are established under I.R.C. §408A, whereas the rules for traditional IRAs are under I.R.C. §408.
2. Treas. Reg. §1.408A-1, A-1(b).
3. I.R.C. §408A(c)(5).
4. I.R.C. §408A(d)(1).
5. I.R.C. §408A(d)(2)(A).
6. I.R.C. §408A(d)(4)(B), Treas. Reg. §1.408A-6, A-9.
7. I.R.C. §691(c).
8. Treas. Reg. § 1.404(a)-3(d).
9. According to a chart compiled by ACTEC in 2018, these states include Alaska, Arizona, Connecticut, Washington, D.C., Delaware, Florida, Idaho, Louisiana, Maryland, Michigan, Minnesota, Mississippi, Missouri, Nevada up to $1 million, probably New Hampshire, New Jersey, probably New Mexico, North Carolina, North Dakota, Ohio, Oregon, Rhode Island, South Carolina, Texas, Washington, West Virginia and Wyoming.

PLANNING FOR AGING AND HEALTH CHALLENGES

CHAPTER 61

61.1 INTRODUCTION

Planning for aging or incapacitated clients will become a major focus of estate planning practices. Those over sixty-five will grow to 19 percent of the population by 2030. This is also occurring as a result of the $5 million inflation adjusted exemption that has made the federal estate tax irrelevant for all but the wealthiest clients. If the estate tax is repealed, as has been proposed, the impact will be more dramatic. The population is aging, five million Baby Boomers a year are retiring. There are approximately 130 million Americans living with chronic disease. Approximately 60 million people (22 percent of the population) suffer from multiple chronic conditions. Approximately 400,000 Americans are living with Multiple Sclerosis. Approximately 1.5 million Americans are living with Parkinson's disease. As clients age, the incidence of chronic disease grows significantly. Thus, planning for aging clients by necessity must incorporate planning for chronic disease.

Specific planning steps are required for aging clients and those with health challenges. Health care documents need to be tailored to address health and aging issues. These are discussed in Chapter 63. Durable powers of attorney are critical. In many instances powers should be tailored to address the specific challenges of the particular client (see Chapter 62). Revocable trusts are strongly recommended for many aging or inform clients (see Chapter 64). For most, if not all aging clients, all of these documents should be prepared: durable power of attorney for financial matters, health care proxy (also called "medical power of attorney"), HIPAA Release (Health Insurance Portability and Accountability Act), pour-over will, and a revocable trust. However, when planning for aging clients in particular, there will be special planning and drafting nuances, that will be discussed in this and the three following chapters.

To address the challenges these clients face more than merely preparing appropriate documents is necessary. Financial planning and personal planning steps (organization, care managers and more) are also important to properly protect these clients from their health challenges, the risks of elder financial abuse, identity theft and other risks. These ancillary steps are often left out in part because of the siloed nature of the planning process. Clients view attorneys as scriveners, CPAs as tax return preparers, and wealth managers as preparing an asset allocation. Many of the ancillary steps, such as consolidating financial accounts so they can more readily be monitored by a client whose capabilities wane with age, fall outside of what may be viewed as "traditional" planning parameters.

Often without a durable power of attorney, health proxy and a revocable living trust, a guardianship or conservatorship must be sought with the court. While proper documents won't assure that a guardianship or other court involvement is not necessary, they will significantly lessen that risk. Perhaps more important, whether or not a court appointed guardian becomes necessary, having proper documents and planning in place will likely safeguard the clients assets before that point is reached. A court may appoint a guardian of a person and a separate guardian of property. A durable financial power of attorney and a revocable trust can avoid the need to appoint a guardian of the person. A health care proxy and living will may avoid the need for a court to appoint a guardian of the person. These steps are not particularly cumbersome and should not materially add to the cost of the estate planning documents. The key, however, is not merely having valid documents, but having the practical aspects of the planning addressed as well.

Example. An elderly client has named her niece as her agent under a well-crafted durable power of attorney. The aunt is injured and rushed to the hospital. The niece arrives to see her aunt but has no idea that she has been named agent. This is not uncommon as many clients never discuss what their documents and planning are with their family. In light of her aunt's condition she searches her aunt's apartment looking for legal and other important documents. It would have cost very little for an adviser to have guided the aunt to save key information in a password App or to have her key legal documents in a secure portal online. Even if the aunt was not technologically able to do any of this, an adviser could have created these and recommended that the aunt inform her niece of these tools. She identifies almost a score of bank and brokerage statements. The aunt's checkbook is generally indecipherable. It takes the niece months of time to sort everything out, and great costs in terms of her time and professional fees. Had the aunt informed her niece in advance of her role, precious time would have been saved. Had the aunt's advisers guided her to consolidate assets into one or two institutions and put her finances on Quicken, and updated them for her every quarter, it could have been seamless for the niece to step in when it became necessary. Having only the necessary documents is a start but not sufficient. The agent should be informed. Financial, legal and other affairs should be organized in a manner that facilitates passing the baton to an agent and simplifying the agent's duties and responsibilities.

Unlike many other tools and techniques discussed in this book, the practice in this area requires the practitioner to deal with a variety of personal problems and decisions of the client or dependent. These range from health care decisions to who will care for these persons if they are unable to care for themselves, and even where they will live. It also requires a great deal of patience and compassion – an important part of the estate planner's duties all too often neglected.

When planning is addressed sufficiently in advance, the client will have time to contemplate the critical life decisions involved, and gain comfort with the process. Unfortunately, in many instances clients do not act until the emergencies have occurred. Planning for these types of individuals is time sensitive and opportunities available currently may be foreclosed quickly. This makes time of the essence in making preparations, in drafting, and in having these documents properly executed, witnessed, and notarized. In even more unfortunate situations the client never addresses planning before the onset of significant health issues that limit or preclude planning. By the time the practitioner is retained the client may lack the capacity to execute documents. In these latter situations it may be feasible to accomplish some of the desired objectives working with existing powers of attorney, guardianship proceedings, and so forth. In these latter cases practitioners should inventory all assets with details as to title, all existing documents particularly noting the powers available to change title or ownership to assets, and so forth. If the existing documents and facts do not support the desired planning it may be feasible to seek a court appointed guardian and request that the court empower the guardian to implement certain estate planning steps.

61.2 PLANNING SHOULD BE ADDRESSED FOR ALL CLIENTS

There is no way to anticipate which client will face which challenge or at which point in time. The age at which cognitive issues begin is often much earlier than most realize. Age sixty has been identified as the optimal age for financial decision making, but capabilities generally decline from that age onward. Therefore, planning for the challenges of aging or incapacity is advisable for all clients. If there is a specific family history, or the client has already been diagnosed with a particular health issue, then planning should be undertaken for that particular mental or physical challenge.

Bear in mind that each health challenge has its own unique symptoms and consequences. A client living with COPD will have different needs from one facing the challenges of Parkinson's disease. Also, each client with a particular challenge, such as Alzheimer's disease will have a different experience than other clients with the same disease. Merely the age at which the client is diagnosed can have a significant impact on planning. The rate of progression of the disease, which can vary considerably from person to person, can have a material impact on planning. Practitioners should request assistance from a client's care manager, or medical personnel to understand these nuances so planning can be addressed accordingly.

61.3 WHAT STEPS SHOULD BE CONSIDERED

The planning scenarios for elderly and incapacitated persons include the following:

1. Provision for management of the financial affairs of the client or dependent in the event they are unable to do so themselves. This employs such techniques as durable powers of attorney, revocable living trusts, and nominations of persons the individual would want to serve as a guardian or conservator in the event the client needs someone to assist in managing his or her financial and legal affairs. This also should include, as discussed above, addressing recordkeeping, consolidation of assets, financial management, budgeting and more.

2. Providing for support of individuals who, due to age and/or health, are no longer self-supporting and have not accumulated sufficient assets to provide for their cost of living. This might include budgeting, planning for government benefits, and more.

3. Planning for long-term health care, including possible institutional care. This might include reviewing existing long term care coverage, having the client and/or the client's spouse obtaining new coverage, revising financial forecasts to factor in more realistic figures for health care costs, and more. In light of the ongoing uncertainty of government programs and health insurance coverage, this issue should be revisited for most clients periodically.

4. Protecting property from claims of the state or federal government for reimbursement of health care costs through Medicaid planning.

5. Planning to minimize overall taxes. Even for clients not subject to an estate tax, minimizing state estate or inheritance taxes, maximizing income tax basis step up on death, and other planning can be beneficial. Also, there is no certainty what future changes will be enacted for any of the various taxes a client may face. Perhaps the only certainty in estate tax planning is that the laws will continue to change. For aging or ill clients there may be a number of special income tax benefits for medical care, home improvements to make a home accessible, deductions for drugs, and so forth. With many elderly clients choosing to age in place rather than move to an institution, some of these costs could be significant. However, in light of tax proposals to restrict itemized deductions, reduce tax rates, etc. it is uncertain what the value of these benefits will be in future years.

6. Coordination with health care providers to understand the current and likely future status of the client's challenges. In many instances this might be through a care manager as an intermediary between the estate and financial planning team and the medical team.

61.4 TAX IMPLICATIONS

The degree to which planning is tax driven will vary dramatically based on the size of the client's estate, the nature of assets and the quantum of appreciation, the continually evolving tax laws, and a range of other factors. There are some special tax benefits available to the elderly or ill client that should not be overlooked:

- If payments are made by a state to a parent to care for taxpayer's disabled child they are taxable income. This is because the intended beneficiary of the welfare payments was the disabled child, not the child's caregiver/parent.[1]

- A car specifically designed to compensate for disabilities, the portion of the price attributable to its special design is a medical expense.[2]

- Cost of a special school for a handicapped dependent may be deductible as a medical expense if principal reason for attendance is special resources for alleviating the handicap. Room and board are included.[3]

- If a taxpayer becomes physically or mentally incapable of self-care, the taxpayer is treated as using such property as his principal residence during any time during a five-year period in which the taxpayer owns the property and resides in any licensed facility (including a nursing home) to care for an individual in the taxpayer's condition.[4]

- Persons over sixty-five and those who are blind are entitled to an increase in their standard deduction in filing their income tax returns.[5]

- Widows and widowers may use joint income tax returns for two years following the death of the spouse.[6]

- Taxpayers who are supporting dependent family members may be entitled to additional dependency exemptions on their income tax returns. These include parents and grandparents, among others.[7]

- There is a dependent care credit available for certain employment-related expenses.[8]

- Taxpayers (of any age) who sell their personal residences are entitled to an exclusion once every two years for up to $250,000 ($500,000 if married filing jointly) of the gain realized on the sale.[9]

- Legal fees may not provide a deduction because of the 2 percent floor on itemized deductions or the AMT trap. The Code, however, may provide a mechanism to obtain a full deduction as an offset to AGI instead of as a miscellaneous itemized deduction. Costs involving discrimination suits, etc. may be deducted from gross income to arrive at AGI. "Any deduction allowable…for attorney fees…paid by, or on behalf of, the taxpayer in connection with any action involving a claim of unlawful discrimination…" Caution: No line exists on Form 1040. Deductibility could have significant impact on net of tax assets client realizes thus affecting all planning.

- Again, as noted above, there are a range of proposals to change the income and transfer tax systems so that these rules may all change. Whatever occurs in the current administration there is no assurance that a future administration will not again change the rules. Thus, practitioners need to be mindful that the rules will continue to evolve and planning actions will have to be evaluated in light of this.

61.5 IMPLICATIONS AND ISSUES IN COMMUNITY PROPERTY STATES

As a general rule, each spouse has a legal duty to support the other spouse, and both community and separate property can be reached to provide for such support. In addition, community assets can be reached to pay the debts and obligations of either spouse incurred during marriage.

If one spouse becomes incompetent, the law may vary on the right of the other spouse to manage community assets. The other spouse may be able to take over complete management, or may in some circumstances be required to share management with a guardian or conservator for the incompetent spouse.

61.6 LONG-TERM CARE PLANNING[10]

Long-term care includes a continuum of services from nursing home care to assisted living to home health care to adult day care. Although a large portion of the overall cost for long-term care may be paid by federal programs, the restrictions and uncertainty of these benefits makes reliance on government assistance unwise. Proper planning for long-term care involves either self-insurance – if retirement assets and income are sufficient – or the purchase of a long-term care insurance contract. It should also be born in mind that the average costs of a couple age sixty-five for medical care for the duration of their lives is approximately $300,000. While that amount would bankrupt the vast majority of American families, for the clients of many practitioners that amount while potentially unpleasant is not ruinous.

Long-term care insurance contracts vary with respect to benefit amounts, elimination (waiting) periods, maximum benefit amounts, inflation protection, and benefit triggers. It is important to choose a combination of policy features that meets a client's needs for protection while remaining affordable enough for the client to maintain the policy in effect until it may be needed. Many clients already have existing long term care coverage and often do not understand the economics and scope of coverage. Practitioners should be certain that someone on the planning team reviews and explains this to the clients. Further, if a client does become incapacitated, someone on the planning team should review existing coverage to identify benefits as well as reporting and other obligations the client/insured may have.

The cost of long-term care in a nursing home and the client's ability to pay a portion of that cost generally determine the benefit amount needed from a long-term care insurance policy. The benefit amount is usually stated in terms of a maximum daily benefit amount. It is also important to factor in the long-term impact of inflation on the real value of daily benefit amount.

The average length of stay in a nursing home for current residents is 2.4 years. A 2010 study however, suggests that, for many clients, the duration of a nursing home stay may be much less. The median length of stay in a nursing home before death was five months. The average length of stay was longer at fourteen months due to a small number of study participants who had very long lengths of stay. 65 percent died within one year of nursing home admission, and 53 percent died within six months of nursing home admission.[11] Home health care providers offer a spectrum of services for those seniors who want to "age in place." Most home care is non-medical care provided by paraprofessionals, and other care is delivered by nurses, therapists or specially-trained home health aides, under the direction of a physician or nurse. They can provide personal assistance or cooking or laundry services and the like.

Forty percent of people who need long term care are working-age adults between eighteen and sixty-four. There is a 68 percent chance that an individual over age sixty-five will become cognitively impaired or unable to complete at least two activities of daily living-including dressing, bathing or eating over their lifetime. On the aggregate, of those who enter a nursing home, 50 percent will stay an average of 2.5 years; 10 percent will stay there five years or longer. 70 percent of single people who enter a nursing home are impoverished within one year. Half of all couples are impoverished within one year of one spouse entering a nursing home.[12]

Benefits offered by a "qualified long-term care insurance contract" – a contract that meets certain federal statutory requirements – are generally not includable in income.[13] However, there is a limit on the amount of qualified long-term care benefits that may be excluded from income. Generally, if the total periodic long-term care payments received from all policies and any periodic payments received that are treated as paid by reason of the death of the insured (under Code section 101(g)) exceed a daily limitation, the excess must be included in income. The daily limitation is equal to the greater of the dollar amount limitation or the actual costs incurred for qualified long-term care services provided for the insured. For 2023, the dollar amount limitation is $300 per day. It is adjusted for inflation annually.

The projected 2023 long-term care insurance federal tax deductible limits are as follows for varying ages of the taxpayer:[14]

- 40 or less - $480;

- More than 40 but not more than 50 - $890;

- More than 50 but not more than 60 - $1,790;

- More than 60 but not more than 70 - $4,770; and

- More than 70 - $5,960.

It has become quite common for clients to purchase a long term care feature or rider on or as part of a life insurance policy. When a long-term care rider is added to a life insurance policy any payout is an acceleration of the life insurance death benefit. The insured may select the long-term care amount and features when buying a policy. The long-term care benefits are paid income tax free after qualifying requirements are met. If the client does not utilize the long-term care feature, beneficiaries will receive an income tax-free death benefit as long as the policy remains in force. Practitioners should be cautious that while life insurance is traditionally held in an irrevocable trust (and perhaps should generally continue to be so held even if the estate tax is irrelevant) a policy with a long term care feature may present tax and legal impediments if held in an irrevocable trust. Will the insured be able to access the benefits under the policy? Might the "benefits" be received by the trust and loaned to the insured? If the insured accesses the benefits, will the proceeds be included in the insureds gross estate (and even if the estate tax is inapplicable, will the policy be reachable by creditors of the insured thereby emasculating the trust)?

61.7 ACCELERATED DEATH BENEFITS AND VIATICAL SETTLEMENTS

Several years ago, partially in response to the growing number of persons with AIDS, some life insurance companies began offering persons with terminal illnesses or long-term medical care needs an "accelerated death benefit," the opportunity to receive a portion of the death proceeds from their life insurance policies prior to the insured person's actual death.

Generally, any amount received under a life insurance contract on the life of a terminally ill insured or a chronically ill insured will be treated as an amount paid by reason of the death of the insured.[15] Amounts received under a life insurance contract by reason of the death of the insured are not includable in gross income. Thus, an accelerated death benefit meeting these requirements will generally be received free of income tax.

However, amounts paid to a chronically ill individual are subject to the same limitations that apply to long-term care benefits. The requirements to qualify are quite stringent and even a client who is quite ill may not qualify for this benefit. Accelerated death benefits paid to terminally ill individuals are not subject to this limit.

A terminally-ill individual is a person who has been certified by a physician as having an illness or physical condition that can reasonably be expected to result in death within twenty-four months following the certification. A chronically ill individual is a person who is not terminally ill and who has been certified as being unable to perform, without substantial assistance, at least two Activities of Daily Living (ADLs) for at least ninety days or a person with a similar level of disability. Further, a person may be considered chronically ill if he requires substantial supervision to protect himself from threats to health and safety due to severe cognitive impairment and this condition has been certified by a health care practitioner within the previous twelve months. The activities of daily living are:

1. eating;
2. toileting;
3. transferring (i.e. from sitting to standing);
4. bathing;
5. dressing; and
6. continence.

There is one exception to this general rule of non-includability for accelerated death benefits. The rules outlined above do not apply to any amount paid to any taxpayer other than the insured if the taxpayer has an insurable interest in the life of the insured because the insured is a director, officer or employee of the taxpayer or if the insured is financially interested in any trade or business of the taxpayer.

Viatical Settlements

A viatical settlement is the sale or assignment of any portion of the death benefit under a life insurance contract on the life of a terminally or chronically ill insured to a viatical settlement provider. In a viatical settlement, the amount paid for the sale or assignment will be treated as an amount paid under the life insurance contract by reason of the insured's death. In other words, such an amount will not be included in income. A viatical settlement provider is defined as "any person regularly engaged in the trade or business of purchasing, or taking assignments of, life insurance contracts on the lives of insureds" who are terminally or chronically ill provided that certain licensing and other requirements, discussed below, are met.

61.8 GOVERNMENT ASSISTANCE PROGRAMS

Several federal programs are available to assist in providing health care for the elderly and disabled, including:

1. Social Security disability benefits where an individual is unable to engage in gainful employment by reason of medically established mental or physical impairment. This impairment must be expected to last until death, or continuously over a period of at least twelve months.

2. Supplemental security income, often called SSI, which provides for needy persons who are elderly, blind, or otherwise disabled.

3. Medicare, which provides medical benefits on the basis of the age of the person, without regard to need.

4. Medicaid, which provides medical assistance regardless of age to the needy.

Medicare

Taxpayers who are sixty-five and eligible for social security, or who are sixty-five and whose spouses are eligible for social security, are eligible for Medicare. Part A of Medicare provides hospital insurance at no cost except for deductible and coinsurance amounts that must be paid by the patient. Part A also provides limited coverage for care in a skilled nursing facility, a hospice, or post-hospital home health services. Part B of Medicare primarily covers physician's services, and is voluntary. Premiums are required under Part B. Certain individuals over sixty-five who are not covered by Part A may elect voluntary coverage by paying premiums if they are enrolled in Part B. Certain disabled persons under sixty-five can also be eligible for Medicare benefits. A person can sign up three months before the month they will turn sixty-five in order to avoid delay in receiving benefits. Accordingly, if a person signs up for Part A or Part B coverage and their birthday is July 20, if they enroll in March, April or May, their coverage will start on July 1. If the person signs up after that, their coverage may be delayed and they may have to pay a higher premium. A client can qualify for Medicare based on their spouse's work record if they are at least age sixty-two and the spouse is at least age sixty-five. A client may also qualify based on the work record of a divorced or deceased spouse.[16] Medicare Part D covers prescription drugs.

Medicaid

Medicaid is a joint federal and state program that provides assistance for health care to certain aged, disabled, or blind individuals. The intent is to provide help to needy individuals. In some cases, this is integrated with the requirements for supplemental security income (SSI) mentioned above. Many states impose an income cap based on SSI requirements. The tests here are largely dependent on state law. There are also special requirements for nursing home benefits. Bear in mind that all these rules may be affected by governmental legislation and may be in flux.

Eligibility

Eligibility for Medicaid depends on the level of one's resources. "Resources" refer to assets owned by an individual or available to an individual. If these exceed a certain dollar value, that individual will be ineligible for various benefits, particularly nursing home care. These generally include assets owned by the spouse of the individual. In addition, the income of the individual and spouse are also available resources.

An individual's personal residence can count as an asset for purposes of Medicaid eligibility depending on state law. For example, in California, the residence is exempt even if the individual is in a nursing home six months or less, because the individual is presumed to intend to return to it.

Congress has imposed and continues to impose strict limits on transfers of assets to achieve Medicaid eligibility. In addition, the Deficit Reduction Act of 2005 made changes designed to thwart planning in this area. For example, the value of any assets transferred within sixty months before the individual makes an application for Medicaid will be considered an available resource.[17] (Under prior law, the look-back period was thirty-six months.) The penalties are in the form of denial of Medicaid benefits for a period of months depending on the value of the property transferred. There are exceptions, including one for transfers to children who are "caretakers" for their parent. There are other exceptions for transfers to spouses, minor children, trusts for disabled children, etc.

For assets transferred to trusts, the look-back period is still sixty months (or five years) from the date the individual makes a Medicaid application or the date the individual enters a nursing home. Assets transferred to trusts within sixty months prior to these dates are considered an available resource.[18] This includes trusts, other than trusts created by will, created by the individual, their spouse, and certain third persons, such as conservators and trustees. The purpose for which the trust was created is not relevant.

Assets in a revocable trust are presumed available resources, regardless of when the trust was created. Further, if any assets are transferred from the revocable trust to another individual within the sixty-month period, which is also a transfer subject to the sixty-month look-back period.

Assets in an irrevocable trust are also deemed to be available resources if payment could be made to the individual from the trust. There are various exemptions, and the statutes are confusing as to the extent of availability.

Social Security Disability Benefits

First and foremost, an individual must have worked in jobs which required contributions into the social security system. An individual who is unable to engage in any substantial gainful activity by reason of a medically determinable physical or mental impairment may be entitled to social security disability benefits if he:

1. is under age sixty-five;

2. has been disabled for twelve months, is expected to be disabled for at least twelve months, or has a disability which is expected to result in death;

3. is "fully insured" under social security (see below);

4. has worked under social security for at least five of the ten years (twenty out of forty quarters) just before becoming disabled, or if disability begins before age thirty-one but after age twenty-four, one may qualify if they have credit for working half the time between age twenty-one and the date of their disability. For example, the Social Security website states that "if you become disabled at age twenty-seven, you would need credit for three years of work out of the past six years."[19]

5. files an application for disability benefits; and

6. completes a five-month waiting period or is exempt from the waiting period.

A person is "fully insured" under social security if he has ten years (forty quarters) of employment under social security or if he has worked under social security for as many quarters as there are years since he reached age twenty-one and before the year in which he became disabled.

61.9 SPECIAL NEEDS TRUSTS

A special needs trust is one established by clients who have children who are under a disability and are receiving supplemental social security (SSI) benefits, or other forms of state or federal assistance. They are intended to permit the parents to furnish some economic benefits to their children without disqualifying them for public assistance. The device may also be used to provide for elderly persons who are disabled, such as a parent.

The purpose of the special needs trust is to permit payments by the trustee to cover needs of the disabled person which do not affect his eligibility for public assistance. The special needs trust deliberately provides that it will not provide for basics such as food, clothing, shelter, and in particular, medical care. It provides only for non-necessaries such as birthday and holiday gifts and comforts of life that cannot be considered basic needs.

The guidelines for what assets may be considered available resources to the disabled person are found in the Program Operational Manual, commonly referred to as POM, which is used by government representatives. If the assets in the trust are available for the basic needs of the disabled person, they may result in denial of public assistance, or the appropriate government agency may even seek to compel reimbursement of public assistance payments from the trust assets.

On the other hand, property held in such a trust does not count as a resource of the disabled person if access to the trust assets is restricted. In general, such trusts should follow a discretionary or protective trust format used for asset protection, but must be even more restrictive. For example, if the trust provided that the trustee could use trust assets only for the "support" of the disabled person, it would count as an available resource.

Such trusts should specifically provide that the trustee may not make any payments that cover items provided by public assistance programs. The trust must be irrevocable and an independent trustee is preferred. It may be part of the basic estate plan of the parents, either in a will or revocable trust that takes effect at death. While the trust could be created irrevocably while the parents are alive, this is generally discouraged. It may have gift tax consequences, and government officials must be informed whenever the disabled person becomes the beneficiary of an irrevocable trust.

To guard against attacks from the providers of public assistance, these trusts may provide for contingent beneficiaries, such as other children, who could become the exclusive beneficiaries of the trust if such an attack is launched. The trust may also have a destruct clause, providing that if the providers do attempt to reach it, or use it to disqualify the disabled person, it will terminate and be distributed entirely too contingent beneficiaries, such as the other children.

When planning for aging parents with adult children with special needs, consider the unique circumstances of these families and adjust planning accordingly. Too often "traditional" planning is provided to these clients and it may not suffice:

- What happens if the elderly parents are caregivers to the adult disabled child?

- Should a guardianship be obtained so that parent has legal authority to act for the adult disabled child?

- If a guardianship is obtained, consider the advantages of naming a successor guardian to address the eventuality of the parent's aging.

- If the parent has a durable power of attorney and revocable trust to manage his or her assets during disability who is named as agent and trustee? Does the financial agent/trustee differ from the successor guardian? Will they cooperate? If it is the same person where are the checks and balances?

- Does the family even need a special needs trust? In some instances, it has automatically been assumed that an adult disabled child should have a supplemental or special needs trust. But for some wealthy families the child may not need or be taking advantages of governmental programs and the family's resources are sufficient that governmental aid is not needed. In these instances the classic supplemental needs trust may unduly restrict the special child's access to benefit from family wealth.

The key point is address the client family's circumstances. Don't merely apply textbook planning.

Special Needs Trusts and Medicaid Eligibility

Both state and federal law provide that if the individual or spouse transfers assets to an irrevocable trust for the benefit of the individual, all of its assets are deemed available resources.[20] However, this will not apply to trusts created by third persons, such as children for their parents, which should be structured as special needs trusts. Many persons who are disabled and have a successful outcome to a lawsuit will place the amount recovered into a special needs trust. This can be established by a parent, guardian or the court. These trusts must include special "payback" provisions providing that the state Medicaid agency will be repaid for medical assistance granted the beneficiary.

61.10 DISABILITY PLANNING

Disability planning should be approached from a very broad perspective depending on the client's circumstances. It might include:

- Disability buy-out insurance to provide for the repurchase of business equity interests when an equity holder is incapacitated.

- Employment agreement provisions. Negotiating salary continuation and other provisions may be critical to later health challenges.

- Shareholder operating or partnership agreements. These may govern salary and benefit continuation, buyout provisions (although often these are contained in a separate buy-out agreement listed above). Some agreements are rather simplistic in their treatment of health challenges. Others might or should contain quite complex treatment of incapacity providing for partial disability, temporary disability and permanent disability. Different types of provisions might be provided for general equity owners and others for founding or senior equity owners.

- General retirement and savings planning. Disability from this perspective can be viewed in a manner similar to early retirement so that general retirement planning is always vital to disability planning.

- A range of estate planning documents, discussed in this and other chapters, are essential to disability planning.

Also, if a client does become incapacitated, practitioners should be careful to identify and then review any contractual or other arrangement that might provide cash flow or other resources to the disabled client. The above checklist can be used in that context as well.

Disability Income Insurance

Disability income insurance provides coverage for lost earnings suffered during the period of a disability that prevents a client from working. Disability policies typically pay benefits equal to a substantial percentage (50 to 70 percent) of regular earnings, providing enough income for a reasonable standard of living.

Disability income policies differ with respect to the elimination (waiting) period, the benefit period, and the definition of disability an insured must meet to qualify for benefits. Some policies only pay benefits if an insured is unable to perform any gainful employment;

other policies may pay benefits if an insured is unable to perform the duties of his particular profession. Policies may pay benefits for life or to a specific age.

The benefits paid by disability income policies are tax-free to the extent the policy premiums were paid by the individual with after-tax dollars.[21] Benefits attributable to policy premiums paid by an employer are fully includable in gross income. Under an individual policy, the premiums paid in the current year are taken into account. Under a group policy, the employee's contributions for the last three years, if known, are considered.

For self-employed individuals or professionals, a disability income policy that pays a percentage of net business income without taking into account on-going business expenses may not be sufficient. For example, a business owner may bring in monthly revenue of $10,000, which pays for $5,000 in monthly business expenses and provides $5,000 in monthly take-home pay. A disability income policy that pays 60 percent or $3,000 per month in tax-free benefits may adequately provide for living expenses, but does not account for any on-going business expenses.

Business overhead expense policies (also called business continuation coverage) are available to fill the gap. Business expense policies pay on a reimbursement basis for actual expenses incurred. These expenses may include fringe benefits paid for by the business for the benefit of the business owner. Business expense policies generally have short elimination periods and offer an open-ended benefit period with a maximum dollar benefit. The policies are generally intended to last for shorter periods, from six months up to three years. After longer periods, presumably, a business will be sold or wrapped up.

61.11 INCAPACITY PLANNING

Before a client is disabled, important steps can be taken to minimize the possible future difficulties. As noted above, if the client has a durable power of attorney for financial matters, a health proxy and a revocable trust, the need for a court appointed guardianship may be reduced. Further, a healthy client can specify who he or she would want appointed as the guardian of the property (in the financial power of attorney) and the guardian of his or her person (in the health care proxy). So advance planning can provide greater individual protection and control.

The most common tools used for incapacity planning are guardianships and conservatorships. Guardianship is a fiduciary relationship created by the law for the purpose of enabling one person, the guardian, to manage the person or estate, or both, of another person, the ward, when the law has determined that the ward is incapable of managing his person or estate himself. Wards fall into two general categories: (1) minors, and (2) adults who have been legally adjudged incompetent to act for themselves.

The term "guardian" is used to refer both to the guardian of the person of the ward and to the guardian of the ward's property. The guardian of the person takes custody of the ward, looks after his personal needs, and in general performs the duties performed by parents of a minor (except the duty of support). The guardian of a ward's property, sometimes known as a conservator, a curator, or a committee, is charged with the responsibility of investing and managing the estate of the ward. One who is appointed a guardian, without any further words of limitation, is held to serve in both guardianship capacities. In this discussion, the term "guardian," without further description, should be taken to refer to a guardian serving in both capacities. A guardian of the property merely will be referred to as a conservator.

Unlike a trustee, a guardian does not take title to the ward's property. Title to the ward's property remains in the ward; the guardian takes custody and control of the ward's property as an officer of the court under whose supervision he acts. While a trustee derives his powers from the trust instrument, a guardian derives his powers from the law.

The court normally having jurisdiction to appoint a guardian is the court in the state of the ward's domicile that has jurisdiction of probate matters. Since a guardian's powers at common law do not extend outside the state in which the guardian is appointed, and since a guardian functions as an officer of the court that appointed him, courts are reluctant to appoint as guardians anyone not a resident within the jurisdiction of the court.

Some states have statutes requiring guardians appointed within the state to be residents of the state. Sometimes, therefore, an ancillary conservator of the estate will be appointed in the state (outside the ward's domicile) where the ward owns property. In many cases, however, the state (outside the ward's domicile) where the ward actually resides or where his property is located will, as a matter of comity, recognize the authority of the guardian appointed by the state of the ward's domicile. But "full faith and credit" requirements of the U.S. Constitution do not appear to hold much sway in guardianship; if a local court thinks the welfare of the ward requires appointment of a local guardian, such action is likely to be taken whether or not a guardian was appointed in the state of the ward's domicile. Some courts will, if necessary, and if statutes permit, appoint nonresident guardians.

61.12 FREQUENTLY ASKED QUESTIONS

Question – What is medigap insurance?

Answer – "Medigap" is a generic name for health insurance which covers some or all of the expenses not covered by either Part A or Part B of Medicare.

Question – May an individual or his spouse waive or forfeit pension rights to become eligible for Medicaid?

Answer – No. Any waiver of pension income, inheritances, or damage claims, as in personal injury suits, is ineffective.

Question – Will amounts paid to family members who are furnishing personal care for an individual be counted as resources?

Answer – While reasonable payments for personal care are not viewed as gifts for Medicaid purposes, payment for past services are viewed with suspicion.

Question – If an individual transfers property by gift, but retains a life estate, what amount will be treated as an available resource?

Answer – According to the federal government, the actuarial value of the life estate, based on the life expectancy of the individual, is subtracted from the value of the property, and the remainder is considered the gift of an available resource.[22]

Question – If an individual purchases a life annuity, will that be subject to the look back gift rules?

Answer – If the annuity is "actuarially sound," based on the life expectancy of the individual, it will not be deemed a partial gift.

Question – Will the transfer of a personal residence to either a revocable or irrevocable trust trigger the look-back rules?

Answer – No. Since the personal residence is an excluded asset under the Medicaid rules, the transfer is not subject to the rule. However, the federal government takes the position[23] that it is a resource. As noted above, the personal residence is often an exempt asset.

Question – Three adult children are contributing equally to the support of their elderly parent. May any of them claim her as a dependent?

Answer – Since no child is furnishing over one half of the parent's support, none of them can claim her as a dependent unless they sign a multiple support agreement. Essentially, this is an agreement that one of the children will claim the mother as a dependent, and the others will not. It may be feasible for the children to create a support agreement that can facilitate maximizing this tax benefit.

Question – When one spouse is in a nursing home, to what extent are the assets of the other spouse protected from claims for reimbursement for public assistance or counted as available resources of the institutionalized spouse?

Answer – The law permits the other spouse, who is called the "community" spouse, to retain assets of a certain value. The amount varies from state to state. In this regard, revocable trusts, may cause substantial problems. If the trust language permits the use of trust assets for the support of the institutionalized spouse, the trust will be considered an available resource. Further, the community spouse may not be able to claim any exemption for the trust assets since they are not in his name. The revocable trust should contain specific language dealing with these issues.

Question – Do children have the obligation to support or maintain an indigent parent?

Answer – Some states, such as Pennsylvania[24] provide that a child of an indigent person, in some situations has a limited responsibility to financially assist or maintain an indigent parent.

With the increased focus on maximizing income tax basis when a client has an elderly parent or other relative that they support this may present an optimal opportunity to grant a general power of appointment to cause trust assets to be included in that financially not well-off parent or family member's estate.

CHAPTER ENDNOTES

1. Carolyn Gay Harper, TC Summ. Op. 2011-56 (U.S.T.C. May 2, 2011).
2. Rev. Rul. 76-80, 1976-1 CB 71.
3. Treas. Reg. §1.213-1(e)(1)(v)(a).
4. I.R.C. §121(d)(7).
5. I.R.C. §63.
6. I.R.C. §2.
7. I.R.C. §§151, 152.
8. I.R.C. §21.
9. I.R.C. §121.
10. See Carol Einhorn, "What Every Professional Should Know About Long Term Care," Leimberg Information Services, Inc. (LISI) Eldercare Planning Newsletter # 14, January 14th, 2013 at http://www.leimbergservices.com.
11. Eric Widera, "Length of Stay in Nursing Homes at the End of Life," Aug. 26, 2010 at https://geripal.org/length-of-stay-in-nursing-homes-at-end/.
12. See Carol Einhorn, "What Every Professional Should Know About Long Term Care," Leimberg Information Services, Inc. (LISI) Eldercare Planning Newsletter # 14, Jan. 14, 2013 at http://www.leimbergservices.com.
13. I.R.C. §7702B.
14. Rev. Proc. 2022-38.
15. I.R.C. §101.
16. An online questionnaire can aide clients in determining eligibility: http://www.medicare.gov/eligibilitypremiumcalc/?AspxAutoDetectCookieSupport=1#eligibility.
17. 42 U.S.C. §1396p(c)(1)(B)(i).
18. Id.
19. There is a chart for other ages at: www.ssa.gov/retire2/credits3.html.
20. 42 U.S.C. §1396A(k).
21. Treas. Reg. §1.105-1.
22. Transmittal No. 64, State Medicaid Manual, Nov., 1994.
23. Id.
24. 23 Pa. C.S.A. 4603.

DURABLE POWER OF ATTORNEY

CHAPTER 62

62.1 INTRODUCTION

A power of attorney is a written document that enables an individual, called the "principal," to designate another person, called an "agent" or an "attorney-in-fact," to act on the principal's behalf. The common use of the term "attorney-in-fact" has caused untold confusion among consumers as it is often interpreted to imply that a lawyer must be named as agent, which is entirely incorrect. The power of attorney grants authority to an agent to act in the place of the principal. According to the Uniform Power of Attorney Act, "Power of attorney" means a writing or other record that grants authority to an agent to act in the place of the principal, whether or not the term power of attorney is used." But remember, while the uniform act is a useful and informative guide, state law will govern each client's power of attorney.

With the aging population and the widespread incidence of chronic illness (approximately 130 million Americans are living with chronic disease (see Chapter 63), powers of attorney should not be a mere "throw-in" when a client has a will or revocable trust completed. Rather, practitioners should educate clients as to the significance of this document and the benefits of really planning and tailoring a power of attorney to each client's particular circumstances. This is particularly important considering the evolution of the circumstances affecting many clients. The estate tax system has changed significantly over time. Many form powers of attorney were created when the estate tax exemption was $600,000 and the annual gift exclusion $10,000. In that environment, many more clients were concerned about maximizing annual gifts. Now for most clients this is irrelevant. At the time most power of attorney forms were created, the phrase "elder financial abuse" had not been coined. Thus, many powers have not yet adapted sufficiently.

The scope of the power can be severely limited and is referred to as a "limited" or "special" power of attorney. One use of a special power is when a client is a solo-practitioner licensed professional and the professional might grant a special power of attorney to another licensed professional to operate the practice in the event of disability (when this is done also consider designating a special executor with similar licensing under the client's will to dispose of that practice if the client dies owning it). It can also be limited to certain specific situations, such as actions regarding the principal's closely-held business or literary works. Such an agent may be a person with special knowledge or particular expertise. Another common use of a special power of attorney is for handling a house closing or similar one-time transaction if the client is going to be unavailable on the particular date. Most powers of attorney tend to be quite broad and are referred to as "general" powers of attorney. These documents tend to provide the agent with all the legal powers the principal might exercise. Since the objective of most powers of attorney is to designate someone to act in a future and unknown emergency the prudent course is to make that grant of authority as broad as possible since the nature of that emergency cannot be predicted. This rationale is likely the correct approach for many clients but also part of the explanation as to how and why powers of attorney are too frequently used in an elder abuse scam to take advantage of a client. Practitioners should be cautious to guide clients creating broad general powers of attorney documents of steps to take to monitor the use of those documents and to create other safeguards.

A "durable" power of attorney is a power of attorney that is not terminated by subsequent disability or incapacity of the principal. At this date, all states have recognized some form of durable power of attorney. The vast majority of such states have either enacted in total the durable power of attorney provisions of the Uniform Probate Code (UPC) or drafted their own statutes in conformity with the provisions of the Uniform Power of Attorney Act. The Uniform Power of Attorney further defines "durable" as meaning "not terminated by the principal's incapacity."[1]

Many states, such as Pennsylvania, provide that unless the document specifically states otherwise, all powers of attorney shall be durable.[2] This is consistent with the Uniform Power of Attorney Act.

While a durable power of attorney should be a part of most estate plans to address issues of aging and disability, in many instances a funded revocable trust is a more powerful tool. Give some consideration to the relationship between the two documents. Should the agent be able to modify or revoke the revocable trust? Should the power expressly state that the agent should not? Few institutional trustees are willing to serve as agents under a power of attorney so that the situation of a family member/friend agent under the power having to work with an institutional successor trustee under the revocable trust is not uncommon. As the population ages these situations will arise with greater frequency. Regular meetings of both fiduciaries and coordination with the planning team will be important to minimize issues.

62.2 WHEN IS A POWER OF ATTORNEY APPROPRIATE?

1. Since no client can predict future health challenges, incarceration or other issues that might necessitate the use of a power of attorney, one should be created for every adult client. While some view powers as a document primarily for elderly or inform clients, these documents should be standard for clients' college bound children since it may be quite useful for a parent to have a power of attorney for a child living at some distance. When the principal is elderly and there is a significant chance that the individual will be incapacitated, the use of a broadly drawn durable power of attorney may negate the necessity of petitioning the local court for appointment of a guardian of the client's property, or a conservator, to handle the principal's assets. However, the combination of a funded revocable trust and durable power of attorney will be a more powerful and comprehensive means of addressing this situation. See Chapter 64.

2. When an individual is living with a physical disability or illness, the effect of which could lead to a permanent or long term incapacity, or could otherwise hinder that client from handling financial and legal affairs.

3. In all situations where an individual desires to provide for the continuity of the management of the individual's assets in the event that the individual is unable to manage those assets for either a short or long duration of time because of physical or mental incapacity, incarceration, or a host of other factors (if provided for in the power of attorney document). The durable power of attorney permits the individual, when competent, to make a determination of who will handle the individual's affairs. This statement, however, over simplifies the incredible array of decisions that may be embodied in a durable power of attorney tailored to address a particular client's circumstances.

4. As a temporary and expedient substitute for a living revocable trust. The trust device is more burdensome and more costly than the durable power of attorney. Also, if the client has a living revocable trust, i.e. one with provisions regarding the trustee's duties during the grantor's lifetime, the assets must be retitled to the trust in order for the trustee to administer them. However, even with a revocable living trust, it is still necessary to have a durable power of attorney for assets which are titled outside of the trust and for handling certain matters that may not be assignable to a trust, such as legal claims and other matters.

5. To provide succession planning for a particular business, professional practice or even a specific assets. If a special or limited power of attorney is used for this purpose then care should be taken to avoid conflict between such a special power and a general power that might be provided to a different person to cover all other matters.

6. To avoid the necessity of legal proceedings to establish a legal guardianship for the property of the person, or conservatorship, for an individual who may face short or long term incapacity.

7. Perhaps some consideration should be given to when a power of attorney may not be appropriate.

If the client/principal has no one really trustworthy or capable to name to serve as agent caution should be exercised. Merely because powers of attorney are ubiquitous in estate plans doesn't mean they are always appropriate.

62.3 WHAT ARE THE REQUIREMENTS FOR A VALID POWER OF ATTORNEY?

1. The principal (the one giving the power) must be of legal age and competent at the time the power is given.

2. The power must be signed by the principal or in the principal's presence by another individual directed to sign his name. It is strongly recommended that the principal sign in the presence of a notary public because, then, there is a strong presumption that the signature is genuine. It is also recommended that two witnesses sign the power of attorney as well. Even if the client's home state has a lesser standard using a higher standard for signing is recommended. In this way if the client has powers in a different state the likelihood of that state accepting the power may be increased with more formality in the signing. Many states will not automatically recognize a power of attorney. This concept is referred to as the "portability" of the power of attorney. Although the Uniform Power of Attorney Act has made some inroads gaps remain. If a client has significant assets in another state it might be advisable to have counsel in that state prepare a power of attorney under that state's laws.

3. The Uniform Power of Attorney Act, as well as applicable state statutes, set forth any additional requirements which must be satisfied. The particular state's statute may also include a form power of attorney that will be valid and acceptable (often called Statutory Form Power of Attorney). While it can be advantageous to use a statutory form power of attorney, those powers are by definition standardized and not tailored to reflect any particular client's circumstances.

4. The attorney in fact (the one receiving the power) must be of legal age, and have sufficient capacity, at the time the power is exercised. While these technical requirements are clear, meeting them does not assure that the named agent has the skills, time or temperament to serve. Practitioners should endeavor to discuss with clients in some detail their choice of agent, and once those choices are made, encourage the client to review with the agent the responsibilities and details of the position.

5. Many states have statutory formalities that must be met for the validity of the power, or in order to have the provisions in the statute governing third party acceptance of it to apply. For example, Pennsylvania requires a preamble to the power of attorney which must appear in capital letters and which is signed by the principal. It does not negate the power of attorney if this preamble is not there. However, if those words are not there, upon challenge, the agent would have the burden of demonstrating that the exercise is proper. This capital lettered preamble warns the principal of the broad powers to handle, sell or dispose of the principal's property without any requirement of prior approval by the principal. By signing this acknowledgement, the principal has been cautioned as to the broad nature of the powers he is giving the agent. Since it is not possible to determine which state a power may have to be used in having two witnesses and a notary is recommended regardless of what the client's home state law provides for.

6. In the event the power of attorney only goes into effect when the principal is incapacitated, it is known as a "springing" power (discussed further in Frequently Asked Questions). A power of attorney that is effective immediately has no particular technical name but might be referred to as an "immediate" power. While many clients prefer a springing power, from the perspective that why should the named agent be able to exercise authority over the principal's assets before needed, using springing powers is fraught with issues. Some states prohibit them. Even where permitted, triggering the mechanism to make the power "spring" into effect can often be quite problematic.

62.4 HOW TO PLAN FOR A POWER OF ATTORNEY – A GENERAL EXAMPLE

Assume your client is in her mid-sixties and single. The average age of diagnosis of Alzheimer's disease is seventy-three. That means fully half of those diagnosed are so diagnosed prior to that age. Taking steps to protect her from the potential risks of aging, dementia, and more is an essential part of any planning. If she has close and reliable friends or family who can serve as agents they should be named. Once named she should be guided as to having some discussion with the first and perhaps next successor agent as to their roles, what steps they might need to take and who they can consult for assistance.

It is also important for practitioners to discuss such financial basics as preparing a budget, consolidating and simplifying asset holdings, creating appropriate records, backups for those records, etc. A budget can be invaluable to a third party stepping in as agent as it provides a roadmap of lifestyle and appropriate expenditures, etc. Consolidating and simplifying asset holdings will make it more management for an agent to take over the client's finances. Too many clients have more than a dozen financial accounts, multiple IRAs and more. The sheer volume makes management a challenge. Recordkeeping is also key. For an agent to decipher a handwritten check register with sparse information will not make it easy to identify what bills to pay or what issues might exist.

Too often planning for powers of attorney has focused on gift provisions. The reality is that with an aging population and the irrelevance of the federal estate tax for most even wealth clients makes that discussion of less or even no importance. In fact, for most clients it might actually be preferable to expressly state in the power that no gift powers are granted. The rationale for an express prohibition is to avoid any ambiguity and perhaps to thereby provide some measure of protection of an agent abusing the financial power of attorney to commit elder financial abuse.

62.5 HOW TO PLAN FOR A POWER OF ATTORNEY – GIFT PROVISION EXAMPLE

Assume your client is on his deathbed on December 28. He could make annual exclusion gifts for this year and if he's alive four days later on January 1 he could make another round of gifts. None of these gifts would be includable in his estate for federal estate tax purposes.

The problem is, he may be mentally competent–and physically able–to act on the 28th of December. But if he becomes either physically or mentally incompetent after that date, the estate tax savings he is legally entitled to will be lost unless someone is entitled by state law to act (specifically to make gifts) on his behalf. The client could name a child or other family member as his attorney-in-fact and give that person the power (in addition to other powers) to make gifts on his behalf. The agent could draw checks on his account to each of the donees (just as if he drew the checks).

For many clients the above gifts may actually prove counterproductive. If the assets given have appreciated, or appreciate post-gift and pre-death, it may have been better to have made no gift and to have instead left the assets in the estate to qualify for a basis step-up on death. For wealthy clients subject to a significant state or federal estate tax the traditional annual gift powers are woefully inadequate. Those powers also do not address the annual inflation adjustments in the lifetime exemption amount. When appropriate, it may be advisable for the power of attorney to authorize gifts of up to the client's remaining gift and GST tax exemption amount.

62.6 HOW TO PLAN FOR A POWER OF ATTORNEY – ILLUSTRATIVE DOCUMENT

An example of a broadly drawn durable power of attorney appears at Figure 62.1. Each state may have its own unique language required for a legal durable power of attorney. For example, Florida has recently adopted a new form for its power of attorney in which it is necessary to include a reference to the Florida statute regarding durable power of attorney.[3] It is important to check for relevant information needed in the state for which clients and advisors reside.

The form illustrated in Figure 62.1 is the form of power of attorney but does not reflect any particular state law. Note that in paragraph 14, it allows unlimited gifting to the spouse. This is limited to the HEMS (health, education, maintenance and support) standard to avoid any argument that it is tantamount to a general power of appointment. Some commentators believe that limitation is not necessary or appropriate. If the gift is made in a fiduciary capacity it may not matter according to other commentators. Also, limiting inter-spousal gifts to a HEMS standard might well hinder important asset protection and personal planning.

Planning considerations are inserted throughout this standard form in brackets to suggest some of the many ways the power of attorney might be tailored for specific client matters.

DURABLE POWER OF ATTORNEY CHAPTER 62

Figure 62.1

POWER OF ATTORNEY

[Illustrative state statutory required statement]

The purpose of this Power of Attorney is to give the person you designate (your "Agent") broad powers to handle your property, which may include powers to sell or otherwise dispose of any real or personal property without advance notice to you or approval by you.

This power of attorney does not impose a duty on your agent to exercise granted powers, but when powers are exercised, your agent must use due care to act for your benefit and in accordance with this power of attorney.

Your agent may exercise the powers given here throughout your lifetime, even after you become incapacitated, unless you expressly limit the duration of these powers or you revoke these powers or a court acting on your behalf terminates your agent's authority.

Your agent must keep your funds separate from your agent's funds. [**Consider whether an exemption should be provided for family members, especially a spouse**]

A court can take away the powers of your agent if it finds your agent is not acting properly.

If there is anything about this form that you do not understand, you should ask a lawyer of your own choosing to explain it to you.

I have read or had explained to me this notice and I understand its contents.

Dated: _____ _____

<u>Principal's signature</u>

KNOW ALL MEN BY THESE PRESENTS, that I, _____, of _____, hereby revoke any general power of attorney [**Comment: Consider whether special powers should be revoked**] that I have heretofore given to any person, and, by these presents, do constitute and appoint _____ my true and lawful Agents. My Agents are hereby authorized to act jointly or severally. I shall refer to them as "my Agent" in the following provisions of this instrument. My Agent shall have full power to transact all my business and to manage all my property and affairs, as I might do if personally present, including but not limited to the following powers:

1. To ask, demand, sue for, recover and receive all sums of money, debts, goods and merchandise, chattels, effects and things of whatsoever nature or description which are now or hereafter shall be or become owing, due, payable or belonging to me in or by any right whatsoever, and upon receipt thereof, to make, sign, execute and deliver such receipts, releases or other discharges for the same, respectively, as they shall think fit.

2. To deposit any moneys which may come into their hands as such Agent with any banks or bankers, to open any accounts, including the right to complete and execute any forms necessary to do so, either in my name or their own name, and any of such money or any other money to which I am entitled, which now is or shall be so deposited, to withdraw as they shall think fit; to sign mutual savings bank and federal savings and loan association withdrawal orders; to sign and endorse checks payable to my order and to draw, accept, make, endorse, discount or otherwise deal with any bills of exchange, checks, promissory notes or other commercial or mercantile instruments; to borrow any sum or sums of money on such terms and with such security as they may think fit, and for that purpose, to execute all notes or other instruments which may be necessary or proper; and to have access to any and all safe deposit boxes registered in my name, including the power to add or remove all or any of the contents thereof.

3. To sell, assign, transfer and dispose of any and all stocks, bonds (including U.S. Savings Bonds), mutual funds, limited partnership interests, loans, mortgages or other securities registered in my name; and to collect and receipt for all interest and dividends due and payable to me.

Figure 62.1 (cont'd)

4. To invest in my name in any stock, shares, bonds (including U.S. Treasury Bonds referred to as "flower bonds"), mutual funds, securities or other property, real or personal, and to vary such investments as they, in their sole discretion, may deem best; and to vote at meetings of shareholders or other meetings of any corporation or company and to execute any proxies or other instruments in connection therewith. To open, operate and maintain a securities brokerage account, wherein any securities may be bought and/or sold on margin, and to hypothecate, borrow upon, purchase and/or sell existing securities in said account. [**Consider whether an exemption from adhering to the Prudent Investor Act should be afforded family or friends serving as agent**].

5. To enter into and upon my real estate[**Consider whether a restriction should be placed on selling the client's home. Particular for older or infirm clients who have invested considerable money and energy transforming a home into an accessible and safe environment, they may not wish the hold sold unless it is essential or until after death**] and to let, manage and improve the same or any part thereof, and to repair or otherwise improve or alter, and to insure any buildings thereon; to sell, either at public or private sale, or exchange any part or parts of my real estate or personal property for such consideration and upon such terms as they shall think fit, and to execute and deliver good and sufficient deeds or other instruments for the conveyance or transfer of the same, with such covenants of warranty or otherwise as they shall see fit, and to give good and effectual receipts for all or any part of the purchase price or other consideration; and to mortgage my real estate, and in connection therewith, to execute bonds and warrants and all other necessary instruments and documents.

6. To acquire, dispose of, repair, alter, store or manage my tangible personal property or any interest in such property, including any intellectual property, electronic property or other intangible property which I may own or have an interest in.

7. To purchase, continue, renew, convert or terminate any type of insurance, including, but not limited to, life, accident, health, disability or liability insurance; to pay premiums and collect benefits and proceeds on any insurance policy; to exercise all powers with respect to insurance that I could exercise, including, amending, adding or changing the beneficiary on any policy, provided my Agent may not name himself or herself as a beneficiary unless my Agent is my spouse, a child or grandchild of mine or my sibling.

8. To contribute, withdraw or deposit funds in any type of retirement plan of mine; to select and change the payment options for the principal; to roll over one retirement plan to another and to exercise all powers that I may have as to any retirement plan, including amending, adding or changing the beneficiary on any plan [**Consider whether the right to change beneficiaries should be prohibited to protect the client's dispositive scheme**], provided my Agent may not name himself or herself as a beneficiary unless my Agent is my spouse, a child or grandchild of mine or my sibling. In all respects, my Agent shall not take any action as to any retirement plan that would disqualify the plan or cause the plan or the distributions to be subject to penalties.

9. To contract with any person for leasing for such periods, at such rents and subject to such conditions as they shall see fit, all or any of my said real estate; to give notice to quit to any tenant or occupier thereof; and to receive and recover from all tenants and occupiers thereof or of any part thereof all rents, arrears of rent, and sums of money which now are or shall hereafter become due and payable in respect thereof; and also on nonpayment thereof or of any part thereof to take all necessary or proper means and proceedings for determining the tenancy or occupancy of such tenants or occupiers, and for ejecting the tenants or occupiers and recovering the possession thereof.

10. To commence, prosecute, discontinue or defend all actions or other legal proceedings pertaining to me or my estate or any part thereof; (to disclaim any part or all of any power or interest in any property to which I or my estate may be entitled); to settle, compromise or submit to arbitration any debt, demands or other right or matter due me or concerning my estate as they, in their sole discretion, shall deem best and for such purpose to execute and deliver such releases, discharges or other instruments as they may deem necessary and advisable; and to satisfy mortgages, including the execution of a good and sufficient release, or other discharge of such mortgage.

Figure 62.1 (cont'd)

11. To represent me in all tax matters; to prepare, sign and file federal, estate and/or local income, gift or other tax returns of all kinds, including all Internal Revenue Service forms, joint returns [**delete if single**], claims for refunds, requests for extensions of time, petitions to the tax court or other courts regarding tax matters, and any and all other tax related documents, including but not limited to, consents and agreements under Section 2032A of the Internal Revenue Code or any successor section thereto and consents to gift tax returns, closing agreements and any power of attorney form required by the Internal Revenue Service including the formal Internal Revenue Service authorization form, No. 2848 or its equivalent, and/or any state and/or local taxing authority with respect to any tax year; to pay taxes due, collect and make such disposition of refunds as my Agent shall deem appropriate; post bonds, receive confidential information and contest deficiencies determined by the Internal Revenue Service and/or any state and/or local taxing authority; to exercise any elections I may have under federal, state or local tax laws; and generally to represent me or to obtain professional representation for me in all tax matters and proceedings of all kinds and for all periods before all officers of the Internal Revenue Service and state and local authorities; to engage, compensate and discharge attorneys, accountants and other tax and financial advisers and consultants to represent and/or assist me in connection with any and all tax matters involving or in any way related to me or any property in which I have or may have any interest or responsibility.

12. To engage, employ and dismiss any brokers, advisors, accountants, counsel or professional personnel, agents, clerks, servants or other persons as they, in their sole discretion, may deem necessary and advisable.

13. To apply for and receive any government, insurance and retirement benefits to which I may be entitled, including the right to act as my representative payee with the Social Security Administration, and to exercise any right to elect benefits or payment options; to terminate, to change beneficiaries or ownership, to assign rights, to borrow or receive cash value in return for the surrender of any or all rights I may have in life insurance policies or benefits, annuity policies, plans or benefits, mutual fund and other dividend investment plans and retirement, profit sharing and employee welfare plans and benefits.

14. To make such limited gifts of my property to any one or more of my spouse, if I am then married, and my descendants [**consider whether gifts to descendants should be permitted**] in such form and amounts as my Agent believes would be in accordance with this paragraph. Notwithstanding any provision herein to the contrary, my Agent may make unlimited gifts to my spouse, if I am then married, [**consider deleting the following phrase/restriction**] for my spouse's health, maintenance and support to maintain my spouse in the station of life to which my spouse is accustomed and after taking into consideration my spouse's other readily available assets and sources of income. [**Evaluate whether the following gift provisions should be retained at all, or in the alternative if gifts up to the principal's remaining exemption amount should be permitted**] Gifts may be made to a Donee either outright or in trust, or under any state's Uniform Gifts or Transfers to Minors Act. In each case of a gift made in trust, my Agent may execute a trust instrument, designating one or more persons (including one or more agents hereunder) as original or successor trustees, or may make additions to an existing trust. In addition to the aforesaid gifts, payments may be made for a Donee which are "qualified transfers" (payments for tuition or medical care) within the meaning of Section 2503(e) of the Internal Revenue Code. In determining the amount of any gifts, my Agent need not treat Donees equally or proportionately, may entirely exclude one or more of my issue, and the pattern followed on the occasion of any gift or gifts need not be followed on the occasion of any other gift or gifts. My Agent shall also have the power to engage in transactions involving any Qualified Tuition Program under Section 529 of the Internal Revenue Code of 1986, as amended, which shall include: the power to establish one or more accounts under one or more Qualified Tuition Programs; make contributions to any such account; select or change the designated beneficiary of any such account; withdraw amounts for my benefit from any such account; direct distributions from any such account to others; roll over any distribution from an account to a different account for the same or a different beneficiary under the same or a different Qualified Tuition Program;

Figure 62.1 (cont'd)

and perform any other act that I could perform with respect to any Qualified Tuition Program account; provided, however, that my Agent may not (a) designate as the beneficiary of an account any person to whom my Agent could not make a gift under this Paragraph, or (b) make any contribution to an account in any calendar year in excess of the amount that could be given in such year outright to the designated beneficiary of the account under this Paragraph.

15. To create a Trust for my benefit, or [**Consider whether the power to create a trust should be granted and the risks to such an action altering the client's intended dispositive scheme**] to make additions for my benefit to any Trust, and specifically to any Revocable Living Trust that I have established, and to withdraw and receive the income or principal of the above Trust or of any Trust over which I have the power to make withdrawals, and to exercise all of the powers over any Trust property that I have given to my Agent to the same extent as if it were my own property, specifically including the powers given to my Agent under paragraphs 5 and 9 in regard to any real estate in my Trust.

16. To renounce and disclaim any property or interest in property or powers to which for any reason and by any means I may become entitled, whether by gift, testate or intestate succession; to release or abandon any property or interest in property or powers which I may now or hereafter own, including any interests in or rights over trusts (including the right to alter, amend, revoke or terminate); and to exercise any right to claim an elective share in any estate or under any will. In exercising such discretion, my Agent may take into account such matters as shall include, but shall not be limited to, any reduction in estate or inheritance taxes on my estate, and the effect of such renunciation or disclaimer upon persons interested in my estate and persons who would receive the renounced or disclaimed property; provided, however, that my Agent shall make no disclaimer that is expressly prohibited by other provisions of this instrument.

17. To renounce any fiduciary positions to which I have been appointed or in which I am then serving, to release any powers I may have with respect to any trust, whether held in fiduciary or non-fiduciary capacity, and to file accountings with a court of competent jurisdiction or settle on a receipt-and-release basis or by such other informal method as my Agent deems appropriate, and to appoint a successor or successors to serve in such fiduciary positions to the extent that I then have the authority to do so.

18. To nominate any person or institution, including my said Agent, as guardian of my estate or of my person, for consideration by the Court if incompetency proceedings for my estate or person are hereafter commenced.[**consider instead indicating that the agents in the order named shall be designated as the guardian of the principal's property if a guardian has to be appointed**]

19. In general, to do all other acts, deeds and matters whatsoever in or about my estate, property and affairs as fully and effectually to all intents and purposes as I could do in my own proper person if personally present, giving to my said Agent power to make and substitute under them an Agent or Agents for all the purposes herein described, hereby ratifying and confirming all that the said Agent or substitute or substitutes shall do therein by virtue of these presents.

20. In addition to the powers and discretions herein specifically given and conferred upon my Agent, and notwithstanding any usage or custom to the contrary, to have the full power, right and authority to do, perform, and cause to be done and performed, all such acts, deeds and matters in connection with my property and estate as they, in their sole discretion shall deem reasonable, necessary and proper, as fully, effectually and absolutely as if they were the absolute owner thereof.

21. In the event of my disability or incompetency, from whatever cause, this power of attorney shall not thereby be revoked.

IN WITNESS WHEREOF, I have hereunto set my hand and seal this _____ day of _____ , _____ .

Witnesses:

Figure 62.1 (cont'd)

> [sample state statutory provision to be executed by an agent] I, have read the attached power of attorney and am the person identified as the agent for the principal. I hereby acknowledge that in the absence of a specific provision to the contrary in the power of attorney, when I act as agent:
>
> I shall exercise the powers for the benefit of the principal.
>
> I shall keep the assets of the principal separate from my assets.
>
> I shall exercise reasonable caution and prudence.
>
> I shall keep a full and accurate record of all actions, receipts and disbursement on behalf of the principal.
>
> Dated: _____ , _____
>
> STATE OF   )
>   ) SS:
> COUNTY OF   )
>
> Before me, the undersigned, a notary public in and for the Commonwealth of Pennsylvania, personally appeared, known to me to be the person whose name is subscribed to the within instrument, and acknowledged that executed the same for the purposes therein contained.
>
> IN WITNESS WHEREOF, I have hereunto set my hand and official seal this ____ day of ____ , ____ .
>
> _____
> Notary Public

62.7 TAX IMPLICATIONS

The holder of the durable power of attorney, if the power is broadly drawn, can be given:

1. the right to execute on behalf of the principal all tax returns including income and gift tax returns;

2. the power to make gifts on behalf of the principal (thereby possibly reducing the principal's estate for federal estate tax purposes, or if not carefully orchestrated resulting in no estate tax savings but a loss in income tax basis step up); and

3. the right to elect to treat gifts made by the competent spouse as split between the competent spouse and the incompetent principal for federal gift tax purposes.

The agent's powers may result in tax implications for the agent. Some states rationalize that broad language relating to gifting powers permits an agent to make gifts to himself or others if the agent is following what the principal has done historically. Other states require that there be specific authorization to make gifts to the agent. This is important because often the agent is the object of the principal's bounty.

If a broad power to make a gift is given to the agent, it could be construed as a general power of appointment. However, there is an exception under Treasury Regulations section 25.2514-3 which states that a power is not considered a general power of appointment if the power of appointment is not exercisable except with the consent or joinder of the creator of the power, i.e. the principal's consent. However, if the principal is incapacitated that consent cannot be given. Consider including language relating to gifts by the agent to himself or herself that are restricted to a health, education, maintenance or support standard so that there is no issue relating to the general power of appointment.[4] Some commentators maintain that if the agent can only make gifts in fiduciary capacity that this restriction would prevent the agent from being considered to hold a general power of appointment over any of the Principal's assets.

62.8 IMPLICATIONS AND ISSUES IN COMMUNITY PROPERTY STATES

Because community property is owned equally by both husband and wife, many transactions require the signature of both spouses in order to be effective. Particularly, in situations where the couple has a community property proprietorship business, the incapacity of one spouse could seriously affect the stability and viability of the business.

Incapacity of one spouse could also prevent the sale of securities or the sale of or even borrowing against real or other property. Because of presumptions of community property status in many instances, title companies and others concerned with the completeness of title transfer usually require the signature (personally or by exercise of a power of attorney) of both spouses even though the property is in the name of only one spouse.

In many cases, a wife will give a power of attorney to her husband if he is the primary manager of the property for the sake of convenience of management. However, consideration should also be given to providing a method of dealing with both halves of the property if either the husband or the wife should suffer any incapacity.

It should be noted that while all states authorize some form of durable power, not all states have adopted the Uniform Durable Power of Attorney provisions.

Some community property states, such as California, provide that if one spouse is legally incompetent, the other spouse will succeed to management of the community property, with court approval required for some transactions. If the attorney-in-fact is not the spouse, there could be serious conflicts between the competent spouse and the attorney-in-fact pertaining to management and investment of community property.

62.9 FREQUENTLY ASKED QUESTIONS

Question – How broad can a durable power of attorney be written?

Answer – The extent of the powers conferred by the principal upon the attorney-in-fact are limited only by the desires of the principal. The example of a broad general power of attorney shown in Figure 58.1 is an attempt by a principal to confer upon the attorney-in-fact the right to act to the same extent the principal could have acted if the principal were present and able to act. Many states require specific language if the agent is to be permitted to make gifts in excess of the gift tax annual exclusion. The real issue is what powers are appropriate given the client's circumstances, the relationship and confidence in the agents named, and other considerations. For example, the power might be as broad as possible under state law but prohibit the agent from changing beneficiaries of retirement plans or life insurance in order to assure that the principal's dispositive scheme cannot be altered.

Question – What is the duration of a durable power of attorney?

Answer – The durable power of attorney, once properly executed, continues until revoked by the principal or until it terminates by its terms on the death of the principal. However, if appropriate the client might limit the duration of the power. Such a limitation might only be advisable for a special power of attorney. In fact, it might be advisable to provide a clause in the power that expressly states that the power of attorney will not lapse until revoked by the principal, state law (e.g., divorce) or death of the principal.

The durable power of attorney, by its very nature, is designed to cover the situation where the principal becomes incapacitated. If the principal is incapacitated it would be impossible for the attorney to obtain a freshly dated power of attorney. Many states and the Uniform Power of Attorney Act include language which requires properly executed powers of attorney to be accepted by financial and other institutions and submit such institutions to civil penalties if they refuse to accept the document.

Question – Can there be more than one attorney-in-fact under a durable power of attorney?

Answer – Yes; however, caution must be taken in drafting the power of attorney. If the power of attorney merely names John Doe and Mary Roe as the holders of the power, then both must act together in order for the power to be operable. If, however, the power is in favor of, "John Doe *or* Mary Roe, either of them to act in place of the principal," then each person can act independently. The practical application of multiple agents should be reviewed with the client. If two or more agents must act in concert that might prove an impossible impediment in the event of an urgent situation. If either agent might sign what if the agents have different perspectives or agendas how can their actions be reconciled? What can a third party do if they receive contradictory instructions from each agent?

Furthermore, the power of attorney can provide for successor attorneys-in-fact in the event of the primary attorney's death or inability to serve.

Question – Does a power of attorney terminate upon disability?

Answer – A power of attorney that is not a durable power of attorney terminates upon disability. However, actions taken by the attorney-in-fact when the attorney-in-fact is unaware of the principal's disability are binding upon the principal. A durable power of attorney by its very definition survives and continues and is not affected by subsequent disability or incapacity of the principal. The default answer should be that every power of attorney should be made to be durable, by inclusion of any required statement mandated by applicable state law (e.g., this power shall remain in force even if the principal is subsequently disabled), unless there is an express reason not to do so.

Question – Does the death of the principal terminate a durable power of attorney?

Answer – Yes. The death of the principal terminates a power of attorney whether or not it is durable. However, as in the case of a power of attorney that is not durable, the durable power of attorney permits the attorney-in-fact who has no notice of the death of his principal to continue to act according to, and under, the power until the attorney-in-fact learns of the death of the principal. Although with the state of communications and technology it is difficult to imagine that this could be a significant period of time absent very unusual circumstances.

Question – What is the relationship between the attorney-in-fact under a durable power of attorney and a court appointed guardian for the incompetent?

Answer – The durable power of attorney may continue to be effective after the appointment of a guardian for the incompetent. However, the law differs by state and even by situation. For example, the guardian of the incompetent appointed by the Court may have the same rights as the principal and may be able terminate the durable power of attorney on behalf of his ward, the incompetent. In some instances the vary appointment of a guardian will terminate the power of attorney. In others, the agent may be able to continue to operate but may have to report to the guardian.

Question – What is a springing power of attorney?

Answer – Most states recognize a particular form of durable power of attorney known as the springing power. A durable power of attorney may become effective upon execution (an immediate power). Clients who are reluctant to grant another person wide powers to act at a time when the principal is capable of acting may prefer to use a springing power. A springing power does not become effective until the occurrence of a specified event such as physical or mental incapacity or disappearance. However, not all states recognize springing power of attorney. For example, Florida has recently repealed the application of this approach.[5]

Some states define the contingencies under which the springing power becomes effective by statute, while other states require that the contingencies be specified in the instrument. All states require that the instrument name the person or persons who are to determine whether the contingency has occurred. For instance, if the contingency is incapacity, a doctor or group of doctors should be named to make such a determination. The attorney-in-fact may be the person making the determination. Obviously, alternate individuals should be named in case the person originally named is no longer able to make such a determination.

A major drawback of a springing power is the potential difficulty in determining whether the contingency has occurred. There may be family disputes over whether a disability has in fact triggered the springing power. This puts a premium on clear and precise language in the instrument defining the contingency and creating an objective mechanism for determining whether it has actually occurred. An even greater potential problem is the reluctance on the part of banks, hospitals, and other organizations to accept a document granting broad powers over property if that document was executed a number of years prior to the date when it "springs." Financial institutions quite often raise the problem of "staleness," even though there is nothing in state law suggesting that the mere passage of time dates a power. For this reason, all powers of attorney should be revised every three years or less. Although banks and other financial institutions should honor a power of attorney, it is good practice to check to see if that institution has its own specific power of attorney form or wording. The restrictions on disclosing private health information, such as those contained in the Health Insurance Portability Accountability Act ("HIPPA"), make it difficult to obtain medical confirmation of incapacity. Thus, it can be time consuming and difficult to trigger a springing power.

Question – Can the attorney-in-fact make gifts on behalf of the principal?

Answer – This is the one area involving the use of durable powers that has resulted in the most tax and legal controversy. In a common situation, the principal is elderly and/or seriously ill, and is not legally competent. The attorney-in-fact proposes to make a series of gifts that fall within the annual exclusion ($17,000 in 2023) to reduce the principal's taxable estate. The IRS has successfully argued that unless gift giving is clearly authorized in the power of attorney itself, or under state law pertaining to the durable powers, the gifts are incomplete for federal tax purposes and still included in the taxable estate of the principal.[6]

Note that if the durable power of attorney is drafted to permit the attorney-in-fact to make gifts, consideration should be given to whether or not the power holder can make gifts to himself or herself. Bear in mind that the attorney-in-fact is often a close family member. As noted above if that person can make gifts to himself or herself, this power could be deemed a general power of appointment for federal tax purposes, and, worse, the failure to exercise the power could be a release of a general power of appointment and treated as a taxable gift.

As noted above the inclusion of a power to make annual gifts is no longer appropriate for most clients and inadequate for wealthy clients.

Question – Does the attorney-in-fact under the durable power assume the same legal liabilities and responsibilities as a trustee?

Answer – The law in this area is unclear, but the attorney in fact assumes significant fiduciary obligations and hence many of the same potential liability risks of a trustee. This includes possible claims the attorney in fact made imprudent investments, or the attorney in fact failed to protect the best interests of the principal. A person who is being considered for such an appointment should be fully informed of his or her potential liabilities.

Question – Who can serve as attorney-in-fact?

Answer – Any trusted person, such as a spouse, relative, or friend. It need not be an attorney. It is a good idea to have an alternative attorney-in-fact to serve if the first choice cannot serve for whatever reason. The real issue for many clients is whether they have someone appropriate to name in this powerful position. One of the most important issues for practitioners to assist clients with is vetting the person to be selected.

Question – What is a durable power of attorney for health care?

Answer – A durable power of attorney for health care (also called a Health Care Power of Attorney or Health Care Proxy) is a document in which the principal confers upon the attorney in fact the power to make health care decisions for the principal in the event the principal is not legally competent. The extent of the permissible powers varies according to state law. In general, the principal authorizes the attorney-in-fact to consent to medical treatment, including surgical procedures. One of the most important and controversial aspects of this document is the extent to which it authorizes the attorney-in-fact to terminate treatment or even terminate life support where the principal is terminally ill or is in what is called "a persistent vegetative state," meaning the principal is in a permanent coma and the best medical opinion is that the principal will never recover.

The durable power of attorney for health care should be a separate legal document.

In appropriate instances, the use of a Physicians Orders For Life Sustaining Treatment ("POLST") may be used in addition to or in lieu of a health care proxy. For isolated clients who may not have someone to name as a health care agent a POLST may be an option.

See Chapter 63 for a more detailed discussion of health care power of attorneys.

CHAPTER ENDNOTES

1. Uniform Power of Attorney Act (2006), available online at: https://www.uniformlaws.org/committees/community-home?CommunityKey=b1975254-8370-4a7c-947f-e5af0d6cb07c.
2. 20 Pa. C.S.A. §5601.1.
3. Fla. Stat. §709.
4. Howard M. Zaritsky, *Tax Planning for Family Wealth Transfers: Analysis with Forms*, Section 2.03 (Thomson Reuters, updated annually).
5. Fla. Stat. §709.2108.
6. *Est. of Casey v. Comm'r.*, 91-2 USTC ¶60,091 (4th Cir. 1991); TAMs 9347003, 9342003.

HEALTH-CARE DOCUMENTS

CHAPTER 63

63.1 INTRODUCTION

There are a number of health care related documents which a client might use:

- A *health care proxy* is a document in which the client designates an agent to make health care decisions. This document will also generally provide a list of powers that are granted to that agent. It is also called a health care power of attorney.

- A *HIPAA release* is a document that appoints a health care representative to have access to a patient's medical information for purposes of monitoring care and to interact with family, the patient and medical providers. This document is intended to address the restrictions on disclosing private health information (PHI) under various laws including the federal Health Insurance Portability and Accountability Act of 1996.

- A *living will* is a statement of health care wishes. While not accepted in every state it is an excellent means of documenting client wishes for an agent even if not binding. A living will should detail client end of life decision making, religious preferences, burial and internment wishes, and more.

- A *Physician Orders Life-Sustaining Treatment (POLST)* is a physician-prepared medical order that addresses end-of-life planning based on conversations between patients, loved ones, and health care professionals. It is intended to ensure that seriously ill or frail patients can choose the treatments they want, and reject the treatments they do not want. A POLTs documents these wishes so that they will be respected. Because POLST is a medical order, a POLST form must be completed and signed by a health care professional and cannot be filled out by a patient. A POLST form is most appropriate for seriously ill persons with life-limiting, or terminal, illnesses; or advanced frailty characterized by significant weakness and extreme difficulty with personal care activities. See www.polst.org for more information and a listing of states permitting this approach.

Practitioners must guide clients to the preparation of one or all of the above documents as is appropriate for their personal circumstances.

63.2 ASSISTED SUICIDE

While this chapter focuses on documentation clients can create to authorize others to make medical decisions when they cannot, it is also important to be aware of a related topic important to end of life decision making, assisted suicide. While the phrase itself may evoke strong emotions on each side of the issue, it is important that practitioners be aware of the developments in this area. As the population ages and medical technology continues to advance the conscious decision of those with terminal conditions and severe pain and/or the loss of quality of life to choose whether to end their life will occur more frequently.

There are now eleven states/jurisdictions that permit what some refer to as "legal suicide." Ten jurisdictions now have statutes that permit this: California, Colorado,

District of Columbia, Hawaii, New Jersey, Maine, New Mexico, Oregon, Vermont, and Washington. Additionally, Montana has a court decision that is viewed as permitting similar actions. Thirty-three states have laws expressly prohibiting assisted suicide, and another three states prohibit assisted suicide via common law. The remaining four states laws, and federal law are silent on assisted suicide.

This is when, after complying with strict procedures, the dying and suffering patient may obtain prescription medication to end their life. These states only permit this for terminally ill individuals who have less than a six-month life expectancy. Requirements of these laws may include:

- The request must be made by the patient from their physician for self-administered aid-in-dying medication.

- Be a resident of the state permitting this. This requirement is an important part of planning that practitioners may be called on to address.

- Be age eighteen or older.

- Be able to communicate an informed decision to health care providers (so that an agent under a health care proxy discussed below may not be permitted to do this for the patient).

- Have a terminal illness with a prognosis of six months or less to live.

- This health status must be confirmed by two physicians, including the individual's primary physician and a second, consulting physician.

- Be confirmed as mentally capable to make this decision by two physicians. They must specifically conclude that the patient understands the consequences of his or her decision.

- To confirm that this the decision is deliberate the patient must make two oral requests, at least fifteen days apart, and one written request in specific to the primary physician. The written request must also be witnessed by at least two other persons who meet certain requirements.

If a client has been diagnosed with a terminal illness and may face severe pain and a loss of quality of life and might wish to avail himself or herself of these laws it is advisable to move to a state permitting assisted suicide in order to take advantage of this option. That move should be made while there is capacity to effectuate establishing residency in the chosen state.

63.3 HEALTH CARE PROXY

A health care proxy or power of attorney is a medical power of attorney in which an individual, the principal, appoints a designated person, the health care agent, to make health care decisions on their behalf. There is a wide disparity in the terminology in this area.

The Uniform Health-Care Decisions Act (Act), adopted in 1993 and as of 2023 enacted in seven states is outlined in the next section. State laws vary significantly in this area, so the estate planner must be familiar with the specific law in the client's domiciliary state. An analysis of clauses from two different types of health-care powers of attorney will be covered in this chapter material, in order to highlight salient points about health-care powers of attorney. Finally, a discussion of the HIPAA authorization form is included, as it is often a very important estate planning document. In all cases, practitioners should be cognizant that these documents are very personal and whatever form may be used as a starting point it should be tailored to the client's particular wishes and circumstances.

Uniform Health-Care Decisions Act

The Uniform Health-Care Decisions Act (the "Act") defines the term advance health-care directive as an individual instruction, which can be either written, oral, or a health-care power of attorney, which must be in writing.[1] From a practical perspective, all adult clients should be encouraged and assisted in creating a written and formally executed instruction. An adult or emancipated minor may give an individual instruction, which is defined as an individual's direction concerning a health-care decision for the individual.[2] An individual instruction may be limited to take effect only if a specified condition arises.[3]

63.4 USING A HIPAA RELEASE

"HIPAA" is the acronym for the Health Insurance Portability and Accountability Act of 1996.[4] Maintaining the confidentiality of Private Health Information (PHI) means protecting info from being made available or being disclosed to unauthorized persons. When might a HIPAA release be useful?

- If your client is ill, can her daughter-in-law, a doctor she wants involved, be able to access your patient chart to monitor care?

- If you're a successor trustee, and the current trustee is forgetting to pay insurance premiums and respond to correspondence, can that person be replaced?

Your partner is disabled and you need to take over your partner's professional practice, how can you obtain the requisite physician letter mandated in your shareholders' agreement to demonstrate incompetence to be able to trigger the replacement provision?

Advise clients to be cautious of the "standard" forms. They may be overreaching or inadequate. Many clients find and sign forms they find on line assuming that they are "standard" with little understanding of the implications.

Requirements for a HIPPA Release

What should be included in a HIPPA release?

- **Writing:** Authorization should be in writing and should acknowledge that it's being made voluntarily.

- **What:** Describe the health information to be disclosed. This could be the entire medical record, or only specified components. Could specify that only medical records between certain dates be released. The HIPAA paradigm is that only as much info should be disclosed as necessary.

- **Who:** Which medical provider should make the disclosure? This could be a specific physician or hospital or a list of providers. A broader approach could be used to indicate a category of providers. For example, "any physicians, hospitals or other medical providers who have provided treatment, other medical services or payment for same, from June 1, 2009 through and including the date of this Authorization."

- **Term:** When does the authorization to disclose PHI expire? This could be: "upon a child attaining age twenty=one." It could be "two years from the signing of this authorization." "Upon the conclusion of my court case" may suffice for a litigation matter, although issues of appeals, etc. might warrant consideration in setting the parameters. "One year from death."

- **Revocation:** A statement that you retain the right to revoke any authorization to disclose your PHI. Any revocation, however, is not binding on a medical provider until they receive it. This minimizes the issue of liability for disclosing information based on an authorization held prior to the revocation.

- **Re-Disclosure:** The release may state that certain information, such as HIV testing results, cannot be disclosed by the person receiving it. However, the release should also acknowledge that once other information is disclosed, it may thereafter be re-disclosed by the person receiving it without the HIPAA safeguards.

- **Purpose:** The purpose for the disclosure should be explained. This might be limited to the minimum information to determine whether you have the ability to function as a trustee or should be replaced, or only that information necessary to underwrite you for life insurance.

- **Signer:** If you are signing the authorization, the signature line should merely state that you are the patient. If, however, another person is signing for you, the authorization should state that that person qualifies as your personal representative under and that they have authority to make health care decisions for you.

When is a HIPAA Release Indicated?

The Health Insurance Portability and Accountability Act of 1996 (HIPAA) is critical to consider in planning for a client's potential health challenges, hospitalizations, etc. Under the HIPAA privacy regulations, a personal representative stands in the shoes of the patient only when that representative has authority to act.[5]

Figure 63.1

SAMPLE HIPAA AUTHORIZATION FORM

HIPAA COMPLIANT AUTHORIZATION FOR THE RELEASE OF PROTECTED HEALTH INFORMATION TO PERSONAL REPRESENTATIVE PURSUANT TO 45 CFR 164.502(g)

TO ALL HIPAA COVERED ENTITIES AND HEALTH CARE PROVIDERS OF: _____

_____

Name of Patient

_____

Street Address

_____

City, State and Zip Code _____

Date of Birth: _____ Social Security Number: _____

I authorize and request the release and disclosure of all protected health information in my file. I expressly request that the designated record custodian of all covered entities under HIPAA identified above disclose full and complete protected health information on me, including, without limitation, the following:

All medical records, meaning every page in my record, including, but not limited to: office notes, face sheets, history and physical, consultation notes, inpatient, outpatient and emergency room treatment, all clinical charts, reports, order sheets, progress notes, nurse's notes, social worker records, clinic records, treatment plans, admission records, discharge summaries, requests for and reports of consultations, documents, correspondence, test results, statements, questionnaires/histories, correspondence, photographs, videotapes, telephone messages and records received by other medical providers.

All physical, occupational and rehabilitation requests, consultations and progress notes.

All disability, Medicaid or Medicare records including claim forms and record of denial of benefits.

All employment, personnel or wage records.

All autopsy, laboratory, histology, cytology, pathology, immunohistochemistry records and specimens; radiology records and films including CT scan, MRI, MRA, EMG, bone scan, myleogram; nerve conduction study, echocardiogram and cardiac catheterization results, videos/CDs/films/reels and reports.

All pharmacy/prescription records, including NDC numbers and drug information handouts/monographs.

All billing records, including all statements, insurance claim forms, itemized bills, and records of billing to third party payers and payment or denial of benefits.

I understand the information to be released or disclosed may include information relating to sexually transmitted diseases, acquired immunodeficiency syndrome (AIDS), or human immunodeficiency virus (HIV), and alcohol and drug abuse. I authorize the release or disclosure of this type of information.

This protected health information is disclosed for the following purposes: _____

_____

This authorization is given in compliance with the federal consent requirements for release of alcohol or substance abuse records of 42 CFR 2.31, the restrictions of which have been specifically considered and expressly waived.

HEALTH-CARE DOCUMENTS CHAPTER 63

Figure 63.1 (cont'd)

You are authorized to release the above records to the following personal representative:

_____
Name of Representative

_____
Representative Capacity (e.g. attorney, records requestor, agent, etc.)

_____
Street Address

_____

City, State and Zip Code _____

I understand the following:

a. I have a right to revoke this authorization in writing at any time, except to the extent that information has been released in reliance upon this authorization.

b. The information released in response to this authorization may be re-disclosed to other parties.

c. My treatment or payment for my treatment cannot be conditioned on the signing of this authorization.

Any facsimile, copy or photocopy of this authorization shall authorize you to release the records requested herein. This authorization shall remain in force and effect until revoked in writing.

_____
Signature of Patient or Legally Authorized Representative/Date

_____
Name and Relationship of Legally Authorized Representative to Patient

_____
Witness Signature Date

Therefore, until the principal is deemed to have lost capacity, as defined above, that personal representative will be barred both from making health-care decisions for the principal and from receiving Protected Health Information (PHI) about the principal pursuant to the general HIPAA privacy rules. This is why it is so important that a written advance health-care directive either be immediate or be coupled with a blanket HIPAA authorization form. Figure 63.1 is a sample HIPAA authorization and release form.

63.5 HEALTH-CARE POWER OF ATTORNEY

The term health-care decision means a decision made by an individual or the individual's agent, guardian or surrogate, regarding the individual's health care, including:

1. selection and discharge of health-care providers and institutions;

2. approval or disapproval of diagnostic tests, surgical procedures, programs of medication and orders not to resuscitate; and

3. directions to provide, withhold or withdraw artificial nutrition and hydration and all other forms of health care.[6]

Any adult or emancipated minor may execute a health-care power of attorney, which may authorize the agent to make any health-care decision that the principal could have made while having sufficient capacity to do so. The term capacity means an individual's ability to understand the significant benefits, risks and alternatives to proposed health care and to make and communicate a health-care decision.[7] A health-care power of attorney must be in writing and signed by the principal.[8] This gives rise to the distinction in the Act between a health-care power of attorney, which must be in writing, and an advance health-care directive, which includes both the health-care power of attorney and the individual instruction, the latter of which can be oral.[9] Regardless, however, practitioners should encourage clients to sign a health care proxy and separately document their wishes in a written, signed and notarized living will.

The written health-care power of attorney remains in effect under the Act, notwithstanding the principal's later incapacity. It may include individual instructions, so all health-care powers of attorney under the Act are durable unless the health-care power of attorney otherwise provides. Unless related to the principal by blood, marriage or adoption, an agent may not be an owner, operator or employee of a residential long-term health-care institution at which the principal is receiving care.[10] Most health-care providers prohibit their employees from witnessing estate planning documents being executed. As a result, it is always prudent to bring along at least one disinterested witness.

Unless the health-care power of attorney otherwise provides, the agent's authority becomes effective only upon a determination that the principal is incapacitated (i.e., no longer has capacity as defined above), and that authority ceases to be effective upon a determination that the principal has recovered capacity.[11] Therefore, unless the individual expressly provides that the power is immediate, a health-care power of attorney under the Act is a springing power of attorney. In contrast to the springing financial power of attorney, discussed in Chapter 62, most or all health-care powers of attorney should be springing.

Unless the health-care power of attorney otherwise provides, the individual's primary physician makes the determination that an individual lacks or has recovered capacity, or that another condition exists affecting individual instruction or the authority of an agent.[12] An agent is required to make a health-care decision in accordance with the principal's individual instruction, as well as the principal's other wishes, to the extent that the agent knows those wishes. Otherwise, the agent is required to make the decision in accordance with the agent's determination of the principal's best interest. In determining the principal's best interest, the agent is required to consider the principal's personal values to the extent that the agent knows the principal's personal values.[13] The Act does not contain a list of factors that the agent could consider in determining what actions would be consistent with the principal's personal values, leaving that up to the agent. The Official Comment to Section 2 of the Act, however, does indicate that several states have enacted a list of such factors.

Maryland is one illustrative state that has enacted a list of factors an agent should consider in the "best interest" of the patient determination. Maryland's factors to consider in the best interest determination are as follows:

(1) The effect of the treatment on the physical, emotional and cognitive functions of the individual.

(2) The degree of physical pain or discomfort caused to the individual by the treatment, or the withholding or withdrawal of the treatment.

(3) The degree to which the individual's medical condition, the treatment or the withholding or withdrawal of treatment results in a severe and continuing impairment of the dignity of the individual by subjecting the individual to a condition of extreme humiliation and dependency.

(4) The effect of the treatment on the life expectancy of the individual.

(5) The prognosis of the individual for recovery, with and without the treatment.

(6) The risks, side effects and benefits of the treatment or the withholding or withdrawal of the treatment.

(7) The religious beliefs and basic values of the individual receiving treatment, to the extent

these may assist the decision maker in determining best interest[14] While the Maryland statute provides instructive guidance that all health care agents should consider, the preferable approach is for clients to have substantive discussions with their agents in advance of an event requiring decision making. Because of the difficulty and unpleasant nature of this type of discussion many clients avoid it. Practitioners should endeavor to guide and encourage clients to have such a discussion.

63.6 LIVING WILLS

Regardless of what state law provides, the preferable approach is for each client to execute a living will that sets forth the client's wishes with respect to key aspects of any of life decision making. In many cases clients do not have conversations with the persons named to serve as agent as to these wishes. Too often the living will signed is a form that clients assume is somehow "standard" and which is therefore not tailored to reflect their specific wishes. One of the most profound issues that warrants carefully addressing in the documentation is religious issues. If the client does not want religious restrictions to apply that must be specified, not ignored. Otherwise, the agent and others may be left wondering whether or not religious restrictions were important and merely forgotten, or intentionally left out.

A health-care decision made by an agent for a principal is effective without judicial approval.[15] A health-care power of attorney may include the individual's nomination of a guardian of the person.[16] An advance health-care directive is valid for purposes of the Act if it complies with the terms of the Act, regardless of when or where executed or communicated.[17]

Before implementing a health-care decision made for a patient, a supervising health-care provider, if possible, is required to promptly communicate to a patient the decision made and the identity of the person making the decision.[18] A supervising health-care provider who knows of the existence of an advance health-care directive, a revocation of an advance health-care directive or a designation or disqualification of a surrogate must promptly record its existence in the patient's health-care record. If that documentation is in writing, the supervising health-care provider must request a copy, and if one is furnished, the supervising health-care provider is required to arrange for its maintenance in the patient's health-care record.[19]

In practical terms, families sometimes intentionally withhold the existence of a health care directive (living will) and even a health proxy. Whether this is done intentionally, or through ignorance of the existence of documents, or for other reasons, the consequences can undermine fundamental wishes of the client. Practitioners should advise clients to have discussions with the persons named agent, with other family members that may have concerns with how decisions are carried out, and provide copies of their documents to their physicians to include in their patient chart.

There are two reasons a health-care provider can refuse an advance health-care directive:

1. A health-care provider may decline to comply with an individual instruction or health-care decision for reasons of conscience.

2. A health-care institution may decline to comply with an individual instruction or health-care decision if the instruction or decision is contrary to a policy of the institution expressly based on reasons of conscience, where that policy was timely communicated to the patient or to a person who is then authorized to make health-care decisions for the patient.[20]

A health-care provider or institution also may decline to comply with an individual instruction or health-care decision requiring medically ineffective health care or health care contrary to generally accepted health-care standards applicable to the health-care provider or institution.[21]

Medical providers and/or facilities can and do sometimes refuse to honor medical decisions communicated by an agent because if violates hospital policy in the particular circumstances. Consideration should be given to including a provision in the health care proxy expressly authorizing the agent to move the client to another health care facility. Further, given the significant differences in state laws with respect to end of life treatments, that provision might authorize the agent to change the domicile of the client to another state in order to facilitate obtaining the desired treatments. An issue with a change in domicile might be that some view domicile as a matter of intent. If the client does not have capacity some commentators suggest that domicile cannot be changed because the client is incapable of changing intent as to where domiciled. Others commentators and court have disagreed and permitted a change in domicile so long as it is in the client's best interests.

Except where the health-care provider has either of the two grounds to refuse to comply with a patient's individual instruction, a health-care provider or institution providing care to a patient is required to:

(1) comply with an individual instruction of the patient and with a reasonable interpretation of that instruction made by a person then authorized to make health-care decisions for the patient; and

(2) comply with a health-care decision for the patient made by a person then authorized to make health-care decisions for the patient to the same extent as if the decision had been made by the patient while having capacity.[22]

A principal may revoke the designation of an agent only by a signed writing or by personally informing the supervising health-care provider.[23] A principal may revoke all or part of an advance health-care directive, other than the designation of an agent, at any time and in any manner that communicates intent to revoke.[24] A decree of annulment, divorce, dissolution of marriage or legal separation revokes a previous designation of a spouse as agent unless otherwise specified in the decree or in a health-care power of attorney.[25] Therefore, it is important that clients execute new health-care powers of attorney immediately upon legal separation or divorce. An advance health-care directive that conflicts with an earlier advance health-care directive revokes the earlier directive to the extent of the conflict.[26] What this also suggests is that if clients are separated and pursuing divorce the medical directives (as well as financial powers of attorney) should be changed. It could be a dire mistake to simply wait for a divorce to be finalized to effectuate the desired change.

If a patient who has lost capacity has not appointed an agent to make health-care decisions, or if the agent or the patient's guardian is not reasonably available (another defined term under the Act), a surrogate may make a health-care decision for a patient.[27] If the patient has not designated an agent under a health-care power of attorney, an adult or emancipated minor may designate any individual to act as surrogate to make the health-care decisions by personally informing the supervising health-care provider. In the absence of a designation, or if the designee is not reasonably available, any member of the patient's family who is reasonably available, in the following descending order of priority, may act as surrogate:

(1) the spouse, unless legally separated;

(2) an adult child;

(3) a parent; or

(4) an adult brother or sister.[28]

Note the conspicuous absence of an unmarried partner, which is why it is so critical that unmarried partners have health-care powers of attorney in place. While some state statutes have addressed this it remains preferable to document the client's intent in this regards. If none of the individuals eligible to act as surrogate in the above list is reasonably available, an adult who has exhibited special care and concern for the patient, who is familiar with the patient's personal values and who is reasonably available, which certainly would include an unmarried partner, may act as surrogate.[29] The Act does not have a list of factors that a surrogate should consider in this determination, leaving that determination up to the surrogate. The list of "best interest" factors previously discussed could be employed in this situation. A surrogate is required under the Act to communicate his or her assumption of authority as promptly as practicable to the members of the patient's family who can be readily contacted.[30] Interestingly, the Act provides no such requirement of notice by an agent. Adding such a requirement to a health-care power of attorney, is particularly important in the blended family context.

The purpose for which clients seek out professional guidance in these matters is to avoid the complications and difficulties apparent in the summary of the rules above. If no documentation is created which sibling would govern under the above common default rule? If the client's parents are divorced, which parent will make decisions? What if siblings and parents disagree? The objective must be to create unambiguous documents that provide the certainty of what the client's wishes are and who specifically should be charged with carrying them out.

A health-care provider or institution declining to comply with an individual instruction or health-care decision is required to:

(1) promptly inform the patient, if possible, and any person then authorized to make health-care decisions for the patient;

(2) provide continuing care to the patient until a transfer to a different health-care provider or institution can be effected; and

(3) unless the patient or person then authorized to make health-care decisions for the patient refuses assistance, immediately make all reasonable efforts to assist in the transfer of the patient to another health-care provider or institution that is willing to comply with the instruction or decision.[31]

A health-care provider or institution may not require or prohibit the execution or revocation of an advance health-care directive as a condition for providing health-care.[32] Unless otherwise specified in an advance health-care directive, a person then authorized to make health-care decisions for a patient has the same rights as the patient to request, receive, examine, copy and consent to the disclosure of medical or any other health-care information.[33] A health-care provider or institution acting in good faith and in accordance with generally accepted health-care standards applicable to the health-care provider or institution is not subject to civil or criminal liability or to discipline under the Act for unprofessional conduct for:

(1) complying with a health-care decision of a person apparently having authority to make a health-care decision for a patient, including a decision to withhold or withdraw health care;

(2) declining to comply with a health-care decision of a person based on a belief that the person then lacked authority; or

(3) complying with an advance health-care directive and assuming that the directive was valid when made and has not been revoked or terminated.[34]

A health-care provider or institution intentionally violating the Act is subject to liability to the aggrieved individual for damages of $500 or actual damages resulting from the violation, whichever is greater, plus reasonable attorney's fees.[35] Any person who intentionally falsifies, forges, conceals, defaces or obliterates an individual's advance health-care directive or a revocation of an advance health-care directive without the individual's consent, or who coerces or fraudulently induces an individual to give, revoke or not to give an advance health-care directive, is subject to liability to that individual for damages of $2,500 or actual damages resulting from the action, whichever is greater, plus reasonable attorney's fees.[36]

63.7 HOW HEALTH CARE DOCUMENTS SHOULD BE CREATED

Drafting Advance Health-Care Directives

Coordination of advance health-care directives with other documents of the client is essential, particularly if different people are agents or power holders. Consider the following:

- The agent under the financial durable power of attorney, and if applicable a trustee under a revocable trust, should be directed to make financial provisions for health care decisions made by the health care agent appointed under the health care power of attorney. This is an important element of coordination to avoid the person designated to handle financial matters dictating medical decision making that has been delegated to a different person. This is particularly important if the client specifies that experimental medical treatments may be approved as these might be quite costly.

- If a living will is completed providing health care directives nothing inconsistent should be drafted in the health care proxy appointing a health care agent.

- If the person named in a HIPAA release to have access to medical information should likely not be different people since the making of health care decisions is generally an extension of or encompassing the powers of the HIPAA Representative to have access to medical information.

Living Wills (Health Care Directives) and Health-Care Powers of Attorney (Health Care Proxies) should be Separate Documents

Living wills and health proxies should be drafted as separate independent documents. Living wills have varying level of legal acceptance in different jurisdictions so that crafting separate documents is more assured to have the client's wishes respected. Also, each document fulfills a distinct purpose. The health proxy designates an agent to make health care decisions. The living will provides statements of health care wishes.

Issues to Consider In Drafting or Reviewing the Health Care Power of Attorney

As is the case with any other documents, client input is essential. Although these matters are of a sensitive nature, a client's feelings and desires are usually impossible to discern without asking questions.

The following issues should be analyzed in the drafting or review of a health-care power of attorney:

1. Identity of agent(s), with alternatives or successors; and governance if there is more than one agent. There are strong opinions as to whether multiple co-agents should ever be used. Some state laws prohibit it. The practical concern of multiple agents is what should be done if in the emotionally turmoil of a very difficult time the agents cannot agree? Practitioners should discuss with clients their choice of agents. Too often clients name, not the person they believe is best equipped emotionally, intellectually or from a perspective of compassion, to serve, but rather the person they believe they are obligated to name (e.g., the eldest child).

2. Statement of the principal's intentions concerning an array of health care and ancillary decisions. This might include any or all of the following:

   - Funeral services. Should religious observances prevail? If so which?

   - Burial or cremation and any details vital to the client.

   - Should last rites or other end of life religious ceremonies be specified?

   - To what degree should pain relief be provided? What if pain relief hastens the onset of death? Can it still be given? Does the client have religious or spiritual end of life rituals or desires so that the provision of pain relief should be tempered to permit these to be observed?

   - Should organ donations be permitted? All organs? Any limitations? Should the body be donated for medical research?

   - Should heroic measures be provided? To what degree and when? What is "heroic?"

   - Should experimental medical treatments be permitted? Mandated?

   - The provision of nutrition and hydration can be quite controversial for religious, emotional or philosophical reasons. Can nutrition and hydration ever be ceased? Must they be provided? Should they be subject to the general provisions in a living will as to when heroic measures might be ceased?

3. Powers that could be considered:

   a. Change or retain domicile or residence (see comments above).

   b. Access and power to disclose medical records.

   c. Consent to, authorize, withhold or withdraw any treatment.

   d. Hire and/or fire medical personnel and institutions as well as others who may be giving assistance.

   e. Give releases.

   f. Authorize and pay medical bills, including, without limitation, insurance premiums. Caution should be exercised about permitting this in a health care related document as it may conflict with financial powers provided in a durable power of attorney or a revocable trust.

   g. Authorize engagement, termination and payment of lawyers to encourage or force medical providers to respect the client's wishes.

4. Releases of agent and health care providers.

5. Third party reliance.

6. Coordination between various power holders and other documents. As noted above it may be preferable to have the agent under a financial power pay all bills and the health care agent direct which medical decisions should be pursued that create those costs.

7. Reimbursement of expenses of agent. It may be advisable to prohibit financial compensation for an agent making health care decisions unless a professional surrogate is hired.

8. A statement of applicable state law. This can be a complex issue when the client has strong ties to two or more states. It is likely inadvisable to create separate health proxies in different states because of the potential for confusion and conflicts.

9. Resignation procedure for a health care agent to resign.

10. Specification of a client's religious persuasion. It is, as noted above, just as important to specify if religious restrictions should not apply, as when they should apply. This is particular important in light of the diversity within even the nuclear family.

The following language is excerpted from a health-care power of attorney, and we include it in Figure 63.2 with accompanying commentary for a discussion of the issues and decisions that must be made. It is not an entire health-care power of attorney.

Figure 63.2

HEALTH-CARE POWER OF ATTORNEY FORM	
	ARTICLE I HEALTH CARE
Commentary: Note that this authorization is broad and allows the agent to copy the principal's medical records at the principal's expense. This clause must be coordinated with the financial power of attorney if someone other than the agent under the financial power of attorney is the agent under the health-care power of attorney. This clause authorizes, but does not require, the agent to disclose the protected health information to anyone whom the agent deems relevant. In a blended family, it is prudent to require the agent to communicate information concerning the principal's care and treatment to all interested parties of both sides of the family, and that is what the bracketed language at the end of this clause addresses. On the other hand, if the agent cannot be relied on to communicate what is appropriate, perhaps a different person should be designated as agent. Another approach is to suggest but not require (to avoid a legally binding restriction) having the agent confer with other successor agents before acting.	The agent shall have the following rights and authority: 1.1 <u>Medical and Other Records</u>. To: (a) have complete access to, examine and, at the Principal's expense, to copy, all medical and other records and/or information pertaining to the Principal's physical or mental condition; and (b) reproduce, disseminate and discuss the same with anyone that the Agent deems relevant, as well as the power to execute such consents and releases as may be necessary to obtain such records and/or information, including, without limitation, all powers necessary for release of information under the Health Insurance Portability and Accountability Act of 1996 (HIPAA), 42 USC 1320d and the private regulations that are contained in 45 CFR 160-164[; provided, however, that the agent shall promptly comply with reasonable requests for protected health information concerning the principal's care and treatment that are made by (NAME OR DESCRIBE THE RELATIONSHIP OF THE PEOPLE WHO ARE ENTITLED TO THE INFORMATION)].

Figure 63.2 (cont'd)

Commentary: This provision allows the agent to deal with all health-care providers just as the principal could, it being understood that this clause must be coordinated with the financial power of attorney and the agent under that instrument. It is recommended that the financial agent solely possess powers over financial matters but be directed to pay for medical decisions made by the health care agent. Consider deleting the bracketed clause. Some clients will not wish to grant the agent named for general medical decision making access to or power over psychiatric and related records and documents. If not, be certain to expressly exclude such powers.	1.2 <u>Engagement and Termination</u>. To: (a) select; (b) contract with; (c) pay and/or terminate employment or discharge physicians other health care providers and health-care organizations, psychologists, social workers, dentists, nurses, therapists, sitters, companions and other professional or nonprofessional medical assistants, hospitals, including surgical care hospitals, insurance companies or other health organizations, institutions, home care, nursing home, custodial care or other places for medical treatment, and also the changing of such selections, decisions as to the manner and nature of treatments, services and care to be performed or delivered by anyone; [and (d) in coordination with the Principal's agent under any durable property power of attorney, to commit the Principal to pay for such, it being understood that the Agent shall not be financially responsible for the Principal's care unless the Agent expressly assumes such personal liability].
Commentary: This is a broad grant of authority to the agent to both consent and withdraw consent to health-care treatment as well as refusal to consent to health-care treatment. If the principal knows in advance what limitations, if any, which the principal would want to place upon the agent, this clause would have to be so modified. It is recommended that nutrition and hydration be addressed in a separate independent provision given the common sensitivity and often controversy accompanying such provisions.	1.3 <u>Consent; Refusal and Withdrawal of Consent; Right to Privacy</u>. To make and execute: (a) all consents; (b) refusals of consents; (c) withdrawals of consent to any care, treatment, service or procedure, including, without limitation, diagnostic tests, surgery, life-sustaining treatment or provision of nourishment and/or hydration (including, for example, all forms of feeding), pain relieving medication or procedures, experimental treatments, cardiopulmonary resuscitation and emergency care; (d) releases from liability for any health care provider or other service provider that acts on behalf of the Principal in reliance upon the Agent, including, without limitation, all documents purporting to be a "Refusal of Treatment" and "Leaving Facility Against Medical Advice;" and (e) such documents and/or actions that are necessary or advisable in order to waive and/or exercise the Principal's right of privacy and right to make decisions on behalf of the Principal, even though these actions may hasten the moment of death, be against conventional medical advice, cause addiction or cause adverse side effects.
Commentary: This is a broad authorization clause intended to comply with the HIPAA privacy regulations. However, because each health-care provider tends to have their own separate form for this issue, it is recommended that the client sign HIPAA authorization forms for the expected health-care providers and use the health-care power of attorney HIPAA authorization to buttress those authorizations and fill in the gaps for any health-care provider for which no HIPAA authorization form was signed.	1.4 <u>HIPAA Authorization</u>. The Principal intends for the Agent to be treated as the Principal would be treated with regard to the use and dissemination of the Principal's individually identifiable health information and medical records ("Protected Health Information") and that in all events the Agent be treated as a HIPAA Representative for the Principal. This authority applies to any information governed by HIPAA. The Principal specifically authorizes: (a) any physician, dentist, other health care professional or medical provider, health plan, hospital, clinic, laboratory, pharmacy or other health care provider, any insurance company and the Medical Information Bureau, Inc. or other health care organization that has provided treatment or services to the Principal or that has paid for or is seeking payment from the Principal for such services, to give, disclose and release such Protected Health Information to the Agent; and (b) to disclose all of the Principal's Protected Health Information regarding any past, present or future medical or mental health condition, including, without limitation, all information relating to the diagnosis and treatment of HIV/AIDS, sexually transmitted diseases, mental illness and drug or alcohol abuse, to the Agent.

HEALTH-CARE DOCUMENTS — CHAPTER 63

Figure 63.2 (cont'd)

Commentary: This clause authorizes the agent to admit the principal into health-care facilities and to transfer the principal out of any such facility. As noted above some clients will not wish to grant the health care agent authority over psychiatric matters. If not, delete/modify the language permitting institutionalization.	1.5 <u>Hospitalization; Institutionalization</u>. To admit the Principal to any health care facility, including, without limitation, hospitals, institutions, substance abuse treatment facilities, homes, residential or nursing facilities, hospice or home care, whether for physical or mental care or treatment; and to remove the Principal from any such facility at any time, even if contrary to medical advice.
Commentary: This clause authorizes the agent to release any party who is asked to rely upon the agent's authority from liability.	1.6 <u>Releases</u>. To release from liability any person who acts on behalf of the Principal in reliance on the Agent and to execute any document in accordance therewith.
Commentary: This clause authorizes the agent to move the domicile of the principal. This clause requires the agent under the health-care power of attorney to coordinate the domicile change with the agent under the property power of attorney. Some clients might prefer to expressly have the health care agent hold this power so that the decision process is focused on moving a domicile, not for tax purposes, but for attaining desired health care treatment, especially end of life decision making. If so, delete bracketed language.	1.7 <u>Change Domicile</u>. [In conjunction with the agent under the principal's property power of attorney,] to establish and change the Principal's domicile.
	ARTICLE II REFUSAL OF MEDICAL TREATMENT
Commentary: This part of the form is optional and is the living will part of the form. This particular clause requires two physicians to certify that the principal's condition is terminal and irreversible. However, applicable state law may only require one physician to so certify, so it is important to know applicable state law in this regard. Consider providing for these type of provisions solely in the living will as a separate document. Practitioners should also be sensitive to religious considerations as withdrawal of life support may have different religious ramifications then withholding such life support.	The Agent has the following powers: 2.1 <u>Withdraw or Withhold Life Support</u>. Assuming that two licensed physicians (one of whom is the Principal's regular attending physician) have personally examined the Principal and have determined that the Principal's condition is terminal and irreversible, or if the Principal is diagnosed as being in a profound comatose state with no reasonable chance of recovery, to sign any documents, waivers or releases that are necessary to withdraw, withhold or cease any procedure calculated only to prolong the Principal's life, including, without limitation, the use of a respirator, cardiopulmonary resuscitation, surgery, dialysis, blood transfusion, antibiotics, antiarrhythmic and pressor drugs or transplants.

Figure 63.2 (cont'd)

Commentary: This clause authorizes refusal and discontinuation of feeding the principal. If the principal desires to continue to be fed, then this clause should be omitted. Consider providing for these type of provisions solely in the living will as a separate document. Practitioners should also be sensitive to religious considerations of nutrition and hydration.	2.2 <u>Nourishment</u>. To refuse or discontinue intravenous or parenteral feeding, misting and endotracheal or nasogastric tubes, if advised that no undue pain will be caused to the Principal.
	ARTICLE III OPERATIONAL PROVISIONS
Commentary: This clause does not compensate the Agent for service as agent. Therefore, if the principal desires to compensate the agent for what can be a burdensome and time-consuming task, then the form would have to be modified. Perhaps the best way to compensate an agent under a health-care power of attorney is time-based (i.e., hourly). It is recommended that compensation, unless for a professional health care surrogate, be considered with caution.	3.1 <u>Expenses; No Compensation</u>. The Agent shall be entitled to reimbursement for all costs and expenses reasonably incurred on behalf, but the Agent shall not otherwise be entitled to compensation for services rendered pursuant to this instrument.
Commentary: This clause would only assess liability to the agent if the agent were determined to have engaged in willful misconduct or acts of gross negligence, which is a standard that is higher than ordinary negligence. If the principal wants to except the agent from all such liability or to even reduce the standard to ordinary negligence (which could be a huge burden on the agent perhaps so much so that no one would serve), then the principal would have to modify the form.	3.2 <u>Release</u>. The Principal releases and discharges the Agent and the Agent's heirs, successors and assigns from any and all liability arising out of any acts or omissions of the Agent pursuant to this instrument, except for willful misconduct or gross negligence.
Commentary: Specifying state law is important because of the disparity in the laws of the various states. Also, because of the portability of patients across state lines all health related documents should be notarized and signed by two independent witnesses to enhance the likelihood of acceptance in other states.	3.3 <u>Applicable Law</u>. This instrument shall be governed by the laws of the state of _____.

Figure 63.2 (cont'd)

Commentary: This clause does four things. First, it expressly provides that the principal retains the right to amend the instrument. Second, the principal retains the power to revoke the instrument. Third, the clause provides a procedure for the agent's resignation. Finally, the clause expressly provides that the principal retains the right to remove the agent and appoint successor(s).	3.4 <u>Revocation, Removal, Amendment and Resignation</u>. The Principal retains the power to amend and/or revoke this instrument in writing. The Principal retains the power to remove the Agent by written document delivered to the removed Agent and to appoint a new Agent, including, without limitation, adding new Agents to serve with any Agent who is then serving, even if the person(s) appointed differ from the successor agents who are named in Section 3.11. If this instrument has been recorded in the public records, then the act of revocation, amendment or removal shall be filed or recorded in the same manner. The Agent may resign in writing delivered to the Principal or, if the Principal is incapacitated, subject to a guardianship or otherwise incapable of communication, by delivery to any person with whom the Principal is then residing or who is responsible for the Principal's care; provided, however, that if, at the time of resignation, the Principal has been formally subjected to a guardianship, then the resigning Agent shall deliver notice of resignation to the Principal's guardian.
Commentary: This clause simply ensures that there is no conflict between any of the principal's other powers of attorney. However, this clause does revoke all prior health-care powers of attorney, including the health-care provisions of a combined property and health-care power of attorney. Therefore, if this is not what the principal desires (i.e., wants to maintain other health-care powers of attorney in existence), then the principal would have to modify the form to cull out which powers of attorney are to remain in existence.	3.5 <u>No Conflict with Property Power of Attorney; Revocation</u>. This instrument is separate and distinct from any other general or special financial or property power of attorney that the Principal may give or have given and shall not revoke or otherwise modify or affect any such power of attorney; provided, however, that this instrument shall revoke all prior health-care powers of attorney and advance health-care directives that the Principal has executed in the past.
Commentary: Even though health-care powers of attorney are intended to be durable, it is good practice to affirmatively state that in the instrument, which is what this clause does.	3.6 <u>Durability</u>. The Principal further declared that this instrument shall not be terminated or otherwise modified or affected by the Principal's incapacity, disability or other condition making express revocation impossible or impractical, including, without limitation, only being subjected to a limited conservatorship for inability to take care of the Principal's property.
Commentary: This provision is important to all health-care providers, who will be concerned about their liability for acting on the agent's representations and/or instructions. This clause provides a blanket release. The clause could be modified to require that the health-care provider be reasonable in their reliance upon the agent. However, the better practice is to give a blanket release because these decisions often require prompt action under pressure.	3.7 <u>Release of Third Persons</u>. No person who relies upon the authority of the Agent pursuant to authority granted in this instrument, whether express or implied, shall be liable to the Principal or his successors and assigns. No person who relies in good faith upon any oral or written representation that the Agent may make as to: (a) the fact that this instrument is then in effect as per the copy that they have been provided; or (b) the Agent's authority pursuant to this instrument in effect shall be liable to the Principal or his successors and assigns.

Figure 63.2 (cont'd)

Commentary: This clause simply gives the agent the right to go to court to enforce the instrument, and it authorizes the agent to pursue any health-care provider who either negligently or willfully refuses to comply with the instrument for damages.	3.8 <u>Judicial Enforcement</u>. With no impact on the effectiveness of this instrument whatsoever, the Agent is expressly authorized, but is not required, on the Principal's behalf and at the Principal's expense, to pursue: (a) a declaratory judgment from any court of proper jurisdiction construing this instrument, including its validity; (b) any action requiring compliance with this instrument; and/or (c) an action for damages against any person who is obligated to comply with this instrument but who negligently or willfully fails or refuses to do so.
Commentary: In blended or fractured families, this clause can be important if the principal desires that persons other than the agent (e.g., the other children) have access to the principal as well as the principal's health-care information, which otherwise might be withheld from those children. This clause is only triggered upon a determination of the principal's incapacity, so if the principal desires to dispense with that requirement, the clause would need to be modified to remove the "upon" part of the clause. The clause does not require constant responses to every request for information and access to the principal and only applies to reasonable requests, because overly wrought individuals may carry it too far and inconvenience or even obstruct the agent's efforts. The clause only requires that the agent respond to reasonable requests and gives a time frame for response that is to be considered reasonable. If the client desires not to provide such a presumption, then the "provided, however" part of the clause would need to be removed.	3.9 <u>Access to Principal and Requests for Information Concerning Health-Care</u>. Upon a determination that the Principal lacks capacity, the Agent shall use his best efforts to make the Principal physically available to [NAME OR DESCRIBE CLASS OF PEOPLE TO WHOM THIS RIGHT APPLIES] and shall promptly respond to reasonable requests for updates on the Principal's health-care condition; provided, however, that [DESCRIBE TIME FRAME, DAILY, HOURLY DURING WAKING HOURS, ETC.] updates will be deemed to be reasonably provided updates for this purpose.
Commentary: The health-care power of attorney should be effectively immediately and not spring into effect only after a subsequent event such as incapacity.	3.10 <u>Effective Date</u>. The Agent's powers and obligations pursuant to this instrument shall be effective on the execution hereof.
Commentary: The principal should name successor agents to act in case the agent is uncomfortable, unwilling or unable to serve.	3.11 <u>Successor Agent[s]</u>. If the Agent is or becomes unwilling or unable to serve, then I appoint [NAME(S) OF SUCCESSOR AGENTS] [in the order selected] as successor agent. If none of the persons appointed above are able or become unwilling to serve, then the immediately last serving Agent shall appoint a successor Agent. If the immediately last serving Agent fails to appoint a successor Agent within [STATE TIME PERIOD FOR APPOINTMENT IN DAYS OR HOURS], then [NAME(S) OF PERSONS WHO SHALL APPOINT A SUCCESSOR AGENT] shall appoint a successor Agent, and any of them may be named as successor Agent, even if it means that they are naming themselves.
A different type of health-care power of attorney, contained in Section 4 of the Act, is outlined and analyzed in Figure 62.3.	

HEALTH-CARE DOCUMENTS CHAPTER 63

Figure 63.3

Uniform Health-Care Decisions Act Form.

The Act contains a specimen form Advance Health-Care Directive,[37] which is set forth below:

PART 1
POWER OF ATTORNEY FOR HEALTH CARE

Commentary: Part 1 (1) of the Advance Health-Care Directive requires only the designation of a single agent, but gives the principal an opportunity to designate alternate agents. This form makes no provision for the designation of co-agents. If co-agents are appointed, then the instrument really must specify that either is authorized to act independently if the other co-agent is not reasonably available. It should specify a method for resolving disagreements between co-agents if those occur. Generally, we caution against appointing co-agents for fear of a lack of consensus at a crucial time in the principal's life. An agent can be encouraged and even required to consult with the rest of the family to get their input, but it is best that only one agent be named to make these calls.	(1) DESIGNATION OF AGENT: I designate the following individual as my agent to make health-care decisions for me: _____ (name of individual you choose as agent) _____ (address) (city) (state) (zip code) _____ (home phone) (work phone) OPTIONAL: If I revoke my agent's authority or if my agent is not willing, able or reasonably available to make a health-care decision for me, I designate as my first alternate agent: _____ (name of individual you choose as first alternate agent) _____ (address) (city) (state) (zip code) _____ (home phone) (work phone) OPTIONAL: If I revoke the authority of my agent and first alternate agent or if neither is willing, able or reasonably available to make a health-care decision for me, I designate as my second alternate agent: _____ (name of individual you choose as second alternate agent) _____ (address) (city) (state) (zip code) _____ (home phone) (work phone)
Commentary: Part 1 (2) of the Advance Health-Care Directive grants the agent authority to make all health-care decisions for the principal, subject to any limitations that the principal may provide in the form. The Advance Health-Care Directive refers to artificial nutrition and hydration and other forms of treatment that keep a principal alive in order to ensure that the principal is aware that those are forms of health care that the agent would have the authority to withdraw or withhold absent specific coverage.	(2) AGENT'S AUTHORITY: My agent is authorized to make all health-care decisions for me, including decisions to provide, withhold or withdraw artificial nutrition and hydration and all other forms of health care to keep me alive, except as I state here: _____ _____ (Add additional sheets if needed.)

Figure 63.3 (cont'd)

Commentary: Part 1 (3) of the Advance Health-Care Directive provides that the agent's authority only becomes effective upon a determination that the individual lacks capacity, but it allows the principal to check a box indicating that the authority of the agent takes effect immediately. As mentioned previously, if the power is not effective immediately, then the HIPAA privacy rules will block access and input by the agent until the crucial incapacity determination is made by a health-care provider, which could negatively impact the principal's health-care, particularly where the health-care provider is slow to make the incapacity determination.	(3) WHEN AGENT'S AUTHORITY BECOMES EFFECTIVE: My agent's authority becomes effective when my primary physician determines that I am unable to make my own health-care decisions unless I mark the following box. If I mark this box [ ], my agent's authority to make health-care decisions for me takes effect immediately.
Commentary: Part 1 (5) of the Advance Health-Care Directive nominates the agent, if available, able and willing to act, otherwise the alternate agents in order of priority stated, as guardians of the principal. This provision apparently was included in the form for two reasons. First, if an appointment of a guardian becomes necessary, then the agent is assumed to be the one whom the individual would most likely want to serve in that role, unless the principal wants the agent under a property power of attorney to serve as guardian or conservator. Therefore, this provision must be coordinated with the property power of attorney. Second, the nomination of the agent as guardian will reduce the possibility that someone other than the agent will be appointed as guardian who could use the position to thwart the agent's authority.	(4) AGENT'S OBLIGATION: My agent shall make health-care decisions for me in accordance with this power of attorney for health care, any instructions I give in Part 2 of this form, and my other wishes to the extent known to my agent. To the extent my wishes are unknown; my agent shall make health-care decisions for me in accordance with what my agent determines to be in my best interest. In determining my best interest, my agent shall consider my personal values to the extent known to my agent. Part 1 (4) of the Advance Health-Care Directive directs the agent to make health-care decisions in accordance with the form, any instructions that the principal gives in Part 2 of the form and the principal's other wishes to the extent that the agent knows those wishes. If the principal's wishes concerning health-care are unknown, then the agent is to make health-care decisions based upon what the agent determines to be in the individual's best interest. In determining the principal's best interest, the agent is to consider the individual's personal values to the extent that the agent knows those values. Section 2(e) of the Act imposes this standard, whether or not it is included in the form, but its inclusion in the Advance Health-Care Directive calls it to the principal's attention, any guardian or surrogate as well as the principal's health-care providers. (5) NOMINATION OF GUARDIAN: If a guardian of my person needs to be appointed for me by a court, I nominate the agent designated in this form. If that agent is not willing, able or reasonably available to act as guardian, I nominate the alternate agents whom I have named, in the order designated.
PART 2 INSTRUCTIONS FOR HEALTH CARE	
Commentary: Because the variety of treatment decisions to which health-care instructions may relate is virtually unlimited, Part 2 of the Advance Health-Care Directive is not comprehensive. It is directed at the types of treatment for which a principal is most likely to have special wishes.	If you are satisfied to allow your agent to determine what is best for you in making end-of-life decisions, you need not fill out this part of the form. If you do fill out this part of the form, you may strike any wording you do not want.

Figure 63.3 (cont'd)

Commentary: Part 2(6) of the Advance Health-Care Directive, entitled "End-of-Life Decisions", provides two alternative choices for the expression of wishes concerning the provision, withholding or withdrawal of treatment. Under the first choice, the principal's life is not to be prolonged if the principal has an incurable and irreversible condition that will result in death within a relatively short time, if the principal becomes unconscious and, to a reasonable degree of medical certainty, will not regain consciousness or if the likely risks and burdens of treatment would outweigh the expected benefits. Under the second choice, the principal's life is to be prolonged within the limits of generally accepted health-care standards. Note that under this choice, it does not require the health-care providers to use all means that possibly could extend life, so if the principal desires heroic and even experimental or research-only options to be used, then the form has to be modified to provide for that result.	(6) END-OF-LIFE DECISIONS: I direct that my health-care providers and others involved in my care provide, withhold or withdraw treatment in accordance with the choice I have marked below: [ ] (a) Choice Not To Prolong Life I do not want my life to be prolonged if: (i) I have an incurable and irreversible condition that will result in my death within a relatively short time; (ii) I become unconscious and, to a reasonable degree of medical certainty, I will not regain consciousness; or (iii) the likely risks and burdens of treatment would outweigh the expected benefits; OR [ ] (b) Choice to Prolong Life I want my life to be prolonged as long as possible within the limits of generally accepted health-care standards.
Commentary: Part 2(7) of the Advance Health-Care Directive provides a box for a principal to mark if the principal wishes to receive artificial nutrition and hydration in all circumstances.	(7) ARTIFICIAL NUTRITION AND HYDRATION: Artificial nutrition and hydration must be provided, withheld or withdrawn in accordance with the choice I have made in paragraph (6) unless I mark the following box. If I mark this box [ ], artificial nutrition and hydration must be provided regardless of my condition and regardless of the choice I have made in paragraph (6).
Commentary: Part 2(8) of the Advance Health-Care Directive provides space for a principal to specify any circumstance when the principal would prefer not to receive pain relief.	(8) RELIEF FROM PAIN: Except as I state in the following space, I direct that treatment for alleviation of pain or discomfort be provided at all times, even if it hastens my death:

Figure 63.3 (cont'd)

Commentary: Because the choices provided in Parts 2(6) to 2(8) do not cover all possible situations, Part 2(9) of the form provides space for the principal to write out his or her own instructions or to supplement the instructions given in the previous subparts of the form. Should the space be insufficient, the principal is free to add additional pages. The health-care instructions given in Part 2 of the form are binding on the agent, any guardian, any surrogate, and—subject to exceptions specified in Sections 7(e)-(f) of the Act—on the principal's health-care providers. Pursuant to Section 7(d) of the Act, a health-care provider also must comply with a reasonable interpretation of those instructions made by an authorized agent, guardian or surrogate.	(9) OTHER WISHES: (If you do not agree with any of the optional choices above and wish to write your own, or if you wish to add to the instructions you have given above, you may do so here.) I direct that: _____ _____ (Add additional sheets if needed.)
	PART 3 DONATION OF ORGANS AT DEATH
Commentary: Part 3 of the Advance Health-Care Directive provides the principal with an opportunity to express an intention to donate bodily organs and tissues at death. The options provided are derived from a suggested form in the Comment to Section 2 of the Uniform Anatomical Gift Act.	(OPTIONAL) (10) Upon my death (mark applicable box) [ ] (a) I give any needed organs, tissues or parts, OR [ ] (b) I give the following organs, tissues or parts only _____ (c) My gift is for the following purposes (strike any of the following you do not want) (i) Transplant (ii) Therapy (iii) Research (iv) Education
	PART 4 PRIMARY PHYSICIAN
Commentary: Part 4 of the Advance Health-Care Directive provides space for the principal to designate a primary physician should the principal choose to do so. Space is also provided for the designation of an alternate primary physician should the first designated physician not be available, able or willing to act.	(OPTIONAL) (11) I designate the following physician as my primary physician: _____ (name of physician) _____ (address) (city) (state) (zip code) _____ (phone) OPTIONAL: If the physician I have designated above is not willing, able or reasonably available to act as my primary physician, I designate the following physician as my primary physician: _____ (name of physician) _____ (address) (city) (state) (zip code) _____ (phone)

Figure 63.3 (cont'd)

| *Commentary:* The Act does not require witnessing of advance health-care directives, but in order to encourage the practice, the Advance Health-Care Directive provides space for the signatures of two witnesses. The Advance Health-Care Directive does not require formal acceptance by an agent. Formal written acceptance by an agent was omitted in the form. Designated agents have no duty to act until they accept the office either expressly or through their conduct. Consequently, requiring formal acceptance reduces the risk that a designated agent will decline to act when the need arises. Formal acceptance also makes it more likely that the agent will become familiar with the principal's personal values and views on health care. While the Advance Health-Care Directive does not require formal acceptance, the explanation to the form does encourage principals to talk to the person they have named as agent to make certain that the designated agent understands their wishes and is willing to take the responsibility. | (12) EFFECT OF COPY: A copy of this form has the same effect as the original.
Commentary: Paragraph (12) of the Advance Health-Care Directive conforms with the provisions of Section 12 of the Act by providing that a copy of the form has the same effect as the original.
(13) SIGNATURES: Sign and date the form here:

_____ _____
(date)   (sign your name)

_____ _____
(address)   (print your name)

_____
(city) (state) (zip)

(Optional) SIGNATURES OF WITNESSES:
First witness   Second witness

_____ _____
(print name)   (print name)

_____ _____
(address)   (address)

_____ _____
(city) (state)   (city) (state)

_____ _____
(signature of witness)   (signature of witness) |

63.8 SOME OPTIONAL PROVISIONS FOR CONSIDERATION

1. Visitation By Partner [Non-blood related persons].

   a. For purposes of visitation in hospitals, nursing homes, or other facilities, it is my express intent that PARTNERNAME be treated and considered for all purposes as an immediate family member, and be given the widest latitude and accommodation as if a member of my immediate family, and if the Agent named is not a member of my immediate family that such Agent be given preference over any blood relatives for visitation and other purposes.

   b. Under no circumstances should an Agent named herein be denied access for visitation or other purposes because such an Agent is not a blood relative.

2. The power to change domicile.

   a. I grant to my Agent the express authority and power to maintain or change my domicile from the State to any other state. I anticipate that if in the future I do not have capacity to change my domicile, I hereby expressly authorize my Agent to change my domicile for any and all purposes. It is my express intent to delegate to and authorize my Agent to so act and to grant my Agent the authority to change my intent as to domicile and to act upon same.

3. The power to address cemetary and related or similar matters.

   a. inquire as to whether the cemetery or cemeteries where my family is buried [interred] are fulfilling their responsibilities under any applicable perpetual care contracts in existence, and to take any actions to assume same, and to direct the Fiduciary under my Last Will and

Testament to make any payments necessary to assure same.

4. Powers of Agent as to Mental Health and Psychiatric Issues.

   a. I specifically grant [do not grant] to my Agent all the powers and rights necessary to effect my Wishes as they pertain to mental health and psychiatric issues.

5. Guardian and Conservator.

   a. To the extent that I am permitted by law to do so, I hereby nominate my Agent to serve as my guardian, special medical guardian, conservator, or in any similar representative capacity, and if I am not permitted by law to so nominate, then I request that any court that may be involved in the appointment of a guardian, special medical guardian, conservator or similar representative for me give the greatest weight to this request.

63.9 FREQUENTLY ASKED QUESTIONS

Question – Is it common to include living will provisions in a health-care power of attorney, and is it advisable to do so?

Answer – A living will should be a separate document independent of the health care power of attorney. The living will should be the primary document that sets forth the client's wishes for health care and end of life. The health care power of attorney should designate the person to make those and other decisions and provide the requisite powers to do so.

Question – What are the risks of making a health-care power of attorney a springing power?

Answer – it is recommended that the health care proxy or medical power of attorney be effective upon execution. The wide range of medical conditions make the application of a springing power for health care problematic. If a client has full capacity he or she will not be in a position to make decisions just prior to, during or after many medical procedures. Is the client really incapacitated and what must be done to corroborate that incapacity and when it ends. The uncertainty can be resolved with an immediately effective power. The definition of incapacity in the health-care power of attorney can be uncertain. It could be an objective determination (e.g., a determination by the principal's supervising health-care provider) or there could be another definition of incapacity. Suppose that the supervising health-care provider is unavailable or, if any health-care provider can make the incapacity determination, they are slow to make the incapacity determination. This loss of time could be very problematic to the principal. It is for these reasons that it is recommended that health-care powers of attorney be immediate in effect. If the principal cannot or does not trust the agent to make the health-care determinations and decisions until the principal loses capacity, then perhaps the principal should revisit the choice of agent.

Question – What are the risks of unmarried partners who fail to execute health-care powers of attorney?

Answer – The risks and associated costs of such a failure could be severe to both partners. The partner who has not been appointed legally could be frozen out of making health-care decisions or even of receiving health-care information about the principal. Indeed, depending upon the partner's relationship with the patient partner's blood family, which often is not good, the partner may even be prohibited from seeing the patient partner at that person's most vulnerable and needful time. This might be the case despite the partner's probable best knowledge of the patient partner's desires and intentions, which family members could sadly and spitefully deem to be irrelevant. For this reason alone, it is imperative that unmarried partners express their intentions and dictates in a health-care power of attorney. See sample clause above.

CHAPTER ENDNOTES

1. See, e.g., Section 1(1), Uniform Health-Care Decisions Act.
2. See, e.g., Section 2(a), Uniform Health-Care Decisions Act.
3. See, e.g., Section 2(a), Uniform Health-Care Decisions Act.
4. Pub. L. No. 104-191, 110 Stat. 1936 (1996); 45 C.F.R. Sec. 164 (2002). HIPAA, as amended (GINA).
5. 45 CFR 164.502(g).
6. See, e.g., Section 1(6), Uniform Health-Care Decisions Act.
7. See, e.g., Section 1(3), Uniform Health-Care Decisions Act.
8. See, e.g., Section 2(b), Uniform Health-Care Decisions Act.
9. See, e.g., Section 1(1), Uniform Health-Care Decisions Act.
10. See, e.g., Section 2(b), Uniform Health-Care Decisions Act.

11. See, e.g., Section 2(c), Uniform Health-Care Decisions Act.
12. See, e.g., Section 2(d), Uniform Health-Care Decisions Act.
13. See, e.g., Section 2(e), Uniform Health-Care Decisions Act.
14. Section 5-601(e), Maryland Health Care Decisions Act.
15. See, e.g., Section 2(f), Uniform Health-Care Decisions Act.
16. See, e.g., Section 2(g), Uniform Health-Care Decisions Act.
17. See, e.g., Section 2(h), Uniform Health-Care Decisions Act.
18. See, e.g., Section 7(a), Uniform Health-Care Decisions Act.
19. See, e.g., Section 7(b), Uniform Health-Care Decisions Act.
20. See, e.g., Section 7(e), Uniform Health-Care Decisions Act.
21. See, e.g., Section 7(f), Uniform Health-Care Decisions Act.
22. See, e.g., Section 7(d), Uniform Health-Care Decisions Act.
23. See, e.g., Section 3(a), Uniform Health-Care Decisions Act.
24. See, e.g., Section 3(b), Uniform Health-Care Decisions Act.
25. See, e.g., Section 3(d), Uniform Health-Care Decisions Act.
26. See, e.g., Section 3(e), Uniform Health-Care Decisions Act.
27. See, e.g., Section 5(a), Uniform Health-Care Decisions Act.
28. See, e.g., Section 5(b), Uniform Health-Care Decisions Act.
29. See, e.g., Section 5(c), Uniform Health-Care Decisions Act.
30. See, e.g., Section 5(d), Uniform Health-Care Decisions Act.
31. See, e.g., Section 7(g), Uniform Health-Care Decisions Act.
32. See, e.g., Section 7(h), Uniform Health-Care Decisions Act.
33. See, e.g., Section 8, Uniform Health-Care Decisions Act.
34. See, e.g., Section 9(a), Uniform Health-Care Decisions Act.
35. See, e.g., Section 10(a), Uniform Health-Care Decisions Act.
36. See, e.g., Section 10(b), Uniform Health-Care Decisions Act.
37. See, e.g., Section 4, Uniform Health-Care Decisions Act.

REVOCABLE TRUSTS

CHAPTER 64

64.1 INTRODUCTION

Revocable trusts are known by a myriad of names. Some of the different names help identify some of the important characteristics of these trusts. Almost universally revocable trusts are touted for their use to avoid probate. While this can be beneficial for clients, this chapter will endeavor to highlight what may be a more important and growing use of revocable trusts, namely providing better security to aging clients.

Many of the consumer names for revocable trusts are rather meaningless, or confusing, but are helpful for practitioners to differentiate the various names to better deal with client questions concerning planning with these trusts:

- These trusts are *inter vivos* **trusts or "living trusts"** in consumer lexicon, because they are created during a client's lifetime. This is to be distinguished from testamentary trusts created on a client's death. The latter are often created under the client's will, but almost all living trusts include provisions creating a range of trusts that only become effective on the client's death.

- They are called **revocable trusts**, the name used in this chapter, because the client can change them at any time. This is an important characteristic of these trusts that differentiates them from the many irrevocable trusts clients create for tax, asset protection and other purposes as part of the estate planning process. This is important because many misinformed clients believe that revocable trusts provide tax and/or asset protection benefits that only irrevocable trusts can provide. During the grantor's lifetime, the grantor retains the absolute right to totally revoke the trust, change its terms to any degree, and/or regain total possession of the property in the trust. This is in fact common, with the client revoking a prior trust by amending and restating it with a new trust when there is a desire to change dispositive terms. Caution must be exercised to assure that the assets held under the predecessor trust remain held in the revised amended and restated trust.

- These trusts have been referred to in some consumer publications as **"loving trusts"** to somehow connote that if you loved your family you would create such a trust to spare them the costs and nightmares (all mostly fictitious) of the probate process. These play on client fears of the purported evils of the probate process.

- Revocable trusts are **grantor trusts** for income tax purposes. This is important as there are no income tax implications to create these trusts. However, given the common use of techniques making irrevocable trusts also grantor trusts for income tax purposes, it is important to differentiate revocable trusts from these other trusts so that clients understand what exactly they are creating.

A revocable trust is a contractual relationship, created during the lifetime of the "grantor" (the person establishing the trust, also called the "settlor"), in which one party (the "trustee") holds property for the benefit of another (the "beneficiary"). In many revocable trusts these parties are all the same, the grantor is the trustee and the primary intended beneficiary. While this might seem an oddity it can nonetheless create a valuable mechanism to protect the grantor from future incapacity, minimize or avoid probate costs, facilitate moving trusts formed on death under the revocable trust to other jurisdictions, segregate and preserve the identity of pre-marital or immune assets, and many other planning objectives. In fact, revocable trusts can be incredibly useful planning tools which are too often either dismissed by many practitioners as simplistic or meaningless, or which are only viewed from the perspective of probate avoidance. With some creativity, they can be incredibly powerful tools, especially with an aging population.

While revocable trust can be established for a limited period of time, such as a specified period of years, that is rarely done. Such a trust can also last until the occurrence or nonoccurrence of a specific event, or it can continue – even after the death of the grantor. The most common use of this technique is a trust that continues for the duration of the client/grantor's lifetime and on death which serves as a primary dispositive document creating trusts for spouses and heirs that might last for as long as applicable law permits.

A revocable trust becomes irrevocable when the grantor, during lifetime, relinquishes title to property placed in the trust and gives up all right to alter, amend, revoke, or terminate the trust. In some instances, revocable trusts grant a third party, such as a family member who is not a beneficiary, the authority to terminate the grantor's power to revoke the trust and right to be a beneficiary. This right can be a powerful tax and asset protection planning tool. If the client becomes incapacitated the client won't be able to relinquish rights to the trust. If the third party can do so it may leave open a valuable planning opportunity. It also becomes irrevocable at the moment the grantor dies. Such a trust effectively becomes irrevocable if the grantor lacks the capacity to amend and restate the trust. With the growing use of revocable trusts as a later life or elder planning tool for aging or infirm clients practitioners will have to exercise considerable caution in determining whether to amend, revoke, or otherwise modify such trusts. Bear in mind that in many jurisdictions a revocable trust requires contractual capacity to modify or revoke, whereas a will may require only testamentary capacity which can be a much lower standard.

64.2 WHEN IS USE OF SUCH A DEVICE INDICATED?

1. Where the grantor wishes someone else to accept management responsibility for all or a portion of the grantor's property. While an investment advisor can be hired by the client and given significant latitude in a discretionary investment account, and a bookkeeper to pay bills, vesting control in a trustee or co-trustee to make decisions provides a greater degree of protection via such transfer of power.

2. Where the grantor wishes to assure continuity of management and income flow of a business or other assets in the event of death or disability those assets could be owned by a narrowly tailored revocable trust. However, it will likely be more efficient to have the business operation owned by an entity, such as a limited liability company ("LLC") and provide for succession of management by naming a successor manager. Similar results can be achieved using a corporate or partnership structure, but the LLC is generally the vehicle of choice. Using an entity rather than trust may prove easier as third parties are more attuned to such mechanism.

3. Where the grantor wishes to protect against the investment and asset management problems that would be brought on by physical or mental incapacity or legal incompetency, or the physical, mental, or emotional incapacity or legal incompetency of beneficiaries. This is becoming the most common and important use of these trusts. A fully funded revocable trust (one to which the client has transferred all appropriate assets, e.g., other than retirement accounts and professional practice interests) can avoid the need for guardianship as a successor trustee can handle all of the client's financial matters when the client can no longer do so.

4. Where the grantor desires privacy in the handling and administration of his assets during lifetime and at death. While many clients assume using a living trust assure privacy this is not the case. A probate contest, for example, may require full disclosure of the revocable trust in the public record if it is the primary dispositive document, or even simply an important dispositive document. That being said, using a revocable trust can avoid having to file a will in the local probate or surrogate's court that has more personal data than the client or his or her family wish disclosed. If there is no issue of a probate litigation then there may be no reason for the detailed dispositive provisions to become public.

5. Where the grantor wishes to minimize estate administration costs and delay at death by avoiding probate. This is often the primary or sole reason most

clients wish to have a living trust. Practitioners need to educate these clients as to the benefits of using a trust to minimize issues as a client ages or develops worsening medical issues. The consumer press has so distorted the view of revocable trusts that many clients will demand them to avoid the anticipated evils of probate. The problems with these common consumer misconceptions is that they can impede professionals from properly advising and guiding clients that have them. For example, having a revocable trust will do little to minimize the post-death cost of dealing with scores of accounts. Rather, consolidating those accounts to the least number of accounts the client actually needs to maintain may eliminate significant administrative costs. Clients who become so focused on a revocable trust to avoid ancillary probate may be reluctant to address the use of an LLC for asset protection that may be far more important than merely probate avoidance. Finally, for really simple estates, joint accounts, pay on death and similar accounts, all avoid probate without the cost of a trust if that is really the appropriate goal.

6. A revocable trust can be a practical way to start "kicking the tires" on a plan while the client is alive. For example, if an aging client will rely on an institutional trustee for assistance, naming that institution as a co-trustee on a revocable trust today may facilitate the client testing the quality and level of service that institution can provide. Where the client would like to evaluate how effective the terms of the trust are, how competent and wise the trust's beneficiaries are at handling the trust's assets, and efficient and/or costly the trust and the trustee are in the operation of the trust during the client's lifetime.

7. Where the client wishes to avoid ancillary administration of assets situated in other states by placing title to those assets in the trustee of a revocable living trust. For example, if a client has a vacation home in another state, and it is titled to his revocable trust, he will not have to engage an attorney in that state to transfer the property or oversee an ancillary administration. This too is often a fallacy. Counsel in that other state should be retained to make the transfer today to the trust so that the cost savings may be insignificant. As noted above, the use of an LLC or other structure might be far more valuable to provide asset protection planning.

8. Where the client would like to reduce the potential for an election against or a contest of the will. However, in some states, the statutory estate that can be elected against is expanded to include revocable living trusts. This too may prove a fallacy. Which state law will govern a right of election against the revocable trust? The laws where the trust is established or the laws of the state where the marriage was sanctified? Perhaps instead the state where the couple resided at death. It may be feasible with careful planning to create a trust in a jurisdiction that has more lenient right of election laws and endeavor to have those apply. However, the home state may view the application of their laws to trust corpus as a fundamental state right to protect the marriage.

9. Where the client would like to select the state law under which the provisions of the dispositive document will be governed, a revocable trust might be created designating that other state's laws. This is actually a relatively new and growing consideration for many larger and more sophisticated clients. It has become popular in recent years to create sophisticated trusts in jurisdictions such as Delaware. Clients with such trusts might/should consider using revocable trusts that expressly provide that Delaware law govern the trusts created under the revocable trust so that there is consistency in planning. This can also have, if effective, an important tax consequence if that living trust reciting other state law can prevent the trusts created on death from becoming subject to state taxation in the client's state of domicile. Certainly, the more secure way to achieve this is to not only designate the desired state law in the revocable trust, but to name perhaps an institutional trustee in that jurisdiction to serve as a trustee (or at least co-trustee from inception) so that situs is arguably in that other jurisdiction from inception.

10. Wealthy clients often create irrevocable trusts in trust friendly jurisdictions. For example, a client residing in a high tax state like New Jersey may prefer to create a trust in a state like Nevada that has a more favorable tax climate, and also a legal climate more supportive of modern trust drafting. If on death the intended plan is to transfer wealth into a trust for the benefit of heirs, the client might prefer that those trusts formed under the will be administered in the same trust friendly jurisdiction. If the trusts for heirs is formed under the client's will, home state court approval may be necessary. If the same trusts are instead formed under a revocable trust the probate court should have no need to be involved.

When is the Use of Such a Device Contra-Indicated?

1. A revocable living trust may not make sense if there is no specific reason to set it up other than to save probate and administration costs – and the certain immediately payable present value cost of drafting the trust and maintaining it will exceed the future possible savings. This calculation is rarely made and it is not clear that these costs can always be known. As a practical matter, a revocable living trust may not be indicated if the client is young and not likely to face probate for many decades, nor is old enough to need the protection a revocable trust can provide from aging. It is less certain whether a revocable trust will be as beneficial if the client is not likely to follow through with the re-titling of property and the other prerequisites and operating procedures. However, if the trust is not funded and the client becomes incapacitated the agent under the client's power of attorney can transfer assets. If the client dies and the trust has not been funded the client's pour over will can transfer assets into the trust. While these latter scenarios are not optimal and forfeit some of the benefits a revocable trust can provide, they still might provide some level of benefits.

2. Stock in a professional corporation may not be able to be transferred to a revocable trust because of the prohibition against ownership by anyone other than a professional.

3. If Code section 1244 stock is held by a revocable living trust, it may not qualify for ordinary loss treatment.

4. The deduction allowed to estates for the amount of income permanently set aside for charitable purposes is not allowed to trusts.

5. A living trust is not necessary if the client's estate is modest, the mortgage paid off, there is no reason to keep probate proceedings private, the executor of the estate is a family member who will probably waive executor's fees, and the client lives in a state where the attorneys' fees are modest.

6. Finally, a revocable trust is not indicated if a less complex and less expensive durable power of attorney can satisfy the need. For instance, a broadly drawn durable power of attorney might enable the holder to do many of the same ministerial tasks (such as preparing and filing tax returns) as the trustee of a trust, but in some situations that may not be the case. A key issue will be whether the client has a person (and preferably a successor) who is appropriate to name under the power of attorney. If the client needs to rely on an institutional trustee a revocable trust will likely be required.

64.3 WHY USE A REVOCABLE TRUST?

If there are no federal income or estate tax savings specifically due to the creation of RLTs, are such trusts so appealing? Some of the many reasons to use revocable trusts include:

1. **To avoid ancillary and even home-state probate.** Assets titled to a revocable trust are not subject to probate. In some states, the probate costs are relatively low and the argument for the use of revocable trusts for avoiding probate is not as strong. However, in some states, the costs of probate can be substantial, with the fees often set by statutory formula. Unfortunately, this one potential benefit has eclipsed more important benefits, such as management of assets through a client's advancing age, chronic illness or disability. The latter has been an underutilized benefit of the revocable trust and one which should become the primary reason as the population continues to age.

2. **To avoid potential guardianship or conservatorship proceeding.** Another area of concern for those persons who decide to use revocable trusts is that, as their capacity begins to wane, the assets maintained in their own name (as opposed to those titled originally or re-titled in the name of the trustee of the revocable trust) could require the appointment of a conservator or guardian by state court and a continuing proceeding and annual charges for the maintenance of the conservatorship or guardianship. Alternatively, if the client has a properly crafted durable power of attorney the agent appointed under that power may be able to management assets. In many instances people have faced considerable hurdles convincing third parties to respect such powers. By having a revocable trust, the potential for guardianship or conservatorship, or the difficulties under a durable power of attorney, might all be avoided since

the trustee can take over the management of the assets if the grantor is incapacitated. However, a revocable trust can provide even greater flexibility and a better safety net by naming a co-trustee to serve with the client as capacity wanes.

3. **Privacy.** Revocable Trusts may provide a measure of privacy as contrasted to a will. This occurs because wills are subject to probate and must be filed with the local probate, orphan's or surrogate's court, and may thereby become a matter of public record. On the other hand, a revocable trust is generally not subject to probate and will remain private, so long as litigation or other issues do not require its introduction. While this potential privacy advantage of revocable trusts is generally true, in some states (i.e. Pennsylvania) a copy of the revocable trust is attached to the state's inheritance tax return, and the tax return is a public document. In these states, the privacy feature of revocable trusts is lost.

4. **Planning for incapacity** though the mechanism of a co-trustee or successor trustee assuming management responsibilities. Also, a care manager provision can be added mandating that an independent care manager evaluate the settlor periodically (e.g., annually or quarterly) and issue a report to the trustee, successor trustee and perhaps a specified family member.

The same revocable trust that is used to avoid probate and potential conservatorship, may contain trusts for a spouse or other heirs, but all these provisions can similarly be included in a will. Thus, the revocable trust usually has provisions for the trust continuing on for the children at the death of both spouses.

The creation of a revocable trust is only the first step and alone will not provide many of the intended benefits. It is necessary to actually transfer the title of assets to the trust in order to be able to avoid probate. This can require deeds for real estate, a bill of sale for personal property, re-titling of brokerage and bank accounts, and so forth.

As long as the grantors are the trustees, no separate income tax return is required to be filed for the trust. Furthermore, a revocable trust is a grantor trust and income is generally taxable to the grantor. Thus, the revocable trust has little impact upon income tax planning or income taxation of the grantors until one of them dies or becomes incapacitated and the trust becomes irrevocable. However, there is another view of this. Consideration should be given to filing a grantor Form 1041income tax return for the trust to create a clear paper trail of the trust's existence and assure assets remain titled in the trust and are accounted for. Further, it can prove quite advantageous to obtain a separate tax identification number for the trust from inception, even if not required under Treasury Regulations. There are a number of reasons for this. First, if the grantor/trustee becomes incapacitated the grantor's Social Security number will no longer be permissible to use and a trust Tax Identification Number will have to be obtained. It will be easier to obtain such a number at inception and title accounts in that number from inception instead of a successor trustee having to deal with this issue at the time of the grantor's injury or illness creating the need for a successor trustee to step in. Given the burgeoning growth in elder financial abuse and identity theft, having significant assets maintained in a trust with a tax identification number different then the grantor's Social Security number can provide an important measure of protection.

Although the revocable trust is a valuable estate and later life planning tool, many attorneys still do not use them with any frequency in their practices.

64.4 DISADVANTAGES OF A REVOCABLE TRUSTS

Recent criticism has focused more on the overuse and misuse of RLTs, than on inherent problems. There has been some valid criticism of books and mass marketing presentations that emphasize the exclusive use of revocable living trusts to avoid probate, mainly because they amount to little more than incredibly expensive one-size-fits-all cookie-cutter "trust mills" that provide little or no advice based on a careful analysis of the client's needs and circumstances. Likewise, all too often, the printed forms and/or web page materials that are provided for "do it yourself trusts" are, generally, not useful (and can even be harmful), since planning for clients must be individualized and based upon their particular goals, estates, and circumstances.

Also, some states, such as Florida have special requirements to maintain the homestead tax exemption and special language may be required. Therefore, it is best to use an attorney practicing in the state where the trust is to be administered.

64.5 WHAT ARE THE REQUIREMENTS?

1. In order for a trust to exist, there must be trust property (also known as trust principal, res, or corpus). Many states have eliminated this requirement so that a trust can be a true "standby" trust effectively awaiting funding on a future date. Not transferring assets to the trust, however, will likely impede the trust from accomplishing its intended objectives. For example, if the revocable trust is intended to be a receptacle to preserve the identity of pre-marital assets, then all such premarital assets (but no marital assets) should be transferred to the trust. Also, if the trust lacks a bank and brokerage account, which a true standby trust will, then those accounts will have to be created by the fiduciary (agent under power of attorney or executor under a pour over will) before assets can be transferred to the trust. Having these formalities in place can make that transition point, less risky.

2. There must be the following parties, although in a few jurisdictions it is possible for the same individual to hold all these positions:

    (a) a "grantor," sometimes referred to as a "settlor," or "trustor" – any person who transfers property to and dictates the terms of a trust;

    (b) a trustee – a party to whom property is transferred by the grantor, who receives legal title to the property placed in the trust, and who generally manages and distributes income according to the terms of a formal written agreement (called a trust instrument) between the grantor and the trustee;

    (c) a beneficiary – a party for whose benefit the trust is created and who will receive the direct or indirect benefit of the use of income from and/or principal of the trust property, as follows:

    (i) income beneficiary – the beneficiary who receives income, generally for life or for a fixed period of years or until the occurrence or nonoccurrence of a particular event;

    (ii) remainder person – the ultimate beneficiary of trust property, who can also be the income beneficiary.

3. The grantor and trustee must be legally competent. Practitioners should be mindful, as noted above, that in many jurisdictions a revocable trust requires contractual capacity which is a higher standard than testamentary capacity. Especially for aging clients this is a reason to create such trusts well in advance of when they will actually be needed.

While many clients might prefer to be the sole trustee that is not a good idea. If the client is aging incapacity is not something that provides advance notice, nor is it generally (baring an acute event) something that occurs at a point in time. Rather the decline from capacity to incapacity is a slope of varying shades of gray that may occur at imperceptible rates over many years. Having a co-trustee from inception can enable the client/grantor/co-trustee to remain actively involved in the management of his or her assets for as long as possible while providing greater protection from potential issues.

64.6 FUNDING A REVOCABLE TRUST

Funding of a revocable trust can occur at the establishment of the trust or at any later date although most states require at least a token funding at the creation of the trust. The holder of a durable power of attorney may be authorized to make transfers of assets or shift the title to property to a previously established revocable trust. In some cases, courts have allowed such transfers even where not specifically authorized by the terms of the durable power although specific authorization is preferable. This court assistance is most likely where the dispositive terms of the revocable trust track closely with the terms of the client's will. A very young client may not feel the need to transfer his or her assets into the trust, while a middle aged or elderly client may feel more secure if the assets are transferred into the trust and the mechanisms are in place to have a successor trustee manage the assets if he or she cannot.

As part of the funding process, it is also important to update any applicable beneficiary designations to coordinate with provisions of the revocable trust. For example, if the revocable trust creates trusts for any beneficiary, it will be important to name the trust as the beneficiary of life insurance or other assets, so that the assets will wind up in the trust for the beneficiary.

64.7 PROVIDING PROPERTY MANAGEMENT DURING THE GRANTOR'S INCAPACITY

If a trust is designed to provide property management during the grantor's incapacity, it should:

1. Provide for income distribution to or for the grantor's benefit. Principal invasion should also be permitted. This could also include specifications as lifestyle or other objectives of the grantor, and name other persons who can or should be supported.

2. Authorize that trust assets could be distributed to others to implement or continue a gift program by a duly-appointed agent. The gift provision could be limited as it often historically was to the limits of the gift tax annual exclusion. However, for most clients this will prove inadequate. For smaller estates gift powers may merely serve as a potential spigot for someone endeavoring to commit elder financial abuse. So for many, even most clients, the trust should expressly negate the power to gift. For clients that are domiciled in a decoupled state, have an estate close to the federal exemption amount, or a large taxable estate, annual gift exclusion limits will be inadequate to accomplish desired tax planning and a broader gift provision could be beneficial.

3. Specify that any pledges already made to a qualified charity be satisfied, and

4. State that the management of a business interest be delegated to certain family members.

Many states have adopted a variation of the Uniform Prudent Investor Act (UPIA). This act is based upon the idea that all trustees should be required to follow the investment concept known as the "Modern Portfolio Theory." The UPIA also requires substantial diversification and recognizes that inflation is a risk. As a result, it is no longer proper for a trustee (assuming no exculpation or specific direction to the contrary in the trust instrument) acting under the rules imposed by this law to invest solely in fixed income assets such as government bonds. The diversification rules are such that, in addition to diversifying the types of assets, it is also necessary to diversify the investments so as to benefit *both* the current income beneficiary and the possible future beneficiaries (the remainder).

Thus, a trustee for a client whose trust becomes irrevocable, or for a surviving spouse, cannot really invest for the benefit of the current beneficiary but must invest in the stock market or some other equity investment to provide growth for future generations. Many trustees object strenuously to these rules being imposed but in many states they have been imposed upon all trusts, both those in existence and those created after the date of the enactment of the law.

Some practitioners provide in their trusts that the trustee is exempt from the rules of the UPIA so as to give the trustee much more flexibility to benefit the current beneficiary as opposed to having to invest so as to benefit the future beneficiaries. The law may be helpful in some circumstances and, for the first time in some state jurisdictions, may permit the shifting away from the trustee the responsibility for investments, so that an investment manager or financial planner may be engaged to manage the assets and thus assume responsibility for them. Another approach to consider is to permit a limited exception to maintain the grantor's investment plan during his or her lifetime and thereafter have the general requirements of the UPIA apply so that the portfolio will be reasonably diversified.

64.8 SHIFTING JOINT PROPERTY INTO A REVOCABLE TRUST

Each spouse in a non-community property state should have a revocable trust. For most couples in community property states, the most effective way may be to create a single revocable trust which has subtrusts for each of the separate property of the husband, separate property of the wife, and for community property. For the latter, by having only one trust, as opposed to two trusts, it is much easier to do planning for estate tax minimization. To the extent that either spouse has separate property or an interest in property held in tenancy in common, those would be held in the subtrust for the person's separate property.

It is possible for the clients to convert property to trust property by merely placing title to the property in the trust. However, even though this can result in the property being controlled by the trust, in most states it is also necessary to go to the probate court in order to actually have the title of the property transferred to the trust in a way that will be accepted by title companies. The result, in this circumstance, is that a failure to actually transfer the title during lifetime results in a much more expensive legal process because the probate court will assume the responsibility to transfer the assets. It also leaves room for doubt or possible argument that is not present if there are actual recorded deeds or other indicia of title that clearly show the transfer to the trust.

Most types of assets may be transferred: stock by reissuance of the certificate or stock power; partnership interests by assignment; even personal property by assignment. The last of these may be very important if the assets of the individual consist mostly of valuable art or other collectibles and the draftsman wishes to assure that the unified credit is utilized. One must consult a partnership or stockholders' agreement to obtain whatever consents may be necessary. Retirement assets or annuities should not be retitled into the name of the trust since this can result in triggering the recognition of income tax. However, while these types of assets may not be retitled into the name of the trust, the trust can be named as the beneficiary. In the case of a young beneficiary, it may be appropriate to structure the trust as a "conduit trust" so that the distributions can be made over the lifetime of the beneficiary. (See "Frequently Asked Questions" below).

64.9 HOW IT IS DONE – EXAMPLES

Example 1. Donna Jones, a highly successful author, worries that if she suffers an accident, or develops Alzheimer's disease or another cognitive impairment in future years, she could become a victim of elder financial abuse. While she believes that her nieces and nephews have both the integrity and knowledge to manage her financial affairs she wants to make the process as seamless as possible for them. So she creates a revocable trust and transfers all her assets other than her IRA to the trust. She has heard horror stories from other family members who have had great struggles caring for an aging parent when banks and other third parties refused to accept a durable power of attorney. She hopes by creating a revocable trust with all assets in it, and having the children named as successor trustees, she will mitigate those concerns.

As years pass Donna realizes that her nieces and nephew's lives are very demanding. They have substantial work and family responsibilities so she wants to make the process of them helping her even less burdensome. Donna amends and restates her revocable trust and names an institutional trustee as successor co-trustee to serve with her nephew (with her nieces named thereafter in age order). The institutional trustee can handle all investments, tax filings and bill paying, freeing up the demands on her children. She believes that this is fairer for the children, will make them less resentful, and will provide her a succession of care plan that will let the family focus on important issues rather than on more pedestrian and time consuming issues the trust company can be paid to handle.

Under different circumstances or to meet different objectives, an irrevocable living trust would be indicated. For example, if Donna were in a high income tax bracket, as well as a high estate tax bracket, she might consider transferring assets to an irrevocable self-settled domestic asset protection trust ("DAPT") for the benefit of herself and all of her heirs. The trust could accumulate income during Donna's lifetime if she had no need for them, and at the appropriate point when she would be confident she would never need some portion of them, distribute income and/or principal to, or use it for the benefit of, her heirs. Donna could name a trust company in her home state to be co-trustee of her revocable trust, and a related entity to that trust company in a jurisdiction that permits self-settled trusts, e.g., Nevada, as trustee of the DAPT. In this way her entire estate plan is coordinated, provides maximum elder planning and significant estate and income tax planning. At Donna's death, the revocable trust would divided into three trusts, one for each heir and the DAPT would do the same. Depending on the GST status of the trusts formed under the revocable trusts it might be possible to simplify the planning by merging the two trusts for each heir into a single GST exempt trust in the trust friendly jurisdiction.

Example 2. James and Gloria Smith, who live presently in a community property state, are moving to a non-community property state. They have decided to secure the income tax advantages of community property when they move to the new non-community property state. They create a joint revocable living trust that expressly states that all assets held are community property assets. They create and fund the trust with only community property before they attach as exhibits to the revocable trust transfer documentation corroborating the community property character of the assets and their transfer to the trust. Following their move to a non-community property state they carefully avoid commingling non-community property assets with the community property assets in the joint revocable trust. In this way they hope to secure a full income tax basis step on all of these assets no matter which spouse dies first.

As long as James and Gloria are competent, each has the right to be able to remove their share of community property from the trust. In many community property states, however, both spouses will need to consent to such withdrawals. While many such trusts incorporate subtrusts: one for the separate property of the husband; one for the separate property of the wife; and one for community property, however, the Smith's opt to create separate revocable trusts for non-community property assets following their move, and leave the community property trust intact as a separate distinct trust.

64.10 TAX IMPLICATIONS

1. For federal income tax purposes, all income of a revocable living trust is taxed directly to the grantor at the grantor's tax rate, since he is considered the owner of the trust corpus.[1]

2. No gift tax is generated by establishing or funding a revocable trust since the gift is not completed until the trust becomes irrevocable.[2] However, it might be useful for some clients to grant express gift powers to trustees so that gifts can be made from the revocable trust. It is also valuable in some instances to grant to a trusteed independent person the right to terminate the grantor's power to revoke the trust. In this way a complete gift of the entirety of the trust corpus can be consummated quickly if advantageous. For example, if the client resides in a decoupled state like New Jersey that has no gift tax, a gift consummated in this fashion of the entirety of the revocable trust could avoid state estate tax.

3. Since the grantor has not irrevocably disposed of any assets, the entire trust corpus will be included in the grantor's estate for federal estate tax purposes.[3]

64.11 IMPLICATIONS AND ISSUES IN COMMUNITY PROPERTY STATES

In dealing with community property, the *inter vivos* trust would have two grantors, the husband and the wife. For a revocable trust, where the grantors intend to retain the beneficial ownership of the property, care must be taken to ensure that accidental gifts under state gift tax law are not made by giving either spouse ownership rights over the other spouse's half of the property. The unlimited gift tax marital deduction eliminates a federal gift tax problem on interspousal gifts. Thus, if the trust is revoked, the property should be clearly indicated as being returned to the husband and wife, as co-owners, and not to one spouse or the other.

One technique used to avoid the inadvertent transmutation of community property into separate property (or separate property into community property) is to clearly spell out in the trust document that community property transferred into the trust retains its character as community property and separate property its character as separate property, and to list in a trust addendum the community property, husband's separate property and wife's separate property in separate schedules (i.e. "subtrusts"). Another method is to establish separate revocable *inter vivos* trusts for each type of property. This latter approach should grow in use with the new focus of estate planning on maximizing income tax basis on death. Separate trusts might require some additional costs and administrative burdens, but as illustrated above it can provide a simpler and more assured means of preserving the community property character of certain assets.

Is the character of community property altered by a transfer to a revocable trust that does not have separate subtrusts for separate property of each spouse and for community property? If the transfer is simply by husband and wife to trustee, and each retains a right to revoke, and the instrument specifically provides that the character of the property remains community in the trust and also if it is withdrawn from the trust, and state law recognizes the ability of the parties to achieve the intended result, the character of the property will remain unchanged. This means that, upon the death of the first spouse, the decedent's one-half and the surviving spouse's one-half interest in the trust will receive a new basis equal to fair market value at death or the alternate valuation date, and only the decedent's one-half of the property in the trust will be included in his estate. There will be no gift at the time the trust is created and there will be no gift upon the death of the first spouse unless, at that time, the trust becomes irrevocable. This is avoided by language that divides the trust into two or three trusts upon the death of either of the donor spouses with the formulas to optimize the "use it or lose it" type of effective exemption provided by the unified credit. This type of revocable trust is used extensively in community property states to deal both with community property and to deal with separate property assets of the spouses.

Caution should be exercised in determining the source and nature of title of property before taking the position that it is community property, as one may when the property is transferred to a trust that indicates that it is held as community property. Taxable gifts under state law may result if the property is the separate property of either spouse or is joint tenancy real property originally acquired with the separate property of one spouse. Although the unlimited marital deduction for federal gift tax purposes reduces the gift tax risks,[4] there still may be state gift tax implications. In addition, it could well inspire litigation in the event of a dissolution if there was not a clear intent between the parties that a gift take place.

Life Insurance

When life insurance has been purchased with community property income or assets (and therefore belongs one-half to each spouse), care must be taken that the terms of a trust, becoming irrevocable at the death of the insured, do not result in a taxable gift by the surviving spouse of all or part of the survivor's half interest in the insurance proceeds. Such gifts are usually to the remainder person(s) of the trust and are not protected by the marital deduction. While in the past it had been preferable to create an irrevocable life insurance trust to hold life insurance, since many people will not be subject to any estate tax they may be more reluctant to incur this extra expense and administrative burden. As such these issues will be more likely to arise, but if the family, even with life insurance, is well below the estate tax exemption amounts there may be little consequence. It may be feasible to name a trust formed under the revocable trust to provide protection for the beneficiary and management of the funds. This will not, however, protect the cash value of the policy in the hands of the insured.

Division of Property at Death

Exercise caution in drafting the provisions regarding the division of property at the death of one community property owning spouse so as to avoid unintended gifts by the surviving spouse. At times, such trusts may be intended to benefit the survivor more if he agrees to have his property also be managed and distributed according to the terms of the trust. Such "election" provisions may also result in gifts by the surviving spouse and, if used, should be drafted carefully by an experienced estate planner.

64.12 WHEN DOES A REVOCABLE TRUST BECOME IRREVOCABLE?

A revocable trust becomes irrevocable upon the earlier of:

- when the grantor gives up the right to revoke the trust;

- when the grantor becomes incapacitated;

- when a person given a power under the trust instrument to revoke the grantor's power does so, or

- upon the grantor's death.

Generally, a grantor lacks the power to revoke a trust during incompetency. But, it is possible to provide in the trust that if the client is deemed to be mentally or physically incompetent, the trust becomes irrevocable. This would block a person acting under a durable power of attorney from changing the plan of disposition in the revocable trust if that agent were in fact expressly granted the power to do so in the power. This would not alone, however, constitute a completed gift of the assets in the revocable trust unless a person was also given the power to do that. It may be possible that if the trust was in a state permitting a self-settled trust that the irrevocability could complete the gift.

Note that the irrevocability of a trust may trigger adverse gift tax implications. A taxable gift is made when a client parts with dominion and control over property. But immediate gift taxation can be blocked. The client could retain a life income in the trust's assets and delay taxation on the gift of the remainder interest (the portion going at his death to the ultimate beneficiaries of the trust) by the reservation of a testamentary power of appointment over that remainder interest. This should work even if the grantor becomes mentally incompetent since it is assumed that he may regain competency at any time before death.

Disposition of Assets upon the Grantor's Death

Assuming a trust is funded at the time of a client's death, assets can be paid directly and immediately to the named beneficiaries and the trust can be terminated. Alternatively, the trust can be continued. However, it should be recognized that if there is any potential estate tax due, the trustee is individually responsible for payment of any estate tax if assets have been transferred out of the trust and there are not sufficient assets left to pay the estate tax. For this reason, in trusts where there may be any potential estate tax due, the trustee may require the retention of a certain amount of assets to deal with any potential estate tax.

The trust, which is now irrevocable, can serve as a receptacle to receive assets poured over into it. It can then continue to exist until its purpose or term has been completed. A third possibility is that the assets in the trust can be poured into trusts provided for under the revocable trust. These can include a credit shelter trust, QTIP trust or others for a surviving spouse and a range of different types of trusts for other non-spouse beneficiaries.

64.13 SELECTING A TRUSTEE

A trustee should possess business judgment (even if there is no business), honesty, and integrity. The trustee must be able and willing to exercise a high degree of care over trust property and avoid (however tempting) investments or acts that are likely to result in losses.

A trustee must have legal capacity to contract. This precludes the appointment of a minor or incompetent adult. Geographical considerations generally contraindicate an individual who lives a considerable distance from the client or his heirs.

The type and size of assets to be placed into the trust, as well as the client's goals, are important considerations in selecting a trustee. Obviously, if the client's primary asset is a business, the trustee will have much more responsibility and must have higher and broader competence than if the trust's assets consisted mainly of cash.

Investment skill is necessary. Under the "prudent person" rule, a trustee will be liable to the beneficiary for losses unless he exercises the same care and skill that a person of ordinary prudence would exercise in dealing with his own property. But the Uniform Probate Code, now in effect in some form in most states, raises this standard for professional trustees by providing: "If the trustee has greater skill than that of a man of ordinary prudence, he is under a duty to exercise such skill." However, the trustee can hire a professional investment adviser to invest trust funds.

Because a trustee must examine and review the trust periodically, administrative and legal skills and knowledge are important. Accountings must be made to the client and eventually to the other beneficiaries. All parties must be advised accurately on the tax and other legal effects. Provisions in the trust must, from time to time, be interpreted.

Family Members, Close Friends, or Business Associates as Trustees

There are significant advantages and disadvantages to naming a family member or business associate as trustee. A nonprofessional trustee is indicated where the minimum fee charged by local professional fiduciaries is higher than it's feasible to pay.

Is it appropriate for a family member, a close friend, or a business associate to serve as trustee? The obvious advantage is that such a person may have a working knowledge of the client, the family, and the finances and business. But selection of a person as trustee must also consider conflicts of interest and ethical problems. For instance, how will a trustee who is also a beneficiary react when faced with a choice that favors him at the expense of other beneficiaries or that favors other beneficiaries at his expense? Will the trustee favor other beneficiaries at his own expense? Will the fees charged by a family member or business associate as trustee be understood and accepted without resentment or will it cause conflict? Will the trustee's "hard choices" be injurious to family relationships? Is the trustee likely to show favoritism or be easily persuaded?

Can an untrained individual deal with the legal, tax, and investment functions of being a trustee? Even though a trustee is legally entitled to hire agents to serve as investment counselors, accountants, and attorneys to assist on special problems, the trustee remains responsible for the ultimate decisions. Would an untrained individual know whom to call? Would the trustee know if the advice he is receiving is both legally and practically correct? Does the trustee understand that he is personally liable for unpaid federal estate taxes if a distribution is made to beneficiaries before the estate tax liability is fully paid (even if the trust specifically allows for immediate distributions from the trust on the grantor's death)? If a distribution is made that can't be recovered, the trustee will be personally liable to the extent remaining trust assets are insufficient to pay the estate's estate tax liability.

Corporate Trustees

A corporate fiduciary (with or without individuals as co-trustees) is clearly indicated when there is no suitable individual or groups of individuals to manage the client's financial affairs. As clients age and there is no family or surviving friends this will become more common. Dynastic trusts of all types, revocable or otherwise can benefit from using an institutional trustee. Corporate fiduciaries are also indicated where the amount placed into the trust is large and/or will require skillful and constant attention. If there is likelihood of family conflict, corporate fiduciaries can make decisions on a more objective disinterested basis than family members.

Trust Protector

Consider also naming a person to serve as trust protector and empowering that person to change trustees, governing law and situs of administration. The protector may also be expressly granted the right to demand an accounting from a trustee. This could be vital as many courts view a revocable trust as the equivalent of a will substitute so that during the settlor's life there may be no right in another person to challenge the trustee's actions.

State Law Issues

A trust will be invalid if it does not meet state law requirements. Planners should be aware of two potential problems: (1) the Doctrine of Merger, and (2) The Passive Trust theory.

In some states, when the same person is both trustee and beneficiary, the trust ceases to exist as a separate entity. Legal title to the property (held by the trustee) merges with the equitable (beneficial) title (held by the beneficiary). The result is that if the sole beneficiary of the trust is also the sole trustee, the beneficiary becomes the absolute owner of the total rights in the trust assets. This is known as a "fee simple" or "fee simple absolute." The trust, as such, ceases to exist. However, in many states the same person may be both trustee and beneficiary.

A second potential problem occurs in the case of a so-called "passive trust." This is a trust that gives the trustee no meaningful duties to perform and gives the beneficiary unfettered enjoyment and management control of assets. The result is a merger of the legal title and the equitable title; the trust ceases to exist. Either through operation of law or through judicial action, where the trustee's duties are purely ministerial and all significant authority and decision making are placed in the hands of the beneficiary, the beneficiary receives total title to the property that was in the trust.

64.14 FREQUENTLY ASKED QUESTIONS

Question – What is a "Pour-over Will?"

Answer – As its name implies, a pour-over trust is one into which assets can be "poured" or funneled from the client's will, into the revocable trust.[5] This type of plan is set up by the client during life and serves as a receptacle for any asset the client would like to pour into it that have not be transferred into the trust during lifetime. While in the past it had been common to create an irrevocable life insurance trust own insurance, as the relevance of the estate tax continues to wane, more clients may now name a trust formed under their revocable trust to hold life insurance. This can provide the asset protection and other benefits for heirs when the client himself or herself does not have any tax or asset protection concerns.

Question – What is a "Contingent Trust?"

Answer – A contingent trust (also known as a step-up or standby trust) is one that takes over and manages and invests assets if and when the client is no longer able to do so. A contingent trust is triggered upon the occurrence of one or more specified contingencies such as the client's physical, mental, or emotional incapacity. It may also be triggered by the client upon an extended trip. Such a trust can be coordinated with the client's durable power of attorney. Specifically, the agent under the power of attorney can pour assets into the trust. While this approach can help avoid the need for probating those assets it defeats many of the other benefits a funded revocable trust can provide as discussed elsewhere in this chapter. The client could appoint himself as trustee. The trust would provide that the grantor (client) would be succeeded by a corporate fiduciary and/or another person if the grantor becomes incompetent.

Incapacity could be defined in a number of ways – as broadly or as narrowly as the client desires. Quite often, the step up trustee takes over (a) upon the decision of a third party such as a child or friend, or (b) upon the trustee's decision that incapacity has occurred but only after a determination of incompetency by one or more specified doctors, or (c) upon a decision solely by the trustee that the grantor is incompetent, or (d) upon a judicial proceeding of incompetency, or (e) upon the determination of an independent arbitrator. Determination by a judicial proceeding is unlikely to be an option many clients will wish, unless they have no close friends or family and are concerned about an institutional trustee taking over management at too early a point in time. The problem with all of these approaches is that incapacity is often not a flip of a light switch, absent a traumatic brain injury or similar acute event. In most cases, the client very slowly over time declines. With the increasing use of revocable trusts to manage assets during aging and incapacity many practitioners will find it prudent to install a co-trustee with the client well before the client is completely incapable of managing his or her own affairs.

Question – What is the effect of a revocable trust on creditors?

Answer – The ability of a revocable trust to protect assets from the claims of the client's creditors will depend on state law and the provisions of the trust document. As a general rule, if the grantor has retained the right to trust assets or the right to alter, amend, revoke, or terminate the trust, there will be little, if any, protection from the claims of creditors. In the typical revocable living trust, the client retains too many rights over the trust assets to put those assets beyond the reach of creditors.

Question – Are there advantages to making the trust the beneficiary of qualified plan benefits?

Answer – First, naming a revocable trust as beneficiary of qualified pension, profit sharing plan, IRA, or HR-10 payments helps to unify the administration of the estate and achieve the client's objectives. Second, a trust serves as a means of deferring the distribution of assets to beneficiaries who may not be ready or able to handle large sums of money. Third, a trust enables the sprinkling of capital and the spraying of income to those beneficiaries who need or deserve it the most or who are in the lowest tax brackets. Fourth, payment of qualified plan benefits to a trustee makes it possible for the trustee to make certain advantageous tax elections on behalf of the estate.

In addition, under IRS regulations, if the trust qualifies as a "designated beneficiary," it is possible to defer the required minimum distribution from the plan over the life expectancy of the beneficiary of the trust. If there are several beneficiaries, the required minimum distributions will be determined based upon the shortest life expectancy of all of the potential beneficiaries of the trust. This result is contrary to the general objective, which is to stretch out the distributions. By taking the distributions over a longer period, the plan assets are permitted to continue growing on a tax-deferred basis. However, there are certain strict requirements that must be met in order for a trust to qualify as a designated beneficiary: (1) the trust must be valid under state law; (2) the trust is irrevocable, or will, by its terms, become irrevocable upon the death of the owner; (3) the beneficiaries of the trust can be identified; and (4), certain documentation is provided to the trustee or custodian.[6]

One drawback of having a trust be named as the beneficiary is that the spouse of the participant cannot elect to be treated as the owner of plan proceeds if a trust is named beneficiary. This prevents the spouse from being able to roll over the retirement proceeds.

If the trust does not qualify as a designated beneficiary, the plan proceeds will have to be paid out either (1) over the participant's remaining life expectancy if the participant died after reaching his required beginning date of age 70½, or (2) no later than the end of the fifth year after the year of the participant's death if the participant died before reaching age 70½.

While a longer period of tax deferral may not be possible if the trust does not qualify, in some cases it may still be more beneficial to name the trust as the beneficiary rather than individual persons. One type of trust which avoids these distribution rules is the "conduit trust." The conduit trust can provide certainty that its beneficiaries will be afforded designated beneficiary treatment. The distinguishing characteristic of the conduit trust is that the Trustee will hold no power to accumulate or hold back IRA distributions. Because of these required distributions, this type of trust may not be ideal for someone with creditor or personal (drug or alcohol) issues, or receiving public benefits. One other consideration is the size of the account at issue. If a young child is the beneficiary, the required minimum distribution may be so large that it is impractical or inadvisable to it, so that the negative income tax aspects of choosing not to include "conduit" provisions should be weighed against this practical consideration. It is, however, the only type of trust that is guaranteed to be treated as a "see through" trust.

Question – Can a revocable trust safely hold the stock of an S corporation?

Answer – To be eligible to elect the "pass through" taxation similar to a partnership, a corporation must meet stringent requirements. The only trusts which qualify as eligible shareholders of S corporations (see Chapter 53) are:

1. Voting trusts

2. A trust receiving stock under a will (but only for the first two years after the stock is transferred to the trust)

3. Code Section 678 trusts (relating to trusts where a person other than the grantor is treated as the owner).

4. Grantor trusts (which includes revocable living trusts over which the grantor has retained all powers or to whom income is taxable under Code Sections 671 to 677, and for 2 years after the grantor's death)

5. A qualified subchapter S trust (QSST)

6. An electing small business trust (ESBT)

If any other type of trust owns stock in an corporation, the S election is automatically nullified. The result is that the corporation would be taxed as a regular corporation and the pass through of income or deductions would be denied.

Question – Are there disadvantages in putting investment real estate in a revocable trust?

Answer – There may be several. The impact on real property taxes must be considered. Some states have provisions for reassessment of real property for property tax purposes if it is transferred. If highly appreciated property is transferred to a revocable trust, this could result in a costly reassessment. Some states, such as California, exempt property transferred to a revocable trust from reassessment. Also, it should be determined whether or not the transfer will accelerate the payment of any mortgage or deed of trust on the property under so-called "acceleration" provisions in the note or mortgage. Again, many transactions are exempt.

Finally, care should be taken to determine if the real property is presently generating losses or will be expected to do so after the death of the owner. Under Code section 469, losses from various activities, including some rental real estate activities, are characterized as passive losses, not deductible except under limited circumstances. However, section 469(i) allows deduction for losses of up to $25,000 per year if the owner is actively participating in the management of the property. Section 469(i)(4) permits continued deduction of such losses for two years after the death of the owner by the owner's estate. It is generally assumed the use of the term "estate" could not be extended to cover revocable trusts. The safer course is to allow such property to pass through an estate, which after two years could distribute it to the trust under pour-over provisions discussed above.

CHAPTER ENDNOTES

1. I.R.C. §671.
2. *Burnet v. Guggenheim*, 288 U.S. 280 (1933).
3. I.R.C. §2038.
4. I.R.C. §2523.
5. It should be noted that retirement plans payable to a trust might not permit distributions to be "stretched-out" over the lifetimes of the beneficiaries. See Treas. Reg. §1.401(a)(9)-4.
6. Treas. Reg. §1.401(a)(9)-4 A-5.

PLANNING FOR UNMARRIED PARTNERS

CHAPTER 65

65.1 INTRODUCTION

In many ways, estate planning for unmarried partners requires much more precision and planning than planning for spouses for both tax and non-tax reasons if the partners intend to plan for each other's benefit. As we have noted elsewhere in this book, it is more important that unmarried partners do estate planning if they want to benefit each other because the laws of intestacy generally are unkind to legally unrelated people, preferring relations by blood, adoption or state approved marriage over persons who have *actual* close relationships with the decedent, even long-term surviving partners.

There are several transfer tax benefits that are only available to *married* spouses, including gift-splitting, portability and the marital deduction. However, there also are some limitations that apply to family members that are not applicable to unrelated persons, even if they are unmarried cohabitants. These include the inapplicability of the Chapter 14 valuation rules because the unmarried couple is not considered to be "members of each other's family" for purposes of that chapter. This makes certain formerly popular estate planning techniques such as GRITs or corporate recapitalization freezes essentially unavailable to legally related families but still available for unmarried couples. So there are some distinct tax opportunities that can only be availed of by unmarried couples.

In this chapter, we will discuss planning options that are available to unmarried partners, including a discussion of the different rules for valuing interests in closely-held entities in buy-sell agreements. We also will discuss cohabitation agreements between unmarried partners, which supplements our discussion in Chapter 67.

65.2 BUY-SELL AGREEMENTS VALUATION

What It Is

We discussed buy-sell agreements in-depth in Chapter 47. However, in that chapter, we focused on the effect of Code section 2703 on the valuation involved in the buy-sell agreement, which applies to entities that are primarily owned by members of the same family. In this chapter, we will discuss the rules of valuation in buy-sell agreements where Code section 2703 is *in*applicable.

Valuation of an interest in a closely-held corporation (and, by implication, interests in other closely-held entities) that are subject to a buy-sell agreement on the fair market value standard begins with Treas. Reg. Sec. 20.2031-2(h), which provides:

> Another person may hold an option or a contract to purchase securities owned by a decedent at the time of his death. The effect, if any, that is given to the option or contract price in determining the value of the securities for estate tax purposes depends upon the circumstances of the particular case. *Little weight* will be accorded a price contained in an option or contract under which the decedent is free to dispose of the underlying securities at *any* price he chooses during his lifetime. Such is the effect, for example, of an agreement on the part of a shareholder to purchase whatever shares of stock the decedent may own at the time of his death. Even if the decedent is not free to dispose of the underlying securities at other than the option or contract price, such price will be *disregarded* in determining the value

of the securities unless it is determined under the circumstances of the particular case that the agreement represents a bona fide business arrangement *and* not a device to pass the decedent's shares to the natural objects of his bounty for less than an adequate and full consideration in money or money's worth. [emphasis added]

As you should be able to see from a review of the regulation, the test for whether a buy-sell agreement will be a factor in the valuation of the subject interest is a *facts and circumstances test*. However, Treas. Reg. Sec. 20.2031-2(h) provides that *little weight* will be accorded to a buy-sell agreement that fixes the price at the owner's death if the owner was able to transfer the shares at any price during lifetime. Moreover, the regulation goes on to provide that a buy-sell agreement will be *disregarded* unless it meets the *conjunctive* test contained therein, i.e., the agreement must represent a bona fide business arrangement *and* it must not be a device to pass the decedent's ownership interests to the natural objects of the decedent's bounty for less than an adequate and full consideration. Note that "adequate and full consideration" in the regulation need not necessarily be fair market value. The two terms are not synonymous. Adequate and full consideration actually may be either higher or lower than fair market value of the subject interest.

That regulation was promulgated in 1958, but it did not help much with the valuation of closely-held corporations. Therefore, in 1959, the IRS issued the seminal valuation ruling, Rev. Rul. 59-60. Section 8 of Rev. Rul. 59-60 provides as follows:

Frequently, in the valuation of closely held stock for estate and gift tax purposes, it will be found that the stock is subject to an agreement restricting its sale or transfer. Where shares of stock were acquired by a decedent subject to an option reserved by the issuing corporation to repurchase at a certain price, the option price is *usually* accepted as the fair market value for estate tax purposes. See Rev. Rul. 54-76, C.B. 1954-1, 194. However, in such case the option price is *not* determinative of fair market value for gift tax purposes. Where the option, or buy and sell agreement, is the result of voluntary action by the stockholders and is binding during the life as well as at the death of the stockholders, such agreement may *or* may not, depending upon the circumstances of each case, fix the value for estate tax purposes. However, such agreement is a *factor to be considered*, with other relevant factors, in determining fair market value. Where the stockholder is free to dispose of his shares during life and the option is to become effective only upon his death, the fair market value is *not* limited to the option price. It is always necessary to consider the relationship of the parties, the relative number of shares held by the decedent, and other material facts, to determine whether the agreement represents a bona fide business arrangement or is a device to pass the decedent's shares to the natural objects of his bounty for less than an adequate and full consideration in money or money's worth. In this connection see Rev. Rul. 157 C.B. 1953-2, 255, and Rev. Rul. 189, C.B. 1953-2, 294. [emphasis added]

Note, again, that the existence of a buy-sell agreement is merely a *factor* to consider in the determination of fair market value of the subject interest. The IRS may consider the relationship of the parties, the relative number of shares that a decedent held as well as other material facts in its valuation determination, which has always struck as somehow violative of the "hypothetical" willing buyer and seller part of the test of fair market value.

The courts have long accepted buy-sell agreements restricting the transfer of securities in family corporations as establishing value for transfer tax purposes.[1] Buy-sell agreements that established a fixed price for a mandatory sale and purchase at death have been recognized as establishing the estate tax value of corporate stock or partnership interests even where there were significant discrepancies between the agreement price and the fair market value of the property in question.[2] Notwithstanding the foregoing, the courts will disregard the price where no bona fide or arm's-length negotiations occurred in determining the fixed price or where the decedent had the effective ability to amend the agreement to alter the price during lifetime.[3]

Many different courts have analyzed and applied the guidelines set out in Treas. Reg. Sec. 20.2031-2(h) and Rev. Rul. 59-60 and its progeny. The principles of Rev. Rul. 59-60 were extended long ago to valuations of interests in partnerships, and, presumably, to LLCs.[4] Under the courts' interpretation, in order for a buy-sell agreement to *fix*, rather than merely *affect*, the fair market value for transfer tax purposes, it must first satisfy five separate requirements:

(1) the price must be determinable from the buy-sell agreement, either an actual fixed price or a formula such as fair market value that produces a fixed price;

(2) the terms of the buy-sell agreement must be binding throughout life and death;

(3) the buy-sell agreement must be legally binding and enforceable;

(4) the buy-sell agreement must be a bona fide business arrangement; and

(5) the buy-sell agreement must not be merely a device to transfer shares to the "natural objects of the decedent's bounty" for consideration that is not adequate and full consideration.

The phrase "natural objects of the decedent's bounty" is not defined in the regulations. However, it was the subject of a Second Circuit opinion in *Gloeckner Est. v. Comm'r*.[5] That decision reversed a Tax Court decision that had expressly found a redemption agreement between a majority shareholder of a closely-held corporation and an unrelated employee to have been a testamentary device to transfer the control of the corporation to an object of the decedent's bounty for less than full and adequate consideration.[6] The Second Circuit discussed the meaning of the phrase "natural objects of the decedent's bounty" at length because it was the main issue on appeal. The court noted that while the phrase was not defined in the regulations, a fair reading of the term from the legislative history is that it is broader in scope than just familial relations. The Second Circuit observed:

> Hence, an intended beneficiary need not be a "relative," in the commonly-understood sense of the word, to qualify as a natural object of a decedent's bounty. Nevertheless, for an agreement to be testamentary, the beneficiary must have enjoyed a relationship with the decedent in which he was considered as though he were in some manner related to the decedent.

Based upon the Second Circuit's interpretation of the phrase, it is highly likely that an unmarried partner will be considered an "object of the decedent's bounty" of a deceased partner. This probably means that a buy-sell agreement between the unmarried partners has to avoid being a mere testamentary device to pass on the business interest to the other partner. Therefore, the price and terms of a buy-sell agreement between unmarried partners probably would have to be similar to those between unrelated co-owners, which significantly reduces the opportunities to transfer ownership of a closely-held business interest at less than fair market value.

65.3 TECHNIQUES THAT ARE NOT GENERALLY AVAILABLE TO RELATED PERSONS

Split Purchases-What It Is

A split purchase is nothing more than where two people purchase temporal interests in an identifiable piece of property. One party (usually the older person) purchases a life estate (the right to receive the income from the property or the right to use, possess and enjoy the property itself for as long as the life tenant lives). The second party (usually the younger person) purchases a remainder interest (the right to the property, whatever it is worth, when the first party's interest terminates. If the first party purchased a life interest, by definition an interest which terminates at death). Each party to a split purchase pays the actuarial value of the interest purchased. The anticipated advantage of this technique is that post-purchase appreciation will not be treated as a transfer for gift tax purposes. So to the extent that the property appreciates after the transaction is consummated, it will not be subject to transfer tax. For example, in August 2018, Ashley, age sixty-five, purchases the income interest, and Carol purchases the remainder interest, in property that has a fair market value purchase price of $1,000,000. Together, the prices of the life income interest, which, under the valuation tables, is worth $ $423,630, and the remainder interest, which is then worth $ 576,370, equal the full fair market value, e.g., purchase price of $1,000,000, of the property. (Calculations courtesy of NumberCruncher Software (610 9240515.) Generally, the values of the income and remainder interests are purely a function of the age of the income holder, i.e., the older the income holder, the smaller the size of the income interest and, consequently, the larger the remainder interest, and vice versa.

The values are determined by using the Code section 7520 applicable federal rate for the month of the purchase and the actuarial tables in the regulations. Nevertheless, if the income purchaser is in precarious health, it may not be possible to use those tables. In that case the *actual* remaining life expectancy of the income purchaser, which probably will be significantly shorter than that under the actuarial tables, would have to be used. This will have the effect of potentially dramatically increasing the size of the remainder interest that the remaindermen are purchasing, and, thus, the purchase price of the remainder interest. Under the Code section 7520 regulations, the tables must be used - *except* as follows:

> For purposes of this paragraph (b)(3), an individual who is known to have an incurable illness or other deteriorating physical condition is considered terminally ill if there is at least a 50 percent probability that the individual will die within 1 year. However, if the individual survives for eighteen months or longer after the date the gift is completed, that individual shall be presumed to have not been terminally ill at the date the gift was completed unless the contrary is established by clear and convincing evidence.[7]

Therefore, where the purchaser of the income interest might not live to actuarial life expectancy, it often is critical to obtain *contemporaneous* medical evidence that the income purchaser does not suffer from an incurable illness or have a deteriorating physical condition of such a magnitude that the income purchaser is not expected to survive for 18 months following the income purchase to enable use of the Code section 7520 mortality tables to value the temporal interests.

Under Chapter 14, persons who are members of the same family have problems doing split-purchases because of Code section 2702(c)(2), which provides as follows:

> If 2 or more members of the same family acquire interests in any property described in paragraph (1) in the same transaction (or a series of related transactions), the person (or persons) acquiring the term interests in such property shall be treated as having acquired the entire property and then transferred to the other persons the interests acquired by such other persons in the transaction (or series of transactions). Such transfer shall be treated as made in exchange for the consideration (if any) provided by such other persons for the acquisition of their interests in such property.

Any term interest in property, such as a life estate or term of years, but not co-ownership, such as tenancy in common or joint tenancy, is treated as if held in trust under Code section 2702. A leasehold is not a term interest if for full and adequate consideration where a good faith attempt is made to determine fair rental value.

In the case of a joint purchase, the amount considered transferred by an individual to family members for this purpose cannot exceed the actual consideration furnished by that individual for the property.[8]

As a result of the limitations imposed on the joint purchase under Code section 2702, the technique will have disastrous gift tax consequences if a related term holder purchases an income interest in the property. Under Code section 2702, that income interest is valued at zero for federal gift tax purposes. The term holder will be treated as if making a gift to the remaindermen, equal to the fair market value of the property, less the actual consideration paid by the remaindermen for the remainder interest. However, the amount of the gift is limited to the actual consideration paid by the term holder.[9] As a result of Code section 2702(c)(2), the family member who purchases the income interest is essentially treated as having made a gift of the income interest that he or she purchased for full fair market value to the remaindermen because the income purchaser is only given credit for the consideration that the *remaindermen* actually pay, not for their *own* consideration paid. This gift tax cost makes split purchases essentially prohibitive for members of the same family. However, as noted above, an *un*married couple is not subject to this limitation.

65.4 WHEN IS THE USE OF A SPLIT PURCHASE INDICATED?

1. When a client would like to improve current income. If a split purchase is used to purchase income producing investment property, the client's income is enhanced by the return provided on the remaindermen's investment.

2. A split purchase may be strong protection against a will contest. Property acquired via split purchase passes by contract and should not be part of the income interest holder's probate estate. So, generally, a disgruntled heir would have no right to property purchased through a split purchase. Likewise, a split purchase offers protection against the claims of a client's creditors and, because it does not pass through probate, it affords the parties confidentiality.

3. When it is desirable to avoid ancillary administration, the split purchase is useful since at the termination of the first party's interest, the remainder person automatically by contract becomes full and complete owner of the property. This means the cost of multiple state probates is avoided.

4. Splits are indicated where federal gift and estate taxes are not a major consideration or will be of relatively minor importance in the overall plan. In some limited circumstances, there may still be some transfer tax advantages using a Split.

5. When the parties are unrelated (as defined in Code section 2702). For example, an unmarried couple should be able to create a split purchase that is not subject to Code section 2702.

65.5 WHAT ARE THE REQUIREMENTS OF A SPLIT PURCHASE?

Ownership of the property is bifurcated into two parts: a "term" interest, which may be either the right to receive stipulated payments from the property for a term of years, or life, or in a very limited situation, the right to use the property for that period. The second part is the "remainder" interest, which will pass to the other joint owner when the term interest expires.

Both the term holder and the remainder holder pay their proportionate part of the purchase price for the property based on government valuation tables setting an actuarial value for the term interest and the remainder interest. It is essential that the purchaser of the life term interest furnish no part of the consideration for the purchase of the remainder interest.

Because the term holder and remainder holder are co-owners of the property, it cannot be sold without the consent of both parties. Because, under most circumstances, the term holder is limited to a fixed dollar payment from the property, the term holder will apparently have no other rights in it. In the limited situations where the term holder can retain full possession and enjoyment of the property for the term, the term holder should have all of the legal rights of a joint tenant in the property. The exact nature of the rights of the term holder and the remainder holder is dependent on state law. Therefore, it is important to divide responsibility for maintenance and capital expenses and taxes at the time of purchase.

65.6 HOW IT IS DONE— AN EXAMPLE OF A SPLIT PURCHASE

Singh, age fifty-seven, and Jorge, age thirty-five, are a couple. Both are in excellent health. They are interested in purchasing a piece of income-producing real estate in March 2017 (when the Code section 7520 rate is 2.0 percent) for $2,000,000. Singh is contemplating retirement and is looking for ways to supplement his income in retirement. Jorge is a young professional. Based upon the Code section 7520 actuarial tables, the value of Singh's income interest is $878,400, leaving the balance of the $2,000,000 purchase price, $1,121,560, as the value that Jorge must pay for the remainder interest. (Calculations courtesy of NumberCruncher Software (610 9240515.)

65.7 GRANTOR RETAINED INCOME TRUST (GRIT)

What It Is

A grantor retained income trust ("GRIT") is an irrevocable trust that the grantor establishes where the grantor retains the right to income for a term of years (or for a period often ending on the first to occur of (1) a term of years, (2) the grantor's death or (3) the trustee's commutation of the income rights). At the expiration of this term (or period), the GRIT assets usually are then distributed outright or continued to be held in trust for the named beneficiaries that the grantor designated at the establishment of the GRIT. If the grantor survives the term of years during which he or she has the income interest, the remaining property in the GRIT passes to the beneficiaries, free of additional gift or estate tax cost.

The only estate or gift tax cost is a gift tax at the time that the GRIT is established equal to the discounted present value of the "remainder" (i.e., the right of the beneficiaries to receive the property after the lapse of the grantor's income interest for a term of years). A GRIT also can pass assets to a less wealthy unmarried partner at a reduced transfer cost, since the latter is not a family member within the definition of Chapter 14, which was added to the Internal Revenue Code in 1990. That chapter essentially eliminated the use of the GRIT technique for a remainder beneficiary who was a family member of the grantor. Because it deals with transfers among traditional family members, other techniques formerly used before its enactment may still be used, since domestic partners, parties to a civil union and other unrelated parties are not in this category. Thus, since an unmarried couple is technically *un*related, a GRIT could be used with the grantor retaining all income from the trust for a fixed term, at the end of which the remainder would pass to the beneficiary.

If the grantor dies before the GRIT term's end, the corpus will be includible in the estate at its fair market value at that time pursuant to Code section 2036. The creation of the GRIT will be a gift equal to the property's fair market value, less the value of the retained income interest. The tax advantage of a GRIT is that if the rate of accounting income is lower than the applicable federal rate, there will be an overvaluation of the income interest, and the remainder will be undervalued. Thus, the grantor will obtain a low discounted value for gift tax purposes. Then, upon trust termination the corpus (including appreciation) will pass transfer tax-free to the other partner.

GRITs are still a powerful tool available to unmarried partners. As with the QPRT, the downside to the GRIT is that assets receive no step-up in basis at the grantor's death if the assets contributed to the GRIT have appreciated in value at the end of the GRIT term if the grantor survives. Additionally, if the grantor does not survive the GRIT term, the GRIT assets are includible in the grantor's estate at their fair market value as of the date of the grantor's death. Also as with the QPRT, such a result is no worse than if the grantor had done nothing.

Nevertheless, the ability to transfer wealth via a GRIT is not unfettered. The IRS maintains that in order to use the valuation tables, the assets transferred to the GRIT must either be currently productive of a reasonable rate of income, or the grantor has to retain the right to force the trustee to make the GRIT property reasonably productive of income.[10] If a GRIT contains a commutation power in the trustee, the grantor must be paid full fair market value for the commuted value of the income interest, or the grantor will be deemed to have made a gift to the remaindermen.[11]

What are the potential downsides of a GRIT? In addition to the uncertainty of whether or not the grantor's property will generate a reasonable rate of return in the opinion of the IRS, if the grantor dies during the term of his or her income interest, there are no transfer tax savings because the full amount of the GRIT property is included in the grantor's gross estate for estate tax purposes.[12] However, the grantor should be no worse off than if nothing were done-that is, the overall gift and estate taxes will be the same as if no GRIT had been formed.

Another downside is that the GRIT must be irrevocable. Therefore once established, the GRIT terms cannot change. This can impact situations like unmarried couples, because a split-up will not defeat the rights of the remaindermen. Because the property will ultimately pass to beneficiaries at the termination of the grantor's income interest, the grantor must be absolutely certain to not need the funds on which to live. Importantly, the property can continue to be held in trust after the grantor's income interest expires. But at that point, the grantor must not have any interest in the continuing trust as a beneficiary and probably not as a trustee unless the trust is very carefully crafted. We recommend against giving the grantor any interest beyond the income interest because of the substantial estate tax risks.

Another downside is that the GRIT property may depreciate in value, which reduces the transfer tax benefits. Presumably, this could be avoided by prudent investment of the GRIT property.

Another downside relates to the administrative inconvenience of having a trust. Someone other than the grantor or the grantor's spouse must be the trustee. The trust terms must be carefully considered and properly drafted. The trust must file income tax returns (Form 1041) each year unless the GRIT is a wholly grantor trust for income tax purposes.

It can be permissible to fund a GRIT with S corporation stock. However, a GRIT cannot be a "qualified subchapter S trust" (QSST) because persons other than the income beneficiary will have an interest in the GRIT during the grantor's life after the termination of the grantor's fixed term income interest. Nevertheless, if the grantor retains a contingent reversionary interest, and if that retained contingent principal interest exceeds 5 percent of the value of the GRIT at inception, then the grantor will then be taxed on all GRIT income pursuant to Code section 673(a). Moreover, since the grantor reserves the income from the GRIT property, the GRIT should be a grantor trust under Code Section 677(a). Therefore, the trust, as a grantor trust, will qualify as a shareholder of an S corporation, at least during the grantor's lifetime, after which it could then convert to a QSST or an electing small business trust (ESBT). Another possibility is to have the grantor retain a "swap" power under Code section 675(4)(C)[13] if the grantor does not retain a contingent reversionary interest. Perhaps a better possibility is to give a swap power to an independent third party.

When is the Use of a GRIT Indicated?

1. When the client is single and has a substantial estate upon which federal estate taxes are certain to be paid. Wealthy widows or widowers, divorced individuals or other unmarried persons can use a GRIT as a "marital deduction substitute."

2. When income producing property is located in more than one state and unification and probate savings are desired. The GRIT would serve to transfer ownership in a manner that would avoid ancillary administration.

3. When the client desires protection from will contests, public scrutiny, or an election against the will if the grantor survives the GRIT term.

4. When the remainder interest of the GRIT passes to someone other than those family members listed in Code section 2702, such as a niece, nephew, a partner or an unrelated friend.

5. When the client wishes to use an alternative to (or be used in conjunction with) a recapitalization or other freezing technique that has the added advantages of gift tax leverage and possible estate tax savings.

6. When there is a high probability that the client will outlive the GRIT term that is needed to obtain a low present value gift to the remaindermen.

7. When the client has assets so substantial that a significant portion can be committed to the remaindermen without compromising his or her own personal financial security.

8. When the client has a high tolerance for complexity and a strong incentive to achieve gift and estate tax savings (rather than taking the direct but potentially more tax costly approach of making an immediate gift).

9. Where the client has property that is expected to appreciate in value, but that might not be producing income that is commensurate with that appreciation.

What are the Requirements of a GRIT?

A few requirements are summarized here.

1. An irrevocable trust must be established. A GRIT must provide that the grantor retains the right to the income for a specified number of years (there is no limit to how few or how many years). As noted below, the longer the specified term of the GRIT, the greater the value of the retained interest and therefore the lower the taxable gift that the grantor is making to the remaindermen.

2. Evidence should be obtained of the value of the assets placed in the GRIT. It is recommended that one or more qualified appraisers value the property at the time of transfer to the trustee of the GRIT.

3. The grantor should be given a mandatory income interest in order to be able to use the actuarial valuation tables. The GRIT instrument should specifically provide that the trustee has no discretion to withhold payments from the grantor (or possession of the trust property from the remaindermen). Payments should be made annually or more frequently.

4. The grantor should be given only the income interest (or possibly a contingent reversionary interest).

5. After the grantor's retained interest has ended, neither the grantor nor any other donor to the GRIT should act as trustee. Retention of an interest as a trustee could lead to estate tax exposure. If the grantor's spouse acts as trustee, consider the potential income tax consequences as a grantor trust, although there may be significant additional benefits to retaining grantor trust status after the end of the term, which would permit the grantor to effectively pay the trust's income tax without a gift tax consequence.

What are the Advantages of a GRIT?

1. GRITs work so well because they are based on two basic principles:

    a. Gift taxes are based on the value of the gift to the donee, and a gift (and therefore the gift tax) must be "discounted" by the time value of money cost incurred by the donee recipient of waiting. The longer the donee must wait, the lower the gift tax value of the asset placed in trust and therefore the lower the cost of the gift. With IRS discount rates (the Code section 7520 rate) that fluctuate from month to month, there can be wide swings in gift tax cost. For instance, if the Code section 7520 rate is 2.0 percent, the taxable gift on a ten year GRIT funded with $1,000,000 by a seventy year old would be $845,450. At a 4.0 percent Code section 7520 rate, the gift would be $719,250, $126,200 less.

b. The federal estate tax does not reach a property interest unless the decedent owned it at death or unless he or she held a "string," a property right that is strong enough to cause it to be pulled back into the decedent's estate. In a GRIT, once the grantor lives longer than the specified term, the grantor neither owns the property in the GRIT nor any rights thereto. Therefore, absent some other factor, the property should escape estate taxation.

2. GRITs are the closest thing to a "no lose" situation; it is a "what have we got to lose?" technique.

a. If the client does not use a GRIT and retains property in his or her sole name, the property plus any appreciation on the property will be includible in his or her estate.

b. If the client who sets up a GRIT dies during the specified term, the result is that an amount not in excess of the value of the property plus any appreciation on the property will be includible in his or her estate (the same result - ignoring legal and accounting and opportunity costs - as if the client had done nothing). However, under regulations finalized in 2008, under Code section 2036 if the grantor dies during the term of a GRIT, the amount included in the estate is limited to an amount necessary to produce the annuity based on IRS interest rates at the time of death.

What are the Disadvantages of a GRIT?

The downside risks, costs or disadvantages of a GRIT include:

1. Attorney fees and the other transaction costs, such as appraisal fees and property titling costs of establishing the GRIT.

2. Lost opportunity cost. The GRIT is an irrevocable trust, so, once assets are placed into the GRIT, the grantor is precluded from taking other planning measures. If the grantor has used up a sizable part of a lifetime applicable exclusion amount to offset the gift of the remainder interest in the GRIT, then the grantor is not in a position to make large gifts of other assets that may substantially appreciate in value. If the grantor dies during the term, the gamble will have been lost. (This risk can be alleviated to some extent by purchasing term life insurance on the grantor's life in an amount equal to the potential estate tax savings).

3. If the grantor does die during the specified GRIT term, the executor may be liable for tax on the includible assets – but the property itself might not be available to pay that tax. (Solutions to this issue are discussed further below.)

4. The property has the transferor's basis in the hands of the beneficiary, so it does not receive a new basis, often a "step up" in basis, at the transferor's death.

5. If the GRIT is funded with low income-producing property, the grantor should retain the right to force the trustee to make the GRIT property reasonably productive of income in order to guarantee use of the Code section 7520 actuarial tables.

How it is Done – An Example of a GRIT

Assume that Georgia, age seventy-five is in a 40 percent gift tax bracket. Assume the Code section 7520 rate is 3.4 percent. She places $10,000,000 into an irrevocable GRIT. The GRIT instrument provides that she will get the income from the GRIT property for a ten year term, and she retains a contingent reversionary interest. At the end of that time, the GRIT property will pass to her partner, Sam.

The present value of her income and contingent reversionary right for ten years is $5,619,900 (.56199 × $10,000,000). Because the entire value of the property placed in the GRIT is $10,000,000 and the value of the interests that Georgia retained is $5,619,900, the value of the future interest gift being made at that point to Sam is the difference, $4,380,100. This entire amount ($4,380,000) is a taxable gift, because the gift tax annual exclusion is allowed only for gifts of a present interest. Of course, if Georgia has not used any of her applicable exclusion amount, the entire gift can be sheltered by the gift tax applicable exclusion amount, which means that Georgia will pay no gift tax unless she has already fully used her gift tax applicable exclusion amount, in which case at a 40 percent gift tax rate, the gift tax would be $1,752,040. If the $10,000,000 property appreciates at an after-tax rate of 4 percent, the property will be worth $14,802,443 by the end of the ten year term. If however, the property appreciated at 8 percent, the property would be worth $21,589,250.

Should Georgia die before the GRIT term expires, the GRIT assets would be included in her estate at their values as of her date of death, and there would be no federal death tax savings.

However, if Georgia survives the ten year term period (no matter by how short a period of time), none of the GRIT assets would be included in her estate. Assuming that the property appreciated at an after-tax rate of 4 percent, at a 40 percent estate tax rate, an approximation of the savings would be $4,168,937 [40% × ($14,802,443 − $4,380,100)]. If the estate tax were discounted to reflect that it would be payable ten years later than the gift tax, then the savings, on a time value of money basis, would be less than that shown. Furthermore, because the property would not pass through probate, probate costs on the asset would be avoided.

GRITs can provide similar gift, estate and GST tax discounts.

What are the Tax Implications of a GRIT?

1. Absent other factors, if the grantor outlives the specified term, none of the GRIT's assets should be included in the grantor's estate. This is because the grantor has retained no interest in trust assets at death. Code section 2036 (retained life estates) applies only if the grantor retained the right to possess or enjoy the property or the income it produces (a) for life, or (b) for a period not ascertainable without reference to the grantor's death, or (c) for any period which does not, in fact, end before the grantor's death.

2. The gift to the remainder beneficiary is a gift of a future interest. Therefore, it cannot qualify for the gift tax annual exclusion.

3. Because a GRIT is a grantor trust, or at least should be structured to be a wholly grantor trust, the grantor will be liable for income tax on ordinary income earned by the GRIT.

4. If the grantor lives beyond the specified term, there should be no further transfer tax because the gift was complete upon the funding of the GRIT.

5. The taxable portion of gifts made after 1976 is considered an "adjusted taxable gift", because the entire present value of the gift to the remaindermen is taxable. However, using a GRIT can transfer a rapidly growing asset at an extremely low transfer tax cost. This results in a significant "leveraging of the applicable exclusion amount." Perhaps more importantly, 100 percent of the appreciation in the property's value occurring after the term ending date escapes estate and gift tax. This makes a GRIT an excellent "estate freezing" device with respect to post-transfer appreciation.

6. When the grantor survives the specified term of the GRIT, no new basis, which often is a step-up, for the property will be allowed under Code section 1014. This is because the property was not acquired from a decedent. The property was acquired by gift when the GRIT was created, so the basis of the donee/remainder beneficiary is generally the same as in the hands of the grantor/donor (i.e., carryover basis). However, the donee's basis is increased by gift tax attributable to the gift in the proportion that the net appreciation (fair market value of gift − basis) bears to the value of the gift.

7. If the grantor dies before the specified term of the trust expires, the date of death value of the property or the value of the corpus necessary to produce the income, will be included in the grantor's gross estate. If there were an estate tax inclusion, (a) there would be no adjusted taxable gift and (b) the applicable exclusion amount utilized in making the gift would be restored to the estate.

It may be appropriate for a beneficiary to purchase insurance on the life of the grantor and carry that life insurance during the period of time in which the death of the grantor would cause estate tax inclusion. The insurance proceeds, received estate tax free, could then be used to purchase assets from the grantor's estate and thereby provide the estate with the liquidity to pay the estate tax.

8. If appreciated property is transferred to a GRIT, the tax on any gain will eventually be paid by (a) the grantor (so long as the GRIT is a grantor trust), (b) the trust (when the GRIT ceases to be a grantor trust), or (c) the beneficiaries (if the property is distributed outright to them on termination of the GRIT). Having taxes paid by the grantor may not, however, be a disadvantage, because the purpose of the GRIT is to "defund" the grantor's estate and shift as much wealth as possible to the remaindermen with minimal gift taxes.

9. GRITs between unrelated parties are not subject to Code section 2702.

65.8 CORPORATE RECAPITALIZATION FREEZES

In the "good old days" before Chapter 14, families used to recapitalize corporations into voting and preferred stock, after which the senior generation would exchange their common stock for preferred stock, and then the parents would give the common stock to the junior generation. By design, the preferred stock would essentially be worth almost the entire value of the corporation, leaving little value for the common stock, resulting in a relatively small gift to the junior generation. The preferred stock would soak up most of the value of the corporation through use of liquidation preferences and other attributes of corporate stock such as put rights and noncumulative dividend rights. However, the preferred stock value would be frozen so that all subsequent appreciation inures to the benefit of the common stockholders, in this case the junior generation. After losing several cases,[14] the IRS prevailed upon the Congress to amend the law, first to add Code section 2036(c) in 1987, and ultimately the enactment of Chapter 14. Code section 2701 applies to entity recapitalizations between "members of the family," and provides very limited preferred interest recapitalization freeze opportunities. However, *un*related parties can still play the freeze game unfettered by Code section 2701, i.e., by engaging in entity recapitalization freeze transactions that are designed to fix the value of the preferred interests, thereby passing the post-recapitalization appreciation to the common interest holders.

65.9 COHABITATION OR PROPERTY AGREEMENTS

While it might not seem obvious, it is just as important for an unmarried couple to have some sort of written agreement at the beginning of their relationship as it is for any couple who are contemplating marriage, if not more so, especially if the couple plans to co-own property or incur debt. The reason is that the law between married couples is much clearer and more pronounced than the law for unmarried partners. For many years, contracts between unmarried partners were not upheld because the courts considered such relationships "meretricious."[15] This began to change with the 1976 California Supreme Court's decision in the celebrated case of *Marvin v. Marvin*.[16] Even though the California Supreme Court did not find the existence of a contract in the Marvin case, the court noted:

> In summary, we base our opinion on the principle that adults who voluntarily live together and engage in sexual relations are nonetheless as competent as any other person to contract respecting their earnings and property rights. Of course, they cannot lawfully contract to pay for the performance of sexual services, for such a contract is, in essence, an agreement for prostitution and unlawful for that reason. But they may agree to pool their earnings and to hold all property acquired during the relationship in accord with the law governing community property; conversely they may agree that each partner's earnings and the property acquired from those earnings remains the separate property of the earning partner. So long as the agreement does not rest upon illicit meretricious consideration, the parties may order their economic affairs as they choose, and no policy precludes the courts from enforcing such agreements.[17]

The partners should engage in full and fair financial disclosure and have separate and independent counsel. The following issues should be considered in a cohabitation or property agreement:

1. The fair distribution of property upon dissolution of the parties' relationship should be the overarching goal of such an agreement. The

agreement should specify what property is separate and the property that will be shared (and on what basis), and it should distinguish between property that is inherited and property that is received as a gift. The agreement also should determine what happens to the increase in value on pre-relationship property that occurs during the period of the relationship. It is usually beneficial to draft specific provisions relating to the ownership and occupancy of the parties' principal residence and contents therein.

2. A clear and unambiguous definition of the terms "time of beginning of the relationship" and "termination of relationship" is essential. The term "termination of the relationship" can be defined to mean when one partner delivers to the other partner a written notice of intent to terminate the relationship, or when a partner vacates the couple's principal residence or requests in writing that the other partner vacates such residence.

3. All debts should be identified, and a determination should be made as to who is responsible for each. These agreements usually provide that each partner retains sole responsibility for the pre-relationship debts and that the other partner is not liable for their payment.

4. The agreement should state if, and the extent of, any obligation to contribute to the support of the household and, upon dissolution of the relationship, the payment and duration of any financial support by one partner to the other.

5. If one of the partners dies prior to a termination of the relationship, the agreement can spell out survivorship rights, such as the right to inherit property and receive retirement, life insurance and other benefits, as well as set forth directives for burial and funeral services.

6. The agreement also should include the right of a partner to be an agent on a durable property power of attorney, serve as a guardian or conservator if a partner becomes incapacitated, make medical decisions on behalf of a partner, and participate in health, disability, life and long-term care insurance plans. The agreement should include HIPAA releases for each partner to be able to discuss the other partner's health-care with health-care providers.

7. The agreement also may provide for non-financial issues such as who will do which household chores, or tend to pets, if, for no other reason, to spell out the understandings of the partners.

8. It is prudent to include a choice of law provision that determines what state law will govern, which can be critical since state law varies so much in this area. There are still a handful of states that will not uphold these contracts.

9. The agreement should provide a method for resolving disputes, such as collaborative law, arbitration or mediation.

10. Often clients want a cohabitation agreement to do double duty as a marriage contract if they ultimately do decide to marry, although some people believe that these two agreements actually are at odds with one another and should not be combined.

11. Consideration is *required* for a cohabitation agreement as in any other contract, whereas, in a marriage contract, the consideration is the marriage itself.

12. How expenses will be handled during the relationship, how assets purchased by the couple will be titled and any post-termination support commitments.

13. The partners often waive the following rights in these types of agreements:

    a. To share in each other's estates upon his or her death.

    b. To "palimony" or other forms of support or maintenance, either temporary and permanent.

    c. To share in the increase in value of the separate property of the other partner during the period of cohabitation.

    d. To the division of the separate property of the partners, whether currently held or thereafter acquired.

e. To any other claims based on the period of cohabitation.

f. To share in the IRA or retirement plans of the other partner.

g. To claim the existence of a common-law marriage.

65.10 FREQUENTLY ASKED QUESTIONS

Question – What are the best assets to place into a GRIT?

Answer – Assets that possess substantial appreciation potential are the best assets to place into a GRIT.

Question – Can the IRS revalue a transfer to a GRIT many years after the GRIT is funded?

Answer – A gift made after August 5, 1997, cannot be revalued for estate or gift tax purposes if the gift was adequately disclosed on a gift tax return and the gift tax statute of limitations (generally, three years) has passed.[18] Therefore, a gift tax return with an adequate disclosure of valuation should be filed with respect to a transfer to a GRIT to start the statute of limitations with respect to valuation of the gift.

Question – Is there an "escape mechanism" that could redirect the remainder interest if the grantor dies during the term? For instance, is there a way to provide that if the grantor's estate has to include GRIT assets, funds in the GRIT return to the grantor's estate rather than going to the remainder beneficiary?

Answer – A reversion to the grantor (or better yet to a revocable trust the grantor established during lifetime to avoid probate), conditioned on the grantor's death within the specified term, could be used. This will reduce the size of the taxable gift.

Question – Is there a cutoff age after which the GRIT no longer is mathematically logical?

Answer – Because the GRIT is a "little to lose – a lot to gain" tool, even clients in their eighties or nineties may want to use such a trust. For instance, assuming a Code section 7520 rate of 2.0 percent and no retained contingent reversionary interest, the value of the income interest retained in a five year QPRT is .079570 of the principal for an eighty year old. Some clients, especially those who are in very good health, may want to gamble with a GRIT. For example, if the eighty-year-old client opted for a ten year term, the value of the income interest jumps to .123940 of the funds placed in the GRIT (and therefore the taxable gift to the remaindermen drops accordingly).

For clients with a slightly lower risk tolerance, consider staggered terms or adding a retained contingent reversionary interest, the latter of which will reduce the size of the taxable gift. For instance, an eighty-year-old client could transfer some property into a two-year GRIT and other property into a three-year GRIT. This technique was used in the *O'Reilly* case.[19]

Question – Are there problems with using closely-held entity interests with a GRIT?

Answer – The major problem with transferring closely held stock or other similarly hard-to-value assets into a GRIT concerns valuation. If the asset is not properly valued and/or not properly disclosed to the IRS, there is a risk of having to pay additional gift tax, penalties, and interest, or of using up more of the lifetime credit against gift tax.

Question – Are there special provisions that should be inserted into a GRIT?

Answer – Yes. Although the GRIT instrument does not have to carefully track the requirements of Code section 2702 and the accompanying regulations, the instrument should contain, at a minimum, what is set forth below.

It is extremely important to document the "completeness" of the transfer at the date that the GRIT is funded. Specifically, the GRIT instrument must provide that the grantor has given up all dominion and control over the property.

The grantor must specifically give up any power to revoke the gift of the remainder. The GRIT instrument should also forbid the grantor to change any beneficial interests in the remainder. Therefore, the grantor can retain no power of appointment (other than, possibly, a power contingent on the grantor dying during the trust term).

The grantor should not be named as trustee after the grantor's retained interest ends. An unrelated, independent trustee or another family member (depending on the terms of any continuing trusts) could be selected.

The GRIT instrument also should specifically deny the grantor any control over the manner or time in which the beneficiaries will enjoy the trust corpus (otherwise, that corpus will be pulled back into the grantor's estate under Code sections 2036 or 2038).

Question – Can stock in an S corporation be placed into a GRIT?

Answer – Under usual circumstances, a GRIT does not qualify to hold S stock because not all of the trust income is payable to the beneficiary. However, because any trust as to which the grantor is treated as the owner for income tax purposes can hold S corporation stock, the solution has been to make the GRIT "defective" for income tax purposes (i.e., taxable under the grantor trust rules).

Question – Assume a grantor, Laura, age seventy established a GRIT in March 2017 for a term of ten years, but with a provision that should she die before the end of the term, it will terminate at her death and revert to her estate. The value of the property placed in the trust is $5,000,000 and the Code section 7520 rate is percent. What is the amount of the gift? What would the amount be if the gift was for a ten year term without a retained contingent reversionary interest?

Answer – There can be a sizable difference between the value of the gift that a grantor would make if he or she retains the contingent reversionary interest versus if he or she does not retain such a right. In Laura's case, that difference is indeed sizable. The amount of the gift where she retains the contingent reversionary interest is $, versus a gift of $, a difference of $where she does not retain such a right. This difference is dramatic in Laura's case given her age when compared to the term of the GRIT. For example, had the GRIT been only for a five year term, the size of the gift with the reversionary interest would have been $, versus a gift of $,

a difference of only $, where she does not retain such a right.

Question – Can an unmarried couple be represented by the same lawyer in the formulation of a cohabitation or property agreement?

Answer – While this may technically be possible, although there are many who would say that it is not ethically possible, we strongly advise and recommend that each partner be represented by separate counsel in the negotiation and formulation of a cohabitation or property agreement.

CHAPTER ENDNOTES

1. See, e.g., May v. McGowan, 194 F.2d 396, 397 (2d Cir. 1952) ("an outstanding option to purchase restricts the market value of stock in the hands of the owner to the option price"); *Lomb v. Sugden*, 82 F.2d 166, 168 (2d Cir. 1936) ("Because of the agreement, the decedent could not have secured a price greater than $69.445 at the time of her death"); and *Wilson v. Bowers*, 57 F.2d 682, 683 (2d Cir. 1932) ("the sale value of the stock during the testator's life could have been no more than the low price at which he was obliged to offer it").
2. *Wilson v. Bowers*, 57 F.2d 682 (2d Cir. 1932); *Fiorito v. Comm'r.*, 33 T.C. 440 (1959), acq. 1960-2 C.B. 3; *Weil Est. v. Comm'r.*, 22 T.C. 1267 (1954), acq. 1955-2 C.B. 3; and *Bischoff Est. v. Comm'r.*, 69 T.C. 32 (1977).
3. *Bommer Revocable Trust v. Comm'r.*, T.C. Memo 1997-380.
4. Rev. Rul. 65-193.
5. 152 F. 3d 208 (2d Cir. 1998).
6. T.C. Memo 1996-148, rev'd and rem'd 152 F. 3d 208 (2d Cir. 1998).
7. Treas. Reg. §25.7520-3(b)(3). See also Rev. Rul. 80-80.
8. Treas. Reg. §25.2702-4(c).
9. Treas. Reg. §25.2702-4(c).
10. See, e.g., PLR 8642028. The courts have agreed with the IRS. See, e.g., *O'Reilly v. Comm'r.*, 973 F.3d 1402 (8th Cir. 1992).
11. See, e.g., TAM 199935003.
12. I.R.C. §2036(a)(1).
13. See, e.g., PLR 8801008.
14. For a case involving pre-I.R.C. §2036(c) and pre-Chapter 14 that illustrates the difficulty that the IRS encountered in fighting recapitalization freeze transactions, see *Lewis M. Hutchens Marital Trust v. Comm'r.*, T.C. Memo 1993-600.
15. See, e.g., Beal v. Beal, 577 P. 2d 507 (Ore. 1978).
16. 557 P. 2d 106 (Cal. 1976).
17. 557 P. 2d 106, 116.
18. I.R.C. §2001(f).
19. 973 F. 3d 1402 (8th Cir. 1992).

COMMUNITY PROPERTY TRUSTS

CHAPTER 66

66.1 INTRODUCTION

Louisiana, California, Arizona, Idaho, New Mexico, Nevada, Texas, Washington, Puerto Rico and Wisconsin have long had a system of married property ownership known as community property, which differs from common law ownership by spouses in other states.

Community property receives an important income tax benefit that non-community property does not – even compared to common law property that is also owned 50/50 by spouses. Community property (even if the title only appears to be in one spouse's name) receives a new date of death (or on rare occasions, an alternate valuation date) basis over the entire property - even though only half of the property is included in a decedent's estate.[1] This is not typically the case for jointly held property owned by spouses under common law, even if it is held in tenancy by the entireties or with right of survivorship – in such cases the basis is typically only 50% adjusted.

In years past, the only option for couples wanting to receive this benefit was to move to a community property state and transmute (convert) their property to community property. Under the Restatement (Second) of Conflict of Laws § 259, when a married couple or a spouse acquires an asset, the fact that the couple or spouse later moves to another state does not affect the character of the property.[2]

Starting in 1998, Alaska established an elective community property regime based on the Uniform Marital Property Act which included a community property trust that out of state residents could use to cause their property to be considered community property under Alaska law.[3] Since then, Tennessee, South Dakota, Kentucky and Florida have also enacted elective community property statutes that include provisions regarding the establishment of community property trusts.[4] Bar association committees in other states like Ohio and Michigan are considering proposing similar legislation. Why shouldn't the rest of the country be able to get the same tax benefit as those in community property states?

Married couples residing in these five states, and probably most other non-community property states, may establish joint revocable trusts under one of these new community property trust laws and should achieve the same income tax advantage after the first spouse's death of a full increase in basis on contributed assets as residents of community property states.

66.2 BASICS OF THE COMMUNITY PROPERTY TRUST

Couples in community property states often establish joint revocable trusts, and couples who move from community property states to common law states often establish such trusts to keep, trace and track their community property as such.[5] This Chapter concerns a completely different use and unique set of statutes that purport to enable a conversion of non-community property to community property.

These new(ish) state community property trust statutes typically have the following requirements:

(1) one or both spouses must transfer property to the trust;

(2) the trust expressly declares that some or all of the property transferred is community property under the state's law;

(3) at least one trustee has a nexus with the state, fitting the definition of a "qualified trustee";

(4) the trust agreement sets forth the powers of the qualified trustee, which include maintaining records and preparing any income tax returns that must be filed by the trust (although these are always grantor trusts that usually do not file a Form 1041);

(5) the trust must be signed by both spouses; and

(6) the trust contains at its beginning a declaration in capital letters giving explicit notice to the settlors about changing the nature of their property rights.

Although no community property trust state has the *requirement* to convert real property outside of that state to personal property (usually by putting it into an LLC before transfer), this may be a good idea to do, since the rules for choice of law often favor the situs of the property and the situs of personal property (such as an LLC interest) is the residency of the owner (here, the trustee residing in the community property trust state).

There is no clear definition of community property, but some court cases have tried to flesh out some general rules.[6]

66.3 ADVANTAGES

The additional basis adjustment for community property afforded to surviving spouses is especially valuable to couples who own farms, real estate, businesses and other highly appreciated assets held outside of retirement plans. It is even more valuable when the surviving spouse can depreciate such assets or would have to sell any assets inherited from their spouse to live on during their lifetime.

Let's start with a simple example of the differences between community property and non-community property vis a vis the basis on the death of a surviving spouse, then walk through the options that a couple has to plan proactively for this, particularly the *community property trust*.

The chart below compares the basis increase at the death of a spouse for community property ("CP") v. jointly held property held in a non-community property state. John and Mary, married, own four mutual funds, a home and a rental property inside of an LLC – at John's death the basis for these assets change as follows, depending on whether these assets are community property or not:

John & Mary's Jointly held assets:	Pre-Mortem Tax Basis	Date of John's Death Value	Basis after John's Death (if not C.P.)	(if C.P.)
Fund Q	$1,400,000	$2,400,000	$1,900,000	$2,400,000
Fund X	$1,000,000	$1,800,000	$1,400,000	$1,800,000
Fund Y*	$1,500,000	$1,300,000	$1,400,000	$1,300,000
Fund Z	$200,000	$800,000	$500,000	$800,000
Home***	$1,000,000	$2,000,000	$1,500,000	$2,000,000
ABC, LLC**	$400,000	$3,000,000	$1,700,000*	$3,000,000*
Total	**$5,500,000**	**$11,300,000**	**$8,400,000**	**$11,300,000**

* Note: Fund Y would not be placed in a community property trust and proactive planning would have the spouses sell, gift or transmute the property to separate property if it is community property, provided there is time to do so before a spouse's death, in order to prevent a double "step down" in basis. However, it is important in understanding basis planning that we show an example of a "loss" asset.

** This chart assumes that husband and wife together own 100% of the LLC and valuation "discounts" are avoided. In order to maximize the basis increase for married couples and avoid discounts, careful attention should be paid to fractionally-owned real estate and business interests in LLCs and their operating agreements. If not careful, a 50% share in an LLC may be valued at a "discount" of 15%-40%, so the value of 50% of an LLC owning $3 million of property in our example might be valued at a 20% discount, $1.2 million rather than $1.5 million, thus increasing total basis to the survivor of $1.2 million plus $200,000 = only $1.4 million, or only $2.4 million for two 50% community property interests.

There is an additional bonus and savings for LLCs owned as CP – there is no requirement to file a Form 1065 partnership income tax return if spouses are sole owners (per Rev. Proc. 2002-69).

*** Similar to above, practitioners should take care to understand that a home held as a 50% tenancy in common or as community property without any right of survivorship may have to be valued at a discount, which would reduce basis.[7] If such property is the equivalent of joint tenancy with right of survivorship, IRC Section 2040(b) may permit *the property to be valued at half of the whole, i.e., without a discount. For more valuable properties, paying attention to this difference in how homes are titled may yield significant savings, since later gain on sale may exceed the $250,000 IRC § 121 capital gains exclusion for the sale of a residence. If a $2 million home that is community property is considered owned 50/50 without any survivorship feature to trigger IRC §2040(b) valuation, and the IRS/courts deem a 25% discount to be appropriate, this would mean the basis becomes only $1.5 million and when the widow sells the home years later a taxable gain can easily occur that exceeds $250,000.*

When Mary, the surviving spouse, sells her property, or calculates the depreciation deduction for any depreciable property, a higher basis saves her income tax. The additional basis afforded to community property in the above example ($2.9 million more in basis in the example above) could easily save $1 million of state and federal income tax for the surviving spouse over her lifetime (depending, of course, on how many of the assets are sold, but there is a beneficial feedback loop in that increased basis reduces income tax burden which reduces the need to sell assets whereas the opposite occurs for couples in common law states – decreased basis means more tax which requires the widow to sell more assets which causes more tax, etc.).

66.4 DISADVANTAGES

There are potential negatives to such trusts: if someone changes their *separate* property (such as property held prior to marriage or received via gift or inheritance) into community property (and the other spouse does not do the same with an equal amount of their separate property) and later divorces, this property converted to community will likely be split 50/50 by a divorce court when it might have been kept separate otherwise.

If there is an intra-spousal gift and a donee spouse dies within one year of funding, the step up in basis may be more limited under Code section 1014(e), the one-year rule, if the gifted funds come back to the donor-spouse upon the death of the donee-spouse within one year of a gift.

The nature of the assets matters – for conservative taxpayers invested largely in cash or cash equivalents or retirement plan assets, the double step up in basis may not matter much. If the property is a primary residence that the surviving spouse cannot depreciate and will have a $250,000 capital gains tax exclusion on later sale that might exceed any gains anyway, there may not be much benefit for a full step up in basis for a home.[8] The couples who benefit the most are real estate investors, many of whom have near-zero-basis property that can adopt a new depreciation schedule.

There may also be an additional cost for not only drafting, but for using an out-of-state professional trustee (if the couple does not already reside in one of the community property trust states). If the clients have disproportionate separate property that would not all be marital upon divorce, counsel may recommend that each spouse have separate counsel, similar to what is done for couples executing pre and post nuptial agreements. This would also drive up costs and complexity.

The age of the couple may matter as well. For couples in their nineties, the second spouse may not survive the first spouse for long enough to get much benefit at all from the earlier step up in basis, and the next generation will often get another step up in basis when the survivor dies shortly thereafter (if inherited outright or in a marital trust, or in an optimal basis increase trust, see Chapter 44).

Furthermore, there is an opportunity cost, both from an estate tax and an asset protection planning standpoint. Having funds in a community property trust means that they cannot go into an irrevocable grantor trust, GRAT, QPRT, CRT or other estate tax planning vehicle. If clients have parents still living, an *upstream optimal basis increase trust* may offer a chance for a basis increase at an older relative's death without waiting for *either* spouse having to die to receive the tax benefit.[9] Other gifting trusts offer more chance to "freeze" an estate and reduce estate tax exposure. From an asset protection perspective, placing funds in a community property trust might preclude having property as tenancy by the entireties, which has significant protection under some states laws.

Unfortunately, there is no ruling or case law explicitly sanctioning the tax effect of such arrangements, even though Alaska passed its elective community property statute over a quarter century ago, in 1998. The IRS has remained noncommittal about whether it will honor these states' elective community property statutes and community property trusts (see IRS Publication 555), perhaps because of the potential state law variances on honoring post-nuptial agreements. While community property trusts should probably "work" in most cases, there is still a level of uncertainty that must be conveyed to clients. The IRS may have more cause to contest the arrangement if the couple resides in a state that restricts the use of post-nuptial agreements, since a community property trust might then be more likely to be found to violate a strong public policy of the couple's state of residence.

There has been no reported case or ruling on any aspect of these statutes since 1998. There are some arguments the IRS could use to deny the step up, but they are far from compelling or convincing. In *Commissioner v. Harmon*, 323 U.S. 44 (1944), the Supreme Court ruled that an Oklahoma statute allowing spouses to elect community property under that state's law would not be recognized for federal income tax purposes (income splitting). The IRS may try to rely on *Harmon* to disallow the full step-up in basis for community property acquired through an opt-in community property state. In Rev. Rul. 77-359, the IRS addressed the tax treatment of community property agreements entered into by a husband and wife residing in the State of Washington (a community property state). It concluded that the conversion of separate property to community property by such residents would be effective for federal gift tax purposes but ineffective for the transmutation of *income* from such property. Citing *Harmon*, the IRS noted, "[t]o the extent that the agreement affects the income from separate property and not the separate property itself, the Service will not permit the spouses to split that income for Federal income tax purposes where they file separate income tax returns."

That said, if a state such as Wisconsin can enact a community property law (which the IRS honors) that allows residents to opt-*out*, why shouldn't the law honor a similar state law like Alaska that allows an opt-*in*? Or states that want to only allow an opt-in under a trust structure? There are some commentators and law review articles that make a good argument that taxpayers can use the law of other states to control their property rights without even using a fancy trust, just as people can establish an LLC in another state and have that state's laws apply to it.[10]

With those caveats, there is still tremendous upside potential with relatively low risk. Community property trusts should be considered for couples with significant low basis-to-value assets, especially business property or real estate (including LLCs/LPs that own such) that is depreciable. If the non-tax negatives are inconsequential, as would be the case for many long-term marriages where most property is considered marital and would be split 50/50 on divorce anyway, such trusts offer the potential to save significant income tax for surviving spouses.

If the courts someday decide (or Congress changes the law) so that community trusts do not "work," it may be a "heads I win, tails I don't lose" proposition, since the spouses establishing such a trust in place of their standard revocable living trust would simply be right back to where they would have been if they had not established the trust in the first place. Unlike many irrevocable trust techniques, community property trusts are typically revocable (although some of the state statutes allow them to be irrevocable), and can easily be changed or undone should the law change or another technique become more enticing.

There is no clear ruling or case law involving these new community property trusts, so don't overpromise the 100% basis increase result, even though there is strong authority for it. Be careful to monitor investments and take funds out of the trust if they go down in value below basis after transfer to the community property trust– otherwise the double "step up" in basis becomes a detrimental "double step down" in basis. For example, the couple buys 1000 shares of Tesla at $260/each for $260,000 in trust, but the stock goes down to $130/share. If one of the spouses dies, the basis in the stock is reduced to $130,000 – whereas if the funds were taken out of trust and transmuted this double step down would be avoided. In a typical joint with right of survivorship account between spouses in a non-community property state (or if it is transmuted to separate property in a community property state), the step down would only be to $195,000 (half the difference). Of course, even a 50% step down in basis could be avoided if the stock were gifted to the non-decedent spouse before death or sold to take a capital loss if it could be used to offset gains.

Dynamic Transmutation. To avoid an inadvertent double step down in basis, could the community property trust agreement provide that any property whose value reduces below its cost basis is *automatically* thereafter held and governed by a subtrust with different terms (i.e., one that is no longer a community property trust)? Perhaps. In theory, such dynamic transmutation should be possible. But until there is clearer precedent, it would be wise to keep community property trusts as simple as possible to avoid further IRS scrutiny and become the test case. Better to simply keep an eye on any highly fluctuating investments and remember to take out any deep losers out of the trust.

Asset Protection Risks and Opportunities – an *Irrevocable* Community Property Trust?

Revocable community property trusts (by far the most common variety) do not provide any asset protection, and there may be an opportunity cost of placing assets in such a trust if the alternative might be to otherwise use tenancy by the entirety, SLATs or other traditional asset protection vehicles.

Most of the state community property trust statutes, however, allow a community property trust to be *irrevocable*.[11] Conceivably in a state such as Alaska, Tennessee and South Dakota, this could double as a domestic asset protection trust (DAPT) that affords some protection to settlors who are beneficiaries of irrevocable trusts. Florida and Kentucky do not have such legislation. If there was ever a "low hanging fruit" tempting the IRS to argue that property in such a trust should not be considered as community property for purposes of state law and IRC §1014(b)(6), however, this would be it. Even if the contribution is not a completed gift (such as through retention of lifetime limited and/or testamentary powers of appointment), it just *smells* a lot different from traditional community property – more so than a joint revocable trust, which the IRS has long recognized as being able to be community property under state law and Code section 1014(b)(6). After all, the trustees own the legal title and the spouses merely retain an equitable interest – but in a typical irrevocable trust they would not retain the entire equitable interest, because an irrevocable trust vests a property interest in both the current beneficiaries and any remaindermen. Equitable interests can indeed be community property, but would it be the *entire* interest? How far can a state deviate and stretch its definitions from traditional community property norms before the IRS and/or courts cry foul? There is no clear and obvious answer. Community property states themselves have dramatic differences in how much creditors can access, whether income earned during the marriage from separate property is community, and other aspects – there is not one clear definition of what community property is – at least not one with any detail.

In conclusion, there is good authority that married couples can choose the state law that applies to their assets and take the position that assets in a community property trust held at death should be treated for Code section 1014(b)(6) purposes the same as for assets held as community property by residents of community property states. There is even authority that it could be done without a formal trust. But don't overpromise your clients when there is still some uncertainty, particularly when you go further and further from traditional community property concepts, such as an irrevocable domestic asset protection community property trust. A conservative client using a community property trust wishing to avoid any risk of interest and penalties after death could simply pay the income tax on later sale as if there were only a 50% step up in basis and then file for a refund of the capital gains tax (and possible net investment income tax) paid as a result. Either the IRS will issue a refund or it will deny it, but in either case there is no chance of additional interest and penalties.

Some may claim that there is nothing to lose in trying, other than attorney and accounting and trustee fees, and a very good chance at a significant upside tax benefit. But remember that there is an opportunity cost and other alternatives that might achieve the same or better goals of increasing basis without the risk of a generous donor-spouse being adversely affected upon divorce.[12]

CHAPTER ENDNOTES

1. I.R.C. §1014(b)(6).
2. Alaska Stat. §§34.77.010 to 34.77.995.
3. Jonathan G. Blattmachr, Howard M. Zaritsky & Mark L. Ascher, *Tax Planning with Consensual Community Property: Alaska's New Community Property Law*, 33 Real Prop. Prob. & Tr. J. 615, 618 (Winter 1999).
4. S.D. Cent. Code §§ 55-17-1 to 55-17-14; Tenn. Code §§ 35-17-101 to 35-17-108; Florida Stat. §§ 736.1501–151; KRS §386.620 et seq.;
5. The Uniform Trust Code §602(b) even has a provision regarding joint trusts holding community property: "(b) If a revocable trust is created or funded by more than one settlor: (1) to the extent the trust consists of community property, the trust may be revoked by either spouse acting alone but may be amended only by joint action of both spouses;"
6. For a tax court case discussing community property, see *Angerhofer v. Comm.*, 87 T.C. 814 (T.C. 1986), analyzing whether property owned by German residents and citizens could be treated as community property, citing in turn the Supreme Court decision of *Poe v. Seaborn*, 282 U.S. 101 (1930) and more recent tax court decision of *Westerdahl v. Comm*. 82 T.C. 83 (1984) for general characteristics of community property, the latter stating: "In making this determination, the Court looked at the spouses' responsibilities, legal obligations, and limitations with respect to one another and to the community property. It regarded several factors as particularly important, but it did not label these factors as requisites for finding a present vested interest. The several factors, when combined and viewed as two broad

attributes, include: Protection of the interest of each spouse in the community property (1) by legally assuring its testamentary disposition or its passage to the decedent's issue rather than to the surviving spouse, and (2) by limiting the managing spouse's powers of management and control so that detriment to the nonmanaging spouse from fraud or mismanagement will be minimized." Since the vast majority of community property states now allow a "right of survivorship" feature to be added, it's uncertain how much this first factor would be relevant today.

7. Although community property did not traditionally have a survivorship feature, states have amended their statutes to permit "community property with right of survivorship": Cal. Civ. Code §682.1 and Cal. Prob. Code §5100 et seq., Alaska Stat. § 34.77.110(e), Ariz. Rev. Stat. § 33-431, Cal. Civ. Code §682.1, Idaho Code §15-6-401 (real property) and Idaho Code §15-6-403 (personal property); NM Stat § 40-3-8(B); Nev. Rev. Stat. §123.250, §111.064, Tex. Est. Code § 112.052(d); RCW 64.28.010 et seq; Wis. Stat. §766.60(5). Apparently Louisiana is a holdout. Property in a joint revocable trust can be treated like jointly held property with right of survivorship for purposes of the I.R.C. §2040(b) valuation loophole if the trust is essentially creating the same administration and survivorship characteristics, see discussion in *Black v. Comm.*, 765 F.2d 862 (9th Cir. 1985).

8. I.R.C. §121 allows a couple (and recent widow/er) $500,000 of capital gains tax exclusion on sale of a primary residence, $250,000 for single taxpayers.

9. See Chapter 44 and *Ed Morrow & The Upstream Optimal Basis Increase Trust*, LISI Estate Planning Newsletter #2635 (April 17, 2018).

10. See, *Community Property for Non-Community Property States*, 24 Quinnipiac Prob. L.J. 260 (2011), by Katherine, Mary and Julie Black, which contains a good historical background on why the system is currently as it is.

11. See, e.g., Tenn. Code §35-17-104(b)(2).

12. For discussion of pros and cons and a comparison chart of different methods of achieving the same, such as using a Joint Exempt Step Up Trust (JEST), Estate Trusts, "Disclaim to Gain" strategies and other techniques, see the white paper titled Optimal Basis Increase Trust (OBIT), by Ed Morrow, downloadable at www.ssrn.com.

MARRIAGE CONTRACTS AND PROPERTY AGREEMENTS

CHAPTER 67

67.1 INTRODUCTION

"[Second marriage is] the triumph of hope over experience."[1]

This chapter will cover the basics of both marriage contracts (both pre-nuptial and post-nuptial) and property (also known as cohabitation) agreements for unmarried couples. It will cover the reasons for and benefits of this type of agreement, as well as what typically is included in such an agreement and the principal reasons why a court might set aside such an agreement. In so doing, this chapter will address the two uniform acts that many states have enacted to cover marriage contracts, the 1983 Uniform Premarital Agreement Act and the new 2012 Uniform Premarital and Marital Agreements Act, and where those acts differ. It will also discuss the laws that state courts most often apply to deal with property agreements among unmarried partners. The chapter will also address issues that pertain to portability and marriage contracts. It is important at the outset of this chapter to underscore the fact that there is no "one size fits all" in this form of agreement; there is no "standard" or "specimen agreement" that can address every issue in a unique relationship between the partners.

The statistics for married and unmarried couples and the need for marriage contracts or property agreements is a mixed bag. According to the 2010 United States Census, approximately 12 percent of couples are unmarried, which represented a 25 percent increase from the 2000 census, so this category of couples is experiencing the most rapid growth of any couples category. Just from 2009 to 2010, the number of cohabiting couples of the opposite sex increased by 13 percent.[2] And, according to other estimates, over 40 percent (and, according to one study, more than 70 percent[3]) of adults cohabited prior to marriage, which perhaps is evidence of changing societal views that formerly referred to cohabiting couples as "living in sin."

Despite the divorce rate, which is estimated to be as high as 50 percent for first marriages, and that, according to a recent Harris Interactive survey, 28 percent believe that marriage contracts are a good idea for people who are contemplating marriage (which grows to 49 percent of divorced people who believe this), it has been estimated that only 1-5 percent of Americans actually have marriage contracts in place. This phenomenon has been studied,[4] and the results indicate that while people generally believe that marriage contracts are a good idea (but more for the rich and famous), despite the divorce statistics, they believe that they do not need one for *their* particular relationship because of "certainty" that *their* relationship will be successful. The reasons that the author of the study propounds for this anomaly generally relate to undue optimism about the success of their marriage despite the odds and that the commencement of a discussion of a marriage contract will send a bad signal to their partner about the prospects for a long-term, successful marriage. Whatever the reason, it appears that far more people could use marriage contracts, and, by extension, property agreements than enter into them, particularly for those who will have blended families.

One or both partners may already have had experience with divorce and the attendant division of marital property. That experience also may keep a partner from marrying again, choosing to couple in unmarried status. Such a client will be acutely aware of the turmoil that is possible – and that may be avoided or reduced by a marriage contract or property agreement. That client often will need little persuasion to enter into such an

943

agreement. In many cases, a marriage contract may be deemed to be mandatory upon the client's remarriage, in accordance with the terms of a separation or nuptial agreement in connection with the client's prior marriage.

If there are children from previous relationships, each client will want to make certain that their children are provided for regardless of which spouse dies first, and that the subsequent remarriage of a surviving spouse will not allow any further diversion of family wealth. The well-known existence of a marriage contract or property agreement may also lessen any perception on the part of the children that a new spouse has entered into the relationship solely to steal their rightful inheritance.

67.2 WHAT IT IS

A marriage contract and a property agreement are legal contracts that can cover a wide range of topics, from finances to what happens if the couple subsequently splits. The process of a couple frankly discussing the issues that could divide them in the future, fosters and promotes discussion of short-term and long-term goals by getting the parties' financial affairs out on the table early in the relationship.

Since finances are so often the reason why couples divorce, it is vitally important that the partners take the time to discuss their assets, their liabilities, their financial problems and their financial goals. Discussions of issues that pertain to marriage contracts and property agreements also can facilitate discussions of important non-financial issues such as each partner's thoughts and desires on children, each partner's expectations about the other partner's post-marital career, i.e., to be a stay-at-home parent, and child-related issues. A good marriage contract or property agreement also can achieve the following:

1. It can reduce uncertainty and unpredictability in the event of split-up or death;

2. It can insulate each partner from the other partner's debts and obligations;

3. It can define what constitutes each partner's separate property and address community property or jointly-owned property;

4. It can eliminate the threat during the relationship of an argument such as "I'm going to split up with you and take you to the cleaners," by clearly setting forth what each party knows going in that they are going to get if the couple splits-up;

5. It can avoid or minimize the cost of litigation if the couple splits-up;

6. It can allow each party to maintain financial independence from the other to the extent of each partner's comfort level; and

7. It can permit a couple who usually is still in an early stage in their relationship to focus their attention on getting to know each other better and toward the very critical non-financial aspects of their relationship by coming to a resolution of the financial issues.

If your client falls into any of the following categories, then the client should consider a marriage contract or property agreement:

1. The client has significantly more wealth and/or income than their partner;

2. The client has significantly less wealth and/or income than their partner;

3. The client's partner has substantial debt obligations;

4. The client intends to leave the current workforce or drop out of school so that the client can stay at home and raise a family;

5. The client stands to inherit substantial assets in the future;

6. The client owns all or part of a closely-held business;

7. The client and/or their partner were previously coupled and/or have children from prior relationships; and

8. The client desires some level of uncertainty about the viability of their estate plan if the client dies first.

67.3 TYPES OF MARRIAGE CONTRACTS AND PROPERTY AGREEMENTS

While experts often refer to them by different names and sometimes have more categories of agreements, there essentially are two types of marriage contracts and property agreements: the so-called "title-based agreement" and the "defined property agreement," each with advantages and disadvantages that we will develop in the next few paragraphs. A *title-based agreement* provides that, upon the termination of the relationship, all of the partners' property falls into one of three buckets – partner 1's separate property, partner 2's separate property or community/jointly-owned property. Generally, this determination will be based solely on how the property is titled at the time of termination of the relationship.

Example. No matter how or when acquired, a car that is titled in Jeremy's name alone will be his separate property, a bank account that is titled in Susan's name alone will be her separate property, and any property that is titled in both partners' names will be jointly-owned property. A *defined property agreement* essentially is any other form of agreement that is not a title-based agreement, i.e., it is a catch-all category.

Title-Based Agreements

A title-based agreement has a number of advantages and disadvantages, which include:

Advantages

1. *Simplicity and Ease of Administration.* One of the biggest advantages of this form of agreement is that it is simple to draft and easy to administer to implement and administer since titling determines ownership of the property.

2. *No tracing of property is required.* Tracing who owns and is entitled to what property often is the most tedious, controversial and expensive process in split-ups. Contrast that clear line of demarcation with an agreement that is not title-based, which may define each of the partner's respective pre-relationship assets, including changes in form during the relationship, to be that partner's separate property. The problem often is that, upon a split-up, a defined property agreement almost always requires the often impossible task of tracing what was owned at the date of commencement of the relationship to property that each partner now owns. Once the partners have split-up, there often are disagreements over interpretations of the agreement, and the courts are clogged with disputes involving these types of agreements.

Disadvantages

1. *Can conflict with partner preferences.* Title-based agreements can conflict with a partner's planning desires in that the partner may want more or less property than what the mere title provides.

2. *Potentially unfair to a partner.* Title-based agreements are rough justice and can be perceived by a partner to be unfair because it arguably does not view the partners' relationship as a partnership and sets the partners up as adversaries during the relationship by encouraging a partner to maintain separate of property.

3. *Requires care during the relationship.* One of the biggest obstacles to title-based agreements is that they require care by the partners during the relationship to keep separate property separate as one of the biggest areas of attack of title-based agreements occurs where the partners commingle separate property and do not maintain the clear line of demarcation of ownership. Courts frequently disregard agreements that the partners themselves do not follow.

Defined Property Agreements

The second category of marriage contracts and property agreements is the defined property agreement, which we defined above by negative implication, i.e., any agreement that is not a title-based agreement, and it has a number of advantages and disadvantages.

Advantages

1. *Flexibility.* A defined property agreement can be made to be extremely flexible, which often appeals to the less-wealthy partner.

2. *Fairness.* A defined property agreement also can address the partners' shared sense of fairness in that the efforts of a partner that enhances the value of the other partner's property can be recognized and compensated upon split-up. Given that equitable division on divorce is the law in many states, the defined property agreement can give the court some room to maneuver in order to reach what the court determines is fair to each former partner.

Disadvantages

1. *Requires significant care in drafting.* Drafting the definitions of what constitutes separate property and jointly-owned property in a defined property agreement requires significant precision and care. A drafting attorney must have substantial knowledge in this area of the law to get the definitions correct as applied to the particular facts of the presenting partners.

2. *Requires property tracing.* Upon termination of the relationship, a defined property agreement can require difficult, expensive and oftentimes impossibly precise property tracing (e.g., to trace pre-relationship property forward to the property in existence at split-up).

67.4 REVIEW OF THE UNIFORM PREMARITAL AND MARITAL AGREEMENTS ACT AND THE UNIFORM PREMARITAL AGREEMENT ACT

The 1983 Uniform Premarital Agreement Act (UPMA) has been enacted in many states. However, the recently enacted 2012 Uniform Premarital and Marital Agreements Act (UPMAA) is expected to replace the UPMA. There are several significant differences between the two uniform acts. One principal difference between the two uniform acts is the scope of each act. The older UPMA only applies to premarital agreements, which are not effective until the partners marry.[5] The UPMAA applies to both premarital agreements and agreements that are executed after the couple is married, where, like the UPMA, a premarital agreement becomes effective upon marriage, whereas a marital agreement is effective upon the signatures of the partners.[6] Neither the UPMA nor the UPMAA applies to couples who either are not married and do not intend to marry.[7] The UPMAA arguably provides better protection than the UPMA for the vulnerable partner. This is because it protects not only against involuntary consent as well as acts under duress and against full disclosure of financial information, as does the UPMA, but it also guards against a partner not being represented by independent counsel unless the agreement contains a notice of waiver of rights.[8]

Pursuant to section 9(f) of the UPMAA, a court may refuse to enforce a term of a marriage contract if, in the context of the agreement taken as a whole, the term was unconscionable at the time of signing; or enforcement of the term would result in substantial hardship for a party because of a material change in circumstances arising after the agreement was signed. Under section 6 of the UPMA, it is irrelevant whether enforcing the agreement at divorce would be unfair or unconscionable.

Even if the agreement was unconscionable when it was signed, under the UPMA, the agreement is enforceable as long as (1) the complaining partner received adequate financial information regarding the other party before the agreement was signed, (2) the complaining partner had already obtained adequate financial information in another manner or (3) the complaining partner knowingly waived the right to receive financial information. Under the UPMA, a complaining partner has to prove that (a) the agreement was unconscionable when it was signed, (b) there was inadequate disclosure of financial information to the complaining partner, (c) the waiving partner did not otherwise possess adequate knowledge of the other partner's financial information, and (d) there was no knowing waiver by the complaining partner of the right to receive that financial information, which proved difficult in many situations. Many states substantially modified section 6 of the UPMA to give more protection to the most vulnerable partner, since section 6 of the UPMA had spawned significant criticism, which led to relaxation of the standard for enforcement in the UPMAA in favor of the more vulnerable partner.[9]

Both the UPMA and the UPMAA essentially invalidate agreements where the effect of the agreement is to force a partner to be eligible to go on governmental assistance by virtue of a waiver of support, and a court can force one partner to provide enough support to avoid that eligibility.[10] The Official Comment to section 9 of the UPMAA describes the following as the factors that many courts have employed to determine whether an agreement was voluntarily signed:

(1) coercion that may arise from the proximity of execution of the agreement to the wedding,

or from surprise in the presentation of the agreement;

(2) the presence or absence of independent counsel or of an opportunity to consult independent counsel;

(3) inequality of bargaining power—in some cases indicated by the relative age and sophistication of the parties;

(4) whether there was full disclosure of assets; and

(5) the parties' understanding of the rights being waived under the agreement or at least their awareness of the intent of the agreement.[11]

The Law of Property Agreements

Property agreements between unmarried partners generally were not enforced because such agreements were thought to contravene public policy that favored marriage. However, beginning with the *Marvin v. Marvin*[12] decision out of California in 1976, courts began to consider that the proliferation of these relationships, together with the easing of divorce requirements and waiting periods under so-called "no-fault divorce" laws and changing societal mores called for a reconsideration of the issue of enforcement of these types of agreements. Today, all states except for Illinois, Georgia and Louisiana will enforce property agreements between unmarried partners.

Since very few states expressly recognize property agreements by express statute, the courts generally employ principles of regular contract law to construe these agreements. While it is far preferable to have a written, express contract, courts have also recognized oral and implied property agreements. Courts have enforced property agreements by finding that a partnership or joint venture existed.[13] Courts also have enforced implied agreements via the quantum meruit theory, which compensates one for the benefits of use of that partner's labor or capital.[14] Courts also have imposed both constructive trusts,[15] which involves the following elements: (a) intent by a grantor to benefit a third person, (b) the transfer of property to another who stands in a confidential relationship to the grantor with the intent that the transferee will transfer the property to the third person and (c) the unjust enrichment of the transferee if the transferee is allowed to keep the property, and resulting trusts,[16] which arise by operation of law at the time of a conveyance when the purchase money for property is paid for by one party but the legal title is taken in the name of another.

67.5 PSYCHOLOGICAL ISSUES THAT ARISE IN THE NEGOTIATION OF MARRIAGE CONTRACTS AND PROPERTY AGREEMENTS

As noted at the outset, many people do not raise the issue of a marriage contract or property agreement for two reasons: an optimistic belief that the relationship will last and a feeling that raising such an issue would send a negative signal about the partner's feeling about the long-term viability of the relationship. Quite often, there is a significant disparity between the relative economic positions of the partners. There can be significant disagreement between lawyers who work in this area about the utility of marriage contracts and property agreements; some lawyers believe that these agreements can be beneficial to a relationship, while others assert that these agreements are "antithetical to romantic commitment."[17]

The partner who has the most wealth must understand that the other partner may feel jammed by the request to sign the agreement, and should simply and gently state the case for the agreement. However, the wealthier partner must be willing to negotiate, or the relationship will suffer, and the agreement might not stand. Likewise, the less wealthy partner must be able to see things through the lens of the wealthier partner and why that partner wants and needs the agreement. Additionally, counsel to both partners must understand that they are working in an area that has strong psychological overtones. They must stay out of conflict with each other during the negotiation of the agreement and be open to the idea that professional psychological assistance and facilitation may indeed be required to do a proper job.[18] If the lawyers treat the situation as adversarial and forget that they are negotiating for what hopefully will be a long-term romantic partnership, they could damage and even destroy the relationship.

Domicile, Governing Law Provisions, Validity and Enforceability

Sometimes a couple's state of domicile will not be formally agreed to prior to them getting together, or they will maintain two households in different states. It is critical that the marriage contract or property agreement confirm the couple's formal relationship domicile and the governing law under the agreement.

Marriage contracts and property agreements are one of the most challenged contracts when a couple split-up. In order to be safe, an estate planner should carefully and completely follow a protocol similar to the following:

1. The partners should fully and honestly disclose all assets and liabilities, together with amounts and values. With respect to values, good-faith estimates of the values of hard-to-value assets are all that is required,[19] i.e., the partner need not to go the expense of obtaining expensive and time-consuming appraisals for purposes of the agreement. This is one of the most common avenues of attack of these agreements, i.e., that a partner failed to substantially disclose all financial information to the other partner, unless the complaining partner knowingly waived their right to this disclosure.

2. The negotiation and/or presentation of the agreement should begin *well before* the date of a wedding or formally getting together. So-called "take-it-or-leave" or "shotgun" agreements that are presented on the eve of the marriage date usually are set aside. A good rule of thumb is that the first draft of the agreement be presented not later than sixty-ninety days prior to the wedding and the agreement signed at least thirty days prior to the wedding.

3. The terms of the agreement must *not* be unconscionable, because a court may be inclined to protect the more vulnerable partner if the couple splits-up. It is commonplace for one partner to have more property and/or income than the other partner. The agreement need not be even-handed, but it must not be construed as a totally one-way agreement. The more negotiation there is, the better. In fact, it probably is advisable for the wealthier partner to give cash consideration to the other partner both for signing the agreement and for some level of support if they are asking the less wealthy partner to waive support.

4. Both partners should have separate representation and/or be given sufficient time to consider waiving a right to counsel. It is not unusual for the wealthier partner to pay the legal fees for the less wealthy partner's counsel to advise on the agreement.

5. Both partners must be given enough time to both engage separate counsel and to meet with and consider the advice of that counsel.

6. Each partner's execution of the agreement must be voluntary.

With respect to agreements that are already in place, it is critical that the estate planner cautiously evaluate whether the agreement could be challenged while the partners are still together. Signs that an agreement might be unenforceable include:

1. Lack of full and honest disclosure by a partner;

2. Agreement executed close in time to marriage or formally getting together, particularly where threats of not going through with the marriage or staying together were made;

3. No right/time to have draft agreement reviewed by separate counsel of the partner's own choosing;

4. Disproportionate bargaining position between the partners;

5. Representation by the same counsel; and

6. The agreement somehow violates public policy, including unfairly limiting a partner's rights to things like child support, child custody/visitation or, in some jurisdictions, alimony. Any other unusual provision that is novel could give rise to a challenge on public policy grounds by itself, which usually is not worth that risk.

If the estate planner is concerned about the enforceability of the agreement, the estate planner should consider advising the parties to revisit and reinstitute the agreement.

67.6 ITEMS TYPICALLY INCLUDED IN A MARRIAGE CONTRACT OR PROPERTY AGREEMENT

Marriage contracts and property agreements can contain a wide range of provisions that are unique to the particular couple. As we noted at the outset of

MARRIAGE CONTRACTS AND PROPERTY AGREEMENTS — CHAPTER 67

this chapter, there is no "standard" agreement of this type. However, partners in most marriage contracts and property agreements waive various rights that they either have or could have in the relationship. Typically, marriage contracts waive the following rights and points:

1. The right to a probate family allowance (in some states, a probate court can award an allowance to a surviving spouse pending settlement of the estate);

2. All community property, quasicommunity property, and quasimarital property rights;

3. The rights or claims of dower, curtesy or any statutory substitute;

4. The right to inherit property from the other by intestate succession;

5. The right to receive property that would pass from the decedent party by testamentary disposition in a will executed before the agreement;

6. The right to take the statutory share of an omitted spouse;

7. Any right created under federal law, including, without limitation, the Retirement Equity Act of 1984;

8. Any right, title, claim or interest in or to the property, income, or estate of the other by reason of the parties' non-marital relationship;

9. All statutory rights to serve as fiduciary, personal representative, etc.;

10. Any right to alimony or other maintenance; and

11. A right to contest the other partner's estate plan.

Agreements of this type also provide the following:

a. Grant of right to occupy property that one partner owns for a certain period of time or for the life of the other partner;

b. Agreement to maintain life insurance and to pay premiums on life insurance or annuities;

c. Agreement to maintain certain will or trust provisions, including income rights, fiduciary positions, etc.;

d. A right of first refusal to acquire the deceased partner's rights in certain property;

e. Grant of certain property to the surviving partner;

f. Family business ownership and participation restrictions;

g. What is separate versus community or jointly-owned property;

h. Compensation for using partner's gift tax annual exclusions and/or the gift tax applicable exclusion amount if the other partner's beneficiaries will benefit from that usage;

i. Agreement to waive spousal rights in retirement plans and IRAs;

j. Provisions about sharing of household expenses;

k. Careful description/delineation of tangible personal property owned by each partner;

l. Agreement to consent to split gifts for federal gift tax purposes and to sign all necessary elections and returns to reflect the same;

m. It is common for marriage contracts and property agreements to deal extensively with where the couple will reside, and what rights each partner has in the residence(s), including upon split up:

   1. Selection or identification of residence(s);

   2. Who will purchase or pay the mortgage and in what amounts;

   3. The manner of title holding, e.g., joint tenants, etc.;

   4. Furniture and fixtures ownership and rights;

   5. If the residence is owned by one partner, who will own or pay for the residence

(mortgage, upkeep and capital improvements, etc.); and

6. If title is to be transferred to the couple, the manner of ownership, the compensation to be paid, if any, to the contributing partner and when the transfer is to take place.

Property agreements among unmarried partners often contain many similar provisions to those contained in marriage contracts. The partners generally usually desire to establish their respective rights and responsibilities regarding each other's current and future income and property, either separate or together, during the period of cohabitation. The partners also normally make a full and complete disclosure of assets and liabilities. Unmarried partners often waive the following rights:

1. To share in each other's estates upon their death;

2. To "palimony" or other forms of support or maintenance, whether temporary or permanent;

3. To share in the increase in value during the relationship in the separate property of either partner;

4. To share in the pension, profit sharing, or other retirement accounts of the other partner;

5. To the division of the separate property of the partners, whether currently held or hereafter acquired;

6. To any other claims based on the relationship;

7. To any rights to serve as the partner's agent under a power of attorney for property or health care;

8. To claim the existence of a common-law marriage; and

9. Sharing of household expenses and responsibilities of the partners.

Perils of Commingling

Commingling is a huge problem when things go south in the relationship, which is why commingling really is the cardinal sin of financial relationships. One cannot reasonably expect a court to untangle a self-created ambiguous mess. Most courts will find that commingling is the death knell to an argument that the property is a partner's separate property because it is easier to rule that the property was transformed by the commingling into jointly-owned property. Just about every professional preaches incessantly about the perils of commingling. However, this advice usually is ignored or forgotten—at least until the couple splits; at that point, a partner remembers this advice and often tries to undo what has been done, usually to little or no success. Community property states have rebuttable presumptions that all property that is acquired during a marriage, with few exceptions, is community property, so in those states, one partner who is asserting that property that was acquired during the marriage was somehow separate property often finds that presumption presents an obstacle to the argument.

Typically, we see commingling asserted as an argument in litigation in one of the following two contexts:

1. **The couple splits during lifetime:** If the couple splits up during lifetime, the claim of commingling usually is brought by the partner who would benefit the most from a finding of commingling. However, in tracing cases, the results are all over the board and are as much a function of the court's patience for the tedious bickering over money as anything else. It is too easy for the court to hold that the commingled separate property lost its status as separate property through the partner's own actions or inactions. Suffice it to say that where the court has sufficient time and patience, the party who is best able to present hard evidence to trace the property usually prevails.

2. **Where the couple splits up because of death:** If the partner who would benefit from the commingling dies first, that partner's separate heirs or legatees frequently argue that the surviving partner, who often is the deceased partner's executor, either misclassified property in which the deceased partner had an interest as that partner's separate property or that commingling converted some of that surviving partner's property into property in which the deceased partner had an interest. This issue highlights yet another potential conflict for the lawyer who both prepares the estate plan but

who also is retained to administer the deceased partner's estate or trust.

Portability and Marriage Contracts

Commentators have posited that a spouse's potential deceased spouse unused exclusion amount (DSUEA) is a valuable asset that should be covered by the marriage contract.[20] The marriage contract could expressly *require* a spouse's executor to make the portability election. In some cases, a deceased spouse's estate would not otherwise be required to file a federal estate tax return. For instance, no federal estate tax return would be required if the estate is under the then-existing applicable exclusion amount. We are suggesting that the marriage contract would require that the estate tax return be filed and that the surviving spouse, who would benefit from the DSUEA, would be responsible for the costs of preparing and filing of the federal estate tax return. Note this possible conflict of interest: If the surviving spouse, who would benefit from the portability election, also is named as executor, then that spouse has a conflict. But this problem could be solved by providing in the marriage contract for the appointment of a special executor to make the portability election in such situations.

In the context of a blended family, if a surviving spouse makes the portability election by electing to have the entire QTIP trust covered — even though the full QTIP election is unnecessary to zero out the estate tax liability — this would preserve the DSUEA of the deceased spouse for the surviving spouse. Unfortunately, this election actually can cost the children of the first spouse to die more money than if the QTIP election is not made. It is becoming common for surviving spouses to appoint a special executor to avoid the conflict of interest in making the QTIP election and to make a compensating adjustment to make the children of the first spouse to die whole.

A lot of marriage contracts require each partner's executor (if other than the surviving spouse) to provide the surviving spouse with a copy of the federal estate tax return that shows how much DSUEA was ported to the surviving spouse. It may also be appropriate to provide a remedy in the marriage contract to the surviving spouse in case the deceased spouse's executor either fails or refuses to make a portability election.

In light of portability, it may be advisable for the partners to disclose in a marriage contract any lifetime taxable gifts that either partner may have made. The marriage contract should also allow the other partner's lawyer the opportunity to review their gift tax returns, to make sure that any taxable gifts were properly reported and to ascertain the audit risks, if any, of those gift tax returns.

This disclosure will be of particular importance if one of the partners is a surviving spouse. A surviving spouse who remarries may only use the DSUEA of his or her *most recently* deceased spouse. Therefore, a surviving spouse's *re*marriage comes at the risk of losing the DSUEA of his or her deceased first spouse, if the second spouse likewise predeceases him or her. For this reason, it will be of extreme importance to a wealthy widow or widower contemplating marriage to determine how much of the other party's applicable exclusion amount has already been exhausted by lifetime taxable gifts. It is not unusual to see partners to make large taxable gifts shortly before remarrying, usually to children who are either concerned about the effect of the pending nuptials on their inheritance rights or just unhappy about the remarriage.

In order to ensure that there will be DSUEA remaining for a surviving spouse, the marriage contract also may require that any future use of his or her applicable exclusion amount by a spouse requires the consent of the other spouse, and that the executors of the first spouse to die must set aside a prescribed minimum amount of DSUEA for the surviving spouse. However, such a provision may only effectively apply to the less wealthy spouse.

Alternatives to Marriage Contracts or Property Agreements

There are some available options to having a marriage contract or property agreement. The three such options are: joint and mutual wills, contracts to make a will and the use of entities, leases and co-tenancy agreements.

Joint and Mutual wills: A joint and mutual will is a single document that serves as the will of two people (usually spouses), under which the surviving joint testator receives the property of the first joint testator to die, and the combined assets of the joint testators pass in a mutually agreed manner on the death of the surviving joint testator. In a joint and mutual will, two (usually married) people execute one document. That will is binding on both parties, becomes effective at the first death of the couple, and cannot be changed during the surviving partner's life. The contractual effectiveness of such a will assumes both parties executed an agreement (with consideration) to provide for such irrevocability at the first death.[21] We find, unfortunately, that these mutual wills are, as two commentators put it, "litigation breeders,"[22] especially in blended family couples, where, after the death of a partner, there may indeed be a strong reason as well as pressure by potential heirs to alter the dispositive provisions. There also may well be a lot of pressure by the partner who expects to survive to receive rights to all of the property of the other partner. We far prefer providing for these matters in a marriage contract or property agreement. Wills can be "reciprocal" without being joint, and wills can be joint without restricting change to the dispositive scheme by the surviving joint testator after the first joint testator's death. If the partners desire to make a joint will that cannot be changed after the death of the first joint testator to die, that joint will should be coupled with a contract to make a will, which we discuss in the next section.

Contract to make a will: Contracts to make a will can take one of three basic forms: a contract to make a particular gift, a contract not to revoke a will or a provision therein and a contract to make no will (i.e., to die intestate). The effectiveness of these contracts differ quite a bit depending upon applicable state law. Like all other contracts, these agreements require acceptance and consideration, and they usually must be in writing. In blended family situations, it is rare to see such a contract separate and apart from a marriage contract or property agreement. They are most often used where a couple does not have a marriage contract or property agreement in place.

Use of entities, leases and co-tenancy agreements: Sometimes, the partners cannot agree to terms on a marriage contract or property agreement or do not want to even bring up such an agreement, but they can readily agree to an alternative means of co-owning and having the right to enjoy property. The first way to do this is to use a formal separate entity such as an LLC or partnership, into which the couple's property is contributed in exchange for entity interests. The partners' rights are governed by the entity governance documents and applicable state law. These terms often grant each partner a right of first refusal over the transfer of the interest of the other partner. Sometimes, the partners enter into a lease whereby the partner who owns the property enters into a formal lease of property such as a residence with the other partner that provides for formal rent terms. Finally, if the partners co-own property, they can enter into cotenancy agreements under which each partner grants the other partner a right of first refusal prior to any attempted sale by that partner. In such cases, the partners often waive the right of partition of the property prior to the formal termination of the relationship.

67.7 HOW IT IS DONE

The following is a checklist of items to consider including in a marriage contract or property agreement:

Recitals

State marital plans, including the date of the wedding (which should ideally be at least sixty days away, but in no event should the agreement be signed less than thirty days away from the wedding absent unusual extenuating circumstances) if any, and if the partners do not plan to be married, affirmatively state that:

1. Give general information concerning the current health and financial independence of each partner.

2. State that neither partner acquired any rights in the property of the other partner during the pendency of their premarital relationship, and both partners waive and release each other with respect to any such rights.

3. If the partners have lived together as an unmarried couple, state the length of time of that relationship and that each partner has been advised by independent counsel of the rights that he or she may have acquired by virtue of living together.

4. State that the partners desire to make a fair and reasonable disclosure of financial information to each other.

5. State the partners' intentions and purposes for the agreement, e.g., to negate community property regime, waive all spousal rights, provide for the end result of termination of the relationship whether by death or divorce, etc.

6. Provide whatever consideration, if any, in addition to mutual agreements and covenants, etc.

Body of Agreement

Incorporate the recitals into the body of the agreement:

1. Provide for the effective date, and, if a premarital agreement, state what happens if the couple does not marry.

2. Provide for the relationship domicile and the governing law under the agreement.

3. Identify independent counsel for each partner, and, if a partner waived his or her right to independent counsel, affirmatively state that fact and that the waiving partner was advised to obtain counsel and is not relying upon the advice of the other partner's counsel, whom the waiving partner understands cannot and does represent him or her and include a notice that is similar, if not identical, to that set forth in section 9(c) of the Uniform Premarital and Marital Agreements Act.

4. State that each partner has had sufficient time to read and carefully consider the entire agreement and to obtain independent counsel, discuss it with independent counsel and to consider that counsel's advice.

5. Affirmatively state that the partners enter into the agreement voluntarily, free from duress, fraud, undue influence, coercion or misrepresentation of any kind and that the agreement was fairly negotiated and represents a fair arrangement.

6. Provide for financial disclosure that both partners admit is substantially complete and accurate but is not precise, with cross-existing confidentiality requirement provisions, which should include a detailed financial statement (but does not have to be audited); copies of income tax returns for at least the past three years; a current monthly statement for every bank account, money market account, certificate of deposit, stock, bond or investment account; identification of all real estate owned, the fashion in which title is held (i.e., joint tenancy, trust, etc.), along with the current mortgage balance(s), home equity loans or lines of credit, appraised value, and appraisals, if any; copies of car titles, loan balances, and estimates of values; most recent statements from any retirement account, whether qualified (ERISA) or not, along with loan balances; and most recent jewelry and personal property appraisals, and each partner should expressly acknowledge the sufficiency of the other partner's disclosure and waive the requirement of any additional disclosure, and this documentation should be attached to the agreement.

7. Each partner should acknowledge that he or she has not contracted with the other partner for any other rights that arise out of the non-marital relationship.

The agreement should clearly provide what property is to remain separate and what property will be co-owned or held as community property, and for the management of separate and jointly-owned/community property; and how inherited property is to be treated:

1. The effect, if any, of the personal or financial efforts of a partner or of the partnership on the property of the other partner.

2. That the agreement does not create any partnership, joint venture, employment arrangement or any other arrangement or claim, including, without limitation, leasehold, license, quantum meruit or quasi community/marital property rights.

3. Rights in employee benefit plans and IRAs, including agreements to waive all rights and to sign all documents after the wedding to waive the rights.

4. The property classification of borrowed funds and property that is acquired with borrowed funds.

5. Waiver of rights in respective estates: The partners should agree that each partner waives and relinquishes, to the fullest extent lawfully possible, all right, title, claim, lien or interest, whether actual, inchoate, vested or contingent, in law and equity, under the laws of any state or under federal law, in the other's separate property, income and estate by reason of the proposed marriage, including, without limitation, the following:

a. Property Rights: All community property, quasicommunity property, and quasimarital property rights;

b. Probate Allowance: The right to a probate family allowance;

c. Probate Homestead: The right to a probate homestead;

d. Dower, Curtesy, Etc.: The rights or claims of dower, curtesy, or any statutory substitute now or hereafter provided under the laws of any state in which the partners may die domiciled or in which they may own real property;

e. Intestacy: The right to inherit property from the other by intestate succession;

f. Testamentary Disposition: The right to receive property that would pass from the decedent partner by testamentary disposition in a will executed before the agreement;

g. Election Against a Will: The right of election to take against the will of the other;

h. Omitted Spouse: The right to take the statutory share of an omitted spouse, notwithstanding the other partner's failure to amend any of his/her existing planning instruments after the partners' marriage to acknowledge the partners' marital status;

i. Administrator: The right to be appointed as administrator of the deceased partner's estate, or as executor of the deceased partner's will, unless appointed pursuant to a will executed after the date of the agreement;

j. Set Aside: The right to have exempt property set aside;

k. No REA Rights: Any right created under federal law, including, without limitation, the Retirement Equity Act of 1984;

l. No Non-marital Rights: Any right, title, claim or interest in or to the property, income, or estate of the other by reason of the parties' non-marital relationship;

m. No Equitable Distribution: Any right to equitable distribution upon termination of the marriage;

n. No Alimony or Separate Maintenance: Any right to alimony or separate maintenance upon termination of the marriage; and

o. No Right to Contest: Any right to contest any of the other party's estate planning documents, including, without limitation, the other party's will or any trust that the other party settles.

6. An affirmative statement of complete testamentary freedom, together with a statement that nothing prevents either partner from leaving a bequest or other provision to the other partner or appointing the other partner to a fiduciary position, but that neither partner has made any such promise to the other partner

7. Estate planning requirements, if any, including powers of attorney for health care and property, living wills and HIPAA authorizations

8. A QTIP information rights provision, if appropriate

9. How the couple's living expenses will be covered and who will be responsible for them

10. The relationship domicile of the partners and the governing law of the agreement

11. Details concerning life insurance policy maintenance and payment requirements, including beneficiary designation requirements, if any

12. Income tax filing-separate returns or joint returns; liability for income taxes; together with a statement that any decision to file a joint income tax return will not constitute any transmutation of any property or the creation of a community/jointly-owned property regime

13. Potential support and/or alimony/palimony in the event of split-up, together with waivers of such rights, if desired

14. Provisions for gift-splitting, if appropriate, and the limits on what the partners will agree to with respect to gift-splitting, i.e., limited to annual exclusion gifts or whether the applicable exclusion amount of the other partner can be used and compensation for that usage

15. Portability

16. Voluntary good faith arm's length negotiations clause

17. Release of premarital liabilities and claims

18. Modifications must be in writing and must be mutually agreed to

19. Dispute resolution provision, i.e., mediation, arbitration, etc., and if alternate dispute resolution is elected, the rules and guidelines for such and how the referee (mediator or arbitrator) will be selected

20. Future attorney's fees in enforcement of the agreement clause

21. Severability clause

22. Certifications by counsel to each partner

67.8 FREQUENTLY ASKED QUESTIONS

Question – Do marriage contracts and property agreements require consideration in order to be effective and enforceable?

Answer – No.[23] However, we believe that the payment of consideration by the wealthier partner in exchange for surrender of valuable future support rights can improve the prospects for future enforcement of the agreement.

Question – What types of things should *not* be included in a marriage contract or property agreement?

Answer – There should be absolutely no reference to personal items such as sex requirements or expectations. Additionally, almost every state prohibits the partners from waiving child support, custody or visitation in an agreement.[24]

Question – Is it ethical for the wealthier partner to pay the fees of counsel who is representing the less wealthy partner to negotiate and draft the marriage contract or property agreement, and what are the ramifications of such an arrangement?

Answer – Yes, provided that the less wealthy partner consents to the payment and gets to select and evaluate the independent advice of their counsel. If these guidelines are followed, the arrangement will be ethical for both lawyers. Payment by the wealthier partner of the less wealthy partner's legal fees should not give rise to any reason to question the enforceability of the agreement.

Question – How can the issue of gift-splitting be best addressed in a marriage contract?

Answer – There are several ways to address gift-splitting in a marriage contract. First, the agreement could be silent as to gift-splitting, which would give each partner an annual right to elect whether or not to split-gifts. Second, the partners could agree that no gifts would be split, which would foreclose gift-splitting as an option unless the less wealthy partner changed his/her mind after the agreement was in effect. Third, the agreement could require gift-splitting of all sizes of gifts, which would allow the wealthier partner to use the less wealthy partner's applicable exclusion amount. Fourth, the agreement could mandate gift-splitting, but the gifts would be limited to annual exclusion gifts, which would limit the wealthier partner's flexibility to make large gifts since the gift-splitting election requires that all gifts be split. Finally, the agreement could require gift-splitting, but the less wealthy partner could be compensated in a number of ways for use of their applicable exclusion amount.

Question – How should income tax filing and liability be accounted for in a marriage contract?

Answer – Typically, the issue is whether the agreement should require joint income tax return filing. If both partners have high income, joint tax return filing may or may not be advantageous in a particular year. So it probably is best to maintain flexibility by only requiring joint income tax filing if the total tax is reduced when compared to each spouse filing as married filing separately or where a spouse requests to file jointly. Where the partners agree to file joint income tax returns, the marriage contract should provide an allocation of the total income tax liability between the spouses. There are a variety of ways to apportion the income tax liability between the spouses, even though filing a joint income tax return makes both spouses jointly and severally liable for all of the income tax. Firstly, the agreement could provide that each spouse would pay a fraction of the joint income tax liability the numerator of which is his or her taxable income, computed as if he or she were filing as married filing separately, and the denominator of which is the taxable income as computed on the joint return. The problem with this approach is that it is possible that the separate taxable incomes of the spouses will not add up to what the joint return taxable income is because of the different operation of ceilings and floors on deductions on their separate and joint incomes and deductions. Secondly, each spouse could pay a fraction of the joint income tax liability the numerator of which is equal to the income tax that a spouse would pay if that spouse filed as a single taxpayer, and the denominator of which is the total amount of income tax that both spouses would pay if they each filed on this basis. Finally, each spouse could pay a fraction of the joint income tax liability the numerator of which is equal to the amount of income tax that he or she would pay if they were not filing a joint income tax return, i.e., as married filing separately, and the denominator of which would be the combined income tax liability that the spouses would pay if each filed as married filing separately. Unlike the first approach, either of the last two approaches should result in apportionment fractions for the spouses that add up to one.

Question – Are there any execution requirements for validity of a marriage contract or property agreement?

Answer – This is a question of applicable state law. If a marriage contract or property agreement contains testamentary provisions or real estate transactions, applicable state law may require that it be executed in conformity with the more stringent requirements for a will (for example, execution in the presence of two witnesses) or for a real estate deed, and in some states, there is a requirement that the marital or property agreement be notarized.

Question – How is the area of waiving rights in qualified retirement plans best handled?

Answer – This issue always is a metaphysical timing problem in that the marriage contract is signed *before* the partners get married, while the waiver cannot be made until *after* the partners are married. At the outset, it is critical that - in the marriage contract -the non-plan participant partner waive *all* rights to the retirement plan benefits and to execute *all* immediate and future waivers *after* the wedding ceremony. It is important to begin with the rights of a surviving non-participant spouse in a qualified retirement plan. If the plan participant dies *prior* to the annuity starting date, then the surviving non-participant spouse must be provided with a qualified preretirement survivor annuity (QPSA). If the participant dies *after* the annuity starting date, then payments to the surviving non-participant spouse must be exclusively in the form of a qualified joint and survivor annuity (QJSA). The QPSA is required to be funded with only one half of the participant's account balance, leaving the remaining half free to be disposed of as the participant may wish, without the need for spousal consent. Once it has begun, a QJSA must continue for the spouse to whom the participant was married on the annuity starting date, even if the spouses subsequently divorce (except as otherwise provided in a QDRO).

The requirements for valid spousal consent are as follows: Only a *spouse* can execute a valid waiver. The implication is that a waiver in a marriage contract that is signed *prior* to the wedding is not valid. The consent to waiver of a QPSA or QJSA must (a) specify the specific non-spouse beneficiary to receive the benefit or, alternatively, expressly agree that the participant may name or change beneficiaries without further spousal consent; (b) acknowledge the effect of the election; and (c) be witnessed by a plan representative or notary public. With respect to timing requirements, the QPSA may be waived only after the participant attains the age of thirty-five. If an earlier waiver is made, it will become ineffective at age thirty-five and have to be redone. The QJSA may be waived only within ninety days of the annuity starting date. Thus, if the non-participant spouse has previously consented to waiver of the QPSA in the course of the estate planning process, once the participant spouse retires and wishes to rollover the plan account balance into an IRA or begin to take regular distributions from the plan (other than a QJSA), another waiver and consent will be necessary.

As a practical matter, the problem only arises in the context of payment of the death benefit from a qualified retirement plan where the participant dies before payments begin, and the spouse survives. If both spouses are alive when payments from the plan begin, and, in violation of their marriage contract, a spouse refuses to waive a QJSA, then the matter can be resolved by the participant spouse divorcing the non-participant spouse. If the parties divorce, the REA waiver requirements need not be met because what is an issue in a divorce is neither a QJSA nor a QPSA, but an ability of the non-participant spouse to obtain a QDRO. Thus, a waiver in a marriage contract of rights in a qualified plan on divorce should be honored. Given that there always is a risk that the non-participant spouse will breach the marriage contract and refuse to execute the waivers after the wedding, the issue then becomes addressing that issue with a proper solution.

One thing that the participant spouse must strongly consider doing is being willing to immediately institute divorce or even annulment proceedings based upon an error and failure of consideration in the marriage contract. Some lawyers have attempted to draft liquidated damages provisions where the non-participant spouse breaches the marriage contract by refusing to execute the waiver, but there is a lingering question about the effectiveness of any attempt to enforce the liquidated damages provision in light of ERISA preemption in this area. The only safe route is to immediately have the newly wedded non-participant spouse execute a valid waiver, immediately following the wedding ceremony if need be. If there is any doubt by the participant spouse-to-be that his or her intended may not execute the valid waiver, another option would be to separate from service, if need be, and roll the plan benefits over into an IRA, to which the REA rights are inapplicable.

CHAPTER ENDNOTES

1. Samuel Johnson, quoted in James Boswell, The Life of Samuel Johnson, LL.D. (1791), Vol. II, p. 182.
2. Rose M. Kreider, "Increase in Opposite-Sex Cohabiting Couples from 2009 to 2010 in the Annual Social and Economic Supplement (ASEC) to the Current Population Survey," Housing and Household Economic Statistics Working Paper (Sept. 15, 2010), p. 1, accessed on March 23, 2013 at http://www.census.gov/population/www/socdemo/Inc-Opp-sex-2009-to-2010.pdf.
3. Galena K. Roahes, et al., "The Pre-Engagement Cohabitation Effect: A Replication and Extension of PreviousFindings," 23 Journal of Family Psychology 1, 107-11 (2009).
4. Heather Mahar, "Why Are There So Few Prenuptial Agreements?" Harvard Law School John M. Olin Center for Law, Economics and Business, Faculty Discussion Paper No. 436 (Sept. 2003).
5. Section 4, Uniform Premarital Agreement Act.
6. Section 7, Uniform Premarital and Marital Agreements Act.
7. Sections 2(2) and (5) and the Official Comment to Section 2, Uniform Premarital and Marital Agreements Act; Section 1(1), Uniform Premarital Agreement Act and Official Comment to Section 1.
8. Compare Section 6, Uniform Premarital Agreement Act, with Section 9, Uniform Premarital and Marital Agreements Act.
9. See J. Thomas Oldham, "With All My Worldly Goods I Thee Endow, or Maybe Not: A Reevaluation of the Uniform Premarital Agreement Act After Three Decades," 19 Duke J. Gender L. & Pol. 8, 84–88 (2011).
10. Section 9(e), Uniform Premarital and Marital Agreements Act; Section 6(b), Uniform Premarital Agreement Act.
11. See, e.g., *Mamot v. Mamot*, 813 N.W. 2d 440 (Neb. 2012).
12. 557 P. 2d 106 (Cal. 1976).
13. See, e.g., *Boland v. Catalano*, 521 A. 2d 142 (Conn. 1987); and *Estate of Thornton*, 499 P. 2d 140 (Wash. 1972).
14. See, e.g. *Burns v. Koellmer*, 527 A. 2d 1210 (Conn. 1987).
15. See, e.g., *Gulack v. Gulack*, 620 A. 2d 181 (Conn. 1993).
16. See, e.g., *Collins v. Davis*, 315 S.E. 2d 759 (N.C. App.), aff'd, 321 S.E. 2d 892 (N.C. 1984).
17. See, e.g., Carlin Flora, "Let's Make a Deal," Psychology Today (Nov. 1, 2004); accessed on March 22, 2013 at http://www.psychologytoday.com/articles/200411/lets-make-deal
18. See, e.g., David W. Belin, Leaving Money Wisely (Scribners 1990), p. 53 and the article noted in footnote 17.
19. Section 9(d)(1), Uniform Premarital and Marital Agreements Act; Section 6(a)(2)(i), Uniform Premarital Agreements Act.
20. See, e.g., George D. Karibjanian and Lester B. Law, "Portability and Prenuptials: A Plethora of Preventative, Progressive and Precautionary Provisions," 2012 Bloomberg BNA Estates Gifts & Trusts Journal 443 (2012).
21. See, e.g., Estate of Helen J. Collins, 619 S.E. 2d 456 (N.C. 1963); and *Higgins v. Stafford*, 866 P. 2d 31 (Wash. 1994). See also Section 2-514, Uniform Probate Code.
22. See, e.g., Frank S. Berall, "Oral Trusts and Wills: Are They Valid?" (2006), accessed on July 6, 2023 at http://www.naepc.org/journal/issue03f.pdf; and Roger W. Andersen, Understanding Trusts and Estates (LexisNexis 2009), section 10.
23. Section 2, Uniform Premarital Agreement Act; and Section 6, Uniform Premarital and Marital Agreements Act.
24. Section 3(b), Uniform Premarital Agreement Act; and Section 10, Uniform Premarital and Marital Agreements Act.

REPRESENTING BLENDED FAMILIES FOR ESTATE PLANNING

CHAPTER 68

68.1 INTRODUCTION

The modern family looks quite different today from the so-called "traditional" family of sit-com television lore, when shows like *The Adventures of Ozzie & Harriet* and *Leave it to Beaver* reinforced perhaps a false notion of what a so-called "regular family" looked like and how they acted and interacted. Changes in laws, including wide spread enactment of so-called "no fault" divorces as well as reductions in the waiting periods for divorces, combined with changes in social mores that reduced the stigma of unmarried couples co-habiting as well as for remarrying after being divorced, have changed the modern family, probably forever (assuming the regular family was ever like that.[1])

This chapter will point out the differences in the rules for legally related versus legally unrelated partners. In particular, see Chapter 65.

68.2 WHAT IS THE DEFINITION OF THE TERM "BLENDED FAMILY"?[2]

A blended family is one in which two people are partners and at least one of the partners has one or more children who are not the children (by birth or adoption) of the other partner. Also known as "stepfamilies," the preferred term is "blended families," even though some criticize the use of that term as problematic and not very descriptive of many families in this category. In fact, the National Stepfamily Resource Center went so far as to describe the term "blended family" as a "catchy media phrase that does not describe either a family relationship or what happens when at least one partner to a marriage brings children from a prior relationship (marriage ended by death or divorce or an unwed parent)."[3]

Realizing that a significant percentage of so-called "blended families" hardly fits within the definition of the word "blended." Therefore, perhaps the choice of terms is aspirational for these families or wishful thinking. This chapter will also discuss planning around blended family difficulties either during lifetime or after death, when relations may not be so cordial, which is why advance awareness of the issues is so mission critical to enable the clients to plan around them.

Explanation

Note that throughout this chapter, it will often be referring to the couple as "partners" rather than "spouses." Likewise, it will often refer to a relationship as a "union" rather than a "marriage." The simple fact is that today, many people are opting, for a variety of reasons, to not become legally married; yet they are living together as a couple. In fact, according to a 2010 study by the Pew Research Center,[4] married households barely comprise a majority (52 percent) of households in the United States today, down from 72 percent in 1960. In fact, that same study indicated that 44 percent of all adults (and over half of people ages thirty-forty-nine) have cohabited at some point in their lives. Some people cannot legally marry. Many who can choose to marry decide, for whatever reason, not to do so. Yet, they live together as a couple and may even have children from that relationship or other relationships.

It is of the utmost importance that the client define the term "family" in their particular situation, whether it is blood/adoption-based or affinity-based. In *Family: The Compact Among Nations*, Jay Hughes defines "family" to include people "who by either genetic lineage *or* bonds of affinity consider themselves related to each other" [emphasis added].[5] In blended families, it has been experienced that, while not a majority, but nevertheless a significant and increasing number of clients include stepchildren and even step-grandchildren within their "family," considering them for both legacies and fiduciary positions. However, the obverse also is true: In many (not so) blended families, the idea of a stepchild somehow inheriting from them or even having anything to do at all with their estates is repugnant to some clients. Therefore, it is important to have that specific conversation with them and not just assume that step relatives should have no role in their estate plans.

68.3 BLENDED FAMILY STATISTICS

More and more, blended families are becoming the norm. In fact, as of 2010, according to United States census data, there are now more blended families than **any** other type of family. Here are some other eye-opening statistics about blended families:

- 50 percent of the children in the U.S. are in one or more blended families;

- 1,300 new blended families are formed **every** day;

- At least **one-third** of the children living in the U.S. are expected to live in a blended family before the age of eighteen;

- 38 percent of marriages in the United States are remarriages for one or both partners;

- 42 percent report having at least one step relative; and

- 25 percent report having been married two or more times by age fifty.

As significantly large as these statistics are, the National Stepfamily Resource Center asserts that the statistics *understate* the number of step or blended families.[6]

68.4 EXAMPLES OF BLENDED FAMILIES

Blended families come in all shapes, sizes and configurations. Perhaps the best known "blended family" is the fictitious "Brady Bunch" of television fame. However, blended families can and do look quite different from the Brady Bunch. Consider the following six different examples, all of which fall within our definition of a blended family:

1. **Brady Bunch:** Mike, age forty, a widower who has three sons, marries Carol, age thirty-eight, a widow who has three daughters. They have no joint children. The children are all minors who live together. Mike owns his own business, and Carol has a substantial separate estate that she inherited from her late first husband.

2. **May/December:** Franklin, age seventy, a wealthy widower who has three grown children in their forties, marries Laurie, age twenty-six, an impecunious dance instructor who has a daughter, age seven, whom she is raising alone. They would like to have a child of their own. Franklin has done a substantial amount of lifetime estate planning and has already passed significant wealth on to his children and grandchildren.

3. **Empty Nesters:** Michael, age seventy-two, is a widower with three grown children, a pension and benefactor of his late wife's life insurance, marries Sophia, age seventy-two, who is long divorced with three grown children and who has no financial experience, has no savings or retirement other than social security, and her only asset is her home. The couple plans to live in Sophia's home, but Michael has a lot more wealth, on which Sophia has become somewhat dependent.

4. **Eat, Drink and Remarry:** John, age sixty-three, marries Judith, age thirty-five, as his fourth wife. John has a son, age thirty-seven. John has some expensive alimony obligations to his first wife. Judith, who has been divorced twice, has two sons, ages eleven and eight, each with a different father, with whom she splits custody. Judith has substantially more wealth than John, while John has far greater income earning potential as a professional. John and Judith have a separate property prenuptial agreement.

5. **Non-Traditional Blended Family:** Marie, age forty-six, and Angela, age thirty-seven, marry. Marie adopted a child, who is now age eighteen, as a single parent. Angela, who has been divorced once, has a child, age ten, whom she is

raising alone with only meager, sporadic child support. Marie stands to inherit money from her parents, but that may be in doubt due to her recent lifestyle choices. Angela has the greater income, and she owns the home that they live in, although both are contributing to payment of the mortgage.

6. **Yours, Mine and Ours:** Bob, age forty-three and divorced once, married Bridgett, age forty-one and divorced once. Each has a child under eighteen from a prior marriage, over whom each has joint custody. Bob and Bridgett also have two children together, ages seven and three. Bridgett is staying at home to raise the young children, while Bob is working to support the family. Bob provides child support to his son's mother, and Bridgett receives child support to a lesser degree for her daughter from her first husband.

These are all examples of what blended families can look like. These examples are not intended to be exhaustive either. There are many other examples of blended families, each of which have valid, vital and unique concerns when it comes to how to make sure the needs of loved ones are addressed in life and after death. Even a quick consideration of each example demonstrates the rich diversity of blended families. In some of the examples, the couples have minor children living with them, others do not. One couple has joint minor children, while also housing part-time their respective separate children. One couple wants to have a child together.

In a few of the examples, the couple has children of a prior union living part-time in their home, while other example couples do not have to deal with part-time resident children. In two of the examples, the new partner is younger than the children of the parent partner. Estate planners who have a narrow focus of what defines a "family" could miss the various ways that individuals in blended families consider all the people who presently are in their lives as part of their "family," and these concerns need to be taken into account in the estate planning process.

Each of these examples presents very different estate planning issues. In some of the examples, one partner makes substantially more income than the other partner. In other examples, one partner has substantially more wealth than the other partner. If the wealthier partner dies first, should the entire estate be held for the benefit of the surviving partner? In some situations, the answer is "perhaps," while in others, the answer may be "no."

This situation becomes even more complicated when taking into consideration the disparate ages of adult children from a prior union and minor children from the current union, all of whom are concerned about how the estate will pan out for them—whether they say so or not. In other examples, one partner has substantially greater earning capacity than the other. Should that earning capacity be cut off because of death and how will the other partner be sustained financially?

In one of the examples, one of the partners has very little financial experience. Who should manage her assets in that example if the financially inexperienced partner is the surviving partner? That partner certainly will be interested in who will do that and will likely want control of their own financial destiny if they survive. One of the couples has a marriage contract, which is becoming far more common, particularly in blended family couples. Is that marriage contract consistent with the couple's other estate planning documents? In one of the examples, one partner has a significant alimony obligation to a former spouse. How will that be affected should that partner die first? How will that partner fare if the other partner dies first?

Simply put, there is no "one size fits all" estate plan for the blended family. Every estate plan for a blended family is different, and the concerns and goals of the families are undoubtedly different also.

68.5 OVERVIEW OF COMMON BLENDED FAMILY ESTATE PLANNING GOALS AND CONCERNS

Blended family partners present some routine and some unique challenges for estate planners. These are the principal concerns that we find blended family partners to have in estate planning:

- Choosing between partner and children;

- Providing for payment/apportionment of estate taxes;

- Hedging bets in the estate planning just in case the union does not work out (average length of subsequent unions is about seven years);

- Dealing with "problem" children, ex-partners and step-children;
- Protecting young/disabled children;
- Caring for elderly parents or siblings;
- Preserving family heirlooms and mementos for their blood/adoption family;
- Selecting the right fiduciaries; and
- Protecting against incapacity.

It is undeniable that single-relationship couples face many of these same issues. What makes the blended family couple's quandaries unique is that there are in essence two sides of a family: the client's children and the client's partner. This affects even simple things like powers of attorney, i.e., the identity of the agent and the scope of the agent's authority, and selection of fiduciaries, e.g., coordinating selection of a successor trustee and an executor with agent under property power of attorney. We'll address powers of attorney issues for blended families in this chapter.

68.6 STARK TRUTH ABOUT BLENDED FAMILY COUPLE RELATIONSHIPS AND LENGTH OF RELATIONSHIPS

Marriage statistics vary a bit depending upon the source. However, according to www.divorcerate.org, approximately 41-50 percent of first marriages, 60-67 percent of second marriages and 73-74 percent of third marriages end in divorce. While there are no known statistics on the breakups of unmarried couples, we suspect that those numbers are even higher since the partners generally (absent unusual circumstances[7]) can simply walk away from each other without legal obstacles and with little financial consequences *unless* there are children of the union. The average length of a subsequent union is seven-eight years.

These statistics are stark and, frankly, somewhat shocking, but those are the facts nonetheless. The estate planner must take these statistics into account in dispensing estate planning advice to couples, particularly with respect to irrevocable lifetime estate planning, and particularly to those who have been in more than one romantic relationship. The estate planner who ignores these statistics does so at professional peril as well as that of the clients.

68.7 CONFLICTS OF INTEREST

This problem comes up routinely in estate planning, and particularly in estate planning for blended family couples. The problem with a conflict of interest is that they almost always look worse with the benefit of hindsight than it does at the time when the estate planner steps into the conflict bog. An LSU Law School ethics professor, the late Warren L. Mengis, used to explain it this way: "In a 'free' case, a lawyer can spot a conflict a mile away, but in a 'fee' case, the lawyer may not see the conflict that is right under the lawyer's nose." In other words, when money and competition for business is involved, estate planners can be blind to obvious conflicts of interest due to personal self-interest. Likewise, in a life insurance situation, the natural desire and need to be compensated for time and effort sometimes competes with the importance of helping a client make the proper decision with respect to type or amount of appropriate coverage.

Business considerations. Conflicts of interest can be good for business in the short run in that they result in current work that does not leave the office for a competitor. But they often are bad for business in the long run even if one successfully navigates the ethical maze. You may have to waste time and money in the future defending yourself against mere accusations of a conflict of interest in an amount in excess of the value of the work. Prudence dictates that you want to avoid becoming the issue in any matter. In that case, the estate planner rarely comes out well.

Ethical considerations. The rules for working with conflicts of interests perhaps are best developed in the legal profession, focus upon those precepts. However, in every other estate planning profession, the analysis should be about the same as for lawyers. In other words, what is an ethical problem for a lawyer probably is an issue for other members of the estate planning team. Resolution of a conflict of interest issues usually requires the estate planner to:

(a) clearly identify the client or clients whose interests either are or potentially are adverse to one another;

(b) determine whether a conflict of interest exists, and whether, despite a conclusion that a conflict does not *presently* exist, joint representation is in the best interests of either the clients or the estate planner;

(c) if a conflict exists, decide whether the estate planner can nevertheless work with the couple, i.e., whether the conflict is "consentable"; and

(d) if the conflict of interest is in fact a consentable one, to consult with the affected clients and obtain their informed consent, confirmed in writing.[8]

The mere *possibility* of subsequent harm to either client does not *itself* require disclosure and consent. What is critical is the likelihood that a divergence in the clients' interests eventually will result and, if one does, whether that divergence will "materially interfere" with the estate planner's independent professional judgment in working with either client in the future.[9] If it is likely that the interests of the clients, including prospective and former clients, will diverge, then the estate planner probably should not attempt to simultaneously represent all interests. Of course, this determination must be made in real time when the estate planner is working for both clients who probably are insisting that there is no conflict. The decision is not an easy one. Therefore, when in doubt, there probably is a conflict to which the clients cannot give adequate consent, so separate representation probably is recommended.

Can't the planner simply get clients to waive a conflict? Too many estate planners blithely believe that if they are faced with a conflict of interest, they can extricate themselves from ethical difficulty simply by having the clients waive the conflict in advance.[10] Unfortunately, the analysis of whether clients who are in actual conflict with one another can waive that conflict is a bit more involved and is deceptively complex. For starters, in order to execute a valid waiver, the clients have to be "adequately informed" that there is an actual or potential conflict of interest between them and be made aware of the potential ramifications of the conflict and available alternatives to the joint representation.[11]

This necessitates a frank discussion with the clients of the pro's and con's of the simultaneous work on behalf of all clients and the possible alternatives to joint representation.[12] In order for clients to even be able to give informed consent, as discussed in the previous section, the conflict must be "consentable."[13] The estate planner must make the "consentable" determination for each client, so that what is a consentable conflict for one joint client may not be consentable for another joint client.[14] Some conflicts are not consentable even if the clients desire to be jointly simultaneously represented by the same estate planner because of the adversarial nature of the conflict.

In determining whether a conflict of interest is "consentable," the estate planner must determine that even where there is no direct *current* conflict between the clients, including prospective clients[15] as well as former clients,[16] a conflict of interest nevertheless exists if there is a "significant risk" that the estate planner's ability to work for the client will be "materially limited" as a result of the estate planner's responsibilities or interests to others.[17] Consentability is determined by considering whether the interests of the clients will be adequately protected if the clients are permitted to give informed consent to representation despite the conflict of interest. Representation is prohibited if the estate planner cannot reasonably conclude that the estate planner will be able to provide competent and diligent representation.[18]

One example of a nonconsentable conflict of interest that immediately comes to mind is where the parties are *directly* adverse to one another in a proposed business transaction, where the clients want the estate planner to simultaneously represent both of them in that negotiation: one seemingly cannot negotiate with oneself.[19] In that instance, a waiver probably would be insufficient to absolve the estate planner of the conflict of interest because of an actual conflict of interest. Additionally, where clients are directly adverse to each other in a pending proceeding, a conflict to allow the same lawyer to represent both clients in that proceeding is non-consentable[20] Another example of a potentially non-consentable conflict of interest includes simultaneously attempting to represent both partners in the establishment of a marriage contract or property agreement.[21]

68.8 NEGATIVE CONSEQUENCES OF CONFLICTS OF INTEREST

Conflicts of interest can be exceptionally troublesome for an estate planner. There are at least six potential negative consequences for estate planners relating to conflicts of interest. Those negative consequences range from loss of both clients to formal disqualification from representing either client to ethics charges to malpractice exposure. Generally speaking, the ethical rules of just about all professional organizations proscribe conflicts of interest because they violate the duty of loyalty that an estate planner owes to each client.[22]

The six potential negative consequences are as follows:

1. **Consequences of conflict: formal disqualification.** The first negative consequence of a conflict of interest is formal disqualification from being able to work with either partner. This consequence is particularly problematic because it often involves a judicial or administrative determination of disqualification, which means that there is some sort of proceeding in which the estate planner has had to defend his or her actions. This consequence also is bad because the estate planner is now the issue in the dispute between the now former partners, a place that no estate planner ever wants to be.[23]

   In the typical disqualification situation, the estate planner is attempting to continue to represent one of the former partners against the interests of a former partner without the consent of the former partner client.[24] Unless disqualified, the estate planner has the potential ability to employ confidential information obtained during the course and scope of the estate planner's work on behalf of the other partner against that partner former client, which is fundamentally wrong and unethical.[25] Secondly, it is entirely possible that the estate planner will be required to be a material witness in the proceeding between the former partners, providing another reason why the estate planner probably should not be permitted to represent either partner.[26]

2. **Consequences of conflicts: damaged reputation.** The second possible consequence of a conflict of interest is the damage to one's professional reputation that may result from the matter coming to light in the public.[27] This could adversely impact the client attraction capabilities of the estate planner both currently as well as in the future. Even if the alleged conflict of interest was not an actual conflict, it is the mere mention that creates the "guilty until proven innocent" problem because you have an unhappy former client who is talking badly about you, which is never good.

3. **Consequences of conflicts: loss of both clients.** The third possible consequence of a conflict of interest is the loss of both clients because both clients may consider the estate planner tainted merely by virtue of having worked with the now ex-partner. Additionally, a conflict of interest also could cause the loss or damaging of a friendship that the estate planner had developed with the client.

4. **Consequences of conflicts: malpractice exposure.** The fourth possible negative consequence of a conflict of interest is malpractice exposure as a direct result of a conflict of interest that caused negligence or a breach of professional fiduciary duty. In Smith v. Hastie,[28] an appeals court reversed a grant of summary judgment that the trial court had granted in favor of a lawyer who had been accused of wrongdoing, and the appellate court remanded the matter for trial on allegations of, among other things, negligence and breach of fiduciary duty of the lawyer.

   In that case, the lawyer had simultaneously represented a husband and wife, who had serious ongoing marital problems and in fact were in marital counseling when the lawyer met with them, in setting up a family limited partnership. In that role, the lawyer allegedly encouraged the wife to transfer assets into the partnership without advising her of the potential conflict that he had in representing the couple. Additionally, the lawyer allegedly failed to inquire into actual conflicts between them, and he did not properly advise the wife of the implications to and of the partnership if the couple were to divorce. In response to two different specific inquiries from the wife about the effect of the partnership on divorce, the lawyer merely said that she would be "fine" if the couple divorced, which happened not too long after the partnership was formed and capitalized.

   See also *Spence v. Wingate*,[29] in which the South Carolina held that, in the context of a blended family where there had been a dispute between the decedent's children and his surviving spouse, the lawyer who represented both the surviving spouse and the decedent's estate breached a fiduciary duty to the surviving spouse former client.

5. **Consequences of conflicts: disgorgement of fees.** It also is quite common for an estate planner who has represented joint clients in a conflict of interest situation to be asked to give back the fees that the estate planner charged.

6. **Consequences of conflicts: discipline.** The final and perhaps most serious ramification of a conflict of interest is exposure to professional discipline. In *in re Plinski*,[30] a lawyer who represented a blended family couple who had adverse estate planning interests was publicly reprimanded.[31] See also *In re Eisel*,[32] a lawyer was reprimanded for failing to disclose to a spouse former client the aspects of the other spouse's estate plan that adversely impacted that spouse.

68.9 TYPES OF CONFLICTS ISSUES OFTEN ENCOUNTERED IN ESTATE PLANNING FOR BLENDED FAMILY COUPLES

Estate planning for blended family couples can present some unique challenges with respect to conflicts of interest between the partners.[33] While the following list of conflicts of interest is not intended to be exhaustive, the list contains some fairly common conflicts of interest between blended family couples:

a. **Classification of property as separate, jointly owned or as community property.**[34] The classification of property is clearly an area of potential conflict between the partners. It is not unusual for one client spouse to benefit from a misclassification of property or from commingling the separate property of the other spouse. These types of disputes can arise if the marital partners subsequently divorce or after the death of a partner, where the descendants or legatees of the deceased partner challenge the classification of property after the partner's death that often is made by the surviving spouse. The best advice we can give to new married partners is to religiously maintain and document separate property as separate. Otherwise, if commingling occurs, the property loses its character as separate property.

b. **What about advice about severing joint tenancies, among other things, to allow for funding of a credit shelter trust?** If the partners are joint tenants but are different in ages, the estate planner has an interesting dilemma. While terminating joint tenancies to enable funding of a credit shelter trust generally is prudent advice, if one partner is significantly younger than the other, query whether terminating a joint tenancy is in the best interests of the younger partner, who, actuarially, is more likely to eventually obtain the asset as the survivor. Can the estate planner who represents both partners in such a situation recommend severance of the joint tenancy, which clearly is in the best interests of the older partner but not necessarily of the younger partner?

c. **Waiver of ERISA/REA spousal rights in a retirement plan.** Spouses have rights in their spouse's ERISA retirement plans. Generally, these rights cannot be waived until the parties are married. It is clear that where one spouse is asked to waive rights under the other spouse's qualified retirement plan, that waiving spouse is surrendering what can be significant rights. Given the potential for tension between new (and second or third time) spouses on this score, estate planners who purport to work jointly with the couple may find themselves in an ethical trick bag.

d. **Effects of commingling that may have already occurred.** Where a partner's rights are protected by a marriage contract or where a partner brought significant assets into a relationship, but that partner has allowed assets to be commingled with those of the other partner, the estate planner may have a conflict pointing out that fact since the commingling is benefitting the other partner. Yet the planner is also obligated to do just that – to properly explain the legal ramifications of both existing and proposed property arrangements.

e. **QTIP trust terms and selection of trustee/executor.** Spouses usually want control of assets after the other spouse's death. This often conflicts with the intentions of the other testator spouse, *particularly* in a blended family. The estate planner who represents the couple jointly may find some uncomfortable conversations about the identity of the trustee for the spouse's benefit and the rights of the spouse, in the trust.

f. **Types of legacies and restrictions on legacies (trust v. outright) to partners in general.** As in the previous section, partners frequently differ over what will be left to the surviving partner and how and under what terms it will be left. It is very easy for the careless estate planner to wander into this conflicts minefield by being co-opted to the cause of one partner.

g. **The right of one of the partners, if married, to elect against the will.** The spousal right of election is a powerful right that surviving spouses have unless they waived that right in a marriage contract.[35] However, where the spouses do not have a marriage contract and the estate planner represents the couple jointly, if one of the spouses leaves the other spouse an amount that, if that partner died today, would not satisfy the spousal share, query whether and how far the estate planner can go to counsel the other spouse about possible rights to elect against the will and obtain a statutory share?

h. **Wealth disparities or economic dependence between the partners.** Where there is a wide disparity between the wealth levels of the partners or where one partner is economically dependent upon the other partner and the estate planner is representing the couple jointly, the estate planner has to be very careful to not allow the wealthier partner to exercise that power to the detriment of the other partner while the joint representation is ongoing.

i. **Interpretation of a marriage contract or property agreement, including whether the agreement would withstand scrutiny.** The partners often have divergent interests in the evaluation and interpretation of marriage contracts or property agreements. It is not unusual for one partner to have required the other partner to enter into the agreement as a prerequisite to going forward with the formal relationship, and for the other partner to have reluctantly entered into an agreement that limited rights upon dissolution of the relationship. It is very common for a marital partner to challenge these agreements after the death of the first of the couple to die.[36]

68.10 WAYS TO WORK WITH BLENDED FAMILY COUPLES

There are three essential ways that an estate planner can work with partners in a blended family: the estate planner could work with the couples jointly, could work with each of the partners and treat them as separate clients or could choose to work with only one of the partners. We believe in a client-centric analysis: what is best for the client ultimately is best for the estate planner too.

Joint Representation

The first way, and we believe the most common way, is for the estate planner to work with the blended family couple as joint clients. Just because the partners have different estate planning goals or beneficiaries does not necessarily mean that there is a conflict of interest between the partners.[37] Query whether the estate planner who undertakes to work with both partners should always obtain a waiver of a conflict of interest.[38]

In our client-centric model, let's analyze the benefits and disadvantages of joint representation to the clients:

1. **Benefits of joint representation.** For all of its potential difficulties for estate planners, joint representation offers a number of significant benefits for client couples, and this is probably why so many clients opt for joint representation despite the potential risks. It also can't be underemphasized that estate planners usually want to represent the couple for fear of losing the work to another estate planner. The biggest issue to some estate planners is whether they will follow the "priestly approach," where they withhold secrets that either partner imparts, or the "show and tell" approach, where the estate planners will not withhold confidential information obtained from one partner from the other partner. Generally, where the duties of confidentiality and loyalty collide, the duty of confidentiality usually prevails.[39] (Consider this issue in your "letter of agreement" that defines the scope of your representation).

The benefits of joint representation to the clients include:

- Cost savings (only one set of estate planners instead of two);

- Efficiency and synergies of time and effort;

- Joint representation could be used to better the communication between the partners; and

- Being treated as real partners, and not as adversaries.

2. **Disadvantages of joint representation.** There also are some disadvantages of joint representation for client couples, including:

- Potential for divided loyalties by the estate planner;

- Potential for domination of the joint representation by one partner to the detriment of the other partner;

- Partners may be reticent to discuss some material controversial topics; and

- A partner may not make full disclosure of sensitive material information to the estate planner.

Concurrent Separate Representation

Despite a lack of express authority, there exists a minority group of very distinguished lawyers who believe that a lawyer can ethically represent related parties such as partners each as separate clients, such that what one partner confides in the lawyer is not going to be shared with the other partner.[40] In this scheme, the lawyer, by carefully tailoring the engagement agreement and obtaining informed consent from the clients, can represent two related parties as if they were separate clients.[41]

The ACTEC Commentaries point out that "[a] lawyer who is asked to provide separate representation to multiple clients should do so with great care because of the stress it necessarily places on the lawyer's duties of impartiality and loyalty and the extent to which it may limit the lawyer's ability to advise each of the clients adequately."[42] The problems are real in that it places upon the lawyer the continuing duty to discern whether a separate representation of related parties like partners can continue in the face of actual conflict between the parties and when that conflict limits the lawyer's ability to continue to provide adequate representation to each client.

Taken all the way to its logical final conclusion, i.e., that the same lawyer can separately represent related parties who have an actual conflict with each other, separate representation seems contrary to the spirit of Model Rules of Professional Conduct Rule 1.7(b)(3), which expressly prohibits concurrent representation of parties who have an actual conflict in the same proceeding. As a real and practical matter, conflicts often are a matter of degree, and it can be very difficult to discern when the conflict has gone too far and now materially limits the lawyer's ability to provide adequate representation to each client. These decisions can look clear only with the benefit of hindsight and are not easily made during the course of the representation.

The problem also is that despite the estate planner's best efforts, the client who waived a conflict and is unhappy with the estate planner can argue that the estate planner's disclosures that obtained the waiver were insufficient. In essence, the estate planner in that tough situation has to prove a negative, i.e., that the disclosures were not insufficient, which is very hard to do.

Separate Representation

The estate planner also can represent only one partner. This is the safest course for the estate planner. However, this often is not what clients want to do (and rarely what the planner wants). In our client-centric model, we review the advantages and disadvantages to each client of separate representation.

1. **Advantages of separate representation.** There are distinct advantages for the partners to each have separate representation, which are:

- Undivided attention and loyalty of the estate planner;

- Total freedom to say what the client feels and wants to have done in his or her estate planning; and

- Generally lower chance of estate plan challenges.[43]

2. **Disadvantages of separate representation.** There are a number of disadvantages to the

partners of each being separately represented. These include:

- Additional cost of two sets of estate planners;
- Potential for treating partners like adversaries;
- Potential for estate planners to put their individual egos in the way of the couple's relationship; and
- The unrepresented partner can still challenge the other partner's estate plan.

68.11 PRE-EXISTING RELATIONSHIPS CAN DETERMINE CLIENT INTERACTION

There are a number of possible scenarios of how the estate planner comes to originally interact with client partners, including:

- You have a **preexisting relationship** (personal or professional) **with one partner** but not the other partner
- You have **separate preexisting relationships** (personal or professional) **with each partner**
- The couple comes to you with you having had **no preexisting relationship** of any kind with either partner

The prudent estate planner will treat each one of these situations differently. We believe that where the estate planner has a preexisting relationship of any kind with one of the partners, that estate planner must tread very carefully and strenuously to avoid showing any favoritism to the client partner with a preexisting relationship. If the partners fall out with one another, the estate planner should anticipate and plan for claims that the estate planner favored one partner over the other. These situations can be exacerbated by the estate planner's continued professional relationship with the partner with whom the estate planner had a preexisting relationship. Again, it is the appearance of impropriety that potentially taints the estate planner. Prudence usually dictates turning both clients loose on other estate planners.

68.12 WHEN IS SEPARATE REPRESENTATION THE WAY TO GO DESPITE WHAT THE CLIENTS SAY?

When separate representation is suggested. The signposts discussed below are relevant when you are trying to decide whether you can work with a couple, and certainly militate in favor of only representing one of the partners. Very few of these signposts are solely determinative of a decision to work with only one partner, but each is a warning sign of potential future problems in working with the couple:

Where one partner is childless, but the other is not. In this situation, the partners have significantly different loyalties. The parent partner often will be torn between his or her children and the other partner, while the other partner has no children to be torn between.

Where one partner does all of the talking or seems to exert control over the other. This issue can come up with single relationship couples. In this instance, you should suggest that you would like to meet with each partner separately as well as jointly. If you are not permitted to meet separately with a partner who clearly demonstrates signs that he or she is either under the control of the other partner or is not permitted to speak during the meeting, then you might be at risk working with the couple jointly.

Length of the relationship. Generally speaking, the shorter the couple's relationship, the more likely it is that you should work with only one partner.

Number of past relationships. If the client has a penchant for having numerous successive relationships, then that is a potential sign of instability that suggests only working with one partner.

Significant age disparity between the partners. Age disparity between partners is not a determinative factor in and of itself to suggest working with only one partner. However, the interests of the parties who are separated by a significant difference in ages may be so divergent that you cannot provide adequate joint representation of the couple.

Significant disparity in wealth or income between the partners. This factor too is not necessarily determinative by itself. However, again, the needs and interests of the partners may be so different that each would be better served by a separate estate planner.

Economic dependence of one partner on the other. Economic dependence by a partner can lead to a loss of autonomy and subservience to the other partner, so this signpost has to be monitored very carefully.

Existence of a pre-nuptial or property agreement. If there is a marriage contract or property agreement, the partners are almost always separately represented in the confection of a marriage contract or property agreement. This suggests that separate representation in their estate planning is still best for the partners because if it was important enough to have such an agreement pursuant to separate representation in the first place, it is still important.

Information held by one partner is off-limits to the other partner, e.g., a secret, etc. This signpost is a serious warning sign of potential problems between the partners, and the estate planner who encounters a client who maintains secrets from the other partner would be best served by treading very carefully working with the couple and should give strong consideration to working with only one partner.

68.13 INITIAL CLIENT INTERVIEW AND ENGAGEMENT LETTER CONSIDERATIONS

In a blended family couple, there usually are some significant differences between the partners because of the assets and obligations that each brings into the relationship. In these situations, in addition to meeting with the couple in each other's presence, it probably is advisable to also meet separately with each partner in order to ferret out any hidden conflicts of interest or sensitive areas that either partner is unwilling to mention in the presence of the other partner.[44]

Most estate planners make their mistakes in working with couples at the initial interview by agreeing right then and there to work with the couple jointly without thinking about it, instead of cautiously feeling the couple out in order to determine whether there are any conflicts between the two partners. For blended family couples, this is especially true, for many of the reasons discussed above.

For initial meetings with these types of clients, it might be prudent to pursue a dual-stage representation model where the estate planner would meet with the couple jointly and separately in order to ferret out any differences between the partners.[45] If the estate planner finds no significant differences between the partners, then the estate planner could work with the couple jointly if that was best for all concerned. However, what happens if the estate planner unearths significant conflicts between the estate planning desires and intentions of the partners? What *should* the estate planner do? What *can* the estate planner do?

That will probably depend upon the written engagement letter that the prudent estate planner had the couple sign before the initial round of meetings. If the estate planner retained the right in the engagement letter to work with only one partner, which a prudent estate planner would include in the engagement letter, then the estate planner who discovers irreconcilable conflicts can do so and proceed with working with only one partner. However, where the estate planner does not retain such a right and there are significant differences between the partners, the estate planner probably has to recuse himself or herself from representing either partner.

The prudent estate planner also should provide in the engagement letter relative to how the planner will treat information that either partner imparts to the estate planner outside of the presence of the other partner where the estate planner is working with the partners jointly. The available options are the "show and tell" approach, in which the estate planner notifies the clients in writing that he or she will not withhold any secret that either client confides in them, and the "priestly" approach, in which the estate planner will retain as confidential any information that either client confides in him or her.

As we pointed out earlier, if the engagement letter is silent on this score, or if there is no engagement letter, the estate planner's duty of confidentiality will prevent disclosing confidential information that one partner imparted outside of the presence of the other partner.[46] If the confidential information adversely impacts the rights of the other partner, then the estate planner probably has to withdraw from working with the couple or either one of them alone.[47] The issue then becomes whether the estate planner can disclose the fact that there is a material conflict between the partners in the estate planner's withdrawal, the so-called "noisy withdrawal," which in all likelihood will tip off the other partner that something is amiss between them.[48] By and large, we believe that the estate planner who alerts the partners to a material conflict between them in withdrawing, but who does not elaborate on or disclose the nature of the material conflict or the confidential information that one partner imparted to the estate planner, has honored professional ethical responsibilities to both partners.[49]

The prudent estate planner could provide for a mix of approaches, i.e., use of a priestly approach for the initial "feeling out" sessions, with a switch to the "show and tell" approach for the joint representation. Whatever the estate planner decides to do, the rules should be expressly set forth in the engagement letter so that there are not any surprises. Assuming that the estate planner is comfortable, as discussed above, the estate planner also could opt to treat the couple as separate clients for the initial "feeling out" sessions. We set out a comprehensive list of provisions that should be in every engagement letter in Chapter 11.

Selected Estate Planning Issues of Concern to Blended Family Couples

Gift splitting. It is not unusual for one partner to have significantly more wealth than the other partner. Through what is known as gift splitting, the wealthier partner could make gifts of the entire amount, but, for gift tax purposes, it is as if both partners made the gifts, thereby doubling the gift. This technique only applies if the partners are married.

Gift splitting often is dealt with in a marriage contract, since Code section 2513 requires a consenting spouse to make an election to split gifts on a gift tax return (Form 709) and also permits revocation of consent to split gifts.

Marriage contracts frequently require spouses to split *all* gifts made, to consent to the filing of a separate gift tax return and to agree not to revoke the consent, but this often is limited to annual exclusion gifts, although the rule applies to *all* gifts made in a calendar year. Therefore, if one spouse makes a large gift, the other spouse may be obligated to split the gift for tax purposes, but not be obligated under the marriage contract to split the gifts.

Because the election under Code section 2513(b) covers all gifts made during a calendar year, including gifts that exceed the annual exclusions that are available to the consenting spouse, thereby necessitating use of that spouse's lifetime gift tax applicable exclusion amount, a pre-nuptial agreement often compensates that spouse in some way for use of that applicable exclusion amount. This often is done through annual exclusion gifts to the children of the consenting spouse.

Example. Nancy and Tom have been married for a few years. Nancy has significantly more wealth than Tom and wants to make annual exclusion gifts of $17,000 (in 2023) to each of her three children. Nancy and Tom have a pre-nuptial agreement that requires the spouses to split all gifts and to cooperate and consent to the filing of all necessary tax returns.

Through gift-splitting, which requires Tom's cooperation but which costs him nothing, Nancy could give each child $34,000, in other words, twice as much. This also requires the filing of a gift tax return and the making of the gift-splitting election.

Now, if Nancy wanted to make larger lifetime gifts to her children, Tom also would join in and double the amount of the gift. However, in this instance, Tom would have to use part or all of his gift-tax applicable exclusion amount, which he may not want to do, especially if he has heirs of his own, but which he would have no choice because of the gift splitting agreement that he made in the pre-nuptial agreement. This large gift situation should be addressed in a pre-nuptial agreement as well.

Sales to intentionally defective grantor trusts. For blended families, sales to intentionally defective grantor trusts must be very carefully designed, even more so than for other families.

The trustee of the purchasing irrevocable trust must be an independent third party because the beneficiaries might be comprised of children from both partners as well as possibly a partner.

This is where it will be imperative to coordinate the selection of an executor of the selling partner's estate, which will be a creditor until the note is paid off, with the selection of the trustee of the purchasing irrevocable trust so that there is not friction after the selling partner's death if the note is not paid off by then.

Intra-family loans and guarantees. At first blush, a loan might not appear to be an estate-planning technique at all. However, if the loan can be made at a favorable interest rate, in other words, below a market interest rate, this can be a very effective estate planning technique, especially if the borrower can invest the loan proceeds to earn more than the interest to be paid on the loan, which would result in a gift tax-free transfer of wealth. Below market loans can be a very effective way to transfer wealth free from gift taxes.

Below market loans can be made to partners or to their children, although the lender must make real sure that there is coordination between the note holder and the personal representative of the lender just in case the lender dies before the loan is repaid.

In blended families, guarantees must be even more carefully considered than usual because there might be resistance by the one partner to a guaranteeing partner's guaranteeing debts of her children since this could impact his financial security if the loan must be paid off by the guaranteeing partner. Moreover, coordination of selection of executors and successor trustees is critical because, for example, if the other partner is the successor trustee or is the executor, that partner may not cooperate with the guarantee, possibly resulting in litigation.

Example. Suppose that Rhett guaranteed a debt for one of his boys, Rex, and then he dies. Rhett named Rex's stepmother, Scarlett, as executrix. Rex is unable to pay the debt, and the creditor calls for Rhett's estate to pay off on the guarantee. Scarlett actually objected to Rhett guaranteeing Rex's debt when he did it. Now, if she won't pay off the debt, she will force the creditor (and Rex) to sue Rhett's estate, which will result in legal fees, delays, and probably some hard feelings on the part of Rex.

QTIP Information Rights. One of the most difficult issues to address in administering blended family estates is dealing with the QTIP estate tax issue of the right of reimbursement for estate taxes on the fictitious inclusion under Code section 2044 because the property is in a trust over which the personal representative or trustee has no control. Valuation can be hard if you don't have access to the property-consider building this right in to both partner's estate plans-also, consider charging the valuation costs to the QTIP trust since the valuation is only being done of that property-but this must be done in advance because, in a blended family, relations might not be good amongst step-siblings at the second death.

Consider adding a clause to the marriage contract that requires certain provisions to be contained in each spouse's will or revocable trust such as the following:

- **QTIP Information Rights.** The parties agree that each shall include the following provisions in their respective wills or revocable trusts and to refrain from removing or in any way modifying these provisions at any time:

- **Cooperation in QTIP Property Valuation.** To cooperate with the executor or trustee of the estate or trust of [NAMED SPOUSE] with respect to the valuation of property in this trust over which a QTIP election was made in my estate ("QTIP Property"), including, without limitation, granting full and complete access to all information concerning the QTIP Property requested by the executor or trustee that is pertinent to the valuation of the QTIP Property at the death of [NAMED SPOUSE] or, if elected in the estate of [NAMED SPOUSE], as of the alternate valuation date permitted under section 2032 of the Internal Revenue Code.

- **Right to Have Access to Valuation Information on QTIP Property.** The Trustee shall have and exercise the right to have access to the property over which a QTIP election was made in the estate of [NAMED SPOUSE] ("QTIP Property") even though the Trustee has no authority or control over the QTIP Property for the limited purpose of valuing the QTIP Property for federal and state estate tax purposes for purposes of including it in my estate.

- **Private Unitrusts and Annuity Trusts.** Where you have a surviving partner as the income beneficiary and the deceased partner's children as principal beneficiaries, as in a traditional trust, the age old conflict is how the trust is to be invested. On the one hand, income beneficiaries want high income, which almost always can be achieved at the cost of growth in the value of the trust's assets. On the other hand, principal beneficiaries always want growth, which can generally be achieved only at the cost of current income.

In a straight unitrust, you can give a partner an interest equal to a percentage of the fair market value of the trust annually for life, which can be payable in monthly or quarterly installments, with the partner's children being the principal beneficiaries and even income beneficiaries (unless a QTIP trust). In order for the unitrust to qualify for QTIP treatment, the surviving spouse partner has to receive the greater of the unitrust amount or the trust's income no less than annually, as well as the other general QTIP requirements.

You also can structure an annuity marital trust that will guarantee a surviving partner a certain amount of money per year, provided the assets hold up. If the partners are married, the trust would have to pay the **greater** of the annuity amount or the trust income if QTIP treatment is desired. Annuity trusts, which operate like charitable remainder trusts, but with a remainder beneficiary being the children, are popular with older couples and where the assets are difficult to value.

QTIP Trusts and Spendthrift Clauses. It is not unusual for the income and principal beneficiaries of a QTIP trust to squabble. It also is not unusual that they simply cannot coexist in the same trust. There are several techniques that are available to assist in the disentangling of a QTIP trust by dividing it between the income beneficiary (the surviving spouse) and the principal beneficiaries (usually the step-children). However, many of these techniques don't work if the spendthrift trust provision prohibits all transfers. Consider an exit strategy in this regard for all blended family QTIP trusts by permitting certain alienations like sales or gifts to certain related people.

A spendthrift trust clause that might work well is:

- **Spendthrift Trust Provision**. The interests of the beneficiaries shall be subject to the spendthrift trust provisions set forth herein. The interests of all beneficiaries shall be subject to the maximum spendthrift restraints permitted by applicable law as to involuntary alienation as well as to voluntary alienation, except, however, that voluntary alienation shall be permitted for transfers, sales or exchanges to or for the benefit of the following persons:

    (1) any descendant, spouse, sibling or ascendant of the beneficiary;

    (2) any other beneficiary of this trust (or of any other separate trust created in this instrument);

    (3) descendants, spouses, ascendants or siblings of any beneficiary of this trust (or of any other separate trust created in this instrument), or

    (4) any trust or entity owned or controlled or held for the beneficial interest by or for any of the foregoing persons named in (1) to (3) hereinabove.

- **Tax apportionment.** See Chapter 25 for an in-depth discussion of these issues.

- **Tangible personal property landmine.** This is a **real** hot button issue—and a source of potential complaint against estate planners if this isn't adequately addressed in the documents. While it is generally not necessary to address tangible personal property in detail and with much attention, blended family estate planning is the exception to this rule.

    In blended families, these issues often are not carefully addressed in estate planning. As a result, the surviving partner gets this property even though the deceased partner may have understood that the surviving partner would give the family property to the children, but there is no guarantee that this wish will be honored.

    If there is any advice that we would give about this type of property, it is to consider having the client give it to the persons that the client wants to have during lifetime. This category can create significant litigation even if the property is not worth much financially. This category of property includes things like family pictures and other family memorabilia, furniture, jewelry, crystal, silverware, and china.

- **Choice of fiduciary issues.** A disinterested, third-party professional (which does not necessarily mean a bank or trust company) is the most strongly recommended option to serve as executor and successor trustee of a living trust in the vast majority of blended family situations in order to reduce rancor between the heirs and to prevent possible shenanigans. We know that this advice will not be taken well either by the other partner or by the various children involved. An excellent and typically more affordable alternative to large institutions is selecting an attorney or a certified public accountant (CPA) who they trust and who does this type of work regularly.

They are much more likely to have a relationship with the family, thereby understanding the specific needs and nuances of the particular blended family scenario, and, the family will less likely be impacted by the ongoing turnover that can often occur in larger institutions.

Despite our strongest recommendations, most people want a family member to serve as executor or trustee. Even in non-blended family situations, this can cause problems, particularly if there are hurt feelings or if the wrong family member is chosen. However, in blended families where the estate will be given to both a partner and the client partner's children from a prior union, family members often have inherent conflicts of interest that make it typically ill-advisable for any of them to serve in either capacity.

There are many drivers to why a partner or their stepchildren may express a strong desire to be executor or trustee, all of which are valid and important to figure out together. It is only human nature to want to take care of oneself. The flexibility that we believe is necessary to the estate plan can't usually be achieved if either a partner or the children serve.

One common underlying concern we have encountered over the years that causes one partner to strongly desire a governance role is anxiety and concern over that partner's care after his or her partner is dead—some will use anything (sex, money, attention, etc.) that will give them power over the selection of fiduciaries—we counsel against it.

On the other side, the children of the wealthier partner will want to be in a position of control as they do not want their stepparent to determine the disposition of what they believe is their due.

We have seen all possible scenarios, including a stepparent and a stepchild as co-trustees. The only way we see these working out well is when there is adequate preparation for the role in advance, and healthy communication throughout life.

For all of the work on a blended family couple estate plan, the most important thing is the selection of the right agents, personal representatives and successor trustees. It is important to coordinate between, for example, the choice of successor trustee or executor with the role of agent under a power of attorney since the latter has to account to the former.

- **Post-death allocations and elections.** There are actually two issues in the allocations of assets in an estate or trust:

    1. What amounts or properties are allocated between the various legatees or beneficiaries; and

    2. Whether a QTIP election will be made, and, if so, what assets will be QTIP'd.

    Both of these issues should always be decided by an independent third party fiduciary in a blended family context. Only an independent third party fiduciary can be "above the fray" when allocating assets between the credit shelter and QTIP trusts.

    If you can't get an independent third party fiduciary to make those calls, one group is going to be unhappy with the calls. Even if the family won't go for an independent third party fulltime fiduciary, the situation cries out for a special trustee to make these calls.

    The issues in QTIP elections in blended families are:

    1. Will there be any QTIP election made?

    2. Who will make the QTIP election?

    3. Who will decide what property is QTIP'd?

    All three of those issues should be determined by an independent third party fiduciary in order to take away the emotional and self-interest aspects. The same is highly recommended as to who decides on the investments in a "traditional" (i.e, non-annuity trust or non-unitrust) QTIP trust; an independent third party should make those calls.

    The planner should consider some "fairly representative" (Rev. Proc. 64-19) language that directs the executor to fund the trusts with assets or cash, or both, and to value all assets at their fair market values determined as of the dates of their respective transfers so that each transfer shares proportionately in the appreciation or depreciation of assets between the date of the decedent's death and the date of transfers, particularly where a "pick and choose" funding formula is used.

The planner should include guidance about considering the income tax consequences of funding and of the assets themselves. Appraisals of subjectively valued assets are a must, especially for interested trustees.

Language such as the following should work to provide guidance on asset allocations: *In funding the trusts established in this instrument, I direct [my Executor/The Trustee] to fund each trust with assets or cash, or both, and to value all assets at their fair market values determined as of the dates of their respective transfers so that each transfer shares proportionately in the appreciation or depreciation of assets between the date of death and the date of transfer. In making the funding decisions, [my Executor/The Trustee] also should consider the short term and long term prospects for appreciation or depreciation in the assets selected, as well as the associated income tax consequences. [My Executor/The Trustee] is strongly advised to obtain independent appraisals from qualified appraisers in making the funding decisions over assets that have no readily ascertainable fair market value on an established public market.*

If you can't convince a client to select an independent third party as trustee or executor, you could give significant guidance in the documents on how the asset allocations should be made. While you would generally give the independent third party fiduciary a blanket indemnification and hold harmless right, you should reduce that right to make it clear that their decisions are subject to review for compliance with their fiduciary duty.

We typically modified the indemnification language to permit liability for breach of the duty of loyalty and impartiality due to conflict of interest in that regard. We think that they have that liability any way, but we like to put it in there to remind them of what they're supposed to be doing and how they're supposed to go about doing it.

Consider language like: *My Executor's decisions with respect to allocations of assets between sub-trusts established hereunder all be final, binding and conclusive on all parties in interest, and my Executor shall have no liability as a result of such decisions except for a breach of fiduciary duty or the duties of impartiality or loyalty.*

- **Portability.** In blended families, it is important that the couple have a frank and honest discussion about portability. The couple should provide instructions relative to it in their estate planning documents and prenuptial agreements. There already have been reported cases in state courts regarding blended family clashes over portability.[50]

An executor who is a child of a prior marriage may choose not to incur the expense of filing an estate tax return and the risk of audit of the DSUE Amount solely to make the portability election for the second spouse. The use of portability with QTIP trust planning in subsequent marriages where the QTIP trust property is going to pass to the descendants of the first spouse to die could visit hardship and federal estate tax exposure to those descendants where the surviving spouse used some or all of the deceased spouse's DSUE Amount and didn't waive reimbursement of the federal estate tax on the QTIP trust, which few spouses in multiple marriage situations will do. The parties could agree to permit the surviving spouse to have the use of any DSUE Amount of the first spouse to die in return for an agreement that the surviving spouse would waive the right of reimbursement for tax due as a result of the inclusion of the QTIP trust in the surviving spouse's estate (or at least for that portion of the QTIP trust equal to the DSUE Amount).

In subsequent marriage situations, portability might offend the decedent's descendants, which is an emotionally charged issue that already has resulted in post-death litigation between step-relations. The federal estate and gift tax statute of limitations stays open for the DSUE Amount, which is another significant disadvantage, particularly where the estate is principally comprised of subjectively valued assets.

Portability is not going away, so couples should affirmatively provide for whether it will be available to the surviving spouse. The parties could agree as follows:

1. The first of the couple to die would require his or her executor to prepare and file a federal estate tax return and make the portability election.

2. The surviving spouse would agree to pay all of the costs of preparing and filing the return to the satisfaction of the executor, who would agree to cooperate and provide all information concerning the deceased spouse's assets and liabilities.

3. The surviving spouse would agree to indemnify, defend and hold the executor harmless from and against any and all taxes, penalties and interest arising out of making the portability election.

4. If a QTIP election is made on the estate tax return of the first spouse to die, the surviving spouse would agree to waive reimbursement of the federal estate tax attributable to inclusion of the DSUE Amount in the surviving spouse's estate in his or her estate planning documents and agree to pay that federal estate tax, together with penalties and interest, if the waiver is ineffective.

Powers of attorney issues. Modifications often are necessary to your regular forms for blended family couples. The power of attorney should not permit an agent partner to significantly alter the principal's estate plan; likewise, the powers of an agent child should be similarly restricted.

The limitations might need to be both affirmative and negative, (negative) e.g., restricting beneficiary changes and gifts that are not in accord with the principal's estate plan; and (affirmative) requiring continuation of annual gifts, etc. In order to dispel uncertainty, the power of attorney should require the agent to give the children of the principal access to financial and medical information, or to the partner, if a child is the agent.

Powers of attorney for blended family couples:

- Should limit giving away precious family heirlooms (e.g., silverware, china and pictures).

- Limit changing beneficiary designations.

- Limit changing distribution provisions in IRAs and retirement plans.

- Should automatically terminate on separation or divorce.

- Should limit the exercise of powers of appointment.

- Should not waive any accountings, and in fact should probably require periodic accountings by the agent, particularly after the principal's incapacity.

- Should affirmatively and broadly restrict self-dealing.

CHAPTER ENDNOTES

1. See, e.g., Coontz, Stephanie, "The Way We Weren't: The Myth and Reality of the 'Traditional' Family," 75 *National Forum*, pp. 11-14 (Summer 1995).
2. Portions adapted from Hood, L. Paul, Jr., and Bouchard, Emily, Estate Planning for the Blended Family (Self-Counsel Press 2012) and expanded.
3. http://www.stepfamilies.info/faq.php.
4. *The Decline of Marriage and Rise of New Families*, Pew Research Center (Nov. 2010); accessible at http://www.pewsocialtrends.org/2010/11/18/the-decline-of-marriage-and-rise-of-new-families/2/.
5. Hughes, James E., Jr., *Family: The Compact Among Generations* (Bloomberg 2007), p. 3.
6. http://www.stepfamilies.info/stepfamily-fact-sheet.php.
7. The unusual case could include a claim for palimony. See, e.g., *Marvin v. Marvin*, 18 Cal.3d 660, 557 P.2d 106 (1976).
8. Comment (2) to Rule 1.7, Model Rules of Professional Conduct.
9. Comment (8) to Rule 1.7, Model Rules of Professional Conduct.
10. See, e.g., Rule 1.7(b)(4), Model Rules of Professional Conduct. Waiver of conflict of interest in an engagement letter in an acrimonious husband and wife setting was held sufficient in *Bishop v. Maurer*, 823 N.Y.S.2d 366 (N.Y. App. 2006).

11. See, e.g., Rules 1.0(e) and 1.7(b)(4), Model Rules of Professional Conduct.
12. Comment (20) to Rule 1.7, Model Rules of Professional Conduct.
13. Comment (2) to Rule 1.7, Model Rules of Professional Conduct.
14. Comment (14) to Rule 1.7, Model Rules of Professional Conduct.
15. Rule 1.18, Model Rules of Professional Conduct.
16. Rule 1.9, Model Rules of Professional Conduct.
17. Rule 1.7(a)(2).
18. Comment (15) to Rule 1.7, Model Rules of Professional Conduct.
19. See, e.g., Comment (28) to Rule 1.7, Model Rules of Professional Conduct.
20. Rule 1.7(b)(3), Model Rules of Professional Conduct.
21. See, e.g., ACTEC Commentaries (5th Ed. 2015), p. 104. cf. Marriage of Drag, 326 Ill. App. 3d 1051, 762 N.E.2nd 1111 (3d Dist. 2002); and In re Marriage of Friedman, 122 Cal. Rptr. 2d 412, 100 Cal. App. 4th 65 (2nd Dis. 2002). But see *McKee-Johnson v. Johnson*, 444 NW 2nd 259 (Minn. 1989), in which the Minnesota Supreme Court observed that it had never held that a lawyer could not ethically represent both prospective husband and wife in a pre-nuptial agreement. See also Cahn, Naomi and Tuttle, Robert, "Dependency and Delegation: The Ethics of Marital Representation," 22 *Seattle University Law Review* 97 (1998).
22. See, e.g., Principle 4, Code of Ethics and Professional Responsibility, Certified Financial Planner Board of Standards, Inc.; Rule 1.7, Model Rules of Professional Conduct; Canon 1, Rule 1.3, Code of Professional Responsibility of the Society of Financial Services Professionals; and Rule 102-2, AICPA Code of Professional Conduct.
23. See, e.g., Matter of Hof, 102 A. D. 2d 591 (1984), in which a lawyer was disqualified from representing a co-fiduciary in an arrangement with a step-son where the lawyer had confidential information obtained from his former client, the step-mother, and used it against her to actually go adverse to her interests on behalf of the step-son without a conflicts waiver.
24. See, e.g., *In re Taylor*, 67 SW 3rd 530 (Tex. App. 2002).
25. See, e.g., Rule 1.9, Model Rules of Professional Conduct.
26. Rule 3.7, Model Rules of Professional Conduct; Estate of Goodman, 2009 N.Y. Misc. LEXIS 2445; 241 N.Y.L.J. 102 (N.Y.S.Ct. 2009), in which a lawyer was disqualified from representing a contestant to appointment of a former client as executor where the lawyer also was expected to be a material witness in the matter and had confidential information about the decedent-spouse's estate plan. See also Iowa Bar Ethics Opinion 07-07 (2007).
27. See, e.g., Comment (29) to Rule 1.7, Model Rules of Professional Conduct.
28. 367 S.C. 410; 626 S.E.2d 13 (S.C. App. 2005).
29. 395 S.C. 148, 716 SE 2nd 920 (2011).
30. 16 DB Rptr 114 (2002).
31. See also Oregon State Bar Association Formal Opinion No. 2005-86, which discusses in *re Plinski* in the context of when a lawyer can represent a couple jointly.
32. 94 CH 878 (Ill. 1995).
33. For an interesting article on the ethics issues of working with couples in non-traditional families, see McGrath, Jennifer Tulin, "The Ethical Responsibilities of Estate Planning Attorneys in the Representation of Non-traditional Couples," 27 *Seattle University Law Review* 75 (2003).
34. See, e.g., *Smith v. O'Donnell*, 288 S.W.3d 417 (Tex. 2009), which was a malpractice case brought by the executor of an estate against the law firm that had advised the executor's decedent in his role as executor of his deceased wife's estate. The Texas Supreme Court held that the executor was in privity with the decedent and could bring the malpractice claim against the decedent's lawyer who had advised him as executor for his late wife. At issue was the law firm's advice about characterizing community property as his separate property and, thus, excluding it from his late wife's estate. After the husband surviving spouse died many years later leaving the bulk of his estate to charity, his jilted and obviously unhappy children sued their father's estate and his executor as beneficiaries of their mother's estate for this mischaracterization, who settled their claims for almost $13 million. The Texas Supreme Court allowed the malpractice claim against the law firm to proceed to trial.
35. See, e.g., Section 2-213, Uniform Probate Code.
36. See *Spence v. Wingate*, 395 S.C. 148, 716 SE 2nd 920 (2011) for an example of a situation where the surviving spouse probably had good grounds to set aside the prenuptial agreement, and that agreement was set aside.
37. See, e.g., State Bar of Montana Ethics Opinion 960731.
38. *Id.*
39. See, e.g., Florida Bar Advisory Opinion 95-4 (1997), discussed in Russell, Hollis F., "Joint Representation of Spouses in Estate Planning: The Saga of Advisory Opinion 95-4," 72 *Florida Bar Journal* 39 (1998); and Russell, Hollis F., and Bicks, Peter A., "Multiple Representation in Estate Planning: Beyond Advisory Opinion 95-4, Part 2," 72 *Florida Bar Journal* 78 (1998). See also Georgia Opinion 2003-02. See also North Carolina RPC 229 (1996), where, in a joint representation of a husband and wife in estate planning, a lawyer may not prepare a codicil to the husband's will that adversely impacts the wife-client's interests outside of the wife-client's knowledge or each spouse agreed not to change their estate plans without the consent of the other spouse.
40. ACTEC Commentaries (5th ed. 2015), p. 123. For a case finding that husband and wife in a blended family context were separate estate planning clients of the same law firm, see Leff v. Fulbright & Jaworski, 2009 NY Slip Op. 31445 (Sup. Ct. NY 2009), aff'd, 78 A.D.3d 531 (NY App. 1st Dept. 2010).
41. For a criticism of separate representation of spouses in estate planning, see, e.g., Hazard, Geoffrey C., Jr., "Conflict of Interest in Estate Planning for Husband and Wife," 20 *The Probate Lawyer* 1 (Joseph Trachtman Lecture) (1994).
42. ACTEC Commentaries (5th Ed. 2015), p. 36.
43. But see *Sindell v. Gibson Dunn & Crutcher*, 54 Cal. App. 4th 1457 (1997), which involved a challenge by step-children on behalf of their subsequent spouse parent to an estate plan of their step-father in a blended family context where the spouses were separately represented and a malpractice lawsuit for failure to obtain a waiver of interests in property that seems to have clearly been the husband's separate property.
44. See, e.g., ACTEC Commentaries (5th ed. 2015), p. 102. See, e.g., *Lovett v. Estate of Lovett*, 593 A.2d 382 (N.J. Super. 1991), which involved a malpractice claim against a lawyer in connection with the preparation of a will for a testator who had children by a prior marriage. The lawsuit alleged that the lawyer failed to meet with the husband-testator out of the presence of his second wife, who would receive a share of his estate outright

under the new will rather than in trust for her, and he rescinded a favorable pre-nuptial agreement that would also benefit the subsequent spouse. Even though the court rejected the charges, it stated that, "[i]n most circumstances, meeting with a client alone would be well advised." 593 A.2d at 387.

45. ACTEC Commentaries, p. 102.

46. See, e.g., Florida Advisory Opinions 92-5 and 95-4; District of Columbia Bar Opinion 296; Georgia Opinion 2003-02; and NY State Bar Op. 555.

47. See, e.g., Comment (31) to Rule 1.7, Model Rules of Professional Conduct.

48. See, e.g., Florida Advisory Opinion 95-4.

49. But see ABA Formal Opinion 92-366, which does not permit a "noisy withdrawal" in a situation where the client was using the lawyer's work to perpetuate a fraud but who stopped that activity. In that instance, the lawyer must simply withdraw. However, where the fraud activity is ongoing, the lawyer may exit via a "noisy withdrawal."

50. See, e.g., *In The Matter of The Estate of Vose*, 2017 OK 3, Case Number: 115424 (Okla. Jan. 24, 2017); discussed in Hood, L. Paul, Jr., "At the Intersection of Portability and Blended Families!" *Steve Leimberg's Estate Planning Newsletter* No. 2523 (March 1, 2017; and Law, Lester and Zaritsky, Howard, "Court Forces the Portability Election - Is Pandoras Box Open?" *Steve Leimberg's Estate Planning Newsletter* No. 2513 (Feb. 8, 2017).

PLANNING FOR DIGITAL ASSETS

CHAPTER 69

69.1 INTRODUCTION

Unheard of twenty years ago, digital assets have become ubiquitous in our society and are now in the trillions of dollars. Estate planners must be able to advise clients on planning and administration of these assets. This chapter covers issues relevant to estate planning including:

(1) what digital assets are,

(2) why they must be considered in modern estate planning, and

(3) how best to create such a plan.

Most, if not all, individuals involved in estate planning will own computers, tablets and smart phones and will have established online accounts to manage email and social media presence. Cryptocurrency is no longer fringe – estimates of U.S. adults owning such assets vary from 20-30 million in 2023 and the market cap of the various cryptocurrencies peaked at nearly $3 trillion in late 2021 (www.coinmarketcap.com). The IRS in Notice 2014-21 provided guidance that digital assets are treated as property under the federal tax rules. The various items of information, such as computer programs, emails or digital photographs stored on personal electronic devices or in online accounts are generally known as digital assets, although many more detailed definitions exist, discussed below. Although, like any other asset, these digital assets fall under the authority of a fiduciary, such as an executor or trustee, for testamentary administration, there are a number of factors that complicate their role. First, even though they are stored on tangible media, such as a cell phone, a hard drive, thumb drive or a CD-ROM disk, the digital assets are intangible. That alone would not cause a problem, as many intangible assets, such as securities and intellectual property rights, are commonly planned for and administered by fiduciaries. However, digital assets are frequently held in accounts administered by third-party providers. Those account providers and the user/owner of the digital assets have entered into a contract through the account provider's Terms of Service (TOS) that governs the user's rights of access to the account. The TOS will frequently limit the ability of third parties, including fiduciaries, to access a deceased user's accounts.

When challenged, account providers may vigorously defend their TOS. One of the first publicized incidents dealt with the email account of a deceased twenty-year old marine named Justin Ellsworth.[1] After Justin Ellsworth was killed in Iraq in 2004, his father, John Ellsworth, contacted Yahoo to access Justin's email account to access journal entries and other writings. Yahoo refused the request based on their Terms of Service, which state that Yahoo email accounts are non-transferrable and subject to termination and deletion upon notification of the user's death.[2] Yahoo maintained that notwithstanding John Ellsworth's interest in having his son's personal writings, Yahoo's policy was necessary to maintain the privacy of its users.

The case was reported by major news outlets and John Ellsworth ultimately obtained a court order from the Oakland County, Michigan probate court directing Yahoo to deliver the contents of Justin's email account.[3] Yahoo complied with the order but did not revise their Terms of Service with regard to decedents' accounts.[4]

In a more recent incident, Canadian widow Peggy Bush tried to re-install a non-working game on her iPad, and discovered that her recently deceased husband carried the Apple ID password to his grave.[5] Her daughter reached out to Apple to obtain access to the account and was rebuffed with requests for a death certificate, a copy of the deceased Mr. Bush's will, and finally a court order. Feeling mistreated, Ms. Bush contacted Go Public, an investigative journalism program on the Canadian Broadcasting Channel. Go Public, which carries the slogan "we hold powers that be accountable," contacted Apple. Apple then changed course and worked with the family to allow Ms. Bush access to the Apple ID without obtaining the court order. The story was widely reported and drew criticism for Apple's behavior.

Why do account providers such as Yahoo and Apple fight so hard to keep email accounts and passwords out of the hands of the deceased account holder's loved ones? One reason is that digital assets are subject to decades-old federal and state privacy laws that limit the ability of account providers to disclose certain digital assets to third parties. These laws subject account providers to civil liability and criminal penalties if they improperly disclose that information.

Many civil liberty organizations and like-minded individuals believe that a decedent's digital assets should be provided with greater privacy protection than other assets due to the personal nature and greater expectation of privacy when using a personal computer or surfing the Internet. For those who believe the digital privacy rights of the deceased should be sacrosanct, even with regard to fiduciaries, the right and ability of an executor or successor trustee to access email accounts, online journals or other digital assets is not comforting.

In light of those privacy concerns, there might be another way to view the prior stories of relatives desperately fighting against coldhearted technology companies. For example, it might be that individuals who open Yahoo email accounts expect that Yahoo will uphold the TOS and ensure that the account is deleted upon the user's death. Some people live private lives online, and the idea of a spouse or a parent having access to their private email accounts after death might be completely against their intent and wishes.

One step forward in the clarification and resolution of these issues is the promulgation of the Revised Uniform Fiduciary Access to Digital Assets Act (RUFADAA),[6] which has been drafted by the Uniform Law Commission (ULC). RUFADAA provides rules confirming the rights and authority of fiduciaries over online digital assets as well the ability of accountholders to decide the fate of their online accounts and designate who should have authority over them after death. As of 2023, some version of RUFADAA has been adopted in every state but Louisiana, Oklahoma and Massachusetts (with the latter two having introduced bills).

In light of these issues, estate planners need to inform clients of the laws that govern digital assets and effectively plan for them so that the client's wishes will be carried out in light of the existing and expected future circumstances. Clients should strongly consider whether their durable power of attorney and will should address whether their fiduciary should have access to all such assets pursuant to RUFADAA, or clarify which ones they would not want them to have access to.

69.2 DEFINITION OF DIGITAL ASSETS

The best definition of digital assets depends on the circumstances. The simplest definition is any electronically stored information that holds value. When speaking to clients, especially those who are not particularly interested in or experienced with technology, it can be helpful to define digital assets in terms of examples. Email accounts are a form of digital asset, as well as Facebook or other social media accounts. Data files that contain written work, photographs, videos, songs, games, programs or other information can be found on personal computers, smartphones or external storage devices (like USB sticks). Other, increasingly common examples include digital currency, such as Bitcoin, or digital property held in video games or online virtual worlds, and nonfungible tokens (NFTs). Although tangible personal property can store or display digital assets, devices like computers or iPhones are not digital assets themselves. Also, even though forms of intellectual property can be stored in electronic form, the IP rights themselves are not digital assets (the same way that a physical book is not the same as the copyright over Its contents). For example, if a client leaves "all tangible personal property" to X, this includes a USB drive or computer, but not necessarily any passcodes or rights to other digital property that it may contain.

When constructing a definition of digital assets in a legal document or statute, the definition must be comprehensive and precise so that it encompasses all property rights within the class, but also not so broad as to inadvertently include other property rights that may be subject to conflicting laws. For example, the copyright of a work created in digital form is a separate (and likely more valuable) intangible asset from the electronic data storing the work. The definition also must also continue to be effective as continued innovation will inevitably result in new forms of technology and ownership rights that may have been specifically describable prior to creation. For example, how would it be to draft a definition of digital asset in 1982 that would include a Microsoft Word document on a personal computer, as well as the rights inherent in a user's Instagram account and the contents of a Bitcoin wallet? Finally, the definition should not be so technical that it cannot be understood by individuals without a technological or legal background.

RUFADAA defines a digital asset as "an electronic record in which an individual has a right or interest. The term does not include an underlying asset or liability unless the asset or liability itself is an electronic record."[7] Record is given the same definition as in the Uniform Probate Code:[8] "information that is inscribed on a tangible medium or that is stored in an electronic or other medium and is retrievable in perceivable form."[9] "Electronic" is further defined as "relating to technology having electrical, digital, magnetic, wireless, optical, electromagnetic, or similar capabilities."[10] RUFADAA's definition is crafted to include all present forms of digital assets and those that are invented in the future. In addition, by excluding non-digital underlying assets, the RUFADAA definition avoids encompassing the underlying intellectual property assets that may be stored in digital form. We recommend incorporating or referencing terms in RUFADAA rather than trying to craft your own definition.

69.3 THE IMPORTANCE OF DIGITAL ASSETS

Although the financial value of digital assets is likely to increase as virtual currencies gain prominence, planners should consider what other types of value may exist. Just like personal property, access to digital assets may be important due to emotional or administrative value. Access is also important so that loved ones or fiduciaries may secure a decedent's digital identity from pranksters or hackers.

Financial Value. Individuals surveyed by McAfee in 2011 valued their digital assets at over $35,000 on average, while average Americans valued their individual digital assets at over $54,000.[11] Admittedly, as the McAfee survey showed that personal writings and photographs were valued at over $18,000, it is not clear that this number represents fair market values.[12] However, certain digital assets, such as digital currencies, domain names, book drafts, online seller accounts (such as eBay), and in-game possessions in video games and online worlds can potentially hold real value. Frequent flyer (or hotel or other provider) points can be valuable. Cryptocurrency in particular has become more widespread and peaked at nearly $3 trillion in 2021 and as of August 2023 has still hovered at around $1 trillion (source: www.coinmarketcap.com), even after several high profile recent scandals.

Personal/Emotional Value. Just as family photographs, photo albums and home videos can be highly valued by a decedent's relatives, so can the same information be valued in digital form. Similarly, email archives, social media postings, and online blogs may provide emotional comfort to relatives.

Administrative Value. Digital assets can contain important information for the administration of a decedent's estate or trust. Personal financial spreadsheets, testamentary documents, business plans and lists of phone numbers or email addresses may all be stored in digital form on the decedent's computer or in various online accounts.

Security Value. Although everyone should be aware of the risk of identity theft or having online accounts hacked, the risk is more pronounced for the dead. This is for the simple reason that dead people don't monitor their online accounts and are not aware when an email or social media account is stolen or compromised. In addition to the potential financial loss of an identity theft, it can be painful for friends and relatives to have to encounter a "digital zombie" of the decedent. One publicized incident was when New York Times columnist David Carr's twitter account @carr2n changed its name to Miranda Davis and started sending out tweets that "'she' loved role playing games and sex."[13]

69.4 RULES GOVERNING DIGITAL ASSETS

Access to digital assets is governed by statutes, including federal law and model statutes that may or may not have been adopted by particular states, as well as the terms of service specified by the commercial entities that have provided the services that are used to create and store the assets.

Federal Law

It is important for planners to understand the Federal criminal and civil laws that affect digital assets. Two laws in particular, the Computer Fraud and Abuse Act and the Stored Communications Act pose problems both for fiduciaries who seek to access a decedent's online digital assets, as well as for Internet service providers who have been asked to provide that access.

Computer Fraud and Abuse Act

The Computer Fraud and Abuse Act[14] (CFAA) was originally enacted in the 1980s as an anti-hacking law.[15] The CFAA *criminalizes* access of a "protected computer" without authorization or in a manner that exceeds authorization. The provisions have been defined and interpreted broadly. A protected computer under the CFAA is defined as any computer "which is used in or affecting interstate or foreign commerce or communication"[16] which includes any computer connected to the Internet, cell phones,[17] and, potentially, almost any device with a microchip.[18]

In a strict reading of the law, a fiduciary that accesses a decedent's digital device or online account without sufficient authorization will be in violation of the CFAA. By that same principal, anyone who logs into a spouse's or child's email account has breached the CFAA as well. Thankfully, at least one Circuit so far (the Ninth Circuit) has held that any permission at all is sufficient to meet the authorization requirement under the CFAA.[19] The fiduciary's legal ownership of the decedent's personal property during the administration period should qualify as such permission from the decedent, as long as no specific prohibitions were made by the decedent. Of course, the presence of language specifically authorizing the fiduciary to access digital information (such as specifically authorizing access pursuant to RUFADAA) will provide significantly more comfort.

It is less clear that the fiduciary's powers and duties, or even specific permission granted by the decedent in estate planning documents or otherwise, will be sufficient to protect a fiduciary that uses the decedent's user information and password to access online accounts. While the deceased user may have provided implicit or explicit permission, that may not be sufficient authorization from the account provider's point of view. In the case of providers with TOS that outright prevent password sharing or account transfer, there is an argument that any such access is unauthorized. Accordingly, it is a possibility that violations of the TOS of Internet service providers in the form of unauthorized fiduciary access are accordingly a violation of the CFAA.[20]

The Stored Communications Act

The Stored Communications Act (SCA) was enacted as part of the Electronic Communications Privacy Act of 1986 (ECPA). The SCA, in part, restricts service providers who provide "electronic communications services" and "remote computing services" to the public by releasing information relating to communications maintained in electronic storage.[21] Electronic communication services include "any service which provides to users thereof the ability to send or receive wire or electronic communications."[22] Remote computing services are defined as "the provision to the public of computer storage or processing services by means of an electronic communications system."[23] The definitions of electronic communications services and remote computing services reflect the age of the SCA and bring to light the difficulty of attempting to precisely define and classify an evolving technology at a fixed point in time. Generally, service providers who provide any messaging services (such as email) to the public are providing electronic communication services and remote computing services, and will be subject to the SCA. A work email account provided by one's employer is not considered to be provided to the public, and accordingly, is not protected by the SCA.

The SCA distinguishes the contents of an electronic communication, defined as "information concerning the substance, purport, or meaning of that communication,"[24] and the record of an electronic communication, which is other, non-content related information. For example, the subject line and text of an email would be considered contents of a communication, while the identities of the sender and recipient or the date and time of transmission of the email would be non-content records of that communication. Absent a statutory exception, the SCA prohibits service providers of electronic communication services from disclosing both content and non-content records. There is an exception that mandates providers to disclose both content and non-content records to government entities under certain circumstances,[25] but no exception mandates disclosure of information to non-government recipients.

The available exceptions for voluntary disclosure of content and non-content records are materially different.[26] In the case of non-content records, an exception is met if the disclosure is made to a person other than a government entity, which would include most fiduciaries.[27] For contents of electronic communications, the only relevant exception for fiduciary access is when the user, sender or communication recipient provides lawful consent to the disclosure.[28] If a fiduciary seeks to gain information about the contents of electronic communications contained within a decedent's account, the service provider may not disclose that information unless the decedent account holder has consented to the fiduciary's access or if the fiduciary is deemed to be the user and provides her own lawful consent under the SCA.

The service provider makes the initial determination as to whether a deceased account holder has given the lawful consent needed to release the decedent's account information. As violations of the SCA may lead to civil liability for service providers,[29] those providers may be reluctant to find that consent has been given without having evidence that can be relied upon in good faith. In 2014 a California appellate court held that a court order could not deem a user to have consented to the release of the contents of electronic communications, but when that same user was ordered by the court to directly provide consent to the service provider, and the user complied with the court order to provide express consent, it would be sufficient for the provider to rely on under the SCA.[30] Although the distinction between being deemed to have consented and being ordered to consent may appear slight, this ruling reinforced the requirement that the user, and only the user, must provide express consent to disclosure of the contents of electronic communications under the SCA, even if that consent was provided under duress.

To date, federal law has not definitively held that an executor, trustee or other fiduciary has obtained the consent of the accountholder by virtue of being appointed in that fiduciary position. Scholars have opined that, so long as the fiduciary has been expressly granted the right to access the decedent's accounts by the decedent during her life, the lawful consent exemption has been met.[31]

It is also unclear whether a fiduciary can provide the required consent in a fiduciary capacity. In one case in the Northern District of California, a magistrate judge quashed a subpoena seeking records of a decedent's Facebook account for the period immediately prior to the decedent's death and refused to issue a declaratory judgment that the executors of the decedent's estate may offer consent under the SCA on behalf of the decedent.[32] However, the court provided in dicta that "nothing prevents Facebook from concluding on its own that Applicants have standing to consent on [the decedent's] behalf and providing the requested materials voluntarily."[33]

Uniform and Model Acts

A number of scholars have proposed that the SCA and the CFAA be amended to clarify that any fiduciary is authorized, or, by virtue of appointment has received, the requisite lawful consent (or is able to provide consent), to access or receive information about a decedent's digital assets under the respective laws.[34] Unfortunately, it appears highly unlikely that the necessary political force can be mustered to make such a change. Establishing a uniform law throughout the states is another alternative, and to date two major uniform laws have been drafted and passed in different jurisdictions.

UFADAA and RUFADAA

The Uniform Fiduciary Access to Digital Assets Act (UFADAA), discussed above, was drafted by the Uniform Law Commission, a nonprofit organization that focuses on drafting uniform state laws.[35] After being approved by the Uniform Law Commission in 2014, UFADAA was amended and revised in 2015 (RUFADAA).[36] According to the Uniform Law Commission, UFADAA was revised to address the concerns of Internet-based businesses and privacy advocates who opposed enactment of the act in various states.[37] UFADAA was enacted in Delaware in 2014 and, as of August 2023, RUFADAA has been enacted in every state but Louisiana, Oklahoma and Massachusetts (with the latter state having introduced a bill).[38]

Both UFADAA and RUFADAA provide a comprehensive solution to the uncertainty surrounding a fiduciary's right to access digital assets. The Acts grant rights to four classes of fiduciaries: personal representatives, trustees of a living trust, conservators, and agents acting under a durable power of attorney.[39] Generally speaking, UFADAA was drafted with the philosophy that a digital asset is no different from a non-digital asset for purposes of fiduciary access and control, and establishes a series of specific rules and procedures that put the fiduciary into the shoes of the user who established the fiduciary relationship. UFADAA was the approach favored by most estate planning professionals seeking to facilitate fiduciary access to the digital assets of a decedent or disabled person.

UFADAA grants each type of fiduciary the right to access all contents, electronic communications, the catalog of electronic communications sent or received, and any other digital asset in which the user held an interest.[40] However, the extent of the access is different for each different type of fiduciary. Personal representatives have access to digital assets by virtue of their fiduciary role, limited only by the provisions of the will or an order of the probate court.[41] Trustees have similar default access limited only by the terms of the trust or court order.[42] Conservators must be specifically authorized by court order to have rights of access.[43] And an agent-in-fact must be *specifically* granted the authority to access digital assets by the principal giving the power of attorney.[44]

Under RUFADAA, the prior grant of full fiduciary access to the user's account has been modified so that a custodian of digital assets, which includes a provider of electronic communication services or remote computing services may instead choose how to disclose the user's digital assets to a fiduciary, either by granting full access to the user's account, granting partial access to the user's account or by providing copy of the digital assets contained in the user's account.[45] These changes were likely made to allay custodians' concerns that under UFADAA they would be forced to allow a fiduciary unrestricted access to a user's account. In addition, under RUFADAA, in order to receive disclosure of the contents of a user's electronic communications, a fiduciary must show that the user expressly consented to that disclosure.[46] This is an extremely important difference from the presumption under UFADAA that a fiduciary, by nature of the fiduciary role, has the consent of the user.[47] Under RUFADAA a user can express consent to disclosure of digital assets to a fiduciary (or deny disclosure) by using an online tool within the account application itself, such as Google's Inactive Account Manager or Faceboo"s Legacy Contact (both discussed below).[48] If the user has not taken advantage of an online tool, or the account does not have that feature, then the user can grant consent to disclosure in a written document, including a will, trust or power of attorney.[49] If the user has not used an online tool and has not explicitly granted content to fiduciary disclosure through estate planning documents or otherwise, the fiduciary's right to access digital assets held by a custodian will be governed by the custodian's TOS.[50]

If the custodian's TOS does not provide for disclosure to fiduciaries, the fiduciary may still seek disclosure of digital assets other than the content of a user's electronic communications.[51] Because the contents of electronic communications – e.g., the body and subject of emails, are likely to be the most important digital assets for administrative purposes, it is important that users who desire such disclosure clearly express their consent either through an online tool or in their estate planning documents.

RUFADAA also granted providers the right to obtain a court order or require a fiduciary to obtain a court order finding that the account in question belongs to the user, that consent to the disclosure has been provided or any other factual finding required by law to facilitate the disclosure.[52]

Both UFADAA and RUFADAA confirm that a fiduciary that has access to an account is subject to any relevant TOS or applicable law, including copyright law.[53] And both Acts confirm that the fiduciary is an authorized user of the account for CFAA purposes and otherwise has the right to access any digital asset not subject to the SCA.[54] These provisions should allow fiduciaries to comfortably administer digital assets without fear of criminal or civil liability provided that they are acting within the limits of their duties.

PEAC

The Privacy Expectation Afterlife and Choices (PEAC) model act was offered as an alternative to UFADAA and RUFADAA and has been promoted by NetChoice, "a trade association of eCommerce businesses and online consumers all of whom share the goal of promoting convenience, choice and commerce on the net."[55] Netchoice members included eBay, Facebook, Google, Overstock.com, Lyft, and Yahoo.[56] PEAC, in its model form, differs substantially from UFADAA and RUFADAA. Rather than confirming rights of access or disclosure for different classes of fiduciaries like UFADAA or RUFADAA, PEAC establishes a judicial procedure to obtain a court order for access to digital assets in the probate court having jurisdiction over a decedent's estate.[57] PEAC only provides access rights to personal representatives who have obtained a court order by satisfying the act's numerous requirements. PEAC only became law in Virginia,[58] but it was repealed in 2017 and replaced with RUFADAA.[59] Thus, we mention PEAC only for background to understand industry lobbying and concerns– RUFADAA is now by far the dominant law and PEAC is more of a historical footnote.

Service Providers' Terms of Service

Although Terms of Service (TOS) are not laws, but terms of a contract between the provider and user, the TOS factor into how the following laws are interpreted and enforced with regard to online accounts. Generally, the relationship between users and service providers are governed primarily by the TOS set forth by the provider. A user will agree to the TOS when the account is established, typically by clicking on the link that indicates consent to the TOS, or what is often referred to as a "clickwrap agreement," and that agreement will be reconfirmed from time to time during the course of use of the provider's services. Relevant to planning for digital assets, many providers' TOS prohibit users from sharing passwords or otherwise allowing third parties to access their accounts. These TOS will change from time to time and the summaries below may become out of date, so it is best to consult those anew (not to mention that new providers and programs such as TikTok or Threads may appear and disappear on the scene). That said, here are a few:

Facebook

Facebook reserves the right to stop providing services to any accountholder who violates the TOS "in letter or spirit," and instructs users that: "[y]ou will not share your password … let anyone else access your account, or do anything else that might jeopardize the security of your account" and that "[y]ou will not transfer your account … to anyone without first getting our written permission."[60]

Providing the password of an account to a fiduciary, even if done in a will or letter of wishes, would violate the letter of Facebook's TOS, which could result in Facebook closing the account upon discovery.[61] If the fiduciary accesses the account using the user's password without notifying the provider, that fiduciary may also be in violation of the Computer Fraud and Abuse Act,[62] a federal criminal statute discussed below. The transfer of a Facebook account to a trustee or a beneficiary would also violate the TOS.

Facebook also has a "Legacy Contact" feature (described below) which allows a user to designate a person to access and have control over the user's account, is considered an "online tool" under RUFADAA, for purposes of granting consent to that access.

Google

Google's TOS do not specifically prohibit password sharing, but instructs users to "keep your password confidential," and reserves the right to "stop providing Services to [the user], or add or create new limits to our Services at any time."[63] Although not presented as a consequence of password sharing or account transfer, Google would be within its rights to terminate any account of a decedent upon learning that the account has been accessed following that user's death. Google's "Inactive Account Manager" (described below) that can be useful for estate planning purposes.

Yahoo

Yahoo's TOS provide that "your Yahoo account is non-transferable and any rights to your Yahoo ID or contents within your account terminate upon your death. Upon receipt [by Yahoo] of a copy of a death certificate, your account may be terminated and all contents therein permanently deleted."[64] Although this termination would be subject to the thirty days' notice restriction discussed above, such notice would not provide much use to a fiduciary who, unable to access a deceased user's Yahoo email account, notified Yahoo of the user's death and requested access to the contents of the account, only to discover that no access would be granted and the account would be deleted in thirty days.

69.5 PREPARING AN ESTATE PLAN FOR DIGITAL ASSETS

Assuming that UFADAA is dead and RUFADAA, or a variation of it, will eventually be the governing law of all states, it is incumbent upon advisors to help clients take digital assets into account while preparing an estate plan. Preparing a plan for a client's digital assets can be organized in the following steps:

1. Identify digital assets.

2. Name a digital fiduciary and grant that fiduciary the necessary powers to lawfully access digital assets.

3. Prepare instructions to accomplish the decedent's intent regarding digital assets.

Step One: Identification of Digital Assets

As many clients may not understand the importance of planning for digital assets, it a good idea to explain some of the risks of failing to plan for digital assets, and some of the benefits of planning. Namely that planning will allow them to decide which accounts and other assets are shared with family members or other individuals (or are deleted), planning will also allow them to name a separate individual to act as fiduciary over digital assets, and that if they fail to plan, it may be impossible for any fiduciary or other individual to ever have postmortem access or receive disclosure of the decedent's digital assets.

Similarly to planning for any other form of assets, it is important to find out what digital assets the client owns. Generally, the best way to do this is to ask the client. Most planners will either do this through a conversation or through a written questionnaire. As most people have not taken inventory or prepared a balance sheet of their digital assets, it may be most helpful to engage in an interview where the client is guided through a systematic series of questions. The following questions may provide a starting point for your conversation:

- *Do you own one or more personal computers?*

- *What important information is stored on your computers?* This might include personal writings, photographs, videos, and financial or other business-related information.

- *How and where is the information stored on your computers?* Some computer users may have complex and difficult to navigate systems of folders or drives with unhelpfully named files. Clients may be prompted to reconsider their data organization, if only to make it easier for their loved ones or fiduciaries to access the data after their death.

- *How can the computers, certain applications, and files be accessed?* Are they password-protected? Clients may have information that cannot be accessed without appropriate passwords. For instance, multi-user computers (such as a shared family computer) may have files, folders or user profiles that are password protected.

- *What other digital devices do you have?* Smartphones and tablets are common digital devices. Any passwords should be listed, and the above questions regarding information and how to access that information are also appropriate.

- *Do you store any data in physical storage mediums such as CDs or backup hard drives?* Although modern computer hard drive space continues to expand in space and reduce in price, some people may use CDs, DVDs, flash memory stick drives, external hard drives or other storage devices to store data. These need to be played by or attached to a computer to access the data stored within.

- *What email and other online accounts do you have?* Common online accounts include email accounts, social media and networking sites, and online bank and brokerage accounts. For each account usernames, passwords and personal verification questions necessary to access them should be listed.

- *What financial accounts do you primarily access online?* Bank, brokerage or other account statements and tax forms may be emailed or accessed through websites. Banks often encourage account holders to communicate with them exclusively through online methods instead of paper statements and other communications. This means that a family member acting as agent/executor/trustee collecting only "snail mail" after death may never receive notice of such accounts.

- *What bills do you pay online?* Utility or other bills may be emailed or paid automatically through the provider's website.

- *Do you use cloud storage accounts?* Cloud storage is the use of third party storage space over multiple servers managed by the hosting company. The data typically can be accessed by the user through any computer or other device, allowing efficient use of local storage space.

- *Do you own any websites or domains names?* Domain names and the websites associated with them can be potentially valuable assets. Generally the owner of a domain has the right to renew ownership on an annual basis for a nominal fee.

- *Do you own any bitcoins or other digital currency?* Digital currency is a medium of exchange that is not regulated by any government. It exists in digital form and is not tied to a specific market. Bitcoin is the most common digital currency, and it keeps track of ownership and transfer through a public ledger known as blockchain, but there are literally thousands of other cryptocurrencies now and ownership has become more widespread.[65]

Step Two: Naming and Authorizing a Digital Fiduciary

Any comprehensive estate plan that covers digital assets should include consideration as to who will be the digital fiduciary that has the right to access and manage digital assets and accounts on behalf of the decedent.

This may very often be the same party who is named as executor or other fiduciary, or may be a separate person who is appointed solely to manage the digital assets. It is not uncommon to name a corporate trustee to be administrative trustee and manage publicly traded stocks and bonds, but appoint an investment manager and have that trustee be directed for unique assets such as real estate, closely held businesses or increasingly common now, assets such as cryptocurrency. In either case, the person who will act as digital fiduciary should be familiar with modern technology, discreet, and able to seek help or hire consultants in situations that require additional technical skills or knowledge. If the digital fiduciary will be the same person as the "regular" fiduciary, then administration of digital assets will be conducted along the rest of the decedent's property.

Because of the CFAA, the SCA and other laws that may increase a fiduciary's liability or impede a fiduciary's access to digital assets, it is important that the digital fiduciary be granted sufficient authority to carry out its duties. For this reason, the will, trust or other document appointing the digital fiduciary should grant specific authority to access and inspect any online accounts, computers, hard drives or other electronic devices that store digital information. It should also be clear that the decedent has granted consent to the disclosure of electronic communications and the contents of electronic communications to the fiduciary under the SCA. Under RUFADAA, discussed above, unless the user consents to disclosure of electronic communications to a fiduciary through the use of an online tool or in estate planning documents (or other written records), the fiduciary will find it very difficult, and likely impossible, to access those digital assets.

Step Three: Preparing Instructions to Accomplish the Decedent's Intent

It follows naturally that after discussing a client's collection of digital assets, it is a good idea to find out what the client would like to happen to them after death. In many cases, digital assets will be treated the same way as the client's personal effects – left to a spouse or other family members. As mentioned above, some individuals consider online or computer-based activities to be inherently private and may not wish to have their online lives examined after death. For this reason, it is important to discuss whether or not the client is comfortable with a fiduciary having access to or receiving disclosure of digital assets.

Instructions to a digital fiduciary should indicate the decedent's intent regarding each digital asset or class of digital assets, if applicable, as well as the means to accomplish that intent. This may be best included in a letter of wishes, rather than in a will or trust to allow the fiduciary more flexibility under unexpected circumstances.

Many digital files or accounts, such as online journals, personal emails to loved ones, digital photographs or videos, contain personal information that a decedent may or may not want to share with others. In that case, it is important to specify who should receive copies of or otherwise have access to those digital assets. Similarly, if there are potentially embarrassing digital assets, the digital fiduciary might be instructed to delete or sanitize those files or accounts prior to sharing them with beneficiaries and other loved ones. If the digital fiduciary is someone other than the decedent's executor, personal representative or trustee, the instructions should include information on how to contact the person appointed as executor, personal representative or trustee, and should explicitly instruct the digital fiduciary to share the necessary information.

Some account providers have established online tools that allow a user to set what will happen to the account following that user's death or extended inactivity. These tools are covered by the provider's TOS and may be modified or removed at the provider's discretion. To the extent that a client has an account with Apple, Google or Facebook, the client should take advantage of the in-application legacy access services provided for those platforms. Sometimes a client may wish to authorize their fiduciary to have general access to their digital assets but restrict or completely prevent access to certain email or social media accounts.

Google Inactive Account Manager

Google's Inactive Account Manager[66] is a service that allows a user to set one or more trusted contacts that will be automatically notified by Google if the original user's account becomes inactive. The user may establish the length of time (a "timeout period") after which her account is deemed inactive, and may set the rights granted to the trusted contacts. Alternatively, the user may instruct that the account be deleted after it becomes inactive. The user may change the settings at any time and as many times as the user likes. The individuals designated as trusted contacts will not be notified until the user's account becomes inactive.

Facebook Legacy Contact

Facebook allows a user to choose a legacy contact for the user's account.[67] Upon Facebook being notified of the user's death, the legacy contact may be granted the right to download an archive of the information the user shared on Facebook, but not the user's private messages. The user may choose to have her profile deleted automatically, or to allow the legacy contact to manage the deceased user's account as a memorial page with limited rights.

Under RUFADAA, a decision made using an online tool will supersede contrary language in that user's estate planning documents. For example, if the user indicates that on her death, the account should be deleted and not disclosed to any fiduciary, those instructions will be binding on the account custodian. Even if the user's will states that her executor should receive disclosure, the instructions in the online tool will trump. Because of the relative importance of instructions given through online tools, it is likely that other internet service providers will release in-application options for posthumous access going forward. It is also important for clients to understand how online tools fit into their estate plans, and for the planner to coordinate the use of online tools with traditional estate planning documents. It is likely that over time other Internet service providers will release online tools to grant or deny consent to posthumous access or disclosure.

Handling Passwords

Online accounts are almost always protected by password. In addition, information on computers, smartphones tablets, and other physical storage mediums may be encrypted and require a password for access. Although many people memorize passwords for security and ease of use, this does not provide much help for anyone else after the accountholder or owner's death. For planning purposes, clients should keep a list of all relevant passwords so a fiduciary or family member can access accounts or encrypted files. If the client does not trust giving the family member such information now, should they trust them to manage their assets in the event of incapacity or death? It is important to remember that under a service provider's TOS and the CFAA, described above, if a fiduciary or family accesses an account without authorization, it may be in breach of the terms of service of the account provider, and more seriously, in violation of federal or civil data protection laws. Before advising a client to use a password to access someone else's account, be sure you understand the potential consequences of that action.

Writing down a list of passwords does raise the risk that someone else might discover it and access the protected account or device. This risk can be mitigated by keeping the list in a place that is safe, but that will be found by a fiduciary or family member after death or incapacity.

It is a bad idea to keep a list of passwords in a formal estate planning document, such as a will or trust. Those documents may be subject to public inspection or otherwise shown to third parties which would expose the decedent's passwords.

A client should update the password list as their passwords change. In the past, computer security experts recommended frequent password changes for security reasons and many account providers or programs suggest or mandate password changes at regular intervals. However, frequent password changes may not actually provide any security benefit when only minor changes are made (i.e. "password8" to "password9").

One alternative is to create a text file or spreadsheet that contains a list of accounts or files and the corresponding passwords. This digital password list would in turn be password protected and that password could be stored in a safe place or given to a trusted individual.

There are many services, both free and fee-based, that maintain a digital list of passwords and will automatically fill in forms for the corresponding online accounts. Again, a single password is used to access the electronic password service. This may be an appealing option for clients who are unlikely to maintain a list of passwords on their own initiative, as the program will automatically store new passwords and note password changes as they happen. Examples of these services include PasswordCaptain, RoboForm, PasswordSafe, Keepass, and LastPass. Browsers increasing include password-saving features as well.

Sample Language

The following sample language uses a broad definition of digital assets and references both the CFAA and the SCA. If RUFADAA or another law governing fiduciary access to digital assets has been enacted in your state, that law should be referenced as well.

> I hereby grant my [trustee / personal representative / executor / digital fiduciary] maximum powers under federal and state law to access, use, share, and control any "Digital Asset" (meaning any electronic communication and its contents or other electronic or digital information however created or stored) that I owned or could have accessed immediately before my death, and I grant my express consent under the Stored Communications Act of 1986, the Computer Fraud and Abuse Act of 1986 and all other state and federal data privacy and criminal laws to allow the [trustee / personal representative / executor / digital fiduciary] to exercise such powers over any Digital Asset.

69.6 ADMINISTRATION OF DIGITAL ASSETS AFTER DEATH

In the administration of a decedent's estate or revocable trust, a fiduciary will be responsible for preparing an inventory of assets, valuing the assets for estate tax purposes and ultimately distributing them to the appropriate beneficiaries. During this process, the fiduciary will be obligated to preserve the value of the estate.

Preparing an Inventory of Digital Assets

To administer an estate consisting of traditional, non-digital assets, a fiduciary typically prepares an initial inventory by carefully sorting through the decedent's paper files. During the first few months following the death, the decedent's mail may provide the fiduciary with information about bank and brokerage accounts or other assets. A thorough search through the decedent's house or apartment may yield personal items and contact information for the decedent's friends and relatives. Once the decedent's financial accounts were identified, a trip to the bank with letters testamentary or a trust certification would be sufficient to gain control of those accounts. Preparing an inventory of digital assets may provide more difficult depending on how much planning the decedent has done and the level of complexity or disorganization in the digital estate. A good first step is to look for any lists of digital assets prepared during the estate planning process. Most individuals do not have such a list. Equally important is a list of passwords, which the decedent may have prepared. Search paper files as well as the decedent's personal computer (assuming you can get in), and any storage or other devices. It is important to prepare a record of digital files discovered – even if the files are likely to have little monetary value, they may contain photographs or other emotionally important items.

A decedent's spreadsheets and financial software can provide information on accounts, investments, debts and businesses of the decedent. Microsoft Excel, TurboTax, Quicken and QuickBooks are examples of these programs.

Searching the decedent's name with an online search engine (such as Google or Yahoo) may discover blogs and other accounts held by the decedent. If the fiduciary has access to the decedent's email account, this will frequently lead to other accounts (such as Facebook or other social media accounts), as an email address is usually tied to non-email accounts. Electronic bank statements or notices of statement availability will generally be emailed. Similarly, if the decedent had signed up for paperless billing, those might be found in the email account. If the digital fiduciary is not also the decedent's personal representative, then the bills should be passed along to the person responsible for paying the decedent's debts.

Accessing Secure or Encrypted Digital Assets

Many individuals may have encrypted digital assets requiring passwords or other means to access them. Without the password, a digital fiduciary may have a difficult time identifying, transferring or otherwise accessing the secure or encrypted asset. Modern encryption technology is sophisticated enough to render encrypted assets essentially inaccessible. However, not all password protected assets are so strongly encrypted.[68] It may be necessary to hire a professional security consultant to analyze and hopefully overcome the encryption. If the decedent did not leave a password list, a digital fiduciary may be able to find clues on a decedent's home computer or smartphone.

Accessing Online Accounts

Generally, if the online account's terms of service do not mandate immediate deletion of the account, the digital fiduciary will be able to gain access or have the contents of the account disclosure to them by directly contacting the account provider and verifying that the decedent consented to the fiduciary having such access. Each account provider has its own terms of service and policies covering third party access to a user's account. The digital fiduciary should carefully review all policies of the service provider, or consult with an expert for advice. Policies governing third-party access can often be found online or in the Licensing or Use Agreement.

If the decedent's state has enacted a law based on RUFADAA, and the digital fiduciary has been explicitly granted consent to access through the decedent's estate planning or other documents, then the process should be relatively straightforward. The digital fiduciary's first step should be to contact the account provider with a request for disclosure of the contents of the electronic communications of the decedent, along with a copy of the decedent's death certificate, evidence of the digital fiduciary's appointment, and evidence of the decedent's consent to the disclosure of such contents to the fiduciary.[69] In many cases, a copy of the decedent's will or revocable trust will provide sufficient evidence of consent.

If the account provider specifically requests it, the fiduciary may also need to provide information linking the account to the decedent, identifying information about the account (such as a username), and a court order finding that:

1. the decedent had an account with the provider;
2. the disclosure of such communications would not violate the SCA;
3. the decedent consented to disclosure; and
4. the disclosure is necessary to the administration of the decedent's estate.[70]

It is anticipated that the account provider would only make these additional requests in cases when it was not clear that the decedent consented to the disclosure, or there is some other issue with the fiduciary's request, as having to obtain a court order will present an additional delay and expense in accessing the decedent's digital assets.

Under RUFADAA, the decedent's use of an online tool (such as Google's inactive account manager) will take priority over any contrary expression in estate planning documents, the provider's TOS, or any other documents.[71] In that case, the fiduciary or other person named in the online tool may be contacted directly by the provider through the tool, or the fiduciary can present evidence of the decedent's use of the tool when contacting the fiduciary.

In cases where the digital fiduciary may not have been granted explicit consent by the decedent to receive disclosure of the contents of the decedent's electronic communication, the digital fiduciary will still be able to receive disclosure of non-content information, also known as the catalogue of the decedent's electronic communications. The catalogue of electronic communications will not contain any information from the body or subject line of the emails or other communications, but will state the sender and recipient of the communication and the date and time when it was sent. This list of communications could be used by the digital fiduciary to determine who the decedent communicated with, and in cases where regular communications were received by financial institutions or other senders, it might provide a lead towards finding additional assets.

To receive disclosure of a decedent's catalogue of electronic communications or any digital asset other than the content of electronic communications, the fiduciary should provide the account provider with a written request for disclosure, a copy of the decedent's death certificate, a copy of an instrument showing the fiduciary's authority, information identifying the decedent's account and linking the account to the user, and an affidavit or court order stating that the disclosure of the information is necessary for the administration of the decedent's estate.[72]

69.7 PRESERVING (AND DISPOSING OF) DIGITAL ASSETS

During the course of administration, a digital fiduciary should take all steps necessary to ensure that the digital assets will continue to be in existence through the period of administration, probate or other necessary time period.

- **Electronic Devices.** Generally, a digital fiduciary should be very cautious when handling a decedent's electronic devices. Care should be taken in turning on unfamiliar computers or smartphones. Although rare, it is possible that the device may be damaged or memory erased upon start up if the device was physically damaged, exposed to water or static electricity, or had undergone some other unfortunate event since it was last used. If there is any suspicion that a device has been damaged or mistreated, it is a justified expense to hire a professional consultant to examine the device to determine whether it is safe for use prior to turning it on. CDs and DVDs can be scratched or broken, and jump drives can be broken or otherwise rendered unusable. All items carrying digital information should be carefully stored in a protective case and in an environment recommended by the manufacturer. A digital fiduciary should consider copying any potentially valuable digital information to a separate back-up location kept separately from the original, so that even if the original source is damaged or lost, the information is still available.

- **Accessing Online Accounts.** If the digital fiduciary attempts to access online accounts by guessing the password, which is not recommended, those accounts may be locked or deleted if multiple unsuccessful attempts are made. A plan of access should be established prior to actually accessing the account. Furthermore, some online accounts may be deleted automatically after a certain passage of time without access, or upon receipt of information indicating that the account holder is deceased. If it is possible that a failure to timely access the account may risk loss of data, the fiduciary will have to weigh the risks of premature access against the risks of a long delay.

- **Intellectual Property Assets.** Intellectual property rights such as copyrights and trademarks relating to digital assets should be monitored and protected. There are procedures under the Digital Millennium Copyright Act of 1998 that allow an individual (or their fiduciary) to protect against the unauthorized use of intellectual property by serving a "takedown notice" to the online service provider that is publishing the unauthorized material.[73] If the alleged infringer immediately removes the unauthorized material, their liability for any copyright infringement is limited.[74] Further legal action (beyond the scope of these materials) may be necessary if the infringing service provider does not remove the unauthorized material.

  For certain copyrighted works, a person's heirs (and not the digital fiduciary) may have legal rights to terminate the person's lifetime copyright transfers or licenses following a certain number of years. These rights can be used, for instance, to renegotiate a publishing contract years after a book was written, especially if the publishing rights have increased in value over that time period.

- **Online Sales Accounts.** If the digital fiduciary is aware of any online sales account maintained by the decedent, such as those on websites such as eBay, Amazon or Craigslist, the digital fiduciary will need to decide whether the online sales business can be continued after the decedent's death. The digital fiduciary should look for any information relating to online sales that had not yet been completed at the time of the decedent's death. Records may include email or text message alerts about recent sales, bank statement or online payment accounts (such as PayPal) for deposits from recent sale transactions. The digital fiduciary should also consider temporarily suspending any further transactions until he or she understands the business and determines the feasibility of continuing to sell products online. Finally, the digital fiduciary should research whether the online sales account may be transferrable. The digital fiduciary must look not only at the relevant user agreement, but also at whether a potential buyer could be located.

Valuing Digital Assets

The digital fiduciary will need to ascertain which, if any, of the decedent's digital assets must be reported on the decedent's federal estate tax return or included on a probate inventory or trust accounting. Digital assets with monetary value must be reported for federal estate tax purposes at their fair market value; "the price at which the property would change hands between a willing buyer and a willing seller, neither being under any compulsion to buy or to sell and both having reasonable knowledge of relevant facts."[75] Examples of valuing specific digital assets include:

- **Digital Currencies.** Most digital currencies are traded through online over-the-counter exchanges, and the historic exchange rate can be found for any date. Exchange rates for digital currencies have fluctuated wildly over the past few years. Unfortunately, simply pulling a value off of one of the various exchanges may not be sufficient for estate, gift or income tax purposes when it's necessary to determine the "fair market value" of a gift or bequest. In the charitable context, a donor is required to obtain a *qualified appraisal* for any asset with a value in excess of $5,000. A gift in excess of this amount also requires the donor to file Form 8283, Noncash Charitable Contributions with the taxpayer's Form 1040, signed by the recipient organization and the qualified appraiser for assets other than cash and qualified appreciated stock contributions over the $5,000 threshold.

- **Domain Names.** Valuable domain names are sold via brokers, who also offer appraisal services. Well-known companies in this field include Afternic or Sedo.

- **Non-Transferable Digital Assets.** To the extent that an online account, license or other digital asset is not transferable and essentially terminates after a person's death, there should be very little or no value for federal estate tax purposes. For example, a decedent has no right to transfer books in his or her Amazon Kindle library, or music on an Apple device, and thus there should be no value to that library (regardless of its size).[76]

- **Personal Emails and Blogs.** Personal assets, such as emails or blogs, will often have little or no value unless the decedent was a celebrity or someone who might inspire people to pay for their otherwise mundane ideas and opinions. Even for celebrities or well-known bloggers, the value of a blog will often evaporate after the person's death. If there is ongoing advertising revenue, the estimated cash flow can be used to establish value.

Disposing of Digital Assets

Ultimately, the digital fiduciary will need to dispose of the decedent's digital assets. This commonly involves distributing them to beneficiaries or deleting or otherwise destroying the digital assets for privacy reasons. The digital fiduciary may also be in the best position to dispose of certain items of tangible personal property holding digital assets, such as computers, hard drives, tablets or smartphones. In that case, the digital fiduciary should be sure to comply with the decedent's instructions regarding the deletion of any data that may be private or embarrassing to the decedent. Securely purging data may require overwriting all of the stored data several times to ensure that it no longer remains in the account or on the computer, hard drive, tablet or smartphone.

If the digital fiduciary has gained access to one or more online accounts, those accounts will ultimately need to be closed at the end of the administration. Generally, the terms of service for most online accounts prohibit transfer to other individuals. However, it is possible that in the future the terms of service may be changed, or a mechanism for transfer could be created by statute or judicial action and in that case, the digital fiduciary would be able to transfer the accounts to beneficiaries.

69.8 CONCLUSION

Planning for digital assets is still evolving. RUFADAA helps provide a framework and solution for many instances and in most states, but there are still likely to be gaps and questions arise. In light of this, a cautious approach is best. Clients should be educated as to the importance of digital assets in their estate plans, and they should understand the importance of granting consent to disclosure in their estate plans. It is incumbent on estate planners to follow developments in this field both on a state and federal level, as best practices may change in the coming years. Finally, it is expected that many planners will begin including language consenting to disclosure to fiduciaries (often referencing RUFADAA) in their standard durable power of attorney, will and trust forms. When doing this, it is important that clients be explicitly notified of these provisions, as some individuals will inevitably prefer that some of their digital assets die with them.

CHAPTER ENDNOTES

1. www.cnet.com/news/yahoo-denies-family-access-to-dead-marines-e-mail/.
2. yahoo.com/us/en/yahoo/terms/utos/.
3. www.cnet.com/news/yahoo-releases-e-mail-of-deceased-marine.
4. *Id.*
5. Marchitelli, Rosa, "Apple demands widow get court order to access dead husband's password." CBC News January 18, 2016. www.cbc.ca/news/business/apple-wants-court-order-to-give-access-to-appleid-1.3405652.
6. Revised U. Fiduciary Access to Digital Assets Act (hereinafter RUFADAA).
7. *Id.* at §2(10).
8. Unif. Prob. Code (2010).
9. *Id.* at §1-201(41) (2010); RUFADAA, §2(22).
10. *Id.*
11. *How Do Your Digital Assets Compare?* (May 14, 2013) blogs.mcafee.com/consumer/digital-assets (as of Jun. 14, 2015); *McAfee Reveals Average Global Internet User Owns More Than $37,000 in Underprotected 'Digital Assets'* (Sep. 27, 2011), www.photoxels.com/mcafee-survey-reveals-we-have-about-37k-of-unprotected-digital-assets (as of Jun. 14, 2015).
12. *Id.*
13. Ohlheiser, Abby "A Question we never thought we would have to ask after someone dies," *The Washington Post*, May 20, 2016. www.washingtonpost.com/news/the-intersect/wp/2016/05/20/what-happens-when-a-deceased-persons-twitter-account-starts-posting-spam.
14. 18 U.S.C. §1030.
15. The CFAA was initially enacted in 1986 as an amendment to 18 U.S.C. §1030 with a limited scope and has since been revised and expanded numerous times resulting in the present law. See generally Kerr, *Vagueness Challenges to the Computer Fraud and Abuse Act*, 94 Minn. L. Rev. 1561 (2010).
16. 18 U.S.C. §1030I(2).
17. *United States v. Kramer*, 631 F.3d 900 (8th Cir. 2011) (holding that a cell phone used only to place calls and send text messages is a protected computer for purposes of applying sentencing enhancements).
18. Kerr, *supra*, at p. 1571 (arguing that the CFFA as interpreted deems any computer to be a protected computer, and that anything with a microchip except a portable hand held calculator meets a definition of a computer under the CFFA).
19. *Id.* at p. 400, citing *LVRC Holdings LLC v. Brekka*, 581 F.3d 1127, 1132-33 (9th Cir. 2009).
20. *Id.* at p. 401 (2014).
21. 18 U.S.C. §§2701-2712. For those interested in learning more about the SCA, Oren S. Kerr's article: *A User's Guide to the Stored Communications Act, and a Legislator's Guide to Amending It* (2004) 72 Geo. Wash. L. Rev. 1208 provides a surprisingly readable primer about this otherwise dense and confusing topic. The article summarizes the SCA and includes suggestions as to how and why it should be changed in light of technological developments and (in Mr. Kerr's opinion) judicial misunderstandings of technology and the SCA.
22. 18 U.S.C. §2510(15).
23. 18 U.S.C. §2711(2).
24. 18 U.S.C. §2510(8)
25. 18 U.S.C. §2703.
26. 18 U.S.C. §2702.
27. 18 U.S.C. §2702(c)(6) ("A provider … may divulge a record or other information pertaining to a subscriber to or customer of such service (not including the contents of communications…) to any person other than a governmental entity").
28. 18 U.S.C. §2702(b)(3) ("a provider … may divulge the contents of a communication … with the lawful consent of the originator or an addressee or intended recipient of such communication, or the subscriber in the case of remote computing service").
29. 18 U.S.C. §2707 (allowing third parties to bring civil actions for violations of the SCA and including provisions for punitive damages in the case of willful or intentional conduct).
30. *Negro v. Superior Court of Santa Clara County*, No. H040146 (Santa Clara Cty. Super. Ct., No. 1-13-CV239634, Oct. 21, 2014).
31. Naomi Cahn, *Probate Law Meets the Digital Age*, 67 Vand. L. Rev 1697, 1711 (2014) ("when a testamentary instrument includes explicit consent [to the fiduciary's access to the decedent's digital assets], then a fiduciary's access should pose no problem under the SCA") (hereinafter *Cahn*).
32. *In re Facebook, Inc.*, 923 F. Supp. 2d 1204 (N.D. Cal. 2013).
33. *Id.*
34. *Digital Death Conundrum*, at pp. 413-414 (as to the SCA: "the SCA could be amended by augmenting [section] 2711 to define 'lawful consent,' thereby eliminating any question about whether or not lawful consent is satisfied through state laws governing fiduciary fields." And as to the CFAA: "Likewise the CFA could be amended by augmenting [section] 1030(e) to define 'authorization,' eliminating any question about whether authorization is satisfied by fiduciary appointments governed under state law."). Cahn, *supra*, at pp. 1719-1720 (as to the SCA: "The legislative fix would be simple: add "or state-recognized fiduciary" to the list of those who can provide lawful consent for disclosure").
35. Fiduciary Access to Digital Assets Act - Uniform Law Commission (uniformlaws.org).
36. Revised Uniform Fiduciary Access to Digital Assets Act (2015) (hereinafter RUFADAA).

37. Proposed Changes to the Uniform Fiduciary Access to Digital Assets Act. On file with author.
38. The ULC maintains a list of states that have introduced and enacted RUFDADAA each year at www.uniformlaws.org.
39. UFADAA §3.
40. UFADAA §§4-7.
41. UFADAA §4.
42. UFADAA §7.
43. UFADAA §5.
44. UFADAA §6.
45. RUFADAA §6.
46. RUFADAA §7.
47. UFADAA §8.
48. RUFADAA §4(a); Google, *About Inactive Account Manager*, support.google.com/accounts/answer/3036546?hl=en; Facebook, *What will happen to my account if I pass away?* www.facebook.com/help/103897939701143.
49. RUFADAA §4(b).
50. RUFADAA §4-5.
51. RUFADAA §6-8.
52. RUFADAA §16(e).
53. RUFADAA §5 and UFADAA §8.
54. UFADAA §8 and RUFADAA §15(d).
55. Privacy Expectation Afterlife and Choices Act (PEAC) *About Us* netchoice.org/about (as of Jun. 14, 2015).
56. *Id.*
57. Privacy Expectation Afterlife and Choices Act (PEAC) §1 netchoice.org/library/privacy-expectation-afterlife-choices-act-peac (as of Jun. 14, 2015).
58. Va. Code, §§64.2-109 through 115.
59. H.B. 1608, 2017 Virginia Legislative Session.
60. *Statement of Rights and Responsibilities* (Jan. 30, 2015) www.facebook.com/legal/terms (as of Jun. 14, 2015).
61. Clearly, as probate proceedings are generally subject to public access, one should not list passwords in a will.
62. 18 U.S.C. §1030.
63. *Google Terms of Service* www.google.com/policies/terms (last modified Apr. 14, 2014).
64. *Yahoo Terms of Service* policies.yahoo.com/us/en/yahoo/terms/utos/index.htm (as of Jun. 14, 2015).
65. Farmer & Tyszka, *Virtual Currency Estate Planning, Bit by Bit* (2014) 40 ACTEC J. 249 contains an excellent discussion of bitcoin that is beyond the scope of this chapter.
66. Google, *About Inactive Account Manager*, support.google.com/accounts/answer/3036546?hl=en.
67. Facebook, *What will happen to my account if I pass away?* www.facebook.com/help/103897939701143.
68. For example, Microsoft Word 95 password protection only uses AES 16 bit key encryption, which can easily be broken by amateurs using password hacking software. Microsoft Word 97 uses a 40 bit key, which is, as expected, more difficult to overcome, and Microsoft Word 2010 uses a 128 bit key which is virtually unbreakable (for now!).
69. RUFADAA §7.
70. *Id.*
71. RUFADAA §4(a), (c).
72. RUFADAA §8.
73. 17 U.S.C. §512(c)(3).
74. 17 U.S.C. §512.
75. Treas. Reg. §2031-1(b).
76. www.amazon.com/gp/help/customer/display.html?nodeId=201014950.

VALUATION PLANNING

CHAPTER 70

70.1 INTRODUCTION

Valuation planning describes any technique used to affect the valuation of property or business interests for gift, estate, or generation-skipping transfer tax purposes. Since the basis for valuation of assets for these purposes is fair market value, which is defined in the regulations as what a willing buyer would pay a willing seller. Assuming both had knowledge of the relevant facts, it may be possible to undertake planning moves that can actually reduce the marketable value of the property, and thus reduce federal transfer taxes.

Valuing property for federal gift, estate, and generation-skipping transfer tax purposes is a complex and often uncertain process. Frequently, the taxpayer's valuation differs widely from the value established by the Internal Revenue Service. Courts are then asked to resolve the valuation question.

Taxpayers utilizing valuation discounts may face unexpected gift tax if their discounts are denied. The courts have been generous in allowing taxpayers to use defined value clauses whereby the taxpayers provide in the trust document that any amount which would exceed what can pass free of gift tax would either not be considered to have been gifted or would divert that portion of the gift to the marital deduction, a charity or back to the grantor.[1]

Value is a variable upon which reasonable minds can and will continue to differ.[2] But value is not determined by a mere flip of the coin. The use of careful and thorough appraisals by qualified experts, documentation of sales of similar property recently sold, and well-drawn arm's length restrictive agreements (such as a buy-sell arrangement) are effective tools in substantiating favorable values.

It is worthwhile at this juncture to lay out **Hood's three rules of valuation in a tax matter**, which are:

(1) actual value is *irrelevant*;

(2) actual value is *unknown*; and

(3) perceived, defensible value is *everything*.

There is no substitute for utilizing a competent, qualified appraiser. Don't ever make that mistake. Clients will often grouse about paying an expert to appraise their property because they almost always believe that they know the value of their own property better than even an educated, third person. Resist the temptation to do that however, or the client will lose, have to pay to fight the matter, including paying the estate planner, and probably pay a significant tax penalty and interest. Keep **Hood's Third Rule of Valuation** at the fore of your mind: Perceived, defensible value is *everything*.

Moreover, an argument for a lower value for estate tax purposes will have a corresponding reduction in the step up in basis and ultimately result in higher income taxes when the property is sold, because valuation discounts are a two-edged sword that cuts both ways. Valuation discounts are an important factor that must be considered when assets are placed into partnerships and tenancy in common. Eventually, the estate's personal representative will have to grapple with weighing and comparing the costs and benefits of saving estate or gift tax with the possible cost of higher income tax payable on capital gains – and the impact that decision will have on various parties.[3]

In 2009, the IRS created the "Discount for Lack of Marketability Job Aid for IRS Valuation Professionals" to assist advisors in their examination of and their

995

independent determination of Discounts For Lack Of Marketability (DLOM) and to help them to better understand the numerous available approaches.[4] After public leaks of the document online, the Service eventually published a copy of the document on its website.[5] The Job Aid does not provide a formula for how to determine DLOM, but it does provide some guidance as to what the IRS believes are important issues to consider.

70.2 WHAT ARE THE REQUIREMENTS?

The client transfers undivided interests in property to other family members, thus reducing the marketable value of the interests in the same property retained by the client. At the client's subsequent death, the reduction in value translates into a lower federal (and, if applicable, state) death tax. In fact, since the interests transferred during life represent less than 100 percent ownership of the property, there are sound and reasonable arguments for claiming that the transferred interests also have a lower marketable value at the time of transfer. By fractionalizing the ownership of the property or business interests through transfers to family members, the client reduces the value of the property or business interests for gift and estate tax purposes.

Example. Your client owns 100 percent of the stock in a closely held corporation, which is engaged in real estate development. He transfers 20 percent stock interests to each of his three children, either outright or in trust. Since the transferred interests are minority interests, the value of the stock for gift tax purposes may be reduced to reflect both the lack of control over the corporation and the fact that there is little if any market for less than a controlling interest in a closely-held business.[6]

Further, the value of the client's retained 40 percent interest may also be reduced, since he is no longer able to sell the entire business unless his children, collectively the controlling shareholders, agree. (Of course, this tax savings must be balanced by the very real control that the client is giving up. A recapitalization followed by gifts of nonvoting common or nonvoting preferred stock may be used in combination with gifts of a lesser percentage of voting common if it is important that the client retain voting control.)

70.3 TAX IMPLICATIONS

The regulations under Code section 2031 discuss factors that are relevant in valuing items includable in the gross estate for federal estate tax purposes.[7] Under the regulations, value is fair market value, "the price at which the property would change hands between a willing buyer and a willing seller, neither being under any compulsion to buy or to sell and both having reasonable knowledge of relevant facts." The courts added a hypothetical description to the willing buyer and willing seller.[8] Thus, the value a particular person would place on property may vary greatly from the measure of worth placed on that same item by the government. In fact, it is neither necessary that there be an established market for an item, nor that there be the "willing buyer and seller" spoken of in the regulations. In the absence of an actual sale, the value is based on a *hypothetical* sale. In the event of an actual sale very close to the death of the owner of the property, the amount realized in that transaction should represent good evidence as to the most appropriate valuation for that particular buyer since presumably the sale was negotiated at arm's length.

Generally, when an organized market does in fact exist, the market price will prevail. The ignorance of a material fact by the buying public or its inability to properly assess the significance of certain events does not form a basis for reducing the price indicated on the organized market. The contrary result applies in the absence of an established market. A purchase or sale is not regarded as determinative of value in situations in which one of the parties was ignorant of a material fact.

The following external factors have had varying effects on the probative value of sales:

- the frequency of sales (the courts tend to disregard isolated or sporadic sales);

- the relationship between the buyer and the seller (it is unusual for sales between parents and children or employers and employees to be given great weight in the light of their almost definitional unequal bargaining positions); and

- offers to purchase or sell (offers as opposed to options present little evidence of value).

Not only should all the factors affecting value be considered, but there should be sound reasoning for the relative weight given to each one.

Determining Value

The Internal Revenue Service would likely consider all the facts and circumstances that a hypothetical buyer and seller would consider. The derived price at which the property would have changed hands between parties "X" and "Y" thus determines the IRS's valuation. By this rule, a forced sale – or a sale outside of regular business channels – would not be determinative of the value.[9] Thus, generally, the IRS's position is that the price at which the item or a comparable item would have been sold at retail is determinative.

Value is basically a question of fact in those situations where there is an established market for identical property. But valuation problems become essentially problems of evidential proof (and often, expert opinion) where:

1. There are different markets for the same property, such as in the case of a property with both wholesale and retail markets.

2. The appraisal of the worth must be made on the basis of comparison with somewhat similar property (posing questions such as: Which properties should be selected? How comparable is it?). What is derived is at best an opinion based upon fact. But it must be much more than an uninformed conjecture or guess if a competent, qualified appraiser issues a conclusion of value.

3. The property in question is unique, such as a patent, copyright or billboard. Here, the data must be analyzed (is the examiner capable of making an adequate analysis?), and an opinion must be formulated as to how much the potential anticipated benefits are worth. In such cases, an appraiser is hired to determine the value.[10]

Since, in practice, valuation problems are frequently viewed by the IRS and the courts as problems of negotiation and compromise, the appraiser's goal should be to derive a fair and sound value that, if litigated, would be sustained by the court. Tax Court judges often re-value and frequently disregard expert testimony.[11] Evidence and proof secured in the form of expert advice through an appraisal, formulated promptly after the gift or the testator's death would likely have a greater probative value than evidence obtained at a later date. (As to the valuation of specific types of property, one must turn to the regulations, rulings, and court decisions.) The appraisal report should properly state the facts associated with *how* the value was determined. After all, this is what a hypothetical buyer of the interest would want to know; then, the appraisal should connect these facts to market evidence. Finally, the report should "tell the story"—a persuasive story as to what the hypothetical buyer would pay for the interest. If the story is not clear, it will likely not be persuasive.[12]

Valuation Date

Generally, federal estate taxes are based either on the fair market value of the transferred property as of the date the decedent died or the value of the property six months after the date of the decedent's death. This later date is known as the alternate valuation date.[13] Once selected for valuation purposes – date of death or alternate valuation – such date applies to all assets in the estate.

If the alternate valuation date is selected and if the property is distributed, sold, exchanged, or otherwise disposed of within six months of the decedent's death, it will be valued as of the date of the distribution, sale, or exchange rather than the date six months after the death of the decedent.[14] Certain types of property diminish in value as time goes on; for example, the present value of an annuity reduces each time a payment is made. Any such property interest or estate whose value is affected by the mere passing of time is valued as of the date the decedent died.[15]

Valuation of Real Property

Because of the uniqueness of land, the value of any real property as of a given date may be subject to widely differing opinions. Absent a market for such property, the greater of (a) the highest price available or (b) the salvage value will control. Where there is a market for real property, the basic factors that affect valuation are:

1. The nature and condition of the property, its physical qualities and defects, and the adequacy or inadequacy of its improvements.

2. The size, shape, and location of the property.

3. The actual and potential use of the property and how the trends of development and economic conditions (such as population growth) affect it.

4. How suitable the property is for its actual or intended use.

5. Zoning restrictions.

6. Size, age, and condition of the buildings (degree of deterioration and obsolescence).

7. The market value of other properties in the area in which the property is located.

8. The value of net income received from the property. Rentals are often capitalized and then adjusted for depreciation. (See discussion of capitalization of income, below.) The same principle can be applied to gross rents. This method, however, must be adjusted to account for operating costs.

9. The value accepted by state probate courts for purposes of state death taxes, if based on appraisals made by qualified real estate experts.

10. Prices at which comparable property in the same area was sold at a time near the applicable valuation date (providing it was an arm's length transaction for the best price obtainable). Usually more than one "comparable property" sale will be used, especially where the property to be valued is a personal residence or undeveloped acreage.

11. How much, taking depreciation into account, would it cost to duplicate the property? The cost or value of land would have to be separated from the total value. The cost of reproducing the building, using present cost figures, would have to be estimated, and then the loss in value due to depreciation would have to be subtracted from the total of the other two figures.

12. Unusual facts.

If a sale of real property occurs within a reasonable period of time after the decedent's death, in such a manner as to insure the highest possible price, the amount received usually will be accepted as its value. Unaccepted offers to purchase the property also will be considered. What of a sale at auction? Usually, this price will be accepted only if it appears that there was no other method that would have obtained a higher price.

Land does not have to produce income or have an active market to attain substantial value. Where lands are in or adjacent to a settled community, owners frequently hold such lands in anticipation of realizing their true value from future sales. For example, a home at the edge of an expanding shopping center might be worth far more to the shopping center developer than it would to a potential buyer in the residential market.

Special Valuation of Certain Farm and Business Real Property

An executor may elect to value qualifying real property on the basis of its actual "special" use rather than its "highest and best" use. This "special use valuation" rule, especially useful where the price of farmland is artificially increased by, or has not kept up with, the price per acre of encroaching housing developments, enables the executor to value the farmland at its value for farming purposes. The maximum reduction of the decedent's gross estate under this provision is $1,700,000 (in 2023).[16] The following are the qualification requirements:

1. On the date of the decedent's death, the property must be involved in a "qualified use." That term is defined by Code section 2032A(b)(2) as use as a farm for farming purposes or in a trade or business other than farming.

2. The value of the qualified property (less debts or unpaid mortgages) in the decedent's estate must equal at least 50 percent of the decedent's gross estate (less debts or unpaid mortgages).

3. At least 25 percent of the gross estate (less debts and unpaid mortgages on all property in the gross estate) must be qualified farm or closely held business real property.

4. Such property must pass to a "qualified heir." This term is defined at Code section 2032A(e) to include the decedent's immediate family plus his ancestors or lineal descendants, his spouse or the spouse of a descendant, or a lineal descendant of a grandparent. A legally adopted child of an individual shall be treated as the child of such individual by blood.

5. The real property must have been owned by the decedent or a member of his family and used as a farm or in a closely held business for an aggregate of five years or more of the eight year period ending on the date of the decedent's death. During this period, the decedent or a member of his family must have been a material participant in the operation of the farm or other business.

If the above conditions are met, the property qualifies for the special valuation rule. The worksheet in Figure 70.1, illustrates how to figure out a special use valuation.

Then if the executor elects to apply Code section 2032A, the farm method of valuing land is generally determined as follows:

A. Average annual gross cash rental for comparable land.

B. Average annual state and local real estate taxes for such comparable land.

C. Average annual effective interest rate for all new Farm Credit Bank Loans.

Formula: $\frac{A-B}{C}$ = value for section 2032A purposes.

This formula provides that the income to be capitalized is the average annual gross cash rental income (for five years prior to the decedent's death) less the average annual state and local real estate taxes (for the same five year period) for that comparable land.

"Comparable land" is (1) land used for farming purposes that (2) must be located in the same vicinity as the farmland to be valued. If there is no comparable land, or if the executor chooses to have the farm valued in the manner of a qualifying closely held business, other factors are applied.

The executor may not use cash rentals from the farm to be valued. The rentals used from comparable farmland must have been the result of arm's length bargaining.

The capitalization rate, the average annual effective interest rate on new Farm Credit Bank loans, is the average billing rate charged on new agricultural loans to farmers in the farm credit district in which the qualified property is located. These amounts are published by the IRS according to the Farm Credit Bank district in which property is located. A reproduction of the relevant parts of the latest ruling on this topic follows.

In order to determine the special use value of a farm under the formula method the average annual effective interest rates on new Farm Credit Bank loans to be used for estates of decedents dying in 2023 are as follows:[17]

Farm Credit System Bank in Which Property is Located	Interest Rates Year of Death 2023
AgFirst, FCB	5.37%
AgriBank, FCB	4.74%
CoBank, ACB	4.53%
Texas, FCB	5.12%

These are the states within each Farm Credit Bank district:

Bank	Location of Property
AgFirst, FCB	Delaware, District of Columbia, Florida, Georgia, Maryland, North Carolina, Pennsylvania, South Carolina, Virginia, West Virginia.
AgriBank, FCB	Arkansas, Illinois, Indiana, Iowa, Kentucky, Michigan, Minnesota, Missouri, Nebraska, North Dakota, Ohio, South Dakota, Tennessee, Wisconsin., Wyoming.
CoBank, FCB	Alaska, Arizona, California, Colorado, Connecticut, Hawaii, Idaho, Kansas, Maine, Massachusetts, Montana, New Hampshire, New Jersey, New Mexico, New York, Nevada, Oklahoma, Oregon, Rhode Island, Utah, Vermont, Washington, Rico.
Texas, FCB	Alabama, Louisiana, Mississippi, Texas.

Figure 70.1

SECTION 2032A SPECIAL USE VALUATION WORKSHEET

(1) Year of Death .... _____

(2) FMV of Gross Estate[1] .... $_____

(3) Debt on Property Includable in Gross Estate[2] .... ($_____)

(4) Adjusted Value of Gross Estate [(2) - (3)] .... $_____

(5) FMV of Qualified Use Property[1,3] .... $_____

(6) Debt on Qualified Use Property[2] .... ($_____)

(7) Adjusted Value of Qualified Use Property [(5) - (6)] .... $_____

(8) 50% of Adjusted Value of Gross Estate [(4) × 50%] .... $_____

If amount of (8) is more than amount of (7), estate is not eligible for special use valuation – STOP.

(9) FMV of Qualified Use Real Property[1,4] .... $_____

(10) Debt on Qualified Use Real Property[2] .... ($_____)

(11) Adjusted Value of Qualified Use Real Property [(9) - (10)] .... $_____

(12) 25% of Adjusted Value of Gross Estate [(4) × 25%] .... $_____

If amount of (12) is no more than amount of (11), estate is eligible for special use valuation. If not, STOP.

(13) FMV of Qualified Real Property[1,5] .... $_____

(14) Debt on Qualified Real Property[2] .... ($_____)

(15) Adjusted Value of Qualified Real Property [(13) - (14)] .... $_____

Amount of (15) must be no less than amount of (12).

(16) FMV of Qualified Real Property [(13)] .... $_____

(17) Tentative Special Use Value of Qualified Real Property .... ($_____)

(18) Tentative Value Reduction [(16) - (17)] .... $_____

(19) Statutory Maximum Special Use Reduction As Indexed .... $_____

(20) FMV of Qualified Real Property [(16)] .... $_____

(21) Reduction in Value [Lesser of (18) or (19)] .... ($_____)

(22) Special Use Value [(20) - (21)] .... $_____

INSTRUCTIONS FOR SECTION 2032A
SPECIAL USE VALUATION WORKSHEET

Definitions

Qualified use means use of the property in farming or other trade or business.

Qualified heir means a member of the decedent's family who acquired the property from the decedent.

Member of the family means, with respect to an individual: (a) the spouse of the individual; (b) an ancestor of the individual; (c) a lineal descendent of the individual, or of the spouse or parent of the individual; or (d) the spouse of a lineal descendant listed in (c).

VALUATION PLANNING   CHAPTER 70

Figure 70.1 (cont'd)

Notes

1. Fair market value (FMV) determined without regard to special use valuation.
2. Where the value of the property has not been reduced by the debt on the property.
3. Real or personal property includable in decedent's estate which: (a) on the date of the decedent's death, was being used for a qualified use by the decedent or family member; and (b) was acquired from or passed from the decedent to a qualified heir.
4. Real property includable in decedent's estate which: (a) was acquired from or passed from the decedent to a qualified heir; (b) was owned by the decedent or family member and used for a qualified use by the decedent or family member for 5 of the last 8 years prior to the decedent's death; and (c) was used in the qualified use in which the decedent or family member materially participated in 5 years out of the 8 years immediately preceding the decedent's death (or retirement or disability).
5. Real property includable in decedent's estate which: (a) is located in the United States; (b) was acquired from or passed from the decedent to a qualified heir; (c) on the date of the decedent's death, was being used for a qualified use by the decedent or family member; (d) was owned by the decedent or family member and used for a qualified use by the decedent or family member for 5 of the last 8 years prior to the decedent's death; (e) was used in the qualified use in which the decedent or family member materially participated in 5 years out of the 8 years immediately preceding the decedent's death (or retirement or disability); and (f) is designated in the Section 2032A election and recapture agreement.

Some of the real property on line 9 may not be eligible for special use valuation because it does not meet requirements (a), (c), and (f) for real property on line 13.

Indeed, with regard to (f), special use valuation can be elected for less than all of the real property that would otherwise be eligible. However, if the election is made, the election must be made for enough real property so that the adjusted value of such property [line 15] is not less than 25% of the adjusted value of the gross estate [line 12].

Example. Assume an average annual gross cash rental for comparable land (in Texas) of $84,000, average annual state and local real estate taxes for such comparable land of $4,000, and a capitalization rate of 5.12 percent.

$$\frac{A-B}{C} = \text{value for section 2032A purposes.}$$

$$\frac{\$84,000 - \$4,000}{5.12\%} = \$1,562,500$$

If there is no comparable land, or if the executor elects to have the farm valued in the manner of a qualifying closely held business, then the following factors shall apply.

1. The capitalization of income that the property can be expected to yield for farming or closely held business purposes over a reasonable period of time under prudent management using traditional cropping patterns for the area, taking into account soil capacity, terrain configuration, and other factors.

2. The capitalization of the fair rental value of the land for farmland or closely held business purposes.

3. Assessed land values in a state that provides a differential or use value assessment law for farmland or real estate owned by a closely held business.

4. Comparable sales of other farms or closely held business land in the same geographical area far enough removed from a metropolitan or resort area so that nonagricultural use is not a significant factor in the sales price.

5. Any other factor that fairly values the farm or closely held business value of the property.

If a farm or a closely held business qualifies for the special valuation rules and its value so determined is used for federal estate tax purposes, then an additional estate tax will be imposed if within ten years after the decedent's death and before the death of the qualified heir, the qualified heir who receives such property disposes of any interest in that property, other than to a qualified family member, or ceases to use that property in the manner in which it was used to qualify for this special tax treatment.

Generally, the additional tax imposed shall be the excess of the tax that would have been imposed on the property if it was valued at its best use over the tax imposed because the property was valued at its "qualified use" value.

If the additional tax is imposed, it is due six months after the date of the disposition of the property or the cessation of its use as a farm or as part of the closely held business. The qualified heir who received such property is personally liable for the additional tax imposed.

Valuation of Life Insurance

Proceeds of life insurance on the life of the decedent receivable by or for the benefit of his estate will be taxed in the insured decedent's estate.[18] In addition, where the decedent held incidents of ownership, such ownership will invoke taxation.[19] The amount includable is the amount receivable by the beneficiary. This includes dividends and premium refunds. In determining how much is includable, no distinction is made between a whole life policy, a term policy, group insurance, or an accidental death benefit.

If a settlement option is elected, the amount that would have been payable as a lump sum is the amount includable. If the policy did not provide for a lump sum payment, the amount includable is the commuted amount used by the insurance company to compute the settlement option payments.

The value of an unmatured policy owned by a decedent on the life of another is included in the policy owner's gross estate where he predeceases the insured.

1. If a new policy is involved, the gross premium paid would be the value.

2. If the policy is paid-up or a single premium policy, its value is its replacement cost, that is, the single premium which that company would have charged for a comparable contract of equal face value on the life of a person who was the insured's age (at the time the decedent-policyholder died).

3. If the policy is an established whole life policy, the value is found by adding any unearned portion of the last premium to the interpolated terminal reserve.

4. If the policy is a term policy, the value is the unused premium.

Valuation of U.S. Government Bonds

Series E bonds are valued at their redemption price (market value) as of the date of death since they are neither negotiable nor transferable and the only definitely ascertainable value is the amount at which the Treasury will redeem them.

Valuation of Promissory Notes

The amount remaining due on an installment note may not represent the true value if the borrower does not have the ability to repay the Note. For example, in a state like Pennsylvania where creditors cannot reach assets held in joint names by husband and wife, such a factor should be taken into account to determine the net worth of the borrower *vis a vis* his ability to repay the Note. This determination may affect how much a hypothetical purchaser of the note would pay for the note.[20]

Valuation of Household and Personal Effects

The general rule for valuing household property and personal effects such as watches, rings, etc., is the "willing buyer-willing seller" rule.[21] But the standard is retail, not wholesale, value.[22] A room by room itemization is typical, especially where household goods include articles of artistic or intrinsic value such as jewelry, furs, silverware, paintings, engravings, antiques, books, statuary, oriental rugs, or coin or stamp collections.

In other than community property states, household goods and the like, personally acquired by and used by husband and wife during marriage, are generally presumed to be the property of the husband. Therefore, in the absence of sufficient evidence to rebut this presumption, household goods and personal effects would be includable in the husband's estate.

Valuation of Annuities, Life Estates, Terms for Years, Remainders, and Reversions[23]

Commercial annuities (annuities under contracts issued by companies regularly engaged in their sale) are valued by reference to the price at which the company issues comparable contracts. A retirement income policy, from the point in time that there is no longer an insurance element, is treated as a contract for the payment of an annuity.

Where the annuity is noncommercial, such as a private annuity, the present value of future payments determines its fair market value. Likewise, for gift and estate tax purposes, the fair market value of life estates, terms for years, remainders, and reversions is their present value.

An annuity is defined as a systematic liquidation of principal and interest. Payments might be made for the life of the annuitant (life annuity) or over a period of years (term certain).

A life estate is a disposition of property in which the primary beneficiary may use the property or receives distributions of only income. Payments might be made for the life of the recipient or could be based on the life of a third party, but the income beneficiary of a life estate receives no right to dissipate the principal. In other words, a life estate is the right of a person for his life, or for the life of another person, to receive the income from or the use of certain property. An example would be, "I give my home to my wife for life." The wife's interest would be a life estate. At her death, the property would go to some other party, called a remainder person, or revert to the grantor. The value of the life estate is based on the life tenant's life expectancy and the appropriate discount rate.

In the case of a term certain arrangement, the present value of income for a given number of years is found in a like manner.

A remainder (the beneficiary gets the principal after a third party has enjoyed the income for life or for a given period of time) is actuarially equivalent to a reversion. An example of a remainder would be "to my son John, for life, remainder to Mary." Instead of coming back to the grantor (a reversion), the property "remains" away from the grantor and goes instead to Mary. Mary is said to have a remainder interest. An example of a reversion is where the principal (after a given beneficiary has enjoyed an income for life or for a given period) reverts to the grantor. If the grantor dies before the person enjoying the lifetime interest, his right to "will" that reversion to his heirs, who will someday receive the principal, is valued under the same rules as annuities, remainders, and life estates.

Annuities, life estates, reversions, remainders, and terms for years are valued according to a discount rate that changes monthly (the Code section 7520 rate). The first step in valuing an annuity based on a life (or on the joint lives of two or more people), a life estate, or a reversion or remainder based on a life (or joint lives) is to convert one of the unknowns (the length of the lifetime involved) to a known (life expectancy). This is done by means of a mortality table, which, based on a study of the longevities of a large number of people over a selected period of time, indicates the expectancy of life (in years) for a hypothetical individual who represents the average experience at each age of life.

The second step is to determine a proper discount interest rate (the second unknown that should be attributed to the interest being valued). When that interest rate is determined, a valuation table can be constructed which converts the two factors to be applied, life expectancy and the rate of interest, into one factor to be applied to the amount of the periodic payment, to determine the present worth or value of the property interest.

The valuation tables are used to do term and life computations. A more detailed explanation for use for the tables can be found there.

Valuation must be based on the so called "Section 7520 rate." This is found with a two-step process. Step one is to compute 120 percent of the Applicable Federal Midterm Rate in effect for the month in which the valuation date falls. Step two is to round the result to the nearest 0.2 percent.

Two qualifications need to be added to this explanation of the law respecting actuarial valuation of term and life computations: First, these valuation provisions do not apply to interests valued with respect to qualified retirement plans (including tax sheltered annuities and IRAs) or in other situations specified in Treasury regulations. Second, if an income, estate, or gift tax *charitable* contribution is allowable for any part of the property transferred, the taxpayer may elect to use the discount rate for either of the two months *preceding* the month in which the valuation date falls. However, if a transfer of more than one interest in the same property is made with respect to which the taxpayer could use the same interest rate, that interest rate must be used with respect to each transferred interest.[24]

Valuation of Listed Stocks[25]

Where a stock has an established market and quotations are available to value the stock as of the date in question, the Fair Market Value (FMV) per share on the applicable valuation date governs for both gift and estate tax purposes.

The FMV is based on selling prices when there is a market for the stock or bond. This would be the mean between the highest and lowest quoted selling price on the valuation date. If there were no sales on the valuation date, but there were sales on dates within a reasonable period both before and after the valuation date, the FMV is determined by taking a weighted average of the means between the highest and lowest sales on the nearest date before and the nearest date after the valuation. The average is then weighted inversely by the respective number of trading days between the selling date and the valuation date.

Where there is a large block of stock that could not be marketed in an orderly manner, the block might depress the market because it could not be converted to cash as readily as could a few shares. Therefore, selling prices and bid and ask prices may not reflect fair market value. Sometimes it may be necessary to value this type of stock as if it were closely held and not actively traded. If this can be established, a reasonable modification of the normal basis for determining FMV can be made. In some cases, a blockage discount is determined by the effect that block would have had on the market if it were sold over a reasonable period of time and in a prudent manner.[26] A similar situation occurs where sales at or near the date of death are few or of a sporadic nature and may not indicate a fair market value.[27]

The converse of the blockage situation above is where the block of stock to be valued represents a controlling interest (either actual or effective) in a business. Here, the price of normally traded shares may have little relation to the true value of the controlling lot. The large block could have the effect of increasing value because of its element of control.

Valuation of Corporate Bonds

The valuation of bonds is similar to that of listed common stock. The mean of the selling prices on or near the applicable valuation date, or, if there were no sales, the mean of bona fide ask prices weighted inversely to the number of trading days from the valuation date will determine the fair market value of the bonds.

In the absence of sales or bid and ask prices, the value must be determined by:

(1) Ascertaining the soundness of the security.

(2) Comparing the interest yield on the bond in question to yields on similar bonds.

(3) Examining the date of maturity.

(4) Comparing prices for listed bonds of corporations engaged in similar types of business.

(5) Checking the extent to which the bond is secured.

(6) Weighing all other relevant factors including the opinion of experts, the good will of the business, the industry's economic outlook, the company's position in the industry and its management.

Valuation of Interests in Closely Held Businesses

The basic principles in valuing interests in closely-held business in the form of partnerships and LLCs are essentially the same as those in valuing closely held stock. So the valuation of such enterprises will be treated under the category of closely held stock.

What exactly is closely held stock? Various criteria have been used to define such stock. Some of these are:

- the number of stockholders;

- restrictions imposed on a shareholder's ability to transfer the stock;

- absence of exchange listing or regular quotation in the "over-the-counter" market; and

- an irregular, limited history of sales or exchanges.

For general purposes, however, stock can be considered closely held where there is some question as to whether its value can be found solely by reference to an established market. The problem of valuing closely held stock is compounded because, by definition, such stock is seldom traded.

The relevant Internal Revenue Code sections and regulations[28] are of little help. They are so vague and general that their application to a specific valuation question is of minimal planning value. The real guidance in valuations of interests in closely-held businesses is set forth in Rev. Rul. 59-60 and the rulings that have amplified it over the years. Rev. Rul. 59-60 looks to eight factors, including:

(a) The nature of the business and the history of the enterprise from its inception.

(b) The economic outlook in general and the condition and outlook of the specific industry in particular.

(c) The book value of the stock and the financial condition of the business.

(d) The earning capacity of the company.

(e) The dividend-paying capacity.

(f) Whether or not the enterprise has goodwill or other intangible value.

(g) Sales of the stock and the size of the block of stock to be valued.

(h) The market price of stocks of corporations engaged in the same or a similar line of business having their stocks actively traded in a free and open market, either on an exchange or over-the-counter.

There are at least seven situations in which the estate planner must value a business or professional practice. Valuation plays a critical role when a planner needs to:

- plan for a client's estate liquidity

- establish a price for buy-sell purposes (should a buy-out be necessitated by death, disability or other health problems, retirement, or lifetime termination of relationship) (e.g., sale of an interest in the business or practice to a third party)

- properly recognize the business's or practice's worth in a client's prenuptial or postnuptial agreement

- apportion assets in a marital dissolution

- ascertain the worth of the business or practice as loan collateral

- perform a fiscal checkup to test the financial health of a client's business or practice, detect adverse financial trends, or uncover opportunities (for instance, a doctor might find that patients are getting older and the business or practice should try to attract younger people or can profitably move into a new area of specialty)

- prepare an estate or gift tax valuation

In the settlement of many estates, the valuation of closely held corporate stock can be a most difficult, time-consuming, and costly problem, especially when a confrontation arises between the executor and the Internal Revenue Service. But careful use of a properly drafted restrictive business agreement can help alleviate and control the problem (subject to the requirements of Code sections 2701 to 2704).

Valuing Stock and Partnership Interests for Estate Planning Purposes

Basic factors to consider. The fair market value of a closely held corporation or partnership is determined in the same manner as stock in a professional practice.[29] In determining the value of a closely held business Revenue Ruling 59-60[30], referenced above, the master guideline for valuing all businesses, requires that eight factors must be considered:

- *Nature of the business and the history of the enterprise from its inception.* This factor measures the risk, stability, depth of management of the business, and the diversity of its operations. With respect to the valuation of a professional practice, the appraiser should review the stability of the practice's financial history, its growth patterns, changes in ownership, market share, marketing approach, and "product" breakdown. For example, is this a law practice that does 70 percent negligence and personal injury work, 20 percent financial and estate planning, and 10 percent real estate? Significant events should be emphasized and events not likely to recur should be eliminated.

- *Economic outlook in general and for the specific industry in particular.* Here, the appraiser must evaluate the "industry" outlook and the position of the practitioner with reference to his competition. The appraiser should consider the cyclical nature of the practitioner's business, the direction of the national economy, and any unique elements in the professional's practice position.

- *Book value of the stock and the financial condition of the business.* The appraiser here must consider the asset value of the professional's practice. Note that the professional's statements are historical-cost based; they should be adjusted to reflect fair market value. Depreciation as recorded under generally accepted accounting principles need not bear any relationship to economic depreciation and the true net value of the assets under consideration.

- *Earnings capacity of the company.* The earnings of a professional practice have been held by many valuation authorities to be the essence of its fair market value, since "everyone knows that the value of shares in a ... company depends chiefly on what it will earn."[31] What is at issue is earnings *capacity*, future income potential, not net income. Adjustments should be made for salaries, travel, and entertainment expenses, nonrecurring items, and potential legal and tax liabilities. In a corporate setting, note that loans to shareholders may represent disguised dividends; loans from shareholders may represent equity rather than debt.

- *Dividend paying capacity.* The emphasis again is on *capacity*, not actual payout. With the professional corporation, the appraiser should focus on cash flow projections and relate dividend capacity to earnings capacity, with due consideration for the need to reinvest in the professional's practice.

- *Goodwill or intangible values.* Goodwill has been extensively discussed above. In its simplest form, goodwill is the excess earnings of the practice over the normal return on tangible assets. Note that the normal return should be the "fair rate of return" earned by comparable practitioners. Tangible assets should be valued at their fair market value rather than at historically based book value.

- *Sales of the stock and the size of the block to be valued.* Here, recent sales are most important. Has the interest in the practice been sold to insiders? What percentage of the practice has been sold? Have there been any recent events since the sale that would affect significantly the value of the practice?

- *The market price of stock of corporations engaged in the same or a similar line of business having their stock traded in a free and open market.* This factor is extremely difficult to apply to professional practices. Few professional practices exist as public corporations. Those that do rarely are comparable to closely held professional practices. A publicly held practice by definition has a value premium for marketability.

However, the six most important words in Rev. Rul. 59-60 are *"common sense, informed judgment and reasonableness."* An appraiser who fails to adhere slavishly to those six important words will miss the valuation mark more often than not. **It is possible to torture the numbers long enough to get them to confess to whatever you want them to say instead of reaching a reasonably defensible conclusion of value.**

The following discussion summarizes four often-used approaches to business valuation: (1) book value, (2) comparable company, (3) capitalization of income, and (4) going concern value.

Book Value

Book value (essentially assets minus liabilities) is a particularly good place to begin the process of valuing a closely held corporation in each of the following situations:

1. Where the business in question is primarily an asset holding company – such as an investment company.

2. Where the company is in the real estate development business and assets are the major profit making factor.

3. Where one person is the sole or major driving force since such businesses are typically worth only their liquidation value upon the death,

VALUATION PLANNING — CHAPTER 70

disability, or termination of employment of such a person.

4. Where the liquidation of the corporation is in process or imminent at the valuation date. The impact of sacrifice sales and capital gains taxation must often be considered since the true value of a liquidating business is only the amount available to shareholders after all expenses and taxes.

5. Where the business is highly competitive, but only marginally profitable. Past profits, thus, become an unreliable tool to measure potential future earnings.

6. Where the assets or the business itself is relatively new.

7. Where some form of merger is likely to occur with another firm.

8. Where the business is experiencing large deficits.

Book value must be adjusted since the assets of most businesses are usually carried on the company's books at historical cost rather than fair market value.

Adjustments are recommended in the following cases:

1. When assets are valued at cost. For instance, the primary assets of a closely held investment company consist of marketable securities. These are typically carried on the company's books at cost. Likewise, land is an asset most companies will carry at cost but which may be worth considerably more on the open market. The result is a book value that bears little or no relationship to the true present worth of the business.

2. When assets have been depreciated at a rate in excess of their true decline in economic value. A good example is the operating company (one which produces or sells products or services to the public) that has purchased machinery or equipment originally costing $1,000,000 but which, on the company's books, has been depreciated down to $300,000. The equipment may be worth a lot more or a lot less than either its cost or the $300,000 figure at which it is presently carried.

3. When items such as potential lawsuits or unfavorable long-term leases have not been shown in the footnotes of the firm's balance sheet.

4. When one or more assets with significant economic value have been completely "written off" – thus reflecting a book value far below the price which they should realistically bring.

5. When the business has carried assets such as franchises and goodwill on the books at a nominal cost.

6. When the business experiences difficulty in collecting its accounts receivable.

7. When the firm's inventory includes goods that are either obsolete or for some other reason are not readily marketable.

8. Where the working capital or liquidity position of the business is poor (low current assets relative to current liabilities).

9. Where the firm is burdened with a substantial amount of long-term indebtedness.

10. Where the retained earnings are high only because they have been accumulated over a long period of time. Such a business may have poor current earnings and the outlook for increased earnings in the future may be dim.

After the adjustments described above have been made, the value of any other class of stock with a priority as to dividends, voting rights or preference to assets in the event of a sale or liquidation must be subtracted. For example, the owner of common stock can't realize the value of the assets until owners of preferred stock have been satisfied.

Once the adjusted book value has been determined for the entire business, it is then necessary to divide the book value by the number of shares outstanding to determine the value per share.

Book value should rarely be used as the only means of valuing a closely held business. It should be used in conjunction with, or as a means of testing the relevancy of, the capitalization of earnings and other methods. (Be sure not to "double count" an asset when combining two or more methods).

Book value should not be used when capital plays a minor role in profit making or where valuing the stock of a party who does not have the voting power to force liquidation, since; in that case, book values have little relevance.

Book Value Calculation

Input:	"Adjusted" Asset Value of Common Stock	$500,000
Input:	Total Adjusted Liabilities	$100,000
Input:	Par Value of Preferred Stock	$50,000
	Total Deductions	$150,000
	Adjusted Book Value of Entire Business	$350,000
Input:	Number of Common Shares Outstanding	$1,000
	Value Per Share of Common Stock	$350.00

Valuation by Reference to Comparable Publicly Traded Companies

A business can sometimes be valued by reference to the value of a comparable company if the stock of that second company is listed, and actively traded, on a securities exchange or on the over-the-counter (OTC) market.

The price per share of the publicly traded stock is divided by its earnings per share. The resulting ratio is then applied to the earnings per share of the business to be valued in order to arrive at the market value per share. Comparable traded securities research should start with federal government publications such as:

- The *North American Industry Classification System (NAICS)* (which categorizes industries)

- The *S.E.C. Directory of Companies Required to File Annual Reports* (which, as its name implies, lists companies which must file reports under various S.E.C. acts)

- The U.S. Department of Commerce, *Census of Business* (which is a compilation of statistics and ratios on various businesses)

- Dun & Bradstreet's *Dun's Review* (which gives key operating and financial ratios)

- Moody's *Investors Service and Manual* (which provides a detailed description of many publicly held corporations)

- Standard & Poor's *Corporation Records* (which provides financial and operating ratios for many corporations).

Be sure to check trade magazines for the industry in question. Many associations also provide detailed information for members of their industry.

In searching for comparable (guideline, in proper appraisal parlance) companies, look for similarities in product line, service, size, marketing and geographic area, growth, profitability, overhead, and competitive position. Examine balance sheets and income statements (use the ratios template) to compare ratios and trends. Seldom, if ever, will a perfect match be found, and many adjustments may have to be made even after a "close fit" is found.

This technique has a number of shortcomings. First, it is difficult to use. Second, an enormous expenditure of time and effort is required to compile accurate and adequate information concerning the business to be valued, the comparable business or businesses, and then to analyze and evaluate the data.

The larger the closely held business, the more likely this approach will be appropriate since the size, corporate capital structure, earnings, liabilities, rate of growth, and diversification are more likely to be comparable to a publicly traded company.

Value Per Share of Closely Held Stock

Input:	Per Share Market Price of Similar Publicly Traded Company	$45.00
Input:	Earnings Per Share of Similar Publicly Traded Company	$4.50
Input:	Earnings Per Share of Business to be Valued	$14.00
	Computed Price/Earnings Ratio	10.00
	Equivalent Capitalization Rate	0.10
	Value Per Share of Closely Held Business	$140.00

VALUATION PLANNING

CHAPTER 70

Capitalization of Income

No formula exists that applies to all assets and that will be accepted by both the IRS and the courts. Converting the projected flow of income from a business or asset into its present value, i.e., "capitalizing the income," provides a simple, reasonably accurate, and commonly accepted way of estimating fair market value.

The concept of income capitalization is simple: determine what amount of income is realistic and proper under the circumstances and then apply a capitalization rate that meets the same criterion. In essence, the capitalization rate is the desired rate of return; the rate of return an investor would be willing to accept for the given level of risk. A high risk investment would equate to a high capitalization rate (which in turn results in a lower value). The asset or business is then presumed to be worth the result when adjusted earnings are divided by the capitalization rate.

The graph in Figure 70.2 illustrates the valuation of a business generating adjusted earnings of $100,000 a year using ten different capitalization rates.

Transforming theory into practice is often complex and frustrating. The brief comments below, pertaining to "adjusting" the earnings and selecting the appropriate rate of return, may help:

(A) Adjustments to income (in the case of a business, use five year average after-tax profits):

Figure 70.2

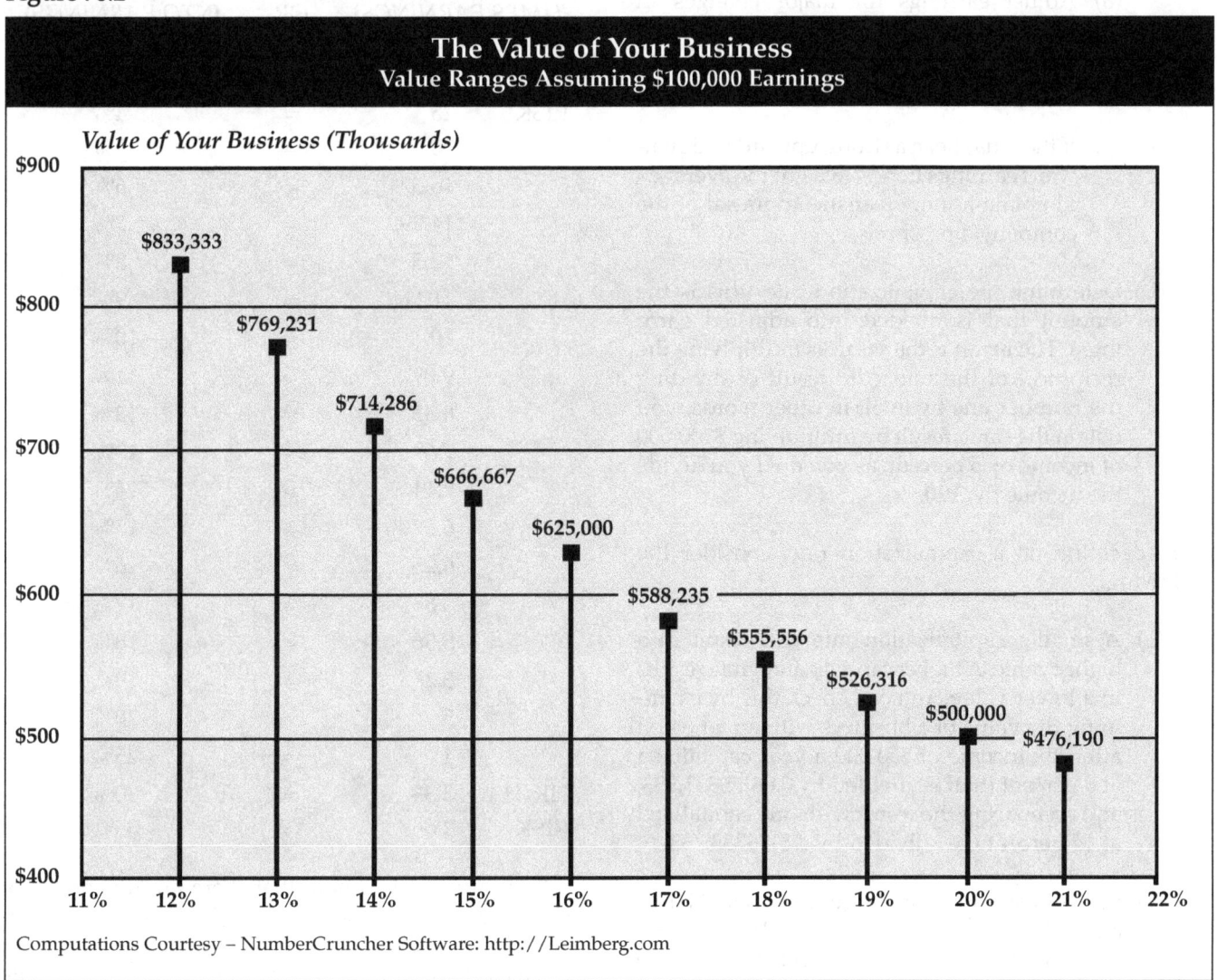

Computations Courtesy – NumberCruncher Software: http://Leimberg.com

(1) Add back excessive salaries

(2) Reduce earnings if salaries were too low

(3) Add back bonuses paid to stockholder-employees

(4) Add back excessive rents paid to shareholders

(5) Reduce earnings where rents paid to shareholders were below what was reasonable in the market

(6) Eliminate nonrecurring income or expense items

(7) Adjust for excessive depreciation

(8) Adjust earnings for major changes in accounting procedures, widely fluctuating or cyclical profits, or abnormally inflated (or deflated) earnings.

(9) If there has been a strong upward or downward earnings trend, "weight the average" to obtain a more realistic appraisal of the company's prospects.

(B) Determine the capitalization rate (this is the amount that is divided into adjusted earnings). The result is the same as multiplying the reciprocal of the rate, (the result of dividing the number one by five). In other words, you obtain the same result by multiplying $100,000 of income by 5 percent, as you do if you divide the income by 0.20.

In deciding on a capitalization rate, consider the following:

(1) A smaller capitalization rate will result in a higher value. A higher capitalization rate results in a lower value. You can check this by examining the value of a business with an adjusted after tax income of $50,000 a year capitalized at 6 percent (that is, divided by 0.06), $833,333, and comparing the result with one capitalized at 15 percent (i.e., divided by .15), $333,333.

(2) Stable businesses with large capital asset bases and established goodwill should be less risky investments, and a lower capitalization rate should be used than if valuing a small business with little capital, financial history, or management depth.

Assign a high capitalization rate to a personal business that depends on the presence of only one or two key people. An investor purchasing this type of business would want a high rate of return as a reward for that risk. (Another way to say the same thing is that such an investor would not make the investment unless a rapid return of capital through a high income stream was expected.)

Comparison Chart

	"MULTIPLIER" (MULTIPLY THIS TIMES EARNINGS)	OR	CAPITALIZATION RATE (DIVIDE THIS INTO EARNINGS)
LOW RISK	28.6	=	3.5%
	25	=	4%
	20	=	5%
	16.67	=	6%
	14.29	=	7%
	12.5	=	8%
	11.11	=	9%
	10	=	10%
	9.09	=	11%
	8.33	=	12%
	7.69	=	13%
	7.14	=	14%
	6.67	=	15%
	6.25	=	16%
	5.88	=	17%
	5.56	=	18%
	5.26	=	19%
	5	=	20%
	4	=	25%
HIGH RISK	3.33	=	30%
	2.86	=	35%

It is important to note that there are no correct or official rates. Even the IRS uses different rates at different times and under different circumstances. It is for this reason that the capitalization of income template provides ten automatic options (which you can modify to provide an infinite number of variations).

Valuation of a Business as a "Going Concern"

A closely held business should (and often does) produce an income in excess of the amount that could be expected from the mere employment of the capital its shareholders have invested. That additional amount of income is derived from an intangible value in the business, a value in excess of the total value of the tangible assets.

By capitalizing earnings attributable to intangibles, i.e., by dividing the additional profits generated by the firm's goodwill, by an appropriate rate, it is possible to estimate goodwill value. If this amount is then added to book (net tangible asset) value, the total business value can be found.

Some of the elements that may comprise a firm's goodwill include:

(1) Location of the business

(2) Reputation of the business

(3) Public recognition of the company's name

(4) Lists of customers and prospects owned by the business

(5) Management effectiveness and depth

(6) Sales, operations, and accounting skills

(7) Employee morale

(8) Position of the business relative to competitors

(9) Other factors that generate income in excess of that amount which could be expected after multiplying the value of tangible assets by a reasonable rate of return.

Note that goodwill does not include the portion of profits attributable to the corporation's ownership of patents, copyrights, formulas, or trademarks, even though they are intangible, since these are all specifically identifiable.

Goodwill, as in the case with other valuation formulas and procedures, should be used only as a guideline and not as the sole determinate of value. Goodwill has minimal relevance to the valuation of most investment companies since they usually do not have large amounts of intangibles. Officially, the IRS does not give strong credibility to goodwill (although the IRS still insists that goodwill must be taken into account in the valuation process).

Going Concern Value

Input: Average Annual Earnings..........................$100,000
Input: Average Annual Asset Value.......................$500,000
Input: Estimated Capitalization Rate..........................0.200
Input: Rate of Return on Tangible Assets......................0.16

Option	Return On Tangible Assets	Earn From Tangible Assets	Earn From Intangible Assets	Goodwill Value	Total Business Value
1	0.160	$80,000	$20,000	$100,000	$600,000
2	0.170	$85,000	$15,000	$75,000	$575,000
3	0.180	$90,000	$10,000	$50,000	$550,000
4	0.190	$95,000	$5,000	$25,000	$525,000
5	0.200	$100,000	$0	$0	$500,000

A reduction in value is often allowed because the shares being valued represent a minority interest in the business. Courts tend to aggregate the lack of marketability inherent in a closely held corporation with the minority interest principle although the minority interest discount arises because such shares have no power to force dividends, compel liquidation, or to control corporate policy. This in turn limits the potential market for such stock to the remaining (and usually controlling) shareholders and reduces the price at which such shares would be purchased.

Conversely, where the shares in question represent a controlling interest, the IRS will generally attempt to apply a premium to the stock's value. "The size of the block of stock itself is a relevant factor to be considered. Although it is true that a minority interest in an unlisted corporation's stock is more difficult to sell than a similar block of listed stock, it is equally true that control of a corporation, either actual or in effect, representing as it does an added element of value, may justify a higher value for a specific block of stock."

Discount for Loss of Key Employee

Both the IRS and the courts have long recognized that the loss of a manager, scientist, salesperson, or other key individual will almost always have a serious effect on the earning power and sometimes on the very stability of a business. Although the principle applies in publicly-held businesses, it is particularly true in a closely held corporation where profits are dependent on the ability, initiative, judgment, or business connections of a single person or small group of owner-employees. A discount in valuation may therefore be appropriate. (This same concept may also be used in determining the amount of key employee insurance a corporation should own.)

There is no universally recognized and accepted formula for computing the economic effect of the loss of a key person. One used in several court cases utilizes a discount approach: a percentage discount is taken from the going-concern value of the business.

Some authorities feel that if the business will survive the death of the key employee, and in time a competent successor can be found, a discount factor of from 15 to 20 percent should be used. Where the business is likely to fail, or be placed in serious jeopardy upon the death (or disability) of the key employee, a discount of from 25 to 45 percent is more appropriate. The exact discount factor should be arrived at through consultation with the officers of the company and the firm's accounting and legal advisers.

Some questions that should be answered in the process of determining the factor (or range of factors) to be used include:

(1) How long will it take for a new person to reach the efficiency of the key individual?

(2) How much will it cost to locate and situate a replacement? Will the new employee demand more salary? How much will it cost to train the new person?

(3) What mistakes is a replacement likely to make during the "break in" period and how much are those mistakes likely to cost the company?

(4) What proportion of the firm's current net profits are attributable to the key employee?

(5) Is the employee engaged in any projects that, if left unfinished at death or disability, would prove costly to the business? How costly? Would a potentially profitable project have to be abandoned or would a productive department have to be closed?

(6) Would the employee's death result in the loss of clientele or personnel attracted to the business because of his personality, social contacts, or unique skills, talents, or managerial ability?

(7) What effect would the key employee's death have on the firm's credit standing?

(8) What proportion of the firm's actual loss is it willing to self-insure, if any?

Key Employee Valuation

Input: Fair Market Value of Business with Key Employee.......................................$750,000

Input: Discount Percent (%) without Employee..

Discount Percent	Value W/O Key Employee	Value of Key Employee
0.16	$630,000	$120,000
0.17	$622,500	$127,500
0.18	$615,000	$135,000
0.19	$607,500	$142,500
0.20	$600,000	$150,000
0.21	$592,500	$157,500
0.22	$585,000	$165,000
0.23	$577,500	$172,500
0.24	$570,000	$180,000

There are a number of ways – other than the approach used in the template – to value a key person's contribution to a corporation's profits. One way is to measure the number of working years remaining to the executive (say ten). Estimate the annual loss of earnings attributable to that person (say $30,000 per year). Then discount (see present value templates) the value of that annual loss (for example, at 10 percent). This will result in the present value of the key person's services, about $184,000.

Alternatively, the goodwill template could be adjusted to measure the goodwill produced through the efforts of the management team and this total would then further be apportioned (perhaps by relative salaries) among the key employees.

For instance, assume a firm had an average annual asset value of $450,000 and an average annual earnings after taxes of $75,000. If 10 percent were thought to be a fair rate of return on tangibles, then $45,000 (10 percent of $450,000) of the $75,000 would be attributable to tangibles. The remaining $30,000 would be attributable to goodwill. Assume 60 percent of this,

$18,000, could reasonably be allocated to management. If it takes five years to replace the entire management team, then $18,000 should be multiplied by five, or a total of $90,000. If the executive in question drew 80 percent of the total salaries of the management team, then that person's worth would approximate $72,000 (80 percent of $90,000).

Buy-Sell Agreements

Most shareholders of closely held corporations restrict the marketability of co-shareholder's stock through "purchase options" or mandatory buy-sell agreements. If the terms of such agreement definitely fix the values of the shares in question, it is not necessary to examine either book value or earnings.

The general rule is that a buy-sell cannot set transfer tax value and that the federal estate tax value will be determined without regard to the price, the formula, or the terms of the buy-sell - unless certain tests are met. These rules govern *all* types of restrictive arrangements with respect to business ownership and, therefore, encompass sole proprietorships, partnerships, LLCs, and corporations and every kind of buy-sell or similar document. Buy sell agreements and Code section 2703 are discussed in detail in Chapter 47.

Reasonable price. The price set in the agreement must be reasonable and determinable. That means the price must be determinable from the agreement itself and is not one that would be worked out between the parties after death. This requirement suggests that the use of a fixed price, a mandate for independent qualified appraisers, or the use of a formula is permissible as long as the value established in the agreement represented full and adequate consideration at the time the agreement was signed – even if there were substantial differences between the date of signing agreement price and the actual date of death value. (Warning: It is not likely the IRS and courts will give much credibility to a price set many years ago and deliberately not updated).

Estate obligated to sell. The estate must be obligated to sell. It can be a binding bilateral agreement (estate must sell/survivors must buy) or a purchase option by the entity and/or other owners, but the estate must be bound to sell at the agreed upon price and/or formula. If the estate *could* but is not *required* to sell, the IRS and the courts are likely to give no or little credibility to the price set in the buy-sell agreement.

Must not be tax avoidance device. If the overall effect and operation of the agreement serves as a device to artificially avoid federal estate tax, i.e., to pass the decedent's shares or other ownership interest to the natural objects of his bounty for less than an adequate and full consideration in money or money's worth, the IRS and the courts will not give credibility to the price set in the agreement for tax purposes.

Lifetime price. The lifetime price can't exceed the deathtime price. The agreement should prevent a sale during lifetime at a price higher than at death; otherwise the IRS will argue the agreement price is a floor rather than a ceiling. If the parties could readily sell the owner's interest at a price much higher during their lifetimes than the agreement specifies at death, the IRS and the courts will presume that the lifetime price is the more realistic and that the deathtime price was designed to shift wealth in a way that was designed to avoid federal estate tax.

Bona fide. There must be a bona fide business purpose for the agreement and the price set in the agreement must have been arrived at in an arm's length manner. Generally, courts will assume this test is met if the parties to the agreement are unrelated. On the other hand, any agreement among family members will be stringently scrutinized to see if these tests are met. Two business purpose arguments that have been successful – when borne out by the facts – are that the agreement was designed to (1) assure continuity of management and (2) maintain family control.

Comparabilty. This is a relatively new and potentially difficult, if not impossible, test for some buy-sell agreements to meet. The terms of the buy-sell must be comparable to similar arrangements entered into by persons in an arm's length transaction. In other words, the parties must be able to show that the terms in the agreement are those that could have been obtained in an arm's length bargain with strangers, and that a similar business in the same line of work would have arrived at essentially the same agreement. This means the terms must be set with an eye to the general practice of unrelated parties. Isolated comparables will not be good enough. Of course, the mere fact that the terms of a buy-sell differ slightly from those of a similar company are not enough, per se, for the IRS to disregard them. More than one valuation methodology can be valid – even within same industry. But this additional requirement has even more than in the past shifted the burden of proof to the taxpayer.

There are grandfather rules with respect to the Code section 2703 tests. These tests do not apply to agreements entered into before October 9, 1990, unless the agreement is substantially modified on or after that date. A substantial modification is one that results in more than a de minimis change to the quality, value, or timing of a party's rights or restrictions. Any discretionary modification (whether or not authorized by the terms of the agreement) that results in a meaningful change to the quality, value, or timing of the rights of any party could be considered substantial. Beware: The failure to update can be considered a substantial modification if the terms of the agreement require periodic (e.g., once a year or once every two years) updating. Adding a family member to the agreement is a substantial modification – unless the addition is required under the terms of the agreement or unless the added family member is in a generation no lower than that of the youngest person who is a party to the agreement before the modification.

A change is not considered substantial if that modification is required by the terms of the agreement itself. Nor is a change considered substantial if the economics of the transaction are not changed; if it modifies a capitalization rate in a manner tied to a specified market interest rate (e.g., Code Section 7520 rate); if a new family member is added to the agreement, assuming the agreement requires such addition, or is in the same generation as the present parties to the agreement (e.g., an agreement between father and son adds father's new wife); or if the "modification results in an option price that more closely resembles FMV."[32] Planners should alert clients that an independent appraisal from a qualified valuation professional is essential to increase the potential for success. Success in establishing a credible value requires that the formula must be appropriate for size/type industry or service, that it is used and recognized by professional appraisers (and preferably one tailored to the client's business by such an appraiser working with client's counsel). The parties should document the basis upon which the price setting formula is created. Ideally, the formula should provide for appropriate adjustments, updated appraisal, and modification whenever the corporation's financial position undergoes a material change. The key to success is for the parties to follow the contemporaneous opinion of a competent independent appraiser, not just for tax valuation purposes, but for purposes of dealing among themselves.

It is quite possible in a case where the IRS is successful in claiming an estate tax value high in excess of the price set in the buy-sell agreement for a seller's estate to receive less cash in payment for the stock than the tax it incurs on that same stock. For instance, if the agreement calls for $50 a share and the stock is taxed at $200 a share, the tax can easily exceed the price the estate receives.

Valuing a Professional Practice

This section explains why estate planners must be able to value professional practices and discusses

- how a professional practice differs from a typical business, and why these differences are important

- considerations in valuing goodwill

- how to value a professional's stock for buy-sell purposes

- a shortcut approach to valuing a professional practice

- how to use the prior transactions, capitalization of billings, and excess earnings valuation methods

- rough rules of thumb

A Complex Task

Valuation of a manufacturing business is difficult enough; the valuation of a professional practice, with its many intangible factors, is more complex still. Productivity, goodwill, and the multitude of other factors that affect a professional practice are difficult to quantify. Rules of thumb may differ widely from one appraiser to another and from one group of professionals to another. Some variables may have greater weight for some buyers than for others. For example, a young doctor seeking to purchase a practice may wish to buy one for about the same costs he'd incur if starting from scratch. Conversely, many hospitals purchase the practices of retiring staff physicians to help insure that the practice will continue to fill hospital beds. The hospital might pay more for the practice if the doctor typically referred patients to it, or if the practice might otherwise be sold to a competing hospital.

The questions asked and the methods used differ depending on the purpose of the valuation and the type of practice in question. For instance, valuations for divorce, one of the most common reasons a professional practice is valued, will emphasize the practitioner's age and health, experience, length of practice, financial success, skills, and reputation. The value of the goodwill these factors might generate could be more important to the divorce court than the factors leading to strong marketability, which would be important for estate tax purposes. Factors established by statute and case law, which tend to vary widely from state to state, must also be taken into account. For example, some states give more weight than others to minority interests or lack of marketability discounts with reference to professional corporations.

Why a Professional Practice is Different

A professional practice differs from other businesses mainly because of:

Expertise. The expertise – or, more important, the *perceived* expertise – of the professionals involved is of paramount importance in determining the fees that can be charged and the income that can be earned from the practice. The education, training, and experience a professional brings to his practice, and the "consumer's" dependence on the delivery of the practitioner's services, are extremely important economic factors that must be considered in determining value. For example, a patient needing brain surgery typically does not shop for a bargain price.

Entry barriers. Higher education, licensing, and certification requirements all serve to slow or limit entrants into professional practice. If, for any reason, licensing or certification is lost, the practitioner can no longer practice. If a professional dies or is permanently disabled, his family members cannot continue to operate the practice unless they are duly licensed and certified in the same profession.

Professional goodwill. Reputation and recommendations are the life blood of the professional practice. Although some professionals obtain significant business from "walk-in" traffic due to location or advertisement, most depend mainly on referrals from peers and the recommendation of present clients to bring in new business. This is particularly true with respect to specialists. For this reason, trust, respect, and "liking" of the practitioner – by peers as well as patients or clients – are crucial to the success of the practice.

Nontransferability. Substitution may be difficult or impossible. Professional skills are to some extent unique and not interchangeable. Consider the relationship between psychiatrist and patient: If the psychiatrist is ill for three weeks and unable to work, an attorney-spouse can't "run the store."

Continuing education. In most professions, information, tools, and techniques become quickly outdated, and the professional must engage in continuous education. This may be through formal course work or by keeping up with professional journals and magazines.

Why the Differences are Important

Most businesses have as part of their value an asset called "goodwill." This can be defined as the quantified expectation of future profits from some source other than mere dollars at work. For instance, if a firm enjoys $80,000 of earnings on a $60,000 capital investment that can reasonably be expected to return 20 percent ($12,000) at a given risk level, then $68,000 of income ($80,000 – $12,000) is attributable to something other than capital. This business-oriented goodwill is an asset of the business that generates value over and above the entity's net asset value.

In a professional practice there are two types of goodwill: business-oriented (stemming from the entity) *and* professional (originating from the individual).

Business-oriented goodwill is attributable to the elements of a professional practice that are similar to those of a regular business: location, operating systems, staff, and patient or client base. Business-oriented goodwill can have significant transferable value, value that can be sold to another licensed practitioner.

Professional goodwill, on the other hand, depends on the unique characteristics of the particular practitioner. At the professional's death, disability, or retirement, that portion of the practice income attributable to professional goodwill will generally leave with the individual. Much of this personal goodwill, however, can be transferred in a sale to another practitioner by creating a well-organized transition in which the departing professional lends credibility to the entering professional.

Valuing Business-Oriented Goodwill and Future Income Flow

Although many sources are available to provide information for valuing a practice's transferable business-oriented goodwill and its likely future earnings, the most accurate source will typically be the firm's own CPA. The CPA should examine ten factors.

Projected earnings. Projected earnings are normally an extension of past earnings. Financial statements and tax returns (specifically income statements, balance sheets, and cash flow statements) should be examined and adjusted to determine:

- *The level of gross income.* Net income figures may be misleading, since principals may be taking profits in the form of perquisites and benefits as well as salaries. The CPA should determine how salaries compare to the "norm" for services performed. Are they too high? Alternatively, if they are lower than comparable payments to similar professionals, does this indicate cash flow or earnings problems?

- *Earnings trend.* At least five years should be reviewed. Measure each year's amount as a percent of a base year. A business trending up indicates the likely presence of growing goodwill. However, the CPA must also consider whether there are unusual or nonrecurring factors that artificially inflate or deflate income. Large pension contributions, malpractice claims, fees or court costs, and salary structures should be studied particularly carefully. The inability of one or more professionals to work during the period examined would obviously have a strong impact on earnings. Did the professional, out of choice, work forty hours per week, or only twenty?

Competition. An increased demand for established practices is typically reflected in an increase in prices. This has occurred in a number of professions due, in large part, to the increase in the number of newly licensed professionals – e.g., dentistry. An appraiser must also consider the number of other practitioners in the area, how thoroughly their practices saturate the market, and the price trend for services similar to those being valued.

Size of patient or client base. The greater the number of satisfied current patients or clients, the greater is the likelihood that a large number of referrals will be made to the practice. More emphasis should be given to this factor when selling the entire practice than when valuing the practice for purposes of appointing assets in a divorce or legal separation. The distribution of the client base should also be evaluated. Consider whether the clients are repeaters, recent additions, referrals from prior clients, young or old, etc. How many patients or clients are seen each day?

Payment sources. How the professional is paid greatly influences both the level and the stability of the practice's income. Measure how likely the practice is to be paid for services rendered, and how soon. Government programs typically pay less per procedure than the usual fee; so the source of payment may also indicate how much will be paid. Questions that should be asked by an appraiser include:

- Is the practice dependent on any particular group of patients or clients for a significant portion of its income?

- What percentage of patients pays bills through private insurance, Medicare, Medicaid, other sources?

- What is the aging of the professional's accounts receivable? Are monthly bills paid in thirty, sixty, ninety days, etc.? (This is a good indication of the financing needs and efficiency of the practice's collection procedures.)

Practitioner's workload. Income figures alone do not tell how many hours it took to generate a given level of profit. A practice that took forty hours of work to generate a given amount of earnings – say $400,000 – may be worth significantly more than one that took seventy hours to develop the same earnings. Factors that must be considered in this area include:

- Is the practice a personal type or mass production type? How much time spent with the patient or client was due merely to the practitioner's work style?

- Does the practitioner spend time on administrative or other problems that could be handled more efficiently and at lower cost by an office manager or other staff?

Fee structure. A great deal can be ascertained by examining the practice's fee structure. A professional who has been consistently and *successfully* charging above-average fees probably has developed significant professional goodwill. If fees are average or below average, perhaps there is an uncovered problem or a potential to increase revenues. An appraiser should ascertain:

- How do this practitioner's fees compare with fees charged in the community by other practitioners of similar reputation and skill?

- When was the last time fees were raised?

- How often have fees been raised in the last five years, and for what reasons?

- Was there measurable resistance to the last increase in fees (a significant drop-off in then current or prospective patients or clients)? Would there be a sizable loss of patients or clients if a fee increase was instituted? How large an increase would the market bear?

- Is billing computerized and how well is the system working?

Staff strength. Second only to the principal(s) in importance to the value of a professional practice is the quality and depth of the staff. Staff includes nonowner professionals (who may or may not carry clientele away if they leave), paraprofessionals, and clerical employees. Questions that should be asked by an appraiser in this area are:

- How long have the various individuals been with the practice; would they be likely to stay if the owner-professional(s) were to die or the practice were sold? What patients or clients (or essential skills) would nonowners take with them if they left? What costs would be involved in recruiting replacements and training them?

- What duties do the nonowners in the practice perform? What percentage of the total practice can be performed without the owner-professional?

- How well are nonowners compensated compared to similar employees in similar practices?

- Are there enforceable employment contracts, covenants not to compete, or special fringe benefits that would tie key employees to the practice even if new ownership takes over?

Location of the practice. In general, practices located in economically vibrant and growing communities are more valuable than those in unattractive and depressed areas, but this is not always true. For example, a dentist may have a higher volume of business in an area where preventive tooth care has not been stressed; a criminal attorney may have more potential business in the inner city than in a suburb.

Ironically, a practice producing a high income isn't necessarily more valuable in a community where there is a shortage of professionals; it would be relatively easy for a new practitioner to take advantage of the demand. Conversely, in a community saturated by and long-settled with professionals, start-up time and expense would be high for a new practitioner; so the value of an established practice with a full appointment book and a well-trained staff would therefore be higher.

Physical and mental health of the professional. Particularly in marital distribution situations, the professional's health is a dominant valuation factor. Significant professional goodwill may exist if the professional is in good health and can repeat or improve upon his past earnings record. But what if past earnings were generated by years of eighty-hour weeks that are no longer feasible? A surgeon who has a blood-pressure problem, or worse yet, an alcohol or other drug problem, may not be capable of sustaining the workload that "built the business."

Age of the professional. Age is another factor that should be given great weight in a valuation for divorce or separation purposes. Age, aside from its tangential relationship to health, can be used to indicate how long a past flow of earnings can reasonably be projected into the future. Although it is logical to project the earnings of a young practitioner for a longer time than a practitioner only a few years from retirement, an appraiser must consider that the earnings of a younger practitioner are lower and less certain.

Shortcut approach to buy-sell valuations. Since nonprofessionals cannot generally hold stock in a professional corporation and since most states require that such stock be bought back by the corporation or its surviving shareholders within a relatively short period of time after the transfer of interest, it is essential that a fully funded buy-sell agreement be utilized to protect the interests of all parties. Quite often the parties to such an agreement are unwilling to hire an independent appraiser to value their stock according to the appropriate sophisticated methods. For this reason, a quick and relatively inexpensive method of determining value is often desired, such as the "one times annual net income" formula all too often used for solo private practices.

Although there is no universal rule or perfect formula for arriving at a price, the simplified worksheet shown in Figure 70.3 provides a quick way to guesstimate the worth of a physician's practice; it can be easily modified to apply to other professional practices.

Figure 70.3

WORKSHEET FOR VALUING A PHYSICIAN'S PRACTICE
WORKSHEET ASSUMPTIONS

ACCOUNTS RECEIVABLE. Sellers sometimes exclude accounts receivable from the sale of the practice to keep the sales price down or to simplify the process; the selling professional collects the revenue from the receivables and the buyer doesn't have to worry about the collectibility or the trouble of collection. Conversely, the purchaser may want a practice with accounts receivable to maintain contact with the patients or clients (similar to purchasing a customer list).

Bills outstanding for more than one year are considered uncollectible; those that have been turned over to collection agencies are not considered as part of accounts receivable. Accounts receivable within 30 days of billing are considered worth between 80% and 90% of their face value. Between 30 and 60 days, the value drops to between 50% and 80%; while in most practices, accounts receivable are worth little after 60 days, *unless* a government agency or private insurer will pay the claim.

Practice point. It is important to view accounts receivable in perspective. Has the professional been "cleaning out" his accounts receivable and living off previous work he's now collecting for? Has he imposed fee increases which create the impression of a constant level of patient volume which is in reality decreasing? Has the professional done a good job of collecting and reporting accounts receivable? In many cases, poor bookkeeping or collection procedures understate the true value of the practice. For instance, a practice may be building its patient volume but, because of inefficiencies or poor pricing of services, hasn't generated a representative cash flow.

BUILDINGS/LAND. The fair market value of the real estate owned by the practice must be used rather than the book value.

EQUIPMENT/FURNISHINGS. A potential purchaser views equipment as capital that will have to be replaced. Equipment depreciates rapidly, partially due to wear and partially to obsolescence caused by the introduction of more effective or efficient (less labor intensive) or easier to use technology.

Some appraisal experts suggest that each item be priced between original cost and present book value. This worksheet suggests that equipment less than five years old be listed at 40% of its cost and older equipment at about 20% of cost. Where appropriate, use an actual fair market value appraisal; for example, certain furniture-say, an antique desk-may have value in excess of its original cost.

DRUGS/SUPPLIES. Most physicians have at least a two-month supply of drugs and other supplies. Divide the annual supply cost by six. Unused disposables are typically worth their cost less 10% to 20%, although a buyer may not choose to use what is currently in inventory, further reducing the practice value.

GOODWILL. Various methods of determining goodwill are discussed throughout this reading. The worksheet rule of thumb-25% of annual gross-can be used as an alternative to another commonly used guideline, $3 to $5 per record of regularly seen patients. Note that these are "quick guess" guidelines; they should not substitute for appropriate financial analysis and evaluation.

Value of Accounts Receivable

	Age	Percent of Face Value	Example	Your Figure
Input:	0-30 days	80-90%	$ 20,000	$_____
Input:	31-60 days	50-60%	50,000	_____
Input:	61 days or more	0 unless insurance	5,000	_____

Buildings and Land
Input: Market value of building and land   1,000,000   _____

Equipment and Furnishings

	Age	Percent of Face Value		
Input:	Less than 5 years	40% of cost	$ 30,000	_____
Input:	5 years or more	20% of cost	4,000	_____
Input:	Drugs, supplies (last 2 month's bills)		12,000	_____
Input:	Cash and market value of invested securities		10,000	_____
Input:	Goodwill (25% of annual gross)		200,000	_____
	Total estimate of practice assets		$ 1,331,000	$_____

Liabilities

Input:	Balance owed on equipment and furnishings	$ 5,000	_____
Input:	Salaries, bonuses, severance pay due	60,000	_____
Input:	Taxes due	40,000	_____
Input:	Accounts payable	23,000	_____
Input:	Insurance premiums due	70,000	_____
Input:	Mortgage balance	80,000	_____
Input:	Other liabilities	3,000	_____
	Total estimate of practice liabilities	$ 281,000	

Total estimate of practice assets	$1,331,000	_____
Total estimate of practice liabilities	281,000	_____
Estimate of value practice	$1,050,000	_____

Warning: Remember that the guidelines in the worksheet are only that; they will vary depending on the circumstances. Be sure to review the list of assumptions accompanying the worksheet. Note that a solo practice is almost always worth less than one where two or more professionals work together. This is why many practitioners bring in one or more associates well before they retire and negotiate a buyout that will effect a long and smooth transition period. This worksheet should be considered only a starting place for a full valuation.

Valuation Methods

Prior transactions method. Perhaps the most reliable method of valuing a practice, when it is available, is to ascertain the price it sold for in a previous transaction. This assumes, of course, that there was a recent sale or exchange and that it was at arm's length. Consideration should also be given to the magnitude of prior transactions – e.g., the purchase of greater than 50 percent of a practice creates a control premium, whereas the purchase of less than a 50 percent interest should involve a minority discount.

Capitalization of billings method. A practice can be valued by dividing the net income by the cost of capital. For example, using this formula, if the practice produced an adjusted net income after the owner's salary of $100,000, and it was assumed that capital should be "costed" at 20 percent (i.e., a buyer with a similar risk opportunity would demand a 20 percent return on his investment), the practice would be worth $500,000 ($100,000 divided by 20 percent).

Another traditional way of arriving at a practice value is by using a multiple of gross billings. The formula for determining the multiple to use is: net income percentage divided by capitalization rate equals percentage of billing factor. For example, assume the firm in our prior example billed $500,000 during the year. Since its adjusted net income was $100,000, its net income percentage on billings was 20 percent ($100,000 ÷ $500,000). Given the 20 percent capitalization rate, its value is $500,000, or 100 percent of billings (20% ÷ 20% = 1, or 100%). If the same firm billed only $400,000 but still netted $100,000 (a percentage of billing factor of 25 percent), it would be worth *more* than 100 percent of the billings. Using the formula, we get a 125 percent multiple: 25% ÷ 20% = 1.25 or 125%. Thus, the practice's value, on these facts, would still be $500,000 (125% of $400,000).

Excess earnings method. This is another simple, widely-used – and often court-blessed – method of quantifying the value of intangible assets. Essentially, earnings (pretax, *including* the professional owner's salary and fringe benefits) are adjusted as discussed above. Then the earnings in excess of that which is earned by similar professionals in similar types of practices are computed and that excess is capitalized (divided by a percentage to arrive at the capital it would take to produce it annually). The result is the estimated value of the goodwill in the practice. This would be added to the fair market value of tangible assets to arrive at a total value.

Example. Assume Doctor Know's average compensation for the last five years – after appropriate adjustments and weighting for its upward trend – was $180,000, but that similar physicians earned only $120,000 during the same period. This indicated that the difference, about $60,000 a year, is due to something other than return on tangible assets.

Excess earnings for most professional practices are capitalized at rates between 20 percent and 100 percent. The wide variation is a result of varying risk levels and differing ages of the professionals in question; the median capitalization rate is 33.3 percent. Here are the goodwill values of Doctor Know's practice at various capitalization rates:

Rate	Adjusted Excess	Value
20%	$60,000	$300,000
25%	$60,000	$240,000
33%	$60,000	$180,000
50%	$60,000	$120,000
100%	$60,000	$ 60,000

This brings up the question asked at the beginning of the discussion on valuations of businesses: what is meant by a "capitalization rate" and how does the appraiser know what capitalization rate to use? The capitalization rate is the projected cost of capital. But there is no fixed and certain answer to the question of "What is the right rate to use?" A good appraiser will consider such things as

- how many more productive years the professional has

- where on the income-producing cycle the professional was as of the valuation date (highest income-producing years for most professionals occur between ages forty-five and fifty-five)

- changes in the profession, the economy, and in government regulation.

For instance, skyrocketing malpractice costs are rapidly changing the practicing environment, causing many professionals to drastically change the way they work.

Most appraisers working with professional corporations will be conservative and use relatively high capitalization rates, 50 to 100 percent (meaning a low multiplier). This is because is more difficult to maintain "excess earnings" than earnings produced by passive income investments and, further, total earnings have been used as a base. If pretax earnings, after reduction for owner's compensation and benefits, is used as the base, a 20 or 40 percent capitalization rate (and thus a higher multiple) would be more appropriate. The table below sets out various capitalization rates and their related multipliers for determining value using the excess earnings method.

Capitalization Rate	Value (multiply adjusted excess by this rate)
3.5%	28.57/1
4.0%	25.00/1
5.0%	20.00/1
6.0%	16.67/1
7.0%	14.29/1
8.0%	12.50/1
9.0%	11.11/1
10.0%	10.00/1
11.0%	9.09/1
12.0%	8.33/1
13.0%	7.69/1
14.0%	7.14/1
15.0%	6.67/1
16.0%	6.25/1
17.0%	5.88/1
18.0%	5.56/1
19.0%	5.26/1
20.0%	5.00/1
25.0%	4.00/1
30.0%	3.33/1

Caveat: As is the case with any valuation method, the excess earnings concept has its limitations. Goodwill can be understated, because even a practice without excess earnings may have considerable worth as a going concern. On the other hand, goodwill can be overstated, because the excess earnings method does not consider whether or not the practice is marketable. Third, many subjective judgments are required (such as the appropriate weight to give the trend of earnings, the adjustments to make to earnings, and the capitalization rate to use).

Rough Rules of Thumb for Valuations

Almost all tax practitioners and financial planners use rules of thumb (often called "SWAG," or Scientific Wild Asset Guesses) that they've developed as the byproduct of practical experience. These estimations lie between calculations and pure conjecture and serve as starting places in the valuation process, later to be abandoned or modified. They can also be used where more precise methods are deemed impractical. The following rough rules of thumb are suggested for valuing various professions:

- *Medical:* Net asset value plus 20 to 40 percent of annual revenue for goodwill (referral practices would be worth less, continuing client base practices worth more).

- *Veterinary:* Net asset value plus 60 to 90 percent of annual revenue for goodwill.

- *Legal:* Because client files can't be sold (traditionally, lawyers are ethically precluded from selling their law practices, but some states have started to permit these sales), personal goodwill typically does not enter into the valuation process. Therefore, net asset value is often the major value determinant. In the case of distribution upon divorce, if there is a buy-sell agreement, the price set in the agreement is usually considered merely an indication of value and is certainly rebuttable. Remember that work-in-progress fees are not reflected in the records of a law firm. So, even if the firm's accounting records are accurate and nonfraudulent, a firm that takes no retainers and sends no bills, but has many contingent fee arrangements, can easily be undervalued. Conversely, fees contingent on events that may not occur must be discounted.

- *Accounting:* Net asset value plus a goodwill payment of from 80 to 130 percent of annual revenue (paid out over time). Another common method uses 20 percent of projected fees for five years, discounted for both attrition and the time value of money. According to the *CPA Handbook*, a third commonly used formula is 40 percent of gross receipts for the prior three years and a percentage of average annual fees as follows: 100 percent for clients served over four years, 75 percent for clients served from three to four years, 50 percent for clients served from two to three years, and 25 percent for clients served from one to two years.

- *Dental:* Net asset value plus 30 to 40 percent of annual revenues for goodwill.

- *Engineering/Architecture:* Net asset value plus 25 to 50 percent of annual revenues for goodwill (firms with few continuing clients would, of course, have little if any goodwill).

Data Needed in the Valuation Process

Valuation experts should review each of the following:

- Last five years' profit and loss statements and balance sheets (certified financial statements by an independent CPA firm are preferable). Five years is a common time frame because it (1) minimizes the possibility of valuation planning, (2) covers a complete business cycle, (3) examines good as well as bad times, (4) permits discounting or elimination of "aberration years," and (5) illustrates the stability and trend of profits. Graphs are particularly useful in identifying and illustrating aberration years or the direction and velocity of a profit trend.

- Last five years' federal income tax returns.

- Any business leases.

- Last five years' fee schedules.

- Brochures on the firm.

- Articles of incorporation and by-laws, and minutes of board of directors' meetings for the last five years.

- Last five years' appointment books.

- State employment research data (particularly information from state professional licensing department).

- Demographic and practice economics information available from state or county professional societies (such as the state or local medical or bar association).

- Studies published in professional journals such as the American Medical Association's "Socioeconomic Characteristics of Medical Practice" (published annually), or by the American Bar Association, or in private publications such as "Medical Economics," or, for the legal profession, "Corporate Law Department Surveys and Survey of Law Firm Economics" (Altman-Weil Management Consultants, Inc., published annually) and "Compensation of Attorneys" (Steven Langer and Associates).

Several professional appraisal groups offer professional designations, including: :

(1) the American Society of Appraisers,

(2) the Appraisal Institute,

(3) National Association of Certified Valuation Analysts,

(4) American Institute of Certified Public Accountants, and

(7) CBV Institute (Canada).

70.4 PLANNING FOR VALUATION DISCOUNTS IN CLOSELY HELD AND FAMILY BUSINESSES

Various other circumstances have substantial impact on the valuation of business, including restrictive agreements, such as cross purchase or redemption plans, and partnership liquidation agreements. Code section 2703 (see Chapter 47) will have a substantial impact on the use of such agreements in many closely held businesses.

Lower valuation for the business interest may result where it does not fully participate in the future growth of the business, i.e., preferred stock and "frozen" partnership interests (see Chapter 49), and long-term installment sales (see Chapter 41).

A failure to undertake proper valuation planning for the family business will leave the estate at the mercy of the IRS, and may make it impossible to retain the enterprise. To be really effective, any plan must contain the following elements:

1. A present transfer of interests in the business from family members in the older generation to those in younger generations, either by sale, gift or both.

2. A shift of all or part of the future growth of the enterprise to the younger generation.

3. The owners of the family business should seriously consider taking full use of their unified credit and even their GST tax exemption during life through transfers of interests in family businesses.

For a good example, see TAM 9131006, where decedent created a family partnership to engage in real estate operations and transferred mostly limited partnership interests to four children and fourteen grandchildren, with one general partnership interest to a son, all covered by the $10,000 annual exclusion. No gift tax returns were filed, and all income was allocated to the decedent for a management fee. Held – no gift or estate tax consequences, profits were to be allocated proportionately to the partners and all limited partnership interests were transferable, subject to a right of first refusal.

On the other hand, retention of value in the estates of the older generation may facilitate stock redemptions, particularly under Code section 303 (Chapter 48); deferred payment of tax under Code section 6166 (Chapter 18); and special use valuation for real property under Code section 2032A (see above).

Regardless of the difficulties, the conclusion is inescapable that lifetime transfers of interests in family business enterprises are almost essential to planning for succession.

The two most common discounts available for family and closely held businesses are the discounts for lack of marketability and for a minority interest (i.e., lack of control). Similarly, an additional discount may be appropriate to reflect those instances in which a limited partner cannot withdraw from the partnership and is locked in to his investment (i.e., a lock-in discount). Also, other discounts may be applied to reflect built in capital gains or key management personnel.

Minority Interest Discounts

The cases have been liberal in permitting substantial discounts in value based on the fact that the decedent's interest in the business is a fractional or minority interest.[33] In some instances, value may be increased to reflect a control premium.

The minority interest discount principle refers to the fact that the owner of less than a majority interest in an enterprise cannot control day-to-day or long range managerial decisions, impact future earnings, control efforts for growth potential, establish executive compensation, or get at the corporate assets through liquidation. Because the owner of a minority interest lacks these benefits of control over the business, an acquiror of a minority interest will pay less for that interest, on a pro-rata basis, than if acquiring a controlling interest in the business. In instances where the owner lacks the ability to exercise control over the operations of the enterprise, the owner's interest may be worth significantly less than its liquidation value.

For many years, the IRS was uncomfortable with the idea that minority interests owned among family members could be valued at a discount even though the collective ownership of the individual family members gave the family control of the corporation. In 1981, the IRS issued Revenue Ruling 81-253,[34] which stated that no minority interest discount would be allowed for intrafamily transfers of shares of stock in a corporation controlled by the family in the absence of discord among the family members (the concept is commonly referred to as the "family attribution" principle.) However, after experiencing a long line of cases in which the family attribution principle was rejected,[35] the IRS announced its abandonment of the family attribution principle in Revenue Ruling 93-12.[36]

But, is the Treasury/IRS rethinking its surrender in Rev. Rul. 93-12? In *Buck v. United States*,[37] the government asserted the following positions in support of its motion for summary judgment:

- *"[A]llowing the discounts would endorse a circumvention of one of the primary purposes of the gift tax, which is to assure that estate tax is not avoided."*

- *Disallowing fractional discounts **where there was no fractional interest beforehand** ensures that "the value of the gift made by the donor, not the measure of enrichment to the donee ... is determinative."*

The government lost the case, but the court made no mention of Rev. Rul. 93-12, which, while not directly on-point, is strongly analogous. Nevertheless, the second position wholly overlooks the very nature of the federal gift tax as an excise tax. Query: Will the IRS start to attempt to assert either of these positions, both of which the court properly rejected?

In determining the size of the minority interest discount to be applied, each case must take into consideration all relevant facts and circumstances.[38] The discount applied in other cases is not normally a determinant as to the proper discount to be applied in a given case.[39] The reference to prior cases and articles discussing discounts is appropriate for demonstrating the existence of a discount, but will not be given any weight for proving the magnitude of discount in a specific case.

A crucial factor in establishing the minority interest discount is the bundle of rights that are possessed by the owner of the corporate or partnership interest. Such rights will be set forth by both a combination of applicable state law, corporate articles and bylaws, partnership agreement, or other rights and restrictions agreed to by the parties. An appraiser who conducts an examination of ownership rights must disregard any provision that constitutes an applicable restriction under Code section 2704(b) and the attorney may have a duty to inform the appraiser of those rights which fall within this definition. Thus, restrictive provisions that are drafted into an agreement should be carefully considered before being implemented.

The courts, IRS, and taxpayers all agree that a minority interest is worth less than a controlling interest on a pro-rata basis. Thus, the issue is not whether a minority interest discount is allowable, but rather the amount of the minority interest discount.

The primary source of data utilized by business appraisers to determine discounts for minority interests in operating entities comes from acquisitions of controlling interests in the public marketplace. This data is utilized because the applicable minority interest discount can be calculated as the inverse of the control premium paid by an investor who acquires various rights that are otherwise unavailable to the minority interest. A number of comprehensive sources that accumulate such information are readily available to the public.[40]

In determining minority interest discounts for privately-held real estate concerns, a different source of empirical data is often utilized. With the decision in *Estate of Berg v. Commissioner*,[41] the Tax Court has specified that a permissible approach for determining minority interest discounts for interests in real estate companies is the "REIT Approach." This approach involves an analysis of publicly traded real estate entities (including Real Estate Investment Trusts, or "REITs") that report the aggregate appraised values of their real estate holdings.

Advanced estate planners and appraisers are quick to point out that the use of REIT data may be inapplicable for valuing smaller, less diverse corporations and partnerships. They argue that the relatively larger size of the typical publicly traded REIT makes such an entity incomparable for discount purposes. A better means of gauging the discount for family limited partnerships and corporations that are of relatively small capitalization (under $25,000,000) may be achieved by making comparison to smaller privately owned limited partnerships traded on the secondary market. These entities typically have partnership agreements which contain similar restrictions to those found in family limited partnerships and usually maintain a less diverse asset base than the typical REIT. Discounts for such entities generally are higher than found in REITs. Data on the trading of such interests may be available through a number of commercial, proprietary sources.

Lack of Marketability Discounts

The lack of marketability principle is well documented and is based on the fact that stock in a closely held business enterprise is less attractive and more difficult to sell than publicly traded stock.[42] Lack of marketability discounts relate to the inherent lack of flexibility in getting in and out of investments with no ready market. Where an active trading market does not exist, then other factors may be used as valuation benchmarks, and the lack of marketability discount becomes operative and applicable.

The IRS issued Revenue Ruling 77-287[43] in order to provide information and guidance to taxpayers, IRS personnel, and others concerned with the valuation, for federal tax purposes, of securities that cannot be immediately resold because they are restricted from resale pursuant to federal securities laws. In valuing restricted securities, Revenue Ruling 77-287 states that the following documents and facts should be reviewed:

1. A copy of any declaration of trust, trust agreement, and any other agreements relating to the shares of restricted stock;

2. A copy of any document showing any offers to buy or sell or indications of interest in buying or selling the restricted shares;

3. The latest prospectus of the company;

4. Annual reports of the company for three to five years preceding the valuation date;

5. The trading prices and trading volumes of the related class of traded securities one month preceding the valuation date;

6. The relationship of the parties to the agreements concerning the restricted stock, such as whether they are members of the immediate family or perhaps whether they are officers or directors of the company; and

7. Whether the interest being valued represents a majority or minority ownership.

The Tax Court will base its analysis of the magnitude of allowable marketability valuation discount on, among other things, the following factors:

1. Comparison of sales prices for private versus public stock;

2. Financial statement analysis;

3. Company's dividend paying policy;

4. Nature of company, position in the industry, economic outlook;

5. Quality of the company's management;

6. Amount of control in transferred interest;

7. Restrictions (if any) on transfer of interest;

8. Holding period for the interest;

9. Redemption policy of company, as shown historically;

10. Costs associated with public offering.

The key is property specific analysis. In other words, in valuing corporations and other entities, value must be determined based upon a comprehensive review of the circumstances of the subject business entity relative to the circumstances of other entities that are being offered for comparison.

The amount of published research data on lack of marketability discounts continues to increase. However, the appraisal profession has been unable to agree upon the method for quantifying lack of marketability discounts. On the one hand, there have been the following studies pertaining to restricted stocks:

Study	Mean Discount
SEC Institutional Investor Study (1966-1969)	24%
Gelman Study (1968-1970)	33%
Trout Study (1968-1972)	33%
Maroney Study	36%
Maher Study (1969-1973)	35%
Standard Research Consultants Study (1978-1982)	45%
Willamette Management Associates Studies (1975-1985)	42%-47%
Silber Study (1981-1988)	34%
FMV Opinions, Inc. Study (1979-1992)	23%
Management Planning Study (1980-1992)	27%
Johnson Study (1991-1995)	20%
Columbia Financial Advisors Study (1996-1997)	21%
Columbia Financial Advisors Study (1997-1998)	13%

Lock-In Discount

For partnerships, consideration should always be given as to whether the interest can be liquidated through the enforcement of withdrawal rights. In some states, if the partnership agreement does not provide a time for when capital will be returned, a limited partner is given the right to withdraw from the partnership no sooner than six months after giving notice to the general partner. In other states, applicable state law prohibits the return of capital to a limited partner except upon the occurrence of certain events specified in the partnership agreement (e.g., upon expiration of the partnership term). California recently amended its limited partnership act to remove withdrawal rights unless specified in the partnership agreement.

If the partnership agreement or state law does not confer upon the limited partner any right to withdraw capital, then the interest may remain in the partnership

VALUATION PLANNING CHAPTER 70

until expiration of the partnership term (often thirty-five to fifty years in length). In such case, the limited partner is "locked-in" to maintaining his investment in the partnership and a lock-in discount is appropriate.

In determining whether a lock-in discount is applicable, Code section 2704(b) must be reviewed. Under this section, a lock-in discount may not exist for federal tax purposes if it constitutes an applicable restriction under state law (see discussion below). In such case, the limited partner may be locked in to the partnership under the partnership agreement but prevented by Code section 2704(b) from considering the effect of the withdrawal restriction if such restriction is more stringent that applicable state law.

Other Discounts

In valuing interests in corporations that hold investment assets (e.g., real property, marketable securities, coins, etc.) consideration should be given as to whether there are potential capital gains that will be taxed at the corporate level.[44] It should be noted, however, that a discount for built-in-gains tax is not automatic.[45]

IRC Chapter 14

Chapter 14 of the Internal Revenue Code must be considered in valuing interests in corporations and partnerships. Chapter 14 presents valuation rules for determining the value of interests in corporations and partnerships that are controlled by family members (generally where more than 50 percent of value is held by the family). The application of these statutes can result in a gift even though no wealth is actually transferred to other family members (e.g., Code section 2701's use of the subtraction method for valuing applicable retained interests) and cause certain restrictive provisions in an agreement to be disregarded for transfer tax purposes (e.g., Code section 2704(b)'s disregard of applicable restrictions).

Section 2701 applies to valuation of corporate and partnership interests designed for estate freeze purposes. In instances where there are capital interests that have a preference as to income distributions, the valuation of transfers (including recapitalizations) among family members may result in gift tax. In instances in which there are no preferences as to capital ownership, Section 2701 generally does not apply.

Code section 2702 applies to interests in trusts (e.g., GRITs, GRATs and GRUTs, split interest purchases) and does not require consideration in valuing a closely held business.

Code section 2703 applies to "any option, agreement, or other right to acquire or use the property at a price less than the fair market value of the property (without regard to such option, agreement or right) or any restriction on the right to sell or use such property." Thus, a right or restriction contained in a partnership agreement, articles of incorporation, corporate bylaws, shareholders' agreement, or any other agreement will fall subject to section 2703.

Similarly, a right or restriction may be implicit in the capital structure of an entity.[46] Such rights and restrictions will have no effect for valuation purposes unless the following three conditions exist:

1. there is a bona fide business purpose;

2. the agreement is not a testamentary device to transfer property to members of the decedent's family for less than full and adequate consideration in money or money's worth; and

3. the terms are comparable to similar arrangements entered into by persons in arm's length transactions.

The IRS has taken an adverse position on the use of investment partnerships for discount purposes, as evidenced by its attempts to use section 2703 to disallow discounts for investment partnerships when an individual died shortly after its formation.[47] Notwithstanding such attacks, many practitioners believe the IRS position on this issue is unfounded and will continue to be defeated in the courts upon presentment.[48]

Code section 2704 applies to lapsed voting and liquidation rights in a corporation or partnership if the individual holding such right immediately before the lapse and members of such individual's family hold, both before and after the lapse, control of the entity. If lapsed voting or liquidation rights exist, then the amount of the transfer is determined by the value of the interest before the lapse minus the value after the lapse.

A voting right means a right to vote with respect to any matter of the entity. In the case of a partnership, the right of the general partner to participate in partnership management is a voting right.[49] A liquidation right

1025

is defined as a right or ability to compel the entity to acquire all or a portion of the holder's equity interest in the entity, including by reason of aggregate voting power, whether or not its exercise would result in the complete liquidation of the entity.[50]

A lapse of a voting right occurs at the time a presently exercisable voting right is restricted or eliminated, while a lapse of a liquidation right occurs at the time a presently exercisable liquidation right is restricted or eliminated. However, a transfer of an interest that results in a lapse of a liquidation right is not subject to section 2704 if the rights with respect to the transferred interest are not restricted or eliminated.

Additionally, Section 2704 allows for the value of property to be determined without consideration of any "applicable restrictions." An applicable restriction is defined as any restriction:

1. that effectively limits the ability of the corporation or partnership to liquidate,

2. with respect to which either of the following applies:

    a. The restriction lapses, in whole or in part, after the transfer [of an interest in the corporation or partnership to (or for the benefit of) a member of the transferor's family], or

    b. The transferor or any member of the transferor's family, either alone or collectively, has the right after such transfer to remove, in whole or in part, the restriction.

Excepted from the definition of applicable restrictions are any commercially reasonable restriction which arises as part of any financing by the corporation or partnership with a person who is not related to the transferor or transferee, or a member of the family of either, or any restriction imposed, or required to be imposed, by any federal or state law. An example of an applicable restriction is where a partnership agreement requires a unanimous vote to liquidate where state law imposes a less stringent requirement (e.g., unanimous consent of the general partners and a majority of limited partners).

As discussed above, a lock-in discount may be negated by section 2704(b) if the lock-in discount is created by an applicable restriction.

Fractional Interest Discounts

The courts have long recognized that the value of a fractional interest in real property may be less than the pro-rata value of the same real property if held as a full fee simple.[51] Among the factors cited by the courts in justifying the application of a discount to the pro-rata value of a fractional interest in real property are the following:

1. The owner of a fractional interest will have greater difficulty in finding a ready market for the sale of the interest due to the fact that a buyer of the interest will have to share ownership with another;

2. The owner of a fractional interest cannot sell the fee interest in the property or lease the property without the consent of the holder of the remaining interest(s);

3. The owner of a fractional interest by himself generally cannot obtain a loan from normal sources of credit secured by only a partial interest in the real property;

4. The owner of a fractional interest may not have the right to exclusive use of the property so as to put it to its highest and best use;

5. An action by an owner of a fractional interest to partition real property does not guaranty that the partitioning co-owner will receive property whose utility is equal to that of the entire parcel from which the partition took place;

6. The cost of bringing an action to partition real property is often substantial and a fee interest in a portion of the property received may be worth less than the proportionate share of the whole property, or the sales proceeds (if the property may not be fairly partitioned) may not equal the property's fair market value; and

7. The existence of an undivided fractional interest is a legal matter affecting title to real property and often cannot be solved without obtaining legal counsel and commencing legal proceedings at significant cost.

For these reasons, many courts have allowed a discount to the proportionate value of real property in order to arrive at the value a willing purchaser would be willing to pay for an undivided fractional interest in real property.[52] If the taxpayer asserts that a discount from the proportionate value of the entire property is warranted, the taxpayer must prove that a willing buyer would purchase the property and a willing seller would sell the property at a price that is less than its proportionate value. Generally, the taxpayer may satisfy this burden by using expert opinion testimony of competent and experienced real estate brokers or appraisers, backed by records of actual sales of fractional interests in the same or similar property.[53]

The IRS valuation manual acknowledges the allowance by courts of decreases in value for partial ownership. The Guide states that the extent of ownership rights in each case is to be determined under state law. Although the IRS Valuation Manual states that the fractional interest discount is generally based on the cost of dividing the land (e.g., survey costs, court costs, legal fees, etc.) the following other factors must be considered:

- Size of the fractional interest
- Number of owners
- Size of tract and likelihood of partition
- Use of land
- Access to financing

Whereas co-owners are free to contract with one another and impose restrictions upon their ownership rights, one means of negating the Service's "cost of partition" argument is through the use of a Co-Ownership Agreement in which each co-owner agrees to waive his right to partition the subject property. Such waivers serve a legitimate business purpose of keeping the property in the immediate family for future generations. It should be kept in mind that a co-ownership agreement is likely to invoke the requirements of Code section 2703 and will not have any effect for federal tax purposes unless the three requirements for the safe harbor are met.

In *Estate of Barge v. Comissioner*,[54] the Tax Court applied a discounted net cash flow approach to value an undivided 25 percent interest in timberland gifted by the donor. The court's analysis reviewed the following factors:

1. time in years to partition;
2. required rate of return;
3. estimated value upon partition date;
4. estimated annual income; and
5. estimated partition costs.

The result produced a 26 percent discount to the otherwise proportionate value of the interest.

Using Fractional Interests with Family Partnerships

Another advanced planning technique is to reduce asset values by applying multiple discounts. This concept is referred to as "double discounting" and permits the use of fractional interests with a family limited partnership to gain the benefits of all four discounts (i.e., fractional interest discount, minority interest discount, lack of marketability discount, and lock-in discount).

Under this planning, the family limited partnership will own less than 100 percent of the real property. Usually, the remaining interest in the property will be owned outside the partnership by children or grandchildren. Ownership of such undivided interests in the form of a generation-skipping trust is often desirable since the income from the fractional interest can be distributed to the child or grandchild and used to pay expenses of education or other expenses (e.g., music lessons, art, dance, and travel to Europe) that are not legal obligations of the parents. The use of a co-ownership agreement to waive the right to partition or cause a forced sale should be included in this planning in order to prevent the child or grandchild from attempting to liquidate his fractional interest.

Although this technique theoretically reduces the value of partnership interests, it can be enhanced by providing empirical data that quantifies the magnitude of last value. To date, the authors are aware of no specific studies that quantify the amount of discount by this planning.

Avoiding Pitfalls

In planning for discounted asset values, watch out for the problem created by *Estate of Smith*,[55] in which the court held that for purposes of computing adjusted taxable gifts on the federal estate return, the value of all lifetime gifts may be reconsidered, even if a gift tax return was filed and the statute of limitations has run.

While additional gift tax cannot be collected, this could force the taxable estate into a higher bracket and alter marital deduction gifts.

Gifts made after August 5, 1997 are no longer revalued for estate tax purposes if the gift tax statute of limitations has run and an appropriate gift tax return has been filed. However, this may very well increase the likelihood of having a gift tax audit because the IRS may no longer revalue such gifts on the estate tax return.

Also, do no overlook *Estate of Murphy*,[56] where eighteen days before death decedent transferred less than 1 percent to each of two children to bring her percentage below 50 percent, and her estate claimed a minority discount. The Tax Court allowed a discount for lack of marketability, but rejected the minority discount, noting that decedent gave up control on paper, but not in reality.

Note that the cases indicate that courts are closely examining the approach used by experts in valuing business interests, and the qualifications of the appraisers. In *Estate of Campbell*,[57] the court emphasized the importance of evaluating both earnings and net asset values in arriving at the actual value, and allowed a substantial discount. In *Estate of Berg*,[58] a 60 percent discount in the value of closely held stock was claimed to represent both minority and lack of marketability discounts. The appraisal was by petitioner's CPA, Mr. Whalen, an experienced practitioner who had served on the faculty of several universities and had testified as an expert witness in several cases on lack of marketability and minority discounts, but as the court noted, with no formal education as an appraiser. The court said: "we find the appraisal by Whalen, who is not a certified appraiser, unpersuasive for two reasons. First, he relies on *Estate of Andrews v. Commissioner*,[59] which does not support petitioner's position. The only other support for Whalen's appraisal is two articles by H. Calvin Coolidge." Although the underpayment penalty that was assessed was later reversed by the Eighth Circuit, this case is a good example of why a formal appraisal, employing a qualified independent full-time appraiser, should always be commissioned.

Control and the Swing Vote Issue

It is well established that if the business interest being valued is a controlling interest, then a premium must be added to the valuation to reflect control. Recently, the IRS has applied this concept to situations where the transfers to individual family members were of minority interests, but they could collectively exercise control over the business entity. A donor owned 100 percent of the stock in a family corporation. He transferred 30 percent to each of three children, and 5 percent to his spouse. The gifts were valued at net asset value less a 25 percent discount for minority interest and lack of marketability.

In Letter Ruling 9436005, the IRS held that even though each gift is valued separately under Revenue Ruling 93-12[60], since the blocks were transferred simultaneously, each had a swing vote characteristic, meaning that the owner of any 30 percent block could join with the owner of any other 30 percent block to exercise control, and that characteristic affected the value of the gift, citing *Estate of Winkler*.[61] The IRS pointed out that had the gifts been sequential, the first 30 percent would not have the swing vote characteristic, but the second would. Further, the transfer of the second 30 percent would increase the value of the first 30 percent, and would be an indirect gift. The same would occur on the transfer of the third 30 percent block.

Costs of Liquidation as a Valuation Factor

Where valuation of interests in corporations is based on the value of the underlying assets of the corporation, should that value be discounted for a hypothetical income tax that would be incurred if the corporation were liquidated to reach the assets? The IRS steadfastly denies such a discount is available.

The Partition Theory

The IRS has also ruled that when valuing undivided interests in property, rather than permitting discounts, the property should be valued under the partition theory. Under that theory, the value of the property in question is reduced by the hypothetical costs of a legal action to partition it. For example, in the case of an undivided one half interest in a farm, the valuation would start with 100 percent of the value of the farm, subtract the legal costs of partitioning it into two farms of equal value, and then divide the result by two.

In what appears to be a blow to the IRS theory of valuation of undivided interests in property based on the cost of partition rather than fractional discounts, the Tax Court has held a fractional interest discount in excess of partition costs is appropriate for a decedent's interest in a farm. In *Estate of Cervin*, TC Memo 1994-550, the court held the farm could not be easily partitioned and a homestead could not be easily sold. In finding higher discounts, the court did not really reject the partition theory, other than with respect to homestead property. It concluded that a partition would involve substantial costs and fees, and the ability of the co-owners to agree on relative values. In other words, it used a discount rather than hypothetical costs of partition. It also rejected reliance by the estate's experts on case decisions and articles, indicating that it is up to the court, not the appraiser, to evaluate the significance of such authorities! A similar discount approach was applied in *Estate of Barge v. Commissioner*, TC Memo 1997-188, in finding a discount based on a number of factors, not just the cost of partition.

The erosion of the IRS's cost-to-partition theory is observed by TAM 9718004, where the IRS recognized fractional interest discounts are not always limited to partition costs. Also, the IRS Valuation Training for Appeals Officers course book states that an appropriate discount for a fractional interest is based on several factors, including:

1. the size of the fractional interest (lower interest indicates a larger discount);

2. the number of owners (higher number of owners indicates a larger discount);

3. the size of the tract and ability to partition (smaller tract indicates a larger discount);

4. the use of the land (less productive indicates a larger discount);

5. the number of owners (more owners indicates a larger discount); and

6. the availability of financing (no financing indicates a larger discount.)

Obtaining Valuation Discounts

First, be reasonable about discounts. Back justifications up, in writing, with an independent qualified third party appraisal that would hold up in court. File that analysis with the gift tax return to start the statute of limitations clock. More importantly, make sure the appraisal satisfies the adequate disclosure provisions of Code section 6501(c).

Second, give the entity a business or investment purpose self-evident from its ongoing activities. An entity must be able to show that the reason for its existence is more than a mere attempt to obtain a transfer tax valuation discount. Build in and document a business or investment reason for the partnership to exist – other than to save transfer tax. Meet state law requirements for the type of entity claimed. The stronger business and investment reasons there are, the more likely the gift and estate tax discounts will be sustained.

Third, the owner must, in reality, treat the entity as separate from himself. In other words, as far as the IRS is concerned, an entity that is the alter ego of the founder isn't an entity. Where the parties intend that nothing of substance will change, except the level of federal transfer tax, expect an IRS challenge. If the IRS can disregard the entity, most if not all of the underlying reason for the discount vanishes.

Fourth, time really is money. Deathbed Family Limited Partnerships (FLP) are an invitation to litigation. So create a FLP before it's needed to save estate taxes.

70.5 ISSUES IN COMMUNITY PROPERTY STATES

The character of a business or investment asset as either community or separate property will have a considerable impact on its valuation. One spouse's undivided 50 percent community property interest in a business or investment asset, which is wholly owned by both spouses, will produce a minority interest discount. On the other hand, a spouse's 100 percent separate property interest in a business or investment asset will not be subject to minority interest discounts. Additionally, any applicable valuation discounts will affect the step up in basis for the surviving spouse which inherits community property.

70.6 THE LEVELS OF VALUE

It is important to be familiar with and understand the so-called levels of value. The chart below depicts one version of the levels of value.

The top level of value is the strategic or synergistic level of value. This level of value is not available to every buyer in the marketplace, because it requires synergies or other intrinsic valuation drivers to be present that only certain buyers possess. For example,

THE TOOLS & TECHNIQUES OF ESTATE PLANNING

a competitor company may be willing to pay a higher price for a competitor firm than someone who is not in the industry yet because of the possibility of achieving synergies by taking steps to eliminate duplicative services, e.g., accounts payable and receivable, sales, etc., within the combined companies that a new entrant into the marketplace could not do. As a result, companies that have these unique valuation drivers are willing to pay more for a competitor in the form of a valuation premium because of the ability to recast the combined financial statements to reflect the elimination of duplicative departments. The strategic or synergistic level of value usually is higher than fair market value and cannot be fair market value because it would require an assumption of a particular buyer, which would violate the hypothetical participant requirement.

This increased value is a strategic or synergistic control premium. Strategic or synergistic value is *not* fair market value. Strategic buyers can operate the combined businesses *differently* than a mere financial buyer who lacks that peculiar characteristic, which opens up avenues of increased value. This is why the strategic buyer usually is willing to pay more than a financial buyer. For example, through a merger and elimination of duplicative departments, e.g., two accounts payable departments, etc., economies of scale can be achieved, and combined financial statements can demonstrate that the combined entity is worth more than the combined value of the two entities standing alone.

The financial control value is the level of value at which the buyer is buying financial control of the

Figure 70.4

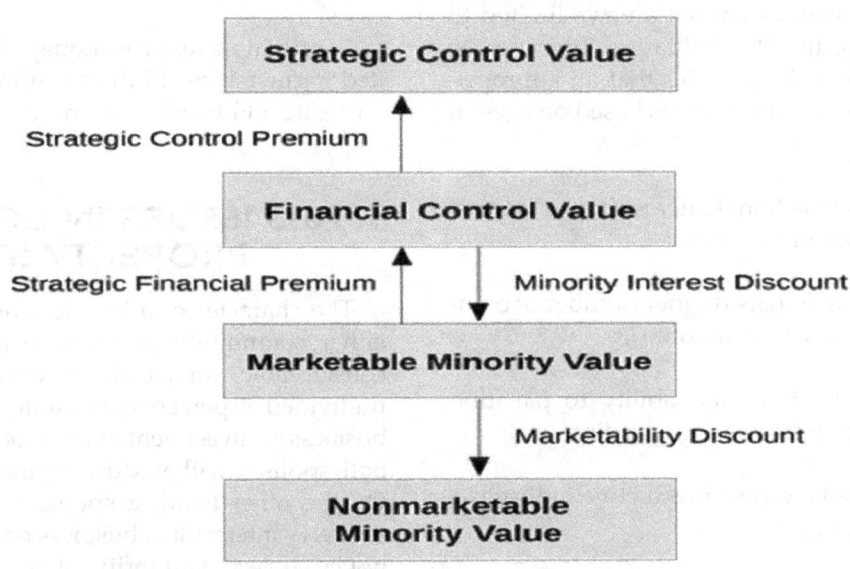

entity, but lacks the synergistic characteristic. The financial buyer is willing to pay more than the buyers at lower levels of value because the buyer is confident that it can operate the company *better* than the prior ownership. For example, the buyer may shorten receipt of accounts receivable or infuse operating capital or additional capital for expansion that the prior owner either didn't or couldn't infuse. Financial control value is considered fair market value of the enterprise or interest.

The marketable minority value is the value of a non-controlling interest where the ownership interest is freely marketable. The majority view in business valuation is that this is the level at which publicly traded stocks generally reside because the vast majority of shareholders hold non-controlling interests.

However, there is a minority school of business appraisers that believes that publicly traded stocks trade at a marketable control value given the small number of corporate takeovers in any given year. This means that these appraisers consider both discounts for lack of control and discounts for lack of marketability for the subject company.

The nonmarketable non-controlling level of value is the lowest level of value, and it generally is a non-controlling interest in a closely held entity. This value takes into consideration a discount for lack of control and a discount for lack of marketability.

The strategic control level, also known as the synergistic control level, may or may not be any higher than the financial control value. If the economies of scale or advantage/characteristic is miniscule or negligible, the strategic buyer may not be willing to pay much more than a financial buyer.

In fact, depending upon the facts, the difference between the financial control value and the marketable minority value or even the non-marketable minority value may be very large or very small.

Example of the Differences in the Levels of Value

Suppose that there is a closely-held operating company that is reflecting net income of $250,000. However, on closer examination, the controlling shareholder is taking out $500,000 per year more in salary than that would be paid to a third party manager. Moreover, there is a lease to the company by the controlling shareholder that calls for rent that exceeds fair market value by approximately $100,000 per year. Additionally, the controlling shareholder's spouse is on the payroll to the tune of $60,000 per year, and all indications are that the spouse is not even reporting for work. A potential control buyer could save $50,000 per year by decreasing inventory turns and by providing additional operating capital. Lastly, a prospective synergistic/strategic buyer of the company could eliminate the accounts payable and accounts receivable departments of the subject company, together with certain executive positions, for a total proposed savings of $300,000 per year. Assume a price-to-earnings multiple of five.

From the standpoint of the levels of value:

1. The unadjusted value of the company is $250,000 × 5 = $1,250,000

2. Normalizing adjustments could be made to the marketable minority level as follows: $250,000 (net income as reported) + $500,000 (excess compensation) + $60,000 (spouse compensation) + $100,000 (excess lease payments) = $910,000 × 5 = $4,550,000

3. Additional adjustments could be made at the control level of $50,000, bringing the value of the company to $4,600,000 (4,550,000 + $50,000)

4. At the strategic level of value, an additional adjustment of $300,000 per year for reduction of expenses of another owned entity due to duplication that could bring the value of the company to $6,300,000 ($4,800,000 + $1,500,000).

Summary of valuation indications:

As reported:	$1,250,000
Marketable minority level of value:	$4,550,000
Control Level of Value:	$4,600,000
Strategic Level of Value:	$6,300,000

70.7 WHERE CAN I FIND OUT MORE?

is an excellent text in the business valuation area. Helpful references are:

1. Valuing a Business: The Analysis and Appraisal of Closely-Held Companies (6th Ed.), Pratt et al, McGraw-Hill (2022).

2. Valuing Fractional Interests in Real Estate 2.0, Dennis A. Webb, Milonguero Press (2022).

3. Valuation: Measuring and Managing the Value of Companies (7th Ed.), McKinsey & Co. (2020).

4. Qualitative Business Valuation: A Mathematical Approach for Today's Professionals (2nd Ed.), Abrams, John Wiley & Sons (2010).

5. Financial Valuation: Applications and Methods (4th Ed.), Hitchner, John Wiley & Sons (2017).

6. Understanding Business Valuation (6th Ed.), Trugman, Business Valuation Resources, LLC (2022).

7. Business Valuation: An Integrated Theory (3rd Ed.), Mercer & Harms, John Wiley & Sons (2020).

70.8 CONCLUSION

The valuation of all business and property interests is an art, not a science. Many variables must be considered and evaluated. The quality of evaluation will be, in part, a function of the appraiser's skill in applying experienced judgment and subjectivity to the objective facts that are gathered. Increasingly, the value of assets must be made within the proper legal framework, and must be supported by a review of all factors, not just those that favor or disfavor a taxpayer.

CHAPTER ENDNOTES

1. *Wandry v. Comm'r.*, TC Memo 2012-088.
2. Back in 1967, the Tax Court, in *Messing v. Comm'r.*, 48 T.C. 502 (1967), wrote "Too often in valuation disputes the parties have convinced themselves of the unalterable correctness of their positions and have consequently failed successfully to conclude settlement negotiations -- a process clearly more conducive to the proper disposition of disputes such as this. The result is an overzealous effort, during the course of the ensuing litigation, to infuse a talismanic precision into an issue which should frankly be recognized as inherently imprecise and capable of resolution only by a Solomon-like pronouncement."
3. See LISI Estate Planning Newsletter No. 1846 (August 9, 2011) available at: www.leimbergservices.com.
4. LISI Estate Planning Newsletter No. 1856 (August 25, 2011) available at: www.leimbergservices.com.
5. Available at: www.irs.gov/pub/irs-utl/dlom.pdf.
6. See TAM 9436005, where the IRS held a control premium should apply to a minority interest on the grounds that it was a "swing vote" that might act in concert with other related shareholders.
7. See Treas. Reg. §25.2512-1 for use of fair market value for gift tax purposes.
8. See, e.g., U.S. v. Simmons, 346 F.2d 213 (5th Cir. 1965).
9. Treas. Reg. §§20.2031-1(b); 25.2512-1.
10. Note that the IRS has the authority to sanction appraisers for unsound valuations under the Pension Protection Act of 2006. See IRC §6695A.
11. *Ludwick v. Comm'r.*, T.C. Memo 2010-104.
12. See LISI Estate Planning Newsletter No. 2008, September 25, 2012.
13. I.R.C. §§2031(a), 2032(a)(2).
14. I.R.C. §2032(a)(1).
15. I.R.C. §2032(a)(3).
16. Rev. Proc. 2017-57.
17. Rev. Rul. 2015-18.
18. I.R.C. §2042(1).
19. I.R.C. §2042(2).
20. Treas. Reg. §20.2031-4.
21. Treas. Reg. §20.2031-6(a).
22. Treas. Reg. §20.2031-1.
23. Treas. Reg. §20.2031-7.
24. I.R.C. §7520.
25. Treas. Reg. §20.2031-2.
26. See *Est. of Smith*, 57 TC 650 (1972), acq. 1974-2 CB 4.
27. Treas. Reg. §20.2031-2(e).
28. I.R.C. §§2031, 2512; Treas. Regs. §§20.2031-1(b), 20.2031-2(b), 20.2031-2(f), 25.2512-2.
29. Treas. Reg. §20.2031-3; Rev. Rul. 80-202, 1980-2 CB 363.
30. 1959-1 CB 237.
31. Judge Learned Hand in *Borg v. Int'l Silver*, 11 F.2d 147 (1925).
32. See Treas. Reg. §25.2703-1(c).
33. See, e.g., *Gallun v. Comm'r.*, 33 TCM 1316 (1974); *Kirkpatrick v. Comm'r.*, 34 TCM 1490 (1975); *Est. of Thalheimer v. Comm'r.*, 33 TCM 877 (1974); *Northern Trust Co.*, 87 TC 349 (1986).
34. 1981-2 CB 187.
35. See, e.g., *Est. of Bright v. U.S.*, 81-2 USTC ¶13,436 (5th Cir. 1981) (community property interest in stock of one spouse not attributed to other spouse to produce a control premium); *Propstra v. U.S.*, 82-2 USTC ¶13,475 (9th Cir. 1982) (fractional interest discount allowed for decedent's community property interest in real property); *Est. of Lee*, 69 TC 860 (1978), nonacq. 1980-1 CB 2 (fractional interest discount allowed for community stock ownership); and *Est. of Andrews*, 79 TC 938 (1982) (discounts permitted for stock in corporation owned by siblings).
36. 1993-1 CB 202.
37. *Northern Trust Co. v. Comm'r.*, 87 TC 349, 384 (1986); See also Treas. Reg. §20.2031-2(f).
38. 38. 563 F. Supp. 3d 8 (D.C. Conn. Sept. 24, 2021).
39. *LeFrak v. Comm'r.*, 66 TCM 1297 (1993).
40. Two well-known sources of control premium data are Mergerstat Review and Mergerstat Control Premium Study.
41. 61 TCM 2949 (1991).
42. *Central Trust Co. v. U.S.*, 62-2 USTC ¶12,092; *Messing v. Comm'r.*, 48 TC 502 (1967), acq. 1968-1 CB 2.
43. 1977-2 CB 319.
44. See *Est. of Jameson v. Comm'r.*, TC Memo 1999-43; *Est. of Simplot*, 2001-1 USTC ¶60,405 (9th Cir. 2001); *Est. of Davis*, 110 TC 530 (1998); *Eisenberg v. Comm'r.*, 98-2 USTC ¶60,322 (2d Cir. 1998).
45. In *Jones v. Comm'r.*, 116 TC 121 (2001), a built-in-gains discount was disallowed for a family limited partnership because the court assumed that a limited partner could transfer a fair market basis to the buyer through an adjustment under I.R.C. §754.
46. Treas. Reg. §25.2703-(3).
47. See TAMs 9736004, 9730004, 9725002, 9719006.
48. See, e.g., *Church v. U.S.*, 2000-1 USTC ¶60,369 (W.D. Tex. 2000). But see *Holman*, 130 TC 170 (2008), aff'd by the 8th Cir. (2010), where IRS won on the tax issue but the court still found discounts to be applicable.
49. Treas. Reg. §25.2704-1(a)(2)(iv).
50. Treas. Reg. §25.2704-1(a)(2)(v).
51. See *Est. of Youle*, 56 TCM 1594; *Est. of Wildman*, 58 TCM 1006; *Est. of Whitehead*, 33 TCM 253 (1974); *Mooneyham v. Comm'r.*, 61 TCM 2445 (1991).
52. See *Est. of Anderson v. Comm'r.*, 56 TCM 78 (1988) (discount of 20 percent allowed to value of undivided one-half community property interest); *Mooneyham v. Comm'r.*, 61 TCM 2445 (1991) (discount of 15 percent allowed to undivided one-half interest in real property owned as tenants-in-common by brother and sister); *Est. of Wildman v. Comm'r.*, 58 TCM 1006 (1989) (discount

of 15 percent allowed to value of undivided one-fifth interest in real property owned as tenants-in-common); *Est. of Feuchter v. Comm'r.*, 63 TCM 2104 (1992) (partnership owning undivided one-half interest in three tracts of land allowed 15 percent discount); *Est. of Baggett v. Comm'r.*, 62 TCM 333 (1991) (decedent's undivided 25 percent interest in real property discounted 35 percent to reflect fractional interest); *Est. of Pillsbury v. Comm'r.*, 64 TCM 284 (1992) (15 percent discount applied to undivided 77 percent and 23 percent fractional interests held in trust).

53. *Stewart*, 31 BTA 201 (1934).
54. TC Memo 1997-188.
55. 94 TC 872 (1990).
56. TC Memo 1990-472.
57. TC Memo 1991-615.
58. TC Memo 1991-279.
59. 79 TC 938 (1982).
60. 1993-1 CB 202.
61. TC Memo 1989-231.

FREEZING TECHNIQUES – CORPORATIONS AND PARTNERSHIPS

CHAPTER 71

71.1 INTRODUCTION

In the most fundamental sense, an estate freeze is any planning device where the owner of property attempts to freeze the present value of the estate and shift the future appreciation to successors, generally the next generation. It may also involve the retention of some form of income stream or cash flow from the property.

This definition of an estate freeze is so broad it includes a variety of techniques, including installment sales of property (see Chapter 41), private annuities (see Chapter 42), a variety of gift planning techniques (see Chapter 8), and buy-sell agreements (see Chapter 47), Grantor Retained Annuity Trusts (GRATs) (Chapter 29) and Intentionally Defective Grantor Trusts (IDGT's) (Chapter 30). The term's general use, however, has been more limited to cover the structuring of family businesses and investments in such a way that the original owners retain much of the present value and control, and some source of revenue, while the growth is shifted. The usual vehicle is the family limited partnership (see Chapter 49), limited liability company (see Chapter 51), or corporation (see Chapters 50 and 53).

In the case of the family corporation, the senior generation typically retains control through the use of voting preferred stock that has a fixed liquidation value, usually par value. Either by forming a new corporation or recapitalizing an existing corporation, one or more classes of common stock are created, which may be nonvoting or at least have limited voting rights. All or part of this common stock is sold or given to the next generation.

The counterpart in the case of the partnership is the formation or restructuring of an existing partnership in such a way that the senior family members retain partnership interests that control the management of the business or investments, from which they receive preferred profit distributions, but which have a fixed liquidation value. Thus, the retained partnership interests resemble preferred stock in a corporation. The remaining partnership interests may then, like the common stock in the case of a corporation, be sold or given to the next generation.

71.2 WHEN IS USE OF SUCH A DEVICE INDICATED?

Where a family business is involved, the freeze has been an important planning tool to assure retention of the enterprise in the family at minimum tax cost. The same may apply to family investments, particularly real estate. It will be used where there is a desire to perpetuate the business or investment within the family, but may also be used to ensure that the value represented by the business passes to the next generation at a reduced tax cost. However the requirements of Code sections 2701 and 2704 (discussed below) limit the use of this planning technique.

Moreover, Congress presumably will be considering restrictions on the favorable aspects of grantor trusts since they were originally part of former President Obama's budget proposal, although it is unknown what President Trump's administration will do in this regard. In a typical sale of appreciated assets to an intentionally defective grantor trust, there is no recognition of gain because the grantor is treated as the owner, the tax "alter ego" of the property in the grantor trust.[1] Under that proposal, these would impose an income tax on appreciated assets that pass to IDGT's through a sale to the IDGT. Moreover, the proposal would have included the assets of the grantor trust in the grantor's gross estate (under the rationale that they are to be considered incomplete gifts). Also, under these proposals, any distributions from a grantor trust would be subject to gift tax. Last, if the grantor trust status toggled off, the assets of the trust themselves would be subject to gift tax.[2] Usually, transactions completed before enactment of laws are not subject to them, so time may be of essence in completing such transactions.

71.3 WHAT ARE THE REQUIREMENTS?

As discussed above, a business entity, either a corporation or a partnership, must be created or altered to structure this form of a freeze. The retained stock or partnership interests of the senior generation must have a limited liquidation value, since that is what makes it impossible for the value of those interests to grow. The retention of preferred dividends or profit distributions is not essential, but adds to the value of the retained interest, which in turn reduces the initial value of the interests transferred to the next generation. Since the transfer of interests may, and probably will, have gift tax implications, the value of the retained interests is very important.

Example. Clive owns 100 percent of the common stock in Acme Corporation, a manufacturing concern. It has been valued at $1,000,000. He wants to bring his two children into the business, give them an incentive to work there by giving them an equity stake in the enterprise, and minimize his own gift and estate taxes.

Clive recapitalizes the corporation with (a) $1,000,000 par value preferred stock with an 8 percent cumulative preferred dividend and (b) common stock. The preferred stock is voting, and in the event of corporate liquidation, the preferred shareholders can receive only par value for it. The common stock is then transferred by gift or sale to the children.

71.4 TAX IMPLICATIONS

1. Code section 2701, titled "Special valuation rules in case of transfers of certain interests in corporations or partnerships" (applicable to transactions entered into after October 8, 1990), focuses on the valuation of retained senior interests in such entities in determining the extent of taxable gifts of other junior interests in the same entity. It also deals with the transfer tax treatment of the retained interests, and how those retained interests will be valued for subsequent transfers during life or at death.

2. Also to be considered in this area is Code section 2704, providing, in general, that most lapsing restrictions on transferred interests in businesses created after October 8, 1990 will be ignored in valuing the interest for transfer tax purposes, or the lapse itself will trigger a transfer tax. This involves situations in which restrictions are imposed on the value of retained stock or partnership interests, which depress the value of those interests. After the owner dies, these restrictions either lapse or can be readily removed by family members.

Section 2701

How Retained Interests Are Valued for Gift Tax Purposes

In order to determine the gift tax consequence of a transfer of a junior interest in a partnership or corporation to a family member, any retained senior interest in the partnership or corporation must be valued under Code section 2701, unless it falls within an exception.

Under section 2701, the value of the junior interests (e.g., common stock or residual units) transferred to "family members" will be determined by subtracting the value of the retained interests in the entity from the total value of the family-held interests in the entity.

For purposes of section 2701, "family members" are the transferor's spouse, any lineal descendant of the transferor or spouse, and the spouse of any descendant.[3]

Other important terms used in section 2701 include:

"Control," which means at least a 50 percent interest in a corporation by vote or value of the corporate stock, or at least 50 percent of the capital or profits in a partnership, or the holding of any partnership interest as a general partner. Control includes interests held by "applicable family members." It also includes attribution through entities and interests held by brothers or sisters or lineal descendants of an individual.[4]

"Applicable family member," which means the transferor's spouse, an ancestor of the transferor or transferor's spouse, or the spouse of an ancestor.[5]

"Qualified payment," which means any periodic dividend on cumulative preferred stock, any comparable payment from a partnership interest, or any other payment where an irrevocable election is made to treat other payments, such as noncumulative preferred dividends, as qualified payments.

Covered transfers include contributions to capital, redemptions, and other changes in capital structure, as well as any transfer that increases the property owned by the entity or the value of the applicable retained interest (defined below) of the transferor or applicable family members, including transfers to a startup entity.[6] A sale is covered by these valuation rules if there is an applicable retained interest (e.g., the sale of common stock in the entity for its full fair market value where the transferor retains preferred stock).[7]

Example. Transferor owns 100 percent of the common stock of a corporation worth $1,000,000. He recapitalizes, taking voting preferred stock with a par value of $1,000,000 and paying a cumulative preferred dividend of 8 percent, and made a gift of the nonvoting common stock to his children. The gift is valued at $1,000,000 less the value of the preferred stock.

Section 2701 applies only if, immediately after the transaction, the transferor or an applicable family member retains an "applicable retained interest," which can be either:

1. Liquidation, put, call, or conversion rights (also referred to in the regulations as "extraordinary payment rights"[8]). A "liquidation, put, call, or conversion right" is defined as any right the exercise or nonexercise of which affects the value of the transferred interest.[9] However, the term does not include any right that must be exercised at a specific time at a specific amount.

    A "distribution right," if the transferor and "applicable family members" "control" the entity.

2. A "distribution right" is defined as a right to distributions from a corporation with respect to its stock or a partnership with respect to a partnership interest, but that term does not include:

    a. Rights in connection with "junior equity interests," defined as common stock or partnership interests under which rights to income and capital are junior to all other equity interests.[10]

    b. "Liquidation, put, call, or conversion rights."

    c. Rights to guaranteed payments from a partnership defined in Code section 707(c), which are certain payments determined without regard to partnership income.[11]

Certain rights, such as the right to mandatory payments fixed as to time and amount are neither extraordinary payment rights nor distribution rights.[12] Thus, mandatory redemption rights (e.g., a requirement that preferred stock be redeemed at a fixed price at a time certain) are not covered. A right to participate in a liquidation is not covered unless the transferor, family members, and applicable family members can compel liquidation.

Nonlapsing conversion rights in a corporation (i.e., the right to convert an equity interest into a fixed percentage of shares of the transferred interest except for nonlapsing differences in voting rights) are not covered.[13] Similar rights in a partnership are also not covered (e.g., where all rights in partnership interests are the same except for nonlapsing differences in management rights and limitation of liability).

In general, the value of an applicable retained interest, other than a distribution right which consists of the right to receive a qualified payment, is zero.[14] The right to a qualified payment is to be valued at fair market value (i.e., what a willing buyer would pay a willing seller for it). Note that an irrevocable election can be made out of qualified payment status, in which case the distribution right will apparently be valued at zero.

If the transferor retains both a qualified payment right and an extraordinary payment right, the value of all rights is determined by assuming the extraordinary payment right is exercised in such a way as to produce the lowest possible valuation, and the qualified payment right is valued at its fair market value.[15]

The section 2701 special valuation rules do not apply to any transferred interest for which market quotations are readily available on the date of transfer from an established securities market,[16] and the following retained interests are specifically excluded from these special valuation rules:

- An interest that can be valued on an established securities market.

- An interest that is of the same class as the transferred interest.

- An interest that is proportionately the same as the transferred interest, except for nonlapsing differences in voting rights or, in the case of a partnership, nonlapsing differences in management and limitations on liability unless the transferor or applicable family member can alter the liability of the transferee.

The rules of section 2701 are complex. Possibly the following summary of how the section works will be helpful:

Section 2701 applies to an interest in a corporation or partnership transferred to a family member where the transferor or "applicable family member" retains a certain interest in the enterprise classified as an "applicable retained interest." If the section applies, the gift resulting from the transfer is determined by subtracting from the value of the family-owned interests in the entity the value of any interests senior to those transferred.

The applicable retained interest consists of the following:

1. An "extraordinary payment right" (i.e., a discretionary liquidation, put, call, conversion, or similar right) valued at zero.

2. A distribution right, also valued at zero unless it is a "qualified payment" right."

3. A qualified payment right, generally a fixed-rate cumulative payment, or a payment which the transferor elects to treat as such a payment, valued as if the rights valued at zero do not exist, but otherwise without regard to section 2701.

If an extraordinary payment right is held in conjunction with a qualified payment right, the rights are valued on the assumption they will be exercised in such a way as to produce the lowest possible value.

The Minimum Value Rule

Since the value of the gift under the above rules is determined by subtracting the value of the retained qualified payment from the value of the entire entity, it is possible the result could be a small amount where the value of the qualified payment is large. However, regardless of the results of the subtraction method, the minimum value that can be assigned to the transfer of a junior equity interest is 10 percent of the total value of all equity interests in the partnership or corporation, plus the total indebtedness of the entity to the transferor, or an applicable family member.[17]

Transfer Taxation of Cumulative Unpaid Distributions

If the corporation or partnership fails to make the required cumulative distributions, or noncumulative distributions the transferor has elected to treat as cumulative distributions, then upon the occurrence of a "taxable event," the taxable gifts or estate of the transferor will be increased by the value of such unpaid distributions. This value will be determined on the assumption all payments are made when due, then compounded as if reinvested at the same discount rate used in valuing the retained interest, less actual distributions paid, based on the date actually paid, but with a four year grace period for late payment.

The total amount subject to tax cannot exceed the transferor's proportionate interest in the excess value of all junior interests in the entity at the applicable date of the taxable event over the value of all such transfers at the original date of transfer. In other words, the additional amount subject to federal transfer tax is limited to the actual growth in the enterprise that was shifted.

A taxable event is the death of the transferor if the applicable retained interest is included in his or her estate, or the transfer of such applicable retained interest. Also, the transferor can elect to treat late payment as a taxable event.[18]

Where the transfer is to a spouse and is not taxable because of the marital deduction or because the transfer was for full and adequate consideration, the above rules will not apply, but the spouse will inherit the tax consequences on a subsequent taxable event.[19] Applicable family members other than the transferor are subject to the same taxable event rule with respect to their retained interests, and if the applicable retained interest is transferred to an applicable family member, such applicable family member is subject to the same rules as to distributions accumulating after the transfer.[20]

Qualified payments can be made in the form of debt instruments if they are for not more than four years and compound interest at a rate no less than the appropriate discount rate is payable from the due date of the payment.[21]

It is important to note that the value of the unpaid distribution is added to the taxable estate or taxable gifts of the transferor along with the value of the retained corporate stock or partnership interest. According to the regulations, the amount subject to transfer tax will be reduced by any amount subject to transfer tax with respect to the same rights to prevent double taxation.

Value of the Retained Frozen Interests for Purposes of Subsequent Transfers

Section 2701 only deals with the value of the retained interest for purposes of valuation of a transferred interest at the time of the transfer of the transferred interest. Apparently, the retained preferred stock or partnership interests would be valued under normal rules for purposes of any subsequent transfers. This means any retained put, call, conversion, or liquidation rights valued at zero under section 2701 will subsequently be valued when the retained interest is transferred. The result is clearly double taxation, since an interest that was valued at zero when retained is subsequently valued at fair market value when the transferor dies or transfers the retained interest.

To avoid this result, there is an adjustment to the decedent's adjusted taxable gifts by reducing them by the lesser of:

1. the amount by which decedent's taxable gifts were increased due to the application of section 2701; or

2. the amount by which the section 2701 value of the retained interest exceeds the section 2701 value of that interest determined at the time of the initial transfer.

The adjustment may also be available to the transferor's spouse.[22]

Is the Freeze a Viable Planning Alternative?

Although a corporate or partnership freeze through the use of common and preferred stock or partnership interests is now available, many commentators believe it has less utility than in the past. In order to avoid a zero valuation for retained interests, it will be necessary to make distributions with respect to the retained interests (subject to the four-year grace period). The income tax will be paid now, while the estate tax is deferred, often until the death of a surviving spouse. Note that the use of the freeze eliminates qualification for the S election, since preferred stock is involved. However, if the entity is a partnership, particularly one with a good cash flow, the freeze may make a great deal more sense — the maximum individual federal income tax rate through 2023 is 37 percent for single persons earning more than $578,126 (and more than $693,751 for joint filers).

If the qualified payments are not made, the resulting inclusion of accumulated distributions in the transferor's taxable gifts or estate could easily exceed the value of the retained interest for federal gift tax purposes.

Example. Assume the applicable discount rate is 10 percent, and the retained dividend is 8 percent. Based on the assumption that the present value of the annual dividend is its fair market value, as required by the regulations, the value of the retained interest is 80 percent of the value of the transferred property. Thus, if the business is valued at $1,000,000, the retained interest is valued at $800,000, the gift at $200,000.

However, if the dividends are not paid for ten years, and the grace period does not apply, the amount of the cumulative unpaid distributions subject to federal gift or estate tax under section 2701(d)(1) would be approximately $1,275,000.

Note: The amount included in the taxable transfers of the transferor cannot exceed the actual growth in the business.

If a freeze is contemplated, can the amount of the taxable transfer be reduced by valuation discounts?

The Congressional Committee Reports acknowledge that all existing discounts are preserved, which means it is possible to argue that the value of the transferred interest for federal gift tax purposes must be reduced to reflect discounts for minority interests, lack of marketability, etc. These discounts often range from 30 percent to 40 percent or more and have served an important purpose in GRAT's and IDGT's, as well as Charitable Lead Annuity Trusts (CLAT's).

The regulations under section 2701 recognize the existence of such discounts, and set forth a four step method to value the taxable gift, taking into account such discounts, as follows:

1. Determine the fair market value of all family-held interests in the entity;

2. Subtract all senior equity interests held by the family other than applicable retained interests held by the transferor or applicable family members, with a pro-rata adjustment for any control premium, followed by the subtraction of the value of all applicable retained interests held by the transferor and applicable family members;

3. Allocate the remaining value among the transferred interests and any other family-held junior (or subordinate) interests;

4. Reduce value for consideration received, and for any minority or similar discounts (presumably including a discount for lack of marketability), determined by subtracting the fair market value of the family-held interests (determined as if voting rights were held by one person who had no other interest in the entity other than the family-held interests of the same class) from the value of the transferred interest determined without regard to section 2701.

Note that if the transfer is to a grantor retained interest trust (i.e., a GRAT or GRUT, see Chapter 29), any reduction in the value of the transfer under Code section 2702 will also be subtracted to determine the net taxable gift.

Alternatives to the Freeze

If the transferor retains common stock or partnership interests, and transfers the preferred interests, section 2701 does not apply. This is sometimes called a "reverse" freeze. When the transferor dies, the value of the common stock will reflect growth, but should be substantially discounted in value because of the burden of the preferred stock with its prior claim to dividends and liquidation proceeds.

Consider the use of a variety of other techniques to freeze growth. This includes installment sales of business interests to family members (see Chapter 40), use of the private annuity (see Chapter 42), and premortem stock redemptions or partnership liquidations of interests of senior family members, giving senior family members a cash flow and transferring the growth in the value of the enterprise to the next generation. Under some circumstances, if the transferor receives a debt instrument issued by a family partnership or corporation, the IRS may seek to treat it as retained preferred stock. See Example 1, Senate Committee Report (OBRA '90), referring to "convertible debt" and treating it as retained preferred stock. IDGT's, GRAT's and Qualified Personal Residence Trusts (QPRT's) are all useful approaches to transfer assets to the lower generation at discounted values. GRATs may still remain available but Congress may subject them to a minimum ten-year term and the remainder interest (the gift portion) may be restricted to a number which is more than zero in value.

Section 2704

Code section 2704 deals with the transfer tax consequences of lapsing rights, and provides that property, in general, will be valued without regard to lapsing restrictions. As a result, the lapse of a voting or liquidation right in a family controlled corporation will have transfer tax consequences.

Example. If a parent and child control a corporation, and parent's stock has a voting right that lapses at parent's death, parent's stock is valued for federal estate tax purposes as if that right were nonlapsing.[23] The Court in *Estate of Smith v. U.S.*,[24] held for the government where the taxpayer argued that the lapse rules of section 2704 applied in respect to Class A shares carrying enhanced voting rights that immediately converted to Class B shares at death.[25] Interestingly, in that case, the estate attempted to argue that the transaction really was an *inter vivos* gift; however, the court's reading of the examples in the regulations did not sway it.

Section 2704 applies if the individual holding such right and members of the family control the corporation, as control is defined in section 2701(b)(2). However, in this case, "family member" includes the spouse of the individual, ancestors and lineal descendants of the individual or spouse, brothers and sisters of the individual, and spouses of any of them.[26]

Under the regulations, the taxable transfer is measured by the reduction in value of all interests in the entity owned by the holder immediately before the lapse unless attributable to other causes. The lapse of the right is deemed to be a transfer subject to transfer tax, at date of lapse, based on the difference between the values of all interests in the entity held by the individual before the lapse and after the lapse.[27] This provision is so broad that any shift of equity or growth could be deemed a lapse, and any contingency that results in lapse of payment, voting, or other rights could have transfer tax consequences.

A voting right is defined as the right to vote on any matter, and in the case of a partnership, includes the management rights held by general partners.[28] A liquidation right is the right to compel the entity to acquire all or a portion of the holder's interest, including a right arising solely by reason of the fact the holder owns sufficient voting rights to compel liquidation.[29]

A lapse occurs whenever a presently exercisable right is restricted or eliminated. However, a transfer with respect to a liquidation right is not a lapse of a liquidation right unless the transfer eliminates the right of that individual to compel liquidation of an interest other than the interest conferring the power.

Example 1. D, who owns 84 percent of the voting common stock of corporation, gives 14 percent each to three children. Even though this reduces D's voting rights to 42 percent, and D loses control, this is not a lapse covered by the statute because the voting rights have only been transferred, not eliminated.

Example 2. Assume D is both the general and a limited partner in a family partnership. As general partner, D can compel liquidation. If D transfers her general partnership interest, she can no longer compel liquidation, but since the successor general partner has the same voting rights, there is no lapse as to D's rights as a general partner. However, there is a lapse as to D's rights as a limited partner, since D has lost the power to compel liquidation of the limited partnership interest, which was an interest other than the interest conferring the power.

A lapse of rights in a retained interest valued under section 2701 is not subject to section 2704 (to the extent necessary to avoid double taxation).[30] Nor is the inability of the family to liquidate after the transfer where the holder could have liquidated before the transfer.[31] If the lapsed right may be restored upon the occurrence of a future event not within the control of the family, there is no lapse so long as the right could be restored.[32]

A voting or liquidation right may arise by state law, corporate charter or bylaws, an agreement, or in any other manner. Similarly, a lapse may occur by reason of state law, corporate charter or by-laws, agreement, or any other means. However, if the lapse is caused only by a change in state law, it is not subject to section 2704.[33]

In addition, an "applicable restriction," which is a limitation on liquidation of an entity that is more restrictive than state law, is to be disregarded if the transferor and family members control the entity, and the restriction either lapses after the transfer or can be removed by the transferor or family members, individually or collectively.[34] However, the term does not include a commercially reasonable restriction imposed in connection with financing if furnished as either a debt or equity contribution by an unrelated person (as defined by Code section 267(b), excluding banks as defined by Code section 581) for trade or business operations.[35] Any buy-sell agreement, option, or restriction covered by Code section 2703 (see Chapter 70), is not subject to section 2704.[36]

Example. D owns all of the preferred stock of corporation, and can compel liquidation after ten years. All common stock is owned by D's children. If D transfers the preferred stock to the children, it is valued without regard to the restriction on liquidation (i.e., as if the right to compel liquidation was immediately exercisable).

The IRS has applied section 2704(b) to disregard liquidation restrictions imposed by a family limited partnership agreement when valuing a partnership interest held by a decedent. The partnership was created on the decedent's deathbed and the partnership agreement's liquidation provisions were more restrictive than state law.[37] However, the courts have held that restrictions imposed by state law in a partnership are not applicable restrictions.[38]

71.5 ISSUES IN COMMUNITY PROPERTY STATES

In a community property state, the business or investment assets may be co-owned by both husband and wife as community property. If so, both must participate in the transaction, and the preferred stock or partnership interests will be held by them as community property. If the common stock or partnership interests are transferred to the children by gift, they may be separate property of the children, depending on state law. However, it is possible that the spouses of the children will obtain a community interest in the transferred property; particularly, if they purchase the stock, its status as community or separate property will depend on what assets they use to pay for it.

Property received in exchange for separate property of a spouse is separate property. For example, if a spouse owns stock and sells the stock for cash and then uses the cash to buy different stock, the new stock is separate property.[39]

Thus, the use of trusts to acquire the stock may minimize or eliminate this potential problem.

71.6 FREQUENTLY ASKED QUESTIONS

Question – Client owns 100 percent of the common stock of X Corporation, which has been valued at $1,000,000. It has been suggested that he recapitalize the corporation to create voting preferred stock with a par and liquidation value of $1,000,000, and a noncumulative preferred dividend of 8 percent per annum, and nonvoting nopar common stock. He would then transfer the common stock to his children. What are the gift tax consequences?

Answer – Under section 2701, unless an election is made, the gift will be $1,000,000. The transaction falls within section 2701, assuming none of the interests involved have a readily ascertainable market value. The common stock is being transferred to "family members," children of the transferor. The transferor has an "applicable retained interest," the preferred stock. It consists of a "distribution right," i.e., the right to the preferred dividend, and a "liquidation right." Under section 2701, the liquidation right is valued at zero. The distribution right is also valued at zero unless it is a "qualified payment." Since a qualified payment is the right to a fixed cumulative preferred dividend, this dividend is not a qualified payment. As a result, under the "subtraction" method required by section 2701, the gift is the entire value of the enterprise, $1,000,000, less the value of the applicable retained interest, zero.

However, the transferor could elect to treat the noncumulative dividend as if it were cumulative. If so, it is a qualified payment and can be valued and subtracted from the value of the enterprise to determine the taxable gift. The regulations indicate the qualified payment is to be valued under general valuation principles, that is, at fair market value.

Question – In 2005, parent transferred undivided interests in the family farm, which was worth $1,000,000, to her children, and simultaneously, parent and children formed a family partnership into which they transferred their respective interests in the property. Parent, who was the general partner, received a capital interest of $1,000,000, and is entitled to an annual distribution of partnership profits of up to $80,000 before any profits are distributed to children. This right to distributions is cumulative, and if not made in one year, carries over to the next. If the partnership liquidates, the parent will receive the first $1,000,000 in liquidation proceeds, and any additional proceeds will be distributed to the children. The children receive limited partnership interests and are entitled to share in any partnership profits and liquidation proceeds not distributed to the parent.

Ten years later, parent dies. No partnership distributions were ever made to parent. Under the terms of the decedent's will, her partnership interest, and all rights to distributions, passes to her surviving spouse outright. The farm was worth $1,500,000 at date of death. What are the estate tax consequences?

Answer – The initial formation of the partnership was covered by section 2701, and the gift tax on the transfers of interests in the farm to the children would be computed by subtracting from the value of the farm in 2003 the value of the right to partnership distributions, which would be "qualified payments."

However, since the qualified payments were never made, they constitute "cumulative unpaid distributions" under the statute. When a "taxable event" occurs, in this case the death of the parent, the value of those unpaid distributions is subject to the applicable federal transfer tax, in this case the federal estate tax. However, since the right to the payments passes to the surviving spouse, the tax will be deferred until the surviving spouse either dies or otherwise transfers the interest.

Note several other points. The maximum amount that could have been taxed in the estate would have been the total growth of the enterprise, $500,000. Also, since there is a four year grace period during which qualified payments can be made to avoid the transfer tax at death, the full unpaid amount may not be subject to tax. When the partnership was formed, parent could have elected to value the qualified payment at zero and pay gift tax on the full value of the farm, $1,000,000. If she had done so, there would be no additional tax on the cumulative unpaid amounts.

Also note that the decedent's estate would in any case include the value of her capital interest in the partnership, arguably worth at least $1,000,000, and her right to unpaid distributions, since those are valuable property rights owned by her estate. The regulations indicate there will be no double tax on the unpaid distributions.

Question – A family corporation is owned equally by two shareholders, parent and child. In 2023, the corporation is recapitalized, with parent and child each receiving voting preferred stock with a fixed liquidation value and a cumulative preferred dividend, and the child also receiving nonvoting common stock. The child then makes a gift of the nonvoting common stock to grandchild. Assume the preferred stock issued to the parent was equal to the full value of his interest in the corporation. What are the potential transfer tax consequences, if any, to the parent?

Answer – The parent did not make a taxable transfer when the corporation was recapitalized, since the parent received full value for his interest in the business and made no gift to the grandchild. However, since the parent is an "applicable family member," the parent or his estate may be vulnerable to a later transfer tax.

In computing the taxable gift to grandchild under the subtraction method, the child may subtract from the value of the corporation the right to all "qualified payments," in this case, the right to cumulative preferred dividends held by both the parent and child. If this is done, the parent is subject to the rules for transfer tax on cumulative unpaid distributions, i.e., if the corporation does not pay the dividends, there will be a gift or estate tax to the parent on a lifetime or deathtime transfer of the parent's preferred stock. As a result, even though the parent was not even a party to the taxable gift, the parent or his estate can incur a substantial transfer tax liability.

Note that the parent can avoid this result if the parent elects not to have his right to the preferred dividend treated as a qualified payment. If the parent does so, the child cannot subtract its value for gift tax purposes, and there would be no later transfer tax to the parent under the cumulative unpaid distribution rules.

Question – Client proposes to form a family partnership to operate a business enterprise. Client will retain a general partnership interest and a limited partnership interest, and sell limited partnership interests to his children for their full value. All partners will participate proportionately in partnership profits and the proceeds of liquidation. Will either section 2701 or 2704 apply to client? Also, See Chapter 49 with regard to the pitfalls relating to family limited partnerships.

Answer – Since the facts indicate all partners will share proportionately in both profits and growth, the gift tax consequences of these transactions are not subject to the provisions of section 2701.[40] As a result, since client sold interests to his children for their full value, there are no gift tax consequences. Note that limitations affecting liability and management do not bring the transaction under section 2701, unless there is a provision for lapse of voting rights and management rights, or the transferor or applicable family member can alter the liability of the transferee partners. Such was not the case here.

However, if client dies or transfers his general partnership interest, client loses the power to compel liquidation of the partnership. Under section

2704, this would be treated as a lapse of the client's power to compel liquidation of his limited partnership interest, subject to gift tax if the client makes a lifetime transfer of his general partnership interest, or estate tax on his death.

CHAPTER ENDNOTES

1. Rev. Rul. 85-13.
2. See LISI (Leimberg Information Services, Inc.) Estate Planning Newsletter No. 1995 (Aug. 7, 2012) at www.leimbergservices.com.
3. I.R.C. §2701(e)(1).
4. I.R.C. §§2701(b)(2), 2701(e)(3).
5. I.R.C. §2701(e)(2).
6. Treas. Reg. §25.2701-1(b)(2).
7. Treas. Reg. §25.2701-1(b)(1).
8. Treas. Reg. §25.2701-2(b)(1), (b)(2).
9. I.R.C. §2701(c)(2).
10. I.R.C. §2701(a)(4)(B)(i).
11. I.R.C. §2701(c)(1)(B).
12. Treas. Reg. §25.2701-2(b)(4).
13. I.R.C. §2701(c)(2)(C).
14. I.R.C. §2701(a)(3)(A).
15. Treas. Reg. §25.2701-2(a)(3).
16. I.R.C. §2701(a)(1).
17. I.R.C. §2701(a)(4).
18. I.R.C. §2701(d).
19. I.R.C. §2701(d)(3)(B).
20. I.R.C. §2701(d)(4).
21. Treas. Reg. §25.2701-4(c)(5).
22. Treas. Reg. §25.2701-5.
23. Treas. Reg. §25.2704-1(f)(Ex. 1).
24. *Estate of Smith v. U.S.*, 109 AFTR 2d 2012-987 (Feb. 13, 2012).
25. See LISI Estate Planning Newsletter No. 1949 (April 12, 2012) at www.leimbergservices.com.
26. I.R.C. §2704(c).
27. Treas. Reg. §25.2704-1(d).
28. Treas. Reg. §25.2704-1(a)(2)(iv).
29. Treas. Reg. §25.2704-1(a)(2)(v).
30. Treas. Reg. §25.2704-1(c)(2)(ii).
31. Treas. Reg. §25.2704-1(c)(2)(i).
32. Treas. Reg. §25.2704-1(a)(3).
33. Treas. Regs. §§25.2704-1(c)(2)(i)(B); 25.2704-1(c)(2)(iii).
34. I.R.C. §2704(b).
35. Treas. Reg. §25.2704-2(b).
36. Treas. Reg. §25.2704-2(b).
37. TAMs 9723009, 9725002, 973003, 9735003.
38. *Knight v. Comm'r.*, 115 TC 506 (2000); *Est. of Strangi v. Comm'r.*, 115 TC 478 (2000).
39. Internal Revenue Manual § 25.18.1.2.16 (02-15-2005), Basic Principles of Community Property Law: Sale or Exchange of Separate Property.
40. See *Church v. U.S.*, 2001-1 USTC ¶60,369 (W.D. Tex. 2000).

NON-U.S. PERSONS IN THE ESTATE PLAN

CHAPTER 72

72.1 INTRODUCTION

Special planning opportunities and problems are present where at least some family members are not U.S. citizens. Techniques will depend largely on the following:

1. The extent to which these individuals have property situated in the U.S.

2. Whether they are classified as either resident or nonresident aliens.

3. Whether they were U.S. citizens who have renounced their citizenship through expatriation to other nations.[1]

4. Whether the spouse of the client is a citizen of the U.S.

Any planning in this area will be contingent on whether or not there is a treaty with the country in question which covers tax issues. The practitioner must always determine if such treaty provisions exist. As of April 28, 2023, the U.S. had estate/gift tax treaties with fifteen countries. Most of the treaties are many years old and may not entirely apply because of changes in the tax laws of the U.S. or the other respective countries. For example, the U.S.-Australia tax treaty was executed in 1954, and Australia no longer imposes an estate tax. Here is the current list of countries with an estate or gift tax treaty:

Country	Estate or Gift Tax Treaty
Australia	Estate & Gift
Austria	Estate & Gift
Canada	Estate *
Denmark	Estate & Gift
Finland	Estate
France	Estate & Gift
Germany	Estate & Gift
Greece	Estate
Ireland	Estate
Italy	Estate
Japan	Estate & Gift

Country	Estate or Gift Tax Treaty
Netherlands	Estate
South Africa	Estate
Switzerland	Estate
United Kingdom	Estate & Gift

* The estate tax provisions are located in Article XXIX B of the United States – Canada Income Tax Treaty.

72.2 WHEN IS USE OF SUCH A PLAN INDICATED?

Special planning will be required in the following situations:

1. Where the client or family member is an alien who is considered to be a resident in the U.S: The tests for determining if an alien is a U.S. resident differ for federal income tax law purposes, from those used for federal estate tax law purposes. Under the income tax rules, the test is strictly objective, i.e., is the alien physically present in the U.S.?[2] If so, the alien is subject to a complex set of tests and rules, usually treated as a resident. On the other hand, the federal estate tax regulations define a U.S. resident as a person who, at the time of death, is "domiciled" in the U.S. Under these regulations, a non U.S. citizen is not domiciled in the U.S. unless intending to remain here indefinitely.[3] Thus, in the case of the estate tax, the test is a subjective test relating to the intent of the person. This section will focus on estate, gift, and generation-skipping transfer tax planning issues.

2. If the alien is treated as a resident for estate tax purposes, it follows that the alien's lifetime transfers are subject to gift and estate taxes in essentially the same manner as U.S. citizens resident in the U.S. The basic gift tax law is that the tax applies to all transfers by any individual, whether resident or nonresident.[4] There is an exception for the transfer of intangible property by a nonresident noncitizen.[5]

3. Where the client or family member is not a citizen or resident of the U.S., but is subject to federal estate tax because the taxable estate includes property situated in the U.S.[6] Property situated in the U.S. includes any stock issued by a domestic corporation (i.e., a U.S. corporation); any property which was situated in the U.S. when it was transferred by the decedent, but which would be included in his estate under Code sections 2035 to 2038; and debt obligations of a U.S. person, the U.S., or a state or any political subdivision thereof or the District of Columbia.[7] It does not include life insurance, certain bank deposits, and other specified debt obligations.[8]

4. Where a surviving spouse is not a U.S. citizen, regardless of such spouse's domicile. The issue is the availability of the gift or estate tax marital deduction for transfers of assets to or in trust for the spouse.[9]

5. Where the client is a U.S. citizen not residing in the U.S. The estate and gift taxes are imposed on all U.S. citizens, regardless of where they live.[10] The generation-skipping transfer tax statutes do not specifically cover this, but since the tax is triggered by a taxable transfer for gift or estate tax purposes, the same rule should apply.

72.3 WHAT ARE THE REQUIREMENTS?

Subject to the foregoing rules, the goal of estate planning for clients in this category is to minimize the impact of U.S. taxes.

1. To avoid federal income tax, an alien who does not hold a permanent U.S. visa can avoid being considered a resident by not being physically present in the U.S. for more than thirty days during the current year or for more than 182 days during the three calendar year period ending with the current year (the substantial presence test).

The 182 day threshold is calculated by multiplying the number of days the individual was in the U.S. in each of the three years by an applicable multiplier, which is one for the current year, 1/3 for the 1st preceding year, and 1/6 for the 2nd preceding year, and adding those three numbers together.[11] For example, an alien who does not hold a permanent U.S. visa can avoid being considered a resident in the current year by not being physically present in the U.S. for more than 120 days in each of the two preceding years and the current year [120 × 1 = 120; 120 × 1/3 = 40; 120 × 1/6 = 20; 120 + 40 + 20 = 180]. This of course will be impossible for most aliens who are actively engaged in business in the U.S., or maintain a home here. If, however, the alien can limit his presence in the U.S. to no more than 182 days in any year, U.S. income tax may be avoided during such year if:

a. The alien has a tax home in a foreign country, and

b. An annual declaration is filed with the IRS with information that shows a closer connection with such foreign country than with the U.S.[12]

2. To avoid federal estate tax, the alien's estate will have to establish the alien's intent, i.e., that the alien's permanent home is outside the U.S. For example, if the alien has a bigger or better residence in the U.S. than in the alien's home country, this will be difficult. Also, the conduct of business and investment affairs should, to the extent possible, be located outside the U.S. Obviously, the alien should avoid signing documents in which the alien is described as a U.S. resident. In addition, such factors as where the alien's doctor is located, and where the alien's spouse and children live and where his children attend school, can be determinative of intent.

3. Where it appears U.S. residency will be unavoidable for either income or transfer tax purposes, the alien should seek to make gifts of assets to non U.S. persons, such as adult children living in foreign countries, before becoming a U.S. resident. This could be done with irrevocable foreign *situs* trusts, and Limited Liability Companies (LLCs) discussed in Chapter 51. Many foreign countries recognize LLCs. This may be particularly useful to reduce the size of the alien's taxable estate. It may also be wise for state income tax purposes to transfer funds to an irrevocable trust sitused in a favorable state in the US without an income tax, if the alien will be moving to a U.S. state with higher state income taxes.

4. Whether or not the alien is deemed a resident under U.S. tax laws, foreign *situs* trusts may be particularly useful to mitigate tax consequences. It will be essential that such a trust be irrevocable and have an independent trustee. However, the alien could retain some powers over the trust to the extent these powers do not cause the alien to be considered the owner of the trust for federal income or estate tax purposes.

5. Where the alien can avoid U.S. residency, the use of foreign *situs* revocable trusts and foreign corporations may be indicated.

6. Where the client is a resident or U.S. citizen, but the client's spouse is not a U.S. citizen, the planner must concentrate on the federal gift and estate tax marital deduction. In general, the gift tax annual exclusion/marital deduction is limited to $175,000 (in 2023, it was $164,000 and $159,000 in 2022 and 2021 respectively) per year where the donee spouse is not a U.S. citizen.[13]

If the surviving spouse is not a U.S. citizen, the estate tax marital deduction is only available if the bequest ends up in a Qualified Domestic Trust (QDOT).[14] This is a trust that meets the requirements for the marital deduction but which must include a series of special provisions relating to the trustee and how the trust is administered. If such a trust is used, the decedent's estate can claim the estate tax marital deduction for transfers to it, but most distributions to the surviving spouse, as well as the value of the assets remaining in the trust at the death of the surviving spouse, will be subject to federal estate tax.[15] Moreover, this estate tax is computed by assuming such assets are added to the estate of the predeceased spouse.[16] A QDOT may be created on a testamentary basis, or by the surviving spouse on a post-mortem basis. It is important that the planner take steps so that the creation of the latter does not result in a taxable gift by the surviving spouse. See Treasury Regulation §20.2056A-4, which provides the procedures for conforming marital trusts and nontrust transfers to the requirements of a QDOT. It specifically preserves the marital deduction for transfers to a QDOT. However, the regulations warn that the transfer tax treatment is solely for such purpose of allowing the marital deduction but not for any other transfer tax treatment, including treatment as a gift. For all other purposes the spouse who made the transfer is considered the transferor.

The basis in a taxable distribution from a QDOT is computed as though the transfer was made by gift. In other words, the initial basis is carried over and increased (but not above fair market value) by the amount of gift tax allocable to the growth in the value of the property occurring after the first spouse's death.

Example. Assume property worth $1,000,000 is placed into a QDOT. It grows to $1,300,000 and is paid out to the surviving spouse and taxed at that time as a distribution. An upward adjustment is allowed in the recipient's hands to account for the gift tax paid on the $300,000 of appreciation.

7. There are also special rules relating to distributions from foreign *situs* trusts to U.S. beneficiaries. For example, there is a special tax, known as the throwback tax, as well as an interest charge if such a trust accumulates income and then distributes the accumulation.[17] This tax, and interest, can cause significant depletion of the trust assets when the trust begins making distributions. If a U.S. person makes an *inter vivos* gift of property to a foreign *situs* trust that has at least one U.S. beneficiary, the trust income is taxed to the grantor.[18] There are significant reporting requirements for such trusts, however.

8. The unified credit and state death tax credit are allowed to the estates of those considered U.S. residents for estate tax purposes, even if they are not U.S. citizens.[19]

9. Foreign death taxes are often imposed on property owned by a resident noncitizen where the property is situated outside the U.S. The estate is permitted a credit for estate, inheritance, legacy, or succession taxes paid to a foreign country in respect of property located in such foreign country and included in the gross estate (or to a U.S. possession). The credit is allowed only for taxes actually paid to the foreign country or U.S. possession and is subject to some limitations.[20]

If the property is to be held by a foreign corporation, it is important to be certain the entity will be recognized as a corporation under U.S. law. Some foreign countries have entities which may nominally be classified as corporations, but which may not be recognized as such in this country. Further, the best procedure to follow is for the alien to transfer the consideration for the purchase of the U.S. real property to the foreign corporation in exchange for stock, and then have the corporation purchase the land. There should always be consideration for the transfer of assets to a foreign corporation. It is also important for the alien to treat the corporation like the separate entity in order to avoid having the IRS pierce the corporate veil and thereby designate the alien as the true owner of the asset.

Example. Your client is the citizen of a foreign country who is not a resident of the United States. He is considering making a substantial investment in real estate in Hawaii. If he makes this investment directly, he will be subject to federal income tax on all of the income since it is U.S. source income. Further, upon his death, the value of the real property will be subject to U.S. estate tax.

If the real property were held through a foreign corporation, there would be little if any income tax advantage, but this would afford complete protection from federal estate and gift taxes. He may also consider holding the real estate through an irrevocable foreign *situs* trust, which will also avoid federal estate and gift taxes, and will not avoid federal income tax. The trust may be a more flexible arrangement. Further, a combination of the corporation and trust may be considered, with a corporation holding the real estate, and the corporate stock held in the irrevocable trust.

72.4 TAX IMPLICATIONS

As discussed above, where a noncitizen becomes a resident of the U.S. under either the income or estate tax definitions, that person will be subject to taxes in essentially the same manner as a U.S. citizen. The critical first step is to determine whether or not the alien is a resident under either tax. If so, the domestic planning options discussed in this book are generally available.

If the alien is not a resident, then the first step is to avoid U.S. gift and estate taxes by structuring the ownership of assets to avoid direct ownership by the alien of U.S. property or business interests. From the income tax standpoint, nonresident aliens are only taxed on income from sources within the U.S. The U.S. source income rules are detailed and complex.[21] Congress somewhat recently added a provision changing some of these rules in the Tax Cuts and Jobs Act of 2017, section 864(c)(8) to the Code, effective for transactions after November 27, 2017. Under section 864(c)(8), if a nonresident alien individual or foreign corporation owns an interest in a partnership which is engaged in any trade or business within the United States, gain or loss on the sale or exchange of all (or any portion of) such interest may be treated as effectively connected with the conduct of such trade or business.

If the nonresident alien does own U.S. *situs* property, then the federal estate tax will apply under the rules discussed in Code sections 2101 and following and the unified credit available is reduced to a maximum of $13,000 (exclusion amount and gross estate filing threshold $60,000) (which is *not* indexed to inflation).[22]

Under the Foreign Investment in Real Property Tax Act, various provisions have been added to the law to insure collection of income tax on the transfer of U.S. real property by nonresident aliens, including withholding.[23]

In addition, property situated in the U.S. is subject to the generation-skipping transfer tax regardless of the fact the transferor is a nonresident alien.

72.5 ISSUES IN COMMUNITY PROPERTY STATES

Most countries in the world, other than those that follow the English common law system, such as most of the United States, do have community property laws. It is very likely assets acquired by noncitizens are community property, and planning should proceed accordingly. In addition, if the alien is a resident in a community property state, that state may seek to impose its community property rules on assets or earnings received while domiciled in the state.

If at least one married spouse is subject to the community property laws of a foreign country, a U.S. state, or a U.S. possession, both spouses generally must follow those laws to determine their income for U.S. tax purposes. But the spouses must disregard certain community property laws if: (1) both are nonresident aliens, or (2) one is a nonresident alien and the other is a U.S. citizen or resident and both do not choose to be treated as U.S. residents. In these cases, both spouses must report community income as explained below:

- *Earned income.* Earned income of a spouse, other than trade or business income and a partner's distributive share of partnership income, is treated as the income of the spouse whose services produced the income. That spouse must report all of it on his or her separate return.

- *Trade or business income.* Trade or business income, other than a partner's distributive share of partnership income, is treated as the income of the spouse carrying on the trade or business. That spouse must report all of it on his or her separate return.

- *Partnership income (or loss).* A partner's distributive share of partnership income (or loss) is treated as the income (or loss) of the partner. The partner must report all of it on his or her separate return.

- *Separate property income.* Income derived from the separate property of one spouse (and which is not earned income, trade or business income, or partnership distributive share income) is treated as the income of that spouse. That spouse must report all of it on his or her separate return. Use the appropriate community property law to determine what is separate property.

- *Other community income.* All other community income is treated as provided by the applicable community property laws.[24]

72.6 PLANNING FOR NONCITIZEN SPOUSES

Lifetime transfers of up to $175,000 (in 2023) per year to a noncitizen spouse qualify for the gift tax marital deduction. The noncitizen spouse could leverage this gift by purchasing life insurance on the life of the citizen spouse. Such insurance would not be included in the estate of the citizen spouse, and through the use of an irrevocable life insurance trust could be excluded from the estate of the noncitizen spouse in the event such spouse is subject to federal estate tax.

Lifetime gifts to a surviving spouse are particularly useful where the surviving spouse is a U.S. resident subject to federal gift or estate taxes. In this case, cumulative gifts of up to the amount of the applicable exclusion amount can be used to take full advantage of the noncitizen spouse's unified credit. Even gifts in excess of that amount can be used to take advantage of the lower estate tax brackets of the noncitizen spouse. This clearly has advantages over the use of a QDOT trust, where the trust assets will eventually be taxed.

Qualified Domestic Trusts (QDOTs)

The use of a Qualified Domestic Trust (QDOT) may allow the spouse of a non-U.S. citizen to achieve the same marital deduction for estate taxes that U.S. citizens have. A QDOT has certain requirements.

1. The trust must meet the same requirements for the marital deduction as a trust for the benefit of a citizen spouse (see Chapter 27 and Treas. Reg. §20.2056A(b)). Thus, it can be a QTIP trust, a trust over which the surviving spouse has the right to all income and a general power of appointment, or an estate trust. In an estate trust, it is not necessary that all of the income be distributed annually to the surviving spouse, so long as all trust distributions must ultimately be made to the spouse or the spouse's estate. Such a trust is often useful where the trust assets are not income producing, such as stock in a closely held corporation. Regulations may provide for arrangements other than trusts in jurisdictions where trusts are prohibited.

2. Except as provided in regulations, at least one trustee must be an individual who is a U.S. citizen or a domestic corporation. If the value of the trust assets exceeds $2 million, at least one U.S. trustee must be a bank or the trustee must furnish a bond or irrevocable letter of credit equal to 65 percent of the value of the trust (Treas. Reg. §20.2056A-2(d)(i)). The actual wording of the bond and letter of credit are stated in the regulations. If the trust is worth less than $2 million, either a bond must be furnished or the trust must contain a clause that not more than 35 percent of its fair market value can be invested in non U.S. real property (Treas. Reg. §20.2056A-2(d)(ii)). Also, an individual U.S. trustee must have a tax home in the U.S. tangible and intangible U.S. property must be in the U.S. or a U.S. brokerage account.

3. No distribution can be made from the trust unless the U.S. citizen or domestic corporation trustee has a right under the trust to withhold from the distribution any tax due on the distribution.

4. The executor of decedent's estate must make a QDOT election. If the qualifying trust is a QTIP, both QTIP and QDOT elections must be made.

5. No marital deduction is allowed unless the property is transferred to a QDOT, or a trust reformed to qualify as a QDOT, or the property is transferred to a QDOT by a surviving spouse, or the surviving spouse becomes a citizen, or there is a treaty. There must be an actual transfer or assignment to a QDOT created by the decedent, executor, or surviving spouse. The rules for conforming marital trusts are contained in Treasury Regulations section 20.2056A-4.

Imposition of the Estate Tax on QDOT Assets

An estate tax is imposed on QDOT assets on the happening of any of the following events:

(1) When any distribution, other than (a) a distribution of income to the surviving spouse or (b) a distribution to the surviving spouse on account of hardship, is made prior to the surviving spouse's death;

(2) When the surviving spouse dies. The entire value of the property in the QDOT at that time will be subject to federal estate tax;

(3) When the QDOT fails to meet any QDOT requirement designed to assure that the IRS will collect the estate tax. The estate tax will be imposed as if the surviving spouse died on the date the trust failed the requirement; or

(4) When the QDOT pays the tax imposed upon the first of the above triggering events, that tax itself is considered a taxable distribution that sets off yet another tax. In other words the QDOT's payment of the estate tax on a distribution is itself a distribution subject to a further estate tax.

The estate tax on the QDOT is computed on an annual basis and reported on a 706 QDT by the Executor as follows:

Step 1: State the amount involved in the taxable event.

Step 2: Add all previous taxable events.

Step 3: Compute the federal estate tax on the estate of the first spouse to die as if the total of #1 and #2 above were included in the decedent's gross estate.

Step 4: Compute the federal estate tax on the estate of the first spouse to die as if only the amount of the previous taxable events were included in the decedent's gross estate.

Step 5: Subtract the tax computed in step #4 from the tax computed in step #3. This is the tax imposed as a result of a current taxable event.

If the surviving noncitizen spouse becomes a U.S. citizen before the decedent's estate tax return is filed, and the surviving spouse was a resident of the U.S. at all times after the decedent's death and before becoming a citizen, the usual marital deduction is available to the surviving spouse (i.e., a QDOT is not required). If the surviving spouse becomes a U.S. citizen after the QDOT is established, the spouse may still be able to treat the balance of the QDOT assets as a conventional marital deduction, as long as the other requirements of Treasury Regulations section 2056A(b)(12) are met. The QDOT may provide that the spouse is permitted to withdraw all of the principal in the trust if he or she becomes a U.S. citizen.

If the estate otherwise qualifies, various tax elections are available upon the death of the surviving spouse, such as stock redemptions under Code section 303 (see Chapter 48), valuation elections under Code sections 2032 and 2032A, and deferred payment of federal estate tax under Code section 6166. Also, a charitable deduction under Code section 2055 may be available.

Joint Tenancy

Under Code section 2040(a), the entire value of the joint tenancy property is included in the estate of the spouse who contributed to the joint tenancy. Section 2040(b) provides a common exception that largely swallows the rule: that qualified joint interests between husband and wife are deemed owned 50 percent by each for estate tax purposes. However, this rule does not apply if the surviving spouse is not a citizen.[25] Accordingly, 2040(a) governs these transfers. Under Code section 20.2040-1(a)(2) the entire value of the property will be included in the decedent's gross estate unless the executor can submit facts to show that the surviving spouse furnished consideration or that it was acquired by gift, bequest, devise or inheritance. There are complicated rules depending on when the consideration was furnished. Also, only the amount which is includible in the decedent's gross estate may be transferred to the QDOT.[26]

72.7 FREQUENTLY ASKED QUESTIONS

Question – What is a controlled foreign corporation, and what is its significance?

Answer – A controlled foreign corporation is a foreign corporation in which either more than 50 percent of the total combined voting power of all classes of stock or more than 50 percent of the total value of the stock is owned by United States shareholders.[27] The net effect of such status is that any income earned by the corporation will be attributed to and taxed to any shareholders who are U.S. residents.[28] This rule will apply even if the corporate stock is owned through a revocable trust. There are complex rules and exceptions.

Question – Is the partnership or LLC a viable form of entity for aliens to hold investments or business interests?

Answer – The partnership has the same advantages to aliens as to other taxpayers in avoiding two levels of taxation on its income. However, if the partnership is making U.S. investments, or carrying on a U.S. trade or business, it is subject to stringent withholding requirements. If a nonresident alien owns an interest in a partnership that is carrying on U.S. business, it appears that the partnership interest will be subject to U.S. estate tax. On sale of the partnership interest, it's possible that some of the income is taxable by the U.S. and some is not – see, e.g., *Indu Rawat v. Commissioner*,[29] holding that gain recognized by a nonresident alien individual partner on a sale of her interest in a U.S. partnership, that was attributable to inventory items, may be treated as U.S.-source income and thus subject to tax in the United States. Congress changed the rules for non-resident aliens selling partnership interests in the Tax Cuts and Jobs Act, by adding section 864(c)(8) to the Code effective for transactions after November 27, 2017 (the above case concerned a transaction before that date). Under section 864(c)(8), if a nonresident alien individual or foreign corporation owns an interest in a partnership which is engaged in any trade or business within the United States, gain or loss on the sale or exchange of all (or any portion of) such interest may be treated as effectively connected with the conduct of such trade or business.

Question – Is an irrevocable foreign trust a viable form of business entity for aliens to hold U.S. investments or business interests?

Answer – Such a trust may be a good planning vehicle, particularly when combined with other entities, such as the foreign corporation or partnership. Again, there are strict withholding requirements on distributions from such trusts. An important advantage of the trust is the potential avoidance of federal estate and gift tax by nonresident aliens. The trust is preferable to any form of direct ownership of U.S. real estate.

Question – A nonresident alien who spends a great deal of time in the U.S. intends to take his daughter, also a nonresident alien, on a shopping trip in this country to purchase expensive jewelry. Is this advisable?

Answer – It would be better for the parent to purchase the jewelry and be the owner, return to the foreign country, and then make a gift of it to his daughter. Otherwise, the transfer is subject to U.S. gift tax.

Question – A decedent is a nonresident alien who was an expatriate from the U.S. four years before her death. Is there any estate tax exposure?

Answer – Code sections 2107 and 877 (expatriation to avoid tax) provide that if citizenship is lost within 10 years of death, an estate tax will be imposed on the estate of the expatriated individual if the individual meets any of the following criteria: (1) The individual earned above a specified annual income in the years before the expatriation, or (2) the individual had a net worth of at least $2,000,000 as of the date of expatriation. For purposes of the estate tax liability, the expatriate's taxable estate would include not only property situated in the U.S. as defined in Code section 2104, but also stock in certain foreign corporations.

Question – A nonresident alien wishes to create a trust for the benefit of U.S. citizens. How can the alien avoid U.S. tax on the trust income?

Answer – If the trust is subject to the grantor trust rules under Code sections 671 to 677, the grantor, not the trust or its beneficiaries, will be taxed on the trust income. This also avoids the tax on accumulations discussed above. If the nonresident alien intends to become a U.S. person (resident or citizen later), the trust should instead be a non-grantor (irrevocable) trust and should require all income be distributed to the beneficiaries in order to avoid the throwback tax.

Question – What is the foreign earned income exclusion for US citizens working abroad?

Answer – This is indexed for inflation and was $112,000 in 2022 rising to $120,000 in 2023.

CHAPTER ENDNOTES

1. Recent changes to the law impose a substantial "exit tax" on assets of those seeking to expatriate. See I.R.C. §877A. Moreover, U.S. citizens and residents who receive certain gifts and bequests from covered expatriates are subject to a 40 percent transfer tax.
2. I.R.C. §7701(b).
3. Treas. Reg. §20.0-1(b).
4. I.R.C. §2501(a)(1).

NON-U.S. PERSONS IN THE ESTATE PLAN — CHAPTER 72

5. I.R.C. §2501(a)(2).
6. I.R.C. §2103.
7. I.R.C. §2104.
8. I.R.C. §2105.
9. I.R.C. §§2056(d), 2056A, 2523(i).
10. I.R.C. §§2001(a), 2501(a).
11. I.R.C. §7701(b)(3)(A).
12. I.R.C. §7701(b)(3)(B).
13. I.R.C. §2523(i).
14. I.R.C. §2056A(b).
15. Income is not subject to the estate tax, nor are distributions for hardship and some miscellaneous items. I.R.C. §2056A(b)(3); Treas. Reg. §20.2056A-5(c)(3).
16. I.R.C. §2056A(b).
17. I.R.C. §§667, 668.
18. I.R.C. §679.
19. I.R.C. §§2010, 2011.
20. I.R.C. §2014.
21. See I.R.C. §871 et seq.
22. I.R.C. §2102(b).
23. I.R.C. §§897, 1445.
24. IRS Pub. 519, *Tax Guide for Aliens*.
25. I.R.C. §2056(d)(1)(B).
26. I.R.C. §20.2056A-8.
27. I.R.C. §957.
28. I.R.C. §954.
29. 29. T.C. Memo 2023-14 (Feb. 7, 2023).

INDEX

All references are to sections.

A

A-B or A-B-Q trust, *See* Marital deduction (trust)
Accumulated earnings tax 50.5
Administrator of an estate 15.3
Alimony payments 57.6
American Taxpayer Relief Act of 2012 .... 20.2
Annual exclusion, *See* Gift tax
Annuity
    charitable remainder annuity trusts 38.1, 38.3
    gifts to children 8.9
    life insurance benefits 34.5
    qualified joint and survivor
        annuity 57.8
    qualified pre-retirement survivor annuity 57.8
    starting date 57.8
    valuation of 70.3
    See also Private annuity
Applicable retained interest 71.4, 71.6
Apportionment rule (property) 47.9
Appraisals
    qualification for 37.3
Attorneys
    attributes of a good attorney 14.7
    duties 14.7
    estate attorneys 14.7, 15.6

B

Bargain sales
    charitable contributions 37.6
Basis
    at death 22.6
    definition 22.6
    property acquired by gift 22.6
    step-up in 22.6

Beneficiary deemed owner trusts (BDOTs) .... chapter 35
    advantages 35.2
    asset protection planning 35.3
    assets best suited for BDOT 35.3
    beneficiary defective inheritor's trust
        (BDIT) compared 35.1
    clients not suited for BDOTs 35.3
    clients well-suited for BDOTs 35.3
    defined 35.1
    disadvantages 35.3
    powers best suited for BDOT 35.3
    settlor 35.1
    situations not well-suited for BDOTs 35.3
    tax risks 35.3
Beneficiary defective inheritor's trust 35.1
Benefits
    deferral of 57.5
    See also Death benefits; Defined benefit plans;
        Disability benefits
Blended families .... chapter 68
    client interview 68.13
    conflicts of interest 68.7
        negative consequences 68.8
        types of issues 68.9
    definition 68.2
    engagement letter considerations 68.13
    estate distribution 22.8
    initial client interview 68.13
    probate 15.12
    representation 68.11, 68.12
    statistics 68.3
    ways to work with 68.10
Bonds
    corporations 50.7
    valuation of 70.3
Buy-sell (business continuation) agreement ... chapter 47
    community property 47.9

Buy-sell (business continuation) agreement (cont'd)
    cross-purchase 47.5
    definition 47.1
    example 47.3
    family 47.8
    first-offer provision 47.4, 47.11
    goodwill method 47.7
    life insurance in 47.3-47.9
    option to buy 47.11
    partnership 47.7
    requirements 47.3
    s corporation 47.6
    stock redemption plan 47.5
    tax implications 47.4
    types 47.1
    use 47.2
    valuation technique 47.10
    "wait and see" approach 47.1, 47.5
Bypass trust, *See* Marital deduction (trust)

C

Call options
    employee stock ownership plan 55.6
Capitalization of income 70.3
Cash
    section 303 stock redemption .... chapter 48
Charitable contributions .... chapter 37
    after-tax savings; calculation 37.9
    bargain sales 37.6
    charitable lead trusts 38.4
    charitable remainder annuity trusts 38.3
    charitable remainder unitrust 38.4
    closely held stock 37.9
    community property states 37.7
    deduction limitations (figure) 37.5
    definition 37.1
    factors (four) in allowable deductions 37.5
    interest in property 37.5
    life insurance 37.8
    methods of giving 38.3, 38.4, 38.7
    partial interest 37.3
    pooled income fund 37.3, 38.4
    property types 37.5
        cash 37.5
        future interest 37.5
        long-term capital gain property 37.5
        ordinary income property 37.5
        rent-free occupancy 37.5
        tangible personal property 37.5
    "qualified" deductions 37.3
    requirements 37.3
    stocks and bonds 37.9
    tax implications 37.5
    use 37.2
Charitable remainder trusts, *See* Trusts

Charitable split interest trusts .... chapter 38
    annuity vs. unitrusts 38.6
    charitable lead trusts 38.4, 38.7
    charitable remainder annuity trusts 38.3
    charitable remainder unitrust 38.4
    community property 38.5
    definition 38.1
    fixed annuity trust 38.1
    life insurance 38.2, 38.4, 38.7
    pooled income fund 38.4
    requirements 38.3
    tax implications 38.7
    use 38.2
    wealth replacement trusts 38.4
Checklist for will .... chapter 11
Child support 57.6
Closely held stock
    charitable contributions 37.9
Collectibles
    IRA investing 56.4
    profit sharing/pension plans 57.11
Community property
    buy-sell agreements 47.9
    charitable contributions 37.7
    conservation easement 39.6
    corporations 50.6
    deferred compensation (nonqualified) 54.8
    disclaimers 13.5
    durable power of attorney 62.8
    elderly and disabled (planning for) 61.5
    employee stock ownership plan 55.5
    family limited partnerships 49.11
    generation-skipping tax 21.7
    gifts and 8.6
    grantor retained interests 29.8
    individual retirement plans 56.10
    installment sales and 41.7
    intentionally defective trust 30.7
    interest-free loans 43.6
    IRA plans 56.10
    irrevocable life insurance 36.4
    life insurance 34.6
    limited liability companies 51.4
    marital deduction 27.8
    non-U.S. persons 72.5
    number of shareholders or partners 19.6
    ownership change to .... chapter 7
    personal holding company 52.6
    power of appointment 12.8
    private annuities 42.7
    profit sharing/pension plans 57.9
    recapitalization 71.6
    S corporations 53.7
    sale (gift) leaseback 46.5
    section 303 stock redemption 48.6
    section 2503(c) trust 28.8
    split interest purchases 45.5
    stepped-up basis 21.5

INDEX

Community property (cont'd)
    survivor's income benefit plan 58.6
    tax basis irrevocable trust 31.5
    transfer of property 7.2
    Uniform Gifts to Minors Act 9.5
    valuation 70.5
    waiver of rights (form) 34.6
    wills 10.8
Community property trusts .... chapter 66
    advantages 66.3
    basics 66.2
    defined 66.1
    disadvantages 66.4
    irrevocable 66.4
    state law 66.1, 66.4
Compensation
    excess 52.4, 53.2
Conservation easement exclusion .... chapter 39
    carryover basis 39.7
    community property states 39.6
    definition 39.1
    requirements 39.3
    tax implications 39.5
    use 39.2
Constructive ownership rules 47.4, 47.5
Corporation(s) .... chapter 50
    accumulated earnings tax 50.5
    alternative minimum tax 50.5
    bonds 50.7
    capital 50.5
    capitalization 50.7
    centralized management 50.1
    "check-the-box" regulations 50.1
    choosing an entity; checklist 50.4
    community property 50.6
    continuity of life 50.1
    corporate control; stock redemption 50.7
    deductions 50.5
    definition 50.1
    disadvantages 50.3
    example 50.4
    fringe benefits 50.2, 50.5
    General Utilities doctrine 50.3
    key person life insurance 50.8
    lending money to 50.7
    leverage 50.7
    limited liability 50.1
    liquidations 50.3, 50.5
    personal holding company tax 50.5
    personal service corporation 50.5
    privacy 50.2
    security: debt or equity 50.7
    taxation of 50.5
    thin capitalization 50.7
    use 50.2
    See also Recapitalization; S corporation
Credit equivalent bypass trust (CEBT) 27.4

Cross purchase agreement
    community property 47.9
    definition 47.1
    example 47.3
    life insurance 47.3, 47.4
    preference over stock redemption plan 47.5
    requirements 47.3
    restriction on transfer of shares 47.11
    tax implications 47.4
    use 47.2
Crummey case/technique/trust .... 8.8, chapter 36
    community property 36.4
    definition 8.8, 36.1
    gifts 8.8
    power of appointment 12.3, 12.6
    requirements 36.3
    tax implications 36.5
    use 36.2
    withdrawal right 30.3
Custodial gifts 9.1, 9.3, 9.6

D

Data gathering
    checklists 2.7
    forms 2.5-2.7
    initial interview 2.1-2.4
Death benefit
    taxation 34.5
Death Benefit Only (DBO), *See* Survivor's
income benefit plan
Death tax apportionment
    community property 25.6
    definition 25.1, 25.2
    federal law 25.2
    frequently asked questions 25.8
    how it is done 25.3
    payment 25.3
    QTIP election 25.3
    requirements 25.5
    state law .... 25.2, chapter 26
    use 25.4
Deceased Spouse Unused Exclusion
    Amount (DSUEA) 13.2, 15.13, 27.2, 27.5
Deductions
    charitable contributions .... chapter 37
        closely held stock 37.9
        determining amount 37.9
        limitations (figure) 37.5
        long-term capital gain property 37.5
    corporations: ordinary and special 50.5
    employee stock ownership act 55.1
    employer contributions
        profit sharing/pension plans 57.3
    marital deduction 27.5
    unfunded deferred compensation payments 54.8

Defective trusts .... chapter 30
    commonly used goals 30.4
    community property 30.7
    definition 30.1
    example 30.5
    requirements 30.3
    tax implications 30.6
    use 30.2
Deferred compensation
    (nonqualified) .... chapter 54
    community property 54.8
    corporate deduction, earliest date 54.10
    definition 54.1
    directors' fees 54.10
    disability benefits 54.9
    ERISA and 54.6
    estate planning 54.3
    income and tax deferral, when not
        appropriate 54.10
    life insurance 54.5
    rabbi trusts 54.4, 54.7
    requirements 54.4
    secular trusts 54.7, 54.9
    securities issues 54.6
    tax implications 54.7
        employees 54.7
        employers 54.7
    use 54.2
Defined benefit plans
    contributions and benefits 57.3
    contribution plans 57.3
    early retirement 57.3
    life insurance in 57.3
    reporting requirements 57.6
    social security integration 57.3, 57.4
Depletion allowances 53.5
Digital estate planning .... chapter 69
    administration of 69.6
    after death 69.6
    common website and social media
        terms of service 69.4
    definition 69.1, 69.2
    disposing of digital assets 69.7
    importance of 69.3
    model acts 69.4
    preparing an estate plan 69.5
    preserving an estate plan 69.5
    preserving digital assets 69.7
    rules governing 69.4
    stored communication act 69.4
    valuing digital assets 69.7
Disability benefits
    deferred compensation plans 54.7
    insurance 61.6, 61.8
    social security 61.8
    total and permanent 57.5
Disclaimer trusts 15.15

Disclaimers .... chapter 13
    community property 13.5
    definition 13.1
    examples 13.3
    generation-skipping transfers (GST) 13.1
    life insurance beneficiaries 13.6
    requirements 13.3
    state requirements 13.3
    surviving spouse 13.2
    tax implications 13.4
    use 13.2
Distributions
    annuity tax rules 57.5
    by corporations 50.5, 50.7, 50.8
    employee stock ownership plans 55.4, 55.6
    prior to age 59½ 56.4
    profit sharing/pension plans 57.3, 57.5
    See also Lump sum distributions
Dividends
    life insurance 34.4
    received deduction 50.5
Divorce
    IRA plans 56.10
Domestic relations order 56.11, 57.6
Durable power of attorney .... chapter 62
    attorney-in-fact 62.1, 62.5, 62.8, 62.9
    community property 62.8
    death of the principal 62.9
    definition 62.1
    duration 62.9
    example 62.4
    extent of powers conferred 62.9
    gifts on behalf of the principal 62.7, 62.9
    guardian for the incompetent and 62.9
    health care 62.9
    how to plan
        general example 62.6
        gift provision example 62.5
        illustrative document 62.6
    requirements 62.3
    springing 62.9
    tax implications 62.7
    terminates upon disability 62.9
    uniform power of attorney 62.9
    use 62.2

E

Earned income 56.2, 72.5
Economic substance test 46.6
Elderly and disabled (planning for) ..... chapter 61
    community property 61.5
    definition 61.1
    disability planning 61.10
    federal programs 61.8
    incapacity planning 61.11
    long-term care planning 61.6

INDEX

Elderly and disabled (planning for) (cont'd)
    medicaid eligibility 61.8
    "medigap" insurance 61.12
    planning scenarios 61.2, 61.3
    special needs trust 61.9
    tax implications 61.4

Employee stock ownership
    plan (ESOP) .... chapter 55
    accumulated earnings tax 55.2
    annual appraisal (valuation) 55.6
    beneficiary designation
        (non-consent) 55.6
    benefits 55.6
    community property 55.5
    definition 55.1
    distributions (taxes) 55.4
    early distribution excise tax 55.6
    "employer securities" 55.6
    ERISA and 55.5, 55.6
    life insurance payments 55.2
    loan interest payments; limits 55.6
    requirements 55.3
    right of first refusal 55.6
    tax implications 55.4
    tax treatment 55.4
    transfers of ownership 55.6
    use 55.2
    voluntary contributions 55.4, 55.6

Endowment insurance 9.6, 34.3

ERISA (Pension Reform Act of 1974)
    employee stock ownership
        plan (ESOP) 55.1
    fiduciary rules 57.6
    nonqualified deferred
        compensation plans 55.4
    protection from creditors 57.6

ESOP, *See* Employee stock ownership plan

Estate/beneficiary attribution rule 47.4

Estate planning
    annual review checklist 2.7
    blended families 1.8, 22.8, 68.13
    checklists 1.9
    client concerns 1.7
    client interview 2.1-2.4
    data gathering for 2.5-2.7
    definition 1.3
    goals 1.6
    L.I.V.E.S 1.3
    malpractice .... chapter 6
    mistakes common in 1.5
    needed by 1.4
    paradigm shift 1.2

Estate tax
    adjusted gross 18.5
    community property states 18.11
    computing federal tax 18.2

Estate tax (cont'd)
    custodial gifts 9.1, 9.3, 9.6
    extensions of time to pay .... chapter 19
        bond for executor .... chapter 19
        closely held business .... chapter 19
        community property 19.6
        election method 19.3
        example 19.4
        installment payments 19.2, 19.3
        losing the right to 19.7
        protective election 19.7
        qualification: the "at least 20 percent
            requirement" 19.3
        reasonable cause 19.1
        requirements 19.3
        tax implications 19.5
        use 19.2
    federal estate tax .... chapter 18
    filing a return 18.10
    gifts and 8.4
    gift tax system and 20.10
    grantor retained interests 29.6
    gross estate 18.3
    inheritance tax, versus 26.2
    inter vivos trust .... chapter 33
    life insurance 34.5
    marital deduction 27.7
    personal holding company cases (figure) 52.4
    portability 18.9
    powers of appointment 12.2
    profit sharing/pension plans 57.5
    qualified conservation easement exclusion 18.4
    QSST or section 678 property 28.6, 53.9
    reimbursement 25.7
    sales (gift) leaseback 46.4
    section 6166 qualifying test 19.3
    state tax 26.3
    tax payable 18.7, 18.8
    taxable estate 18.6
    valuation of assets for 70.1-70.3
    voluntary DBO plan 58.1, 58.3, 58.5, 58.7
    See also Gift tax

Estate trust, *See* Marital deduction (trust)

Estates, Income Taxation of .... chapter 22

Ethics .... chapter 5
    code of ethics 5.1
    conflict of interest 5.2
    practical ethics 5.2

Executors
    attributes of a good executor 14.2
    checklist of primary duties 15.12, 15.13, 16.2
    conflicts of interest 14.2
    duties 14.2
    election (option) 31.3
    estate tax duties 16.2
    income tax duties 16.2
    powers of attorney 14.3

Executors (cont'd)
   primary duties......................................chapter 16
   probate 15.2, 15.3, 15.12, 15.13
   role of.. 15.2, 15.3
   selecting an executor 14.2
Extensions, *See* Estate tax
Extraordinary payment rights................................ 71.4

F

Fair market value.. 41.4, 41.5
Family limited partnership ....chapter 49
   asset protection 49.8
   "check-the box" regulations 49.16
   community property 49.11
   compared to C corporation
      (figure) 49.13
   compared to limited liability company
      (figure) 49.13
   compared to S corporation
      (figure) 49.13
   definition.. 49.1
   detriments.. 49.12
   family ownership..................................... 49.5
   family partnership.................................... 49.1
   guaranteed payments 49.16
   income tax aspects 49.9
   life insurance 49.12
   management and control......................... 49.4
   minor as partner 49.16
   reducing transfer tax 49.6
   requirements.. 49.3
   success (hints) 49.14
   tax implications 49.10
   use.. 49.2
   valuation methods................................... 49.7
Family-owned interest 71.4
Family/trust/corporation attribution
   rule 47.4
Fiduciary responsibility.. 57.6
First-to-die insurance... 34.3
Fixed term of years... 42.3
Fringe benefits
   corporations................................... 50.2, 50.5
   deductible 50.2
   personal holding company 52.4
   S corporations 53.6

G

General utilities doctrine.............................. 50.3, 52.1
Generation-skipping transfer
   (GST)...chapter 21
   basis adjustment 21.5
   community property 21.7
   creation of 21.4

Generation-skipping transfer (GST) (cont'd)
   defined 21.1
   direct skips... 21.5
   requirements.. 21.3
   tax 13.1, 21.5, 21.6, 36.2, 36.5
   use.. 21.2, 21.4
   wills 21.4
Generation-skipping trust............ 21.1, 21.2, 21.4, 21.8
Gift leaseback, *See* Sale (gift) leaseback
Gift tax.. 8.1-8.4
   accidental gifts 8.6
   annual exclusions
      estate or GST tax advantage.............. 8.4
      requirements summarized 8.4
      section 2503(c) trust 20.7, 28.3
      Uniform Gifts to Minors Act......................... 20.7
      Uniform Transfers to Minors Act 20.7
      value; computation................................ 8.4
   basis 8.4
   buy-sell agreement; valuation 47.10
   community property 8.6
   corporations... 50.2
   Crummey gifts 8.8
   custodial gifts 9.1, 9.3, 9.6
   estate tax system 20.10
   exempt gifts 20.5
   filing requirements 8.10
   future interests 8.4
   gain or loss; computation 8.4
   grantor retained interests ....chapter 29
   income tax aspects 20.11
   interest-free loans 43.5
   inter vivos trust....................................chapter 33
   life insurance 8.7
   marital deduction 8.4, 67.6
   net gifts... 8.4
   power of appointment 12.3, 12.5, 12.6
   property: factors in planning a gift 20.4
   purchase of property in joint names.......... 8.10
   reverse gift technique............................. 8.10
   S corporations 53.6
   sale (gift) leaseback................................. 46.3
   shifting wealth and income to children
      annuities... 8.9
      convertible planning 8.9
      employ your children 8.9
      life insurance 8.9
      Savings Bonds 8.9
      UGMA or UTMA funds 8.9
   split gift.. 8.4
   split interest purchase 45.4
   true tax on net gift 8.4
   unified credit against 8.4
   use of gifts... 8.1-8.2
   valuation of property for 20.6
Gifts ....chapter 8
   best time to make gifts 8.10

INDEX

Gifts (cont'd)
    best type of property to give.................................. 8.5
    completed transfer.. 20.6
    definition, for gift tax purposes................... 20.1, 20.3
    elements.. 20.3
    estate tax... 8.4
    gratuitous transfers.. 20.4
    income tax reduction.. 8.2
    life insurance trust... 36.5
    lifetime... 20.2
    net gift.. 8.4
    of property... 8.5
    outright gifts.. 8.5
    reporting... 20.8
    requirements.. 8.3
    sham gifts... 20.4
    split gifts... 8.4, 8.6
    trust or custodial account... 8.9
    types of.. 20.3
    use.. 8.2
Going concern value... 70.3
Gold coins
    IRA investing.. 56.4
Grandfathered elective deferral SEP...................... 56.6
Grantor retained interests
    (GRAT, GRIT, GRUT, QPRT).................... chapter 29
    advantages.. 29.4
    closely held stock.. 29.9
    community property... 29.8
    definitions... 29.1, 29.2
    disadvantages... 29.5
    estate tax.. 29.5
    example.. 29.6
    property in more than one state............................. 29.2
    requirements... 29.3
    reversion to the grantor... 29.7
    section 2702... 29.7
    special provisions in.. 29.9
    tax implications... 29.7
    unified credit equivalent.. 29.7
    uses.. 29.2
    valuation issue.. 29.7
Grantor trusts.. 30.1, 30.2, 30.3, 53.8
Guardianship... 61.9

H

Health-care documents................................. chapter 63
    assisted suicide... 63.2
    creating documents... 63.7
    health-care power of attorney................................ 63.5
        sample form.. 63.5
    health-care proxy... 63.3
    HIPAA release... 63.4
        requirements for.. 63.4
        sample form.. 63.4
    living wills... 63.6
    provisions... 63.8

Health-care documents (cont'd)
    types of documents... 63.1
    Uniform Health-Care Decisions Act....................... 63.3
        sample form.. 63.7
Human side of estate planning..................... chapter 3
    countertransference.. 3.2
    death... 3.1, 3.3
    fears... 3.4
    frequently asked questions..................................... 3.5
    good estate planning... 3.3
    transference... 3.2

I

Incapacity
    durable power of attorney..................................... 61.9
    living will... 63.6, 63.7
    resuscitate, do not.. 63.5
Income tax
    basis... 22.6
    blended families.. 22.8
    community property states..................................... 22.7
    distributable net income (DNI)..................... 22.3, 22.5
    estates.. 22.3, 22.4
    fiduciary accounting basics.................................... 22.2
    frequently asked questions................................... 22.9
    gifts.. 8.4
    group term life insurance plans................... 34.3, 37.8
    income in respect of a decedent (IRD)................. 22.4
    inter vivos trust.. chapter 33
    interest-free loans....................................... chapter 43
    net investment income tax (NIIT)......................... 22.5
    profit sharing/pension plans....................... 57.3, 57.5
    sales (gift) leaseback................................... chapter 43
    trusts.. 22.3
Individual retirement plans
    (and SEPS).............................. chapter 56, chapter 59
    active participant... 56.4
    AGI threshold... 56.4
    beneficiary
        bypass trust.. 59.2
        charitable remainder trust................................ 59.2
        charity... 59.2
        children... 59.2
        credit shelter trust... 59.2
        designated beneficiary..................................... 59.2
        designation forms... 59.3
        QTIP-able trust.. 59.2
        revocable living trust....................................... 59.2
        surviving spouse... 59.2
    blended families.. 59.3
    checklist.. 59.3
    collectibles.. 56.4
    community property.. 56.10
    death of account holder.. 59.2
        death after required beginning date................ 59.2
        death *before* required beginning date............. 59.2
    definitions... 56.1

Individual retirement plans (and SEPS) (cont'd)
    distributions from; beginning 56.4
    distributions prior to age 59½ 56.4
    divorced spouse 56.11
    employer contribution; time limit 56.4, 56.6, 56.7
    exceptions to early withdrawal
        penalty tax 56.8, 56.9
    inherited 56.11
    lump sum distributions 56.8
    non-working spouse 56.4
    planning with .... chapter 59
    required minimum distributions 59.1, 59.2
    requirements 56.3
    rollovers 56.9
    Roth IRAs 56.5, 60.2
    SECURE Act 59.1, 59.2
    SECURE Act 2.0 .... 59.1, 59.2, 60.1, 60.2, 60.3
    SIMPLE IRAs 56.7
    Simplified Employee Pensions (SEPs) 56.6, 60.3
    spousal consent 59.3
    surviving spouse 56.11
    tax implications 56.8
    traditional 56.4

Inheritance tax
    favorable state treatment 27.2
    how it works 27.5
    QTIP elections 27.3
    See also Estate tax

Inherited IRA 24.2, 56.11
Installment sales and SCINs .... chapter 41
    community property 41.7
    computing tax free, gain, and
        interest elements (figure) 41.3
    definition 41.1
    down payment in year of sale 41.8
    private annuities 41.8
    related party rules 41.4, 41.8
    related purchaser 41.8
    requirements 41.3
    "second disposition" rule 41.4, 41.8
    self-cancelling installment notes
        (SCINs) .... chapter 41
    special depreciable property rule 41.4
    tax implications 41.4, 41.5
    taxation of seller under (figure) 41.3
    use of 41.2

Insurance
    gifts of 8.8, 9.1, 9.6, 37.8
    See also Life insurance

Intentionally defective trust
    community property states 30.7
    how it is done 30.5
    powers 30.4
    requirments 30.3
    tax 30.6
    uses 30.2

Interest
    charitable contributions 37.3, 37.5, 37.9
    free transferability of 49.16
    S corporations, tax exempt .... chapter 53

Inter vivos QTIP trust
    advantages 33.3
    contrast with other marital trusts 33.2
    creating 33.4
    definition 33.1
    floating spouses 33.4
    one-year rule 33.4
    QTIP-able trust 59.2
    reverse QTIP 33.4
    S corporation 33.4
    taxation 33.4

Inter vivos trust .... chapter 64
    community property 64.11
        division of property at death 64.11
        life insurance 64.11
    definition 64.1
    disadvantages 64.4
    examples 64.9
    funding 64.6
    incapacity 64.7
    requirements 64.5
    shifting joint property 64.8
    tax implications 64.10
    uses 64.2

Interest-free (or below market
    rate) loans .... chapter 43
    community property 43.6
    definition 43.1
    demand loans 43.5
    examples 43.4
    exceptions and limitations 43.5
    foregone interest 43.3
    gift loans 43.3
    gift taxes 43.6
    key employee loan 43.7
    tax implications 43.5
    term loans 40.5
    use of 43.3

Intestate succession 7.4
Intra-family loans .... chapter 40
    cautionary tale 40.6
    definition 40.1
    example 40.4
    frequently asked questions 40.7
    requirements 40.3
    tax implications 40.5
    use 40.2

IRA, *See* Individual retirement plans (and SEPs)
Irrevocable election 15.5, 20.7, 71.4
Irrevocable life insurance trust
    community property states 36.4
    Crummey trust .... chapter 36
    frequently asked questions 36.8

INDEX

Irrevocable life insurance trust (cont'd)
    generation skipping transfer tax 36.5
    requirements 36.3
    tax implications 36.5
    trustee 36.7
    use 36.2
Irrevocable trust, See Tax basis irrevocable trust

J

Jointly held property 1.5
Junior interests 71.4

K

Key employees
    definition 57.3
    discount for loss of 70.3
Key person life insurance 34.8, 48.4, 53.9
Kiddie tax 8.2, 28.5

L

Law
    unauthorized practice of .... chapter 4
Leaseback, See Sales (gift) leaseback
Leverage 50.7
Life estate(s)
    split arrangement 45.2
Life insurance
    accumulated earnings tax problem 50.5
    actuarial assumptions 57.3
    alternative minimum tax 47.4
    annual renewable term 34.3
    basic ownership rights 34.4
    buy-sell agreements 47.3, 47.4
    charitable contributions 37.8
        current gifts 37.8
        group term life insurance 37.8
        premium payments 37.8
        splitting proceeds 37.8
        valuation 37.8
    charitable split interests 38.2, 38.4, 38.7
    community property 34.6
        inception of title doctrine 34.6
        premium tracing doctrine 34.6
        prenuptial agreement 34.6
        separate property status 34.6
        waiver of interest 34.6
        waiver of rights (figure) 34.6
    convertible term 34.3
    custodian as beneficiary 9.6
    decreasing term 34.3
    definition 34.1
    disability waiver premium 34.4
    disclaimers by beneficiaries 13.6

Life insurance (cont'd)
    distributions 34.4
    dividend provisions 34.4
    employee stock ownership plan 55.2
    endowment insurance 34.3
    expected return multiples (figure) 34.5
    federal estate taxes
        discount 34.2
        gross estate 34.8
    first to die 34.3
    gift taxes and 8.7, 34.8
    group life insurance 34.8
    guaranteed insurability 34.4
    improperly arranged 1.5
    level term 34.3
    modified life insurance 34.3
    profit sharing/pension plans 57.3, 57.5, 57.10
    re-entry term 34.3
    S corporations; tax 53.9
    salary increase ("selective")
        pension plan 34.8
    section 303 stock redemption 47.5, 47.9
    section 6166 installment payout 19.3-19.7
    single premium whole life 34.3
        borrowing against 34.3
        tax advantages 34.3
    split benefits 37.8
    "split-dollar" life insurance 34.7
        estate tax free 34.7
    survivor's income benefit plan 58.3
    survivorship life 34.3
    tax implications 34.5
        annuity rules 34.5
        death benefits 34.5
        deductibility of policy loan
            interest 34.5
        dividends 34.5
        living benefits 34.5
        lump sum cash settlement 34.5
        premiums 34.5
    transfer-for-value rule 34.5
    types 34.3
    Uniform Gifts to Minors Act 9.1, 9.6
    Uniform Transfers to Minors Act 9.1, 9.6
    universal life 34.3
        first year expense 34.3
        "stop and go" features 34.3
    uses of 34.2
    valuation of 70.3
    variable life 34.3
    variable universal life 34.3
    whole life (permanent) insurance 34.3
        characteristics 34.3
        limited payment life 34.3
        straight life 34.3
    See also Key person life insurance
Lifetime transfer 42.2

Limited liability companies............................chapter 51
   centralized management 51.3
   "check-the-box" regulations 51.2
   classification...51.2
   community property 51.4
   compared to C corporation 51.1
   compared to family limited partnership...........51.5
   compared to S corporation 51.1
   definition..51.1
   estate planning..51.1
   family business 51.5
   free transferability of interests 51.3
   professional practices...51.6
   requirements..51.2
   tax implications...51.3
Limited liability partnership 51.1
Liquidations.............................50.3, 50.5, 51.1, 51.5
Living trust, *See* Inter vivos trust
Loans
   demand loans..43.5
   employee stock ownership plan........................55.1
   housing loans 57.8
   IRA plans: borrowing from 56.4
   mortgage loans..57.8
   pension plan participants 57.8
   repayment within five years 57.8
   term loans 43.5
Long-term capital gain property
   charitable contributions 37.5
Lump sum distributions
   IRA rollover...56.8
   life insurance 34.5
   profit sharing/pension plans.............................57.5

M

Malpractice..chapter 6
   advisors 6.5
   avoiding problems..6.6, 6.12
   compound liability..6.3
   costs of malpractice...6.14
   defined 6.1
   documentation, importance of 6.7, 6.9
   external communication.....................................6.11
   malpractice insurance...6.13
   quality control...6.10
   relationship limits..6.8
   simple liability..6.3
   targets of opportunity 6.2
Marital deduction (trust)
   A-B or A-B-Q trusts 27.1, 27.5
      disadvantages 27.9
      example 27.5
      right to appoint...27.9
      typical estate (models).................................27.5
   community property 27.8
   credit equivalent bypass trust...........................27.4

Marital deduction (trust) (cont'd)
   definition..27.1
   distributable net income 22.2, 22.5
   estate trust...27.1-27.2
   family trust 27.1, 27.4
   fractional share bequest 27.9
   funding formula...27.4, 27.9
   inter vivos trust..27.2, 27.3
   joint tenancy 27.8
   life insurance 27.1, 27.4, 27.5, 27.9
   maximum qualification.......................................27.9
   models (figures) 27.5
   pecuniary formula clauses 27.9
   planning...27.1
   pourover will...27.1
   power of appointment trust...............27.1, 27.3, 27.4
   probate 27.2, 27.4
   qualified terminable interest
      property (QTIP) trust 27.1-27.9
   qualifying for...27.9
   requirements..27.3
   right of withdrawal 27.4
   "spray" or "sprinkle" clause 27.4
   survivor's property trust 27.4
   tax implications...27.7
   trustee functions 27.9
   unified credit 27.1
   uses 27.2
   zero tax 27.5
Marriage contracts and property
   agreements...chapter 67
   alternatives 67.6
   checklist..67.7
   commingling 67.6
   definition...67.1, 67.2
   frequently asked questions 67.8
   items included...67.6
   psychological issues 67.5
   types of...67.3
   Uniform Premarital Agreement Act 67.4
   Uniform Premarital and Marital
      Agreements Act...67.4
Married couples, *See* Community property
Maximum payout provision 42.3, 42.4
Minors
   qualified disclaimers 13.6
   See also Uniform Gift to Minors Act
Money-purchase pension plan..........................57.3
Mortgage loans 57.8
   sale-leasebacks 46.7

N

National Service Life Insurance...........................34.6
Non-citizen residents, planning for ....chapter 72
Non-citizen spouse 15.15, 33.4
Nongrantor-Owner (Section 678) Trust 53.9

INDEX

Non-U.S. persons .... chapter 72
    children 72.3
    community property 72.5
    definition 72.1
    generation-skipping 72.2
    gifts 72.2, 72.6
    income tax 72.2, 72.4
    joint tenancy 72.6
    life insurance 72.2, 72.6
    qualified domestic trusts (QDOTs) 72.6
    requirements 72.3
    tax implications 72.4
    transfer tax 72.3, 72.4
    trusts 72.3, 72.6, 72.7
    uses 72.2
Non-voting stock 53.8

O

One person LLC 51.3
Optimal basis increase trusts (OBITs) .... chapter 44
    advantages 44.2
    asset protection 44.3
    defined 44.1
    disadvantages 44.3
    tax risks 44.3
Ordinary income property
    charitable contributions 37.5
Ownership of property
    community property 7.2
    joint tenancy with right of survivorship 7.2
    life estate/remainder 7.2
    outright ownership 7.2
    tenancy by the entirety 7.2
    tenancy in common 7.2

P

Partnership
    choosing an entity; checklist 50.4
    corporations 50.2
    freezing techniques .... chapter 71
Passive loss rules 53.10
Pension Benefit Guarantee
    Corporation (PBGC) 57.6
Pension plan(s) .... chapter 57
    actuarial assumptions 57.3
    age-weighted 57.3
    annuity rules 57.5
    automatic survivor benefits 57.8
    collectibles 57.11
    community property 57.9
    contributions and benefits 57.3
    death benefits; taxes 57.5
    deduction of contributions 57.3
    defined benefit plan 57.3

Pension plan(s) (cont'd)
    defined contribution plans 57.3
    definition 57.1
    disability 57.3, 57.5, 57.8
    distributions (early) 57.5
    domestic relations order 57.6
    eligibility 57.3
    employee's cost 57.5
    ERISA compliance 57.6
    estate tax implications 57.5
    excess contributions 57.7
    fiduciary responsibility 57.6
    financial hardship 57.8
    funding 57.3, 57.4
    income tax implications 57.5
    life insurance limitations 57.3, 57.10
    loans 57.8
    nondiscriminatory 57.3, 57.7, 57.8
    planning with .... chapter 56
    protection from creditors 57.6
    reporting and disclosure
        requirements 57.6
    requirements 57.3
    retirement age 57.3
    safe harbor 401(k) 57.7
    social security integration 57.3
    summary plan description 57.6
    surviving spouse benefits required 57.8
    target benefit pension plan 57.3
    tax implications 57.5
    termination insurance 57.6
    thrift and savings plan 57.3
    top heavy plans 57.3
    types of plans 57.3
    uses 57.2
    vesting 57.3
    voluntary employee contributions 57.3, 57.5
    See also Defined benefit plans; Profit sharing
        /401(k) plans
Pension Protection Act of 2006 .... 57.3, 59.2
Personal holding company
    cases involving estate tax discount
        (figure) 52.4
    community property 52.6
    definition 52.1
    examples 52.1
    income shifting, to child 52.7
    life insurance 52.5
    requirements 52.3
    stepped-up basis 52.6
    tax implications 52.4
    uses 52.2
Personal service corporation 50.5
Pooled income funds
    definition 38.4
    requirements 38.4
Portability 18.9, 24.2, 26.3, 27.2, 27.9

Post mortem tax elections
    checklist 15.15, 24.2
    closely held corporations 24.2
    defined 24.1
    disclaimers 24.2
    estate tax elections 24.2
    income tax elections 24.2

Power of appointment .... chapter 12
    community property 12.8
    Crummey power 12.3, 12.6
    de minimis rule (five-and-five
        power) 12.6, 12.7
    definition 12.1, 12.2
    discretionary authority to
        invade principal 12.9
    estate tax, federal 12.5
    examples 12.5
    five-and-five powers 12.6, 12.7
    general power 12.6
    hanging 12.7
    lapse 12.4
    limited power; gift taxes 12.6
    marital deduction 12.3, 12.8, 27.1, 27.3, 27.4
    perpetuities, rule against 12.9
    release 12.4
    requirements 12.4
    tax consequences 12.6
    tax implications 12.6
    uses 12.3

Power of attorney
    agents under 14.3
    definition 62.1
    springing 14.3
    See also Durable power of attorney

Practice of law, unauthorized .... chapter 4
    defined 4.2
    lawyer-client relationship 4.1
    non-lawyers and law firms 4.3
    regulations 4.1

Private annuity .... chapter 42
    alternatives to 42.2
    community property 42.7
    definition 42.1
    examples 42.3
    joint and last survivor 42.1, 42.4
    life expectancy outlived 42.2
    life insurance 42.5
    payments tied to income from
        property 42.6
    property in escrow 42.9
    requirements 42.3
    stock redemption 42.8
    tax basis 42.2, 42.4
    tax implications 42.4
    trusts 42.6
    types (two) 42.1
    uses 42.2

Probate .... chapter 15
    administrator 15.3
    attorney for the estate 15.6
    avoiding 27.2
    collecting assets 15.7
    debts 15.10
    distributing assets 15.11
    executor 15.2, 15.3, 15.12, 15.13
    expenses 15.10
    funeral arrangements 15.4
    handling the business 15.8
    investing assets 15.9
    personal representative 15.5
    post mortem tax elections 15.14, 15.15
    protecting assets 15.9
    remaining assets 15.11
    successor trustee 15.2
    taxes 15.10, 15.14, 15.15

Profit-sharing / 401(k) plans .... chapter 57
    actuarial assumptions 57.3
    collectibles 57.11
    community property 57.9
    contributions and benefits 57.3
    deduction of contributions 57.3
    definition 57.3
    eligibility 57.3
    estate taxes 57.5
    401(k) plan 57.3
    life insurance 57.10
    plan features 57.8
    planning with .... chapter 59
    protection from creditors 57.6
    requirements 57.3
    retirement age 57.3
    SIMPLE 401(k) plan 57.7
    social security integration 57.3
    tax implications 57.5
    top heavy plans 57.3
    uses 57.2
    vesting 57.3

Property
    apportionment rule 47.9
    basis determination 22.6
    future interests in 37.5
    gift, as
        basis of 20.9
        best type to give away 8.5, 8.10
        computing basis 8.4
        gain or loss; computation 8.4
        net gift 8.4
        outright gifts 8.5
        planning properly 20.6, 20.11
        purchase of property in joint names 8.10
        types that should not be given 8.5
    ownership of .... chapter 7
        community property 7.2
        joint tenancy with right of
            survivorship 7.2

INDEX

Property (cont'd)
  ownership of (cont'd)
    life estate/remainder 7.2
    outright ownership 7.2
    tenancy by the entirety 7.2
    tenancy in common 7.2
  private annuities and 42.8
  transfer of .... chapter 7
    at death 7.4
      intestate succession 7.4
      limitations 7.4
      survivorship 7.4
      wills 7.4
    lifetime 7.3
    trusts 7.4
      rule against perpetuities 7.4
      spendthrift provisions 7.4
  valuation of 70.3
  See also Community property

Proprietorship
  choosing an entity; checklist 50.4

Publicly traded companies 70.3

Purchase price
  establishing, for a business 47.10

Put 71.4

Q

Qualified business income deduction .... chapter 23
  calculation 23.1
  choice of entity 23.9
  definition 23.4
  eligible taxpayers 23.1
  mechanics 23.2
  phase out 23.3
  qualified trade or business 23.5
  rationale 23.1
  section 199a 23.7, 23.8
  special rules 23.6
  specific service trade or business limitation 23.3
  tax planning 23.8
  unadjusted basis limitation 23.3

Qualified domestic trusts (QDOTs) 72.6

Qualified payments 71.4, 71.6

Qualified retirement plan
  See Retirement plan, qualified

Qualified Subchapter S trust (QSST) 28.6, 53.9

Qualifying Terminable Interest Property (QTIP) 12.3, 18.6, 27.1-27.9
  marital deduction 12.3, 27.3-27.6

R

Rabbi trusts 54.4, 54.7

Real property, *See* Property

Realty transfer tax 46.3

Recapitalization
  community property 71.5
  definition 71.1
  estate freeze 71.1
  example 71.3
  requirements 71.3
  tax implications 71.4
    estate tax problems 71.4
    gift tax problems 71.4
  uses 71.2

Rent-free occupancy
  charitable contributions 37.3

Retirement
  age requirements 57.3
  income 57.3
  non-top heavy plans 57.3

Retirement plan
  funding 57.3
  See also Pension plan

Retirement plan, qualified
  exclusive benefit rule 57.3, 57.6
  life insurance in 57.10
  planning with .... chapter 59

Revocable trusts
  advantages 64.3
  community property 64.11
  definition 64.1
  disadvantages 64.4
  examples 64.9
  frequently asked questions 64.14
  funding 64.6
  grantor trusts 64.1
  inter vivos 64.1
  irrevocable comparison 64.12
  joint property 64.8
  living trusts 64.1
  requirements 64.5
  tax implications 64.10
  trustee 64.13
  use 64.2

Rollover
  IRA provisions 56.4, 56.7, 56.9

Roth IRA
  advantages 60.2, 60.4
  conversion to 60.4, 60.5
  defined 60.1
  disadvantages 60.5
  funding 60.1
  maximum age 60.2
  SECURE Act 60.1, 60.2
  SECURE Act 2.0
    changes 60.3
    distribution rules 60.3
    Roth IRA 60.3
    SEP IRAs 60.3
    SIMPLE IRAs 60.3

S

Safe deposit box
   checklist 2.7
Sale (gift) leaseback .... chapter 43
   community property 46.5
   definition 46.1, 46.2
   donor/trustee bargaining position 46.3
   economic substance test 46.6
   examples 46.3
   grantor taxed on trust income 46.4
   IRS treatment of 46.3
   mortgage and 46.3
   related parties 46.3
   requirements 46.3
   safe harbor test 46.3
   sale-leaseback 46.3
   tax implications 46.4
   transaction as a loan 46.3
   uses 46.3
Savings Bonds Series EE 8.9
S corporation .... chapter 53
   choosing an entity; checklist 50.4
   community property 53.7
   deferred compensation plan in 53.10
   definition 53.1
   doing business in several states 53.6
   electing small business trust 53.9
   election 53.6
      advantages 53.6
      consent of all shareholders 53.6
      disadvantages 53.6
      effective date 53.6
      states recognizing federal election 53.6
      states requiring state election 53.6
      termination of election 53.6
   fringe benefits 53.6, 53.9
   life insurance; taxes 53.10
   outright gift to minor child 53.8
   passive loss rules 53.10
   requirements 53.3
   section 678 trust 28.6, 53.9
   section 2503(c) trust 28.6
   state income taxes 53.6
   state law, and election decision 53.6
   stock (one class only) 53.3
   "straight debt instrument" 53.3
   tax implications 53.5
      computation of taxable income 53.5
      corporate tax rate 53.5
      depletion allowances 53.5
      net operating loss 53.5
      tax exempt interest 53.5
   termination of election 53.6
   transferring ownership, shifting wealth 53.8
   uses 53.2
Section 199A, tax planning under 23.8

Section 303 stock redemption .... chapter 48
   agreement for 48.4
   cash distribution 48.7
   community property 48.6
   constructive ownership rules 48.5
   corporate control, loss of 48.4
   death taxes and estate expenses 48.1
   definition 48.1
   estate settlement costs 48.3, 48.7
   examples 48.4
   insurance premiums 48.4
   IRS audit, and dividend treatment 48.7
   key person life insurance proceeds 48.4
   life insurance, and accumulated
      earnings 48.4
   "more than 35 percent" test 48.6
   requirements 48.3
   step-up-in-basis rules 48.5
   stock left to a specific legatee 48.7
   stock other than that held by
      executor 48.7
   tax implications 48.5
   time limits 48.4
   uses 48.2
Section 678 trust 28.6, 53.9
Section 2503(b) trust
   definition 28.1, 28.7
   gift treatment 28.6
   income distribution 28.7
   tax to minor 28.7
   use 28.2
Section 2503(c) trust
   community property 28.8
   definition 28.1, 28.3
   disadvantages 28.4
   qualified subchapter s trust
      (QSST) 28.6
   requirements 28.2, 28.3
   retain property for child past 21 (age) 28.3
   S corporation stock 28.6
   section 678 trust 28.6
   tax implications
      donor acting as trustee 28.5
      father places trust for minor son 28.5
      kiddie tax 28.5
   Uniform Gift to Minors Act
      as alternative 28.1, 28.6
   Uniform Transfers to Minors Act
      as alternative 28.1, 28.6
   uses 28.2
Secular trust 54.7, 54.9
SECURE Act 56.1, 59.1, 60.1, 60.2
SECURE Act 2.0
   Roth IRAs 60.1, 60.3
   scope 56.1, 59.1
   SEP IRAs 60.3
   SIMPLE IRAs 60.3

INDEX

Securities
    charitable contributions 38.1-38.4
    "employer securities" 55.2, 55.3
    installment sale rules 41.1, 41.2
Self-cancelling installment notes (SCINs) 41.1
    tax implications 41.4
Self-employment
    HR-10 retirement plans 56.4
Servicemen's Group Life Insurance 34.6
Simplified Employee Pensions (SEPs)
    definition 56.6
    limit on contributions 56.6
    participation in other plans 56.6
    requirements 56.6
    SECURE Act 2.0 .... 60.3
    social security integration 56.6
Social Security
    integration with
        profit sharing/pension plans 57.3
        SEPs 56.6
    offset plan 57.3
Sole proprietor 53.2
Sole proprietorship 50.1, 50.2, 50.4
Split-dollar plan 34.7
Split interest purchase of property .... chapter 45
    community property 45.5
    definition 45.1
    depreciation deductions 45.4
    joint purchased property 45.6
    requirements 45.3
    tax implications 45.4
    term of years or life estate, for 45.4
    uses 45.2
Spousal lifetime access trust (SLAT)
    advantages of 32.3
    asset protection 32.6
    assets best suited for 32.6
    charitable beneficiaries 32.7
    definition 32.1, 32.2
    disadvantages of 32.4
    domestic asset protection trust jurisdictions 32.7
    donor spouse
        as beneficiary 32.7
        death income tax basis 32.7
        loans to 32.7
    dynasty SLAT 32.2
    floating spouse 32.2, 32.3
    frequently asked questions about 32.10
    grantor trust 32.7
    independent valuation 32.6
    intervivor QTIP trust, difference 32.2
    joint SLAT 32.8
    lifetime credit shelter trust 32.1
    reciprocal trust doctrine 32.8
    rule against perpetuities 32.2
    transfer 32.6
    uses 32.5

Springing power of attorney 14.3, 62.3, 62.9
Step-down in basis 22.6
Step-up in basis 22.6
Stock(s)
    S corporations 53.1, 53.2, 53.3, 53.4, 53.5
    valuation of 70.3
    See also Stock redemption (plan);
        Section 303 stock redemption
Stock bonus plans 55.1, 55.6
Stockholders
    corporate control 48.4
Stock redemption (plan)
    buy-sell agreement .... chapter 47
    dividends, as 47.4
    preference over cross-purchase plan 47.11
    restriction on transfer of shares 47.11
    tax implications 47.11
    See also Section 303 stock redemption
Subchapter S, *See* S corporation
Substantial presence test 72.3
Surviving spouse 1.5, 42.9, 57.8
Survivor annuity
    qualified joint and 57.8
    qualified pre-retirement 57.8
Survivor's income benefit plan
  (S.I.B.) .... chapter 58
    community property 58.6
    death benefits in estate 58.6
    definition 58.1
    ERISA, funding 58.5
    marital deduction 58.7
    tax implications 58.4
        beneficiary's position 58.4
        employee's position 58.4
        employer's position 58.4
    use 58.2
Survivorship life insurance 34.3

T

**Tangible personal property charitable
  contributions** 37.5
Target benefit plan 57.3
Tax basis irrevocable trust
    community property 31.5
    definition 31.1
    frequently asked questions 31.6
    requirements 31.3
    tax implications 31.4
    use 31.2
Tax option corporation, *See* S corporation
**Tax Reform Act of 1986 (TRA '86) General
  Utilities Doctrine repealed** 52.1
Tax Relief Act of 2010 .... 11.1, 18.9
**Tax Relief and Health Care Act of
  2006** 43.5

Taxes
  alternative minimum tax 47.4
  See also Death tax apportionment; Estate tax;
    Generation-skipping
    transfer tax; Gift tax; Income tax
Tenancy by the entirety 7.2, 27.8
Term insurance 34.3
Thin capitalization 50.7
Thrift and savings plan 57.3
Throwback tax 72.3, 72.7
Top heavy
  combination of plans 57.3
  contributions and benefits 57.3
  distribution age 57.3
  HR-10 plans 57.3
  profit sharing/pension plans 57.3
Transfer-for-value rule 47.4
Transfer of property
  at death 7.4
    intestate succession 7.4
    limitations 7.4
    survivorship 7.4
    wills 7.4
  lifetime 7.3
  trusts 7.4
    rule against perpetuities 7.4
    spendthrift provisions 7.4
Trust protector
  defined 14.5
  duties 14.5
Trustees
  attributes of a good trustee 14.4
  co-trustees 14.5
  duties of 14.4
  marital trusts 27.3
  selecting a trustee 14.4
Trusts
  charitable lead trusts 38.4, 38.6, 38.7
  charitable remainder annuity
    trusts 38.3
  charitable remainder unitrusts 29.7
  defective 29.9
  ESBT 17.7
  income taxation of 22.3
  power of appointment 12.2
  property, transfers of 7.2
  rabbi 54.3, 54.5
  revocable .... 17.7, chapter 64
  S corporation trust 17.7
  section 678 trust 53.9
  tax basis irrevocable .... 30.5, 30.6, chapter 31
  See also Grantor retained interests
    (GRAT, GRIT, GRUT, QPRT); Inter vivos trust;
    Marital deduction (trust);
    Section 678 trust; Section 2503(b) trust;
    Section 2503(c) trust, Tax basis irrevocable
    trust

Trusts, in general .... chapter 17
  administrative trust 17.8
  anatomy 17.2
    administration 17.2, 17.7
    duties and powers, trustees 17.2
    general provisions 17.2
    generation-skipping provisions 17.2
    grantor trust provisions 17.2
    nature of the trust 17.2
    office of trustee 17.2
    players 17.2
    property placed in trust 17.2
    protectors 17.2
    separate investment 17.2
    trust protectors 17.2
  charitable remainder trust 17.1
  common types 17.7
    ESBTs 17.7
    intervivos QTIP 17.7, 59.2
    revocable living 17.7, 59.2, 64.1
    S corporation trusts 17.7
    section 678 .... 17.7
  contingent trust 17.8
  defined 17.1
  directed trusts 17.3
  grantor retained annuity trust (GRAT) 17.1
  QSST trusts 17.7
    advanatages 17.7
    disadvantages 17.7
  selecting a jurisdiction 17.4
  selecting a trustee 17.5
  tax implications 17.7
  trust protectors 17.6
    as fiduciaries 17.6

U

Unauthorized practice of law .... chapter 4
Undistributed income 28.3
Uniform Gifts to Minors Act (UGMA) ...... chapter 9
  community property 9.5
  custodial property 9.4, 9.6
    if minor dies 9.6
    life insurance beneficiary 9.6
  definition 9.1
  disclaimers 13.6
  estate taxation of donee 9.4
  estate taxation of donor 9.4
  example 9.3
  gift tax exclusion 9.3, 9.4
  income shifting 9.2
  insurance policies 9.6
  minor's death, disposition of property 9.6, 53.8
  property: types to transfer 9.6
  requirements 9.3
  S corporations 53.8
  section 2503(c) trust and 28.6

INDEX

Uniform Gifts to Minors Act (UGMA) (cont'd)
    successor custodian 9.5, 9.6, 53.8
    support obligations 9.5
    tax implications 9.4
    uses 9.2

Uniform Transfers to Minors Act (UTMA)
    custodial property 9.4, 9.6
    definition 9.1
    disclaimers 13.6
    estate taxation of donee 9.4
    estate taxation of donor 9.4
    minor's death, disposition of
        property 9.6, 53.7
    requirements 9.3
    successor custodian 9.5, 9.6, 53.7
    support obligations 9.5
    tax implications 9.4
    use 9.2

United States government bonds
    valuation of 948

Universal life insurance 34.3

Unmarried partners, planning for .... chapter 65
    buy-sell agreements 65.2
    cohabitation 65.1, 65.9
    definition 65.1
    frequently asked questions 65.10
    grantor retained income trust (GRIT)
        advantages 65.7
        definition 65.7
        disadvantages 65.7
        example 65.7
        tax implications 65.7
        use 65.7
    property agreements 65.9
    recapitalization freezes, corporate 65.8
    split purchase
        definition 65.3
        requirements 65.5
        use 65.4

V

Valuation
    basis 70.1
    closely held business interests 70.3, 70.4
    community property 70.5
    definition 70.1
    discounts 70.4
    family business 70.4
    federal estate tax 70.3
    federal gift tax 70.3
    Hood's rules of valuation 70.1
    levels of value 70.6
    methods 70.3
    property for gift tax purposes 20.6
    requirements 70.2

Valuation (cont'd)
    tax implications
        annuities 70.3
        bonds 70.3
        closely held business 70.3
        determining value 70.3
        farm 70.3
        life insurance 70.3
        methods 70.3
        professional practice 70.3
        stock 70.3
        valuation date 70.3
        valuation of real property 70.3
    transferred property 18.4

Variable life insurance 34.3
Variable universal life 34.3
Vesting
    profit sharing/pension plans 57.3
    top heavy plans 57.3

W

Wealth replacement trusts 38.1
Will(s) .... chapters 10 and 11
    appointment of fiduciaries clause 11.10
    attestation clause 11.12
    bequests 11.7
    cash 11.7
    change 10.6
    checklist 11.2
    community property implications 10.8
    debts clause 11.3
    death tax implications 10.7
    definition 10.1, 11.1
    errors or problems 1.5
    fractional share bequests 27.9
    intangibles 11.7
    intestate succession 10.3
    introductory clause 11.2
    power of appointment 10.9
    powers clause 11.9
    property, transfer of 10.3
    real estate clause 11.6
    requirements 10.4
    residuary clause 11.8
    revocation 10.6
    tangible personal property clause 11.5
    tax clause 11.4
    tax implications 10.7
    terms 10.5
    testator's signing clause 11.11
    use 10.2

Z

Zero tax marital deduction 27.5